P9-CNB-539

Catharina Day

IRELAND

'When you're in Ireland, you can be
certain that the irritations and
annoyances that can accompany one
through everyday life will disappear,
and your desires for a good day's walking
in the mountains, a spot of fishing or
a good read before a warm fire
will be become realities.'

CADOGANguides

1

1 Atlantic Drive, Co. Mayo

3

4

2 Lough Doo, Co. Mayo
3 Clochans, Co. Kerry
4 Boat maintenance, Kinvarra, Co. Galway

5

5 Ring of Kerry
6 Connemara, Co. Galway
7 Dingle Peninsula, Co. Kerry

8 Rock of Cashel, Co. Tipperary

13

12

9 10

11

14 Kenmare, Co. Kerry
15 City Hall, Dublin
16 Bar life, Dublin
17 Georgian door, Dublin

18 Crown Liquor Saloon, Belfast
19 Graveyard, Co. Mayo
20, 21 Republican and Loyalist murals,
   Belfast
22 Clonmacnoise, Co. Offaly

23 Birr Castle Gardens, Co. Offaly

About the author

Catharina Day comes from a long-established Irish family. She was born in Kenya but moved to County Donegal as a small child. She attended school in Ireland, and then went to university in England. She was married in County Donegal, and visits frequently with her husband and four children from her home in Scotland. She has compiled an anthology of Irish literature. Her acknowledgements can be found below.

About the updater

Mary O'Neill was born in Cork and grew up in Dublin. She moved to Oxford in 1988, where she worked as an editor/project manager at the University Press. She is now a freelance editor, and the author of *Pick Your Brains about Ireland*, one of Cadogan's eight illustrated travel books for children. A keen observer of developments in her home country, she returns regularly with her family and 'loves her oul' Dublin'.

Author acknowledgements

Numerous people helped me compile this book, and to them I wish to say many thanks. It would take many pages to mention all but a few by name, for through my researches on the guide I have met many delightful people who have given me an insight into their locality. In particular I would like to thank Tourism Ireland, who have always been extremely generous with information, advice and goodwill. My family have over the years been very supportive and a great help. My mother has been an enthusiastic gatherer of information and her wide general knowledge has been invaluable. My sister Angelique has been a great help, especially with Ulster, as has my sister Georgina with Co. Laois and Co. Offaly. My husband Simon helped me in countless ways, acting as my agent and trying out hotels and restaurants on his business trips to Dublin. I am indebted to the late Araminta Swiney, who advised me on what to leave out, Brian Walker for help with the historical background, Flora Armstrong for her initial help with South Ulster and Co. Armagh and John Colclough, who recommended places to stay and eat. Special thanks to Mary O'Neill, who updated this sixth edition. A big thank-you to all Cadogan readers who have written in with their recommendations. Finally, thanks to Paula Levy, who first gave me the opportunity to explore and write about this lovely country.

Contents

Cadogan Guides
2nd Floor, 233 High Holborn,
London WC1 7DN
info@cadoganguides.co.uk
www.cadoganguides.com

The Globe Pequot Press
246 Goose Lane, PO Box 480, Guilford,
Connecticut 06437–0480

Copyright © Catharina Day 1990, 1993, 1995,
1998, 2002, 2006

Cover photographs: © Doug Pearson/Jon Arnold;
© Susannah Sayler
Photo essay: © Alex Robinson
Maps © Cadogan Guides, drawn by Maidenhead
Cartographic Services Ltd.
Maps of the Republic of Ireland based on
Ordnance Survey Ireland, Permit No. 8190
© Ordnance Survey Ireland and Government of
Ireland. Maps of Northern Ireland based on
Ordnance Survey Northern Ireland mapping
with the permission of the Controller of HMSO,
Permit No 60103 © Crown Copyright 2006

Art director: Sarah Gardner
Managing Editor: Natalie Pomier
Editor: Rhonda Carrier
Editorial Assistant: Nicola Jessop
Proofreader: Mary O'Neill and Pat Bulhosen
Indexing: Isobel McLean

Printed in Italy by Legoprint
A catalogue record for this book is available
from the British Library
ISBN 10: 1-86011-327-3
ISBN 13: 978-1-86011-327-7

Introduction

Ireland is the perfect place to take a holiday. This lovely island has physical and spiritual qualities that are seldom found in the western world. The pace of life is relaxing, the scenery beautiful and varied, with the sea never far from sight. Dublin, the capital, is cultured, attractive and easy to explore. The people of the country are easy to meet and almost invariably courteous and friendly. The climate is good and, although it's often damp, when the sunshine comes in soft shards it intensifies the already lovely colours of the landscape. Forget sun culture and all its paraphernalia; travel with stout shoes and a warm jersey.

There is no such thing as a tiresome, hot journey in Ireland. Country roads are usually empty, and traffic jams are still an exception in most places. Some visitors bent on 'doing' Ireland get from one end of the country to the other in a day's drive, but this is not the way to travel. If you rush, the charm of the country and the people will pass you by, and the Irish do not approve of rushing.

Whatever direction you decide to go in, it is possible to stay in tranquil country houses, where the proportions and furnishings of the rooms are redolent of a more gracious age. Not only is the food delicious – fresh seafood, local meats, game and vegetables – but you can also taste well-chosen wines and, of course, decent whiskey and beer. You will find the owners and staff of these places keen to help with any request you have, whether it's finding the origins of your great-granny, or directing you to the best fishing, golf, beaches, crafts and sites of historical interest.

It is so easy to travel in a country where you can explain your needs in English, and find yourself understood. Dry archaeological and historical facts suddenly become much more fascinating when you can ask for the local version of events, and hear for yourself the wonderful stories that make up history. Hearing the sound of spoken Irish is another pleasure that's in store. You'll discover a race who can express themselves with great character, humour and precision.

When you're in Ireland, you can be certain that the irritations and annoyances that can accompany one through everyday life will disappear, and your desires for a good day's walking in the mountains, a spot of fishing or a good read before a warm fire will become realities. However, it is important not to stick rigidly to a plan and become irritated when it has to be delayed, for nothing in Ireland can be planned right down to the last detail. Sometimes information can only be found out on the spot, since opening times, timetables and other schedules tend to be more subject to change than in other countries.

Ireland remains largely agricultural, with relatively few areas of industrial development. There are few motorways, endless suburbs, belching factories, marching powerlines, and little of the ugly side-effects of industry. Hopefully, the Irish will ensure things stay that way. Its population is relatively small, at about 5 million, and the Six Counties which form part of the United Kingdom, make up 1,556,000 of that total. The differences between the Six Counties, colloquially referred to as 'the North', and the Republic of Ireland, 'the South', are explored in the '**History**' section later in the guide, and will become apparent as you read the chapter on each county.

For years there has been a commonly held misconception that it was dangerous to travel in the North. Violence was confined to very small areas and no tourist has even been harmed by the Troubles within Ireland. Sensible, unprejudiced travellers will soon discover that, with the exception of a few well-known areas, the North is actually a quiet, unspoilt and attractive region. If your sympathy for the ordinary people of the province and your admiration for their courage and forbearance has been stirred by their problems, one of the most positive things that you can do is visit the province itself.

Both North and South share a fascinating past; as Yeats wrote, 'Behind all Irish history hangs a great tapestry even Christianity had to accept, and be itself pictured there.' The Irish race has a long memory and a poetic imagination, which gives each hill, lough and pile of stones a background or story. The history of Ireland has been turbulent, and its telling fraught with prejudice and misunderstandings. But it is fascinating to approach it through its literary tradition. Ireland had its Golden Age of learning roughly between the 6th and 11th centuries; Frank O'Connor described it as the civilization of 'the little monasteries'. Monks transcribed the Celtic oral culture, wrote poetry and honoured God during the Dark Ages, when the rest of the Continent was in the hands of the Barbarians.

Ireland also had a strict bardic tradition, according to which members of the poets' guild had to study for a duration of up to 12 years before they were qualified. From that disciplined environment came mature poetry that is as evocative and delicate as poetry from China: stirring epics such as *The Tain*, which chronicles the wars of a heroic race, and moving love laments. Most of us can only read these poems in translation from the Gaelic, but luckily the translators, often present-day Irish poets, bring them close to us. From the 18th century onwards, the ability of the Irish to express themselves in the language of the Saxon has been apparent from the works of Jonathan Swift through to W. B. Yeats and the marvellous poets of today, such as Seamus Heaney. Poetry, theatre and the novel have continued to thrive since the heady days of Ireland's cultural renaissance and the uprising against the British in 1916; arts and music festivals flourish throughout the country today. Go if you can to the Abbey Theatre in Dublin or the Druid Theatre in Galway to see a play by Sean O'Casey or Brian Friel.

Modern Ireland conjures up a romantic idyll of whitewashed cottages set against a mountainous landscape, and it is true that, in places, this is still possible to find. But a great deal has changed; many technological companies have been attracted to the country's highly educated young population, and these have brought wealth, prosperity and transformation to the land. As a traveller in Ireland you will be able to enjoy all the conveniences of modern-day Europe and still lose yourself in its wilderness and beauty.

By the end of your holiday, you may feel tuned in to the country and its people to the point where that famous saying can be aired yet again: that (the English) are more Irish than the Irish themselves: *Ipsis Hibernis hiberniores*.

A Note on Names

You will find that there are occasions when place names vary in spelling from those in this guide book. This is because different translations from the Gaelic exist, and there is no completely standardized map to follow. Bartholomews, Ordnance Survey, the RAC and the AA produce very good and detailed maps.

The Gaeltacht

This is the name given to several areas in Ireland where (Irish) Gaelic is spoken as the everyday language. These areas are mainly in the west, in counties Donegal, Mayo, Galway and Kerry. You can expect all the signposts to be in Irish.

A Guide to the Guide

After a brief **Introduction** to this island and its people, and a selection of the Best of Ireland, there is a **History** from pagan times, which outlines the main events and problems that constitute the complex Ireland of today. This is followed by a brief résumé of the **religious** background and a selection of the country's most famous saints. Next are features on the **Old Gods and Heroes**, and ancient sites and early architecture in **From Stone Circles to Castles**. The next section, **Topics**, gives brief insights into notable features of Ireland and Irish life. These include some fascinating pieces on the Fairy People and Historic Houses and Gardens, and useful information for genealogists in 'Trace your Ancestors'. Then there is a comprehensive and important **Travel** section, followed by the **Practical A–Z**. This is packed with information that will help you get the best from your visit, including advice on where to stay and eat, sports and leisure activities.

The 32 counties are divided into the provinces of **Munster, Connacht, Ulster** and **Leinster**, with Belfast and Dublin featuring separately from the rest of the counties. This constitutes a gazetteer of the whole country, with lots of local history and anecdotal knowledge together with descriptions and details of the places of interest. Full, practical lists of transport facilities, tourist information centres and festivals are given at the beginning of each county section in grey boxes. Where counties are divided into smaller areas, then the listings for shopping and leisure activities, places to stay and eat and entertainment are found in grey boxes near to each area's heading (e.g. 'The Ards Peninsula' in County Antrim).

At the end of the book there is an essay on **Language**; a **Glossary** of archaeological, architectural and associated terms; a brief **Chronology**; a recommended **Further Reading** list; and a comprehensive **Index**.

Chapter Divisions

80 km
50 miles

N

Atlantic

Ocean

North Channel

Derry

NORTHERN

IRELAND

Belfast

Donegal

13
ULSTER

Sligo

Irish

Sea

12
CONNACHT

REPUBLIC

Galway

Dublin

OF

14
LEINSTER

Wicklow

IRELAND

Limerick

11
MUNSTER

Wexford

Waterford

St. George's Channel

Cork

Celtic

Sea

The Best of Ireland

Art galleries: The Glebe Gallery, Co. Donegal; National Gallery, Dublin; Crawford Gallery, Cork; Chester Beatty, Dublin.

Beaches: There are many beautiful, unspoilt strands; in particular, Portsalon, Co. Donegal; Magilligan, Co. Londonderry; Keel, Achill Island, Co. Mayo; Inch, Co. Kerry; Streedagh, Co. Sligo; Ballyconneely, Co. Galway; White Strand and Spanish Point, Co. Clare; White Park Bay, Co. Antrim.

Carved high crosses: Moone, Co. Kildare; Cardonagh, Co. Donegal.

Castles: Carrickfergus and Dunluce, Co. Antrim; Parke's Castle, Co. Leitrim; Cahir Castle, Co. Tipperary; Trim Castle, Co. Meath; Doe Castle, Co. Donegal.

Craft shops: Ballycasey Workshops, Co. Tipperary; Nicholas Mosse Pottery, Bennetsbridge, Co. Kilkenny; Craft Park, Roundstone, Co. Galway.

Equestrian events: Dublin Horse Show; Ulster Harp National; Galway Races.

Festivals: Wexford Opera Festival; Kilkenny Arts Week; Galway Film Festival; Galway Oyster Festival; Belfast Arts Festival; Dublin Drama Festival; Feis na nGleann, Co. Antrim; Music Festival in Great Irish Houses; Willie Clancy Summer School, Co. Clare; Puck Fair, Co. Kerry; Boley Fair, South Down.

Fine houses: Castletown, Co. Kildare; Bantry Bay House, Co. Cork; Castle Coole, Co. Fermanagh.

Folk parks: Cultra Park, Co. Down; Bunratty, Co. Clare; Ulster American Folk Park, Co. Tyrone.

Gardens: Birr Castle, Co. Offaly; Mountstewart, Co. Down; Annestown, Co. Cork; Glenveagh, Co. Donegal.

Golf courses: Bundoran; the Royal County Down, Newcastle; Royal Portrush; Portmarnock; Lahinch; Ballybunion; Killarney; Galway City; Rosses Point; Portsalon.

Landscapes: Most of the coastal and mountain stretches of Connacht, especially between Westport and Clifden; views from the top of Croagh Patrick; and Achill Island. Wild bog between Mulrany and Bangor Erris; coastal and mountain stretches in Co. Donegal, especially from Lough Salt and from the top of Muckish Mountain. The Antrim Coast, the Burren, Bantry Bay, Knockmealdown Mountains, the Ring of Kerry, the Ring of Beara, the Sperrin Mountains.

Museums: Ulster; National Museum, Dublin.

Pubs: Dick Macks, Dingle; Mary Anne's, Castletownshend; Crown Liquor Saloon, Belfast; The Stag's Head, Dublin; Rita's, Portsalon; Moran's on the Weir, Clarinbridge; Rotterdam Bar, Belfast.

Round towers: Glendalough, Co. Wicklow; Devenish Island, Co. Fermanagh; Ardmore, Co. Waterford.

Ruined friaries and churches: Cong, Co. Mayo; Killaloe, Co. Clare; Dysert O'Dea, Co. Clare; Clonfert Cathedral, Co. Galway; Moyne, Co. Mayo.

Unusual activities: Seaweed baths, Enniscrone; Sham Fight, Scarva; hurling matches, anywhere in Ireland; Donegal Motor Rally; Puck Fair, Killorglin; Lammas Fair, Ballycastle; visit to Doon Well, Co. Donegal; Lough Derg Gourmet Ride.

7

History

I found in Munster, unfettered of any
Kings and queens, and poets a many –
Poets well skilled in music and measure,
Prosperous doings, mirth and pleasure.
I found in Connaught the just, redundance
Of riches, milk in lavish abundance;
Hospitality, vigour, fame,
In Cruachan's land of heroic name
I found in Ulster, from hill to glen,
Hardy warriors, resolute men;
Beauty that bloomed when youth was gone,
And strength transmitted from sire to son.
I found in Leinster the smooth and sleek,
From Dublin to Slewmargy's peak;
Flourishing pastures, valour, health,
Long-living worthies, commerce, wealth.

from *Prince Alfrid's Itinerary* (James Clarence Mangan's version)

If you happen to fall into conversation with an Irishman in a bar, the subjects of religion and politics are bound to arise. With luck you'll have a cool glass of Guinness in your hand, for discussions on Ireland are inevitably emotional. The Irish are good talkers and have very long memories, so it's worth having some idea of their history.

Many of Ireland's troubles have stemmed from its geographical situation; too far from Britain to be assimilated, too near to be allowed to be separate. Elizabeth I poured troops into the country because she appreciated the strategic importance of Ireland to her enemies. Over the centuries Ireland has been offered help in its fight for independence, but it was never disinterested help; whoever paid for arms and fighting men in Ireland wanted to further their own military, political, religious or ideological cause. France in the late 18th century supplied arms to Ireland to distract England from other policies; and in Northern Ireland the IRA were supplied with some guns by foreign powers. Most recently, more than 30 years of European Union (EU) membership has paid dividends for Ireland. The economic disparity with the UK has narrowed considerably, and Ireland has gained in self-confidence in a union where the centre of power is not London, but Brussels. The shared economics of EU membership are helping to undermine political and religious differences.

General History

Pre-Celtic Ireland

The hills and river valleys are scattered with monuments from the Stone, Bronze and Iron ages. Most have some kind of religious significance, and they have been swathed in romance and heroism by the Celtic storytellers or *shanachies* in the cottages and castles. Sadly, only a few of these traditional oracles survive as 'memory men'.

The earliest record of humans in Ireland is dated to 8,700– 8,600 years ago, from fragments found at a camp in **Mount Sandel** near Coleraine. The people of this time lived a nomadic life, hunting and trapping; they could not move around easily, as the countryside was covered by forest, interrupted only by lakes and rivers. They used *curraghs*, similar to the boats used today by fishermen in the west of Ireland, and built lake-dwellings, or *crannógs*. No one is sure where these people came from, but they had the island to themselves for 3,000 years. Then came **Neolithic** humans, who were perhaps the **Fir Bolg** of Celtic mythology: at this stage everything is vague. These farming people gradually spread over all of Ireland, clearing the forest as best they could with their stone tools. They evidently practised burial rites, for they built very sophisticated chambered tombs, decorated with spirals and lozenge shapes. For example, the Great Burial Chamber at Newgrange in the Boyne Valley, from 2500 BC, has a chamber large enough to contain thousands of cremated bodies. These people must have been very well organized, with the energy and wealth to spare for such an ambitious project – similar in its way to the pyramids, and 1,000 years older.

Around 2000 BC yet another race appeared, of skilled miners and metal-workers. They were called the **Beaker People**, or the **Tuatha Dé Danaan**, as they are known in legend. They opened up copper mines and started to trade with Brittany, the Baltic and the Iberian Peninsula. They had different beliefs about burial: their dead were buried singly in graves lined with stone slabs and covered with a capstone. Other peoples with different burial habits and funeral rituals also arrived at this time, though it is not clear in what order, or to what extent they intermingled. They are named after objects associated with their culture, hence we have Bowl Food Vessel People, Urn People and Vase Food Vessel People. There are around 1,000 chambered graves, ring-shaped cairns, standing stones, rows and circles of stones left from these times, concentrated in the Boyne Valley; they hint at various rituals and, it has been suggested, at observations of the stars. They are often called 'fairy stones', and the chambered graves have been nicknamed 'Dermot and Grania's bed'.

The Celts

The first arrival of the Celts cannot be precisely dated; a few may have come as early as 900 BC, though the main waves of Celtic invaders occurred between 700 BC and 400 BC. These people had iron weapons and defeated the Beakers, whose legendary magical powers were no defence against the new metal. Known as the **Celts** or **Gaels**, the new invaders had spread from southern Germany, across France, and as far south as Spain. Today everybody in Ireland has pride in the 'Celtic' past: epic tales sing the praises of men and women who were capable of heroic and superhuman deeds, and their beautiful gold jewellery is carefully preserved as proof of their achievements. The Celts brought to Ireland a highly organized social structure, and the La Tène style of decoration (its predominant motif is a spiral or a whorl). Ireland was divided into different clans with three classes: the **free**, who were warriors and owned land and cattle; the **professionals**, such as the jurists, Druids, musicians, storytellers and poets, who could move freely between the petty kingdoms; and, finally, the **slaves**. Every clan had a petty king, who was under the authority of a high king at Tara, Co. Meath.

The Gaels made use of many of the customs and mythology that had existed before their arrival, so their 'Celtic' civilization represented a unique mix. They were also very fortunate, for although they were probably displaced themselves by the expanding **Roman Empire**, once they got to Ireland they were protected to some extent by England, which acted as a buffer state. The Romans never extended their ambitions to conquering Ireland, so the Gaels were able to develop their traditions, unlike Celts elsewhere in Europe. They spent most of their time raiding their neighbours for cattle and women, who were used as live currency. In their religion, the human head was all-important as a symbol of divinity and supernatural power – even when severed from the body it would still retain its power. Warriors used to take the heads of slain enemies and display them in front of their houses. The Gaels also believed firmly in an afterlife, and would lend each other money to be repaid in the next world.

The Arrival of Christianity

Christianity was brought to Ireland in the 5th century AD by **St Patrick**, and quickly became accepted by the kings. **Cormac MacArt**, who ruled in Tara about a century and a half before St Patrick arrived, had already seen the light and told his court of Druids and nobles that the gods they worshipped were only craven wood. The Druids put a curse on him and soon afterwards he choked to death on a salmon bone; just before he died he ordered that he was not to be buried in the tomb of Brugh (Newgrange) but on the sunny east point by the River Rosnaree. When St Patrick lit a fire that signalled the end of Druid worship, legend has it that he was looking down from the Hill of Slane on to Rosnaree. The Christians skilfully reconciled their practices and beliefs with those of the pagans; a famous saying of St Columba was 'Christ is my Druid'. The early Christians seem to have been very ascetic, building their monasteries in wild and inaccessible places. You can still see their beehive-shaped dwellings on **Skellig Michael**, a windswept rocky island off the Kerry coast. The Irish monasteries became renowned for their scholarship throughout Europe, which was submerged in the Dark Ages, and produced beautiful manuscripts such as the famous *Book of Kells*.

The Viking Invasion

The tranquillity of Ireland, 'land of saints and scholars', was brutally interrupted by the arrival of the **Vikings** or **Norsemen**. They were able to penetrate right into Ireland through their skilful use of the rivers and lakes. They struck for the first time in 795, but this was only the start of a 300-year struggle. Much treasure from the palaces and monasteries was plundered, for the buildings had no defences, so the monks built round towers in which to store their precious things at the first sign of trouble. Eventually the Norsemen began to settle down; they founded the first city-ports – Dublin, Wexford and Waterford – and started to trade with the Gaels. Military alliances were made between Celts and Vikings whenever it helped a particular native king in the continuous struggle for the high kingship. After a short period of relative calm another wave of Norsemen invaded and the plundering began again; but **Brian Boru**, who had usurped the high kingship from the O'Connors, defeated the Vikings at Clontarf in 1014 and broke their power permanently. Unfortunately for the Gaelic

people, Brian Boru was murdered by some Vikings in his tent just after the victory at
Clontarf. Havoc and in-fighting became a familiar pattern, as the high kingship was
fought for by the O'Briens, the O'Loughlins (or O'Loghlens) and the O'Connors. The
Gaelic warriors wasted themselves and their people, because no single leader
seemed strong enough to rule without opposition. The next invaders saw that their
opportunity lay in the disunity of the Irish.

The Norman Invasion and Consolidation

In the mid 12th century the Pope gave his blessing to an expedition of **Anglo-Normans**
sent by **Henry II** to Ireland. The Normans were actually invited over by the King of
Leinster, **Dermot MacMurragh**, who had made a bitter enemy of **Tiernan O'Rourke**
of Breffni by running off with his wife, Devorgilla. He also backed the wrong horse in
the high kingship stakes, and the united efforts of the High King Rory O'Connor and
O'Rourke brought about a huge reduction in MacMurragh's kingdom. So he
approached Henry II, offering his oath of fealty in exchange for an invasion force of
men with names such as Fitzhenry, Carew, Fitzgerald and Barry – names you still see
in Irish villages. The Normans were adventurers and good warriors: in 1169 several
Norman nobles decided to try their luck in Ireland, and found it easy to grab huge
tracts of land for themselves. The Gaels had faced so few attacks from outside their
country that they were unprepared for battle – yet although their weapons were
inferior, they had the advantages of greater numbers and a deep knowledge of the
countryside. The Normans had a well-equipped cavalry who rode protected by a
screen of archers. Once they had launched a successful attack, they consolidated their
position by building moats, castles and walled towns. **Strongbow**, one of the most
powerful of the Norman invaders, married MacMurragh's daughter and became his
heir, but his successes and those of the other Norman barons worried Henry II. In 1171
Henry arrived in Ireland with 4,000 men and two objectives: to secure the submission
of the Irish leaders and to impose his authority on his own barons. He achieved both
aims, but the Gaelic lords still went on fighting. In fact, the coming of the Normans
began a military struggle that was to continue over four centuries.

The Bruce Invasion

In 1314 **Robert Bruce of Scotland** decisively defeated English forces at Bannockburn,
and was in a position to try and fulfil his dream of a united Celtic kingdom by putting
his brother **Edward** on the throne in Ireland. At first his invasion was successful, but
he left a trail of destruction. The year 1316 was marked by famine and disease exacerbated
by the war. His dream brought economic and social disaster to Ireland, and when
Edward Bruce was defeated and killed at Dundalk, few of his allies mourned his death.
The Normans' control fluctuated within an area surrounding Dublin known as the
Pale, and they became rather independent of their English overlord; in some cases,
such as the De Burgos (Burkes), they became more Irish than the Irish. In the north
and west the Gaelic lords continued to hold their territories. To do so they imported
Scottish mercenary soldiers, **gallowglasses**, who prolonged the life of the independent
Gaelic kingdoms for more than two centuries after the defeat of Edward Bruce.

The Nine Years' War: Elizabethan Conquest and Settlement

Ever since the Norman invasion, Ireland had been ruined by continual fighting. By the late 16th century, **Queen Elizabeth I** was determined to bring the Irish more firmly under English control, especially the Ulster lords who had so far maintained almost total independence. Elizabeth took over the Irish policy of her father that had never been fully implemented; her government decided that all the Gaelic lords must surrender their lands to the Crown, whereupon they would be regranted immediately. At this time Ulster, today the stronghold of Protestantism, was the most Gaelic and Catholic part of Ireland, and it was from here that the great **Hugh O'Neill** and **Red Hugh O'Donnell** launched a last-ditch struggle against Elizabeth. Initial successes bolstered the rebels' morale. Elizabeth, recognizing the gravity of the situation, sent over her talented favourite soldier, the Earl of Essex. Most of his troops died from disease and guerrilla attacks, and with no reinforcements he had little alternative other than to make a truce with O'Neill. Disgrace and execution were his reward.

In February 1600 Lord Mountjoy arrived in Ireland with 20,000 troops. Risings in Munster were crushed, and with them the aspirations of Connacht and Leinster. The Gaelic chiefs were ruthless in their allegiances. They had hailed O'Neill as Prince of Ireland but now, anticipating defeat, they deserted him. O'Neill's hopes were raised by the long-promised arrival of Spanish troops at Kinsale in 1601, but they only numbered 4,000. When they did do battle against Mountjoy, the Irish were left confused when the Spaniards failed to sally out as arranged.

The Flight of the Earls

O'Neill returned to Ulster on 23 March 1603 and made his submission to Mountjoy, only to learn in Dublin later that Queen Elizabeth had died the very next day. He is said to have wept with rage. Amongst all the nobles, only he might have been able to unite the Irish and beat Elizabeth. O'Neill had his titles and lands returned to him, but the Dublin government, greedy for his property, began to bait him. It took his land at the slightest excuse and forbade him to practise Catholicism; abandoning hope and his followers, he sailed to Europe. This 'Flight of the Earls' took place on 14 September 1607, from the wild and beautiful shores of Lough Swilly. It symbolizes the end of Gaelic leadership and a new period of complete domination by the English. The Irish lords took themselves off to the courts of France and Spain or into the foreign armies. They had spent most of their energies warring among themselves, and at the last moment deserted their country, and left the Irish peasants with no leadership.

The Confederation, Cromwell and the Stuarts

By the 1640s, Ireland was ready for rebellion again – there were plenty of grievances. **James I**, a staunch Protestant, dispossessed many Gaelic and old English families in Ireland because they would not give up Catholicism, and he began the '**plantation**' of the most vehemently Catholic province, Ulster, with Protestant settlers. Previous plantations had not worked because of inclement weather, but James knew the Scots could skip about the bogs as well as the Irish. When **Charles Stuart** came to the throne, many Catholic families hoped that they might be given some religious freedom and retain their estates, but nothing was legally confirmed. In 1633 **Black Tom**, the Earl of Strafford, arrived with the intention of making Ireland a source of profit rather than loss to the king. In his zeal to do so he succeeded in alienating every element in Irish society. His enemies amongst the Puritans in Ireland and England put pressure on the king to recall him and he was eventually executed. English politics became dominated by the dissension between the Roundheads and the Cavaliers and the hopeless Irish took note. Their maxim was 'England's difficulty is Ireland's opportunity'. Charles attempted to deal with the growing unrest in Ireland by giving everybody what they wanted, but he no longer had enough power to see that his laws were carried out. The Gaelic Irish decided to take a chance and rebel; many of them came back from the Continental armies hoping to win back their old lands. In October 1641 a small Gaelic force took over the whole of Ulster and there were widespread uprisings in Leinster. In Ulster, the Gaelic people had been burning for revenge and the new planted families suffered terribly. This cruel treatment has never been forgotten by Ulster Protestants.

The Dublin government was worse than useless at controlling the rebels, who continued to be successful. While the government waited for reinforcements from England, they managed to antagonize the old English, because they made the mistake of presuming that they would be disloyal to the Crown, and so viewed them with suspicion. The old English families decided to throw in their lot with the rebels since they were already considered traitors, but with one condition: a declaration of loyalty from the Gaelic leaders to the (Catholic) English crown, which was now seriously threatened by the Puritans.

The Confederation of Kilkenny

By February 1642 most of Ireland was in rebel hands. The rebels established a provisional government at **Kilkenny**, and Charles began to negotiate with them, hoping to gain their support against the Puritans. Things were too good to last. The destructive factors that have ruined many Irish uprisings, before and since, came into play: personal jealousy and religion. The old English were loyal to the king and wanted a swift end to the war; the Gaelic Irish were only interested in retrieving their long-lost lands and were ready to fight to the bitter end. This disunity was exacerbated by the rivalry between the Gaelic commander, **Owen Roe O'Neill**, and the commander of the old English army, **Thomas Preston**. In October 1645 the Papal Nuncio arrived and the unity of the Confederates was further split: he and O'Neill took an intransigent stand over the position of the Catholic Church, to which Charles I could not agree.

The rebels won a magnificent victory over the Puritan General Munro at Benburb, but O'Neill did not follow it up. The confederates, torn by disunity and rivalry, let opportunities slip past and they lost the initiative. Eventually they did decide to support the king and end their Kilkenny government, but by this time Charles I had been beheaded and his son had fled into exile. The Royalists were defeated at Rathmines in 1649 and the way was left clear for the Puritan leader, **Cromwell**, who landed in Dublin soon after. Cromwell came to Ireland determined to break the Royalists, break the Gaelic Irish, and to avenge the events of 1641 in Ulster. He started his campaign with the

Siege of Drogheda, and there are the most gruesome accounts of his methods. When his troops burst into the town they put Royalists, women, children and priests to the sword; 3,552 dead were counted, while Cromwell only lost 64 men. Catholics curse Cromwell to this day. The same butchery marked the taking of Wexford. Unsurprisingly, he broke the spirit of resistance by such methods and there were widespread defections from the Royalists' side. Owen Roe O'Neill might have been able to rally the Irish but he died suddenly. Cromwell's campaign only lasted seven months, but he took all the towns except Galway and Waterford. These he left to his lieutenants.

By 1652 the whole country was subdued, and Cromwell encouraged all the Irish fighting men to leave by granting them amnesty if they fled overseas. The alternative to exile was, for many families, something that turned out to be even worse: compulsory removal to Connacht and County Clare. Some families had been neutral during all the years of fighting, but that was never taken into account. Cromwell was determined that anyone suspect should go 'to Hell or to Connacht'. The government had lots of land to play with after that. First of all they paid off 'the adventurers', men who had lent them money back in 1642. Next, the Roundhead soldiers, who had not been paid their salaries for years, were granted Irish land instead. In this manner, the Cromwellian Settlement parcelled out even more land to speculators, foreigners and rogues.

Stuart and Orange

After the **Restoration of the Monarchy** in 1660, the Catholics in Ireland hoped for toleration and rewards for their loyalty to the Stuart cause. They felt threatened by the fast-expanding Protestant community, but Charles did not restore many Catholic estates because he had to keep in with the ex-Cromwellian supporters, although Catholics were given a limited amount of toleration. However, with the succession of Charles' brother **James II**, a Catholic, in 1685 things began to brighten up. In Ireland, the Catholic Earl of Tyrconnell became commander of the army and, later, chief governor. By 1688 Roman Catholics were dominant in the army, the administration, the judiciary and the town corporations, and by the end of the year Protestant power in Ireland was seriously weakened. James frightened all those Protestants in England who had benefited from Catholic estates. They began to panic when he introduced sweeping acts of toleration for all religions. His attempts to re-establish the Catholic Church alienated the country to such a great extent that the Protestant aristocracy eventually invited **William of Orange** over to England in November 1688 to relieve his father-in-law of his throne. James fled to France but soon left for Ireland, a natural base for the launch of his counter-attack. By the date of his arrival in March 1689, only Enniskillen and Londonderry were in Protestant hands.

The Siege of Londonderry and Battle of the Boyne

The subjugation of the Protestant city of Londonderry was James' first aim. In a famous incident celebrated in Orange songs, a group of apprentice boys shut the city gates to the Jacobite (English Catholic) army. So began the famous **Siege of Londonderry**. The townspeople proved unbreakable, even though food supplies ran very low and they were reduced to eating rats and mice, and chewing old bits of leather. Many died of starvation during the 15 weeks of the siege, but just as they were about to give in, the food ship *Mountjoy* forced its way through a great boom built across the Foyle. This military and psychological victory was of enormous significance in the campaign. When William himself arrived at Carrickfergus in June 1690, James confronted him at the Boyne. William of Orange had an army of about 36,000, comprised of English, Scots, Dutch, Danes, Germans and Huguenots (French Protestants), against James' army of about 25,000, made up of Irish and French. William triumphed, and James deserted the battlefield and left Ireland in haste.

In the **Battle of the Boyne** James seems to have completely lost his nerve. The Jacobite forces had to retreat west of the Shannon to Limerick, and William promptly laid siege to it. So weak were its walls that it is said they could be breached with roasted apples. The Catholic defence of Limerick was as heroic as that of Londonderry. Patrick Sarsfield slipped out with a few followers, intercepted William's siege train and destroyed it. William then gave up and departed for England, leaving Ginkel in charge. The next year the French King Louis XIV sent over supplies and men to fuel the Jacobite cause, hoping to divert William in Ireland for a little longer. The Jacobite leader St Ruth, who landed with them, proved a disaster for the Irish; Sarsfield would have been a better choice. Ginkel took Athlone and Aughrim in June and July of 1691, after two battles that gave rise to stories of Jacobite courage that have inspired patriot poets and musicians. The last hope of the Catholic Irish was now Limerick.

The Treaty of Limerick

Sarsfield skilfully gathered together what Jacobite troops were left and got them back to Limerick. (St Ruth had been killed by a cannonball and, rather typically, had appointed no second-in-command.) Ginkel tried to storm the town from both sides, but still Limerick held out and he began to negotiate with Sarsfield. Honourable terms were made for the Jacobites, and Sarsfield signed the famous **Treaty of Limerick** in October 1691. The next day a French fleet arrived and anchored off the Shannon estuary, but Sarsfield stood by the Treaty that seemed to guarantee quite a lot: Catholics were to have the same rights as they had had under Charles II and any Catholic estates that had been registered in 1662 were to be handed back; Catholics were to be allowed free access to the bar, bench, army and parliament; and Sarsfield was to be given a safe passage to the Continent with his troops. But the Treaty was not honoured, except for the last clause that got all the fighting men out of the country. This was one of the dirtiest tricks the English played; to be fair to William of Orange he wanted the treaty to be enforced, but being new and unsure of his support he complied with the treachery. Eleven thousand Irish Jacobites sailed away to join the French army, forming the Irish Brigade. Over the years many came to join them from Ireland, and were remembered in their native land as the **Wild Geese**.

The Orange/Stuart war still lives vividly in the imagination of the people of Ireland. The Siege of Londonderry has become a sign of Protestant determination: 'no surrender 1690' is scrawled, usually in bright red paint, on the walls and street corners of Loyalist areas in Northern Ireland. The Battle of the Boyne is remembered in a similar way.

The Penal Laws

The defeat of the Catholic cause was followed by more confiscation of land, and the **Penal Laws**. A bargain had been struck with the Protestant 'planters', who were allowed to keep a monopoly of political power and most of the land, in return for acting as a British garrison to keep the peace and prevent the Catholics from gaining any power. To do this they passed a series of degrading laws, which were briefly as follows: no Catholic could purchase freehold land; any son of a Catholic, turning Protestant, could turn his parents off their estate; families who stayed Catholic had their property equally parcelled out amongst all the children, so that any large estates soon became uneconomic holdings; all the Catholics were made to pay a tithe towards the upkeep of the Anglican Church; all priests were banished; no Catholic schools were allowed and spies were set amongst the peasants to report on 'hedge schools', a form of quite sophisticated schooling that had sprung up (priests on the run taught at these schools and celebrated Mass); a Catholic could not hold a commission in the army, enter a profession or even own a horse that was worth more than £5. These anti-religious laws had the opposite effect to that intended – Catholicism took on a new lease of life in Ireland. In addition, **economic laws** were introduced that put heavy taxes on anything that Ireland produced – cloth, wool, glass and cattle – so that the country could not compete with England. The trading regulations were particularly disadvantageous to the non-conformist Ulster Protestants, and many of them left.

Gradually, however, things began to relax. The Catholics had been well and truly squashed. The Protestants began to build themselves grand and beautiful houses, leaving the damp and draughty towerhouses to decay. Irish squires were famous for their hard drinking; the expression 'plastered' comes from the story of a guest who was so well wined and dined at a neighbour's housewarming party that he fell asleep against a newly plastered wall. He woke up next morning to find that his scalp and hair had hardened into the wall.

As the 18th century progressed, however, there were signs of aggression amongst the peasantry; agrarian secret societies were formed with names such as the **White Boys,** the **Hearts of Oak,** and the **Molly Maguires**. They were very brutal, meting out rough justice to tenants and landlords alike. If any peasant paid rent to an unfair landlord, he was likely to be intimidated or have his farm burnt down. In Ulster, peasant movements were dominated by sectarian land disputes. The Catholics were called the **Defenders** and the Protestant groups the **Peep-O'Day Boys**. In the 1770s, the Penal Laws were relaxed a little; Catholics were allowed to bid for land, and they incensed the Protestants by bidding higher. After a particularly bad fight between the two sides that the Protestants won, the **Orange Order** was founded in 1795. A typical oath of one of the early clubs was, 'To the glorious, pious and immortal memory of the great and good King William, not forgetting Oliver Cromwell, who assisted in redeeming us from popery, slavery, arbitrary power, brass money and wooden shoes.'

The **American War of Independence** broke out in 1775 and Ireland found itself undefended. There were fears of an invasion by France or Spain, and a general feeling that some sort of defence force ought to be put in place. The **Volunteers** were organized with officers from the Protestant landowning class. As the fears of invasion receded, however, these turned their considerable muscle to the cause of political reform, and the British began to fear that they might follow the example of the American colonies. Irish Protestants and Catholics alike watched the war with approval, particularly since many of the rebel Americans were of Ulster–Scots blood. The landowners had their own parliament in Dublin, but all important matters were dealt with by London.

A group of influential landowners began to think that Ireland would be much better off with an independent Irish parliament. In 1783, the British government, influenced by the eloquence of the great speaker **Henry Grattan**, acknowledged the right of Ireland to be bound only by laws made by the King and the Irish parliament. Trade, industry and agriculture began to flourish, and the worst of the Penal Laws were repealed or relaxed.

Grattan's Parliament

Grattan's Parliament was really an oligarchy of landowners, but at least these understood the problems of the economy and tried to bring a more liberal spirit into dealings with Catholics and dissenters. Grattan wanted complete Catholic emancipation, but for that the Irish had to wait. Trinity College was made accessible to those of all religious persuasions, though Catholics were forbidden by their bishops to go there. The great Catholic Seminary at Maynooth was founded and endowed with money and land from the Protestant aristocrats, who were worried that the priests educated at Douai might bring back with them some of those frightening ideas of liberty and equality floating around France. Dissenters were given equal rights with the Established Church at this time.

Dublin was now a handsome Georgian city, a centre for the arts, science and society. To pay for all this pleasure, landowners began to sublet their estates to land-hungry tenants. In the early 1790s, fear and anger swept through Europe in the form of the French Revolution, and the governments of Europe, whether Catholic or Protestant, drew nearer together in mutual fear. Many who at first were delighted with the revolution in France became disgusted by the brutality of its methods. The Irish government disbanded the Volunteers and got together a militia and part-time force of yeomanry. It was nervous of a French invasion and increasingly of a middle-class organization, the 'United Irishmen', who were sick of a government that only spoke for a tiny proportion of the population.

Wolfe Tone and the United Irishmen

The aim of the United Irishmen was to throw open the Irish parliament to all Irishmen, irrespective of their rank or religion. Many United Irishmen were from Ulster non-conformist backgrounds. Initially, the movement was supposed to be non-violent, but when war broke out between England and France, all radical societies were forced to go underground. No liberal ideas could be tolerated during the war effort. **Wolfe Tone** was a Dublin lawyer and a prominent United Irishman; he crossed over to France to try and persuade the French Directory to help.

The Protestant Wind

Wolfe Tone brilliantly argued a case for French intervention and, on the night of 16 December 1796, the last great French invasion force to set sail for the British Isles slipped past the British squadron blockading Brest, anchoring off Bantry Bay five days later. They waited for a clear, calm day for the frigate carrying the Commander-in-Chief to arrive; then the wind changed and blew from the east, remembered in all the songs as a 'Protestant Wind'. The fleet endured the storm for three days, then the ships cut cable and headed back for France. Only Wolfe Tone and his ship, *The Indomitable*, remained and, as Tone put it, 'England had not such an escape since the Armada'.

Meanwhile, in the Irish countryside, increasingly brutal attempts were made by the militia and the yeomanry to stamp out sedition. In Ulster, where the United Irishmen were strong, efforts were made to set the United Irishmen against the Orangemen, many of whom had joined the yeomanry. This continual pressure forced the society to plan rebellion. However, government spies had infiltrated its ranks, and two months before the proposed date many of the leaders were arrested. By this time many Irish peasants had joined the United Irishmen, inspired by the heady doctrine of Tom Paine's *Rights of Man*. The increased power of the Irish parliament had not meant more freedom for them – on the contrary the heretics and alien landlords now seemed to have more power to persecute them in the forms of tithes and taxes. Yet the Gaelic-speaking peasants had little in common with the middle-class agitators either, and their anger was even more explosive.

The 1798 Rebellion

In May 1798 the rebellion broke out. The United Irish leaders had planned a rebellion believing they could count on an army of more than 250,000. However, the absence of leadership and careful planning resulted in local uprisings with no central support; even those that achieved some success were quickly crushed. In Ulster there were two main risings, under **McCracken** and **Munro.** They both enjoyed brief success, during which time the rebels treated any Loyalist prisoners well – a marked contrast to what had happened in other counties. However, the sectarian battles between the Peep-O'Day Boys had already soured the trust of the Catholics, and many of them did not turn up to help the mixed bunch of United Irishmen. Poor Wolfe Tone and others who had started the society with such hopes for affectionate brotherhood saw their ideals drowned in a sea of blood.

Nugent, commander of the government forces in Ulster, appealed to the rebels who had property to lose, especially in the rich eastern counties, and proclaimed a general amnesty if the County Antrim rebels gave up their arms. The rebels of County Down did not get off so humanely: when they had been routed and shot down, they were left unburied in the streets for the pigs to eat. McCracken and Munro were executed.

The Races of Castlebar

As the war between France and England became more embittered, Wolfe Tone succeeded in raising another invasion force. On 22 August 1798, the French **General Humbert** arrived in Killala Bay with 1,000 men and more arms for the rebels, although most of them had dispersed. Humbert captured Ballina and routed 6,000 loyalist troops in a charge called the 'Races of Castlebar'. But there were not enough rebels, and Humbert had to accept honourable terms of surrender in September. Only a few weeks later, another French expedition arrived with Tone on board and entered Lough Swilly. It was overcome by some British frigates, and Wolfe Tone was captured. He appeared before a court martial wearing a French uniform and carrying a cockade. The only favour he asked was the right to be shot, which was refused, whereupon he cut his own throat with a penknife and lingered in agony for seven days.

In the space of three weeks 30,000 people, mostly peasants armed with pitchforks and pikes, women and children, were ruthlessly cut down or shot. The rebellion of 1798 was one of the most tragic and violent events in Irish history, horrifying people to such an extent that they desperately began to search for ways of bringing about change in a non-violent way. Ideas of political and religious equality were totally discredited, as a result of the deaths and destruction of property. The British government found that an independent parliament was an embarrassment to them, especially since the 'Protestant garrison' had not been able to put down the peasant rising without their assistance.

The Union

William Pitt ('Pitt the Younger'), the British Prime Minister, decided that union between Great Britain and Ireland was the only answer. First he had to bribe the Protestants to give up their power; many earldoms date from this time. Then the **Act of Union** was passed, with promises of Catholic emancipation for the majority. Pitt really did want to give them equality, for he saw that it was a necessary move if he wished to make Ireland relatively content.

Unfortunately Pitt was pushed out of government, and **King George III** lent his considerable influence to those who were opposed to Catholic emancipation: he claimed that the idea of it drove him mad. The Union did not solve any problems, as the Catholics felt bitterly let down and the temporary Home Rule of Grattan's Parliament was looked back upon as an example. Irreconcilable nationalism was still alive and kicking. Union with England was disadvantageous to Ireland in the areas of industry and trade, and many poorer Protestants were discontented – although from now on the Ulster non-conformists supported the Union, for many had been disillusioned by the vengeance exacted on Protestants by the Catholic peasantry. The terms of the 1801 Act were never thought of as final in Ireland, although the English failed to understand this.

The Liberator: Daniel O'Connell

Catholics still could not sit in parliament or hold important state offices or senior judicial, military or civil service posts. Finally, they found a champion among themselves: a Catholic lawyer called **Daniel O'Connell**, who believed that 'no political change is worth the shedding of a single drop of human blood'. O'Connell founded the **Catholic Association** that, among other things, represented the interests of the tenant farmers. Association membership was a penny a month, and brought in a huge fighting fund. Most important of all, the Catholic priests supported him, and soon there were branches of the association everywhere. A turning point for Irish history and the fortunes of Daniel O'Connell came with the Clare election in 1828, when the association showed its strength. O'Connell had an overwhelming victory against the government candidate when all the 40-shilling freeholders (the Catholic electorate) voted for him. The whole country was aflame: they wanted Daniel at Westminster. **Wellington**, the prime minister of the day, was forced to give in, and the **Emancipation Bill** was passed in April 1829. But this was not a gesture of conciliation, for at the same time he raised the voting qualification from 40 shillings to a massive £10. Protestant fears had been raised by the power of such a mass movement, for tenant farmers had dared to vote in opposition to their landlords, even though voting was public. To English Catholics, Daniel was also a 'Liberator'.

For 12 years O'Connell supported the Whig Government and built up a disciplined Irish party whose co-operation was essential to any government majority. He was then able to press for some very necessary reforms, and when the viceroy and his secretary were sympathetic, much was achieved. However, with the return of the Conservatives in 1840, O'Connell decided it was time to launch another popular agitation campaign, this time for the repeal of the Union. His mass-meetings became 'monster meetings', each attended by well in excess of 100,000 people. The government refused to listen on this issue; British public opinion was firmly against it and in Ulster there was a distinct lack of enthusiasm. Daniel O'Connell arranged to have one of his biggest meetings yet, at Clontarf, where Brian Boru had defeated the Vikings. The Government banned it and O'Connell, unwilling to risk violence, called it off. He himself was arrested for conspiracy and sentenced by just the sort of packed jury he had been trying to abolish. Luckily for him, the House of Lords was less frightened and more just; they set aside his sentence. But by then O'Connell's influence had begun to fade, and some Irish began to look to violence to achieve their aims.

The Young Irelanders

Within the Repeal Association was a group of young men who called themselves the **Young Irelanders**. They had founded *The Nation* newspaper to help O'Connell, but they soon began to move in a different direction. They believed that culturally and historically Ireland was independent of England, and fed their enthusiasm on the painful memories of 1798, composing heroic poetry that they set to old ballad tunes. They were useless at practical politics and did not have the support of the clergy. In 1848 they responded to the spontaneous and romantic uprisings in Europe with one of their own. It was a dismal failure and alienated many people who had been in favour of the Repeal of the Union. The Nationalist movement was not to become respectable again until 1870.

The Great Hunger

The diet of an ordinary Irish person consisted of six pounds of potatoes and a pint of milk a day, and they lived in miserable conditions. The Cromwellian and Williamite plantations, together with the effect of the Penal Laws, left the Catholics with only five percent of the land. Except in the North, where a thriving linen industry had grown up, people had to make their living from farming. Absentee landlords became more of a problem after the Union, their agents greedier and their rent demands even higher. From 1845 to 1849 the **potato blight** struck, with tragic results.

The population of Ireland, as in the rest of Europe, had begun to rise quickly in the late 18th century, perhaps because the potato could feed large families on small plots of land. The most deprived and populated area of Ireland was the west, where the potato was the only crop that would grow; it alone sustained the fragile equilibrium of large families on tiny holdings. The scene was set for agricultural and social catastrophe. As the blighted potatoes rotted in the ground, people ate cabbage, wild vegetables, turnips and even grass, but these could not supply more than a few meals. Gradually, thousands of people began to die of starvation, typhus fever, relapsing fever and dysentery. Even so, corn and cattle were still leaving the country; nothing was done that might interfere with the principle of free trade and private enterprise. The government's attitude was rigid, though they did allow maize in – a crop nobody had any vested interest in. Food distribution centres were set up, and some relief work was paid for by the government. But this was not very sensible sort of work – mostly digging holes only to fill them in again. Something constructive, such as laying a network of railway lines, might have interfered with private enterprise. Out of a population of 8.5 million, 1 million died and another 1 million emigrated.

Emigration

The Irish had been emigrating for years, first to escape persecution by fleeing to the Continent, and then as seasonal labour for the English harvests. The Ulster Scots had set the first pattern of emigration to America. They had found that Ireland was not the promised land, after being lured over there by grants of land and low rents. Bad harvests, religious discrimination and high rents sent them off at the rate of 4,000 a year. Not many Catholics followed, for there were still restrictions on Catholic emigration. Many Irish went to Australia as convicts or free settlers. But the heaviest years of emigration were just after the famine, especially to the USA. People travelled under appalling conditions in boats called 'coffin ships'. It took six to eight weeks to get to America in those overcrowded and disease-ridden conditions. By 1847 nearly a quarter of a million were emigrating annually.

Irish priests followed their flocks out to America and Australia and founded churches wherever they were needed, so a distinct Irish Catholic Church grew up. Such an influx of starving, diseased Irish Catholics was quite another thing to the steady flow of a few thousand Ulster Scots, and initially a lot of people were prejudiced against them. Most of the emigrants left Ireland loathing the British in Ireland. Their children grew up with the same hatred, and sometimes became more anti-British than the Irish left in Ireland. This bitterness was soon transformed into political activity, aided by the Young Irelanders who had fled to America. Many of the emigrants had come from the west where the Gaelic language and culture survived relatively undisturbed. The rest of Ireland, especially the east, was quite anglicized and became more so with the development of education and transport.

America and Irish Politics

In 1858, **James Stephens** founded a secret movement in Ireland called the **Irish Republican Brotherhood** (IRB). Shortly afterwards, he and **John O'Mahony**, a comrade from the uprising of 1848 who had fled to America, reorganized the Irish Catholics in America into a twin movement called the **Fenian Brotherhood**. The Fenians called themselves after the legendary Fianna Warriors and were dedicated to the principle of Republicanism. Because of the need for secrecy, the IRB was generally known at this time under the name of the Fenians, the American part of the organization, which was able to function openly. In Ireland, aided by money from America, the Fenians started up a newspaper, *The Irish People*, which was aimed at the urban worker. When the American Civil War was over, many Irish-American soldiers came over to help the Fenians in Ireland, although their military operations were always dismal failures. But Fenianism remained a potent force. The unfortunate execution of Allen, Larkin and O'Brien, who became known as the Manchester Martyrs, in England in 1867 became further powerful propaganda for the Fenian cause.

John Devoy in America and **Michael Davitt** of the **Irish Land League** were imaginative enough to see that violence was not the only way to fight high rents. They made a loose alliance with **Charles Stewart Parnell**, the leader of the **Irish Party** in the House of Commons. John Devoy was head of **Clan na Gael**, an organization that cloaked Fenianism. In America, through the Fenians, Parnell was able to collect money for the land agitators. John Devoy gave money and moral support to the revolutionaries in their fight for independence. Clan na Gael created good propaganda for the Nationalists and, between the death of Parnell and the rise of **Sinn Féin** (the new Nationalist party), did everything it could to drive a wedge between the USA and England, and to keep the States neutral during the First World War. It even acted as an intermediary between Germany and the IRB, who were negotiating for guns.

The Irish-Americans played such an important part in Irish politics that it is worth jumping forward in time for a moment to recount subsequent events. In 1918 **Éamon de Valera**, born in America, was elected by Sinn Féin as head of a provisional government. He came to America with high hopes during the War of Independence in Ireland. He wanted two things: political recognition from the government for Dáil Éireann – the Irish parliament set up in Dublin in 1919 – and money. He failed in his first aim: he was rebuffed by President Wilson, who was himself of Ulster–Scots blood, and very proud of it too. However, De Valera got plenty of money – $6 million, in the form of a loan – but he fell out with Devoy. He founded a rival organization called the **American Association for the Recognition of the Irish Republic** (AARIA). When Ireland split over the solution of partition and there was a civil war, the Republicans, who rejected the partition, were supported by the AARIA, whilst the Free Staters had Devoy and Clan na Gael behind them. The leading spirit of the AARIA was **Joseph McGarrity**, who later broke with De Valera when he began to act against the IRA. His group and their successors continued to give financial support to the IRA during the troubles in Northern Ireland.

Now to return to the efforts of the British government to forestall the repeal of the Union, and the efforts of various organizations to bring it about.

Tenants' Rights and the Land War

The British Government was blamed by many in Ireland for the tragic extent of the famine, but the government was blind to the lessons it should have taught them. The famine had only intensified the land war, and the 1829 Act simply enabled the impoverished landlords to sell their estates, which the peasants had no money to buy. So the speculators moved in, seized opportunities for further evictions and increased the rents. Tenant resistance smouldered, stimulated by the horrors of the famine. Michael Davitt organized the resistance into the **National Land League**, with the support of Parnell, the leader of the Irish Party in the House of Commons. In the ensuing **Land War** (1879–82), a new word was added to the English language – 'boycott'. The peasants decided not to help an evicting landlord with his crops and he had to import some loyal Orangemen from Ulster to gather in the harvest. The offending landlord was a Captain Boycott. The tenants wanted the same rights that tenants had in Ulster and fair rent, fixity of tenure and freedom to sell at the market value. They also wanted a more even distribution of the land – at that time three percent of the population owned 95 percent of the land.

Behind all the agitation at this time, and all the obstruction that the Irish Party caused in parliament, was a desire for the repeal of the Union. But the politicians saw the problem as religion, over-population, famine – anything but nationalism. It did not enter English heads that the Irish might not want to be part of Britain – with the Union, in their eyes, Irishmen were on an equal footing with the rest of Great Britain; they were part of the Empire. The Union was also a security against foreign attack and had to stay. Only one man said anything sensible on the subject and he was not listened to. **J. S. Mill** said that England was the worst qualified to govern the Irish, because English traditions were not applicable in Ireland. England was firmly *laissez-faire* in her economic policies, but Ireland needed economic interference from the government. This the English politicians had resolutely refused to do during and after the famine. **Gladstone** and other Liberals were aware of the discontent. They tried to take the sting out of Irish nationalism by dealing with the problems individually, believing that then the nationalist grievance would disappear.

Killing Home Rule with Kindness

One of the first things to be dealt with was religion, for that could not be kept out of politics. The Protestant Ascendancy still monopolized powerful positions, despite Catholic emancipation. There may have been no legal barriers any more, but there were some unofficial ones. The Anglican Church of Ireland remained the Established Church until 1869, and until then the Irish peasants had to pay tithes to it. The Catholic hierarchy wanted state-supported Catholic education, but the government attempted to have inter-denominational schools and universities. This never satisfied the Catholic Church, and consequently, much later on, it supported the illegal nationalist organizations. Unfortunately, the government was unwilling to establish the Catholic Church in Ireland as they would have had problems with the Protestants in Ulster, so although the Catholic Church had consolidated its position, it was not conciliated.

The distress of the peasant farmers had, by this time, become identified with nationalism, so the government set out to solve the economic problems, thinking that this would shatter the nationalists. But they acted too late. Only in 1881 were the demands of the tenants met. Large amounts of money were made available to tenants to buy up their holdings and, by 1916, 64 percent of the population owned land. (Many of these new owners had the same surnames as those dispossessed back in the 17th century.) But Britain was remembered not for these Land Acts, generous as they were, but for the Coercion and Crime Acts that the minister for Ireland, **Balfour**, brought in to try to control the unrest and anarchy that existed in some parts of the country. The **Land Purchase Acts** took away the individual oppressor and left only the government against whom to focus discontent. The peasants had been given more independence and the landlords were virtually destroyed, therefore the Union became even more precarious. The Nationalists could not be bought off.

Home Rule for Ireland?

Parnell forced the government to listen, often holding a balance of power in the House of Commons, and for a while he rallied the whole Nationalist movement behind his aggressive leadership. The bait of universal suffrage was enough for the Fenians to try to overthrow the Union from within. The **Secret Ballot Act** in 1872 made this even more attractive than abortive rebellions. But the **Home Rule League** did not succeed, even though Gladstone and the Liberals, in Opposition at that time, had promised to support it. Parnell's aggressive tactics alienated many Englishmen, and his Protestant origins upset some of the Catholic hierarchy, who thought he should have concentrated a little more on pushing the Catholic university they wanted. Also, his affair with Kitty O'Shea and involvement in a divorce case shocked many Victorians and non-conformists in the Liberal Party. They demanded that Parnell be dropped from the leadership of the Irish Party, and when the Catholic hierarchy heard this, they also began to openly scold 'the named adulterer' and turned their congregations against him.

Another reason for the failure of the Home Rule Bill was that the mainly Protestant and industrial North of Ireland had no wish to join the South. The North thought it would be overtaxed to subsidize the relatively backward, agrarian South, and the Protestants feared being swamped by the Catholics. Their fear produced in them a siege mentality; Parnell's divorce case was like a gift from heaven, giving the Protestants a reprieve. English opinion was still against Home Rule, and it was only because the Irish Party had made a deal with the Liberals that there was any hope of their succeeding. With the fall of Parnell, the Irish Party split and lost much of its importance.

Parnell's fall in 1891 and the failure of the 1893 Home Rule Bill initiated a resurgence of revolutionary nationalism. The younger generation was shocked by the way the Catholic Church within Ireland condemned Parnell over the O'Shea case. And, as the moral authority of the Church was cast aside, so was one of the barriers to violence. Parnell's failure to work things out through Parliament seemed to indicate that only violence would work. Young people started to join the Irish Republican Brotherhood, and even the Church began to show more sympathy, because at least nationalism was preferable to the atheistic socialism that was creeping into Dublin.

Gaelic Cultural Renaissance

There was a new mood in Ireland at the end of the 19th century. The people were proud of being Irish and of their cultural achievements. Unfortunately only 14 percent of the population spoke the Gaelic language (the famine and emigration that followed had seriously weakened its hold); English was taught in schools, knowledge of it led to better jobs and opportunities, and Irish music and poetry were neglected except by a few intellectuals. However, it was in the stories of Ireland's past greatness, her legends and customs, that many diverse groups found a common ground. In 1884 the **Gaelic Athletic Association** started to revive the national game, hurling. In 1893 the **Gaelic League** was formed. Its president was **Douglas Hyde**, who campaigned successfully for the return of Gaelic lessons to schools and Gaelic as a qualification for entry to the new universities. He never wanted the League to be a sectarian or political force, but it did provide a link between the conservative Catholic Church and the Fenians and Irish Nationalists. 'The Holy Island of St Patrick' developed an ideal: that of the Catholic, devout, temperate, clean-living Irishman. The Gaelic League and the Gaelic Athletic Association were used by the IRB as sounding boards or recruiting grounds for membership.

The Liberals returned to power in 1906 and things began to look brighter for Home Rule. In 1910 **John Redmond** led the Irish Party and held the balance of power between the Liberals and the Conservatives. In 1914 Asquith's **Home Rule Bill** was passed, although it was suspended for the duration of the First World War. But six years later Ireland was in the middle of a war of independence and the initiative had passed from the British into the hands of the revolutionary nationalists. This happened because the British Government had left Home Rule too late; the time lag between when it was passed and when it actually might be implemented gave the Irish public time to criticize it and see its limitations. The nationalists began to despair of ever finding a parliamentary solution, for the British could now not force the North into Home Rule and were shutting their eyes to the gun-running which had been going on since the formation of the Ulster Volunteers (*see* below).

The Irish people were rather lukewarm about organizations such as the IRB and its associated, new **Sinn Féin** Party, founded by Arthur Griffith. In fact, military recruitment, relative prosperity and the nominal achievement of Home Rule brought Ireland and the rest of Britain closer together during the War. The IRB's military council wanted to do something to stem the fragmentation of their movement. An event on Easter Monday in 1916 meant all was 'changed utterly'. (W.B. Yeats).

Easter Rebellion 1916

Plans for a national rising with German support were made. The support did not arrive but, despite the confusion, the IRB leaders were determined that the rising should go ahead in Dublin. It happened very quickly – suddenly the tricolour of a new Irish Republic was flying from the General Post Office in Dublin. Two thousand Irish Nationalist volunteers, led by **Patrick Pearse** of the IRB, stood against the reinforcements sent from England and then surrendered about a week later. People were horrified at first by the waste of life, but then the British played into the hands of Patrick Pearse.

All 14 leaders were executed after secret trials. The timing of the uprising was no coincidence. Pearse and the others wanted it to be a blood sacrifice in order to breathe new life into the nationalist cause.

The executions happened before there could be any backbiting as to why the whole thing had been a muddle. Suddenly they were dead, and pity for them grew into open sympathy for what they had been trying to achieve. The Catholic Church was trapped in the emotional wave that advocated revolution. The party that gained from this swing was **Sinn Féin**; it was pledged to non-violent nationalism and was the public front of the IRB. John Redmond, the leader of the Irish Party at Westminster, had urged everybody to forget their differences with England and fight the common enemy, Germany, but the Irish Nationalists, who were negotiating with the Germans, saw things in a very different light. Many Irishmen did go and fight for Britain: approximately 200,000 men enlisted, but the feeling grew that Redmond was prepared to compromise over Home Rule and shelve it until it suited the British. Sinn Féin, under the influence of American-born Éamon de Valera, set out to mobilize popular support through propaganda and electioneering.

When conscription was extended to Ireland in 1918, even more people decided that Sinn Féin was the only party that could speak for them. It won all the Irish seats bar six. Redmond's party was finished. The only problem was that 44 of the Sinn Féin members were in English jails; those that were not met in Mansion House and set up their own Dáil Éireann. Éamon de Valera made an audacious escape from Lincoln prison and was elected the first President of the Irish Republic in 1919. The Irish Volunteers became the **Irish Republican Army**, and war was declared on Britain.

The North

In the North a leader had been found to defend the Union in Dublin-born **Edward Carson**. A leading barrister in London (he cross-examined Oscar Wilde in that notorious lawsuit), he was openly supported by the Conservatives in England. In 1912, as Home Rule was discussed in Parliament, a solemn **Covenant of Resistance to Home Rule** was signed by hundreds of thousands of Northern Unionists. The **Ulster Volunteers** were formed, and pledged to use all means possible to not come under an Irish parliament in Dublin. After the Easter rising of 1916, Carson was assured by **Lloyd George** that the six northeastern counties could be permanently excluded from the Home Rule Bill of 1914. When the **War of Independence** broke out in the South, the British offered them partition with their own parliament whilst remaining within Britain. Today they still feel their ties are with a liberal Britain, not the Catholic South. (Remember that, until recently, in the Republic there was no divorce, limited contraception, and mixed marriages were discouraged, while the Welfare State is still comparatively undeveloped.)

The War of Independence

The British Government had been caught out by the Dáil's Declaration of Independence. The British were busy trying to negotiate a peace treaty at Versailles, and the Americans made it clear that they sympathized with the Irish. Ammunition raids, bombing, burning and shooting began in Ireland, mainly against the Irish

Constabulary. The British Government waited until the Versailles Conference had come to an end and then fought back. The **Black and Tans** were sent over to reinforce the police, and Lloyd George tried to play it down as a police situation. Their methods were notoriously brutal and it seemed that their reprisals were more vicious than the IRA incidents that had provoked them. It became a war of retaliation. **Michael Collins** was in charge of military affairs for the IRA; he waged a vicious, well-thought-out campaign against the Black and Tans. By July 1921 a truce was declared because the British public wanted to reach a compromise. In October an Irish delegation, which included Griffith and Collins, went to London to negotiate with Lloyd George. They signed a treaty that approved the setting up of an Irish Free State with Dominion status, similar to Canada. The British were mainly concerned with the security aspect and they made two stipulations; that all Irish legislators take an oath of allegiance to the Crown and that the British Navy could use certain Irish ports, Treaty ports.

Civil War

The Republicans (or anti-treaty side) in the Dáil were furious. They regarded it as a sell-out. They did not like the oath, or the acceptance of a divided Ireland. Michael Collins saw it as a chance for 'freedom to achieve freedom' and when it came to the debate on it in the Dáil, the majority voted in favour of the treaty. De Valera was against, and, as head of the Dáil, he resigned; **Arthur Griffith** succeeded him. In June, when the country accepted the treaty, civil war began. The split in the Dáil had produced a corresponding split in the IRA; part of it broke away and began violent raids into the North. The remainder of the IRA was reorganized by Michael Collins into the Free State Army. When he was assassinated, a man just as talented took over, **Kevin O'Higgins**. This period is remembered as the **War of Brothers**, and it was bitter and destructive. Men who had fought together against the Black and Tans shot each other down. Finally, the Republicans were ready to sue for peace. De Valera, who had not actively taken part in the fighting but had supported the Republicans, ordered a ceasefire. The bitterness and horror of the Civil War has coloured attitudes to this very day. The differences between the two main parties, **Fine Gael** (pro-treaty) and **Fianna Fáil** (anti-treaty), are historical rather than political, although perhaps in foreign policy Fianna Fáil has taken a more anti-British line. Fine Gael held power for the first 10 years and concentrated on building the 26-county state into something credible and strong. In 1926 De Valera broke with Sinn Féin because they still saw the Dáil and the government in power as usurpers, as bad as the British, and refused to take up their seats. De Valera, the master pragmatist, founded his own party, Fianna Fáil; the new state wanted a change, and in 1932 he formed a government. He soon made it clear that Ireland was not going to keep the oath of allegiance or continue to pay the land annuities (the repayment of money lent to help tenants pay for their farms).

De Valera

In 1937 De Valera drew up a new **Constitution** that named the state Éire, or Ireland. It declared Ireland a Republic in all but name and seemed a direct challenge to the Northern Ireland Government. Article 5 went like this: 'It is the right of the Parliament

Government established by the Constitution to exercise jurisdiction over the whole of Ireland, its Islands and territorial seas'. Article 44.1.2. recognized 'the special position of the Holy Catholic, Apostolic Roman Church as the guardian of the Faith professed by the great majority of its citizens'. De Valera would not go so far as to 'establish' it, as the Church of Ireland had once been, and as the Catholic hierarchy wanted. (This article was removed from the Constitution in the 1970s). Both parties had trouble with extremists in the 1930s; Fine Gael had to expel General O'Duffy of the Fascist Blueshirt Movement, and Fianna Fáil were embarrassed by their erstwhile allies in the IRA. De Valera dealt with the situation by setting up a military tribunal and declaring the IRA an illegal organization in 1936. The IRA did not die but went underground and continued to enjoy a curious relationship with the government and the public. When it got too noisy it was stamped on; but the IRA continued to be regarded nervously and with respect for its ideals, and its members' intransigence seemed to be in line with Ireland's dead patriots. In 1939 Éire declared itself neutral during the Second World War, which further isolated it from the rest of the British Isles. In 1949, Costello's Interparty Government finally inaugurated a Republic and broke Commonwealth ties. Relations between the North and the South remained cool until the tentative *rapprochement* in 1965 between Lemass (the Taoiseach of Éire) and O'Neill (the prime minister of Northern Ireland.) But relations cooled again rapidly as the Troubles (1968–1970) began and two members of Taoiseach Jack Lynch's Fianna Fáil ministry were implicated in gun-running for the IRA.

Northern Ireland

The North Today

It is very difficult to be impartial about the Troubles in Northern Ireland – they have been tragic and frightening. With the ceasefire holding at the time of writing, the interparty Assembly elections in June 1998 have provided a structure of government on which to try to build a stable society, so there is hope for the future, albeit a very cautious one. The basic reason for the start of the Troubles is that the Catholic minority in the North did badly with the division of Ireland in the 1920s, and once the Northern Ireland State was set up they were treated as second-class citizens. The series of events that lead up to the present situation is discussed in more detail below. Before you read on, you may find it useful to look at the glossary of Northern Irish political parties and terms at the end of this chapter.

Discontent Amongst Ulster Catholics, 1921–69

The Ulster Protestants made up two-thirds of the population of Northern Ireland, and the Catholics the remainder. Under the leadership of Edward Carson and James Craig, the Ulster Protestants had managed to wrest their bit of Ulster from the rest of Ireland, and preserve the Union with Britain. They repudiated the idea of a Catholic, Gaelic Republic of Ireland, and held themselves aloof from events in the Free State, (later the Republic). No attempt was made to woo the Catholic Nationalists, perhaps because the Protestant leaders, ever-anxious about being turfed out of the Union with Britain and into the Republic of Ireland, directed all their energies into preserving the Union. The **Government of Ireland Act** in 1920 gave Westminster supreme authority over Northern Ireland, which was run internally from a separate Parliament at Stormont Castle. The **Ireland Act** of 1949 enshrined the constitutional guarantee that gave the Stormont Parliament the right to decide whether Northern Ireland would remain in the UK or not.

All Catholics were regarded as supporters of the **IRA**, an organization that was indeed a real menace to this shaky state. It was seen as imperative that Catholics should never be allowed into positions of power and influence. **Sir Basil Brooke** (1888–1973) was typical of the type of blinkered cabinet minister who ran the government for years. He, along with **James Craig** (1871–1940), first prime minister of Northern Ireland, encouraged Protestants to employ only Protestants, for he, like others, believed that the Catholics were 'out to destroy Ulster with all their power and might'. He became prime minister in 1943 and played an active role in linking the Orange Order, of which he was a leading member, with the government of the time. Protestant businesses tended to employ Protestants and Catholics employed Catholics. There were few mixed housing areas or marriages. The Catholic priests fiercely defended their right to run Catholic schools – as they still do.

Government went on at a mainly local level through county and town councils. The Loyalists ensured that they always had a majority on the councils through the use of **gerrymandering**. The local voting system also favoured Protestants, who were often wealthier, for the franchise was only granted to house-owners or tenants, and the number of votes allocated to each person could be as high as six, depending on the value of their property. Because the Protestant rulers controlled housing schemes and jobs, the working-class Protestants were given the lion's share of any existing housing or jobs. Northern Ireland had a much lower standard of living than the rest of the UK, and any advantages were eagerly grasped by these workers, who displayed little feeling of worker solidarity with their fellow Catholics. They never could escape from their religious prejudices to unite against the capitalists, although the ruling class had feared their alliance during the 1922 riots over unemployment.

The Catholics themselves were ambiguous about the State; in the 1920s most of them were Republicans, and they never gave up hope that the Dublin Government might do something about this situation. Many believed that the Six Counties could not survive and, in the beginning, Nationalist Republican representatives refused to sit at Stormont. On the other hand, others had watched with horror the bloodshed and bitterness that resulted from the Civil War in the Irish Free State. After being educated, many of the bright ones emigrated rather than fight the system. The IRA attempted over the next 50 years to mount a campaign in the North but gained little support; a big campaign in 1956–62 that killed 19 people failed miserably. The local Catholics did not back them, and the **B Specials** (a Protestant-dominated special police force) zealously pursued the culprits – often at the expense of law-abiding Catholics, who were left resentful and disgruntled. For the time being, the Protestant Unionists were able to dominate Catholic Nationalists in elections in a proportion of about four to one. This gave them a feeling of security, which was also bolstered by the gratitude of the British government for their loyalty and help during the Second World War, when the North of Ireland had been a vital bulwark for the rest of the UK.

The Civil Rights Movement – British Troops Move In

Yet things had to change. As young, educated Catholics and Protestants grew up, they began to agitate about the obvious injustices, and the **Civil Rights Association** was formed in 1967. Unfortunately, the marches that drew attention to their aims also attracted men of violence on both sides and, as the marches turned into riots, the Protestant Loyalists, including the **Royal Ulster Constabulary** (RUC) and B Specials, seemed to be in league with the Protestant mobs against the Catholics. At this point the discredited IRA failed to seize their opportunity to woo the Catholics, who were both confused and frightened.

The Catholics initially welcomed the British troops, who were brought in to keep the peace in August 1969 after the Loyalists and police beat up Civil Rights marchers at Burntollet, and later the inhabitants of the Bogside in Londonderry. At that time, **Terence O'Neill** had taken over from Lord Brookborough as prime minister at Stormont. Although of the same Unionist Ascendancy stock, he realized that something must be done to placate the Nationalists. The few liberal gestures that he made towards the Catholics and the Republic opened up a Pandora's box of fury and opposition amongst the Protestant Unionists, the most extreme of whom found a leader in the **Reverend Ian Paisley**. The reforms O'Neill planned over housing and local government had come too late, and he was swept away by the Protestant backlash when he called a General Election in April 1969. The brutality with which the police had broken up the Civil Rights marches had stirred support for the IRA, and the Summer Marching Season was marked by even more violence.

The IRA Exploit Events

The IRA organized itself to exploit the situation. It split into two after an internal struggle, and the murders and bombings that dominated events after this time are mainly the work of the Provisional IRA, which is best known today as the IRA. The British Army lost the confidence of the Catholic community it had come to protect through heavy-handed enforcement of security measures. Besides, the IRA posed as the natural guardians of the Catholics, so there were cheers amongst the Catholic Nationalists when the IRA killed the first British soldier in October 1970. The IRA aimed to break down law and order; to them any method was legitimate, and any member of the army or police a legitimate target.

The Stormont Government hastened to pass some much-needed reforms between 1969 and 1972. The RUC was overhauled, and the B Specials abolished. A part-time security force was set up within the British Army, called the **Ulster Defence Regiment (UDR)**. In 1971 a Housing Executive was set up to allocate houses fairly, irrespective of religious beliefs. The IRA conducted a bombing campaign in the cities – innocent civilians were killed or injured and buildings destroyed. British soldiers responded to rioting in the Bogside in January 1972 by killing 13 people on what has become known as **Bloody Sunday**. A cycle of violence begetting violence began to spiral, and society divided along even more sectarian lines than before. The legacy of hatred, psychological distress and bitterness that has built from this time is terrible to contemplate.

UK Attempts to Solve the Problem

In 1972 the Stormont Government and Parliament were suspended by the British government, which had always retained full powers of sovereignty over it, and Direct Rule from Westminster was imposed. The head of government was a **Secretary of State for Northern Ireland**, appointed by the prime minister of the UK and a member of the British Cabinet. The Secretary governed through ministers and civil servants. Members of Parliament from the constituencies of Northern Ireland, elected from various parties, sat in Westminster, where they tried to bring Northern Irish issues to the attention of the House. **Internment** was introduced in August 1971, and many terrorist suspects were imprisoned without trial. This hardened Catholic opinion against British justice, and the practice was gradually phased out after a couple of years. Subsequently, the **Diplock System of Criminal Courts** was introduced, which means alleged terrorists are tried by judges who sit alone without juries. It was justified by the amount of intimidation to which the jury could be subjected. Various power-sharing initiatives between the largely Protestant Unionist parties and the Catholic and Nationalist SDLP did not get off the ground, so Direct Rule continued. The suspension of the Stormont Parliament removed the constitutional guarantee of the 1949 Act but it was renewed in the 1973 **Constitution Act**, which established the principle that any change in the status of Northern Ireland would have to have majority consent.

The Sunningdale Agreement

In December 1973 the leaders of the Northern Irish parties, a new Executive, and ministers from the United Kingdom and, for the first time, the Republic of Ireland, met at Sunningdale in England. They agreed to set up a **Council of Ireland** to work for cooperation between Northern Ireland and the Republic. The Agreement provided for a new type of Executive in Northern Ireland, in which power was to be shared as far as possible between representatives of the two communities in a joint government. It was the dawn of a new hope for the province, but the Unionist masses and the Republican terrorists did not want this new cooperation to work. Faced with a general strike called by the Ulster Workers' Council, which paralysed the province, the government did not use the army to break the strike, but allowed intimidation by 'Loyalist' paramilitary organizations to win the day. The Unionist members of the Executive resigned, and Direct Rule had to be resumed. Many people believe that if the Sunningdale Agreement had been implemented, much suffering could have been avoided, and Northern Ireland might have become a more stable place sooner.

The Victims of the Troubles

The province suffered sectarian killings, bombings, and the powerful propaganda of the hunger strike campaign by IRA prisoners in the early 1980s. The economy was struggling and well-educated members of society, Protestant and Catholic, left in droves.

However, since the first ceasefire in 1994, things have improved. The economy has picked up and foreign investors are looking again at Northern Ireland. Ulster people have suffered the gradual erosion of their society through violence and intimidation, and the subtler psychological effects that violence induces. On the positive side, the spirit and bravery of the people remains unbroken, and manufacturing businesses continue to compete in international markets. But the statistics in such a small population are grim. Between 1969 and 1994, 3,168 people lost their lives and around 3,300 people were injured and maimed, including 2,200 civilians. Feelings of despair, fear and outrage in both communities led to extreme attitudes in the 1980s. The Reverend Ian Paisley and his colleagues had a huge following, while support for Sinn Féin increased considerably at the expense of constitutional nationalists in the SDLP.

The Anglo-Irish Agreement

In 1985, after initial efforts by **Garrett Fitzgerald**, the Fine Gael prime minister of the Republic, and **Margaret Thatcher**, the British prime minister, the **New Ireland Forum** met in Dublin. It was agreed that Northern Ireland would remain in the United Kingdom as long as the majority so desired, but that the Dublin government should have an institutionalized consultative status in relation to Northern Irish affairs.

The effect of the Agreement was largely positive, though gradual. Both governments made progress in the complicated area of extradition and cross-border security, especially after the general revulsion in the Republic against the IRA bomb attack in Enniskillen in 1987. The British government grasped the nettle of injustice over the conviction of the 'Guildford Four' and the 'Birmingham Six', prisoners wrongly convicted of bombings in Britain. The re-opening of these cases and the subsequent acquittal of the prisoners dissipated much bad feeling in the Republic of Ireland, where there is great scepticism about British justice in relation to the Irish. One of the most important achievements of the agreement was that the Irish government formally accepted 'the principle of consent' by the people of Northern Ireland. Any change in the Constitution Act of 1973 had to have majority consent. The Unionists were not mollified by this, for it was enshrined in the Constitution of the Republic that the Irish Republic claimed the whole island, and this claim had not been given up. The agreement made the world realize that the 'Brits out' solution would mean forcibly transferring a million-strong Protestant population into a united Ireland that did not really want them, and the probability of bloody civil war.

The strength of the emotional link between the rest of the UK and the Northern Irish has changed since the beginning of the 20th century. The Union was no longer regarded as a cause in itself; many English, Welsh and Scots know little about the North of Ireland, and questioned the lives lost and money spent maintaining the Union. The Unionists understood this very clearly and felt increasingly threatened. The Nationalists had not rejected the IRA, who continued to work for the destruction of the Six-County state through murder and bombing campaigns in Ulster. In Britain and Europe, the IRA followed a campaign of bombing 'soft' British military targets, and assassinating British politicians and industrialists to turn British public opinion against the Union with Northern Ireland.

1990–93

Inter-party talks began in Northern Ireland and, before they broke down, some progress was made in defining the three complicated relationships between the North and the UK, the North and the Republic, and the Republic and the UK. This meant there was a set of negotiating mechanisms for the peace process to be furthered. British policy continued to try to find the middle ground between opposing parties in the North, and it was hoped that the politics of the extremists would wither away. In 1992 and 1993, the IRA carried out bombing attacks in the financial heart of London and elsewhere. One such attack in a shopping centre in Warrington killed two children; there was worldwide revulsion, and a peace movement was launched in Dublin. The IRA could continue their campaign of violence indefinitely, but there were signs that key elements in the IRA wanted to try to change things through political action. In April 1993, **John Hume** of the SDLP started a dialogue with **Gerry Adams** of Sinn Féin. Both the British and the Irish governments reacted furiously to this, but popular nationalist support for the dialogue, in both the North and South, forced the governments to rethink their policy. The British prime minister, **John Major**, and his Irish counterpart, **Albert Reynolds**, began a new policy of trying to draw the extremists into the political process and to aim at all-party talks for a lasting constitutional settlement that would bring peace. In October 1993, the IRA planted a bomb in a Belfast fish and chip shop killing 10 people; a terrible revenge was exacted by extremist loyalists who shot 14 people in a pub in Greysteel. Both acts horrified the people of Northern Ireland.

The Downing Street Declaration

On the 15th December 1993, the Irish and British prime ministers presented a **Joint Declaration** that successfully managed to address the competing claims of the Nationalists and the Unionists. The British Government declared in the document that Britain 'had no selfish strategic or economic interest in Northern Ireland' and recognized the right of the people of Ireland, North and South, to self-determination. Both governments affirmed that the status of Northern Ireland could only be changed with the consent of 'a great number of its people'. In the event of an overall political settlement, the Irish government declared it would drop its claim to the Six Counties contained in articles 2 and 3 of the Irish Constitution. The Irish government would establish a forum for peace and reconciliation at some later date. Both governments offered a place at the negotiating table to the extremists on both sides if they renounced violence.

Ceasefire

After a disappointing reaction to the Declaration and prevarication for several months, the IRA eventually announced 'a complete cessation of military operations' on 31 August 1994. In the following weeks, the extremist Unionist forces of the UFF, the UVF and the Red Hand of Ulster announced a ceasefire, conditional upon the IRA's continuing ceasefire. This ceasefire brought great opportunities for eventual peace, and the people of the North became increasingly convinced that they must find politicians who were prepared to find new ways of settling their differences.

The end to the day-to-day killing came as an enormous relief to everybody who lived there. Unfortunately, the main protagonists continued to disagree over major issues such as the release of prisoners, the withdrawal of the British Army, the decommissioning of arms amongst terrorist groups, the future of community policing in Northern Ireland, and the role of the Southern Irish Government in the future of the province.

The British and Irish governments produced two important framework documents in 1995. These sought to provide a basis for discussion in a **Northern Irish Forum** with elected delegates from all the different parties. The framework documents proposed a new assembly elected by proportional representation, a new relationship between North and South and between all the countries surrounding the Irish Sea. However, the discussions met stalemate over the **decommissioning of arms**. The IRA and Sinn Féin wanted the British Army to withdraw first and all political prisoners to be released before they gave up any of their weapons. The Unionists wanted the IRA to give up their arms first as a sign of their good intentions. In February 1996, the IRA declared their part in the ceasefire over with a bomb attack on Canary Wharf in London, which killed two people. The talks continued without Sinn Féin, little progress was made, and things looked very gloomy.

In the UK, the Conservative government under John Major was replaced in May 1997 by a Labour government with a huge majority. The new prime minister, **Tony Blair**, was no longer reliant on the Unionist vote in the House of Commons that gave him a freer hand all round. The Official Unionists, under the leadership of **David Trimble**, were breaking out of their reactionary 'Ulster Says No' mould, and it seemed as if the influence of Ian Paisley and his DUP was on the wane.

In the British elections, Sinn Féin's **Gerry Adams** and **Martin McGuinness** were voted into Westminster, although they did not take up their seats. In the Irish Republic, a general election brought a victory for Fianna Fáil, and their leader, **Bertie Ahern**, said he was willing to talk to Sinn Féin about a new ceasefire. The new Northern Ireland Secretary of State, **Mo Mowlam**, also promised to admit Sinn Féin to the talks if they called a new ceasefire. The American senator **George Mitchell**, who had been given the delicate task of brokering all-party talks, suggested the talks on the decommissioning of arms should take place at the same time, but separately, as the talks on the future of the province.

Sectarian tension was heightened in the mid-1990s when Orange marchers insisted on taking their traditional routes, which often lay in Catholic areas. In July 1997, at Drumcree in Portadown, violence flared up and spread throughout the province when an Orange Order march was forced down the Garvaghy Road, centre of the local Nationalist community, on its way from Drumcree Church. The reaction within the community was intense in the face of what they saw as sectarian intimidation. The head of the Orange Order Lodges decided to cancel and reroute some of the potentially violent 12th July marches. Tension in the province was running high after events at Drumcree, but this gesture from the Orange Order helped. Horrible sectarian murders added to the tension, but the restoration of the IRA's ceasefire in August improved matters considerably. In September 1997 the leaders of Sinn Féin joined the all-party talks. The Official Unionist Party dropped its demand that the decommissioning issue must be settled before any negotiations could begin. Instead, an independent commission on illegal arms decommissioning was set up.

At last, negotiations between all the concerned parties could begin; both the Irish and British prime ministers emphasized that there was now a clear agenda and timescale, and that the talks must not get lost in prevarication. The talks consisted of three interlocking and interdependent strands: the internal settlement of the province; North-South relations; and Anglo-Irish relations.

On 11 April 1998, after many vicissitudes, the world was told that there had been an historic agreement. The **Good Friday Agreement** mapped out radical new arrangements for a devolved Ulster Assembly, a council of ministers linking Northern Ireland and the Republic, and limited cross-border bodies who would work things through together. A new Council of the Islands would be set up that would link all the devolved assemblies in the UK, and in Dublin and London. The Irish government promised to amend Articles 2 and 3 of its Constitution that lay claim to the Six Counties. In return, the British Government stated that it would replace the Government of Ireland Act.

The people of Ireland from both sides of the border voted their approval of the Agreement in a **Referendum** in May 1998. However, the slow progress towards implementation of the terms of the Agreement is frustrating and has suffered some discouraging setbacks. Many Unionists are against the Agreement, and their vote is split, as was very apparent in the Assembly elections in June 1998 and the UK elections in June 2001. The new Assembly requires representatives to classify themselves as either Unionist, Nationalist or 'Other'. Certain legislation requires the consent of all three groups. The various Unionist parties make up the largest group in the Assembly. The SDLP is the dominant Nationalist Party, followed by Sinn Féin. The principal 'other' party is the Alliance, who polled badly.

David Trimble of the UUP was appointed the Assembly's First Minister, with **Seamus Mallon** of the SDLP as his deputy, and with executive authority in the hands of 12 ministers who, along with 98 others, make up the **Northern Ireland Assembly**. The Assembly decides on the internal affairs of state, while security, justice, and taxation remain the province of the Secretary of State and government in Westminster. One of the Assembly's initial tasks has been to decide on the areas of cross-border cooperation between the North and South. (At the time of writing, the Assembly remains in suspension following claims of IRA intelligence gathering at Stormont in 2002. David Trimble stepped down as UUP leader after a disastrous UK election result in which the party lost four of their five seats in Westminster, including Trimble's own, to the DUP and Sinn Féin.) Slowly, new structures and organizations have been created to fulfil strand one of the Good Friday Agreement. The Unionists are aware that, over the next 25 years or so, the population will become more balanced, and thus their negotiating position will weaken. The Nationalists too, are weary of the Troubles, and have seen their status within the province improve significantly over the years, while Sinn Féin and other Republican groups are experiencing the many dividends of joining the democratic process.

There are major problems ahead over the question of arms still held by the IRA and Loyalist terrorist groups, and the resolution of the Drumcree parades issue, which each year is banned by the cross-party Parades Commission, set up to arbitrate over controversial parades. The future of community policing in Northern Ireland is also problematic. The IRA has been policing Catholic West Belfast for many years, to protect their own financial empire, and to control lawless youths. Historically, there has always been Catholic hostility towards the RUC and few Catholic recruits into the force because of their fear of the IRA. In order to create a more representative force, in July 2001 its name was changed to the **Police Service of Northern Ireland** (PSNI), with a new uniform and oath of allegiance. This was necessary if the rule of law was to be reimposed on criminal activities and extortion rackets run by terrorist groups. Punishment beatings and sectarian beatings have not ceased. The **Omagh bombing** on 15 August 1998 was horrific in terms of civilian deaths, with 28 people killed and hundreds injured. This was perpetrated by the **Real IRA**, a splinter group of the Provisional IRA that has emerged since the Sinn Féin leadership agreed to the ceasefire and the Good Friday Agreement.

Since 1998, both Nationalists and Unionists have benefited greatly from the relative peace and stability that the agreement has brought. At the same time, the difficulty of implementing its terms fully has contributed to a polarization of politics. The anti-agreement DUP has become the largest Unionist party, while Sinn Féin has overtaken the moderate SDLP as the largest Nationalist party. Peace appears to have fed the extremes.

The implications of these developments for the peace process are as yet unclear. On the positive side, neither Sinn Féin nor the DUP appears to want to repudiate the agreement. Indeed, in December 2004, a deal on weapons decommissioning between them was almost brokered, although it ultimately foundered on the largely symbolic issue of photographic evidence. On the negative side, the agreement has yet to foster real trust between the political leaders or their respective supporters. Northern Ireland remains a deeply divided society. Suspended between war and peace, the politics of transition may continue for some time yet.

The Republic Today

The Irish Republic has a titular head of state, a **president** who is elected for seven years by the vote of the people. The president is empowered on the recommendation of the Dáil to appoint the prime minister (**Taoiseach**, pronounced 'tee-shookh'), sign laws and invoke the judgement of the Supreme Court on the legality of bills. S/he is also supreme commander of the armed forces. The Irish Parliament consists of the president and two Houses: the Dáil and the Senead or Senate. The Dáil is made up of 166 members (TDs) elected by adult suffrage through proportional representation. The Senead has 60 members: 11 are nominated by the Taoiseach; 49 are elected by the Dáil and county councils from panels representative of the universities, labour, industry, education and social services. The average length of an Irish government is three years.

In the 1970s and 1980s each Irish government had to face unemployment, growing emigration and a huge national debt. In 1988, incomes measured by GDP per head were just 63 percent of those in the UK. However, by 1998, the Republic had overtaken the UK, and today its GDP is one of the healthiest in the European Union. The forecast for the future is that the Republic's economy could grow annually by more than five percent a year. European investment in technology, food processing, pharmaceuticals and the marketing industries has benefited Ireland enormously. This is partly because of its young, well-educated population and skilled workforce. Emigration has almost halted. In fact, growing numbers of economic migrants, particularly from Eastern Europe, are entering the country, causing a worrying upsurge in racism. On the positive side, a recent US survey of 22 countries found that Ireland was overall top for feelings of national pride. The Republic is a major supporter of the EU and has been famously described as 'Europe's best pupil'. Ireland has done very well economically from EU funding, and it is now becoming a net contributor to the EU after years of being a net recipient. It easily met the criteria for joining the Euro zone.

The principle of neutrality so long adhered to in foreign affairs is no longer certain. Developments within the EU may see a watering down of Irish neutrality, as they include a commitment by all members to a common security policy and involvement in the 60,000-strong Rapid Reaction Force. The traditional lines of Irish parties are also changing from the pro- and anti-treaty (of 1921) stances. **Mary Robinson**, when Head of State (1990–97), brought a new flexibility and dynamism into politics here. Her policies continued with the election of **Mary McAleese** in 1998.

Irish Political Parties

The origins of the two major Irish political parties, Fianna Fáil and Fine Gael, hark back to the violent differences between those against the Free State Treaty and those for it in the turbulent 1920s.

Fianna Fáil: has established itself as the dominant ruling party.

Fine Gael: the second largest party in the country, is close to other Christian Democrat parties in Europe and has strong European inclinations.

The Labour Party: has found it difficult to gain popular support, as people have tended to be very conservative and voted as their family do – either Fine Gael or Fianna Fáil. This is changing, as Labour has increased its power base in the last 15 years in Dublin and Cork, and formed coalition governments either with Fianna Fáil or Fine Gael.

Sinn Féin: is a political expression of militant republicanism. Since the commencement of the peace process, its support has grown substantially in Northern Ireland. It has also gained electoral support in the Republic.

Other Parties in the Dáil

The Progressive Democrats: founded in 1985 by former members of Fianna Fáil after a split in that party, this is currently in a coalition partnership with Fianna Fáil.

The Green Party: is allied to Greens in 28 other countries.

Glossary of Political Parties and Terms

The following labels and identities crop up constantly during discussions on Northern Ireland:

Alliance: a label used for a party composed of moderate Unionists, both Protestant and Catholic. It loses out to the more extreme parties.

B Specials: a special, part-time reserve force within the RUC with powers to search out IRA members, operating from the 1920s until the 1970s. Catholics maintain that its members beat up alleged IRA members and intimidated ordinary Catholics.

Catholic: according to the 2001 Census, 678,462 people belonged to the Roman Catholic Church in Northern Ireland.

Civil Rights Movement: this was begun in the 1960s, inspired by the American Civil Rights campaigner Martin Luther King. The Civil Rights Association, which was founded in 1967, called for jobs, for houses and for a system of one man, one vote. It was supported by both Catholics and Protestants, and the leadership of the Association has been described as 'middle aged, middle class and middle of the road'. The Civil Rights Movement was hijacked by a more Republican and Socialist element and the mob violence that attended the Civil Rights marches. It eventually lost out to the IRA.

Direct Rule: The Government of the United Kingdom of Great Britain and Northern Ireland had always retained full powers of sovereignty on all matters over the Northern Ireland Government at Stormont. Thus, when the riots and bloodshed began to get out of control, and the Stormont government seemed unable to implement reforms or control the police, Direct Rule was imposed in 1972. It was suspended in 1998 with the creation of a new Northern Ireland Assembly.

Fenian: a term for a Catholic that suggests s/he is a Republican.

Gerrymandering: refers to the policy of concentrating large numbers of Catholics with Republican views in unusually big electoral districts, while Protestant Unionists were in smaller districts. This meant the Protestant Unionists were always certain to win a larger number of representatives, district by district. Gerrymandering gradually became the norm from the late 1920s until the electoral reforms at the beginning of the 1970s.

Internment: the arrest of alleged terrorist suspects for an indefinite period of time without trial.

IRA: this was the label used to describe the Irish Republican Army, which did not disband after the Civil War in Ireland ended (1920–21). The IRA is outlawed in the Republic of Ireland and the United Kingdom. The objective of its members is to fight by the gun and bomb until the whole of Ireland is free of the British, and the Six Counties reunited with the rest of Ireland. In 1969, with the start of civil disturbances, the IRA was reinvigorated. Firstly it reorganized itself and split into two. The Marxist Socialist-inspired members call themselves the Official IRA (OIRA), whereas the traditionalists call themselves the Provisional IRA (PIRA) after the 'Provisional' government of Ireland that was set up in the GPO after the Easter Rising of 1916. The ideal of the 'Provos' is straightforward: a United Republic of

Ireland, whatever the cost in terms of violence. The Provisionals are generally referred to as the IRA, since the Officials have dropped out of the action, and declared a ceasefire in 1972.

Loyalist: refers to a Protestant who is prepared to use violence to prevent a United Ireland and maintain the Union with the UK.

Nationalist: refers to anyone who supports a united Ireland.

Protestant: refers to Church of Ireland members, Presbyterians and other non-Catholic denominations. In the 2001 census, the Church of Ireland numbered 257,788 people, and Presbyterians numbered 348,742.

PSNI: Formerly the Royal Ulster Constabulary (RUC), which has now become the Police Service of Northern Ireland. This police force manages much of the security of Northern Ireland in cooperation with the British Army. The Catholic Nationalists in Northern Ireland traditionally regarded the RUC with dislike and suspicion, believing it to be biased by its largely Protestant Unionist membership. Catholics who joined it were singled out for death by the IRA, but it still managed to have eight percent of (mainly English) Catholics in its ranks. The PSNI now has a different uniform and oath of allegiance.

Orange Order: a sectarian and largely working-class organization that originated as a secret Protestant working-class agrarian society known as the Peep-O'Day Boys. William of Orange (William III of England) became their hero, and the society changed its name to the Orange Order in 1795. Its members have a traditional fear of the Catholic majority in Ireland and are Unionist in politics. Orange Lodges are still active in Northern Ireland.

Republican: a supporter of a united Ireland. The term is used as a synonym for a supporter of the IRA.

Republican Movement: this covers both Sinn Féin and the IRA.

Socialist, Democratic and Labour Party (SDLP): Formed in 1970 in Northern Ireland. It is committed to achieving a United Ireland through peaceful and democratic means. It is not linked, except through its aims, to Sinn Féin, the political wing of the IRA, which is less choosy about its methods.

Summer Marching Season: the Orange and Hibernian marches that take place during July and August. Each side commemorates opposing events in the history of Ireland. In the past, drums and equipment were lent between the two sides, but the present conflict has distilled into bitterness and hatred, so the practice has ceased. The Orange marchers in particular frequently take provocative routes through Catholic areas.

Taig: an offensive term used by Loyalists to describe Catholics.

Unionist: refers to supporters of the Union with Great Britain, who have no wish to share an Irish nationality with the Republic of Ireland. There are two main Unionist parties in Northern Ireland. The Official Unionists (UUP) were the original party and are, at least on the surface, more willing to discuss options to try to solve the crisis in the State. The Democratic Unionist Party (DUP), led by Ian Paisley, is more radical and Protestant. It is very anti any cooperation with the Irish Republic, and anti the Pope.

UVF, UDA, UFF and **LVF**: The Ulster Volunteer Force and the Ulster Defence Association are illegal Protestant terrorist organizations that recruit from the working class. They're usually involved in revenge sectarian killings and assassinations of IRA members. The Ulster Freedom Fighters and Loyalist Volunteer Force are illegal Protestant paramilitary organizations that engage in bloody sectarian and Republican killings, and also they feud among themselves.

UDR: was the Ulster Defence Regiment regiment of the British Army, many of whose soldiers were part time, and were drawn from the Protestant population in Ulster. More than 200 UDR soldiers were killed by the IRA during the Troubles, often when they were off-duty.

Religion

Despite a small decline in the last few years, Ireland still has the largest number of regular churchgoers in Western Europe, and although many of the social factors that generally undermine religion are present, they do not seem to be having a huge effect as yet. The reminders and symbols of a religious faith and deep love of God are to be seen everywhere throughout the country.

The images that fill my mind are a child in white, showing off her dress after her first Holy Communion; rags caught in brambles around a holy well; cars parked up a country lane, everybody piling out for Mass, umbrellas held high and skirts fluttering. The Catholic people of Ireland invoke and refer to the Virgin Mary and to Jesus often in their everyday talk. Roadside shrines to the Virgin are decorated with shells and fresh flowers, and some people still stop what they are doing to say the Angelus at noon and at sunset. Grey neo-Gothic churches dominate the small country towns, whilst in the smaller villages the chapel or church is a simpler building, planted around with dark yews and beeches, above which the ceaseless cawing of the rooks can be heard.

In Ireland, most people will want to know what religion you are – whether Catholic, Presbyterian, Church of Ireland, Baptist, Methodist or Quaker. If your religion is still a mystery, they will very soon find out, not by a direct question, but in a very roundabout way of conversation and enquiry. There has long been a strong, although small, Jewish community in Ireland, and recently there has been an increase in Islam and Buddhism. In the past, the Christian clergy would have encouraged their congregation to feel sorry for these 'poor heathens', and the greatest pity was reserved for those who did not believe in a God at all. This huge Catholic complacency is less obvious as Ireland develops into a more liberal and democratic society.

The history of Ireland has had much to do with this feeling of religious identity, and unfortunately in the North this mix of politics and religion has produced individuals whose extreme Catholic or Presbyterian attitudes are reminiscent of those in 17th-century Europe. The bigotry that characterizes such attitudes has been a major factor in the political situation in the North today. Great efforts are made by some of the clergy to organize ecumenical meetings, but mostly their congregations ignore them. The challenges to the clergy in the North are enormous because, in this welcome period of peace, they must try to work together against sectarianism, and to promote reconciliation between the different Christian traditions.

Church leaders in Ireland realize that for the present position of religion in Ireland to continue, they will have to adapt to the many social trends that are changing Christian Ireland. Among the factors driving the trends are prosperity and an increase in materialism, a young, well-educated population, and a rise in the feeling that the individual should decide for him- or herself on many of the moral issues on which the churches used to pronounce. This is especially true in matters of sex, marriage and family life. Under pressure from many groups, and a national referendum, the Republic has brought in divorce (albeit with many restrictions), and birth control measures are more widely available. The respect usually accorded to those in religious life has been shaken by a number of church scandals, and many people feel that the churches must become more open and accountable.

Pre-Christian Ireland

The Irish have been religious for 5,000 years; there are plenty of chambered cairns (mounds of stones over prehistoric graves) to prove it. The Celts who arrived in waves, mostly between 500 BC and 300 BC, seem to have been very religious, and had a religious hierarchy organized by Druids. These people worshipped a large number of gods, and central to their beliefs was the cult of the human head. They believed that the head was the centre of man's powers and thoughts. Their stonemasons carved two-headed gods, and the style of their work has a continuity that can be traced up to the 19th century. There are heads in the Lough Erne district that are difficult to date. They could be pagan, early-Christian or comparatively modern. The origins of the earlier Tuatha Dé Danaan are lost in legend: they may have been pre-Celtic gods or a race of invaders, themselves vanquished by the Celts. They are believed to have had magical powers and heroic qualities. Today they are remembered as the 'wee folk' who live in the *raths* and stone forts. Here they make fairy music that is so beautiful that it bewitches any human who hears it. The wee folk play all kinds of tricks on country people, from souring their milk to stealing their children, and so a multitude of charms have been devised to guard against these fairy pranks. I can remember being told about the fairies who used to dance in magic rings in the fields; the trouble was, if you tried to get near they would turn into yellow ragwort dancing in the wind.

Early-Christian Ireland

Christianity is believed to have come to Ireland from Rome in the 4th century, though St Patrick is credited with the major conversion of the Irish in the 5th century. The Irish seem to have taken to Christianity like ducks to water, although much of our knowledge of early-Christianity comes through the medieval accounts of scholarly (but possibly biased) clerics. One explanation for the ease with which Christianity took over is that the Christians didn't try to change things too fast, and incorporated elements of the Druidic religion into their practices. An example of this assimilation by the Christians is the continuing religious significance of the holy wells. Ash and rowan trees, both sacred to the Druids, are frequently found near the wells, and Christian pilgrims still leave offerings of rags on the trees as a sign to the Devil that he has no more power over them. *Patterns* (pilgrimages) and games used to be held at the wells, although they often shocked the priest, who would put the well out of bounds and declare that its healing powers had been destroyed. There are many everyday signs that the spiritual life of the Irish people harks back to pagan times. In cottages you might see a strange sign like a swastika, made out of rushes. This is a St Brigid's Cross, hung above the door or window to keep the evil spirits away. Fairy or sacred trees are still left standing in the field even though it is uneconomic to plough round them – bad luck invariably follows the person who cuts one down.

Monasteries in Early-Christian Ireland

The first Christian churches were built of mud and wattle, and later of oak wood; the larger ones were painted inside with frescoes and decorated with linen hangings. The need for chalices, altar vessals, bells and bible covers stimulated craftsmen to produce filigree and enamel work and carvings. By the end of the 5th century, a monasticism of the kind associated with the communities of the Desert Fathers in the Near East and Eastern Europe came to Ireland, and many place names with *disert* in them are indicative of each. Larger, more relaxed monasteries also flourished, and became the most important centres in the region. Each one followed the rule established by its founder. The episcopal organization set up by St Patrick was replaced by one in which the abbots were the more effective leaders in the Church.

By the end of the 6th century the Church was firmly monastic, with great monasteries such as Clonmacnoise in County Offaly and Clonfert in County Galway. These centres were responsible for big strides in agricultural development and were important for trade; they also became places where learning and artistry of all sorts were admired and emulated. The Ireland of 'Saints and Scholars' reached its peak in the 7th century. The monks sought an ascetic and holy way of life, although this was pursued in a warlike manner. The ultimate self-sacrifice was self-imposed exile, and so they founded monasteries in Scotland, England, France, Italy and Germany. The abbots, by the 8th century, had become all-powerful in Irish politics; many were tied by kinship to petty kings, and so were involved in their territorial disputes. Missionaries continued to leave Ireland and contribute to the revival of Christianity in Europe, and there was a blossoming of the arts with wonderful metalwork and painted manuscripts. By the 9th century, the monasteries were commissioning intricately carved stone high crosses, such as you can see at Ahenny in County Tipperary.

Religious Discrimination

Religious discrimination is long established in Ireland. Over the centuries, Catholics and Protestants have suffered by not conforming to the established church, although Catholics have undoubtedly been subjected to the greatest share of discrimination and persecution. The Huguenots (French Protestants), who were skilled workers and established the important linen industry, arrived when Louis XIV revoked the Edict of Nantes in 1686. The biggest group of dissenters were the Presbyterians: most of them were Scots who settled in Ulster during the 17th century. They had been persecuted in Scotland because of their religious beliefs and now they found that Ireland was no better; the Presbyterians were as poor as the native Irish, and many found life so hard that they emigrated to America. Quakers, Palatines (German Protestants), Moravians, Baptists and Methodists also settled in Ireland, but their numbers have declined through emigration and intermarriage.

Religion in Ireland Today

The 1991 population census revealed that, overall, 75.1 percent of the Irish are Catholic, 14 percent are Protestant, and the rest is made up of people who either were not inclined to state their religion, or who did not have any religion at all.

In the Republic, the Catholic majority of 88.4 percent is obviously the controlling force in political and social life, and the Protestant minority has bowed out gracefully. The Protestants used to represent almost 10 percent of the population but this figure has declined to 3.1 percent through mixed marriages and emigration.

In theory the modern state does not tolerate religious discrimination, and it is true that both Jews and Protestants have reached positions of importance and wealth in industry and banking. However, the Protestant classes had it so good during the hundreds of years of British rule that it is not surprising that for a short time there was a legacy of antipathy towards anyone connected with the mainly Protestant ascendency. Happily, the antipathy has nearly disappeared now. The Church is still very powerful; the bishops' exhortations on divorce, contraception, AIDS and so on are listened to with great earnestness by the politicians, and the sanctity of the family is held to be of the greatest importance. In Northern Ireland, the laws of the land are quite secular, being laid down by the British government, but divorce is still quite unusual there, too, and the principal UK legislation on abortion, the 1967 Abortion Act, has not been extended to the province.

The parish priest, of great importance in Irish society, is usually very approachable. You might meet him in the village bar having a drink and a chat. Nearly every family has a close relative who is a priest or a nun, and they leave in great numbers to serve overseas, taking their particular brand of conservative Catholicism with them. Schooling is mostly in the hands of the Church (incidentally, Ireland has a very high standard of literacy and general education), and thankfully the days of the cane and the cruel sarcasm of the priest-teachers described by so many Irish writers has disappeared. The people in the top positions in Ireland today mostly went to Christian Brothers Schools (look in the Irish *Who's Who*). So did many county councillors and petty officials who organize Ireland's huge bureaucracy. The old-boy network still gets favours done, grants approved and planning permission granted.

In Northern Ireland, there is a divided system – although all schools are eligible for 100 percent state funding, most Catholics attend Catholic 'maintained' schools and more Protestant children attend state 'controlled' schools. There's a small but growing number of mixed religion primary and secondary schools, attended by around two percent of children. Irish people practise their religion faithfully in rural areas. The churches are full on Sundays, and visits to Knock, Croagh Patrick and Lough Derg are made many times in a person's lifetime. Holy wells are still visited, and Stations of the Cross go on even in ruined churches and friaries. But in the cities more and more young people and disillusioned individuals have moved away from the Church, and some religious orders are forced to advertise for new priests. The numbing censoriousness of Catholicism and Protestantism in Ireland has become part of the island's image, just like the green hills and constant rain, but it is a theme that has been overplayed. Great community involvement and care comes directly from the churches, and the social events are great fun. The Irish are among the most generous when it comes to raising money for world disasters, and this charity work is usually channelled through the Church.

Death and weddings are always occasions for a bit of *craic*, and there is also a party held whenever the priest blesses a new house. Irish couples spend more on their engagement rings and weddings than their English counterparts; it is a really big occasion. The Irish wake for the dead has lost many of its pagan rituals – mourning with keening and games involving disguise, mock weddings, jokes and singing.

Nowadays, the deceased person is laid out in another room and people come to pay their last respects, and then they spend the rest of their evening drinking, eating and generally reminiscing.

In 2001 a reliquary containing half the bones of Saint Thérèse of Lisieux came to Ireland on a three-month tour, attracting huge crowds: according to the organizers, as many as 3 million people turned out to see the holy relics. Without a doubt, religious faith is alive and well in Ireland.

Irish Saints

Every locality in Ireland has its particular saint. The stories that surround him or her belong to myth and legend, not usually to historical fact. One theory is that all these obscure, miraculous figures are in fact Celtic gods and goddesses who survived under the mantle of sainthood. Included below is a short account of the lives of some of the most famous saints, about whom a few facts are known.

Brendan (c. 486–575), Abbot and Navigator

This holy man is remembered for his scholastic foundations, and for the extraordinary journey he made in search of Hy-Brasil, believed to be an island of paradise, which he had seen as a mirage while looking out on the Atlantic from the Kerry Mountains. His journey is recounted in the *Navigatio Brendan*, which was a treasure of every European library during the Middle Ages. The oldest copies are in Latin and date from the 11th century. The account describes a sea voyage that took Brendan and 12 monks to the Orkneys, Wales and Iceland, and to a land where tropical fruits and flowers grew. Descriptions of his voyage have convinced some scholars that he sailed down the east coast of America to Florida. Tim Severin, a modern-day explorer, and 12 others re-created this epic voyage between May 1976 and June 1977. In their leather and wood boat, they proved that the Irish monks could have been the first Europeans to land in America (the boat is at the Lough Gur Interpretative Centre, County Limerick; see p.138). Christopher Columbus probably read the *Navigatio*, and in Galway there is a strong tradition that he came to the west coast in 1492 to search out stories about St Brendan. The saint's main foundation was at Clonfert, which became a great scholastic centre. Brendan is buried in Clonfert Cathedral, and he is honoured in St Brendan's Cathedral (see p.270) in Loughrea, County Galway, where the beautiful mosaic floor in the sanctuary depicts his ship and voyage.

St Brigid (died c. 525), Abbess of Kildare

Brigid, also known as Bridget, Bride and Brigit, and the most beloved saint in Ireland, is often called Mary of the Gael. Devotion to her spread to Scotland, England and the Continent. The numerous traditions and stories surrounding her describe her generous and warm-hearted acts to the poor, her ability to counsel the rulers of the day, and her great holiness. Her father was a pagan from Leinster and she was fostered by a Druid. She decided not to marry and founded a religious order with seven other girls.

They were the first formal community of nuns and wore simple white dresses.
St Brigid has her feast day on 1 February, which is also the date of the pagan festival
Imbolg, marking the beginning of spring. She is the patron saint of poets, scholars,
blacksmiths and healers, and is also inevitably linked with Brigid, the pagan goddess
of fire and song. There is a tradition that St Brigid's Abbey in Kildare contained a
sanctuary with a perpetual fire, tended only by virgins, whose high priestess was
regarded as an incarnation and successor of the goddess. The two women are further
linked by the fact that Kildare in Irish means 'church of oak', and St Brigid's church
was built from a tree held sacred to the Druids. There's a theory that Brigid and her
companions accepted the Christian faith, and then transformed the pagan sanctuary
into a Christian shrine.

Kildare was a great monastic centre after Brigid's death, and produced the now lost
masterpiece of the *Kildare Gospels*. Tradition says that the designs were so beautiful
because an angel helped create them. The St Brigid's nuns kept alight the perpetual
fire until the suppression of the religious houses during the Reformation. Brigid was
buried in Kildare Church, but in AD 835 her remains were moved to Downpatrick in
County Down, because of the raids by the Norsemen. She is supposed to share a grave
with St Patrick and St Colmcille, but there is no proof of this. In 1283 it is recorded that
three Irish knights set out to the Holy Land with her head; they died en route in Lamiar,
Portugal, and in a church there her head is enshrined in a chapel to St Brigid. The
word 'bride' derives from St Brigid. It is supposed to originate from the Knights of
Chivalry, whose patroness she was; they called the girls they married their 'brides'.

St Columban (died 615), Missionary Abbot

Columban, also known as Columbanus, is famous as the great missionary saint. He
was born in Leinster and educated at Bangor in County Down under St Comgall, who
was famed for his scholarship and piety. Columban set off for Europe with 12 other
religious men to preach the gospel and convert the pagans in Gaul (France) and
Germany. He founded a monastery at Annegray, which is between Austria and
Burgundy, in AD 575, and his rule of austerity attracted many. Lexeuil, a larger
monastery, and Fontaines were both established within a few miles of Annegray.
When Columban was exiled by the local king, he and his followers founded Bobbio in
the Apennines, between Piacenza and Genoa. Bobbio became a great centre of
culture and orthodoxy from which monasticism spread. Its great glory was its library,
and its books are scattered all over Europe and regarded as treasures.

St Colmcille or St Columba (c. 521–97), Missionary Abbot

Along with St Patrick and St Brigid, Colmcille, also known as Columba and Columcille,
is probably the most famous of the Irish saints. This charismatic personality was a
scholar, poet and ruler, and spread the gospel to Iona and hence to Scotland. Colmcille
was a prince of Tyrconnell (County Donegal), and a great-great-grandson of Niall of
the Nine Hostages, who had been High King of Ireland. On his mother's side he was
descended from the Leinster Kings. He was educated by St Finian of Movilla, in
County Down, and also by Finnian of Clonard and Mobhi of Glasnevin. He studied

music and poetry at the Bardic School of Leinster, and the poems he wrote that have survived are delightful. A few are preserved in the Bodleian Library, Oxford. He chose to be a monk, and never to receive episcopal rank. He wrote of his devotion: 'The fire of God's love stays in my heart as a jewel set in gold in a silver vessel.'

In AD 545 he built his first church in Derry, the place he loved most. Then he founded Durrow and later Kells, which became very important in the 9th century when the Columban monks of Iona fled from the Vikings and made it their headquarters. In all, he founded 37 monastic churches in Ireland, and he also produced the *Cathach*, a manuscript of the Psalms. At the age of 42 he set out with 12 companions to be an exile for Christ. They sailed to the island of Iona, off the west coast of Scotland, which was part of the Kingdom of Dalriada ruled over by the Irish king Aidan. He converted Brude, King of the Picts, founded two churches in Inverness, and helped to keep the peace between the Picts and the Irish colony. The legend that he left Ireland because of a dispute over the copy he made of a psalter of St Finian is very dubious. Apparently the dispute caused a great battle, although the high king of the time, King Diarmuid, tried to settle the dispute and had ruled against Colmcille, saying: 'to every cow its calf, to every book its copy'. The saint is supposed to have punished himself for the deaths he caused by going into exile. Colmcille was famous for his austerity, fasting and vigils; his bed and pillow were of stone. He died at Iona, and his relics were taken to Dunkeld (Scotland) in AD 849.

St Enda of Aran (died *c.* 535), Abbot

Famous as the patriarch of monasticism, Enda is described as a warrior who left the secular world in middle life. He had succeeded to the kingdom of Oriel, but decided to study for the priesthood. Granted the Aran Islands by his brother-in-law, Aengus, King of Cashel, he is said to have lived a life of great severity, and never had a fire in winter, as he believed that 'hearts so glowing with the love of God' could not feel the cold. He reputedly taught 127 other saints, who are buried close to him on the islands.

St Kevin of Glendalough (died *c.* 618), Abbot

Many stories surround St Kevin, but we know that he was one of the many Irish abbots who chose to remain a priest. He lived a solitary, contemplative life in the Glendalough Valley. He played the harp, and the Rule for his monks was in verse. He is supposed to have prayed for so long that a blackbird had time to lay an egg and hatch it on his outstretched hand. His monastery flourished until the 11th century. In the 12th century St Lawrence O'Toole came to Glendalough and modelled his life on St Kevin's, bringing fresh fame to his memory. The foundation was finally destroyed in the 16th century.

St Kieran (*c.* 512–49), Abbot

St Kieran, also known as Ciaran, is remembered for his great foundation of Clonmacnoise, where the ancient chariot road through Ireland crosses the River Shannon. Unlike many Irish abbots he was not of aristocratic blood, for his father was a chariot-maker from County Antrim, and his mother from Kerry. St Kieran attracted craftsmen to his order, and Clonmacnoise grew to be a great monastic school, where, unusually for Ireland, the position of abbot did not become hereditary. Kieran died within a short time of founding the school. Many kings are buried alongside him, for it was believed that he would bring their souls safely to heaven.

St Malachy (1094–1148), Archbishop of Armagh

Malachy is famous as the great reformer of the Irish Church. He persuaded the Pope, Eugenius III, to establish the archbishops of Ireland separately from those of England. He also ensured that it was no longer possible for important ecclesiastical positions to be held by certain families as a hereditary right. For example, he was appointed Bishop of Armagh, although the See of Armagh was held in lay succession by one family. It was an achievement to separate the family from this post without splitting the Irish Church.

The saint was educated in Armagh and Lismore, County Waterford, and desired only to be an itinerant preacher. His great talents brought him instead to be Bishop of Down and Connor, and in 1125 Abbot-Bishop of Armagh. He travelled to France, where he made a lasting friendship with Bernard of Clairvaux, the reforming Cistercian. The Pope appointed him papal legate in Ireland, and while abroad he made some famous prophecies; one was that there will be the peace of Christ over all Ireland when the palm and the shamrock meet. This is supposed to mean when St Patrick's Day (17 March) occurs on Palm Sunday.

St Patrick (*c.* 390–461), Bishop and Patron Saint of Ireland

St Patrick was born somewhere between the Severn and the Clyde on the west coast of Britain. As a youth he was captured by Irish slave-traders and taken to the Antrim coast to work as a farm labourer. Controversy surrounds the details of Patrick's life. Popular tradition credits him with converting the whole of Ireland, but nearly all that can be truly known of him comes from his *Confessio* or autobiography, and other writings. Through these, he is revealed as a simple, sincere and humble man who was full of care for his people; an unlearned man, once a fugitive, who came to trust God completely. Tradition states that after six years of slavery, voices told him he would soon return to his own land, and he escaped. Later, other voices called to him from Ireland, entreating him 'to come and walk once more amongst us'.

It is believed that he spent some time in Gaul (France) and became a priest; perhaps he had some mission conferred on him by the Pope to go and continue the work of Palladius, another missionary bishop who worked among the Christian Irish. It is believed that some confusion has arisen over the achievements of Palladius and Patrick. Patrick, when he returned to Ireland, seems to have been most active in the north, whilst Palladius worked in the south. He made Armagh his primary see, and it has remained the centre of Christianity in Ireland. He organized the church on the lines of territorial sees, and encouraged the laity to become monks or nuns. He was very concerned with abolishing paganism, idolatry and sun-worship, and he preached to the highest and the lowest in the land. Tradition credits him with expelling the snakes from Ireland, and explaining the Trinity by pointing to a shamrock.

One of the most famous episodes handed down by popular belief is that of his confrontation with King Laoghaire at Tara, known as the seat of the high kings of Ireland, and the capital of Meath. It was supposedly on Easter Saturday in 432, which that year coincided with a great Druid festival at Tara. No new fire was allowed to be lit until the lighting of the sacred pagan fire by the Druids. St Patrick was camped on the Hill of Slane, which looks onto Tara, and his campfire was burning brightly; the Druids warned King Laoghaire that if it was not put out, it would never be extinguished. When Patrick was brought before Laoghaire, his holiness melted the king's hostility and he was invited to stay. Although Laoghaire did not become a Christian, his brother Conal, a prince of the North, became his protector and ally.

Certain places in Ireland are traditionally closely associated with St Patrick, such as Croagh Patrick in County Mayo, where there is an annual pilgrimage to the top of the 2,510ft (765m) mountain on the last Sunday of July; and Downpatrick and Saul in County Down. The cult of St Patrick spread from Ireland to many Irish monasteries in Europe, and in more modern times to North America and Australia, where large communities of Irish emigrants live. The annual procession on 17 March, St Patrick's Day, in New York has become a massive event, where everybody sports a shamrock and drinks green beer. However, quite a few Irish believe St Colmcille should be the patron saint of Ireland, not this mild and humble British missionary.

Oliver Plunkett (1625–81), Archbishop of Armagh and Martyr

This gentle and holy man lived in frightening and turbulent times, when to be a practising Catholic in Ireland was to court trouble. He was born into a noble and wealthy family whose lands extended throughout the Pale. He was sent to study in Rome, and was a brilliant theology and law scholar. He became a priest in 1654 and in 1669 was appointed Archbishop of Armagh.

Oliver was one of only two bishops in Ireland at that time, and the whole of the laity was in disorder and neglect. Apart from the hostility of the Protestants, the Catholics themselves were divided by internal squabbles. Oliver confirmed thousands of people, and held a provincial synod. He did much to maintain discipline amongst the clergy, to improve education by founding the Jesuit College in Drogheda, and to promulgate the decrees of the Council of Trent.

Oliver managed to remain on good terms with many of the Protestant gentry and clergy, but was eventually outlawed by the British government. The panic caused by the false allegations made by Titus Oates in England about a popish plot was used by Plunkett's enemies, and he was arrested in 1678. He was absurdly charged with plotting to bring in 24,000 French troops, and levying a charge on his clergy to support an army. No jury could be found to convict him in Ireland, so he was brought to England, where he was convicted of treason for setting up 'a false religion which was the most dishonourable and derogatory to God of all religions and that a greater crime could not be committed against God than for a man to endeavour to propagate that religion'. He was hanged, drawn and quartered at Tyburn in July 1681. His head is in the Oliver Plunkett Church in Drogheda, County Louth, and his body lies at Downside Abbey, Somerset.

The Old Gods and Heroes

04

The Celts

Nobody knows exactly when the first Celts arrived in Ireland, but it was some time before 1000 BC, with the last wave of people coming around the 3rd century BC. The Greek chroniclers were the first to name these people, calling them *Keltori*. Celt means 'act of concealment', and it has been suggested that they were called 'hidden people' because of their reluctance to commit their great store of scholarship and knowledge to written records. Kilt, the short male skirt of traditional Celtic dress, may also come from this word.

The Celtic civilization was quite sophisticated, and much of the road-building attributed to the Romans has been found to have been started by the Celts. The Romans frequently built on their foundations. In Ireland, ancient roads are often discovered when bog is cleared.

Ireland's ancient and rich epic story tradition was strictly oral until the Christian era. Even then, it was well into the 7th century before the bulk of it was written down by scribes, who often added to or changed the story in order to give it some moral Christian interpretation. The reluctance of the Celts to commit their knowledge to writing is directly related to the Druids and their power, because the Druidic religion was the cornerstone of the Celtic world, which stretched from Ireland to the Continent and as far south as Turkey. Irish mythology is therefore concerned with the rest of that Celtic world, and there are relationships with the gods and heroes of Wales, Scotland, Spain and central Europe.

The *Book of the Dun Cow* and the *Book of Leinster*, the main surviving manuscript sources, date from the late 11th century. Many earlier books were destroyed by the Viking raids, and entire libraries were lost. The various sagas and romances that survived have been categorized by scholars into four cycles. First, the **mythological cycle**: the stories that tell of the various invasions of Ireland, from Cesair to the Sons of Milesius. These are largely concerned with the activities of the Tuatha Dé Danaan, the pagan gods of Ireland. Next there is the **Ulster Cycle**, or deeds of the Red Branch Knights, which include the tales of Cú Chulainn and the *Táin Bó Cuailgne*. Then there is the **Cycle of Kings**, mainly stories about semi-mythical rulers; and finally the **Fenian Cycle**, which relates the adventures of Fionn MacCumhaill (Finn MacCool) and the warriors of the Fianna. Only qualified storytellers could recite these sagas and tales under Brehon (Celtic) laws, and they were held in great respect. Several qualities emerge from these sagas and tell us a great deal about the society of Iron Age Ireland, and indeed Europe. The stories are always optimistic, and the Celts had evolved a doctrine of immortality of the soul.

The heroes and gods were interchangeable – there were no hard and fast divisions between gods and mortals. Both had the ability to change shape, and they often reappear after the most gruesome deaths. The gods of the Dé Danaan were tall, beautiful and fair, although, later, in the popular imagination, they became fairies or the 'little people'. They were intellectual as well as beautiful, but as gullible as mortals, with all our virtues and vices. They loved pleasure, art, nature, games, feasting and heroic single combat. It is difficult to know whether they are heroes and heroines made into gods by their descendants. In the 11th century, Cú Chulainn was the most admired hero, particularly by the élite of society. Then Fionn MacCumhaill took over. He and his band of warriors became very popular with the ordinary people right up to the early 20th century. The English conquests in the 17th century and the resulting destruction and exile of the Irish intelligentsia meant that much knowledge was lost, though the peasantry kept it alive in folklore recited by the *shanachie* or village storyteller. Then, with the famines and vast emigration of the 19th century, the Irish language came under great threat and, with it, the folklore.

The stories were anglicized by various antiquarians and scholars at the end of the 18th century and into the 19th century. These did a great deal in terms of recording and translating the Irish epic stories into English and of preserving the Gaelic; many of them were Ulster Presbyterians. Names that should be remembered with honour are William Carleton, Lady Wilde, T. Crofton-Croker, Standish James O'Grady, Lady Gregory and Douglas Hyde. Their writings and records of Irish peasant culture have become standard works.

The question of where Irish myth ends and history begins is impossible to answer. Historical accounts are shot through with allegory, supernatural happenings and fantasy. In this, nothing at all has changed, as a similar mythical process is applied to modern Irish history.

Directory of the Gods

Amergin: a Son of Milesius, and the first Druid of Ireland. Three poems are credited to him in *The Book of Invasions*.

Aonghus Óg: the God of Love, son of Dagda. His palace was by the River Boyne at Newgrange. He is also known as Aengus.

Ard Rí: the title of High King.

Badhbha or *Badh*: goddess of battles.

Balor: a god of death, and one of the most formidable Fomorii. His one eye destroyed everything it gazed on. He was destroyed by his own grandson, Lugh.

Banba, Fotla and Éire Dé Danaan: sister goddesses who represent the spirit of Ireland, particularly in Irish literature and poetry. It is from the goddess Éire that Ireland takes its modern name.

Bilé: god of life and death. He appears as Cymbeline in Shakespeare's play.

Bran: 'Voyage of Bran'. This is the earliest voyage poem, which describes through beautiful imagery the Island of Joy and the Island of Women. It is also the hound of Fionn MacCumhaill.

Brigid: goddess of healing, fertility and poetry. Her festival is one of the four great festivals of the Celtic world. Brigid is also a Christian saint (*see* p.46) who has become confused in popular folklore with the goddess.

Caílte: cousin of Fionn MacCumhaill, and one of the chief Warriors of the Fianna, as well as a poet. A Christian addition to his story has returned him from the Otherworld to recount to St Patrick the adventures of the Fianna.

Conall Cearnach: son of Amergin, a warrior of the Red Branch, and foster brother and blood cousin of Cú Chulainn. He avenged Cú Chulainn's death by slaying his killers.

Conchobhar MacNessa: king of Ulster during the Red Branch Cycle. He fell in love with Deirdre (*see* below) and died from a magic 'brain ball' that had been lodged in his head seven years before by the Connacht warrior, Cet.

Conn: one of the Sons of Lir, the ocean god, who was changed into a swan by his jealous stepmother Aoife. There is also a Conn of the hundred battles, High King from AD 177 to 212.

Cormac MacArt: High King from AD 254 to 277 and patron of the Fianna, who reigned during the period of Fionn MacCumhaill and his adventures. His daughter Gráinne was betrothed to Fionn MacCumhaill but eloped with one of Fionn's warriors, Diarmuid. His son succeeded him and destroyed the Fianna.

Cú Chulainn: the hound of Culann, also called the Hound of Ulster. He has similarities with the Greek hero, Achilles. He was actually called Setanta until he killed the hound belonging to Culann, a smith god from the Otherworld. He promised to take its place and guarded his fortress at night. He became a great warrior whose battle frenzy was incredible. Women were always falling in love with him, but Emer, his wife, managed to keep him. He is chiefly famous for his single-handed defence of Ulster during the War of the Tain (Bull of Cuailgne) when Ailill and Medb of Connacht invaded (*see* pxxx, Medb). He was acknowledged as champion of all Ireland, and was forced to slay his best friend, Ferdia, during a combat at a crucial ford. Later Cú Chulainn rejected the love of the goddess of battles, Mórrigan, and his doom was sealed; his enemies finally slew him. During the fatal fight he strapped his body to a pillar stone because he was too weak to stand. But such was his reputation that no one dared to come near him until Mórrigan, in the form of a crow, perched on his shoulder, and finally an otter drank his blood.

Dagha: father of the Gods and patron god of the Druids.

Diarmuid: foster son of the love god, Aonghus Óg, and a member of the Fianna. The goddess of youth put her love spot on him, so that no woman could resist loving him. He eloped with Gráinne, who was betrothed to Fionn MacCumhaill, and the Fianna pursued them for 16 years. Eventually the couple made an uneasy peace with Fionn, who went out hunting with Diarmuid on Ben Bulben, where Diarmuid was gored by an enchanted boar who was also his own stepbrother. Fionn had the power to heal him with some enchanted water, but he let it slip through his fingers. Aonghus Óg, the god of love, took Diarmuid's body to his palace and, although he did not restore him to life, sent a soul into his body so that he could talk to him each day.

Deirdre: Deirdre of the Sorrows was the daughter of an Ulster chieftain. When she was born, it was forecast by a Druid that she would be the most beautiful woman in the land, but that, because of her, Ulster would suffer great ruin and death. Her father wanted to put her to death at once, but Conchobhar, the Ulster King, took pity on her and said he would marry her when she grew up. When the time came, she did not want to marry such an old man, particularly as she had fallen in love with Naoise, a hero of the Red Branch. They eloped to Scotland. Conchobhar lured them back with false promises, and Naoise and his brothers were killed by Eoghan

MacDuracht. Deirdre was forced to become Conchobhar's wife. She did not smile for a year, which infuriated her husband. When he asked her who she hated most in the world, she replied, 'you and Eoghan MacDuracht'. The furious Conchobhar then said she must be Eoghan's wife for a year. When she was put in Eoghan's chariot with her hands bound, she somehow managed to fling herself out and dash her head against a rock. A pine tree grew from her grave and touched another pine growing from Naoise's grave, and the two intertwined.

Donn: king of the Otherworld, where the dead go.

Emain Macha: the capital of the kings of Ulster for six centuries, which attained great glory during the time of King Conchobhar and the Red Branch Knights.

Emer: wife of Cú Chulainn. She had the six gifts of womanhood: beauty, chastity, eloquence, needlework, a sweet voice and wisdom.

Female champions: in ancient Irish society women had equal rights with men. They could be elected to any office, inherit wealth and hold full ownership under law. Cú Chulainn was instructed in the martial arts by Scáthach, and there was another female warrior in the Fianna called Creidue. Battlefields were always presided over by goddesses of war. Nessa, Queen of Ulster, and Queen Medb of Connacht were great warriors and leaders. Boadicea of Britain was a Celtic warrior queen who died in AD 62, and this tradition survived with Grace O'Malley of County Mayo into the 16th century.

Ferdia: the best friend of Cú Chulainn, killed by him in a great and tragic combat in the battle over the Brown Bull of Cuailgne (or Cooley).

Fergus MacRoth: stepfather of Conchobhar, used by him to deceive Deirdre and Naoise and his brothers. He went into voluntary exile to Connacht in a great fury with the King, and fought against Conchobhar and the Red Branch. But he refused to fight against Cú Chulainn, which meant the ultimate defeat of Queen Medb and her armies.

The Fianna: known as the Fenians, a band of warriors guarding the high king of Ireland. Said to have been founded in about 300 BC, they were perhaps a caste of the military élite. Fionn MacCumhaill was their greatest leader. In the time of Oscar, his grandson, they destroyed themselves through a conflict between the clans Bascna and Morna. In the 19th century, the term was revived as a synonym for Irish Republican Brotherhood, and today it is used as the title for one of the main Irish political parties, Fianna Fáil, which means 'Soldiers of Destiny'.

Fintan: the husband of Cesair, the first invader of Ireland. He abandoned her and survived the Great Deluge of the Bible story by turning into a salmon. Fintan is also the Salmon of Knowledge, who ate the Nuts of Knowledge before swimming to a pool in the River Boyne, where he was caught by the Druid Finegas. He was given to Fionn MacCumhaill to cook. Fionn burnt his finger on the flesh of the fish as he was turning the spit, sucked his thumb, and acquired the knowledge for himself.

Fionn MacCumhaill: anglicized as Finn MacCool. He was brought up by two wise women, then sent to study under Finegas the Druid. After acquiring the Knowledge of the Salmon, Fintan, he became known as Fionn, the Fair One. He was appointed head of the Fianna by Cormac MacArt, the High King at the time, in place of Goll

MacMorna, who had killed his father. His many and magical exploits include creating the Giant's Causeway, in County Antrim. His two famous hunting hounds were Bran and Sceolan, who were actually his own nephews, the children of his bewitched sister. His son, Oisín, was the child of the goddess Sadb, but he suffered unrequited love for Gráinne. In the story of the Battle of Ventry, Fionn overcomes Daire Donn, the King of the World. He is said not to be dead, but sleeping in a cave, waiting for the call to help Ireland in her hour of need.

Dé Fionnbharr and Oonagh: gods of the Dé Danaan who have degenerated into the king and queen of the Fairies in folklore.

Fionnuala: the daughter of Lir. She and her brothers were transformed into swans by her jealous stepmother, Aoife. The spell was broken with the coming of Christianity, but they were old and senile by then.

Fir Bolg: 'Bagmen', a race who came to Ireland before the Dé Danaan. They do not take much part in the myths.

Fomorii: a misshapen and violent people, the evil gods of Irish myth. Their headquarters seems to have been Tory Island, off the coast of County Donegal. Their leaders include Balor of the Evil Eye, and their power was broken for ever by the Dé Danaan at the second Battle of Moytura, in County Sligo.

Gaul: Celt, a Gaulish territory that extended over France, Belgium, parts of Switzerland, Bohemia, parts of modern Turkey and parts of Spain.

Geis: a taboo or bond that was usually used by Druids and placed on someone to compel them to obey. Gráinne put one on Diarmuid.

Goibhnin: smith god, and god of handicraft and artistry.

Goll MacMorna: leader of the Fianna before Fionn MacCumhaill.

Gráinne: anglicized as Grania. Daughter of Cormac MacArt, the high king, she was betrothed to Fionn MacCumhaill but thought him very old, so she put a *geis* on Diarmuid to compel him to elope with her. Eventually he fell in love with her (*see* Diarmuid, p.54). After Diarmuid's death, although she had sworn vengeance on Fionn, she allowed herself to be wooed by him and became his wife. The Fianna despised her for this.

Laeg: charioteer to Cú Chulainn.

Lir: ocean god.

Lugh: sun god who slew his grandfather, Balor, and the father of Cú Chulainn by a mortal woman. His godly status was diminished into that of a fairy craftsman, Lugh Chromain, a leprechaun.

Macha: a woman who put a curse called *cest nóiden* on all Ulstermen, so that they would suffer from the pangs of childbirth for a period of five days and four nights in times of Ulster's greatest need. This curse would last nine times nine generations. Macha did this because her husband boasted to King Conchobhar that she could beat the king's horses in a race, even though she was pregnant. She died in agony as a result.

Medb: anglicized as Maeve. Queen of Connacht, and wife of Ailill, she was famous for her role in the epic tale of the cattle raid of Cuailgne (Cooley), which she started when she found that her possessions were not as great as her husband's. She wanted the Brown Bull of Cuailgne, which was in Ulster, to outdo her husband's bull, the White-Horned Bull of Connacht. This had actually started off as a calf in her herd but had declined to stay in the herd of a woman. She persuaded her husband to join her in the great battle that resulted. The men of the Red Branch were hit by the curse of the *nóiden* (*see* Macha), and none could fight except Cú Chulainn, who was free of the weakness the curse induced and singlehandedly fought the Connacht champions. Mebh was killed by Forbai, son of Conchobhar, while bathing in a lake. The bulls over which the great battle had been fought eventually tore one another to pieces.

Milesians: the last group of invaders of Ireland before the historical period. Milesius, a Spanish soldier, was their leader but it was his sons who actually carried out the Conquest of Ireland.

Nessa: mother of Conchobhar. This strong-minded and powerful woman secured the throne of Ulster for her son.

Niall of the Nine Hostages: High King from AD 379 to 405, and progenitor of the Uí Néill dynasty. There is a confusion of myth and history surrounding him.

Niamh: of the Golden Hair. A daughter of the sea god Manannán Mac Lir, she asked Oisín to accompany her to the Land of Youth and live there as her lover. After three weeks, he discovered that 300 years had passed.

Nuada of the Silver Hand: the leader of the Dé Danaan gods, who had his hand cut off in the great battle with the Fomorii. It was replaced by the god of healing.

Ogma: god of eloquence and literature, from whom ogham stones were named. These upright pillars carved with incised lines that read as an alphabet from the bottom upwards probably date from AD 300.

Oisín: son of Fionn and Sadb, the daughter of a god, and leading champion of the Fianna. He refused to help his father exact vengeance on Gráinne (to whom Fionn was betrothed) and Diarmuid (with whom Gráinne eloped), and went with Niamh of the Golden Hair to Tír na nÓg, the Land of Youth. Oisín longed to go back to Ireland, so Niamh gave him a magic horse on which to return, but warned him not to set foot on land, as 300 years had passed since he was there. He fell from his horse by accident and turned into an old, blind man. A Christian embellishment is that he met St Patrick and told him the stories of the Fianna, and they had long debates about the merits of Christianity. Oisín refused to agree that his Ireland was better off for it. His mood comes through in this anonymous verse from a 16th-century poem translated by Frank O'Connor.

Patrick you chatter too loud
And lift your crozier too high
Your stick would be kindling soon
If my son Osgar stood by.

Oscar or Osgar: son of Oisín. He also refused to help Fionn, his grandfather, against Diarmuid and Gráinne. The high king of the time wished to weaken the Fianna and allowed the two clans in it, Morna and Bascna, to quarrel. They fought at the battle of Gabhra. Oscar was killed and the Fianna was destroyed.

Partholón: the leader of the third mythical invasion of Ireland. He is supposed to have introduced agriculture to Ireland.

Red Branch: a body of warriors who were the guardians of Ulster during the reign of Conchobhar MacNessa. Their headquarters were at Emain (*Eamhain*) Macha. The Red Branch cycle of tales has been compared to the *Iliad* in theme. The main stories are made up of the *Táin Bó Cuailgne* (the Brown Bull of Cuailgne or Cooley). Scholars accept that the cycle of stories must have been transmitted orally for nearly 1,000 years, providing wonderful descriptions of the remote past.

From Stone Circles to Castles

05

Ireland is fascinatingly rich in monuments, and you cannot fail to be struck by the number and variety of archaeological remains all over the country. They crown the tops of hills or stand out, grey and mysterious, in the green fields. Myths and stories surround them, handed down by word of mouth. Archaeologists too have their theories, and they are as varied and unprovable as the myths!

Humans are known to have lived in this country since the Middle Stone Age (roughly from about 6000 BC). There are no structures left from these times but, following the coming of Neolithic or New Stone Age peoples, some of the most spectacular of the Irish monuments began to be built.

Here is a brief description of the types to be seen in order of age.

Stone Circles

Stone circles served as prehistoric temples and go back to Early Bronze Age times. Impressive examples may be seen at Lough Gur, County Limerick, and on Beltany Hill, near Lifford, County Donegal. Earthen circles probably served a similar purpose. One example is the Giant's Ring at Drumbo near Belfast, which surrounds a megalith. They have been variously interpreted as ritual sites and astronomical calendars. They are mainly found in the south-west and north. Associated with them are standing stones.

Megalithic Tombs

Neolithic colonizers with a knowledge of agriculture came to Ireland between 3000 and 2000 BC and erected the earliest megalithic chambered tombs. They are called the court cairns, because the tombs are made up of a covered gallery for burial with one or more unroofed courts or forecourts for rituals. Pottery has been found in these tombs. Court cairns are mainly found in the northern part of the country – north of a line between Clew Bay in the west and Dundalk Bay in the east. Good examples are the full-court cairns at Creevykeel, County Sligo, and Ballyglass, County Mayo (one of a group on the west shores of Killala Bay).

Linked to the court cairns is the simple and imposing type of megalith – the dolmen or portal dolmen. This consists of a large, sometimes enormous, capstone and three or more supporting uprights. The distribution of the dolmens is more widespread but tends to be eastern. There is one with a huge capstone at Browne's Hill, just outside Carlow town. Another variety of megalith is the wedge-shaped gallery. There are numbers of such tombs in the Burren area in County Clare, where they are built from the limestone slabs so common in the region. Most excavated wedges belong to the Early Bronze Age – 2000 to 1500 BC. They are now largely bare of the cairns or mounds that covered them. The people who built them advanced from being hunters to growing crops and keeping domestic animals.

The most spectacular of the great stone tombs are the passage graves. The best known is Newgrange, one of a group on the River Boyne, to the west of Drogheda, County Louth, which by its construction and the carvings on the stones is among the most important megalithic tombs in Europe. The graves belong to a great family of structures found from eastern Spain to southern Scandinavia. The decorative carving that covers many of the stones consists of spirals, lozenges and other motifs, and is thought to have some religious significance. Unchambered burial mounds also occur throughout the country. They date largely from the Bronze Age, but earlier and later examples are known.

Standing Stones

These are also known as gallauns. They are single pillar stones that also have a ritual significance, and that occasionally mark grave sites. Others carry inscriptions in ogham characters.

Ring forts

The most numerous type of monument to be seen throughout Ireland is the ring fort, which is known also as *rath, lios, dun, caher*, and *cashel*. There are about 30,000 of these in the country. They originated as early as the Bronze Age and continued to be built until the Norman invasion. The circular ramparts, varying in number from one to four, enclosed a homestead with houses of wood, wattle-and-daub, or partly stone construction.

Well-preserved examples of stone forts are those at Staigue, County Kerry, the royal site at Grianan of Aileach, near Derry, and the cashels of the Aran Islands. Collections of earthworks identify the royal seats at Tara, County Meath, and Emain Macha, County Armagh, where earthen banks are now the only reminders of the timber halls of kings. They, like Tara in County Meath, lie at the centre of a complex tangle of myth and tradition in the ancient Celtic sagas.

Hill forts

Larger and more defensive in purpose are the hill forts, the ramparts of which follow contour lines to encircle hilltops. To this class belongs the large green enclosure at Emain Macha known as Navan Fort, in County Armagh.

Crannógs

Crannógs, or artificial islands, found in lakes and marshy places, are defensive dwelling sites used by farmers, with even earlier origins than the forts, but that continued in use sometimes until the 17th century. The Craggaunowen Centre in County Clare has a very good example, and many were found at Lough Gara, near Boyle, County Roscommon.

Early Irish Architecture

Before the Norman invasion, most buildings in Ireland were of wood. None of these have survived. In the treeless west, however, tiny corbelled stone buildings shaped like beehives and called *clochans* were constructed. They were used as oratories by holy men. Some, possibly dating from the 7th century, still exist. *Clochans* are particularly common in County Kerry: there are many on the Dingle Peninsula and some very well-preserved examples in the early monastic settlement on the Skellig Rock, off the Kerry coast. Also in Kerry is the best-preserved example of an early boat-shaped oratory, at Gallarus.

Most of the early mortared churches were modelled on wooden prototypes. They were very small, and from an early stage were built with stylistic features that have remained characteristic of Irish buildings: steeply pitched roofs, inclined jambs to door and window-openings. Many of these small churches would have been roofed with wood, or tiled or thatched, but some were roofed with stone. The problem of providing a pitched roof of stone over a rectangular structure was solved by inserting a semi-circular arch below the roof. The small space over the arch forms a croft. A fine example is St Kevin's Church at Glendalough, County Wicklow. These buildings lack features by which they can be accurately dated; a conservative dating would be from the beginning of the 9th century onwards.

Round Towers

Contemporary with these early Irish churches, and very characteristically Irish, are round towers, of which approximately 120 are known to have existed in Ireland. These tall, gracefully tapering buildings of stone, with conical stone roofs, were built as monastic belfries, with the door about 12ft (3.5m) from the ground. This is a clue to their use as places of refuge or watch-towers during the period of Viking raids between the 9th and 11th centuries. Food, precious objects and manuscripts were stored in them. The ladder could then be drawn up. There are about 70 surviving examples in varying degrees of preservation. A good example is the one on the Rock of Cashel, County Tipperary.

The monk who wrote these beautiful lines expresses the tensions of those days:

Bitter the wind tonight,
Combing the sea's hair white:
From the North, no need to fear
the proud sea coursing warrior.
                    version by John Montague

High Crosses

These carved stone crosses, usually in the typical 'Celtic' ringed form, contain a great variety of biblical scenes and ornament. They are found in most parts of the country in early monastic sites. The earliest type are simple crosses carved on standing stones. They are most common in the west and on the Dingle Peninsula, County Kerry. The development of low-relief carving began in the 7th century, and it gradually became more complex, as can be seen in the cruciform slab at Carndonagh, County Donegal, carved with scenes of the Crucifixion, and interlaced ornament.

The ringed high cross first appears at a later date; the earliest group of high crosses, dating from the 8th century, are in southern Kilkenny and Tipperary. Good examples can be seen at Ahenny, County Tipperary, and Kilkieran, County Kilkenny. Also close are the Ahenny Crosses in County Tipperary. In this group the cross-shafts and heads are carved in sandstone with spirals and other decorative forms derived from metalwork, with figure-carvings on the bases. To the north, in the Barrow Valley, is another group, later in date and more roughly carved in granite. The Barrow group has an interesting innovation: the faces of the shafts and heads are divided into panels, in which a scene, usually biblical, is portrayed. The best of these crosses is at Moone, County Kildare.

Sandstone was used again for crosses in the 10th century; they still grace monastic ruins scattered across the Central Plain. The West Cross and Muiredach's Cross at Monasterboice in County Louth are the best examples. In each case the east and west faces are carved with scriptural scenes, while the north and south faces have spirals, vine-scrolls, and other decorations. Favourite subjects for the carver were the Crucifixion; the Last Judgment; Adam and Eve; Cain and Abel; and the arrest of Christ. Later elaborate crosses may be seen at Clones, County Monaghan, Drumcliff, County Sligo, Ardboe, County Tyrone, and Donaghmore, County Down.

By the end of the 11th century the cross had changed; the ring was often left off, and the whole length of the shaft was taken up with a single figure of the crucified Christ. Ecclesiastical figures often appear on the opposite face and the base, and the decoration of the north and south faces usually consists of interlaced animals. Crosses of this style were being carved up until the mid 12th century. A good 11th-century cross exists at Roscrea, County Tipperary, and a good 12th-century cross at Tuam, County Galway.

Romanesque Architecture

Characteristics of this decorative style appear in Irish buildings of the 12th century. While remaining structurally simple, the Irish churches of the period have carved doorways, chancel-arches or windows, with ornament in an Irish variation of the style. The most impressive example of the style is the arcaded and richly carved Cormac's Chapel on the Rock of Cashel, County Tipperary, consecrated in 1134. The use of rib-vaulting over the chancel here is very early, not only for Ireland, but for the rest of Europe. Many of the characteristic features of the early churches, such as antae and sloping jambs, were kept throughout the Romanesque period. The use of the chevron, an ornamental moulding, is common in Irish Romanesque work, and it is nearly always combined with rows of beading. The use of carved human heads as capitals to the shafts in the orders of the doorway may be seen in the portal at Clonfert, County Galway, which has some of the most richly carved Irish Romanesque decoration. This style is also referred to as Hiberno-Romanesque.

Transitional Architecture

At the time the Romanesque style was so popular, a plainer type of church building was being introduced by the Cistercian order, whose first church in Ireland, Mellifont Abbey in County Louth, was influenced by Continental churches, with simple, carved decoration. Examples of the 12th-century churches of this transitional style are at Baltinglass, County Wicklow; Boyle, County Roscommon; and Jerpoint, County Kilkenny.

Gothic Architecture

With the coming of the Normans and the changes they wrought, the native tradition in building declined, and Gothic architecture was introduced in the 13th century. The Irish Gothic cathedrals were on a smaller scale than their English and Continental counterparts; the grouping of lancets in the east window and south choir wall is typical of the Irish buildings of this time, such as the ruined cathedral of Cashel, County Tipperary. The restored cathedrals of St Canice, Kilkenny, and St Patrick, Dublin, are also good examples. Gothic parish churches in the plain Early English style were built only in anglicized parts of the country, for example at Gowran, County Kilkenny.

Because of the turbulent times during the 14th century, very little building was done in Ireland. This changed in the 15th and 16th centuries, when a native Gothic style began to emerge, particularly in the west. It is best seen in the Franciscan friaries and the rebuilt Cistercian abbeys of the period. A good example of the Franciscan style, with narrow church, a tall tapering tower, carved cloister and small window openings can be seen at the well-preserved ruin at Quin, County Clare. The Cistercian style, with a larger church, a huge square tower topped by stepped battlements, and a large carved cloister, can be seen at Kilcooly and Holycross, County Tipperary.

Castles

Although the Normans had built many castles before they came to Ireland, in the first years of the invasion they built fortifications of wood, usually taking over the sites of ancient Irish forts. The remains of these can be seen all over the eastern half of the country in the form of mottes and baileys. At the end of the 12th century, the construction of stone fortifications on a large scale began. An early example of Norman building skill is at Trim, County Meath. It has a great square keep in a large bailey, defended by a high embattled wall, with turrets and barbicans. Other examples of this type are at Carlingford, County Louth, and Carrickfergus, County Antrim.

A very attractive feature of the Irish countryside is the ruined 15th- or 16th-century towerhouse, which became common from about 1420. These fortified farms consisted of a tall, square tower that usually had a small walled *bawn* or courtyard. In most cases the *bawn* has disappeared, but well-preserved examples can be seen at Doe Castle near Creeslough, County Donegal; Pallas, County Galway; and Dunguaire (Dungory), near Kinvara, County Galway.

Topics

06

The People

The people are thus inclined: religious, frank, amorous, sufferable of infinite paines, verie glorious, manie sorcerers, excellent horsemen, delighted with wars, great alms-givers, passing in hospitality.
                                    Holinshed's *Chronicles*, 1577

This description so aptly fits the Irish today that there remain only a few superficial remarks on the subject. Conditions have changed radically. For a start, almost half of the population lives in the spreading cities. Still, compared to its near-neighbour, England, and to many other European countries, Ireland is a very rural place, and even city-dwellers have close links with their country background. Wherever they live, though, Irish people have a healthy disdain for time and the hustle and bustle of business. As you travel around, bear in mind the old Irish saying, 'When God made time he made plenty of it.' You will become aware of a great sense of shared identity and neighbourly feeling, particularly towards those in trouble, or the very old.

The traits peculiar to the Irish that always reassert themselves, wherever they are in the world, are numerous. Amongst them is a delight in words and wordplay (reading anything by Flann O'Brien or James Joyce will give you a taste of it); a love of parties and *craic* (a good time), music, dancing and witty talk; a ready kindness that never fails; great hospitality and an interest in your affairs that is never mere inquisitiveness but a charming device to put you at your ease.

The Irish do however have a certain irascible spirit, quickly roused in the face of bland priggishness. They never forget an insult or a wrong, and this memory will go back for generations; it might have been a quarrel over land or the meanness of the local gentry. Oliver Cromwell is still remembered with hatred for his savage campaign in the 1650s. The Irish can also be untidy – in their houses and in the countryside, and ignorance or indifference towards aesthetic matters exists. Old buildings often go to rack and ruin, and vile ribbon development chokes the towns and the countryside around them. There is a phenomenon of rusty cars dumped in lonely glens, litter in any old place, and general messiness. Not for the Irish the freshly painted doors and gateways of the Anglo-Saxon.

Each province and county of Ireland produces further individual traits. Northerners have a reputation for direct speech and a certain fighting spirit. The Munster people are held in respect for their poetry. A Dubliner might be considered a bit of a know-all. The people of Connacht are famous for their hospitality and strength.

Finally, one last word in this briefest of outlines: the Irish still have a great sense of the spiritual. The Catholic Church is very strong (despite recent sex scandals, the secularization of the schools and the introduction of divorce) but so is the faith of Church of Ireland members and of the Presbyterians, to judge by the large numbers who attend their churches on Sundays. Religion is the great anchor that pervades all aspects of living. This, perhaps, partly explains why in Ireland there is sometimes little thought for the future, and life is lived for the moment.

The Fairy People

The Fairy People, or *Daoine Sidhe*, are a rich part of Irish folklore. According to peasant belief, they are fallen angels who are not good enough to be saved and not bad enough to languish in Hell. Some say they are the gods of the Earth, as is written in the *Book of Armagh*, or the pagan gods of Ireland, the Tuatha Dé Danaan (the Tuatha may also have been a race of invaders whose origins are lost in the mists of time). Antiquarians have different theories but, whatever they surmise, these fairy people persist in the popular imagination and are kept alive in tradition and myth.

The Fairy People are quickly offended, and must always be referred to as the 'Gentry' or the 'Good People'. They are also easily pleased, and will keep misfortune from your door if you leave them a bowl of milk on the windowsill overnight. Their evil seems to be without malice, and their chief occupations are feasting, fighting, making love and playing or listening to beautiful music. (The only hardworking person amongst them is the leprechaun, who is kept busy making the shoes they wear out through dancing.) It is said that many of the beautiful tunes of Ireland are theirs, remembered by mortal eavesdroppers. Apparently, Carolan, the last of the great Irish bards, slept on a *rath* that, like the many prehistoric standing stones in Ireland, had become a fairy place in folk tradition; for ever after, fairy music ran in his head and made him the great musician he was.

Some of the fairy types are not very pleasant. The following are brief descriptions of a few:

The **banshee**, from *bean sidhe*, is a woman fairy or attendant spirit who follows the old families, and wails before a death. The *keen*, the funeral cry of the peasantry, is said to be an imitation of her cry. An omen that sometimes accompanies the old woman is an immense black coach, carrying a coffin and drawn by headless riders.

The **leprechaun**, or fairy shoemaker, is solitary, old and bad tempered; he's the practical joker among 'the Good People'. He is very rich because of his trade, and buries his pots of gold at the end of rainbows. He also takes many treasure crocks, buried in times of war, for his own. Many believe he is the Dé Danaan god Lugh, the god of arts and crafts, who degenerated in popular lore into the leprechaun.

The *leanhaun shee*, or fairy mistress, longs for the love of mortal men. If they refuse, she must be their slave; if they consent, they are hers and can only escape by finding another to take their place. The fairy lives on their life while they waste away, and death is no escape. She has become identified in political song and verse with the Gaelic Muse, for she gives inspiration to those whom she persecutes.

The **pooka** lives in solitary mountain places and old ruins, and is of a nightmarish aspect. It is a November spirit, and often assumes the form of a stallion. It comes from water and is only easy to tame if you can keep him away from the sight of it. If you cannot, he will plunge in with his rider and tear him or her to pieces at the bottom. Some authorities have linked the pooka with a he-goat from *púca* or *poc*, the Gaelic for goat. Others maintain that it is a forefather of Shakespeare's Puck in *A Midsummer Night's Dream*.

Tracing Your Ancestors

If you have any Irish blood in you at all, you will have a passion for genealogy. The Irish seem to like looking backwards. When they had nothing left – no land, no Brehon laws, no religious freedom – they held on to their pride and their genealogy. Waving these before the eyes of French and Spanish rulers ensured that they got posts at court or commissions in the army. There is thus no such thing as class envy in Ireland: everyone is as good as the next man, and everyone is descended from some prince or hero from the Irish past. It is the descendants of the Cromwellian parvenues who had to bolster up their images with portraits and fine furniture. Now the planter families have the Irish obsession with their ancestors too.

Information and sources for research are rather fragmented, and it would be best to write to the Genealogical Office in the National Library in Dublin before you come, to ask their advice, or contact the Irish Genealogical Project, which is also very helpful. For Ulster families, try the Ulster Historical Foundation. You must have first found out as much as possible from family papers, old relatives, and the records of the Church and State in your own country; your local historical or genealogical society might be

Sources of Genealogical Information

Genealogical centres within the various counties are also listed in 'Sports and Activities' in the grey boxes in the relevant sightseeing chapters, as well as in the main text of the book.

Calgagh Heritage Centre, Butcher St, Derry City, Co. Londonderry, t (028) 7137 1967. This holds genealogical data from 1663 in its heritage library. There is an extensive computerized genealogical database, which currently holds more than 2 million records. Admission is free.

Clare Heritage Centre and Genealogical Society, Church St, Corofin, Co. Clare, t (065) 683 7955, *http://clare.irish-roots.net*. This holds parish records for Co. Clare (post-1864); staff will research family history. *Closed Sat and Sun.*

Cobh Heritage Centre, Cobh, Co. Cork, t (021) 481 3591, *www.cobhheritage.com*. This offers a record-search service for approximately €25.

Eneclann, Unit 1, Trinity College Enterprise Centre, Pearse St, Dublin 2, t (01) 671 0338, *www.eneclann.ie*. Staff here will undertake genealogical and historical research on your behalf. An initial search assessment costs around €21.

Heraldic Artists Ltd, 3 Nassau St, Dublin 2, t (01) 679 7020, *www.heraldicartists.com*. A Dublin bookshop that stocks a lot of useful genealogical publications.

Genealogical Office, National Library, 2 Kildare St, Dublin 2, t (01) 603 0200, *www.nli.ie*. This handles enquiries into heraldry, genealogy and family history for the whole of Ireland, and staff will make searches for you for a small fee. It also publishes a useful leaflet, *Getting Started*, that introduces you to the records it holds. This is also the contact address for a list of research agencies in the Republic. Consultations are by appointment only. *Closed Sat pm and Sun.*

General Register Office (Births, Marriages and Deaths), Government Offices, Convent Rd, Roscommon, t (090) 663 2900, *www. groireland.ie*. Staff here will supply birth, marriage or death certificates. Marriages of non-Catholics were recorded from 1845, of all faiths from 1864. The search fees are reasonable. *Closed Sat and Sun*. There's a second office at 49–55 Chichester St, Belfast BT1 4HL, t (028) 9025 2000, *www.groni.gov.uk*.

Irish Family History Foundation, Pat Stafford, Yola Farmstead, Tagoat, Co. Wexford, t (053) 32611, *www.irish-roots.net*. A cross-border umbrella organization for local genealogical and historical societies.

able to help. Find out the full name of your emigrant ancestor, the background of his or her family, whether rich, poor, merchants or farmers, Catholic or Protestant. The family tradition of remembering the name of the parish or townland is a great help.

In America, immigrant records have been published by Baltimore Genealogical Publishing Company in seven volumes, and lists the arrival of people in New York between 1846 and 1851. In Canada, the Department of Irish Studies at St Mary's University, Halifax, is very helpful. In Australia, the Civil Records are very good: try the National Library, Canberra, the Mitchell Library, Sydney, and the Society of Australian Genealogists, Richmond Villa, 120 Kent Street, Sydney.

Music

Traditional Irish music is played everywhere in Ireland: in the cities and in the countryside. Government sponsorship helped to revive it, especially through **Radio na Gaeltachta** (Irish-language radio) in the west. Now there is great enthusiasm for it: a nine-year-old will sing a lover's lament about seduction and desertion without

Its research centres all over Ireland have computerized information on Irish families; parish and appropriate civil records are being collected and filed. An initial search costs around €75. Enclose an international reply coupon if contacting by post.
Irish Genealogical Project, 7–9 Merrion Row, Dublin 2, *www.irishgenealogy.ie*. This is a source of information and advice for researchers and for those commissioning research.
Irish Genealogical Research Society, c/o The Irish Club, 82 Eaton Square, London SW1W 9AJ, England, *www.igrsoc.org*. A charity that promotes research and has a valuable library containing manuscripts of family histories, memoirs and pedigrees, useful for those whose research is pre-1864. It also publishes an annual journal, *The Irish Genealogist*. Staff cannot undertake research for you. Admission is £10. *Closed exc Sat 2–6*.
National Archives, Bishop St, Dublin 8, t (01) 407 2300, *www.nationalarchives.ie*. The Public Record Office in Dublin burnt down in 1922, and with it many of the Church of Ireland registers. This houses Griffith's *Primary Valuation of Ireland, 1848–63*, which records the names of those owning or occupying land and property, rebellion reports and records relating to

1798; it also holds records of transportees to Australia. You need to bring along some form of ID in order to obtain a Reader's Ticket. *Closed Sat and Sun*.
National Library, Kildare St, Dublin 2, t (01) 603 0200, *www.nli.ie*. This holds many sources: books, newspapers and manuscripts, including Griffith's *Primary Valuation of Tenements*, the Tithe Applotment Books, microfilm copies of Roman Catholic parish registers up to 1880 and a collection of landed estate records. *Closed Sat pm and Sun*.
Public Records Office of Northern Ireland, 66 Balmoral Ave, Belfast BT9 6NY, t (028) 9025 5905, *www.proni.gov.uk*. Tithe applotment records, valuation and church records, pre-1864.
Registry of Deeds, Henrietta St, Dublin 7, t (01) 670 7500, or lo-call t 1890 333001, *www.irlgov.ie/landreg/*. This holds records of land matters from 1708 onwards. Visitors can carry out research for a small fee. *Closed Sat and Sun*.
Ulster Historical Foundation, 12 College Square East, Belfast, t (028) 9033 2288, *www.uhf.org.uk*. This undertakes searches and has published a useful guide, *Ulster Libraries, Archives, Museums and Ancestral Heritage Centres – A Visitor's Guide*.

batting an eyelid to a grandfather whose generation scarcely remembered the Gaelic songs at all. Traditional music has strengthened its hold on the cultural life of the country, rather than sadly declining as it has done in England. Today Ireland has one of the most vigorous music traditions in Europe, and this is a big pull for many visitors. Irish ballads are sung the world over: many emigrants consider themselves exiles still, and the commercial record industry churns out the ballads. Most record covers tend to be decorated with grinning leprechauns and a few shamrocks for good measure.

Serious traditional music is not in this folksy style. Listening to it can induce a state of exultant melancholy or infectious merriment. Whatever way, it goes straight to your heart. The lyrics deal with the ups and downs of love, failed rebellions (especially that of 1798), soldiering, dead heroes, religion and homesick love for the beauty of the countryside. Not surprisingly, comparatively few deal with occupations or work.

The bard in pre-Christian society was held in honour and a great deal of awe for his learning and the mischievous satire in his poetry and music. After the Cromwellian and Williamite wars, he lost his status altogether; music and poetry were kept alive by the country people, who cheered themselves up during the dark winter evenings with stories and music. Sadly, nowadays the traditional Irish harp is scarcely used, except when it is dragged out for the benefit of tourists. The main traditional instruments used are the *uilleann* pipes, which are rather more sophisticated than the Scottish bagpipes, the fiddle (violin) and the tin whistle. The beat and rhythm are provided by a hand-held drum made from stretched goat hide, called the *bodhrán*. The accordion, the flute, guitar and the piano are used by some groups as well, and are played singly or together. A popular feature of the traditional music scene are the *seisiúns* – informal sessions of music, *céilís* and cabaret.

The airs, laments, slip jigs, reels and songs all vary enormously from region to region, and you might easily hear a Cork man or a Leitrim fiddler discussing the interpretation of a certain piece with heated emotion. Pieces are constantly improvised upon, and seldom written down; inevitably some of the content gets changed from generation to generation. Traditional fiddle music from County Donegal has long been among the best in the land. A form of singing that had almost died out by the 1940s is the *Sean-Nós*, fully ornamented and sung, unaccompanied, in Gaelic. Today the *Sean-Nós* section in music festivals is overflowing with entrants.

Today Ireland is producing some good musicians of a completely different type from the folk groups. The local bands that play in the bars play jazz, blues and a rhythmical and melodious combination of pop and traditional instruments. Look in the local newspaper of any big town or ask in a record shop; they will know what gigs are on and probably be able to sell you a ticket as well. Some big names on the rock and pop scene have come from Ireland, including Van Morrison, U2, The Corrs, The Cranberries, Westlife and Sinéad O'Connor. The phenomenal success of *Riverdance*, which toured the world and sold out in every venue, has given traditional music and dance the glamour of Broadway.

You will have no difficulty hearing traditional ballads or folk music in bars or hotels; players usually advertise in the local newspaper, or by sticking a notice in the window. They are usually only too happy to let you join. In 1951 **Comhaltas Ceoltóirí Éireann** was set up to promote traditional music, song and dance. It now has 200 branches around the country, and their members have regular *seisiúns*, which are open to all. Ask at a tourist office or write to Comhaltas Ceoltóirí Éireann, 32 Belgrave Square, Monkstown, County Dublin, **t** (01) 280 0295.

Boglands

Ireland is literally rich in boglands, formed over many hundreds of years. In the past, boglands were despised, except as a source of fuel, but nowadays we know how rich they are in flora, fauna and also history: underneath the bog, well-preserved bodies, jewelled crosiers for bishops, golden cups, giant elks' antlers and brittle pots of butter have all been revealed as the turf is cut away. A vast quantity of folklore has grown up around them too, beautifully described in *Irish Folk Ways* by E. Estyn Evans. In many fairy stories, humans are lured off their path and into the bog by strange lights at night. Indeed, walking on bogs can be very mucky and sometimes dangerous, so keep to the few paths and try to go with a local to guide you.

Many writers describe the great peace and wellbeing to be had from a day on the bogs, cutting turf. Even now, Dubliners cling to their cutting rights on a piece of Wicklow hill, for there is something eminently satisfying about cutting the sods of rich blackness, and then, during the bitter cold winter nights, heaping them onto the open fire.

About 14 percent of Ireland's land surface is bog. The brooding immutability and the drizzling rain and winds that sweep it have surely contributed towards the Irish philosophy of fatality. There are two types – blanket and raised. The latter are mainly to be found in the midlands. In Ireland, wetness is a key factor in the formation of peat, which begins in lakes and ponds as plants invade the water. Sphagnum moss is the vital plant because it holds water like a sponge and has a great capacity for trapping nutrients. Peat builds up because the moss releases acid that inhibits the breakdown of dead plants.

The Irish economy has been bolstered by the boglands. The government-owned turf company, Bord na Móna, was set up in 1946 and has drained vast areas of peat, cutting it by machines and using the fuel to generate electricity. The sphagnum in the upper layers is baled as horticultural peat and sold for use in gardens all over Britain. But the draining of the bogs has consequences for rivers, and for those living near them in valleys, for the bogs act like huge natural sponges that soak up rainfall and release it very slowly. Thus, if the bog is stripped away, there is danger of flooding. Stripping is also ecologically costly, as gully erosion results. Some hand-cut bogs, when left, show signs of being colonized and healed by the bog-forming plants themselves, but this is unlikely to happen in machine-cut bogs. Sheep-grazing and burning also do damage. A balance must be found between economic needs and conservation needs, because at the rate the machines can cut the turf, there will be no more left within the next 20 years. All the insects, birds and animals that find a home in the bog will disappear if nothing is done, and we will lose the flight of the golden plover and the special mosses and flowers.

Historic Houses and Gardens

If you want to try to understand the Anglo-Irish, who have a very muddled status amongst most shades of opinion, the best thing to do is to look round one of their houses. The expression 'Anglo-Irish' has political, social and religious connotations. It is used to describe the waves of English settlers and their descendants who became so powerful in the land after the success of the campaigns of Elizabeth I of England. An optimistic view is held by some that 'Anglo-Irish' is a tag that should only be applied to literature, and indeed it does seem ridiculous that, after 300 years of living in a place, these land-owning families are not counted as truly Irish. On the one hand, it is a fact that the sons of the Ascendancy were educated in England, served the British Empire as soldiers or civil servants, and saw themselves as different from the native Irish; whilst on the other, many of these people felt a great and patriotic love for Ireland, led revolts and uprisings against British rule and, starting with the Normans, became 'more Irish than the Irish themselves', as the Latin saying goes.

Ireland's Big Houses were built by families who would be most offended if you called them English, although as far as the Gaelic Irish are concerned, that is what they are. 'The Big House' is another very Irish expression; it is applied to a landowner's house regardless of its size or grandeur. In fact, if you look through Burke's *Guide to Irish Country Houses* and the rather depressing, but fascinating, *Vanishing Houses of Ireland* (published by the Irish Architectural Archive and the Irish Georgian Society), you will get a very good idea of the variety and huge number of houses that belonged to the gentry. (Valerie and Thomas Pakenham's book *The Big House in Ireland* also gives fascinating and witty insights into life behind doors.)

The English monarchs always financed their Irish wars by paying their soldiers with grants of land in Ireland, and, as the country was so unruly, during the 17th century the settlers lived in fortified or semi-fortified houses. There are only a very few examples of Tudor domestic architecture. Portumna Castle, in County Galway, is a ruined mansion of this type, but the most famous of them is Ormonde Castle in Carrick-on- Suir, in County Tipperary, which has the remains of some 16th-century stuccowork, including a plasterwork portrait of Elizabeth I. Look out also for the early-17th-century plasterwork if you visit Bunratty Castle, in County Clare. Another interesting house that it is possible to visit is Huntington Castle in County Carlow, a fortified Jacobean house constructed in 1620. The most impressive and the first Irish building in the grand Renaissance style is the late-17th-century Royal Hospital at Kilmainham in Dublin, which has been rescued from dereliction and restored. It now houses the Irish Museum of Modern Art, and its state rooms are once more decorated with rich and costly furnishings.

The majority of Big Houses were built in the 100 years following the Penal Laws in the 1690s, when the Protestant landowners settled down to enjoy their gains. The civil and domestic architecture that survives from these times is both elegant and splendid, and is to be found in every county. The chief centre of this 18th-century architecture was, of course, Dublin. Even before the unfortunate Union of Ireland with England in 1801, it was a confident, learned and artistic capital. Today, in spite of the building developers, it has held on to its gracious heritage. When you are in Dublin, make a point of walking around the elegant residential squares of St Stephen's Green, Merrion Square and Fitzwilliam Square to the south of the city, and, on the north side, Parnell and Mountjoy squares. The two great masterpieces of public building, the Custom House and the Four Courts, were built by James Gandon towards the close of the century, and they still dominate the skyline. A few distinguished buildings were added to the city in the 19th century, including Gandon's King's Inns, but after the Union, building in Dublin tended to stagnate.

A Big House usually consists of a square, grey stone block, sometimes with wings, set amongst gardens and parkland with stables at the back, and a walled garden. Sometimes it is called a castle, although sometimes the only attribute of a castle it may have is a deep fosse. A lingering insecurity must often have remained, for many of them are almost as tall as they are wide, with up to four storeys, rather like a Georgian version of the 16th-century towerhouse. The buildings are completely different in atmosphere here from their counterparts in England. They have not undergone Victorian 'improvements' or gradually assumed an air of comfortable mellowness over the centuries. It was an act of bravado on the part of the Anglo-Irish to build them at all, for they always had to be on the alert against the disaffected natives, who readily formed agrarian groups such as the White Boys. They never had enough money to add on layer after layer in the newest architectural fashion; their houses remained Palladian splendours or Gothick fantasies that were constructed during the Georgian age, when the old fortified house could at last be exchanged for something more comfortable.

The Big Houses that remain are full of beautiful furniture, pictures, *objets d'art* and the paraphernalia of generations who appreciated beauty, good horses, and hard drinking and eating, and were generous and slapdash by nature. It is against this background of grey stately houses looking onto sylvan scenes and cosseted by sweeping trees that one should read Maria Edgeworth, supplying some details oneself on the Penal Laws, the famine, the foreignness of the landlords and their loyalties. The literature on the 'Big House' is huge, and if you read Thackeray, Trollope, Charles Lever, Somerville and Ross, and more Maria Edgeworth on the subject, you will not only be entertained but well informed. The Big House, the courthouse, the jail and the military barracks were all symbols of oppression, and not surprisingly many of them got burnt out in the 1920s. But these houses echo with the voices of talented and liberal people: the wit of Sheridan, Wilde, the conversations of Mrs Delany, the gleeful humour of Somerville and Ross, whisper through the rooms as you wander around.

In England there is a whole network of organizations and legislation to protect the historic house. In the Republic of Ireland there are no exact equivalents of the National Trust or the Historic Building and Monuments Commission, and no National Heritage fund. This means that there are no grants for repairs to buildings, and no effective legislation to protect them from dereliction or neglect. Even now the Big House is persistently regarded by the powers that be as tainted with the memories of colonialism and an oppressive age. They are labelled as 'not Irish', although the artisans who built and carved the wonderful details of cornicing, stuccowork and dovetailing, elegant staircases and splendid decoration were as Irish as could be. There are many desolate shells to glimpse on your travels, though it is still possible to go around quite a selection of well-cared-for properties.

The Heritage Council is allocated a little money to help a few architecturally important buildings each year. It was set up by Charles Haughey and has helped to change official attitudes. But it is the Irish Georgian Society (*74 Merrion Sq, Dublin,* **t** *(01) 676 7053, www.archeire.com/igs/*) that has so far done most to secure the future of the Big House. Founded in 1958 to work for the preservation of Ireland's architectural heritage, the society has carried out numerous rescue and restoration works on historic houses. Other influential organisations include An Taisce, The National Trust for Ireland (*Tailor's Hall, Back Lane, Dublin 8,* **t** *(01) 454 1786, www.antaisce.org*); they have saved much of Georgian Dublin from the demolishers.

Later Architectural Forms

Palladian: used to describe a pseudo-classical architectural style taken from the 16th-century Italian architect, Palladio. Sir Edward Lovett Pearce introduced the style to Ireland, and it was continued by his pupil, Richard Cassels, also known as Castle. Carton and Castletown in Co. Kildare, and Russborough in Co. Wicklow are good examples of the Palladian style, in which the central block of each house is flanked by pavilions. One of the most perfect Palladian houses in the British Isles is Bellamont Forest in Co. Cavan, designed by Pearce, which is unfortunately closed.

Neoclassical: a style of building that is similar to that of Palladio but was more directly inspired by the civilization of Ancient Rome. It became popular in the 1750s until the Gothic Revival.

Gothic Revival: From the 1830s, many houses and churches were built in a style harking back to the Tudor and perpendicular forms; their popularity gradually gave way to the more severe style of the Early-English and Decorated Gothic. English architect Augustus Pugin (1812–52) equated the Gothic with the Christian, and Classicism with the pagan. He designed some Irish churches and cathedrals, including St Mary's Cathedral in Killarney. J. J. McCarthy (1817–82), an Irish architect, was very strongly influenced by Pugin; see his work at St Patrick's (RC) Cathedral, Armagh.

Gothick: an amusing and romantic style that was popular in the late 18th century. It is spelt with a 'k' to distinguish it from the serious, and later, Gothic Revival. Gothick castles were built by Francis Johnston and the English Pain brothers, who came over to Ireland with John Nash during the 1780s.

Hiberno-Romanesque: A style that was popular in Catholic church architecture from the 1850s onwards. It fitted in with growing national feelings to lay claim to an 'Irish style' that existed before the Anglo-Norman invasion. A good example of it can be seen at the RC Church in Spiddal, Co. Galway.

Irish Rococo Plasterwork: The great period of rococo plasterwork in Ireland began with the Swiss-Italian brothers Paul and Philip Francini, who came to Ireland in 1739 to decorate the ceiling at Carton, Maynooth, for the Earl of Kildare. They were great *stuccodores* and modelled magnificent combinations of plaster figures, trophies, fruit and flowers. See their work at Castletown House, Celbridge, Co. Kildare and at

Newman House, 85–6 St Stephen's Green, Dublin. Irish craftsmen quickly learned the technique, and between 1740 and 1760 many beautiful ceilings were created. They tended to leave out figures, and concentrate on birds, flowers, and musical instruments. The ceilings are graceful yet lively, with a swirling gaiety that makes Adam ceilings, which later became the fashion, seem rather stilted. A fine example of a rococo ceiling and staircase is at 20 Lower Dominick Street, Dublin, where the composition of birds, flowers and fruits is perfect. Other splendid examples of this rococo exuberance can be seen at Russborough, Co. Wicklow, the Rotunda Hospital Chapel, Dublin, and Newman House, 85–86 St Stephen's Green, Dublin.

Selected Architects

Richard Cassels, also known as Castle (*c.* 1690–1751). Cassels was responsible for some of the most beautiful country houses in Ireland. He was of Huguenot origin (his family came from Germany to England), and was part of the circle surrounding Lord Burlington, the wealthy and scholarly aristocrat who did so much to bring neoclassicism to Britain. Cassels came to Ireland in the 1720s and designed Powerscourt House, in Co. Wicklow, which so sadly was burnt down in the 1970s. He also designed Carton House in Co. Kildare, the Rotunda Hospital in Dublin, many houses on St Stephen's Green, and Leinster House. He is credited with the designs for Parliament House (now the Bank of Ireland building) on College Green. Cassels was also involved in designing the Newry Canal, begun in 1730, which linked the coalfield of Coalisland in Co. Tyrone to Newry, a distance of 18 miles (28.8 km). It was the first major canal in the British Isles. He designed the Doric Temple and the Dining Halls in Trinity College, Dublin.

James Gandon (1743–1823). Born in London of Huguenot origin, and apprenticed to William Chambers, the Scottish architect, Gandon was invited to Ireland to build a new Custom House in Dublin. He arrived in 1781 and it was completed the same year. He was later commissioned to make extensions to Parliament House on College Green, and his Classical Four Courts were finished in 1802. He also designed the King's Inns, although he resigned from the project in 1808 because of irritation with the Lord Chancellor, and it was completed by his partner, Baker. His buildings – original and harmonious combinations of elegant neoclassical and Palladian Baroque styles – set the seal on Dublin's character at the time of Grattan's Parliament.

Francis Johnston (1760–1829). An architect in Armagh, he was responsible for many of the fine buildings there, such as the Observatory. He moved to Dublin in 1793, where he designed the Chapel Royal in Dublin Castle, and the GPO in O'Connell Street. He also supervised the rebuilding of the House of Commons. He made a huge contribution to founding the Royal Hibernian Academy of Painting, Sculpture and Architecture in 1823, and he was its president for many years. He designed some Gothick castles such as Charleville Forest in Co. Cork.

Sir Charles Lanyon (1813–89). Born in Belfast, Lanyon built the Custom House in the city in 1857. Lanyon was adept at creating country houses in the Italian style; imposing and florid buildings adapted from Italian palaces and villas of the High Renaissance Period.

Sir Richard Morrison (1767–1849). A Regency architect from West Cork who designed the neoclassical Fota House, in Co. Cork, where the estate buildings, including a huntsman's lodge, are scaled-down versions of the house. You can also see his fine courthouse in Galway City.

John Nash (1752–1835). An English architect who designed grand country houses, among them Killymoon Castle and Caledon in Co. Tyrone. His elegant neoclassical style can be seen in the planned terraces of Regent's Park, London, and in the Royal Pavilion, Brighton.

Sir Edward Lovett Pearce (1699–1733). Born in County Meath, he served as a soldier. While visiting Italy in his early 20s, he made drawings of the buildings in Venice and other Italian cities. He was the leader of the Irish Palladians, and he designed the interior of the largest and most splendid of all Irish country houses, Castletown in Co. Kildare. Pearce became an MP and, in 1730, Surveyor-General. He worked on the Irish Houses of Parliament on College Green (the first purpose-built parliament house in the world, and now the Bank of Ireland), together with his pupil Richard Cassels (*see* p.75).

Robert West (*c.* 1730–90). A Dublin architect and *stuccodore* responsible for many of the fine houses in the Georgian squares of Dublin, including 20 Lower Dominick Street, which it is possible to visit, and No.85 St Stephen's Green, Dublin.

Gardens and Arboreta

If you love the colours, shapes, textures and scents of peaceful and mature gardens, you can have a marvellous time touring the many gardens of Ireland. The climate is a fortunate one for plants and trees because it is temperate and rainy; there is a variety of rocks and soils; and the winter is so mild it allows for the cultivation of tender plants. The grass grows well and makes generous areas of green, interacting with the formal hedges, herbaceous borders, impressive trees and romantic stretches of water that nearly always enhance the parkland of these gardens.

Gaelic Ireland does not have a long horticultural tradition. It began when the Anglo-Normans and later settlers introduced the idea of a pleasure garden, with its flowers and fruits. The unsettled state of Ireland, with its many hundreds of years of internal fighting and conquest, left little time for gardening until the 18th century. By then the country was calmer and the new 'Ascendancy' began to build themselves comfortable houses, formal gardens and parklands. They planted their estates with fine oak and beech woods, and it is usually fairly obvious today where the lands around you formed part of a demesne, because of the trees. Inevitably, these parks and gardens were regarded as symbols of conquest, and they were often attacked by the landless peasants. An attitude still prevails in Ireland that does not value trees, except as firewood, and very few non-sacred ones are left to grow on the lands of the small farmer.

That said, one of the most attractive features of the Irish landscape is the way your eye is drawn to the top of ancient *raths* or ring forts that are crowned by graceful trees. These grow undisturbed because of their association with the fairies. Many landlords planted exotic species of trees around these forts and on small hillocks in the 19th century, and they do much to beautify the landscape. The Huguenots who came to Ireland with William of Orange brought with them new fashions in evergreens, topiary, and flowers such as tulips, pinks and auriculas. Mazes were laid within clipped hedges, and there are still a few examples, as at Birr Castle in Co. Offaly and Kilruddery, near Bray, Co. Wicklow.

Most of the Irish gardens that survive were started in the 18th and 19th centuries. The Dublin Florists' Club, which was founded in 1746, was a great stimulus to the propagation of flowers and trees. It sounds like a very convivial society whose members (mainly aristocrats, army men and clergy), met in taverns and drank endless toasts to the King, the Royal Family and 'the glorious memory' (of William III). After these loyal toasts, exhibits of carnations and auriculas were passed around to be admired by the assembled company. Specimens were named and premiums were offered to plantsmen by the society.

More recently, Ireland has become famous for its roses, which are cultivated by very famous breeders such as Dickens and McCredy's, and for its daffodils, bred by Guy Wilson near Broughshane, Co. Antrim and Lionel Richardson of Waterford.

The mid 18th century saw the fashion for naturalized parkland take over from formal gardening. In the 19th century William Robertson, who started life as an Irish garden boy in County Laois, led the revolution against bedding plants and artifice and became the advocate of wild gardens – where the plant was suited to the situation and the garden to the nature of the ground. Mount Usher in County Wicklow and Anne's Grove Gardens in County Cork are fine examples of his style.

For those who love rock gardens designed as miniature mountain landscapes, the garden at Rowallane in County Down is a delight. Mount Stewart, also in County Down, is full of the bizarre, including fanciful topiary. There is a charming Japanese garden at Tully (part of the National Hunt Stud), and Kilruddery and Powerscourt in County Wicklow are lovely examples of Italianate gardens with beautiful ironwork and classical statuary. The arboreta at Castlewellan, Fota, Birr and Powerscourt are very famous; and at Derreen in County Kerry the Australian tree fern has become naturalized. Howth Castle Gardens in County Dublin and Rowallane in County Down have superb rhododendron trees.

Glenveagh Castle in County Donegal and Glin Castle Gardens in County Limerick are special favourites. Both are a happy mixture of formal and wild gardens, with huge walled gardens filled with flowers, vegetables and herbs. Both have wonderful natural settings. Another great favourite is Birr Castle Gardens, in the heart of Ireland. If you are in Dublin, do not neglect to go to the superb Botanical Gardens in Glasnevin.

The list of treasures and rare species in Irish gardens open to the public is very impressive, and there are too many to mention here. Useful publications are *The Gardens of Ireland* by Tourism Ireland, *The Hidden Gardens of Ireland* by Marianne Heron (Gill & Macmillan) and *Irish Gardens* by Terence Reeves-Smyth (Appletree Press). The Royal Horticultural Society of Ireland (*Swanbrook House, Bloomfield Ave, Morehampton Rd, Dublin 4, t (01) 668 4358, www.rhsi.ie*) holds flower shows, lectures, and garden visits. The Ulster Gardens Scheme (*contact the Northern Irish Tourist Board*) organizes open days in many gardens.

Potatoes and the Famine

Potatoes were the principal form of food for Irish peasants during the 19th century. The whole family would sit around a *kishawn* (basket) made of willow placed on the three-legged iron pot in which the spuds had been boiled. The summer months were known as the hungry months, because the old crop of potatoes was finished. The last Sunday in July, or the first Sunday in August, was the ancient feast of *Lughnasa* (Lammas), which was a celebration of the start of the new harvest. Sometimes a delicious mixture of new potatoes, milk, onion, spices and melted butter would be eaten from the first digging of the new potatoes, known as *colcannon*.

The potato crop enabled large families to live on tiny, subdivided holdings on the poorest land. The vegetables were grown in lazy beds, the farmers using spades to build up ridges of soil on these stony hillside farms. You can still see the traces of lazy beds in hillside parts of Munster. Today they are no longer cultivated; many were abandoned in the famine times.

The potato blight, a fungal disease that struck between 1845 and 1849, had fatal consequences for the peasants who were living in this subsistence economy, especially those in the west and southwest of the country. Enormous suffering, death and disease followed, as well as the departure of millions of folk for Britain, Australia, Canada and America.

The consequences of the famine and emigration were enormous, and in fact still affect Ireland today. The population of Irish-speaking small farmers declined dramatically from 1847; nearly a quarter of a million emigrated every year. The landscape was emptied of people, villages became deserted, and the more prosperous farmers increased their land holdings. Very often all but the eldest son in a family emigrated; he was left to carry on with the farm, and he did not marry until very late in life, usually when his parents were dead. The wandering labourer who had an important place in society gradually died out as a class after the famine. These labourers had once gone to hiring-fairs all over the provinces to be taken on by 'strong' or 'comfortable' farmers, as the better-off were called. Many were poets and storytellers and as such helped to keep oral traditions alive. The spade was the essential tool that each labourer carried with him, and every region in Ireland had its own variation of spade that was made by the blacksmith to suit local conditions. A Munster spade, for instance, is typically a very long, narrow blade with fishtail ends.

'Clonakilty God help us' is an expression that originates from the time when that area westwards through Rosscarbery and Skibbereen, in County Cork, suffered terribly. At Knockfierna in west County Limerick there is a village that has been preserved as a memorial to the famine. Before it struck, about 1,000 people lived on the hill overlooking the Golden Vale. Afterwards, only 300 remained. These people lived in terrible conditions, doing back-breaking work to survive. Today there is no one left; only the huts remain. The Knockfierna Heritage and Folklore Group has developed the National Famine Commemoration Park here, which includes 15 dwellings on their original sites, around which you can still see the potato ridges.

Gaelic Games

Hurling (or hurley) and Gaelic football are uniquely Irish games, which are played widely in the counties of south-west Ireland. Both games are extremely fast and demand expert coordination, quick thinking, brawn, bravery and sure-footedness. It is probably fair to say that hurling requires the most skill and practice; Dr Johnson described it as 'hockey without the rules'. The game has been played all over the world wherever Irish migrants have settled. In Scotland it is called Shinty, and was introduced by Irish missionaries, along with Christianity. To watch a match in Dublin, Derry, Cork City, Galway or another of the 32 county grounds in Ireland would give you a huge buzz and some insight into Irish culture (matches are advertised in the local newspapers, or you can get details from the local tourist office). Gaelic football, which uses the same pitch as hurling, is often described as a mixture of soccer and rugby, although it is much older than either of these games.

The first recognized version of hurling was recorded in County Meath in 1670, though it has existed in Ireland since pre-Christian times; the hero Cú Chulainn – the hound of Cullen – was named thus after killing a guard dog by driving a hurling ball down his throat. Skill on the hurling field in these ancient times was equated with ability on the battlefield. By the 17th and 18th centuries the games were sometimes wild and violent, the rules were not set, and many regional variations existed.

Games are organized under the auspices of the GAA (Gaelic Athletic Association; *www.gaa.ie*), which has been described as the 'greatest single bonding force in the Gaelic nation'. The GAA was founded in 1884 by Michael Cusack and Maurice Davin in a hotel meeting in Thurles. The Association standardized the rules in order to preserve the traditions of the games, in particular hurling, which was in danger of being gentrified and becoming a variant of hockey. Rugby was also becoming the accepted alternative to Gaelic football, especially amongst the middle classes. After the horrors of the Great Famine, many Irish customs and pastimes had fallen into decline, yet hurling was still very popular in much of southwest Ireland. The founding of the GAA was part of a general movement within the country, initiated by largely middle-class intellectuals, to promote and esteem all things Irish. The literary revival and the language movement were part and parcel of this, but they did not achieve the mass following that grew up around the GAA, which was built on rural and Catholic support. Influential patrons of the GAA in its infancy were Dr Croke, the Archbishop of Cashel and Emly, Charles Stewart Parnell and Michael Davitt.

The GAA organizes the two sports on a parish, county and provincial level. Among the most famous of the many different leagues and championships are the All-Ireland Club Championship, the finals of which are played in Croke Park in Dublin on St Patrick's Day; the Railway Cup in early spring; and the Sam Maguire Cup.

Cork and Tipperary have a famous rivalry that has built up over the years and makes matches between them especially electric. Christy Ring of Cloyne, County Cork, and Nicholas English, who played brilliantly for Tipperary, spring to mind as hurling heroes; heroes indeed are the players in the minds of their parish, county and province. People line the roads and streets to welcome home their teams, and bonfires are lit to celebrate great victories. All the players are unpaid, participating for the game and the glory.

Hurling is played with a *camán* or curved stick, and is variously known as *cambuc, camack, camac, crabsowl, shinney, hockie, hockey* or *hawkey* throughout the Celtic fringes of Britain. The Galway Statutes of 1527 include it as a prohibited game, describing it as 'the horlinge of the litill balle with hockie stickes or staves'. The Irish hurling stick is short with a wide blade and is used to hit the ball in the air, to bounce it along on the stick or to balance it there while the player is running and being tackled aggressively. The stick is also used to hit the ball along the ground, although the breadth of the Irish stick means that the players cannot be as dextrous as their Scottish neighbours across the water, who play with a narrower stick. (The Ireland versus Scotland matches at Croke Park are legendary, the strengths and shortcomings of each method of hurling adding up to a match of equals.)

The ball in Gaelic football and hurling can be dribbled, punched or kicked and carried in the hand for not more than four steps, after which it must be either bounced or 'solo-ed'. This means dropping the ball on to the foot or *camán* and kicking it back into the hand. In hurling you are not allowed to catch the ball more than twice. The goalposts for both games are the same shape as for rugby, although the crossbar is lower than on a rugby post. The ball used in Gaelic football is smaller than a soccer ball, while in hurling it is hard and leather-covered, like a hockey ball with raised ridges, and is known as a *sliotar*.

The growing popularity of soccer all over Ireland is seen as something of a threat to hurling and Gaelic football, as both these sports need commitment and training from an early age. The willing involvement of the religious orders, who used to run many of the educational establishments and helped train players after school, has not been replaced within the more secular organization. The dominance of Munster and the modern cult of counting success above everything is discouraging clubs that have never been very successful. The GAA once imposed Rule 21, which forbade any member of the RUC (now known as the PSNI) from participating in GAA events – unsettling for people who were worried about sectarianism and the politicization of sport. However, the GAA have now abolished this rule, and the Irish government gave them a grant of £20 million towards the refurbishment of Croke Park.

Food and Drink

Beyond the Potato

Eating out in Ireland can be a memorable experience – if the chef gets it right. The basic ingredients are among the best in the world: succulent beef, lamb, salmon, seafood, ham, butter, cream, eggs and wonderful **bread** – which is often home-made, and varies from crumbly nutty-tasting wheaten bread to moist white soda bread, crispy scones, potato bread and barm brack, a rich fruity loaf that is traditionally eaten at Hallowe'en. Irish **potatoes** are light and floury, and best when just off the stalk, and crispy carrots and cabbages are sold in every grocery shop, often bought in from local farms. If you stay in a country-house hotel, the walled garden will probably produce rare and exotic vegetables and fruit.

The history of Ireland has quite a lot to do with the downside of its cuisine: overcooked food, few vegetables, and too many synthetic cakes. The landless peasants had little to survive off except potatoes, milk and the occasional bit of bacon, so there is little traditional 'cuisine'. **Fish** was until recently regarded as 'penance food', to be eaten only on Fridays. Local people talk with amusement of those who eat oysters or mussels, and most of the fine seafood harvested from the seaweed-fringed loughs and the open sea goes straight to France, where it appears on the starched linen tablecloths of the best restaurants. But do not despair if you love fat oysters or fresh salmon, because they can always be had either in the bars, the new-style restaurants that are really excellent, or straight from the fisherman. Remember that everything in Ireland works on a personal basis. Start your enquiries for any sort of local delicacy at the local post office, grocer or butcher, or in the pub.

Having got over the trauma of the famine, and since the relative prosperity of the 1960s, many people in Ireland like to eat **meat**, hence the number of butchers or 'fleshers' in every town. Steak appears on every menu, and if you stay in a simple Irish farmhouse, huge lamb chops with a minty sauce, Irish stew made from the best end of mutton neck, onions and potatoes, and bacon and cabbage casserole baked in the oven are delicious possibilities. Fish, however, is becoming more readily available.

The standard of **restaurants** in Ireland is getting much better. This is especially true of those run by people from other European countries, many of whom set up here because of the beauty of the country and quality of the raw ingredients. There are Irish cooks, too, who combine local specialities and traditional recipes with ingredients and cooking methods from other cultures. Ballymaloe House in County Cork (*see* p.209) and Drimcong Restaurant in County Galway (*see* p.281) spring immediately to mind. Serious cooking is still a recent phenomenon, though, and many places will be trying to impress you (and the restaurant guides) with showy creativity, so expect to come across some bizarre sauces and combinations of ingredients.

Eating out here can be a massive disappointment. Too many restaurants still serve up musty, watery vegetables, overcooked meat, frozen fish, and salads of the limp lettuce and coleslaw variety. Also, eating out is not cheap, unless you have a pub lunch. To compete with the pubs, many restaurants do charge considerably less for lunch than dinner, so if it is convenient you can save a lot by having your main meal of the day in the afternoon.

To get around the serious problem of eating cheaply in Ireland, fill up on the huge breakfasts provided by bed and breakfast places. If the lady of the house also cooks high tea or supper for her guests, take advantage of that too: this is usually delicious and very good value. Irish people love their food, and are generous with it: huge portions are normal in the home and often in restaurants. It is a sign of inhospitality to provide a spartan meal. (They say, 'It was but a daisy in a bull's mouth'.)

Bakeries usually sell tea, coffee and soft drinks along with fresh apple pies, doughnuts, cakes and sausage rolls. Roadside cafés serve the usual menu of hamburgers, chicken 'n' chips and so on. In the North take-away joints do a tearing trade: most of the big towns have Chinese restaurants, pizza places and fish-and-chip shops. Vegetarians will find that there is an increasing number of restaurants in Dublin and the larger towns that cater specifically for their needs. Also, vegetarians will find that even where no special menu exists for them, people are generally keen to provide suitable fare. If you are staying in a country house, you should telephone in advance to let them know you are vegetarian.

You can sample the many delicious cheeses of Ireland by finding a good deli or wholefood shop, buying some bread and salad and taking yourself off to eat a picnic in some wonderfully scenic place. If it is drizzling, warm yourself up afterwards with a glass of Irish coffee in the local pub.

Restaurant Listings

You will normally find that the service in Ireland is friendly and helpful. A variety of good eating places are listed in the grey boxes within the sightseeing chapters; in the various culinary deserts that exist, places that we have listed are the best of an indifferent lot. The establishments are categorized in the following cost brackets, which are based on an average three-course meal without wine. Bear in mind that proprietors and places change, so it is always best to phone before you arrive.

Luxury

More than €66/UK£45 a head, but cost is no object These restaurants serve creative food, cooked with fine ingredients. They are often in the dining rooms of stately country houses or castles, where silver and crystal sparkle and you are surrounded by fine pictures and furniture. Or they may be smart, fashionable places in cities.

Expensive

Between €45 and €66 (UK£31–45) a head. Many country-house hotels come under this category, as do seafood restaurants around the coast and city establishments. Lunch in expensive places is often a very reasonably priced set meal, so ask about this if you do not want to fork out for dinner.

Moderate

Between €22 and €44 (UK£15–30) a head. The quality of the food in such places may be as good as more expensive establishments, but the atmosphere is informal and, sometimes, less stylish.

Inexpensive

Less than €22 (UK£15) a head. This category includes bar food, lunchtime places and cafés. You can usually be sure of good home-made soup.

Eating Hours and Etiquette

Most restaurants do lunch and dinner, but check before you go. A few do only dinner and Sunday lunch. Some country places only open at the weekend in winter.

Service is usually included in the bill at restaurants. In country towns, and sometimes even in Dublin, you may find it difficult to pay by credit card, so you are advised to check before you order your meal.

If there is no liquor licence, managers are usually happy to let you bring in your own wine or beer, if you ask. (Publicans – pub landlords – have a monopoly on licences, and many restaurants cannot get them without having to fulfil ludicrous requirements).

Legal and Illicit Drinks

'The only cure for drinking is to drink more' goes the Irish proverb. Organizations such as the Pioneers exist to wean the masses off 'the drink' – alcohol costs an arm and a leg, what with the taxes and the publican's cut. Yet an Irish bar can be one of the most convivial places in the world. The delicious booze, the cosy snugs and the general hubbub of excited conversation, which in the evening might easily spark into a piece of impromptu singing, makes the business of taking a drink here very pleasant. On the other hand, pubs can also be as quiet as a grave, especially in the late afternoon when a few men nod over their pint, and an air of contemplation pervades.

You are bound to have been lured into trying **Guinness** by the persuasive ads you see all over the world (Guinness got to be what it is by the same sort of massive and diabolically clever advertising that made an institution of Coca-cola). Stout, or porter, is a beer that is made by drying the malt at a high temperature: browning it in effect, and providing the characteristic colour and taste, though there's considerably more to the art than just that. The export trade is thriving; but the place to get a real taste of the creamy dark liquor is in an Irish bar. It is at its most delicious when it is draught and drunk in a bar around Dublin, where it is made. Guinness does not travel well, especially on Irish roads. It is said to get its special flavour from the murky waters of the River Liffey, and you can go and find out for yourself if this is so by visiting the brewery at St James' Gate (*see* p.562). The quality of taste once it has left the brewery depends on how well the publican looks after it and cleans the pipe from the barrel, so it varies greatly from bar to bar.

If it's obvious that you are a tourist, your Guinness may be decorated with a shamrock drawn on its frothy head. They've finally managed to get Guinness into a can, though it's only a pale reflection of the real thing. If you are feeling adventurous, try something called black velvet – a mixture of Guinness and champagne. And note that it isn't just Guinness – down in Cork, Murphy's and Beamish make stout that's just as good, and is available everywhere.

Whiskey has been drunk in Ireland for more than 500 years, and the word itself is derived from *uisce beatha*, the Irish for water of life. It is made from malted barley with a small proportion of wheat and oats, and occasionally a pinch of rye – so it's a blended whiskey, though without the distinctive taste of blended Scotch. On the whole, Irish is better than American blended, and as good as Canadian. There are several brands: Jameson's, Paddy, Power, and Bushmills (from the North) are all good.

Irish coffee is a wonderful combination of contrasts – hot and cold, black and white – and is very intoxicating. It was first dreamed up in County Limerick in the 1940s. It's made with a double measure of Irish whiskey, one tablespoon of double cream, one cup of strong, hot black coffee, and a heaped tablespoon of sugar. To make it, first warm a stemmed whiskey glass. Put in the sugar and enough hot coffee to dissolve the sugar. Stir well. Add the Irish whiskey and then pour the cream slowly over the back of a spoon. Do not stir the cream into the coffee; it should float on top. The hot whiskey-laced coffee is drunk through the cold cream.

Poteen (pronounced 'pot-cheen') is illicit whiskey, traditionally made from potatoes, although nowadays it is often made from grain. Tucked away in the countryside are stills that no longer bubble away over a turf fire but on a Calor gas stove. Poteen is pretty disgusting stuff unless you get a very good brew, and it probably kills off a lot of brain cells, so it's much better to stick to the legal liquid.

If you happen to stay in that wonderful country house, Longueville, near Mallow (*see* p.212), order a bottle of dry fruity white **wine** from Ireland's only vineyard. It is delicious, and rare, because of Ireland's fierce frosts and the uncertainty of sunshine.

Bars

The old-fashioned serious drinking bar with high counter and engraved glass window, frosted so the outside world couldn't intrude, is gradually changing. It used to be a male preserve. Farmers on a trip to town can be heard bewailing the weather or recounting the latest in cattle, land prices or gossip. What the inns have lost in character they compensate for, to a degree, with comfort. The bar of the local hotel is the place to find the priest when he is off-duty. My own favourite drinking establishment is the grocery shop that is also a bar, where you ask for a taxi/plumber/undertaker only to find that the publican or his brother combine all these talents with great panache.

Licensing Hours

In the Republic, public houses are officially open Mon–Wed 10.30am–11.30pm, Thur–Sat 10.30–12.30am, and Sun and St Patrick's Day 12.30–11pm. In winter they close half an hour earlier. Plenty of places stay open later, although you'll have to get in before closing time, since they lock the doors and then carry on. The Gardaí don't seem to mind. There is no service on Christmas Day or Good Friday.

In Northern Ireland, pubs are open Mon–Sat 11am–11pm, Sun 12.30–10pm. Also, you can always get a drink on Sundays at a hotel, though you are supposed to justify it by having a meal as well if you are not staying there. In the Republic, children are nearly always allowed to sit in the lounge bar with packets of crisps and fizzy orange to keep them happy, and they often appear in the evenings too when there's music.

If you do get into a conversation in a bar, a certain etiquette is followed: men always buy everybody in your group a drink, taking it in turns to buy a round; women will find they are seldom allowed to. If there are 10 people in your group, you will find yourself drunk from social necessity and probably out of pocket as well. The price in the Republic for wine, whiskey and beer is higher than in the UK. If you are bringing a car from France or the UK, it might be as well to bring some booze in with you, or you could stock up in Northern Ireland. The customs allowance is 1½ litres of distilled beverages or spirits, 12 litres of beer and (if the alcohol is bought duty-paid) 4 litres of wine per person. Customs enforcement is not systematic.

Travel

08

Getting There

By Air

Most flights to the Irish Republic go to **Dublin**, but there are also international airports at **Cork**, **Shannon** (Limerick), **Galway**, **Sligo**, **Kerry** (Killarney), **Knock** (in Co. Mayo) and **Waterford**. The main airport in Northern Ireland is **Belfast International** (aka Belfast Aldergrove), but there is also another, smaller, more central airport, **Belfast City**. There are also flights to **Derry** (Eglinton Airport) and

Enniskillen. There are no direct flights from Dublin to Belfast – the two towns are 3hrs apart and well connected by road and rail.

From Britain

The Irish Republic's national airline, **Aer Lingus**, handles an enormous number of flights to the Republic from British and European cities. If you are going to immerse yourself in all things Irish, you might start with this airline and its bright green planes. Aer Lingus will take you to Dublin, Shannon or Cork from at least one of the following: Birmingham, Bristol, Edinburgh, Glasgow,

Airlines

From the UK

Aer Arann, t 0800 587 2324, *www.aerarann.ie*. Flights to regional airports in Ireland: Birmingham, Edinburgh and Southampton to Cork; Luton and Manchester to Galway and Waterford. Also Manchester to Kerry.

Aer Lingus, t 0845 084 4444, *www.aerlingus.com*. Flights from Birmingham, Bristol, Edinburgh, Glasgow, Heathrow, Jersey, Liverpool and Manchester to Dublin. Flights from Heathrow to Cork and Shannon.

Air France, t 0870 142 4243, *www.airfrance.co.uk*. London City to Dublin.

Air Southwest, t 0870 241 8202, *www. airsouthwest.com*. Flights from Bristol and Newquay to Dublin.

Air Wales, t 0870 777 3131, *www.airwales.com*. Cardiff, Norwich and Plymouth to Dublin. Plymouth to Cork.

British Airways (BA), t 0870 850 9850, *www.ba.com*. Gatwick to Dublin, Heathrow to Shannon and Cork; Manchester to Belfast, Derry, Cork and Shannon.

British Midland (BMI), t 0870 607 0555, *www.flybmi.com*. Heathrow to Dublin and Belfast. Glasgow and Edinburgh to Dublin and Cork. Leeds/Bradford to Cork and Dublin.

bmibaby, t 0870 264 2229, *www.bmibaby.com*. Nottingham to Dublin, Cork and Belfast; Birmingham, Cardiff, Leeds/Bradford, Manchester, Teeside to Cork; Birmingham and Manchester to Knock (Connacht).

easyJet, t 0905 821 0905 (65p/min), *www.easyjet.com*. Gatwick to Cork, Shannon, Knock and Belfast.

Euromanx, t 0870 787 7879, *www.euromanx. com*. Isle of Man to Dublin.

Flybe, t 0871 700 0123, *www.flybe.com*. Norwich and Southampton to Dublin.

Luxair, t 0800 389 9443, *www.luxair.lu*. Manchester to Dublin.

Ryanair, t 0871 246 0000 (10p/min), *www. ryanair.com*. Flights from most UK regional airports and from Gatwick, Stansted and Luton to Dublin; Bristol, East Midlands, Glasgow and Liverpool to Shannon; London and Liverpool to Cork. Also flights from London to Derry, Kerry and Knock.

Thomsonfly, t 0800 000 747, *www.thomsonfly. com*. Doncaster/Sheffield to Dublin.

From the USA and Canada

Aer Lingus, USA t 1 800 IRISH AIR, *www. aerlingus.com*. Boston, Chicago, Los Angeles, New York and Orlando to Dublin, and New York, Chicago and Boston to Shannon.

American Airlines, USA t 1 800 433 7300, t 1 800 543 1586 (TDD), *www.aa.com*

Air Canada, Canada t 1 800 567 4160, USA t 1 800 268 0024, *www.aircanada.ca*

British Airways, USA t 1 888 AIRWAYS, *www.ba.com*

Continental Airlines, USA t 1 800 231 0856, *www.continental.com*. New York/Newark to Dublin and Shannon.

Delta, USA and Canada t 1 800 241 4141, t 1 800 831 4488 (TDD), *www.delta.com*. Atlanta, New York and Chicago to Dublin, and Atlanta to Shannon.

United Airlines, USA t 1 800 538 2929, t 1 800 323 0170 (TDD), *www.united.com*. Flights from major US centres to London.

Liverpool, London or Manchester (*see* below). Other airlines also fly direct to Dublin, Cork and Shannon from the 4 main London airports (Heathrow, Gatwick, Luton and Stansted), and there are numerous additional flights to Irish cities from British regional airports. Budget carrier **Ryanair** has regular flights connecting Dublin with Birmingham, Cardiff, Glasgow, Leeds, Liverpool, Stansted, Luton and Manchester, as well as services from Glasgow and Stansted to the other Irish airports. Most British airlines run regular flights to Belfast from the UK.

Prices are always in a state of flux but are reasonable by European standards; however, there is a bewildering array. As a guideline, an economy return from London to Dublin should cost around £40, London to Belfast around £22. The no-frills, low-cost carriers such as **easyJet** offer very low prices, and **Ryanair** offers extremely competitive fares, especially if you book online. London's *Time Out* and the Sunday newspapers are good places to start hunting for bargains. A travel agent or bucket shop can also help you to find the best deal.

From the USA and Canada

The main airports for transatlantic flights are **Dublin** and **Shannon**, which are served by direct scheduled flights from Atlanta, Boston, Chicago and New York. The main carriers flying direct to Ireland are Delta Airlines and Aer Lingus, but of course many others fly to European destinations, where you can pick up connecting flights. Often you can get a better price on these flights than you would pay if you flew direct.

Since **prices** are constantly changing and there are numerous kinds of deals on offer, the first thing to do is find yourself a travel agent who is capable of laying the current options before you. The time of year you choose can make a great difference to the price and availability of tickets. Expect to pay more and to have to book earlier if you want to travel at peak times, especially between June and August. Prices can range from around $500 for the best bargain deals to well over $1,000 for a plain ticket on a regular flight, so do some shopping around. A number of companies offer cheaper charter flights to Ireland – look in the Sunday travel sections of *The New York*

Internet Travel

A good place to start looking for flights and bargain deals is on the Internet. There are countless websites; those listed below are a good starting point.

UK and Ireland
www.cheapflights.co.uk
www.expedia.co.uk
www.lastminute.com
www.skydeals.co.uk
www.sky-tours.co.uk
www.thomascook.co.uk
www.travelocity.com
www.travelselect.com

USA and Canada
www.air-fare.com
www.expedia.com
www.flights.com
www.orbitz.com
www.priceline.com
www.travellersweb.com
www.travelocity.com
www.xfares.com (carry-on luggage only)
www.smartertravel.com

Times, Los Angeles Times, Chicago Tribune, Toronto Star or other big-city newspapers. Remember to read all the small print, as there are often catches, such as big cancellation penalties or restrictions about changing the dates of your flights; sometimes charter contracts include provisions that allow charter companies to cancel your flight, change the dates of travel and add fuel surcharges after you have paid your fare.

Shannon Airport, by the way, offers a variety of duty-free goods and Irish specialities: cut crystal glass, Connemara rugs, Donegal tweed and so on. If you don't want to get burdened with lots of presents and packages during your stay in Ireland, you can get everything here at the last minute.

Student and Youth Discounts

If you can produce an **International Student Identity Card** (ISIC), you can expect to get discounts of at least 25% on standard passenger rates for travel. There are student/under-26 rates for flights between

Airline Offices in Ireland

Aer Lingus, t 0818 365 000
American Airlines, t (01) 602 0550
bmibaby, t (01) 890 340 122
British Airways, t 1 890 626 747
British Midland, t 0870 607 0555
Continental Airlines, t 1 890 925 252
Delta Airlines (Dublin), t (01) 844 6139
Shannon, t (01) 844 6139
easyJet, t 1 890 923 922
Euromanx, t 0870 787 7879
Flybe, t 1 890 925 532
Ryanair, t 1 530 787 787
United Airlines, t 0845 844 4777

Britain and Ireland, and similar concessions for transatlantic flights. You can get your card from the agencies below, who can also help you to find student deals.

STA Travel, USA, 205 East 42nd St, New York, NY 10017, t 212 822 2700 and branches across the States, or t 1 800 781-4040, *www.statravel.com*. Student flights.

STA Travel, UK, 86 Old Brompton Rd, London SW7, t (020) 7581 4132, and branches in all main university towns and campuses, *www.statravel.com*. Flights and more.

Travel Cuts, Canada, 187 College St, Toronto, Ontario M5T, t (416) 979 2406 and branches across Canada, *www.travelcuts.com*. Canada's largest student travel specialist.

Getting To and From the Airports

Trains and/or buses run between the main airports and city centres. They're comfortable, frequent and economical; taxi drivers, by contrast, tend to ask a dramatically high price for a ride into the city.

Dublin Bus runs Airlink services (routes 747 and 748) between **Dublin Airport**, the Central Bus Station (Busáras), Connolly and Heuston railway stations and O'Connell St every 10–15mins from 5.45am to 11.30pm. Aircoach also runs a service to city-centre hotels and landmarks every 15mins from early morning to 10.20pm. You can also catch the cheaper but slower Citybuses (routes 41, 41B and 16A), which circulate between the airport and Eden Quay, outside Busáras.

There is a daily Airbus service from **Belfast International Airport** into Belfast's Europa Buscentre (Mon–Sat every 30mins, Sun every 30–60mins), and a regular train service from **Belfast City Airport** to Belfast Central Station, as well as a regular Citybus (route 21). One way to get from Belfast International Airport to Derry City is to take the Antrim Airlink bus service (Mon–Sat 7.45am–7.45pm) to Antrim's railway station, from where you may catch one of the 6 daily trains to Derry. You can also use the Airporter scheduled service, which runs 4–10 coaches Mon–Fri (t 028 7126 9996, *www.belfastairport.com*).

Bus Éireann runs similar services from **Cork Airport** to Cork City, and from **Shannon Airport** to Limerick, 15 miles (25km) away.

By Sea

The **ferries** from the British west coast cross the Irish Sea at the shortest possible crossing points. Which port and crossing you choose will depend on where you are starting from, and where you wish to go in Ireland – which is not as obvious as it may seem. The Irish Sea is notoriously rough, and some crossings may be cancelled due to gales in winter.

The main crossings are as follows:

Rosslare Harbour (near Wexford) and south-east Ireland is served by Fishguard and Pembroke in South Wales, as well as regular services (every other day) from Cherbourg and Roscoff in northern France.

Dublin Port and **Dun Laoghaire** are served by Holyhead, in North Wales, and Liverpool. Since early 1994 the Holyhead route is also served by a high-speed catamaran that crosses the Irish Sea in 1hr 40mins. There is also a seasonal service to the Isle of Man.

Belfast and nearby **Larne**, in the North, are served by ferries and catamarans taking the short crossing from Cairnryan and Stranraer in south-west Scotland, and by ferries taking the longer journey from Liverpool. There is also a seasonal service to the Isle of Man.

Cork, the port for the southern Republic, is reached via Swansea, in south Wales, and from Roscoff, in France.

All the ferry ports are well connected to rail and coach transport (*see* opposite), and all the ferry services have drive-on/drive-off facilities for cars. **Prices** depend on time of year and length of crossing, how long you intend to stay in Ireland and, if you are taking your car,

Ferry Companies

Irish Ferries, Dublin t 0818 300400; Liverpool t 0870 517 1717; London t 0870 517 1717, *www.irishferries.com*. Holyhead–Dublin, 2 sailings daily all year, 3¼hrs; 3 catamaran sailings daily all year, 2hrs. Pembroke– Rosslare, 2 sailings daily all year, 3½hrs.

Isle of Man Steam Packet Company, Isle of Man, t 0870 552 3523; Dublin, t (01) 624 661 661, *www.steam-packet.com*. Seasonal services from Isle of Man to Dublin and Belfast, operating mid-Mar to end of Dec. Crossing to Dublin 4½ hours; Sea Cat, 2hrs 40mins; to Belfast 2hrs 45mins.

Norse Merchant Ferries, UK t 0870 600 4321, *www.norsemerchant.com*. Birkenhead–Belfast, 1 daily, all year, 8½hrs. Birkenhead–Dublin, 1 daily, all year, 7½hrs.

P&O European Ferries, UK t 0870 2424 777, Ireland t (01) 407 3434, *www.poirishsea.com*.

Cairnryan–Larne, 3 sailings daily, all year, 2hrs; 5 catamaran sailings daily Apr–mid-Oct, less than 1½hrs.

Stena Line, reservations in the UK t 0870 570 7070; Dublin, t (01) 204 7777, *www.stenaline.ie*. Holyhead–Dun Laoghaire, 4 sailings daily all year, 3½ hrs; 2 catamaran sailings, 1½ hrs. Fishguard–Rosslare, 3–6 ailings daily all year, 3½hrs; by catamaran 1½hrs. Stranraer–Belfast, 4 ferry sailings daily, 1hr 45mins or 3½hrs; 4 catamaran sailings daily, 1¾hrs.

Swansea Cork Ferries, Swansea, UK t (01792) 456116; Cork Ferryport, Ringaskiddy, t (021) 427 1166, *www.swanseacorkferries. com*. Swansea–Cork, 10hrs (overnight crossing from Swansea, every day or every other day). Taking you all the way to the west coast, it costs about the same as the shorter crossings.

the number of passengers, car size and so on. Schedules can be complex too. Find a good travel agent and let them explore the options.

Note that at some peak times of the year – Easter, Christmas and especially around spring and autumn bank holidays – and on all sailings from Liverpool, the number of passengers on certain ferry crossings is controlled. All non-motorist passengers must have a **'sailing control ticket'** to board the ship at these times. These can be obtained when you book your crossing, or if you change your booking or have an open ticket, from the ferry offices. It is worth checking whether you need a control ticket before you start your journey.

Otherwise, crossings are easygoing. Unless they are packed, there is usually no problem if you happen to miss a boat, even if you have a car. Staff will just put you on the next one – but do ring ahead and let them know if you are delayed.

By Train

All the ferries crossing back and forth between Britain and Ireland are scheduled to link up with **trains** that go frequently and speedily from London to Fishguard, Liverpool, Holyhead and Stranraer. You can buy your **tickets** at any train station or booking office,

or from National Rail, t 08457 484 950, *www.nationalrail.co.uk*. You can get couchettes on the night trains, or when it is quiet you can stretch out along the seats.

London (Euston) to Dublin via Liverpool/ Dublin and Holyhead/Dun Laoghaire takes 6–11hrs; London (Paddington) to Wexford via Fishguard and Rosslare takes approximately 12½hrs; London (Euston) to Belfast via Liverpool takes about 16hrs; and London (Euston) to Belfast via Stranraer and Larne takes about 13hrs.

By Coach

Travelling by coach/ferry to Ireland is quite an endurance test. The journey seems endless, with lots of stops through Britain and Ireland to pick up other travellers, but it is cheap and takes you straight to destinations in the provinces, without changing on arrival in Ireland. The small coaches that go to and fro across the Irish Sea are flourishing private enterprises in the hands of local individuals. They leave all parts of Ireland for the chief cities of England, Scotland and Wales, full to the brim with Irish people returning to work or coming home on leave. Look for the smaller companies in Irish newspapers, which you can buy fairly easily in Britain.

Coach Companies

Eurolines, t 0870 580 8080, Victoria Coach Station, Buckingham Palace Rd, London SW1, *www.eurolines.co.uk.* Connected with Bus Éireann and National Express, this has regular services. London–Dublin: 3 daily, 11–12hrs. London–Waterford/Cork/Killarney (via Rosslare): 1 daily, overnight, 18hrs. London–Waterford/Limerick/Tralee (via Rosslare): overnight, 18hrs. Glasgow–Dublin: 1 daily, overnight, 10hrs. Leeds–Dublin: 1 daily, 11hrs. Bristol–Dublin: 3 daily, overnight, 12hrs. Birmingham or Bristol–Waterford/Cork/ Killarney: 3 daily, 19–21hrs.
Ulsterbus, Belfast **t** (028) 90 66 66 30, *www.ulsterbus.co.uk.*

London services leave from Victoria Coach Station. **Fares** from London can be as low as £39 return, or as high as £55. Ask about special student rates. The major coach companies for **Northern Ireland** are Eurolines/National Express and Ulsterbus in Belfast.

Entry Formalities

Passports and Visas

Although British citizens do not require a passport to enter the **Republic**, it is worth taking a passport or some form of identification with you for completing formalities, such as hiring a car. Citizens of the USA and Canada must have a valid passport to enter the Republic, but no visa is required.

For **Northern Ireland**, entry formalities are exactly as they are for entry to the United Kingdom. US and Canadian citizens require a passport, but no visa. UK citizens do not need any form of identity documents, but it's as well to carry some since, if you are stopped in a security check, quick identification will speed the process.

Citizens (other than UK citizens) of the European Union, Australia and New Zealand need a full passport or identity card for entry into both the Republic and Northern Ireland. Passports are also required for visitors from other countries, and citizens of some may need visas too. Check with your nearest Tourism Ireland office, or see *www.foreignaffairs.gov.ie* for details.

Customs

There is no customs inspection carried out on travellers between the Republic and Northern Ireland or Britain. Travellers do not have to pay tax or duty in the UK or Ireland on goods that have been bought in other EU countries, as long as they are for personal use or to be given as gifts.

Guidelines are issued for quantities of tobacco and alcohol that are regarded as reasonable for personal use; if you bring more than these amounts, you must be able to satisfy customs officers that they are genuinely for your own use. The current limits are: 800 cigarettes, 400 cigarillos, 200 cigars, 1kg of smoking tobacco, 10 litres of spirits, 20 litres of fortified wine, 90 litres of wine and 110 litres of beer. Note that travellers aged under 17 are not allowed to import tobacco or alcohol.

Duty free no longer exists within the EU borders. If you are arriving from outside the EU, however, duty free remains, as do customs allowances, which are: 200 cigarettes or 100 cigarillos or 50 cigars or 250 grams of tobacco; 2 litres of still table wine; 1 litre of spirits or strong liqueurs over 22% alcohol, or 2 litres of fortified wine, sparkling wine or other liqueurs. The limit on all other goods including gifts and souvenirs is £145 for Northern Ireland, €92 for the Republic. Anything above these limits must be declared and tax paid.

Residents of the USA may each take home $400-worth of foreign goods without paying duty, including tobacco and alcohol allowances. Canadians can take home $500 worth of goods in a year, plus their tobacco and alcohol allowances.

Dog- and cat-owners can bring their pet with them to Ireland, as long as it comes directly from Britain, the Channel Islands or the Isle of Man, and has been there for a period of at least 6 months.

Customs Information

Irish Republic: t (067) 44000, *www.revenue.ie*
UK: t 0845 010 9000, *www.hmce.gov.uk*
USA: t (202) 927 6724, *www.customs.ustreas.gov*
Canada: t 800 461 9999, *www.ccra-adrc.gc.ca*

VAT Refunds

Any non-EU visitor can claim back the **VAT** (Value Added Tax) on goods bought in Ireland. To claim a tax refund, you must complete a **Cashback voucher** provided by the shop and present the form and goods to Customs when you leave. You must take your purchases home with you, within 3 months of purchase.

Railway Companies

Iarnród Éireann, t 1850 444 2222 or t (01) 836 6222, *www.irishrail.ie*. Information, timetables and tickets in the Republic.

NIR Travel Shop, Great Victoria Street Station, Belfast, t (028) 9066 6630; reservations t (028) 9089 9409, *www.nir.co.uk*. Rail travel in Northern Ireland.

Getting Around

By Air

It is possible to fly from one city to another in Ireland. However, this is a small island and the main destinations are well covered by rail and bus. **Aer Lingus** and **Ryanair** fly from Dublin to Cork, Shannon, Galway, Knock Airport in Co. Mayo, Sligo, Kerry (near Killarney) and Waterford (*see* pp.88–90 for details). **Aer Arann Express**, Ireland, t 0818 210210, UK t 0800 587 2324, *www.aerarannexpress.com*. Dublin to Donegal, Sligo, Galway, Kerry and Cork, and to the Aran Islands from Galway.

By Train

In the Republic, trains are operated by **Iarnród Éireann** ('Iron Road Irish Rail'). Routes radiate out from Dublin and take you through sleepy little stations and green countryside. The system is rather like the British system of 50 or 60 years ago, with old signal boxes that still need people to operate them and keep an eye on things. People are always friendly on trains, and the ticket inspectors are far from officious. Services are reliable, and the fares are reasonable. Just the same, the network is not extensive, and especially lacking in the west and north; you will find trains useful mostly for getting to and from Dublin. Fares are nearly always more than those of buses, especially for one-way trips.

If you are planning an itinerary with lots of train trips in a short time, ask about the special rail cards, allowing unlimited travel over a given period of time. There are **Faircard** and **Weekender** deals for students, especially on return trips to or from Dublin (one of these even includes a free laundry service) as well as

various discount tickets. The **Irish Explorer** ticket can be used for 5 days out of 15, is valid on the Republic's entire intercity and suburban rail network and costs €127. The **Irish Rover** has similar conditions and can also be used in Northern Ireland (€157.50). The **Irish Explorer Rail and Bus** also includes travel on Bus Éireann; a ticket covering both north and south is €194. At the top of the range is the **Emerald Card**, which can be used for 15 days out of 30 and is valid for both trains and buses in both countries, costing €375. Children's tickets are all half-price.

Rail travel in Northern Ireland is run by **Northern Ireland Railways** (NIR), with services connecting Belfast to Coleraine and Derry and the ports. This system is fully integrated with Iarnród Éireann, and lines between Belfast and Dublin are operated jointly by Iarnród Éireann and NIR. It takes 2hrs to reach Dublin on the Belfast–Dublin non-stop express, and there are 8 trains a day (5 on Sundays).

Ireland is part of the **Eurail Pass** and **Inter-Rail Pass** networks, which allow unlimited rail travel on European railways, including the Republic of Ireland but excluding the UK, and free ferry crossings from France to Ireland. To obtain the Eurail Pass you must be resident of a non-European country and buy it outside Europe; check *www.raileurope.com* for details. The Inter-Rail Pass is available to European residents, including the over-26s, and can be purchased in the UK from Rail Europe, t 08708 371 371, *www.raileurope.co.uk*. There are also discount rates for under-26s.

For **steam train** enthusiasts there are plenty of places in Ireland where you can travel on one, as narrow-gauge lines are reopened. The Northern Irish Tourist Board publishes a guide to steam railways that covers the whole of Ireland, and the Steam Traction Museum in Stradbally, Co. Laois, hosts 'steam rallies' in summer (*see* p.516).

By Bus

The bus service throughout Ireland is efficient and goes to the most remote places. The main companies are **Bus Éireann/Busáras** in the Republic, and **Ulsterbus** in Northern Ireland. Rail and bus transport generally in Northern Ireland is operated by Translink. Prices are reasonable, although on Bus Éireann they can be irrational, with a 20-mile (32km) journey sometimes costing as much as a 100-mile (160km) one. The best deals are on midweek return tickets between the main cities.

Bus Éireann offer discount **Irish Rambler** tickets for 3, 8 or 15 days, costing €45, €100 and €145 respectively. There's a similar **Irish Rover** ticket, which is also good on Ulsterbus; again, the options are 3, 8 or 15 days and the respective prices are £37/€60, £84/€135 and £120/€195. They also operate chatty 1-day and half-day tours throughout the Republic from many cities; ask for details at any of their Travel Centres, located in the bus company offices in Cork, Dublin and Galway. Addresses and phone numbers for individual bus stations are given in the 'Getting Around' sections of the relevant chapter. Local transport in Dublin and most places in Co. Dublin is handled by **Dublin Bus, t** (01) 873 4222.

The most convenient and reliable source for bus information is always the local tourist office. Bus Éireann have offices only in the largest towns, and there are many other smaller independent bus companies around. Two of the largest are **Nestor Bus**, which runs a Galway–Dublin service, or **Suirway**, which serves the south-east. Some private lines stop running in summer, as they depend on students for much of their income. You can pick up a Bus Éireann timetable at tourist offices and at some newspaper stands. Note that, in the Republic, bus destinations posted on the front of the bus are often given in Irish; Dublin, for example, may be seen as *Átha Cliath*, Galway *Gaillimh*, or Waterford *Port Láirge*. If in doubt, ask.

Ulsterbus runs frequent services to all parts of Northern Ireland. You can pick up timetables at any Ulster bus station, or the tourist office in Belfast. The Ulsterbus head office is at the Europa Buscentre, on Great Victoria St; the other main bus station is in Oxford St. Metro operates the city bus services in Belfast only. Ulsterbus offers **Freedom of Northern Ireland** tickets for a day or a week, good on buses and trains in the North, and Irish Rover tickets that are also good on Bus Éireann.

For further details of special fares and bus excursions, see *On the Move*, published by the Northern Ireland Tourist Office.

Student and Youth Fares

You can expect to get discounts of at least 25% on standard passenger rates for travel with an ISIC card. You can also buy a **Travel Stamp** for around €8, which gets you some big savings: 50% off single adult tickets on B&I Line ferry crossings between Britain and Ireland, 33% discount off mainline rail fares in Ireland, 30% off single adult CIE provincial bus journeys and 50% off the return fare to the Aran Islands by boat. The stamp is available from USIT (Union of Students International Travel), from student travel offices in the UK, USA or Canada (*see* p.90), and at Irish and Northern Irish universities.

Usit, 19 Aston Quay, Dublin 2,
t (01) 602 1600; University of Limerick,
t (061) 332 079, *www.usit.ie*

By Car

To explore Ireland with minimum effort and maximum freedom, bring a car. If you fill it up with people who share the ferry and petrol costs, it won't be too expensive. Buy a detailed road map and, if you have time, choose a minor road and just meander. It is along these little lanes that the secret life of Ireland continues undisturbed. The black and red-brown cows still chew by the wayside while the herdsman, usually an old man or a child, salutes you with an upward nod. You will come upon castles, and the ruins of the small,

---

Bus Companies

Bus Éireann/Busáras, Store St, Dublin,
t (01) 836 6111, *www.buseireann.ie*
Metro, Belfast, **t** (028) 9066 6630
Nestor Bus, Galway, **t** (091) 797 144
Suirway, Waterford, **t** (051) 382 209
Ulsterbus, Europa Buscentre,
Great Victoria St, Belfast, **t** (028) 9066 6630,
www.ulsterbus.co.uk, www.translink.co.uk

circular buildings called *clochans*, still breathing with memories, tumbled even further by the local farmer in search of stone; and there are views of hills that have never reached the pages of any guide book.

Once upon a time, one of the best things about driving in Ireland was the lack of other cars, and the absence of ugly, if efficient, motorways with their obligatory motor inns and petrol stations. With the Republic's new prosperity, this has changed in many places. Traffic around the towns, especially Dublin, can be ferocious, while the government is committed to a big programme of new roads and road widenings that are guaranteed to make the problem worse, while eroding the country's natural beauty and its way of life. Car ownership in Ireland has risen in keeping with most European countries, but for now, some country roads are serene enough.

Watch out for the country driver who tends to drive right in the middle of the road, never looks in their mirror to see if anyone is behind, and probably won't indicate if they suddenly decides to turn left or right. The ones wearing old tweed caps are usually the worst offenders. There is also the other extreme: people who drive at crazy speeds on narrow roads. Cars frequently pull out of a side road in front of you and, just as you are getting up enough steam to pass, suddenly turn off down another side road. Don't be alarmed by the sheepdogs that appear from cottage doorways to chase your car – they are well skilled at avoiding you.

If your car **breaks down** in any part of Ireland you will always be able to find a mechanic to give you a hand; whether it's late at night or on a Sunday, just ask someone. He or she will sweep you up in a wave of sympathy and send messengers off in all directions to find you someone with a reputation for mechanical genius. If it is some small and common part that has let you down, he will either have it or do something that will get you by until you come to a proper garage. One thing you will notice is that the Irish have a completely different attitude to machinery from most nationalities. In England, if you break down, it is an occasion for embarrassment; everybody rushes by hardly noticing you or pretending not to. In Ireland, if your car has broken down

the next passing car will probably stop, and the problem will be readily taken on and discussed with great enjoyment. The Irish can still laugh at the occasional failure of material affairs.

Facts and Formalities for Car Drivers

In Ireland you **drive on the left** (when you are not driving in the middle of the road); the government has installed signs in seemingly random places around the country to remind us: *Conduire à gauche! Links fahren!* **Petrol stations** stay open until around 8pm, and the village ones are open after Mass on Sundays. If you are desperate for petrol and every station seems closed, you can usually knock on the door and ask somebody to start the pumps for you. Prices are roughly the same as in Britain, 3 or 4 times as much as in the US.

The **speed limit in the Republic** is 100kph (60mph) on ordinary roads, 110kph (70mph) on motorways, and 50kph (30mph) through the villages and towns, as posted. Note that speed limit signs in the Republic are now given in kilometres. Road signs showing distances to the next towns are also usually in kilometres (the older, white signs with black borders are in miles; newer, enamelled aluminium signs in green or white are usually in kilometres). Otherwise, directional signs are mainly notable for their absence; out in the country you will get lost, and probably stay lost. Some signs, especially in Gaeltacht areas, will be written in Irish; of these, the most important to know is *Go Mall* – slow down. *An Lár* is the city centre, while *Gach treo eile* signifies 'all routes'.

The **speed limit in Northern Ireland** is 70mph (112 kph) on dual carriageways, 60 mph (96 kph) on country roads, 40 mph (64 kph) in built-up areas and 30mph (48 kph) in towns.

Drivers and front-seat passengers must always wear a **seat belt** – it is illegal not to. Children under 12 should travel in the back. There are strict drink-driving laws in the Republic as in the North, and the police will use a breathalyzer test if they suspect you 'have drink taken'; the legal limit is roughly 2 pints of Guinness.

There are some excellent **motoring maps**: Bartholomew's quarter inch, obtainable from the AA and Bord Fáilte, gives good details of minor roads. The principal roads in Northern Ireland are marked A, lesser roads B; in the Republic they are N (national) and R (regional). Scenic routes are signposted and marked on the Bord Fáilte map. Place names on signposts in the Republic are usually given in English and in Irish; in the places where Irish only is used a good map will be useful.

Residents of the Republic of Ireland, Northern Ireland and Great Britain who are using private cars and motorcycles may cross the borders with very little formality. A **full, up-to-date licence** is all you need. Under EU regulations, private motor insurers will provide the minimum legal cover that is required in all EU countries, although they

Motoring Organizations

American Automobile Association,
t 1 800 AAA HELP, www.aaa.com
British Automobile Association,
t 0870 600 0371, www.theaa.com
Irish Automobile Association, Dublin
t (01) 617 9540, Cork t (021) 52444,
www.aaireland.ie
RAC, UK only t 08705 722 722

Car Hire Firms

These are only some of the bigger firms whose staff will meet you at the airports and the ferry ports.
Argus Rent A Car Ireland, t (01) 490 6173, www.argus-rentacar.com
Avis, Shannon t (061) 715600; Cork t (021) 428 1171; Cork Airport t (021) 432 7460; Dublin t (01) 605 7500; Aldergrove Airport, Belfast t 02894 422 333; Larne t 02828 260 799; www.avis.ie
Budget, Shannon t (061) 471361; Cork t (021) 314000; Dublin t (01) 837 9611; www.budget.ie
Dan Dooley Rent-a-Car, central reservations t (062) 53103, www.dandooley.com
Hertz, Dublin t (01) 844 5466; Aldergrove Airport, Belfast t 02894 422 533; www.hertz.ie
Murrays Europcar, Dublin t (01) 812 0410; Belfast t 02894 423164, www.europcar.ie
National Car Rental, Shannon t (061) 472633; Cork t (021) 431 8623; Dublin t (01) 844 4162, www.nationalcar.com
For further details contact the **Car Rental Council**, 5 Upper Pembroke St, Dublin 2, t (01) 676 1690, www.carrentalcouncil.ie

may need to be told before you travel. Remember to always carry the **vehicle registration book**. If you have hired a car, be sure to tell the rental company that you plan to cross borders, and that you have all the necessary papers; the rental company should also deal with all the insurance headaches.

Parking meters are used to control car parking in the central zones of Dublin. The meters are in operation during specific hours Mon–Sat, when street parking is prohibited at non-metered sites. Yellow lines along the kerbside or edge of the roadway indicate waiting restrictions. In some large towns a **disc system** is used to control parking in the centre. Parking discs can be bought, usually in books of 10, at shops and garages near the car parks. Unexpired time on a parking disc can be used at another parking place.

In **Belfast** it's best to head for a car park; in Northern Ireland, for security reasons, parking is not permitted in central city areas marked off as 'Control Zones', which are clearly indicated by yellow signs saying 'Control Zone. No Unattended Parking'.

Car Hire

All of the big car-hire chains will meet customers at the airports and the ferry ports of the Republic, but you can do better to wait and get a cheaper deal with a city-centre branch, or even better, with one of the **local budget firms**. If you can book in advance you can get a car for as little as €154 (UK£110) a week subject to availability. Otherwise, rates for the smallest cars can go as high as €311 (UK£500) or more.

In Northern Ireland, the story is much the same. The chains all operate from both of Belfast's airports but it's much less expensive to hire a car from their city-centre branches. Local firms (see phone book) can offer even better deals. Renting a car in Ireland is never cheap, but you might be able to bargain if business is slack. Look out also for fly-drive, or rail-sail-drive **packages** offered by some of the airlines and ferry companies: these usually represent major savings. Note that to hire a car you should normally be over 23 and in possession of a licence that you have held for at least two years without endorsement. The car-hire company will organize **insurance**, but do check this. If you do not take out extra collision-damage waiver insurance you can be liable to damage up to €1,700 (UK£2,790). Check that your contract covers both the North and the Republic if you plan to drive in both areas.

By Bicycle

Ireland is one of the most pleasant countries in which to cycle. Once you escape the main highways, the roads are quiet, there are still many birds and animals who live around the hedgerows, and in many places there is no pollution to spoil the air. This means that you'll encounter all the whiffs and pongs of the countryside, and in-between the delicious gorse and honeysuckle perfumes will waft the strong, healthy smell of manure.

You can take your own bike onto the ferry for free, or you can rent one when you arrive. In the Republic the **Raleigh Rent-A-Bike** network connects some 70 centres throughout the country, with tandems, racing bikes, and ordinary touring bikes available for hire. For full details get the *Cycling Ireland* leaflet from the nearest Bord Fáilte office. This gives details of the main hire companies, lists Irish cycling holiday specialists, and also describes 23 suggested routes. Alternatively, contact the Raleigh Rent-A-Bike Division direct (*see* below). Raleigh network members and other bike-hire shops are listed within the 'Getting Around' sections in each chapter.

The Northern Ireland Tourist Board produces a leaflet on cycling, which lists tours, routes and events for cyclists, plus a number of cycle-hire companies. Rental rates are comparable to those in force in the Republic. You can also hire bikes at some youth hostels in the North; contact the HINI for details. Note that bicycles hired in the Republic cannot be taken into Northern Ireland, and vice versa. Irish Cycling Safaris run well-organized, enjoyable holidays bicycling through scenic parts of the country.

Eurotrek Raleigh Ireland, t (01) 465 9659, *www.raleigh.ie*

HINI (Hostelling International NI), Belfast t (0289) 032 4733, *www.hini.org.uk*

Irish Cycling Safaris, t (01) 260 0749, *www.cyclingsafaris.com*

On Foot

If you enjoy **walking** in the countryside, Bord Fáilte and the Northern Ireland Tourist Board produce useful leaflets on public footpaths. The website *www.irishwaymarkedways.ie* is a mine of information for those wanting to walk in the Republic of Ireland.

From all accounts, **hitch-hiking** in the countryside seems to be a fairly safe but rather slow method of transport round the South. In the North you might find that people will not pick you up because years of the Troubles have made them cautious. It would be unwise to hitch around border areas anyway, and there are plenty of buses that will take you through. (**Women**, as always, should be especially cautious, and it is advisable, if they are determined to hitch-hike, for them to travel with a companion; *see* 'Women Travellers', p.122.)

On major roads, write your destination on a bit of cardboard and hold it up. You will find you have to compete with local people who hitch regularly from town to town. Tony Hawkes made a wager in a pub that he could hitch-hike a circuit of Ireland carrying a refrigerator. He won the bet (and wrote a book about it; *see* **Further Reading**, p.619).

Getting to the Aran Islands

The Aran Islands situated to the west of Galway are probably the most famous of the islands lying off the west coast of Ireland, but there are many others, each with its own charms. You can reach most of these by boat services from the nearest mainland port – these range from regular car-ferry lines for some of the larger islands, to asking on a dock for a friendly fisherman to take you over to the smallest ones. For more details, *see* p.93 and p.288.

Tour Operators

There are hundreds of tour companies offering all manner of enticing holidays in Ireland. Tourism Ireland has lists of the main operators in their brochures. Alternatively, contact your travel agent.

Special-interest Holidays

Travellers who want holidays with a focus – ancestor-hunting, angling, bird-watching, farm and country, gastronomy, gardens, golf, riding, sailing, a mixture of these or none of them – are well catered for in Ireland. The main specialist companies are listed in tourist board brochures. Bord Fáilte also has brochures with organizations offering holidays 'designed to enable participants to acquire new leisure skills' – sports, gardening, cookery, arts and crafts – 'in a relaxed and green environment'.

Specialist Tour Operators

See also 'Summer Schools', pp.115–16.

In the UK

Angler's World Holidays, 46 Knifesmithgate, Chesterfield, Derbyshire, S40 1RQ, t (01246) 221 717, www.anglers-world.co.uk. Game fishing for salmon and sea-trout, dollaghan, gillaroo, sonaghen and ferox trout, and coarse fishing for bream, roach, rudd, tench and monster pike in rivers, lakes and loughs.

Back-Roads Touring Co., 14A New Broadway, London W5 2XA, t (020) 8566 5312, www.backroadstouring.co.uk. Tours of Dublin, Killarney, Galway, Sligo and Donegal.

Enjoy Ireland, t (01254) 692 899, www.enjoyireland.com. Golfing, riding, angling and walking holidays.

HF Holidays, Imperial House, Edgware Rd, London, NW9 5AL, t (020) 8905 9556, www.hfholidays.co.uk. Dingle Way and West of Ireland guided walking holidays, or stays in Killarney National Park, Co. Kerry.

On Course Travel, t (01372) 451 910, www.ireland-oncourse.co.uk. Horse-racing holidays.

In Ireland

Ardress Craft Centre, Kesh, Co. Fermanagh, t (028) 6632 3319. Holidays based around courses in arts and crafts.

Colclough Tours, 71 Waterloo Rd, Dublin 4, t (01) 660 7975, www.tourismresources.ie. Tailor-made itineraries, cars with driver-guides, and accommodation ranging from traditional farmhouses to the grandest castles. Tours can take in gardens, genealogy, ghosts, gourmet meals and historical sites.

Emerald Star Line Ltd, The Marina, Carrick-on-Shannon, Co. Leitrim, t (071) 962 7633, www.emeraldstar.ie. Cruising on the Shannon.

Go Ireland, Killorglin, Co. Kerry, t 0800 3698 7412 (Ireland), t 0800 783 8359 (UK), www.goireland.ie. Guided and independent walking and cycling holidays in Co. Kerry.

Irish Country Holidays, Old Church, Mill St, Borrisokane, Co. Tipperary, t (067) 27789, www.country-holidays.ie. A firm giving you the chance to live as part of a small, rural community for a week, in Ballyhoura, Co. Limerick, the Barrow/Nore area, Lough Corrib country, or west Cork. All of the communities offer something special in the way of landscape, customs and amenities.

Irish Cycling Safaris Ltd, Belfield Bike Shop, University College Dublin, Belfield House, Dublin 4, t (01) 260 0749, www.cyclingsafaris.com. Leisurely 1-week cycling holidays (bikes supplied) in many areas, especially the Cork/Kerry and Connemara regions.

Kerry Holidays, c/o Kerry Airport, Farranfore, Killarney, Co. Kerry, t (066) 976 3222 (Ireland), t 0800 039 0088 (UK), www.kerryholidays.com. Fly-drive, B&B, self-catering and golf holidays.

Oideas Gael, Glencolumbcille, Co. Donegal, t (0749) 730248, www.oideas-gael.com. A workshop-type course in Irish culture and language, which includes folklore, singing, storytelling, set dancing and local history.

In the USA and Canada

Backroads, 801 Cedar St, Berkeley, CA 94710-1800, t 1 800 GO-ACTIVE, or t 462 2848, www.backroads.com. Multi-sport: golf, walking and biking, with packages in counties Kerry, Cork and Galway.

CIE Tours International Inc, 100 Hanover Ave, PO Box 501, Cedar Knolls, NJ 07927-0501, t 1 800 CIE-TOUR, or t 973 292 3438, www.cietours.com. Escorted coach, self-drive or independent holidays, including 'Irish Pub and Folk' and 'Irish Legends' tours.

Classic Adventures, New York State, t 1 800 777 8090, www.classicadventures.com. Guided biking holidays in the south-west.

Golf International Inc., 14 East 38th St, New York, NY 10016, t 1 800 833 1389, www.golfinternational.com. A great variety of golf courses on customized or escorted tours.

Practical A–Z

Children

You will find that Irish bed and breakfast establishments welcome children. Many have family rooms with 4 or 5 beds, and charge a reduced price for them. Most supply cots and highchairs and offer a babysitting service, but always check beforehand. Some farm and country houses keep a donkey or pony and have swings and play areas.

Irish people love children, and easily tolerate seeing and hearing them in bars and eating places during the daytime. Children's menus are offered at a cheaper price and generally people will be helpful, but in some places they will not be so happy if you turn up with kids in the evening for dinner. If you are contemplating staying in some of the smart country-house hotels, which are full of precious antiques, please check that it is a suitable place for children beforehand.

Climate

Ireland lies on the Gulf Stream, which makes the climate mild, equable and moist. No temperature of more than 90°F or less than 0°F has ever been recorded. Rainfall is heaviest in the high western coastal areas, where it averages more than 80 inches (203cm) a year. On the east coast and over the central plain, rainfall averages between 30 and 40 inches (76 and 101cm). Rain is Ireland's blessing, yet, from the reputation it has in its own country and abroad, you might imagine it was a curse. It keeps the fields and trees that famous lush green, and the high level of water vapour in the air gives it a sleepy quality and softens the colours of the landscape. The winds from the east increase the haziness and mute the colours, but these are nearly always followed by winds from the northwest that bring clearer air and sunshine. So the clouds begin to drift and shafts of changing light touch the land. Nearly every drizzly day has this gleam of sunshine, which is why the Irish are always very optimistic about the weather. The driest parts of the country are counties Carlow,

Wexford and parts of Kilkenny and Waterford, the 'Sunny Southeast' as the tourist office imaginatively puts it, averaging fewer than 200 days with rain a year. Donegal, Tyrone, Londonderry, Sligo, Galway and coastal parts of Cork, Clare and Kerry average more than 250.

Snow is rare and seldom severe. Spring tends to be relatively dry, especially after the blustery winds of March, and the crisp colours and freshness of autumn only degenerate into the cold and damp of winter in late December. You can hope for at least 6 hours of sunshine a day over most of the country during May, June, July and August.

Disabled Travellers

Bord Fáilte produces useful booklets advising travellers with disabilities. Particularly commended is *Accessible Accommodation in Northern Ireland*. Useful advice for travelling in the North can also be obtained from Disability Action in Belfast.

The tourist board also publishes a comprehensive list of accommodation with access in its annual guides, available from its offices. In Dublin the National Rehabilitation Board can offer you information and assistance. The Irish Wheelchair Association can supply wheelchairs for the disabled.

In Britain, RADAR is an excellent source of information. The Holiday Care Information Unit offers advice for all travellers with special needs, and publishes a short information sheet on the Irish Republic.

Specialist Organizations in Ireland
Comhairle, 44 North Great George's St, Dublin 1, t (01) 874 7503, *www.comhairle.com*
Disability Action, Belfast, t (028) 9029 7880, *www.disabilityaction.org*
Irish Wheelchair Association, Blackheath Drive, Clontarf, Dublin 3, t (01) 818 6400, *www.iwa.ie/*. Services for disabled travellers, plus guides for disabled holidaymakers.
National Disability Authority, Dublin 4, t (01) 608 0400, *www.nda.ie*

Specialist Organizations in Britain
Holiday Care Service, 2nd Floor, Imperial Buildings, Victoria Rd, Horley, Surrey RH6 7PZ, t (01293) 774 535,

Average Daily Temperatures	
Jan	4–7°C (39–45°F)
July and Aug	14–24°C (57–75°F)

www.holidaycare.org.uk. Up-to-date information on destinations, transport and helpful tour operators.

RADAR (Royal Association for Disability and Rehabilitation), 12 City Forum, 250 City Rd, London EC1V 8AF, **t** (020) 7250 3222, *www.radar.org.uk.* Useful books for travellers with disabilities, including 'Access to Air Travel' and several holiday 'factpacks'.

RNIB (Royal National Institute for the Blind), 105 Judd St, London,WC1H 9NE, **t** (020) 7388 1266, *www.rnib.org.uk.* The RNIB's mobility unit offers a 'Plane Easy' audio-cassette that advises the blind or visually impaired on air travel. It also advises on accommodation.

Specialist Organizations in North America

American Foundation for the Blind, 11 Penn Plaza, Suite 300, New York, NY 10001, **t** (212) 502 7600, or **t** 800 AFBLINE, *www.afb.org.* The best source of information in the USA for visually impaired travellers.

Mobility International USA, PO Box 10767, Eugene, OR 97440, **t** (541) 343 1284, *www.miusa.org.* Information on international educational exchange programmes and voluntary services for the disabled.

SATH (Society for the Advancement of Travelers with Handicaps), 347 Fifth Ave, Suite 610, New York, NY 10016, **t** (212) 447 7284, *www.sath.org.* Travel and access information, including a good website.

Eating Out

You will normally find service in Ireland friendly and helpful. A variety of good eating places are listed under 'Eating Out' in each chapter; in the culinary deserts that do exist, those listed are the best of an indifferent lot. Restaurants are categorized in the price ranges below. For further details on eating habits, *see* **Food and Drink**, pp.81–86.

> **Restaurant Price Categories**
>
> Categories are based on an average 3-course meal for one person, without wine.
>
> *luxury* more than €66/UK £45
> *expensive* €45–66/UK£31–45
> *moderate* €22–44/UK£15–30
> *inexpensive* less than €22/£15

Electricity

The current is 220 volts AC, so bring a current converter if you have US appliances/computers. Wall sockets take the standard British-style 3-pin (flat) fused plugs, so Americans and other Europeans will need a plug adaptor too.

Embassies and Consulates

Australian Embassy, Fitzwilton House, Wilton Terrace, Dublin 2, **t** (01) 664 5300, *www.australianembassy.ie*

Australian High Commission, Australia House, The Strand, London, WC2 B4L, **t** (020) 7379 4334, *www.australia.org.uk*

British Embassy, 31 Merrion Rd, Dublin 4, **t** (01) 269 5211, *www.britishembassy.ie*

Canadian Embassy, 65 St Stephen's Green, Dublin 2, **t** (01) 417 4100

Canadian High Commission, Grosvenor Sq, London W1, **t** (020) 7258 6600

New Zealand Consulate General, 37 Leeson Park, Dublin 6, **t** (01) 660 4233

South African Embassy, Earlsfort Court, Dublin 2, **t** (01) 661 5553

US Embassy, 43 Elgin Rd, Dublin 4, **t** (01) 668 8777, *http://dublin.usembassy.gov/*

US Consulate, Danesfort House, 223 Stranmillis Rd, Belfast BT9 5GR, **t** (028) 9038 6100, *www.usembassy.org.uk*

Emergencies and Hazards

Emergencies

If you fall ill, have an accident or are the victim of a crime in Ireland, people will rush to your aid. Whether they bring quite the help you need is another matter. If in doubt, get the advice of your hotel, local tourist office or the police. In serious cases (medical or legal), contact your embassy or consulate (*see* above). Try to keep your head: in the case of medical treatment, take your insurance documents, inform the people treating you of your cover, and make sure you keep all receipts (or at least get someone reliable to do this for you).

The **emergency telephone number** (to call any of the emergency services) in both the Republic and the North is **t** 999. In the Republic you can also call **t** 112.

Beasts

If you decide you want to have a picnic in an inviting green field, just check that there is not a bull in it first. High-spirited bullocks can be just as alarming; they will come rushing up to you to have a good look, and knock you over in the process.

Midges

Toads and adders are said to have fled from Ireland at the sound of St Patrick's bell tolling from the top of Croagh Patrick mountain; unfortunately, the voracious midges of the west coast did not take their cue. They are very persistent on warm summer evenings, so remember to arm yourself with an insect repellent. There is plenty of choice in the chemist if you forget. Wasps, hornets and horseflies also emerge in summer.

Motorists

Motorists in Dublin should always lock their cars, and leave them in authorized car parks. Many cars are stolen and taken for 'joy rides' by young boys. Do not leave luggage or valuables in the car.

The Sea

A major hazard can be strong currents in the sea. One beach may be perfectly safe for bathing but the one beside it positively dangerous. Always check with locals before you swim. There are lifeguards on most of the resort beaches; few elsewhere.

Also, don't eat the seaweed. No matter how clean the water looks, beware! It may make you sick to your stomach.

Walkers

Walkers who intend to go through bog and mountainous country should be warned that, even though it looks dry enough on the road, once you are into the heather and moss you will soon sink into waterlogged ground. Wear stout boots and bring at least an extra jersey. Sudden mists and rain can descend, and you can get very cold. You should not rely on mountain rescue teams to find you; if you do intend to go walking on a mountain range, leave word at your hotel or put a note on your car as to where you plan to go. During the **shooting season** (grouse and snipe from Aug to 3 Jan, duck from Sept to 31 Jan and pheasant

Calendar of Events

March

Dublin Film Festival, t (01) 661 6216, *www.dubliniff.com*. New Irish cinema.
Irish Grand National, Fairyhouse, Co. Meath, *www.hri.ie*. The famous horse race.
St Patrick's Week, *www.stpatricksday.ie*. Events centre around St Patrick's Day (17 Mar), with parades, music, dance and theatre, especially in Dublin, Cork, Galway and Limerick.
World Irish Dancing Championships, t (01) 475 2220. The biggest event in the Irish dancing calendar.

May

Fleadh Nua, Ennis, Co. Clare, **t** (01) 280 0295, *www.fleadhnua.com*. Traditional music, song and dance.

June

Castlebar International Four-day Summer Walk, t (094) 902 4102, *www.castlebar4dayswalks. com*. Walking and traditional, pop and classical music, late June–July.

**IIB Music in Great Irish Houses Festival,
t** (01) 664 2822, *www.musicirishhouses.com*. International soloists and orchestras performing in grand houses through summer.
Irish Derby, The Curragh, Co. Kildare,
t (045) 441205, *www.curragh.ie*. Another famous horse race.
The Cat Laughs Comedy Festival, Kilkenny, *www.thecatlaughs.com*. A well-received comedy event held over 5 days.

July

Galway Arts Festival, t (091) 562655, *www.galwayartsfestival.com*. One of the biggest and most popular festivals in the country, with theatre, arts and music.
RDS Kerrygold Irish Oaks, The Curragh, Co. Kildare, **t** (045) 441205, *www.curragh.ie*. A big event in the horse world calendar.

August

Connemara Pony Show, Clifden, Co. Galway,
t (095) 21863, *www.cpbs.ie*. A famous show that marks the culmination of a week-long festival celebrating the Connemara pony.

from 1 Nov to 1 Jan), be careful of wandering into stray shot on the hilly slopes or in marshy places.

The Fairies

There is just one last possible hazard that you might only have dreamt about: the mischievous fairies might put a spell on you so that you never want to return to your own country. It's not a joke, for Ireland is an enchanting country that is difficult to leave. As a rule, it's no use enquiring about charms against this enchantment, or any other; the answer is always the same: 'There used to be a lot of them in the old days, but the priests put them down.' You'll hear the same about *poteen*. Underneath, people have a sneaking belief in fairies – why, in a perfectly modern housing estate outside Sligo, is there a ragged mound that escaped the bulldozer and cement? Perhaps it is a fairy *rath*?

Have you ever heard where the fairies come from? Padraic Colum (1881–1972), the Irish-American author, found out from a blind man he met in the west, who believed in them as firmly as in the Gospels. Apparently, when the Angel Lucifer rebelled against God, Hell was made in a minute. God swept Lucifer and thousands of his followers down to it, until the Angel Gabriel said, 'O God Almighty, Heaven will be swept clean.' God agreed, saying, 'Them that are in Heaven let them remain so, them that are in Hell, let them remain in Hell; and them that are between Heaven and Hell, let them remain in the air.' And so the angels that remained between Heaven and Hell became the fairies.

Festivals

Tourism Ireland's annual *Calendar of Events*, available from tourist offices and at *www. tourismireland.com*, presents you with a dazzling array of international festivals and small town extravaganzas, where everyone has a ball: jolly music pours into the street, farmers and tradesmen parade their goods and machinery, and there are endless bouncing baby competitions, discos and poteen, whiskey and stout drinking bouts.

See 'Calendar of Events', below, for details of some of the main annual festivals.

Dublin Horse Show, RDS, Dublin 4, t (01) 668 0866, *www.rds.ie*. A major equestrian event.
Fleadh Cheoil na hÉireann, t (01) 280 0295, *www.comhaltas.com*. Up to 5,000 traditional musicians playing impromptu sessions, usually in summer (venues change).
Kilkenny Arts Festival, t (056) 63663, *www.kilkennyarts.ie*. A festival comprising music recitals, poetry, art, theatre and children's workshops.
Puck Fair, Killorglin, t (066) 976 2366, *www. puckfair.ie*. Lots of drinking and wildness revolving around a captured goat.
Rose of Tralee International Festival, t (066) 712 1322, *www.roseoftralee.ie*. An event to which girls of Irish parentage and birth from all over the world come to compete for the title 'Rose of Tralee'. There are carnival parades, street dancing, fireworks, music, and the Tralee races.

September
Dublin Theatre Festival, t (01) 677 8439, *www.dublintheatrefestival.com*. The opportunity to see work by Irish writers and productions by a variety of well-known international theatre companies, late Sept–Oct.
International Festival of Light Opera, Theatre Royal, The Mall, Waterford, t (051) 872639, *www.waterfordfestival.com*. A dozen light operas, performed one after the other in Waterford's lovely old theatre.
Matchmaking Festival, Lisdoonvarna, Co. Clare, t (065) 707 4005, *www.matchmakerireland. com*. A festival for local bachelors (and ladies in search of a husband), accompanied by drinking, noise and crowds.

October
Ballinasloe Horse Fair, t (090) 964 3453, *www.ballinasloe.com*. One of Europe's oldest horse fairs, which can get wild, in early Oct.
Belfast Festival at Queen's, t (028) 9097 1034, *www.belfastfestival.com*. Music, theatre, dance, film and more.
Wexford Opera Festival, Theatre Royal, Wexford, t (053) 22400, *www.wexfordopera.com*. Rare operatic masterpieces with supporting events, Oct–Nov.

Health and Insurance

If you need **medical** or **dental** treatment in the Republic, you are expected to pay for the treatment then claim back the costs from your insurance company. This may not be something you can discuss on the operating table. *In extremis* the international emergency services offered by firms such as Europ Assistance or Travel Assistance International, which are often incorporated into travel-insurance packages, are blessings. For all kinds of medical care, EU citizens can benefit from mutual agreements between EU member countries. British citizens travelling to the Republic can use any GP who has an agreement with the Health Board, but to benefit from this you need your **EHIC card** (which has replaced the E111 form) with you; application packs are available from post offices, but it's quickest to apply online at *www.dh.gov.uk*. The same scheme also applies to dentists and to hospitals.

The best advice is to always **insure** your holiday, and do so as soon as you book your ticket. Standard travel insurance packages issued by major insurance companies cover a broad range of risks, including cancellation due to unforeseen circumstances, transport delays caused by strikes or foul weather, loss or theft of baggage, medical insurance and compensation for injury or death. The cost of insurance may seem substantial, but it is negligible when compared to almost any claim, should misfortune befall you. That said, it is worth checking to see if any of your existing insurance schemes cover travel risks: certain British household insurance schemes, for example, include limited travel cover.

To **claim** for loss or theft of baggage, you need evidence that you have reported the incident to the police. Check your insurance details for what is required of you in such circumstances. It is, by the way, useful to have more than one copy of your insurance policy – if your baggage is stolen, the document may go with it.

Heritage and Interpretative Centres

The last decade or so has seen a huge increase in the number of these centres all over Ireland. The larger ones incorporate local history, flora and fauna, using audio-visuals as an aid, or life-size models and actors dressed in period costume. The Office of Public Works have built a few interpretative centres in places of great natural beauty and fragile ecology. Controversy was provoked by the siting of one in the middle of the Burren, Co. Clare. Inevitably such places destroy some of the beauty and peace with huge car parks, WCs, craft centres etc., however sympathetic the architecture and landscaping may be. Many of the small heritage centres double as **genealogical centres** and are set in fine old buildings (mainly in towns) that have been restored by the efforts and enthusiasm of the local people.

Money

Currency

The **Republic of Ireland**, part of the European Monetary System, has the **euro** (€) as its official currency. In **Northern Ireland** the currency is still the **UK pound** (£). For current exchange rates and online conversions, see *www.xe.com*.

Euro notes are in denominations of 5, 10, 20, 50, 100, 200 and 500, with coins for €1 and €2. Each single euro consists of 100 cents; coins are used for 1, 2, 5, 10, 20 and 50 cents.

As everywhere, the best exchange rates are available at banks, the worst at hotels. Rates will also be less good at bureaux de change, though these are useful when banks are closed. They can be found in city centres, key tourist areas such as Killarney, ferry terminals and the international sections of airports, including those at:

Cork: *open Mon–Fri 6.45am–8pm*
Dublin: *open daily 5.30am–9pm*
Shannon: *open daily 6.30am–9.30pm*

Getting Cash and Using Credit Cards

You can obtain **cash** in local currencies from bank ATMs, usually sited in airports as well as towns and cities. Check with your bank or building society as to whether charges will be applied to your withdrawals, and which ATMs you may use. Leading **credit** and **debit cards** (Visa, Mastercard/Access, American Express and Diner's Club) are widely accepted in major hotels, restaurants and shops, but always check that your card will be accepted before you buy anything.

Traveller's Cheques

The main brands of traveller's cheques (American Express, Visa and Thomas Cook) are accepted by banks throughout the Republic of Ireland and Northern Ireland.
American Express Foreign Exchange Bureau, 41 Nassau St, Dublin 2, **t** (01) 890 205511, *open Mon–Fri 9–5*; also at International Hotel, East Avenue Rd, Killarney, Co. Kerry, **t** (066) 35722, *open Mon–Fri 9–5*.
Going Places, 57 Donegall Place, Belfast, **t** 0870 853 0515. American Express traveller's cheques are cashed here on a commission-free basis.
Thomas Cook, 11 Donegall Place, Belfast, **t** (028) 9088 3940

Banks

Small towns in Ireland have at least one bank. These are open Mon–Fri 10am–12.30pm and 1.30–4pm in the Republic. Banks in the larger towns will usually have 1 day each week – normally market day or Thur – when they will stay open until 5pm. Larger branches do not close for lunch.

In the North, banks also open at 10am and close at 4pm, but in Belfast and Derry City they do not close at lunchtime.

The bank usually occupies the grandest building in town – the various banking groups seem to have some sort of conscience about historical buildings, which is very rare in Ireland. The moving of money is accompanied by massive security, which looks very out of keeping with the happy-go-lucky attitude in Ireland but is necessary because bank raids have become so common.

Tipping

Tipping is not really a general habit in Ireland, except in taxis and in eating places where there is table service. Taxi-drivers will expect to be tipped at a rate of approximately 10% of the fare; porters and doormen expect 50 cents or so. There is no tipping in pubs, but in hotel bars where you are served by a waiter it is usual to leave a small tip. A service charge of 12%, sometimes 15%, is usually raised automatically on hotel and restaurant bills. Where this is not the case, a tip of this magnitude would be in order, if you feel that the service merits it.

Newspapers

The best newspaper to read while you are in Ireland is the *Irish Times* (*www.ireland.com*), followed closely by the *Irish Independent* (*www.unison.ie/irish-independent*) and the *Irish Examiner* (*www.examiner.ie*). The Saturday edition of the *Irish Times* runs a 'What is on' list of exhibitions, festivals and concerts around the country.

In Northern Ireland, the *Newsletter* has a Unionist slant, while the *Irish News* (*www.irishnews.com*) sells mainly to the Nationalist community. The *Belfast Telegraph* (*www.belfasttelegraph.co.uk*) is middle of the road. Every small Irish town and county has its own newspaper; wherever you're staying, make sure to have a read and watch the community life unfold.

Image (*www.image.ie*) is a glossy women's magazine along the lines of *Harpers & Queen*, filled with fashion features, interior decoration restaurant reviews, short stories and more. *Phoenix* (*www.phoenix-magazine.com*) is the Irish equivalent of *Private Eye*, and *The Village* (*www.villagemagazine.com*) is a monthly news and current affairs magazine with excellent investigative journalism.

Packing

Whatever you do, come expecting rain – wellington boots, umbrellas and raincoats are essential unless you want to stay inside reading a book all day. Once you get out into the rain, though, it is never as bad as it looks, and the clouds soon begin to clear. Bring warm jumpers, trousers, woollen socks and gloves for autumn, winter and early spring. The best thing to do is to expect the cold and wet and then get a pleasant surprise when it's sunny and hot – so sneak in a few T-shirts, just in case. Sometimes the sun shines furiously in March and April and you can end up with a very convincing tan.

If you like walking, bring a pair of fairly stout shoes or boots – trainers end up bedraggled and let the water in. Fishing rods and swimsuits are worth packing, if you think you may have cause to regret leaving them behind. Bring a sleeping bag if you plan to stay at youth hostels.

Post Offices

Letterboxes are green in the Republic and red in the North. Some villages in the Republic list them among the historic monuments in their brochures – old ones with the monogram of Queen Victoria, now painted green. As you would expect, you have to put British stamps on letters posted in the North.

If you do not have a fixed address in Ireland, letters can be sent *Poste Restante* to any post office and picked up with some proof of identity. There is a post office in every village, often in the village shop. In general the Irish Post is admirably efficient; the gentlemen behind the counters will sometimes be amateur poets and historians. Remember that Ireland's most glorious battle was fought from a post office – the 1916 Rebellion.

Post offices are open 9am–5.30pm Mon–Fri and 9am–1pm Sat, and closed Sun and public holidays. Sub-post offices often close on 1 day a week at 1pm. The GPO in O'Connell St, Dublin, is open 8am–8pm Mon–Sat, except bank holidays.

Shopping

Shopping in Ireland is one of the most relaxing pastimes imaginable. High-quality design and craftsmanship make for goods that will last you a lifetime. You can find them easily in the craft centres that have been set up all over the country. The **Crafts Council of Ireland**, which is based at Castle Yard, Kilkenny, **t** (056) 776 1804, *www.ccoi.ie*, has given a great boost to many talented craft workers and helped them to market their wares and join forces in studios and workshops, sometimes in IDA (Industrial Development Authority) parks.

Crafts are not cheap, because of the artistry and labour involved, but you can find bargains at china, crystal and linen factory shops if you are prepared to seek them out. Grinning leprechauns, colleen dolls, Guinness slogan T-shirts and shamrock mugs are stacked high in most gift shops if you want something cheerful and cheap, but do not ignore the real products from Ireland.

Opening Hours

Shops in Ireland are usually open Mon–Sat from 9 or 9.30am to 5.30 or 6pm. Craft shops in scenic areas are usually open on Sun as well, especially if they have a tea-room. In some towns there is an **early-closing day**, when businesses close at 1pm; this is normally Wed, though it differs in some areas.

You shouldn't have much trouble finding food or petrol on Sun; these days the majority of supermarkets open for at least a few hours in the morning.

Irish Specialities

Connemara Marble: a natural green stone, found in the west, which ranges from bright field-green through to jade and oak-leaf colour, sometimes with stripes of brown. It is worked into jewellery and sold with other locally made objects, such as paperweights or chess sets.

Food and Drink: Soda, wheaten and potato breads are found everywhere in Ireland – McCambridge's brown bread is even available in airport shops. Smoked salmon and farmhouse cheese is sold in every shape, size and texture.

Irish whiskey (note the 'e' in the Irish spelling) is slightly sweeter than Scotch; try Bushmills, Paddy, Power and Jameson's. Cork gin is considered to have a delicious tang of juniper. Popular liqueurs are Irish Mist, which contains whiskey and honey, Tullamore Dew and Bailey's Irish Cream.

Public Holidays

January: New Year's Day (1st).
March: St Patrick's Day, Republic only (17th).
March/April: Good Friday, which is widely observed as a holiday but is not an official one; Easter Monday.
May: May Day (1st or early May); Spring Holiday, N. Ireland only (end May).
June: June Holiday, Republic only (first Mon in June).
July: Orange Parades, N. Ireland only (12th).
August: August Holiday, Republic only (first Monday in Aug). Summer Holiday, N. Ireland only (end Aug).
October: October Holiday, Republic only (last Mon in Oct).
December: Christmas Day (25th); Boxing Day/St Stephen's Day (26th)

Glass: Waterford Crystal is world-famous for its quality and design. Attractive crystal glass can also be bought at the factories in Cavan, Tyrone, Sligo and Cork. The hand-blown glass from the Jerpoint Glassworks in Co. Kilkenny is worth collecting.

Hand-knits and Aran Sweaters: Connacht, Donegal and the coastal stretches of Munster have the greatest variety. In the Clifden/Leenane region of Connemara, you can buy soft, striped wool rugs and cured sheepskins, which make good bedside rugs. Aran sweaters are made from tough wool, and are lightly coated in animal oils so that they are water-resistant and warm. They have differing patterns; in the past there were family patterns so that drowned fishermen could be recognized. Make sure you buy one that has the hand-knitted label.

Jewellery, Silver and Antiques: Claddagh rings (*see* p.273) are still the loveliest of all love tokens, and are very evocative of the west. Try to go to the July Antiques Fair at the RDS in Dublin.

Lace: Irish lace is one of the lightest and most precious of all the specialities to take home. It is fun if you can visit the convents and cooperatives where the lace is made. Try the Lace Cooperative, Carrickmacross, t (042) 966 2506; the Good Shepherd Convent, 9 Good Shepherd Ave, Limerick, t (061) 317522; and Kenmare Lace and Design Centre, Kenmare, t (064) 41491.

Linen: you can buy excellent Irish linen teacloths and fine linen sheets in Belfast. Hand-embroidered handkerchiefs and tablecloths are for sale in Co. Donegal.

Pottery and China: talented potters work in rural communities all over Ireland; the best places to find their work for sale is at IDA centres and craft shops. Look for Roundstone in Connemara, Co. Galway, Belleek in Co. Fermanagh, Arklow in Co. Wicklow, and the work of Nicholas Mosse, sold at the Kilkenny Design Centre (*www.kilkennydesign.com*).

Traditional Musical Instruments: for *bodhráns* (a type of drum), try John McNeill, 140 Capel St, Dublin, t (01) 872 2159, or try Malachy Kearns, Roundstone Musical Instruments, IDA Craft Centre, Roundstone, Co. Galway, t (095) 35808, *www.bodhran.com*. To get hold of uilleann pipes and bodhráns,

pay a visit to The Bodhrán Maker, Spiddle Rd, Spiddal, Co. Galway, but make sure to phone ahead (Mon–Fri 9–5, t (091) 589 094, *www.irishpipesandbodhrans.com*).

Tweed: hand-woven from wool, tweed keeps you warm but also lets your skin 'breathe'. Donegal tweed is particularly attractive, with its subtle shades. In Ardara and its environs you will still find thick, naturally dyed tweed. Báinín (pronounced 'bawneen') is an undyed tweed, and is often used for upholstery. For more information, see the Blarney Woollen Mills website, *www.blarney.com*.

Woven Baskets: you can buy baskets made of willow or rush all over Ireland: bread baskets, turfholders, place mats and St Brigid Crosses – charms against evil.

Smoking

In an unprecedented move, smoking was banned from pubs and restaurants in the Republic of Ireland in March 2004. All public premises must comply by law.

Currently, Northern Ireland retains British laws about smoking, which is not yet completely banned in pubs and restaurants. If you require a smoking or non-smoking bedroom, check when you book that what you want is available.

Sports and Activities

Adventure Sports

The House of Sport, Longmile Rd, Dublin 12, t (01) 450 7376, *www.mountaineering.ie*, can give you information on mountaineering, canoeing and many other sports. In the North, contact the Sports Council for Northern Ireland, t (028) 9038 1222, *www.sportni.org.uk*.

Birdwatching

You can still hear the corncrake amongst the fields of Rathlin Island, or the choughs calling from the rocky headlands. Walking along the coastal mudflats in winter, whether you are in Co. Down or Co. Wexford, you will very likely see whooper swans.

Ireland has more than 60 bird sanctuaries; contact the **National Parks & Wildlife Service**, 7 Ely Place, Dublin 2, t (01) 647 2300. Field trips are organized by branches of **Bird Watch Ireland**, **t** (01) 281 9878, *www.birdwatchireland.ie*; you can also contact them at the **RSPB** (Royal Society for the Protection of Birds), Belvoir Park Forest, Belfast, **t** (028) 9049 1547, or the **National Trust** (NI), Rowallane, Saintfield, Co. Down, BT24 7LH, **t** (028) 9751 0721.

Canoeing

This is an exciting and compelling way to tour Ireland via the Liffey and the Barrow rivers, with their smooth-flowing stretches, rapids and weirs. The other principal rivers are the Nore, Boyne, Slaney, Lee, Shannon, Suir and Blackwater. You can always camp by the waterside as long as you get permission from the owner. Contact Michael Scanlon, **House of Sport**, Longmile Rd, Dublin 12, **t** (01) 450 7376; **AFAS**, **t** (0749) 152800, *www.adventuresports.ie*, or the **Canoe Association of Northern Ireland**, **t** 0870 240 5065, *www.cani.org.uk*.

Caving

This activity has become more organized of late with the setting up of the **Speleological Union of Ireland** (*www.cavingireland.org*) at the House of Sport (*see* above). The caving possibilities in the Cavan/Fermanagh area and in Co. Sligo are numerous. For more information, contact the Speleological Union, the **Irish Orienteering Association**, **t** 1809 923490, *www.orienteering.ie*, or AFAS, as above

Cruising the Inland Waterways

This is an unforgettable and exciting way to travel around Ireland. The main waterways are the **River Shannon**, which is navigable from Lough Key to Killaloe, and the **River Erne**, which has 2 huge island-studded lakes and is navigable for more than 50 miles (80km) from Belturbet to the little village of Belleek. The 2 are now linked due to the recent restoration and opening of the Shannon-Erne Waterway, along with the Grand Canal and the River Barrow (the canal links Dublin with the Shannon and the Barrow). Along the waterways you pass peaceful, lush scenery: tumbledown castles, abbeys and beautiful flowers and birds. In the evening you can moor up your boat for a meal and a jar and listen to some good traditional music.

The Erne waterway is beautifully wooded, with nature reserves and little islands to meander amongst. Lough Erne in all covers 300 square miles (777 sq km) of water. Cruiser-hire companies operate around the lakes; contact the Erne Charter Boat Association. The Shannon-Erne waterway links the North and South and makes it possible to navigate along a 190-mile (300km) stretch. For 1-way rental, contact Erincurrach Cruising.

On the **Shannon** there are several companies offering luxury cabin cruisers for self-drive hire, ranging from 2 to 10 berths. All are fitted with fridges, gas cookers, hot water and showers; most have central

Boat Cruise Companies

Athlone Cruisers Ltd, Athlone, **t** (09064) 72892
Celtic Canal Cruisers Ltd, Tullamore, Co. Offaly, **t** (0506) 21861
Corrib Cruises, Cong, Co. Mayo, **t** (092) 46029/46292, or **t** (091) 552808, *www.corribcruises.com*. A company specializing in cruising and exploring Lough Corrib.
Derg Marine Cruisers, Killaloe, **t** (061) 376364
Emerald Star Line Ltd, The Marina, Carrick-on-Shannon, **t** (071) 962 7633, or **t** (078) 20234, *www.emeraldstar.ie*
Erne Charter Boat Association, Fermanagh Tourism, Enniskillen, **t** (028) 6632 3110
Erincurrach Cruising, Blaney, Enniskillen, **t** (028) 6864 1737, *www.boatingireland.com*

Riversdale Barge Holidays, Riversdale, Ballinamore, Co. Leitrim, **t** (071) 964 4122, *www.riversdalebargeholidays.com*
Shannon Castle Line, Williamstown Harbour, Whitegate, Co. Clare, **t** (061) 927042, *www.shannoncruisers.com*
Shannon Sailing Ltd, Dromineer, Nenagh, Co. Tipperary, **t** (067) 24499, *www.shannonsailing.com*

Day trips and **pleasure cruises** are also available on the Shannon. Contact:
Destination Killarney, **t** (064) 32638.
It is possible to take the *Killarney Waterbus* through the famous lakes on a trip lasting 1½ hours.
Jolly Mariner Marina, Athlone, Co. Westmeath, **t** (0902) 72892/72113

heating. A dinghy, charts, binoculars and safety equipment are included on the river and lough routes. Groceries and stores can be ordered in advance and collected when you arrive. Skippers must be over 21, and the controls must be understood by at least 2 people in a group, but no licence is necessary. You receive an hour of tuition, more if you need it. The average price for a 6-berth cruiser ranges from €700 per week in Apr to about €1,800 in July and Aug. Ask for details from your travel agent or Irish tourist office.

You will find that there are some excellent **pubs and restaurants** catering for the needs of the cruisers; ask at the local tourist office. Good pubs along the River Shannon include Hughes Pub, Northgate St, Athlone; Conlins, Church St, Athlone; Garry Kennedy's, Portrow; Hough's Pub and Killeen's in Shannonbridge; the Sail Inn, Scarriff; the Jolly Mariner, Sean's Bar and the Green Olive, Athlone; the Crew's Inn in Roosky.

Some of the companies listed opposite also operate river cruises. Many others exist, wherever there are rivers and loughs; these are listed in the 'Sports and Activities' sections for each county.

Useful reading: *The Shell Guide to the Shannon, The Guide to the Grand Canal*, and the *Guide to the River Barrow*. Available from Eason and Son Ltd, 40 Lower O'Connell St, Dublin 1, t (01) 858 3800 (*www.buy4now.ie*).

Fishing

We are most grateful to Antony Luke for the following personal account. Antony has been returning on holiday to Ireland since 1963. He acts as a consultant on fishing matters to the corporate entertainment company Country & Highland, gives fly-fishing instruction, and organizes salmon-fishing parties. He has a cottage on one of the northern isles of Orkney, where he keeps a lobster boat, and from where he runs a business exporting fish and shellfish.

Whatever the catch, one always returns from Ireland with a story and happy memories. The sport is excellent, and all visitors are treated with the usual great Irish hospitality and charm. Tackle shops are very helpful, and Tourism Ireland, the tourist board for the whole of Ireland, issues a wealth of information, including dates of angling competitions and an excellent brochure on angling in Ireland.

In general, fishing in Ireland is more available to the general public and less restricted than in Scotland. Notably, fishing on Sunday is permitted. Unlike the UK, there is no closed season for coarse fishing. Seasons for other types of fishing vary according to region and sometimes specific rivers. Costs are also comparatively low. Government licences are not hefty, but they are required for salmon and sea-trout fishing.

For the purposes of licensing, fishing in the **Republic** can be divided into 4 categories: game, for salmon and sea-trout (migratory); trout (non-migratory); coarse, for perch, roach, rudd, bream, tench, etc., and pike; and sea-fishing. Visitors require a licence for the first. It is possible to purchase individual or composite licences from Tourism Ireland offices in your country of residence. In the Republic, they can be bought from any Tourist or Fisheries Board office, from all government-run fisheries, and from many tackle shops.

One of the finest aspects of the sport in Ireland is the variety of different fishing techniques that are to be found in quite small areas. It is possible to fish a lake system – either dapping or wet-fly – and a river on the same day. In the UK, this is only possible in a few places on the west coast of Scotland, and to some extent in the Hebrides.

The great Irish limestone lakes such as Carra, Conn, Mask and Corrib offer some of the best trout-fishing in the world, especially at the time of the mayfly (mid-May to early June). On Corrib there is also salmon. A ghillied boat is necessary if you wish to fish these beautiful lakes scattered with many hundreds of small islands; Irish ghillies have a great knowledge of the shoals and bays where fish lie. They are often also highly entertaining.

Coarse fishing is immensely popular in the Republic, particularly with visitors from the UK, where there is a closed season from mid-Mar to mid-June. Vast expanses of water throughout the centre of the country are open to visitors, and pike-fishing here is amongst the best in Europe.

It would take a book longer than this one to list all the rivers and loughs for visiting game-fishers. On the whole, salmon-fishing is privately owned, but good association water is available for the general public. On the east coast, the Boyne, Liffey and Slaney rivers have early runs of salmon, and grilse run later – from mid-June. On the south coast, the Nore, Suir, Barrow and the Blackwater also have early runs of salmon, and grilse later. On the southwest coast, there are a number of rivers and lake systems, notably Lough Currane at Waterville and the Maine and Laune, including the Killarney Lakes. In the mid-west the list is endless, numbering such famous places as Ballynahinch, the Newport, which drains Lough Beltra, Delphi, the Moy and the mighty Shannon. Fishing on the Shannon was badly affected by the introduction of the hydro-electric scheme in 1929, but the Castleconnell beats are still worth a visit. The Corrib River drains the Corrib system and the famous Galway Weir. Thousands apply every year for a permit to fish here, but you may be lucky in the ballot for selection. If not, join the crowds at the Galway Salmon Weir Bridge and watch the ranks of salmon stream past.

Also in the mid-west, one of my favourite spots is the River Erriff, administered by the Central Fisheries Board. Running through a glacial valley in the heart of Connemara, it has a wild beauty, culminating in a cascade over the Aasleagh Falls and into the sea at Killary Harbour. Beats are on both banks and generous. Given good conditions, the Erriff can be as prolific as some of the most famous rivers. Visitors can either take a cottage or stay in the Aasleagh Lodge, which offers both dinner and B&B. Book early through the Manager, Erriff Fishery, Aasleagh Lodge, Leenane, Co. Galway.

Sea-trout have been in decline over the past decade, especially on the west coast, and some well-known sea-trout fisheries have suffered badly due to 'sea lice' (which many claim is due to salmon farming). Considerable research is now being done by the Salmon Research Trust at Newport, and things have shown a slight improvement. By contrast, runs of salmon and grilse have held up well recently.

Sea-angling is increasingly popular with the hardy fisherman. The Central Fisheries Board issues a comprehensive booklet. More boats are available for hire than ever before, though they can be expensive for the individual; it is best to organize a group of 4 or more. Kinsale is a main centre for sea-angling. Here, when the sea warms a degree or so, odd species of tropical fish arrive. Out of Kinsale there is also good shark-fishing, and many other species such as conger, skate and, for the less choosy, huge bags of large pollack can be caught. On the west coast, Cleggan is another small port where boats can be hired. The area round Connemara is startlingly beautiful, and many self-catering cottages can be rented.

Other main sea-fishing stations are Rosslare and Dungarvan in Co. Waterford; Youghal, Ballycotton, and Baltimore in Co. Cork; Cahirciveen and the Dingle Peninsula in Co. Kerry; Westport, Achill Island, Newport and Belmullet in Co. Mayo; and Moville in Co. Donegal. As a rule, all stations will be able to supply boats for hire, rods, tackle, etc.

Northern Ireland has a wealth of lakes, rivers and tributaries, and fine sport can be had in all areas. Seasons vary, as they do in the south, and costs are not high.

Lough Erne is well known for quality in all types of fishing. The upper water is mostly for coarse fish, while the lower holds salmon and trout. The River Foyle and its tributaries, some running into Lough Foyle, have good runs of salmon and sea-trout. The River Bann divides into two; the lower drains Lough Neagh and is famous for its salmon-fishing, but the lower beats are expensive. The Upper Bann rises in the Mountains of Mourne and fish run later. The popularity of **sea-fishing** has grown immensely in recent years; 24 species of sea-fish are caught regularly. The main centres boats can be hired from are Portrush,

Fishing Information

Central Fisheries Board, t (01) 884 2600, *www.cfb.ie*. The board to contact to find out how to get the necessary fishing licence for the area in which you wish to fish.

Fermanagh Lakeland Tourism, Enniskillen, Co. Fermanagh, **t** (028) 6634 6736

Foyle Fisheries Commission, 8 Victoria Rd, Derry City, **t** (028) 7134 2100. Game-rod licences.

Northern Regional Fisheries Board, Station Rd, Ballyshannon, Co. Donegal, **t** (071) 985 1435, *www.nrfb.ie*

Golf Courses

Eastern Ireland

Carlow: an exceptional course.
Delgany: one of the nurseries of Irish golf. It has produced several famous players, including Harry Bradshaw and Eamon D'Arcy.
Howth: clings precipitously to the hill's southern slopes. It offers high-quality golf and spectacular views.
Island Golf Course: on a peninsula across the water from Malahide, among rolling dunes.
Co. Louth Golf Course/Baltray, Drogheda: home to the East of Ireland Championships, reputed to have the finest greens in Ireland.
Luttrelstown: quality greens and beautiful landscaping 15 mins west of Phoenix Park.
Mount Juliet: host to the Murphy's Irish Open several years running. This is probably the best inland course in Ireland.
Mullingar: the scene of several international tournaments in recent years.
Open Golf Centre, at Newtown House, St Margaret's. This has 27 holes, plus a driving range with 4 pros available for lessons.
Portmarnock: the jewel of the Republic's crown, less than 30 mins' drive from Dublin.
Royal Dublin: hosts the Irish Open Championship, along with the above.

Woodenbridge and **Courtown**: 2 courses not far from the sea, and well worth a visit.

Northern Ireland

Ballyliffin Golf Club: set amid daunting sand hills and surrounded by the Atlantic on 3 sides, yet still inland in character.
Luttrelstown: a beautifully landscaped course south of Belfast.
Portsalon and **Rosapenna**: 19th-century courses that still test the the giants, with stunning views of the Donegal coastline.
Royal County Down Golf Course, Newcastle: quite possibly the best links course in the world. Scenically stunning, the Royal County Down lies right at the base of the Mourne Mountains.
Royal Portrush: near the Giant's Causeway; the only Irish course ever to have hosted the Open Championship. Only the most competent should tackle it on blustery days.
Valley Course: an entertaining few days can be spent in the Portrush and Portstewart area, for there are no less than 5 courses within a mile (1. 6km) or so of one another.

Western Ireland

Ballyconneely Golf Club: another for a calm day, in the western reaches of Connemara.

Glenarm, Larne and Whitehead in Co. Antrim; and Bangor and Donaghadee in Co. Down.

Rod licences are issued by the Fisheries Conservancy Board (FCB) or the Foyle Fisheries Commission (FFC). Permission to fish from the owner of the water – often the Department of Agriculture, the ultimate authority for fisheries in the North – takes the form of a permit. Angling clubs that own waters not held by the Department issue daily tickets. All permits and licences for fishing in Northern Ireland, and a lot more details, are available from the Northern Regional Fisheries Board in Donegal. The Lakeland Visitors' Centre at Enniskillen is also helpful. Tackle shops throughout the province issue permits and tickets for, or have details on, angling clubs (*see* box left for contacts).

Golf

We are most grateful to Bruce Critchley for this expert guide to Ireland's golf courses. Bruce is now a TV golf commentator, following a successful amateur international career in the 1960s. A consultant to golf-course developers, he also, in association with his wife's company, Critchley Pursuits, arranges tours of British, Irish and Continental courses for both British and American enthusiasts.

With the possible exception of Scotland, Ireland can boast more courses per head of population than any other country in the world. As with Scotland, quality is in no way diminished by quantity and, in common with the rest of the British Isles, the greatest courses are situated at the seaside.

As host to the British Open Championship, names such as St Andrews, Muirfield and Royal Birkdale are famous around the world. The likes of Portmarnock, Mount Juliet and Royal Portrush suffer nothing by comparison. But they are just the tip of Ireland's golfing iceberg, and no discerning golfer's experience is complete without a taste or two of what's littered around the shores.

Bundoran Golf Club: a delightful clifftop course.
Donegal Golf Course, Murvagh: a splendid challenge, 7,000 yds (6,400m) off the back.
Galway Club: a more gentle test.
Lahinch: traditionally the home of the South of Ireland Championships.
Rosses Point: the prince of courses in this area, in the shadow of Benbulben. It has hosted most of the country's major events.
Strandhill and **Inniscrone**: seaside courses.
Westport Golf Course: a test for the itinerant golfer, on the shores of Clew Bay.

Southwestern Ireland

Ballybunion: a real treasure. A second 18 of equally high quality has recently been added.
Bantry: no trip to this neck of the woods should miss this little 9-hole gem, overlooking the famous bay.
Dooks at Glenbeigh and the mighty links of **Waterville**: 2 widely differing courses on the Ring of Kerry. Glenbeigh, which is only 5,750 yards (5,260m) in length, is supposedly the 3rd-oldest course in the country and follows the undulating dunes. Waterville is much more recent and, as the ocean is on 3 sides of it, the wind is an ever-present factor.

Killarney: can there be any more beautiful setting for golf anywhere in the world? Perhaps the 2 courses don't quite match up to the view, but then very few would.
Shannon Golf Club: near the airport. A modern course, inland in character, with lovely views down to the River Shannon.
Tralee: an outstanding Arnold Palmer course on Kerry's coastline.

Southern Ireland

Away from the pounding of the Atlantic Ocean, the courses in the south don't have the sand dunes out of which links courses are traditionally carved. Nonetheless, the natural beauty of the countryside lends a great backdrop wherever courses are constructed.
Bandon Golf Course: southwest of Cork city, set in the grounds of Castlebernard Castle.
Clonmel: has spectacular views over the plains of Tipperary.
Doneraile: is a little 9-holer that should not be passed up.
Little Island, Cork. The most spectacular here, with holes alternating between the edge of the huge quarry and views over the estuary.
Midleton: to the east, well worth a visit.
Thurles: a parkland setting complete with fine old oaks and elms.

Wherever you go in Ireland, golf courses abound, and whatever your standard you'll find something to enjoy. With facilities getting ever more crowded around the major cities of the world, Ireland offers golf as it used to be – the ability to get on a course in the hours of daylight, and green fees that are not going to break the bank. Bord Fáilte publishes golfing guides, or see *www.globalgolf.com/ireland*.

If you are thinking of a golfing holiday, some of the courses do get busy in summer and it is always advisable to check with clubs in advance and, where necessary, get a confirmed tee time. Also, every travelling golfer should carry a handicap certificate as proof of competence. Trolleys will be for hire at most clubs and quite a few will be able to lay on caddies if ordered in advance.

Hang-gliding

Ireland is a hang-glider's paradise: shaped like a saucer with a mountainous rim. The wind blows from the sea or from the flat central plains. Most of the hills are bare of power-lines and trees, and the famous turf provides soft landings. Flying in the Republic is controlled by the Irish Hang-Gliding Association, *www.ihpa.ie*. In Northern Ireland, contact the Ulster Hang Gliding & Paragliding Club, *www.uhpc.f9.co.uk*, or the Sports Council for Northern Ireland, *www.sportni.org*.

Horse-racing

Irish people are wild about horses; they breed very good ones, and they race them brilliantly. You can go and watch them being exercised on the Curragh in Co. Kildare, a nursery of some of the finest racehorses in the world. Classic flat races that take place on the Curragh are the Airlie/Coolmore Irish 2000 Guineas, and Goffs Irish 1000 Guineas in May, the Budweiser Irish Derby in June, far and away the premier International flat race of the year; the Kildangan Stud Irish Oaks in July, and in Sept the Jefferson Smurfit Memorial Irish St Leger. Close to the Curragh is the Irish National Stud, with its magnificent and authentic Japanese Garden.

The flat racing season runs Mar–Nov, with occasional Sun meetings; other important flat racing is held at the modern Leopardstown course on the south side of Dublin. The main National Hunt (steeplechasing and jumping courses) are at Leopardstown, Punchestown, Navan, Gowran, Galway and Fairyhouse, where you can watch the exciting Irish Grand National on Easter Monday. The most fashionable event is the 3-day meeting at Punchestown near Naas, Co. Kildare, in the last week of Apr. The Dublin Horse Show, a major sporting and social event, includes showjumping competitions for the Aga Khan Trophy, the Nations Cup and the Grand Prix.

The weekly *Irish Field* and daily *Racing Post* and *Sporting Life* publish form, venues and times of all race meetings and point-to-points. Tourism Ireland's *Calendar of Events* also shows some racing fixtures. See also *www.hri.ie*.

Hurling
To read about this sport, *see* **Topics**, p.79.

Polo
The All-Ireland Polo Club in Phoenix Park, Dublin, is one of the oldest clubs in the world. Matches take place Wed evenings, Sat and Sun afternoons, from May to the middle of Sept, plus sponsored 4-day tournaments from June to Aug.

Riding Holidays
There are many new residential schools and companies offering ponytrekking holidays. The Irish are putting their natural love of horses to good use, and the areas of beauty where you can ride include empty beaches that stretch for miles, heathery valleys, forests, empty country roads and loughside tracks. Accommodation and food are arranged for you. Tourism Ireland can provide full details.

Sailing
The Irish coastline is uniquely beautiful, with diverse conditions and landscapes. The waters are never crowded, and the shoreline is completely unspoilt. On one of those sublimely beautiful evenings when the light touches each hill and field with an exquisite clarity, you will think yourself amongst the most privileged in the world. And if you want a bit of *craic*, there are many splendid bars and restaurants to be visited in the sheltered harbours. But the peace and calm of the sky, the land and the sea in the many inlets is deceptive, for the open seas in the north-west can be rough and treacherous, exposed as they are to the North Atlantic. A journey around the whole coastline should only be attempted by experienced sailors.

Ireland has a long sailing tradition, with more than 125 yacht and sailing clubs around the country. The Royal Cork Yacht Club at Crosshaven is the oldest in the world, founded in 1720 as the Water Club of the Harbour of Cork. Many of these clubs have preserved their original clubhouses, and exude a feeling of tradition and comfort. Visitors are made extremely welcome, and are encouraged to use the club facilities.

If you don't have your own yacht, it's possible to charter a variety of craft. If it is your ambition to learn to sail, there are several small, friendly schools. In Ulster, information on yachting facilities, sailing schools and charter companies can be had from the **Sports Council for Northern Ireland** in Belfast (*see* p.107). In the Republic, contact the **Irish Sailing Association**, 3 Park Rd, Dun Laoghaire, Co. Dublin, **t** (01) 280 0239, *www.sailing.ie*.

Where to Sail
The South-west: Ireland's south-west coast, bordering the counties of Cork and Kerry, is a favourite with Irish sailors, and it has a good selection of charter companies, sailing schools and windsurfing facilities. The harbours are charming, and the peninsulas and islands around which you can sail are magnificent.

The West: Further west, in County Galway and Co. Mayo, there is exciting sailing around the Aran Islands, Clifden, Renville and Clew Bay and the many deserted islands with haunting, beautiful names.

The North: Here is the glorious coastline of Sligo and Donegal. You need to be an experienced sailor to sail in these waters, for charts are outdated and inaccurate, currents and shallows are sometimes treacherous, and there are few facilities for sailors.

The East: More wonderful sailing can be had on Strangford and Carlingford Loughs in Co. Down, and around the Antrim Coast. Just north of Dublin there are several excellent sailing centres that retain the charm of fishing villages. Inland is the huge freshwater expanse of Lough Derg in the River Shannon system, where you can anchor in a sheltered bay or in one of the charming canal harbours.

Practicalities

There is no tax or duty if you bring in your **own yacht** for a holiday; a special sticker is issued by customs officials on arrival. Mariners should apply to the harbourmaster of all ports in which they wish to anchor. On arrival at the first port of entry, the flag 'Q' should be shown. Contact should then be made with the local customs official or with a *garda* (policeman or -woman), who will be pleased to assist. Fees are very reasonable in marinas and harbours. Note that it is illegal to land any animals without a special licence from the Department of Agriculture, but this does not apply to pets from Britain.

The main centres for **charter** are the south-west coastline, Clifden and Lough Derg. Private charter can be arranged at leading sailing centres elsewhere. Bare-boat and crewed charters are available on boats ranging from 4- to 7-berth. The average cost of chartering a 4-berth yacht ranges from €130 per person per week in the low season to €165 per person per week in the high season. For a complete list of yacht charter companies, contact Tourism Ireland.

Most of the **sailing schools** are residential and located in areas of scenic beauty. Many offer other outdoor sports such as boardsailing (wind-surfing), canoeing and sub-aqua. A full list of schools is available from Bord Fáilte in Dublin and from the **Irish Association for Sail Training**, Confederation House, 84–86 Lower Baggot St, Dublin 2, **t** (01) 660 1011.

Useful Media

The **Irish Cruising Club** (*www.irishcruisingclub. com*) publishes *Sailing Directions*, which covers the entire coast of Ireland, and includes details of the coast, sketch plans of harbours, tidal

information and details of port facilities. The *Directions* come in 2 volumes – one for the south and west, and one for the north and east. It's available from most Irish booksellers. Also recommended is *Sailing Around Ireland* by Wallace Clark (Batsford), and *Islands of Ireland* by D. McCormick (Osprey, 1977). The BBC issues gale warnings and shipping forecasts on Radio 4 and the World Service.

Sub-aqua

Ireland's oceans are surprisingly warm and clear, because they are right in the path of the Gulf Stream. So it would be very difficult to find a better place for underwater swimming or diving. *Subsea* is the official journal of the **Irish Underwater Council, t** (01) 284 4601, *www. scubaireland.com*, which publishes information about the affiliated clubs, articles on diving, etc. Centres for experienced divers and equipment hire are in counties Mayo, Donegal, Galway, Kerry, Clare, Wexford, Down. Ask for information in any tourist office. By the way, you should know that it is illegal to remove shellfish from the sea.

Surfing

Due to the geographical position of Ireland, great swells endlessly pound the west coast, producing waves comparable to those in California. The entire coastline of Ireland is thus ideal for surfing when the beach, tide and wind conditions are right. Many of the beaches in counties Donegal, Sligo, Kerry, Waterford and Clare are considered first-rate

Walking and Mountaineering Centres

The House of Sport, Upper Malone Rd, Belfast, **t** (028) 9038 1222. Details on climbing in the Mournes. It also handles grants and serves as an advice centre.

Irish Ways, Ballycanew, Gorey, Co. Wexford, **t** (055) 27479, *www.irishways.com*

National Mountain and White Water Centre, Tiglin, Ashford, Co. Wicklow, **t** (0404) 40169, *www.tiglin.com*. Details of training courses in mountaineering.

Tullymore Mountain Centre, Bryansford, near Newcastle, Co. Down, **t** (028) 4372 2158. Climbing in the Mourne Mountains.

Youth Hostel Association, *An Óige*, 6 Mountjoy St, Dublin 1, *www.irelandyha.org*

for breakers. Hire centres are not numerous, although you can occasionally hire equipment from hotels and adventure sports centres, but it's best to bring your own board and wetsuit. Contact the **Irish Surfing Association, t** (096) 49428, *www.isasurf.ie*, for details of beaches and surfing centres.

Swimming and Beaches

There are lovely beaches (which are also called strands) wherever the sea meets the land – north, south, east or west. If you wish to go sea-bathing (it can be surprisingly warm because of the Gulf Stream), you need to bear in mind that swimming is not a regulated sport, and that there are lifeguards only on the most popular beaches, if at all. Be aware of the possibility of a strong undertow or current, and always ask locally about the safest ones for swimming.

Walking and Mountaineering

Irish mountains and hill areas are not high (few peaks reach more than 3,000ft/915m), but they are rugged, varied, beautiful and unspoilt. There are quartz peaks, sandstone ridges, bog-covered domes and cliff-edged limestone plateaux. Excellent walking trails have been or are being developed. General advice, information and a list of hill-walking

and rock-climbing clubs can be obtained from the Mountaineering Council of Ireland at the House of Sport (*see* box opposite), who can send a list of guides. Tourism Ireland offices also stock hill-walking info sheets for individual areas. The website *www.irishwaymarkedways.ie* is a mine of info on walking in the Republic.

The Ordnance Survey ½-inch-to-a-mile maps and a compass are essentials for serious walkers. Maps and guidebooks can be bought at some bookshops or sports shops in popular walking areas, or from the National Map Centre, 34 Aungier St, Dublin 2, **t** (01) 476 0471.

Remember that there are very few tracks on Irish mountains; always let your hotel know where you are climbing or walking, or leave a note in your car. Mountain rescue in the Republic is co-ordinated by the Gardaí (Police) and in the North by the Police Service of Northern Ireland (PSNI). There are mountain rescue teams in the main mountain areas.

Summer Schools

The phrase 'Ireland, land of saints and scholars' is a delightfully apt one when it comes to the tradition of learning. You can study and learn some fascinating subjects in a beautiful environment in this country, and yet still feel as if you are on holiday.

Summer Schools

Art/Painting
Achill Island School of Painting, Co Mayo; **t** (058) 56182. Early July–Aug.
Burren Landscape Painting, Co. Clare, **t** (065) 707 4208

Irish Studies
Douglas Hyde Summer School, Ballaghaderreen, Co. Roscommon, **t** (094) 986 0170, *www.ballaghaderreen. com/culture.htm*. July.
Humbert Summer School, Ballina, Co. Mayo, **t** (096) 22034, *cooneyjohn@eircom.net*. Aug.
Parnell Summer School, Avondale, Rathdrum, Co. Wicklow; **t** (01) 285 2113, *www.parnellsociety.com*
University College Dublin, International Summer School for Irish Studies; **t** (01) 475 2004, *www. ucd. ie/summerschool*. July.

Literature
Bard Summer School, Clare Island, Clew Bay, Co. Mayo, **t** (01) 490 4879, *www.bard.ie*. July.
Brian Merriman Summer School, Lisdoonvarna, Co. Clare; **t** (086) 382 0671, *www.merriman.ie*. Late Aug.
Goldsmith Summer School, Abbeyshrule and Ballymahon, Co Longford, **t** (0902) 32374, *linesend@iol.ie*. June.
James Joyce Summer School, UCD International Summer School Office, Newman House, 86 St Stephen's Green, D2; or contact Dept of English, University College Dublin, D4, **t** (01) 7168 8159, *www.artsworld.ie/joyce-school*. July.
John Hewitt International Summer School, The Market Place Theatre, Armagh, **t** (028) 3752 1821, *www.johnhewitt.org*. A school named after an Ulster poet, with lectures, music, poetry and plays, July and Aug.

Synge Summer School, Whaley Lodge, Rathdrum, Co. Wicklow; t (0404) 46597, *www.wicklow.ie/syngesummerschool*. July.
Shakespeare Summer School, Ely House, Ely Place, Dublin 2; t (01) 832 1897. Late Aug.
William Carleton Summer School, Clogher, t (028) 8776 7259. Aug.
Yeats International Summer School, Yeats Memorial Building, Douglas Hyde Bridge, Sligo; t (071) 914 2693, *www.yeats-sligo.com*. A programme of lectures, seminars, readings and tours.

Music

Joe Mooney Summer School, Drumshanbo, Co. Leitrim, t (078) 41213/41426. Traditional music, song and dance, late July.
O'Carolan Traditional Irish Music Summer School, Keadue, Co. Roscommon; t (071) 964 7204; *www.harp.net/keadue/*. Late July–early Aug.

Scoil Éigse; Comhaltas Ceoltóirí Éireann, 32 Belgrave Sq, Monkstown, Co. Dublin t (01) 280 0295, *www.comhaltas.com*. Traditional music and dancing; late Aug.
South Sligo Summer School, Tubbercurry; t (071) 912 0912. Music and dance; mid-July.
Willy Clancy Summer School, Miltown Malbay, Co. Clare, t (065) 708 4281. Mid-July.

Other Courses

Achill Archaeological Summer Field School, Dooagh, Achill Island, Co. Mayo, t (098) 43564, *www.achill-fieldschool.com*.
Oideas Gael **Irish Language and Summer School**, Glencolmcille, Co. Donegal; t (073) 30248, *www.oideas-gael.com*. Culture, flute and bodhrán-playing, dancing, Irish language, pottery, hill-walking and archaeology, summer.
Taipéis Gael, Malinbeg, Glencolumbcille, Co. Donegal, t (073) 30325, *taipeisgael@ eircom.net*. Tapestry and weaving, summer.

The Irish Tourist Board (*www.ireland.ie*) will send you an up-to-date list of programmes if you contact them and request the *Live and Learn* brochure.

The courses that are on offer range from the seriously intellectual to activity holidays. You can study for a period of 1 month, 2 weeks or a few days, and the variety is tremendous. Some of them are run by Ireland's universities, and offer courses on literature, history, Gaelic, and archaeology. Various private companies run arts and crafts courses, painting, English-language courses and classes in traditional music and dancing.

One of the most enjoyable summer schools is the Yeats International Summer School in Sligo, which is well run and set in wonderful countryside. Enjoyable lectures and tours are also offered by the Irish Georgian Society. Contact the Society at 74 Merrion Square, Dublin 2, t (01) 676 7053, *www.igs.ie*.

For other courses, *see* below.

Telephones and Internet

The **country code** for the Republic is t 00 353; for Northern Ireland t 00 44, if calling from outside the UK. However, if you call Northern

Ireland from the Republic of Ireland, all 8-digit numbers can be prefixed with just t 048.

It is more expensive to telephone during working hours than outside them. Note that if you telephone from your hotel you are liable to be charged much more than the standard rate. Phonecards, sold by most newsagents, are a much cheaper, more convenient option.

Ireland has the same **time zone** as Great Britain, and follows the same pattern of seasonal adjustment in the summer (i.e. Greenwich Mean Time plus 1hr, from the end of Mar to the end of Oct).

The **Internet** has a wealth of information to help you prepare all the practical details for your holiday, such as accommodation, especially in the busy summer months, when festivals make rooms hard to come by in even the smallest of towns. It can also enhance your knowledge of Ireland's history, politics and culture before you leave home.

Internet cafés are blossoming in Ireland; airports and libraries also usually provide public access points and local tourist offices can direct you to the nearest.

Irish Tourist Offices Abroad

UK
London: Tourism Ireland, Nations House,
103 Wigmore St, W1U 1QS, UK only
t 0800 039 7000, or t (020) 7518 0800,
www.tourismireland.com
Glasgow: 98 West George St, 7th Floor,
G2 1PJ, t (0141) 572 4030

USA
New York:345 Park Ave, NY 10154,
t (212) 418 0800, *www.shamrock.org*,
www.tourismireland.com

Canada
Toronto (written and telephone enquiries),
160 Bloor St West, Suite 1501, Ontario, M4W
3E2, t (416) 925 6368, *www.tourismireland.com*

Toilets

Public loos – *leithreas* – are often labelled in
Irish: *Fir* (men) and *Mná* (women). They're
usually pretty grim. Nobody minds if you slip
into a lounge bar to use the loo, though it's a
good excuse to stop for a drink as well.

Tourist Boards

Tourism Ireland (*www.tourismireland.com*)
runs tourism services for both the Republic
and Northern Ireland. Staff at its offices are
incredibly helpful and will organize whatever
is practical. They can supply you with a wealth
of beautifully produced maps and leaflets,
most free, as well as reasonably priced fuller
booklets on, for example, accommodation.
They can also find a hotel or B&B in your price
range and book it for you.

The most useful office if you are in Dublin is
the Dublin Tourism Centre on Suffolk St, just
off Grafton St, t (01) 605 7799, *www.visitdublin.
com*. You can contact Tourism Ireland in the
North through the NITB, on t (028) 9023 1221,
www.discovernorthernireland.com.

There are some 80 tourist information
offices scattered around the Republic; see
www.ireland.ie. Some of these open only
during the summer season, though most are
open all year (some may close for a few days

each week in winter). Addresses are given in
the grey boxes at the beginning of each
county, and when counties are divided, at the
beginning of that area.

Where to Stay

Whether you are a traveller with plenty
of loot to spend, or one who is intent on
lodging as cheaply as possible, Ireland offers
lots of choice. Places to stay range from
romantic castles, graceful country mansions,
cosy farmhouses, smart city hotels and hostels
that, although spartan, are clean and well run.
Many of these hostels have double or family
rooms, are independently owned and require
no membership cards.

At the beginning of each county chapter
(and where counties are divided, at the
beginning of each area), there is a list of
recommended accommodation, split into
price categories (explained below). With this
list as a guide, it is possible to avoid the many
modern and ugly hotels where bland comfort
is doled out for huge prices, and to avoid the
shabby motels and musty bed-and-breakfast
establishments. Some counties are favoured
with many desirable hotels and B&Bs, whilst
a few are meagerly served. If that is the case
where you are, your best bet for a pleasant stay
is to stick to the farmhouse accommodation,
which is usually adequate.

One thing you can be sure of is that the Irish
are among the friendliest people in Europe,
and when they open their doors to visitors

Weights and Measures

1 kilogram = 2 lb
1 litre = 1.76 Imperial pints = 2.11 US pints
1 centimetre = 0.39 inches
1 metre = 39.37 inches = 3.28 feet
1 kilometre = 0.621 miles
1 hectare = 2.47 acres
1 lb = 0.45 kilograms
1 Imperial pint = 0.56 litres
1 US pint = 0.47 litres
1 Imperial gallon = 4.54 litres
1 US gallon = 3.78 litres
1 foot = 0.305 metres
1 mile = 1.609 kilometres
1 acre = 0.404 hectares

Accommodation Price Ranges

*Prices listed here and elsewhere in the book
are for bed and breakfast per person per night.*
  luxury more than €110/UK£75
  expensive €74–110/UK£51–75
  moderate €37–73/UK£25–50
  inexpensive less than €37/UK£25

they give a great welcome. The many
unexpected kindnesses and the personal
service that you will experience will contribute
immeasurably to your visit. The countryside is
beautiful, and there are many sights to see,
but what adds enjoyment and richness,
above all, to a tour of Ireland is the pleasant
conversation and humour of the people.

Prices

Tourism Ireland registers and grades
hotels and guesthouses, and divides the many
B&B businesses into Farm, Town and Country
Houses. All of this is very useful, but apart from
indicating the variety of services available and
the cost, you really do not get much idea of
the atmosphere and style of the place. The
establishments that are listed in this book are
described and categorized according to price,
and include a variety of lodgings ranging from
a luxurious castle to a simple farmhouse – all
have something special to offer a visitor. This
may be the architecture, the garden, the food,
the atmosphere and the chat, the distance you
are from a special tourist site, or simply the
beauty of the surrounding countryside. The
most expensive offer high standards of luxury,
and the cheapest are clean and comfortable.
Most are family-owned, with a few bedrooms,
and none fits into a uniform classification, but
they are all welcoming and unique places to
stay. The price categories (*see* above) are of
necessity quite loosely based, and some of the
more expensive establishments do weekend
deals that are very good value. Please, always
check prices and terms when making a
booking. Rates in the Republic are quoted in
euros. Sterling (UK£) is the currency used in
Northern Ireland.

Luxury

Expect top-quality rooms with style and
opulence. Furnishings will include priceless
antiques, while the facilities and service

provide every modern convenience you could
wish for. Many of the 4-star hotels in Dublin
fall into this category, but there are also some
delightful castles and mansions, set in
exquisite grounds, all over Ireland.

Expensive

All bedrooms have their own bathroom,
direct-dial telephone, central heating, TV
and the other mod cons, but many have
something else as well – charm, eccentricity,
and a feeling of mellow comfort. There are
places where you might sleep in a graceful
4-poster hung with rich cloth, and wake
up to the sort of hospitality where the smell
of coffee is just a prelude to a delicious cooked
breakfast, and the sharp, sweet taste of
home-made jam on Irish wheaten bread.

Moderate

Most of these places have private bathrooms
and extremely good cooking and service. Again,
some have a wonderful atmosphere combined
with attractive décor, which is sometimes all
the more atmospheric for its touch of age.

Inexpensive

Whitewashed farmhouses, Georgian
manses, rectories, old manor houses, modern
bungalows and fine townhouses come under
this heading, along with the increasing
numbers of holiday hostels. They are all very
good value, good *craic*, and you will often get
marvellous, simple cooking. Not all bedrooms
will have central heating or ensuite facilities,
but there will be perfectly good bathrooms
close by and washbasins in the room.

Websites for Accommodation

The Blue Book: *www.irelands-blue-book.ie*
Friendly Homes of Ireland:
  www.tourismresources.ie
The Hidden Ireland: *www.hidden-ireland.com*
Independent Holiday Hostels:
  www.hostels-ireland.com
Irish Hotels Federation: *www.beourguest.ie*
Irish Tourist Board:
  www.ireland.ie/accommodation
Town and Country Homes:
  www.townandcountry.ie

Reservations

Reserve directly with the establishment in question, or via Tourism Ireland offices in Ireland, Northern Ireland and Great Britain, who operate an enquiry and booking service. (Offices in other countries operate an enquiry service only.) Offices throughout Ireland will reserve a room for you for the price of a phone call, but will only book you into registered and approved lodgings. A 10% deposit is payable, plus a charge of €4 for the service.

Make sure that you book early for the peak months of June, July and Aug. At other times of the year it is usually quite all right to book on the morning of the day you wish to stay (except in Dublin, which can be crowded in any season). Also, good places soon get known by word of mouth, so they are always more likely to be booked up in advance.

Literature

Tourism Ireland offices keep plenty of booklets on various types of accommodation. There is an illustrated hotels and guesthouses guide called *Be Our Guest*; a *Farmhouse Bed and Breakfast Guide*; an *Illustrated Town and Country Homes* guide for B&Bs and a *Caravan and Camping Guide*. Other useful publications are the *Ireland Self-catering Guide*, *The Hidden Ireland Self-catering Guide* and *The Hidden Ireland Guide*, with accommodation in listed heritage houses, and *Friendly Homes of Ireland*. All these are available from any tourist office. The Northern Ireland Tourist Board stocks similar publications, including a comprehensive list of accommodation, *Where to Stay*.

Hotels

Tourist boards register and grade hotels in five categories: **A* grade** stands for the most luxurious bedrooms and public rooms with night service, very good food and plenty of choice. Most bedrooms have their own bath, and suites are available. These are the sort of places where delicious snacks are automatically served with cocktails. This grading includes baronial mansions in exquisite grounds or the plush anonymity of some Dublin hotels.

A grade stands for luxury hotels that don't have quite so many items on the *table d'hôte*, nor do they have night service; but the food is just as good and the atmosphere is probably less restrained.

B* grade stands for well furnished and comfortable; some rooms have a bath, cooking is good and plain. **B grade** and **C grade** are clean, comfortable but limited, with **B grade** offering more in the line of bathrooms and food.

All Tourism Ireland graded hotels have heating and hot and cold water in the bedrooms. If you come across a hotel that is ungraded, it is because its grading is under review or because it has just opened, or does not comply with Tourism Ireland's requirements.

The prices of hotels vary enormously, no matter what grade they are, and the grading takes no account of atmosphere and charm. Many of the most delightful and hospitable country houses come under B or C grades, while some of the A grade hotels are very dull. All graded hotels are listed in the Tourism Ireland booklets. Northern Irish hotels are listed in their *Where to Stay* guide.

Guesthouses

These are usually houses that have become too large and expensive to maintain as private houses. The minimum number of bedrooms is 5. The top grade houses are just as good as their hotel equivalent, as are those graded lower down the scale, though the atmosphere is different. Some of the best places to stay are guesthouses, particularly in Dublin.

If you decide to vary your accommodation from guesthouse to townhouse, country house or farmhouse, you will discover one of the principles of Irish life: that everything in Ireland works on a personal basis. If you are on holiday to avoid people, a guesthouse is the last place you should book into – it is impossible not to be drawn into a friendly conversation in a guesthouse, whether about fishing or politics. You will get a large, thoroughly uncontinental breakfast, and delicious evening meals with a choice within a set meal. Dinner is usually very punctual, at 8pm, after everyone has sat around by the fire over very large drinks. Lunch or a packed lunch can be arranged.

All grades of guesthouse have hot and cold water, and heating in the bedrooms. **A grade** guesthouse rooms have private bathrooms, but their reputation is based on scrumptious food and comfortable surroundings. You can get full details of many of the finest guesthouses in Tourism Ireland's booklets *Be Our Guest* and *Where to Stay in Northern Ireland*. As a general guide, a comfortable, even luxurious, night's sleep will cost between €22 (UK£15) and €73 (UK£50). A meal, where available, ranges from €10 to €26 (UK£7–18) on average. Sometimes the owners provide high tea; sometimes the only meal they do is breakfast.

Farmhouses, Townhouses and Country Houses

Often these family homes make your stay in Ireland, for you meet Irish people who are kind, generous and intelligent. This is also the most economical way to stay in Ireland if you don't want to stay in a tent or in a youth hostel. If you are not going to a place that is recommended, it is largely a matter of luck whether you hit an attractive or a mediocre set-up, but always watch out for the shamrock sign, Tourism Ireland's sign of approval.

Wherever you go, you should have a comfortable bed (if you are tall, make sure it is long enough; sometimes Irish beds can be on the small side), and an enormous breakfast: orange juice, cereal, eggs, bacon, sausages, toast, marmalade and a pot of tea or coffee.

Bed and breakfast per person ranges from around €26 to €44 (UK£18–30) throughout the Republic and the North if you are sharing a bedroom. You can get much cheaper weekly rates, with partial or full board. Very often you can eat your evening meal in the dining room of the B&B. Again, there will be masses to eat and it will be piping hot – so much better than many restaurants and cafés. There is often great flexibility about breakfast and other meals: they happen when it suits you, but you should give notice before 12 noon if you want dinner.

Some houses serve **dinner** for around €10–26 (UK£7–18), and some offer a cheaper 'high tea' (€7–10, UK£5–7), a sensible meal that evolved for the working man who begins to feel hungry at about 6pm. You get a plate of something hot, perhaps chicken and chips, followed by fresh soda bread, jam and cakes and a pot of tea. Some houses provide tea and biscuits as a snack for late-night nibblers at around 10pm.

More and more establishments have ensuite bathrooms, for which you usually pay about €2.50 (UK£1.70) extra. If there is just a communal bathroom, you may be charged a little for hot water, though this is now rare.

For those hitch-hiking or using public transport, townhouses are the easiest places to get to and find, but the real favourites are farmhouses and country houses. The farms concentrate on dairy, sheep, crop farming or beef cattle, or often a mixture of everything. Tucked away in lovely countryside, they may be traditional or modern. The farmer's wife, helped by her children, usually makes life very comfortable and is often ready to have a chat and advise you on local beauty spots and good places to hear traditional music, or to go for a *ceili*. Some of the town- and country houses are on fairly main roads, but they are generally not too noisy as there is so little traffic. The type of house you might stay in ranges from Georgian to Alpine-style bungalows, from a semi-detached to a 1950s dolls' house. There are a bewildering number of architectural styles in the new houses beginning to radiate out from small villages.

Renting a House or Cottage

This is very easy. Every regional office of Tourism Ireland has a list of houses and apartments to let, as well as the national *Self-Catering Guide*, with photographs and descriptions of a wide choice of houses and flats. There is also a short list of self-catering houses at the back of the booklet *Guest Accommodation*. Places to rent range from converted stable blocks to modern bungalows.

In the North, ask the NITB for their self-catering bulletin or look in the back of the accommodation booklet and in newspapers. The Republic has a very popular 'Rent-an-Irish-Cottage' scheme (*www.rentacottage.ie*) with

Big House Rentals

Country House Tours, 71 Waterloo Rd, Dublin 4, **t** (01) 660 7975, from the US **t** 1 800 894 5712, *www.tourismresources.ie/cht*. Tours of public and private houses and castles.

Elegant Ireland, 15 Harcourt St, Dublin 2, **t** (01) 475 1665/475 1632, *www.elegant.ie*

The Hidden Ireland, PO Box 31, Westport, Co. Mayo, **t** (01) 662 7166, *www.hidden-ireland.com*

National Trust, **t** 0870 458 4400, *www.nationaltrust.org.uk*

centres in counties Limerick, Galway, Mayo, Tipperary and Clare. The cottages are thatched, whitewashed and traditional; inside they are well designed, with an electric cooker, fridge and kettle – all the mod-cons you need. There are built-in cupboards and comfy beds and linen. Simple, comfortable, Irish-made furniture and fittings make it a happy blend of tradition and modern convenience. Cottages vary in size: some take 8 people, others 5.

Easter and May, June, July and Aug are the most expensive times, with weekly prices hovering around €345–556 (UK£235–312), but in Oct, sometimes the nicest month in Ireland weather-wise, a cottage can be very reasonable at around €230–330 (UK£155–290) per week. Local people take a great interest in you and do their best to make you content because they are shareholders in the scheme.

Renting Big Houses

There is a growing demand to stay in or rent an Irish castle, and some are surprisingly reasonable in price. There are some exclusive and attractive country houses where you can stay as the guest of friendly, interesting hosts, and where you can be sure of good food.

The National Trust has several gloriously restored properties in Northern Ireland. Castle Coole in Co. Fermanagh and Springhill in Co. Londonderry are favourites. You can also to rent holiday properties on some NT estates.

Youth Hostels

The Irish YHA is called *An Óige* and has 44 hostels. These are distributed all over the Republic; there are a few in the Six Counties, often in wild and remote places, which are doubly attractive to the enterprising traveller. Members of the International Youth Hostel Federation can use all of these hostels in Ireland. You can join for €20 (UK£13); there is no age limit, and your card can be used worldwide. Buy an International Guest Card, by purchasing 6 welcome stamps costing €2 (UK£1.40) each. The stamps may be bought one at a time at 6 different hostels.

Youth hostels are sometimes superb houses; sites range from cottages to castles. They are great centres for climbers, walkers and fishers, and are not too spartan; many also have a comfortable laxity when it comes to the rules. You must provide your own sheet and sleeping bag. A flap or pocket to cover the pillows can be bought at the *An Óige* office, and the hostel provides blankets or sheet bags. All hostels have fully equipped kitchens, and most also provide breakfast, packed lunches and an evening meal on request.

Charges vary according to age, month and location; in July and Aug it is slightly more expensive, and it is vital to book. This applies also to weekends. All *An Óige* and HINI (Hostelling International Northern Ireland) hostels may be booked from one hostel to another, or centrally by contacting the head office listed below. Most hostels open all year.

There are several rail/cycling holidays on offer to hostel members. The average cost of staying overnight is around €13 (UK£9). All information, an essential handbook and an excellent map can be obtained from the *An Óige* head office at 61 Mountjoy St, Dublin 7, t (01) 830 4555, *www.anoige.ie/ www.irelandyha.org*. For Northern Ireland, contact HINI, 22 Donegall Rd, Belfast, BT12 5JN, t (028) 9032 4733, *www.hini.org.uk*.

Besides the youth hostels, a large number of independent hostels have appeared in recent years. These are friendly, open to everyone (children are welcome in most), and most have double and family rooms; some even have single rooms. They are also less likely than the youth hostels to have bothersome rules, such as curfews and no access to rooms in the daytime. All will rent you sheets and provide duvets and blankets. The average price for a dormitory bed in high season is €13 (UK£9). These hostels are listed in Tourism Ireland's

Horsedrawn Caravans

You get a trustworthy and solid horse and a barrel-shaped caravan sleeping 4. You can travel at a relaxing pace, usually about 9 miles (15km) a day. The cost per week is from around €260 in the low season to €700 in July and Aug. Contact Tourism Ireland, or:

Dieter Clissmann Horsedrawn Caravans, Carrigmore Farm, Wicklow, Co. Wicklow, t (0404) 48188

Kilvahan Horsedrawn Caravans, Portlaoise, Co. Laois, t (0502) 27048, *www.horsedrawncaravans.com*

Slattery's Horsedrawn Caravans, 1 Russell St, Tralee, Co. Kerry, t (066) 712 2364

Accommodation Guide, or get a list from the Independent Holiday Hostels of Ireland (IHH), 57 Lower Gardiner St, Dublin 1, **t** (01) 836 4700, *www.hostels-ireland.com.*

Camping and Caravanning

Camping and caravan parks that meet the standards set by the tourist boards are listed in a booklet available from tourist offices, *Caravan and Camping in Ireland*. Sites are graded according to amenities, and many are in beautiful areas. Laundry rooms, excellent showers and loos, shops, restaurants, indoor games rooms and TV make camping easy and also more civilized, especially if you have kids.

You can also **hire** caravans and motorhomes; see the *Caravan and Camping* booklet or *www.camping-ireland.ie*. Overnight charges in camping parks are around €7–12 (UK£5–8), with a small charge per person at some parks and for electrical linkup. If you bring your own caravan or camping equipment and have Calor gas appliances, the only compatible ones on sale in Ireland are those supplied by Gaz. Some caravan parks accept dogs on a leash.

Farmers usually say yes to people asking if they can camp or park their caravan in a field, but you must ask permission first and tell them how long you want to stay. Be polite and do not get in the way, and they will give you drinking water, lots of chat, and perhaps even some garden vegetables.

Women Travellers

Irish men have an attitude towards women that is as infuriating as it is attractive. They are a grand old muddle of male chauvinism with a dash of admiration for and fear of their mothers, sisters and wives. Irish women, meanwhile, have a sharpness and wit that makes them more than a match for 'your man' in an argument, but at the same time they work their hearts and guts out.

If you are a lone female traveller, Irishmen will often help with your luggage and your flat tyre, and will stand you a meal or a drink without any questions. If a man tries to chat you up in a bar, or at a dance, this is usually just a bit of *craic* and is not to be taken too seriously – the game is abandoned at once if you get tired of it. You might encounter a prevailing attitude that you ought to be travelling with somebody else – but it's only the women who will say so, remarking, with a smile, that it must be a bit lonesome.

If you walk into an obviously male preserve, such as a serious drinking pub, don't expect to feel welcome unless everybody is drunk, and by that time you should scarper anyway. A bit of advice, which does not apply just to women, was pithily put by an Irish politician: 'The great difference between England and Ireland is that in England you can say what you like, so long as you do the right thing. In Ireland you can do what you like, so long as you say the right thing.'

Women travellers are advised against hitch-hiking, whether alone or in a group (*see* also p.97). If you do hitch-hike on your own, or with a female companion, you will get plenty of lifts and offers to take you out dancing that night. Exercise caution and use your common sense.

The Province of Munster

Munster

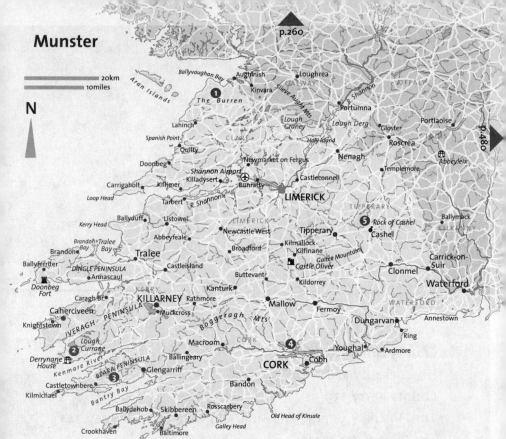

20km
10miles

N

Aran Islands
Ballyvaughan Bay
Aughinish
Loughrea
GALWAY
Kinvara
Slieve Aughty Mts
The Burren ❶
Portumna
R. Shannon
OFFALY
Lough Graney
Lough Derg
Gloster
Portlaoise
LAOIS
p.480
Lahinch
CLARE
Holy Island
Roscrea
Spanish Point
Quilty
Newmarket on Fergus
Nenagh
Templemore
Abbeyleix
Doonbeg
Shannon Airport
Castleconnell
Carrigaholt
Killadysert
Killimer
Bunratty
LIMERICK
TIPPERARY
Loop Head
Tarbert
R. Shannon
Ballymack
Kerry Head
Ballyduff
Listowel
LIMERICK
Rock of Cashel ❺
KILKENNY
Abbeyfeale
Newcastle West
Tipperary
Cashel
Brandon–Tralee Bay
Brandon
Tralee Bay
Tralee
Castleisland
Broadford
Kilmallock
Kilfinane
Galtee Mountains
Carrick-on-Suir
Ballyferriter
DINGLE PENINSULA
Annascaul
Buttevant
Castle Oliver
Clonmel
Waterford
Doonbeg Fort
Kanturk
Kildorrey
KERRY
Caragh Br.
KILLARNEY
Rathmore
Mallow
Fermoy
WATERFORD
Caherciveen
IVERAGH PENINSULA
Muckross
Boggeragh Mts
Dungarvan
Annestown
Knightstown
Lough Currane ❷
Macroom
CORK
Youghal
Ring
Ardmore
Derrynane House
Kenmare River
Ballingeary
Cobh
BEARA PENINSULA ❸
Glengarriff
CORK
Castletownbere
Bandon
Kilmichael
Bantry Bay
Ballydehob
Skibbereen
Rosscarbery
Old Head of Kinsale
Crookhaven
Baltimore
Galley Head

NORTHERN IRELAND
ULSTER
CONNACHT
REPUBLIC OF IRELAND
LEINSTER
MUNSTER

Highlights

1 The unique flora, limestone and ancient sites of The Burren, Co. Clare
2 Lovely walks at Derrynane House and Beach, Co. Kerry
3 The Beara Peninsula's stunning coast and brooding mountains, Co. Cork
4 Culture and shopping in Cork City
5 The imposing Rock of Cashel, ancient capital of Munster, in Co. Tipperary

Munster (*Cúige Mumhan*) is the largest province in Ireland, and it is a mixture of everything that one generally considers Irish. The purples of the mountains melt into chessboards of cornfields, in which the stooks stand like golden pieces. Houses are whitewashed, glens are deep and the coastline is made ragged by the force of the Atlantic, with sandy bays and rocky cliffs. It is a land of extremes: a large, placid, fertile plain, brooding mountain scenery, luxurious vegetation, and harsh barren land. The stately River Shannon flows along the border of Tipperary and on out to the sea between County Clare and County Limerick. The extreme south-westerly coast is swept by westerly gales, and trees have been distorted into bent and twisted shapes. The moonscape of the Burren contrasts with the softness of Killarney; the dairy-land of Cashel of the Kings, where the lordly and the holy worshipped on a rock above the plains, contrasts with the thrashing sea around Dingle and the Iveragh Peninsula.

The Burren is the youngest landscape in Europe, and its carboniferous limestone hills have been shaped by intense glaciation. Spring gentian, mountain avens, hairy primrose, milkwort and orchids are among the wonderful variety of plants that flourish here. Wild goats still range it and keep at bay the ever-invasive hazel scrub. A great collection of southern and northern plants grow throughout the province. The best time to visit for them is May.

This is the land of the Mumonians; the 'ster' suffix is a Scandinavian addition to the ancient name of Muma, as it is with Ulster and Leinster. The people are warm, relaxed and musical; however, they can also be backward-looking and quarrelsome. Dubliners say that Munster is a little England. The Anglo-Normans certainly had a part in moulding the towns, as did some of the adventurer types of the Elizabethan times, but Cork city has created many lively Irish minds, whether Celts or later arrivals.

Munster has always been cut off geographically from the rest of Ireland – by the mountains of Slieve Bloom, the bogs of Offaly and the River Shannon. This has helped to develop a great mythological tradition, with mother-goddesses figuring prominently in legend and placenames. There is Aire of Knockaney in County Limerick, and Aibell of Crag Liath. Anu is Mother of the Gods, whose breasts are represented in the Pap Mountains on the Kerry border. Most primitive of all is the ancient Hag of Beare, who spans many centuries and to whom many megalithic monuments are attributed. She is supposed to have written the marvellous 9th-century poem *The Hag of Beare*, which is a lament for lost beauty and the struggle between bodily pleasure and salvation through the Christian way of repentence:

> Yet may this cup of whey
> O! Lord, serve as my ale-feast –
> Fathoming its bitterness
> I'll learn that you know best.

Also strong in the mythological tradition is Donn Firinne, the ancestor-god to whom all the Irish will journey after death. His house is believed to be somewhere in this province. Munster has been commonly accepted as being divided into two parts – between the ancient O'Brien Kingdom of Thomond and the MacCarthy Kingdom of Desmond. This was certainly a political reality between the 12th and 17th centuries.

County Limerick

A limerick is a nonsense verse, and Limerick is also a lovely county in Ireland. The county existed long before the five-line stanza, but since Edward Lear popularized them in his nonsense book, limericks have become world-famous. The origin of these poems is intriguing and open to debate, but it is claimed that in the 18th century a group of poets known as the Poets of Maigue, who lived near Croom, wrote these witty verses in good-natured sparring and as drinking songs. James Clarence Mangan, who was himself a great poet, translated them into English in the 1840s, and they became popular in England.

One of the poets, a tavern-keeper named Sean O'Tuama, wrote:

I sell the best brandy and sherry
To make my good customer merry
But at times their finances
Run short as it chances
And then I feel very sad, very.

One of his customers, Andy MacCraith, replied:

O Tuomy! you boast yourself handy,
At selling good ale and bright brandy,
The fact is your liquor
Makes everyone sicker,
I tell you that – I, your friend, Andy.

County Limerick itself is a quiet farming community, dotted with the ruins of hundreds of castles and bounded on the north by the wide River Shannon, which flows into the sea. On its other sides lie a fringe of hills and mountains: the peaks of the Galtees in the south-east, the wild Mullaghareirk Mountains in the south-west

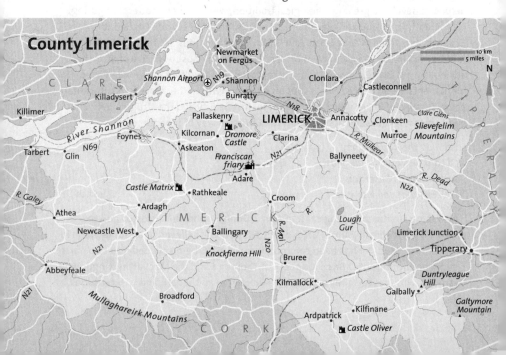

County Limerick

Arrival and Getting Around

By Air
Shannon Airport (*www.shannonairport.com*) lies about 15 miles (24km) north of Limerick City in Co. Clare, off the N19. A regular **airport bus** runs to and from Limerick City bus station (45mins; at least 1 per hr 7am–midnight, fewer on Sun; €7). There's also a 24hr **taxi desk** in the Arrivals hall (fares around €30).

By Train and Bus
Limerick City's train and bus stations sit together on Parnell St. **Bus** services (**t** (061) 313333) go to Cork, Ennis, Tipperary, Dublin and Waterford; **train** services run to Dublin, Cork and Clonmel/Waterford/Rosslare.

By Bike
Emerald Alpine, 1 Patrick St, Limerick, t (061) 416983. Bike hire.

By Car
Traffic is a big problem in Limerick City, and most of the centre is a disc parking zone.

Shannon Car Ferry
See **County Clare**, p.239, for information on the Tarbert–Killimer car ferry.

Festivals

Dates of festivals vary, and some towns have one-off festivals. Contact the tourist office, t (061) 317522, for details of all of the following.

January
UnFringed. An alternative theatre, dance, cabaret, comedy and arts festival.

February
Kate O'Brien Weekend. An annual festival for Limerick's famous author.

March
EV+A – Exhibition of Visual + Art. Irish and international contemporary art, selected by a leading curator (Mar–May).
Limerick Spring Festival (weekend nearest 17th). An event including the huge **St Patrick's Day Parade**, with marching bands and street entertainers; **Limerick International Band Recital Competition**, with jazz ensembles, concert bands and orchestras; and the **International Marching Band Parade and Competition**, where Irish and international bands compete on the streets.

April
Ballyhoura Walking Festival. A 3-day event with graded walks, near Kilfinane.
Fresh Film Festival, *www.freshfilmfestival.net*. A young people's film festival .

May
Fleadh by the Feale, Abbeyfeale, *www.fleadhbythefeale.com*. Traditional music, song and dance, including a bones-playing competition, on the May Bank Holiday weekend.

July
Irish Coffee Festival, *www.irishcoffeefestival. com*. A celebration of Irish coffee, which was invented by local Foynes Airport chef Joe Sheridan in 1942.
Shannon International Music Festival, *www. icorch.com*. Five days of classical music, with acclaimed guests – in 2005 they included soprano Emma Kirkby.

August
Galbally Garden Fete. Pipe bands, carnival, fun and games, and music from a top Irish band.
Limerick Agricultural Show, *www.limerickshow. com*. Showjumping, horticulture, craft exhibitions and family entertainment.

September
Éigse Michael Hartnett Literary Festival, Newcastle West. Irish and international poets and writers, singing and lectures.

October
Castleconnell Craft Fair. Irish-made crafts.
Limerick International Poetry Festival, Cuisle. Poetry slams, readings and book launches.
Lough Gur Storytelling Festival, Bruff. Storytelling, drama, music and singing.

November
Sionna Festival of Dance and Music. Three weeks of traditional music and dance.

and the rich Golden Vale in the east. There are lovely forest walks in all these places and good sailing on the Shannon. The visitor will be fascinated by Lough Gur, with its wealth of archaeological remains, and the many ruined Norman castles and monasteries that survive among the green fields and old farmhouses, lying snugly in the valleys. The best dairy cattle come from County Limerick, and it is also famous for its horse-breeding, due largely to the county's fertile pastures.

Limerick likes to call itself the 'Birthplace of the Celtic Tiger'. When Taoiseach Seán Lemass liberalized Ireland's economic policies in the 1950s, the county was one of the first to take advantage. The Shannon Development and the Free Trade Zone still provide a lot of jobs. Limerick City has a reputation for its vibrant cultural life; it has a good university, excellent museums, art galleries and classical music concerts.

History

Unsurprisingly in such fertile countryside, the monks founded important monasteries here. That they were rich is proved by the bejewelled Ardagh Chalice, found in a ring fort in 1868 and now in the National Museum in Dublin. The Vikings, in search of new territory and loot up the Shannon Estuary, destroyed many centres of learning. They founded a colony here, which later became the City of Limerick.

Next came the Anglo-Normans, also attracted by the rich lands. Among the principal families were the Fitzgeralds, the De Burgos, the De Lacys and the Fitzgibbons. But the earls of Desmond, the heads of the Fitzgeralds, owned the most; they ruled like independent princes, and eventually quarrelled with their Tudor overlords in England. (They and their supporters are known as the Geraldines.) The Tudors attempted to centralize their authority in the 16th century, and consequently the Geraldines, who by now were completely Gaelicized, started a revolt in 1571 and maintained a constant guerrilla war against the Crown and its agents. This ended in savage wars, repression and ruin for their house.

Throughout the following centuries up to the present, Limerick has played a significant role in uprisings against English rule. In 1650 there was the 12-month siege of Limerick by Cromwell, which ended in capitulation. The Jacobite-Williamite war (1689–91) saw two more sieges in which the heroic General Patrick Sarsfield played his role (see p.131). William Smith O' Brien, a Limerick man, was one of the leaders of the abortive 1848 Rebellion, and three of the leaders of the 1916 Rising in Dublin were from the county. Edward Daly and Con Colbert were executed, but Éamon de Valera escaped that fate because of his American birth. Later, he was one of the leaders of the War of Independence (1919–1921) and President of Ireland from 1959 to 1973.

Limerick City

Limerick City, at least at first sight, has something rather drab about it. The famous novelist Kate O'Brien came from the respectable middle class that moulded this city in the course of the 19th century, and she described it as having 'the grave,

Tourist Information

Limerick City: Arthur's Quay, t (061) 317522,
www.shannonregiontourism.ie
Shannon Airport: t (061) 471664,
touristofficeshannon@shannondev.ie

Tours

An *Angela's Ashes* **Walking Tour** takes you around scenes from Frank McCourt's memoir (daily at 2.30pm from St Mary's Action Centre, 44 Nicholas St, t (061) 318106).

The **Great Limerick Tour** travels in an open-top bus (mid-June–mid-Aug daily at 11am and 2.30pm; t (061) 313333).

Shopping

The best **shopping streets** in Limerick are Cruises St, Arthur's Quay, Patrick St, William St and O'Connell St. The daily **Milk Market** sits on the corner of Ellen St and Wickham St; on Fri stalls sell arts and crafts, on Sat mornings it becomes a busy farmers' market.
Greenacres Deli, Carr St, Milk Market, Limerick. Good picnic items, with a feast of Mediterranean and local food.
Irish Handcrafts, 26 Patrick St, Limerick. Woollens and tweeds.
Niamh Hynes, Newgarden Rd, Lisnagry, t 377331. Hand-thrown porcelain decorated with colourful creatures.

Sports and Activities

Golf

Limerick Golf Club, Ballyclough, t (061) 415146, *www.limerickgc.com*
Limerick Golf and Country Club, Ballyneety, t (061) 351881, *www.limerickcounty.com*. A championship-quality course.

Rathbane Golf Club, off R512 Lough Gur road, t (061) 313655, *www.rathbanegolf.com*

Horseracing

Limerick Racecourse, Patrickswell, t (061) 320000, *www.limerick-racecourse.com*

Where to Stay

Limerick City

Radisson SAS Hotel, Ennis Rd, t (061) 326666, *www.radissonsas.ie* (*expensive–luxury*). A plush but not completely bland modern hotel with landscaped gardens and many facilities (a swimming pool, a sauna, a solarium, a gym, tennis courts and a beauty salon, and a spa opening in 2006). There's an expansive hot or cold buffet breakfast and a good dinner menu.
Castletroy Park Hotel, Dublin Rd, t (061) 335566, *www.castletroy-park.ie* (*expensive*). A modern 4-star hotel with an uninspiring exterior but surprisingly good accommodation and a reputation for its good food.
Kilmurry Lodge Hotel, Castletroy, t (061) 331133, *www.kilmurrylodge.com* (*moderate–expensive*). An inviting-looking vine-clad hotel with 4-acre gardens, comfortable rooms and a very pleasant restaurant where fresh, local food is cooked by award-winning chefs.
Hanratty's Hotel, 5 Glentworth St, t (061) 410999 (*moderate*). A hotel established in 1796, with atmosphere and good facilities.
Railway Hotel, Parnell St, t (061) 413653, *www.railwayhotel.ie* (*moderate*). An old-fashioned and very comfortable family-run hotel.
Woodfield House Hotel, Ennis Rd, t (061) 453022, *www.woodfieldhousehotel.com* (*moderate*). A cosy hotel within walking distance of the centre, with a steakhouse restaurant.

grey look of Commerce'. It is largely Georgian in character: a grid pattern of streets was superimposed onto the older town, which was built following the curve of the River Shannon.

Limerick is doing its best to forget the hard times of the 1940s–60s, and it has recently been given a substantial facelift. It has a reputation for smart clothes shops, and the Art School here has produced some talented fashion designers. Also, it has the much-lauded Hunt Collection of art treasures, which is worth making the journey

Alexandra Guest House, 5–6 O'Connell Ave, t (061) 318472 (inexpensive). An attractive Victorian house with ensuite rooms, only 5mins' walk from the city centre.

Mount Gerard B&B, O'Connell Ave, t (061) 314981 (inexpensive). A family B&B within a lovely Victorian house, in a convenient location for the centre.

Eating Out

Moll Darby's, 8 George's Quay, t (061) 411511 (moderate). An atmospheric original stone building right in front of King John's Castle, serving hearty food, including steaks and seafood. Closed lunch.

The Parlour Restaurant, inside Thady O'Neills, Ennis Rd, t (061) 322777 (moderate). A finely decorated place with a cosy atmosphere and classic, creative dishes.

Quenelle's Restaurant, Steamboat Quay, t (061) 411111 (moderate). Gourmet dining in crisp surroundings with a view over the quays. Fine meat, fish, game and vegetarian dishes are offered. Closed lunch Sat–Wed, and Sun eve.

Ducarts, in Hunt Museum, Rutland St, t (061) 312662 (inexpensive–moderate). A pleasant lunch spot where you can have a meal or just a snack on the terrace, with a view over the Shannon. Closed eves.

Green Onion Café, inside Limerick's, Ellen St (inexpensive). A popular café serving veggie options and good Italian coffee.

Greene's Café-Bistro, 63 William St, t (061) 314022 (inexpensive). A central carvery-bistro with beautiful stained glass and wholesome Irish dishes. Closed eves and Sun.

Matt the Thresher, Birdhill, t (061) 379227 (inexpensive). A delightful country pub situated on the road into Limerick (and therefore technically in Tipperary), serving excellent food and home-made bread, which you can enjoy together with views across the Shannon.

Ruben's Café and Wine Bar, 17 Denmark St, t (061) 312599 (inexpensive). A great place for wholesome food and vegetarian dishes, set in a pleasant renovated stone building. Closed eves and Sun.

The Wild Onion Bakeshop and Café, High St, (inexpensive). Scrumptious breakfasts and lunches, including home-made vegeburgers, cakes and breads. Closed eves, and Mon and Sun.

Entertainment and Nightlife

Pubs and Clubs

The Old Quarter, Little Ellen St. A relaxed Art Deco-style bar, with outdoor seating and regular jazz ensembles.

Schooners, Steamboat Quay, t (061) 328147. A place on the banks of the Shannon, popular for its live local bands.

Traditional Music

Belltable Arts Centre, 69 O'Connell St, t (061) 319866, www.belltable.ie. A great arts centre that hosts especially good events during festivals.

Dolan's, 3–4 Dock Rd, t (061) 314483, www. dolans-pub.ie. A lively venue situated in the old docklands area, with music played by accomplished musicians. It's a good place for food too.

Irish World Music Centre, University of Limerick, t (061) 202917, www.iwmc.ie. Lunchtime concerts on Tue and Thur.

The Locke, George's Quay, t (061) 413733. A bar dating back to 1724, with a very relaxed atmosphere.

for alone. For a city of its size (the population is 87,000), Limerick also has a buzzing nightlife. The high levels of unemployment and emigration have decreased significantly as new industries have been set up, and its cultural life is healthy. The city is very proud of its musical heritage, with a strong choral tradition, chamber music and marching bands. Mezzo-soprano Suzanne Murphy was born here, the 1990s saw local band The Cranberries gain international stardom, and there's an Irish World Music Centre (see above). The people of Limerick are not so proud, however, of

Frank McCourt's descriptions of their city in *Angela's Ashes* (a memoir of his childhood), even though a walking and bus tour (*see* p.129) points out some of the places mentioned in his grim, exuberant and funny portrait of life in 1930s–40s Limerick.

History

Like Londonderry, Limerick is a symbolic city full of memories, and there is lots to see that reveals Limerick's more ancient past. It was founded in AD 922 by the Norsemen, and has always been an important fording place on the River Shannon; in 1997 the city celebrated the 800th anniversary of its royal charter. More concrete evidence of the past is the massive round tower of King John's Castle, built in 1200, which sits on the river guarding Thomond Bridge and is one of the best examples of fortified Norman architecture in the country. The motto of the city is *Urbs antiqua fuit studiisque asperrima belli*, 'An ancient city inured to the arts of war'.

The history of the city is certainly stirring. In the wars of 1691 it was eventually surrendered to the Williamite Commander Ginkel after a fierce battering from his guns. The siege that preceded the surrender is stored away in the psyche of Irishmen. During the 1690s there were three struggles going on: the struggle of Britain and its Protestant allies to oppose the ascendancy in Europe of Catholic France, the struggle of Britain to subdue Ireland, and the struggle between the Protestant planter families and the Catholic Irish for the leadership of Ireland. The French supplied money and commanders to help Catholic James II wrest his crown back from the Protestant William of Orange. The majority of the Catholic Irish supported the Jacobite cause, and many joined up.

It is part of Irish folk memory that the French commander St Ruth and King James were asses, and that the Irish commander Patrick Sarsfield was intelligent, daring and brave. The Irish army had been beaten at the Boyne under St Ruth and had retreated to Limerick, where the walls were said to be paper-thin. William began a siege while he waited for the arrival of big guns, but Patrick Sarsfield led a daring raid on the siege train from Dublin and destroyed it. Sarsfield rode through the night with 600 horses into the Clare Hills, forded the Shannon and continued on through the Slievefelim Mountains. Finally, he swooped down on William III's huge consignment of guns and blew them skywards. His action saved Limerick from destruction for a time, when the siege was abandoned. When William did break through Limerick's walls he sent in 10,000 men to wreak havoc, but the women and children of the city fought alongside their men and beat them back.

The second siege began the following year, and this time heavy losses were inflicted when the Williamite leader, Ginkel, gained control of Thomond Bridge. The promised help never came, and there was nothing to do but negotiate an honourable treaty. This Sarsfield did, and he agreed to take himself and 10,000 Irish troops off to France, in what became known as 'The Flight of the Wild Geese'. But the terms of the treaty were not carried out. The stone beside Thomond Bridge, where it was supposed to have been signed, is known as 'The Stone of the Violated Treaty'. In the Catholic Cathedral of St John is the Sarsfield Monument by sculptor John Lawlor (1820–1901).

The City Centre

The old Viking town of Limerick sits on an island formed by the Shannon and the Abbey River (a branch of the Shannon). Known as **English Town**, it's one of the most interesting parts of Limerick to wander in, along with its Irish counterpart across the water. The Vikings and later the Normans tried to keep the native Irish from living and trading in the city area, so the Irish settled on the other side – in **Irish Town**. A short circular walk will take you around the main places of interest.

In the centre is the tourist office and Arthur's Quay Park, between the Shannon and the city's sparkling modern shopping district. From here, cross the river by Sarsfield Bridge, then turn right up Clancy's Strand, which gives you a good view of the city.

This passes by the **Limerick Treaty Stone** and leads to Thomond Bridge and the Old Town. You also pass **King John's Castle** (*open daily Apr–Oct 9.30–6, Nov–Mar 10.30–4.30, last adm 1hr before close; adm; t (061) 360788*), which has a two-floor interpretative centre that explains the castle's history through displays and an audio-visual show. Outside, you can explore the battlement views, excavations of pre-Norman buildings and a reconstruction of the courtyard as it might have looked in medieval times. The **Limerick Museum**, next door in Castle Lane (*open Tue–Sat 10–1 and 2.15–7 exc public hols; adm; t (061) 417826*), houses an impressive collection of items from the Neolithic, Bronze and Iron Ages, as well as the city's mace and sword. Other civic treasures include the famous 'Nail': a pedestal that was formerly in the Exchange (once in Nicholas Street; only a fragment of the façade remains) where the merchants of Limerick used to pay their debts. (Most trading centres in England had one of these, hence the expression 'to pay on the nail'.)

Walk down Nicholas Street to **St Mary's Cathedral**, the only ancient church building left in the city, built in 1172 by Donal Mor O'Brien, King of Munster. Inside, it has plenty of atmosphere, monuments and impressive furnishings, including some superb 15th-century oak misericords carved into the shapes of fantastic beasts, such as the cockatrice and griffin. They are known as 'mercy seats' because although it looked as if the singers were standing, they could instead use them to half-sit or lean on. The acclaimed **cathedral choir** can be heard here regularly (*Sept–July most Suns at 11.15am and evensong, 1st Sun of month 7pm*). The oak for the misericords and barrel-vaulted roof came from the Cratloe Woods in County Clare. The cathedral was vandalized by Cromwell's soldiers, although it still has its pre-Reformation limestone high altar. Note the spectacular chandeliers. The Hiberno-Romanesque doorway on the west side is splendid, and the graveyard and garden surrounding the cathedral are charming. In summer there's a **son et lumière** show about Limerick (*nightly, 9.15*).

A few minutes' walk down Bridge Street and over the little Abbey River brings you to the best thing in Limerick: the Old Custom House in Rutland Street. This restored 18th-century building is now home to the **Hunt Museum** (*open Mon–Sat 10–5, Sun 2–5; t (061) 312833, www.huntmuseum.com*) and is a rare example of architecture by Davis Ducart. John Hunt was a noted art historian and Celtic archaeologist who died in the 1970s. He and his wife Gertrude gathered together a remarkable European collection of more than 2,000 objects, part of which comprises a hoard of archaeological finds that are considered the second most important in Ireland today. There's also 18th-century silver; jewels, including early-Christian brooches; paintings (one by Picasso); and Egyptian, Roman, Greek and medieval carved statues and artefacts, including the 9th-century bronze **Cashel Bell**, the largest in Ireland, found near Cashel town in 1849. As self-portraits go, the one by Robert Fagin with his half-naked wife is rather stunning; so, in a different way, is the bronze horse by Leonardo da Vinci.

After the 1760s, when the city walls were dismantled, English and Irish town merged and Georgian streets and squares were built. St John's Square has the lofty spire of the Victorian Gothic **St John's Cathedral**, as well as a number of lovely old buildings of the mid 18th century. From here, a walk up Brennan's Row and a right on Sean Heuston Place brings you to the **Milk Market** (*see* 'Shopping', p.129).

More fine Georgian streets can be found on the southern edge of the city centre, around the **Crescent**, a development of the early 1800s at the southern end of O'Connell Street, and around **People's Park**. Close to the entrance of the park, off Pery Square, the **Limerick City Gallery of Art** (*open Mon–Fri 10–6, Thur 10–7, Sat 10–1; t (061) 310633, www.limerickcity.ie*) has a collection of modern Irish paintings, and holds some very interesting exhibitions of contemporary art.

The **Belltable Arts Centre** (*69 O'Connell St, t (061) 319866, www.belltable.ie*) is situated to the southwest; various travelling theatre companies stop off here and it's well worth seeing what's on. There is also a small gallery that shows the work of many local artists and is part of the international EV+A festival (*see* p.127). The University of Limerick, on the edge of the city off the main Dublin road (N7), houses several art collections; the **National Self-Portrait Collection** (*open Mon–Fri 9–5; t (061) 333644, www.ul.ie/campuslife/arts/arts.html*) is the most worthwhile. The university is also home to the Irish Chamber Orchestra (*www.icorch.com*) and has a fine concert hall. Classical, traditional and world music concerts take place here regularly, especially during the International Music Festival (*see* p.127).

Limerick is the great bastion of rugby in Ireland, and one of the many local clubs wins the All-Ireland League almost every year. Hurling is also a very popular and successful sport in Limerick, in which local clubs have their own style of playing.

Around County Limerick

Down the Shannon to Glin

From Limerick City, the N69 follows the Shannon Estuary. Sitting between the road and the Shannon are two very prominent landmarks: the crumbling 15th-century **Carrigogunnell Castle** at Clarina, superbly set on a volcanic rock with a commanding view of the river, and, four miles (6.4km) farther west, the romantic silhouette of **Dromore Castle** (*private*), designed by E.W. Godwin for the Earl of Limerick in 1870.

In the vicinity of Kilcornan is the gutted ruin of **Curragh Chase**, which burnt down in 1942. The minor Victorian poet Aubrey de Vere lived most of his long life here, and was often visited by Tennyson. One visit produced the poem 'Lady Vere de Vere'. Aubrey de

Tourist Information

Adare: Adare Heritage Centre, Main St,
t (061) 396255. *Closed Jan.*

Shopping

Lucy Erridge Crafts, Main St, Adare,
t (061) 396898. Knitwear and unusual crafts.
Orchard Pottery, Castleconnell, t (061) 377181.
Stoneware with colourful Celtic designs.

Sports and Activities

Golf
Adare Manor Golf Club, Adare, t (061) 396566,
www.adaremanor.ie. See hotel listing, below.
Newcastle West Golf Club, Rathgoonan,
Ardagh, t (069) 76500
Abbeyfeale Golf Centre, Dromtrasna Collins,
Abbeyfeale, t (068) 32033

Ponytrekking
Clonshire Equestrian Centre, Adare,
t (061) 396770
Yerville Stables, Pallasgreen, t (061) 351547

Where to Stay

Adare Manor Hotel and Golf Resort, Adare,
t (061) 396566, *www.adaremanor.ie (luxury).*

The original house of the earls of Dunraven,
a mix of Victorian, Gothic and Tudor Revival
fantasy, with beautiful grounds, horseriding,
shooting and an 18-hole golf course.
Dunraven Arms Hotel, Adare, t (061) 396633,
www.dunravenhotel.com (luxury).
An olde-worlde option, with appealing
interiors, friendly staff, a pool and a garden.
Its **Maigue Restaurant** serves top-rate food;
the **Inn Between** is a more informal choice
in a thatched cottage.
Glin Castle, Glin, due west of Adare by the
Shannon, t (068) 34173, *www.glincastle.com
(luxury).* The home of the present Knight of
Glin and his wife, with 15 exclusively decorated
rooms, plus a sitting room, library, drawing
room and gardens. The **dining room** offers
Irish country-house cuisine, with organic
fruit and veg picked from the walled garden.
See also opposite. *Closed Dec–Feb.*
The Mustard Seed, Ballingarry, t (069) 68508,
www.mustardseed.ie (expensive).
A 19th-century house on a hill, with
characterful rooms, a great dining room (*see*
opposite) and pretty, lovingly kept gardens.
Ash Hill House, Kilmallock, t (063) 98035,
www.ashhill.com (moderate). A crenellated,
turreted Georgian house with 3 large,
comfortable rooms and a 2-bedroom
apartment, fascinating plasterwork ceilings
and shades of Anglo-Irish splendour. It's also
a stud and working farm; dogs are welcome.

Vere did many good works during the famine and is buried in Askeaton. The ruin is in
a very romantic setting; the demesne is now **Curragh Chase Forest Park** (*open daily;
www.coillte.ie*) and footpaths are laid out in the arboretum and around the reed-filled
lake. Also in Kilcornan is the **Celtic Park and Gardens** (*open Mar–Oct daily 9–6;
no under-13s;* t *(061) 394243*), a fascinating collection of original and re-created Celtic
structures, such as a dolmen, a lake dwelling, a stone templar church and extensive,
well-planned gardens. Just west, **Askeaton Friary** is a preserved 14th-century complex
endowed by the earls of Desmond, with fine ancient stone carvings.

At **Foynes**, Limerick's little port, is the diverting **Flying Boat Museum** (*open Apr–Oct
daily 10–6; adm,* t *(069) 65416, www.flyingboatmuseum.com*). Between 1939 and 1945
Foynes was famous as a base for seaplanes crossing the Atlantic. The radio and weather
room with original transmitters, receivers and Morse code is fascinating. Many high-
ranking British and US officers passed through Foynes during the Second World War
and Irish coffee was concocted then, by the restaurant's chef (*see* 'Festivals', p.127).
Boyce's Garden (*open May–Sept daily 10–6;* t *(069) 65302*), at Mount Trenchard, is a
superb one-acre garden overlooking the Shannon, with a rock garden and a pergola.

Castle Oaks House, Castleconnell, t (061) 377666, *www.castleoaks.ie (moderate)*. A Georgian house by the Shannon, handy for golf and angling, with an award-winning restaurant.
Courtenay Lodge, Newcastle West, t (069) 62244, *www.courtenaylodgehotel.com (moderate)*. A comfortable if uninspiring choice near some of Ireland's best golf courses.
Millbank House, Murroe, t (061) 386115, *www.millbankhouse.com (moderate)*. A welcoming Georgian house on a farm. Fish for trout and salmon on the Mulcair flowing through it.
Ivy House, N21, Craigue, Adare, t (061) 396270 *(inexpensive)*. Three rooms in an ivy-covered 18th-century house. *Closed Nov–Feb.*
O'Driscolls B&B, Glin, t (061) 386115, *www.odriscolls-accommodation.com (inexpensive)*. Four homely rooms with views onto a garden and a lounge with an open fire in winter.
Reens House, near Rathkeale, Ardagh, t (069) 64276 *(inexpensive)*. A 17th-century Jacobean house on a dairy farm. *Closed Nov–Mar.*

Self-catering
Ballyteigue House, Rockhill, Bruree, t (063) 90575, *www.ballyteigue.com (inexpensive)*, A gracious Georgian house for 9 with country-style interiors, plus a beautiful cottage for 6.
Finniterstown House, Adare, t (061) 396232, *www.tourismresources.ie/cht/finn.htm (inexpensive)*. The 19th-century home of the O'Grady clan, in farmland with tennis courts, sleeping 10.

Springfield Castle, Drumcollogher, t (063) 83162, *www.springfieldcastle.com (inexpensive)*. A fabulous historic home for holiday lets, sleeping 14, plus 4 in a cottage in the grounds.

Eating Out

See also the hotel listings, above.
The Wild Geese Restaurant, Main St, Adare, t (061) 396451 *(luxury)*. An award-winning mix of classic French and modern Irish food.
The Mustard Seed, Echo Lodge, Ballingarry, t (069) 68508 *(expensive)*. Delicious and imaginative food from organic sources; try the smoked salmon with walnut oil.
M. J. Finnegan's, Dublin Rd, Annacotty, t (061) 337338 *(moderate)*. Excellent food in an 18th-century pub, with weekend *céilí* music.
Worrall's Inn, Castleconnell, t (061) 377148 *(moderate)*. A popular family-run restaurant specializing in fish, steak and Med-style fare.
The Blue Door Restaurant, Adare, t (061) 396481 *(inexpensive)*. Simple modern Irish food.

Pubs
Duggan's, Bridge St, Newcastle West.
The Gables, Colbert St, Athea. Traditional music.
Paddy the Farmers, Annacotty. A cosy, vibrant and award-winning pub.
The Ramble Inn, Church St, Abbeyfeale. A good place for Irish music.

At **Glin**, which is a lovely village on the Shannon, it is possible to visit **Glin Castle** (and also stay in it; *see* box opposite page). This is still the ancestral home of the Knights of Glin, who are part of the Fitzgerald tribe. The present Knight is an art historian by profession and a stalwart campaigner on behalf of Ireland's historic buildings, which are so often left to decay. The castle is Georgian Gothic with castellations, and has been noted for its flying staircase, its plasterwork and its 18th-century furniture, portraits and landscape paintings. The gardens (*visitors welcome by prior arrangement*) are beautifully planned and tended, and form a fitting extension to this romantic house. Exotic plants and the dark-leaved myrtle with its creamy, scented flowers love the mild climate; the walled garden is large and sloping and filled with fruit, herbs and vegetables for the house. The hens have Gothic-style quarters and a headless Ariadne stands in a rustic temple.

By the castle gates is the **Glin Heritage and Genealogical Research Centre** (*open June–Sept Tue–Sun 10–6; t (068) 34001*). Tarbert, to the west of Glin in County Kerry, is the site of the **car ferry** across the Shannon (*see* p.239), which makes a very useful short cut into County Clare.

Following the border with Kerry, southwards from Glin, you come to **Athea**, a pretty centre for traditional music. All around are lovely hill walks and drives. **Abbeyfeale**, on the N21 south of Athea, surrounded by rolling hills, is another centre of traditional music, song and dance. It is also the gateway to Killarney and Tralee. To the east are the **Mullaghareirk Mountains**, which are forested mainly with the uniform evergreens so beloved of the Forestry Commission.

Adare and the Maigue Valley

About 10 miles (16km) from Limerick, south-west on the N20/N21, **Adare** (*Áth Dara*: ford of the oak) is set in richly timbered land through which the little Maigue river flows. This village has attracted visitors for many years. There is only one wide street, Main Street, bordered by pretty thatched cottages, many of which are antique shops, craft shops or restaurants. The village is noted for its fine ecclesiastical ruins, but there's also a restored washing pool opposite Trinitarian Abbey, just off Main Street. Imagine the stories and scandal exchanged here as the women washed their clothes.

The finest ruin is the **Franciscan friary** (*in grounds of Adare Manor Golf Club; ask at entrance for permission to visit*), founded in 1464 by Thomas, Earl of Kildare, and his wife. (The village belonged to the Kildare branch of the Fitzgeralds, or Geraldines.) The friary was attacked and burned by Parliamentary forces in 1539 and 1581, but its ruins are beautifully proportioned, and can be seen from the long narrow **bridge** of 14 arches (*c.*1400) on the outskirts of the village (on the N20 going north).

The modern village has grown up around the rest of the ecclesiastical buildings. The **Augustinian priory**, now the Church of Ireland Church, was founded in 1315 by the Earl of Kildare and restored in 1807 by the first Earl of Dunraven. He and his family did much to protect the old buildings, and built the thatched cottages in Main Street in the 1820s. His family used to own the Gothic Tudor Revival-style **Adare Manor** (now a luxury hotel, *see* p.134), the lush parklands and elegant formal gardens of which surround the village. The **church** has some interesting carvings of animals and human heads, and gives a good idea of what an Irish medieval church must have looked like.

The ruined **Desmond Castle**, on the banks of the Maigue beside the bridge, was built in the 13th century on the site of an earlier ring fort. It is a fine example of feudal architecture with its square keep, curtain walls, two halls, kitchen, gallery and stables.

The area around Adare is known as the Palatine because of the number of Lutherans (refugees from southern Germany) who settled here in the 18th century under the patronage of Lord Southwell. The British government encouraged them to come and paid their rents for a number of years. **Rathkeale**, 17 miles (27km) west of Adare, has a small **Irish Palatine Heritage Centre** (*open mid-May–mid-Sept Tue–Fri 10–12 and 2–5, Sun 2–5; adm; t (069) 64397*) devoted to their history. The Palatines are credited with introducing crop rotation, and their descendants, bearing such names as Ruttle, Shier, Teskey and Switzer, are still numerous in the area. Rathkeale is one of the largest towns in County Limerick and is in the centre of the dairy farming region. It is notable for its fine early-19th-century courthouse and doorways in the main street.

Castle Matrix (*open June–Aug daily 11–4; adm; t (069) 64284*), pronounced '*mat*trix' and located about a mile (1.6km) to the south-west, is a fine Geraldine towerhouse built *c.*1410. The poet Earl of Desmond, whose style epitomized the courtly love genre, lived here in the 1440s. The restored castle houses a unique collection of documents relating to the Wild Geese – Irish soldiers who served nobly in the Continental armies of the 17th and 18th centuries. Castle Matrix has the reputation of being the first place in Ireland where the potato was grown (though Youghal makes that claim too). According to local history, the poet Edmund Spenser met Walter Raleigh here in 1580, and they became great friends. When Raleigh returned from his successful voyage to America, he presented some potatoes to their host, Lord Southwell, who cultivated them. The Methodist movement in North America was initiated at Castle Matrix: Palatine refugees on the estate were converted by John Wesley, and in 1760 Philip Embury and Barbara Ruttle Heck sailed to New York and founded a church there.

A short distance to the south-west is **Ardagh**, which is famous for the chalice, brooches and bronze cup discovered in an ancient ring fort (now displayed in the National Museum in Dublin). The chalice is wrought of gold, silver and bronze, and ornamented with enamel, amber and crystal. The 15th-century medieval **Desmond Hall** (*open mid-June–mid-Sept daily 9.30–6.30; adm; guided tours; t (069) 77408, www.heritageireland.ie*), in the square, is where the earls of Desmond would have held banquets. The hall has a fine oak musician's gallery and limestone hooded hearth, with a vaulted lower chamber and tower.

Croom, right in the middle of County Limerick in a charming position on the River Maigue, is celebrated as the meeting place of the 18th-century Gaelic poets of the Maigue. Here the light verse of the limerick was first popularized and later taken up by Edward Lear. (Their poetry is available in translation; it is unforgettable for its wit and feeling.) There is an old Geraldine **castle** hidden behind a wall on the southern approach to the village. Croom was frequently attacked by the O'Briens, whose territory it bordered. Their battle cry was 'The strong hand forever!' ('*Lamh laidir abú!*') and it was always met by the rallying cry of the Geraldines, 'Croom forever!' ('*Cromadh abú!*'). The old grain mill at **Croom Mills** (*open Apr–Oct daily 10–5; café and craft shop open all year; t (061) 397130, www.croommills.com*), with its 16ft (4.8m) waterwheel, has been restored as a working mill and heritage centre.

Knockfierna Hill, 6 miles (10km) south-west of Croom, is a fine place for a walk. It is held sacred to the *Dé Danaan*, King of the Other World, or Death, *Donn Forinne*, and translates as 'the hill of truth'. From the summit you can see a great expanse of blue mountains and the pale Shannon Estuary. This area was badly affected in the famine, and you can see restored cottages at the **Famine Park** near Ballingarry.

Lough Gur

Lough Gur, 11 miles (17km) south of Limerick City, is guarded by the remains of two **castles** built by the earls of Desmond. Legend holds that the last of the Desmonds is doomed to hold court under Lough Gur and to emerge, fully armed, at daybreak on every morning of the seventh year in a routine that must be repeated until the silver shoes of his horse are worn away. As if to echo the story, the lake is horseshoe-shaped. Lough Gur is rich in field antiquities, revealed when the water level was lowered by drainage in the 19th century. Humans have lived here since 3000 BC and you can see **stone circles**, wedge-shaped **graves**, a **crannóg**, a **ring fort** and **Neolithic house sites**. The impressive **Interpretative Centre** (*open May–Sept daily 10–6; guided tours; adm; t (061) 385186, www.shannonheritage.com*), built as two Neolithic dwellings with steeply pitched, thatched roofs and wattle fences, has an excellent audio-visual exhibition explaining the history of the Lough Gur area from the Stone Age.

Kilmallock, about 11 miles (17km) south of Lough Gur on the R512, is in the rich land of the Golden Vale. It was founded by St Mocheallog and received a charter in the time of Edward III, during which period it was heavily fortified. Built by the Geraldines (Fitzgeralds), it was a centre of Desmond power between the 14th and 16th centuries, and was partially destroyed during the Desmond Rebellion. It was also used during the Cromwellian and Williamite wars, when its fortifications were destroyed. The 15th-century **King's Castle** still stands in the centre of town; it has the appearance of a towerhouse, but as well as being a citadel it has been used as an arsenal, a school and a blacksmith's. **Blossom's Gateway** is a surviving remnant of the town's medieval walls, and one of the best examples of its kind in Ireland.

Kilmallock Museum (*open daily 1.30–5; guided town tours available; t (063) 91300*), near the castle, holds a small collection of relics from the town's past and some models of medieval Kilmallock and its Stone Age counterpart, which was recently excavated nearby. There is a beautiful ruined 13th-century **Dominican priory** (known locally as 'the abbey') across the river, dating from the 13th century. A pillar in its aisle arcade shows a ball flower ornament, which is very rare in Ireland, though it was common in England during the 14th century.

South of Kilmallock are the **Ballyhoura Mountains**, which straddle the border with County Cork and provide pleasant farming country, with opportunities for ponytrekking and walking. The slight remains of a **round tower** can be seen beside a **holy well** at **Ardpatrick**. Two miles (3.2km) south of Ardpatrick, in the demesne of Castle Oliver, Marie Gilbert was born in 1818. She became Lola Montez, mistress of Ludwig I of Bavaria.

Approximately 12 miles (18km) to the east, outside the village of Galbally, a lovely walk may be made up **Duntryleague Hill**, where you can explore a megalithic **passage tomb** and the remains of a **stone circle**.

Bruree, 4 miles (7km) to the west of Kilmallock on the R518, is the place where Éamon de Valera grew up. His mother came from here; his father was a Spaniard. De Valera was born in Manhattan, but when his father died his mother sent him back here at the age of two to be reared by his grandmother. The school he went to is now the **De Valera Museum and Bruree Heritage Centre** (*open Mon–Fri 10–5, Sat and Sun 2–5; adm; t (063) 90900*). He became a maths teacher and joined the Gaelic League, beginning his lifelong championship of the Irish language. He is referred to affectionately in Ireland as 'Dev'.

An old cornmill with a huge **millwheel**, the second largest in Ireland, is a striking view as you enter the village from the west.

East of Limerick

Castleconnell, 6 miles (9km) from Limerick, is a pretty Georgian spa town on the Shannon. **Murroe** (also spelt Moroe) and the Clare Glens are on the north-eastern borders of Limerick, about 10 miles (16km) from Limerick City on the R506. Murroe lies under the foothills of the **Slievefelim Mountains**, and is dominated by the 19th-century mansion of **Glenstal**, which was built by the Barrington family as a massive Norman Revival castle. The Barringtons left it in 1921 after Winifred, a daughter of the house, was shot dead in an ambush while travelling with an army officer and a district inspector of the RIC. Now a Benedictine monastery, **Glenstal Abbey** (*www.glenstal.org*) is the only Benedictine boys' school in Ireland, and is a centre for the promotion of ecumenicalism. It has a remarkable collection of Russian icons, and the church is open to the general public for Mass and Benediction. The monks will always make you welcome; they sell beautiful hand-turned wooden bowls, books by Glenstal monks and others, and music in their shop. The wooded grounds are very beautiful in May and June when the rhododendrons are out.

The Barringtons donated the **Clare Glens** to the county councils of Limerick and North Tipperary for the public's pleasure. The Glens, 3 miles (5km) north of Murroe, are not so much glens as a scenic gorge with sparkling waterfalls and a nature trail.

Four miles (6.4km) west, at **Clonkeen**, is a small rectangular church from about the 12th century, with a richly decorated Irish Romanesque doorway and north-wall window.

County Kerry

Kerry is packed with some of Ireland's most beautiful scenery and friendliest folk. It is a kingdom all of its own, whose people love to use words with skill, flamboyance and humour. An irregularly shaped county with long fingers of land reaching into the sea, it boasts the opulent lakes of Killarney at its centre, set amongst the wooded slopes of the Macgillycuddy's Reeks, the grandest mountain range in the land. To the west are the peninsulas of Iveragh and Dingle, where mountains and sea are jumbled together in a glory of colour. The Beara Peninsula, which Kerry shares with County Cork, has an equal beauty but is relatively unexplored. Every year small farmers create a pattern of golden hay ricks and cornfields, and wild flowers grow in the hawthorn hedges and handkerchief fields where the black Kerry cow grazes – when she's not creating a jam in the narrow country lanes. One exotic plant that has colonized the south-west to its advantage is the scarlet-blossomed fuchsia; other subtropical plants thrive too, due to the warming effects of the Gulf Stream.

Off the coast are some fascinating islands that it is possible to visit, with some perseverance. On the Skellig Rocks, the word of God has been praised and celebrated for 600 years. Valentia is a soft, easy island by comparison, connected to the mainland by a causeway. The Blaskets, three miles (5km) out to sea, are beautiful but deserted: the community of subsistence farmers and fishing folk that the islanders recorded in a couple of lyrical biographies is sadly gone.

County Kerry

The possibilities for enjoying yourself in County Kerry are numerous. If you're driving around the narrow country lanes you'll see the most superb views of seascape, hill and valley. (But don't try to cover too much ground in one day, for the roads are very twisty and each bend holds more alluring beauty – you can end up driving too much and exploring too quickly.) County Kerry's hotels and restaurants are generally of a very high standard, and the seafood and salmon are all that could be desired. Sailing, deep-sea fishing, diving and water-skiing are all easy to arrange, as are golf, game fishing, horseriding and walking in the heathery mountains. For those who most like to wander among gardens and around historic buildings, there are several properties open to the public. (One of the most famous is Derrynane House, the house of Daniel

O'Connell, 'the Great Liberator'.) For those interested in the ancient past, Kerry is scattered with ogham stones, standing stones, forts and beehive-shaped cells called *clochans*, the stone huts of holy men. Interpretative centres have opened to educate those interested in local history and cater for the coach tours.

Expect some rainy weather and cloud – County Kerry is notoriously wet and warm.

History

A brief historical outline starts back in the Bronze Age, some 4,500 years ago. Miners from Spain and Portugal were attracted by the precious metals found in the mountains, and it is still possible to find traces of their mines and assembly places,

Getting There and Around

By Air

Kerry airport is about 12 miles (19km) north of Killarney on the N23. There is no shuttle bus service from the airport. A **taxi** to Killarney town centre costs approximately €20. **Kerry Airport**, t (066) 976 4644, *www.kerryairport.ie*

By Bus or Train

The rail and bus **stations** are next to each other by the Great Southern Hotel on Park Rd, a few minutes from the town centre.

Kerry is linked to Dublin by a good **train** line from Killarney (t (064) 31067).

Bus Éireann (t (064) 30011) provides a good **bus service** to many parts of the county. In July and Aug it runs daily **coach tours** round the Ring of Kerry and the peninsula from Killarney and Tralee.

By Ferry

If you're driving from Shannon Airport, you can save yourself some time by avoiding Limerick City and taking the **Killimer–Tarbert car ferry**; *see* **County Clare** p.239.

By Bike

Killarney Rent-a-Bike, Old Market Lane, Main St, Killarney, t (064) 32578. Free maps with rentals.
O'Sullivan's Bike Shop, Bishop's Lane, New St, t (064) 31282
Trailways Outdoor Centre, College St, t (064) 39929. A hire place that also arranges tours and accommodation.

Car Hire

National, Kerry Airport, t (021) 432 0755, *www.carhire.ie*
Randles Irish Car Rental, Kerry Airport, t (064) 31232, *www.irishcarrentals.com*

Getting to Islands off Kerry

Bring something to eat and drink with you, as well as some all-weather gear. Note that all trips are weather-dependent.

Blasket Islands

The **Blasket Island Boatmen** sail from Dunquin Pier in summer every half-hour from 10am, t (066) 915 6422.

The *Peig Sayers*, t (066) 915 1344, *www.greatblasketisland.com*, sails from Dingle. Its owners offer an overnight package that includes dinner, B&B and the return trip to the islands (€70pp).

Skellig Islands

The fragile environment on Great Skellig means a limit is set on how many people can visit, so reservations are essential in high season. Fares cost around €32 and the average journey time is 50mins.
Ballinskelligs Watersports, from Ballinskelligs Pier, t (066) 947 9182.
Michael O'Sullivan, from Waterville, t (066) 947 4255
Pat and Des Lavelle, from Portmagee or Valentia, t (066) 947 6124. A husband-and-wife team of experts on the Skelligs.

A **water bus tour** is available from the Skellig Experience Heritage Centre on Valentia Island, t (066) 947 6306.

marked with stone circles, rock carvings and wedge tombs. From the wealth of legend that remains of the later Bronze Age and early Iron Age (500 BC), it is possible to build up a picture of society as it was then: hierarchical, aristocratic and warlike. There were no towns, and cattle-raising and raiding dominated everything. Farmers lived in ring forts and on *crannógs* for defensive reasons. Writing was confined to an archaic form of Irish, which you can see on the ogham stones scattered around the county. Kerry beaches were the landing places for many of the legendary invasions, voyages and battles of Ireland's past. The miners who sailed into the bays from Spain are recorded in legend, as are the other waves of settlers.

Christianity came in the 5th century, and great changes began. The old tribal centres went into decline, and powerful new kingdoms emerged, often with an abbot-prince at their heads. A strong monastic structure grew up and some monasteries became

Valentia Island

You can get here over the **bridge** at Portmagee, or a **car ferry** runs in season between Reenard Point and Knightstown (cars €4 return, pedestrians €3; journey 5mins; **t** (066) 947 6141).

Festivals

March
St Patrick's Week, *www.corkkerry.ie*. A huge celebration including a Great Parade (17th) and Roaring 1920s Festival.

April
Samhlaíocht **Easter Arts Festival**, Tralee, *www.samhlaiocht.com*. A programme of music, dancing and street entertainment.

May
Féile na Bealtaine, Dingle and Ballyferriter. *www.feilenabealtaine.ie*. May Day festivals.
Killarney Races, Racecourse, **t** (064) 31125
Listowel Writers' Week (*www.writersweek.ie*).
Siamsa Tíre, National Folk Theatre of Ireland, Tralee (*www.siamsatire.com*). Music, folklore and dance (May–Sept).
Walking Festival, Kenmare (*www.kenmarewalking.com*). Late May–early June.

June
International Bachelor Festival, Ballybunion, *www.corkkerry.ie*
Kerry Festival of Music, Kenmare, **t** (064) 41233. Traditional music.
Tralee Races, Ballybeggan, **t** (066) 712 6490, *www.traleehorseracing.com*

July
Caherciveen Festival of Music and the Arts, *www.celticmusicfestival.com*
Castlegregory Summer Festival, *www.corkkerry.ie*. Mid-July.
Féile Lughnasa, Cloghane and Brandon. *www.irishcelticfest.com*. A festival including a pilgrimage to Mt Brandon.
Killarney Races, Racecourse, **t** (064) 31125

August
Blessing of the Boats, Dingle Pier, *www.corkkerry.ie*. Sun late Aug or early Sept.
Fleadh Cheoil na hÉireann, Clonmel *www.clonmelfleadh.com*. A celebration of Irish culture, music, song and dance.
Puck Fair, Killorglin, *www.puckfair.ie*. See p.160.
Races and Regatta, Dingle, *www.corkkerry.ie*
Rose of Tralee Competition, Tralee, *www.roseoftralee.ie*. A big festival/beauty contest.
Tralee Races, Ballybeggan, **t** (066) 712 6490, *www.traleehorseracing.com*

September
Listowel Harvest Festival and Races, *www.corkkerry.ie*. An event including the Harvest Queen competition, street entertainment, races and marching bands.

October
Patrick O'Keeffe Traditional Music Festival, Castleisland, *www.corkkerry.ie*

December
Wren Boys' Festival, Dingle and Listowel, *www.corkkerry.ie*. Parades, music and fireworks in an ancient tradition, 26th.

great centres of learning. The monks learnt the art of writing and recorded the sagas and legends. Many of these centres were in inhospitable locations – the 'dysart' of some place names. In Kerry there is the wonderfully preserved 7th-century foundation on Skellig Michael.

In the upheavals and faction-fighting of the 11th and 12th centuries, three ruling families emerged in Kerry as definite clans: the MacCarthys to the south of Killarney; the O'Donoghues around Killarney; and the O'Sullivans around the Kenmare rivers. These are names that crop up again and again in Kerry's history, right up to today. In the 13th century, with the arrival of the Anglo-Normans, the Fitzgeralds and other closely related fighting men established strongholds throughout the region. They became the Palatine earls of Desmond (*Deas Mumhan*, West Munster) and brought with them many tenants and fighting men who introduced the common Kerry names of Walsh, Browne, Chute, Landers, Ashe and Ferriter. The earls of Desmond became so powerful that they were able to maintain an independence from the centralizing efforts of the English monarchs right up until the reign of Elizabeth I. They adopted many of the old Irish traditions, language, laws and dress; and poetry and music flourished under their patronage. The last earl took part in a rebellion against Elizabeth and lost his lands and his life, and even in this remote part the Gaelic way of life began to disappear.

Another branch of the Fitzgeralds who crop up again and again in Irish history were the earls of Kildare, eventually the dukes of Leinster. The son of the first duke, Lord Edward Fitzgerald, was a United Irishman and was highly involved in the plans for the Rising of 1798, though he died in prison, after the organization was infiltrated by informers. The county was reorganized in 1606 into the shape we know today, and the new landowners were largely English Protestants. The political destruction of the 17th century is wonderfully recorded in the laments and satires of the poets of Munster. The following short verse written by David O'Bruadair (c. 1625–98) sums up what the poets felt:

Sad for those without sweet Anglo-Saxon
Now that Ormonde has come to Erin
For the rest of my life in the land of Conn
I'll do better with English than a poem.
Version by John Montague

Kerry produced perhaps the greatest Irish leader there has ever been in the shape of Daniel O'Connell, who in 1829 won Catholic emancipation, not only for the Irish, but for all Catholics under British rule. He came from an old Gaelic family who had managed to hold on to their lands and get along with their Protestant neighbours.

The famine of 1847 and the emigration that followed reduced the population of Kerry as it did all over Ireland. Nowadays Kerry is a land of small farmers and relies on the tourist industry. Other industries include food processing, the manufacture of animal feed, pharmaceutical and small-engine manufacturing, dairying and automotive manufacture. The population of County Kerry is approximately 132,500, although this swells considerably during the tourist season.

The Northern Beara Peninsula, Kenmare and Killarney

The route into County Kerry via County Cork is spectacular. However, instead of going straight to the large town of Killarney, you might start by exploring Kerry's portion of the quiet Beara Peninsula. Around **Lauragh** and the **Cloonee Loughs**, the waterfalls and lakes are lovely and relatively free of tourists. An unmarked road off the R571 will take you up to a wonderful view over the Beara Peninsula, the Cloonee Loughs and Inchiquin Lough. Across the lough is **Uragh** (or Lauragh) **Wood**, a survivor of the primeval oak woods that once covered most of Ireland. Uragh is a mixture of native oak and sessile oaks that are distinguished by their curious hunched branches.

There is a beautifully planted garden at **Derreen Gardens** (*open 10–6 Apr–Oct Fri–Sun, Aug daily; adm; t (064) 83588*), near Lauragh on the R571, where the moist climate gives the plants a tropical vigour. As you walk through the winding paths and tunnels of deep shade cast by the delicate bamboo, blue eucalyptus and tousled rhododendrons, there are glorious glimpses of sea and wild mountain country. Stately North American conifers and New Zealand tree ferns also decorate the garden. The land, and thousands of acres around it, used to belong to Sir William Petty, who was responsible for the mapping of two-thirds of Ireland after the Cromwellian Conquest. He is blamed for denuding many of the oak woods over a large area, especially around Caragh, as fuel for his ironworks, although his descendants (who were further ennobled with the marquisate of Lansdowne) planted the gardens and woods you see today, and also laid out Kenmare.

Leave yourself at least a couple of hours to wander around **Kenmare** (*Neidín*), a pretty, colourful 19th-century market town at the head of the River Kenmare's broad estuary. The town is full of excellent cafés, pubs, restaurants and shops. The colours of woven rugs, jerseys and tweeds on sale here echo the beautiful surrounding countryside perfectly. Fine silver jewellery and good-quality ceramics by local artists are to be found in the many craft shops, and there is a wide range of books of local interest to enhance your background knowledge.

It is worth seeking out the Neolithic **stone circle**, reputedly the biggest in south-west Ireland, along the banks of the River Finnihy. To get there, walk up the road to the right of the Market House (home to the tourist office); the stone circle is signposted, and you'll see it on the right overlooking the river.

Back on the town square and above the tourist office is the **Heritage Centre** (*open Easter–Sept Mon–Sat 10–6, July and Aug Sun 11–5*), where an exhibition explores the career of Sir William Petty and the history of the area. Another attraction of note is the **Kenmare Lace Centre** (*open Mon–Sat 10–5.30; adm; t (064) 41491*), also on the square, where you can look at a display of the point lace made locally, and even see demonstrations. The shop sells some wonderful examples of delicate Irish laceware.

This is marvellous walking country, and you can base yourself in Kenmare to savour the views of the rolling Kerry Hills, the Macgillycuddy's Reeks and the Caha Mountains on the Cork border. It's an ideal location because two of Ireland's long-distance walking routes, the Kerry Way and the Beara Way, converge in the town. In May, Kenmare is busy with keen walkers taking part in the **Walking Festival** (*see* p.142). This also links to the West Cork Walking Festival (see p.177), which takes place in different locations in West Cork each year.

Tourist Information

Kenmare: Kenmare Heritage Centre, **t** (064) 41233, *www.corkkerry.ie. Open June–Sept.*

Shopping

Art and Crafts

Anam Cré, Rusheens, Ballygriffin, Kenmare, **t** (064) 41849, *www.kenmare-pottery.com.* Beautiful hand-made ceramics and crafts.

Avoca, Moll's Gap, *www.avoca.ie.* Woven fabrics and knitwear in a selection of beautiful colours.

Black Abbey Crafts, 28 Main St, Kenmare, **t** (064) 42115. A place selling unusual, tasteful handcrafts.

Cleo's, 2 Shelbourne St, Kenmare, **t** (064) 41410. Top-quality, modern tweeds, linen and rugs.

De Barra, Main St, Kenmare. A silversmith producing unique Celtic jewellery.

Kenmare Lace Centre, The Square, Kenmare, **t** (064) 41491. Locally made lace.

Michael J Quill Centre, **t** (064) 85511, Kilgarvan. A charity-run centre selling hand-made crafts.

Nostalgia, 27 Henry St, Kenmare, **t** (064) 41389. New and antique linen and lace.

Quill's, Kenmare **t** (064) 41078. Aran sweaters, golfing gear, shoes and gifts.

Books

Noel and Holland Books, 3 Bridge St, Kenmare, **t** (064) 42464

Food and Drink

The Pantry, 30 Henry St, Kenmare, **t** (064) 42233. Organic produce, home-made bread and Capparoe goat's cheese for picnics.

Sports and Activities

Golf

Kenmare Golf Club, Killowen, Kenmare, **t** (064) 41291, *www.kenmaregolfclub.com*

Ring of Kerry Golf & Country Club, Templenoe, **t** (064) 42000, *www.ringofkerrygolf.com*

Ponytrekking

Dromquinna Stables, Kenmare, **t** (064) 41043

Spas

Sámas, The Park Hotel (*see* below), *www.samaskenmare.com.* A stylish, modern day spa offering facials, massage, body wraps and thermal treatments, plus an outdoor 'infinity' pool with views over Kenmare Bay.

Sheen Falls Lodge Health Spa (*see* below). Massage, body wraps, beauty treatments and fitness facilities, including a small pool.

Watersports

There is excellent deep-sea fishing in the Kenmare River Estuary. Brown trout fishing takes place on the Kenmare River.

Seafari, 3 The Pier, Kenmare, **t** (064) 42059, *www.seafariireland.com.* Guided cruises introducing local marine wildlife. Other activities include fishing expeditions, kayaking and water-skiing.

Kenmare Bay Diving Centre, Kenmare, **t** (064) 42238

Dromquinna Manor, Kenmare, **t** (064) 41657. Fishing, water-skiing, tube riding, windsurfing, canoeing and tennis.

Where to Stay

Kenmare

The Park Hotel, High St, **t** (064) 41200, *www.parkkenmare.com* (*luxury*). A château-style hotel with a deluxe spa (*see* above), and modern comforts in rooms furnished with antiques. The dining room (*see* p.146) serves an outstanding seafood-oriented menu.

Sheen Falls Lodge, **t** (064) 41600, *www.sheenfallslodge.ie* (*luxury*). A beautifully located option with sunny, low-key décor. Rooms are elegant, the **restaurant** is lavish, and there is a spa (*see* above) and a helipad.

On the main road to Cork is the village of **Kilgarvan** (*Cill Gharbháin*), just outside of which is the **Michael J. Quill Centre** (*t (064) 85511*), a training centre for people with learning difficulties, with a gift shop selling handcrafts, some made by the trainees. It also provides guided walks of the area.

Sallyport House, t (064) 42066, *www. sallyporthouse.com* (*expensive*). A spacious, modernized 1930s house in peaceful surrounds overlooking Kenmare Harbour.

Brook Lane Hotel, t (064) 42077 (*moderate*). A rather characterless if pleasant 'boutique' hotel with reasonable prices.

Dromquinna Manor, t (064) 41657 (*moderate*). A very comfortable Victorian manor with lovely views over the water, and water-skiing and horseriding nearby.

Hawthorne House, Shelbourne St, t (064) 41035 (*moderate*). A comfortable, modern house with ensuite rooms and delicious, lavish food.

Lansdowne Arms, William St, t (064) 41368 (*moderate*). A friendly, family-run hotel.

The Lodge, Kilgarvan Rd, t (064) 41512, *www. thelodgekenmare.com* (*moderate*). Ten rooms, one wheelchair-adapted, in a smart modern guesthouse opposite Kenmare Golf Club.

Muxnaw Lodge, t (064) 41252, *www. muxnawlodge.com* (*inexpensive–moderate*). An attractive 1801 house overlooking Kenmare Bay, close to town. There is an all-weather tennis court and good gardens and walks.

Shelbourne Lodge, t (064) 41013 (*inexpensive–moderate*). A Georgian farmhouse with rooms with antiques and wooden floors. Run by two of Kerry's best restaurateurs, it serves scrumptious home-made breakfasts.

Atlantic Lodge, t (064) 42666, *www. atlanticlodge-kenmare.com* (*inexpensive*). A newish, family-run hotel set in fields, 5mins' walk from the town. It has large rooms and a relaxed atmosphere.

Driftwood, Killowen, t (064) 89147, *www. driftwoodkenmare.com* (*inexpensive*). A lovely B&B with bright, airy rooms, stripped pine furniture and a log fire in the guest lounge.

Lake House, Cloonee, Tuosist, t (064) 84205 (*inexpensive*). A friendly pub and restaurant with guest accommodation, in a beautiful lakeside setting. *Closed Nov–Easter.*

Rose Cottage, t (064) 41330 (*inexpensive*). A family-run B&B in an old stone cottage in the town centre.

Eating Out

Kenmare

The Park Hotel (*see* p.145) (*luxury*). Delicious French cuisine in grand surroundings.

An Leath Phingin, 35 Main St, Kenmare, t (064) 41559 (*moderate*). Fresh pasta, *risotti*, scrumptious sauces and stone-oven pizzas prepared by a north-Italian chef.

The Boathouse Restaurant, Dromquinna Manor, The Quay, Kenmare, t (064) 41788 (*moderate*). A place for fine seafood and sweeping views down by the harbour.

Darcy's Old Bank House, Main St, Kenmare, t (064) 41589 (*moderate*). A local favourite with innovative specialities and colourful décor.

The Lime Tree, Shelbourne St, Kenmare, t (064) 41225 (*moderate*). An American-style café with plenty of atmosphere.

Packies, 35 Henry St, Kenmare, t (064) 41508 (*moderate*). Excellent but unpretentious seafood cooking made from the best ingredients. Reservations are essential.

Café Indigo, The Square, Kenmare, t (064) 42356 (*inexpensive*). A trendy daytime haunt for beautiful young locals and tourists, with an esoteric seafood menu and minimalist decoration. The pub beneath, **The Square Pint**, is good for traditional entertainment on summer evenings.

The Horseshoe Bar and Restaurant, 3 Main St, Kenmare, t (064) 41553 (*inexpensive*). A friendly, informal bistro with a charcoal grill.

The New Delight, 18 Henry St, Kenmare, t (064) 42350 (*inexpensive*). A wholesome café serving imaginative vegetarian and vegan food and organic wine.

The Purple Heather, Henry St, Kenmare, t (064) 41016 (*inexpensive*). Good lunchtime snacks, home-made soups and seafood. There is a cosy fire in the bar to relax in front of.

The Wander Inn, 2 Henry St, Kenmare, t (064) 42700 (*inexpensive*). A perfect venue for the classic combination of a plate of Irish stew, a pint of Guinness and traditional Irish music.

The family-run **Kilgarvan Motor Museum** (*open Tue–Sat 9.30–6; adm;* **t** *(064) 85346, www.kenmare.net/jjmitchell*), which is located at Slaheny, contains a passionately amassed collection of classic and vintage cars, including some examples by Rolls Royce, MG and Alvis.

The N71 leading from Kenmare to Killarney is a very twisty and very steep road, but you'll discover that the landscape is quite spectacular as you find yourself borne high aloft green fields and rock-strewn hills. On the way, outside Kenmare, you can go and take a look at **St Mary's Holy Well**, which is still much visited, since the waters are reputed to have strong healing powers. Once you have climbed to the top of the mountain and through Moll's Gap, you'll be rewarded by wonderful views of Killarney's lakes and woods.

Killarney

Killarney (*Cill Áirne*, church of the sloes) is a resort town that only began to grow up in the 1750s, when tourism in Kerry first became popular. The town itself is not the attraction, but rather the combination of lakes, woods, mountains and the stunning light and skies in the surrounding countryside, which remain beautiful and unspoiled. If you are prepared to walk in the mountains and the National Park, away from well-worn tracks, you will find that the luxuriant green of the woods, the soft air, the vivid blue of the lakes and the craggy mountains above will have the same charm for you as they have for countless travellers since the 18th century.

Killarney does have one thing to offer sightseers: the Gothic Revival **St Mary's Cathedral**, built in silvery limestone by Augustus Pugin in the 1840s. You will find it in Cathedral Place, a continuation of New Street, possibly on the site of the 'church of the sloes' from which Killarney takes its name. It is a successful building: austere and graceful, with good stained glass. The cathedral was not finished completely until 1908, partly because it served as a hospital during the famine. Pugin's fine interior plasterwork was almost completely destroyed, except in one small chapel. Killarney's fine **Franciscan Friary** (completed 1867), built by Augustus Pugin's eldest son, Edward, lies in College Street. It has a simple style with a vaulted, oak-beamed ceiling and a Flemish-style altar (1871) by a Belgian, J. Janssen. Look out for the vivid south window from the studio of Harry Clarke (1930). Facing the church is the **Sky Woman** monument (1940) to four great Kerry poets: Pierce Ferriter, Geoffrey O'Donoghue, Aodhagán O'Rahilly and Owen Roe O'Sullivan, who lived in the 17th and 18th centuries. (It is worth reading their poetry; the translated versions are excellent.)

It is fun to wander down some of the old lanes branching off the main street that survive from Killarney's Victorian era. There are plenty of shops, pubs and restaurants, but avoid staying in the centre, as it gets quite crowded. Expect to be approached by the **jarveys**, who gather with their ponies and traps on the street corner as you enter town on the N71; they will guide you around the valley and take you for as long or as short a trip as you want. Negotiate the price for the ride beforehand, and be prepared for a certain amount of chat; most have a host of stories about the landmarks that

Tourist Information

Killarney: *Áras Fáilte*, Beech Rd, t (064) 31633, *www.corkkerry.ie*

Shopping

Crafts

Brian de Staic, 18 High St, Killarney, t (064) 33822, *www.briandestaic.com*. A good place for craft jewellery.

Bricín Craft Shop & Restaurant, 26 High St, Killarney, t (064) 34902

Blarney Woollen Mills, Main St, Killarney, *www.blarney.com*

Kerry Crafted Glass, Kilcummin, t (064) 43295, *www.irishkerryglass.com*

Kerry Woollen Mills, Beaufort, t (064) 44122. The real thing – a woollen mill producing proper scratchy blankets. *Closed Sat and Sun Nov–Feb.*

Sports and Activities

Golf

Killarney Golf and Fishing Club, Mahony's Point, t (064) 31034, *www.killarney-golf.com*. Championship golf courses situated next to Lough Leane.

Beaufort Golf Club, Churchtown, Beaufort, t (064) 44440, *www.beaufortgolfclub.com*

Spas

Killarney Park Hotel (*see* opposite) *www.killarneyparkhotel.ie/thespa*. This spa within a luxurious hotel has 8 therapy suites, offering a range of beauty, massage and relaxation treatments, as well as a swimming pool, an outdoor hot tub and a fitness suite.

Touring Around the Gap of Dunloe

Tours in Killarney National Park and through the Gap of Dunloe on the outskirts of Killarney (*see* p.149 and p.151) can be booked in town or at the Gap. You can take a horse-drawn 'jaunting car' from Killarney or Kate Kearney's. The cost depends on the distance (€30–50). During the trip, the jarveys (drivers) will regale you with stories; they have gained a reputation for telling visitors what they expect to hear: stories of legends, leprechauns… you name it.

If the expense of a **boat trip** down the three lakes doesn't appeal, you can hire a **bike**, walk or catch a bus. There are half- or full-day **coach** trips, and **ponies** can be hired to explore the Gap (only advised for experienced riders).

Castlelough Vintage Tours, 17 High St, Killarney, t (064) 32496. A combined day tour of the area by bus, jaunting car and boat.

Lily of Killarney, 3 High St, Killarney, t (064) 31068. Covered 'water coach' tours of Lough Leane with commentary; daily departures in summer from Ross Castle 10.30–5.45.

Killarney Stables, Ballydowney, t (064) 31686, *www.horsevacationireland.com*. Pony treks around Killarney National Park.

O'Sullivan's Cycles, Bishop's Lane, New St, t 31282. Bicycle hire.

Tangney Tours, Kinvara House, Muckross Rd, t (064) 33358. Jarvey tours from Kenmare Place, opposite the International Hostel.

Walking

Killarney National Park and the country around the Macgillycuddy's Reeks has some of the best, most arduous ridge-walking country in Ireland. The **Glen of Cummeenduff** leads to the heart of the Reeks, or there's the equally desolate and stunning **Glen of Owenreagh**. The **Kerry Way** hiking trail begins in Killarney and passes Muckross Lake before climbing to some dramatic scenery around Torc Mountain

have been polished and embroidered since Killarney became a tourist destination in the 18th century. Some is tongue in cheek, as is the hoary old phrase about the constant rain: "Twasn't rain at all, but just a little perspiration from the mountains!'

Some geography of the area: the underlying rock varies from old red sandstone to limestone, while the scooping action of glaciers in the Ice Age created the precipitous mountain corries. Lower down, the indented lakes are softened by oak, holly and arbutus, interspersed with the mauve of the alien *rhododendron ponticum* in late spring.

and Windy Gap. It goes on to Kenmare and from there clean round the Iveragh Peninsula – the hiker's version of the Ring of Kerry. Take waterproof gear as the weather comes straight in off the Atlantic. Visibility is often very poor, with wreaths of mist on the hills.

Where to Stay

Killarney

Cahernane House Hotel, Muckross Rd, **t** (064) 31895, *www.cahernane.com* (*luxury*). A 19th-century residence built for the earls of Pembroke, now an elegant hotel with well-reputed dining rooms.

Killarney Park Hotel, Kenmare Place, **t** (064) 35555, *www.killarneyparkhotel.ie* (*luxury*). Glamour in the heart of Killarney – marble floors, antiques, a spa (*see* opposite) and huge suites.

Killarney Royal Hotel, College St, **t** (064) 31853, *www.killarneyroyal.ie* (*luxury*). A small boutique hotel with attentive staff and excellent dining-room and bar menus. Rooms have marble bathrooms.

Hotel Árd na Sidhe, Lough Caragh, **t** (066) 976 9105, *www.killarneyhotels.ie* (*expensive–luxury*). A beautiful 1913 manor on Lough Caragh, with antiques, chintz and fresh flowers. The dining room serves international and Irish cuisine.

Castlerosse Hotel, **t** (064) 31144, *www. castlerossehotelkillarney.com* (*expensive*). A hotel with great lake and mountain views, catering well for disabled guests. Golf packages are available, and the inviting leisure centre offers Swedish massage.

Coolclogher House, Mill Rd, **t** (064) 35996, *www.coolclogherhouse.com* (*expensive*). A Victorian house in a walled estate, with tranquil rooms and a great conservatory.

Killarney Great Southern Hotel, **t** (064) 31262, *www.gshotels.com* (*expensive*). A stylish hotel with landscaped gardens and good facilities.

Gleann Fia Country House, Deerpark, **t** (064) 35035, *www.gleannfia.com* (*moderate*). A Victorian-style guesthouse in a wooded valley.

Killeen House Hotel, Aghadoe, **t** (064) 31711, *www.killeenhousehotel.com* (*moderate*). A friendly, cosy little hotel up in the hills. The restaurant, **Rozzers**, serves very good food.

Carriglea House, Muckross Rd, **t** (064) 31116 (*inexpensive*). Comfortable rooms with ensuite bathrooms, close to Muckross House.

Crab Tree Cottage, Mangerton Rd, Muckross, **t** (064) 34193, *www.crabtreebnb.com* (*inexpensive*). A gaily decorated B&B with an attractive, plant-filled garden.

Hillcrest Farmhouse, Gearahmeen, Black Valley, **t** (064) 34702, *www.hillcrestfarmhouse.com* (*inexpensive*). A homely place in the wilds.

Eating Out

Killarney

The Strawberry Tree, 24 Plunkett St, **t** (064) 32688 (*expensive*). Imaginative Irish fare.

Blue Door Bistro, High St, **t** (064) 33755 (*moderate*). A casual space with wooden floors and simple, well-cooked dishes.

Foley's Seafood and Steak Restaurant, 23 High St, **t** (064) 31217 (*moderate*). Delicious seafood, lamb and good vegetarian dishes.

Gaby's Restaurant, 27 High St, **t** (064) 32519 (*moderate*). A Med-style café with delicious seafood. No bookings are taken so arrive early.

The Granary Restaurant and Bar, Touhills Lane, Beech Rd, **t** (064) 20075 (*inexpensive– moderate*). Hearty food and live music.

Stonechat Restaurant and Café, Flemings Lane, **t** (064) 34295 (*inexpensive*). Very good home-made soups and organic dishes.

Killarney National Park, the Gap of Dunloe and Around

The Killarney Valley runs roughly north to south through a break in the great Macgillycuddy's Reeks. **Killarney National Park** (*visitor centre at Muckross House, see p.150; t (064) 31440, http://homepage.tieircom.net/~knp*) covers a large part of the valley. It was once the Muckross Estate: its 11,000 acres, including Muckross House and Abbey, were given to the nation by Mr Bowers Bourne of California and his son-in-law, Senator Arthur Vincent, who had owned the property for 31 years.

The Reeks rise up to the west of three famous lakes. The **Upper Lake** (*An Loch Uachtarach*) is narrow, small and very impressive; it is enclosed by mountains and scattered with wooded islands, on which cedars of Lebanon stand high among the trees. A narrow passage leads into a connecting stretch of water that is called the **Long Range**, which flows under the Old Weir Bridge and rushes over some rapids, giving a frisson of fear and excitement to those taking a boat tour. The river then divides at the 'Meeting of the Waters': the left branch flows into the Lower Lake, **Lough Leane** (*Loch Léin*), and the right branch empties into Middle Lake, **Lough Muckross** (*Loch Mhucrois*). The limestone that underlies Lough Muckross has been worn away to form a series of fantastically shaped rocks and cliffs. Situated on Lough Leane's western side is **O'Sullivan's Cascade**, which, with all the blessed rain, is always a pretty sight.

Ross Castle (*open Apr daily 10–5; May and Sept daily 10–6; June–Aug daily 9–6.30; Oct Tue–Sun 10–5; guided tours only; adm adults; t (064) 35851, www.heritageireland.ie*) is situated 1½ miles (2.5km) to the southwest of Killarney, on a peninsula with pretty, wooded paths running to the edge of Lough Leane. The castle is a fine ruin dating from the 15th century, consisting of a towerhouse surrounded by a *bawn*. The castle was built by the O'Donoghues and taken by the Cromwellians; it was one of the last strongholds to fall. It has been restored and there are guided tours that provide a good deal of historical information. Evidence of copper deposits can be seen in Lough Leane's green waters here; these deposits were worked in the Bronze Age and the 18th century. On its south side is an 18th-century house built by the Brownes, who became earls of Kenmare.

From Ross Castle you can hire a boat to **Innisfallen Isle** (*book in advance during high season; a return trip costs around €5*), an isle like a country in miniature, with hills, valleys and dark woods. Holly and other evergreens grow very thickly here. Near the landing stages are the extensive ruins of **Innisfallen Abbey**, founded about AD 600 as a refuge for Christians during the Dark Ages in Europe. *The Annals of Innisfallen*, a chronicle of world and Irish history written between 950 and 1380, are now in the Bodleian Library, Oxford. The monastery lasted until the middle of the 17th century, when the Cromwellian forces held Ross Castle.

At the centre of Killarney National Park you will also find **Muckross House** (*house open daily 9–6 July and Aug, 9–5.30 Sept–June; working farms open Mar, Apr and Oct Sat, Sun and bank hols 1–6, May daily 1–6, June–Sept daily 9–7; adm to house; extra fee for farms; t (064) 31440, www.muckross-house.ie*), which was constructed in the Tudor style in 1843. On the death of the last MacCarthy (the family who were landlords of this area) in 1770, the Muckross lands passed to an Anglo-Norman family, the Herberts, who had already leased it for 200 years. This, their fourth house, was built for Henry Arthur Herbert, who hosted a visit by Queen Victoria in 1861. The main rooms are furnished in splendid Victorian style; the rest of the house has been transformed into a museum of Kerry folklore with a craft shop in its basement. You can see a potter, a weaver, a bookbinder and a blacksmith at their trades. There is a very informative film on the geology and natural beauties of the park, which is shown every half-hour. It is worth paying the extra to tour the **traditional working farms,** especially if you are accompanied by children; they are bound to love the chickens, the pigs and little black Kerry cows, which give such sweet milk. The gardens that surround the house are delightful; here you can see the native Killarney strawberry tree (*arbutus unedo*), an evergreen with creamy white flowers that are followed by strawberry-like fruit.

Close by, overlooking Lough Leane, is **Muckross Abbey**, a graceful early English ruin founded in 1448 for the Observatine Franciscans. After being dispossessed by Cromwell in 1652, the Franciscans had to go into hiding, but they returned in more tolerant times and set up a boys' school and a new church in Killarney. In fact, the abbey area is almost like a stage set for everything the tourist wishes to see, and its natural beauty is enhanced by the superb gardens and arboretum. There is a gigantic yew tree in the centre of the cloister. The walks laid out in the park lead you through a mature oak and yew wood and to the very end of the peninsula, to the cliff known as Eagle Point, named after the golden eagles that used to be seen here. The path crosses the wooded Dinis Island. You are now 2.3 miles (3.7km) from Muckross House; if you do not want to retrace your steps, join the N71 Kenmare road (about a mile or 1.6km away).

The **Gap of Dunloe** (*Bearna an Coimin*), 6 miles (9.5km) west of Killarney and about 8 miles (13km) in length, is a wild gorge bordered by the dark Macgillycuddy's Reeks, the Purple Mountain and Tomies Mountain. The **Macgillycuddy's Reeks** (*Na Cruacha Dubha*) include **Carrantuohill** (*Corrán Tuathail*), at 3,414ft (1,040m) the highest mountain in Ireland. Cars are not welcome on the dirt track until after 7pm during the tourist season, as the route is taken up with horses, cyclists and walkers. However, taking in the sights by pony and trap, also known as a jaunting car, or joining a boat trip along the lakes, is great fun (*see* p.148).

The mouth of the Gap starts at **Kate Kearney's Cottage** (*t (064) 44146, www. katekearneyscottage.com*). Kate was a local beauty renowned for her potent brew of poitín, though some say she was a witch. Today her cottage has grown to become a café, restaurant and shop. The road continues through to **Moll's Gap**, on the Kenmare road (N71). The journey through the Gap is spectacular, with steep gorges and deep glacial lakes. It can be a good idea to approach the Gap from the opposite way to the crowds, especially if you are walking or biking. Take the main Killarney–Kenmare road (N71); there is plenty to stop for en route. Notice the strawberry tree, or *arbutus*, growing among ferns and oaks, and the pink saxifrage on the wayside.

All of the following sights are well signposted.

You can stop and take an easy walk up the woodland path to the **Torc Waterfall**, found by following a rough road on the left just before a sign cautioning motorists about deer. The walk is very short, leading you through splendid fir trees to the 60ft (18m) falls. It is also possible to drive there and park.

Back on the main road, for another little detour to some falls, continue on past the Galway Bridge, where you can follow the stream up into the hills to the **Derrycunnihy Cascades**. Maybe you will come upon a few sika (Japanese deer) or native red deer. The cascades are set in primeval oak woods, and this is a rich botanical site of ferns and mosses. This area has its own Killarney fern, *trichomanus speciosum*.

Go back to the main road again (N71) and continue for 6 miles (9.5km) to **Ladies' View**, which gives you a marvellous view of the Upper Lake. Now turn off right before Moll's Gap and right again along the dirt track. You are now close to the Gap of Dunloe. A path leads you along the river to **Lord Brandon's Cottage** (*refreshments available*), where tour groups coming from the Gap join the boats back to Killarney.

To the west is a continuation of the Gap: the **Black Valley**, a wild and remote corner of Kerry. Almost the entire population died off here during the potato famine, and the place counts only a few inhabitants today.

Other Excursions

To see a fine example of **ogham stones**, take the R562 road towards Killorglin, past the Dunluce Castle Hotel. Turn right down a hill to a T-junction, then right again, and go over the bridge and up the hill. A signpost points left to a collection of ogham stones in a wired enclosure high on the bank. This is the best place in Kerry to see the weird ogham writing, which was the only form that existed in Ireland before the arrival of Christianity. The lateral strokes, incised into the stone and crossing a vertical line, give the name of a man long, long dead.

The **Dunloe Castle Hotel gardens** (*ask at hotel reception; **t** (064) 44111*) are worth a visit. It is claimed that your walk will take you around the world in a botanical sense, such is the variety of plants. The very pretty village of **Beaufort** has a good golf course.

Another fine view of the Killarney lakes and mountains can be seen from **Aghadoe Hill**, about 2½ miles (4km) west of Killarney. It is not at all touristy. In pagan times, the hill was believed to be the birthplace of all beauty, and lovers still meet here. The legend goes that whoever falls in love on Aghadoe Hill will be blessed for a lifetime. From here you can see the voluptuous pair of hills known as the **Paps of Anu** (Danu), the mother of the gods. (James Stephens is said to have remarked jokingly, 'I think those mountains ought to be taught a little modesty.') Lower down the hill are the ruins of a round tower, a castle and the remains of a 12th-century church with a Romanesque doorway. To get there from the centre of Killarney, take the Tralee road until you see a sign for Aghadoe Heights Hotel. The view opens up around the hotel. One of the youth hostels is also in this direction.

Halfway between Killarney and Killorglin are the **Kerry Woollen Mills** (*see p.148*), established in the 17th century. The mill shop sells some of what it produces.

The Ring of Kerry

The narrow Ring of Kerry is 112 miles (180km) long, and takes about three hours to drive without any detours. Starting at Kenmare (*see p.144*), you can take the N70 and follow the coiling road south round the coast, stopping to enjoy the views or going down the tiny R roads to get a better look at St Finan's Bay, Bolus Head and Doulus Head. The Ring ends at Killorglin. You can travel anticlockwise if you prefer, starting from Killarney on the Killorglin road. The views are equally good but the route gets clogged with tourist traffic in July and August – coaches usually tour this way.

The Southern Ring, to Waterville

Parknasilla is a sheltered wee place on the Kenmare River, where it widens out into a sea inlet of islands and lovely bathing places fringed by woods and flowers. The coves are favoured sunning places of the Atlantic seal. A lovely climb can be made up Knocknafreaghane (1,350ft/412m), and also the less demanding Knockanamadane Hill. **Sneem** (*An Snaidhm*) is a quiet village out of season, divided by the Sneem River. It has a good pub and was attractively laid out by an 18th-century landlord around a green, through which the river runs. On the green is a **monument** to Charles de Gaulle, who once spent two weeks here. Locals refer to it affectionately as the 'De Gallstone'. Other modern sculptures are positioned around the place, the most memorable being the modern beehive huts beside the church, which have some stained-glass panels by James Scanlon.

About 10 miles (16km) to the west of Sneem, continuing on the N70, you will come across a signpost right to **Staigue Fort**, which is isolated at the head of a desolate valley, and is between 1,500 and 2,000 years old. This circular stone fort rises out of a field (*the farmer who owns it requests a donation from those crossing his land*), and a large bank and ditch surround it. Its thick dry-stone walls are in good condition, and the place has a tremendous atmosphere of ancient strength. It was probably constructed by late Bronze Age people, but it has never been excavated or restored. Elaborate stairways lead to the defensive platform; it is fun to climb to the top, look out over the coast and wonder where it fits in among the myths and legends of these parts. Two miles (3.2km) away, at the Staigue Fort Hotel, there is a small exhibition centre about the fort. Beyond Castlecove village on the N70 is **White Strand**, which is a superb beach for bathing.

West again on the N70, a mile (1.6km) from **Caherdaniel** (*Cathair Donall*), is **Derrynane House** (*open May–Sept Mon–Sat 9–6, Sun 11–7; Apr and Oct Tue–Sun 1–5; Nov–Mar Sat and Sun 1–5; adm; t (066) 9475113, www.heritageireland.ie*), which was the home of Daniel O'Connell, 'the Great Liberator', who won Catholic emancipation in 1829. It still contains many of his possessions, including his desk, his duelling pistols and his rosary, in amongst the plain furniture that he seems to have favoured. It is beautifully kept as a museum, although part of the house had to be demolished, having got beyond repair. The mellow simplicity of what survives is very appealing, with its low ceilings and tiny Gothic-style chapel. The video of O'Connell's life is worth watching, and the historical background very interesting. O'Connell believed that 'no political change whatsoever is worth the shedding of a single drop of human blood'. The grounds have exceptionally fine coastal scenery and form part of a national park of hundreds of acres.

Derrynane Bay has one of the most glorious strands in the country, which is a wonderful place for a long walk. A shorter walk can be taken to **Abbey Island** and its ruined 10th-century abbey, along a cliff path with the rocky outline of the Skelligs framed by the sea and sky. Nearer to land are the isles of **Deenish** (*Dúinis*) and **Scariff** (*An Scairbh*). Access to the abbey is only possible at low tide. Several O'Connell graves can be seen in the graveyard.

Tourist Information

Caherciveen: RIC Barracks, t (066) 947 2589
Waterville: t (066) 947 4646.
Open June–mid-Sept.

Shopping

Crafts

Boyle's, Langford St, Killorglin, t (066) 976 1110.
A hardware shop that also sells pottery and angling gear.
Cill Rialaig **Project**, Dungeagan, Ballinskelligs, t (066) 947 9277. An art gallery that also runs drawing, ceramics and painting workshops. *Closed Oct–Mar.*
Fuchsia Cottage Pottery, Dooneen, Caherciveen, t (066) 947 3456, *http://fuchsiacottagepottery.com*. A family business selling watercolours, pottery, sculpture and gifts.
Waterville Craft Market, t (066) 947 4212

Sports and Activities

For information on **boat trips** to the **Skelligs**, *see* 'Getting to Islands off Kerry', p.141.

Fishing

There is excellent **deep-sea fishing** available on Valentia Island and **shore-angling** all round the Ring of Kerry. **Sea trout** fishing is available on the Inny River; **salmon** fishing is also very popular here. There's excellent fishing on Lough Currane, near Waterville, and **brown trout fishing** takes place on Lough Leane and Lough Avaul.
Contact one of the following:
Butler Arms Hotel, Waterville, t (066) 947 4144, *www.butlerarms.com*
Glencar Hotel, Glencar, t (066) 976 0102.
This is the place if you want to fish on the River Laune and the River Caragh.
Michael O'Sullivan, Waterville, t (066) 74255

Golf

Dooks Golf Links, Glenbeigh, t (066) 976 8205, *www.dooks.com*
Killorglin Golf Club, Stealroe, Killorglin, t (066) 976 1979, *www.killorglingolf.ie*
Waterville Golf Links, Waterville, t (066) 947 4102, *www.watervillegolflinks.ie*

Ponytrekking

Burkes Activity Centre, Faha, Rossbeigh Rd, Glenbeigh, t (066) 976 8386, *www.burkesactivitycentre.ie*. A centre right on Rossbeigh Strand, with treks across the sand.

Walking

Countryside Tours, Glencar House, Glencar, t (066) 976 0211. Walking and hiking tours.
Into The Wilderness Tours, The Climbers' Inn, Glencar, t (066) 976 0101, *www.climbersinn.com*. Walking, boating and biking tours.

Watersports

Activity Ireland, Caherdaniel, t (066) 947 5277, *www.activity-ireland.com*. Scuba diving lessons and equipment, plus sea-angling and guided hill-walking on the Kerry Way.
Ballinskelligs Watersports, t (066) 947 9182, *www.skelligsboats.com*. World-class diving off the Skellig Islands; packages available include accommodation.

Where to Stay

Caragh Lodge, Caragh Lake, t (066) 976 9115, *www.caraghlodge.com* (*luxury*). A pleasant, well-furnished country house overlooking the lake, with a fine garden. Try to get rooms in the main house, not the yard.
Parknasilla Great Southern Hotel, Parknasilla, t (064) 45122, *www.gshotels.com/parknasilla* (*luxury*). A comfortable hotel in a mansion on the banks of Kenmare River, with a garden. Ask for a room in the older part.

Waterville

A few miles further round the coast, **Waterville** (*An Coireán*) is the main resort of the Ring; palm trees and fuchsia imbue it with a Continental air, and hotels line the waterfront. Some people speak Gaelic here (the Munster variety), and Ballinskelligs Bay is a favourite place for Gaelic-speaking students. The beach here and at St Finan's Bay is very beautiful, with splendid views.

Carrig House, Caragh Lake, t (066) 976 9100, www.carrighouse.com (*expensive*). Good food and friendly accommodation in a delightful, historic country house on the shore of Caragh Lake.

Butler Arms Hotel, Waterville, t (066) 947 4144, www.butlerarms.com (*moderate–expensive*). An intimate, family-run, pleasantly old-fashioned hotel. It's a lovely place to stay if you like salmon or trout fishing.

Glanleam House, Valentia Island, t (066) 947 6176 (*moderate–expensive*). The Knight of Kerry's elegant old manor, surrounded by splendid sub-tropical gardens. Antiques adorn the interior with its slate fireplaces and grand library.

Glencar House Hotel, Glencar, t (066) 976 0102, www.glencarhouse.com (*moderate*). A remote, comfortable, clean and efficient country-house hotel in stunning surrounds.

Glendalough House, Caragh Lake, Killorglin, t (066) 976 9156, www.glendaloughhouse. com (*moderate*). A lovingly furnished house boasting great views over the lake and a wonderful hostess.

Iskeroon, Caherdaniel, t (066) 947 5119, www. iskeroon.com (*moderate*). A large bungalow in a very remote setting – you have to drive across a beach to get to it – and affording spectacular views over Derrynane Harbour. It offers great seafood, turf fires, interesting books and a semi-tropical garden leading to a private pier. Children are not allowed.

Smugglers' Inn, Cliff Rd, Waterville, t (066) 947 4330, www.welcome.to/thesmugglersinn (*moderate*). A friendly place on the beach.

Tahilla Cove, near Sneem, t (064) 45204, www.tahillacove.com (*moderate*). A 1960s flat-roofed guesthouse with a Caribbean feel on the Ring of Kerry shore.

The Climbers' Inn, Glencar, t (066) 976 0101, www.climbersinn.com (*inexpensive*). Cottage-style bedrooms and a hostel behind, plus a walking, cycling and climbing centre offering wilderness tours. It's in a wild mountain location, 30mins and a million miles from Killarney.

The Moorings Guesthouse, Portmagee, t (066) 947 7108, www.moorings.ie (*inexpensive*). Comfortable rooms in a cosy guesthouse, with views over the harbour, plus a restaurant and friendly bar (*see* below).

Mount Rivers, Carhan Rd, Caherciveen, t (066) 947 2509 (*inexpensive*). Comfortable rooms with ensuite bathrooms in a Victorian house.

Eating Out

Nick's Restaurant and Pub, Lower Bridge St, Killorglin, t (066) 976 1219 (*expensive*). A very friendly and great fun place serving large portions of seafood and steaks, and often packed with local people singing round the piano.

The Blue Bull, South Square, Sneem, t (064) 45382 (*moderate*). Good-quality seafood served in an old-style building, including delicious seafood platters.

Stone House, Sneem, t (064) 45188, www.sneem.net/stonehouse (*moderate*). Reasonable Irish food, including fresh oysters and lobsters. *Closed lunch*.

The Moorings Restaurant and **The Bridge Bar**, Portmagee, t (066) 947 7108, www. moorings.ie (*inexpensive–moderate*). Two welcoming venues in the same building, serving mouthwatering fresh seafood – simple dishes in the bar and heartier fare in the restaurant. There's an Irish Night in the bar on Tue, and set dancing and music every Fri and Sun.

The Blind Piper, Caherdaniel, t (066) 947 5126 (*inexpensive*). A lively place in a pretty hamlet, with substantial dishes.

QC's Seafood Bar Restaurant, 3 Main St, Caherciveen, t (066) 947 2244 (*inexpensive*). Good Spanish-style local meat and fish grills.

The *Cill Rialaig* **Arts Centre** (*t (066) 947 9297*) in **Ballinskelligs** (*Baile an Sceilg*) is a small gallery and tea-room in a thatched building. It's associated with an artists' retreat (*see* 'Shopping', box opposite page) in the restored pre-famine village of *Cill Rialaig* nearby, where the revered folklorist and storyteller Sean O'Connell was born in 1853. Inland is **Lough Currane** (Loch *Luioch*), popular with anglers; the mountain streams that feed it are well known for brown trout.

This area is a rich source of legend. It was near Waterville that Cesair, grand-daughter of Noah, landed with her father, two other men and 49 women. They were hoping to escape the Great Flood of the Bible story. The year, apparently, was 2958 BC. The women divided the three men amongst them, but two of them died and the third, Fintan, was so reluctant to remain with the women that he fled and later turned himself into a salmon.

The peninsula was also the landing point of another invasion; the coming of the Celts. The 12th-century manuscript *The Book of Invasions*, or *Lebor Gabala*, describes it as follows: the Milesians arrived in Spain, where they built a watchtower from which they saw Ireland, and it looked so green and beautiful that they set sail for it. Their poet, Amergin, sang a poem of mystical incantations when he first touched the Irish shore. The poem itself is rather beautiful, and this is part of what he sings:

I am the womb: of every holt,
I am the blaze: on every hill,
I am the queen: of every hive,
I am the shield: for every head,
I am the grave: of every hope.

Version by Robert Graves

The Book of Invasions states that the Celts arrived on 1 May, 1700 BC. As you enter Waterville on the N70, on the skyline to your right is an alignment of four **stones**. This is supposed to be the burial place of Scene, wife of one of the eight leaders of the Milesians. Perhaps Staigue Fort has something to do with them.

The Skellig Islands

A trip to the Skellig Islands, which takes up a whole day, is a highpoint of any visit to this part of the country. These jagged, rocky islands lie out to sea from St Finan's Bay and rise dramatically from the sea.

Little Skellig (*An Sceilg Bheag*) is home to thousands of gannets and other sea birds, and you'll see that its dark surface is splashed white – a mixture of birds and droppings. This is a nature reserve, so the boats do not land here. **Skellig Michael** (*Sceilg Mhichil*, or Great Skellig) has on it an almost perfect example of an early monastic settlement, which was in use between the 6th and 12th centuries. The Gaelic word *sceilig* means 'splinter of stone', and you can only wonder at the skill of those who cut and shaped that stone. The remains – seven beehive huts and oratories that convey something of the indefatigable striving of this community – still impress one with their simplicity

A sea cruise around the islands can be taken from Caherciveen or Dingle, or from the Skellig Heritage Centre (*see* opposite and 'Getting to Islands off Kerry', p.141). If you wish to go yourself and stop off at the island for a couple of hours, boats can be hired at several places around the coast: from Waterville, the closest point, from Portmagee and also at Caherdaniel or Derrynane Pier. (The boats only go out there between mid-March and October, and whether you get there will be determined by the weather. Take a waterproof jacket, flat shoes, a picnic and, if you are keen on birdlife, a pair of binoculars.) The trip out there can be very rough even on a fine day, and the boat will soon be riding great valleys of jade, iridescent water. It illuminates something of the hunger for solitude that those holy men felt. Shearwaters glide past; they are known locally as 'mackerel cocks' for their knowledge of where the shoals are. Kittiwakes abound, and you may get a chance to see a huge gannet bomb into the water after a fish.

You land to the noisy fury of the seabirds, and approach the monastery up a **stairway** made up of about 600 steps, 165m (540ft) long and hacked out of stone more than 1,000 years ago. It is thought that St Finan founded the monastery on this barren rock, half a mile (0.8km) long and three quarters of a mile (1.2km) wide, in the 7th century. There was little these holy men could do there except pray and meditate, fish and grow vegetables. The way of life must have been hard; sometimes the waves crashing around the rock reach enormous heights.

You can see **clochans**, **stone crosses**, the **holy well**, **cisterns** for storing rainwater, two **oratories** and **cemeteries**, and the ruins of **St Michael's Church** which, although it is of medieval origin, has not lasted as well as the cells. These are laid out close together on a small plateau and enclosed by a strong wall. The oratories and medieval church are separated from the six cells or beehive huts by the holy well. Fresh water on this desolate island is provided by the rock fissures, which hold rainwater. The Vikings raided the monastery in 812 and 823; but in 995 Olaf Trygveson, son of the King of Norway, is reputed to have been baptized here. When he became king he introduced Christianity to Scandinavia. The addition of 'Michael' to the name of the island happened sometime in the 10th century. Since St Michael is the leader of the Heavenly Host against the spirit of wickedness in high places, his name is invoked in many places throughout Europe, for instance at Mont St-Michel in Brittany.

The monastery here grew independent of the authorities in Rome, as did the clerics in Ireland as a whole. The Celtic church refused to follow a 7th-century ruling about the time of Easter, and it was not until medieval times that the Skelligs fell into line. The monastic community appears to have withdrawn from the island in the 13th century, maybe because the weather got harsher or because it was attracting too many pilgrims. It remained a place of penitential pilgrimage, especially during the 18th century. The automated **lighthouse** dates from 1865.

The **Skellig Heritage Centre** (*open daily Apr, May and Sept–Nov 10–6, June–Aug 10–7; adm; exhibition and Skellig cruise extra, t (066) 947 6306, www.skelligexperience.com*), situated on Valentia Island, beside the road bridge that links the island to Portmagee, interprets the life of the monks on Skellig Michael through film, graphics and models. It also gives information about the birdlife, the waterlife and the lighthouse service, and has books, crafts and snacks for sale. It is worth visiting for the background knowledge it gives, before you go out to see for yourself. There are environmental concerns about the number of visitors to the islands, so you may prefer simply to circle the island in one of the tour boats run by the centre.

Inside the Ring: The Iveragh Peninsula's Interior

The Ring does not venture deeply into the interior of the Iveragh Peninsula, but you could do just that by travelling to the lake area of Caragh, Glencar and Lough Cloon, which will take at least half a day. This wild, mountainous landscape was the hunting ground of the legendary giant Finn MacCool (of the Giant's Causeway in County Antrim) and it is absolutely delightful. Myriad little roads lead up to these parts. Perhaps the simplest is the lonely, unnumbered road through the **Ballaghisheen Pass** (*Bealach Oisín*), which runs between Killorglin and Waterville. It branches off the N70 just north of Waterville, by Inny Bridge. The River Caragh is famous for its early salmon, and the Macgillycuddy's Reeks cast their great height against the skyline all the way. There is an interesting walk to be had at the north end of **Lough Cloon** (*Loch Cluanach*), where up a small road to some farmhouses and then right along a track you will find an **ancient settlement** with ruined clochans and terraced fields.

Farther up in this wild country, turn right at Bealalaw Bridge and carry on until you come to a right fork over the Owenroe River, which takes you into the **Ballaghbeama Gap** and joins a larger road to Sneem. You travel along a tortuous and breathtaking channel between two mountains, Knocklomena and Knockavulloge, named in Irish after the golden gorse that grows on their slopes. Traces of the early Bronze Age Beaker People have been found here in rock carvings.

Alternatively, follow the Caragh River to Caragh Bridge and on to Killorglin. All these single track roads are lonely but so beautiful; huge boulders lie scattered like sheep on the slopes of the hills. Some were old turf tracks, or led to communities long gone since the famine times. The **Kerry Way**, a signed route for walkers, starts at Glenbeigh and follows a beautiful, desolate route through the Reeks. If you have come for the walking and climbing, note that the summits are challenging; don't attempt them without a good map and take sensible precautions (*see* also 'Walking', p.154).

The Northern Ring: Caherciveen to Killorglin

A rather theatrical **tower** guards the bridge and the inlet at **Caherciveen** (*Cathair Saidhbhín*), sometimes spelled Cahersiveen. It used to be the Royal Irish Constabulary barracks but is now a **heritage centre** (*t (066) 947 2777*). The design is grandiose Victorian and was used for many other police barracks all over the British Empire; this one was built to take police reinforcements after the 1867 Fenian Uprising and was burnt down in 1922 by anti-Treaty forces during the Civil War. Now restored through a community project, it houses exhibitions that have clearly had a lot of local input. From the barracks there is a three-mile (4.8km) floral walk along the coast to *Cuas Crom*.

Daniel O'Connell was born in Caherciveen, and the Catholic church has a dedication to him. The long main street has more pubs than you could believe possible, but not of the old-fashioned shop-cum-bar type: these are fast disappearing all over Ireland. It is often difficult to get a meal in any, especially off season. This area is marked by turf-cutting and dominated by **Knocknadobar,** the holy mountain, also known as 'the hill of wells'. From the summit at 2,267ft (690m), you get a wonderful view of the Dingle Peninsula and Blasket Islands. **St Finan's Well**, on its slopes, was reputed to cure sick cattle. People still take water from **St Fursey's**, at its foot. Once upon a time, on the last Sunday in July, a festival of dancing and singing would take place at the summit in preparation for the harvest festival, *Lughnasa*, but the custom has died out.

Valentia Island (*Dhairbhre*)

Closer to the sea, **Valentia Island** and its quiet little harbour village of **Knightstown** (*an Chois*) is a pretty place to stay. The village was named after the Knight of Kerry, an improving landlord who owned most of the island. He opened a slate quarry in 1816, and the blue-grey slates were used to roof, among other famous buildings, the British Houses of Parliament. The quarry gave work to 400 men and women, even during the famine. You can still see the old workings and spoil, though an enormous cavern has been converted into a grotto, with Our Lady of Lourdes placed high and St Bernadette gazing up at her. Another industry the knight set up was weaving; the small but excellent **Heritage Centre** (*open Apr–Oct daily, call for times, **t** (066) 947 6411; adm*) in the old schoolhouse details the natural dyes that were used, many from plants. The knight also planted a garden at **Glanleam House** (*open June–Sept daily 11–7; adm; **t** (066) 947 6176*). Tree ferns, bamboos and other subtropical species love it here, as the harbour is very sheltered by Beginish and Church Island. Himalayan poppies and candelabra primulas give intense colour in summer, and paths take you down to the sea. You can get a map from the tourist office, on the pier, with marked walks. One of the best is along the **Cliffs of Fogher**; massive slaty shelves pounded by huge waves.

You might decide to get out to the little islands in the bay. Shell middens and the remains of an ancient iron smelting industry have been found on the golden strand and dunes at the eastern end of Beginish. Deep-sea fishing and diving can be organized on the island. In Victorian times this sleepy place was right at the hub of action, for Valentia was chosen as the site for the first transatlantic cable in 1858 – after which locals could get in direct contact with New York but not with Dublin. The views across to the mainland are magnificent. A very short ferry trip links Knightstown with Reenard Point, 3 miles (4.8km) west of Caherciveen.

Onwards to Killorglin

The N70 continues around the peninsula, passing close to Knocknadobar Mountain and along **Kells Bay**, a good place to bathe. This wildly romantic landscape is peopled with heroes from Ireland's legendary past; Fionn MacCumhaill and the warrior band the Fianna hunted these glens. Close by, in the locality of Rossbeigh and **Glenbeigh** (*Gleann Beithe*), the landscape is rich in memories of Oisín, son of Fionn, who returned after his long sojourn in the Land of Youth. He came back to the desolate glens of the Ballaghisheen Pass looking for his companions in the Fianna, and from this great height surveyed the glens and mountains. He did not understand that 300 years had passed whilst he was enchanted, and that they were long dead. This area is also strongly associated with the story of Diarmuid and Gráinne (*see* p.54 and p.56), who stayed in a cave at Glenbeigh.

A fascinating visit can be made to the **Kerry Bog Village Museum** (*open Mar–Nov daily 9–6; adm; t (066) 976 9184*) just to the east of Glenbeigh, which depicts life as it was in the rural 1800s. The areas of bogland hereabouts support a wealth of plant and insect varieties; the acid-rich soil and rich, coloured mosses, including the sphagnum mosses, soak up the water and help to create the bog itself. Sundews and bog asphodel, dragonflies and butterflies flourish.

A walk may be made to **Lough Coomasaharn** and beyond. Branch off the N70, south-west of Glenbeigh, by turning left and crossing over the Beigh River, then turn right through the townland of Ballynakilly Upper. This leads you into a landscape of purple mountains and to the tarn itself, full of trout and char. A walk around the lough brings you to **Coomacarrea Mountain** (2,541ft/772m). From its summit you can see a host of mountains – peak after peak, starred with lakes and ribboned with silver rivers draining into Dingle Bay.

An easier walk on the strand of **Rossbeigh** (Rossbehy on some maps) might be appealing; the sand here often looks gold against sapphire in the glancing sun. There are other walks around **Lough Caragh** (*Loch Cárthai*), a place popular with visitors since Victorian times. It is strange to think that the bare bogland here was once covered in oak and holly trees; they were mostly destroyed by Sir William Petty, who used them as fuel for a successful ironworks he created in the 17th century. Only a fringe of trees survive around the lough now. South of the lough is **Glencar** (*Gleann Chárthaigh*), a little village, and a wild glen. The Gaelic ruling family in these parts were the MacCarthys. It was from here that the head of the clan decided to take his title when he submitted to Elizabeth I, and became the Earl of Glencar.

Back on the N70, the Ring of Kerry ends with the attractive town of **Killorglin** (*Cill Orglan*), which grew up around an Anglo-Norman castle on the River Laune. The castle is now ruined, but you can explore a similar one nearby at **Ballymalis**. This has been partly restored, and you can climb to the top of the 16th-century tower, which is great fun. Killorglin is famous for its cattle and horse fair, known as the **Puck Fair** and held in August (*see* p.103 and p.142), when vestiges of an ancient rite are enacted. A wild goat from the mountains is captured and enthroned in a cage in the centre of town. He is a symbol of the unrestricted merrymaking to follow. The event may date from the worship of the Celtic God, Lugh. The *craic* is certainly good; book well in advance if you want to stay overnight in the town at this time.

The Dingle Peninsula

This slender peninsula, the northernmost arm that Kerry stretches out into the sea, has become one of the most popular tourist destinations of the west. Dingle could be the Iveragh Peninsula in miniature, one with an equal helping of natural beauty. There is the same sort of spectacular coastal road; girdling impressive, grand, encircling mountains, and an even greater wealth of ancient remains and localities associated with Irish mythology. At the tip, instead of the Skellig Islands, there are the Blaskets. To the west of Dingle is wonderful, austere country, battered by Atlantic wind and sea.

Tourist Information

Castlegregory: Visitor Centre, Tailor's Row, Strand St, **t** (066) 713 9422

Dingle (An Daingean): t (066) 915 1188

Shopping

Crafts

Annascaul Pottery, Green St, Dingle, **t** (066) 915 7186. Pottery with sea motifs.

Brian de Staic, Green St, Dingle, *www.briandestaic.com*. A silversmith.

Dingle Craft Village, *Ceardlann na Coille*, out of Dingle towards Milltown

Irish Wild Flowers Ltd, 132 The Wood, Dingle. Wildflower seeds and gifts.

Lisbeth Mulcahy, Green St, Dingle, *www.lisbethmulcahy.com*. Designer wall hangings, scarves, table linen and throws.

Louis Mulcahy Pottery Workshop, Clogher, Dingle, *www.louismulcahy.com*. Large, distinctive pieces with a Grecian influence.

NU (Niamh Utsch) Goldsmith, Green St, Dingle, *www.nugoldsmith.com*. Contemporary designs using precious and semi-precious stones.

Penny's Pottery, Ventry, **t** (066) 915 9962. Lots of chunky lavender-blue pottery.

Food and Drink

Noreen Curran, Green St, Dingle. A place selling delicious smoked bacon and black pudding.

Ted Browne, Kilquane, Ballydavid, **t** (066) 915 5183. The place to come for wonderful smoked salmon.

Sports and Activities

Fishing

There is excellent **deep-sea fishing** off Ballydavid Head, and **shore-angling** is possible all round the Dingle Peninsula. *An Tiaracht*, Dingle, **t** (066) 915 5429. A boat sailing from Smerwick harbour, Ballydavid.

Golf

Castlegregory Golf and Fishing Club, Stradbally, **t** (066) 713 9444. A 9-hole golf course that also has a freshwater lake filled with brown trout, available to those with their own boat and equipment.

Dingle Links/*Ceann Sibeal*, Ballyferriter, **t** (066) 915 6255, *www.dinglelinks.com*

Ponytrekking

Most centres offer beach trekking and rides through woodlands and hills. *Coláiste Íde* **Stables**, *Baile an Ghoilin*, Burnham, Dingle, **t** (066) 915 9100, *www.colaiste-ide-stables.com*

Dingle Horse Riding, Ballinaboula, Dingle, **t** (066) 915 2199, *www.dinglehorseriding.com*

Longs Horse Riding, Kilcolman, Ventry, **t** (066) 915 9034, *www.longsriding.com*

This area is a government-protected **Gaeltacht**, and many local people speak Irish among themselves, though you will find that they switch to English when you are around for courtesy's sake. Signposts are in Gaelic, so it's a good idea to have a map with both the Irish and the anglicized place names on, although we have included both where possible in this section. The full name for Dingle is *Daingean Uí Chúis*, usually abbreviated to *An Daingean*.

Annascaul to Dingle Town

From the Ring of Kerry, Dingle is reached by continuing along the N70 to Castlemaine and then heading for Annascaul on the R561, which passes the vast, beautiful sandy beach at Inch (*Inse*). The most spectacular way to get to Dingle, however, is via **Camp** (*An Com*; west of Tralee on the R559) and the **Glennagalt Valley** (*Gleann na nGealt*, 'glen of the madmen'). It's fascinating to learn that lunatics used

Tours

Hidden Ireland Tours, Dingle, t (087) 221 4002, *www.hiddenirelandtours.com*. Walking tours. *Sciúird* Archaeology Tours, Dingle, t (066) 915 1606. Guided tours.

Walking Routes

The **Dingle Way** is a circular route around the Dingle Peninsula (110miles/178km). The **Pilgrims Route** goes from Dingle to Cloghane (40miles/64km). The *Ryan's Daughter* **Route** is at Dunquin.

Watersports

You can **dive** in Ventry and Dingle Bays. In the latter you can swim with a **dolphin** called Fungi (*see* p.164); walk just east of Dingle to the bay, or join a boat trip at Dingle harbour.

Good places to **swim** are Slea Head, Smerwick Strand, near Ballyferriter, and Stradbally. You can also **surf** at Inch Strand and Srudeen Strand, near Dingle, but bring your own board. **Dingle Boatmen's Association**, t (066) 915 1163 **Waterworld**, Castlegregory, t (066) 713 9292, *www.waterworld.ie*. A scuba centre, offering visits to the Blasket and Magharee islands.

Where to Stay

Dingle

Dingle Skellig Hotel, Dingle, t (066) 915 0200, *www.dingleskellig.com* (*expensive–luxury*). A family-friendly hotel with good facilities.

Dingle Benners Hotel, Dingle, t (066) 915 1638, *www.dinglebenners.com* (*expensive*). A hotel in the centre, with 52 well-appointed rooms and spectacular views.

The Captain's House, The Mall, Dingle, t (066) 915 1531, *http://homepage.eircom.net/ ~captigh* (*moderate*). A B&B with a seafaring tradition, plenty of awards adorning the walls and wonderful turf fires. A self-catering seaside bungalow is also available.

Doyle's Townhouse, John St, Dingle, t (066) 915 1174, *www.doylesofdingle.com* (*moderate*). One of the most enjoyable, comfortable places to stay in the country. Rooms are full of individuality: shelves and tables groan with interesting books that you can linger over by a warm fire. The restaurant next door is known for its conviviality and food.

Gorman's Clifftop House, *Glaise Bheag*, Ballydavid, t (066) 915 5162, *www. gormans-clifftophouse.com* (*moderate*). A breathtakingly sited choice, with rooms with waxed wooden furniture, locally made artworks and weavings, and views over the sea or mountains. Some even have Jacuzzis. Home-made bread is served for breakfast.

Aisling House, Castlegregory, t (064) 31112, *www. aislinghouse.com* (*inexpensive*). A clean and comfortable choice, with delicious breakfasts.

Emlagh Lodge, Emlagh West, Dingle, t (066) 915 1922, *www.emlaghlodge.com* (*inexpensive*). Large bright rooms in a great position overlooking Dingle Bay harbour, with wooden furniture and polished floors.

to be brought to Glennagalt for recovery, aided perhaps by the magnificent scenery between the Beenoskee Massifs. It was also once believed that many lunatics would find their own way to this place, no matter what part of Ireland they hailed from. This is the way that the old railway used to go, dropping down to Annascaul on its way over to Dingle.

Entering the peninsula from **Castlemaine** (*Caisleán na Mainge*), the coastal road (the R561) passes beneath the **Slieve Mish Mountains** (*Sliabh Mis*), where you will discover not only wild beauty but a fund of archaeological remains. The light glancing off the surface of the sea and the traditional field patterns with silvery stone walls and grey ribbed hills make this a scenic drive. Some big new houses have been built looking out to sea in recent years; this is happening all around the coastal parts. Not only are the locals better off than they have ever been, with emigration tailing off, but many newcomers are moving in, attracted by the beauty and the way of life here in the south-west.

The Phoenix, Shanahill East, Castlemaine, t (066) 976 6284, *www.thephoenixorganic. com* (*inexpensive*). A B&B in a dear little stone cottage, with organic gardens growing vegetables that go on the menu in its vegetarian restaurant. Camping is also possible here.

Self-catering

Cois Cuain, Cooleen, t (066) 915 5151, *www.coiscuain.com* (*inexpensive*). A lovely 3-bedroom house near the harbour, with wooden floors, gaily decorated rooms and a courtyard garden to the rear.

Criomhthain, Ballinknockane, Ballydavid, t (066) 718 5662 (*inexpensive*). A traditional stone cottage with 3 rooms and views over the sea or Mt Brandon.

The Old Stone House, Cliddaun, Dingle, UK t +44 (0) 1423 860246, *www.irishholidayrentals.com/ property.html?id=342* (*inexpensive*). A farmhouse cottage, with open fires and well-decorated interiors, sleeping 6.

Eating Out

Dingle

Beginish Restaurant, Green St, Dingle, t (066) 915 1588 (*expensive*). Wonderful seafood served by enthusiastic staff. There's a rear conservatory.

The Chart House, The Mall, Dingle, t (066) 915 1205 (*expensive*). Memorably good food.

Doyle's Seafood Bar and Restaurant, John St, Dingle, t (066) 915 1174 (*expensive*). A room reminiscent of an old Irish kitchen, serving deliciously prepared seafood.

Armada, Strand St, Dingle, t (066) 915 1505 (*moderate–expensive*). A traditional west coast restaurant with a good reputation.

Fenton's Restaurant, Green St, Dingle, t (066) 915 2172 (*moderate–expensive*). Locally sourced produce such as lamb from the restaurant's own farm, or fresh lobster.

Gorman's Clifftop Restaurant, *Glaise Bheag*, Ballydavid, t (066) 915 5162 (*moderate– expensive*). A welcoming place for such delights as crab claws in butter, wild Atlantic smoked salmon, and Dingle Bay prawns.

The Forge, Holy Ground, Dingle, t (066) 915 2590 (*moderate*). Steaks and seafood.

The Half-door, John St, Dingle, t (066) 915 1600 (*moderate*). Excellent, imaginative food.

An Café Liteartha, Dingle, t (066) 915 2204 (*inexpensive*). A bookshop and café serving delicious open sandwiches.

Dick Mack's Pub, Green St (*inexpensive*). The kind of rapidly disappearing place where you can buy a pint or a pair of shoes.

Lord Baker's, Main St, Dingle, t (066) 915 1277 (*inexpensive*). Good-quality bar food.

O'Riordan's, Castlegregory, t (066) 713 9379 (*inexpensive*). An atmospheric lunch spot with unusual dishes and memorable breads.

Whelans, Main St, Dingle, t (066) 915 1620 (*inexpensive*). Very good Irish stew and other traditional dishes.

The Phoenix B&B and organic restaurant (*see* above) may catch your eye as you drive along; such enterprises are indicative of the way of life many young Irish people and foreigners come here to enjoy. In the little towns you will often spot organic food shops with adverts for yoga classes in the windows, and the Saturday-morning markets selling crafts, local vegetables and cheeses go from strength to strength.

The great **Strand of Inch** (*Inse*) offers views across the bay and over the mountains. This immense sheet of sand holds the water after the tide goes out; to walk on it as it reflects the sky is a remarkable experience. Around the sadly littered entrance is a car park and café-cum-craft shop. In the pubs, after 10pm, you can listen to traditional music or singing, which only happens when the locals get together.

At **Annascaul** (*Abhainn an Scail*) you can get a drink at the **South Pole Inn** (*t (066) 915 7388*) , so-called because a former proprietor, Tom Crean, was part of that brave team with Scott in the Antarctic. **Dan Foley's Bar** (*t (066) 915 7252*) is another excellent drinking house, and Dan himself is a great source of local knowledge and folklore.

To the northeast of Annascaul, on the right summit of Caherconree Mountain, is a rare example of an inland promontory **fort**. It dates from about 500 BC and is associated with Cú Chulainn, the great Ulster hero. Notorious for his attraction to women, he rescued Bláthnait (a damsel who had been kidnapped by Cú Roí) from here and carried her off to the north of Ireland. A drive or a walk of a few miles can be made to tranquil **Annascaul Lake**; the little tarred roads to it are empty of all but a few tractors, and you scarcely pass a house.

Dingle Town (*An Daingean*, fortress – though nothing remains of one now), a big fishing port and the westernmost town in Europe, has developed in a very attractive way. The population is only about 1,500, but this can treble in summer. Gaily painted houses and busy streets lead you to the harbour, where the fishing boats move gently in the swell of the tide. The catches off this part of the coast are terrific; the boats are small and high-tech methods have not yet arrived. This adds greatly to the charm of the scene. The Roman Catholic church in the centre of the town is a calm place enlivened by narrow stained-glass windows, and is full of welcome. The cafés and bars also invite one to linger, and give the town a delightful holiday atmosphere. The choice of restaurants, pub food and traditional music is excellent; there are also several very good craft shops and bookshops to browse in. While you're here, it is worth buying a good map that shows all the ancient sites in this area.

The local celebrity and major attraction is undoubtedly **Fungi**, a playful bottle-nosed dolphin who wandered into the bay in 1983 and decided to stay. Boats in the harbour take tourists out to visit Fungi daily (*see* p.162); you can swim with him, wetsuits are for hire and there is a life-size model of him on display at the **Dingle Aquarium** (*open daily 10–6; adm; t (066) 915 2111, www.dingle-oceanworld.ie*). This is not just a tourist attraction but an informative and well-laid-out exhibition of the wonders of the deep. The highlight is a walk-through aquarium with all the stars of Kerry marine life in attendance, including small sharks.

Continuing west, **Ventry** (*Ceann Trá*) has a lonely white strand on which, it is said, the King of the Other World, Donn, landed to subjugate Ireland. He had come to help the King of France avenge his honour, as Fionn had run off with his wife and daughter. The great Fionn MacCumhaill and his Fenian knights won the day, of course (*see* **Old Gods and Heroes**, p.55). On the road to Slea Head, just off the R559 at Fahan (*Fán*) and about 3 miles (5.8km) past Ventry, there is a group of early-Christian **clochans**, 414 in all. Some were built by hermit monks, others are 19th-century. Until recently, farmers still built clochans as stables for animals, and the continuity of style with the unmortared stone is such that it is difficult to tell the old from the new.

Farther on, at **Slea Head** (*Ceann Sléibhe*), you will see an old stone and mud cottage, the **Famine Cottage** (*open Apr–Oct daily 10–6; adm; t (066) 915 6241, www.faminecottage. com*). Once the home of the Kavanagh family, who emigrated to the United States, the cottage has been re-created to look as it would have when the family lived there in the 19th to early 20th century. It's a fascinating place, and it's quite chastening to see what harsh lives such people in the west of Kerry would have lived. At the back is a clochan, latterly named *Puicín na Muice* (the pig pen); other buildings nearby were also part of the farm.

Strewn all over the slopes of **Mount Eagle** (*Sliabh an Iolair*) are 19 **souterrains**, 18 **standing stones**, two **sculptured crosses** and seven **ring forts**. The most prominent is the powerful-looking **Doonbeg Fort**, which can be seen from the road, surrounded by the sea on three sides. The fort is dated between 400 and 450 BC. It was well protected by several defensive earthen walls and an inner stone wall. Inside, local people and livestock would have gathered when under threat by rival tribal groups. There is a souterrain leading from the inside of the fort to the entrance.

The road leading from Fahan winds around the countryside from Mount Eagle to Slea Head, from where you have views of the Blasket Islands. The viewing places here allow you to stop and savour the views of traditional sheep fields, walls and dramatic headlands, dark against the ever-changing light of the seas and skies. Aerial photographs have revealed how the traditional land-holding patterns of these small farms are changing, and with them the landscape that we all cherish. Signs invite you to visit the well-known Louis Mulcahy Pottery (*see* p.161), where you can watch a pot taking shape and perhaps make a purchase from the good selection of ceramics on sale.

The Blasket Islands (*Na Bhlascaodaí*)

The Blaskets are made up of several tiny islands plus the Great Blasket, all now uninhabited. Charles Haughey, the former Taoiseach and a fellow still surrounded by seemingly eternal investigations, owns one of them (Inisvickillane) as a holiday retreat. Plans to protect the islands (involving compulsory purchase) were proposed a few years ago – although interestingly, Haughey's island was not included. Great Blasket was established as a national historic park in 1989.

Some beautiful writing has sprung from the **Great Blasket** (*An Blascaod Mór*), produced just before the island way of life collapsed in the 1940s (see *www.blasketislands.com*). The young emigrated because of the harsh living conditions, and the Great Blasket has been uninhabited since 1953. Accounts of island life left to us through the writing record the warmth and the fun, as well as the misery and heartbreak, of their hard way of life. Their acceptance of death and life has great dignity, as does their sense of comradeship with the others on the island. There are three autobiographies written in the 1920s and 1930s: *The Islandman* by Tomás O'Crohan, *Twenty Years a-Growing* by Maurice O'Sullivan, and the autobiography of Peig Sayers, often taught in schools. All are worth reading for the humour, pathos and command of the Gaelic language, which comes through even in translation.

You can visit the Blaskets from Dingle or Dunquin Harbour (*see* 'Getting to Islands off Kerry', p.141). Regular ferries take about 25 minutes from Dunquin. You might be lucky and persuade a local to take you out there in a *currach*, the boat used for centuries by the island men to catch the shining mackerel found in these waters. When you arrive, you will see that the Great Blasket is full of memories. If you have read the literature, you will recognize the White Strand where the islanders played hurling on Christmas morning. Sadly, the stone walls around the intensively farmed fields have now tumbled and the village is a ruin. Tomás O'Crohan wrote at the end of his account, 'Somewhere there should be a memorial of it all... For the like of us will never be again'. It is a pleasant walk up to the ruined hill fort, and there are wonderful views. You might also catch a glimpse of Blasket's new inhabitants – red deer, recently transplanted from Killarney.

In **Dunquin** (*Dún Chaoin*), the **Blasket Centre** (*open daily Easter–June and Sept 10–6, July and Aug 10–7; adm; t (066) 915 6444*) focuses on the story of the Blasket Islands. Unlike Horace's inn, the interior is better than the exterior; even though it looks like an oversized public convenience from the outside (its primary function for the many coach tours that find their way there), the exhibition is excellent. An unusual children's attraction in Dunquin is **The Enchanted Forest** (*t (066) 915 6234*), a fairytale museum full of fantasy, fun and friendly bears taking a journey through a mythical forest of the seasons in search of holidays. Dunquin became famous after the film *Ryan's Daughter* was filmed here, and there's a *Ryan's Daughter* walking route around Dunquin (*see* p.162), as well as mementoes from the film *Far and Away* (1991).

Ballyferriter to Tralee

Back on the mainland again, heading north up round the peninsula, you arrive at **Ballyferriter** (*Baile an Fheirtéaraigh*), a small village popular with holiday-makers because of the good beaches close by. It was named after the Anglo-Norman family of Ferriter who built the nearby ruined Castle Sybil. The most famous of that family was Pierce Ferriter, who wrote courtly love poetry; a soldier who was executed in Killarney when Cromwell and his forces rampaged through Ireland. The locals are very keen on preserving their heritage, namely the Irish Gaelic language, antiquities and beautiful scenery. Displays on the archaeology, flora and fauna of the area can be seen at Ballyferriter's **Corca Dhuibhne** **Regional Museum** (*open Apr–Oct daily 10–6; adm; t (066) 915 6333, www.corca-dhuibhne.com*).

At **Ballydavid** (*Baile na nGall*), the ancient industry of currach-making goes on. The beaches around here are magnificent, in particular **Smerwick Strand**. In any of these you might find 'Kerry diamonds' – sparkly pieces of quartz that make a more attractive souvenir than anything you could buy. Everywhere are signs of past wars and struggles. One such ruin is **Dún an Óir**, or Fort de Oro, built by Spanish forces in 1579 when they and some Irish dug themselves in during the rebellion against Elizabeth I. Lord Grey, her deputy, took the fort, and the garrison was massacred. The road that leads past Castle Sybil towards Ferriter's Cove has many potholes and is not recommended if you are in a car; it is more comfortable to stroll among the superb views of the sea cliffs and Smerwick Harbour.

East of Ballyferriter, signs point the way to the oratory of **Gallarus** (*Visitor Centre, t (066) 915 5333*), the most perfect relic of early Irish architecture, and a sight not to be missed. You approach through a fuchsia-lined path amongst the green fields. This tiny, inverted, tent-shaped church may go back as far as the 8th century; no one knows. There is more art in it than meets the eye; despite their accidental appearance, all the stones in it were carefully shaped, and they fit together so well that not a drop of rain has got in for more than 1,000 years. The only missing parts of the original building are the crosses that stood at each end of the roof ridge. A visit here, along with a look at the reconstructed plans of the monastery at Ardfert (*see* p.171), provides a vision of the remarkable aesthetic of Irish building in the early medieval golden age – round, walled settlements, round huts and towers, and strange but striking shapes. It's fascinating to speculate how Irish architecture would have evolved had the local traditions not been destroyed by the Vikings and supplanted by foreign forms under the English.

At the crossroads above Gallarus, take a sharp left for **Kilmalkedar Church** (*Cill Maolceadair*), built in Irish Romanesque style in the 12th century. There must have been an earlier pagan settlement here as there are some ancient carved stones around the site, including an ogham stone and an early sundial. Nearby, close to a ruined house for the clergy, is the Saint's Road up **Brandon Mountain** (*Cnoc Bréanainn*, 3,127ft/950m). This ancient track leads up to **St Brendan the Navigator's Shrine**. St Brendan climbed up to its summit to meditate and in a vision saw Hy-Brasil, the Island of the Blessed. Afterwards he voyaged far and wide looking for this ideal land, possibly even as far as America. People still climb up here on the last Saturday in June to pray. An easier climb can be made from the village of **Cloghane** (*An Clochán*). The views from it are magical – it's not surprising St Brendan saw Utopia from here.

The main (unnumbered) road from Dingle to Stradbally and then on to Tralee (R560) takes you over the **Connor Pass** (*An Chonair*, 1,500ft/497m) to reveal great views over Dingle Bay and Tralee Bay. There are dark loughs in the valley and giant boulders strewn everywhere. At the foot of the pass, a branch road leads off towards Cloghane and Brandon, both good bases for exploring and climbing the sea cliffs around Brandon Point and Brandon Head. **Brandon Bay** looks temptingly calm at times, but it is a dangerous anchorage. Mountains encircle it, and the road is high above the sloping fields that edge the long beach. **Tomasin's Bar** in **Stradbally** (*Sráidbhaile*) has framed newspaper cuttings that record the sinking of *The Port of Yorrock*, a barque from Glasgow returning from America that tragically went down with all hands. There is a memorial to the crew on Kilcummin Strand.

This area is well worth spending some time in if you base yourself in or near **Castlegregory** (*Caisleán Ghriaire*). You could explore the sandy spit of the peninsula that ends at Rough Point, whilst the **Magharee Islands** (*Oileán an Mhachaire*), made of limestone and sometimes called The Seven Hogs, are scattered even farther north. To the south towers **Beenoskee Mountain** (*Binn os Gaoith*) and beside it the slightly smaller Stradbally. Beenoskee summit gives you sublime views in every direction.

Surfing and swimming are excellent here, and an interesting trip can be made to **Illauntannig**, one of the Magharee islands (*see* 'Watersports', p.162). On it are the remains of an old monastic ruin surrounded by a cashel. The limestone gives the coast distinctive, rough-ridged and fluted shapes. On the spit is Lough Gill, a shallow, brackish lagoon where the Bewick's swan and other waterbirds have made their home. A variety of flowers thrive on the water's edges and in the lough itself are large yellow waterlilies. On the main road into Tralee you will pass Blennerville (*see* p.170).

Tourist Information

Tralee: Ashe Memorial Hall, t (066) 712 1288

Shopping

Antiques
Antiques & Interiors, 15 Princes St, t (066) 712 5635. A Georgian house furnished with books, prints and antiques, all of which are for sale.

Crafts
Carraig Donn Knitwear, 17 Bridge St, www.carraigdonn.com
John J Murphy Weavers, Currow Rd, Farranfore, www.killarneyweavers.com. Contemporary scarves, wraps, capes, hats, throws and more.
Úna Ní Shé, Cathair Bó Sine, Ventry, www.unanishe.com. A place where you can buy unusual felt sculptures.

Food
Sean Cara, 5 Abbey Court. A purveyor of a range of excellent cheeses, home-made breads and lemon curd.

Sports and Activities

Golf
Kerries Golf Course, The Kerries, t (066) 712 2112
Tralee Golf Club, West Barrow, Ardfert, t (066) 713 6379, www.traleegolfclub.com

Open Farms
Farmworld, Slieve, Camp, t (066) 915 8200. An 160-acre hill farm with rare breeds.

Watersports
The Aqua Dome, Ballyard, t (066) 712 8899, www.discoverkerry.com/aquadome. An indoor water themepark.
West Kerry Angling and Fenit Sea Cruise Centre, Fenit Pier, t (066) 713 6049. A centre running trips to the Magharee Islands.

Where to Stay

Tralee
Ballygarry House Hotel, Killarney Rd, t (066) 712 3322, www.ballygarryhouse.com (luxury). An elegant hotel in well-kept gardens, renowned for its food (see opposite) and service.

Tralee (Trá Lí)

Tralee, the chief town and administrative capital of County Kerry, is invariably jam-packed with cars and shoppers. It is famous for the sentimental Victorian song 'The Rose of Tralee'.

Tralee was the chief seat of the Desmond family, but nothing remains of their castle. In 1579 the Earl of Desmond was asked to aid the Commissioners of Munster against the Spanish, who had landed at Smerwick. But the Desmonds had no love for the English, and that night Elizabeth's representatives and their entourage were put to death by the Earl's brother. In the following year a ruthless campaign of retribution was waged against the Desmonds. Tralee was threatened and the Earl set the town afire rather than leave anything that might be claimed as a prize by the Queen's men. In 1583 the Earl of Desmond, then an old man, was hunted from his hiding place in Glanageenty woods and beheaded. His head was put on a spike on London Bridge, as was customary in those times. The old Dominican priory that the Desmonds founded was completely destroyed by Sir Edward Denny, the Elizabethan courtier-soldier, who was granted the town when the Desmond estates were seized.

The town has suffered continually from wars and burnings, and today is largely mid 19th century in character, although there are some elegant Georgian houses in the centre. The courthouse has a fine Ionic façade, and in Denny Street there is an

Meadowlands Hotel, Oakpark, t (066) 718 0444, *www.meadowlands-hotel.com* (*expensive*). A comfortable hotel with charming, elegant interiors. The superb restaurant, *An Pota Stóir*, offers seafood freshly caught by the hotel proprietor.

Castlemorris House, Ballymullen, t (066) 718 0060 (*moderate*). A large 18th-century house in extensive gardens, with a pleasant drawing room, spacious bedrooms, open fires and a friendly atmosphere.

Collis Sandes House, Oakpark, t (066) 712 8658, *www.colsands.com* (*moderate*). A Victorian country house hosting wonderful, traditional musical entertainment in the evenings. There are both dorms and private rooms.

The Grand Hotel, Denny St, t (066) 712 2877, *www.grandhoteltralee.com* (*moderate*). A plush, comfortable option, though it's more 'smart' than 'grand'.

Tralee Townhouse, High St, t (066) 718 1111, *www.traleetownhouse.com* (*inexpensive–moderate*). A convenient spot with plain rooms.

Finnegan's Hostel, 17 Denny St, t (066) 712 7610, *www.finneganshostel.com* (*inexpensive*). An 18th-century townhouse B&B.

The Willows, 5 Clonmore Terrace, t (066) 712 3779, *www.thewillowsbnb.com* (*inexpensive*). A B&B in a pretty terrace.

Eating Out

Tralee

Brooks Restaurant, Ballygarry House Hotel (*see* opposite) (*expensive*). A hotel restaurant offering a gourmet menu with a great choice of chargrilled meats or seafood, including yellowfin tuna and Atlantic oysters.

Restaurant David Norris, Ivy House, Ivy Terrace, t (066) 712 9292 (*expensive*). Creative global cuisine, organic where possible.

The Tankard, Kilfenora, t (066) 713 6164 (*moderate*). A cheerful pub and restaurant with great views over Tralee Bay, extremely popular with locals for its beef and seafood.

Nightlife and Entertainment

Duchas House, Edward St, Tralee, t (066) 712 4803. Irish music, song and dance, July/Aug.

impressive 1798 memorial of a single man armed with a pike. In Ashe Street the Dominican **Church of the Holy Cross** is by Pugin, built after the monks had managed to re-establish themselves here, long after Sir Edward Denny destroyed their priory. The priory garden contains some ancient carved stones, amongst them the White Knight stone and the Roche slab that date from 1685, proof that the foundation was at least partly in existence in the reign of James II. The interior is very fine, especially the Chapel of the Blessed Virgin, with exquisite mosaics and altar charts by that great artist Michael Healy, who worked at the turn of the 20th century. In Abbey Street there is a modern **church** with a lovely chapel dedicated to the Blessed Virgin Mary, which contains some fine stained-glass work, also by Healy.

The **Ashe Memorial Hall**, an imposing 19th-century building off Denny Street, houses the very fine **Kerry County Museum** (*open Jan–Mar Tue–Fri 10–4.30, Apr–May Tue–Sat 9.30–5.30, June–Aug daily 9.30–5.30, Sept–Dec Tue–Sat 9.30–5; adm; t (066) 712 7777*). The display, entitled 'Kerry, The Kingdom', traces the history of Kerry from 5000 BC and the exhibits include archaeological treasures found in Kerry. There is some fascinating film footage taken during the War of Independence and after up to 1965. Thomas Ashe, for whom this building is named, was a native of Tralee and was active in the 1916 Uprising and the IRB. He was arrested and imprisoned in Mountjoy Prison, where he went on hunger strike in protest at being treated like an ordinary convict and not as a political prisoner. After he was force-fed roughly, fluid got into his windpipe and then his lungs, and he died a few hours later. He was a close friend and ally of Michael Collins, who described him as 'A man of no complexes. Doing whatever he did for Ireland and always in a quiet way'. Another attraction in the museum is a life-size reconstruction of a street in medieval Tralee – you travel through it in a 'time car', seeing and smelling what street life was like in the walled Desmond town, so different from the Tralee of today with its supermarket, multi-screen cinema complex and aqua-dome fun centre. The town park surrounding the museum and tourist office is well maintained with pretty trees and, of course, there is a rose garden, which blooms at its best during the Rose of Tralee Festival.

Past the rose garden is the headquarters of **Siamsa Tíre** (*t (066) 712 3055, www. siamsatire.com*), the National Folk Theatre, which presents performances of song, dance and mime in an idealized version of rural life. Those with children can carry on around the corner to Godfrey Place and the **Science Works** (*t (066) 712 9855*), an interactive science museum.

The **Tralee Steam Train** (*runs May–Oct, on the hour 11–5; t (066) 712 1064*), a relic of the old Tralee and Dingle narrow-gauge railway, leaves from Ballyard station. The two-mile (3.2km) jaunt takes you to **Blennerville Windmill** (*open Apr–Oct daily 10–6; adm; t (066) 712 1064*), the largest in the British Isles (1780), complete with restaurant and craft shops. Here there is access to the **Irish Famine Ship Records** (*on a trial basis at the time of writing; small charge*) – a database of 19th-century emigrants who travelled to the USA before and during the Great Famine.

Blennerville used to be the port for Tralee, though it is now silted up. The shipyard includes a **visitor's centre** (*open daily 9–6; adm*), with exhibits on traditional shipbuilding and the emigrant experience. Blennerville was the initial site for the reconstruction of the *Jeanie Johnston*, a replica 18th-century sailing ship built from original plans. *Jeanie* was a passenger ship that carried emigrants to America in the years of the famine. The vessel was completed in 2002 and the project team and crew successfully re-created the voyage to the USA and Canada in 2003.

It is interesting to look at the intricate family tree of the Blennerhassetts, a family who ruled over these parts in the 18th century and renamed the place in their honour. One of them tried to abolish Puck Fair in Killorglin, but locals refused to comply. One of their old homes is at Ballyseedy Castle (now a hotel). To the north of Tralee near Castleisland is **Crag Cave** (*signposted off N21 Limerick–Tralee road; open daily mid-Mar–June and Sept–Nov 10–5.30, July and Aug 10–6; adm; t (066) 714 1244; www.cragcave.com*), an underground cave system at least two and a half miles (4km) long, discovered in 1983 and now a big tourist attraction.

North Kerry

North Kerry has none of the splendour of Dingle, but it does boast rather a quiet charm, a taste of which you will get if you drive between Tralee and Tarbert on your way over to County Clare. Places worthy of a visit in north Kerry include the village of **Spa**, which was once famous for its sulphur waters, and **Fenit**, a small fishing port,

Tourist Information

Listowel: St John's Church, t (068) 22590.
Open Apr–Sept.

Shopping

Art and Crafts

Blue Umbrella Gallery, 21 Church St, Listowel, t
087 611 0499. A local arts/crafts cooperative.

Sports and Activities

Fishing

John Deady, Fenit, t (066) 713 6118.
The *Kerry Colleen* running from Fenit.
Keltoi Lodge, Ballybunion, t (068) 25222, *www.
deepseacharters.ie*. Sea angling from Tarbert.

Golf

Listowel Golf Club, Feale View, Listowel,
t (068) 21592. A 9-hole course.
Old Course and **Cashen Course**, Ballybunion,
t (068) 27146, *www.ballybuniongolfclub.ie*

Open Farms

Beal Lodge Dairy Farm, Asdee, Listowel, t (068)
41137. Watch farmhouse cheese being made.

Ponytrekking

Curragh Cottage, Spa, Tralee, t (066) 713 6320

Seaweed Baths

Collins Family, North Beach, Ballybunion,
t (068) 27469. *Open June–early Oct.*
Daly's Baths, Ladies' Strand, Ballybunion,
t (068) 27559. *Open June–end Sept.*

Where to Stay and Eat

Barrow Country House, near Ardfert, t (066)
713 6437, *www.barrowhouse.com* (*moderate*).
A beautiful 1723 house, once home to the
knights of Kerry, located right on Barrow
harbour. Rooms are large and luxuriously
appointed; some suites have a Jacuzzi.
Burntwood House, Listowel, t (068) 21516,
burntwoodhouse@hotmail.com (*moderate*).
A Georgian house attached to a dairy farm
on the Ballylongford road, offering B&B.
Listowel Arms Hotel, The Square, Listowel,
t (068) 21500, *www.listowelarms.com*
(*moderate*). An old-fashioned country hotel
with elegant interiors. The dining room
(*expensive*) serves very good fresh local
produce amidst restrained classical décor.
Mount Rivers, Listowel, t (068) 21494,
www.mountriverslistowel.com (*moderate*).
A comfortable 19th-century family home
just outside Listowel (off the R555), with a
family suite and 2 double rooms.
White Sands Hotel, Ballyheigue, t (066) 713
3102, *www.cmvhotels.com* (*moderate*).
A hotel surrounded by wonderful beaches.
Its **Jimmy Browne's Pub** hosts regular
traditional music sessions.
Listowel has a few award-winning restaurants
and is a good place to find gourmet food.
The Oyster Tavern, The Spa, Fenit, t (066) 713
6102 (*expensive*). Award-winning seafood,
game and steaks (as well as vegetarian
meals) in a beautiful setting.
Allos Bistro, 41 Church St, Listowel,
t (068) 22880 (*moderate*). Great European
food served in a casual ambiance.
The Literary Café, *Seanchaí* Centre, The Square,
Listowel, t (068) 22212. Good café food.

from where the coastal views on a bright day are stunning. On a fine day, the
fishing trips and the barbecues that are held on the Magharee Islands in Tralee Bay
(*see* p.167) are bracing.

A very well-known ecclesiastical site built on St Brendan's original foundation is
Ardfert Cathedral on the R551, a noble Norman building dating from the 13th century
and partially restored (*open May–Sept daily 9.30–6.30; guided tours; adm; www.
heritageireland.ie*). Exhibits inside detail Ardfert's history as a monastic centre from
the earliest times. The great nave remains without a roof, and the authorities have
had to put up a sign to forbid locals from making any new burials inside. Besides the
cathedral, the grounds contain a picturesque graveyard with those vault-like graves

that are common here, and the remains of the early Romanesque church that the cathedral replaced, which has a beautiful carved south window. Beside it is *Temple na Griffin*, a late Gothic ruin. Ardfert was an important settlement in the early Middle Ages, and probably long before then. The surrounding countryside is full of ring forts and other ancient relics, along with an austerely handsome 15th-century **Franciscan friary and church** just down the road from the cathedral.

Banna, about 6 miles (9.6km) north-west of Ardfert, is a place of dunes, caravans and a beach that is at least 6 miles (9.6km) long. **Ballyheige** is a small village on a continuation of Banna Strand; the white sand and views of Kerry Head make it popular with holiday-makers. Inland, signposted after the village of Ballyduff, is **Rattoo Round Tower** and ruined priory, rising from among the flat fields. The tower is one of the most perfect examples of its kind and is in good condition. The graveyard has the usual mixture of old and new gravestones and is overgrown with delicate ivy and hart's-tongue fern. **Rattoo Heritage Complex** (*t (066) 713 1000; adm*) has a display on the local archaeology, history and folklore of north Kerry.

On the main road between Tralee and Listowel at Kilflynn is A Day in The Bog (open daily 9–7; t (066) 713 2555). With a thatched roof, pets' corner, café and audio-visual show, it re-creates a farmer's life in the boglands. There's also an exhibit on the work of the North Kerry Writers. Someevenings it hosts traditional music sessions.

Listowel has ambitions as a cultural centre and puts on a Writers' Week every spring, with a book fair, art and photography exhibitions and writing workshops. This attractive town is situated on the River Feale, on the flat Kerry plain, with a ruined 15th-century castle in the square. It belonged to the Fitzmaurice family, Anglo-Normans who later showed consistent disloyalty to the Crown. Also in the square is a handsome Catholic church, and on the outskirts of town is a racecourse.

Many writers came from this area. Of particular note are Bryan MacMahon, whose novel *Children of the Rainbow* is entrancing, with its descriptions of the Kerry countryside, and prolific novelist and playwright John B. Keane, whose pub is on William Street. His novel *The Field* became an Oscar-winning film. Listowel has some remarkable plaster shopfronts by Pat McAuliffe (1846–1921), **The Maid of Erin** on Church Street being the most rococo. **St John's Theatre and Arts Centre** (*open daily 9.30–6; t (068) 22566*), on the square in the late Georgian Church of Ireland church, has a weekly programme of theatre, music, dance and exhibitions and occasional evening shows.

On the coast, some 10 miles (16km) northwest of Listowel on the R553, is the delightful and popular resort of **Ballybunion**. The golden sand is divided by a black rocky promontory, upon which perch dramatically the remains of a 14th-century castle. Besides good sea bathing, you can have a relaxing hot **seaweed bath** (*see* p.171), which leaves your skin feeling like silk and seems to take away any aches and pains. It is very popular with jockeys after the Listowel races. The seaweed is hand-picked from the Blackrocks every day.

The views of Kerry Head and Loop Head in County Clare are magnificent from Ballybunion, and there are long, bracing walks along the cliffs to **Beal Point**, which overlooks the Shannon Estuary. See if you can persuade a boatman to take you out to the intricate and connecting caves within the cliffs; the largest is known as the Pigeon

Cave. Most people come here for the beach and the golf, and B&Bs line the road towards the golf course. Slap bang next to the smart-looking clubhouse is the parish burial ground, among the dunes and cropped grass. It's an odd sight, especially when funeral mourners meet golfers. **Ballybunion Heritage Museum** *(adm; t (088) 654127)*, on Church Road, has some interesting relics of the Marconi Station and the Lartigue monorail system, which between 1888 and 1924 ran to Listowel.

Carrigafoyle Castle, north of Ballylongford, is a 16th-century O'Connor castle that stands by the shoreline; it was built of carboniferous sandstone and has weathered well. It's always accessible, and you can walk to the battlements by a winding raised stone path (this may be submerged during spring tides) to get a stunning view. Rather than take the main road to Ballylongford, you could go on the winding (unnumbered) coastal road, bordered by quiet farms and the lapping sea, where waders pick their way across the shore. This will take you eventually to Carrigafoyle.

If you are taking the car ferry across to County Clare from **Tarbert** *(see p.239)*, you can stop to see the **Bridewell Courthouse and Jail** *(open Apr–Oct daily 10–6; adm; t (068) 36500)*. The buildings have been restored with tableaux, exhibits and documents to show what justice and prison were like for local people in Victorian times when the British still ruled. Especially interesting are the accounts of life on transportation ships going to Australia, and the verse of the neglected poet Thomas MacGreevy (1894–1967), who came from around here.

A short, signposted walk leads from the courthouse through mature mixed woods, part of the demesne of **Tarbert House** *(open May–Aug Mon–Sat 10–12 noon and 2–4, Sun 10–12 noon; adm; t (068) 36198)*, a fine, grey Georgian Queen Anne house that has been the residence of the Leslie family since it was completed in 1730. Many of the paintings and pieces of furniture inside date from the 18th century. Visitors to the house included Benjamin Franklin, Jonathan Swift, Dan O'Connell, Lord Kitchener and Winston Churchill.

County Cork

Imagine quiet flowing rivers in green wooded valleys, a coastline that combines savage rock scenery with the softest bays, hill slopes that are purple with heather in the late summer, and an ivy-clad castle standing amongst hayricks in a field, and you have captured something of County Cork. This is Ireland's largest county, and it includes some of the richest agricultural land (in the north-east), the third largest city in Ireland and the important ocean port of Cobh, as well as the most beautiful coastal and mountain scenery in the country and a famously mild climate because of the warm Gulf Stream. It is also the most suitable spot to indulge in the relaxing pastimes of eating and drinking: you'll find some of Ireland's best hotels and restaurants located in attractive settings all over the county. There is wonderful sailing, deep-sea angling, and salmon- and trout-fishing amongst its 680 miles (1,088km) of indented coastline, with beautiful stately homes and gardens to visit, and, of course, the Blarney Stone to kiss. The growth of tourism has not yet spoilt the

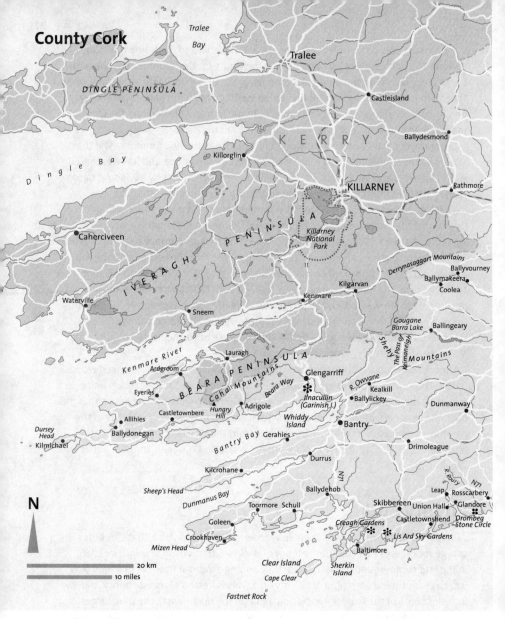

County Cork

Tralee Bay

Tralee

DINGLE PENINSULA

Castleisland

Ballydesmond

Dingle Bay

Killorglin

KERRY

Rathmore

KILLARNEY

Caherciveen

Killarney National Park

Derrynasaggart Mountains

Ballyvourney

Ballymakeera

Coolea

IVERAGH PENINSULA

Kilgarvan

Kenmare

Gougane Barra Lake

Ballingeary

Waterville

Sneem

Kenmare River

Lauragh

Ardgroom

BEARA PENINSULA

Caha Mountains

Glengarriff

Beara Way

The Pass of Keimaneigh

Mountains

Eyeries

Ilnacullin (Garinish I.)

R. Owvane

Kealkill

Ballylickey

Dunmanway

Allihies

Castletownbere

Hungry Hill

Adrigole

Whiddy Island

Bantry

Dursey Head

Ballydonegan

Gerahies

Bantry Bay

Drimoleague

Kilmichael

Durrus

Kilcrohane

R. Roury

N71

Sheep's Head

Dunmanus Bay

Ballydehob

Leap

Rosscarbery

Glandore

Toormore

Schull

Skibbereen

Union Hall

Castletownshend

Drombeg Stone Circle

N

Goleen

Creagh Gardens

Lis Ard Sky Gardens

Crookhaven

Mizen Head

Baltimore

20 km

10 miles

Clear Island

Sherkin Island

Cape Clear

Fastnet Rock

coast, but it has encouraged better restaurants, hotels, pubs and shops. Many of the most discerning visitors are the Corkonians themselves, who work hard in the city and enjoy their free time in pretty coastal resorts such as Kinsale and Crosshaven.

The city is something else: country people may be more laidback, but city folk have produced a cosmopolitan centre humming with energy and confidence, full of grand buildings and shops, industry and culture, aided by a wit and business sense that is hard to beat. Dubliners alternate between jealousy and heavy sarcasm in trying to describe the place – the best I've heard is, 'God's own place with the devil's own

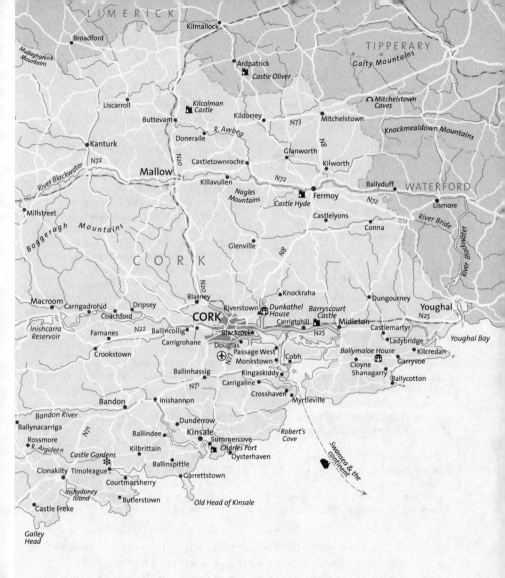

people'. Corkonians think nothing of nipping across to Paris for the weekend, and there is an air of sophistication here that seriously challenges Dublin as the cultural capital. The Triskel Arts Centre in the city centre is excellent and puts on a great variety of events all year, while the Crawford Art Gallery has a memorable collection of Irish and English works.

Corkonians are a mixed bunch, consisting of the down-to-earth working class and the moneyed middle class – which includes a rather genteel Protestant element whose forebears manned the British Empire – as well as quite a few 'blow-ins':

Getting There

A wide selection of airlines flies to Cork from various UK cities; *see* **Travel** pp.88–90. You can also get to Cork by **ferry**: Fishguard–Rosslare, or Swansea–Cork; *see* **Travel** pp.90–91.

From the Airport

Cork Airport is south of the city on the N27; there is a regular **shuttle service** from the airport to the bus station on Parnell Place, which takes 20mins and costs €4. A **taxi** to Cork City centre costs approximately €15. **Cork Airport**, **t** (021) 431 3131, *www.cork-airport.com*

Getting Around

Trains include a suburban service to Fota and Cobh. For enquiries call **t** (021) 450 6766, or see *www.irishrail.ie*. **Kent Station** is a 5min walk northeast of the city centre on Lower Glanmire Rd. The **bus station** is central, in Parnell Place, with city and rural services. City-centre fares are a flat rate; a day pass costs about €6. Call **t** (021) 450 8188 or use the travel planner on *www.buseireann.ie*. A central **taxi rank** can be found in the middle of St Patrick's St; **Cork Taxi Coop, t** (021) 427 2222.

Car Hire

Alamo/National, t (021) 432 0755, *www.carhire.ie*
Thrifty, t (021) 434 8488, *www.thrifty.ie*
Murrays, t (021) 491 7300

Bike Hire

Irish Cycle Hire, Cork rail station, **t** (021) 455 1430
Rothar Cycle Tours, 55 Barrack St, **t** (021) 431 3133

Getting to Islands off County Cork

Sherkin Island: from Baltimore, 8 daily sailings in summer (about 10mins, €5); **t** (028) 20125, *www.baltimore-ireland.com*
Cape Clear Island: there are 2 ferries, one from Schull and one from Baltimore (both 45mins). The **Baltimore** *Naomh Ciarán II* runs at least once daily, **t** 086 346 5110, *www.capeclearferry.info*; the **Schull** *Karycraft* sails daily June–Sept (and May if sufficient demand), **t** (028) 28138, *www.westcorkcoastalcruises.com*
Ilnacullin: the Glengarriff passenger ferry *Harbour Queen*, Mar–Oct daily every 20mins; **t** (027) 63116, *www.garnishislandferry.com*
Bere Island: 2 ferries operate services to Bere; **Bere Island Ferries** sail the *Misneach* or *Morvern* from Castletownbere, **t** (027) 75009, *www.bereislandferries.com*; **Murphy's Ferries** sail daily from a pontoon 2 miles (3km) east of Castletownbere, **t** (027) 75014, *www.murphysferry.com*
Whiddy Island: off Bantry in Bantry Bay, **t** (027) 50310.
Heir Island: from Cunamore Pier, off Bantry Rd, Skibbereen, or from Baltimore. Contact **Danny Murphy, t** 086 888 7799, or **Richard Pyburn, t** 086 809 2447.
Shearwater Cruises: cruises from KYC Marina in Kinsale, **t** (023) 49610

Britons, Europeans and North Americans who have settled down to enjoy the way of life. You will notice them particularly in west Cork, where some have restored traditional cottages and farms, and produce their own vegetables, art and crafts.

The Cork accent is very strong, slow and sing-songy – you may have to concentrate to understand it.

History

The well-watered and fertile lands of Cork attracted settlement as far back as 6000 BC, when people lived by hunting, fishing and gathering roots and berries. From the megalithic period, stone circles, standing stones and wedge tombs have survived, as farmers did not touch them, believing them to be fairy places.

Festivals

Cork City expanded its events calendar after it was named European Capital of Culture in 2005. For more events info, call **t** (021) 425 5100.

March

Celtfest: Celtic art, music, dance, language and culture, held by Cork University.
St Patrick's Day Festival: in most Cork towns.

April

Cork International Choral Festival, City Hall, *www.corkchoral.ie*

May

Baltimore Wooden Boat and Seafood Festival, *www.baltimorewoodenboatfestival.com*
Bantry Mussel Fair, *www.bantrymusselfair.ie*.
Denis Murphy's Weekend: in Knocknagree.
Rosscarbery Arts & Literature Festival, *www.rosscarbery.ie/arts_and_literature*
West Cork Walking Festival, *www.westcork.ie*

June

Bandon Music Festival, *www.bandonmusicfestival.com*
Cork Midsummer Festival, *www.corkfestival.com*. Twelve days of events and performing arts.
Eurochild, *www.tighfili.com*. Children's poetry.
Innishannon Steam and Vintage Rally, *www.isvrally.com*. A bank-hol weekend event.
Murphy's Uncorked, *www.murphysuncorked.com*. Irish and UK stand-up comedians.
West Cork Garden Trail, *www.westcorkgardentrail.com*

West Cork Literary Festival, Bantry, *www.westcorkmusic.ie*

July

Bandon Summer Carnival
Cahirmee Horse Fair, Buttevant. An ancient fair.
Wild Boar Festival, Kanturk
Youghal Maritime Festival

August

Ballabuidhe **Races and Horse Fair**, Dunmanway, *www.ballabuidhe.com*. An ancient race.
Ballingeary Agricultural & Horticultural Show, Animals on show in a Gaeltacht village.
Courtmacsherry Harbour Festival: Sandcastle competitions, talent contests and races.

September

Cork Folk Festival, *www.corkfestival.com*
Frank O'Connor Festival of the Short Story, *www.munsterlit.ie*. Cork City.
International Storytelling Festival, Cape Clear Island (*http://indigo.ie/~stories*)
Midleton Food & Drink Festival, *www.irelandcork.com/midleton*
Youghal Through the Ages Heritage Week, *www.youghalchamber.ie*. Irish heritage.

October

Cape Clear Storytelling Workshop, Cape Clear Island, *http://indigo.ie/~ckstory*
Cork Film Festival, *www.corkfilmfest.org*
Cork Jazz Festival, *www.corkjazzfestival.com*
Kinsale Festival of Autumn Flavours, *www.kinsalerestaurants.com*. A festival of fine food.

Waves of invaders brought different peoples, with the Celts arriving between 800 and 500 BC. Written history dates from the coming of Christianity and later clerics recorded the sagas, annals and laws of this Celtic culture, which had been left intact on the edge of the Roman Empire. St Ciaran of Cape Clear is titled 'first-born of the Saints of Ireland'; it is claimed he arrived before St Patrick in the 5th century AD.

Early church sites abound, and the metalwork and carved stone that survive from the 11th and 12th centuries testify to the mastery and skill of the Celtic artist. With the invasion of the Anglo-Normans in 1169, the Continental religious orders were set up in rich and beautiful abbeys. Some of their ruins remain. The Norsemen or Vikings mounted many raids on the early-Christian settlements from the late 8th century onwards. They soon founded their own ports, settling down to trade with the native Irish, accepted Christianity, and so gradually became amalgamated into Gaelic society, especially in the south-east.

The Anglo-Norman invasion brought advanced building techniques to Ireland: the Norman warlords built a number of sophisticated castles, usually on defensive sites that had been used before. Their followers lived in moated farmhouses. The Gaelic ruling families – the MacCarthys, the O'Sullivans, the O'Mahonys, the O'Driscolls and the O'Donovans – generally lost out to the Norman Barrys and their followers. In the 15th century, the ruling families built towerhouses, and many of these grand ruins remain, to add drama and interest to the countryside and coastline (Blarney Castle is one of the best examples).

Comfortable domestic architecture did not develop until the 17th and 18th centuries, because until then the county was very unsettled, as the Celts and Anglo-Normans fought, made alliances with and against each other, and largely ignored the laws issued from London. It was only the area around Dublin, known as 'the Pale', that was really under the thumb of the English.

After the Elizabethan wars of the late 16th century, the land was colonized with families loyal to the Crown, who supported the administrators sent to implement English rule. Huge tracts of land were granted to adventurers; men such as Richard Boyle, who became Earl of Cork, and Sir Edmund Spenser, who wrote *The Faerie Queene* at Kilcoman Castle. Beautiful Georgian houses survive from the 18th century, especially in the richer farmlands of Cork, when the new landowners began to feel secure in their properties and to build, plant and garden. It is possible to stay in many of these fine houses, which are not huge but perfect in proportion and decoration. Nowadays, many have been bought up by the increasingly prosperous Irish and by foreign buyers. There is a new regard for the craftsmanship of the mainly Irish workers who created them, and a reassessment of the landed gentry, who were not necessarily all as bad as they have been portrayed.

By contrast, the oppressive laws introduced to control the Catholic population in the 1690s, the Rising of 1798 and the ghastly famine of the 1840s all combined to create a peasantry that was poverty-stricken. Large families relied almost totally on the potato, and the failure of the crop in successive years brought starvation, disease and death to thousands in County Cork. The fight for fair rents and fixity of tenure was pursued vigorously in the 1880s. The Irish War of Independence was fought with ferocity in County Cork, with burnings and cruelties on both sides. The Civil War split family loyalties in two, and it was especially bitter in County Cork, where anti-Treaty forces were in control. Michael Collins (1890–1922), the dynamic revolutionary leader and one of the men responsible for negotiating the Anglo-Irish Treaty of December 1921, was the son of a small farmer from Clonakilty. During the Civil War he was shot in the head by the anti-Treaty forces, in an ambush between Macroom and Bandon.

Today, the memories of the Civil War are still alive, but the people are forward-looking. Industries such as whiskey-making, brewing, clothing, food-processing, computers and pharmaceuticals have boomed around Cork Harbour. The drug Viagra, among others, is made in Ringaskiddy for Pfizer, as well as artificial hips and knees produced for Johnson & Johnson (as you can imagine, a good many jokes circulate in the local bars). A large proportion of the population, which presently stands at about 473,000, is involved in the tourist industry.

Cork City (Corcaigh)

The name Cork comes from the Gaelic *Corcaigh*, meaning 'marshy place'. Ireland's second city, with a population of 140,000, is built on marshy land on the banks of the River Lee and has crept up the hills. Over the years, nearly all the islands in this marsh have been reclaimed, their watercourses built over and the city walls removed. The river flows in two main channels, crossed by bridges, so that central Cork is actually on an island. (It can be confusing if you are driving there for the first time, with its one-way roads and the crossing and recrossing of the river.)

Until the Anglo-Norman invasion in 1169, Cork City was largely a Danish stronghold. It was famous from the 7th century for its excellent school under St Finbarr. The Cork citizens were an independent lot and, though after 1180 English laws were nominally in force, it was really the wealthy merchants who were in charge. In 1492 they took up the cause of the Yorkists and Perkin Warbeck, and went with him to Kent, where he was proclaimed Pretender to the English crown (by claiming he was Richard IV, King of England and Lord of Ireland). They lost their charter for that piece of impudence, but Cork continued to be a rebel city – although, rather curiously, it offered no resistance to Oliver Cromwell. William III laid siege to it in 1690 because it stood by James II, and it had to surrender without honour. In the 17th and 18th centuries it grew rapidly with the expansion of the butter trade, and many of the splendid Georgian buildings you can still see were built during this time. By the 19th century it had become a centre for the Fenian movement, which worked for an independent republic. During the War of Independence (1919–21), the city was badly burned by the Auxiliaries, known as 'the Black and Tans' after the colours of their uniform, and one of Cork's mayors died on hunger strike in an English prison. But Cork is also famous for a more moderate character, Father Theobald Matthew (1790–1856), who persuaded thousands of people to go off the drink, though the effect of his temperance drive was ruined by the potato famine and the general misery it brought.

Cork still has a reputation for clannish behaviour amongst its businessmen and for independence in the arts and politics, but it would be hard to find a friendlier city to wander around, and you can easily explore it on foot.

City Centre

Cork's business and shopping centre is crowded onto an island between the twin channels of the River Lee, with elegant bridges linking the north and south sides of the city. The city's elegant skyline is still, like Derry's, 19th-century. Cork has spires and gracious wide streets, and many of its fine buildings, bridges and quays are of a silvery limestone. **St Patrick's Street** curves close to the river; one side of the street is lined with old buildings, the other by uninspiring modern offices, shopfronts and an opera house built since the burning in 1920. Here you will find a statue of Father Matthew. The covered **English Market**, hidden behind the facades of St Patrick's Street, is rather like Smithfield Market in London and displays great pig carcasses and drisheen (a type of black pudding), as well as fresh fish, piles of vegetables, tasty bread and olives of every description. It also has some superb eating places.

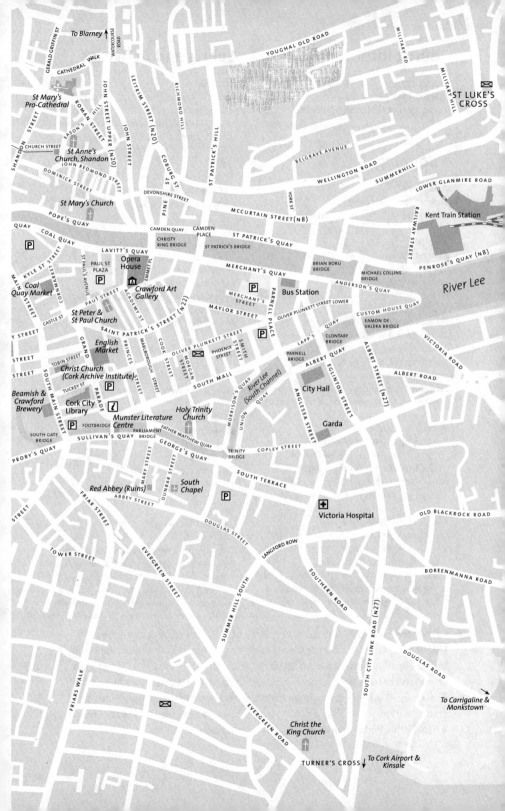

To Blarney ↑

GERALD GRIFFEN ST
WATERCOURSE ROAD

CATHEDRAL WALK

MILITARY RD

MILITARY RD

✉ ST LUKE'S CROSS
ST LUKE'S HILL

YOUGHAL OLD ROAD

St Mary's Pro-Cathedral

ROMAN STREET

JOHN STREET UPPER (N20)

JOHN STREET

LEITRIM STREET

RICHMOND HILL

ST PATRICK'S HILL

BELGRAVE AVENUE

WELLINGTON ROAD

SUMMERHILL

LOWER GLANMIRE ROAD

SHANDON STREET

EASON'S HILL

CHURCH STREET

St Anne's Church, Shandon

JOHN REDMOND STREET

JOHN STREET (N20)

COBURG ST

PINE ST

DEVONSHIRE STREET

YORK ST

RAILWAY STREET

Kent Train Station

DOMINICK STREET

St Mary's Church

POPE'S QUAY

MCCURTAIN STREET (N8)

PENROSE'S QUAY (N8)

QUAY

COAL QUAY

CAMDEN QUAY

CAMDEN PLACE

ST PATRICK'S QUAY

River Lee

P

KYLE ST QUAY

LAVITT'S QUAY

CHRISTY RING BRIDGE

ST PATRICK'S BRIDGE

MERCHANT'S QUAY

BRIAN BORU BRIDGE

MICHAEL COLLINS BRIDGE

ANDERSON'S QUAY

PAUL ST PLAZA

Opera House

EMMET PL

ST PAUL'S AVENUE

MAIN STREET

Coal Quay Market

CORNMARKET STREET

PAUL STREET

ACADEMY ST

Crawford Art Gallery

MERCHANT'S STREET

P

Bus Station

PARNELL PLACE

OLIVER PLUNKETT STREET LOWER

CUSTOM HOUSE QUAY

EAMON DE VALERA BRIDGE

CASTLE ST

St Peter & St Paul Church

SAINT PATRICK'S STREET (N22)

MAYLOR STREET

QUAY

LAPP'S QUAY

VICTORIA ROAD

Y STREET

GRAND

PRINCES STREET

MARLBOROUGH STREET

COOK STREET

OLIVER PLUNKETT STREET

P

PHOENIX STREET

SMITH STREET

CLONTARF BRIDGE

ALBERT QUAY

English Market

TOBIN STREET

MORGAN STREET

PARNELL BRIDGE

EGLINTON STREET

ALBERT STREET (N27)

ALBERT ROAD

STREET

Christ Church (Cork Archive Institute)

TUCKEY ST

P

PARADE

SOUTH MALL

MORRISON'S QUAY

River Lee (South Channel)

City Hall

ANGLESEA STREET

Beamish & Crawford Brewery

SOUTH MAIN STREET

Cork City Library

i

FOOTBRIDGE

P

Munster Literature Centre

Holy Trinity Church

FATHER MATHEW QUAY

UNION QUAY

Garda

SOUTH GATE BRIDGE

PARLIAMENT BRIDGE

SULLIVAN'S QUAY

GEORGE'S QUAY

TRINITY BRIDGE

COPLEY STREET

PROBY'S QUAY

MARY STREET

DUNBAR STREET

SOUTH TERRACE

STREET

Red Abbey (Ruins)

ABBEY STREET

South Chapel

P

OLD BLACKROCK ROAD

✚ Victoria Hospital

DOUGLAS STREET

LANGFORD ROW

SOUTHERN ROAD

BOREENMANNA ROAD

FRIAR STREET

TOWER STREET

EVERGREEN STREET

SUMMER HILLS SOUTH

SOUTH CITY LINK ROAD (N27)

DOUGLAS ROAD

To Carrigaline & Monkstown →

FRIARS WALK

✉

EVERGREEN ROAD

Christ the King Church

✝

TURNER'S CROSS ↓

To Cork Airport & Kinsale

Tourist Information

Cork City
Blarney: t (021) 438 1624
Cork City: *Áras Fáilte*, Grand Parade,
t (021) 425 5100

Shopping

Antiques
Flea market, Cornmarket St
McCurtain St. Antiques and bric-à-brac.

Books
Mercier Bookshop, 18 Academy St.
A wealth of books of Irish interest,
and novels by Irish authors.

Crafts
Blarney Castle Craft Shop, Blarney
Blarney Woollen Mills, Blarney,
www.blarney.com
Cork Crystal, Kinsale Rd, t (021) 431 3336,
www.corkcrystal.ie
Shandon Craft Centre, The Butter Exchange,
Shandon. A wide selection of quality crafts.

Food and Flowers
The English Market, between St Patrick's St,
Grand Parade and Oliver Plunkett St.
Foodstuffs from all over the world.
Natural Foods, 26 Paul St. A place worth
seeking out for its delicious bread.

Musical Instruments
Crowleys Music Centre, 29 McCurtain St,
t (021) 503426. A centre selling bodhráns
and other musical instruments.
The Living Tradition, 40 MacCurtain St, t (021)
450 2564, *www.thelivingtradition.com*.
A specialist Irish traditional music store.

Sports and Activities

Cruises
Cork Harbour Cruises, t (021) 481 1485.
Daily departures in summer, from Penrose
Quay in Cork and the main Kennedy Pier in
Cobh (adults €4, children €2.50).

Fishing
Angling Charters, Kayville, Carrigaloe, Cobh,
t (021) 481 2435, *www.anglingcharters.ie*.
Day or evening trips.

Golf
Cobh Golf Club, Ballywilliam, Cobh,
t (021) 481 2399
Cork Golf Club, Little Island, t (021) 435 3451,
www.corkgolfclub.ie
Douglas Golf Club, Douglas, t (021) 489 5297,
www.douglasgolfclub.ie
Fernhill Golf and Country Club, Carrigaline,
t (021) 437 2226, *www.fernhillcountryclub.com*
Fota Island Golf Club, Carrigtohill,
t (021) 488 3710, *www.fotaisland.ie*
Harbour Point Golf Complex, Little Island, t (021)
435 3094, *www.harbourpointgolfclub.com*
Monkstown Golf Club, Monkstown,
t (021) 484 1376
Muskerry Golf Club, Carrigrohane,
t (021) 438 5297
Ted McCarthy Municipal Golf Course,
Mahon, t (021) 429 4280,
www.corkcorp.ie/ourservices/rac

Tours
OLGA (Official Local Guiding Association)
organizes guided tours all over the county.
They also run 2 **walking tours** in Cork City: the
Cork City Trail (*June–Sept, Sat 11am; 90mins; €7*)
takes in most of the city's highlights, and the
Literary and Historical Tour (*June–Aug, Tue
and Thur, 7pm; 90mins; €7*) explores the city's

Paul Street, which is located to the north of St Patrick's Street, once the city's Huguenot quarter, is now the trendy corner of Cork, with cafés, bookshops and buskers jostling for space in an attractive pedestrianized area. Paul Street joins **Cornmarket Street** with its open-air fleamarket, which is usually known as the **Coal Quay** – here you can bargain for trifles and observe the sharp-tongued stallholders in action. Also off Paul Street you'll find **St Peter and St Paul Church**, a neo-Gothic building by the younger Pugin, Augustus.

literary heritage and rounds off with refreshments in *An Spailpín Fánach*. **OLGA Cork**, t (021) 488 5405. Walking tours depart from outside the tourist office.

Watersports

International Sailing Centre, 5 East Beach, Cobh, t (021) 481 1237, *www.sailcork.com*

Where to Stay

Cork City

Hayfield Manor, Perrott Ave, College Rd, t (021) 484 5900, *www.hayfieldmanor.ie* (*luxury*). A modern building designed in a traditional style, graciously appointed, with a lovely pool, air conditioning and various self-pampering facilities.

The Metropole Ryan Hotel, McCurtain St, t (021) 450 8122, *www.ryan-hotels.com* (*luxury*). Old-fashioned charm and excellent facilities, including 3 pools, 2 dining areas with great views over the River Lee, and the Met Tavern.

Jury's Hotel, Western Rd, t (021) 494 3000, *www.jurysdoyle.com* (*expensive*). A modern, slightly dull but practical hotel with sports facilities and a riverside garden.

Maryborough House, Douglas, t (021) 436 5555, *www.maryborough.com* (*expensive*). A beautiful 18th-century house with large, comfortable rooms and very good service.

Hotel Isaacs, 48 McCurtain St, t (021) 450 0011, *www.isaacs.ie* (*moderate–expensive*). Cheerful rooms and serviced apartments in a converted warehouse.

Commodore Hotel, Cobh, t (021) 481 1277, *www.commodorehotel.ie* (*moderate*). An old-fashioned seaside hotel.

Lotamore House, Tivoli, t (021) 482 2344 (*moderate*). Comfortable ensuite rooms.

Garrycloyne Lodge, Garrycloyne, Blarney, t (021) 488 6214 (*inexpensive*). A welcoming B&B just north of Blarney, on a 145-acre dairy and sheep farm.

Maranatha Country House, Blarney, t (021) 438 5102, *www.maranathacountryhouse.com* (*inexpensive*). Bizarrely – some might say delightfully – frilly and floral B&B rooms in a lovely 19th-century house.

Sheila's Hostel, 4 Belgrave Place, Wellington Rd, t (021) 450 5562, *www.sheilashostel.ie* (*inexpensive*). A conveniently central hostel north of the river.

Eating Out

Cork City

The Ivory Tower, Exchange Buildings, Princes St, t (021) 427 4665 (*expensive*). An upstairs restaurant in the heart of the city, with a talented chef–patron.

Bawnleigh House Restaurant, Ballinhassig, south of city on N71, t (021) 477 1333 (*moderate*). Don't be put off by the rather grim décor; food here is delicious and creative.

Greene's, Hotel Isaacs (*see above*), t (021) 455 2279, *www.isaacs.ie/greenes* (*moderate*). A hotel-restaurant serving global fare.

Jacques Restaurant, 9 Phoenix St, t (021) 427 7387 (*moderate*). A place serving imaginative cooking, including particularly good vegetarian dishes.

Oyster Bar, Market Lane, off St Patrick's St, t (021) 427 2716 (*moderate*). A place with the atmosphere of a gentlemen's dining room, with white-aproned waitresses and an excellent seafood menu.

Café Paradiso, 16 Lancaster Quay, Western Rd, t (021) 427 7939, *www.cafeparadiso.ie* (*inexpensive–moderate*). Great vegetarian food made with all-organic ingredients.

The **South Mall**, to the south of the island, and adjoining **Grand Parade** have some pretty buildings. In Washington Street, east of the Grand Parade, is the magnificent Corinthian façade of the 19th-century **Court House**. Just off South Mall is **Holy Trinity Church**, on **Father Matthew Quay**, with a wonderful stained-glass window dedicated to Daniel O'Connell, 'the Great Liberator'. Between South Main Street and Grand Parade is the fine 18th-century **Christ Church**, now housing the county archives. At the south end of the Grand Parade is a monument to Ireland's patriot dead.

Clancy's Bar and Bistro, 15–16 Princes St, t (021) 427 6097 (*inexpensive*). A useful address if you are shopping or visiting the city centre, relaxed and friendly.

Crawford Art Gallery Café, Emmet Place, t (021) 427 4415, *www.crawfordartgallery.com* (*inexpensive*). A café run by one of the Allen family of Ballymaloe Restaurant fame, serving light, original food for lunch or early suppers. The fresh orange juice and gooey cakes are particularly good.

Eastern Palace, in English Market (*see* p.182), t (021) 427 6967 (*inexpensive*). A Chinese restaurant serving up zesty and imaginative cuisine, including an excellent lunch menu.

The Gingerbread House, Paul St Plaza, t (021) 427 6411 (*inexpensive*). A good place for takeaway or eat-in sandwiches, croissants and cakes.

Gino's, Winthrop St, t (021) 427 4485 (*inexpensive*). Fabulous pizzas that are famous amongst Corkonians, designed for big appetites.

Oz Cork, Grand Parade, t (021) 427 2711 (*inexpensive*). An establishment offering a taste of Australia in the heart of the city. It's extremely popular, so make sure to book a table in advance.

Quay Co-op, 24 Sullivan's Quay, t (021) 431 7026, *www.quaycoop.com* (*inexpensive*). A good wholefood, vegetarian restaurant, open for lunch and dinner. It's also a wholefood shop and bookshop.

Triskel Arts Café, Triskel Arts Centre, 15 Tobin St, t (021) 427 2022, *www.triskelart.com* (*inexpensive*). An arts café offering a wide variety of filling lunchtime dishes, including very good soups.

The Vineyard, Market Lane, off St Patrick's St, t (021) 427 4793, *www.vineyard.ie* (*inexpensive*). A traditional, old-fashioned bar that's ideal for a quiet drink.

Entertainment and Nightlife

Pubs and Clubs

An Spailpín Fánach, South Main St. A great venue for traditional music.

Bodhrán Bar, 42 Oliver Plunkett St. Traditional Irish music.

City Limits, Coburg St. A place offering different styles of music, and occasional comedy and disco nights.

Clancy's Bar and Bistro, Princes St. A Victorian-style bar and restaurant, lined with gold-leaf advertising mirrors

The Lobby Bar, Union Quay. A place to sample a decent pint of Murphy's Stout.

Theatre, Music and Film

There is plenty to choose from in the evenings. Check the *Cork Examiner* or *Evening Echo* for current listings.

Cork Opera House, Emmet Place, t (021) 427 0022, *www.corkoperahouse.ie*. This is open for about 8 weeks every summer.

Everyman Palace Theatre, McCurtain St, t (021) 450 1673, *www.everymanpalace.com*. A theatre that does not restrict itself in any way, hosting tragedy, farce or comedy by any author as long as they're good. If you go prepared for anything, chances are you won't be disappointed.

Granary Theatre, Mardyke, t (021) 490 4275, *www.granary.ie*. A place for new and experimental work.

Kino Cinema, Washington St, t (021) 427 1571, *www.kinocinema.net*. First-run and classic films catering for all tastes.

Triskel Arts Centre, Tobin St, t (021) 427 7300, *www.triskelart.com*. A venue for a wide range of events – music, exhibitions, drama, film seasons and poetry readings.

Crawford Art Gallery (*open Mon–Sat 10–5; t (021) 427 3377; www.crawfordartgallery. com*) in Emmet Place has a stunning collection of works by Irish artists such as Seán Keating, Orpen and Walter Osbourne. There are also some very good 18th- and 19th-century paintings – look out for two magnificent ones by James Barry, a native of the city. Don't miss the gallery's excellent **café** (*see* above), or the nearby craft shops. Opposite North Mall, on Cork Island still, the **Old Maltings** buildings have been adapted for the university and include a small theatre, **The Granary** (*see* above).

Swans, which are the symbol of Cork City, are fed near here, so you can often see large flocks of them. Close to the Maltings is the large Mercy Hospital, in Prospect Row, off Grenville Place, which incorporates the 1767 **Mayoralty House**, built as the official residence of the Mayor of Cork, with some fine rococo interior plasterwork. It was designed by Davis Ducart, a Sardinian whose work can also be seen in the Limerick Customs House.

Follow the river westwards along Dyke Parade and leafy Mardyke Walk, and then cut south across Western Road, to come to the Oxbridge-style **University College Cork**, with its buildings grouped around a 19th-century Gothic square. There is an important collection of **ogham stones** here, which you can see in the Stone Corridor. The only modern building within the complex is the **Boole Library**, which opened in 1985. It is named in honour of George Boole (1815–64), who was the first professor of mathematics here and who is credited with working out the principles of modern computer logic.

The Roman Catholic **Honan Chapel** is a period piece of Celtic revivalism, copied from Cormac's Chapel on the Rock of Cashel and adorned with some exquisite Irish revival stained glass.

Close to the university is **Cork City Museum** (*open Mon–Sat 9–6; t (021) 427 0679*), a pleasant Georgian house with an ultra-modern wing in the gardens of **Fitzgerald Park**, north of the Lee. It is worth visiting for local information and history, particularly on the War of Independence. There are displays of silver, glass and lace and, on the first floor, the Garryduff bird, a tiny wren of exquisite gold filigree dating from the early-Christian period. Bus number 8 from the centre will drop you nearby.

Cork is the home of two Irish stouts that rival Guinness – Murphy's and Beamish. The **Beamish Brewery** (*open May–Sept Tue and Thur 10.30 and 12 noon, Oct–Apr Thur 11am; adm; t (021) 491 1100; www.beamish.ie*), on South Main Street, offers brewery tours throughout the year.

North of the River

St Patrick's Street leads to St Patrick's Bridge. Once over it, you enter a hilly part of the city. Some of the 19th-century streets here are literally stairways on the steep slopes, and so are accessible only to those on foot.

Off Shandon Street, **St Anne's Shandon** church belltower, with its two faces in white limestone and two in red sandstone, topped by a cupola and distinctive salmon weather vane, looks down into the valley. It is nicknamed the 'four-faced liar' because the clock often tells a different time on each side. The church, open daily, was built between 1722 and 1726 to replace a church destroyed during the Williamite siege. The peal of eight bells, which were made in Gloucestershire in 1750, are dear to every Corkonian heart. You may ring the bells of Shandon for a small fee, and conjure up Father Prout's lyrical poem about the spells they wove for him 100 years ago:

'Tis the bells of Shandon
That sounds so grand on
The pleasant waters of the River Lee.

Skiddy's Almshouse, founded in 1584, stands in the churchyard. In about 1620, the Vintners Company of London settled a perpetual annuity of IR£24 (€30) on 12 Cork widows. Part of the 18th-century Butter Exchange is now the **Shandon Craft Centre,** but once it was the largest butter market in the world. The **Cork Butter Museum** (*open Mar–Oct daily 10–5; t (021) 430 0600*), on O'Connell Square, explains the history of butter-making in Cork and Kerry up to the present day through displays of traditional tools, including a 1,000-year-old keg of 'bog butter'. By the Exchange is the **Firkin Crane Centre** (now used by the Institute for Choreography and Dance), built in 1855 as the market expanded. The cattle slaughterhouse was also once in this area; the salted meat provided for the British Navy and many European ships making the voyage to America. By the river is **North Mall**, with some fine 18th-century doorways.

The Dominican **St Mary's Church**, by the River Lee, was completed in 1839 and has a magnificent classical façade. It is in a very prominent position, which allows us to date it as post-Catholic Emancipation (Catholic churches built before that time were built away from the main centre of towns and cities). Farther north is **St Mary's Pro-Cathedral**, begun in 1808, which has a fine tower.

To the west of the city is the neogothic **Cork City Gaol** (*open daily Mar–Oct 9.30–6, Nov–Feb 10–5; adm; t (021)430 5022, www.corkcitygaol.com*), off Sunday's Well Road. It has been restored as a museum and depicts the life of a 19th-century prisoner, and the social history of the period. Upstairs is the **Radio Museum** with a collection of old-time radios and an exhibition on the impact of radio on our lives.

South of the River

South of the river, between Bishop and Dean streets, is **St Finbarr's Cathedral**, which was built in the 19th century by wealthy Church of Ireland merchants on the site of the ancient church founded by St Finbarr. (If you don't have time to do much visiting in Cork, this building and the Art Gallery are essential sights.) The cathedral's great spires dominate the city, and it has a beautiful west front, with three recessed doors, elaborate carving and a beautiful rose window. The building itself is in the Gothic style of 13th-century France and was built between 1867 and 1879 by a committed medievalist, the English architect William Burges. His eye for detail was meticulous as well as humorous, and the whole effect is vigorous – a defiant gesture to Catholic Ireland. Also on the south side, off Douglas Street, is the grey limestone tower of **Red Abbey**, a remnant of a 14th-century Augustinian friary. Close by, on Dunbar Street, is **South Chapel**, built in 1766 on an inconspicuous site. At this time, the penal laws may have relaxed, but a show of Catholicism was discouraged and disliked by the ruling classes. It contains most of its original fittings and furniture, and a sculpture of 'The Dead Christ' by John Hogan.

Back on Sullivan's Quay, the **Munster Literature Centre** (*Tigh Litríochta; t (021) 431 2955; www.munsterlit.ie*), at 84 Douglas Street, has an interesting multimedia exhibition of well-known writers from Cork City and County. Authors such as Elizabeth Bowen, Frank O'Connor, William Trevor and Patricia Lynch (who wrote enchanting children's stories) are all represented. The centre also promotes young poets and writers and is a focus of literary activity in the south.

The Suburbs

The **Church of Christ the King** on Evergreen Road, to the south at Turner's Cross, was designed by an American architect, Barry Byrne, in the 1930s. The carved figure of Christ crucified with his arms spread above the twin entrance doors is very striking.

Riverstown House (*open May–mid Sept Wed–Sat 2–6, or by appointment; adm; t (021) 482 1205*), near Glanmire, 3 miles (4.8km) from the city centre off the old Cork–Dublin road, was built in 1602, and has exquisite plasterwork by the Francini brothers. The brothers were Swiss-Italian stuccoers who came to Ireland in 1734 and adorned the ceiling of the dining room with allegorical figures, representing Time rescuing Truth from the assaults of Discord and Envy. Dr Browne, the Archbishop of Cork, was responsible for remodelling the original house in the 1730s and it remained in his family until the early part of the 20th century. It has been beautifully restored by its present owners, Mr and Mrs Dooley, with the help of the Irish Georgian Society.

This area is well endowed with large houses overlooking the Lee Estuary. One you can visit is **Dunkathel House** (*open May–mid-Oct Wed–Sun 2–6; adm; t (021) 482 1014*), also in Glanmire. It is a fine Georgian Palladian house, worth visiting; afternoon tea here is very pleasant too. The house was built by a wealthy Cork merchant in 1790 and has a wonderful bifurcated staircase of Bath stone. A permanent display of watercolours by Elizabeth Gubbins, a daughter of the house, is on the walls. She was a deaf-mute who travelled widely, recording her experiences and the scenery as she went. There is a rare 1880s barrel organ that is still played for visitors.

Across the Glanmire Valley from Dunkathel is Brian Cross's attractive **Lakemount Gardens** (*open by appointment; adm; t (021) 482 1052, www.lakemountgarden.com*), on Barnavara Hill, Glanmire.

Twenty minutes' walk from the city centre, via Barrack Street and Bandon Road, is the **Lough**, a freshwater lake with wild geese. **Douglas Estuary**, via Tivoli (15 minutes from the centre by car) is home to hundreds of black-tailed godwits, shelducks and golden plovers. The **Cork Heritage Park** (*open daily May–Sept 10.30–5; adm; t (021) 435 8854*) in Blackrock illustrates the maritime history of the city and its burning during the War of Independence, as well as the history of a Quaker merchant family, the Pikes, who lived there. Other interesting buildings on the estuary are **Blackrock Castle**, designed by the Pain brothers, and Father Matthew's **Memorial Tower**, on the other side of the water, a neo-Gothic folly.

Around Cork City

About 5 miles (8km) south-west of Cork City on the N22, at **Ballincollig**, you can visit the 19th-century **Royal Gunpowder Mills** (*open Easter–Sept daily 10–6; adm; t (021) 874430*) on the banks of the Lee. This produced huge quantities of gunpowder for the British army. The restored visitor centre has an exhibition gallery, craft shop and café.

Blarney is 5 miles (8km) north-west of the city on the R617. This small village has a fame out of all proportion to its size because it is the home of the **Blarney Stone**. According to legend, whoever kisses it will get the 'gift of the gab'. This magic stone is high up in the ruined keep that is all that is left of **Blarney Castle** (*open May and Sept Mon–Sat 9–6.30, Sun 9.30–5.30, June–Aug Mon–Sat 9–7, Sun 9.30–5.30, Oct–Apr Mon–Sat 9–6/sunset, Sun 9.30–sunset; adm; t (021) 438 5252, www.blarneycastle.ie*). It is a magnet for almost every visitor to Ireland, so expect to find the place (and the entire town of Blarney) crowded and full of knick-knacks. In the days of Elizabeth I, the castle was held by Dermot MacCarthy, the lord of Blarney, who had the gift of *plámás*, the Irish word for soft, flattering or insincere speech. Elizabeth had asked him to surrender his castle, but he continued to play her along with fair words and no action. In the end the frustrated Queen is supposed to have said, 'This is all Blarney – he says he will do it but never means it at all'. The MacCarthys forfeited their castle in the Williamite wars of 1690, and it was later acquired by the St John Jefferyes family.

To kiss the Blarney Stone, climb the stone steps up five flights to the parapet, where an attendant will hold your feet while you drop your head down to the stone. The stone is probably a 19th-century invention, and today you can even buy yourself a certificate that guarantees you have kissed it. The castle is well worth seeing for its own sake, as it is one of the largest and finest towerhouses in Ireland, built in 1446 by the MacCarthy clan. The landscaped gardens surrounding it are also superb.

You might also like to visit **Blarney House and Gardens** (*open for guided tours June–mid-Sept Mon–Sat 12 noon–6; adm; t (021) 438 5252*), a Scottish baronial mansion that was built by Charles Lanyon, with a charming garden, ancient yew trees, scattered rocks and a lake.

Fota House and Estate (*open Apr–Sept Mon–Sat 10–5.30, Sun 11–5.30, Oct–Mar daily 11–4; adm; t (021) 481 5543; www.fotahouse.com*) is on magical little Fota Island in the River Lee Estuary. The arboretum surrounding the house is luxurious and mature, with one of the finest collections of semi-tropical and rare shrubs in the British Isles. The restored house, which is mainly Regency in style, was built as a hunting lodge, and has a splendid neoclassical hallway. There is also a bee garden and a **wildlife park** (*open Mon–Sat 10–6, Sun 11–6, last adm 1hr before close; adm; t (021) 481 2678, www. fotawildlife.ie*). The park is an ideal expedition for children as the animals (giraffes, zebras, ostrich, antelope, kangaroos, macaws and lemurs) roam freely – only the cheetahs are in a large pen. The splendid scimitar-horned oryx, extinct in its native North Africa, is being bred here.

Cobh

Cobh (*An Cóbh*, pronounced *Cove*) is situated 15 miles (24km) to the southeast of Cork City, on the R624 off the N25, and is served by regular trains. The shortest and most interesting way to reach it, however – if you can managed to find your way through Cork's southern suburbs, that is – is by the little car ferry at **Passage West**, which makes an inexpensive five-minute crossing to Carrigaloe, just beside **Cobh**. Cobh is the great harbour of Cork and handles enormous ships. During the 18th century, it served as a great naval base for the British; later, nearly all the transatlantic ships and liners stopped here – it was the last port of call for the *Titanic*, and the destination of the *Lusitania* when it was torpedoed nearby off Old Head. For many thousands of people, it was the embarkation port for the new worlds of North America and Australia.

Despite the industry that surrounds it, Cobh is a rather pleasant place to stay, near the city but without its bustle. The colourful centre, almost entirely 19th-century, is dominated by the Gothic **St Colman's Cathedral**, the work of Pugin and Ashlin. It dates from 1868 but was not completed until 1919, and has a soaring spire and glorious carillon of some 40 bells – the largest in the British Isles – which can be heard at 9am, 12 noon, 4pm and 6pm. Between 1848 and 1950 2.5 million people emigrated to America from here, with many a sad scene enacted by the quay. The history of the port and the story of the emigrants is recorded at the **Cobh Heritage Centre** (*open daily 10–6; t (021) 481 3591, www.cobhheritage.com*), a converted Victorian railway station. There's a genealogical information centre for those with Irish antecedents.

There is a long, proud yachting tradition here: the Royal Yacht Club, founded in 1720, is the oldest in Ireland and Great Britain, though it moved from its original home near the railway station to Crosshaven. It has a very good summer regatta. The old Yacht Club in Cobh is now the **Sirius Arts Centre** (*open Wed–Fri 11–5, Sat and Sun 2–5; t (021) 481 3790, www.iol.ie/~cobharts*), home to contemporary art exhibitions and a permanent exhibition on local maritime history.

The view from the hill above Cobh facing south on to the harbour, peppered with islands (one a prison) and edged with woods, is superb. If you want a stroll, make for the old **churchyard of Clonmel**, a peaceful place where many of the dead from the *Lusitania* are buried. Also buried here is the Rev. Charles Wolfe, 1791–1823, remembered for 'The Burial of Sir John Moore', a stirring poem extravagantly praised by Byron. Sir John Moore died a hero in the Peninsula Wars, but he was closely linked to Ireland through his role in quelling the 1798 Rebellion. Unlike many of his superiors, he was successful in disarming parts of the south with restraint, and he is remembered for his clemency and humanity; he found the behaviour of his own Irish troops disgraceful.

Not a drum was heard, not a funeral note
As his corpse to the ramparts we hurried
Not a soldier discharged his farewell shot
O'er the grave where our hero we buried.

One of the finest public monuments in the country is the **Lusitania Memorial** in Casement Square. It depicts two mourning sailors and, above them on a stone pedestal, the Angel of Peace. It was sculpted by Jerome Connor (1876–1943), born in County Kerry but raised in Massachusetts. Also in Cobh, the former Presbyterian church, known as the **Scots Church**, is a museum with many interesting artefacts from former industries, including the Belvelly Brickworks. Models of Cork harbour coasters, marine paintings and maritime photographs are also in the collection.

Crosshaven, 13 miles (21km) south-east of Cork city on the Cork Harbour Estuary, a crescent-shaped bay filled with yachts and boats of every description, is the playground of the busy Cork businessmen and their families. There are delightful little beaches at Myrtleville and Robert's Cove, farther along the coast.

Around County Cork

West of Cork: The Lee Valley and Gougane Barra to Bantry Bay

Heading west from Cork for Killarney, the N22 and the more scenic R618 meet at **Macroom** (*Maigh Chromtha*: 'sloping plain'), a busy market town on the Sullane River. Macroom once belonged to Admiral Sir William Penn, whose son founded Pennsylvania, and it has a small folk **museum** (*t (026) 41840*).

This is a gorgeous part of Ireland, with green pastures and bright fuchsias and heather. The Lee and Inishcarra reservoirs swell the river. The R618 follows the lovely River Lee from Cork City through Dripsey and Coachford. Just beyond Macroom,

Tourist Information

Macroom: Castle Gates, The Square, t (026) 43280. *Open May–Sept.*

Shopping

Macroom Country Market. This is best visited on a Tue morning, when the stalls are in full swing and you can stock up on delicious farm-produced cheese.

Milmorane Basketry, Milmorane, Ballingeary, Macroom. The place to come to buy quality hand-made baskets.

Prince August Toy Soldier Factory, Kilnamartyra, Macroom, t (026) 40222, *www.princeaugust.ie*. Ireland's only lead soldier factory, in a wild setting well off the beaten track.

Sports and Activities

Golf

Lee Valley Golf and Country Club, Clashenure, Ovens, t (021) 433 1721, *www.leevalleygcc.ie*
Macroom Golf Club, Lackaduve, Macroom, t (026) 41072

Open Farm

Muskerry Farm Museum, Ryecourt Meadows, Farnanes, t (021) 733 6462. This museum on the Cork–Killarney road hosts displays of horse-drawn machinery.

Watersports

Carrig Water Ski Club, Carrigadrohid, Macroom, t (021) 487 3027. A club with wheelchair facilities. *Closed Nov–Apr.*

Where to Stay

Farran House, Farran, Macroom, t (021) 733 1215, *www.farranhouse.com* (*expensive*). An elegant country house set in 12 acres of mature beech woods. Guestrooms have huge bathrooms.

Bridelands Country House, Crookstown, Macroom, t (021) 733 6566, *bridelands@eircom.net* (*moderate*). Comfortable accommodation in an attractive old house.

The Castle Hotel, Macroom, t (026) 41074, *www.castlehotel.ie* (*moderate*). A welcoming hotel with impressive service, its own leisure centre and an award-winning restaurant.

Gougane Barra Hotel, Ballingeary, t (026) 47069, *www.gouganebarra.com* (*moderate*). A quiet hotel in a perfect setting on the shores of the beautiful Gougane Barra Lake.

Eating Out

The Auld Triangle, Killarney Rd, Macroom, t (026) 41940 (*moderate*). This restaurant is popular among locals because of its extensive à la carte dinner menu.

Café Muesli, South Square, Macroom, t (026) 42455 (*inexpensive*). An interesting selection of vegetarian and Italian cuisine.

south off the R584, is a marshy area of water, **The Gearagh**, a haven for waterbirds, and woodlands of oak, ash and birch. It forms part of the Lee hydroelectric works and is an expansion of the river into a maze of rivulets. The overall effect is of dreary flooded land, but it is a bird-watcher's dream.

If you are heading for Killarney, try to include the **Pass of Keamaneigh**, 5 miles (8km) west of Ballingeary on the R584, which takes you on a loop into the wild countryside.

Follow the N22 up the Sullane Valley through Ballymakeera (*Baile Mhic Íre*) and Ballyvourney (*Baile Bhúirne*), passing the ruins of **Carrigaphuca Castle**, a MacCarthy towerhouse. Turn off the N22 where it is signposted Kilgarven and Kenmare on the left. In **Ballyvourney**, stop at the **shrine and holy well of St Gobnait**, who established a monastery here in the 6th century, after being led to this spot by a vision of nine white deer. She is said to have kept the plague away from the village by consecrating the ground so the disease could not pass. She is also known as the patroness of bees. In the church is a wooden 13th-century statue of Gobnait, displayed to pilgrims on her feast day (11 February). *Tomhas Ghobnata* (Gobnait's measure) is still observed: a length of wool is measured against her statue, then used for curing ailments.

Nearby, in **Killeen**, is **St Gobnait's Stone**, an early cross pillar; carved on one face is a figure bearing a crozier. If you turn left off the N22, the road climbs up to tiny Coolea (*Cúil Aodha*), home of Sean O'Riada (1931–71), a composer and musician who helped awaken interest in Irish musical heritage by reviving traditional dances and tunes.

Continuing through the moorland, you come to a fork in the road: make a sharp left and you will ascend steeply to **Ballingeary** (*Béal Atha an Ghaorthaidh*) via Inchee Bridge. From here it is a short distance to **Gougane Barra**, 'the rock cleft of Finbarr'. This is a dramatic glacial valley with a shining lake in its hollow into which run silvery streams, and the source of the River Lee. In the lake is a small island, approached by a causeway, where St Finbarr set up his oratory in the 6th century. At the entrance to the causeway are **St Finbarr's Well** and an ancient cemetery. The island has a few 18th-century remains, some Stations of the Cross, and a tiny modern Irish Romanesque chapel that is often used for weddings. A popular pattern (pilgrimage) is made here every year on the Sunday nearest to the feast day of St Finbarr (25 September).

After the **Pass of Keamaneigh**, strewn with massive boulders, you come into the colourful valley of the Owvane River, with a view of Bantry Bay. At **Kealkill**, 5 miles (8km) before you reach Bantry, there is an ancient **stone circle**, reached by an exciting hilly road just off the R584. Ask someone locally for directions, as it isn't easy to find.

South of Cork: Kinsale to Mizen Head

Kinsale and Around

Kinsale (*Cionn tSáile*: 'tide head') is 18 miles (29km) south-west of Cork City on the R600. A sheltered port on the Bandon Estuary, it has long been famed as a quaint seaside town with excellent restaurants and carefully preserved 18th-century buildings, often clad with grey slates to keep out the damp, or painted cheerful colours.

Tourist Information

Bantry: t (027) 50229. *Open June–Sept.*
Kinsale: Pier Head, t (021) 477 2234
Skibbereen: North St, t (028) 21766

Shopping

Books
Fuchsia Books, Schull

Crafts
Adrigole Arts, Droumlave, Adrigole
Bandon Pottery, St Finbarr's Place, Lauragh
Bantry House Craftshop, Bantry
Courtmacsherry Ceramics, Courtmacsherry
Great Barrington Pottery, Eyeries
Ian Wright, Corsits Pottery, Kilnaclasha,
  Skibbereen
Jagoes Mill Pottery, Farrangalway, Kinsale
Keane on Ceramics, Pier Rd, Kinsale
Kinsale Crystal Glass, Market St, Kinsale
Leda May Studios, Main St, Ballydehob
Norbert Platz, Ballymurphy, Inishannon,
  near Bandon. Unique hand-made baskets.
Rory Connor, Ballylickey. Hand-made knives.
Rossmore Country Pottery, Clonakilty

Food
Adele's, Schull. Cakes and breads.
Durras Farmhouse Cheese,Croomkeen, Durras.
  Semi-soft raw milk cheese.
Gubbeen Cheeses, Gubbeen House, Schull.
  Wonderful soft cheese made on a farm.
Manning's Emporium, Ballylickey, Bantry.
  Local cheeses and whiskey cake.
Milleens Cheese, Eyeries, t (027) 74079. Good
  cheese, garlic or plain semi-soft. Call ahead.
Quay Food Co., Market Quay, Kinsale.
Twomey's Butchers, 16 Pearse St, Clonakilty.
  Famous Clonakilty black pudding.
Ummera Smoked Products, Ummera House,
  Timoleague, Bandon, t (023) 46187. Delicious
  smoked salmon sausage. Call before visiting.

Markets
Bandon: Fri 2–4.
Bantry: Fri mornings; fair in market square
  on first Fri of month.
Carrigaline: GAA Hall, Fri 10–11.
Skibbereen: Fri 12 noon–2.

Sports and Activities

Art Galleries
Harling Gallery, Cotter's Yard, Main St, Schull,
  t (028) 28165
Kent Gallery, Quayside, Kinsale, t (021) 477 4956,
  www.kentgal.com
West Cork Arts Centre, North St, Skibbereen,
  t (028) 22090

Courses and Tours
Ballydehob Historical, Archaeological and
  Landscape Tours, *Teach Dearg*, Ballydehob,
  t (028) 37282
The Ewe Art Centre, Glengarriff, near Mizen
  Head, t (027) 63840, *www.theewe.com*. An
  art retreat with pottery courses and a shop.

Fishing
Bandon Angling Association, Bandon,
  t (023) 41674. Fishing in the Bandon River.
Baoite Mara Teo, Cape Clear, Skibbereen,
  t (028) 39146. Chartered trips.
Fallon's Sport Shop, North St, Skibbereen,
  t (028) 22246. State licences and permits.
The Kinsale Angling Co-op, 1 The Ramparts,
  Kinsale, t (021) 477 4946, *www.kinsaleangling.
  com*. Angling on the Blackwater River.

Golf
Bandon Golf Club, Castle Bernard, t (023) 41111
Bantry Golf Club, Bonenark, Bantry,
  t (027) 50579, *www.bantrygolf.com*
Fernhill Golf and Country Club, Carrigaline,
  t (021) 437 2226, *www.fernhillcountryclub.com*
Glengarriff Golf Club, Glengarriff, t (027) 63150
Kinsale Golf Club, Kinsale, t (021) 477 4722,
  www.kinsalegolf.com
Old Head Golf Links, Kinsale, t (021) 477 8444,
  www.oldheadgolflinks.com. Closed Nov–Mar.
Skibbereen and West Carbery Golf Club,
  Skibbereen, t (028) 21227, *www.skibbgolf.com*

Ponytrekking
Ballinadee Pony Trekking, t (021) 477 8152
Bantry Horse Riding, Coomanore South, Bantry,
  t (027) 51412, *www.eventingireland.com*

Spas
Inchydoney Island Spa, Clonakilty, t (023) 33143,
  www.inchydoneyisland.com. Thalassotherapy
  beauty and massage treatments.

Walking

The Beara Way. A (122-mile) 196km circle round the Beara Peninsula from Glengarriff.
The Sheep's Head Way. A (56-mile) 90km circular route from Bantry.

Watersports and Cruises

Aquaventures, Lifeboat Rd, Baltimore, t (028) 20511, *www.aquaventures.ie*. An impressive dive centre offering trips to see abundant marine life and wrecks, including a German U-boat and the infamous Kowloon Bridge.
Baltimore Diving Centre, Baltimore, t (028) 20300, *www.baltimorediving.com*
Baltimore Sailing School, The Pier, Baltimore, t (028) 20141, *www.baltimoresailingschool. com*. Courses on ketches and day boats.
Glenans Irish Sailing Club, Baltimore, t (028) 20154, *www.glenans-ireland.com*. Residential sailing courses.
Kinsale Dive Centre, Castlepark Marina, Kinsale, t (021) 477 4959
Kinsale Harbour Cruises, t (021) 477 8946, *www.kinsaleharbourcruises.com*
Kinsale Outdoor Education Centre, Kinsale, t (021) 477 2896, *www.kinsaleoutdoors.com*. Instruction in all watersports.
Oysterhaven Holiday and Activity Centre, Kinsale, t (021) 477 0738, *www.oysterhaven.com*
Sail Ireland Charters, Kinsale, t (021) 477 2927, *www.sailireland.com*. Bare or skippered trips.
Schull Watersports, Schull, t (028) 28554. Dinghies and windsurfing.

Where to Stay

Inchydoney Island Lodge, Clonakilty, t (023) 33143, *www.inchydoneyisland.com* (*luxury*). A luxurious hotel with a thalassotherapy spa (*see* opposite).
Seaview House Hotel, Ballylickey, near Bantry, t (029) 58900, *www.cmvhotels.com* (*luxury*). A luxuriously appointed Victorian house with spacious bedrooms, antique furniture, and an excellent dining room.
Sovereign House, Newmans Mall, Kinsale, t (021) 477 2850, *www.sovereignhouse.com* (*luxury*). A striking converted Queen Anne house, on cobbled streets leading down to the harbour.

Blairs Cove House, Durrus, near Bantry, t (027) 61127 (*expensive*). A Georgian house in a spectacular setting on Dunmanus Bay, with 3 courtyard suites and a self-catering cottage in the grounds (available Mar–Nov).
The Blue Haven, Kinsale, t (021) 477 2209, *www.bluehavenkinsale.com* (*expensive*). The best hotel in Kinsale: small, cosy and comfortable, with excellent food.
Casey's Hotel, Baltimore, t (028) 20197, *www. caseysofbaltimore.com* (*expensive*). The best type of small hotel: welcoming, comfortable and with excellent food.
Perryville House, Kinsale, t (021) 477 2731, *www.perryvillehouse.com* (*expensive*). Sophisticated accommodation, with stunning views and superb breakfasts.
Westlodge Hotel, Bantry, t (027) 50360, *www.westlodgehotel.ie* (*expensive*). A scenically located option just outside town, with a leisure centre and gym.
Bantry House B&B, Bantry, t (027) 50047, *www.bantryhouse.ie* (*moderate*). The converted wing of an interesting country pile (*see* p.204), with a library, billiard room and extensive gardens at guests' disposal.
Butlerstown House, Butlerstown, south of Courtmacsherry, t (023) 40137 (*moderate*). A Georgian country house with fine rooms and excellent breakfasts.
The Castle, Castletownshend, t (028) 36100, *www.castle-townshend.com* (*moderate*). A B&B in a gentrified 18th-century castle. It also has some apartments in its towers, and 3 terraced cottages in the village (sleeping 2–6).
Castle Salem, near Rosscarbery, t (023) 48381, *www.castlesalem.com* (*moderate*). An atmospheric B&B in an impressive 15th-century castle where William Penn once slept. Donations are gratefully received to preserve the building.
Fortview House, Gurtyowen, Goleen, t (028) 35324, *www.fortviewhousegoleen.com* (*moderate*) A friendly farmhouse in a remote setting, with airy rooms and fresh, tasty breakfast options: home-made bread and preserves, pancakes and freshly laid eggs.
Glebe Country House, Ballinadee, Kinsale, t (021) 477 8294, *http://indigo.ie/~glebehse* (*moderate*). A family-run Georgian rectory, informal and relaxed.

Grove House, Skibbereen, **t** (028) 22957, *www.grovehouse.net* (*moderate*). A pleasant Georgian house with 4-poster beds. Room 3 has a 200-year-old bath.

Kilbrogan House, Bandon, **t** (023) 44935, *www.kilbrogan.com* (*moderate*). A lovingly restored Georgian B&B home with 5 airy ensuite rooms with wooden floors, sash windows and inviting beds.

Marine Hotel, Glandore, west of Rosscarbery, **t** (029) 58900 (*moderate*). A simple hotel with lovely views of the cove. The restaurant has a good reputation (*see* opposite).

O'Donovans Hotel, 44 Pearse St, Clonakilty, **t** (023) 33250, *www.odonovanshotel.com* (*moderate*). A wonderful, old-fashioned hotel situated in the town centre, with a fine public bar.

Duvane Farm, Ballyduvane, Clonakilty, **t** (023) 33129, *www.duvanefarm.com* (*inexpensive–moderate*). A B&B in a working farmhouse, with lovely country-house décor. Fresh eggs are served for breakfast. *Closed Dec–Feb.*

Dromcloc House, Relane Point, 1mile (1.6km) south-west of Bantry, **t** (027) 50030, *www.dromclochouse.com* (*inexpensive*). A B&B on a dairy farm, offering a warm welcome in a wonderful location. Fishing and boat trips can be arranged.

Grove House, Ahakista, Durras, **t** (027) 67060 (*inexpensive*). A pretty old farmhouse on the Sheep's Head Peninsula. You can sample its own delicious honey and free-range eggs.

Heron's Cove, The Harbour, Goleen, near Mizen Head, **t** (028) 35225, *www.heronscove.com* (*inexpensive*). A well-run B&B right on the water, with a superb seafood restaurant (*see* opposite).

Hillcrest Farm, Ahakista, Bantry, **t** (027) 67045, *www.ahakista.com* (*inexpensive*). A traditional farmhouse with lovely views.

Kilfinnan Farm, Glandore, **t** (028) 33233 (*inexpensive*). A traditional farmhouse.

Leighmoneymore House, Dunderrow, Kinsale, **t** (021) 477 5312, *www.leighmoneymore.ie* (*inexpensive*) A friendly farmhouse looking out over the River Bandon.

Maria's Schoolhouse, Glandore, **t** (028) 33002, *www.mariasschoolhouse.com* (*inexpensive*). A very hospitable hostel with striking interior decoration.

Schull Central B&B, Schull, **t** (028) 28227 (*inexpensive*). An efficiently run, comfortable, central B&B. All rooms are ensuite.

Seacourt, Butlerstown, **t** (023) 40151 (*inexpensive*). A beautiful 1760 house with views of the Seven Heads Peninsula.

Seamount Farm, Goat's Path Rd, Glenlough West, Bantry, **t** (027) 61226, *www.seamountfarm.com* (*inexpensive*). A well-kept farmhouse B&B overlooking Bantry Bay.

Shiplake Mountain Hostel, Dunmanway, **t** (023) 45750, *www.shiplakemountainhostel.com* (*inexpensive*). A traditional farmhouse hostel in the mountains, with a kitchen where you can make meals from organic vegetables sold by the owners (who also offer wholemeal bread and delicious pizzas).

Travara Lodge, Courtmacsherry, **t** (023) 46493 (*inexpensive*). Comfortable rooms with views of the bay and good home-cooking.

Self-catering

Courtmacsherry Coastal Cottages, **t** (023) 46198 (*moderate*). Eight luxury cottages overlooking Courtmacsherry Bay.

Grove House Courtyard Cottages, Skibbereen, **t** (028) 22957, *www.grovehouse.net* (*inexpensive*). Three stone cottages for 2–7.

Hollybrook Cottages, Hollybrook House, Skibbereen, **t** (028) 21245 (*inexpensive*). Some 19th-century properties on a wooded estate.

Lumina Farm Cottages, Cahermore, Rosscarbery, **t** (023) 48227, *www.luminafarm. com* (*inexpensive*). Five cottages sleeping 4–8

Eating Out

Liss Ard Lake Lodge, Liss Ard, Skibbereen, **t** (028) 22635 (*luxury*). Refined cuisine, ranging from Mediterranean to Oriental, in a lovely location.

Blairs Cove House, Durras, **t** (027) 61127 (*expensive*). A restaurant in the stable building of a Georgian mansion, run by a French–Belgian couple. Steaks and fish are cooked on an open wood-fired grill. *Closed lunch, Mon and Nov–mid-Mar.*

The Blue Haven, 3 Pearse St, Kinsale, **t** (021) 477 2209, *www.bluehavenkinsale.com* (*expensive*). A very good restaurant in a cosy hotel. Seafood is a speciality, but the steaks are good too.

Good Things Café, Durras, Ahakista Rd,
t (027) 64126, *www.thegoodthingscafe.com*
(*moderate–expensive*). A Michelin
award-winning café-style restaurant
with a fantastic modern Irish-Continental
menu based on the freshest local produce.

Mews Bistro, Baltimore, t (028) 20390
(*moderate–expensive*). Impressive, upscale
contemporary cooking. *Closed lunch.*

The Rectory, Marine Hotel, Glandore
(*see* opposite) (*moderate–expensive*).
Excellent food in elegant surroundings,
with views over the harbour.

The Altar Restaurant, Toormore, Schull, t (028)
35254 (*moderate*). Tasty pâtés and seafood.

Annie's Restaurant, Main St, Ballydehob,
t (028) 37292 (*moderate*). Good-value set
meals and special portions for children.

Casey's, Baltimore, t (028) 20197, *www.
caseysofbaltimore.com* (*moderate*). A bar and
seafood restaurant with a wide choice of
freshly caught fish, and music on Saturdays.

Casino House, Coolmain Bay, Kilbrittain,
near Kinsale, t (023) 49944 (*moderate*).
A restaurant in a lovely old house,
specializing in Continental dishes using
seasonal ingredients where possible.

Customs House Restaurant, Baltimore, t (028)
20200 (*moderate*). An elegant restaurant
that conjures up imaginative, excellent
seafood dishes in a seaside setting.

Heron's Cove Restaurant, Goleen, near Mizen
Head, t (028) 35225, *www.heronscove.com*
(*moderate*). A cosy restaurant in a harbour
setting, serving very good fish and shellfish
dishes, plus meat and vegetarian options.

Island Cottage Restaurant, Heir Island,
Skibbereen, t (028) 38012 (*moderate*). Great
cooking in an unlikely, remote setting at the
only restaurant in Cork you need a boat to
reach (for which there's a fee). *Closed lunch.*

Larchwood House, Pearson's Bridge,
Bantry, t (027) 66181 (*moderate*).
Good home cooking in a friendly and
informal atmosphere.

Lawrence Cove House, Bere Island,
Castletownbere, t (027) 75063 (*moderate*).
A fabulous fish restaurant on the island,
with its own ferry service.

Max's Wine Bar, 48 Main St, Kinsale,
t (021) 477 2443 (*moderate*). A wine bar in an
attractive old house, offering a varied menu.

The Old Bakery, West End, Castletownbere,
t (027) 70869 (*moderate*). A place that
boasts of having the last espresso machine
before New York.

Kicki's Cabin, 53 Pearse St, Clonakilty,
t (023) 33384 (*inexpensive–moderate*).
A maritime-themed restaurant with
unusual menus.

The Baybery, Union Hall, Glandore Bay,
t (028) 33605, *www.churchillandco.com/
baybery* (*inexpensive*). Wholesome food,
hand-crafted pine furniture and pottery.

La Brasserie, O'Donovan's Hotel, 44 Pearse St,
Clonakilty, t (023) 33250, *www.odonovanshotel.
com* (*inexpensive*). Simply-cooked hearty
grub. The bar has a huge Guinness mural
and a collection of old bottles and glasses.

The Courtyard Restaurant & Deli, Main St,
Schull, t (028) 28390 (*inexpensive*).
A combined restaurant, bar, craft shop and
deli, serving simple but delicious lunches.

Dillon's Pub, Mill St, Timoleague, t (023) 46390
(*inexpensive*). A Continental-style bar/café
with good snacks.

Holly Bar, Ardgroom, Beara Peninsula,
t (027) 74433 (*inexpensive*). Decent soup
and sandwiches. A holly tree grows in the
middle of the bar.

Levi's Bar, Main St, Ballydehob, t (028) 37118
(*inexpensive*). This is the old-fashioned
type of bar that used to be common in
Ireland, consisting of a dimly lit, friendly
room with two long counters; on one
side are the bottles and glasses, on the
other are groceries.

Mary Anne's Bar, Castletownshend,
t (028) 36146 (*inexpensive*). Excellent
bar food served in a friendly atmosphere.
Beware of the rather boisterous Hooray
Henrys at the height of the summer season.

The Snug, The Quay, Bantry, t (027) 50057
(*inexpensive*). An eccentric bar opposite the
harbour, with simple home-cooked dishes.

Entertainment and Nightlife

Traditional Music

The Lord Kinsale, 4 Main St, Kinsale
The Shanakee Bar, Market St, Kinsale

A few far-sighted people restored the dilapidated buildings in the 1960s, so that Kinsale avoided the usual fate of a town with a lot of ancient history and decaying houses – piecemeal demolition. In recent years it has become the smartest, poshest and most expensive corner of rural Ireland, with music and cinema stars bidding up local property values, and wealthy Cork folk dining out in its restaurants. It can become quite crowded in the summer, and some new holiday homes jar a little, but for all that it's still a very agreeable place. There is a lot to see in the area, as well as good-quality craft shops, delis, restaurants, antique shops and art galleries.

Kinsale was once an important naval port. In 1601 the Irish joined forces with Spain against the English after the Ulster chieftain Hugh O'Neill called for a national rising and support of the Catholic cause. He met with success at first, and appealed to Spain for help. In September 1601, a Spanish fleet anchored here with 3,500 infantry aboard. They planned to meet with the Gaelic lords O'Neill and Tyrconnell, who were marching south to meet them. In November, the forces of O'Neill met with the forces of Mountjoy, Elizabeth's deputy, who was besieging the Spaniards. Within hours, the Gaelic army had been defeated at the disastrous Battle of Kinsale, which led to the Flight of the Earls and put an end to the rebellion against Queen Elizabeth I, which in turn led to her reconquest of Ireland. It was the beginning of the end for Gaelic Ireland; anglicization was now inevitable, and though the peasantry still spoke Irish, the language of power was English.

Afterwards, Kinsale developed as a shipbuilding port. It declared for Cromwell in 1641, but James II landed and departed from here after his brief and unsuccessful interlude fighting for his throne between 1689 and 1690.

St Multose Church is the oldest building in town, with parts of it dating from the 12th century. Inside, take a look at the Galway slab, in the south aisle, and the old town stocks. The churchyard has several interesting 16th-century gravestones that in spring are covered in whitebells and bluebells, and in summer red valerian grows out of crevices in every wall. **Desmond Castle** (*open mid-Apr–mid-June Tue–Sun 10–6, mid-June–Oct daily 10–6; adm;* **t** *(021) 477 4855, www.heritageireland.ie*), a towerhouse from the 1500s, was once used as a customs house and later as a prison for captured American sailors in the War of Independence as well as for the French. The castle now accommodates an **International Museum of Wine** that details the Irish links of some major vineyards in Europe. There is also the **Kinsale Regional Museum** (*open Sat 10–5, Sun 2–5; adm; town tours for groups of 8+;* **t** *(021) 477 7930, http://homepage.tinet.ie/ ~kinsalemuseum*) in the Dutch-style old courthouse and market building, with an interesting collection of material associated with the life of the town and port through the centuries, especially the Siege and Battle of Kinsale.

By the harbour are the ruined remains of **King James Fort**, built some time after 1600. A much better example of a military fort can be seen on the opposite shore near the attractive village of Summercove, 2 miles (3.3km) away from Kinsale: the spectacular **Charles Fort** (*open mid-Mar–Oct daily 10–6, Nov–mid-Mar Sat and Sun 10–5; adm;* **t** *(021) 477 2263, www.heritageireland.ie*) was built in the 1670s (during the reign of Charles II) as a military strongpoint. It is shaped like a star, and you can wander round its rather damp nooks and crannies. It was breached by Williamite forces under Marlborough after a 13-day siege. The severe 18th- and 19th-century houses inside were used as barracks for recruit training, and the fort was burned by the IRA in 1921. It is possible to walk to Charles Fort: follow the Scilly Walk from the middle of Kinsale. It takes about 45 minutes. Farther east is the little port of **Oysterhaven**.

To the south-west, on the R604, near **Ballinspittle**, is a **ring fort** built around AD 600. This tiny village is now famous for its **shrine** to Our Lady: the statue of her is said to have moved in 1985; since then thousands of people have come to pray here and, already, miracles have been associated with the statue. Unfortunately, also in 1985, the statue was attacked and badly damaged by a Christian sect from California. It has been repaired but apparently has not moved since.

There are some superb sandy beaches at the resort of **Garrettstown** on the wide expanse of Courtmacsherry Bay, a little farther south on the R604, and splendid cliff scenery at the **Old Head of Kinsale**, at the end of the road (to see the cliffs and an old lighthouse on the point, you'll need to pay an admission fee to the golf course, which occupies most of Old Head). The *Lusitania* was sunk off here, with 1,198 lives lost. Round the Old Head the remains of a 15th-century De Courcy castle, known as **Ringnone Castle**, overlooks the blue and white-flecked sea.

A good drive or cycle ride can be made along the River Bandon from Kinsale to **Inishannon**, once an 18th-century Huguenot weaving village. You will pass several ruined castles on the way. Take the unnumbered route via Ballinadee by crossing the Western Bridge. From Inishannon you can get to Bandon on the N71.

Bandon to Clonakilty

The market town of **Bandon**, 20 miles (32km) south-west of Cork City on the N71, was founded in 1608 by Richard Boyle, the Earl of Cork. Over the gate of the then-walled town it is said that there were once the words, 'Turk, Jew or atheist may enter here, but not a papist'. A Catholic wit responded, 'He who wrote this wrote it well, the same is written on the gates of hell'. The ownership of the town passed to the dukes of Devonshire through marriage and they constructed most of its public buildings. The Maid of Erin Monument commemorates the Rebellions of 1798, 1848 and 1867. West of Bandon, the river skirts the demesne of **Castle Bernard**, originally called Castle Mahon. It was a large mansion with a Gothic façade, but it was burnt down in the summer of 1921, one of 15 houses burnt around Bandon in the same week. The owner, Lord Bandon, was kidnapped by the IRA but released a few days later after talks between De Valera, Arthur Griffith and the leaders of the Southern Unionists, during which safeguards for the Protestant and Unionist minority were agreed. The River Bandon and its tributaries make for good fishing and walking and, if you want to explore, Kilbrittain, Timoleague and Courtmacsherry Bay are unspoilt.

Courtmacsherry, a peaceful place with a lovely setting on the bay, is a sea-angling centre. Motorists can get a good view of the wooded valleys and rolling fields, which do not have the high hedges you find in Tipperary. **Timoleague** is dominated by the ruins of a **Franciscan Abbey** founded in 1312 overlooking the mud flats of the estuary. It has a fairly complete cloister and an outer yard, and is always accessible to the public. The mud flats are the temporary home of birds from the far north, Russia and beyond. On the banks of the Argideen are the varied, lush **Timoleague Castle Gardens** (*open June–Aug Mon–Sat 11–5.30, Sun 2–5.30; adm,* **t** *(023) 46116*), with many rare and tender plants. The 13th-century Barry Castle is in ruins, but the more modern house sits comfortably amid the landscaped gardens. Both the Catholic and Protestant **churches** are worth seeing in the village, the latter for its Harry Clarke window, the former for its richly decorated walls covered in mosaic decorated by a Maharajah. **Dillon's Pub** in Timoleague (*see* p.195) is a good stopping place for a coffee or lunch.

Clonakilty (*Cloich na Coillte*), birthplace of Michael Collins (*see* below), received its first charter in 1292. It was a thriving linen town in the 18th century but was given the label 'Clonakilty, God help us' during the Great Famine, such was the horror and suffering of the people there. Nowadays it is an attractive place, with traditional hand-painted signs swinging from the pubs and shops. You could linger in the **West Cork Regional Museum** (*open daily May–Oct, call for times,* **t** *(023) 33115; adm*) on Main Street, or in the craft centre, or look at the statue of the pikeman, a monument to 1789. A **model railway village** (*open Mon–Fri 11–5, Sat and Sun 1–5; adm;* **t** *(023) 33224, www.clon.ie/mvillage.html*) has been built on the Inchydoney Road and re-creates the world of the long-closed West Cork Railway. Clonakilty is also famous for its black puddings, sold at **Twomey's** (**t** *(023) 33733*), the butcher's shop in Pearse Street.

Lisnagun Ring Fort (*Lios na gCon:* 'fort of the hound'; *open Mon–Fri 9–5, Sat and Sun 10–5; adm*), a reconstructed 10th-century defensive farm, is signposted on the N71, just outside town on the Cork Road. Just off the N71 near Ballinascarty are **Lisselan Gardens** (*open daily Jan, Feb, Nov and Dec 8–5, Mar, Apr and Oct 8–6, May, June and Sept 8–7, July and Aug 8–8; adm;* **t** *(023) 33249, www.lisselan.com*). Mature rhododendrons and unusual, exotic trees and plants are cultivated here in an informal 25-acre landscape, around a simple French-château-style house built in 1851.

Other attractions include a small **stone circle** at **Templebrian**, north of the village off the N71, and a fine, broad beach at **Inchydoney** (it is becoming a bit overdeveloped, but there are plenty of other coves and inlets around Clonakilty). Inland from here, if you fancy a drive or bike ride away from the coast, follow small, uncrowded roads going north-west amongst scenic farmland, past wooded demesnes, to **Ballynacarriga Castle** south-east of Dunmanway (*Dún Mánmhaí*), a well-preserved ruin on the edge of a small lough, with a *sheela-na-gig* on the outside wall and fine stone carvings within.

The reputation of Michael Collins, much-loved strategist of the War of Independence, is growing with the years, rather as Dev (De Valera) himself prophesied . He was born a few miles outside Clonakilty, and bus tours now run from Clonakilty to **Woodfield**, the family homestead near Pike's Cross with a small memorial to him. Only the older building remains, as the new farmhouse was burnt down in a revenge attack by a regular army officer, Major A.E. Percival, and his troops in 1921 after an IRA attack on Rosscarbery. Michael Collins went to see the ruins on the last day of his life, and met up with friends and relatives in his cousin's bar. He was confident that he would not be attacked in his own county despite the warnings of friends who told him that something was planned; later he was ambushed by anti-Treaty forces and shot in the head on the road between Bandon and Clonakilty. A little further west is **Sam's Cross**, where there is a bronze roundel of him by Seamus Murphy.

Rosscarbery to Glandore

The N71 now leads to **Rosscarbery**, a charming old-fashioned village with a pretty square, famous for its eating houses, lively pubs, and a strange saying – 'Rosscarbery, where they buried the elephant' – which nobody seems to understand. It had a famous school of learning founded by St Fachtna in the 6th century, and a medieval Benedictine monastery. The very attractive 17th-century **Protestant church** is on the site of the old cathedral; it was mostly rebuilt in the 19th century, although the tower dates from 1612. It was raised to a bishopric in the 12th century. Inside the church is a marble statue of the sixth Baron Carbery in Elizabethan dress, and a fine carving on the west doorway. The nationalist Jeremiah O'Donovan Rossa (1831–1915) was born in the grounds of the Celtic Ross Hotel (which has delicious bar food). He was active in the Fenian movement, arrested in 1865, and sentenced to penal servitude, but was freed in 1871 on the condition that he left Ireland. He went to America, where he published, among other things, recollections of his prison life. When O'Donovan Rossa died, he had an enormous funeral in Dublin, at which Patrick Pearse proclaimed, in his famous oration, 'The fools, the fools, they have left us our dead, and while Ireland holds these graves, Ireland unfree shall never be at peace'.

Castle Freke, the home of the barons of Carbery, is a sad Gothic ruin to be found on the road out to **Galley Head**. It was in fine shape for the 10th baron's coming-of-age ball in 1913, for it had just been restored, after a fire, with reinforced steel window frames and reinforced concrete between the walls. The 10th Lord Carbery was rather a spoiled young man who is remembered for his daring looping of the loop in his monoplane, his beautiful wife Jose, and his devilment in shooting out the eyes of his neighbours in a group painting of the Carbery Hunt that used to hang in the hall of Castle Freke. After the end of the First World War he, like many Anglo-Irish, left, sold the estate and settled elsewhere, in his case in Kenya, where he married twice more. The castle just grew more dilapidated with the passing years.

Inland to the west, in the valley of the little River Roury, stands **Coppinger's Court**, an Elizabethan or Jacobean mansion burned out in 1641, which shelters cows in winter. To the left off an unclassified road between **Leap** (pronounced 'lep') and Rosscarbery, it was built by Sir William Coppinger, who sprang to prominence after the defeat of the Irish chieftains and Spaniards at the Battle of Kinsale. At that stage he was valet to one of the O'Driscolls, but used the time and position to amass an empire from the confiscated lands of the defeated chieftains, only to lose it to Cromwell in his old age.

North-west of Rosscarbery, signposted off the N71 Skibbereen road, is **Castle Salem** (*tours by appointment; adm; t (023) 48381, www.castlesalem.com*), a 15th-century towerhouse built for the MacCarthys, known as Benduff. It was confiscated from Florence MacCarthy in 1641 and given to a Cromwellian soldier, a Major Apollo Morris, who became a Quaker and renamed it Castle Shalom, meaning 'peace', which over the years has become Salem. During the 17th century, a farmhouse was built into the thick castle walls, and now the entrance into the first floor of the castle is through a small door at the top of the farmhouse stairs. It is slowly crumbling away, but perhaps your entrance money will help to keep its roof on. It also offers B&B (*see* p.193). The graves of a community of Quakers are in the grounds.

From Roury Bridge, a country road (R507) winds to **Drombeg Stone Circle**, from where you can see across pastures and cornfields to the sea. Erected between the 2nd century BC and 2nd century AD, it may have been used for some kind of fertility rite and worship of the sun. A cremated body was discovered in the centre of the circle when it was excavated. Close beside the circle are the remains of an open-air roasting oven and cooking pit, so it must have been a place of feasting. The cooking pit would have been filled with water and hot stones added to bring the water to boiling point.

The beaches of Owenahincha and, to the east, the Longstrand have wonderful sand. **Union Hall** and **Glandore** are two pretty and colourful resort villages on a narrow inlet 5 miles (8km) west of Rosscarbery, with harbours filled with painted boats. Their grey-steepled Protestant churches add to their prettiness, though the congregations have dwindled to a handful. Union Hall was named after the 1800 Act of Union, which the British government and most of the Ascendancy sought after the eruption of 1798. Glandore is fashionable with the rich; its south-facing seaside houses form a street known as 'millionaire's row'. Jonathan Swift was a visitor to Glandore while writing *Rupes Carberiae*. Hardy fuchsia adorns the hedges here as it does in so much of west Cork; the bright red-and-purple-flowered plant was brought from Chile.

Castletownshend to Cape Clear Island

Round the next headland, **Castletownshend** is a neat Georgian village on a steep hill, in the middle of which grows a huge sycamore tree. The bar and restaurant **Mary Anne's** (*see* p.195) is a popular tourist spot, with a beer garden at the back. The village's claim to fame is that it used to be the home of Edith Somerville (1858–1949), author of *The Real Charlotte* and the humorous *Reminiscences of an Irish RM* and other novels. She is buried in the pretty Church of Ireland graveyard here, with her cousin and co-author Violet Martin (1862–1915), who wrote under the pen name Martin Ross. In their day, Castletownshend was made up of 'the gentry', who were all vaguely related to each other: the Coghills, the Chavasses and the Alymers all lived in good stone houses at various points throughout the village. At one end lived the Somervilles in Drishane House and, in the castle on the shore, lived the Townshend family. They still do to this day – you can even stay in **The Castle** (*see* p.193).

Park your car in the village and walk up to **St. Barrahane's Church** to visit the graves of Edith Somerville and Violet Martin, and look down on the wooded Castlehaven shore. It is one of the prettiest graveyards in the country, planted with autumn-flowering cyclamen, gnarled cherry trees and the stately yew. The church itself has a very fine Harry Clarke window and a four-spired turret. The history of these Protestant families reveals itself in the gravestones and memorials in the church. They hoped for service to the British Empire and retirement to Ireland for their sons and, if they were lucky, intermarriage with local families for the daughters. Edith Somerville did not put her energies into marriage and children, and we are all the better off for it. She and Violet Martin managed to collaborate to produce brilliantly funny yet serious novels. Their talent for remembering and polishing the well-turned word or phrase, as well as the idiosyncrasies of their neighbours, is irresistible. Edith was the organist in the church and at one time master of the Carbery Hunt (still going strong). Her brother, Admiral

Boyle Somerville, was shot dead on his doorstep in 1935, in a sad afternote to the War of Independence. The Somervilles got on well with all the locals but, after the establishment of the Irish Free State, the IRA were operating spasmodically against the status quo. The admiral had been asked what life was like in the British navy by young local men and had also provided them with references. The IRA accused him, in a note that was thrown in the door by his murderer, of being a British recruiting agent. In response to this outrage, De Valera reinstated the ban on the IRA that he had lifted in 1932.

On the outskirts of the village is a pleasant Catholic church on the road to Skibbereen, and farther on is **Knockdrum Fort**, a stone-built cashel. Opposite the fort is an alignment of standing stones known as 'the fingers' – a prehistoric calendar. A road follows the coast westwards to Castlehaven where, in the little glen leading up to the 18th-century rectory (of the first Somerville to come to Cork), there's a holy well dedicated to St Barrahane. It is still venerated: locals hang threads from the branches of the tree that overhangs it, and as the thread rots, their ailment disappears.

Skibbereen, linked to Castletownshend by the R596, is a market town famous for its weekly newspaper, the *Southern Star*, previously called the *Skibbereen Eagle*. It's a good read and sheds light on local preoccupations. The old phrase, 'Skibbereen, where they ate the donkey', came about during the Famine. From 1846 to 1848 more than a million people died in Ireland, yet foodstuffs worth £17 million were being exported to England every year. The soup kitchens run by the gentry could not possibly feed the thousands of starving people who poured into Skibbereen from the countryside.

Between Skibbereen and Drimoleague, off the R593, is an exciting and thoughtful enterprise, **Liss Ard Gardens** (*open summer Sun–Fri 10–8, winter Wed–Sun 1–6; adm; t (028) 22368, www.lissard.com*). This is a combination of artistic spaces, water and wildlife gardens extending for 40 acres. The 'Sky Garden' was designed by the American James Turrell.

Three and a half miles (5.6km) to the south of Skibbereen on the Baltimore Road are the **Creagh Gardens** (*open daily 10–6; adm; t (028) 22121*) – romantic and informal gardens planted amongst woods that lead to the river estuary. They are best seen between April and June, although the grounds are lovely all year. The walled garden is cultivated organically and contains a variety of hens and other fowl.

All around Skibbereen, and particularly to the west, is some lovely countryside where knuckles and fingers of land reach out into the sea, breaking off into islands such as Sherkin and Clear. **Baltimore** is an attractive fishing village that is perched at the end of one of these fingers. It looks out on to the humpy shape of Sherkin Island, and beyond that to the wonderful expanse of Roaringwater Bay and Carbery's Hundred Isles. In summer, the trawlers are outnumbered by the sailing boats, and the place buzzes with visitors who come for the sea sports, the hotels, the bars and the eating places, and to visit the islands. Holiday cottages have been built here, as they have in many of these coastal villages; they jar slightly among the local architecture, but thankfully there are not yet enough of them to spoil the area. This is also the place to get a boat for the islands – negotiate a fare with the local fishermen, or hop aboard the regular ferryboat.

The O'Driscolls ruled all this area, but by 1200 their power had dwindled and their chief kept up his revenues by plundering ships and exacting harbour dues. You will notice that many people you come across here have the surname O'Driscoll, and in August, in the week before the annual regatta, there is always an O'Driscoll get-together. The O'Driscolls built nine castles around Baltimore in order to secure themselves; these are now all dramatic ruins, especially those on Cape Clear and on Sherkin Island. This area has many tales of blood and treachery – one such story describes a retaliatory attack on Baltimore in 1537 by some soldiers from Waterford, after the O'Driscoll chief of the time had plundered a ship loaded with Spanish wine bound for Waterford City. Another recounts the disappearance of 150 people who were carried off as slaves by Algerian pirates in 1631. A number of them were English settlers who arrived in 1607 during the time of Sir Fineen O'Driscoll (who was on good terms with the English). The pirates had been guided into Baltimore by a man from **Dungarvan**, just up the coast. The abducted settlers and the native Irish who were also taken were never seen again. Thomas Davis speculated on their fate in his poem *The Sack of Baltimore*:

Oh! Some must tug the galley's oar and some must tend the steed,
This boy will bear the sheik's chibouk; and that a bey's jereed.

Not surprisingly, people moved farther inland and Skibbereen was founded. Baltimore later became a rotten borough in the gift of Lord Carbery, sending two MPs to the English Parliament. After the Famine, during which time people here suffered terribly, a boat-building industry was set up, and there are still two or three boat-builders locally. You can learn to sail at the sailing schools based here, or even better, if you have your own boat, arrive that way and explore the islands with their sandy beaches and tranquil green fields. Diving, windsurfing and deep-sea fishing are all easy to organize. There are also regular ferries to the islands.

East of Baltimore on the mainland is the beautiful **Lough Ine**, just the place for a walk or picnic. Or you could walk from the village up to the navigational beacon at the tip of the peninsula – a beautiful spot, with dramatic cliffs of shiny slate, which breaks off in big sheets and piles up on the shore below. Lough Ine is a remarkable stretch of saltwater connected to the sea by a very narrow channel partially blocked by a sill of rock, which prevents the lough from ever dropping below the halfway mark. Very little fresh water flows into it, and it is extremely deep, especially on its western side. This unusual geography has produced a marine life more typical of the Mediterranean Sea: the red-mouthed goby fish, a variety of sponges, coral and the purple sea urchin thrive in its warm waters. Seawater rushes in and out of the channel with the pull of the tide, and the water is very clear. In the shallows you can see the spiky sea urchins and the pearly saddle oyster in profusion. The lough is a nature reserve and divers have to obtain a government permit. The water is scattered with humpbacked islands, and the road that leads down to the car park is edged in September with arches of brilliant red fuchsia. The hilly woods behind are often hung with dramatic wisps of cloud, great conifers mixed with beech give way to oaks and holly, and the walks are edged with ferns and bell heather.

Sherkin Island (*see* 'Getting to Islands off County Cork', p.176) encloses Baltimore harbour. It is very small with three sandy beaches. Murphy's Bar on the island hires out bikes, and you can head off to visit one of the excellent sandy beaches on the far side of the island or the ruins of a 15th-century Franciscan abbey that was destroyed by the expeditionary raid from Waterford in 1537. There are several B&Bs on the island and bars serving food.

St Ciaran was born on **Cape Clear Island** (*see* 'Getting to Islands off County Cork', p.176), where the remains of a cross and holy well mark the site of his church. There are several other ancient stones at the eastern end of the island, in the townland of St Comillane; one is known as the trysting stone because of the hole bored through it. About 140 people live on the island, which is Irish-speaking. There is a B&B, a campsite, a couple of hostels, three bars, a small heritage centre and a pottery. Of special note here is Ed Harper's goat's cheese and, even better, his ice cream (*t (028) 39126*). The cars that the islanders use are very ancient, and a lot of dead cars litter up the place. A visit to the island makes a wonderful day trip (it takes about 45 minutes on the ferry), but you might like to stay for a day or so to go walking or bird-watching. There is an important **bird observatory** here by the harbour, and it is worth asking about organized bird-watching trips, as the island is on a major bird migration route and many birds are blown in by the autumn gales. You may see Manx shearwaters that live on the rocky islands off the Kerry coast; in the mornings and evenings during July and August, huge numbers fly past, skimming the water on their way back and forth from their feeding grounds.

The familiar **Fastnet Rock**, mentioned in the shipping forecasts, is just off Cape Clear, and you can get a fine view of it from the hill of Clear and its south-facing sea cliffs. This is especially dramatic in the winter, when the wind often reaches force 10 and the seas are huge with waves and spume. The list of ships lost in these waters makes chilly reading, but it is a divers' paradise. The diving centre in Baltimore organizes diving around the reefs of Fastnet.

Ballydehob to Mizen Head

Ballydehob is on the next finger of land, stretching into Roaringwater Bay and the Atlantic. It is a colourful little village 10 miles (16km) from Skibbereen on the N71, distinguished by a fine 12-arch railway bridge, now defunct, which lies at the head of Roaringwater Bay. Quite a few 'blow-ins' have come to live around here: Germans, Dutch and English who have bought up neglected cottages in spectacular situations. About 2 miles (3.2km) south at **Rossbrin Cove**, the ruin of an O'Mahony castle stands by the sea, home of 14th-century scholar Finin. **Gurtnagrough Folk Museum** (*open daily in summer, call for times, t (028) 37274; adm*) , 3 miles (5km) north of Ballydehob, contains a delightful, haphazard collection of bygone agricultural and domestic tools.

Schull (pronounced 'skull'), west of Ballydehob on the coast, is a small boating and tourist centre with a deep harbour; ferries (*see* p.176) run out to Clear Island and along the coast to Baltimore. Schull has a good selection of craft shops, food shops, restaurants and cafés. It also has a wonderful second-hand bookshop, Fuchsia Books, in which you could while away hours on the many books of Irish and local interest.

It also has the small **Schull Planetarium** (*call for opening times, **t** (028) 28552; adm, www.westcorkweb.ie/planetarium*), in Schull Community College, since the night skies here are so free of light pollution. Diving and sailing are also offered in the village.

A spectacular road runs from Schull up to **Mount Gabriel** (1,339ft/407m). If you climb it, be careful of the prehistoric copper mines dug into the slopes. The view is out of this world. The R591 curls round the head of lovely **Toormore Bay** and past **Goleen** with its sandy beach (the Gulf Stream means that swimming is quite feasible here) and the Ewe Art Centre nearby (*see* 'Courses and Tours', p.192). The road winds on in its spectacular way to **Crookhaven** with its boat-filled harbour. O'Sullivans Bar is a good place for a jar, its walls decorated with sketches of well-known locals. This was once a busy anchorage for fishing and sailing fleets. Marconi built the first transatlantic telegraph station here in 1902, before moving it to Valentia Island in Kerry.

Farther on, **Barley Cove**, one of the best beaches in the south-west, stretches down to the splendid, sheer heights of **Mizen Head**, the southwesternmost point of Ireland. The soft red sandstone cliffs banded with white fall down to the sea, while flurries of birds glide on the air currents beneath you. The cliffs are high and nearly vertical, so be careful. A lighthouse on the islet below is linked to the mainland by a suspension bridge. Many ships have been wrecked here in the past. The old fog signal station, now controlled automatically, has been opened to visitors (by the former keeper) as the **Mizen Head Signal Station Visitor Centre** (*open daily mid-Mar–May and Oct 10.30–5, June–Sept 10–6, Nov–mid-Mar 11–4; adm; **t** (028) 35115, www.mizenhead.ie*).

Farther around is **Three Castle Head**, where on the edge of the sheer cliffs is a dramatic ruin, an O'Mahony castle. On its other side is a supposedly haunted lough. You can walk out to it, but do not bring any dogs, and ask permission at the farmhouse first. (From the Barley Cove Hotel car park turn right, then left at the T-junction, right at the next junction, ignoring the sign for the B&B on the left. Pass through the farm gate and on up the track.)

From Mizen Head, the R591 goes to **Durrus** at the head of Dunmanus Bay, which has another ruined medieval castle. The drive to Kilcrohane and Sheep's Head, over Seefin Pass then on to **Gerahies**, is magnificent and untouristy. Views extend across Bantry Bay and the Beara Peninsula. The **Sheep's Head** peninsula is relatively unvisited; stand on the hilliest parts of the rocky promontory and look down on the little farmhouses built into the side of the slopes. The small village of **Kilcrohane** is famous for its early potatoes. You can walk or cycle along the Goat's Path and north side of the peninsula. From Durrus, an amazing route (part-road part-track but quite drivable) leads past the Durrus Cheese Farm and over the top of the peninsula down into Bantry.

Bantry (*Beanntraí*) has one of the finest views in the world, out over the bay. There is a deep-water harbour between the Beara and Dunmanus peninsulas, which in 1796 attracted a French fleet of 47 ships and 14,000 troops under General Hoche, with Wolfe Tone on board. They were all set to support the planned United Irishmen's uprising, but what became known as the 'Protestant wind' foiled their attempt to land and they had to return to France. Don't miss **Bantry House** (*open Mar–Oct daily 10–6; adm;* see also '*Where to Stay*', *p.193; **t** (027) 50047, www.bantryhouse.com*), which has a glorious view and is directly above the town, so you do not see the ugly petrol stations below it. You can tour the house on your own (accompanied by the faint strains of classical music), with a detailed guide written by the owner. Rare French tapestries, family portraits and china still have a feeling of being used and loved.

The house and garden have definitely seen better days, yet this is one of the most interesting houses in Ireland open to the public, and certainly one of the least officious. The house was built in 1740, and added to in 1765. The owner, Mr Egerton Shelswell-White, is always at work on various restoration projects in and around the house. He is an enthusiastic patron of music, and many fine concerts are held in the library. The dining room is a stunning shade of bottle-blue, against which the gold-framed portraits and the china and silver look magnificent. Two of the portraits are of King George II and Queen Charlotte. They were painted at the sovereign's order and given to the first Earl of Bantry, from whom Mr Shelswell-White is descended, as a token of thanks for his efforts in helping repel the French invasion force of 1798. In the side courtyard of the house is an **Armada Exhibition** devoted to the 1796–78 Bantry Bay Armada. There is a 1:6 scale model of a frigate in cross-section and extracts from Wolfe Tone's journal. The house also has a tea-room and craft shop.

Offshore is **Whiddy Island**, now used for long-term oil storage by Gulf Oil, which brought prosperity in the 1970s (some of the bungalows along the shore of Bantry Bay were built then). Gulf Oil suspended their operations in 1979, when 50 people were killed when a tanker exploded.

To the west of the town you can view the 9th-century **Kilnaruane Pillar Stone** (take the N71 Cork road and turn left by the West Lodge Hotel), carved with figurative and interlaced panels, including one of a boat with oarsmen that some people think is a depiction of St Brendan.

Glengarriff's (*An Gleann Garbh*) humpy hills and wooded banks look over still water and isles. The average annual temperature here is 11°C (52°F). **Ilnacullin Gardens**, alias Garinish Island (see *p.176 for details of ferry; open Mar and Oct Mon–Sat 10–4.30, Sun 1–5; Apr Mon–Sat 10–6.30, Sun 1–6.30; May, June and Sept Mon–Sat 10–6.30, Sun 11–6.30; July and Aug Mon–Sat 9.30–6.30, Sun 11–6.30; adm; t (027) 63040, www. heritageireland.ie*), used to be covered only in rocks, birch, heather and gorse, until it was made into 37 acres of garden by a Scotsman, John Allen Bryce, in 1910, and designed by Harold Peto. Now it is a dream island full of subtropical plants, complete with a formal Italian garden, rock gardens and a marble pool full of goldfish. It is an exceptional place, perfectly structured and full of outstanding plants, and well worth the return boat fare from Glengarriff. George Bernard Shaw often stayed here. You will find that there are many boatmen willing to take you out to the island.

The village itself consists of a main street lined with craft shops selling woollen items of every description, and soft sheepskins. Wonderful walks can be taken in the **Glengarriff Forest**, full of every shade of green – mossy trees and stones, ferns growing in every crevice and on the trees, mostly oak, beech and holly. Also growing in wild profusion is *Rhododendron ponticum*; here, as in Killarney, it has become a threat to native plants. There is a steep drive to **Barley Lake** (*Loch na hEornan*), up in mountainous bogland crossed by rushing streams. The tourist office stocks a local walking map.

You might walk in **Glengarriff Valley**, 'the bitter glen', and up to the hills hidden in the Caha Range, or continue westwards into the **Beara Peninsula** – one of the less touristy parts of the western coasts. The Beara presents rougher, rockier landscapes than its neighbours to the north and south, under the sombre peaks of the **Caha Mountains**, some of the highest in Ireland. From **Adrigole**, the first town west of Glengarriff, you can drive up the **Healy Pass Road**, with its lovely mountain scenery gazing down on the indented sea line and the green woods. It is quite a testing zigzag drive following the R574 road to Lauragh in County Kerry (*see* p.144).

Castletownbere, the only town of any size, is a fishing village constructed around a deep-water harbour where you can get a boat across to Bear Island (Bere on some maps). It is busy in the summertime with sailors, walkers and cyclists and festivals, especially during the regatta on the first weekend of August. Hungry Hill (2,251ft/ 686m) and Sugarloaf Mountain (1,887ft/575m) are very popular with climbers and hill-walkers, offering beautiful views in every direction. To the west are the looming **Slieve Miskish Mountains** with equally lovely views. Bear Island is used by the Irish army for training; it has a pub, a shop, a splendid restaurant and a B&B, and the opportunity for long, peaceful walks.

Just outside Castletownbere is the ruined castle of **Dunboy** (*on private land; adm may be charged*), on a small wooded peninsula. In fact there are two buildings here: the ancient ruin was the castle of Donal O'Sullivan Bere, the powerful chief of the O'Sullivans, who played a leading role in organizing the revolt against English rule. He fought in the disastrous Battle of Kinsale, and his castle was besieged by Sir George Carew. It held out bravely under the leadership of MacGeoghegan, a subsidiary chief, but was eventually stormed and its inhabitants hanged. Donal waited in hiding for more help from the Spanish but, when he learnt that Philip III of Spain had abandoned all thoughts of another expedition, he decided Ulster was his safest refuge. He set off from Glengarriff in late December 1602 with 400 fighting men, 600 women and children and servants. They were continually attacked by the English and other hostile chiefs; only 35 survived to reach the protection of the O'Rourke chief in Leitrim Castle. Donal hoped for a pardon from James I in 1603 but got none, so he sailed to Spain with his family. Philip gave him honours and a pension, but he was murdered in Madrid by John Bathe, an Anglo-Irishman. J.A. Froude based his Irish historical romance *The Two Chiefs of Dunboy* (1889) on this story.

The other ruin on the peninsula is a 19th-century **Puxley Mansion** in the Scottish Baronial style, built by the Puxleys, a family who became very wealthy through copper-mining. They were burned out in 1921, although they had lived latterly mainly in England. Daphne du Maurier used them as an inspiration for her novel *Hungry Hill*. Exotic garden escapees grow wild in the hedgerows and roadsides here – gunnera, buddleia, orange monbretia – and every garden sports spiky New Zealand flax and the pretty myrtle with its cinnamon-coloured bark.

A scenic drive can be made to the end of the Beara Peninsula, where another sparsely inhabited island, **Dursey Island**, at the tip of the peninsula, is connected to the mainland by a **cable car** (*open Mon–Sat 9–11, 2.30–5 and 7–8, Sun 9–10.30, 1–2.30 and 7–8; also June–Aug Sun 4–5; arrive 30mins before departure*) at Ballaghboy.

The cable car was set up in the 1970s and is designed to take six passengers, or one person and a cow, and is said to be the only working example of its kind in Ireland. The islanders graze cattle and try to earn a living through fishing. About 20 people live on the island full time, but Irish is no longer spoken here although it was recorded in 1925 as being a Gaeltacht area. A road leads through the village of **Kilmichael** and across the middle of the island to a Martello tower. Tracks lead around the cliffs to **Dursey Head**, which has wonderful views: from here you can see the three rocks in the ocean known as the Bull, the Cow and the Calf.

As the road winds around the coast, there is barely a tree to be seen; only thorn and fuchsia hedges, and astonishingly beautiful coastal views all the way through Allihies, Eyeries and Ardgroom. Between Castletownbere and Allihies, at the junction where the road goes left for Dursey, is a wedge **grave** in a field, and from here you can see the beach at Ballydonegan.

The village of **Allihies** is a tiny place along one street, with a fine hostel and friendly pubs. Fresh fish is fried up in the simple Atlantic restaurant, bikes can be hired from O'Sullivan's, and the beach at Garinish is of white crystalline sand. There is a café and camp site by the beach, and as yet the place is unspoiled. Allihies has always been a fishing village, but during the 19th century it was also a busy copper-mining centre that formed part of the Puxley empire. The mines closed in 1930 but used to employ 1,200 people, some of whom were skilled workers brought in from Cornwall to oversee the locals. This caused great resentment, and the community boycotted the Cornish workers – their food supplies had to come from Wales on the boats that took the copper ore to Swansea. Their ruined stone cottages and the remains of a Nonconformist chapel are still there. There is easy walking around the copper mines, which are above the village. Part of the **Beara Way** runs above Allihies; a track continues from the copper mine, and it is a glorious walk to Eyeries. (Read *West Cork Walks* by Kevin Corcoran.)

Back on the tarmac road to Eyeries, you pass a sign for globe artichokes (pick your own), a treat for self-caterers. The café on the beach sells hand-made crafts, and you might want to stop in at **Great Barrington Pottery** (*shop open afternoons, but they are flexible*). The drive to Eyeries is as different as the weather; you might be impressed by churning seas, black rocks, rough bracken and wind-torn skies, or, if the weather is fine, by idyllic cerulean water, brilliant green fields, wildflowers and silvery rocks. Massive rocks are scattered around this area; recent archaeological research has shown that many date from the earliest days of Christianity in Ireland. Some also date from penal times, when Catholics had to hold their services in secret places. The scenery is barren and hard, with exciting juxtapositions of colour, and the Slieve Miskish Mountains are a constant brooding presence.

The village of **Eyeries** is painted in strong Mediterranean colours; behind it rises Maulin Mountain (2,044ft/620m). Above **Ballycrovane Harbour**, on a little hill, looms the country's tallest **ogham stone**, at more than 5m (17ft). Milleens, a farmhouse cheese, is made around here. As you approach **Ardgroom** the seas are calmer, and in the bay the lines of seaweed-covered ropes and rafts indicate mussel farming. The road continues to Lauragh and Derreen Gardens (*see* **County Kerry**, p.144).

East of Cork: Midleton and Youghal

Approximately 11 miles (18km) from Cork City, east on the N25, is the attractive town of **Midleton** (*Mainistir na Corann*), which has benefited from the restoration of an 18th-century whiskey distillery, the **Old Midleton Distillery**, off Distillery Road (*open for guided tours Mar–Oct daily 10–6, Nov–Feb Mon–Fri 11.30, 2.30 and 4; adm; t (021) 461 3594, www.whiskeytours.ie*). It's a fine building, self contained within 11 acres, and you can tour all the major parts – mills, maltings, cornstores, stillhouses and kilns. The waterwheel is in perfect order, and you can see the largest potstill in the world, with a capacity of more than 30,000 gallons, and sample some of the delicious stuff. There is a mass of information charting the history of Irish whiskey.

South-west of Midleton is the impressive 15th-century **Barryscourt Castle** (*open June–Sept daily 10–6, Oct–May Fri–Wed 11–5; adm adults; t (021) 488 2218/3864, www.heritageireland.ie*) at Carrigtohill, which contains an exhibition on the history of the Barrys and the castle. It is a quadrangular keep with square towers surrounded by a lawn, overlooking the inner reaches of Cork harbour. The 18th-century farmhouse in its *bawn* sells crafts, antiquarian books and teas.

The fast main road (N25) to Midleton and Youghal means that many people don't explore the peninsula opposite Crosshaven. Turn off at Midleton and follow the R629 to *Cluain Uamha* ('meadow of the cave'), where an ancient bishopric was founded by St Colman in the 6th century. There are some large limestone caves close to the village, but it is chiefly interesting for its vast and ancient cathedral. This dates from the 13th century, and the round tower beside it is one of the only two surviving round towers in the county. You are allowed to climb to the top, from which the view is superb; its castellated top is more modern. Among the monuments in the cathedral is an alabaster tomb to George Berkeley, the philosopher who was bishop here from 1734 to 1753, and a 17th-century Fitzgerald tomb. The carved decoration on the north door represents the pagan symbols of life.

The R629 from Cloyne leads down to **Ballycotton**, a little fishing village in a peaceful, unspoiled bay. There is a pretty view out to the Ballycotton Islands, which protect the village from the worst of the sea winds, and a bird sanctuary on the extensive marsh by the estuary. Close by is the welcoming **Ballymaloe House** (signposted in Castlemartyr on the Cork–Waterford road), famous for its hotel, restaurant, cooking school and kitchen/craft shop (*see* p.209). The **gardens** (*open daily 9–6; adm; t (021) 465 2531*) are modern, though laid out within the old grounds, and are designed to resemble a series of 'rooms', including a potager in geometric patterns, a formal fruit garden, a herb garden, a rose garden and herbaceous borders.

At Ladysbridge, near Garryvoe, are the ruins of a grand fortified house built of local limestone, **Ightermurragh Castle**. Over one fireplace is a Latin inscription that tells that it was built by Edmund Supple and his wife, 'whom love binds in one', in 1641.

Two miles (3.2km) south-east in **Kilcredan**'s 17th-century Church of Ireland church are some fascinating limestone headstones with a variety of imaginative motifs. Sadly, the church has suffered the fate of many of that faith and is without a roof, and the carved tomb of Sir Robert Tynte has been ravaged by the weather.

Tourist Information

Midleton: Jameson Heritage Centre,
t (021) 461 3702. *Open June–Sept.*
Youghal: Market House, on harbour,
t (024) 92447, *www.youghalchamber.ie.*
Open June–mid-Sept.

Shopping

Ardsallagh Goat's Cheese and Milk,
Ardsallagh, Youghal. Local dairy produce.
Some of the cheese is bottled with olive oil.
Ballymaloe Craft & Kitchen shop, Shanagarry.
Hand-made kitchen knives.
Stephen Pearce Pottery, Shanagarry,
www.stephenpearce.com

Sports and Activities

Activity Centres
Trabolgan, Midleton, **t** (021) 466 1551,
www.trabolgan.com. Indoor and outdoor
fun for children.

Courses and Tours
Ballymaloe Cookery School, Shanagarry,
Midleton, **t** (021) 464 6785, *www.
cookingisfun.ie.* Cookery, gardening and
wine courses at the famous Ballymaloe
House hotel (*see* opposite).

Golf
East Cork Golf Club, Gurtacrue, Midleton,
t (021) 463 1687, *http://homepage.eircom.
net/~eastcorkgolfclub*
Water Rock Golf Course, Midleton, **t** (021)
461 3499, *www.waterrockgolfcourse.com*
Youghal Golf Club, Knockaverry, Youghal,
t (024) 92787, *http://homepage.eircom.net/
~youghalgc*

Open Farms
Cnoc A Ceo **Leahy's Open Farm and Museum,**
Condonstown, Dungourney, **t** (021) 466 8461.
Feed the animals, play games or visit the
agricultural museum. *Closed Oct–Easter.*

Spas
**Midleton Park Wellness Centre
and Spa**, Midleton, **t** (021) 463 5153,

www.midletonpark.com/wellness. A range
of treatments and alternative therapies
(facials, hydrotherapy, wraps, reflexology,
hot stone massages and reiki), plus state-of-
the-art facilities: a pool, gym, steam room,
outdoor hot tub, sauna and aerobics room.

Where to Stay and Eat

East of Cork
Aherne's Hotel and Seafood Restaurant,
North Main St, Youghal, **t** (024) 92424,
www.ahernes.net (*expensive–luxury*).
Well-appointed rooms in a good atmosphere.
Wonderful fresh fish, local meat and
produce are used in the restaurant.
Ballymaloe House, Shanagarry, **t** (021) 465
2531, *www.ballymaloe.ie* (*expensive*).
A beautiful Georgian house near the fishing
village of Ballycotton, with elegant rooms,
friendly service and generous helpings of
fabulous food that may inspire you to take
a cookery course (*see* above).
Midleton Park Hotel, Midleton **t** (021) 463 5100,
www.midletonpark.com (*expensive*).
A luxurious option for the price. The décor
is beautiful, the atmosphere relaxed and
the restaurant food superb.
Glenview House, Ballinaclasha, Midleton,
t (021) 463 1680, *www.glenviewmidleton.com*
(*moderate*). An 18th-century house with
homely décor, good food, lovely grounds and
2 self-catering mews apartments.
The Old Parochial House, Castlemartyr, **t** (021)
466 7454 (*moderate*). An elegantly restored
Victorian house on the edge of the village.
**Spanish Point Seafood Restaurant
and Guesthouse**, Ballycotton, **t** (021) 464
6177, *www.spanishpointballycotton.com*
(*moderate*). Comfortable rooms in a
Georgian house with wonderful views.
John Tattan catches the fish and Mary
cooks it for their wonderful restaurant.
The Clean Slate, Midleton, **t** (021) 633655
(*moderate*). Adventurous food served in a
striking building.
Finin's Restaurant and Bar, Main St, Midleton,
t 463 2382 (*moderate*). An attractive pub
with an excellent restaurant.
The Farm Gate, Broderick St, Midleton, **t** (021)
463 2771 (*inexpensive–moderate*). Traditional
fare made with largely local ingredients.

Just to the south is **Shanagarry**, famous for Stephen Pearce's pottery (*see* p.209), and the old home of the father of William Penn, founder of Pennsylvania. You can buy simple earthenware and glazed pottery from his studio and tea-rooms or at the Ballymaloe House craft shop, one of the best kitchen shops in the country (*see* p.209).

Youghal (pronounced 'Yawl'; *eochaill*, 'yew wood'), about 30 miles (48km) east of Cork City on the N25, is an important medieval town that used to be a centre for the carpet industry but has become one of the most attractive seaside towns in Ireland. Set on the estuary of the River Blackwater, it has many fine bathing places and a long sandy beach. The river scenery between here and Cappoquin is memorable for its pretty woods, the silver twisting Blackwater and the attractive houses along its banks.

Youghal was founded by the Anglo-Normans in the 13th century and destroyed in the Desmond Rebellion of 1579. The Fitzgeralds, earls of Desmond, were a powerful Anglo-Norman family who joined forces with the Gaelic lords from Ulster to try to repulse the armies of Elizabeth I. Ruthless coercion and martial law put down the rebellion – 'man, woman and child were put to the Sword' wrote Raleigh's half-brother. The ruined town was handed over to Sir Walter Raleigh, since he had played an important part in the suppression, along with 42,000 acres of the Earl's forfeited estate in the Elizabethan plantation period. Raleigh became an 'undertaker', agreeing to repopulate his lands with English settlers and drive out the native Irish. He became mayor of the town and lived in the gabled **Myrtle Grove House** (*private*) at the end of William Street. He later sold Youghal to Richard Boyle, who became the Earl of Cork. Thereafter, it was a prosperous place, supporting Oliver Cromwell and so avoiding another sacking. Raleigh reputedly planted the first potato in the garden – an act that was to have far-reaching consequences for Ireland's population.

In nearby Church Street is the 15th-century Church of Ireland collegiate **Church of St Mary**. Inside this large cruciform church are some interesting monuments, including one to the Earl of Cork, Richard Boyle, looking very smug, surrounded by his mother, his two wives and nine of his 16 children. A memorial stands to an extraordinary lady, the Countess of Desmond, who apparently died in 1604 at the age of 147 after falling out of a tree when gathering cherries. The church was built around 1250, rebuilt in 1461 by Thomas, the 8th Earl of Desmond, and restored in 1884, after lying partially derelict since the Desmond Rebellion. The most notable features are its early English west doorway, the massive pulpit with its canopy of carved bog oak, and the large stained-glass east window (*c*.1468) with the arms of the Desmonds, Sir Walter Raleigh, the Earl of Cork and the Duke of Devonshire. Nearby, on Main Street, is a ruined 15th-century towerhouse, **Tynte's Castle**. Large sections of the old town walls still stand, up on the crest of the hill, but even in 1579 they were in a bad state, and were easily breached by the rebellious Earl of Desmond.

The old part of town lies at the foot of a steep hill; the modern part has grown along the margin of the bay. The main street is spanned by Youghal's landmark, a tower known as the **Clock Gate**, erected in 1771. Other buildings of note are the **Red House**, an early-18th-century Dutch-style brick building, and, on the corner of Church Street, a group of restored medieval **almshouses**. Youghal's harbour is close by. When you see it, try to imagine it fixed up with picket fences and clapboard siding to look like New Bedford, Massachusetts – that's what John Houston did to it when he filmed *Moby Dick* here in 1954, with Youghal's old salts, housewives and children pressed into service as extras. Paddy Linehan's Moby Dick bar facing the harbour is full of photos and mementoes. The tourist office, in the old market house, includes a heritage centre with exhibits on Youghal's rich history, and in summer it offers walking tours of the town. Across the road in Foxes Lane is a small folk museum.

Leaving Youghal for the east, you might wish to take a detour up the lovely **Blackwater Valley**, which has some of the best driving and walking country in Ireland – if you like wooded banks, green fields, old buildings and twisting, unfrequented roads. You may be tempted to follow the Blackwater River to **Lismore** in County Waterford: its cathedral is very impressive, with fine monuments, Georgian glass, Gothic vaulting and a window by Edward Burne-Jones, made by William Morris. The town itself shows the planned approach of the local landlord family, the dukes of Devonshire, who inherited the castle and estates through the Boyles. The 14th child of Richard Boyle, Earl of Cork, is famous for establishing Boyle's law, a basic tenet of physics. To the east is the Great Rath (*Lios Mór*), after which the town is named. The demesne of **Lismore Castle** dominates the town; when it was being rebuilt between 1812 and 1821, the 13th-century Lismore Crosier and 15th-century *Book of Lismore* were found built into the walls of the castle. Both are now in the National Museum, Dublin. The castle can be rented, and the general public can visit the gardens edging the river, with a stately 800-year-old yew walk.

To the west, along the R666, back towards Fermoy, you will pass the turreted Gothic tower gatehouses and bridge of **Ballysaggartmore** (1834) – all that is left of the Kiely estate. This folly was built to the design of their gardener; locals say that after building it, the Kielys ran out of money and had to live in a less significant house on the estate (demolished in the 1930s.)

North of Cork: Fermoy to Mallow

Fermoy (*Mainistir Fhearmuighe*, abbey of the plantations), 30 miles (48km) north of Cork City on the N8, used to be a garrison town for the British army. People here are familiar with every fascinating detail of salmon-catching. The town, built along both sides of the dark River Blackwater, has seen more prosperous days and retains an air of shabby gentility. Lord Fermoy, an ancestor of the late Princess of Wales, is said to have gambled away his Fermoy estates in an evening. The Protestant church, built in 1802, contains some grotesque masks; however, the Catholic church is rather elegant: it was designed by E.W. Pugin in 1867, with an interior by the Pain brothers.

Just outside Fermoy, overlooking the river to the west, is one of the most beautiful houses in Ireland, the late-Georgian mansion, **Castle Hyde**, now owned by Michael Flatley of 'Riverdance' fame (*no access to public*). This was the ancestral home of Douglas Hyde, the first president of the Irish Republic and the founder of the Gaelic League, though he was born at French Park in County Roscommon. **Castlelyons**, a few miles outside the town (turn left off the N8 going towards Cork), is a quiet, pretty

Tourist Information

Fermoy: Brian Toomey Sports, McCurtain St,
t (025) 438 1624
Mallow, Bridge St, t (022) 42222

Shopping

Ardrahan Cheese, Ardrahan House, Kanturk
Mitchelstown Market, Thurs 10.30–4.

Sports and Activities

Fishing

Ballyvolane House, Castlelyons, near Fermoy,
t (025) 36349, *www.ballyvolanehouse.ie*
Speycast Ireland, Ghillie Cottage, Kilbarry Stud,
Fermoy, t (025) 32720, *www.speycast-ireland.
com*. Salmon fly-fishing tuition.

Golf

Doneraile Golf Club, Doneraile, t (022) 24137
Fermoy Golf Club, Corrin, Fermoy, t (025) 32694
Kanturk Golf Club, Kanturk, t (029) 50534
Mallow Golf Club, Ballyellis, Mallow, t (022) 21145
Mitchelstown Golf Club, Limerick Rd,
t (025) 24072, *www.mitchelstown-golf.com*

Open Farms

Kanturk Rural Farm Museum, Mealehara,
Kanturk, t (029) 51319
Millstreet Country Park, Millstreet, t (029) 70810,
www.millstreetcountrypark.com. Nature trails
and archaeological reconstructions.
Rambling House Farm Museum and Folk Park,
Mallow, t (029) 76155. *Closed Oct–Apr.*

Ponytrekking

Green Glens Equestrian Centre, Millstreet,
t (029) 70707. One–6-day trail rides.

Walking

The Ballyhoura Way: Limerick Junction–John's
Bridge near Kanturk (56miles/90km).
The Blackwater Way: Knockmealdown
Mountains–Muckross Park (105miles/168km).

Where to Stay

Castlehyde Hotel, Fermoy, t (025) 31865,
www.castlehydehotel.com (*luxury*).
A beautiful, renovated 18th-century
woodland hotel. There's bar food, or the
dining room offers bistro-style lunches and
richer modern Irish dinners. In summer, you
can eat on a terrace in the woodland garden.
Longueville House, Mallow, t (022) 47156,
www.longuevillehouse.ie (*luxury*).
A stylish manor with views to the river and
Callaghan Castle ruin. The luxurious rooms
are decorated in warm hues, the food is
superlative, and the service is attentive.
Assolas Country House, Kanturk, t (029) 50015,
www.assolas.com (*expensive*). A country
house among mature trees leading down to
the river, offering tennis, fishing and croquet
in the grounds, and delicious food.
Ballyvolane House, Castlelyons, near Fermoy,
t (025) 36349, *www.ballyvolanehouse.ie*
(*expensive*). A Georgian house in beautiful
grounds, serving local seasonal produce,
cheese and meats in its dining room. The
self-catering cottage sleeps 6.
Glanworth Mill, Glanworth, Fermoy, t (025)
38555, *www.glanworthmill.ie* (*expensive*).
A riverside inn with excellent food and rooms
named after writers linked with the area,
including one room cut into the cliff face.
Hibernian Hotel, Mallow, t (022) 21588, *www.
hibhotel.com* (*moderate*). A comfortable
family-run option.
Springfort Hall, Mallow, t (022) 21278, *www.
springfort-hall.com* (*moderate*). A simple but
comfy 18th-century manor in woodlands.

Self-catering

Cashman Thatched Cottage, Garrison, t (029)
50197, *www.irelandselfcateringguide.com*
(*inexpensive*). A charming thatched cottage
with gardens to front and rear, sleeping 6.

Eating Out

La Bigoudenne, 28 McCurtain St, Fermoy,
t (025) 32832 (*moderate*). A French bistro,
with filled crêpes a speciality.
Paki Fitz's, Cork St, Mitchelstown, t (025) 84926
(*moderate*). A café, bar serving food and
sophisticated restaurant.
Glanworth Mill, Glanworth, Fermoy,
t (025) 38555 (*inexpensive–moderate*).
A café serving delightful soups, salads and
desserts, and a formal restaurant for dinner.

hamlet where intimations of past history compel you to stop. Here is the great ruined house of the Barrys, a Norman family, burned down in 1771, and the remains of a 14th-century Franciscan friary. In the graveyard of Kill St Anne is a roofless 15th-century church; within it is the ruin of an 18th-century parish church. The classical **Barrymore Mausoleum** is impressive, especially the white marble bust of the Earl of Barrymore.

To the north, **Mitchelstown** is famous in Ireland for butter and cheese, an industry that employs a lot of people, though its cheese is rather boring – Cheddar and a sort of soft bland spread. It is also famous for its limestone **Mitchelstown Cave** (*open daily 10–6; adm; t (052) 67246*), which have good examples of stalactites and stalagmites, and are very extensive. They are a further 10 miles (16km) to the north on the Cahir road (N8). The Lord of Kingston planned Mitchelstown in the grand manner, with important buildings at the end of vistas. If you have time, walk through **Kingston Square** with its 18th-century almshouses for decayed Protestant gentlefolk, and a central chapel designed by John Morrison of Cork. His son and grandson were also architects and were responsible for some of the finest buildings in the county. A tree-lined street leads to the Church of Ireland church, designed by G. R. Pain.

The castle, which was the focus of all this grandeur, has unfortunately been demolished and replaced with a huge dairy factory. The old castle was founded by the White Knights of Desmond, and passed to the Kingstons through marriage around 1660. The old castle was replaced with a Gothic mansion by G. R. Pain in 1823, but the estates were heavily mortgaged owing to the extravagance of the Regency earl. Mary Wollstonecraft (1759–97), who wrote *Vindication of the Rights of Women* and was the mother of Mary Shelley, spent time as a governess here; her libertarian and feminist ideas were deeply disapproved of by the family.

By the reign of Anna, Countess of Kingston, the land wars were brewing; her tenants wanted their rents reduced and refused to pay her. Her finances were already straitened; it was well known that you would get barely a raisin in her barmbrack if you were invited to tea. In 1880, some 1,600 of her tenants demanded a rent reduction, and there was a huge demonstration in Mitchelstown in 1881. The dispute ended with evictions; most tenants paid up and were reinstated by the summer of 1882. But the whole thing started up again in 1887, and a meeting in Mitchelstown of Land Leaguers, tenants, nationalist MPs and Radicals from England turned into a riot that ended when two people were killed and 20 were seriously wounded by police shots. There is a statue of John Manderville, a leader of the agitation for fair rents, and stone crosses to commemorate the dead in the Market Square. Elizabeth Bowen describes the last garden party at Mitchelstown in her recollections, *Bowen's Court* (*see below*).

The countryside around becomes richer as you travel west and enter the Golden Vale, a fertile plain that extends north of the **Galty Mountains**. At Kildorrey, turn right off the N73 on to the R512 to go to **Doneraile**. Near here was the home of novelist Elizabeth Bowen (1899–1973) whose works so beautifully describe the shades and subtleties of the Anglo-Irish. Her house, Bowen's Court, a beautiful 18th-century mansion, was demolished in the 1960s – a victim of the government's lack of interest in historic buildings at that time. The farmer who bought it was only interested in the land and the timber.

Doneraile and Buttevant are in Edmund Spenser country, 40 miles (64km) north of Cork City, between the Blackwater and the **Ballyhoura Mountains**. Here the poet served the Crown in various positions, and wrote most of *The Faerie Queene*, trying (unsuccessfully) to flatter Queen Elizabeth I enough to get the grant of a bigger manor, one closer to London. While spinning his learned Renaissance fantasies he also found time to write *A View of the Present State of Ireland*, in which he advocated a policy for the island uncomfortably close to genocide. Spenser had just been appointed Sheriff of Cork when a revolt broke out in 1598, and the Irish repaid him by sacking and burning his home and chasing him back to England, where he died the following year. His home, **Kilcolman Castle**, is now a sombre ruin, hard to find, in a field beside a reedy pool north-east of Doneraile.

From 1895 to 1913 Doneraile was the parish of Canon Sheehan, who wrote wise and funny books about Irish rural life. His statue stands outside the Catholic church. **Doneraile Court and Wildlife Park** (*open mid-Apr–Oct Mon–Fri 8am–8.30pm, Sat 10–8.30, Sun 11–7, Nov–mid-Apr Mon–Fri 8–4.30, Sat and Sun 10–4.30; adm; t (022) 24244*) has a wonderful Georgian house saved from ruin by the Irish Georgian Society (*under restoration at time of writing*). Here, Elizabeth Barry, wife of the first Viscount Doneraile, hid in a clock case to observe a masonic lodge meeting in the house. Perhaps she laughed, but whatever happened she gave herself away, and all the masons could do to keep her quiet was elect her as a mason – the only woman mason in history. A sadder story concerns a 19th-century viscount who kept a pet fox, which bit him and his coachman one day. The fox was found to have rabies, and both men travelled to Paris to be treated by Pasteur, but though the coachman continued with his treatment, Lord Doneraile gave it up. He soon developed the disease and died a terrible death in 1887. The beautiful surrounding parkland has been developed for tourists, and there are nature walks, cascades, and herds of deer in the park.

Nearby is the unique alkaline **Kilcolman Bog**, home to many birds; you can visit it if you are involved in bird study (contact the tourist office). At **Buttevant** during July is the **Cahirmee Horse Fair**, which has been held here for hundreds of years and is always good *craic*, with lots of other events happening at the same time.

Mallow, 10 miles (16km) south, was a famous spa where the gentry of Ireland came. The old spa house in Spa Walk is now privately owned and the once-famous water gushes to waste. The town has some pretty 18th-century houses and a timbered, decorated Clock House. **Mallow Castle** is a still-impressive, though roofless, ruin of a fortified 16th-century towerhouse. The Catholic **St Mary's Church** has a pretty interior and Romanesque revival façade. Davis Street is named after poet and nationalist Thomas Davis (1814–45), born in No. 72. The **Mallow Races**, held intermittently through spring, summer and autumn, are the only times the place really comes alive, though it is frequented by anglers, and the **Folk Festival** in July is very cheerful.

At **Castletownroche** on the N72, 10 miles (16km) east of Mallow, notice the pretty Church of Ireland church on a rise above the river and wander around the ruins of Bridgetown Abbey, founded by FitzHugh Roche in the 13th century. North of the church is **Anne's Grove** (*open Easter–Sept Mon–Sat 10–5, Sun 1–6; adm; t (022) 26145*), with tranquil woodlands and a walled garden. The sloping grounds surrounding the beautiful 18th-century house are planted in the style made popular by William Robertson in the late 19th century. Nothing is contrived, and the massed plants lead along winding paths to the river and gardens.

Just south of the Blackwater River at Castletownroche is **Killavullen**, where **Ballymacmoy House**, original home of the Hennessys of cognac fame (now in their ownership again), is being restored. The extensive caves beneath the estate are open in summer. North-east of Castletownroche is **Glanworth**, a sleepy village dominated by the imposing remains of Roche's castle above the River Funchion, on which stands an 18th-century watermill converted into an attractive inn.

From Mallow, the country lanes that take you through the **Boggeragh Mountains** have a wild mystery, heightened by the green glow from the overgrown hedges forming an arbour overhead. The road from Mallow to Killarney meanders past the haunted shell of the O'Callaghan's castle at Dromaneen. **Kanturk**, north of the main road, is an attractive 18th-century planned town. **Kanturk Castle** is a huge building, begun around 1609 but never finished. It is said that the Privy Council ordered work to stop and the owner, McCarthy, flew into a rage and ordered that the blue glass tiles with which the castle was to be roofed be thrown into the river.

A little diversion to the north-west will take you to **Liscarroll**. This small and remote village has the third-largest **Norman castle** in Ireland, which was probably built by the Barrys. It also has the largest concentration of donkeys in the country, for outside the village is a **donkey sanctuary** (*open Mon–Fri 9–4.30, Sat and Sun 10–5; t (022) 48398, www.thedonkeysanctuary.ie*).

Back on the main road (N72) to Killarney (which bypasses **Millstreet**, famous for its equestrian centre), the second road to the left after Rathmore, about a mile (1.6km) from the town, goes to the base of the **Paps Mountains**, dedicated to the ancient fertility goddess Danu. At the end of that road, by the school, turn left and then first right where a small signpost points to 'The City'. This extraordinary site, enclosed by a dry-stone cashel 10ft (3m) high, is the setting for what may be the oldest uninterrupted religious ceremony in Europe. Certainly since the early Iron Age, people have gathered here in May. Time stands still; uninterpreted and without a gift shop in sight, this is the sort of place that makes a tour of Ireland memorable.

County Waterford

Waterford is a fertile county, with rugged mountain beauty and a pretty coastline dotted with fishing villages-cum-holiday resorts and interesting ruins. The south-east coast also has a reputation for being sunny. The county is traversed by two mountain ranges, the Comeragh and the Monavullagh, which are set with tiny lakes and planted conifer forests. The valley in which Waterford City lies is watered by the River Suir, which flows into the River Barrow, which in turn is fed by the River Nore. These sister rivers cross the county, which is furthermore bordered by the Blackwater and the great Atlantic sea. In *The Book of Invasions* (or *Lebor Gabala*), a mythological account of the pre-history of Ireland, the first Celts described the site where

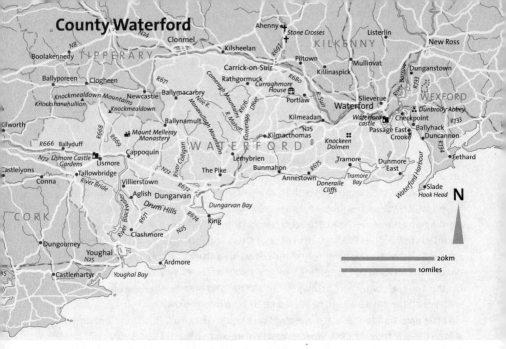

Waterford City grew up as 'a sweet confluence of waters, a trinity of rivers'. It was, however, Norsemen who founded the city of Waterford in about AD 850 and used it as a base from which to raid up the rivers to the rich valleys of Tipperary and beyond. The name 'Waterford' is of Danish origin.

History

A brief sketch of the county's history must start with the great race of builders from the Boyne Valley who built Newgrange in County Meath. They spread down to Waterford and left a number of impressive monuments to their civilization. The manner of their decorative carvings, which is unmistakable, has been tagged the 'Boyne Valley style'. Their tombs and portal dolmens are particularly concentrated around the seaside resort of Tramore; human remains that date from approximately 9000 BC have been discovered to the east of Cappoquin. When the Celts invaded in about 500 BC, the main tribe in Waterford seems to have been the Deisi, who launched successful raids on Roman Britain. They held territory between the Blackwater and the Suir, and such was their impact that Waterford county is still referred to as 'the Decies'.

The Norsemen kept to their patch round *Vadrafjord*, or Waterford city, occupying themselves with raiding and establishing trade links. The early-Christian monks made a great impact on the Decies. St Declan of Ardmore is supposed to have pre-dated St Patrick's mission in the first half of the 5th century. The Monastic foundation at Lismore dates from AD 635 and became famous throughout Europe as a centre of learning, with 20 centres of study within its complex. It was constantly raided and burned by the Norsemen from about AD 833.

In the 1120s, Lismore became the centre of a reformation movement under Saint Malachy, who wanted to bring the Gaelic church under the domination of the Pope. The Anglo-Normans entered into this scene in about 1167 because of an alliance that Dermot MacMurragh, King of Leinster, made with them against the Norsemen of Waterford. This was part of a larger quarrel that he was having with O'Rourke of Breffni. Waterford was besieged by the Norman commander Richard de Clare (also called Strongbow) and his men, and eventually fell. Strongbow married the King of Leinster's daughter, and many of his followers also married Irish girls. So the invaders stayed, intermarried with the Gaelic nobility and created a race who, as the years went by, abandoned their allegiance to the kings of England and became Gaelic in their customs. Religion and Reformation brought the English armies back to the shores of Waterford because the city merchants chose to support the Catholic faith. They got further involved in the overspill of the English Civil War, suffering several sieges that ended at last in 1690 with surrender to William III (William of Orange).

Getting There and Around

By Air
Aer Arann, t 0800 587 2324. A daily service between London Luton and Waterford City.

By Rail
Mainline train services from Plunkett Station, just across the bridge from the city centre, connect Waterford City with Dublin, Limerick and Rosslare.
Iarnród Éireann, Waterford, t (051) 873401, www.irishrail.ie

By Bus
Bus Éireann has at least 12 buses a day to Dublin and along the coast to Cork, less frequent services to the smaller towns, and a regular connection to the beaches at Tramore. Towns along the River Suir can be reached by Suirway. Buses leave from the Quay opposite the tourist office – take a taxi or walk across the bridge from the rail to the bus station.
Bus Éireann, Waterford, t (051) 879000, www.buseireann.ie.
Suirway, Waterford, t (051) 382209

By Bike
Bikes can be hired from:
Altitude, 22 Ballybricken, Waterford, t (051) 870356/850228, www.altitude.ie
Wright's Cycle Depot, 19–20 Henrietta St, Waterford, t (051) 874411

Festivals

April
Sean Dunne Writers' Festival, Waterford, t (051) 849856, arts@waterfordcity.ie. A series of readings, workshops and musical performances held to celebrate the Waterford writer.

May
Féile na nDéise, Dungarvan, t (058) 45273. A traditional Irish music festival.

June
Immrama Festival of Travel Writing, Lismore, t (058) 54975/54855, www.lismoreimmrama.com. A festival with writer and Lismore resident Dervla Murphy as patron, hosting readings by national and international travel writers, exhibitions and a range of fringe activities.

August
Spraoi Street Festival, Waterford, t (051) 841808, www.spraoi.com. 'Ireland's biggest street festival', held on bank-holiday weekend.

September–October
Waterford International Festival of Light Opera, Theatre Royal, Waterford, t (051) 375437, www.waterfordfestival.com. A music festival.

Waterford City

Waterford is snugly situated on a curve of the River Suir before it opens out into the sea. It has a reputation for good wine bars, and the old parts of it are attractive, although the modern surrounds are very ugly, as is too often the case. A quick tour of the city should perhaps start with the **Waterford Crystal Glass Factory** (*open for guided tours Mon–Fri Jan, Feb, Nov and Dec 9–3.15, Mar–Oct 8.30–4; t (051) 332500, www.waterfordvisitorcentre.ie*), a mile or so (about 1.6km) west of the city on the Cork Road (N25). There are organized tours around the factory. Most visitors will have heard of Waterford Crystal, which has a worldwide market, and its beautifully patterned cut glass with many different styles. The industry was started in 1783, and pieces dating from that time are now extremely valuable. You can see a wonderful example in the cut-glass chandelier that hangs in the City Hall in the Mall.

Tourist Information

Waterford: 41 The Quay, t (051) 875823, *www. waterfordtourism.com*. Also at Waterford Crystal Tourist Centre, Cork Rd, t (051) 358397

Internet Access

Voyager Internet Café, Parnell Court, Parnell St, Waterford t (051) 843843. *Closed Sun.*

Shopping

General
City Square, Arundel Sq, Waterford, t (051) 853528, *www.city-square.ie*. A central mall.
Kelly's Ltd, The Quay, Waterford, t (051) 873557. A ladies' fashion store.

Crafts
Aisling Crafts and Sweaters, 61 The Quay, Waterford, t (051) 873262
Ardmore Pottery, The Cliff, Ardmore, t (024) 94152, *www.ardmorepottery.com*
Dyehouse Gallery & Waterford Pottery, Dyehouse Lane, Waterford, t (051) 844770, *www.dyehouse-gallery.com*, *www.waterfordpottery.com*. Pottery.
The Waterford Treasures Shop; *see p.220*

Crystal
Joseph Knox Ltd, 3–4 Barronstrand St, Waterford, t (051) 875307, *www.josephknox.com*

Waterford Crystal Gallery and Factory, N25 west, Kilbarry, Waterford, t (051) 332500, *www.waterfordvisitorcentre.ie*

Sports and Activities

Golf
Faithlegg Golf Club, Faithlegg House, Waterford, t (051) 382000, *www.faighlegg.com*
Waterford Castle, The Island, Ballinakill, t (051) 878203, *www.waterfordcastle.com*

Ponytrekking
Callaghane Riding Centre, Dunmore Rd, Waterford City, t (051) 382154

Tours
Walking Tours of Historic Waterford, t (051) 873711. City tours from the Granville Hotel.

Where to Stay

Waterford City
Waterford Castle, The Island, Ballinakill, Waterford, t (051) 878203, *www. waterfordcastle.com* (*luxury*). A very luxurious Anglo-Norman castle 2 miles (3.2km) downstream from Waterford City, with a range of excellent sporting facilities.
Dooley's Hotel, 30 The Quay, Waterford, t (051) 873531, *www.dooleys-hotel.ie* (*expensive*). An old-established hotel. *Closed 25–28 Dec.*
Granville Hotel, The Quay, Waterford, t (051) 305555, *www.granville-hotel.ie*

The Mall is right in the heart of Waterford, and from here you can see most of the buildings of interest in the city. A tour could include the crystal factory, a quick look in at the City Hall, and then a browse in **Reginald's Tower** (*open Easter–Oct daily 10–6, Nov–Easter Wed–Sun 10–5; adm; t (051) 304220, www.heritageireland.ie*), which guards the end of the Mall by the river. A massive circular fortress with a wall 10ft (3m) thick, it was built in 1003, and named after the Norse governor of the time. When the desperado Strongbow landed in 1170 and took the city, Reginald's Tower became a Norman stronghold and has since then served as a royal residence, a mint, a military barracks and a city prison. It now holds a very interesting display of old artefacts and memorabilia from Waterford's past.

Just down the Quay on Greyfriars Street is the **French Church**, which was originally a Franciscan foundation built in 1240. It got the label 'The French Church' because it was used by Huguenot refugees who came to Ireland after the Revocation of the

(*moderate–expensive*). A smart, olde-worlde and conveniently central option.

Brown's Townhouse, 29 South Parade, t (051) 870594, www.brownstownhouse.com (*moderate*). A late-Victorian house with ensuite rooms. Breakfast is served at a large table; fresh fruit salad and home-made breads and jams accompany a fry-up.

Sion Hill House, Ferrybank, Waterford, t (051) 851558, www.sionhillhouse.com (*moderate*). An early 19th-century house with a lovely 4-acre garden and 4 ensuite bedrooms.

Eating Out

Chez K's Steak & Seafood Restaurant, John St, Waterford, t (051) 844180, www.chez-ks.com (*expensive*). A busy steak and seafood restaurant. *Closed lunch and Mon.*

Waterford Wine Vault, High St, Waterford, t (051) 853444, www.waterfordwinevault.com (*moderate*). A well-stocked wine bar, perhaps the finest in Ireland, in the cellars of an 18th-century wine merchant. The small, deservedly popular restaurant has a good nouveau-vegetarian and seafood selection, substantial entrees and friendly service. *Closed lunch.*

Poppy's Restaurant, Park Rd, Waterford, t (051) 304844 (*moderate*). Fresh local seafood, Mediterranean salads and chargrilled specialities; popular with locals. *Closed Mon.*

The Bowery Bar and Bistro, 2 The Mall, Waterford, t (051) 855087 (*inexpensive*). A vibrant place with its own nightclub.

The Brasserie, Arundel Sq, Waterford, t (051) 857774 (*inexpensive*). An informal budget option.

Haricots Wholefood Restaurant, 11 O'Connell St, Waterford, t (051) 841299 (*inexpensive*). Vegetarian, vegan, meat and fish dishes, plus – a rarity in Irish restaurants – freshly squeezed juice. *Closed Sun and from 8pm.*

The Olde Stand, 45 Michael St, Waterford, t (051) 879488 (*inexpensive*). Excellent pub food and a good upstairs restaurant.

Entertainment and Nightlife

Arts
Waterford Arts Centre, Garter Lane, 22A O'Connell St, Waterford, t (051) 855038, www.garterlane.ie

Waterford Show, City Hall, The Mall, Waterford City, t (051) 875788. A presentation of Irish music, story, song and dance, held May–end Sept Thur, Fri and Sun at 9pm.

Traditional Music
The Gingerman, Arundel Lane, Waterford, t (051) 879522. Traditional music (Mon–Wed) and ballads (Thur).

The Mansion House, Johnstown, Waterford, t (051) 857574. A stylish traditional bar, well suited to family and group occasions.

T&H Doolan's, George's St, Waterford, t (051) 841504. An ancient pub hosting music most nights.

Edict of Nantes in 1686. It has a lovely east window and some interesting carvings; the keys are kept in the adjacent **Waterford Treasures at the Granary** (*open summer Mon–Sat 9–6, Sun 11–6, winter Mon–Sat 10–5, Sun 11–5; adm; **t** (051) 304500, www. waterfordtreasures.com*), in the same building as the tourist office . This museum has a good collection of artefacts from Viking and Norman times and, in 'The Waterford Viking Show', tells of the city's heritage through music, dance and storytelling (*mid-June–mid-Sept Mon, Wed and Fri 8pm; for all ages; lasts 90mins*). Turn third left after the French Church and you come to **St Olaf's Church**, founded by the Norsemen in about AD 980 and rebuilt by Normans.

At the end of Greyfriars Street in Cathedral Square is the Church of Ireland **Christ Church Cathedral**, which was built in 1779 and is classical Georgian in style. Inside are several older monuments, one of them in remembrance of the 15th-century Lord Mayor Rice, who chose to depict himself in a state of decay with frogs, toads and other wriggling things emerging from his entrails. The cathedral was restored after fire in 1779 to plans created by a local architect, John Roberts. It was redecorated again in 1891. Another lovely building is the Chamber of Commerce in George Steet, built by the same architect as the cathedral. You can ask to see inside it. In September the Theatre Royal hosts the Waterford International Festival of Light Opera (*see p.217*). Waterford City produced some great actors whose names are still revered in the acting world: Mrs Jordon in 1767, and Charles Kean in 1811. It is also where the Christian Brothers opened their first scholastic establishment in 1802. Edmund Ignatius Rice had his first foundation at Mount Sion in Barrack Street, since when the order has spread all over the world. **Mount Congreve Estate and Gardens** (*open Thur Apr–Sept, call for times, **t** (051) 384115; adm*) at Kilmeadan, 5 miles (8km) west of Waterford city, covers more than 110 acres with one of the world's largest collections of rhododendrons.

Around County Waterford

Portlaw to Annestown

Portlaw, on the River Clodagh, north-west of Waterford on the R680, was founded as a model village by a Quaker family, the Malcolmsons, who had started up a cotton industry in the 19th century. Unfortunately many of the quaint houses have been modernized and become dull in the process. Beside the town is **Curraghmore House and Gardens** (*open 9–1 Jan Mon–Fri, May–mid-July Mon–Sat, and by appointment; adm; **t** (051) 387101*), the family home of the Marquis of Waterford. The family name is Beresford, and they were once noted for their dominance in the Church and the government; one of them was called 'Sand Martin' because of his skill in picking sinecures and plum jobs for his many friends. (A characteristic of the sand martin is to share his nest with a numerous extended family.) Curraghmore is worth visiting just to see the splendid, grey 18th-century house in its parkland setting, with gentle hills rising behind. The specimen trees have reached a magnificent size; they were mainly planted in the 19th century. It is worth seeking out the 18th-century shell house made by the Countess of Tyrone.

Nearby on the Waterford Harbour is the village of Crooke. Roughly opposite and a little further down is Hook Head, interesting because the two – so it is claimed – are immortalized in the saying 'By Hook or by Crooke', a phrase first used by sailors. There is nothing much to see at Crooke, but **Passage East**, further up the estuary, is an atmospheric village that has been a ferry crossing for centuries and an important port. It was here that Strongbow landed in 1170, and here too that Henry II landed a year later with 4,000 men in 400 ships to make sure that Strongbow did not set up a rival kingdom and step into the shoes of his father-in-law Dermot MacMurrough, who had just died. He formally declared Waterford a Royal City, and tradition holds that it remained loyal to him and his heirs until the 16th century and the English Reformation. Today there is a car ferry across from Passage East to County Wexford.

Dunmore East, 10 miles (16km) south-west of the city, is a little seaside place, rather like a Devon fishing village, with beautiful little headlands made of old red sandstone carved into cliffs and safe bathing beaches. Sea pinks grow along the cliff edges, where there are some peaceful places to walk. Follow the coast path leading along to Brownstown Head, where there are the remains of a fort. You will meet colourful fishermen in the bars, although they can be quite clannish. Dunmore was the centre of a thriving herring industry and the Irish terminal for a mail service from England in the early 19th century.

Tramore, 10 miles (16km) around the coast to the west, is the place to go if you want to meet Irish people on holiday rather than fellow foreigners. Its 3 miles (4.8km) of sand are swept by the Gulf Stream, which makes the sea fun for bathers and surfers. It has a well-developed amenity complex beside the promenade, a miniature railway and boating lake, attractions such as 'Laserworld' and 'Splashworld', and a first-class racecourse. A quick and pleasant walk to the west of the town leads by a coastal path to some steep cliffs known as the Doneraile Cliffs.

The remarkable **Knockeen Dolmen** is nearby but quite difficult to find. Follow the signs off the Tramore to Carrick-on-Suir road (R682). Drive until you come to a three-forked road. Take the right fork and drive uphill until you come to a white farmhouse. Opposite is a field gate and stile. The dolmen is in the shadow of the hedge on the far side of the field. It probably marks the grave of a local Deisi chieftain. This sort of tomb-building was going on when people moved from being hunter-gatherers to keeping domestic animals and growing their own food. Two large matching upright stones mark the entrance, with three smaller standing stones behind. The uprights support the heavy capstone, which is thought to have been raised up by a system of propping and levering.

Annestown, on the R675 nearby, also has a lovely beach. So does **Bunmahon**, further west, a small fishing village that is perched above some magnificent cliffs.

Dungarvan and Ardmore

Dungarvan is a pleasant seaside town where the River Colligan broadens into Dungarvan Bay. There are the remains of an old Norman castle and a pretty arched bridge. In the graveyard of the Church of Ireland church by the river is a curious 'holed' gable with circular openings. Two and a half miles (4km) north-west of the town, on

Tourist Information

Ardmore: t (024) 94444. *Open summer only.*
Dungarvan: The Courthouse, Bridge St,
    t (058) 41741, *www.dungarvantourism.com*
Lismore: Courthouse, t (058) 54975.
    Open Apr–Oct.
Tramore: Railway Sq, t (051) 381572,
    www.tramore.ie. Open June–Sept.

Shopping

Crafts
Ardmore Pottery and Craft Gallery,
    Ardmore, t (024) 94152
Waterford Woodcraft, Dunabrattin,
    Annestown, t (051) 396110

Crystal
Criostal na Rinne (Eamonn Terry), Ballinagoul,
    Ring, t (058) 46174, *www.criostal.com*

Sports and Activities

Fishing
For **sea-angling**, contact:
Dungarvan East Angling Charters,
    Fairybush House, Dunmore East,
    t (051) 383397
Dungarvan Sea Angling Club, Dungarvan,
    t (058) 41298

Golf
Dungarvan Golf Club, Knocknagranagh,
    Dungarvan, t (058) 43310/41605,
    www.dungarvangolfclub.com
Faithlegg Golf Club, t (051) 382241
West Waterford Golf and Country Club,
    Dungarvan, t (058) 43216,
    www.waterfordgolf.com

Indoor Leisure Centre
Splashworld, Tramore, t (051) 390176

Ponytrekking
Melody's Riding Stables, Ballymacarbry,
    t (052) 36147

Walking
Walk through the Comeraghs on the
Munster Way marked trail, or St Declan's Walk,
a popular pilgrimage route that goes from
Lismore to Ardmore; ask at the tourist office
for details. Orienteering, bird-watching, hill-
walking and other activities are also organized
through the tourist offices in summer.
Shielbaggan Outdoor Education Centre,
    Ramsgrange, t (051) 389550

Watersports
Excellent swimming beaches are at Tramore
(also a popular spot for surfing), Dunmore
East, Ardmore and round Dungarvan.
Dunmore East Adventure Centre,
    harbour, Dunmore East, t (051) 383783,
    www.dunmoreadventure.com.
    Sailing, windsurfing and canoeing.
Oceanic Manoeuvres, 3 Riverstown, Tramore,
    t (051) 390944, *www.oceanicmanoeuvres.com*
T–Bay Surf Centre, Tramore beach, t (051)
    391297, *www.surftbay.com.* Surf hire, beach
    facilities and activity camps.

Where to Stay

Ballyrafter House, Lismore, t (058) 54002,
    www.waterfordhotel.com (*expensive*).
    A comfortable Georgian house and ideal
    base for fishing or exploring the lovely
    Blackwater Valley.
Richmond House, Cappoquin, t (058) 54278,
    www.richmondhouse.net (*expensive*).

the fork of the R672 and N72, is the **Master McGrath Memorial** erected in 1873 –
a plain stone structure with an elegant spire. The tablet is engraved not with the
name of some famous Victorian but with the image of a greyhound – the locals
claim it is the first monument in the world to be dedicated to a dog. (Master McGrath
won the Waterloo Cup for coursing on three occasions during the 19th century.) The
animal is still remembered in ballads and by a brand of superior dog food. About
5 miles (8km) south on the R674 is the famous Irish-speaking village of **Ring**, the only
Gaeltacht area in the south-east, where students take summer courses in Irish.

A comfortable Georgian country house with a very good restaurant. *Closed 23 Dec–10 Jan.*

Blackwater Lodge, Upper Ballyduff, t (058) 60235, *info@ireland-salmon-fishing.net* (*moderate*). A snug place in which fishermen swap stories.

Castle Country House, Milstreet, Cappagh, near Dungarvan, t (058) 68049, *www. castlecountryhouse.com* (*moderate*). A very homely castle with a lovely restored 15th-century wing. Walking and fishing are available.

Clonanav Farm Guesthouse, Nire Valley, Ballymacarbry, , t (052) 36141, *www. clonanav.com* (*moderate*). A guesthouse and 4-bedroom self-catering bungalow. The hosts are experts on local walks and angling.

O'Shea's Hotel, Strand St, Tramore, t (051) 381246, *www.osheas-hotel. com* (*moderate*). A small family-run hotel close to the beach. *Closed 25 Dec.*

Round Tower Hotel, College Rd, Ardmore, t (024) 94494, *rth@eircom.net* (*moderate*). Simple accommodation in an old convent, with a restaurant that's a good place for Sun lunch (it's also open for lunch and dinner daily late May–late Sept). *Closed 25–29 Dec.*

Aglish House, Aglish, t (024) 96191, *www. aglishhouse.com* (*inexpensive–moderate*). A pleasant stone farmhouse near the River Blackwater, with a restaurant. *Closed Dec–mid-Mar.*

Bennett's Church, Old School House, Clonmel–Dungarvan road, Nire Valley, Ballymacarbry, t (052) 36217 or t 0882 571203, *richiem@tinet.ie* (*inexpensive*). An old converted school in a pretty setting, furnished with antiques.

Self-catering

Cappagh House, Kilcannon Wood, Cappagh, Dungarvan, t (058) 68396, *www.cappagh-house.com* (*inexpensive*). A old mews and a former lodge house, both with a double bedroom and 2 twin rooms. A cot is available.

Kate's Cottage, Riverside, Tarr's Bridge, Dungarvan, t (058) 41040 (*inexpensive*). A modern but cosy thatched cottage in its own grounds, just over a mile (1.6km) from Dungarvan town centre.

Eating Out

The Ship Restaurant and Bar, Dunmore East, t (051) 383141 (*expensive*). A casual, fun place offering good seafood. *Closed Nov–Apr Mon and Tue, and Sun eve.*

Richmond House, Cappoquin, t (058) 54278 (*moderate–expensive*). Multi-award-winning globally influenced modern Irish cuisine. *Closed Mon.*

Hartley's Bistro, 21 Queen St, Tramore, t (051) 390888 (*moderate*). Seafood and steak. *Closed lunch.*

Barron's Bakery and Coffee House, The Square, Cappoquin, t (058) 54045 (*inexpensive*). A good place for lunch.

McAlpin's Suir Inn, Cheekpoint, north of Passage East, t (051) 382220, *www.macalpins. com* (*inexpensive*). Good pub grub. *Closed lunch.*

Entertainment and Nightlife

Traditional Music

Bean a Leanna **Pub**, 86 O'Connell St, Dungarvan, t (058) 44882

Marine Bar, N25 west of Dungarvan, t (058) 46520, *www.marinebar.com*

Seanachie, N25 west of Dungarvan, t (058) 46285

Ardmore, west along the coast on the R673, combines a long, popular beach with an important ecclesiastical site. Just outside the village are the remains of a 7th-century monastic settlement founded by St Declan, possibly as early as the 5th century. Some say St Declan was converting the pagans to Christianity while St Patrick was still a slave herding cattle. The ancient remains are spread over a small area and interspersed with more modern gravestones and memorials. They include the most graceful **round tower** in Ireland, built in the 11th century of cut stone. Its entrance door is 10ft (3m) above ground, so the monks could store precious things up there: in times of trouble, they entered it via a retractable ladder. There is also the remains of a 12th-century Romanesque **cathedral**, with a wealth of figure-sculpture over almost the whole of the west gable. The figures are badly weathered, but you can just make out the Judgement of Solomon, Adam and Eve with the Tree and the Serpent, and the Adoration of the Magi. In the nave and chancel are some ogham stones from c. 400 AD, which suggests this was a burial place even before St Declan arrived. The lower portion of the building is believed to incorporate part of an earlier 7th-century church.

St Declan's Oratory in the eastern part of the graveyard is reputed to be where he is buried; on 24 July many locals still make a pilgrimage to it. St Declan's Oratory is typical of the small, dark dwellings in which the early fathers used to live. Apparently this preference for separate cells grouped together comes from the Coptic Egyptian influence in the Irish Church, along with a rejection of the bodily senses and a deep suspicion of women. (St Declan's Oratory was not in fact built until the 9th century, but Irish architecture seems to advance very slowly.) This foundation was the recognized seat of a bishop as early as AD 1111.

About half a mile (0.8km) east, St Declan's **Holy Well** was renovated in 1789, and many people still visit it. There is a stone chair, three stone crosses and a stone basin for pilgrims to wash in. Down on the strand is a *crannóg*, visible only when the tide is out. There too lies **St Declan's Stone**, at the end of the strand. It was supposed to have been used by the saint to carry his bell and vestments across the sea from Wales. It is reputed that if you crawl beneath it your aches and pains will be cured (though, of course, this manoeuvre is impossible for sinners). **St Declan's Way**, the old pilgrims' route between here and Cashel in County Tipperary, is popular with walkers.

Inland: Cappoquin to Ballymacarbry and the Nire Valley

An unmarked road runs from the south-west corner of the county, through Clashmore and Aglish to Cappoquin, following stretches of the Blackwater lined by stately grey houses. It also passes through **Dromana Wood**, a small bit of ancient forest embellished with a domed gatehouse at the northern end, a Victorian folly in a style of architecture described as 'Hindu-Gothic'; indeed, it resembles a miniature Taj Mahal. **Cappoquin**, famous for chickens, is at the head of the tidal estuary of the River Blackwater. Wooded hills surround it, the northern slopes of the Knockmealdown Mountains rise to the north. This is an excellent place to fish for trout or roach.

Four miles (6.4km) north, off the R669, is the Trappist Cistercian abbey of **Mount Melleray** (*t (058) 54404*). The monastery is modern, but in its precincts are five ogham stones. The order has built up an almost self-sufficient community that still keeps the old rule of monastic hospitality: everyone is welcome for a meal.

The N72 from Cappoquin to Lismore follows the Blackwater, overlooked by gracious houses. **Lismore** has one of the finest **castles** in Ireland, dating back in parts to an 1185 construction by King John. It belonged to Sir Walter Raleigh in 1589 and he sold it to the adventurer Richard Boyle, later the first Earl of Cork, who apparently said: 'I arrived out of England into Ireland, where God guided me hither, bringing with me a taffeta doublet and a pair of velvet breeches, a new shirt of laced fustin cutt upon taffeta, a bracelet of gold, a diamond ring, and twenty-seven pounds three shillings in monie in my purse.' His 14th child, Robert, is remembered as the father of chemistry, having established Boyle's Law in the late 17th century, which proves that air has weight – a milestone in the dissociation of chemistry from alchemy. In 1814 the Lismore Crozier and the 15th-century manuscript *The Book of Lismore* were discovered here in one of the walls (both are displayed in the National Museum in Dublin). Eventually the castle passed through the female line to the Devonshire family, who still own it. The present castle was rebuilt in the mid 19th century by the 6th Duke of Devonshire. *Lios mór* means 'great fort' in Irish, and this great pile of grey castellated stone hanging over the Blackwater lives up to all one's expectations of what a castle should be. It is not open to the public, though it can be rented. However, the **gardens** (*entrance in Lismore; open mid-Apr–mid Oct daily 1.45–4.45, from 11am in high season; adm; **t** (058) 54424, www.lismorecastle.com*)are very lovely, especially the stately 800-year-old Yew Walk. Edmund Spenser may have written part of *The Faerie Queene* here.

Lismore is an ancient place of renown, both for learning and piety. Under St Colman in the 8th century, it won the title of 'Luminary of the Western World', and men came from all over Europe to study here. The Norsemen, of course, were attracted to it like bees to honey, and looted the place frequently, but the monastery and abbey were finally destroyed by Raymond le Gros and his Norman mercenaries in 1173. The Gothic **Cathedral of St Carthach** is one of the loveliest in Ireland, approached by a tree-lined walk. It dates from medieval times but was restored by the Earl of Cork in 1633. The graceful limestone spire was added in 1827. There is an interesting 1557 MacGrath tomb and a window by Edward Burne-Jones, made by William Morris. The **Heritage Centre** in the Courthouse details the town's ancient history.

On the R668 a few hundred yards to the north of the castle there is a fine walk to **Ballysagartmore Towers**, a Gothic-style gateway and tower that guards the entrance to a three-arched bridge; a waterfall adds to the beauty of the scene. To the west of Lismore, the nearby village of Ballyduff on the Lismore–Fermoy road (R666) is another possible base for salmon or roach fishers. To the north-east, the **Nire Valley** is fantastic for views, ponytrekking and walking. On either side of it are mountain slopes, clear tumbling streams and woods. (It lies between the Comeragh and Knockmealdown ranges and can be approached from Clonmel to Ballymacarbry, or from the R671 off the N72 near Cappoquin.)

Ballymacarbry is a welcome spot for ponytrekkers and walkers exploring the Nire Valley and heather-covered slopes of the Comeragh Mountains. The friendly local bar hires out ponies, as does Melody's Stables (*see* p.222). A superb car trip awaits you if you head for the village of Lemybrien at the junction of the Waterford/Carrick-on-Suir road and Dungarvan roads (R676 and N25). Just north of it is a highly scenic road through the mountains, the **Comeragh Drive**, which takes you up to the Mahon waterfall. It is well signposted. Locals call the road to the falls the 'Magic Road'; at just the right spot, if you can find it, you can take your car out of gear and enjoy the bizarre impression you are rolling uphill.

Rathgormuck, on the R678 about 6 miles (10 km) from Clonmel, is a lovely little village on the northern side of the Comeragh mountains. It is a popular hiking centre, and boasts the remains of an early-medieval church and castle.

County Tipperary

To get a clear idea of the beauty of Tipperary – and it is very beautiful, even though it lacks a stretch of coastline – walk to the top of Slievenamon, which in early summer is scented with the almond fragrance of gorse blossom. Slievenamon is a county landmark; a conical mountain north of Clonmel that rises to 2,358ft (719m). Up here, you get the feeling of space and a wide, splendid view: to the south are the Comeraghs and silver ribbon of the Suir; to the west, the Galtees; and to the north, the Rock of Cashel rising out of the flat, rich farmland.

Slievenamon in Irish means 'mountain of the fairy women'. The story relates how Fionn and the Fianna warriors had dallied with fairy women, so when Fionn decided to wed, to prevent any of them becoming jealous, he said he would marry the one who reached the summit of the mountain first. However, the wily man had set his heart on Gráinne, the daughter of King Cormac, and so he whisked her up to the top the evening before the race. When the panting winner reached the top, 'there sat the delicate, winsome Gráinne, and not a feather of her ruffled'. So much for legend.

The refrain 'It's a long way to Tipperary' entered the battlefields of the Somme as a favourite British marching song during the First World War. So many people have heard of the county without knowing of its glorious countryside and its wealth of

Getting There and Around

By Rail
Mainline routes (Waterford–Limerick and Cork–Dublin) pass through the county and stop at Thurles, Cahir, Clonmel, Carrick-on-Suir and Roscrea. The 2 main lines cross at busy Limerick Junction station, which is just outside Tipperary town.
Iarnród Éireann, Tipperary, t (062) 51206, Limerick Junction, t (062) 51824, www.irishrail.ie

By Bus
Bus Éireann services are limited to a few daily Tipperary–Waterford runs via Cahir, Clonmel and Carrick-on-Suir. Clonmel, Cahir and Cashel also have some direct connections to Dublin and Cork. A competing line, Kavanagh's, connects Dublin with Thurles, Cashel and Tipperary.
Bus Éireann, Waterford, t (051) 879000, www.buseireann.ie
JJ Kavanagh's, Clonmel, t (052) 29292

By Bike
The Raleigh Rent-a-Bike network operates throughout the county.
Moynan, 61 Pearse St, Nenagh, t (067) 31293
OK Sports, New St, Carrick-on-Suir, t (051) 640626

Worldwide Cycles Bike Rental, 4 Market House, Clonmel, t (052) 21146

Festivals

June
Clonmel Show, t (052) 22611.
A horse show that includes jumping.

July
Clonmel Junction Festival, t (052) 29339, www.junctionfestival.com. Performing arts.
Kilcommon Festival, t (062) 78103.
An 8-day affair in the rural highlands between Nenagh and Thurles, with traditional music and dance, Gaelic games, sheepdog trials and street entertainment.
Munster Fleadh Cheoil, t (01) 280 0295.
Traditional Irish music, song and dance.

August
Aonach Paddy O'Brien, Nenagh, t (067) 42900.
A traditional music and arts festival, held in the name of a local composer/accordionist.

November
Cashel Cultural Festival, t (087) 055 2179 or t (052) 34455, www.cashelartsfest.com

12th- and 13th-century church buildings and castles. For the angler there are rivers of brown trout; for the archaeologist, plenty of Stone Age and Iron Age sites. Horse lovers will be attracted by the hunting and the gourmet riding holidays around Lough Derg. This is also a fine place for the breeding of horses, gun-dogs and greyhounds. But for passing travellers, it is the story of Cashel of the Kings and the strength of Cahir Castle that hold the imagination. Another treasure is the County Offaly town of Birr, to the north, where the gardens and arboretum of the castle are amongst the finest on the island, and there is soon to be a splendid scientific centre.

History

The history of this county is very closely linked to that of the great Ormonde family. The founder of the family in Ireland was Theobald Fitzwalter, who came over in 1185 with Prince John, and was later appointed to high office as Chief Butler to the Lord of Ireland. Thenceforth, the family surname was Butler, and its members generally remained faithful to the interests of the British Crown. This was in direct contrast to their kinsfolk and arch enemies, the Geraldines. The Geraldines were close neighbours and split into two branches, Desmond and Kildare. Tipperary was divided into two Ridings; with Clonmel as the capital of the South Riding, and Nenagh as the capital of the North Riding. This division dates from some early administrative peculiarity.

Tipperary has always been a rich prize for the winners of battles and uprisings, because of its fertile farms and pastures. In the 18th century it was a county of landlords and relatively prosperous peasants. The region was settled during this time by Palatines who were fleeing religious persecution. The potato famine hit hard in the 1840s, and, later, during the uncertain times leading up to Independence, many landlords were burnt out.

Southern Tipperary

Clonmel and the Southeast

Clonmel ('The Honeyed Meadows'), in the south of the county on the N24, has a lovely setting by the River Suir and the Comeragh Mountains. An important town when the Norman family of Butler were all-powerful, today it is the largest in the county, with bustling shops and industries that produce everything from cider to computer parts. It has a prosperous, bright look about it, which is not surprising as most of Tipperary, particularly its central region around the Suir and the Golden Vale, is particularly fertile. The restored Franciscan friary in the town centre has retained its old tower and a 15th-century Butler tomb with stone effigies of a knight and lady. **South Tipperary County Museum** (*open Tue–Sat 10–1 and 2–5; adm; t (052) 34551*), in the civic centre, has town memorabilia and a gallery with some 20th-century paintings.

Parts of Clonmel's medieval walls still stand around William Street and Kickham Street; though picturesque, they weren't strong enough to keep Oliver Cromwell out in 1650, despite a spirited defence under Hugh Duff O'Neill. Laurence Sterne, who wrote one of the first English experimental novels, *Tristram Shandy*, was born in

Tourist Information

Cahir: Castle St, **t** (052) 41453.
Closed Sun exc July and Aug.
Cashel: Main St, **t** (062) 61333/62511.
Closed Sat and Sun Nov–Feb.

Internet Access

The Olde Church, Bansha, **t** (062) 54980.
Closed Sat and Sun.

Shopping

Crafts
Craft Granary, Church St, Cahir, **t** (052) 41725
Kylathea Traditional Crafted Baskets,
  Mullinahone, **t** (051) 647056
Rossa Pottery, Cashel, **t** (062) 61388
Sarah Ryan Ceramics, Palmers Hill, Cashel,
  t (062) 61994

Glass
Tipperary Crystal, Ballynoran, N24, Carrick-on-
  Suir, **t** (051) 640543, *www.tipperarycrystal.com*

Food and Drink
The Honey Pot, 14 Abbey St, Clonmel,
  t (052) 21457. A health food shop and
  restaurant with an organic vegetable
  market Thur and Fri.

Sports and Activities

Fishing
Brown trout and salmon fishing are good
on the River Suir and its many tributaries.
Cashel Golden Tipperary Anglers Association,
  Cahervillahow, Cashel, **t** (062) 72354

Clonmel Salmon and Trout Anglers,
Kavanagh's Sport Shop, Upper O'Connell St,
Clonmel, **t** (052) 21279
Reiska Cahir, Cahir, **t** (052) 42729

Golf
Ballykisteen Golf and Country Club, Limerick
  Junction, near Tipperary, **t** (062) 33333
Clonmel Course, 3 miles (5km) outside Clonmel
  at Lyreanearla, **t** (052) 21138. A pretty course.
Tipperary Golf Club, Rathanny, Tipperary,
  t (062) 51119/52061
Slievenamon Golf Club, Lisronagh, Clonmel,
  t (052) 32213

Horseracing
This takes place in Tipperary, Thurles and
Clonmel throughout the year.

Ponytrekking
Cahir Equestrian Centre, Grangemore, Cahir,
  t (052) 41426
Davern's Equestrian Centre, Tannersrath Lower,
  Clonmel, **t** (052) 22991 or **t** (086) 252 0752
Hillcrest Equestrian Centre, Galbally,
  t (062) 37915. Trekking, lessons, etc.
Lisfuncheon Equestrian Centre, Lisfuncheon,
  Ballyporeen, **t** (052) 67617
Lissava House Stables, Cahir, **t** (052) 41117

Walking
The **Cahir Way** is a signposted walking route
from Cahir to Ballydavid through the Galtee
Mountains. There are also trails between
Carrick-on-Suir, Clonmel and Clogheen near
'The Vee', in the Knockmealdown Mountains.
Jane Toomey, t (062) 33360.
  Information on the above routes.
Margaret O'Keefe, t (052) 33456.
  Details on trails around Slievenamon.

Clonmel (in 1713); as was George Borrow, another English novelist (1803–81). The
enterprising Italian pedlar Charles Bianconi, who gave Ireland its first public transport
service when he ran his celebrated Bianconi long cars from Clonmel to Cahir in 1815,
came to Clonmel as a poor vendor of holy pictures, and stayed. Close to his original
headquarters, at Richmond Mill in Emmet Street, is Clonmel's **Museum of Transport**,
(*open Mon–Sat 10–6, also June–Sept Sun 2.30–6; adm; t (052) 29727*). The Parish Church
of St Mary has a fine east window.

About 2 miles (3km) east of town, off the N24 and near Marlfield, is **St Patrick's Well**.
This is a noted local beauty spot, in a pretty glen and near the Scillogues twin lakes.

Where to Stay

County Tipperary has really got its act together when it comes to well-run bed and breakfast in lovely country houses. The following establishments are in beautiful places, have comfortable rooms, and produce delicious food for breakfast and dinner.

Aherlow House Hotel, Glen of Aherlow, t (062) 56153, *www.aherlowhouse.ie (expensive)*. A popular local hotel in the middle of a forest.

Cashel Palace Hotel, Main St, Cashel, t (062) 62707, *www.cashel-palace.ie (expensive)*. Elegant living in an historic and beautiful 18th-century house.

Dundrum House, Dundrum, near Cashel, t (062) 71116, *www.dundrumhousehotel.com (expensive)*. A country hotel furnished with Victorian furniture, with good food and excellent sporting facilities. Lifts make access easy for the disabled. *Closed 24–26 Dec.*

Lismacue House, Bansha, t (062) 54106, *www.lismacue.com (expensive)*. A beautiful avenue of lime trees leads you to this gracious 17th-century house. The owners offer you a warm welcome, with excellent dinners and breakfasts and a real sense of Anglo-Irish tradition – not to mention tons of local advice. *Closed Nov–Feb.*

Mobarnane House, Fethard, t (052) 31962, *www.mobarnanehouse.com (expensive)*. A renovated 18th-century family house with a late Georgian addition, not recommended for those with young children. The friendly owners offer a very high standard of service: excellent dinners and breakfasts are served with clockwork efficiency, and they are a mine of local knowledge. *Closed Nov–Feb.*

Bansha House, Bansha, t (062) 54194, *www.tipp.ie/banshahs.htm (moderate)*.

A comfortable Georgian home in 100 acres of farmland where brood mares and foals roam among the beech and lime trees. Its hospitable owners encourage visitors to relax or explore the 'walkers' paradise' surrounding the house. They also let a self-catering cottage nearby, and serve dinner with advance request.

Carrigeen Castle, Cork Rd, Cahir, t (052) 41370 *(moderate)*. Lovely cosy rooms.

The Glen Hotel, Aherlow, t (062) 56151 *(moderate)*. A family-run hotel set among trees, near the Galtee Mountains.

Knocklofty House, Clonmel, t (052) 38222, *knocklofty@eircom.net (moderate)*. A central and very comfortable place overlooking the River Suir.

Cappamurra House, Cappamurra, Dundrum, t (062) 71127 *(inexpensive)*. Well-furnished rooms in a 300-year-old farmhouse. Horseriding is available. *Closed Dec–Feb.*

Cashel Holiday Hostel, John Street, Cashel, t (062) 62330 *(inexpensive)*. A cheerful hostel in an old town house. Tours can be arranged.

Indaville, Cashel, t (062) 62075 *indaville@ eircom.net (inexpensive)*. Friendly, comfortable accommodation. *Closed Oct–Mar.*

Self-catering

Lismacue, Bansha, t (062) 54106, *www.lismacue. com (luxury)*. A very comfortable 17th-century coachhouse sleeping 6. *Closed Nov–Feb.*

Anner Castle, Ballinamore, Kilsheelan, near Clonmel, t (052) 33365, *www.annercastle.com (inexpensive)*. Accommodation in a romantic 19th-century folly in landscaped parkland.

Ballyslateen, Golden, Cashel, t (062) 72287 *(inexpensive)*. A lovely farmhouse.

Cooper's Cottage, Raheen, Bansha, t (062) 54027, *cooperscottage@esat.clear.ie*

Further downriver, still following the N24, is the old town of **Carrick-on-Suir**, a thriving market town that had a big wool industry, founded by the Duke of Ormonde in 1640. His family, the Butlers, had long made Carrick their stronghold, and Black Tom, the 10th Earl of Ormonde, built himself the fortified Elizabethan mansion home you can see, **Ormond Castle** (*open for guided tours mid-June–Sept daily 10–6; adm; t (051) 640787*). He was loyal to Elizabeth I, and was evidently hoping for quieter times. There is nothing quite like this Tudor mansion in Ireland – when it was built the transition from the fortified castle to the undefended house had not yet begun, and when it did, the Tudor style gave way to other architectural fashions. It has been well restored.

(*inexpensive*) A 19th-century cottage that is in a convenient location for exploring the Glen of Aherlow.

Killaghy Castle, Mullinahone, **t** (052) 53112, *killaghycastle@eircom.net* (*inexpensive*). An 18th-century manor farmhouse with a Norman castle attached, available for up to 18 people, self-catering, in a quiet location to the north of Slievenamon, with horseriding close by. The village of Mullinahone is noted for its memorabilia and for the grave of 19th-century novelist and revolutionary Charles J. Kickham.

EcoBooley, Clogheen, **t** (052) 65191, *www. ecobooley.com* (*inexpensive*). A pioneering eco-friendly cottage.

Eating Out

Bishop's Buttery, Cashel Palace Hotel, Cashel (*see* opposite), **t** (062) 62707 (*expensive*). Modern Irish cuisine, accompanied by the resident pianist Fri and Sat.

Chez Hans, Moore Lane, Cashel, **t** (062) 61177 (*expensive*). Excellent food by a German chef, served in a former church. There's an adjoining daytime café. *Closed lunch, and Sun and Mon.*

Dundrum House, Dundrum, **t** (062) 71116 (*expensive*). Simple but excellently prepared Irish dishes.

Clifford's Restaurant, 29 Thomas St, Clonmel, **t** (052) 70677 (*moderate–expensive*). Modern Irish cuisine made from locally sourced organic ingredients, by an award-winning chef. *Closed lunch and Mon.*

The Glen Hotel, Glen of Aherlow, **t** (062) 56151 (*moderate–expensive*). Pub meals served daily in a spectacular position overlooking the wooded valley. *Closed eves exc Sat.*

Legends and The Kiln, Cashel, **t** (062) 61292, *www.legendsguesthouse.com* (*moderate–expensive*). A place offering a French and Irish menu, together with a pre-theatre option for the benefit of those attending Brú Ború next door (*see* below). *Closed lunch exc Sun, and Wed.*

Mulcahy's Restaurant, 47 Gladstone St, Clonmel, **t** (052) 25054, *www.mulcahys.ie* (*moderate*). The place to come for steak and seafood, or for a Sunday carvery.

Angela's Restaurant, 14 Abbey St, Clonmel, **t** (052) 26899 (*inexpensive*). A good choice for vegetarians, offering eclectic cuisine, fresh ingredients and speciality baked items. *Closed eves and Mon.*

Baileys of Cashel, Main St, Cashel, **t** (062) 61937, *www.baileys-ireland.com* (*inexpensive*). Reasonable lunches and dinners served in a guesthouse.

Crock of Gold, 1 Castle St, opposite Cahir Castle, **t** (052) 41951 (*inexpensive*). A small restaurant above a craft shop, handy for snacks and afternoon tea.

Granny's Kitchen, St Patrick's Rock, Cashel, **t** (062) 61861 (*inexpensive*). A traditional establishment welcoming children and vegetarians. *Closed winter.*

Honeypot, 14 Abbey St, Clonmel, **t** (052) 21457 (*inexpensive*). A wholefood restaurant providing crunchy salads and tasty bakes.

Entertainment and Nightlife

Brú Ború, beside Rock of Cashel, **t** (062) 61122, *bruboru@comhaltas.com*. A traditional Irish music and dance show held in summer, Tue–Sat 9pm.

Ahenny ('Ford of Fire'), about 3½ miles (6km) from Carrick-on-Suir off the R697 and the border with County Kilkenny, boasts two elaborately carved stone crosses from the 8th century in a sleepy churchyard . The bases are carved with wonderful figures, the crosses with spiral, interlaced and fret designs. The art of the high cross has developed here from abstract decoration to storytelling in stone. A message on the base of the larger North Cross depicts Christ giving the Apostles their mission; on the base of the South Cross is the scene of Daniel in the lion's den. Around the area are some extensive slate quarries. Their vast spoil-heaps and water-filled holes are softened by many kinds of orchids and yellow irises, known locally as *felistroms*.

Near Fethard, about 6 miles (10km) north of Clonmel on the R689, is **Kiltinane Castle** and **Kiltinane Old Church**, where you can see some *sheela-na-gigs* smothered in ivy. **Fethard** itself, 3 miles (5km) further north, has a lovely old church with fine 15th-century windows and a square tower. There is also a 14th-century Augustinian abbey, which has a fine collection of gravestones and beautiful arches beside the sanctuary. It is always open to view. On the Cashel road (R692) just outside the village is a **Folk and Transport Museum** (*open May–Sept Mon–Sat 10–6, Sun 11.30–5, Oct–Apr Sun 11.30–5; adm; **t** (052) 31516*) with some interesting items from the agricultural past, including a man-trap, for catching poachers. Three miles (4.8km) to the north-east of Fethard is the ruined **Knockelly Castle**, with a fine 16th-century tower. Five miles (8km) south of the town is the ancient **Church of Donaghmore**, in a very ruined state, though it still has a very beautiful carved Irish-Romanesque doorway.

Travelling north from Fethard towards the Slieveardagh Hills is **Killenaule**, on the R689. This village has an impressive Gothic-style Catholic church. There is a good view of Slievenamon from here. Ten miles (16km) further north, again following the R689, you come to **Kilcooly Abbey** (*always accessible*), on an unnumbered road that follows the wall of Kilcooly estate. (Park your car outside the entrance gate and walk a few hundred yards up the avenue. Take a path to the right, past the Church of Ireland church, and go through a field with a marvellous stone dovecote.) Kilcooly Abbey is one of the most outstanding examples of Cistercian building in County Tipperary. It was founded in 1183 and nearly ruined in 1445, with subsequent reconstruction. Despite being a muddle, it is a very handsome ruin, with a superb six-light east window. The south doorway is set in the midst of a highly ornamented screen with a carved crucifixion and a scene of St Christopher bearing Jesus over a river, symbolized by a shoal of fish. Among the other carvings is one on the doorway of the south transept, of a coy mermaid holding a looking-glass – a motif also found in Connacht.

Cashel

South of Kilcooly, towards the middle of the county, is one of the landmarks of Ireland, the **Rock of Cashel** (*open daily mid-Mar–mid-June 9–5.30, mid-June–mid-Sept 9–7.30, mid-Sept–mid-Mar 9–4.30; adm; **t** (062) 61437, www.heritageireland.ie*). This steep outcrop of limestone rising out of the rich agricultural land of the Golden Vale is crowned with the imposing ecclesiastical ruins of the ancient capital of the kings of Munster. The grouping of the bare, broken buildings against the sky is memorable and worth travelling many miles to see. There is an 11th-century round tower; a small chapel known as St Cormac's Chapel; a grand cathedral that was built in the 1230s; and a Vicars' Choral Hall, built around 1420. The Vicars' Choral Hall has some exhibits, including St Patrick's Cross. Outside on the rock is a replica of this cross, which was moved inside to protect it from erosion.

The Rock was the seat of ancient chieftains and later the early Munster kings, and upon this naturally well-defended high place there was very likely a stone fortress or *caiseal*. Legend records that in AD 450 St Patrick came to Cashel to baptize either Corc the Third or his brother and successor, Aengus. During the ceremony, Patrick is supposed to have driven the sharp point of his pastoral staff into the king's foot by mistake, and the victim bore the wound without a sign, thinking that such pain was all part of becoming a Christian. From that time onwards, Cashel was also called St Patrick's Rock. Brian Boru, High King of Ireland, was crowned here in 977. In 1101 King Murtagh O'Brien granted the Rock to the Church, for its political importance had declined, and it became the See of the Archbishopric of Munster.

The Rock itself and the buildings are now under the care of the Office of Public Works, and the guided tour lasting 40 minutes or so is very interesting. If you prefer to walk around on your own, however, you will find **Cormac's Chapel** on your right as you face the main bulk of the cathedral buildings, in the angle that is formed by the choir and south transept of the cathedral. It was built during the 1130s by the Bishop-King Cormac MacCarthy and is a fascinating building from an architectural point of view, constructed in a style that has been described as Hiberno-Romanesque. The most Irish thing about Cormac's Chapel is its steep stone roof. As for the rest – the twin towers, the storeys of blank wall arcading, the high gable over the north doorway and most of the stone-cut decoration – it could be German. Inside is a splendid but broken stone sarcophagus of 11th-century work. The ingenious pattern of ribbons and wild beasts with which it is decorated is believed to have been reintroduced into Ireland by the Vikings. A gilt copper crozier head was found inside the sarcophagus. The head, which is now preserved in the National Museum in Dublin, is late-13th-century French, and is richly ornamented with animal and fish forms in enamel, turquoise and sapphire.

The French and German influences at Cashel are not surprising: there are documented links between Cashel and the Irish monasteries of Cologne and Ratisbon; before the chapel was constructed, monks were always travelling to and from the Continent. The fascinating carved-stone heads are a feature of Romanesque architecture, also originating in France. One is reminded of the Celtic head cult, and perhaps both Irish and French carvings derive from ancient Celtic monuments, such as can be seen in Roqueperteuse and Entremont in southern France.

As you enter the complex of buildings through the restored **Vicar's Choral Hall**, you will see the Cross of St Patrick, probably of the same date as the sarcophagus. Christ is carved on one side and an ecclesiastic, perhaps St Patrick, is carved on the other. The massive base on which it is set is reputed to be the coronation stone of the Munster Kings. The immense ruins of the cathedral built beside Cormac's chapel date from the second half of the 13th century, and were the scene of two deliberate burnings in the Anglo-Irish wars of the Tudors and Cromwell. In 1686 the cathedral was restored and used by the Church of Ireland, but then it was left to decay until Cashel became a National Monument and everything was tidied up. What remains is a fine example of austere Irish Gothic architecture with a rather short nave, the end of which is taken up with what is known as **The Castle**, a massive tower built to house the bishops in the 15th century. Everything about the cathedral is superbly grand and delicate – in marked contrast to Cormac's Chapel.

The round tower is roughly 11th-century. You can see the top of it perfectly if you climb to the top of the castle, and you get a wonderful view of the Golden Vale, the hills to the east and west, and Slievenamon in the south. There is a gap in the hills to the north that is said to correspond exactly to the size of the Rock. Legend tells that the Devil bit off the Rock and spat it onto the plain below, hence the name of the mountain: Devil's Bit. Just below, on the plain, is **Hore Abbey**, built by the Cistercians from Mellifont. It is always accessible if you want to visit it. The Rock looks superb at night, particularly during the summer when it is floodlit. You should also visit the nearby **Cashel Folk Village** (*open daily 10–7.30 in high season; adm; t (062) 62525*), which recreates an Irish village of a century ago.

Cashel Town is a thriving place with a very good hotel, the Cashel Palace (*see* p.230). It used to be the residence of the Church of Ireland archbishops and was constructed in gracious Queen Anne style in 1730. The architect, Edward Lovett Pearce (1699–1733), also built the Irish Houses of Parliament in Dublin. It is worth having at least a coffee here, so that you can get a glimpse of the panelling and carving. The **GPA Bolton Library** (*adm; t (062) 61232*), situated within the precincts of the St John the Baptist **Cathedral**, has one of the finest collections of 16th- and 17th-century books in Ireland. There are several on display, but you have to contact the Dean if you want to get inside the cathedral. The Roman Catholic **Church**, which was also called after St John the Baptist, is in direct contrast to the simplicity of the cathedral – exotic and full of statues. The shopfronts in Cashel's main street are very colourful and the plastic age has not made too much impact.

Cahir

Cahir ('Stone Fortress'), 8 miles (12.8km) south of Cashel at the meeting of the N8 and N24, is the loveliest sort of Irish town, on the River Suir, with old-fashioned shops, colourful houses and a wide main square, with plenty of space to walk and park. It has a magnificent, fully restored 15th-century castle on an island in the river, the largest of its period in Ireland. **Cahir Castle** (*open daily mid-June–mid-Sept 9–7.30, mid-Mar–mid-June and mid-Sept–mid-Oct 9.30–5.30, mid-Oct–mid-Mar 9.30–4.30; guided tours; adm; t (052) 41011, www.heritageireland.ie*) was granted to James Butler, the third Earl of Ormonde, in 1375, and through many vicissitudes it remained in that family until Victorian times. The Ormonde Butlers were a Norman family who became all-powerful in the county. They also became rather too independent of their monarch in England, and the massive fortifications of the castle came under fire from the cannon of the Earl of Essex in 1599. It was the only important success of his Irish Campaign. A visit to the castle is memorable, as the guides are enthusiastic and really bring the defensive tactics of the Butlers to life. One's head is set spinning by the ingenuity of the portcullis and the holes for pouring burning oil. The Great Hall and other rooms within the castle are furnished and there is plenty of information about the lifestyle of the day. There is also an excellent audio-visual show outlining the archaeological and ecclesiastical sites of importance in the area. The town of Cahir has several old buildings, including the townhouse of the last Butler, the Earl of Glengall, in the square. This is now a typical Irish country hotel, the Cahir House Hotel.

On the outskirts of Cahir is the restored **Swiss Cottage** (*open for guided tours May–Sept daily 10–6, mid-Mar–Apr, Oct and Nov Tue–Sun 10–1 and 2–4.30; adm; t (052) 41144*), a delightful folly designed by John Nash for Lord and Lady Cahir in the early 19th century. It is the epitome of the rural idyll, with a higgledy-piggledy thatched roof and grotto chairs. The Church of Ireland church here was also by Nash.

The **Vee Road** (R668) from Cahir passes through some beautiful wrought-iron gates then plunges you deep in the countryside, eventually taking you through the Knockmealdown Gap and over the county border into Waterford. Ten miles (16km) south of Cahir you pass through Clogheen, before the road curves up the slopes thick with pine forest; then it turns back on itself in a wide hairpin, or 'V', and there's the most fabulous view over a patchwork of fields. It is sometimes quite misty, and as you go down towards Lismore in County Waterford, you look through the rain and sparks of sunlight at shifting vales. Just before Lismore the trees are tropically thick, festooned with moss and ferns, then suddenly the spires of Lismore Cathedral appear against the skyline. Off the Vee Road, just west of Clogheen on the R665, **Ballyporeen** has become famous for its connection with the family of Ronald Reagan: his great-grandfather was baptized in the church here, and there is a pub named after him.

Four miles (6km) away at Coolagarran Roe, Burncourt, is the **Mitchelstown Cave** (*open daily Feb–Oct 10–6; adm; t (052) 67246*) with fantastical dripstone formations, stalactites, stalagmites and columns. Well signposted from Ballyporeen, it is 2 miles (3km) off the N8 Mitchelstown/Cahir road. The caves were often used by rapparees, or rebels on the run. The prominant rebel, the Sugane Earl of Desmond, took refuge in them in 1601 but was betrayed to the English by his kinsman Edmond, the last White Knight, who received £1,000 for his treachery. A rare species of spider, *Porrhomma myops*, is found in the network of caves. You must explore with the guide, who is a fascinating source of stories and information.

The **Glen of Aherlow**, between the Galtee mountains and the Slievenamuck Hills, is not really a glen but a lush, colourful valley. The R663 runs parallel with the River Aherlow, and signs point to many tarns and lakes set in the beautifully shaped Galtees.

Tipperary and the Galtees

Tipperary, which lies in the Golden Vale, is a great farming centre. The town has a fine bronze figure of Charles Kickham (1828–82), patriot and novelist. Read his novels *Knocknagow* and *The Homes of Tipperary* if you can. The Manchester Martyrs and John O'Leary (1830–1907), a Fenian leader and journalist, also have memorials worth looking at. The town's Catholic **church** is a Gothic limestone building.

The Galtees are a magnificent huddle of peaks formed from a conglomerate of old red sandstone and silurian rocks, and stretch from Tipperary into Limerick, where they merge with the Ballyhoura Hills bordering Cork. The ridge-walking is fantastic, especially around Lyracappul. The splendour between the Silvermine Mountains (which are still mined for silver and zinc) and Toomyvara, on your way to Nenagh, is worth exploring. Around here you will hear stories of Ned of the Hill, the local Robin Hood, who plundered the English planter families and composed the lovely song 'The Dark Woman of the Glen'.

Northern Tipperary

Thurles and Nenagh

Deep in the countryside between Thurles and Cashel, on the banks of the lazy Suir, and reached by a road (R660) hemmed in by hawthorn hedges, is **Holycross Abbey**. The abbey was built so that a portion of the True Cross presented by Pope Paschal II in 1110 to Murtagh O'Brien, King of Munster, might be properly enshrined. In 1182 the abbey was transferred to the Cistercians, who embellished it so magnificently that it became a popular place of pilgrimage. It was rebuilt and changed over many centuries, though most of the finest work belongs to the 15th century. Inside is a sedile of perfect workmanship, so delicate that it resembles the work of a woodcarver rather than a mason working in limestone. The abbey is in full use today, having been restored by skilled workmen, who had to give their best to equal the standard of past centuries. It is open for prayer all day, and there is a craft shop in the courtyard.

Three miles (5km) north of Holycross on the R660 is **Thurles**, a busy market town situated on a plain by the River Suir. It was important as a strategic base during the Anglo-Norman conflict. It is also famous for its sugar-beet factory, and for the founding of the Gaelic Athletic Association (GAA) in 1884 by Archbishop Croke: there is a statue of him in Liberty Square. He is buried in the fine cathedral in the town centre; this was modelled on the cathedral in Pisa, and has a pretty belltower. It is the centre of the Catholic archdiocese of Cashel, one of the four into which Ireland is

Tourist Information

Nenagh: Connolly St, t (067) 31232

Shopping

Crafts
Farney Castle Knitwear and Porcelain
    Visitor Centre, Holycross, t (0504) 43281
Hanly Woollen Mill Shop, Ballyartella, Nenagh,
    t (067) 24278
McQuaid's Traditional Music Shop,
    38 Pearse St, Nenagh, t (067) 34166

Food and Drink
Cooleeney Cheese, Cooleeney House, Moyne,
    Thurles, t (0504) 45112. Delicious Camembert-
    style cheese. Call ahead for availability.

Sports and Activities

Cycling
Premier Cycling Holidays, Nenagh,
    t (090) 974 7134, www.premiercycling.com

Fishing
Dromineer Bay Hotel, Nenagh, t (067) 24114
Lough Derg Angling Holiday Centre, Killaloe,
    t (061) 376777, www.loughderg.net
Otway Lodge, Dromineer, t (067) 24273/24133

Golf
Nenagh Golf Club, Beechwood, Nenagh,
    t (067) 31476, www.nenaghgolfclub.com

Horseracing
Ballintoher Equestrian Centre, Nenagh,
    t (067) 31400

Watersports
Shannon Sailing Centre, New Harbour,
    Dromineer, t (067) 24295. Lough Derg cruises,
    boat hire, sailing, windsurfing and canoeing.

Where to Stay

Ballycormac House, Aglish, Borrisokane,
    t (067) 21129, www.ballyc.com (*moderate*).
    A 300-year-old farmhouse, with exceptional
    breakfasts. Activities can be organized.

divided. The town has a racecourse and the remnants of two keeps, **Bridge Castle** (guarding the south side of the bridge) and **Black Castle** (in the town centre). There is also a modern exhibition centre on Slievenamon Road, the **Tipperary Institute GAA Club** (*open Mon–Fri, plus Sat Apr–Sept, call for times, t (0504) 23579, http://tipperary.gaa.ie*), devoted to Gaelic games such as hurling, football, camogie and handball.

Nenagh is the administrative capital of the north riding of Tipperary. It has an impressive 100ft (33m) circular keep called the **Nenagh Round**, which was built as part of a strong pentagonal castle in 1200 by the first of the Ormonde line, and is one of the best examples of its kind in the country. The Bishop of Killaloe did it an injustice in 1858 by adding a castellated crown, but it is still beautiful. Across the road in the 19th-century gaol and governor's house is the **Nenagh Heritage Centre** (*t (067) 33850*). Permanent displays and temporary exhibitions are on view here; one, 'The Hurler', gives you an insight into that very national sport. The centre also provides a genealogical service.

Terryglass and **Lorrha** are pretty villages beside Lough Derg. The former has a good craft shop. Lorrha's architecture is still that of an unspoilt Irish village, with a smithy, an old school and some single-storey buildings. There are remnants of 9th-century high crosses, a Norman motte, and a finely decorated doorway in the Norman church of the Canons Regular. At the other end of the village is an attractive Roman Catholic church. Nearby is a splendid towerhouse and the remains of a 13th-century **Dominican priory** with some lovely carved tombs about 350 years old.

Kylenoe, Terryglass, **t** (067) 22015 or **t** (088) 2756 0000, *ginig@eircom.net* (*moderate*). An attractive stone farmhouse with excellent breakfasts and dinners.
Otway Lodge, Dromineer Harbour, Dromineer, **t** (067) 24133/24273, *flannery@eircom.ie* (*inexpensive*). A comfortable, convenient choice for those exploring Lough Derg.
Tír na Fiuise, Terryglass, **t** (067) 22041, *www.tirnafiuise.com* (*inexpensive*). A quiet, pretty farmhouse on an organic farm, with extremely hospitable hosts who also offer self-catering stone cottages.

Self-catering
Riverrun House, Terryglass, **t** (067) 22125, *www.riverrun.ie* (*inexpensive*). Cottages in a beautiful village.

Eating Out

Dwan's Brewery Pub and Restaurant, The Mall, Thurles, **t** (0504) 26007 (*moderate*). A place offering food, home-brews and special beers, brewery tours and live music at weekends.

Matt the Thresher's, Birdhill, southwest of Nenagh, **t** (061) 379227 (*inexpensive*). A place serving superior pub food, including organic bread, seafood and Limerick ham, thoughout the day.
Paddy's Pub, Terryglass, **t** (067) 22147 (*inexpensive*). A good spot for a pub lunch or dinner, with traditional music at night and in the Derg Inn next door.
The Whiskey Still, Dromineer, **t** (067) 24129 (*inexpensive*). A traditional old pub offering good grub and music.

Entertainment and Nightlife

Traditional Music
Hickey's Bar, Silvermines, **t** (067) 25003
Larkins, Garrykennedy, Portroe, **t** (067) 23232. Music 4 nights a week.
The Lucky Bags, Kilruane, **t** (067) 41444. Music Tue, Sat and Sun.
Stapleton's Bar, Pallas Cross, Borrisoleigh, **t** (0504) 51281

Five miles (8km) from Nenagh is the holiday centre of **Dromineer** on the edge of Lough Derg. It has a fine ruined castle by the harbour, and the place has been sympathetically developed as a sailing, fishing, cruising and water-skiing resort. The wooded islands that cluster in the 25-mile (40km) long lough are fun to explore, and there are regular cruises if you do not want to navigate a boat yourself.

Roscrea and Surroundings

Two wonderful artefacts from the early-Christian era have been found in these parts: the early-9th-century silver Roscrea Brooch, with its gold and amber decoration; and the mid-8th-century *Book of Dimma*, which contains the four Gospels and is enclosed in a shrine of bronze with silver plates ornamented with Celtic interlacing. Both treasures are now in Dublin: you can see the *Book of Dimma* in Trinity College, and the brooch in the National Museum.

At the entrance to the little town of Roscrea, St Cronan's Church and Round Tower is all that remains of a monastery founded by St Cronan in the early 600s. The west façade of this 12th-century Romanesque church has survived; the rest was demolished to make way for an 1812 Church of Ireland church in the churchyard. There is also a 12th-century high cross there. The Roman Catholic **Church of St Cronan** in Abbey Street is built on the site of a 15th-century Franciscan friary, of which the square tower and part of the church remain. The altarpiece is very attractive. Don't miss the **Roscrea Heritage Castle Complex** in Castle Street, which contains **Damer House** (*open June–Sept daily 10–6; adm; for info on other opening hours and special exhibitions call t (0505) 21850, www.heritageireland.ie*). This early-18th-century townhouse is in the curtilage of a 13th-century Norman castle built by the Ormondes. It was rescued by the Georgian Society and has a wonderful carved pine staircase that took years of loving care to restore. The panelling and proportions of the rooms are very attractive. The town Heritage Society now runs the centre, with an annexe for cultural and historical exhibitions; it also has a craft and book shop and tourist information.

County Clare

Until the 4th century Clare was part of Connacht, after which it became known as the Kingdom of Thomond. It is a wild and beautiful county, still marked with signs of a tempestuous past; there are 2,300 stone forts or cahers dating back to pre-Celtic times. Clare is bounded by water on three sides – the silvery Shannon Estuary and River widen into Lough Derg on its south and east side, its western side is edged by the pounding Atlantic Ocean, and on its northern border it meets County Galway. It is unspoilt by tourism, even though it has some unattractive ribbon development and the urban sprawl of huge Shannon Airport in the flatlands of the River Shannon and its estuary to the south. The locals earn money from farming, tourism and fishing; the airport and the industries that have grown up around it also give a lot of employment to the surrounding area. It benefits further from the Shannon Scheme, the largest hydroelectric scheme in the country. The population is approximately

103,000, with most people living in the flat central plain from which the county takes its name, *An Clár*. It is separated by the Shannon Estuary from County Kerry, its neighbour in the south, though there is a car ferry from Tarbert to Killimer.

Most people go inland, almost to the centre of Ireland, to find the Limerick bridge, then only shoot through Clare on their way to the delights of Connemara. But Clare has its plunging cliffs and strange limestone karst landscapes to attract the more adventurous. The west Clare coast ends in the dramatic Cliffs of Moher, and besides gazing at the splendid seascapes you can sea-fish, dive, walk, rock-climb, play golf and dolphin-watch along this part of the coast. To the north, overlooking Galway Bay, the Barony of the Burren looks like a misplaced section of the moon, white, crevassed and

Getting There and Around

By Air
Shannon Airport (**t** (061) 471 444, *www.shannonairport.com*) is 15 miles (24km) south of Ennis town. *Bus Éireann* runs a regular **airport bus** to Ennis (30mins, around €5).

By Bus and Rail
Buses leave Ennis from the station (**t** (065) 682 4177) in the centre, with connections to Shannon Airport, Limerick, Galway and Dublin. Ennis **train station** (**t** (065) 684 0444) is in Station Rd; services mirror the bus lines. You can get to most smaller towns by bus.
For guided tours of the Burren, contact **Burren Coaches**, **t** (065) 707 8009.

By Ferry
The **Shannon Car Ferry** (**t** (065) 905 3124, *www.shannonferries.com*) sails between **Tarbert** in Kerry and **Killimer** in Clare. There are daily, hourly crossings (May–Sept half-hourly). Cars €14 single/€22 return; pedestrians €4 single.

By Bike
Irish Cycle Hire, train station, Ennis, **t** (065) 682 1992, *www.irishcyclehire.com*
Michael Tierney, 17 Abbey St, Ennis, **t** (065) 682 9433, *www.ennisrentabike.com*

Getting to Islands off Clare
The following operate ferry services to the Aran Islands:
Aran Islands Fast Ferries, **t** (065) 707 4550, *www.aranislandsfastferries.com*.
Twenty-minute sailings between Doolin and Inisheer thoughout the high season, costing €20 return.

Doolin Ferries, **t** (065) 7074455, *www.doolinferries.com*. Ferries from Doolin or Galway to Inishmore, Inisheer and Inishmaan by request, all year.
Willie O'Callaghan, **t** (065) 682 1374. Cruises in summer from Liscannor Pier.
The following operates a daily ferry service to Scattery Island from Kilrush marina:
Shannon Dolphins, **t** (065) 905 1327, *www.discoverdolphins.ie*

Festivals

May
Clare Festival of Traditional Singing, Miltown
Maylaby Fleadh Nua Ennis, *www.fleadhnua.com*
Iniscealtra Festival of Arts, Mountshannon

June
Clare County *Fleadh*, Ennis.
Spancil Hill Fair. A traditional horse fair.

July
Féile Brian Ború, *www.killaloe.ie*. A 5-day event on a Viking theme in Killaloe.
Scariff Harbour Festival, *www.scariff.com*

August
Éigse **Mrs Crotty**, **Festival of Concertina Music**, Kilrush, *www.eigsemrscrotty.com*
Feakle International Traditional Music Festival, *www.feaklefestival.ie*
Lisdoonvarna Matchmaking Festival, *www.matchmakerireland.com*. Until Oct.

September
Dan Furey Weekend, *www.labasheeda.net*.
Set and step dancing in Labasheeda.

County Clare

Galway Bay

Black Head

Inishmore

Aran Islands

Inishmaan

Fanore

Ballyvaughan Bay

Ballyvaughan

Burren Way

Corkscrew Hill

Aillwee Caves

The Burren

Inisheer

N67

Poulnabrone Megalithic Tomb

Lisdoonvarna

10 km

5 miles

N

Doolin

Ballykinvarga Stone Fort

O'Brien's Tower

Kilfenora

Cliffs of Moher

R. Dealagh

Leamaneh Castle

Hags Head

Liscannor

St Brigid's Holy Well

Lahinch

Ennistymon

Liscannor Bay

R. Cullenagh

Atlantic

N67

Miltown Malbay

Ocean

Spanish Point

Slievecallan

N85

Quilty

The Hand Cross Roads

Lake Boolynagreana

Doonbeg

N68

Corbally

R. Doonbeg

Cooraclare

Kilkee

N67

Kilrush

Killadysert

Carrigaholt

Killimer

Loop Head

Scattery Island

River Shannon

Tarbert

barren; but springy turf and calcium-loving plants grow in the earth-filled fissures, and cattle graze happily around the cracks. The archaeological and botanical interest and mysterious charm of this rocky place make many converts. There are numerous places to bathe and fish, whilst the scenery and walking around the lakes and hills of Slieve Bernagh, which rise on the west side of the long stretch of Lough Derg, and the Slieve Aughty Mountain Range, are some of the best in the county.

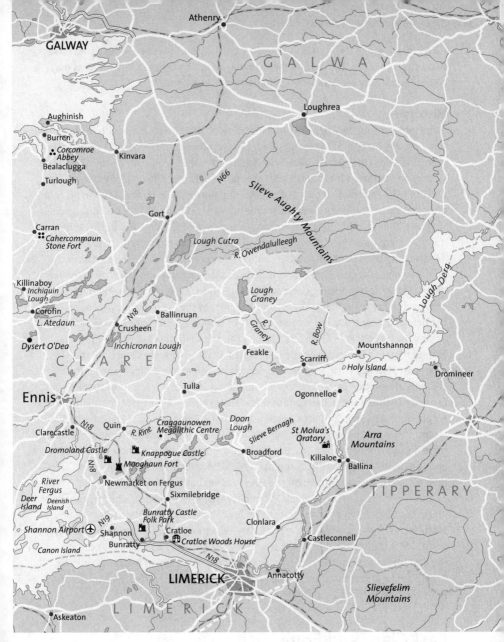

Walking and caving attract the more active visitors, but many regard County Clare as the best place in Ireland in which to hear traditional music. Doolin, a little fishing village and port for boats to Inisheer, one of the Aran islands, became the place to hear it in the late 1970s, and continues to attract European and American backpackers. But spontaneous creativity and musical excellence has long moved on from Doolin to other places in Clare.

Recently, a few of the wonderful carved stone heads in the ancient holy sites have been stolen, apparently hacked off and driven away. The Office of Public Works may have to substitute replicas for the originals if this continues.

History

The 12th-century *Book of Invasions*, or *Lebor Gabala*, connects Clare with the Fir Bolgs, but we know little about these shadowy people. Many centuries later, it was a Clare man, Brian Boru of the clan O'Brien, who conducted a vigorous campaign against the Vikings and defeated them at Clontarf in 1014. He became High King of Ireland in 1002, and built the Palace of Kincora as his residence in 1012. Sadly, he was killed in his tent after the battle of Clontarf, and the fragile national unity he had created disappeared very fast. There is nothing left of Kincora, that palace of feasting and music; in fact, nobody is really sure exactly where it was located (it was probably close to Killaloe).

In the tales of ancient Ireland, the countryside was fraught with the battles of the landowning Celtic clans: the O'Briens, O'Deas, MacNamaras and MacMahons, who, when they were not waging fierce war on foreigners, passed the time fighting amongst themselves. In 1172 the incumbent chief of the O'Briens, Donal Mór, enlisted the help of a new group of invaders, a party of Norman mercenaries, in his war against the O'Conors of Connacht. Despite this initial foothold in the country, the Norman-English forces did not make much of a mark in County Clare until the accession of Henry VIII in 1534 and his acknowledgement as King of Ireland. The O'Briens were made Earls of Thomond, and remained more or less loyal to the English crown until the Cromwellian conquest (*see* **History**, p.14). After that time, Clare and its neighbouring region, Connacht, became a seat of rebellion against English rule. Clare is part of the wild west of Ireland; when Cromwell heard that a substantial part of Clare had no trees on which to hang a man, nor enough water to drown him, nor enough earth to bury him, he thought it would be just the place to banish the rebellious Irish he had thrown off the land in other parts of the country.

Later, in the 19th century, Daniel O'Connell was able to exploit this burning sense of injustice and channel it into his campaign for Catholic emancipation in which he was enthusiastically supported by the peasantry, who gave his organization the 'penny a month' that they could afford. He became the MP for Ennis and used his position in the English Parliament to campaign for the repeal of the Union with England. The Great Famine and emigration hit the population of Clare very hard: its population fell from 286,000 in 1841 to less than half this number 30 years later.

East Clare and Ennis

Around Lough Derg

Broadford, **Tulla** and **Feakle** are all pleasant villages where you can stay in farms or town- and country houses and explore the Clare Lakelands. **Lough Graney** is especially beautiful, with its wooded shores. Most of the loughs are well stocked with bream, brown trout and pike. Near Feakle, the witty and often outrageous

18th-century poet Brian Merriman earned his livelihood as a schoolmaster. Here also is the cottage of Biddy Early, the wise woman about whom at the turn of the century Lady Augusta Gregory collected stories for her book, *Visions and Beliefs of the West of Ireland*.

From the neat and pretty village of **Mountshannon** on Lough Derg it is possible to get a boat to **Holy Island**, which is also known as *Iniscealtra*, about half a mile (o.8km) from the shore. Regular ferries run in summer, or you could hire a boat at the harbour, which is a main stopping place on the lake for hire-cruisers and sailing boats. The view of Tountinna Mountain from the lough is magnificent. The giant cross on its summit was erected to the Irishmen who fell in 'the Troubles' of 1916–22. This mountain is in County Tipperary; the Gaelic meaning of the name *Tul tuinne* is 'the hill above the wave'.

The Christian settlement on the island is attibuted to St Cairmin, who lived here c. AD 640. Today there are five ancient churches, a round tower, a saint's graveyard, a hermit's cell and a holy well. St Cairmin's Church, beside the incomplete round tower, has a wonderful Hiberno-Romanesque chancel arch, impressive in its simplicity. St Mary's Church, much altered in the 16th century, contains a monument to Sir Turlough O'Brien and his wife. This O'Brien was infamous for butchering the Spanish Armada survivors who were washed up on the coast of Clare. The festival at the holy well was famous for the bacchanalian revelry that accompanied it. It was stopped by the priests some time in the 19th century, because the local squireens would seduce the girls attending. The memorial stones are still in place in the saint's graveyard for the period covering the 8th to the 12th centuries. Unfortunately the whole effect is rather spoiled by modern tombstones and garish plastic wreaths.

Around Killaloe and Bunratty

Killaloe is situated right on the great Shannon River and is surrounded by the **hills of Slieve Bernagh** and the **Arra Mountains**. It is connected to Ballina in Tipperary by an elegant bridge of 13 arches. Not far from the bridge, on the west bank of the river, is the gem of Killaloe, **St Flannan's Cathedral**, a fine 12th-century building built by Donal O'Brien on the site of an earlier church that was founded in the 6th century by St Lua. There is a magnificent Hiberno-Romanesque door that is better than anything else of its kind in Ireland, and that is said to be the entrance to the tomb of Murtagh O'Brien, King of Munster, who died in the same century in which the cathedral was built. The bold and varied carvings of animals and foliage on the shafts and capitals, and the pattern of the chevrons on the arches, are not merely decoration; they are modelled to make the entire conception an organic whole.

Nearby is **Thorgrim's Stone**, the shaft of a cross bearing a runic and ogham inscription dating from about AD 1000. The view from the top of the square cathedral tower is superb: you can see all the mountains that crowd round the gorge of Killaloe, and the beautiful Lough Derg. In the grounds of the cathedral is **St Flannan's Oratory**, with a lovely high stone roof; its Gothic doorway is a splendid contrast to the cruciform cathedral. The oratory, which dates from the 12th century, has a Romanesque west door, but the inside is quite dark and gloomy.

Tourist Information

Ennis: Arthur's Row, **t** (065) 682 8366
Killaloe: The Bridge, **t** (061) 376866.
Open Mar–Sept.
Shannon Airport: t (061) 471664

Shopping

Crafts
Ballymorris Pottery, Cratloe
Bunratty Folk Park, Bunratty Castle.
   Woven clothing, candles and prints.
Bunratty Village Mills, Bunratty. A shopping
   complex including a Tipperary Crystal shop
   and a Meadowes & Byrne clothing store.
Clare Craft and Design, Parnell St, Ennis. A
   place displaying and selling the art, pottery
   and crafts of a number of Clare craftspeople.
Cratloe Woods House, north-west of Limerick,
   t (061) 327028.
Peadar O'Loughlin, Clare Business Centre, Ennis.
   Fiddles and violins.

Food and Drink
Bunratty Winery, Bunratty. Very good mead.
Open Sesame, 35 Parnell St, Ennis.
   Organic vegetables and local cheeses.

Sports and Activities

Cruising
   Mountshannon Harbour, on Lough Derg, is a
great place to begin boat trips up the lovely
River Graney (also known as the Scarriff).

Shannon Castle Line, Williamstown Harbour,
Whitegate, **t** (061) 927042, *www.*
shannoncruisers.com. Cruiser hire for
3 nights or more. Instruction is available.

Fishing
O'Callaghan Angling & Cruising, Ennis, **t** (065)
   682 1374, *www.ocallaghanangling.com*

Golf
Dromoland Castle Golf Club, Newmarket on
   Fergus, **t** (061) 368144, *www.dromoland.ie*
East Clare Golf Club, Scarriff, **t** (061) 921322,
   www.scariff.com/east.htm
Ennis Golf Club, Drumbiggle, Ennis, **t** (065) 682
   4072, *http://homepage.tinet.ie/~egc.*
Shannon Golf Club, Shannon Airport,
   t (061) 471551, *www.shannongolf.com*
Woodstock Golf and Country Club,
   Woodstock House, Ennis, **t** (065) 682 9463,
   www.woodstockgolfclub.com

Ponytrekking
Cahergal House, Newmarket on Fergus,
   t (061) 368358, *www.cahergal.com*
Carrowbaun Farm Trekking Centre, Killaloe,
   t (061) 376754
Clare Equestrian Centre, Ennis, **t** (065) 684 0136,
   www.clareequestrian.com
Clonlara Equestrian Centre, Clonlara,
   t (061) 354172, *www.clonlaraequestrian.com*

Walking
   The **Mid-Clare Way** is a waymarked circular
route from Quin, covering 62 miles (100km),
and passing through nature reserves at
Dromore Woods and historic Dysert O'Dea.

The Roman Catholic **church** standing high above the town is believed by some to be on the site of Kincora, the great palace of Brian Boru, where riotous banquets were the order of the day. (Others believe Kincora to have been at Beal Boru, an ancient earthen mound to the north of the town.) Inside the church are fine stained-glass windows by Harry Clarke, who worked on many church windows in the early decades of the 20th century. His style is fantastical and fairy-like, in the manner of the English illustrator Aubrey Beardsley, and the colours are exceptionally vivid. In the grounds is **St Molua's Oratory,** a very ancient ruin reconstructed here after being removed from an island in the Shannon before it was flooded by the Shannon Hydroelectric Scheme in 1929. Killaloe is a centre for fishing and boating; there are facilities for water-skiing and sailing, and a large marina (*see* 'Watersports', box opposite). **Ballina,** over the bridge, has better bars and restaurants.

Watersports

The **swimming** is good in Lough Graney.
University of Limerick Adventure Centre, Killaloe, **t** (061) 376622, *www.ulac.ie*. Watersports facilities and instruction.

Where to Stay

Dromoland Castle, Newmarket on Fergus, **t** (061) 368144, *www.dromoland.ie* (*luxury*). A hotel owned by the same consortium as Ashford Castle, with beautiful grounds, a golf course and delicious food. The atmosphere can be a bit impersonal.

Bunratty Castle Hotel, Bunratty, **t** (061) 478700, *www.bunrattycastlehotel.com* (*expensive*). Excellent accommodation and traditional music every night, though the bar can be so full of people it's difficult to get served.

Old Ground Hotel, O'Connell St, Ennis, **t** (065) 682 8127, *www.flynnhotels.com* (*expensive*). Well-appointed rooms in an 18th-century building in Ennis. Good food is served in the café and **O'Brien Room** restaurant, and the **Poets' Bar** hosts traditional music sessions.

Thomond House, Dromoland, Newmarket on Fergus, **t** (061) 368304, *www.thomondhouse. com* (*expensive*). This Georgian-style house belongs to Conor O'Brien, the 18th Baron Inchiquin and the O'Brien of Thomond. It overlooks Dromoland Castle and its lake, the original home of the O'Briens, which is also now a hotel (*see above*). Salmon-fishing, deerstalking, riding and golf need to be arranged in advance.

Tinarana House, Killaloe, **t** (061) 376966, *www. tinaranahouse.com* (*moderate–expensive*). A B&B in a beautifully decorated Victorian mansion and health farm in a park. Horseriding and boating can be arranged.

Ardsollus Farm, Quin, **t** (065) 682 5601 (*moderate*). Rooms in a 300-year-old farmhouse overlooking Dromoland estate.

Carrygerry House Hotel, Shannon, **t** (061) 360500, *www.carrygerryhouse.com* (*moderate*). A spacious 18th-century house with elegant yet homely décor, only 5mins from Shannon Airport. The restaurant serves delicious meals (*see below*).

Smyths Country Lodge Hotel, Feakle, **t** (061) 924000, *www.iol.ie/~smythvil* (*inexpensive–moderate*). A cosy fishing hotel.

Mooghaun Farmhouse, Newmarket on Fergus, **t** (065) 682 5786, *mooghaunfarmhouse@ eircom.net* (*inexpensive*). A family farmhouse B&B in a great location.

Rathmore House B&B, Ballina, Killaloe, **t** (061) 379296, *www.rathmorehouse.com* (*inexpensive*). A welcoming, comfortable B&B.

Self-catering

Ballyhannon Castle, near Quin, **t** 086 814 5837, *www.ballyhannon-castle.com* (*moderate*). A stunningly restored and decorated 15th-century castle with massive stone walls and crafted stout oak beams, sleeping 8.

Strasburgh Manor Holiday Homes, Inch, Ennis, **t** (065) 683 9125, *http://homepage. eircom.net/~strasburgh* (*inexpensive*). Restored 18th-century stone-cut cottages in woodland, sleeping 4 or 9.

A mile (1.6km) or so out of Killaloe on the R463 is **Crag Liath** (*always accessible*), which is known locally as the Grianan, overlooking the road northwards to Scarriff. It was written in 1014 in the annals of *Loch Ce* that this fort was the dwelling place of Aoibheal (also known as Aibell), the celebrated banshee of the Dalcassian Kings of Munster, the O'Briens. (In Irish, *Dal gCais* means sept or tribe of Cas.) A banshee (*bean-sidhe*), or fairy woman, is a ghost peculiar to people of old Irish stock; her duty is to warn the family she attends of the approaching death of one of its members. Thus it was that Aoibheal appeared to Brian Boru on the eve of Clontarf and told him that he would be killed the next day, though not in the fury of the battle. This is exactly what happened, for he was murdered in his tent when the battle was over and the victory his. It is a lovely, short climb to the fort. All around you is beauty: woods, water and mountain.

Eating Out

The Conservatory, Carrygerry Country House, Newmarket on Fergus, **t** (061) 360500, *www.carrygerryhouse.com* (*expensive*). Marvellous, rich local meat, fish and vegetarian dishes served amidst country-house charm. *Closed lunch and Mon.*

Muses Restaurant, Bunratty House Mews, Bunratty, **t** (061) 364082 (*expensive*). A restaurant in the cellars of an attractive 1846 house, its décor and atmosphere reflecting a feeling of a long-gone leisurely way of life. The menu is based on fresh local produce, and there's a good wine list. *Closed lunch and Mon.*

Castle Banquets, **t** (061) 360788 (*moderate*). Medieval banquets at Bunratty and Knappogue castles (*see* below and p.248).

Gallagher's Seafood Restaurant, Bunratty, **t** (061) 363363 (*moderate*). A charming, thatched cottage specializing in local seafood. *Closed Mon.*

Galloping Hogan's, Ballina, near Killaloe, **t** (061) 376162 (*moderate*). The place for relaxed alfresco dining on the shores of tranquil Lough Derg.

Game Keeper's Restaurant, Smyth's Country Lodge Hotel, Feakle, **t** (061) 924000 (*moderate*). Impressive fare in an intimate setting.

Goosers Bar and Eating House, Ballina, near Killaloe, **t** (061) 376791 (*moderate*). A popular, award-winning restaurant serving local produce, meat and fish, with plenty of intimate character and inviting open fires. The bar serves some of the best pub grub in the area.

Lantern House, Ogonnelloe, south of Scarriff, **t** (061) 923034 (*moderate*). Excellent home cooking in a lantern-lit room overlooking Lough Derg. *Closed lunch.*

Mac's Pub, Main St, Bunratty, **t** (061) 360788 (*moderate*). Good seafood, plus music in the evening, in the middle of Bunratty Folk Park.

Cloister Restaurant and Bar, Abbey St, Ennis, **t** (065) 682 9521 (*inexpensive–expensive*). A olde-worlde bar by day, offering good soups, local cheeses and nutty brown bread, and a more formal restaurant at night.

Durty Nelly's, Bunratty, **t** (061) 364861, *www.durtynellys.ie* (*inexpensive–expensive*). A pub and eating house popular with both locals and visitors. The Loft is a quiet venue offering à la carte, mostly meat, dishes; the **Oyster Restaurant** specializes in seafood

Flappers, Tulla, **t** (065) 683 5711 (*inexpensive–moderate*). Interesting, tasty food, including veggie dishes, in a simple setting.

Entertainment and Nightlife

Traditional music

Clare is particularly famous for its music sessions. **Ennis** boasts a number of good venues; try:

Brogan's, O'Connell St

May Kearney's Bar, 1 Newbridge Rd

Tailor Quigley's Pub, Auburn Lodge, Galway Rd, **t** (065) 682 1247. A venue named after the famous local tailor from the song 'Spancil Hill', with music and song nightly in summer.

If you cross the Shannon at Limerick, you will find yourself heading for **Bunratty Castle and Folk Park** (*open daily June–Aug 9–6, Sept–May 9.30–5.30; adm; t (061) 360788, www.shannonheritage.com*) on the Newmarket road (N18). Allow the best part of a day to tour the castle and folk park – it is very interesting and well conceived. Bunratty is a splendid towerhouse beside a small stone bridge over the River Ratty; a perfect Norman-Irish castle keep. The present castle dates from 1460, but it is at least the fourth built on the same spot. It was constructed by the McNamaras, a sept of the O'Briens, and remained an O'Brien stronghold off and on until 1712, playing an important part in the struggle between the Anglo-Norman De Clares and the Thomonds. It was then occupied by the Parliamentarian Admiral Penn, father of Pennsylvania founder William Penn. After years of neglect it was bought by Lord Gort in 1954, who restored it with the help of *Bord Fáilte* and the Office of Public Works.

They have managed to recreate a 15th-century atmosphere, and there is a wonderful collection of 14–17th-century furniture, tapestries and early portraits. The stairs to the upper apartments are very narrow and steep, which can be annoying when the place is crowded, but you do get a real feeling of what it was like to be one of the privileged during those times, and the mellow simplicity of the furnishings is very attractive. In the evenings, the castle provides a memorable setting for some medieval-style banquets (*see* box opposite); some people dismiss these as 'paddywhackery' but they are great fun, though certainly not cheap.

The folk park has gradually grown up in the castle grounds, with examples of houses from every part of the Shannon region; many of them were re-erected here after being saved from demolition during the Shannon Airport extension. The various types of cottage range from the wealthier small farmer's house, with a small parlour, down to the cabin of a landless labourer. They are all furnished with authentic cottage pieces; one constant is the dresser-cum-henhouse, keeping the fowl snug in the house at night. Patchwork quilts, utensils, ornaments and pictures tell a million stories about life in the olden days, while outside the cottages you can wander around the vegetable patches and hay stooks, and watch the pigs, donkeys, doves and chickens. Inside some of the cottages there are people who can tell you about the old life that has all but disappeared now; you may even get a taste of the scones baking on the open turf fire. The teashop here sells these fresh scones and delicious home-made apple pie. You can see butter-making, basket-weaving and all the traditional skills that made people nearly self-sufficient in days gone by. Village life too is depicted; the school, the musty-smelling doctor's house with its oilcloth on the floor, the post office selling stamps and sweets, and various shops selling crafts and old linens, as well as a bar where you can have a good glass of creamy Guinness. Further into the park there is also an excellent collection of agricultural machinery. There are good craft centres close to the folk park and at the Ballycasey Workshops about 3 miles (5km) west on the N18.

It is also worth making an expedition to **Cratloe Woods House** (*open June–mid-Sept Mon–Sat 2–6; adm; t (061) 327028*), on the main Limerick/Shannon–Ennis road (N18), about 5 miles (8km) from Limerick. Cratloe Woods is an ancient O'Brien house, and the only surviving example of an Irish long house that is still lived in as a home. It is packed with interesting history, and there is a good tea and craft shop. The woods themselves are a remnant of the only primeval oak forest left in Ireland, and if you climb Woodcock Hill you will get a fine view. Timber from these woods was used for the roof of Westminster Abbey in London in 1399, and further back in the mists of time we know that the men of Ulster came down and cut the oaks and carried them back to make a roof for the Grianan of Aileach, near Derry.

Towards Ennis

Beyond Bunratty is the entirely modern sprawl of buildings that makes up Shannon town and airport. The roads around here are large and busy, but they soon get smaller and more attractive as you get further into the county. On the road to Newmarket on Fergus, you will pass by **Kilnasoolagh Church**; if you can get in, it is worth it to see the exuberant baroque monument (*c.* 1717) by William Kidwell. It is a sculptured figure of an obese O'Brien – this time Sir Donat, the son of Máire Ruadh, who is rather a legend in Clare; a tough, hatchet-faced woman who kept her castle at Leamaneh in the Burren against all the odds. Their descendant was Lord Inchiquin, who built **Dromoland Castle**. This line of O'Briens became loyal servants of the Crown, and they were rewarded well. But in the 19th century William Smith O'Brien (1803–64) of Dromoland bucked the trend, became a leading member of the Young Irelanders and planned a revolt. He and others decided on an armed rising, despite the fact that many of them had been arrested and the preparations for the rising were not complete. In July 1848, O'Brien and a small party clashed with 46 policemen in the widow McCormack's cabbage patch at Ballingarry, in County Tipperary. That was the end of the uprising; O'Brien was sentenced to death, but this was commuted to penal servitude, and later he was given an unconditional pardon.

Newmarket on Fergus takes its name from a 19th-century O'Brien, Lord Inchiquin, who was very enthusiastic about horses. In the grounds of his neo-Gothic mansion, which is now a luxury hotel (*see* p.245), is **Mooghaun Fort** (also spelled Maughaun), one of the largest Iron Age hill forts in Europe, enclosing 27 acres with three concentric walls. Maybe it was people from this fort who buried the enormous hoard of gold ornaments that was discovered nearby in 1854 by workmen digging the way for a railway line. Unfortunately, much of it was melted down, probably by dealers, but a few pieces of 'the great Clare gold find' have found their way to the National Museum in Dublin. You can reach the fort through Dromoland Forest. Access is by foot via a forestry car park signposted to the left off the N18 road between Newmarket on Fergus and Dromoland.

At **Craggaunowen** off the Quin–Sixmilebridge Road (R469), there is a reconstructed Bronze Age *crannóg* or lake dwelling, including a ring fort and farmers' houses, which was built on a pond next to a four-storey towerhouse. This house contains an important collection of medieval art donated by John and Gertrude Hunt, who were involved in setting up **Craggaunowen, the Living Past** (*open daily Apr, Sept and Oct 10–6, May–Aug 9–6; adm; t (061) 367178, www.shannonheritage.com*). This fascinating centre gives visitors a good idea of how our ancestors lived. On display is the *Brendan*, a replica of the original boat that was used by St Brendan on his voyages. Tim Severin, a modern-day adventurer, sailed it to North America via Iceland and Greenland, with the purpose of demonstrating that St Brendan could have been the first person to discover America, in the 6th century. Some rare and ancient breeds of poultry and livestock, including Kerry cattle, graze in the reconstructed pens and fields. The valley surrounding it is beautiful, and if you are there at teatime, make sure to try one of the delicious scones at the reception cottage.

Not far away, at **Quin** (about 8 miles/13km to the north-west of Bunratty), you will find **Knappogue Castle** (*open Apr–Oct daily 9.30–7.30; adm; t (061) 368103, www. shannonheritage.com*), which is run on the same lines as Bunratty Castle, with medieval banquets in the evening (*see* p.246). The ribbon development that lies between Sixmilebridge and Quin may disappoint you; this is a feature around all expanding towns in Ireland.

At the following crossroads, to the east of the town, a right turn will lead you to **Quin Abbey** (*always accessible*), which is well preserved and is subject to visits by countless coach tours. The abbey was founded for the Franciscans in 1402 and subsequently incorporated into a great castle that was built by one of the De Clares. The monastic buildings are grouped together around an attractive cloister, and there is a graceful tower. Buried here is a famous duellist who went by the wonderful name of Fireballs MacNamara.

North-east of Quin, on the unmarked road between the R469 and the R352, you can walk up to the **Mound of Magh Adhair**. This was the crowning place of the kings of Thomond, and a battle was fought here in 877 between Lorcan, the Thomond king, and Flan, High King of Ireland.

Ennis

Ennis (*Inis*, river meadow), the busy and attractive county capital, is situated on a great bend of the River Fergus. The streets are narrow and winding, and in the centre is a hideous monument to the great Daniel O'Connell, who successfully contested the Clare seat in 1828, even though the repressive laws of the time disqualified Catholics from standing. Right in the middle of town is the substantial ruin of **Ennis Friary** (*open Apr–May and mid-Sept–Oct Tue–Sun 10–5, June–mid-Sept daily 10–6; adm; t (065) 682 9100, www.heritageireland.ie*). The friary was founded for the Franciscans by Donnchadh O'Brien, King of Thomond, just prior to his death in 1242. It is rich in sculptures and decorated tombs, although the building itself has been rather mucked about, with various additions and renovations. On one of the tombs you can see the sculptured device of a cock crowing. The story goes that, standing on the rim of a pot, he cries in Irish, 'the son of the Virgin is safe' – a reference to the story of the cock that rose from the pot in which it was cooking to proclaim that 'Himself above on the Cross will rise again', to the astonishment of the two Roman soldiers who had questioned the prophecy.

There is also the small **Clare Museum** (*open Mon–Fri; adm; t (065) 684 2119*) in a former convent in Arthur's Row, which specializes in objects associated with famous Clare people. De Valera has strong connections with this place, as he represented Clare from 1917 to 1959. Fans of Percy French (1854–1920), painter and entertainer, can look at the old steam engine immortalized in his 'Are you right there, Michael, are you right?' This song about the West Clare Railway, and the engine's habit of stopping at places other than stations, led to a libel action with the directors.

North-east of Ennis are the **Slieve Aughty Mountains**, and it is really worthwhile to drive up into the foothills for the view – perhaps to **Ballinruan**, a small village with a stunning panorama. The huge plain of Clare, interspersed with loughs, bright green fields of irregular shapes, bogs, woodland and tracts of limestone, is spread before you, with the odd church spire or tumbled castle adding romance. Beyond this rises the barren limestone mass of the Burren, stretching as far as Galway Bay, while to the south are the wide Shannon River and the hills of Limerick.

The Burren and the Clare Coast

North of Ennis

On the way from Ennis to Corofin (off the N85 to Ennistymon, and 2 miles/3.2km off the R476) is the religious settlement of **Dysert O'Dea**. It was started in the 7th century by St Tola, but he probably lived in a cell of wattle and daub. The present ruin is a much-altered, 12th-century Hiberno-Romanesque church with a badly reconstructed west doorway that now stands in the south wall. The door is sumptuously carved, and the arch has a row of stone heads with Mongolian features, the idea for which came from northern France. Beside the church is the stump of a round tower, and just east of it is a high cross from the 12th century, with Christ shown in a pleated robe, and below him a bishop with a crozier. A decisive battle fought here in 1318 drove the Anglo-Normans out of the surrounding area for several centuries, when the O'Brien chief of the time defeated Richard de Clare of Bunratty and expelled him. Dysert O'Dea Castle (*adm*; **t** *(065) 683 7401*) with its heritage centre is the start of a short signposted walk around the archaeological remains of the vicinity.

Corofin village lies between two pretty lakes, the Inchiquin and Atedaun. There is good game and coarse fishing here, and plenty of caves, for this is marginal shale and limestone countryside in which the River Fergus plays some tricks. The **Clare Heritage and Genealogical Centre** (*open Mon–Fri 9–5.30*; *t (065) 683 7955*) offers a 'trace your ancestors' service (*fee*) and has very interesting displays on rural Ireland 150 years ago.

About 2 miles (3km) further up on the R476 is **Killinaboy** ('Kilnaboy' on some maps), a small village close to the northern tip of Lough Inchiquin. The remains of a round tower rest in the graveyard of a ruined church from the 11th century. Over the south door is a *sheela-na-gig*, a grotesque, erotic female figure. These are often carved and fixed to ecclesiastical buildings, probably as a sort of crude warning to the monks and laity of the power of female sexuality. There are many gallery graves round here. One mile (1.6km) north-west of Killinaboy, at Roughan, over a stile and in a field, is the Tau Cross, shaped like a T with a carved head in each arm. Several like this were found in a Celtic sanctuary at Roquepertuse in France; it is likely that this is pre-Christian. The minor roads around **Lough Inchiquin** are a real delight to walk or cycle along.

Several little roads from Killinaboy meander right into the heart of the Burren. Take the first road to the right after leaving Killinaboy, between Glasgeivnagh Hill and Mullaghmore. The **Cappaghkennedy** megalithic tomb is near the summit of Glasgeivnagh. At the next junction take a left and continue back in a wide circle to Carran, passing the great stone fort of **Cahercommaun**. To get to it, turn left in Carran village and left again at the next junction. Look out for an avenue to the left that leads to a car park. From here you go a short way on foot. The fort is situated on a cliff edge across some ankle-breaking country, but while you pick your way across, notice the flower life between the stones. A Harvard excavation team reached the conclusion that the fort was occupied during the 8–9th centuries by a community that raised cattle, hunted red deer and cultivated some land for growing grain. This route brings you back to the main road (R480).

On the main road leading to Kilfenora (R476) is the lovely, ruined **Leamaneagh Castle**. It has a 1480 tower and early-17th-century fortified house. Sir Conor O'Brien, who built it, had a strong-minded wife, *Máire Ruadh* ('Red Mary'). After he died, she married an influential Cromwellian to ensure the inheritance of her son, Donat, and prevent the expropriation of her lands. The story goes that when one day he made an uncalled-for remark about her first husband, she pushed him out the window.

The Burren

This district is generally called 'the Burren' after the ancient Barony of that name. Burren (in Gaelic, *An Bhoireann*) means 'the stony district'. It extends some 25 miles (40km) from east to west and 15 miles (24km) from north to south, between Galway Bay and the Atlantic, with the villages of Doolin, Kilfenora, Gort and Kinvara forming its south-eastern border. It is dotted with signs of ancient habitation – stone forts, walls and megalithic tombs that blend perfectly with a landscape strewn with strangely shaped rocks, left behind as the glaciers retreated.

You have to get out of your car and walk here – the Burren's appeal is gradual rather than dramatic. The Burren is a plateau riven by valleys, some of which lead to the sea; others go nowhere, only into themselves. The **Aran Islands** (*see* 'Getting to Islands off Clare', p.239) rise from Galway Bay, sometimes appearing dark and close to shore, at other times in a shimmering misty haze, far away. They were part of the Burren many ages ago and share its geology and flora. In late May the place is starred with sky-blue gentians, bloody cranesbill, geraniums and orchids. Arctic-alpine mountain avens sprawl lavishly over the rocks and Irish saxifrage tufts cover sea-sprayed boulders. In the damp clefts of limestone are shade-loving plants such as the maidenhair fern. The plentiful rainfall disappears into the limestone pavements and down into a subterranean maze of passages and caverns. No rivers meander through these valleys. Impermanent lakes, known as turloughs (from the Irish *tur*, dry), appear when the groundwater floods through the fissures after a lot of rain. No one has been able to explain fully how such a profusion of northern and southern plants came to grow together, some of them unknown in continental Europe; seeds must have survived from a warmer age, despite the actions of the glaciers and fracturing movement of the earth that shaped this rock. The present temperate winters and warm limestone beneath the turf suit the plants, and their colonies have grown up unhindered because the arid land has never been cultivated, only grazed by cattle.

The Burren is rich in antiquities – portal and megalithic tombs, *cahers* and cooking places left by Stone Age farmers who cleared the hills of forest. How to maintain the traditional ways of farming that have preserved the unique character of the Burren is an unresolved issue. Bulldozers are clearing the mythical landscape of ancient stone patterns, and mechanized spraying creates a sward of modern flowerless grasses. The farmers are encouraged in this by EU grants: after all, they have to make a living, and there is no support system in place to stop the destruction, only the opportunities for profit that farmers can make in opening up their land and houses to tourists.

Tourist Information

Cliffs of Moher: Liscannor, **t** (065) 708 1565.
Open Mar–Oct.
Kilkee: The Square, **t** (065) 905 6112.
Open June–Aug.
Kilrush: Moore St, **t** (065) 905 1577.
Open May–Sept.
For background information on the geology, heritage, agriculture and ecology of **the Burren**, see *www.burrenbeo.com*.

Shopping

Crafts

The Burren Perfumery, Carron, **t** (065) 708 9102, *www.burrenperfumery.com*. A still-room, herb garden, shop and organic tea-room that can organize trips to the Burren by local experts.
Doolin Crafts Gallery, Doolin, **t** (065) 707 4309, *www.doolincrafts.com*. Batik, books, fine art, glass, clothing and an excellent café.
Eugene Lambe, Fanore. *Uilleann* pipes.
Kenny Woollen Mills, Main St, Lahinch. Designer woollens, tweeds, Arans, Waterford crystal and Belleek china.
Manus Walsh Craft Shop, Ballyvaughan. Paintings, silver, jewellery and enamels.
The Rock Shop, Liscannor, **t** (065) 708 1930, *www.therockshop.ie*. Liscannor stone and common, semiprecious and precious stones.
Whitethorn Crafts, Ballyvaughan. Ceramics, glass, jewellery and clothes.

Food and Drink

The Burren Smokehouse, Lisdoonvarna. Home-smoked salmon and other local produce, and guided tours.
The Farmshop, Aillwee Caves. Food for picnics or to take home – spring water from the caves, honey, cheeses, pickles and preserves.
Unglert's Bakery, Ennistymon. German rye breads and strudels.

Sports and Activities

Courses

Berry Lodge, Miltown Malbay, **t** (065) 708 7022, *www.berrylodge.com*. Weekend cookery courses, including 'a taste of Irish cooking'.
Willie Clancy Summer School, Miltown Malbay, **t** (065) 708 4281, *www.setdancingnews.net/wcss*. A summer school comprising lectures, concerts and workshops in Irish dance and traditional music.

Fishing

Atlantic Adventures, Cappa, Kilrush, **t** (065) 905 2133. Deep-sea fishing.
Burke's Shop, Main St, Corofin, **t** (065) 683 7677. Brown-trout fishing on the lakes.
O'Callaghan Angling & Cruising, Liscannor, **t** (065) 682 1374, *www.ocallaghanangling.com*. Deep-sea fishing and trips to the Aran Islands.

Spas and Seaweed Baths

Spa Wells Centre, Lisdoonvarna, **t** (065) 707 4023. A little-changed Victorian spa well, with sulphur water available by the glass.
Thalassotherapy Centre, Gratton St, Kilkee, **t** (065) 905 6742, *www.kilkeethalasso.com*. Seaweed baths and other treatments.

Golf

Kilkee Golf Club, Kilkee, **t** (065) 905 6048, *www.kilkeegolfclub.ie*
Kilrush Golf Club, Ballykett, Kilrush, **t** (065) 905 1138, *www.kilrushgolfclub.com*
Lahinch Golf Club, Lahinch, **t** (065) 708 1003, *www.lahinchgolf.com*

Ponytrekking

Burren Riding Centre, Fanore, **t** (065) 707 6140
Willie Daly Riding Centre, Ennistymon, **t** (065) 707 1385, *http://homepage.eircom.net/~williedaly*. Riding holidays at a horse whisperer's centre.

Get out of your car to see and feel the Burren's magic. Walk in its moss-softened hazel woods and see close up the profusion of colour and scented plants in early summer that somehow thrive on the thin soil of the limestone pavements. The black wiry fronds of the maidenhair ferns and the bright green hart's tongue hide in the shelter of the grikes, while wild goats and rabbits nibble at the succulent grass. Many of the stone ring forts where the ancients kept their cattle for safety are covered in

Walking

The best walking **map** of the Burren, by local cartographer Tim Robinson, is sold around the area. The **Burren Way** runs for 26 miles (42km) between Liscannor and Ballyvaughan.

Burren Hill Walks, Ballyvaughan, **t** (065) 707 7168, *http://homepage.eircom.net/~burrenhillwalks*

Burren Outdoor Education Centre, Bell Harbour, Turlough, **t** (065) 78033, *www.oec.ie*

Watersports

Swimming is good at Fanore, **Lahinch** (in the sea or at the leisure centre on the promenade), **Spanish Point** and **Doonbeg**. *See also* p.239 for information on **cruises** to the Aran Islands.

Dolphinwatch, Carrigaholt, **t** (065) 905 8156, *www.dolphinwatch.ie*. Two-hour cruises in the Shannon Estuary to observe the large colony of dolphins living there and listen to them with underwater microphones.

Kilkee Dive Centre, The Pier, Kilkee, **t** (065) 905 6707, *www.diveireland.com*. Highly reputed scuba-diving, snorkelling and boat-handling courses.

Lahinch Surf School, Lahinch Promenade, **t** 087 960 9667, *www.lahinchsurfschool.com*. Lessons with an Irish surfing champion.

Where to Stay

Gregan's Castle, near Ballyvaughan, **t** (065) 707 7005, *www.gregans.ie* (*luxury*). An old manor house, with wonderful food and beautiful rooms. It's set at the top of Corkscrew Hills amidst verdant gardens, in fantastic contrast to the Burren moonscape, with wonderful views over Galway Bay.

Ballinalacken Castle Hotel, Coast Rd, Lisdoonvarna, **t** (065) 707 4025 (*moderate*). A beautifully situated hotel in front of the castle, overlooking the beach, with open fires and an award-winning restaurant, for which booking is essential.

Clifden House, Corofin, **t** (065) 683 7692, *www.clifdenhouse-countyclare.com* (*moderate*). A highly eccentric, characterful house, associated with Richard Burton, translator of the *Arabian Nights*.

The Falls Hotel, Ennistymon, **t** (065) 707 1004, *www.fallshotel.net* (*moderate*). A large hotel with a spectacular view right over the river, full of atmosphere and faded charm. The spa and leisure centre was added in 2006 and features a children's pool.

Fernhill Farmhouse, Doolin Rd, Lisdoonvarna, **t** (065) 707 4040, *www.fernhillfarm.net* (*moderate*). A welcoming, comfortable B&B on a working cattle farm close to the Burren, with 9 rooms and characterful décor.

Halpin's Hotel, 2 Erin St, Kilkee, **t** (065) 905 6032, *www.halpinsprivatehotels.com* (*moderate*). Good service and plain but comfy rooms.

Sheedy's Country House Hotel, Lisdoonvarna, **t** (065) 707 4026 (*moderate*). A friendly, family-run hotel with a popular restaurant.

Berry Lodge, Miltown Malbay, **t** (065) 708 7022, *www.berrylodge.com* (*inexpensive–moderate*). A Victorian house with pretty rooms, several with iron bedsteads and shutters, and excellent food in the **restaurant** (*moderate–expensive*); the owner also runs a cookery school (*see* opposite).

Crotty's Bar, Kilrush, **t** (065) 905 2470, *www.crottyskilrush.com* (*inexpensive–moderate*). A cosy traditional bar with accommodation above. Rooms are a little small, and it can be noisy, but it's a great place for atmosphere.

The Old Parochial House, Cooraclare, **t** (065) 905 9059, *www.westclare.net/parochialhouse* (*inexpensive–moderate*). A wonderful old house with spacious rooms, wooden floors and old furniture, including 4-poster beds. The quaint self-catering cottages in the old stables sleep 2–4.

Fergus View, Kilnaboy, Corofin, **t** (065) 683 7606 (*inexpensive*). A farmhouse offering good home cooking.

brambles or hazel, and you could easily pass them by. The farmers still practise 'booleying' (*see* p.257), though here it is the opposite of the usual transhumance: because of the mild climate and the summer warmth stored in the limestone, the grass grows well, so cattle are brought to the uplands in the winter, whereas in the summer months the Burren is a desert with no surface pools or streams, and the cattle are brought back down to be close to the farmhouses and water.

Inchiquin View, Kilnaboy, Corofin, t (065) 683 7731, *bkellinchfmho@eircom.net* (*inexpensive*). A farmhouse overlooking the Fergus River and Lake Inchiquin.
Lismactigue, Ballyvaughan, t (065) 707 7040, *mike-g.keane@analog.com* (*inexpensive*). A thatched farmhouse in a ring fort on a green road in the Burren.

Self-catering

Clifden House, Corofin, t (065) 683 7692, *www.clifdenhouse-countyclare.com* (*inexpensive*). Two charming apartments in the stable wing of a Georgian manor, also a hotel (*see* p.253). One sleeps 6, the other 8.
Oughtdarra Thatch Cottages, Doolin/ Lisdoonvarna, t (065) 707 4154, *www. harbourviewthatchedcottages.com* (*inexpensive*). Three thatched cottages in the heart of the Burren, with bright décor, wood floors and furniture, and exposed beams.

Eating Out

The Gairdin, Market St, Corofin, t (065) 683 7425 (*expensive*). A small restaurant with delightful, award-winning modern cooking.
Orchard Restaurant, Sheedy's Country House Hotel, Lisdoonvarna, t (065) 707 4026 (*expensive*). Surprisingly sophisticated food in a family-run hotel, plus pub lunches.
Barrtrá **Seafood Restaurant**, Lahinch, t (065) 708 1280 (*moderate–expensive*). A simple but good seafood restaurant just outside Lahinch, with views of the bay.
The Cape Restaurant, Armada Hotel, Spanish Point, t (065) 708 4110 (*moderate–expensive*). Hearty, traditional Sunday roasts or bar food in a variety of settings, with uninterrupted views over the Atlantic.
Corkscrew Bar, Gregan's Castle Hotel, Ballyvaughan, t (065) 707 7005, *www.gregans.ie* (*moderate–expensive*).

Delicious food served all day, in a cosy bar with a fire and low-beamed ceiling.
The Black Oak Restaurant, Rineen, near Miltown Malbay, t (065) 708 4403 (*moderate*). An extensive, international menu served in a restaurant perched on the coast road, with beautiful views down on to Liscannor Bay.
The Long Dock, Carrigaholt, t (065) 905 8106 (*moderate*). A traditional pub in a beautiful fishing village, with flagstone floors and a good reputation for its local fresh seafood.
Mr Eamon's Restaurant, Lahinch, t (065) 708 1050 (*moderate*). An unpretentious, popular steak and seafood house.
O'Looney's, Promenade, Lahinch, t (065) 708 1414 (*moderate*). Good seafood and bar food, plus sandwiches and music nightly.
Trí na Chéile, Ballyvaughan, t (065) 707 7029 (*moderate*). A small, unpretentious place with lots of seafood. It's very popular and has a great atmosphere.
The Cottage Restaurant, St Brigid's Well, Liscannor, t (065) 708 1760 (*inexpensive–expensive*). Lunch and serious evening dining in a rustic setting.
Linnane's Lobster Bar, New Quay, Burren, t (065) 707 8120 (*inexpensive–moderate*). An authentic Irish pub overlooking Galway Bay, specializing in seafood: chowder, lobster and oysters.
Roadside Tavern, Kincora Rd, Lisdoonvarna, t (065) 707 4494 (*inexpensive–moderate*). A wood-panelled pub-cum-smokehouse, with delicious smoked salmon and chowder.
Aillwee Cave Restaurant, Ballyvaughan, t (065) 707 7036/77067 (*inexpensive*). Delicious soups, pies and cakes served in a cave. *Closed eves.*
Cassidy's, Carron, Burren, t (065) 708 9109 (*inexpensive*). A remote pub in the wildest part of the Burren, with tasty lunches of local produce, such as farmhouse cheeses.
Monk's Bar, Ballyvaughan, t (065) 707 7059 (*inexpensive*). A place for delicious mussels and brown bread, plus traditional music at night.

Kilfenora, a place of ancient importance on the fringe of the Burren, houses the **Burren Centre** (*open daily mid-Mar–May, Sept and Oct 10–5, June–Aug 9.30–6; adm;* **t** *(065) 708 8030, www.theburrencentre.ie*) explaining local flora, fauna and rock formations. In the graveyard of its ruined church are four excellent 12th-century, carved high crosses. A fifth cross with elaborate carvings, including that of the crucifixion, stands in a field to the west. Close to it is a holy well.

On the R480 to Ballyvaughan, 6 miles (9.7km) past Leamaneagh Castle, the great dolmen of **Poulnabrone** ('pool of sorrows') with its massive capstone is one of the Burren's most photographed sites. Excavations in 1986 produced the remains of 14 adults and six children and dated the tomb as middle Neolithic. The farmer will probably ask you for a donation. Also on the road to Ballyvaughan, a mile (1.6km) out of Kilfenora, is one of the finest stone forts in Ireland, **Ballykinvarga**. This has a very effective trap for those trying to launch an attack: a *cheval-de-frise*, sharp spars of stone set close together in the ground.

At **Ballyvaughan**, an attractive fishing village on the north edge of the Burren, rent an Irish cottage and explore **Black Head**, which looks over shimmering Galway Bay, with clear views of the Aran Islands and the Cliffs of Moher. The islands are made of the same grey limestone as the Burren and have the same bright flowers in spring. Ballyvaughan village, in a green wooded vale, has good craft shops, and its harbour is the starting point for boat trips to the islands. There are a couple of 16th-century towerhouses: Gleninagh, signposted between Ballyvaughan and Lisdoonvarna, was occupied by the O'Loughlins until 1840. Close by is a deserted, ruined village that in the 1930s still had a thriving community and 85 men fishing from their curraghs out in the bay. Another O'Loughlin stronghold, **Newtown Castle** (*open daily Easter–early Oct 10–6; adm; t (065) 707 7200*), down a lane off the N67 2 miles (3.2km) south of Ballyvaughan, is unusual in that it is round with a square base. Tours take about 40 minutes; a trail around the surrounding area includes bardic poetry recitals and extracts from ancient annals, as well as archaeology and geology.

While in Ballyvaughan, explore the Burren uplands and the inlets of **Ballyvaughan** and **Aughinish Bays**, quiet beaches where the oystercatcher whistles. A long tramp can be made into the stony fastness of Turlough Hill or the higher Slievegarron, where all the Burren features make their appearance. The pass between Turlough and Corcomroe Abbey is called Mám Chatha, the Pass of Battle. This is the path Donagh O'Brien took on his way to battle against his rival and kinsman Dermot O'Brien in 1317. He was forewarned of defeat by the Hag of the Burren as he passed Lough Rask, close to Bealaclugga; washing a pile of heads and limbs in the waters, she told Donagh that his head was in the pile. After raining foul curses upon his head, she disappeared. Later that day he and his followers were dead. Dermot O'Brien went on to defeat Richard de Clare, which kept the Normans out of the Burren for nearly 200 years. **Corcomroe Abbey** was founded by the Cistercians in 1195; in the north wall of the choir is an effigy of King Connor O'Brien. To the south, on a hill, are the remains of the three ancient churches of Oughtmama.

All over the Burren there are hundreds of caves formed by underground rivers. The **Aillwee Cave** (*open for guided tours daily 9.30–5.30; adm; t (065) 707 7067/36, www.aillweecave.ie*) 2 miles (3.2km) to the south-east of Ballyvaughan on the N67 has caverns festooned with stalagmites and stalactites, dating back to 2 million years BC. When the river dried up, or changed its course, they became the dens of wild bears and other animals. The food shop and craft shop here are excellent, and the centre itself is built sympathetically to blend in with its surroundings, although there is a charge to enter even the car park.

The Clare Coast

Taking the corkscrew road to **Lisdoonvarna** (*Lios Dúin Bhearna*, 'the enclosure of the gapped fort'), you get a series of lovely views of Galway Bay. Since the decline of Mallow, Lisdoonvarna is Ireland's most important spa. The waters are said to owe much to their natural radioactivity; there are sulphur, magnesium and iron springs, a pump room and baths. Hotels, guesthouses and B&Bs have sprung up everywhere, and though the town could not be described as attractive, it has a certain energy when it is very crowded in summer. Traditionally it was the place moderately prosperous farmers came to to arrange marriages for their children; and there is still much courting. Excitement peaks in August with the Matchmaking Festival (*see* p.239).

The sandy cove at **Doolin**, 3 miles (4.8km) away, is good for fishing but dangerous for bathing. This long straggling little fishing village became famous for its traditional music in the late 1970s, and is still a mecca for music-lovers. Several hostels cater for the visitors, and the pubs do a fine trade, with traditional music nightly in summer. On the outskirts is the very fine Doolin Crafts Gallery (*see* p.252). You can get a boat from here to Inisheer, the smallest of the Aran Islands (*see* p.239).

In this area are curious mineral nodules formed by limestone and shale that look just like tortoise shells; three are built into the wall beside the Imperial Hotel in Lisdoonvarna. From here, the coast road (R478) leads to the **Cliffs of Moher**, which drop down vertically to the foaming sea. Seabirds somehow nest on the steep slopes: guillemots, razorbills, puffins, kittiwakes, various gulls and choughs, and sometimes even peregrines. The cliffs stretch for nearly 5 miles (8km) and are made of the darkest yellow sandstone and millstone grit. On a clear day there is a magnificent view of the Twelve Bens, the mountains of Connemara and the three Aran Islands. **O'Brien's Tower**, on the cliff edge, was constructed in 1835 by local landlord Cornelius O'Brien, as an observation post from which to watch the turbulent seas. He also got his peasants to build a three-mile (4.8km) wall of limestone flags to prevent visitors being sucked over the edge of the cliffs by the downdraughts. Behind it is an **Information Centre** (*open daily Mar–May, Sept and Oct 9.30–6, June–Aug 9.30–8, weather permitting*).

On the R478 southeast of the cliffs is **Liscannor**, a little fishing village where a few of the fishermen still use *currachs*. It is on the north shore of Liscannor Bay. The famous limestone flags of Clare were exported from here; it is easy to spot the lovely striated stones propping up a gateway, or used as lintels, roofing slates or paving. Down on the shore of Liscannor Bay (just off the R478) is the tumbledown ruin of St Macreehy's Church (he was a destroyer of plagues, eels, and dragons), and there is also a holy well. John P. Holland (1841–1914), who invented the submarine, was born here, but Liscannor is more famous locally for the **Holy Well of St Brigid**, about 2 miles (3.2km) to the north-west of Liscannor on the R478, near the Cliffs of Moher. The well is an important place of pilgrimage: on the last Saturday in July a vigil is held there, and the 'patron' (celebration) continues on into Lahinch on the Sunday with racing and sports on the strand. It was the end of the 'hungry month' and the beginning of the festival of *Lughnasa*, when all the crops were harvested, so the 'patron' was celebrated with a feast of new potatoes.

Lahinch, a mile (1.6km) south of Liscannor, is a small seaside resort with a pretty arc of golden sand and waves big enough for surfing, plus a fine promenade that is home to the **Lahinch Seaworld Centre** (*open daily 10–6; adm; t (065) 708 1900, www.iol.ie/ ~seaworld*), where you can see the underwater life of the Atlantic Coast and unusual Clare coastline. The promenade also has a large indoor pool, a children's pool and a soft play area. Lahinch's golf course is championship-standard but guests are most welcome. The clubhouse barometer is very basic: players scan the links for goats, and if there are none, it is not worth going out to play – you will get too wet!

Ennistymon, with its colourful shopfronts, is 2 miles (3.2km) inland on the N85, in a wooded valley beside the cascading River Cullenagh. The Falls Hotel (*see* p.253), which was previously known as Ennistymon House, was the home of Francis MacNamara, a bohemian character and a friend of Augustus John, whose daughter Caitlin married Dylan Thomas. MacNamara was a supporter of Sinn Féin and an advocate of free love. He generally shocked local sensibilities – the parish priest let fly at him from the pulpit for letting his children play naked on the beach at Doolin. In 1919 his father, who was an ardent unionist, was shot in the neck when one of his shooting parties was ambushed; later Francis' own house at Doolin was burnt down by the Black and Tans.

Southwards, following the N67 down the coast from Lahinch, you come to **Spanish Point** (just off the R482), a good spot for surfing, where a great number of ships from the Spanish Armada were wrecked. Those sailors who struggled ashore were slaughtered by the locals on the orders of the Governor of Connacht, Sir Richard Bingham, and a local man, Sir Turlough O'Brien. **Miltown Malbay**, opposite Spanish Point on the N67, is noted for its Willie Clancy Summer School in July (*see* 'Courses', p.252). It is a splendid time to visit for all the fun; the standard of traditional music in the bars is good all year round.

From Miltown Malbay, which used to be a rather smart Victorian resort, you can have a swim at the silver strand of **Freach**, just to the north of the town, or climb **Slievecallan**, the highest point in west Clare, which has a megalithic tomb on its south-east slopes. On the way you could rest at the little lake at **Boolynagreana**, which means 'the summer milking place of the sun'. To get there, follow the R474 southwards for 6 miles (9.6km) to the Hand Cross Roads, and then walk over rough land for about a mile (1.6km). All round these foothills the ancient agricultural practice of transhumance was pursued. This is known in Ireland as 'booleying' and involves moving livestock to mountain pasture during the summer months. Booleying has fallen into disuse with modern feeding methods.

Back on the coast road (N67) you will find **Quilty**, which is a strange name for an Irish village: it comes from the Irish *coillte*, woods, but there are no trees on this flat part of the coast. The great lines of stone walls are bestrewn with seaweed being dried for kelp-making. The seaweed is either burned, and the ash used for the production of iodine, or exported for the production of alginates that produce the rich, creamy head on Guinness. The church here is reminiscent of the early-Christian churches, but in fact it was built in 1907, with money given by some French sailors who were rescued by the villagers when their ship was wrecked one stormy night.

Southwest Clare

Kilkee (*Cill Chaoidhe*, 'church of St Caoidhe'), about 12 miles (19km) south on the N67, is a favourite resort among the Irish, though tasteless buildings have rather spoilt its Victorian ambience. It is built along a sandy crescent-shaped beach; the Duggerna Rocks, acting as a reef, make it safe for bathing at any stage of the tide. Within the rocks are natural swimming pools, and further to the south is a large sea cave. A cliff walk starts from the seafront, from where you can get a good view of these sights. Diving off the Duggerna Rocks is organized by a watersports centre at the harbour.

The coast south-west for about 15 miles (24km), as far as **Loop Head**, is a succession of caverns, chasms, sea stacks and weirdly and wonderfully shaped rocks. Between Kilkee and Loop Head runs a walking path of some 15 miles (24km). There is a colourful legend about Ulster's hero Cú Chulainn, who was being pursued by a termagant of a woman called Mal. He came to the edge of the cliffs on Loop Head and leapt on to a great rock about 30ft (9m) out to sea. Mal, not to be outdone, made the same leap with equal agility and success. Cú Chulainn leapt back to the mainland and this time Mal faltered, fell short, and disappeared into the raging ocean. Out of this legend came the name Loop Head (Leap Head in Irish).

The R487 takes you close to Loop Head, but you really need to branch off down the minor roads to get a view of all its splendour. If dolphin-watching appeals, head for **Carrigaholt**, where boat trips (*see* p.253) go out to a resident population of 60 bottlenose dolpins who hang around the Shannon Estuary; they also go from Kilrush.

Kilrush (*Cill Rois*, 'church of the promontory') is a busy market town overlooking the Shannon Estuary, with a large marina and a heritage centre that explores the role of the landlords, the Vandeleurs, in shaping the town. At the restored **Vandeleur Walled Garden** (*open daily summer 10–6, winter 10–5; adm; t (065) 905 1760*), you can walk through 420 tranquil acres of woodland. The Catholic **church** has some windows by Harry Clarke, who was part of the movement to revive the art of stained glass in Ireland. About a mile (1.6km) away is the harbour, centred around Cappagh Pier.

Two miles (3.2km) out into the estuary, **Scattery Island** (Cathach's Island), founded by St Senan in the 6th century, has some interesting monastic remains. An island in the broad Shannon was easy meat for the Vikings, who raided it several times. The round tower is very well preserved and has its door at ground level, so the unsuspecting monks must have been surprised by the aggressive Norsemen. The five ruined churches date from medieval times. Boat trips from Kilrush to Scattery Island are available in summer (*see* 'Getting to Islands off Clare', p.239), and the **Scattery Island Centre** (*open daily mid-June–mid-Sept 10–1 and 2–6; t (065) 905 2139, www.heritageireland. ie*), situated on the marina on Merchant's Quay in Kilrush, offers an introduction to the island before you go.

The **Fergus Estuary**, where the mouth of the River Shannon gapes its widest, is a paradise of forgotten isles, untouched and deserted, with names such as **Deer Isle**, **Canon Isle** and **Deenish**. You can base yourself near **Killadysert**, on the R473 going north to Ennis, and have great fun exploring them. If you make enquiries you may find someone to take you out there in a boat.

The Province of Connacht

11

Connacht

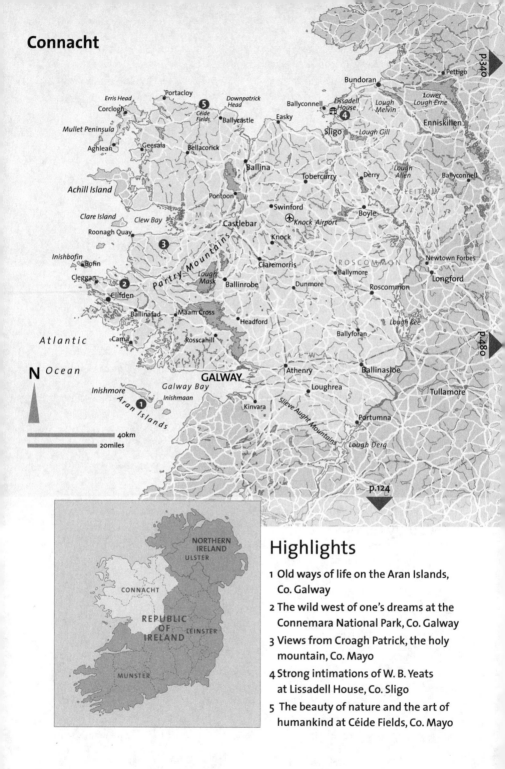

p.340
p.480
p.124

Pettigo
Bundoran
Lower Lough Erne
Erris Head
Portacloy
Downpatrick Head
Ballyconnell
Lissadell House
Lough Melvin
Corclogh
Céide Fields
Ballycastle
Easky
Enniskillen
Mullet Peninsula
Sligo
Lough Gill
Aghlean
Geesala
Bellacorick
Ballina
S L I G O
Tobercurry
Derry
Lough Allen
Ballyconnell
Achill Island
Pontoon
L E I T R I M
Clare Island
Clew Bay
M A Y O
Castlebar
Swinford
Knock Airport
Boyle
Roonagh Quay
Knock
Newtown Forbes
Inishbofin
Bofin
Claremorris
R O S C O M M O N
Cleggan
Lough Mask
Ballymore
Longford
Clifden
Ballinrobe
Dunmore
Roscommon
Ballinafad
Maam Cross
Headford
Lough Ree
Cama
Rosscahill
Ballyforan
Atlantic
G A L W A Y
Ballinasloe
N Ocean
Athenry
Inishmore
Galway Bay
GALWAY
Loughrea
Tullamore
Inishmaan
Aran Islands
Kinvara
Slieve Aught Mountains
Portumna
Partry Mountains
Lough Derg

40km
20miles

NORTHERN IRELAND
ULSTER
CONNACHT
REPUBLIC OF IRELAND
LEINSTER
MUNSTER

Highlights

1 Old ways of life on the Aran Islands, Co. Galway

2 The wild west of one's dreams at the Connemara National Park, Co. Galway

3 Views from Croagh Patrick, the holy mountain, Co. Mayo

4 Strong intimations of W. B. Yeats at Lissadell House, Co. Sligo

5 The beauty of nature and the art of humankind at Céide Fields, Co. Mayo

The province of Connacht (*Cúige Chonnacht*), also spelt Connaught, is made up of counties Galway, Mayo, Roscommon, Sligo and Leitrim. Oliver Cromwell thought of Connacht as a Siberia to which he could banish the troublesome Catholic landowners. It was here, on the crowded, stony farms that the famine struck the hardest in the 1840s. Today, it seems a wild paradise of mountains, heather and lakes into which the Atlantic makes spectacular entrances with black cliffs, golden beaches and island-studded bays. This is the wild west, which was for centuries remote from Dublin and fashionable values; where in some parts the local people still speak Gaelic, and where they have clung to their traditions in spite of the past invaders and the more insidious advance of modern life.

On a bright day in this region, you might think Cromwell did those 'transplanted Irish' a good turn: your aesthetic feelings are satisfied, and you can be sure that a good meal is waiting at the next hotel. The grey rocks, the scraggy sheep, the turf ricks and misty mountains are transformed into a tumble of brownish purple, with streaks of silver and blue where deep valley lakes reflect the sky. This is why the monks in early-Christian times turned their backs on the court of Tara and the rich Celtic princes, and built their tiny churches on the windswept islands off the coast.

Farming and fishing is a risky business here, and the history of Connacht reflects the barren countryside closely. The Norman invaders seem to have been less successful, or less persistent, here than in other provinces; or else they became Irish themselves, like the De Burgo family, who changed their name to Burke. It is rather ironic that the Connacht people, who so strongly ignored outside influences for hundreds of years, should be more Anglicized now because of TV and the tourist trade than they ever were under the British. But the areas known as the *Gaeltachta*, where Gaelic is still the first language, are protected by the government, and incentives by way of grants have encouraged people not to move off to America or England for jobs.

It would be a mistake, though, to think that all Connacht is wild mountain scenery. A large part of it belongs to the limestone plain that covers the centre of Ireland, making it saucer-shaped, with its mountains on the rim. The whole of Roscommon, part of Leitrim, South Sligo and much of Galway is made up of neat fields, trees and heather, dotted with lakes and watered by the lovely River Shannon. The Shannon rises in the Iron Mountains of Cavan and flows south-west into Leitrim, where it curves to form a moat round the eastern boundary of Connacht. This part of the province is wonderful, but it lacks the instant splendour of Connemara or the Joyce Country. The Shannon widens to engulf huge lakes, rather like a snake swallowing down its prey whole, and continues to coil down the countryside.

The climate of the west is mild, though a misty rain often falls, leaving you soaked. The mountains seem to nudge the clouds above them into rain, but there is always a glimmer of sunshine about, and in summer it can get superbly warm. Scarlet fuchsia grows along the coast roads in place of the overbearing hawthorn hedges. In parts where you would be hard put to find a blade of grass, a giant hogweed plant will grow in early summer; purple rhododendron grows here profusely. All of Connacht, but especially Connemara, is rather like a piece of tweed cloth with a thread of grey running through it – a speckled look, given by its thousands of little stone walls.

History

Connacht has a lion's share of heroes, legends and battles. Back in the mists of pre-history, tradition holds that the Fir Bolgs, who had thought themselves alone on the island, bumped into the tall, fair Tuatha Dé Danaan, and the resulting battle was fought on the plain of Moytura. The Fir Bolgs were defeated and had to retreat to the islands and mountains of the west. Here they built themselves the marvellous ring forts of *Dun Aonghasa* and *Dubh-Chathair* on the Aran Islands, and clung on while the centre of power shifted from the Dé Danaans to the invading Celts. The legendary Dé Danaans are supposed to have brought with them the *Lia Fáil*, or Stone of Destiny, which was used in Ireland as the coronation seat, and which, some people claim, can still be seen at Tara in County Meath.

Connacht has produced two infamous queens. One of them told Queen Elizabeth I not to patronize her, and was a sea pirate who ruled from Clare Island. Her name was Grace O'Malley (*see* p.300). The other was Maeve (or Medb), a legendary queen who is remembered in the epic tale of 'The Cattle Raid of Cooley' (*see* p.56). On the slopes of the hauntingly beautiful Ben Bulben, the legendary hero Diarmuid met an untimely death in a boar hunt that was arranged by his enemy Fionn MacCumhaill (*see* **Old Gods and Heroes**, p.54).

County Galway

County Galway (*Gaillimh*) is the second-largest county in Ireland, and 50 percent of its population continue to speak Gaelic as their first language. The county stretches from the wild and beautiful region known as Connemara in the west, to the banks of the Shannon and Lough Derg in the east, and includes the island-studded Lough Corrib. It is truly a county of contrasts. There is bog and rich farming land that a Meath man would not turn up his nose at, while amongst the mountains and along the coastline the tiny *clochans* of whitewashed stone cottages tell of a different way of life, where the Atlantic winds blow strongly and red hens scratch away at a soil that is made fertile by seaweed.

For those of you who have come in search of peace and solitude, miles of lonely valleys and hills and enormous golden beaches await you. Anglers will be in paradise fishing on Lough Corrib, the other countless lakes and the salmon rivers of Owenglin and Dawros. Some very good restaurants have been established that serve delicious fresh seafood prepared in imaginative ways. As for drinking, the bars here are the friendliest that you could hope to come across. Ancient Stone Age fortifications and early monastic churches add more fascination to the county. A trip to the Aran Islands is not only an adventure in itself but gives you a chance to see Conor Fort on Inishmaan, constructed of massive great stones. Romantic ruins of 15th-century castles add their charm and stories to the landscape; some have been restored for the public to look around. Galway City is an attractive and civilized place, with plenty of cultural life: music, theatre, good bookshops and cosy bars in which to discuss everything you have seen and heard.

History

The names that crop up again and again in the history of County Galway are O'Flaherty, De Burgo, and Lynch. They each represent a different and conflicting group who battled it out for centuries. The O'Flahertys were a warlike Gaelic tribe from Connemara, also known as *Iar-Chonnacht*. The De Burgos were Norman adventurers who were granted the land around Galway City in 1226, at which time it was a small fort. Richard de Burgo fortified it strongly to keep out the O'Flahertys, but over the years the De Burgos became Irish in their ways and lost their allegiance to the Crown. During the reign of Edward I at the end of the 13th century, 14 Anglo-Norman and Welsh families had settled in the town, and were passionate Royalists. They controlled all the civic powers and kept themselves to themselves, excluding any Irish from the town, including the De Burgos or Burkes as they were now called. (Quite when this name change happened is not recorded.) In 1518 the Corporation resolved that no inhabitant should receive into his house, 'at Christmas, Easter, no feast else, any of the Burkes, MacWilliams, Kellys, nor any *sept* else without licence of the Mayor and Council, on pain to forfeit £5, that O nor Mac shall strut nor swagger through the streets of Galway'. The chief of these 14 families, or 'tribes' as they were known, were the Lynches, and through the enterprise and resourcefulness of such families Galway City became rich, trading in wine and other commodities with Spain. The tribes of Galway were able to hang on to civic power in their city until 1654, when Cromwellian forces took the city after a siege lasting several months and shattered it. The Williamite wars in the 1690s brought about another siege and spelt the end of Galway's independence.

Galway City was the administrative centre for the west of Ireland during British rule in the 18th and 19th centuries. The famine years of 1845–49 bought desolation and horror to the countryside, and massive emigration followed for several generations. However, the Congested Districts Board that was set up in 1890 to promote the development of traditional crafts and fishing industries started to improve matters. At the turn of the century, Nationalists used the west of Ireland as a powerful symbol of 'Real Ireland', because the people remained un-Anglicized and still spoke Gaelic despite widescale emigration and the national school system, which between 1831 and 1904 taught no Irish. After the establishment of the Irish State, the Congested Districts Board evolved into the *Roinn na Gaeltachta* (the Department of State responsible for Irish-speaking districts), and special grants were made available to encourage people to stay in the county. The IDA (Industrial Development Authority) has also had great success in attracting sophisticated industrial companies. Galway City has its own university, the second largest regional technical college in the country, and a flourishing arts community. The attempts to preserve the Irish language are bolstered by *Radio na Gaeltachta* and Irish summer colleges, where students from all over Ireland speak Gaelic, learn *céilí* dancing and stay in the houses of Irish-speaking families. The struggle to preserve the Gaelic-speaking districts is always present: tourism and television undermine it, and the young continue to emigrate to other parts of Ireland and abroad. Many people have a sister or brother working in North America or England.

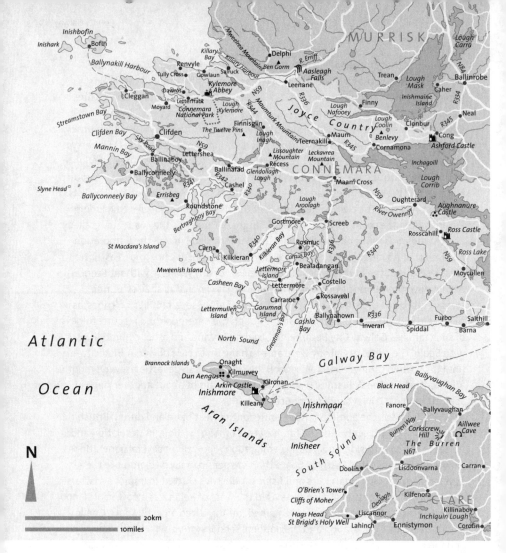

East Galway

Gort (*Gort Inse Guaire*: 'Field on Guaire's Island'), the main town on the road from Galway to Ennis, Shannon, Limerick and the south, stands in a natural gap between the Slieve Auchty mountains and The Burren – the traditional road between Munster and Connacht. Guaire was the name of the 7th-century king who built a castle here; he was supposed to have been so generous that his right hand – his giving hand – was longer than his left. One day, as he sat down to a sumptuous meal, the plates of food suddenly flew out of the windows; he naturally followed his meal on horseback, intrigued by such magic. After a few miles he came upon St Colman, who had just that minute finished a seven-year fast by gobbling up the feast. Instead of being angry, the king was impressed; he was even more so when he found Colman was a

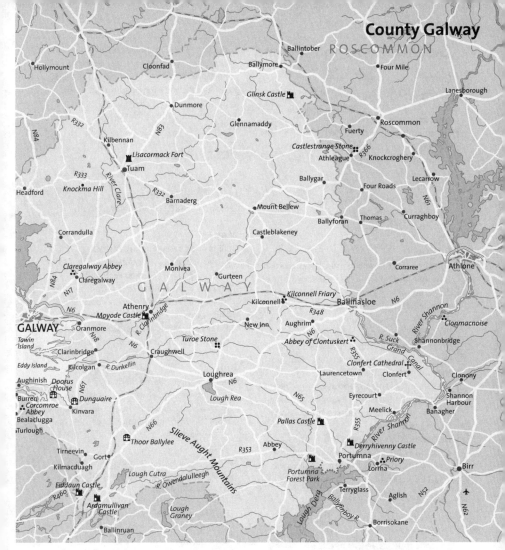

relation, and granted to him the lands of Kilmacduagh, where the saint founded a monastery. About 4 miles (7.4km) south-west of Gort on the R460, **Kilmacduagh** has one of the most interesting collections of church buildings in Ireland. There is a 12th-century monastic church that is called a 'cathedral'. Though it is roofless today, it retains some good carvings; one on the jamb of the door is an incised comic face with earrings. The round tower near the small lake was built in the 11th or 12th century. It is one of the most perfect in Ireland; its angle has something in common with the Leaning Tower of Pisa. The monks used to build the door of such towers about 25ft (7.6m) from the ground, so that when marauders attacked they could whip up the ladders once they were safely installed with their treasures.

In **Tirneevin**, just to the north of Kilmacduagh, is a small church with a very fine stained-glass window of Christ the Sower, by George Campbell.

Getting There and Around

By Air
Galway Airport has daily flights to Dublin on Aer Lingus, and some to London. There is a bus connection from the rail/bus station in Galway City that is scheduled to meet flights.
Galway Airport, Carnmore, **t** (091) 755569, *www.galwayairport.com*

By Rail
Galway Train Station, t (091) 562730, *www.irishrail.ie*. There are a few daily trains to Dublin.

By Bus
Buses depart from the train station, which is right in the centre, off Eyre Square. Galway City is one of Bus Éireann's main hubs, and you can get to almost every town in Galway and the surrounding counties conveniently. For Dublin, you can do better with Nestor Bus; other private operators provide economical services to Co. Galway towns, especially during the summer months.
Bus Éireann, t (091) 562000, *www.buseireann.ie*. This company also offers day tours around Connemara and The Burren from Galway City in summer.
Galway Bus Information, t (091) 562000
Nestor Bus, t (091) 797144, *www.busnestor. galway.net*. Returns trips from Galway to Dublin, costing €15.

By Bike
Europa Bicycles, Earls Island, Galway City, **t** (091) 563355. A company that arranges bicycle tours as well as hire.

Irish Cycle Hire, Victoria Place, Eyre Sq, Galway City, **t** (091) 561498, *www.irishcyclehire.com*
John Mannion, Bridge St, Clifden, **t** (095) 21160
Kearney's Bicycle Hire, Headford Rd, Galway City, **t** (091) 563356
Renvyle Stores, Tully, **t** (095) 43485

Festivals

April
Cúirt Literary Festival, Galway City, **t** (091) 565886, *www.galwayartscentre.ie*

May
Ballinasloe Coarse Angling Festival, **t** (0909) 644474, *www.irelandholidays.co.uk*
Fleadh na gCuach ('Cuckoo Festival'), Kinvara, *www.kinvara.com*. A traditional music and song festival incorporating art and drama.
Galway Early Music Festival, Galway City, **t** (087) 930 5506, *www.galwayearlymusic.com*

June
Bloomsday, Nora Barnacle House, Bowling Green, Galway City, **t** (091) 564743, *www.norabarnacle.com*. Open-air readings from the writings of James Joyce, held on 16 June at 6.30pm.

July
Galway Arts Festival, t (091) 509700, *www.galwayartsfestival.ie*. The biggest arts festival in Ireland.
Galway Film *Fleadh*, Town Hall Theatre, Galway City, **t** (091) 751655, *www.galwayfilmfleadh.com*

Around Gort are many little streams that suddenly disappear into the limestone. The River Beagh emerges to flow through a ravine, the Ladle, into the Punchbowl: a huge funnel-shaped hollow surrounded by trees, with water swirling dangerously at the bottom. It is only a few yards from the road, and not difficult to see even if you are in a hurry. The Gort area is full of literary associations: in 1917, W. B. Yeats bought a ruined towerhouse for £35 and called it **Thoor Ballylee** (*open June–30 Sept daily 10–6; adm; t (091) 631436/537700*). Tourism Ireland restored it, and many rare first editions of Yeats' work are on exhibit there. He lived here until 1929, whereupon it fell into ruin once more. You will find it just off the N66 north of Gort. It is a romantic building with a wonderful view from the top. An audio-guide to the tower and grounds is available in different languages. Lady Gregory's old home, **Coole Park**, is about 2 miles (3.2km)

Galway Races, Ballybrit Racecourse, 2 miles (3.2km) from city, t (091) 753870 *www.galwayraces.com*. Horseracing held late-July–early Aug. The most exciting meetings, which are those at the end of July, feature the Galway Plate and the Galway Hurdle – a mixture of high society and sweet-talking bookies.

Kiltartan Hedge School, Coole Park and Yeats Tower, Gort, t (048) 9064 9010, from UK t (028) 9064 9010. An informal exploration of W.B. Yeats' Coole and Ballylee in the landscape that inspired his writing.

August

Connemara Pony Show, Clifden, t (095) 21863, *www.cpbs.ie*. An annual show of Connemara ponies, organized by the Connemara Pony Breeders' Society.

Crinniú na mBád ('Gathering of the Boats'), Kinvara, t (091) 637579, *www.kinvara.com*. A traditional boat festival, with *currach*-racing, arts, sports, children's events and traditional music.

September

Clarinbridge Oyster Festival, t (087) 251 7155, *www.clarinbridge.com*. Lots of drinking, oyster-opening competitions, traditional music, dance and fun.

Clifden Community Arts Festival, t (095) 21163, *www.clifdenartsweek.ie*. Top-quality arts events, poetry, lectures, recitals and exhibitions.

Galway Oyster Festival, Galway City, t (091) 522066, *www.galwayoysterfest.com*. An event focused around an oyster-opening championship attracting international

participants. There are also dances, dinners, shows and speeches from local worthies, and maybe a celebrity or two.

Lady Gregory of Coole: An Autumn Gathering, t (091) 521836, *rogorman@galwayadvertiser.ie*. A weekend of lectures, a play and discussions about the folklorist, dramatist and joint founder of the Abbey Theatre.

October

Baboro International Arts Festival for Children, t (091) 562667 or t (087) 7970019, *www.baboro.ie*. Irish and international theatre, dance, music and workshops for 3–12-year-olds, held in Galway City and around the county.

Ballinasloe October Horse Fair and Festival, t (09096) 43453, *www.ballinasloe.com*. A traditional festival dating back to 1772.

Celtic Spirit/Culture Week, Inis Mór, Aran Islands, t (099) 61424, *www.celticexperience. net*. A 7-day programme of set/*céilí* dancing, old Gaelic songs, sessions and partying with islanders, boat trips, walks, etc.

Cooley-Collins Traditional Music Festival, Gort, t (091) 632370. Traditional music, *céilí* and storytelling for kids (adults welcome).

Maam Cross October Fair, Maam Cross, t (095) 22622. The sale of sheep, cattle and ponies from stalls, trailers and cars.

Tulca Season of Visual Arts, t (087) 6430244; *www.tulca.ie*. Exhibitions in venues across Galway city and county.

December

Woodford Mummers' *Féile*, t (0909) 749248. Music, singing and dancing in traditional dress on 26 and and 27 Dec.

north-east of Gort (*park open all year; visitor centre open daily June–Aug 10–6, Apr, May and Sept 10–5; adm; t (091) 631804, www.coolepark.ie*). She was a writer and co-founder, with Yeats, of the Abbey Theatre in Dublin. Many remarkable people from the Irish literary scene stayed here, including Yeats, who found it a refuge when he was ill and little known. Nothing is left of the house, demolished for its stone, but the spreading copper chestnut that served as Lady Gregory's visitors' book still grows in the walled garden: you can make out the initials of A. E. (George Russell, mystical painter), Jack Yeats, Sean O'Casey and a bold G. B. S. – George Bernard Shaw. Mementoes of Lady Gregory and the Celtic Revival can be seen at the **Kiltartan Gregory Museum** (*open June–Aug daily 11–5.30, Apr, May, Sept and Oct Sun 1–5; adm; t (091) 631069/632346, www.gortonline.com/gregorymuseum*), at Kiltartan Cross north of Gort.

Tourist Information

Ballinasloe: **t** (090) 974 2604. *Open July and Aug.*
Thoor Ballylee: north of Gort, **t** (091) 631436.
Open June–Sept.
Tuam: **t** (093) 25486/24463. *Open July and Aug.*

Shopping

Crafts
Clarinbridge Crystal, Clarinbridge, **t** (091) 796178
Dunguaire Castle, Kinvara, **t** (061) 360788
Thoor Ballylee, **t** (091) 631436 or **t** (091) 537700
Tuam Mill Museum Craft shop, Shop St, Tuam,
   t (093) 24141 or **t** (087) 4121201

Sports and Activities

Fishing
There is coarse fishing for brown trout on
the River Clare and Lough Rea, and on the
River Suck for bream, rudd, perch and pike.
   For tackle and information, contact:
Mr Salmon, Main St, Ballinasloe, **t** (0905) 42120
Sonny Martyn, Tuam, **t** (093) 24151

Golf
Galway Bay Golf and Country Club,
   Oranmore, **t** (091) 790711/790712
   www.galwaybaygolfresort.com.
   A championship course.

Ponytrekking
Aille Equestrian Centre, Aille Cross, Loughrea,
   t (091) 841216, *www.aille-cross.com.*
   A firm organizing week-long trails in
   Connemara, among other outings.
Clonboo Riding School, Corrandulla,
   t (091) 791362
Rockmount Riding Centre, Claregalway,
   near Galway City, **t** (091) 798147

Where to Stay

Lynch Haydens Gateway Hotel, Dunlo St,
   Ballinasloe, **t** (0909) 642347, *www.*
   lynchotels.com (*expensive*). A lovely hotel
   with landscaped gardens and 50 rooms.
Oranmore Lodge, Tuam Rd, Oranmore,
   t (091) 794400, *www.oranmorelodge.com*
   (*expensive*). A comfortable choice offering
   good food.
Cregg Castle, Corrandulla, **t** (091) 791434,
   creggcas@indigo.ie (*moderate–expensive*).
   A 17th-century castle, friendly and ideal for
   those with children. Traditional music is
   hosted in the evenings.
Ballindiff Bay Lodge, Luimnagh, Corrandulla,
   t (091) 791195, *www.mickrey@gofree.indigo.ie*
   (*moderate*). A hotel on the edge of Lough
   Corrib, with good angling facilities.
   Closed Nov–Mar.
O'Deas Hotel, Bride St, Loughrea, **t** (091)
   841611, *odeashotel@eircom.net* (*moderate*).

Five miles (8km) south of Gort are the ruins of the 16th-century **Ardamullivan Castle**, an O'Shaughnessy stronghold. They were the ruling *sept* in these parts before they were dispossessed by Cromwell. Another of their strongholds is **Fiddaun Castle**, also ruined but with a fine *bawn*, 5 miles (8km) south-west of Gort.

Around Kinvara

Kinvara is a charming fishing village at the head of a bay with a restored 16th-century castle called **Dunguaire**, also known as Dungory (*open daily May–6 Oct 9.30–5.30; adm; medieval banquets twice-nightly May–early Nov;* **t** *(061) 360788 or* **t** *1800 269811*). It is sited on a little jutting promontory beside the bay; a towerhouse stands within the strong walls of its close-fitting *bawn*. On summer evenings you can savour the delights of a medieval banquet as you listen to readings from Irish literature (*see* box opposite). The Great Hall is rather bijou but the Irish dancing and singing are fun. To the north, through the windows of the castle, you look over the waters of Galway Bay to the hills of Connemara. To the south you can make out the grey and hazy hills of The Burren in County Clare (*see* p.250). The road from Kinvara goes past the head of

A comfortable, unpretentious, family-run option in a Georgian townhouse.

Doorus House Youth Hostel, Doorus, Kinvara, t (091) 637512 (*inexpensive*). A hostel on the site of Yeats' and Lady Gregory's famous conversation, which led to the creation of the Abbey Theatre.

Hazel House Farmhouse, Mausrevagh, Headford, t (091) 791204, *hazelhouse@esatclear.ie* (*inexpensive*). A modern bungalow where you get a traditional Irish welcome, including tea and scones when you arrive. If you like, the host will play the accordion, banjo and fiddle for you. *Closed Oct–Mar*.

Eating Out

Dunguaire Castle Medieval Banquet, Kinvara, t (061) 360788, or t 1800 269811, *www.shannonheritage.com* (*luxury*). Typical Irish fare, accompanied by poetry readings.

Meadow Court Restaurant/Bar, Loughrea, t (091) 841051, *www.meadowcourthotel.com* (*expensive*). A hotel offering international dishes and seafood.

The Moorings Restaurant, Main St, Oranmore, t (091) 790462 (*expensive*). Food cooked by an award-winning chef, including fish specialities such as Asian seared tuna. Don't miss the warm chocolate pudding. *Closed Sun eve and Mon*.

Oranmore Lodge, Tuam Rd, Oranmore, t (091) 794400 (*expensive*). A hotel-restaurant serving rich Irish cooking.

Aughrim School House Restaurant, Aughrim, Ballinasloe, t (0909) 673936 (*moderate*). Simple but good food.

The Blackthorn, Crowe St, Gort, t (091) 632127 (*moderate*). A bar and upstairs restaurant, with live music on Sat nights.

Cré na Cille Public House, High St, Tuam, t (093) 28232 (*moderate*). A good place for well-priced game, meat and seafood dishes. *Closed lunch and Sun*.

Lynch Haydens Gateway Hotel, Dunlo St, Ballinasloe, t (0909) 642347 (*moderate*). A hotel (*see* opposite) serving good pub snacks and excellent restaurant food.

Paddy Burke's, Clarinbridge, t (091) 796226, *www.paddyburkesgalway.com* (*moderate*). A good place for oysters, ideally accompanied by a glass of creamy stout, and other seafood.

Sullivans Royal Hotel, The Square, Gort, t (091) 631257, *www.irelandmidwest.com*, (*moderate*). Home-cooked food.

Imperial Hotel, The Square, Tuam, t (093) 24188 (*inexpensive*). A place for hearty and good-value lunches.

Moran's Oyster Cottage, Kilcolgan, near Clarinbridge, t (091) 796113, *www.moransoystercottage.com* (*inexpensive*). A seafood bar in an old cottage overlooking its own oysterbeds in Galway Bay.

the peninsula, on which is **Doorus House**, where Yeats and Maupassant each stayed. (It is now a youth hostel; *see* above) Northwards from Kinvara the N67 runs inland, with little sideroads turning west to the island waters of Galway Bay. One such leads to the ancient monastic site of Drumacoo, which is dedicated to a nun, Sister Sorrey. Here there is a very beautiful south doorway decorated in early-Gothic style, c. AD 1200. There is also a very weedy holy well outside the churchyard wall.

At **Clarinbridge**, on the main Galway–Limerick road (N18), the bars come alive in September with enthusiasts gathered there for the Oyster Festival (*see* p.267). Whatever the time of year, though, take the tiny signposted sideroad to Moran's on the Weir in Kilcolgan (*see* above), for delicious Guinness and seafood of all sorts.

Around Portumna

Fifteen miles (24km) east of Gort on the R353 is **Portumna** (*Port Omna*: 'Landing Place of the Tree Trunk'). This market town stands at the head of the huge and intricate Lough Derg, the furthest downriver of the Shannon lakes and a major cruising centre, with plenty of shops and bars. To the west of Portumna is good walking country on the forested slopes of **Slieve Aughty**. The R353 from Gort bisects the mountain, and there are numerous unnumbered roads from which you can climb to a vantage point and see the extensive views of Lough Derg and the surrounding countryside. The climb up the Slieve Aughty mountains is not too strenuous an exercise, for the highest point is 1,207ft (368m). On the edge of the town is the forested demesne of the earls of Clanrickarde, now a lovely **forest park** (*car park adm*) with nature trails and picnic spots bordering Lough Derg. The 17th-century **Portumna Castle** (*open mid-Apr–Oct daily 10–6; adm; t (0909) 741658, www.heritageireland.ie*), which is being restored by the Office of Public Works,is probably the best example of Jacobean art in Ireland. A stone set in the crumbling walls of the double staircase bears an affectionate epitaph to a dog that died in April 1797:'Alas poor Fury, she was a dog taken all in all, I shall not look upon her like again'. Near the castle is a Dominican friary, founded in 1410, with beautiful windows.

There are two castles in this area you should go out of your way to see (though neither is open to the public): Derryhivenny and Pallas. **Derryhivenny Castle** is 3 miles (4.8km) north-west of Portumna. Built in 1653 by Donal O'Madden, it is well preserved and one of the last towerhouses built in Ireland. **Pallas Castle** is about 6 miles (9.7km) from Portumna on the Loughrea road (N65). Built in the 16th century by the Burkes, it has defensive lower storeys, and any openings are few and purely utilitarian – making it a terrible place to have actually lived in.

Amongst the lush and peaceful Shannon valley, about 15 miles (24km) north-east of Portumna and 10 miles (6km) north-east of Eyrecourt off the R355/6, is a monastery founded by St Brendan the Navigator in AD 563. There is a superb example of Irish Romanesque art in the doorway of the minuscule 12th-century church known as **Clonfert Cathedral** (*open daily*). Six receding planes are decorated with heads, foliage and abstract designs; within the pediment, sculptured heads peer down at you. The 15th-century chancel arch is decorated with angels, rosettes, and a mermaid admiring herself in a mirror. **Clonfert Catholic Church** houses a 13th-century wooden Madonna and child, found in a tree hole. It was probably hidden during Cromwell's time. **Meelick**, close by on the River Shannon, has mooring facilities for boats.

Around Lough Rea

Loughrea ('Town of the Grey Lake') is a bright, colour-washed town on lovely **Lough Rea**. Its pubs host fine traditional music, which is very popular here. It started life as a stronghold of Richard de Burgo, whose family turned into Burkes, then Clanrickardes; you will often come across the name. The town is very affluent because at Tynagh there are lead and zinc mines. Don't miss **St Brendan's Catholic Cathedral**; it is not very inspiring from the outside, but inside the decoration epitomizes the development of ecclesiastical arts and crafts in Ireland from 1903 to 1957. The stained-glass windows are by Sarah Purser and other members of her Tower of Glass. This was a stained-glass workshop founded in 1903 in Dublin that attracted other talented artists, such as Evie Hone. The statue of the Virgin and Child is by John Hughes, and the embroidered sodality banners are by Jack Yeats. The Carmelite monastery is a fine early-14th-century ruin, and next door to it is an active Carmelite abbey.

A most impressive curiosity is the **Turoe Stone**, which is found 4 miles (6.4km) north of Loughrea, signposted from the hamlet of Bullaun. It is a rounded pillar about 3ft (1m) high. A swirling mass of opposed spirals is carved upon the upper part. It must have had some ritual purpose; dating from the 1st century AD at the latest, it is the finest of its type in Ireland, and its decoration has been linked with the Celtic *La Tène* style of decoration found in Brittany, and also with the Omphalos Stone in Delphi that was seen as the navel or centre of the world by the ancient Greeks. The stone was moved to its present position from a ring fort called Rath of the Big Man.

The family who live in the house close by have sought to benefit from the tourists by opening the **Turoe Pet Farm and Leisure Park** (*open Easter–Sept daily 10–7, Oct, Nov and 24 Dec –Easter Sat and Sun 2–6, 1–23 Dec Thur and Fri 6–8, Sat and Sun 2–8; adm; **t** (091) 841580*), which changed the ambience somewhat. There's a duck pond, small animals, a playground with swings and a collection of old farm machinery.

At **Kilreekill**, near Loughrea, you can visit an **equestrian museum** at Dartfield (*open daily 10–6; adm; **t** (091) 843968, www.dartfieldhorsemuseum.com*).

Around Ballinasloe

Ballinasloe (*Béal Átha na Sluaighe:* 'Town of the Ford of the Hostings'), 20 miles (16km) east on the N6, is famous for its **Horse Fair** in early October, when the quiet streets suddenly bustle with eight days of carnival events and show-jumping competitions (*see* 'Festivals', p.267). Horses are still put for sale on the fair green but not in the number that the ballads reminisce about. (Horse fairs used to be common all over Ireland up until the 1950s, when the tractor and car took over.) A tower is all that remains of the castle, which used to command the bridge over the River Suck. The Suck is excellent for coarse fishing, and Ballinasloe Angling Week, one of the biggest coarse angling competitions in Ireland, takes place here annually. **St Michaels Church** contains some of the best stained glass by Harry Clarke (1889–1931) and Albert Power (1883–1945), both highly regarded artists.

Kilconnell village, about 6 miles (9.7km) away on the R348 to Galway, has a Franciscan friary, founded in 1353 by William O'Kelly. In the 17th century it was unsuccessfully besieged by Cromwell. In the north wall of the nave are two 15th- to 16th-century tomb chests, one with flamboyant tracery. The west tomb is divided into niches with the carved figures of saints John, Louis, Mary, James and Denis. Under the tower the corbel shows a little carving of an owl in high relief. Tradition alleged that the incompetent French general, St Ruth, who led the Irish against King William in 1691, was buried here after the Battle of Aughrim. West of Ballinasloe on the N6 is the site of the battle, and the **Battle of Aughrim Interpretative Centre** (*open June–Aug Tue–Sat 10–6, Sun 2–6; tea-room; adm; **t** (0909) 673939*). The main causes and results of the battle are explored in displays, documents and an audio-visual show.

The well-preserved ruins of the **Abbey of Clontuskert** on the way to Laurencetown (R355) are on the site of a 9th-century monastery rebuilt by industrious Augustinian monks in the 14th century with money from the sale of 10-year indulgences. The monks ignored the Reformation and carried on until Cromwell finally wrecked the place. It has an unusual west door of 1471, with saints, a mermaid and other creatures.

Around Athenry

Athenry (*Baile Átha an Rí*: 'Town of the King's Ford') is pronounced 'Athenrye' and was founded by Meiler de Bermingham, a Norman warlord, in the last half of the 13th century. The strong walls that were later built round it still remain in fragments. In the central square stands the remains of a 15th-century cross showing the Crucifixion on one side and the Virgin and Child on the other. **St Mary's Parish Church** was built in 1289, if not before. It became collegiate in 1484, and was suppressed in 1576 and burnt by Clanrickarde's sons (even though the mother of one of them was buried there). The graceful spire in the grounds dates from 1828. Now ruined but full of interest is the **Dominican priory** founded by De Bermingham in 1241. It has been a university and a barracks, and has been tidied up by the Office of Public Works. The tracery work of the east window, dated 1324, is very fine. The church was the burial place of the earls of Ulster and many of the chief Irish families of the west, but their graves were destroyed by Cromwell's soldiers. In a recess a small carving of a monk grins forever, and there is an grave slab dated 1682 to Thomas Tannain, on which are carved the bellows, anvil, auger, pinchers and horseshoes of his blacksmith's trade. In North Gate Street is a **heritage cottage** (*access through tourist information point*), a re-created traditional cottage furnished as it would have been in the early 20th century.

Moyode Castle, 2 miles (3.2km) south-west of Athenry, is a ruined mansion with an ancient castle in its grounds. Here in 1770 the nucleus of what was to become the Galway Blazers Foxhounds was formed. The Big House, which is now a ruin, was taken over in the Nationalist cause by Liam Mellows and his Galway followers for several days during the Easter Rising in 1916. Mellows was a Socialist leader who was executed during the Irish Civil War in 1922. **Claregalway** on the River Clare is now a suburb of Galway, where you'll find the remains of a 13th-century **Franciscan abbey**.

Around Tuam

Tuam ('Grave Mound'), pronounced 'Choom', is a very uninspiring place: the streets smell of beer and chips. But it has a long history, and during the 12th century was the seat of the O'Connor kings of Connacht. A fine 12th-century cross in the town square and imposing **Church of Ireland cathedral** are reminders of its past glory. Though the latter is a Gothic-revival structure, it still has a splendid, lavishly carved 12th-century chancel arch of rosy sandstone. The imposing church door is surrounded by carved decoration; on one of the splays, the Devil pulls Adam's ears. In Shop Street, **Tuam Mill** (*open mid-June–mid-Sept Mon–Sat 10–5.30; adm; **t** (093) 24141*), one of the county's last mills, is a museum and heritage centre, and provides tourist information in summer.

Four miles (6.4km) north of Tuam is **Tollenfal Castle**, ancestral home of the Lallys – one of whom was French general Baron de Lally, whose name is inscribed on the Arc de Triomphe in Paris. **Lisacormack Fort**, 1 mile (1.6km) north-east on the Dunmore road (N83), is the largest earthwork in this area. Neither is open to the public. On the Ballinrobe road (R332), 2½ miles (4 km) from Tuam, is **Kilbennan Church**, in Gothic style with 16th-century detail. Beside it is a 10th-century round tower. **Barnaderg Castle**, 4 miles (6.4 km) south-east of Tuam on the R332 to Barnaderg, is believed to be one of the last castles built in Ireland. On the keystone over the door is a *sheela-na-gig*.

Headford (*Áth Cinn*: 'Ford Head'), 10 miles (16km) west of Tuam, is set in countryside divided by stone walls. It is neat and tidy and a favourite angling centre, where you may stock up with fishing tackle and groceries. The surrounding countryside contains the ruins of many Norman castles. **Knockma Hill**, about 7½ miles (12km) east of Headford on the R333, is traditionally held to be the home of King Finbarr and his Connacht fairies, and the burial place of Queen Maeve (one of several, including Knocknarea Mountain in Sligo). It is the only hill for miles. **Ross Errilly Abbey**, just outside Headford, is an important and well-preserved 14th-century ruin; the cloister remains intact, although not ornate, and the domestic buildings are complete, exhibiting perfectly the arrangements of a Franciscan friary in the Middle Ages. There is a round hole in the floor of the kitchen: it is not a well but a fish tank, built so the monks would always have fresh fish on Fridays. Notice that often the Abbot knew how to choose the best architects, the finest land and best-stocked rivers for himself.

Galway City

Galway is a bustling city that has been the centre of trade for the whole of Connacht since the 13th century, despite a decline in the 18th and 19th centuries. The wine trade with Spain and enterprise of its citizens has given it an independence and character that marks it out from the other provincial towns of Ireland. In recent times that character has become even more pronounced. With new hi-tech industries and its growing prominence as a tourist centre, Galway has become the boom town of Ireland, and one of the fastest-growing cities in Europe. The mixture of Celtic tradition and cosmopolitan modernity make it a unique place indeed.

History

There has always been some sort of settlement here because of the ford on the Corrib River, but it never achieved any importance until the arrival of the Anglo-Normans. The De Burgos built a castle here in 1226. By the end of the 13th century, many Welsh and English families had been encouraged to settle here, and they built themselves strong stone walls to keep out the now dispossessed and disgruntled De Burgos and the wild O'Flahertys. There were 14 main families, and they became known as the tribes of Galway. Fiercely independent, they created an Anglo-Norman oasis in the middle of hostile Connacht. In 1549 they placed this inscription over the west gate: 'From the fury of the O'Flaherties, good Lord deliver us'. (It is no longer there.) They also put out edicts controlling the presence of the native Irish in the town. An Irish settlement thus grew up on the west side of the Corrib following completely different traditions. They spoke only Gaelic and earned a livelihood through fishing. The settlement is now renowned for the Claddagh Ring, which you will notice on the fingers of many Irish exiles: it is a circle joined by two hands clasping a heart, often used as a marriage ring. Nowadays the romantic but poverty-stricken Claddagh settlement that appealed to Victorian travellers is gone, and the thatched and whitewashed one-storey cottages have been replaced by a modern housing scheme.

Tourist Information

Galway: *Áras Fáilte*, Forster St, **t** (091) 537700, *info@irelandwest.ie*

Shopping

Antiques

Antique shops in Galway City cluster around Cross St.

Cobwebs, 7 Quay Lane, **t** (091) 564388, *www.cobwebs-galway.ie*. A jewellery specialist.

Tempo Antiques, 9 Cross St, **t** (091) 562282

Twice as Nice, 5 Quay St, **t** (091) 566332

Books

Charlie Byrnes Bookshop, Middle St, **t** (091) 561766, *www.charliebyrne.com*

Kenny's Bookshop, High St, **t** (091) 709350, *www.kennys.ie*

Crafts

Fadu, Middle St, **t** (091) 564429. Modern and traditional hand-made pottery, wood, wrought-iron and slate items.

Galway Woollen Market, 21 High St, **t** (091) 562491

Meadows and Byrne, Lower Abbeygate St, **t** (091) 567776. Crafts.

O'Máille's, 16 High St, **t** (091) 562696, *www.omaille.com*. Tweeds and knitwear.

Royal Tara China, Mervue, Galway, **t** (091) 751301, *www.royal-tara.com*. Showrooms, guided tours (Mon–Fri) and a tea-room.

Crystal

Galway Irish Crystal, Merlin Park, **t** (091) 757311, *www.galwaycrystal.ie*. Tours, a showroom and a restaurant.

Food and Drink

Food For Thought, 5 Abbeygate St, **t** (091) 565854. Health foods.

Goya's Pastry Shop, 3 Kirwans Lane, **t** (091) 567010. An establishment selling some of the best *pâtisseries* this side of Paris, plus a small coffee shop (*see* p.276).

Loughnane's Food Hall, Forster Court, **t** (091) 564437. A well-established butcher's shop.

McCambridge's Grocery, 38 Shop St, **t** (091) 562259. A good place to stock up on cheese and preserves.

Jewellery

Claddagh Jewellers, Eyre Square, **t** (091) 563081 or **t** 1800 473 3259, *www.thecladdagh.com*

Markets

Saturday Morning Market, by Church of St Nicholas. A wonderful array of cheese, herbs, vegetables, sausages and home-made jams, sold 8.30–4.

Traditional Music

Mulligan, 5 Middle Street Court, **t** (091) 564961, *www.mulligan.ie*

Zhivago's, 5–6 Shop St, **t** (091) 564198

Sports and Activities

Fishing

Corrib Tackle, Kilkerrin Park, Galway, **t** (091) 769974, *www.corribtackle.com*

Duffy's, 5 Mainguard St, **t** (091) 562367

Freeney's, 19 High St, **t** (091) 562609

Galway Fishery, Nun's Island, Galway, **t** (091) 563118, *www.wrfb.ie*

The chief tribe of Galway was the Lynch family, and there is a colourful story about the Lynch who was mayor in 1493. The tribe had grown prosperous through trading in wine with Spain and Bordeaux; this Lynch had the son of a Spanish merchant staying in his house who aroused the jealousy of Walter, his son. Walter stabbed the young guest to death, but because he was so popular nobody could be found to hang him. So his father, having pronounced the sentence, did the deed himself and, filled with sadness, became a recluse. Near the Church of St Nicholas, in a built-up Gothic doorway on Market Street, is a tablet commemorating the event, which gave the verb 'to lynch' to the English language.

Golf

Galway Golf Club, Blackrock, Salthill,
t (091) 522033, www.galwaygolf.com

Horseracing

For details of the Curragh Races, contact the
tourist office in Galway, t (091) 537700.

Indoor Leisure Centres

Leisureland, Salthill, t (091) 521455. Watery fun.

Pleasure Cruises

Corrib Tours, Furbo, t (091) 592447,
www.corribprincess.ie

Ponytrekking

Feeney's Riding School, Tonabrockey,
Bushypark, near Salthill, t (091) 527579

Killeen House, Bushypark, t (091) 524179,
www.killeenhousegalway.com
(moderate–expensive). A luxurious modern
guesthouse in manicured gardens within
walking distance of Lough Corrib, run like a
small hotel. Immaculate outside and in, it
has themed bedrooms such as Edwardian
and Regency. Closed Christmas period.
Skeffington Arms Hotel, 28 Eyre Sq, Galway,
t (091) 563173, www.skeffington.ie
(moderate). A small, central hotel with a
restaurant (see p.276) and pub.
Barnacle's Quay Street Hostel, 10 Quay St, t (091)
568644, www.barnacles.ie (inexpensive).
A hostel in the heart of the action.
D'Arcy's B&B, 92 Fr. Griffin Rd, t (091) 589505
(inexpensive). A good modern B&B, with
all-ensuite rooms and parking.

Where to Stay

Galway

There are B&Bs galore in Salthill, including a
large selection on Fr. Griffin Road, within easy
walking distance of the centre.

Ardilaun House Hotel, Taylors Hill, Galway,
t (091) 521433, www.ardilaunsunhousehotel.ie
(expensive). A large, attractive mansion with
wooded grounds, serving good food.

Great Southern Hotel, Eyre Square, t (091)
564041, www.greatsouthernhotelgalway.com
(expensive). A rambling Victorian hotel in
the centre, with comfortable rooms and a
rooftop spa and health centre.

Brennan's Yard Hotel, Merchant's Rd,
t (091) 568166, www.brennansyardhotel.com
(moderate–expensive). A comfortable option
with friendly service and pleasant bedrooms
with lots of stripped pine and local pottery.

Eating Out

Galway

Oyster Room, Great Southern Hotel, Eyre Sq,
t (091) 564041 (expensive). Good seafood.

Park Restaurant, Foster St, Eyre Square, t (091)
564924, www.parkhousehotel.ie (expensive).
A hotel restaurant that's served some of
Galway's best food for the past 30 years.

Ard Bia, 2 Quay St, t (091) 539891, www.ardbia.
com (moderate). A delightful restaurant with
an eclectic menu featuring the likes of garam
masala duck breast with green beans and
cherry chutney. Try the chocolate ricotta tart
with ice cream for dessert, and round it all
off with one of the unusual teas or coffees.
The daytime café has great sandwiches and
specials, and weekend brunches.

Cactus Jack's, Courthouse Lane, t (091) 563838
(moderate). Irish-Cajun-TexMex fare.

Galway City Centre

Galway was an important administrative centre during the days of the British, from
the 17th century until Independence. It now has a strong cultural identity, with its
own university where courses are followed in Irish and English, a large technical
college, and vigorous and high-quality theatre, traditional music and song. The city
itself is small enough to walk around in a day. The planned 18th-century part centres
around Eyre Square, which you come into immediately when approaching the city
from the east. The Galway tourist office, Áras Fáilte, in Victoria Park, is just a block
away, close to the railway and bus station. The **Gardens** in Eyre Square are dedicated

McDonagh's Seafood Bar, 22 Quay St, t (091) 565001, www.mcdonaghs.net (inexpensive–moderate). Excellent eat-in and take-away fish and chips.

Nimmo's, Spanish Arch, t (091) 561114 (moderate). An atmospheric downstairs café and an upstairs restaurant, serving seafood in a lovely location. Closed Mon.

Pierre's Restaurant, 8 Quay St, t (091) 566066, www.pierresrestaurant.com (moderate). Excellent-value French food. Closed lunch.

Royal Villa, 13 Shop St, t (091) 563450 (moderate). Good-quality Chinese food.

The Malt House, High St, t (091) 567866, www.malt-house.com (inexpensive–moderate). Excellent soups and snacks. Closed Sun.

Skeffington Arms Hotel, 28 Eyre Sq, t (091) 563173 (inexpensive–moderate). Sandwiches, light meals and sophisticated dinners.

Tigh Neachtain, 17 Cross St, t (091) 566172 (inexpensive–moderate). A great pub with good bar food. Closed lunch Sat and Sun.

Da Tang Noodle House, 2 Middle Street Mews, t (091) 561443 (inexpensive). An authentic noodle joint.

Fat Freddy's, The Halls, Quay St, t (091) 567279 (inexpensive). An invariably packed place serving up first-rate pizza and a variety of innovative dishes.

Food For Thought, 5 Abbeygate St, t (091) 565854 (inexpensive). A vegetarian restaurant beside a health food shop.

Goya's Pastry Shop, 3 Kirwans Lane, t (091) 567010 (inexpensive). Delicious cakes and coffee.

McSwiggan's, 3 Eyre St, t (091) 568917, www.mcswiggans.com (inexpensive). Seafood and veggie dishes.

Taafe's Bar, 19a Shop St, t (091) 564066 (inexpensive). A pub with good food.

Entertainment and Nightlife

For current entertainment listings, see www.galway.net/galwayguide.

Jazz

Blue Note, 3 William St, t (091) 589116

King's Head, 5 High St, t (091) 566630

Quays Bar, Quay St, t (091) 568347

Theatre

Druid Theatre, Flood St, t (091) 568660, www.druidtheatre.com. A venue with an international reputation for its exciting, mostly contemporary repertoire.

Taibhdhearc na Gaillimhe, Middle St, t (091) 562024/563600, www.antaibhdhearc.com. Interesting Irish-language theatre plus traditional music and bilingual folk presentations. The venue hosts the acclaimed Siamsa Festival of music, dance and drama in July and Aug.

Town Hall Theatre, Courthouse Sq, t (091) 569777, www.townhalltheatregalway.com

Traditional Music

There's ballad-singing and traditional music in the local bars. In the summer months try the following:

The An Púcán Bar, Foster St, t (091) 561528

The Crane Bar, 2 Sea Rd, t (091) 587419

Lisheen Bar, Bridge St, t (091) 563804

The Quays, Quay St, t (091) 568347. Mon and Tue nights.

The Roisin Dubh, 8 Dominick St Upper, t (091) 586540, www.roisindubh.net. Sat and Sun.

The Snug, William St

Taaffes, 19a Shop St, t (091) 564066

Taylor's, 7 Dominick St Upper, t (091) 587239

to John F. Kennedy, who received the freedom of the city only a few months before his assassination. In the gardens are captured Russian cannons, brought home from the Crimean War by a famous regiment in the British Army, called the Connaught Rangers, as well as a fine steel sculpture by Eamon O'Doherty based on the sails of the Galway 'hookers' or fishing boats; and a statue to Padraic O'Conaire (1883–1928), who wrote short stories in Gaelic and pioneered the revival of Gaelic literature.

The liveliest part of Galway is the medieval centre, with narrow streets winding down from Eyre Square to the river. **Shop Street/High Street/Quay Street** is the spine of the district; lined with the city's most popular bars, restaurants and shops, it jumps day and night. Fragments of buildings and mutilated stone merchant houses still exist amongst the fast-food signs and modern shopfronts. You have to go and seek out the strange and memorable animal carvings and the fine doorways and windows that have survived. The best example is **Lynch's Castle** in Shop Street, which now houses a branch of the Allied Irish Bank.

The **Church of St Nicholas** in Market Street is rather attractive, and worth a visit for its fine carvings. You may hear the eight bells peal, which make a lovely sound over the city. A proud tradition exists that Christopher Columbus stopped at the church for Mass on his way to discover America. No.8 Bowling Green, close by, is the **Nora Barnacle House Museum** (*open May–Sept Mon–Sat 10–5; adm; t (091) 564743, www.norabarnacle.com*), once the home of James Joyce's wife. The little museum contains memorabilia of the couple and their links with County Galway. A Saturday market of organic vegetables, German sourdough breads and local cheeses is held in its shadow, with an atmosphere that revives shades of medieval Galway. The modern **Catholic cathedral**, beside the salmon weir on the river, is an imposing hotchpotch of styles that dominates the skyline. It was completed in 1965. The weir is in fact one of the best places to go and idle away the hours. Shoals of salmon making their way up to the spawning grounds of Lough Corrib lie in the clear river – the only entrance from the sea to 1,200 miles (1,930km) of lakes.

Elizabeth Tudor confirmed the city's charter in 1579, and appointed the mayor as admiral with jurisdiction over Galway Bay and the Aran Islands. The town was fully walled with 14 towers, but now there is only a fragment left near the quay, called the **Spanish Arch**. The office of Mayor, which had been in decline and abolished in 1840, was restored and given statutory recognition in 1937. The mayor's silver sword and great mace dating from the early 17th century are on display in the Bank of Ireland, at No.19 Eyre Square. The mace, a fine piece of Galway silver, was returned to the city by the Hearst Foundation in the USA in 1961.

Near the Spanish Arch, the **Galway City Museum** (*open Mon–Sat 10–1 and 2–5; adm; t (091) 567641*) has displays on the history of Galway and folk life. The **Kenny Art Gallery** in the high street holds exhibitions of ceramics, sculptures and paintings by contemporary artists. The **Grain Store** on Lower Abbeygate Street shows work in wood and metal. The **University of Galway Gallery** (*t (091) 24411*) also holds occasional exhibitions. The local newspapers, the *Galway Advertiser*, Connacht *Tribune* and *Galway Sentinel* (which is free), as well as the tourist office, have details of what's on. Good traditional music is played in the city's bars; the atmosphere can verge on the raucous. Galway City is always lively, partly due to the youthfulness of its inhabitants, but the week of the famous **Galway Races**, in late July, the **Arts Festival** (also July) and the **Oyster Festival** in September bring an extra sparkle (for all, *see* pp.266–7).

Salthill is a seaside resort that merges with the city. Many local people holiday here or come on day-trips. Hotels, fun-parks and bingo halls line the seafront; it's a bit rundown, like many old seaside resorts all over the British Isles. But at night the place lights up as the strip opens up its clubs and discos, catering primarily to the population of Galway City. Children can splash about all day at **Leisureland** (*see* p.275), with funfair rides and amusements, or visit Ireland's national aquarium, **Atlantaquaria** (*t (091) 585100, www.nationalaquarium.ie*), in the same complex.

Connemara

Connemara is not an area firmly drawn by boundary lines; it is the name given to the western portion of County Galway that lies between Lough Corrib and the Atlantic, bounded in the north by Killary Harbour.

Lough Corrib and Around

Here at **Moycullen** the real splendours of the west begin, although it is worth stopping only when you get to **Oughterard**. A pretty river, the Owenriff, runs through the charming town, which is right on the upper shores of Lough Corrib and a good place to base yourself if you are keen on salmon and trout angling. If you are coming from Costelloe on the coast road or going there from Oughterard, take the mountain road, which joins the two towns cross-country and gives you a vast panorama of watery landscape as you go up through a small hill pass.

Aughnanure Castle (*open 25 Mar–end Oct daily 9.30–6; key with caretaker rest of year; guided tours on request; adm; t (091) 552214*), situated 3 miles (4.8km) to the south-east of Oughterard, is an O'Flaherty building that is believed to have been one of the strongest fortresses at the time that Cromwell was blockading Galway. The six-storey tower stands on an island of rock. In the days of its prosperity, a portion of the floor of the hall was made to collapse: one of the flagstones was hinged downwards and an unwelcome guest might well find himself tipped into the fast-flowing stream below. Nothing of the hall stands today: it too collapsed into the stream, as did the cavern over which it was constructed. But the castle has been restored, and you can climb right to the top.

Ross Castle (*not open to the public*), located 5 miles (8km) to the south-east of Oughterard beside the shores of Ross Lake, was the home of the Martins, who bankrupted themselves trying to help out in the famine times of the 1840s. You can follow the road from the village down to Lough Corrib for a lovely drive along its wooded shores. It leads you to the Hill of Doon and a good view of the largest island on the lake, **Inchagoill** (*Inis an Ghaill*: 'Island of the Devout Stranger'). This really is the prettiest and most interesting of the hundreds of islands on Lough Corrib. There is a 5th-century church, **Teampall Pháraic**, and another of 10th-century origin further to the south, which was reconstructed in 1860. There is also the **Stone of Lugna**, named after the navigator of St Patrick. This 2ft (72cm) high obelisk bears engraved Roman characters. It is fancifully claimed to be the earliest Christian inscription in Europe after the catacombs.

Clonbur is a centre for fishermen, situated on the limestone isthmus between Lough Mask and Lough Corrib. If you decide that you want to climb the Connemara, Maumturk or Partry mountains, Clonbur is well placed. One mile (1.6km) to the west rises the lovely mountain area that is known as Joyce Country, where it is said that the Fir Bolgs assembled before they made their last stand against the Dé Danaan at the Battle of Moytura. In the foothills leading up to the highest peak, Benlevy (1,370ft/ 418m), is Lough Coolin, a peaceful, dreamy sort of place. You can drive there, but be warned that the road is very narrow.

Tourist Information

Clifden: Galway Rd, **t** (095) 21163. *Open Mar–Oct.*
Oughterard: **t** (091) 552808

Internet Access

Two Dog Café, Church Hill, Clifden,
t (095) 22186

Shopping

Crafts

An Tinteán Crafts Workshop,
Katie and Ann Hand Knits, Camus,
Connemara, **t** (091) 574076.
Rugs, Aran sweaters, hats and crafts
hand-made by local weavers and knitters.
Avoca, Letterfrack, **t** (095) 41058, *www.avoca.ie.*
Woodwork, design and a great tea-room.
The Celtic Shop and Tara Jewellers,
Clifden, **t** (095) 21064
Connemara Heritage and History Centre,
Lettershea, Clifden, **t** (095) 21808
Connemara Pottery, Ballyconneely Rd,
Clifden, **t** (095) 21254
Craft Centre, Spiddal, **t** (091) 553376.
Crafts, an art gallery and a coffee shop.
Leenane Cultural Centre, **t** (095) 42323.
Knitwear, tweeds, crystal, pottery, jewellery,
a restaurant and a handicrafts exhibition.
Rosmuc Knitwear, Gort Mór, Rosmuc,
t (091) 574172. Hand-woven sweaters.
Roundstone Ceramics, Roundstone, **t** (095)
35874. Hand-crafted pottery decorated with
mythical fishes and other wonderful designs.
Standún Gift Shop, coast road, Spiddal, **t** (091)
553108, *www.standun.com.* Knitwear and
Irish fashions, pottery, glass and crafts.

Crystal

Connemara Celtic Crystal,
outskirts of Moycullen, **t** (091) 555172

Food and Drink

Carabay Seaweed, Kylebroghlan, Moycullen,
t (091) 555112. Health foods.

Traditional Music

Roundstone Musical Instruments,
IDA Craft Centre, Roundstone, **t** (095) 35808.

A place selling hand-crafted goatskin
bodhráns. It also has a summer shop in
Main St, Clifden.

Sports and Activities

Beaches

It is possible to bathe in the various inlets
and coves all along the coast. There are fine,
sandy beaches at Ballyconneely and Tullycross.

Fishing

For brown trout, sea-trout and salmon
fishing on Lough Corrib, call the tourist office
in Galway City for details and regulations.
Delphi Lodge Fishery, Leenane, **t** (095) 42211
Erriff Fishery, Leenane, **t** (095) 42252
Thomas Tuck, Western Garage, Oughterard,
t (091) 552335. Help with boat hire and fishing.
For **sea-angling**, contact the Western Region
Fisheries Board (**t** (091) 563110, *www.wrfb.ie*).
Several boat owners take out fishing trips in
Clifden, including: **John Brittain, Blue Water
Fishing**, **t** (095) 21073; **John Ryan**, **t** (095) 21069.

Golf

Connemara Golf Club, Ballyconneely,
Clifden, **t** (095) 23502
Oughterard Golf Club, **t** (091) 552131

Outdoor Activities

Delphi Adventure Centre, Delphi, Leenane,
t (095) 42208. Canoeing, rock-climbing,
surfing, hill-walking and snorkelling.
Killary Adventure Company, Leenane, **t** (095)
43411. Canoeing, sailing and rock-climbing.

Pleasure Cruises

Corrib Tours, Furbo, **t** (091) 592447. Lough tours.
Sea Cruise Connemara, Leenane, **t** (091) 566736

Ponytrekking

Aille Cross Centre, Loughrea, **t** (091) 841216
Cashel House Hotel Riding Centre,
Cashel, Connemara, **t** (095) 31001
Connemara Pony Stud and Riding Centre,
Errislannan Manor, Clifden, **t** (095) 21134

Spa Treatments

The Mountain Lodge and Spa at Delphi,
Leenane, Galway, **t** (095) 42987

Where to Stay

Ballynahinch Castle Hotel, Ballinafad, Recess, t (095) 31006, *www.ballynahinch-castle.com*, (*luxury*). A former Indian maharajah's residence in a magnificent setting at the base of one of the Twelve Bens. The ambiance is relaxed and informal.

Cashel House Hotel, Cashel, t (095) 31001, *www.cashel-house-hotel.com* (*luxury*). A very luxurious yet cosy house, full of fine furniture and *objets d'art*. The superb garden overlooks a beautiful sea inlet, and horseriding can be arranged.

Rosleague Manor Hotel, Letterfrack, t (095) 41101, *www.rosleague.com* (*luxury*). A pretty, friendly, first-class hotel overlooking Ballinakill Bay, with delicious food.

Delphi Lodge, Leenane, t (095) 42296, *www.delphilodge.ie* (*expensive*). This 1,000-acre estate includes mountain, water and bog, and is an ideal spot for fly-fishing (courses are run for novices). The hospitable owner makes every dinner an occasion, with excellent food and old-fashioned service that has won the seal of approval of none less than Prince Charles. Rooms are elegantly comfortable. Lunch/packed lunches are available.

Connemara Gateway Hotel, Oughterard, t (091) 552328, *www.connemaragateway.com* (*moderate–expensive*). A pleasant, modern hotel with a heated indoor swimming pool and tennis facilities.

Sweeney's Oughterard House Hotel, Oughterard, t (091) 552207, *www.sweeneys-hotel.com* (*moderate–expensive*). An ivy-covered Georgian house by the river, complete with a good restaurant.

The Ardagh Hotel, Ballyconneely Rd, Clifden, t (095) 21384, *www.ardaghhotel.com* (*moderate*). A small, Dutch-run hotel offering wonderful food (*see* opposite).

Ben View House, Bridge St, Clifden, t (095) 21256, *www.benviewhouse.com* (*moderate*). A pleasant, old-fashioned B&B in the centre of Clifden, offering a choice of breakfasts and ensuite rooms with TVs.

Crocnaraw House, Moyard, t (095) 41068, , *www.crocnaraw.co.uk* (*moderate*). A cosy little country house with tasteful rooms and striped Connemara wool rugs strewn about. The food is delicious and well prepared.

Currarevagh House, Oughterard, t (091) 552312 (*moderate*). A country house in the most beautiful setting on the edge of Lough Corrib. A charming and friendly atmosphere reigns in the cosy Victorian rooms. The passages are crammed with books, stuffed fish and fishing tackle. The food is comforting in an old-fashioned way. The extremely helpful hosts have some of the best wild brown trout fishing in Europe, which they will organize for guests.

Day's Hotel, Inishbofin Island, t (095) 45809 (*moderate*). A well-established, clean and friendly, family-run hotel right on the pier; the son runs musical evenings. Children are welcome, and there are facilities for divers.

Doonmore Hotel, Inishbofin, t (095) 45804, *www.inishbofin.com/doonmorehotel.htm* (*moderate*). A simple, clean choice with a restaurant offering good local seafood.

Moycullen House, Moycullen, t (091) 555621, *www.moycullen.com* (*moderate*). An Edwardian sporting lodge in the Arts and Crafts style, set in a lovely woodland garden overlooking Lough Corrib. Fishing and boating can be organized by the hosts.

The Quay House, Beach Rd, Clifden, t (095) 21369, *www.thequayhouse.com* (*moderate*). The old harbourmaster's house, with a friendly, relaxed atmosphere.

Zetland House Hotel, Cashel Bay, t (095) 31111, *www.zetland.com* (*moderate*). A converted hunting lodge in an isolated setting with views over the bay. The manager trained at the Ritz in Paris. The food is superb, and there is tennis, billiards and other activities.

Ard Aoibhinn, Cnocan Glas, Spiddal, t (091) 553179, *aoibhinn@gofree.indigo.ie* (*inexpensive*). Comfortable ensuite rooms close to the sea.

Camillaun, Eighterard, Oughterard, t (091) 552678, *camillaun@ eircom.net* (*inexpensive*). A comfortable, modern wooden-floored home with its own boats that you can take from the River Owenriff (next to the garden) and float out on Lough Corrib to fish or explore Inchagoill Island. Dinner (*moderate*) is available by arrangement.

Col-Mar House, Salahoona, Spiddal, t (091) 553247 (*inexpensive*). A friendly, old-fashioned option in a lovely setting, with especially good breakfasts.

Fáilte, Ardbear, off Ballyconneely Rd, Clifden, t (095) 21159 (*inexpensive*). A pleasant B&B with good breakfasts.

Killary House, Leenane, t (095) 42254 (*inexpensive*). A friendly farmhouse in a superb situation.

Mallmore Country Guest House, Ballyconneely Rd, Clifden, t (095) 21460, *www.mallmore.com* (*inexpensive*). A comfortable, friendly country house.

Self-catering

Delphi Cottages, Leenane, t (095) 42222, *www.delphilodge.ie* (*inexpensive*). Five adorable cottages in the grounds of the Delphi Lodge Estate (*see* opposite)

Fermoyle Lodge, Costello, Connemara, t (091) 786111, *www.fermoylelodge.com* (*inexpensive*). A former fishing lodge (some say a fairy's house) near a lake, hidden among trees, rhododenrons and a Victorian garden, with a stone staircase leading to a wooded area. Dinner (*expensive*) is available by arrangement. With the adjoining mews, the lodge sleeps up to 13. It's a good stopping point if taking the ferry to the Aran Islands.

Ireland West Tourism, Inveran, Galway Bay, t (091) 537777, *www.irelandwest.travel.ie* (*inexpensive*). A thatched cottage with sea views.

Island Holiday Cottages, Annaghvaan, Lettermore, t (091) 572212, *www.conamaracottages.com* (*inexpensive*). Thirteen relaxing cottages on Gaeltacht Island off Leitir Mór, which is joined to the Connemara mainland by bridge. Each sleeps up to 6 people, and there is a communal games room and tennis court.

Renvyle Thatched Cottages, Renvyle, Tullycross, t (095) 43464, *www.irishcottageholidays.com* (*inexpensive*). Nine modernized thatched cottages of various sizes.

Eating Out

The Ardagh Hotel, Clifden, t (095) 21384, *www.ardaghhotel.com* (*expensive*). A place offering delicious Continental food and good-value open sandwiches.

Cashel House Hotel, Cashel, t (095) 31001 (*expensive*). Superb food in country-house surroundings unsuitable for children. Booking is essential. *Closed lunch.*

Erriseask House Hotel, Ballyconneely, Clifden, t (095) 23553 (*expensive*). Unexpectedly imaginative cooking. *Closed out of high season (exc Easter).*

Zetland House Hotel, Cashel Bay, t (095) 31111 (*expensive*). Wonderful seafood.

O'Grady's on the Pier, Barna Pier, Barna, t (091) 592223, (*moderate–expensive*). Breton and French-style seafood. *Closed lunch Mon–Fri.*

The Signal Restaurant, Clifden Station House, Clifden, t (095) 21699 (*moderate–expensive*). A varied menu featuring local produce.

Destry's, Main St, Clifden, t (095) 21722 (*moderate*). A laid-back, lively bistro-style restaurant named after a Marlene Dietrich film, with delicious modern cooking.

Drimcong House Restaurant, Moycullen, t (091) 555115 (*moderate*). A lovely 17th-century house offering the most delicious and original taste combinations, using the best seasonal offerings. Vegetarian and children's meals are available, and there are always turf fires in the rooms. *Closed Mon.*

High Moors Restaurant, Doneen, Clifden, t (095) 21342 (*moderate*). Very good home-cooking, featuring mostly home-grown ingredients. Booking is essential. *Closed Nov–Apr.*

Portfinn Lodge, Leenane, t (095) 42265, *www.portfinn.com* (*moderate*). Great seafood.

O'Grady's Seafood Restaurant, Market St, Clifden, t (095) 21450 (*inexpensive–moderate*). A traditional seafood restaurant. *Closed Sun.*

Boat Inn, The Square, Oughterard, t (091) 552196 (*inexpensive*). Good pub food.

Boluisce Seafood Restaurant, Spiddal Village, t (091) 553286 (*inexpensive*). Delicious seafood.

Day's Hotel Bar, Inishbofin, t (095) 45809 (*inexpensive*). Good seafood and soups.

Peacocke's/Quiet Man Restaurant, Maam Cross, Recess, t (091) 552306. Good lunches.

Entertainment and Nightlife

Traditional Music

Day's Hotel, Inishbofin, t (095) 45809. Wed–Sun nights in summer.

Doonmore Hotel, Inishbofin, t (095) 45804. Wed–Sat nights in summer.

Mannion's Bar, Market St, Clifden, t (095) 21780

Teach Ceoil, Tullycross, t (095) 43446. Summer.

The Joyce Country

Cornamona on the northern corner of Lough Corrib on the Dooras Peninsula is in one of the most popular Irish-speaking districts in North Connemara, on the edge of the Joyce Country. This area is named after a race of Welshmen who settled in Connacht after Richard de Burgo conquered it in the 13th century. The native O'Flahertys and Joyces eventually got on well and used to rough up the 'plainsmen' on the isthmus, which became known as the Gap of Danger. Not one road around here is dull, and the fishing on the loughs is good. On the R345 to Maum is the spectacular **Hen's Castle**, built by the O'Connors on an island in the Corrib. It is said to have fallen into ruin after an O'Flaherty ate the hen given to his family by a witch.

At **Maumeen** (*Maimean*) in the Corcogemore Mountains (part of the Maumturk range) is **St Patrick's Bed and Holy Well**, reached by a footpath off the R336. Pilgrims have travelled here for centuries, as the well is reputed to have strong healing powers. The annual pilgrimage, on the last Sunday of July, has undergone a revival recently, with many people attending. **Lough Nafooey** ('Lake of the Spectre') is one of the most beautiful in Connemara. It is off a mountain road that leads up the Finny River, and can also be approached by another road halfway between Maum and Leenane off the R336. Lots of little streams run into the lake: the music of gurgling water plays continually in early summer, accompanied by the smell of gorse and pine trees.

Connemara's Southern Coast

This section includes most of the Irish-speaking parts and stretches along the north of Galway Bay, and from there along the Atlantic to Carna. Its northern boundary runs from Gowlaun (*Gabhla*) through Maam Cross to Barna (*Bearna*). This part of the world is hilly and remote, for there are very few roads into it. From Galway to Spiddal (R336) it is disappointingly built-up, although you do get glimpses of the Aran Islands, looking far or near according to the clarity of the weather.

Rossaveal (*Ros An Mhíl*) at the mouth of Galway Bay has a cabin-cruiser that runs regularly to Aran, doing a brisk trade in turf, as Aran has no fuel resources of its own. You may have noticed the black beetle-like boats fishermen in Connacht use. The type of *currach* you see in Ireland varies considerably from the Donegal coast to the Kerry coast in the south. Here they are very light and need a skilful man to handle the long, heavy, bladeless oars. It is astonishing how much they can carry: a load could include cement, or pigs and sheep with their legs tied and muffled.

From Rossaveal follow the road north for just a few miles to **Costello**, which has a wonderful coral strand and good salmon-fishing river. There is quite a meeting of the roads here; you can either to Maam Cross or follow a little road to Carraroe (*An Cheathrú Rua*). Back on the main road, you come to Screeb (*Scríb*); a left here brings you to Lough Aroolagh and Gortmore (*An Gort Móro*). Here, on a ledge of hillside above a small lake in the townland of Turlough, you can tour the whitewashed **Pearse's Cottage** (*Teach an Phiarsaigh; open Easter and mid-June–mid-Sept daily 10–6; guided tours on request; t (091) 574292, www.heritageireland.ie*), where the patriot wrote plays and poems. Patrick Pearse built it as proof of his interest in Irish language and culture. He believed that if the Irish language died, the nation would too.

Back on the R340, 4 miles (6.4km) further on, is the village of **Kilkieran**. Here is scenery typical of the west: scattered houses with no nucleus nor clear distinction from the next village. You can see the brooding island of Lettermore and, if the wind is in the right direction, smell the rich seaweed that is dried in a factory here. Kilkieran and **Carna** are lobster-fishing centres, and there is a research station for shellfish, but you will find it difficult to buy a lobster for yourself – most of the seafood that is caught goes abroad or to the hotels. A side-road from Carna over a bridge takes you to **Mweenish Island** with its beautiful sandy beaches.

You can get a boat from Carna to **St MacDara's Island** for a marvellous view across Bertraghboy Bay. MacDara was a 5th-century saint who was greatly honoured by the people of Iar Chonnachta – so much so that in the age of sailing boats, the fishermen used to dip their sails three times before passing the island.

Western Connemara

This is the district west of Maam Cross to the Atlantic, extending northwards to Killary Harbour and the Partry Mountains. It is a superb part of the world, much more exciting and untouched than the road that leads you round South Connemara.

Maam Cross to Roundstone

Maam Cross is a place that you see signposted constantly. In fact it is the most unprepossessing place, but it is the centre of magnificent scenery and everybody travelling round Galway ends up here. If you climb Leckavrea Mountain (1,307ft/402m) there are great views of the Twelve Bens, Maumturks and Lough Corrib. From Maam Cross you could take the N59 past Recess, and then the N59/R341 for Roundstone. **Recess** is a pretty village where suddenly you come upon woods and Glendollagh Lough after driving through some spartan scenery. Lissoughter Mountain at 1,314ft (400m) is worth climbing: you can see over to Lough Inagh and the mountains either side. This is where the green Connemara marble is quarried. It was formed millions of years ago by the action of strong compressive forces and heat on limestone. The oldest rocks in the county are exposed in this central area: the Twelve Bens (or Pins) and the Maumturk Mountains.

Cashel village is on a minor road (R342) right on Cashel Bay, an inlet of Bertraghboy Bay. It became famous overnight when General de Gaulle spent his holidays here. All these inlets and the mountain roads leading into the interior are bathed in the most superb colours. The luxurious Cashel House Hotel (*see* p.280) is worth stopping at for a walk around the wonderful sub-tropical gardens or tea on the lawn.

Roundstone is a pleasant 19th-century village. The name is an awful English corruption of the Irish *Cloch na Rón*, which means 'Rock of the Seals'. There is a pretty harbour that looks across the water to the low-lying islands in Bertraghboy Bay and a friendly bar, O'Dowd's, where the fishermen contrast starkly with the Dubliners in their smart Aran sweaters. **Errisbeg Mountain** (987ft/300m) towers above the village. It is a short climb, but the views are superb; look out for the flowers and plants, for this is a place beloved of botanists as well as artists. Two miles (3.2km) on towards Ballyconneely are two of the best beaches in Connacht. You will have seen their silver lines beside the blue sea if you climbed Errisbeg. They are called **Gorteen** and **Dog's Bay**. The latter is another terrible mistranslation from *Port na Feadóige*: 'Bay of the Plover'. **Ballyconneely** is on the isthmus about 9 miles (14.4km) from Roundstone. The coast road is called 'the brandy and soda road' because of the exhilarating air. Beside the wide Mannin Bay is Coral Strand, so-called because of the white sand-like debris of a seaweed that looks like coral. Four miles (6.4km) south of Clifden is the site where Alcock and Brown came to ground after the first ever transatlantic flight.

Clifden (*An Clochan*: 'Stepping Stones') is generally called the 'capital' of Connemara. It actually has a population of only just over 1,000, but it is the biggest place around in a countryside of scattered hamlets and farms. The town sits in a sheltered bay, and if you walk half a mile (0.8km) to the Atlantic shore and gaze out from it, you are looking straight towards America. It is a well-planned early-19th-century town founded in 1812 by John D'Arcy, and the two spires of the Protestant church and the Catholic cathedral give it a distinctive outline. There are plenty of places to eat, and much going on, including bands and craft and cookery exhibitions, and the wide streets overflow with people speaking Gaelic as well as an English that uses the idioms and expression of Gaelic.

When travelling around this part of Connemara, you will pass through lakes, rivers, forests and mountains where there is little hint of pollution or industry. Even the machinery that is used on the farms is still fairly traditional. At **Dan O'Hara's Homestead Farm**, part of **Connemara Heritage and History Centre**, just off the N59 in Lettershea (*open Apr–Oct daily 10–6; adm; t (095) 21808, www.connemaraheritage. com*), you can see an eight-acre farm that is being run as it would have been in the 19th century. It's also an all-organic farm.

There is a lovely road signposted 'Sky Road' that takes you further north round the indented coast. Amidst sprays of fuchsia it climbs high above Clifden until it is over **D'Arcy's Castle**, the baronial-style ruin of the D'Arcy who founded the town. From here you can watch the waves crashing onto the rock islets of Inishturk and Inishbofin, while beyond to the north is Clare Island. The road continues into quiet, seaweed-fringed Streamstown Bay, where white Connemara marble is quarried.

Inishbofin Island

Inishbofin Island can be reached by boat, with the journey taking 45 minutes each way. The boats leave Cleggan pier two or three times daily April to October, or once a week in winter. Sailings depend on the weather, so always check ahead. There are two boats: the *Queen* (*tickets from King's Ferries, King's Shop in Cleggan, t (095) 44642*), and the *Inishbofin Experience Dun Aengus* (*t (095) 45806/44750*).

Inishbofin has a very varied history. In the 7th century St Colman founded a monastery here, remains of which can still be seen. In the 13th century the O'Malleys won the island from the O'Flahertys, adding to their seaboard empire. Grace O'Malley is said to have fortified it, although the locals say she could not dig through the rock to finish the deep ditch she was making. In 1652 Inishbofin was surrendered to the Cromwellians and was used as a sort of concentration camp for monks and priests. The fortress Cromwell built above the harbour has room for six cannons, but now there are only red-beaked choughs to sound the alarm. Inishbofin has two hotels (*see* p.280), so it is easy to get something to eat while you are there (both hotels also hire out bikes). There is a small **Heritage Centre** (*open summer noon–5pm*) near Day's Hotel. The island's beaches are beautiful.

Letterfrack to Leenane

Letterfrack, a pretty village, was founded by the Quakers. There are wonderful bays for swimming and, along the coastal approach from Moyard onwards, some excellent craft shops. Nearby is the sparkling Diamond Hill (1,460ft/445m). On the Renvyle peninsula to the north of Letterfrack, the **Connemara Sea Leisure: Oceans Alive Visitor Centre** (*open daily Mar–Sept 9.30–7, Oct–Apr 10–4; adm; t (095) 43473*) includes an aquarium, a marine museum and sightseeing cruises. **Connemara National Park** (*open all year*), extending over an area of 3,800 acres (1,540ha), is of outstanding ecological value, as well as being very beautiful. There is a **Visitors' Centre** (*open Apr–mid-Oct 10–5.30, July and Aug 9.30–6.30; adm; t (095) 41054/41006*), with exhibits and an audio-visual room describing the geology, the flora and fauna of the area. Short- and long-distance walks have been laid out.

The Kylemore Valley lies between the Twelve Bens and the forested Doughruagh Mountains in the north. The Twelve Bens and Maumturks, with their beautiful varying shapes, are not much above 2,000ft (610m) at their highest. (If you are going climbing, note that even though it may be sunny and dry at sea level it will be very wet underfoot in the mountains.) On the floor of the valley, trees and rhododendrons grow beside the three lakes and the Dawros River, which are well stocked with salmon and sea trout. There is a splendid lakeside mock castle in the woods at **Kylemore Abbey**, which is now a girls' school and a convent for the Benedictine nuns of Ypres. The nuns run a restaurant and an excellent craft shop, and cultivate the beautiful grounds around which you can wander, including a restored Victorian walled garden (*abbey and tea-room open all year; craft shop and restaurant open mid-Mar–Nov daily 9.30–5.30; gardens open daily Easter–Oct 10.30–4.30; adm; t (095) 41146, www.kylemoreabbey.com*. The wealthy Liverpudlian merchant who built the castle also built a fine mock-Gothic chapel, with pillars of Connemara marble. Nearby is a pre-Christian chamber tomb.

The road to the mouth of Killary Harbour (R334) is set between the dark blue fjord and stream-scored green hillsides, which give the effect of crushed velvet. This is one of the safest natural anchorages in the world, keeping an almost constant depth of 13 fathoms, and sheltered from the wind by the mountains around. The Erriff River comes tumbling over the Aasleagh Falls at the bridge just to the north of **Leenane**. This village, situated at the head of Killary Harbour, has plenty of accommodation (*see* pp.280–81) if you want to base yourself here for walking or fishing.

The **Leenane Cultural Centre** is just above the village on the N59. Besides acting as an outlet for local knitters, it also has information on local history and places of interest, and a **Sheep and Wool Museum** (*open Apr–Oct daily 9.30–6; t (095) 42323/ 42231*). Leenane featured as the location for the film *The Field*, and you will find constant references to it all over the village.

The Aran Islands

The people and the islands of Aran were described sensitively by the playwright John Millington Synge in his notebooks and in his play *Riders to the Sea*. If you read them, you will long to visit these windswept islands in Galway Bay. Liam O'Flaherty, another great Irish writer, was born here in 1897, two years before Synge first came to the islands. He describes the hard life of the island people in his short stories, *The Landing* and *Going into Exile*. Tim Robinson, a stranger who came and lived on the islands a few years ago, wrote a wonderful book called *Stones of Aran*, which is well worth searching out in Kenny's bookshop in Galway City (*see* p.274). The Aran Islands today are much the same as they were in John Synge's time, although in the summer the irritations that tourism always brings diminishes some of their peace and unique culture, particularly on Inishmore.

The Islands

There are three Aran Islands: Inishmore ('Great Island'), Inisheer ('East Island') and Inishmaan ('Middle Island'). They can be reached by air from Galway City, by a regular ferry boat from Galway Harbour or Doolin in County Clare, or by motorboat from Rossaveal. Most tourists come here for the rugged beauty and sweeping views, and to visit the prehistoric and early monastic ruins. The landscape, which is similar to that of The Burren in County Clare (*see* p.250), is made up of porous limestone. You will notice as you approach by boat that it is eroding into great steps. Gentian, maidenhair fern, wild roses and saxifrage blossom on the 11,000 acres (4,450ha) that make up the three islands, but only six percent of the land here is rated as productive. The soil has been built up over the years with layer upon layer of seaweed, animal manure and sand from the beaches, so that these limestone rocks can support a few cattle, donkeys and rows of potatoes.

The Aran Islands currently have a population of approximately 1,450: 900 people on Inishmore, 300 on Inishmaan and 250 on Inisheer. The young people tend to disappear to the mainland or further for jobs, and seldom come back. When John Millington Synge came to the islands between 1899 and 1902, he felt very aware that they were the hinterland of European culture, and he was strongly drawn to the islanders' faith in God. This is what he wrote of a young girl on Inishmaan: 'At one moment, she is a simple peasant, at another she seems to be looking out at the world with a sense of prehistoric disillusion, and to sum up in the expression of her grey-blue eyes, the whole external despondency of the clouds and the sea.'

There are seven stone forts on the islands; four on Inishmore, two on Inishmaan and one on Inisheer, all believed to go back as far as the early-Celtic period 2,500 years ago. Mythology states that they were built by the Fir Bolg after they were defeated by the Tuatha Dé Danaan at the Battle of Moytura (*see* **Old Gods and Heroes**, p.56). The people who lived on the islands became Christians in the 5th century, converted by St Enda. Monastic schools were set up that became famous over the centuries, and people came from far and wide to study there. In the Middle Ages, the O'Flahertys of Galway and the O'Briens of Clare fought endlessly over the ownership of the islands.

The English finally ended the dispute by constructing and garrisoning a fort, called **Arkin Castle**, in the late 16th century. It is situated along the shore of the bay as you arrive at Inishmore. It was occupied at various times by Royalists, Cromwellians, Jacobites and Williamites.

The Aran Islands are wild and rugged, with so many attractions that you might wish to stay for months. The views around the forts and churches are magnificent, and you can wander around the rough roads, amongst the limestone rocks, watching for the little flowers and plants that somehow manage to grow. There are beaches on Inishmore and Inisheer, and the water is comparatively warm. It is best to ask locally about the various beaches, and about sea-angling, which can be done from a *currach* or the cliffs. Every summer evening there are ballad sessions in the public houses.

Inishmore

Inishmore is the largest of the islands, being about 8 miles (12.9km) in length. When you get off the steamer you can hire either a bicycle or a sidecar and jarvey to see the sights. The capital, **Kilronan**, has become rather touristy, but the people remain cheerful and courteous. **Ionad Árainn** (*open daily June–Aug 10–7, mid Apr, May, Sept and Oct 11–5; adm; t (099) 61355, www.visitaranislands.com*), a museum of folklife in Kilronan, displays material about the Gaelic League.

Kilronan is linked by road to a chain of villages. If you want to relax in a friendly drinking house after the gruelling voyage, Daly's pub in **Killeany** (*Cill Éinne*) is the place to go. Amongst the fields separated by loose stone walls (the effect is rather maze-like), you will come upon some ancient ecclesiastical sites and the forts. The people of Aran, who could be descended from the Fir Bolgs, never bother with gates – they are too expensive to import. Instead, if they are herding livestock through different fields, they take down the stone walls and then calmly build them up again when the animals have got through.

Dún Aonghasa or Dun Aengus (*open daily Mar–Oct 10–6, Nov–Feb 10–4; t (099) 61008*) is on the south coast, on the summit of a hill that rises straight up from the sea. It covers some 11 acres (4.5ha) and consists of several concentric ramparts, 18ft high and 13ft deep (5.5m by 4m), which form a semi-circle with the two edges ending on the brink of the cliffs that fall nearly 350ft (107m) to the Atlantic. The approach is designed to cripple you if you do not advance with caution, for outside the middle wall, sharp spars of stone set closely in the ground form a *chevaux-de-frise*. Be warned that the site is not enclosed and you could quite easily fall from the cliffs.

Dun Eoghanacha, another stone ring fort, is located to the south of the village of Onaght on the north-east coast, and is circular in shape. The fields to the west and south of it are full of ancient remains. One and a half miles (2.5km) to the west of Killeany is **Dubh Chathair**, some of which must have disappeared over the steep cliffs, for it was once even larger than Dun Aonghasa. At Kilchorna, Monasterkieran and Teampall an Cheathrair are more evocative ruins.

Monasterkieran, just to the north-west of Kilronan, has the ruins of a transitional period church, early cross slabs, an ancient sundial and a holy well. Kilchorna, about one mile (1.6km) south-west of Kilronan, has two *clochans*. **Teampall an Cheathrair**

Getting There and Around

By Air

Aer Arann, which flies to all 3 islands, operates several daily flights all year from Connemara Regional Airport in Inverin (19 miles/30km west of Galway, with connecting buses to the city centre for all flights). Actual flying time is about 10mins, and fares are about twice those of the ferry, though special packages including a night's B&B accommodation on the island make it a much better deal, especially if you want a look at the islands from the air. Scenic flights for groups can also be arranged.

Aer Arann, Dominick St, Galway, t (091) 593034, *www.aerarannislands.ie*; also Galway Airport, t (091) 755569;and Inverin, t (091) 593034

By Sea

The main port of call is Kilronan on Inishmore.
Aran Ferries, t (091) 568903, *www.aranislandferries.com*. A fast modern fleet of 6 vessels, offering up to 4 services a day in the peak season. Timetables are available from the Galway Tourist Office, t (091) 537700, where you can also book.

Aran Islands Direct, t (091) 566535, *www.aranislandsdirect.com*. Services between Rossaveal and Inishmore year round; in summer there may be 6 boats a day. Coaches depart from Galway 90mins before boat departures, and the crossing takes 40–60mins.

Doolin Ferries, t (065) 707 4455, *www.doolinferries.com*. Services to Inisheer and Inishmore from Doolin, in Co. Clare, Easter–Sept. You can usually arrange a through ticket to make the islands a stepping stone from Clare to Galway.

O'Brien Shipping (Doolin Ferries), t (091) 567283/567676, *obrienshipping@eircom.net*. Services to all 3 islands June–Sept daily, rest of year Tue, Thur and Sat, departing Galway docks at 10am and Aran at 5pm. Return tickets on all lines are about €20.

By Minibus

The regular public bus on Inishmore, leaving from Kilronan, can take you to most villages. A number of islanders also offer inexpensive mini-bus tours of the island from Kilronan.

By Bike

Bicycles can be hired at several places in Kilronan, including:
Aran Bicyle Hire, t (099) 61132

By Jaunting Car

Contact Galway or Kilronan tourist office for details of jaunting cars – small horse-drawn carts that have run since Victorian times, and can be hailed like taxis when you disembark from your boat.

Festival

June–early July
Festival of Saints Peter and Paul, Inishmore, t (099) 61263. Music and *currach* races.

Tourist Information

Comharchumann Forbartha Arann, t (099) 61354, *www.visitaranislands.com*
Inishmore: Kilronan, t (099) 61263

Shopping

Crafts

An Púcán Craft Shop, Kilronan, Inishmore, t (091) 757677
Carraig Donn, Kilronan, Inishmore, t (099) 61033. Knitwear and gifts.
Inis Meain Knits, Inishmaan, t (099) 73009, *www.inismeain.ie*. Some of the best traditional jumpers in the country (huge numbers are exported to Italy).
Snámara Craftshop (Islanders' Co-operative), Main St, Kilronan, Inishmore, t (099) 61359

Sports and Activities

Watersports

Aran Deep Sea Angling, t (091) 68903. Fishing charters.
Aran Islands Dive Centre, Inishmaan, t (099) 73134
Aran Watersports, Kilronan, Inishmore, t (087) 904 2777. Fishing and boat hire (including a *currach*). *Closed Oct–Apr*.

Where to Stay

Aran Islands

There are plenty of choices on Inishmore, mostly in and around Kilronan, but in summer you'd do well to have a booking before you get on the boat. Note that some places outside Kilronan send people to meet visitors coming off the ferries.

For more information, see *www.irishislands.ie*.

Ard Einne, Kilmurvey, Inishmore, t (099) 61126, *www.ardeinne.com* (*moderate*). A guesthouse overlooking its own beach, serving fine dinners at reasonable prices and offering bike hire and tours.

Kilmurvey House, Kilronan, Inishmore, t (099) 61218, *www.kilmurveyhouse.com* (*moderate*). An old stone house with friendly owners a 20min walk from Dún Aonghasa, serving good, simple meals. It's a highly recommended place to unwind.

Man of Aran Cottage, overlooking Kilmurvey Bay, Inishmore, t (099) 61301, *www. manofarancottage.com* (*moderate*). A cottage that appeared in the famous film before it became a B&B. The owners are enthusiastic organic gardeners.

Tigh Chonghaile, Moore Village, Inishmaan, t (099) 73085 (*moderate*). B&B in a comfy, spacious house with organic cooking.

Ard Alainn, Inishmaan, t (099) 73027 (*inexpensive*). A typical Aran farmhouse where you get a warm welcome.

Ard Mhuire, Inisheer, t (099) 75005 (*inexpensive*). A long-established B&B.

Dun Aengus Hostel, beach, Kilmurvey, Kilronan, Inishmore, t (099) 61318 (*inexpensive*). A good hostel.

Mainistir House Hostel, Kilronan, Inishmore, t (099) 61169, *www.mainistirhousearan.com* (*inexpensive*). Great-value accommodation with multilingual, friendly staff, good music and an excellent veggie restaurant (*see* below).

Ms Maura Sharry, West Village, Inisheer, t (099) 75024, *radharcnamara@hotmail.com* (*inexpensive*). A B&B attached to *Radharc Na Mara* Hostel.

Radharc An Chláir, Castle Village, Inisheer, t (099) 75019 (*inexpensive*). A cosy, friendly establishment where you can feast on heart-warming cooking.

Radharc na Mara Hostel, West Village, Inisheer, t (099) 75087 (*inexpensive*). A decent hostel.

Tigh Ui Chathain, Inisheer, t (099) 75090 (*inexpensive*). A friendly B&B in a family home.

Eating Out

Aran Islands

An tSean Chéibh ('The Old Pier'), Kilronan, Inishmore, t (099) 61228 (*moderate*). Good home-baking and fresh fish. There's a good fish and chip shop in the same building. *Closed Nov–Apr*.

The Aran Fisherman, Kilronan, Inishmore, t (099) 61104, *www.aranfisherman.com* (*moderate*). Local crab, lobster, salmon, monkfish and other seafood, plus meat and vegetarian dishes, pizzas, salads and home-baking. Traditional Irish music, song and dance shows are hosted.

Man of Aran Cottage, Kilmurvey Bay, Inishmore, t (099) 61301 (*moderate*). Soup, sandwiches and lobster lunches, plus dinner. *Closed mid-Oct–Feb*.

Dun Aengus Restaurant, Kilronan, Inishmore, t (099) 61104 (*inexpensive*). A traditional stone house serving seafood, steaks, global and vegetarian dishes. *Closed lunch*.

Joe Watty's Pub, Kilronan, Inishmore, t (099) (099) 61155 (*inexpensive*). Good chowders. *Closed outside high season*.

Mainister House Hostel, Kilronan, Inishmore, t (099) 61322 (*inexpensive*). A place popular for its wonderful vegetarian buffets; be sure to book and turn up by 8pm, as it disappears all too quickly.

Organic and Wild Café, South Aran Centre, Fisherman's Cottage, near pier, Inisheer, t (099) 75073, *www.southaran.com* (*inexpensive*). A member of the Slow Food movement, using organic produce and local seafood.

Teach Osta, Inis Meáin, Inishmaan, t (099) 73003 (*inexpensive*). The only pub on the island, with good bar food and a convivial atmosphere.

Entertainment and Nightlife

Tigh Ned, near pier, Inisheer, t (099) 75104. Traditional music, nightly in summer.

('The Church of the Four Comely Saints'), is near the village of Cowrugh. It is a small 15th-century building outside which four great flagstones mark the supposed graves of the saints.

Teampall Bheanain, just to the south of Killeany, is 6th-century. Measuring only 10ft by 7ft (3m by 2m), it is a unique example of an early-Christian church. With the coming of Christianity and St Enda in AD 483, the island became known as Aran of the Saints: at Killeany, 2 miles (3.2km) to the south-east of Kilronan, there are the graves of 120 of them. All Enda's followers seem to have reached the glorious state of sainthood after living their lives in the narrow confines of *clochans*. The site also contains the remains of a small, early church and the shaft of a finely carved high cross. A few yards to the north-west of the doorway you can see a flagstone that is claimed to cover the grave of St Enda.

Inishmaan

Inishmaan is not usually visited by tourists, who tend to go to Inishmore if they're only coming to the islands on a day-trip. If you do go to Inishmaan or Inisheer, see if you can go by *currach* – it is an exciting experience to drop into the frail-looking craft and leave the security of the mail boat. (*Currachs* are made of laths and canvas, which is then tarred over.)

You can see the huge **Fort of Dun Conor** (*Dun Chonchúir*) from the sound as you approach the shore of Inishmaan. It is in the middle of the coastline and faces out to Inisheer. Its three outer walls have disappeared, with the exception of the remnants of the inner curtain, but the massive fortress wall, built of stones that only a race of giants could lift easily, is almost intact. Nearby is a freshwater spring that never dries up, called **St Chinndheirg's Well**. It is supposed to have curative properties. In the same area is one of the most interesting churches on the island, **Cill Ceann Fhionnaigh** ('Church of the Fairheaded One'). It is one of the most perfect primitive Irish churches in existence, and there is another holy well here.

Inisheer

As you come through Foul Sound towards **Inisheer**, you will see **O'Brien's Castle** on the rocky hill to the south of the landing place – a 15th-century tower set in a stone ring fort. Inisheer is the smallest of the three islands, at only about 2 miles (3.2km) in width, but it greets you with a broad, sandy beach. It also boasts a tiny **10th-century church** dedicated to St Gobhnait – the only woman who was allowed on the islands when the saintly men ruled these shores. Situated to the south-east of the landing place is the **Church of St Kevin** (*Teampall Chaomham*). This ancient building is threatened by shifting sand, but the locals clear it every year on the saint's feast day, 14 June. It has a Gothic chancel, and an earlier nave. Islanders are still buried in the ground around the church.

Synge wrote this of the men of Inisheer: 'These strange men with receding foreheads, high cheek bones, and ungovernable eyes seem to represent some old type found on these few acres at the extreme border of Europe, where it is only in the wild jests and laughter that they can express their loneliness and desolation'.

County Mayo

Mayo is a large county that towards the east is made up of limestone plains. These are interrupted by the sandstone hills of the Curlews and, further north, by the Ox Mountains or Slieve Gamph. From Ballinrobe in the south-eastern corner to Ballintobber and Claremorris, heading for the central plains around Lough Mask, you might turn a corner and see the most unexpected things: perhaps a hedgehog or an otter, a beautiful shining lake, or a vast grey dolmen. If you stray to the south-west of the county, to the stunningly beautiful coastline, and explore right up to the Mullet Peninsula and Portacloy, you will find yourself amongst some of the most spectacular and lonely scenery in the entire west. Quartzite, schist and gneiss rocks form dramatic mountains and cliffs, and the Atlantic Ocean provides a wonderful backdrop for the fuchsia-covered inlets, the beaches, the soft green *drumlins* and the stretches of wild boggy countryside.

Mayo is one of the loveliest Irish counties, especially the loughs of Furnace and Feeagh, the hillside country looking to the Holy Mountain, Croagh Patrick, and the wild Nephin range. Between the lonely mountain bogs are some charming villages, excellent eating places and comfortable houses in which to stay.

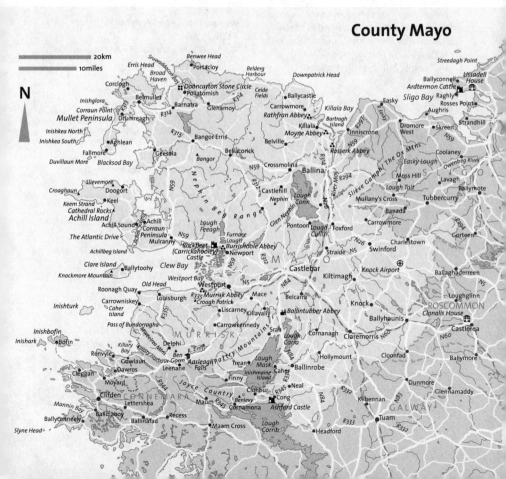

County Mayo

Getting There and Around

By Air

Knock International Airport, which is south of Charlestown, receives 7 flights a week from Manchester, Luton, Stansted, Gatwick and Birmingham (bmibaby, easyJet and Ryanair). **Knock Airport, t** (094) 936 7222, *www.irelandwestairport.com*

By Rail

Each of the following has 3 train services daily to Dublin.
Ballina Station, t (096) 71820, *www.iarnrodeireann.ie*
Castlebar Station, t (094) 21222
Westport Station, t (098) 25253/25329

By Bus

You can get around by bus to almost anywhere within Mayo, or points beyond, but services are never as frequent or convenient as they might be. There are a number of obscure local lines; as always, the tourist offices are the best source for bus information.
Bus Éireann, Ballina, **t** (096) 71800, *www.buseireann.ie*

By Bike

Achill Sound Hotel, Achill Island, **t** (098) 45245
Bike World, Castlebar, **t** (094) 25220
O'Connor's, Main St, Cong, **t** (092) 46008
O'Malleys, Keel, Achill Island, **t** (098) 43125
Sean Sammons, The Fuel Yard, James St, Westport, **t** (098) 25471

Getting to the Islands

To Clare Island: O'Malley Ferries make a total of 5 runs a day from Roonagh; **t** (098) 25045, *www.omalleyferries.com*; you can also purchase tickets from Westport Tourist Office, **t** (098) 28288. Clare Island Ferries (**t** (098) 28288, *www.clareislandferry.com*) operates the island's largest ferry, *The Pirate Queen*, from Roonagh quay, with up to 5 crossings a day in summer.
To Inishturk and Caher: Somewhat informal services, also from Roonagh point; negotiate with local fishermen, or ask Chris O'Grady at the Bay View Hotel (**t** (098) 26307). The

Caher Star and *Lady Marilyn* make trips during the summer, from Roonagh via Inishturk, **t** (098) 45541.
To Inishglora and Inishkea: There are no regular services to these islands; you'll have to find someone with a boat to take you over, such as Matthew Geraghty in Belmullet, **t** (097) 85741.

Festivals

May

Castlebar International Blues Festival, **t** (094) 902 3111. May–June.
Fleadh, Newport, **t** (094) 926 7009. Traditional music and dance.

June

Achill Yawl Sailing Festival, t (098) 36287. Races with traditional sailing boats, June–Sept.
Westport Horse and Pony Show, **t** (098) 26206
Westport International Sea Angling Festival, **t** (098) 27297/27344. Late June.

July

Ballina Festival and Arts Week, **t** (096) 79814/79815
Croagh Patrick Pilgrimage, Westport, **t** (098) 28871. An annual climb to the top of the mountain, at the end of the month.
International Four-day Walking Festival, Castlebar, **t** (094) 902 4102
Mulranny **Mediterranean Heather Festival**, **t** (098) 36287. Sheepdog trials, community sports, angling and other entertainment.

August

Geesala Festival, Ballina, **t** (097) 86742. A traditional festival hosting equestrian sport events.

September

Westport Arts Festival, t (098) 25711
Westport Horse Fair, t (098) 25616/26206

October

Roola Boola, Castlebar, **t** (094) 902 3733. A children's arts festival.

History

Historically, County Mayo ('Plain of Yew Trees') has its fair share of fascinating archaeological remains – mainly court cairns in the north-west of the county. The legendary battle of Moytura, which took place between the Tuatha Dé Danaan and the Fomorians, was fought on the Mayo plains in the 303rd year of the world. The written history of Mayo starts, as it does for the whole of Ireland, with the coming of Christianity and St Patrick, who fasted for 40 days on the mountain that is now called Croagh Patrick in his honour. Important monastic remains are scattered about the county. Their names, such as Cong and Ballintubber, reverberate with past associations of learning and devotion to God. Ballintubber Abbey has celebrated Mass daily since it was founded in 1216, and was a stopping place for pilgrimages on their way to climb the holy mountain of Croagh Patrick.

The Celtic people arrived in about 300 BC, and gradually evolved into *septs* with identifiable surnames such as O'Connor and O'Malley. The Anglo-Norman invasion in the 12th century bought a new influx of peoples with names such as Joyce, Burke (originally De Burgo), Walsh and Prendergast. In time they became more Irish than the Irish, often marrying the Celtic Irish and allying themselves with various factions. The English monarchs eventually determined to subjugate Ireland, since most of the Anglo-Normans had lost their loyalty to the Crown. From 1600 English rule was firmly established. The county was 'shired' in about 1570 and called Mayo after a small hamlet within its eastern borders.

After the Cromwellian victories of the 1640s, many Irish people from all over the country were dispossessed of their fertile lands and sent 'to hell or Connacht'. Many hundreds of small landowners arrived in Mayo and had to make a living out of the bleak moorland and bogs. In the following century, the Rebellion of 1798 brought great hope and ultimately great loss of life to Mayo. The whole country rose up against English rule, and the French Directory in Paris, who were eager to export their revolution, sent more than 1,000 French troops to join the United Irishmen. The French General Humbert landed in Killala and inflicted a humiliating defeat on the English General Lake at Castlebar. The Irish peasants were armed only with pitchforks and other rudimentary weapons, but in the euphoria of victory a 'Republic of Connacht' was set up with John Moore (an ancestor of George Moore, the novelist) as its president. But massive English reinforcements soon put an end to the new Republic, and the uprising all over Ireland was vigorously put down. A large number of people were hanged.

During the Napoleonic Wars, all horses were commandeered for the British army, and that was when the donkey, which is so associated with this part of the country, was introduced. The potato blight between 1845 and 1847 bought huge suffering and loss of life. The peasants barely survived in a good year, but several years of partial crop failure and then the complete loss of their staple crop meant that families died in their thousands. In the years that followed, many emigrated. Great bitterness and loss of hope followed, until the land-leaguers started to organize tenant resistance to evictions and land clearance in the 1860s. (Speculators had moved in to buy land off impoverished landowners, and they had few scruples about evicting peasants.)

Michael Davitt, a Mayo man from Straide, and Charles Stewart Parnell were the leaders of the land agitation, and eventually the government bought huge tracts of land and redistributed it to the people who worked it. An incident during this time of agitation gave a new word – 'boycott' – to the English language. What happened was as follows. In 1880, the local people refused to co-operate with Lord Erne's land agent at Lough Mask House. The harvest was ripe for cutting, but nobody would lift a hand to help him. The agent's name was Captain Boycott, and the affair drew a lot of attention to the issue of land rights.

Today much of the population of County Mayo earns money from tourism, in some form or another, and from keeping hill-sheep and fishing. Foreign companies have been encouraged by the state to set up here, and at Killala, in north Mayo, there is a huge Japanese chemical textile plant. The land is sparsely populated, and people are very friendly and helpful. The Mayo Gaeltacht covers parts of north-west Mayo, including Curraun, parts of Achill and the Mullet Peninsula, plus a small area around Tourmakeady – the centre of the Gaeltarra Éireann knitwear industry.

Tourist Information

Castlebar: t (094) 902 1207. *Open May–Sept*
Cong: t (094) 9546542. *Open May–Sept*
Knock: t (094) 938 8193. *Open May–Sept*
Knock Airport: t (094) 936 7222. *Open June–Sept*

Shopping

Crafts
Foxford Woollen Mills, Foxford,
t (094) 925 6104. This firm also has
an outlet in Westport.
Hats of Ireland, Breaffy Rd, Castlebar,
t (094) 902 1144
The Sun House, Swinford Rd, Foxford,
t (094) 56506. A place selling porcelain,
stoneware and jewellery.

Food and Drink
Stauntons Health Shop, Cavendish Lane,
Castlebar, t (094) 902 3959. Health foods.

Sports and Activities

Fishing
The salmon and brown trout fishing is
superb on loughs Mask, Carra and Corrib.
For further information, contact:
North Western Regional Fisheries Board,
Ballina, t (096) 22788, *www.nwrfb.com*

Golf
Ashford Castle Hotel, Cong, t (094) 954 6003.
A very plush hotel (*see* opposite) with a golf
course in its grounds.
Ballinrobe Golf Course, Clooncastle,
Ballinrobe, t (094) 954 1118

Ponytrekking
Ashford Riding Centre, Cong, t (094) 954 6507
Claremorris Equitation Centre, Galway Rd,
Claremorris, t (094) 936 2292
Turlough Equitation Centre, Castlebar,
t (094) 902 2310

Sailing
Glenans Sailing Centre, Collanmore Island,
Westport, t (098) 26046,
www.glenans-ireland.com

Tours
Clew Bay Heritage Centre, The Quay, Westport,
t (098) 26852, *www.museumsofmayo.com*.
This organizes historical walking tours in
the summer months.

Walking
The **Western Way** (t (094) 902 4444),
the 45-mile (73km) signposted trail over the
mountains to Westport, starts at Oughterard.
It is linked to the **Foxford Way** (t (094) 925
6488), leading through the mountains to
loughs Conn and Cullin.

Eastern Mayo

Cong to Ballinrobe

Mayo has many holy sites. One of them, **Cong** ('Isthmus'), is beside the island-studded Lough Corrib, just over the border from County Galway. The Corrib and Mask lakes are connected by a river that flows underground for part of its course. At some stage a canal was built so that you could take a boat between the lakes, but the water never stayed in the porous limestone.

Cong is a very friendly place with a reconstructed medieval **market cross**, one of the best ancient **abbeys**, and an attractive modern Catholic **church**, all by the tree-lined river. The abbey, founded in the 7th century by St Feichin, became the favourite place of the O'Connors, Kings of Connacht, who for a time were also high kings of Ireland. There are four fine doorways left and the cloisters, restored in the late 19th century by Benjamin Lee Guinness. The monks became very rich here because they possessed a fragment of the True Cross (it is now in the National Museum in Dublin).

Where to Stay

Ashford Castle, Cong **t** (094) 954 6003, *www.ashford.ie* (*luxury*). A very comfortable hotel with stunning grounds and opulent Victorian furnishings, although the large rooms can make it seem rather impersonal. There is Irish entertainment in the Dungeon Bar, a choice of dining options, a health club and sauna, and sailing on Lough Corrib. Alternatively, try equestrian pursuits, golf, falconry or trail walking.

Belmont Hotel, Knock, **t** (094) 938 8122, *www.belmonthotel.ie* (*moderate*). A reasonably priced choice with an award-winning restaurant. Ask about the natural-health therapy packages.

Knock House Hotel, Ballyhaunis Rd, Knock, **t** (094) 938 8088, *www.knockhousehotel.ie* (*moderate*). A modern hotel in parkland, offering golf breaks. The large restaurant offers both local and international dishes.

Self-catering

Mary Hennelly's Cottage, Rocksborough, Ballinrobe, **t** (094) 9541316, *www.irelandwestholidayhomes.com* (*inexpensive*). An original stone cottage sleeping up to 5, with an open turf fire.

The Old Granary, Culduff, Foxford, **t** (094) 9251183, *www.culduffcottages.com* (*inexpensive*). Three well-restored farmhouses, not suitable for those with children.

Eating Out

Ashford Castle, Cong, **t** (094) 954 6003 (*expensive*). Irish food served in a sumptuous, impressive setting (*see above*).

The Fennel Seed Restaurant, Main St, Cong, **t** (094) 954 6243, *www.ryanshotelcong.ie* (*moderate*). A hotel restaurant offering top-quality local produce. *Closed Mon out of season.*

Mulberry Restaurant, Breaffy House Hotel, Breaffy Rd, Castlebar, **t** (094) 9022033 (*moderate*). Another good hotel-restaurant.

Tulsi Restaurant, Lower Charles St, Castlebar, **t** (094) 902 5066 (*moderate*). An Indian restaurant with good vegetarian dishes.

Lantern Restaurant, Thomas St, Castlebar, **t** (094) 902 3502 (*inexpensive–moderate*). Cantonese, Thai and northern Chinese cooking. *Closed lunch.*

Mulligans Pub, James St, Claremorris, **t** (094) 71792 (*inexpensive*). A traditional Irish pub serving good steaks.

Entertainment and Nightlife

Traditional Music

Padraic Horkan's, Main St, Swinford, east of Castlebar, **t** (094) 925 1189. A wonderful old-fashioned place.

Also in Cong, on Abbey Street, is the **Quiet Man Cottage** (*open Mar–Nov daily 10–5; rest of year by appointment; adm; t (094) 954 6089, www.quietman-cong.com*), which was used as a set in the 1951 John Ford film starring John Wayne. Filming was a major event in these parts – partly because they had to bring electricity to the town to make filming possible. Cong was a busy place in Neolithic times; you can see a tomb called **The Giant's Grave** off the R345 west of town and a **stone circle**, also off the R345, on the way to Neal. The demesne of **Ashford Castle** (*t (094) 954 6003*), built by Benjamin Lee Guinness, borders the river here. Ashford is a mid-19th-century fantasy castle, with castellated towers, overlooking Lough Corrib. It is now a hotel (*see* p.295), but anyone may walk in the beautiful grounds for a small fee. The underground tunnel through which the river flows can be reached by various openings with intriguing names; **Pigeon Hole** is the most impressive. You climb down steep steps to reach the underground stream, which is said to contain two white trout, supposed to be an enchanted maiden and her lover. **Captain Webb's Hole** was named after an individual who pushed his unfortunate mistresses down it. Apparently the 13th mistress had the sense to push him into the hole instead.

Between Cong and Ballinrobe on the R345/R334 is a bizarre site, the **Neale** (pronounced 'nail'). It is approached through the gates of an old estate set in an area that is rich in ring forts. The Neal demesne contains a medieval tomb-carving with a 19th-century inscription claiming that 'the gods go back to the year of the world 2994'. To get a glimpse of the private ruin of **Lough Mask House**, 4 miles (6.4km) south-west of Ballinrobe, turn right off the R334 just as you leave town, and go through the little hamlet of Ballinchalla. This was the home of the Charles Boycott, who was ostracized by his tenants during the land agitation of the 1880s. About 2 miles (3.2km) away from town is the great stone fort of **Cahernagollum**, and a mile (1.6km) further on is **Killower Cairn**, dating from the Bronze Age.

Castlebar to Knock

On the N84 travelling north to Castlebar, you pass by the fretted shores of Lough Carra. On the eastern shore is the ruin of **Moore Hall**, burned down in 1923; it was the home of George Moore (1852–1933), the novelist. He was something of a terror in Irish literary circles, and fell out with W. B. Yeats and Lady Gregory, moving to England for the last 20 years of his life. He is buried on an island in the lake. The demesne is now a forest park with a picnic site, walks and lakeside scenic views.

A mile (1.6km) south of Castlebar is **Ballintubber Abbey** (*open daily 9am–12 midnight; donation; t (094) 9030934, www.ballintubberabbey.ie*), off the N84 to the east. Known as 'the Abbey that Refused to Die', it's the only one founded by an Irish king that has survived intact. The fame of Ballintubber goes even further back to the time of St Patrick, who baptized his converts in a holy well there and founded a church. In the early 13th century the king of Connacht, Cathal of the Wine-red Hand, built the abbey for the Augustinian order. When the guesthouse to the abbey was excavated, many burnt stones were found near the stream over which it was built, revealing how the monks had heated their water: by throwing in red-hot stones. There is a pilgrim path from here to Croagh Patrick, 20 miles (32km) away to the west. The foot-weary pilgrims must have been in need of a good wash when they returned. Nearby, at Mary Moran's Cottage, a crafts and information centre on the N84, you can visit **The Celtic Furrow** (*open May–Oct daily 10.30–5; adm; t (094) 903 0934*), a guided tour/exhibition on the Celtic calendar, festivals and folklore .

Another noted place of pilgrimage is **Knock**, situated in the Plain of Mayo, 7 miles (11.3km) from the freshwater fishing centre of Claremorris. In 1879 the Virgin Mary, St Joseph and St John appeared here to 14 people. Although it rained heavily on the witnesses, the area round the apparition remained dry. The quiet little village of Knock has become very commercialized, with chapels, monuments and a huge basilica; holy water comes from chrome taps and there are endless car parks. More than 750,000 visitors and pilgrims see the shrine annually – it even has its own airport. At **Knock Folk Museum** (*for opening times call t (094) 938 8100, www.museumsofmayo.com*) you learn about the Knock Apparition and see displays on local customs from the 1870s.

Castlebar is the administrative centre of Mayo and is busy enough to have a small airport. The town started as a settlement of the De Barrys. It became more important in 1611 when James I granted it a charter, and it is remembered for the ignominious scattering of the British garrison in 1798, when the French general Humbert advanced with a motley crowd of French and Irish troops. The event is known today as the 'Races of Castlebar'. John Moore, the first and only president of the Connacht Republic, is buried in the Mall and there is a memorial to 1798 beside his grave.

Western Mayo

Delphi Valley to Louisburgh

At the head of the Killary inlet separating Galway and Mayo are the handsome **Aasleagh Falls**. Here you can take a beautiful and lonely route up to Louisburgh through the pass of Bundorragha (R335), with the Mweelrea Mountain on your left and Ben Gorm on your right. You soon come to **Delphi**; it's an apt name, for the mountains and the wilderness have a sort of wisdom that you can sense in the peace around you. Lord Sligo was so impressed by its resemblance to Delphi in Greece that he renamed it from Fionnloch. Three loughs lie beside the road: Fin Lough ('Bright Lake'), Doo Lough ('Dark Lake') and Glencullin Lough ('the Lake of the Holly Tree Glen').

Louisburgh (pronounced 'Lewisburg') is a pretty village near Clew Bay. The purple-blue mountain ranges give it a marvellous backdrop; and it has numerous pubs hosting traditional music. The story of Grace O'Malley (*see p.300*) is documented in the **Granuaile Centre** (*open May–Oct Mon–Sat 10–7; adm; t (098) 66341*) here. There are fine sandy **beaches** at Old Head and further to the south-west at Carrowniskey.

If you take a minor road from Louisburgh and travel west for a couple of miles over some low hills, you will come to **Roonah Quay**. There are some pleasant places to stay here, and quite a lot to see. **Kilgeever Abbey** 2 miles (3.2km) east has an ancient well and church. Pilgrims to Croagh Patrick still include it in their itinerary. **Murrisk Abbey**, founded by Tadhg O'Malley in 1457, is 7 miles (11.3 km) further to the east on the R335 to Westport, and has a beautiful east window.

Tourist Information

Achill: t (098) 45384. *Open June–Aug*
Westport: James St, **t** (098) 25711,
www.visitmayo.com
The Westport Heritage Centre, also located
here, traces the history of the town.

Internet Access

Dunnings Cyber Café, The Octagon,
Westport, **t** (098) 25161

Shopping

Crafts

There are many good shops in Westport,
particularly on the High St, the Mall, Shop St
and Bridge St.
Carraig Donn, Bridge St, Westport, **t** (098) 26287,
www.carraigdonn.com. Knitwear and gifts,
including Aran sweaters.
The Linenmill, The Demesne, Westport,
t (098) 29500, *www.linenmill.ie*
The Long Acre, Bridge St, Westport,
www.thelongacre.com. A shop selling
antiques, collectables, ephemera, and
what it tantalizingly describes as 'the odd
and the bizarre from all over Ireland'.
Waterfront Gallery, The Harbour, Westport,
t (098) 28406. Woollen goods.
Westport Pottery, Liscarney, Westport,
t (098) 21239, *www.anu.ie/westportpottery.*
Fine local pottery.

Food and Drink

On Thursday mornings there is a **farmers'
market** in the Town Hall in Westport.

Sports and Activities

Fishing

For information about **sea-fishing,** contact
one of the following:
Mary Gavin-Hughes, Newport, **t** (098) 41562
Peter McGee, Newport, **t** (098) 41313
Tony Burke, Achill Island, **t** (098) 47257
V. Keogh, The Helm Bar, The Quay, Westport,
t (091) 26194, *www.thehelm.info*

There is **coarse fishing** for salmon and trout
near Newport. For tackle and advice, contact:
Delphi Fishery, Leenane, **t** (095) 42222,
www.delphi-salmon.com
Newport House Hotel, t (098) 41222,
www.newporthouse.ie

Golf

Achill Island Golf Club, Keel, Achill Island,
t (098) 43456, *www.members.achilltourism.
com/golfclub*
Westport Golf Club, t (098) 28262. A lovely
course between the sea and Lough Patrick.

Horsedrawn Caravans

Mayo Horsedrawn Caravan Holidays,
Belcarra, Castlebar, **t** (094) 9032054.
Self-catering caravans (*see* also p.121).

Otter-watching

Island Otterwatch, Claggan, Kilmeena,
Westport, **t** (098) 41048. Outings to spot
otters, dolphins and seals around Clew Bay.

Outdoor Activities

McDowell's Hotel & Activity Centre,
t (0908) 43148, *www.achill-leisure.ie.*
A centre offering canoeing, wind-surfing,
snorkelling, rock-climbing, hill-walking
and orienteering.

Ponytrekking

Drummindoo Stud and Equitation Centre,
Castlebar Rd, Knockranny, Westport,
t (098) 25616
Carrowholly Stables, Carrowholly, Westport,
t (098) 27057, *www.carrow-hollystables.com*

Spa Treatments

Rosmoney Spa and Seaweed Baths,
Rosmoney, Westport, **t** (098) 28899

Walking

Croagh Patrick Walking Holidays, Westport,
t (098) 26090, *www.walkingguideireland.
com*. Guided hill-walking tours.

Watersports

Glenans Irish Sailing School, Collanmore
Island, Kilmeena, Westport, **t** (098) 26046.
Sailing and other watersports facilities.

Where to Stay

Newport House Hotel, Newport, t (098) 41222, *www.newporthouse.ie* (*luxury*). A superb country-house hotel overlooking the river. Irish 18th-century furniture adds to the elegance and beauty: notice the rococo Chippendale mirror over the fireplace in the dining room. Guests enjoy old-fashioned formal service and delicious food.

Delphi Lodge, Leenane, t (095) 42222 (*expensive*). A comfortable converted sporting lodge in a wild position, with its own salmon fishery.

Bay View Hotel, Clare Island, t (098) 26307 (*moderate*). The only place on the island to stay: friendly and comfortable.

McDowell's Hotel, Slievemore, Dugort, Achill Island, t (098) 43148, *www.achill-leisure.ie* (*moderate*). An atmospheric family-run place.

Rosturk Woods, Mulranny, Westport, t (098) 36264, *www.rosturk-woods.com* (*moderate*). A comfortable, elegant family house on Clew Bay, welcoming children. Self-catering is also available (*see below*).

Achill Isle House, Newtown, Keel, Achill Island, t (098) 43355, *achillisle@eircom.net* (*inexpensive*). A simple choice near the beach.

Cuaneen House, Carramore, Louisburgh, t (098) 66460 (*inexpensive*). A modern farmhouse in a beautiful location overlooking Clew Bay, run by a friendly family offering good home-cooking.

Carrabaun House, Westport, t (098) 26196 (*inexpensive*). A pleasant bed and breakfast.

Island House, Dookinella, Keel, Achill Island, t (098) 43180 (*inexpensive*). More than adequate lodgings.

Teach Mweewillin, Corraun, Achill Island, t (098) 45134 (*inexpensive*). A modern bungalow on a hillside overlooking Achill.

Self-catering

Rosturk Woods, t (098) 36264, *www. rosturk-woods.com* (*expensive–luxury*). Two houses on Clew Bay, with paths to the water's edge, one with 2 bedrooms, the other with 4.

Westport House Caravan and Camp Site, Westport, t (098) 25430/27766, *www. westporthouse.ie* (*inexpensive*). Camping and caravanning in the grounds of the estate.

Eating Out

The Lemon Peel, The Octagon, Westport, t (098) 26929, *www.lemonpeel.ie* (*expensive– luxury*). A modern bistro-style restaurant. *Closed lunch, Mon, and Sun out of season.*

Newport House, Newport, t (098) 41222 (*expensive*). An elegant hotel (*see above*) with good food, especially the home-cured fish.

La Bella Vita, High St, Westport, t (098) 29771 (*moderate–expensive*). A bistro serving authentic Italian food. *Closed Mon.*

JJ's Bar and Weir Restaurant, Chapel St, Louisburgh, t (098) 66140 (*moderate*). Bar food and a popular seafood restaurant. *Closed Mon, plus Tue–Fri Nov–Feb.*

McDowell's Hotel, Slievemore Rd, Dugort, Achill Island, t (098) 43148 (*moderate*). Tasty home-cooking.

Quay Cottage, The Harbour, Westport, t (098) 26412, *www.quaycottage.com* (*moderate*). A cosy, folksy seafood restaurant with good bread. There's a vegetarian menu as well. *Closed lunch and Mon.*

The Boley House, Keel, Achill Island, t (098) 43147 (*inexpensive–moderate*). Well-prepared well-thought-out menus served in a stone cottage, including salmon and steaks. *Closed lunch and out of season.*

Calvey's Restaurant, Keel, Achill Island, t (098) 43158, *www.calveys.com* (*inexpensive– moderate*). Good vegetarian dishes, seafood, beef and lamb from the owners' own farm.

The Asgard Tavern and Restaurant, The Quay, Westport, t (098) 25319 (*inexpensive*). Good-value restaurant meals and pub food .

The Chalet, Keel, Achill Island, t (098) 43157 (*inexpensive*). Fine fish and chips.

Entertainment and Nightlife

Traditional Music

Matt Molloy's Bar, Westport, t (098) 26655. A bar owned by a member of Irish folk group The Chieftains (if you can't get in, there are plenty of other choices in summer).

McDowell's Hotel, Slievemore Rd, Doogort, Achill Island, t (098) 43148. Entertainment hosted by a family-run hotel (*see above*).

Croagh Patrick is a sacred and beautiful mountain where St Patrick is believed to have spent 40 days and nights in fasting and prayer. For this feat of endurance he is said to have extracted a promise from God that the Irish would never lose the Christian faith he had brought them. The mountain is made up of quartzite, which breaks up into sharp-edged stones, so it is not very comfortable walking – some pilgrims do it in bare feet. Even if you are not interested in the religious aspects of the mountain, climb it just to see the magnificent views of Clew Bay below. The **Croagh Patrick Information Centre** (*open daily 17 Mar–Oct, call for times* **t** *(098) 64114, www.museumsofmayo.com*) is at Teach naMiasa, Murrisk; tired walkers will find the café, craft shop and shower facilities particularly welcome.

The Islands of Clare, Inishturk and Caher

Clare Island (population: 140) has more land given over to farming than the other islands, though its higher slopes are covered in heather. It has superb cliffs up to 300ft (91m) high, but even these are overshadowed by the Knockmore Mountain, which drops from 1,550ft (472m) in a few hundred yards to join the cliffs. You could easily spend a couple of days on Clare, although there's not a huge amount to occupy you – you may just come and have a picnic. As you come into the small stone pier, you see **Grace O'Malley's Castle**, converted into a coastguard station in the 19th century but now a ruin. The large, square stone tower still dominates the bay. There is a holy well at **Toberfelabride**, but the gem of Clare is its abbey, about 1½ miles (2.5km) west of the harbour. **Clare Abbey**, a 15th-century church with a tower, is believed to be a cell of the Cistercian monastery of Abbeyknockmoy in County Galway. The most notable thing about the **friary** (*always accessible*) is the trace of fresco painting on the plastered ceiling of the vaulted roof; they seldom survive in medieval Irish churches.

Grace O'Malley, Warrior and Pirate Queen

This part of the coast and the islands off it are associated with the warrior woman who outshone all her male contemporaries in qualities of leadership: Granuaile, otherwise known as Grace O'Malley. A pirate captain whose symbol was the seahorse, her territory included Clare, Caher, Inishturk and Inishbofin. Her family had been lords of the Isles for 200 years, and in the 40 years that it took the Tudors to extend their power to Ireland, Granuaile was the mainstay of the rebellion in the west. At the age of 45 she gave birth at sea to her first child, Toby. An hour later, her ship was boarded by Turkish pirates. The battle on the deck was almost lost when she appeared wrapped in a blanket and shot the enemy captain with a blunderbuss. Her men rallied, captured the Turkish ship and hanged the crew. She was also in the habit of mooring her ships by tying them together, passing the main rope through a hole in her castle walls and retiring to bed with the rope wound round her arm, in order to be ready at the first alarm.

Grace was forced, aged 63, to sail up the Thames to parley with Elizabeth I, who offered her a title; Grace replied that she was a queen in her own right. Finally, they made a deal: Grace would retain some of her old lands, including Clare, and in return would keep down piracy. People still talk of Grace today, though she died in 1603.

Grace O'Malley is buried here: on a plain arch leading from the roofless nave to the chancel is a coat of arms topped by a horse rampant with the words '*Terra Marique potens O'Maille*' ('O'Malley powerful on land and sea'). You can walk to the **lighthouse** at the north end, where there are spectacular views from the cliffs.

Inishturk has a wonderful beach on its south side, and its little farms are full of wildflowers. About 90 people live here and make a living from fishing. **Caher Island** evokes the mood of early monastic settlements better than any other, especially since it is now uninhabited. It is a lovely grey-green place of walls, donkeys, sheep and green pastures. The **church** here is small and roofless. Around it are 12 stone crosses, the most recent of which is not less than 1,000 years old. One on the hilltop shows a human face, another a pair of dolphins. In the graveyard is **St Patrick's Bed**, with impressions said to be the mark of his hands, feet and hips. Few pilgrims come nowadays to lie in his bed and hope for a miraculous cure.

Clew Bay: Westport and the Corraun Peninsula

From Louisburgh, the R335 winds its way to Westport, with lovely views of Clew Bay. The sea-angling grounds here are among the best in Europe. **Westport** is an attractive 18th-century planned town – unusual in the west. James Wyatt, a well-known Georgian architect, designed it for the Marquess of Sligo, and included a pretty walk called the Mall that runs beside the River Carrowbeg and is overhung with trees. In summer the place is overflowing with people attracted by the town's many festivals. Here too, you can walk around one of the few stately homes of the west of Ireland – **Westport House** (*open 11.30–5 Easter–June Sat–Mon, July and Aug daily, Nov Sat and Sun; adm;* **t** *(098) 27766/25430, www.westporthouse.ie*). The house, to the west of the town, is full of old Irish silver, family portraits and lovely furniture, and there is a miniature zoo in the grounds. It was built by Colonel John Browne and his wife, ancestors of the present Marquess of Sligo. He was a Jacobite, and she was the great great grand-daughter of Grace O'Malley.

Newport, on the N59, has a superb country-house hotel overlooking the river (*see* p.299). Newport House used to be the home of the O'Donnells, once the earls of Tir Connell, who were often in the forefront of opposition to English rule. The modern Irish Romanesque style **church** of St Patrick has some Harry Clarke stained-glass windows depicting the Last Judgement.

The coastline around here is full of little islands and inlets. About ½ mile (0.8km) outside Newport on the N59, take a little road signposted to Furnace; this leads you into the wild mountain country of the **Nephin Beg** range. When it's sunny, the lakes go a deep, sparkling blue; and the air is bracing, rather like that of Switzerland. If you decide to explore the wild territory of the interior between Glen Nephin and Bangor Erris, follow the old mountain road on past the lakes and past Glennamong Mountain (2,063ft/629m), until it joins the R312. Then turn northwards until it joins the N59 at Bellacorick. The route is very beautiful; fuchsia and rhododendron mingle with the stone walls and rock.

Continuing along the N59, turn off to **Burrishoole Abbey**, a 15th-century ruin (*always accessible*), and a very charming and peaceful place where the sea laps all about.

The next stop-off is further along the coast, at **Rockfleet Castle** (which is also known as Carrickahooley), a complete towerhouse that stands on seaweedy rock overlooking Newport Bay. This four-sided 15th-century castle was built by the Burkes and passed to Grace O'Malley by means of a trick: she married Richard Burke on the understanding that either of them could end the marriage after a year. She used the year to garrison the castle with her own men and kept it when she declared the marriage ended.

When you get to **Mulranny** on the neck of the **Corraun Peninsula**, you will find a long strand looking out to Croagh Patrick across Clew Bay. This area is very popular in the summer months, for the climate is mild. Rhododendrons bloom luxuriously, and myriads of yellow flags grow in the fields, which are another common and lovely sight in Connacht – although the local farmers wouldn't agree. The Corraun Peninsula is a wild knob of land through which you can pass on the way to Achill Island. The single-track road around it provides a fine introduction to Achill Island, which has all the most attractive characteristics of Connacht, including the sleepy whitewashed cottages you can see across the water and the smell of burning turf floating on the breeze. Placid-looking donkeys are everywhere.

Achill Island

Achill is connected to the mainland by a bridge, and because it is one of the easiest islands to reach, it is the most touristy. The island covers 53 square miles (137.25 sq km) and is the largest of the Irish islands. The best introduction to it is to take the **Atlantic Drive**. This is signposted clearly as you leave the little hamlet of Achill Sound beside the causeway. You pass a small, ruined 12th-century church and then a charming towerhouse, **Kildownet**, which is supposed to have belonged at some time to Grace O'Malley. The road follows the line of the shore round the south tip and passes **Achillbeg Island**, which contains the remains of an old hermitage.

Keel is a big village with restaurants and craft shops and a large, sandy beach. The west-facing **Cliffs of Menawn** to the south of Keel have been wrought by the sea and wind into fantastic shapes, which are best viewed from a boat. Particularly noteworthy are the **Cathedral Rocks**, covered in fantastic fretwork. If you walk 3 miles (4.8km) to the end of Menawn Strand, you come to a holy well; and if it is low tide you can see the arches and pillars of the rocks clearly. Above, Mweelin Mountain rises up. It is an easy climb, if approached from Dookinelly. **Keem Bay** is a lovely sandy cove obvious from the cliff road, and a favourite haunt of the basking shark.

Doogort is a little fishing hamlet in the shadow of Slievemore Mountain (2,204ft/ 672m). The hamlet has a contentious history. In the early 19th century, a Protestant missionary outpost was established here in order to convert the local Catholics. The Mission acquired title to the rights of three-fifths of Achill in a short time, and resentment amongst the Achill people ran high. This was intensified when, apparently, soup and bread was given out to islanders during the famine only if they became Protestants. The Mission closed down in the late 19th century but it did help start the first hotel on the island. Along the coast here are the **Seal Caves**. You can hire a boat to get to them and enjoy the superb bathing beaches.

Northern Mayo

From Mulranny, the N59 runs over a vast bog; the edges are enlivened by splashes of purple rhododendrons and a few fir trees. Turf, which for hundreds of years has been cut from the bog, is used much less in heating and cooking now bottled gas has made domestic life a lot easier. But many farmers and country people have rights to turf turbaries, which they cut every year. The tool used to cut the neat sods from the bog is called a slane; as they are cut the sods are arranged in little piles to dry. The pattern of the piles varies from area to area, but they often resemble little *clochans*.

Bangor Erris is a small place on the long, lonely road to Belmullet. This region is still known as Erris, one of the ancient Norman baronies of Ireland. **Belmullet** is one of the loneliest towns in Connacht. It stands on a slender piece of land just wide enough to prevent the Mullet from becoming an island. All the commerce of the peninsula is channelled through this town, so on market day it is surprisingly full. If you want to base yourself here before exploring the wild and lonely peninsula, there is plenty of accommodation (*see* p.304). Belmullet is famous for sea-angling, and there is an international fishing festival here in August. The Mullet is almost divided into little islands by the deep bays that cut into it on either side. The beaches and fishing are excellent, and there are superb views of Achill, the Nephin Beg range, and the mystical islands of Inishglora and Inishkea. The grey and red-necked phalarope nests in the crevices and rocks along the coast, and the peninsula is scattered with prehistoric remains. Out in Blacksod Bay lies the wreck of *La Rata*, a large Spanish galleon that went down in the wild seas of September 1588 – part of the Armada that threatened England. The islands of Inishglora and Inishkea are uninhabited and hardly ever visited by tourists. Getting out to them is a matter of negotiation with local fishermen, and they can only be reached in calm weather. A walk around each one takes at least an hour. Always bring your own picnic and drinks.

Along the spectacular coastline from Blacksod Bay to Ballina you can follow the **North Mayo Sculpture Trail**. Fifteen contemporary works, based on aspects of Irish folklore and the landscape, are scattered on various sites. The tourist office can furnish you with a list of them.

Inishglora and the Islands of Inishkea

On **Inishglora** ('Island of the Voice'), the Children of Lir regained their true form after being turned into swans by their jealous stepmother. The spell was to be broken when St Patrick's bell was heard ringing out over Ireland, but, unhappily for the Children of Lir, their immortality only lasted whilst they were swans. They came ashore, blind, senile and decrepit, to die almost at once.

Inishglora has been a sacred island for thousands of years. It is only one mile (1.6km) from the Mullet Peninsula, and its ecclesiastical remains are associated with St Brendan the Navigator. Some of the buildings definitely date from the 6th century. The most complete is the 12th-century **St Brendan's Chapel**, built of dry-stone masonry. Close by are the ruins of a church for men and a church for women. The holy well here is supposed to turn red if the water is touched by a woman's hand.

Tourist Information

Ballina: t (096) 70848. *Open late Mar–Sept.*

Shopping

Crafts

Terrybaun Pottery, Bofeenaun, near Pontoon, Ballina, t (094) 9256472. Earthenware.

Clothing

Flannery Knitwear, Graughill, Pullathomas, Belmullet, t (097) 84607
Gaeltarra Knitwear, Tourmakeady, t (094) 954 4015, *www.gaeltarra.ie*

Sports and Activities

Fishing

Coarse-fish on the Moy, one of the best salmon rivers anywhere, or loughs Conn and Cullin.
Lough Conn, Healy's Hotel, Pontoon, t (094) 905 6443
Moy Fishery, Ridge Pool Rd, Ballina, t (096) 21332
Sea-angling is also possible:
Vincent Sweeney, Blacksod, Ballina, t (097) 85774

Golf

Ballina Golf Club, Mossgrove, t (096) 21050

Where to Stay

Enniscoe House, Castlehill, near Crossmolina, Ballina, t (096) 31112, *www.enniscoe.com* (*expensive*). A Georgian house in parklands on the shores of Lough Conn. Its grand, spacious rooms are filled with family furniture and there are huge log fires. The superlative cooking uses seasonal ingredients. The grounds include ornamental and organic gardens (*adm*), adjoined by Mayo North Heritage Centre (*see* p.306). Woodcock shooting is available in winter for small groups, and boats and ghillies to get out on the lough can be arranged. There are self-catering apartments in the grounds for short lets. *Closed Nov–Mar.*
Pontoon Bridge Hotel, Pontoon, t (094) 925 6120, *www.pontoonbridge.com* (*expensive*). A well-known lakeside hotel with a waterfront

bar and 2 restaurants (see *below*). Tuition is available in fishing, cooking and painting, and golf packages are available.
Healy's Hotel, Pontoon, t (094) 925 6443, *healyspontoon@eircom.net* (*moderate*). A quiet place with a lovely setting on the shore of the lough, making it great for anglers, and a restaurant.
Breege Padden, Quignalegan House, Sligo Rd, Ballina, t (096) 71644 (*inexpensive*). A family B&B recommended by readers of this guide.
Highdrift, Haven View, Ballina Rd, Belmullet, t (097) 81260, *anne.reilly@ireland.com* (*inexpensive*). B&B accommodation in a modern bungalow with turf fires.
Kilmurray House, Castlehill, Crossmolina, Ballina, t (096) 31227 (*inexpensive*). A friendly, cosy farmhouse with good food. *Closed Nov–Mar.*

Self-catering

See also Enniscoe House, above.
Rathoma Cottage, Rathoma, Killala, t (096) 31340, *www.rathomacottage.com* (*inexpensive*). A restored country cottage in the heart of Mayo, sleeping 6–8.

Eating Out

Restaurants in this area are generally pretty dismal; it's best to head over to Westport, Cong or Castlebar (*see* p.295).
Pontoon Bridge Hotel, Pontoon, t (094) 925 6120 (*moderate–expensive*). The best place for food, with lake views.
Dillon's Bar and Restaurant, Dillon Terrace, Ballina, t (096) 72230 (*moderate*). A place famous locally for its salmon. *Closed lunch, and Mon and Tue out of season.*
Western Strands Hotel, Main St, Belmullet, t (097) 81096 (*moderate*).Seafood specialities, and pub grub and snacks all day.
The Anchor Bar, Georges St, Killala, t (096) 32050 (*inexpensive*). Pub lunches.

Entertainment and Nightlife

Traditional Music

The Broken Jug, O'Rahilly St, Ballina, t (096) 72379

Once it was believed that the more serious a dead man's crimes, the more important it was to have him buried on an holy island. This not only improved his chances of salvation but ensured that he could not come back to haunt you, since the spirits of the dead cannot pass over water. It is said locally that on Inishglora lots of bones are uncovered where the soil is washed away by rain and sea-spray.

South-west lie the islands of **Inishkea** ('Isle of the Lonely Heron'). Legend tells of Mulhenna, who was unfaithful to her husband and was banished here for 1,000 years, condemned to take the form of a heron. South Island has a little deserted hilltop village, though fishermen camp here when they are working offshore. The islanders moved to the mainland after 10 men drowned in 1927 during a freak gale. Moondaisies, grass, sheep and sandy beaches will be your reward if you come out here. Both islands have the remains of ancient churches, incised stone crosses and some prehistoric signs of occupation. **Duvillaun More**, the most distant of this chain of islands, lies off the southern tip of the Belmullet peninsula and is only accessible when the sea is calm. There are remains of monastic settlements here too, including a holy well.

The Northern Coast

On the mainland again, make your way up to the fishing hamlet of Pollatomish on Sruwaddacon Bay. Take the unnumbered road west of Barnatra on the R314. Close to the cliff edge you will see **Dooncarton Stone Circle** and megalithic tomb. Further north is the little harbour village of **Portacloy**, which is surrounded by high cliffs. **Céide Hill** and the surrounding area is probably one of the world's most extensive stone age monuments. The **Céide Fields Visitor Centre** (*open daily mid-Mar–May 10–5, June–Sept 9.30–6, Oct and Nov 10–3; open Dec–mid-Mar by advance booking; adm; t (096) 43325, www.heritageireland.ie*) just off the R314 explains the archaeology and geology of the area. Hidden in the bogs is evidence of a well-organized farming community dating from more than 5,000 years ago, and extensive patterns of stone-walled fields and corrals have been revealed.

On the R314 in the north-eastern corner of the county, **Ballycastle** is typical of the villages in the west. The streets are wide, the air smells faintly of turf, and everybody seems to be asleep. The cliffs of **Downpatrick Head** are full of wheeling birds, terns, gulls, skuas, razorbills and guillemots, plus less active ones such as puffins; all seem to have nests somewhere on the edges of the cliffs. There are picnic tables set out overlooking the Atlantic, but it does not look as if anyone has ever eaten off them, and now the birds and seapinks have taken over, visited by the occasional hare. There is wire fencing on the head to prevent you from falling into the crevasses and holes around the cliff edge.

One of the most spectacular holes is a puffin hole called Poulnachantinny. Once upon a time St Patrick was having a fight with the Devil, and dealt him such a blow with his crozier that the Devil was hammered clean through the rock and down into the sea-cave below. In their fight they also knocked a bit of the headland off into the sea – the stack of **Doonbristy** is proof. An old promontory fort was built on Doonbristy, before it separated from the headland. It is a ruin now. There is a *pattern* (pilgrimage) to the holy well and ruined church of St Patrick on Garland Sunday in May.

About 2 miles (3.2 km) north-west of Ballycastle on the R314 is **Doonfeeney Graveyard**, where there is a ruined church and a standing stone about 18ft (5.5m) high, with a cross carved on it. A large ring fort stands close by, where, according to old beliefs, fairies hold their revels. The graveyard is scattered with ancient stone slabs, and it is a quiet, secret place. In spring, east towards **Killala Bay** (still following the R314), the banks of the roadside are covered in daisies and primroses. Killala was the scene of the landings in 1798, when Humbert brought 1,100 French soldiers, plus supplies and artillery, from France to support the rebels. The bay is rather like a lagoon, having calm sheltered waters. Before you get to the town, a road to the left leads you past **Rathfran Abbey**, a ruined but fine Dominican friary dating from 1274. **Killala** town is very pretty and rather higgledy-piggledy, with a round tower rising from the middle. The tower is of a later date than the abbey, and the doorway is almost 13ft (4m) from the ground. It is now thought that such towers were the work of skilled builders who moved around the country from site to site. This tower is of a blue limestone with a greenish cap.

Two miles (3.2km) west is a 15th-century ruin called **Moyne Abbey** – it was in fact a friary – on the estuary of the lovely salmon river, the Moy, reputedly one of the best in Europe. Just a mile or two upstream is another abbey, **Rosserk**, which is rather more complete and is regarded as one of the finest Franciscan friaries in the country. It has some good carvings on the double piscina, one of which is of a round tower. The buildings include a square tower, a nave, a chancel, a south transept, a cloister and some conventional buildings. There is a lovely arched doorway and east window.

Ballina and the Loughs

Ballina (pronounced 'bally-nah'), a port town on the estuary of the River Moy, is a good place to stay if you are here for the fishing. It is an excellent shopping centre as well, especially after the remoteness and lack of choice in Erris – though these days Ballina is perhaps best known as the home town of former president Mary Robinson. West of Ballina at Enniscoe, Castlehill, is the **Mayo North Heritage Centre** (*open June–Sept Mon–Fri 9–6, Sat and Sun 2–6, Oct–May Mon–Fri 9–4, Sat and Sun 2–6; t (096) 31809*), off the R315 and 2 miles (3km) south of Crossmolina. It is in the outbuildings of Enniscoe House, which is also an attractive and comfortable place to stay (*see p.304*).

Foxford, which is located 10 miles (16km) due south of Ballina, is a convenient place to stay if you are fishing on loughs Conn and Cullin. Its thriving wool and tweed mill in St Joseph's Place operates the **Foxford Woollen Mills Visitor Centre** (*open Mon–Sat 10–6, Sun 12 noon–6 (from 2 in winter); t (094) 925 6104, www.foxfordwoollenmills.ie*), where you can watch rugs, blankets and tweeds being made . This area is highly attractive; the summit of Nephin Mountain is of whitish quartzite, which means that it looks perpetually snow-capped, and when the sun is shining it provides a lovely background for the deep-blue waters of Lough Conn. **Pontoon** is on the isthmus between the two loughs, and there are two hotels there (*see p.304*).

It is worth stopping at **Straide**, if you are going to Castlebar. This is the birthplace of Michael Davitt (1846–1906), who started the Land League. His family were evicted from their small farm when he was five, and they emigrated to Lancashire, where he worked as a child in the cotton mills and lost his right arm in the machines. The **Michael Davitt National Memorial Museum** (*open daily 10–6; adm; t (094) 9031022*) here has a large collection of historical documents and photographs relating to the League. Opposite is a ruined **Franciscan abbey**, founded in the mid 13th century, which has a wonderful series of sculptures. The *Pietà* is especially good; the Virgin sits with the limp body of Christ in her lap, guarded by two angels. There is an elaborate 15th-century tomb chest in the same style with figures of saints.

County Roscommon

Roscommon is a wonderfully green and fertile county, with shining sheets of water encircling it and scattered throughout. It is the only county in Connacht without a seashore, but its many lakes and rivers give it a different charm from that of its windswept Atlantic neighbours. The placid River Shannon forms its eastern boundary, engulfed as it is by the beautiful Lough Ree for several miles. The River Suck, which is beloved of coarse fishermen, forms the boundary with County Mayo in the west, and Lough Key, Lough Gara and Lough Arrow encircle the county in the north. In the east and west there is bogland, but in the centre rich pastureland divides into fine cattle and sheep farms. The flood meadows on either side of the Suck provide a perfect environment for bird-watching. Great flocks of widgeon come here to graze, as do whooper swans, golden plovers, black-tailed godwits and white-fronted geese. Snipe, curlew and lapwing are also common. The familiar, beautiful cry of the curlew, as it turns and wheels above the green fields, is a sound that is peculiarly reminiscent of the Irish countryside.

There are many prehistoric monuments to see – burial mounds, megalithic tombs and ring forts – and the most powerful Norman and Gaelic leaders of the medieval period built strong castles and abbeys here that have survived, although they're in a ruined state. The Cistercian abbey in Boyle is perhaps the most impressive, but the countryside is scattered with charming Church of Ireland churches dating from the 17th and 18th centuries, which nowadays have hardly a congregation at all.

The Protestant English and Scottish invaders who built these churches also planned and constructed impressive estates. The wealth of design and craftsmanship that went into making these large houses and their parks is only just beginning to be appreciated today; for years they were branded as the symbols of oppression by a race that has a long memory for wrongs and past injustices. One such great house, near Boyle, belonged to the King family of Rockingham.

You could spend a melancholy few days touring the ruined Big Houses of County Roscommon, as you can everywhere in Ireland. The list of sad remains in this county is long: Kilronan Castle near Ballyfarnon, Mantua near Castlerea, Mount Plunkett near Athlone, Mount Talbot, Athleague, the Bishop's Palace in Elphin, and Ballanagare House in Ballanagare. The latter was built by the O'Connors, who were high kings of Ireland in pre-Norman times. Their principal seat at Clonalis near Castlerea – an attractive late-19th-century house – is open to the public, and houses a collection of

County Roscommon

N

20km
10miles

SLIGO

Lavagh
Achonry
Tubbercurry
Banada
Charlestown

Ballymote
Castlebaldwin
Derry
Carrowkeel
Lough Arrow
Kesh
Riverstown
Ballyfarnon
Keadue
Drumshanbo

Lough Allen

LEITRIM

N4

Ballinafad

Curlew Hills

Lough Meelagh

R294

Gorteen
Mullaghroe
Boyle
Lough Key
Lough Key Forest Park

Drumcong

Leitrim

R284

Lough Gara

Knock Airport

MAYO

Ballaghaderreen

Ballinameen

Carrick-on-Shannon

Killukin
Jamestown
Drumsna

N4

Drumod

Frenchpark

Hill Street
Clougher

N5

Elphin

Roosky

R202

Ballyhaunis

Lough O'Flynn

Clonalis House

Castlerea

N60

Rathcroghan

Kilglass Lough

Dromod

N60

Tulsk

R367

Carnfree

Strokestown

N5

Lough Forbes

Termonbarry

Cloonfad

Ballymore

Ballintober

ROSCOMMON

Four Mile House

Cloondara

Lanesborough

Dunmore

Glinsk Castle

N83

Glennamaddy

Roscommon Castle
Roscommon

Fuerty

Ballymurray

LONGFORD

Castlestrange Stone
Athleague

R366

Knockcroghery

Inishcloraun
Newtown Cashel

R332

Barnaderg

Ballygar

Galey Castle
Lecarrow

Saint's Island

Four Roads

Mount Bellew

GALWAY

Ballyforan

Thomas

Curraghboy

N61

Lough Ree

Inchmore

WESTMEATH

Glassan

Monivea

Gurteen

Castleblakeney

Killinure Lough

Corraree

Athlone

Bealin

Kilconnell

Ballinasloe

R348

Killogeenaghan

N6

New Inn

Aughrim

N6

Old Town

River Shannon

Clonmacnoise

OFFALY

Abbey of Clontuskert

R355

R. Suck

Shannonbridge

Blackwater Bog

Ferbane

Loughrea

N6

Laurencetown

Clonfert

Grand Canal

Clonony

Getting There and Around

By Rail
Trains between Dublin and Sligo pass through Boyle. The Dublin–Westport–Ballina line passes through Roscommon Town and Castlerea; both lines have about 3 trains a day.
Roscommon Train Information, t (090) 662 6201

By Bus
Express bus services run from Dublin to Roscommon Town, Strokestown, Elphin, Ballaghaderreen, Ballanagare and Boyle. There is also a good local bus network.
Bus Éireann Information, Athlone,
t (090) 648 4406

By Bike
Bicycle hire, as well as sales and repair, are available at:
Brendan Sheerin, Main St, Boyle,
t (071) 966 2010
Buckley's Cycles, Astor Buildings, Roscommon, t (090) 662 7318
Riverside Cycles, Bridge St, Boyle, t (071) 966 3777

Festivals

May
Strokestown International Poetry Festival, t (066) 947 4123. Poetry competitions, international poets performing readings, and workshops.

July–August
Boyle Arts Festival, t (071) 966 3085, www.boylearts.com
Boyle Music Fest, (071) 966 2145. Music, arts, culture and street entertainment.
Castlerea International Rose Festival, t (094) 962 1186. Top bands performing in the street.
Country and Western Carnival, Boyle, (071) 966 2145. A very popular event.
O'Carolan Harp and Traditional Irish Music Festival and School, Keadue, Boyle, t (071) 964 7247

October
Féile Frank McGann, Strokestown, t (078) 33289, www.feilefrankmcgann.com. A traditional music festival.

Tourist Information
Athleague: t (090) 666 3602
Boyle: t (071) 966 2145. Open May–Sept.
Roscommon: t (090) 662 6342, www.roscommon.ie, www.visitroscommon.com. Open mid-May–mid-Sept.

Shopping

Crafts
The Bastion Gallery, 6 Bastion St, Athlone, t (090) 649 4948
Eight 'Til Late, Market Sq, Roscommon
Rainbow End, Bridge St, Boyle, t (071) 966 3026
Time Pieces, Main St, Roscommon, t (090) 662 5408. Clocks, jewellery and crafts.
Una Bhan Craft Shop, Main St, Boyle, t (070) 966 3033, www.unabhan.net

Sports and Activities

Cycling
For details of cycle routes in County Roscommon, contact Athleague Visitor Centre, t (090) 666 3602, or see www.suckvalley.com.

Fishing
There is **coarse fishing** on the River Suck and its tributaries at Glinsk, Castlecook, Ballygar and Ballyforan, as well as on Errit Lake, Hollygrove Lake, and in the Ballyhaunis area, Eaton's Lake, and Lakehill Lake.
Fishing for **brown trout** takes place on the upper stretches of the River Suck, the River Derryhipps and limestone lake O'Flynn. For more information, contact Roscommon tourist office (see above) or one of the following:
Angling and Visitor Centre, Athleague, t (090) 666 3602
Ballaghaderreen and District Angling Club, t (094) 986 0077
Bodo Funke, Angling Services Ireland, Boyle, t (071) 96 63660, www.anglingservicesireland.com
Cavetown Angling Club, t (071) 966 8037
Christopher Wynne, Main St, Boyle, t (071) 966 2456. Fishing information, ghillies and supplies of tackle and bait.
Ireland West Tourism, t (091) 563081

Golf

Boyle Golf Course, t (071) 966 2594
Roscommon Golf Club, t (090) 662 6382

Open Farms

Glendeer Open Farm, between Roscommon and Athlone, t (090) 643 7147. *Closed Oct–Mar.*

Pleasure Cruises

There are summer cruises on Lough Key; see *www.visitroscommon.com* or contact local tourist offices for more information.
Shannon-Erne Waterway Holidays, Cootehall, near Carrick-on-Shannon, Co. Leitrim, t (071) 966 7028
Tara Cruisers, The Moorings, Lough Key, Boyle, t (071) 966 7777
Viking Tours, Athlone, Co. Westmeath, t (090) 647 3383, *vikingtours@ireland.com*

Ponytrekking

Kiltoom Stables, near Athlone, t (090) 648 9511
Munsboro Riding Holidays, Munsboro Lodge, Sligo Rd, Roscommon, t (090) 662 6449
Una Bhan Tourism Centre, King House, Military Rd, Boyle, t (071) 966 3033, *www.unabhan.com*. This also organizes fishing, bike tours and other activities, such as farmhouse skills.

Where to Stay

The Abbey Hotel, Galway Rd, Roscommon, t (090) 662 6240, *www.abbeyhotel.ie* (*expensive*). An attractive little Georgian hotel.
Clonalis House, Castlerea, t (094) 962 0014, *www.clonalis.com* (*moderate–expensive*). An opportunity to stay with descendants of Ireland's last high kings in their Victorian-Italianate house on a lovely wooded estate. Shooting and fishing can be arranged, as can dinner (*luxury*; 24hrs notice required). There are mews houses to rent on the estate too.
Gleeson's Townhouse, Market Sq, Roscommon, t (090) 662 6954, *www.gleesonstownhouse.com* (*moderate*). A central option with well-appointed rooms and a restaurant.
Glencarne House, Ardcarne, near Carrick-on-Shannon, t (071) 966 7013 (*moderate*). A fine Georgian farmhouse with comfortable rooms, lovely old furniture and well-cooked meals (book in advance for dinner).

Royal Hotel, Bridge St, Boyle, t (071) 966 2016 (*moderate*). An inn on the river in the town centre, established more than 200 years ago.
Riversdale House, Knockvicar, near Boyle, t (071) 966 7012 (*inexpensive*). A period farmhouse in the middle of the countryside, with its own lake and river fishing.

Self-catering

See also Clonalis House, above.
Abbey House, t (091) 966 2385 (*inexpensive*). Lovely old houses to rent in the grounds of Boyle Abbey.
Rookwood, Athleague, t (090) 666 3810 (*inexpensive*). An old gate lodge by the river.

Eating Out

Cromleach Lodge, Lough Arrow, Castlebaldwin, t (071) 916 5155, *www.cromleach.com* (*expensive*). Fine cuisine in the hills above Lough Arrow (in Co. Sligo, but near Boyle).
Italia, Knockvicar, Boyle, t (071) 9667788 (*moderate–expensive*). Italian cuisine served in an attractive location near Knockvicar marina. Booking is advised. *Closed Mon.*
The Abbey Hotel, Abbeytown, Galway Rd, Roscommon, t (090) 662 6240 (*moderate*). Excellent French-style cooking in an 18th-century house.
Donnellan's, Clarendon House, Knockvicar, Boyle, t (071) 966 7016 (*moderate*). A pleasant restaurant with a good children's menu. *Closed Mon and Tue.*
Gleeson's Townhouse, Market Sq, Roscommon, t (090) 662 6954 (*moderate*). A hotel (*see* above) with a daytime café and a restaurant serving Irish and European country fare.
Keenan's, Tarmonberry, near Strokestown, t (043) 26052/26098; *www.keenans.ie* (*moderate*). An ideal spot for anglers, steps away from the Shannon, comprised of a 19th-century pub and restaurant.
Royal Hotel, Bridge St, Boyle, t (071) 966 2016 (*inexpensive–moderate*). A coffee shop serving salads and snacks, a restaurant serving carvery lunches, and an adjoining Chinese, The Royal Palace, t (090) 663 0648.
James Clarke, Patrick St, Boyle, t (071) 966 2064 (*inexpensive*). A traditional pub serving delicious Irish coffees.

early Irish papers and books (*see also* 'Where to Stay', opposite). Stokestown Park House, the ancestral home of the Mahons, will lift your spirits. In 1979 the owner of the local garage bought it in partnership with the present curator, and they began an extensive programme of restoration. It is one Big House with a bright future, full of hope and boasting plenty of community involvement to sustain it. The other great Gaelic family of Roscommon were the MacDermotts; the head of the family was known as the MacDermott Prince of Coolavin. They survived as property-owners right up to the early 20th century.

Northern Roscommon

Keadue to Boyle

Keadue is near the Sligo and Leitrim borders. It is in one of the most attractive parts of the county, with the **Slieve Anierin Range**, also known as the Arigna Mountains, rising to the east. The R284 mountain road from Sligo to Ballyfarnon, further north, gives one a magnificent view over **Lough Meelagh** and Lough Skean. Between Keadue and Ballyfarnon the same road passes close to the edge of Lough Meelagh, where on the shore there is an ancient church site and a holy well called **Kilronan**. Both are associated with St Lasair and St Ronan. St Lasair was the daughter of St Ronan, who founded the original church in the 6th century. It has been burned down twice, and was last rebuilt in the 17th century. You are far away from the bustle of life here in the enchanted and weed-high graveyard. In the ruined church is a modern monument to Turlough O'Carolan, who died in 1733, the last in a line of harpists and poets who used to have such status in the Gaelic kingdoms. He is supposed to have composed the melody that is used for 'The Star Spangled Banner'. He was born blind, and somehow came to the home of Mrs MacDermott Roe of Alderford, Ballyfarnan, who befriended and educated him. She provided him with a horse so he could wander the country playing his harp at the Big Houses. He is buried in the graveyard, and to commemorate his memory the O'Carolan Festival is held annually in August (*see* p.309).

Nearby, surrounded by the ash trees so sacred to the Druids in ancient times, is a clear **well** that flows into the lough. Rosaries and rags ornament the ground, and a large rectangular stone slab is supposed to heal those suffering from backache. The cure entails crawling under the slab, which is balanced on two other stones. A *pattern* is made to the well on the first Sunday of September every year.

Boyle is an attractive town between Lough Key and Lough Gara. The Curlew Hills rise to the north-west and the River Boyle flows through it. The main street was once the avenue to the castle of the King family, who later moved to Rockingham House (*see* p.312). By the river bank is **Boyle Abbey** (*open early Apr–Oct daily 10–6, rest of year key with caretaker in Abbey House B&B; adm; **t** (071) 966 2604*), a ruined Cistercian abbey, founded in 1161 and closely associated with its brother house, the great Mellifont Abbey in County Louth (*see* p.493). It was not completed until 1218 and reflects the change of fashion from the round arches of the Romanesque period to the pointed lancet of the early English Gothic style. There is a mix of different styles of arches and lavishly decorated capitals. The monastery was suppressed in 1569 and occupied by Cromwellian soldiers later on; you can see their names carved on the door of the porter's room. Looking onto the River Boyle is **Frybrook House** (*open June–Sept daily 2–6; adm;* **t** *(071) 966 3513*), with beautiful 18th-century plasterwork. It is right next to the Main Street, where another 18th-century house, **King House,** was restored and opened as an Interpretative Centre (*open daily Apr–Sept 10–6; adm;* **t** *(071) 966 3242, www.roscommoncoco.ie/kinghouse.htm*). It was once the seat of the King family. An exhibition explores the history of Celtic chiefs, such as the MacDermotts, and the 17th-century English families who amassed huge estates.

East of the town is the great demesne of **Rockingham House**, which belonged in the 18th century to the King family of Rockingham. The Kings later became the earls of Rockingham and abandoned the house, which subsequently served as a military barracks for the Connaught Rangers, a British army regiment, and then later the Irish army. The house burnt to a shell in 1957 but has now become a tourist attraction. Unfortunately, the character and splendour of the place has been rather lost. The park is now planted with conifer trees that form part of the beautiful **Lough Key Forest Park** (*open daily Apr–Oct, call for times,* **t** *(071) 966 2363; car park adm; www.coillte.ie/ tourismandrecreation*), 4¾ miles (7.6km) east of Boyle on the N4. Here there are walks, a bog garden, picnic sites, a caravan and camping park, boating, fishing and cruising.

About 2 miles (3.2km) away at **Drumanone** is one of the largest dolmens in Ireland, known locally as **Druid's Altar**, which may have been a monument to someone living in the Bronze Age. It is beside the R294, just beyond the railway line, and is found by following a grassy lane to a railway crossing. Close by, on the waters of Lough Gara, 300 *crannógs* (artificial islands) have been found. These were used by Iron Age farmers as defensive sites for themselves and their cattle. Some were in use up until the 17th century. Thirty-one dug-out wooden boats were also excavated here.

Frenchpark and Around

South-east of Lough Gara is **Frenchpark**, birthplace of Douglas Hyde (1860–1949), founder of the Gaelic League and the first president of Ireland. His great cultural and social achievement was to collect stories and folklore from the peasantry. Some of the stories were at least 1,000 years old, and had been transferred orally from generation to generation. They were in grave danger of being lost altogether, as the use of Gaelic was declining. He was born in the rectory here and retired to **Ratra House** (*not open to public*) in his old age. You pass the house as you enter Frenchpark from the direction of Ballaghaderreen on the N5. The Church of Ireland church and graveyard in which he is buried is typical of many: it is a grey, simple Planter's Gothic with a garden of gravestones, flowers and grasses. It is now the **Douglas Hyde Interpretative Centre** (*open May–Sept Tue–Fri 2–5, Sat and Sun 2–6; donation requested;* **t** *(094) 987 0016*).

Frenchpark House was built to the designs of Richard Castle (or Cassels), who was Ireland's greatest Palladian architect (*see* p.75). Its interior was dismantled in the 1950s, and the ruin was demolished in the 1970s. In the grounds is a five-chambered souterrain. Like all souterrains, it is difficult to date, but it was used between the Bronze Age and the 5th century AD.

Six miles (9.7 km) south-east of Frenchpark is the **Hill of Rathcroghan**, a beautiful place just off the N5 going south-east to Tulsk. Rathcroghan is a flat-topped, almost circular mound about 68 yards (62m) in diameter. In the 1st century AD the legendary Queen Maeve, or Medb, also known as a warrior and earth goddess (*see* p.56), had a palace here. A little south of the mound is an enclosure known as the **Graveyard of the Kings**. This contains the remains of stone sepulchral chambers and, along with Kells in County Meath and Brugh (Newgrange) in County Louth, is well known as one of the three royal burial places of prehistoric Ireland. In the graveyard is an old redstone pillar known as the **Pillar Stone of Daithí**. Daithí was a pagan king of Ireland who, according to the *Book of Leinster*, conquered Scotland, invaded the Continent and died in the Alps from a stroke of lightning in about AD 428. Forts are scattered all around this area, to a radius of 3 miles (4.8km).

Three miles (4.8km) to the south-east of Rathcroghan, just outside Tulsk, is **Carnfree**, the inauguration mound of the O'Connors, kings of Connacht. It is not much to look at – a grassy mound of earth and stones about 8ft (2.4m) high and 40ft (12m) in circumference – but the views from it are wonderful. It is reputed to be the burial ground of Conn of the Hundred Battles and the three Tuatha Dé Danaan queens: Éire, Fotla and Banba. Here at Croghan, Queen Maeve launched her expedition to capture the Brown Bull of Ulster (*see* p.57). It is difficult to imagine these legendary figures and this place as the seat of power, for the plain is crisscrossed by stone walls and modern farms.

In the village of **Tulsk** itself is the ***Cruachan Aí*** **Visitor Centre** (*open June–Sept Mon–Sat 9–6, Sun 1–5, Oct–May Mon–Sat 9–5; **t** (071) 963 9268, www.cruachanai.com*), an educational museum that arranges tours of the *Cruachan* ('Royal Palace') of Queen Maeve. The tours evoke a sense of the importance of this burial place for the kings of Connacht, said to be one of the most significant of Europe's Celtic royal sites.

Castlerea to Roosky

Just north-west of **Castlerea**, a market town on the attractive wooded land near the River Suck, stands **Clonalis House** (*open June–Aug Mon–Sat 11–4; adm; **t** (094) 962 0014*), ancestral home of the O'Conor clan. The family can trace itself back to Feredach the Just, a petty king who reigned in AD 75. The O'Conors produced 24 kings for Connacht, and 11 high kings for Ireland. At Clonalis an inauguration stone, not unlike the Stone of Scone, symbolizes the O'Conors' royalty and prestige. The existing Victorian house was built in 1880; the old 18th-century house is now derelict after storm damage in 1961. The land itself has belonged to the O'Conor family for at least 1,500 years, in spite of war and the Penal Laws. Besides furniture and family portraits, the house contains a unique collection of early Irish documents. Among them is a copy of the last Brehon (Gaelic) Law judgement, handed down in about 1580. Also on show is the harp of Turlough O'Carolan, who composed beautiful and haunting airs and three *planxtys* (lively pieces of dance music) for his O'Conor patrons. Within Castlerea itself, **Hell's Kitchen Railway Museum and Bar** (*open Mon–Sat 12 noon–6; **t** (094)*

9620181, www.hellskitchenmuseum.com) makes for an amusing diversion. Sean Browne's private collection of railway memorabilia has spilled over into the bar, with a restored A55 locomotive built into the wall.

Four miles (6.4km) to the south-east of Clonalis on the R367 is **Ballintober of Bridget** (named after St Bridget's Well), where you can see a ruined **O'Conor castle** (*always accessible*) that withstood many sieges, including one by the Cromwellians. The 13th-century castle was the O'Conor's principal seat after the Anglo-Norman invasion in the 12th century until the beginning of the 18th century, when they moved to Clonalis. It is now an extensive ruin, quadrangular in shape, with towers at each corner and two other towers defending the main entrance on the east.

Glinsk Castle (*always accessible*), south of Ballintober and just over the border into County Galway, is well worth a visit. Glinsk is the shell of one of the best fortified houses in Connacht, with four storeys of mullioned and transomed windows and stacks of chimneys, now used by the starlings and crows. Sir Ulric Burke, who died in 1708, is supposed to have built it, but its machicolated appearance suggests an earlier design. It is approached on an unnumbered road, between the R360 just south of Ballymore or the R362. Turn left at the Kilcroan crossroads.

Returning north-east via the R367, going through Tulsk and onto the N5, you will come to **Strokestown**. It sits at the foot of Slieve Bawn, which at 864ft (263m) is quite something in this low-lying countryside. The town is very handsome, with a wide main street laid out by Maurice Mahon, who was created Baron Hartland in 1800, and was impressed by the Ringstrasse in Vienna. Inside the former Church of Ireland church is **Roscommon Heritage Centre** (*open Mon–Fri 2.30–4.30; **t** (071) 963 3380*). The church was built in 1819, reputedly to the design of Sir John Nash, and has a fine octagonal nave. If you want to trace your Roscommon ancestry, the centre offers a research service (*www.roscommonroots.com*).

One of the most fascinating Big Houses that has survived intact is **Strokestown Park House** (*open 16 Apr–31 Oct daily 11–5.30; adm; **t** (071) 963 3013, www.strokestownpark.com*), on the eastern outskirts of the town. Strokestown was the ancestral home of the Mahon family from 1660 to 1979. Most of the house was designed by Richard Cassels in the 1730s, but it contains both 17th- and 19th-century interiors. The house and lands were bought by the present owners intact, with all its centuries-old paraphernalia; there is a still-room where the mistress of the house dried herbs and concocted remedies for minor illnesses, and the nursery is full of lovely old toys. The kitchen gallery is a very unusual thing to find in Ireland. From here, the mistress of the house could observe and communicate with her cooks and underservants without having to trail down to the kitchen herself. Weekly menus were dropped from the balcony every Monday. The ballroom-cum-library still has its original furniture. The stables, with magnificent groin-vaulted ceilings and Tuscan pillars, now house a Famine Museum – a startling contrast after the splendours of the mansion. In the parkland surrounding the house pheasants and sheep graze, unconcerned by the occasional car and village boys who have made it their own adventure land. A modern pleasure garden has been made within the walls of the old, with a richly coloured herbaceous border, yew arbours, walks and a maze.

Roscommon and Around

Roscommon is the county town and the main shopping centre of the county, as well as a popular angling resort. It is dominated by the castle, the friary and the **old jail** in the Main Street. The last hangman of the jail was not a man but a woman known as Lady Betty, who was supposed to have agreed to do this grisly job to save her own head from the noose. The Georgian **courthouse**, opposite, has lovely rounded windows rescued by the Bank of Ireland. In the 8th century St Coman founded a monastery here from which the town gets its name, but there is sadly nothing left of it today. South of the town centre, off Abbey Street, is the ruined **Dominican friary** founded by Felim O'Conor, king of Connacht in 1253. His tomb is sculptured with figures representing gallowglasses – fierce warriors from the west of Scotland, hired by the Irish kings to fight the Norman and English invaders.

Roscommon Castle, north of the town off Castle Street (*always accessible*), was built in 1269 by Roger d'Ufford, Lord Justice for Ireland. Four years later it was razed to the ground by the Irish, built anew, and taken again by the O'Connors in 1340, who held it for more than 200 years. It is a typical Anglo-Norman fortress, quadrangular, with a tower at each angle and one on each side of the gateway. It began to fall into decay in the last years of the 17th century. The Roman Catholic **Church of the Sacred Heart** off Abbey Street is built of local cut limestone and was completed in 1925. Over the main door are some lovely glass mosaics constructed by the famous Italian firm of Salviati & Co. It also has a replica of the famous processional Cross of Cong, made in Fuerty in 1123 of oak decorated with animal designs in bronze gilt.

Five miles (8km) to the west of Roscommon on the R366 is the village of **Fuerty** itself, with the remains of a Franciscan church in which at least 100 priests were massacred in Cromwellian times by a Colonel Ormsby. The colonel, who is buried here, was known as *Riobard na nGligearnach* ('Robert of the Jingling Harness'), whose cruelties are still remembered in local stories. Between Fuerty and Athleague, on an unnumbered road by the River Suck, is the **Castlestrange** demesne. The house is a ruin, but under some trees is an egg-shaped Iron Age boulder, the Castlestrange Stone. It is covered in whorls and spirals that seem to have been potent ornamental symbols and were often used in the pre-Christian Celtic *La Tène* style. The land is privately owned, but it is unlikely that anyone will object to you visiting the stone.

The N61 from Roscommon to Athlone stays close to Lough Ree, but not close enough to get a proper look at it. If you cut down a small country lane to **Galey Castle**, just beyond Knockcroghery village, you will see the island of Inishcloraun in Lough Ree, where the legendary Queen Maeve retired to ponder on her eventful life and to find some peace (*see* **Old Gods and Heroes**, p.56). She used to bathe in a clear, fresh pool here, but an enemy pursued and killed her with a stone.

From **Lecarrow** another minor road leads you down to the **Castle of Rindown** (*always accessible*), a great fortress in the 13th century, with a rectangular keep within curtain walls. In the shelter of its stone walls a medieval Norman village grew up. A defensive ditch was built across the peninsula on which it was built, and it became one of the bases for the conquest of Connacht. Now it is an ivy-covered ruin and place of peace.

County Sligo

Writing in the 19th century about a tour of Ireland made with her husband, Mrs S. C. Hall dismisses Sligo in a few words with these lines: 'In scenery and character it so nearly resembles the adjoining county of Mayo that we pass over Sligo'. Nothing could be further from the truth. Sligo is somehow civilized, unlike the other counties in Connacht: there is order among the lakes and the glens, among the great table mountains and the open beaches.

From an artistic standpoint, Sligo is Yeats just as Wessex is Hardy, for there is hardly a knoll or stream in the county that did not stir his imagination. His brother Jack (1871–1957) used paint instead of words to capture the faces of old men at the Sligo races, or the special quality of the light that bathes figures on the beaches – a light that is very like that which plays around the coast of Brittany. Jack is always quoted

Getting There and Around

By Air
There is a Sligo–Dublin flight Mon–Fri.
Sligo Airport, Strandhill, t (071) 916 8280, www.sligoairport.com

By Rail
There's a daily service from Sligo to Dublin via Boyle; call t (071) 69888.

By Bus
Bus Éireann operates daily from Sligo to Dublin, Ballina, Derry and Galway. Local bus services also link the villages of Inniscrone and Tobercurry.
Sligo Bus Station, Lord Edward St, t (071) 916 0066

By Bike
Contact North West Tourism, t (071) 916 1201, www.irelandnorthwest.ie, for details of its Hiking and Biking Guide. For bike hire and equipment, try one of the following:
Bicycle Hire Conways, 6 High St, Sligo, t (071) 916 1370
Gary's Cycles, 5 Quay St, Sligo Town, t (071) 45418, gary@iol.ie

Festivals

January–February
Yeats Weekend Winter School,
t (071) 916 0291, www.yeats-sligo.com

June–July
Sligo Arts Festival, Sligo Town, t (071) 914 2693
Sligo County *Fleadh*, Strandhill, t (071) 916 7650
South Sligo Summer School of Traditional Music and Dancing, Tubercurry, t (071) 918 2151, www.ssschool.org

August
Ballymote Heritage Weekend, t (071) 918 3380
Gurteen Agricultural and Horse Show, Gurteen, t (071) 916 5082. End of month.
James Morrison Traditional Festival, Castlebaldwin, t (071) 916 5880
Michael Coleman Traditional Festival, Gurteen, t (071) 918 2599
Warriors' Festival, Strandhill, t (071) 916 8339. This incorporates the **Culleenamore Horse and Pony Races** and the **Warriors' Run** to Queen Maeve's legendary grave, on Knocknarea Mountain.
Yeats International Summer School, Sligo Town, t (071) 9142693, www.yeats-sligo.com

October
Ballintogher Feis, Ballintogher, t (071) 916 4250
Sligo International Choral Festival, Sligo Town, t (071) 917 0733

November
Sean Nós **Singing**, Coleman Heritage Centre, Gurteen, t (071) 918 2599, www.colemanirishmusic.com

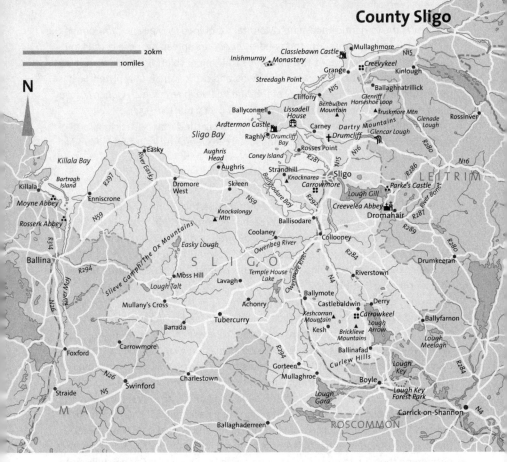

20km
10miles

N

as saying, 'Sligo was my school and the sky above it', and it was William Butler Yeats' wish that he should be buried under 'bare Ben Bulben's head'. All the places that inspired Yeats are still largely untouched; they are brought to your notice occasionally by discreet Tourism Ireland notices that quote the name and the line from the poem in which they are mentioned.

The two brothers became intimately bound up in Sligo through their maternal grandparents, the Pollexfens, who were millers and small shipowners. They used to spend their school holidays with them, travelling from London where their father, John, tried to earn a living as a portrait painter. They occupy such an important part in the artistic and literary history of Ireland in the early 20th century that one can hardly do justice to them in a guide book. Suffice it to say that if you obtain a copy of William Butler's collected poems, and make sure you visit the county museum in order to see the paintings by Jack, you will know why.

Besides being so beautiful, Sligo is famous for its traditional fiddle music, for fishing and for its fabulous hoard of prehistoric remains. In the vicinity of Carrowmore there is a huge cemetery with tombs dating from the Mesolithic and Neolithic Stone Ages.

Close by is the romantic Knocknarea Mountain, crowned by Maeve's Cairn, one of the highlights of a Sligo tour. Ring forts and *crannógs* are spread over the county and date from the Bronze Age. At this time, the local king or chieftain would have lived in and ruled from the fort. There were no towns, and cattle were highly prized. So it is understandable that the epic story of the *Táin Bó Cuailnge*, in which Queen Maeve plays such a central part, should describe a war over a bull (*see* p.57).

The people in these parts are mainly sheep- and cattle-farmers. The climate is similar to that in the rest of Ireland; and it has the wonderful light that is found all along the west coast.

History

The chief Gaelic families of Sligo were the O'Haras, the O'Conors and the O'Dowds; and since the Anglo-Normans did not reach Sligo until the mid 13th century, these families continued with their own private quarrels and territorial struggles. When the Normans did arrive, in the persons of the Fitzgeralds and the Burkes and their followers, they failed to maintain their grants of land. Therefore, up until the early 17th century, the Celtic culture and native Brehon laws continued to function alongside the English administrative structure.

From 1585 onwards there was a gradual change in land ownership and in the Celtic order of society. Elizabethans and later Cromwellian soldiers were granted lands, which in numerous cases were unoccupied church lands, or lands that had never been permanently settled. The population of Ireland was extremely small at that time, and many of the farmers moved their cattle from one pasture to another. Of course, some tribal lands were confiscated and granted to new settlers, but on the whole, English families settled into Sligo fairly peacefully. The names Phibbs, Crofton, Perceval, Ormsby, Parke, Irwin, Gore, Jones and Cooper date from these times. Today their descendants farm the land and maintain their wonderful homes by opening them up to guests. You can stay with the O'Haras at Coopershill House or the Percevals at Temple House (*see* 'Where to Stay', p.325). Each family represents a strand of Sligo's history.

Sligo Town was badly sacked and burned during the 1641 Rebellion, and later was held for the Jacobites in the wars of the 1690s. The whole county suffered terribly during the famine of the 1840s. Thousands died or emigrated to the New World; this struck the death knell for the Gaelic peasant culture, which had so far survived the vicissitudes of the centuries since the English invaded. Gaelic ceased to be the everyday language of the peasants, and many of the folk stories and traditions would have been lost forever if it had not been for enthusiasts and antiquarians such as Lady Gregory (1852–1932) and Yeats. They and others collected much folk material and later, in 1904, they and J. M. Synge (1871–1909) set up the Abbey Theatre in Dublin, which produced many Irish sagas.

During the 18th and 19th centuries, Sligo Town was a large port. Its industries were distilling, brewing, linen manufacture, milling, and rope- and leather-making. The famine hit the economy very hard, and it took many years to recover. Today, the county is prosperous again, with most people working in agriculture.

Sligo Town and Environs

Sligo, with only 20,000 souls, is the largest town in north-west Ireland. It has a great deal of colourful charm, and a feeling of centuries-old importance and prosperity. People come from their farms in the countryside to shop, socialize, go to the cinema or theatre and to attend the large hospital. The town centres around two bridges over the River Garavogue. There are attractive 18th-century buildings and some rather ugly 20th-century office blocks, hotels and supermarkets. The streets are always busy and quite congested with traffic, so if you have a car it would be wise to leave it in the car park off Wine Street.

In the **Anglican cathedral** in St John Street, designed by Richard Cassels, is a brass memorial to Susan Mary Yeats, mother of William and Jack. The cathedral itself dates from the 14th century and has been restored several times. It is a cruciform shape, in the perpendicular style, with a huge tower. The **Catholic cathedral**, made out of local limestone, is next door. This Romanesque building has a beautiful high altar, and a fine peal of bells. It was completed in 1874. **Sligo Abbey**, a graceful ruined Dominican priory off Abbey Street, was founded in 1252 but reconstructed in the 15th century after being burnt. It then suffered the usual fate of Irish monasteries, and was destroyed by the Cromwellians. The abbey ruins have been tidied up and some conservation work has been carried out by the Office of Public Works. Inside are monuments to the local Gaelic nobility, and some fine cloisters. The tower and the cloister, the east window and the high altar were added during the 15th century. The key to the abbey is available at any time from the caretaker; directions to his house are on the entrance gate.

Sligo Town Hall and **Courthouse** were built in the late 19th century, and you can visit them in the course of an interesting walking route devised by and available from the tourist office. As you wander, you may notice the shabby backyards of the houses sloping down to the River Garavogue, although the owners of the shops and pubs in the streets have made an effort to look after their handsome Edwardian frontages.

You can easily spend a delightful couple of hours in the **County Museum and Art Gallery** housed in the County Library building in Stephen Street; the custodians are charming, and the collection of pictures by Jack Yeats, Paul Henry, Nora McGuinness, Sean Keating and others is inspiring. The **Sligo County Museum** (*open June–Sept Tue–Sat 10.30–12 noon and 2–4.50, Oct–May daily 2–4.50; adm; t (071) 914 1623*) in the building attached to the library has exhibits of prehistoric interest and items on folk life and on the Anglo-Irish war of 1919–1921. It also has a section on the Yeats family – William, Jack and sisters Lily and Holly. At one time they set up a publishing press and started different cottage industries. W. B. Yeats won the Nobel Prize in 1923, and this is proudly displayed. The **Sligo Art Gallery** (*same hrs as museum; t (071) 9145847, www. sligoartgallery.com*), in the Yeats Memorial Building at Hyde Bridge, holds impressive travelling art shows by national and international artists. It also contains papers and books of special interest to Yeats scholars. There is another gallery, the **Model Arts and Nilard Gallery** (*t (071) 9141405, www.modelart.ie*) on The Mall, which hosts travelling exhibitions and is developing its own art collection.

Tourist Information

Sligo: Temple St, t (071) 9161201, and
Yeats Building, Hyde Bridge, t (071) 9142693
See also *www.discoversligo.com*.

Internet Access

Cygo Internet Café, 19 O'Connell St, Sligo,
t (071) 914 0082. *Closed Sun.*
Galaxy Cyber Café, Millbrook, Riverside,
Sligo, t (071) 914 0441

Shopping

Books

Book Nest, Rockwood Parade (beside river),
t (071) 914 7306, *www.booknest.ie*
Keohane's, Castle St, Sligo, t (071) 914 2597.
Irish-interest books.
The Winding Stair, Hyde Bridge,
t (071) 914 1244

Crafts

Benbulben Pottery, Branley's Yard,
Rathcormac, t (071) 914 6929
Carraig Donn, O'Connell St, Sligo, t (071) 914
4158. Aran sweaters and other knitwear.
The Cat & the Moon, 4 Castle St, Sligo, t (071)
914 3686, *www.thecatandthemoon.com*.
Pretty handicrafts and jewellery.
Dolly's Cottage Craft Centre,
Strandhill, t (071) 9160839
Michael Kennedy Ceramics,
Market St, Sligo, t (071) 916 2586
Michael Quirke, Wine St, Sligo, t (071) 914 2624.
Sculptures in wood on mythological themes.
Mullaney Bros, 9 O'Connell St, Sligo,
t (071) 914 0718. A good place to get hold
of tweeds and cashmeres.
Sligo Crystal and Giftware, 2 Hyde Bridge,
Sligo, t (071) 914 3440

Food and Drink

Cosgrove's, 32 Market St, Sligo, t (071) 914 2809.
An old-fashioned deli crammed with goodies.
Gourmet Parlour, Bridge St, Sligo, t (071) 914
4617. Delectable chocolate cakes and breads.
A catering service is available.
Tír Na nÓg, Grattan St, Sligo, t (071) 916 2752.
Fresh vegetables, Irish cheeses, seaweed,
herbs, shampoos and soaps.

Sports and Activities

Boat Hire

Blue Lagoon Bar, Sligo, t (071) 914 2530.
Boat hire on Lough Gill.

Fishing

For advice on **coarse fishing** in the River
Owenbeg and Lough Glencar, and for tackle
and equipment, contact the following:
Barton Smith, 4 Hyde Bridge, Sligo Town,
t (071) 914 2356, *www.bartonsmith.ie*
Irish Angling Services, Ballyconnell,
Co. Cavan, t (049) 952 6258
Shannon Regional Fisheries (Angling Section),
t (0509) 21777. Northern Fisheries waters
information and share certificates.

For **sea-angling** advice and boat hire, call:
Lomax Boats and Angling, Mullaghmore,
t (071) 916 6124
Tommy McCallion, Rosses Point, t (071) 914 2391

Golf

County Sligo Golf Club, Rosses Point,
t (071) 917 7134, *www.countysligogolfclub.ie*.
A championship links course.
Strandhill Golf Club, Strandhill,
t (071) 916 8188, *www.strandhillgc.com*

Pleasure Cruises

Wild Rose Waterbus, t (071) 916 4266 or t 0872
598869. Cruises on Lough Gill accompanied

The large municipal **Doorly Park** bordering the River Garavogue has lovely walks with
wonderful views of Lough Gill and the mountains. Inside, **Sligo Racecourse** hosts races
in April, June and August. A highlight of a tour of Sligo is a boat ride past the wooded
scenery of Lough Gill (*see* above). You can drive round Lough Gill, taking the R286 to
Dromahair in County Leitrim then the R287 to the N4, going back into Sligo Town.
Don't forget to go around **Parke's Castle**, over the border in County Leitrim (*see* p.334).

by recitations of Yeats' poetry, visiting the Lake Isle of Innisfree and Parke's Castle. The 60min tour departs from Doorly Park or Parke's Castle in Sligo Town, Mar–Oct.

Ponytrekking
Sligo Riding Centre, Carrowmore, t (071) 916 1353, *www.irelandonhorseback.com*

Seaweed Baths
Celtic Seaweed Baths, Strandhill, Sligo, t (071) 916 8686, *www.celticseaweedbaths.com*. A treat not to be missed.

Surfing
Catch some waves at **Strandhill**. For advice, information and equipment contact:
Call of the Wild, Stephen St, Sligo, t (071) 914 6905
Perfect Day Surf Shop & School, Strandhill, t (071) 9128488, *www.perfectdaysurfing.com*

Tours
There are signposted **walking tours** around Sligo Town and **guided tours** every weekday in summer; contact the tourist office for details.

Where to Stay and Eat

Sligo Town
Aisling, Cairns Hill, Sligo, t (071) 916 0704, *aislingsligo@eircom.net* (*inexpensive*). A B&B overlooking Sligo Bay.
Lissadell View, Tullyhill, Rathcormac, Drumcliffe, t (071) 914 3892 (*inexpensive*). A peaceful B&B with scenic views.
Bistro Bianconi, 44 O'Connell St, Sligo, t (071) 914 1744 (*moderate*). Pasta and pizza to take away or eat in a pleasant modern interior.
Coach Lane Restaurant, 1 Lord Edward St, Sligo, t (071) 916 2417 (*moderate*). Imaginative modern cuisine.

Fiddlers Creek, Rockwood Parade, Sligo, t (071) 914 1866 (*moderate*). The place to come for variety of traditional or Louisiana-style steaks, or globally inspired dishes such as crispy honey roast duckling, wild mushroom tagliatelle, salmon, sole and vegetarian offerings. There are in-house DJs and live bands 4 evenings a week, so this is not the place for a romantic tête-à-tête.
Le Montmartre, Market Yard, Sligo, t (071) 916 9901 (*moderate*). A French-run restaurant with a wide-ranging menu, including locally sourced seafood dishes. *Closed Mon.*
Hargadon's, O'Connell St, Sligo, t (071) 70933 (*inexpensive*). An atmospheric pub with cosy snugs, old adverts and mirrors decorated with gold-painted slogans of whiskey and Guinness. *Closed eves.*
Kate's Kitchen, 3 Castle St, Sligo, t (071) 914 3022 (*inexpensive*). Deli salads and sandwiches to take away.

Entertainment and Nightlife

Theatre
The Factory, Sligo, t (071) 917 0431, *www.blueraincoat.com*. Productions by the Blue Raincoat Theatre Company.
The Hawk's Well Theatre, Temple St, Sligo, t (071) 916 1526, *www.hawkswell.com*. A venue hosting both revivals and pieces of contemporary Irish theatre.

Traditional Music
Fureys, Bridge St, Sligo, t (071) 914 3825. Tue–Sat evenings.
Leitrim Bar, The Mall, Sligo, t (071) 914 3721
McGarrigle's Bar, O'Connell St, t (071) 71193. Thur and Sun evenings, plus lunch sessions.
McLaughlin's, t (071) 914 4209. Nightly.

Strandhill and Carrowmore
If you take the R292 going west of Sligo Town, after 3 miles (4.8km) you come to **Strandhill**, a popular village resort on the rocky coast (also reached by city bus from Sligo). It has rather too much concrete and is not greatly attractive, but the strand is superb. The hard sand stretches for miles and the waves are good for bodysurfing. Huge dunes dominate the shore to the south-west of the seafront car park, and you

might find beach pebbles with interesting fossil remains. Just as you enter Strandhill on the R292 is **Dolly's Cottage** (*open July and Aug daily 2–6; t (071) 9167564*), a typical early-19th-century rural dwelling. It consists of a few simply furnished rooms, a mud floor and a thatched roof.

From every direction in this area you can see **Knocknarea Mountain**, which is topped by Maeve's Cairn. To climb it, continue along the R292 for a few miles and take the little road marked 'Glen', which ascends the lower slopes. (You will know if you have gone too far because just beyond the turning for the Glen road is a restaurant called Glen Lodge.) From the Glen road, you get a lovely view of the hummocky green fields down to the shore. You will come to a farm where it is possible to leave your car, as long as you are tactful and polite. The walk to the summit (1,978ft/603m) is along a track of curiously moulded limestone, with orchids and primroses growing either side. The cairn itself is 33ft (10m) high by 197ft (6m) wide, a huge mound of weather-beaten stone. It is reported to be the burial place of Maeve, Queen of Connacht, who challenged the forces of Ulster to a battle over a bull. The famous story is contained in the *Táin Bó Cuailgne*, the longest and most important of the Ulster cycle of heroic tales (*see* p.57). The origins of the *Táin* are ancient and pre-Christian, though it was actually written down by monks in the 12th century. Maeve is thought to have lived around the time of Christ, but the cairn may well be Bronze Age. Archaeologists believe that within it may be a passage tomb similar to that at Newgrange in County Meath, which was built by Stone Age farmers in about 3000 BC. As yet no one has excavated it, probably because it would be very expensive to undo its massive structure – and it would be very sad if they did.

Continue on through the crossroads at Knocknarea Church, and instead of rejoining the R292 take the turn south-east. You are now on the right road for **Carrowmore**, about 3 miles (4.8km) further on. This amazing megalithic Stone Age cemetery spreads over many small fields. The excavated burial chambers contain cremated remains dating from 3000 BC. There are circles, passage graves and dolmens – each has a little notice warning that it is a national monument, but unfortunately since the 19th century more than 100 have been destroyed, and only 40 remain.

Heading back towards Sligo town you see **Cummeen Strand**, which stretches up to Rosses Point. This expanse of sand and water is mentioned in Yeats' poem *Red Hanrahan's Song*; here the River Garavogue flows into the sea. You can walk or drive out to **Coney Island** from the Strandhill side when the tide is out. (Coney is supposed to have given its name to the New York pleasure island.) Only a few people live on it, and the beaches surrounding it are tranquil. You will be able to watch wild duck and waders; during the winter months brent geese feed on the mudflats.

Rosses Point to Glencar

Rosses Point, a seaside village and resort that lies 5 miles (8km) to the north of Sligo, is reached by city bus from Sligo or by following the R281 along the curve of Sligo Bay. The village is long and straggling, with plenty of pubs and pleasant places to eat. It has a first-class golf course that is used for the West of Ireland Amateur Open Golf Championship every year during the Easter weekend. At Dead Man's Point the yacht club and an open-air swimming pool are a hive of activity and colour and, during the summer, pleasure boat trips around Sligo Bay leave daily from Rosses Point pier. There are many Dead Man's Points all over this part of the coast, probably because the tides are so very treacherous. This one is supposed to owe its name to a long-dead foreign seaman who was buried rapidly at sea because the boat had to be away before the tide changed. He slid into the water accompanied by a loaf of bread, just in case he was not quite dead.

A trip to **Glencar** is a very pleasant excursion if you are staying in Sligo Town. Leave Sligo on the N16 for Manorhamilton, and after about 10 miles (16km) a left turn will signpost you to **Glencar Waterfall**. The road takes you along the edge of Glencar Lough, and steep-sided mountains rear up against the sky. The Differeen River feeds the lough while the Drumcliff River runs out the opposite end. This spot is popular with salmon and sea-trout anglers. A small car park marks the path to the waterfall, which drops 49ft (15m); it is particularly impressive after heavy rains. In Yeats' poem 'The Stolen Child', he talks of the Glencar pools 'that scarce could bathe a star'. The pools are now bordered by a concrete path but are still very beautiful, with the noisy stream and a mass of rhododendrons around them.

Around County Sligo

North Sligo

Drumcliff and Lissadell House

If you follow the N15 northwards towards Donegal, after a distance of about 5 miles (8km) you will find yourself in **Drumcliff**. This ancient Christian monastic site still has the remains of the old monastic enclosure and a fine 10th-century high cross that is carved with biblical scenes. St Columba (*see* p.47 and p.338) founded a monastery at Drumcliff during the 6th century, before sailing away to Iona. The road divides the site in two, with the cross on your right and the stump of a round tower on the left. The graveyard of the Church of Ireland church, which you will also see to your right, contains the **grave of W. B. Yeats**. Yeats' great-grandfather was the rector of this simple Georgian Protestant church, and the poet is buried here, under his beloved Ben Bulben. He has a very plain headstone with his own epitaph 'Cast a cold eye on life, on Death/Horseman, pass by'.

Just past Drumcliff, to the west an unnumbered road via Carney leads you to **Lissadell House** (*open May–mid-Sept daily 11–6; guided tour; adm; t (071) 916 3150, www.lissadellhouse.com*), with its grounds swallowed up by Forestry Commission conifers. The house is the home of the Gore-Booths, a family who came to Sligo during the early 17th century. Like many of the Irish gentry, the Gore-Booths were great travellers and worked all over the British Empire. They brought home all sorts of weird and wonderful things, and Lissadell is a rich repository of furniture, pictures and books. Sir Robert Gore-Booth built the house during the troubled years that culminated in the famine of the 1840s, and mortgaged the estate to help the poor during the famine. His son Sir Henry is famous for sailing to the rescue of the Arctic explorer Leigh Smith. The following generation included Eva and Constance, both of whom were great friends of W. B. Yeats, who stayed in the house frequently during the second decade of the 20th century. Constance married a Polish artist and became Countess Markievicz, and became deeply involved with the struggle for Irish independence. Having won a seat for the Sinn Féin party, she, like the rest of them, refused to take up her seat in Westminster and sat instead for the Revolutionary Parliament called the *Dáil Éireann* as the minister for Labour.

The building is in plain Georgian style with a cavernous porch. It is in a lovely situation looking onto the sea, Knocknarea and Ben Bulben, but it is also very large and a little rundown. In the centre is a two-storey hallway lined with Doric columns leading to a double staircase of Kilkenny marble. Downstairs in the vast kitchen you can have tea and coffee made under conditions reminiscent of the 1920s; there is no drinking water or electricity in this part of the house, and buckets of water have to be lugged down the stairs. The forestry lands around Lissadell House have picnic sites, and in the winter months you may be lucky and see skeins of barnacle geese wheeling in the sky, since there is a huge colony of them here. The two south-facing beaches that border the forest are reputedly the warmest in the county.

Tourist Information

Enniscrone Tourist Office, Unit 2, Castle Park House, t 096 36746, *www.enniscroneonline. com*. Open summer.

Shopping

Crafts and Antiques

Benbulben Pottery, Rathcormac, t (071) 914 6929
Mews Art Gallery, Rathcormac, t (071) 914 3689
Yeats' Country Antiques,
    Rathcormac Craft Village, t (071) 914 5589

Sports and Activities

Fishing

Coarse and game fishing can be had on the Owenmore River and lakes in its system, which produce great pike, bream and rudd. The sister of the Owenmore, the Owenbeg, is known for its sea-trout, as is Glencar Lough.

Sea-angling can be done from the shore at Enniscrone Strand, Enniscrone Pier, Easky Quay, Kilrusheighter Strand, Mullaghmore Pier, Mermaid's Cove and Milk Haven.

Brendan Merriman, Mullaghmore, t (072) 41874
Gerry Sheerin, Grange, t (071) 91 66472
Lough Arrow Boats, t (071) 916 5491. Boat hire.

Golf

Enniscrone Golf Club, Enniscrone, t (096) 36297, *www.enniscronegolf.com*. A high-quality course amid magnificent scenery.
Tubercurry Golf Club, t (071) 918 5849

Pleasure Cruises

There are waterbus tours on Lough Gill, and excursions to Inishmurray Island Apr–Oct. Call:
Peter Power, Mullaghmore, t (0872) 576268
Rodney Lomax, Mullaghmore, Cliffony,
    t (071) 916 6124
Tommy McCallion, Rosses Point, t (071) 914 2391
Wild Rose Waterbus, t (071) 916 4266. Tours of Lough Gill (*see also* p.334).

Ponytrekking

Ard Chuain Equestrian Centre, Corballa,
    near Ballina, t (096) 45084
Horse Holiday Farm Ltd, Temple Mount, Grange,
    t (071) 916 6152, .*www.horse-holiday-farm.com*.
    Daily pony hire or 7- to 14-day trail rides through the mountains and along the coast, staying in B&Bs or country-house hotels.

Raghly and the Gleniff Horseshoe Loop

The road past Lissadell continues west towards the tiny fishing harbour of **Raghly**, which is surrounded by stunning views of Drumcliff Bay and the mountains all around. On the way there you will pass **Ardtarmon Castle**, built in the 17th-century as a semi-fortified manor house by an ancestor of the Gore-Booths. It is privately owned and has been restored.

Continuing along the coast on this tiny unnumbered road, on your left you will see **Knocklane Hill**. This was the site of a Celtic promontory fort and a Martello tower, built as a lookout post in the uncertain times of the Napoleonic era. It is a short and exhilarating climb to the top of the hill, and on a fine day you will be rewarded by unsurpassable views. The beaches along this stretch of coastline are very isolated and there is much bird-life. Sand covered much of the headland until bent grass was sown in the 19th century by Lord Palmerston, the British prime minister. The beach at **Streedagh**, signposted to the left, has magnificent sand dunes, and the limestone rocks contain fossil coral formed about 4 million years ago. All around the coast are wrecks of the warships of the Spanish Armada. 'The Rock of the Spaniards', just to the north of Streedagh, was the place where, in 1588, three Armada ships foundered. Contemporary accounts tell us that 1,100 bodies were laid out on the beach at a time, and that most of the men who reached the shore were stripped and killed.

Woodlands Equestrian Centre, Tubercurry, t (071) 918 4207

Seaweed Baths

Kilcullen's Seaweed Baths, Cliff Rd, Enniscrone, t (096) 36238. *Closed Mon–Fri Nov–Apr.*

Surfing

Easkey and Enniscrone are good spots. For advice, information and equipment contact: **Easkey Surf and Information Centre**, Easkey, t (096) 49428

Where to Stay

Coopershill House, Riverstown, t (071) 916 5108, *www.coopershill.com (expensive)*. A Georgian mansion in its own wooded parkland, with the most delightful aspects of a gentleman's residence, including spacious rooms filled with furniture and books and warmed by crackling log fires. Dinner is available.

Cromleach Lodge, Castlebaldwin, t (071) 916 5155, *www.cromleach.com (expensive)*. A very comfortable option. Delicious breakfasts are accompanied by charming views over Lough Arrow. *Closed Nov–Jan.*

Markree Castle, Collooney, t (071) 916 7800, *www.markreecastle.ie (expensive)*. A grand country-house hotel with a castellated façade and reception rooms with tall mirrors and Louis Philippe-style plasterwork dating from 1845. Guestrooms are very comfortable, the views over the countryside are superb, and formal gardens lead down to the River Unsin. The **Knockmuldowney Restaurant** (*see* p.326) has a good reputation.

Temple House, Ballymote, t (071) 918 3329, *www.templehouse.ie (expensive)*. A rambling mansion made even grander in the 1860s by a nabob ancestor of the present family who own it. It has a lovely, slightly faded Victorian feel. The owners are organic farmers, and the breakfasts are particularly delicious. Fresh produce is served in the dining room (*luxury*; dinner with advance notice), including lamb and beef from the estate farm and dishes such as Cashel blue cheese tart followed by pear croustade. Boats are available for pike and perch fishing on Temple House Lake, and shooting for woodcock, snipe and duck on the estate can be arranged. Note that scented cosmetics and perfumes must not be worn, as the owner is chemically sensitive. *Closed Dec–Mar.*

It is not surprising that the people of **Inishmurray**, 4 miles (6.4km) off the coast, abandoned their lands and houses in the 1950s, for life here was very hard. This island used to be famous for its brand of *poteen*. Now it is famous for the early-Christian relics that have survived: beehive huts, small rectangular stone oratories, open-air altars, pillars and tombstones are dotted all over the island. The **monastery** in the middle of the island was probably built on a Druidic site, for one of the oratories is known as the Temple of Fire, and round about are quite a few stones, known as 'cursing stones', that are thought to have been used in Druidic rituals. Trips out to the island can be organized easily throughout the summer months from Mullaghmore (*see* 'Sports and Activities', p.324).

North of Cliffony, a rock peninsula projects into Donegal Bay. Its sandy beach has encouraged the growth of the small resort of **Mullaghmore**. On the headland is a Victorian Gothic castle – **Classiebawn** (*not open to public*), once the home of Earl Mountbatten of Burma. In 1979 the Earl and members of his family were killed by an IRA bomb on their boat in the bay below.

Return to the N15, and at the hamlet of **Creevykeel** by the crossroads stop to look at a court tomb regarded as one of the finest in Ireland. It consists of a circular ritual court bounded by upright stones. Opposite the entrance are two burial chambers under a lintel that date from between 3500 and 3000 BC.

Ardtarmon House, Ardtarmon, 11 miles (18km) northwest of Sligo on Drumcliff–Raghly road, t (071) 9163156, *www.ardtarmon.com* (*moderate*). A peaceful country house with mountain views, a 19th-century ambiance, and simple breakfasts (plus dinners with advance notice). There is an easy walk to the sea nearby. *Closed mid-Dec–early Jan.*
Beach Hotel, The Harbour, Mullaghmore, t (071) 916 6103, *www.beachhotelmullaghmore.com* (*moderate*). A comfortable old hotel on the seafront, with a pool, gym and sauna.
Ross House, Riverstown, t (071) 916 5140 (*moderate*). Comfortable and friendly farmhouse accommodation. It's good for children – there's lots of activity on the farm.

Self-catering
William Coleman, Lavagh, Tubercurry, t (071) 918 4053 (*moderate–expensive*). A 2-bedroom thatched cottage near the mountains.
Ardtarmon House, Ardtarmon, t (071) 916 3156, *www.ardtarmon.com* (*inexpensive*). Five cottages attached to the estate (*see above*).
North West Tourism, Sligo, t (071) 916 1201, *www.irelandnorthwest.ie* (*inexpensive*). Cottages on Lissadell House estate, plus other properties in the area.

Eating Out

Cromleach Lodge, Castlebaldwin, t (071) 916 5155, *www.cromleach.com* (*expensive*). A Michelin-rated hotel-restaurant (*see* p.325).
Eithna's Seafood Restaurant, The Harbour, Mullaghmore, t (071) 91 66407 (*expensive*). A good fish place; try a seafood platter.
Knockmuldowney Restaurant, Markree Castle, Collooney, t (071) 916 7800 (*moderate*). Tasty food, an excellent wine list and friendly service in a hotel in an atmospheric early-19th-century castle (*see* p.325).
Yeats Tavern, Drumcliff, t (071) 916 3117 (*moderate*). A bar-café and a restaurant with facilities for children. The salads are good.

Entertainment and Nightlife

Traditional Music
Beach Bar, Aughris, t (071) 916 6703
Ellen's Pub, Maugherow, near Grange, t (071) 916 3761. A tourist attraction in its own right, with a thatched roof and frequent *seisiúns*.
The Thatch, Ballisodare, t (071) 916 7288. A place well known for its *seisiúns*.

Cross over the N15 and continue for 5¾ miles (9km) along the unnumbered road leading to Ballaghnatrillick Bridge. Cross the bridge and take the right-hand turn onto the **Gleniff Horseshoe Loop**. This road runs into the heart of the Dartry Mountains, with their tumbling streams and desolate limestone cliffs. A left turn takes you to Truskmore Mountain, which rises to 2,115ft (645m). From the car park for the RTÉ transmitter station, a short walk takes you to the top for a wonderful view. Close to the summit are the entrances to Ireland's highest caves. These form part of an ancient underground system truncated by the glacier that formed the Gleniff valley. One of these caves is supposed to be where Diarmuid and Gráinne slept when they were fleeing from the wrath of King Fionn MacCumhaill. Diarmuid and Gráinne are the Irish equivalent of Tristan and Iseult: every cave, dolmen and *cromlech* seems to be named after them (*see* **Old Gods and Heroes**, p.54 and p.56). From here, you can follow the loop road around to Cliffoney and back on to the N15, or turn left along the old route and rejoin the N15 at the Mullaghnaneane crossroads.

West Sligo

Killala Bay, Sligo Bay and into the Ox Mountains

The western parts of County Sligo make up a variety of handsome seascapes, mountainous bogland and pretty lakes. The coastal stretch has been developed for holiday-makers, whilst the mountains behind are wild and relatively unexplored. The R297 branches off the N59 between Sligo and Ballina in County Mayo and meanders through the villages along the coast. **Enniscrone** (or Inishcrone) is a holiday resort on Killala Bay with a long, sandy strand that is ideal for bathing. It also has a marina with berths for yachts and deep-sea fishing boats for hire. There is an excellent bath-house offering saltwater seaweed baths and steam baths in your own little wooden box (*see* 'Sports and Activities', p.325). The pier and breakwater provide excellent fishing and bird-watching opportunities, and there is lovely walking country up the Moy estuary to Ballina. At the north end of town and in ruins is **Nolan's Castle**, an early-17th-century semi-fortified manor house.

This area is dotted with the ruins of castles, some of which have romantic associations. **O'Dowd's Castle**, 3 miles (4.8 km) to the south of Enniscrone, is one such ruin. A local story tells of how one of the O'Dowds captured a mermaid and stole her magic cloak, and so was able to change her into a mortal woman. She bore him seven children but always longed to return to the sea. When she at last regained her cloak she changed back into a mermaid, took her children to a place called Cruckacorma, in Scurmore, and transformed them into pillar stones. She then returned to the sea. (The pillar stones are actually on a tumulus, and are known locally as 'the Children of the Mermaid'). Two miles (3.2km) north of Enniscrone is **Castle Firbis**, the ruined stronghold of a family well known for their poetry and annals. The MacFirbis Clan were the hereditary poets and historiographers to the O'Dowds between the 14th and 17th centuries. They had a school of learning here where many important manuscripts were compiled. The most important to survive are *The Yellow Book of*

Leacan (*c.* 1391), now in Trinity College, Dublin; *The Great Book of Leacan*, compiled between 1416 and 1480, now in the Royal Irish Academy, Dublin; and *The Book of Genealogies of Ireland*, compiled between 1585 and 1671, and now in University College, Dublin. One of the last MacFirbis scribes was employed by Sir James Ware (1594–1666) to prepare transcripts and translations from the Gaelic. Ware, an antiquary and historian, was responsible for preserving and collecting valuable historical material on Gaelic Ireland. As a member of parliament and the auditor-general for Ireland, he was in a good position to help native Celts such as the MacFirbis clan.

Easky is a fishing village 8 miles (12.9km) from Enniscrone on the coast road. The village is guarded by two Martello towers, built to raise the alarm if Napoleon tried to invade. It is famous for its waves in winter and it has become something of a surfer's hangout, although there are also other watersports facilities. Two miles (3.2 km) east on the R297, by the roadside, is the split rock also known as **Fionn MacCumhaill's Fingerstone**. This is said to have been split by MacCumhaill's sword – Irish heroes always have superhuman strength – and is very impressive. It may in fact have been created in the Ice Age. Legend tells that the rock will close on anybody who dares to pass through the split three times.

From Dromore West the R297 road joins the N59. Take the mountain road, signposted on the left, along a scenic route to Easky Lough. If you continue on into the Ox Mountains, then just after the hamlet of Moss Hill you can turn right for Gleneask and **Lough Talt**. The views in this wild and isolated country are fabulous, and it is possible to walk from Lough Easky to Mullany's Cross. Ask in the local tourist office for *Irish Walks Guide 3, Northwest*, by Simms and Foley, which details this route. The R294 traverses the region and leads to the market town of Tubercurry (*see* p.329). Just before you reach it, at **Banada** is the ruin of **Corpus Christi Priory**, beautifully situated on the River Moy. The priory was the first Irish house of the Augustinian Friars of the Regular Observance and was founded by the O'Haras in 1423.

Skreen to Coolaney

Another lovely route can be taken into the Ox Mountains from **Skreen**, which is a tiny little place just off the N59 between Ballisodare and Dromore West. It is worth stopping off at the **Church of Ireland graveyard** to see the carved box tombs that date from between 1774 and 1866. The Black family tomb is a masterpiece of carving. On the north side it shows a ploughman in a top hat, tail coat, buckled shoes guiding a plough. The west end has a cherub's head and a skull and crossbones carved in high relief. The minor road leads you past tumbling streams and grand mountain scenery, past Lough Achtree and on to the scenic route signposted 'Ladies Brae'. Reforestation has changed the face of the mountains: the subtle browns, greens and purples have given way to the standardized green of the sitka spruce and lodgepole pine. But the skies and the shapes of the mountains are still magnificent, and the forests will one day yield a good cash-crop. As you journey closer to **Coolaney** the road runs close to the Owenbeg River, which makes a very pleasant picnic spot. And as you enter Coolaney you might notice the Pack Horse Bridge, which has many arches but is in a very bad state of repair, with several trees growing up in it.

Just outside Coolaney, about 1½ miles (2.4km) east on an unnumbered road leading to Collooney, is the **Holy Well of Tobar Tullaghan**, also known as Hawk's Well. This tranquil place used to be a place of pilgrimage for many; during the medieval period it was regarded as one of the Wonders of Ireland, apparently gushing forth freshwater at one moment and saltwater at another. It is still thought that the water in the well ebbs and flows with the tide.

Close to Collooney and just off the N4 is **Markree Castle**, which was until recently a huge and derelict Gothic-style pile. Now beautifully restored, it is a hotel (*see* 'Where to Stay', p.325). This is an especially satisfactory state of affairs because the current owner, Charles Cooper, is a descendant of the Coopers who acquired the estate in the 17th century. The castle was built in 1802, when the 18th-century house was transformed by the designs of Francis Johnston (1760–1829).

Aughris to Ballisodare

The coastal stretch between Ballisodare and Skreen is very pretty. Make sure to visit the little fishing harbour of **Aughris** and walk around Aughris Head, then have a jar in the Beach Bar (*see* p.326), which is famous for its Saturday-night traditional music sessions. Though it has been badly modernized, you can admire the views from a cosy bench outside.

The cliff ledges of Aughris Head hold the nesting places of many different bird species, and Dunmoran Strand to the east is a lovely sandy beach. **Ballisodare** is a bit of a thoroughfare for traffic leaving Sligo Town for Ballina, but it's worth a stop to see the remains of a pre-Romanesque church here, and a 7th-century monastery that was founded by St Feichin of Fore in County Westmeath. The church overlooks the wooded edge of Ballisodare Bay. Close by is the ruin of a 15th-century church, almost buried in rubble from the quarry.

South Sligo

Tubercurry and Ballymote

Tubercurry (also known as Tobercurry) is a busy market town that hosts the Western Drama Festival. The festival is very well thought of for the quality of the productions and the range of different styles and interpretations. The town is also a good centre for anglers, being close to loughs Gara, Key, Arrow, Easky and Talt. Brown trout, pike and perch are the usual catches. Another excellent fishing centre to the north is **Ballymote**, which also has a ruined square Norman **castle** (*always accessible*) that was used as a major defensive post up until the 1690s. You get to it through the car park of the St John of God's Nursing Home near the railway station. While in the area, you could take the opportunity to stay in the intriguing 18th-century **Temple House**, situated off the N17 about 5 miles (8km) to the north-east (*see* 'Where to Stay', p.325).

Close by is **Achonry**, an early-Christian monastic site in a very ruined state that boasts a cathedral, the **Church of St Nathy** (CI). It dates from 1823, and on its east side are the ruins of a 15th-century church with a lofty square tower.

Gorteen and Lough Gara

Southeast of Tubercurry is the village of **Gorteen** (or Gurteen), which is recognized by traditional music-lovers as the centre of the distinctive Sligo flute-and-fiddle style. Sometimes you can hear the evocative airs and dancing tunes at the **Traditional Restaurant** and the **May Queen** in the centre of the town. Impromptu dancing may start up, which is the greatest fun. Courses are offered in traditional musical styles, songwriting, instrument playing and *sean-nós* singing at the **Coleman Heritage Centre** (*t (071) 918 2599, www.colemanirishmusic.com*) in Gorteen.

On the R294, 2 miles (3.2km) south-east of Gorteen at the Mullaghroe crossroads, is a 16th-century square stone **castle** consisting of a walled enclosure with six square towers and the remains of a curtain wall. It was the stronghold of the O'Garas, a ruling Gaelic family of that time. Fergal O'Gara, a patron of the monks, compiled the *Annals of the Four Masters* between 1623 and 1626. **Lough Gara** itself is set with tiny islands, some of them man-made *crannógs* that were inhabited by Iron-Age farmers.

Keshcorran and Carrowkeel

Over wooded and boggy lands to the north-east of Gorteen is the summit of **Keshcorran**, from where there are fantastic views of the surrounding countryside. (Get there by travelling cross-country on the minor road from Mullaghroe to Kesh. Just before you get to Kesh, cross the R295 running between Ballymore and Boyle.) Keshcorran has many caves on its west face, all associated with legendary characters such as Cormac MacArt, the wise and generous high king who ruled over the heroes of the Fianna (*see* p.54). On Garland Sunday (the last Sunday in July), locals still gather by the caves for prayers and chat in a tradition that stretches back thousands of years to celebrations in honour of the Celtic God Lugh.

Close by on a hill-top of the Bricklieve Range are the Bronze Age passage graves of **Carrowkeel**. You reach these via an untarred mountain road, just off the N4 between Castlebaldwin and Ballinafad, which takes you round the base of the hilltop on an approach from the north-west for a couple of miles (3.2km). The burial chambers were elaborately planned and set in round cairns, with commanding views of the land. The cruciform passage graves are narrow and roofed with large lintel stones, whilst the larger chambers are roofed with corbelled stone.

County Sligo has many interesting archaeological remains that possibly link up with the mythological stories of Ireland's past. The great and legendary battle between the Fomorians and the Tuatha Dé Danaan, which is related in the *Book of Invasions*, or *Lebor Gabala*, is reputed to have taken place near here, and it is said that the slain were buried here. Fourteen cairns are located on the spurs of promontories, but there is also a 'village' of 14 *clochans*. It is possible to enter a few of the tombs, one of which is lit up by the setting sun on the longest day of the year. This contrasts with the great passage tomb at Newgrange in County Meath, which is lit by the sun at sunrise on the shortest day of the year. Also in the area, at Riverstown, is **Sligo Folk Park** (*open May–Oct daily, call for times, t (071) 916 5001; open Nov–Apr by appointment; adm; coffee shop; www.sligofolkpark.com*), a community of traditional houses and cottages portraying a bygone Irish lifestyle.

County Leitrim

Leitrim is a very individual county, with a secret, forgotten feel to it; it is a good place for a quiet holiday. The region is long and narrow, having a foothold in the sea and stretching back to mountains, hills and streams. It is divided in two by Lough Allen, one of the many lakes of the Shannon river. It shares the beauty of Lough Gill and Lough Melvin with County Sligo, and has countless lakes of its own. The lakes are, by all accounts, teeming with bream, pike, perch, salmon and trout. The renovation of the 19th-century Ballinamore and Ballyconnell canal provides the link between the Shannon and the Erne, and cruisers are able to travel for 470 miles (750km) along tranquil inland waterways.

If you are a walker and anxious to be alone, the mountains around Manorhamilton are full of beauty; you will pass the remains of many deserted cottages on slopes where only sheep and cattle graze. The people of Leitrim are mainly small farmers, and the land has attracted quite a few outsiders or 'blow-ins', who are keen to own a smallholding and try organic methods. Trees thrive here, and the district immediately north of Lough Allen is planted with conifers. South of Slieve Anierin the county is covered by a belt of *drumlins*. These teardrop-shaped hills were left behind by retreating glaciers and are composed of gravel debris. Most of the Leitrim boundary with County Roscommon to the west is formed by the winding River Shannon.

History

Before County Leitrim was 'shired' in around 1585 by Elizabethan administrators, it was known as West Breffni. The principal *sept* of this area was O'Rourke, whose members lived around the tiny settlement of Leitrim. In the centuries leading up to the Anglo-Norman conquest, the O'Rourkes were continually involved in dynastic struggles for the high kingship of Ireland. In the 12th century, Tighernan O'Rourke was allied to Rory O'Connor, the high king. Dermot MacMurragh, the King of Leinster, coveted his position, and a struggle broke out. MacMurragh raided Breffni in 1152 and stole Devorgilla, O'Rourke's wife. This led to the banishment of MacMurragh in 1166, and the arrival of the Normans in 1169 to help him win his kingdom back. For Ireland, it was the beginning of a long and traumatic relationship with England. However, Breffni was hardly affected by the Normans, who kept themselves to the south, and the Gaelic system under the lordship of the O'Rourkes lasted until Elizabeth I mounted her conquest of Ireland.

Brian O'Rourke, the chieftain of the time, was one of the few Irish recorded who tried to rescue some of the Spanish sailors wrecked off the Sligo-Leitrim coast after storms drove the 1588 Armada onto the rocks. As a reprisal he was taken prisoner and hanged at Tyburn in 1590. His son, Brian of the Battleaxes, fought endlessly against the English and joined in the Nine Years' War against the Elizabethan Conquest with the Ulster lords O'Neill and Red Hugh O'Donnell. Their defeat at the Battle of Kinsale in 1601 spelled the end of their power, and the O'Rourke estate and castles were handed over to English and Scottish planters. The names Hamilton, St George, Harrison, Gore and Clements date from that time.

County Leitrim

The Gaelic system took a long time to break down. Turlough O'Carolan, the famous blind harper, composer and poet (1670–1733), lived in Mohill for a while, succoured by the Gaelic system of patronage and welcomed into the houses of peasants and gentry with his music. The Irish people everywhere still spoke Gaelic and remained fervent Catholics, which set them far apart from the new colonialists. The 1798

Rebellion bought bloodshed to Leitrim as the peasants joined in the French general Humbert's march to Ballinamuck, County Longford, from Mayo. Many of them were slaughtered. The potato famine and emigration took its toll during the 1840s, and by 1851 the population had dropped from 155,000 to 43,000. Today the population is about 28,000. One of the heroes of the Irish struggle for independence came from Leitrim: Seán MacDiarmada (1884–1916), who was born in Kiltyclogher, was one of the seven signatories of the proclamation of the republic in Easter Week 1916. He was court-martialled and executed in May 1916.

North Leitrim

Around Manorhamilton

Manorhamilton is situated at the meeting of four valleys in a setting of steep limestone hills and narrow ravines. It was built by Sir Frederick Hamilton, whose fine 17th-century mansion, now a ruin and cloaked in ivy, overlooks the town. At **Manorhamilton Castle Heritage Centre** (*open May–Sept Tue–Sat 11–6, Sun 2–7; craft shop, café, herb garden, picnic area; adm; t (071) 985 5249*) you can find out about the O'Rourke, O'Conor and Maguire clan revolt against Sir Frederick in 1641. It's also a good place from which to explore the various roads that spiral out from Manorhamilton. You can take a boggy little road signposted right, a few miles down the main road to Belcoo (N16). It leads to some *cashels* known as **Tallyskcherny**, built in about 500 BC. The land around here belonged to the O'Rourke chieftains who took part with O'Neill and O'Donnell in the last great rebellion of the Irish nobility against Elizabeth I, in the last decades of the 16th century.

North of Manorhamilton, the Bonet Valley narrows towards the source of this pretty river into an equally pretty lake, the **Glenade**. This is a superb example of a glacial valley. The R280 runs beside its waters, thickly edged with trees. The hills are high in the east, and to the west a line of crags rise from the grassy slopes. The road slopes down to **Kinlough**, a neat little village on Lough Melvin only 3 miles (5km) from the sea. If you want to taste the delights of **Bundoran**, a highly developed seaside resort in Donegal, it is only a few miles further on. The many-islanded Lough Melvin extends for 8 miles (13km), and a scenic road follows its southern side from Kinlough to Rossinver. A sign by the road points to **Rossclogher Abbey and Castle**. The small ruined abbey was founded by St Mella, and the deserted castle was a stronghold of MacClancy, a sub-chieftain of the O'Rourkes. In 1588 nine survivors of the Spanish Armada took refuge here. You have to leave your car or bicycle and walk over long grass to reach both buildings, but it is worth it, for the view of the lough is superb. Notice the line of rushes, probably a causeway, going out to the castle, which is on a little island or *crannóg*. The abbey is easy to wander around, but you have to cross shallow water to reach the castle and it is easiest viewed from the shore.

At **Rossinver** at the head of the southern end of the lake are the remains of a 13th-century church and a 6th-century monastery of St Mogue, with a holy well nearby. The modern gravestones look somewhat out of place.

The road that leads south from here to Kiltyclogher passes over the ancient earthwork that is known as the Worm Ditch or the **Black Pig's Dyke**, which extends intermittently from Bundoran in the west to Newry in County Down. It was probably built by the Scotti, people who lived in the north between 300 and 200 BC, to prevent encroachment from the south. Legend, as usual, tells a much more colourful story: the ditch was formed by the slithering of a huge serpent over the land; or if it was not a serpent, then it was a monstrous pig that snuffled and rooted around, throwing up the earth as it went.

In the centre of **Kiltyclogher** village you can stand and admire Albert Power's statue of Seán MacDiarmada, who was executed for his part in the 1916 uprising. The cottage where he was brought up (*open to the public by arrangement; t (071) 9853249*) is a short distance away, in the townland of Corranmore .

Follow the R283 to a rock at **Laughty Barr** where people used to go to hear Mass during the times of the Penal Laws. Signposted from the road is **Kiltyclogher megalithic tomb**, a court cairn that was built between 2000 and 1500 BC and is known locally as Prince Connell's Grave.

Around Dromahair

Dromahair is a very pretty village about 8 miles (12.9 km) from Manorhamilton, through which the River Bonet flows until it gets to Lough Gill. The N16/R286 road from Manorhamilton has the most beautiful views of Lough Gill, and in the wooded country around (approached from the R286/R287) are the ruins of **Creevelea Abbey**, founded in 1508 by Margaret, wife of Owen O'Rourke. The abbey has a pretty pillar with a carving representing St Francis talking to birds in a tree. The branches and roots of the tree grow in Celtic patterns.

In the middle of the town you can see the sparse remains of **Breffni Castle**, stones from which were used to build another mansion known as The Old Hall beside it in 1630. The old castle was the chief stronghold of the O'Rourkes, and it was from here that, in 1152, Devorgilla, the wife of Tighernan or Tiernan O'Rourke, eloped with Dermot MacMurragh at the age of 44. But she regretted her action, for Dermot turned out to be even crueller than Tiernan, and one day she slipped back to be reconciled with him. Her elopement was the turning point in Irish history, for it led to the flight of Dermot MacMurragh and his alliance with Henry II, which resulted in the Anglo-Norman invasion of Ireland.

On the scenic R286 that runs around Lough Gill, on the way to Sligo, there are plenty of lay-bys where you can park and look out over the water to the many islands. Following this route you pass the 17th-century **Parke's Castle** at Fivemilebourne (*open 29 Mar–May Tue–Sun 10–5, June–Sept daily 9.30–6.30, Oct daily 10–5; guided tours; adm; t (071) 916 4149*), a fine example of a planter's insecurity. The manor house was well fortified against the Irish and is surrounded by high *bawn* walls with picturesque turrets and steep sloping roofs. It has been restored and contains a permanent exhibition with information about many of the monuments in the area. You might also want to take a cruise on the *Wild Rose* waterbus that operates on Lough Gill (*see* p.320).

Getting There and Around

By Rail
Carrick-on-Shannon links with Boyle, Sligo and Dublin. There are 3 daily trains Mon–Sat, 2 Sun. **Carrick Station, t** (071) 962 0036

By Bus
Expressway buses link Carrick-on-Shannon with Dublin/Sligo. There is a good local network. **Sligo Bus Depot, t** (071) 916 0066

By Bike
Gerharty's, Main St, Carrick-on-Shannon, t (071) 962 1316. Bike hire.

Festivals

May–June
Community Arts Festival, Carrick-on-Shannon, t (071) 962 2245

July
Joe Mooney School of Traditional Music, Song and Dance, Drumshanbo, t (071) 964 4095
Mohill Arts Festival, t (071) 963 1174
Newtown Gore Festival, t (049) 433 3582

August
Ballinamore Annual Festival, t (071) 964 4095.
Michael Shanley Traditional Weekend, Kiltyclogher, t (071) 985 4200

September
Carrick-on-Shannon Fishing Festival, t (071) 962 0489
Green Festival Northwest, www.thegreenfestival. com. County-wide events.

October
North Leitrim Walking Festival, t (071) 985 6063

Tourist Information

Carrick-on-Shannon: The Marina, t (071) 962 0170, www.leitrimtourism.com, www. northwest.travel.ie. Open mid Mar–Oct.

Internet Access

Gartlans Cybercafé, Bridge St, Carrick-on-Shannon, t (071) 962 1103

Shopping

Crafts
Leitrim Design House, Market Yard, Carrick-on-Shannon, t (071) 965 0550
The Sculpture Centre, Manorhamilton, t (071) 985098

Food and Drink
Oasis Health Foods, Main St, Carrick-on-Shannon, t (071) 962 1560

Sports and Activities

Boat Hire
Crown Blue Line, The Marina, Carrick-on-Shannon, t (071) 962 7634
Emerald Star Line, The Marina, Carrick-on-Shannon, t (071) 962 7685
Riversdale Barge Holidays, Ballinamore, t (071) 964 4122

Cycling
For information on the **Kingfisher Cycle Trail**, log on to www.cycleireland.com, or contact North West Tourism, t (071) 61201.

Fishing
For details on **coarse fishing**, contact:

From Dromahair you need to take the R289, which joins the R280, to reach Drumkeeran and Drumshanbo. This road twists and winds through the hills, taking you past Lough Belhavel and Lough Allen. Along the roads you will notice signposts naming the various lakes and the sort of fish that you are likely to catch in them. Lough Allen is noted for its large pike; fish weighing more than 30lb (13.6kg) are not uncommon. There is good bream fishing from the banks of the 20 lakes within the 5-mile (8km) radius of Drumshanbo.

The Creel, Main St, Carrick-on-Shannon,
t (071) 9620166. Tackle and information.
The Drowes/Lareen Fisheries, Kinlough,
t (071) 984 1055
North West Regional Fisheries Board,
t (096) 22788, www.northwestfisheries.ie
Northern Regional Fisheries Board,
t (071) 985 1435
Rossinver Fishery, Eden Point, t (071) 9841 4511

Golf
Ballinamore Golf Club, t (071) 964 4346
Carrick-on-Shannon Golf Club, t (071) 966 7015

Outdoor Activity Centres
Lough Allen Adventure Centre, Ballinaglera,
t (071) 964 3292

Ponytrekking
Hayden Equestrian Centre,
Carrick-on-Shannon, t (071) 963 8049
Moorlands Equestrian Centre,
Drumshanbo, t (071) 964 1792

Steam Train Rides
Cavan and Leitrim Railway, Dromod,
t (071) 963 8599, www.irish-railway.com

Walking
There is good walking to be had in Cairns Hill
Forest Park near Dromahair.

Where to Stay
For the luxurious Cromleach Lodge
situated just over the border in Co. Sligo, see
p.325. For Glencarne House in neighbouring
Roscommon, see p.310.
The Bush Hotel, Carrick-on-Shannon, t (071)
967 1000, www.bushhotel.com (moderate).
A small, friendly, central choice with solid
Irish cooking.

Glebe House, Ballinamore Rd, Mohill, t (071)
963 1086, www.glebehouse.com (moderate).
A 19th-century rectory. Fishing and riding
can be arranged, and there's a pony for
children. There's a minimum 2-night stay.
Riversdale Farm Guesthouse, Ballinamore,
t (071) 964 4122 (moderate). An Edwardian
farmhouse with light and spacious rooms,
a swimming pool and sauna, a squash court,
good home-cooked food, and delightful
hosts who also run Riversdale Barge Holidays,
so you can take a trip up the Shannon–Erne
Waterway. Closed Dec and Jan.
Stanfords Village Inn, Main St, Dromahair,
t (071) 916 4140 (inexpensive). Comfortable,
clean rooms away from the craic in the
traditional Irish bar with its bottles stacked
high to the ceiling, hard stools and cosy fire.

Eating Out
Al Mezza, Old Dublin Rd, Jamestown,
t (071) 962 5050 (moderate). A Lebanese
restaurant where you can share meze
platters. Closed Mon Nov–Mar, Tue Apr–Oct.
The Courthouse Restaurant, Kinlough,
t (071) 984 2391, www.thecourthouserest.com
(moderate). Good Italian cooking.
Glenview, Ballinamore, t (071) 964 4157
(moderate). A restaurant forming part of a
B&B in a lovely setting beside the Woodford
river. You need to book in advance.
Cryan's Pub, Bridge St, Carrick-on-Shannon,
t (071) 962 0409 (inexpensive). Basic pub
lunches, and quiche and pizza in the
adjoining coffee shop.
Lough Rynn Estate Restaurant, Mohill,
t (071) 963 1427 (inexpensive). A restaurant
with traditional food, and a fast-food outlet
offering snacks. There is also a craft shop,
nature trails, guided tours and angling on
the estate. Closed mid-Sept–late Apr.

Drumshanbo itself is a tidy and well-kept town, and one that keeps close to its
culture and traditions; you can learn about many of these at the interesting Visitors'
Centre, *Sliabh an Iarainn* (open Easter–Oct Mon–Sat 10–6, Sun 2–6; adm; t (071) 964
1522). The Slieve Anierin range, or Iron Mountains, dominate the landscape in these
parts. Iron was mined here two centuries ago, but the industry ceased when the
timber in the neighbourhood, which was the source of fuel for the smelting furnace,
was used up.

South Leitrim

Carrick-on-Shannon was always an important crossing place. During the plantation of Leitrim in the reign of James I it was fortified and garrisoned to protect the new settlers. It is the county town, a pretty place and the centre of river cruising on the Shannon. Within 6 miles (9.6km) there are 41 lakes; and fishing is free and unrestricted. Many coarse fishermen make it their base.

Worth a look is the **Costelloe Memorial Chapel**, the second smallest chapel in the world, erected by Edward Costelloe in 1877 in remembrance of his wife. Both are now buried there in crumbling coffins, which are visible behind glass in sunken pits at either side of the entrance. Drop into Armstrongs next door, which sells drink amongst all the shoes and jumpers. It looks like nothing has changed here since Edward Costelloe passed away.

Following the N4 over the border into County Roscommon, you will come to the **Lough Key Forest Park** (*open all year; restaurant and mooring facilities for boats; car park adm; t (071) 966 2363*). The park is very beautifully laid out with bog gardens and nature trails, and there are boat trips on the lake.

Still following the N4 towards Dublin, keep close to the Shannon and pass through **Jamestown**, founded in the reign of James I. The next village of interest is **Drumsna**, on a hill overlooking the Shannon. The river scenery is lovely. When the Shannon was used to transport produce, Drumsna was quite an important trading centre. Anthony Trollope lived here for some time and wrote his novel *The MacDermotts of Ballycloran*.

Dromod and **Roosky** are pretty little villages on the edge of the Shannon. If you retrace your steps to Dromod and take the R202 to **Mohill**, you come into *drumlin* country, a place of little hills the hollows of which are filled with lakes. Mohill is a favourite angling centre. Between here and Dromod, 6 miles (9.6km) off the N4 Sligo–Dublin road on the shores of Lough Rinn, is a lovely estate that was once owned by the earls of Leitrim. The Victorian walled, terraced gardens of **Lough Rynn House** (*usually open mid-June–mid-Sept daily 10–7 but call t (071) 916 1201 in advance to check; adm includes tours*) are very attractive, with many beautiful redwoods and rhododendrons as well as 600 fishable acres (243ha) of Lough Rinn. The estate was rescued by an American, Mike O'Flaherty, who saw it advertised in a real estate office in the USA, and flew over and bought it.

Fenagh, up in the hills, has the ruins of two medieval Gothic churches. They are all that remain of the monastery that St Columba (*see* p.338) founded and that, under the rule of his close friend St Caillin, became internationally famous as a school of divinity. This is a lovely lake-starred area where you can fish to your heart's delight.

Close to the little village of **Drumcong** on the R210, on an island in Lough Scur, is a ruined Elizabethan castle that was often attacked by the O'Rourkes of Breffni. Above the lough is **Sheebeg**, a small hill with a prehistoric mound on its summit. It is one of the many resting places that were accorded to the legendary Fionn MacCumhaill.

On the road (R209) back to Carrick-on-Shannon is the sister hill of **Sheemore**, which also has a prehistoric cairn and a huge cross that was erected to mark Holy Year 1950. Both are easy to climb.

St Columba the *Enfant Terrible*?

Colourful stories have grown up around the lives of all Irish saints that have no historical foundation. The following is one such story about St Columba.

Among saints, St Columba seems to have been a bit of a rebel. Once, while he was a guest of St Finian, he borrowed a psalter and secretly copied it out. Finian found out and said that the copy should be his, but Columba refused to hand it over. The high king was asked to settle the dispute, and he ruled in favour of Finian, saying that just as every calf belongs to its cow, so every copy belongs to the book from which it is made. St Columba did not accept the king's judgement and gathered an army. He fought the king and won, but with the loss of 3,000 lives. Columba's friend, St Molaise of Inishmurray, advised him to leave Ireland forever as a penance, and convert as many people as he had caused to die.

For more about St Columba, or Colmcille, *see* p.47.

The Province of Ulster

12

Ulster

Highlights

1 Spectacular basalt columns rising out of the sea at the Giant's Causeway
2 Peaceful Devenish Island in Co. Fermanagh
3 Characterful gardens at Mount Stewart House, Co. Down
4 Glorious boat trips to Tory Island
5 A satisfying foray into history at the Ulster Museum, Belfast

The Ulster border has meant much through the ages: Cú Chulainn, the Hound of Ulster, was perhaps its most famous guard when he defended it against the host of Ireland during the epic battles of the Brown Bull of Cooley. Myth has always been used throughout Ulster's history by those keen to validate their points of view, and the boundaries of Ulster (or *Ulaid*) have shifted continuously up until the 16th century.

However, it is interesting to contemplate how myth and history support each other over this enmity between North and South. Irish archaeologists concluded that a great earthen wall was built 2,000 years ago to separate Ulster (*Ulaidhstr*: Land of the Ulstermen) from much of the south of Ireland. It consisted of two pairs of double ramparts – the largest of which was 90ft (27m) wide, 18ft (5.5m) high and 1½ miles (2.8km) long, and formed part of a defensive border along the line of the upper reaches of the Shannon River. It is thought that the wall was built by tribal rulers in central Ireland to prevent the warlike tribes of Ulster from crossing two of the major fords across the Shannon, at Drumsna and Carrick in County Leitrim. The Drumsna wall cuts off a loop of the Shannon and is broken only by an entrance complex that formed a huge gateway into tribal territory – probably the Kingdom of Connacht.

Another earthwork, built in the third or second century BC and known as the Black Pig's Dyke, stretches intermittently from Donegal Bay to the Dorsey and Newry Marshes in the east. This time the defence was built by the Ulstermen against the Southerners. It is likely that the two earthworks reflect stages in the armed conflict between these two major prehistoric tribal groupings. The legendary Connacht Queen Maeve may have built the defences during the great battles over the Brown Bull of Cooley (*see* p.56).

The Northern Ireland you will see today has suffered most in the towns from the last 30 years of the Troubles. This has paradoxically brought about planned and attractive public housing and buildings for the most part, although, as with the rest of Ireland, there are few exceptionally pretty towns. But the countryside is as beautiful and has been made accessible through the development of forest parks and the guardianship of bodies such as the British National Trust. The North is also different because it was industrialized during the 19th century, and so endured the uglier stages of capitalist development, while southern Ireland is only now building factories and pulling itself out of its agriculturally based economy.

Having said all that, the visitor should not ignore Northern Ireland, thinking it is a foreign and probably dangerous country within Ireland – it certainly is not. One great plus point for the North is its teeming lakes and rivers; coarse fishermen find nothing like it anywhere else in the British Isles.

The vast majority of Northern Irish people are friendly, hard-working, witty and kind. The North and the South, as the states of Ireland are colloquially referred to, cooperate in many areas, especially the arts and tourism. A major example was the reopening of the 19th-century Ballinamore and Ballyconnell canal, linking the Shannon and Fermanagh lake systems. It fell into disuse more than 100 years ago, and restoration has been funded by both governments, the EU and the International Fund for Ireland.

The six counties that make up the North are Antrim, Armagh, Down, Fermanagh, Londonderry and Tyrone. They are included in the ancient province of Ulster together with Cavan, Monaghan and Donegal, which are part of the Irish Republic.

History

Some experts on the Irish race maintain that in ancient times the North was full of Picts and the South full of Milesians – another Celtic tribe from Spain whose invasion is recorded in the ancient manuscript, the *Lebor Gabala*, or *Book of Invasions*. They probably arrived in about 200 BC. What is more sure is that later, in the 17th century, Ulster was the most systematically planted province because of its continued fierce resistance to the English, and the hardy Scots were introduced into the province to provide a loyal garrison.

The sign of Ulster is the Red Hand. This symbol is the result of the race for the overlordship of Ulster between the Gaelic MacDonnells and the Norman De Burghs in the 12th century. The first to reach land would take the prize, and, as the contestants struggled through the shallows off the Antrim coast, MacDonnell, fearing that De Burgh who was leading the race would win, cut off his own hand and threw it far onto the strand, where it lay covered in blood. The symbol of this fair land is thus oddly prophetic of the many bloody struggles for its conquest.

The two great clans of the west are descended from the sons of the great High King of Ireland, Niall of the Nine Hostages (AD 379–405). Their names were Conal and Eoghan, and they each gave their name to a district in this part of the province: Tyrconnell and Tyrone. When Brian Boru, who was the high king in the 11th century, instituted surnames in Ireland, the followers and descendants of Conal and Eoghan took the names O'Donnell and O'Neill respectively, and it was they who rebelled against English rule.

County Fermanagh

This is the lakeland of Ireland, bounded with limestone mountains in the south-west and scattered with *drumlins* that speckle the lakes with islands. A third of the county is underwater, covered by the lake system of the Erne with its mass of lakelets in the upper lough, and the great boomerang of Lower Lough Erne. Then there are the two Lough MacNeans in their mountain fastness, which together with the county's share of Lough Melvin have until recently discouraged incoming populations, so it is a place of long-lasting traditions and folklore. Even today, few strangers settle in this area, although the lakes attract summer visitors.

The countryside in which these beautiful lakes are scattered is mostly composed of little rushy farms where sheep and cattle graze. The higher ground is covered in hazel scrub, while in the limestone upland to the western edge of the country the soil is so poor that natural species have survived undisturbed by the tractor or fertilizers of the farmer. There are some lovely ash woods at Hanging Rock and Marble Arch. Here too are the famous Marble Arch Caves on Cuilcagh Mountain, which you can explore with a guide. The county also has two exquisite Georgian mansions under the care of the National Trust – Castle Coole and Florence Court. The coarse fishing is legendary, and every year in May fishermen have great fun at the Guinness Classic Fishing Festival, which spreads events all over the myriad lakes. You can explore the lakes by

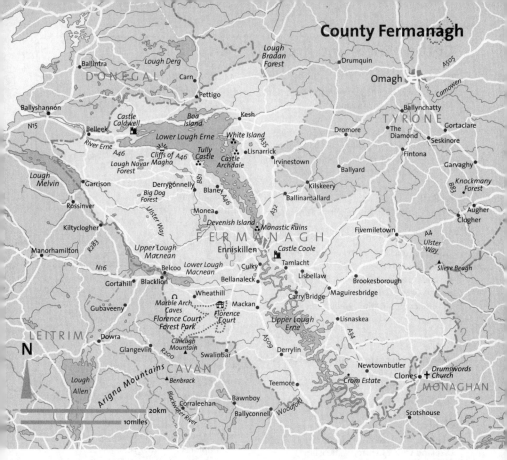

County Fermanagh

chartering a cabin cruiser, and there are plenty of opportunities for water-skiing. The waterways of the Upper and Lower Erne are now connected to the great waterway of the Shannon by the Ballyconnell and Ballinamore canal, which passes through some very unspoilt scenery.

History

The history of this county is similar to that of the rest of Ulster. The Maguires were the chief Gaelic family here before the Plantation. In the 17th century, Scottish 'undertakers' arrived (this name is derived from their 'undertaking' a pledge to provide a population loyal to the English Crown). Many grand houses were built by landowners in the 18th century. Fermanagh has a vast and largely unrecorded ancient history, which you will get glimpses of through the beautiful carvings and stone statues still to be seen in graveyards and the Enniskillen Museum.

Those of a reflective turn of mind will be fascinated by the pagan idols; their impassive stone heads are to be found on the islands and peninsulas of Lough Erne. Usually they are mixed up with the gravestones of the newer religion, Christianity. The two seem to mingle quite happily. There are many remains of Christian hermitages; on Devenish Island, on Lough Erne, there is a superb collection of

Getting There and Around

By Air

Air traffic is handled by Belfast International Airport and Enniskillen Airport.

Enniskillen Airport, St Angelo, Trory, Enniskillen, **t** (028) 6632 9000. Four miles (6.4km) from Enniskillen, this has flights to Jersey and Zürich. Plans are afoot to develop further routes to the UK and Europe.

By Rail

There is no train service within Fermanagh.

By Bus

Six Ulsterbus express buses run daily from Belfast to Enniskillen, 2 from Dublin. There are good local bus links from Enniskillen to country areas; see *www.ulsterbus.co.uk*.

Enniskillen Bus Station, Wellington Rd, **t** (028) 6632 2633

By Car

Lochside Garages Ltd, Tempo Rd, Enniskillen, **t** (028) 6632 4366. Car hire.

M & N Car Rental, Irvinestown Rd, Enniskillen, **t** (028) 6632 4712.

By Bike

Bicycle hire is available from:

Lakeland Canoe Centre, Castle Island, **t** (028) 6632 4250

Marble Arch Cycle Hire, Tarmon, Blacklion and Florencecourt, **t** (028) 6634 8320

Festivals

There are lots of tiny festivals and sporting events in villages thoughout the summer; ask at the tourist office. The following are among the most interesting:

May

Fermanagh Classic Fishing Festival, **t** (028) 6632 3110

Scottish Pipe Band Competition, **t** (028) 6638 8202 or **t** (028) 6632 4078

June

Border Trek Cycle Event, **t** (028) 9032 1462 or **t** (028) 6632 3110. A 50mile (80km) cycle for peace.

Fiddlestone Festival, Belleek, **t** (028) 6865 9701. A traditional festival.

Lisnaskea Feis, **t** (028) 6772 1610. A celebration of Irish musical culture.

July

Lady of the Lake Festival, Irvinestown, **t** (028) 6862 1656, *www.ladyofthelakefestival.com*. An event named after a mystical woman said to have made her way among the islands of Lower Lough Erne in a flowing gown, filled with light and carrying wildflowers.

Summer Drama Season, Ardhowen Theatre, Enniskillen, **t** (028) 6632 5440

August

Enniskillen Agricultural Show, **t** (028) 6632 2509

Kesh Carnival/Maid of Glendurragh Festival, **t** (028) 6863 2545

Lough Melvin Open Trout Angling Championships, **t** (028) 6865 8194

October

Antique and Fine Art Fair, Enniskillen, **t** (028) 6632 7360

Eddie Duffy Traditional Music Festival, **t** (028) 6864 1679

December

International Mummers' Festival, Enniskillen, **t** (028) 6632 5050. Historical drama.

ecclesiastical ruins dating from the 6th century. The headlands of the loughs are wooded and often enough their interest is enhanced by the ruins of Plantation castles from the 17th century.

This county and the town of Enniskillen suffered greatly after the Troubles began in 1969. The most notable tragedy was an IRA bomb in 1987 that killed 11 people in Enniskillen. Today there is much hope here for a new era, ushered in by the Good Friday Agreement and the Northern Ireland Executive. Fermanagh has never been a rich county. Its population has always lived by farming and fishing, and now tourism.

Enniskillen and Around

Enniskillen is built on a bridge of land between Upper and Lower Lough Erne. At first sight the medieval conglomeration of town and castle makes you think this is a very ancient town, but modern shops, supermarkets and offices soon spoil the illusion. Before the plantation the Maguires held sway over this lakeland area and used it as the centre for their watery dominions. Enniskillen's name comes from Cathleen, one of the women warriors of the Fomorian invaders. Her husband Balor was head of a pirate gang quartered on the rock island of Tory, off the Donegal coast. He resurfaced as the Celtic god of darkness, whose one eye could strike you dead (*see* **Old Gods and Heroes**, p.53). Enniskillen is famous for its home regiments – the *Air of the Inniskillings* became the tune of 'The Star Spangled Banner'. Visit the **County Museum** (*open Mon 2–5, Tue–Fri 10–5, plus May–Sept Sat 2–5, July and Aug Sun 2–5; adm; t (028) 6632 5000, www.enniskillencastle.co.uk*), housed in the 15th-century Maguire's Keep. One of the best and friendliest local museums, it displays some of the strange head sculptures found in the locality, and explains the history of Fermanagh from the Middle Stone Age to the end of the early-Christian period. There is also an audio-visual show on the Maguires of Fermanagh. British regiment enthusiasts will be interested in the soldiering relics of the Royal Inniskilling Fusiliers in the same building. Attached to the museum is the fairytale **Water Gate**, with towers and fluttering standards.

Tourist Information

Enniskillen: Fermanagh Tourist Information Centre, Wellington Rd, t (028) 6632 3110

Shopping

Crafts

Belleek china, fishing-fly brooches and Irish lace are sold in giftshops in central Enniskillen.
Ann McNulty Pottery, Unit 1, The Buttermarket, Down St, Enniskillen, t (028) 6632 4721
Belleek Pottery, Belleek, t (028) 6865 8501, *www.belleek.ie*. Ireland's most famous pottery, producing fine glazed porcelain.
Fermanagh Craft Consortium and Design Centre, The Buttermarket, Down St, Enniskillen, t (028) 6632 4499, *www.fermanaghcraft.com*

Sports and Activities

Cycling

The waymarked **Kingfisher Cycle Trail** covers 230 miles (370km) through counties Fermanagh and Leitrim, Cavan, Donegal and Monaghan. The Tourist Centre in Enniskillen has details.

Fishing

The Tourist Information Centre in Enniskillen (*see* above) stocks permits, licences and booklets on local waters.

Golf

Castle Hume Golf Club, Enniskillen, t (028) 6632 7077
Enniskillen Golf Course, Castle Coole Estate, t (028) 6632 5250, *www.enniskillengolfclub.com*. An excellent course with a good clubhouse.

Watersports

Lakeland Canoe Centre, Enniskillen, t (028) 6632 4250. Canoeing.

Where to Stay

Killyhevlin Hotel, Dublin Rd, Enniskillen, t (028) 6632 3481, *www.killyhevlin.com* (*expensive*). A comfortable, modern hotel with wonderful views over Lough Erne. The bar is a great chatting place among fishermen, and you can also enjoy a very good lunchtime carvery and excellent evening meals.

You should take a walk through the centre of Enniskillen, which is rather a jumble: the winding main street takes on about six names during its course. You might be impressed enough to buy the local souvenir brooches, made from fishing flies. In the old **Buttermarket** you can buy a variety of hand-crafted goods (*see* 'Shopping', p.345). The **Church of Ireland cathedral** dates from the mid 17th century but was extensively remodelled in the 19th. In the chancel and choir hang the colours of the Royal Inniskilling Fusiliers together with the pennons of the Inniskilling Dragoons, which were recruited in the town. Close by is St Michael's Catholic Church, which was built in 1875 to plans by John O'Neill, although the spire (designed by the original architect) dates from 1992. Inside are some fine paintings depicting scenes from the life of Christ. Four are by the Scottish artist Charles Russell (1852–1910), while the Holy Family scene is by Michael Joseph Healy (1873–1941). For a good view of the town and surrounding area, you could climb the 108 steps to the top of the **Coles Monument** (*open May–Sept daily 2–6; adm; t (028) 6632 5050*). It was built between 1845 and 1857 in Forthill Park at the eastern end of town.

Just outside Enniskillen to the north-west is the **Portora Royal School**, founded in 1608. As a public school it had Oscar Wilde and Samuel Beckett among its more famous pupils. About 1¼ miles (2.4km) south-east of the town, on the main Belfast road (A4), is **Castle Coole** (*house open 12 noon–6pm 16 Mar–May Sat, Sun and bank*

Killyreagh House, Tamlaght, Enniskillen, **t** (028) 6638 7221 (*moderate*). A comfortable 19th-century country house where fishing, riding and tennis can be arranged.

Dromard House, Dromard, Tamlaght, Enniskillen, **t** (028) 6638 7250 (*inexpensive*). Comfortable rooms in a converted stable loft.

Corrigan Shore, Clonatrig, Bellanaleck, Enniskillen, **t** (028) 6634 8572 (*inexpensive*). A modern guesthouse welcoming anglers.

Riverside Farm, Gortadrehid, Culkey, Enniskillen, **t** (028) 6632 2725 (*inexpensive*). A friendly and comfortable farmhouse. The River Sillies at the bottom of the farm holds the record for coarse fishing.

Saddler's, 66 Belmore St, Enniskillen, **t** (028) 6632 6223 (*moderate*). Lovely pub food.

Scoff's, Belmore St, Enniskillen, **t** (028) 6634 2622, *www.scoffsuno.com* (*moderate*). A popular place for ostrich steaks and *nouvelle cuisine*. Booking is essential at weekends.

Blakes of the Hollow, 6 Church St, Enniskillen, **t** (028) 6632 2143/5388 (*inexpensive*). A pub with original Victorian décor, serving snacks.

Crow's Nest, 12 High St, Enniskillen, **t** (028) 6632 5252 (*inexpensive*). Oysters, cottage pie and ham, plus live music every evening (it can get noisy).

Pat's Bar, 1 Townhall St, Enniskillen, **t** (028) 6632 7462 (*inexpensive*). Good lunches.

Eating Out

Franco's Restaurant, Queen Elizabeth Rd, Enniskillen, **t** (028) 6632 4424 (*moderate*). A good place for reasonably priced pasta, pizza, fish and vegetarian dishes.

Oscar's, Belmore St, Enniskillen, **t** (028) 6632 7037 (*moderate*). A popular restaurant with a good atmosphere (children are made very welcome) and good food, including salmon and other seafood specials.

Entertainment and Nightlife

Theatre
Ardhowen Theatre, Enniskillen, **t** (028) 6632 5440

Traditional Music
Blakes of the Hollow, 6 Church St, Enniskillen, **t** (028) 6632 2143/5388. A fine pub hosting weekend sessions.

*hols, June Fri–Wed, July and Aug daily, Sept Sat and Sun; parkland open daily Apr–Sept,
10–8, Oct–Mar 10–4; adm; t (028) 6632 2690, www.ntni.org.uk)*, an assured neoclassical
house restored by the National Trust, who replaced the Portland stone blocks of the
façade. It was built between 1790 and 1797 with an agreeably simple symmetry;
the main block with its colonnaded wings was designed by James Wyatt. Inside,
18th-century furniture is still in the rooms for which it was made. English plasterer
Joseph Ross, who had worked for Adam at Syon and Harewood, made the long
journey to supervise the creation of the ceilings. The building accounts of the
house survive, and, since the cost of the construction exceeded the estimates,
some restraint may have been exercised in the decoration, keeping it elegant but
simple. In the surrounding parkland there is a lake that has a very long-established
colony of greylag geese. It is said that if they leave Castle Coole, so will the Lowry-
Corrys, earls of Belmore, whose seat it is.

Northern Fermanagh

The Islands in Lower Lough Erne
Lower Lough Erne stretches in a broad arc with a pattern of 97 islands, with Belleek
at one end and Enniskillen at the other. Ripe for exploration, Lough Erne's scattered
islets hold many treasures. You should not miss **Devenish**; here St Molaise founded a
monastic community in the 6th century, which was probably a more perilous venture
than usual in that remote water kingdom, where paganism persisted long after
Christian practices had taken hold in more accessible parts.

However, there is a legend that credits these parts with a visitation by a character
from the Old Testament, for the prophet Jeremiah is said to have his grave in the
waters of Lough Erne. His daughter Hamutal was married to the son of a high king
of Ireland, and she brought as her dowry the Stone of Destiny, the coronation stone
of Scone – the same stone that Fergus, who also cropped up in County Antrim (*see*
p.379), took to Scotland.

Devenish island has a complete round tower, with an elaborately decorated
cornice. Another ruin on the island incorporating some outstanding decoration is the
12th-century Augustinian **Abbey of St Mary**. Here St Molaise rested from his labours,
listening spellbound to birdsong that, it was said, was the Holy Spirit communicating.
The reverie lasted 100 years, and when he looked around the abbey had been built.
You will find it a few miles outside Enniskillen off the main road to Omagh (the
A32). (For transport to the island, *see* 'Sports and Activities', p.349.)

Another island with more tangible supernatural associations is **White Island**, in
Castle Archdale Bay, north of Enniskillen, famous for its eerie statues. All eight of
them are lined up in a row against the wall of a 12th-century church. Like many of the
sculptures found in Fermanagh and nearby districts, there is a pagan quality about
these objects. There are conflicting theories about just what they represent. Possibly
they are of Christian origin employing archaic pre-Christian styles, dating from
between the 7th and 10th centuries.

Shopping

Crafts

Ardess Craft Centre, Kesh, **t** (028) 6863 1267.
A range of local pottery, woven rugs and other crafts. Spinning and weaving workshops are available.

Belleek Pottery Visitor Centre, t (028) 6665 8501, *www.belleek.ie.* A pottery offering 20min guided tours. Its parian china and early designs are collectors' items; you can even eat off the stuff in the Pottery Restaurant.

Fermanagah Crystal, Main St, Belleek, **t** (028) 6865 8631. Fermanagh's only crystal factory, where you can watch glasses, vases and lamps of lead crystal being hand-cut. A mail-order service is available.

Sports and Activities

Birdwatching

The waterways here are the home of kingfishers and great crested grebes. The Erne basin is an important breeding ground for redshank, snipe, lapwing and curlew.

Eddie McGovern, Fermanagh Tourist Information Centre, Wellington Rd, Enniskillen, **t** (028) 6632 3110

Boat Hire

The area comprises more than 300 sq miles (800 sq km) of island-studded lakes and rivers, with more than 70 free jetty-moorings and only one lock. Many companies hire out cruisers by the day or week. Prices range from around £385 a week for a 4-berth cruiser in the low season and £1,000 for an 8-berth in the high season. Firms welcome complete novices and give free lessons on how to handle boats. You can get a complete list from the tourist office in Enniskillen; *see* p.345.

Carrickcraft, Blaney, Enniskillen, **t** (028) 3834 4993, *www.cruise-ireland.com.* One-way boat hire between the Erne and the Shannon.

Manor House Marine, Killadeas, **t** (028) 6862 8100, *www.manormarine.com*

Cycling

Kingfisher Cycle Trail Tour, t (028) 6632 0121/ 6632 3110, *www.cycletoursireland.com.* A 30–40-mile (48–64km) ride along the trail from Belleek, over Boa Island to Kesh, down through Irvinestown to Enniskillen and over to Florence Court.

Fishing

The Fermanagh lakelands are renowned for their coarse fishing. Brown trout and salmon fishing are also excellent in the rivers and loughs. Lough Melvin is notable for housing 3 unusual species of trout: the gillaroo, the sonaghan and the ferox.

Lough Melvin Holiday Centre, Garrison, **t** (028) 6865 8142. Angling holidays.

Pleasure Cruises

The *Kestrel* leaves from the Round 'O' Quay in Enniskillen for cruises round the islands every day July–Sept, and includes a stop at Devenish Island. You can hire the *Kestrel* for private groups. Boats over 10hp must be registered with the Portora Locks Warden. You could also try: *Inishcruiser,* Share Centre, Lisnaskea, **t** (028) 6772 2122. This is equipped with a bar and facilities for up to 60 people.

Boa Island, joined to the mainland by a bridge at each end, is the largest island. Its name comes from *Badhbha,* war goddess of the Ulster Celts, and traditionally it stayed the centre of the Druidic cult long after Christianity had arrived in Ireland. In the old cemetery, **Caldragh,** at the west end, is a strange 'Janus' figure with a face on each side. Such figures (several were found in the Fermanagh area and in Cavan) are thought to have had ritual significance; a hollow in the head may have held sacrificial blood.

The Northern Shore of Lough Erne

Killadeas is a fishing village that looks out on to Lough Erne. In the graveyard of the chapel you can see a number of ancient, sculptured stones. One of these, called the Bishop's Stone, depicts a man with a crozier and bell. It certainly dates back to

Ferry to White Island from Castle Archdale. *Apr–June Sun 2–6, July and Aug daily 11–6.*
Ferry to Devenish Island from Troy point, 3 miles (5km) north of Enniskillen (A32/B82). *Easter–Sept daily 10, 1, 3 and 5.*

Ponytrekking
Equestrian sports practically stopped in much of Co. Fermanagh after the foot-and-mouth epidemic in 2001. The nearest horse-riding centre is in Fivemiletown, Co. Tyrone (*see* p.360).

Watersports
Water-skiing and canoeing is available through the cruiser-hire companies listed opposite, or from:
Drumrush Watersports Centre, Drumrush Lodge, Lough Erne, Kesh, t (028) 6863 1578
Tudor Farm, Goal Island Road, Kesh, t (028) 6863 1943

Rossfad House, Killadeas, t (028) 6638 8505 (*moderate*). A Georgian country house in a scenic location by Lower Lough Erne.
Castle Archdale Youth Hostel, Irvinestown, t (028) 6862 8118 (*inexpensive*). Family rooms and group accommodation in an historic listed building.

Self-catering
Shannon-Erne Luxury Cottages, Teemore; t (028) 6774 8893, *info@shannon-erne.co.uk* (*expensive*). Six traditional-style cottages on the banks of the canal. Each sleeps 4.
Innish Beg Cottages, Innish Beg, Blaney, Derrygonnelly, t (028) 6864 1525 (*inexpensive*). Five cottages with views over Lower Lough Erne and a private shoreline. A rowing boat can be hired.
Lusty Beg Island Chalets, Boa Island, t (028) 6863 3300, *www.lustybegisland.com* (*inexpensive*). Self-catering chalets sleeping 6, or B&B (*moderate*).

Where to Stay

Ardess House, Kesh, t (028) 6863 1267, *www.ardesshouse.co.uk* (*moderate*). A guesthouse offering wholefood cooking. The craft centre in the grounds hosts courses.
The Cedars, Castle Archdale, Irvinestown, t (028) 6862 1493 (*moderate*), *www.cedarsguesthouse.com*. A relaxed and inviting guesthouse with views of the Lough Navar Mountains.
Lakeview House, Drumcrow, Blaney, t (028) 6864 1263 (*moderate*). A farmhouse with lough views.

Eating Out

The Cedars, Castle Archdale, Drumall, Lisnarrick, t (028) 6862 1493 (*moderate*). Excellent steaks.
The Waterfront, Irvinestown, t (028) 6862 1938 (*inexpensive–moderate*). A restaurant offering a small menu comprising very good traditional dishes.
Mahon's Hotel, Irvinestown, t (028) 6862 1656, *www.mahonshotel.co.uk* (*inexpensive*). A limited choice of meals, served all day.
Fiddlestone Bar, Belleek (*inexpensive*). A good place for sandwiches.

pre-Norman times. There is also a carved stone figure in the churchyard that dates back to the 9th century. The country around the lough is full of the dips and hollows of the glacial-drift *drumlins*. Just beyond the lough you can visit the **Castle Archdale Country Park** (*open daily early morning–dusk*), located on the B82. It is an old demesne that has now been opened up for walking in the beautiful forest along nature trails, and for camping, boating and fishing. The old castle itself is a pretty ruin that is worth a stroll around.

From the jetty you have good views over to White Island and **Davy's Island**; this is a good place for making a boat trip over to some of the nature reserve islands. Perhaps the loveliest aspect of this part of the shoreline is the flowers that decorate the water's edge.

Kesh is a busy little fishing village on the A35 where you can hire cruise boats. There is a boat-building industry here specializing in traditional broad-beamed eel boats, as this is a centre for eels (though subsidiary to Lough Neagh). From Kesh you can make your way to the pretty little island of **Lusty Beg**, which has holiday chalets for hire and B&B accommodation (*see* p.349). Another 'Janus' figure was discovered here, which is now in the Enniskillen Museum.

Following the curve of the shoreline west you reach **Pettigo**, which is just in County Donegal, with newer houses straggling on and over the border into Fermanagh. Pettigo is an angling village that has grown up by the River Termon about a mile (1.6km) from where it flows into Lough Erne. It was on the pilgrims' route to Lough Derg, which lies in Donegal, about 4 miles (6km) away, so it is busy in summer. The ruins of the 17th-century **Castle Magrath**, with its keep and circular towers at the corners, are on the outskirts of the village, next to the rectory. The B136 joins up with the A47 here and leads you to the ruined **Castle Caldwell**, which is situated on a wooded peninsula jutting out into the lough – a romantic situation for a romantic and enterprising family. One of the Caldwells had a barge on which music used to be played for his pleasure. Unfortunately, a fiddler overbalanced on one of these occasions and was drowned. You can see his fiddle-shaped monument with its warning:

On firm land only exercise your skill
There you may play and safely drink your fill.

During the 19th century the Caldwells promoted the original porcelain industry at nearby Belleek, using clay found on their estate. Visitors can wander in their gardens above the shore, admiring the view that in 1776 made Arthur Young, the well-known agriculturalist, exclaim that there was 'shelter, prospect, wood and water here in perfection'. You can use the wildfowl hides to watch the plentiful ducks, geese and other birds; these grounds also have the largest breeding colony of black scooters in the British Isles.

At **Belleek** (*Beal Leice*: 'Flagstone Ford'), you reach another border village. Anglers have a joky saying that you can hook a salmon in the Republic and land it in Northern Ireland. But it's more famous for its lustreware, which is produced for ornament rather than anything utilitarian. The 19th-century **pottery** (*see* p.348) is very attractive; it has a small museum and offers guided tours. Also in Belleek is **Explorerne** (*open May–Sept daily 11–5; adm; t (028) 6865 8866*), an exhibition centre detailing the history of Lough Erne through exhibits and video.

The Southern Shore of Lough Erne

On your way along the southern shore the road (the A46) hugs the waterline, for limestone cliffs loom overhead, rising to a height of 2,984ft (909m) at Magho. From the **Lough Navar Forest** (inland via Derrygonnelly on the B81) viewpoint you can take in the splendid sight of the lough spread out in front of you, with the hills of Donegal in the distance, and the ranges of Tyrone, Sligo and Leitrim in a grand panorama. The forest entrance, opposite Correl Glen, is about 5 miles (8km) west of Derrygonnelly. It takes you on a 7-mile (11km) scenic road that is full of nature trails and little lakes, and has a campsite. The Ulster Way footpath runs through the forest up to a height of 1,000ft (305m), and runs down to Belcoo, between Upper and Lower Lough MacNean. This mountainous area is full of caves.

The plateau on the southern shore is covered with forest lands, and behind them are the Cuilcagh Mountains rising to the south. If you stick to the loughside you will pass the plantation-era **Tully Castle** (*open Apr–Sept Tue–Sat 10–7, Sun 2–7, Oct–Mar Tue–Sat 2–7; adm*) and, further inland towards the south, a better-preserved castle at **Monea** (*always accessible*). Both show the Scottish style brought to this country by settlers. Monea's front shows two circular towers that are square on the top storey, and the crow-stepped gables add to its Scottish air.

Southern Fermanagh

Up into the Western Mountains

For spectacular sights, nature has more on her side than architecture, so head towards the mountains in the west. You can take winding roads cross-country from Monea, but for a simpler route take Enniskillen as a starting point and follow the A4. At **Belcoo** you reach a village lost in the mountains, situated on a narrow strip of land separating the two Lough MacNeans. In this place *patterns* to St Patrick's Well are held on Bilberry Sunday, the last Sunday in July and also the date of the Celtic *Lughnasa*, or festival of fertility; a lingering tradition that gave Brian Friel the name for his play *Dancing at Lughnasa*.

If you go back by **Lower Lough MacNean**, you will see the **Hanging Rock** from the minor road that goes to Blacklion across the border. Limestone has endowed this place with caverns. They stretch in a sort of underground labyrinth running through the Cuilcagh Mountains, and some remain to be explored. **Marble Arch Show Caves** (*open Mar–Sept daily from 10am, weather permitting; last tour 4.30pm; adm; call ahead before setting out, t (028) 6634 8855, www.fermanagh-online.com/tourism*) at Marlbank, Florencecourt, have been designated a European Geo-Park in recognition of their geological importance. The 1¼-hour tour includes an underground boat trip. Take a jumper and flat shoes.

The wooded demesne of Florence Court is situated under the steep mountain of **Benaughlin**, which means 'peak of the horse'; the white limestone showing through the scree at the foot of the eastern cliff did indeed once portray the outline of a horse, though it has now become difficult to distinguish. **Florence Court** (*house open Apr, May and Sept Sat and Sun 1–6, June–Aug Wed–Mon 1–6; grounds open daily 10–7; adm; t (028) 6634 8249*), home of the Coles, earls of Enniskillen, is about 8 miles (13km) south-west of the town they helped to fortify in Plantation times, on the A4 and A32 Swanlibar road. Built in the mid 18th century for Lord Mountflorence, the house has sadly suffered fire damage, but there is still some fine rococo plasterwork. It is beautifully situated in woodland with views across to the Cuilcagh Mountains. In the gardens is the original Florence Court yew, from whose seedlings grew *Taxus baccata fastigiata*, now found all over the world.

Shopping

Antiques

Forge Antiques, Circular Rd, Lisbellaw
Sheelin Irish Lace Museum/Sheelin Antiques,
Bellanaleck, t (028) 6634 8052, www.
irishlacemuseum.com. An award-winning
antique lace museum and an antiques shop.

Sports and Activities

Birdwatching

Waterways here are home to kingfishers
and great crested grebes, and the Erne basin
is a breeding ground for redshank, snipe,
lapwing and curlew.
Eddie McGovern, Fermanagh Tourist
Information Centre; see p.345.

Fishing

The Fermanagh lakelands are renowned for
their coarse fishing. Brown trout and salmon
fishing are also excellent in the rivers and
loughs. See 'Sports and Activities' in Northern
Fermanagh, p.348, for more information.

Golf

Enniskillen Golf Club, Castle Coole Estate,
t (028) 6632 5250

Pleasure Cruises

Carrybridge Boat Company, Lisbellaw,
t (028) 6638 7034
The Share Centre, Lisnaskea, t (028) 6772 2122.
Tours of Upper Lough Erne on the *Inishcruiser*.
A Viking longship is available by request.
Closed Oct–Easter.

Potholing

Marble Arch Caves, Florence Court; see p.351.

Where to Stay

Lanesborough Arms, High St, Newtownbutler,
t (028) 6773 8866 (*moderate*). A refurbished
18th-century townhouse.
Tullyhona House, Marble Arch Rd, Florence Court,
t (028) 6634 8452, www.archhouse.com
(*inexpensive*). A old house in its own grounds
beside Upper Lough Erne, with children's
play areas. Fine home-cooking is provided.

Self-catering

Crom Cottages, Crom Estate near Lisnaskea,
t (028) 6773 81118 or t UK (01225) 791199,
www.nationaltrust.org.uk (*expensive*).
Seven converted cottages situated on a
National Trust Estate.
Rose Cottage, Florence Court, t UK (01225)
791199, www.nationaltrust.org.uk (*expensive*).
A cottage on Florence Court demesne.
Belle Isle Estate Cottages, Lisbellaw,
t (028) 6638 7231, www.belleisle-estate.com
(*inexpensive*). Traditional cottages – a garden
cottage, a coachhouse and bridge house –
on a lovely estate at the northern end of
Upper Lough Erne, sleeping 4–6, with
spacious, modern interiors.

Eating Out

The Sheelin, Bellanaleck, t (028) 6634 8232
(*inexpensive–moderate*). An excellent choice
for lunch or dinner, set in a traditional
cottage with climbing roses round the door,
and offering a delicious and original menu.
Florence Court House, t (028) 6634 8249
(*inexpensive*). The place to come for
well-priced lunches of quiche, stews and
wheaten bread. *Closed eves.*
Wild Duck Inn, Lisbellaw, t (028) 6638 5032
(*inexpensive*). Pub grub.

Upper Lough Erne

Upper Lough Erne and the maze of waters from the Erne river system require a good
map. This area bridges less water-strewn east Fermanagh, some of whose pretty towns
bear names of founder planter families. **Brookeborough** is on the A4, near the home of
the Brookes, who were prominent in Northern Irish affairs. Basil, the first Viscount
Brookeborough (1888–1973), was Prime Minister of Northern Ireland, and is remembered,
perhaps unfairly, for his *laager* mentality towards Roman Catholics. **Maguiresbridge** is
named after the reigning chieftains, who were deposed by the planters.

This area is rich in folk tradition; you might meet someone with the secret of a cure, either for animal or human ailments. If you are interested in the distinctive sculptures you may have seen at the Enniskillen Museum or elsewhere, search out **Tamlaght Bay** near Lisbellaw on the A4, where at **Derrybrusk Old Church** you can see some more strange carved heads on a wall. At nearby **Aghalurcher Churchyard**, near Lisnaskea on the A34, you can see gravestones carved with what seems to be a rather macabre funerary motif, typically found in Fermanagh: the skull and crossbones.

The Crom Estate (*open Apr–end Sept Mon–Sat 10–6, Sun 12–6; car park fee;* **t** *(028) 6773 8118*) on the shores of Upper Lough Erne is a huge acreage of woodland, parkland and wetland. Under the protection of the National Trust, it is an important nature conservation area. You approach it on a minor road off the A34 in Newtownbutler.

Lisnaskea, also on the A34, is rather an interesting market town with a restored market cross the ancient shaft of which has fine carving. In the middle of the town is a ruined 17th-century castle built by Sir James Balfour, which was burnt down in the 19th century. On the main street is a folklife display at the **library** (*open Mon, Tue and Fri 9.15–5, Wed 9.15–7.30, Sat 9.15–12.30;* **t** *(028) 6772 1222*). A cruise boat leaves from the jetty here for 1½-hour tours of Upper Lough Erne (*see* opposite).

The upper reaches of Lough Erne are scattered with 58 little 'islands'. These prettily named islands are really tiny districts or townlands, and not islands at all. Some of them are inhabited, though on an increasingly part-time basis. A sad story illustrates the difficulties associated with island living: a postman living on **Inishturk Island** froze to death when his boat was trapped in ice during the hard winter of 1961. **Cleenish Island** can be reached from Bellanaleck on the A509 by a bridge. There are some remarkable carved headstones in the graveyard. Even more interesting is the collection of carved slabs on **Inishkeen**, accessible by causeway from Killyhevlin.

Belle Isle is a townland that claims to be the spot where the *Annals of Ulster* were compiled in the 15th century by Cathal MacManus, Dean of Lough Erne. **Galloon Island** is large, with another ancient graveyard where you may, if you persevere, discern the curious carvings on the 9th- or 10th-century cross shafts depicting a man hanging upside down. Some think that this might be Judas Iscariot, or perhaps St Peter.

County Tyrone

This is the heart of Ulster, the land named after Eoghan (Owen), one of the sons of High King Niall of the Nine Hostages, who lived in the 4th century AD and was the progenitor of the O'Neill dynasty. The least populated of the six counties, Tyrone is celebrated in many a poignant song by emigrant sons. The Sperrin Mountains cover a large part of the north, the highest, at 2,240ft (678m), being Sawel, which is on the border with County Londonderry. In these lonely hills, locals have panned for gold for hundreds of years – excitement has recently been generated by the discovery of large deposits. Lough Neagh forms Tyrone's eastern border for a few miles in the east, but the county's attractions are its chattering burns, its flora and fauna and its peaceful glens. There is much to attract the walker and naturalist in the Sperrin Mountains.

In the south-eastern area it is well wooded, and there is a much quoted tag about 'Tyrone among the bushes, where the Finn and Mourne run'. The land in this region is more fertile and well-planted with trees; farmers here keep cattle and sheep. Many of the farmhouses are still of whitewashed stone with gaily painted doorways. The linen industry is important at Moygashel, and there are many small businesses in the main towns, such as milling and crafts. The Plantation families have their traditions and Big Houses in the south-east too. Some of the loveliest, such as Caledon, are still occupied by their original families; the most unusual, Killymoon Castle, was saved from ruin by a farmer who bought it for £100 in the 1920s. Neither is open to the public.

Tyrone is an undiscovered county for many tourists, but it inspires pride in natives. Tyrone people are known for their music and their talent with language, both the spoken and written word. Many writers and poets come from this part of the world: William Carleton, John Montague, Brian Friel and Flann O'Brien.

Getting There and Around

By Air
Belfast International Airport and Dublin Airport are about 70 miles and 86 miles (112km and 137km) from Omagh respectively. Enniskillen Airport (*see* p.344) is not very far away, and nor is the City of Derry Airport, t (028) 7181 0784. Belfast City Airport, t (028) 9093 9093, also has services. (An airbus service operates to and from Belfast city centre, t (028) 9033 3000.)

By Rail
There is no train line in Co. Tyrone. The nearest stations to the county are Portadown, t (028) 3835 1422, and Derry City, t (028) 2565 2277.

By Bus
Translink/Ulsterbus runs a good service to all parts of the county. Express Coach and Bus Éireann link Co. Tyrone to other parts of Ireland. Bus Éireann, t (074) 21309 Derry City bus station, t (028) 7126 2261 Omagh bus station, t (028) 8224 2711 Strabane bus station, t (028) 7138 2393

By Car
Gallen Vehicle Hire, 96 Drumlegagh Rd South, Omagh Town, t (028) 8224 6966 P.G. McGillion, 132 Melmount Rd, Sion Mills, t (028) 8165 8275 Tattyreagh Car Hire, 110 Tattyreagh Rd, Fintona, t (028) 8284 1731

By Bike
Conway Cycles, 1 Market Place, Omagh, t (028) 8224 6195, and 157 Loughmacrory Rd, Carrickmore, t (028) 8076 1258. Bike hire.

Festivals

May
Magherafelt and District Mad May Festival, t (028) 8224 7831 West Tyrone *Feis*, t (028) 8224 7831. Dance/music.

June
Fair Day Carnival, Strabane, t (028) 7138 2204. Street entertainment in vintage Strabane. The Strawberry Fair, Sion Mills, Strabane, t (028) 8165 8350. A traditional village fête.

July
Clogher Valley Agricultural Show, Augher, t (028) 8224 7831 Omagh Agricultural Show, t (028) 8224 7831 Ulster American Folk Park Festival, t (028) 8225 6330. *See* also p.357.

August–September
Glenelly Sheep and Dog Trials, Plumbridge, Strabane, t (028) 8164 8744 Johnny Crampsie Weekend, Strabane, t (074) 41106. Traditional music and workshops. Magherafelt Folk and Hillwalking Festival, (028) 8224 7831 Storytelling Festival, Rural College, Draperstown, t (028) 7962 9100

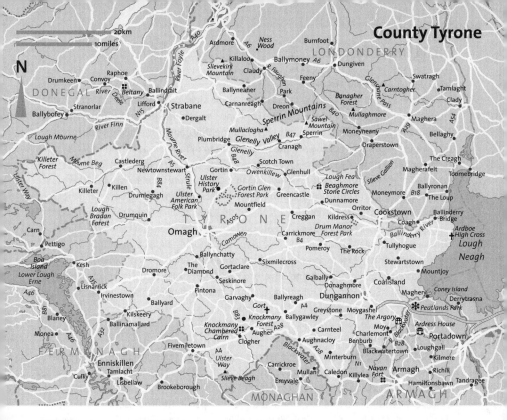

History

County Tyrone's past can be illustrated by concentrating on the lands and estate of Caledon, a small village that lies close to the border with County Monaghan. This was O'Neill territory, and the natives fought the English vigorously from the mid 17th century onwards, but by the 18th century the region had been planted with Scottish undertakers. The story of Captain William Hamilton is typical of many of the new landlords. A Cromwellian soldier and one of the Hamiltons from Haddington in East Lothian, William was granted the Caledon estate of Sir Phelim O'Neill after the Battle of Benburb in 1646. By 1775 the Hamilton line, which had intermarried with the Osserys – earls of Ossery and Cork – had become very extravagant. As a result of their debts, the property was sold to a Derry merchant's son, James Alexander, who had acquired a vast fortune in the service of the East India Company. The most distinguished member of this family (which still owns the estate) was Viscount Alexander of Tunis.

Tyrone's history lives on in its language: some expressions recall Gaelic, although it is no longer spoken here, and a few turns of phrase will take you back to the days of Elizabeth I. For example, a 'boon' is a company of people in the house, to 'join' is to begin, to 'convoy' is to accompany, and 'diet' is the word for food. The small farmers in this area are for the most part descended from Scottish Presbyterians, although in the Sperrins there are many Catholic descendants of the O'Neills and their *septs*.

Northern Tyrone

Strabane and Environs

Strabane (*An Srath Ban*: 'The White Holm') is a border town and almost the twin of Lifford, across the Foyle in Donegal. The Finn and the Mourne join to form the Foyle here as well. Strabane is a bustling town with friendly people. It is also the birthplace of John Dunlap, printer of the American Declaration of Independence. You should try to visit **Grays Printers' Museum** (*open Apr–end Sept Tues–Sat 2–5; adm; t (028) 7188 4094*), the 18th-century printing shop in Main Street where Dunlap worked. There is a collection of 19th-century hand-printing machines in full working order. Another Strabane-born notable is that curious wit Brian O'Nolan, alias Flann O'Brien. He wrote *The Poor Mouth, At-Swim-2-Birds* and other stories, and his column in *The Irish Times* between 1937 and 1966 became a byword for a debunking type of humour.

Just to the north-east of Strabane, at **Dunnamanagh** (also spelled 'Donemana'), on the town's outskirts, you'll find **Silverbrook Mill** (*Brook Rd; t (028) 7139 7097*), which comprises an 18th-century cornmill and a 19th-century flaxmill. You might also visit the **Tom Agnew Mill Pottery**, nearby (*see* opposite).

The Tyrone Hills

East of Strabane you pass into the **Tyrone Hills**, which consist mainly of the Sperrin mountain range and extend into County Londonderry. This is perfect walking country, full of glens and mountain passes to beyond Plumbridge (which is at the western end of the beautiful Glenelly Valley) and Cranagh. The **Sperrin Heritage Centre** (*open daily Apr–Oct, call for times, t (028) 8164 8142; adm*) is situated on Glenelly Road, between the villages of Cranagh and Sperrin. Here there is a comprehensive and interesting display of Sperrin wildlife, showing all the animals, birds and plant species that you might see while walking in the glens around here, such as the hen harrier or the cloudberry, which grows on a single patch west of Dart Mountain.

One of the great saints of Ireland, St Brigid, is strongly associated with this area; there are not many houses that do not have a St Brigid cross hanging above the door to ward off evil. These crosses look rather like the ancient symbol of the swastika, and are made of rushes. The B48 from Gortin to Omagh passes through the wild and beautiful **Gortin Glen Forest Park**, where there are nature trails among the conifer trees. The Ulster Way also passes through. The country lanes around about are bright with gorse and primroses in spring, and the lambs make a very pretty sight. The **Ulster History Park** at Cullion traced human settlement and society from 8000 BC to the 17th century; it is currently closed but there are hopes that a new buyer will reopen it in the not too distant future.

A couple of miles to the south-east of Strabane, on the pretty, unnumbered Plumbridge road, at Dergalt, is the **Wilson Ancestral Homestead** (*open July and Aug Tue–Sun 2–5, rest of year call for hours, t (028) 7138 2204; adm*). This comparatively humble dwelling is where President Woodrow Wilson's grandfather (among many other children) was reared before he set off for the United States, where he became a newspaper editor.

Tourist Information

Castlederg: 26 Lower Strabane Rd,
t (028) 8167 0795. *Open Easter–Oct.*
Cranagh: Sperrin Heritage Centre, 274 Glenelly Rd,
Plumbridge, t (028) 8164 8142. *Open Apr–Oct.*
Omagh: 1 Market St, t (028) 8224 7831
Strabane: Abercorn Sq, t (028) 7188 3735.
Open Apr–Sept.

Internet Access

Omagh Library, 1 Spillar's Place (off Dublin Rd),
t (028) 8224 4821

Shopping

Antiques
Kelly's Antiques, Old Mountfield Rd, Omagh
Melmount Auctions, Unit C, Ballycolman
Industrial Estate, Strabane, t (028) 7138 2223
Tom Agnew Mill Pottery, Brook Rd, Donemana/
Dunnamanagh, t (028) 7139 8377. Useful
objects for daily living in muted stoneware.
Viewback Antique Auctions, 8 Castle Place,
Omagh, t (028) 8224 6271

Sports and Activities

Fishing
Fishing is good on the River Blackwater, near
Omagh, for brown trout, sea trout and salmon,
and on the Mourne River system, which
includes the Strule, Owenkillew and Glenelly.
Licences are available from Foyle Fisheries
Commission or local fishing tackle shops.
Baronscourt Estate, Newtownstewart, t (028)
8166 1683. This also offers pike fishing in the
estate's lakes. Book well in advance.
C.A. Anderson and Company, 64 Market St,
Omagh, t (028) 8224 2311. A hardware
merchant providing fishing permits.
Department of Culture, Arts and Leisure,
Inland Fisheries Division, Strabane District
Council, t (028) 9025 8861. Fishing permits.
Foyle Fisheries Commission, Derry,
t (028) 7134 2100

Golf
Fintona Golf Club, Fintona, t (028) 8284 1480.
The best parkland 9-hole in Ireland.
Newtownstewart Golf Club, t (028) 8166 1466
Omagh Golf Club, t (028) 8224 3160.
An 18-hole parkland course.

Ponytrekking
Ardmourne House Stables, t (028) 8167 0291
Ashlee Riding Centre, t (028) 7188 2708
Clanabogan Riding Stables, 85 Clanabogan Rd,
Omagh, t (028) 8225 2050
Tullywhisker Riding School, t (028) 8165 8267

Shooting
Rough and clay pigeon shooting is available
over the Sperrin Mountains. You need to book
well in advance.

Newtownstewart, on the A5 10 miles (16km) south of Strabane, is a 17th-century
Plantation town. It is attractively laid out on a large main street. Nearby on the B84
lies the **Baronscourt Estate,** which has a fine mansion house and gardens that you
can tour (*by appointment only, t (028) 8166 1683*). There is coarse and game fishing
available on the estate, and ponytrekking and golf nearby.

The **Ulster American Folk Park** (*open Easter–Sept Mon–Sat 10.30–6, Sun 11.30–5,
Oct–Easter Mon–Fri 10.30–5; last entry 3.30; adm; t (028) 8224 3292, www.folkpark.com*)
is between Newtownstewart and Omagh, sandwiched between the A5 and the
Plumbridge road, on Mellon Road, Castletown. Visitor Attraction of the Year 2000–2001,
it was developed to illustrate the life that emigrants left in Ireland and the life they
encountered in their new land, by reconstructing the buildings they inhabited. The
ancestral home of the Mellons and the boyhood home of Archbishop John Hughes of
New York are very spartan and simple, and established showpieces. There is a fair bit
of outdoor walking, so take along some good strong shoes and a raincoat.

Baronscourt Estate, Newtownstewart,
 t (028) 8166 1683
Collow Quarry Shooting Grounds,
 44 Bradan Rd, Drumquin, t (028) 8283 1521.
 Clay pigeon shooting.

Walking

There is fine walking in the valleys of the Glenelly, Owenreagh, Owenkillew and Camowen rivers; in the 12 Sperrin forests; and in Gortin Glen Forest Park with its nature trails and wild deer. The **Ulster Way**, a signposted walking trail, goes through the Sperrins.

Strabane Tourist Information, Castlederg Visitor Centre (for both, see p.357) and the Sperrin Heritage Centre (see p.356) sell maps and guides to the area for walkers and cyclists Apr–Oct; the rest of the year you can get them from the Department of Culture, Arts and Leisure of Strabane District Council, t (028) 7138 2204.

Where to Stay and Eat

Mellon Country Hotel, Castletown, Omagh, t (028) 8166 1224, *www.melloncountryhotel. com* (*moderate*). Pleasant modern rooms and a restaurant serving good steaks.
Clanabogan Country House, 85 Clanabogan Rd, Omagh, t (028) 8224 1171, *www.clanaboganhouse.freeserve.co.uk/* (*inexpensive*). A B&B in a restored period house with its own gardens and woodlands.

Golden Hill, 32 Tattykeel Rd, Omagh, t (028) 8225 1257, *www.goldenhill-guesthouse.com* (*inexpensive*). A very welcoming choice in a lovely scenic location.
Sperrin Restaurant, 88 Beltany Rd, Omagh, t (028) 8225 0200 (*moderate*). A grill bar and an à la carte menu. Book ahead.
Badoney Tavern, 16 Main St, Gortin, t (028) 8164 8157 (*inexpensive*). Good pub lunches and snacks.

Self-catering

An Creagán, Creggan, Omagh, t (028) 8076 1112, *www.an-creagan.com* (*inexpensive*). Eight traditional-style cottages; each sleeping 6.
Aughalane *Clachan*, Aughalane, Omagh, t (028) 8164 8000 (*inexpensive*). Cottages for 2–5.
Mote Cottage, Omagh, t (028) 8224 5689 (*inexpensive*). Traditional whitewashed cottages with flowers around the door, sleeping 2 people.

Entertainment and Nightlife

Traditional Music

An Creagan Visitor Centre, t (028) 8076 1112
Dún Uladh Heritage Centre of Ulster, Ballinamullan, Omagh, t (028) 8224 2777
Teach Ceoil (Rouskey) and **Fernagh** *Céilí* House, t (028) 8224 2777. Evenings of *craic*, traditional music, dance, stories and poetry.

East of Omagh, at Creggan, you will find the **An Creagán Visitor Centre** (*open daily Apr–Sept 11–6.30, Oct–Mar 11–4.30; adm; t (028) 8076 1112, www.an-creagan.com*), with bog trails, archaeological exhibits and a restaurant. Several archaeological walks and events are held throughout the year.

Omagh

Omagh, the capital of Tyrone, is separated from the other large town of the county, **Cookstown**, by the Black Bog. This accounts for the turfcraft souvenirs you may find, which make an alternative to the more usual Irish linen hankies or crochet. Some people tell you that there is something French about this town, with its twin-spired church and its reputation for liveliness. Brian Friel, the playwright, is a native. (Any of his plays are worth making a special effort to see; he gives a profound and lyrical insight into Irish culture.). Other writers from this area are Benedict Kiely, Alice

Milligan and William Forbes Marshall. The town is a good spot for fishing on the Camowen and Owenreagh rivers. Those wanting to hear musical talent should time their visit to coincide with the West Tyrone *Feis* in May, also known as the Omagh *Feis*, which has plenty of Irish music and dancing.

Since 15 August 1998, Omagh has been known foremost as the site of the most devastating single act of violence in the history of the Troubles: 29 people were killed by a bomb that day in the city centre. There is now a small memorial garden at the site, on Drumragh Avenue beside Strule Bridge, where one may spend some time in quiet reflection.

Southern Tyrone

From Omagh to Cookstown

Omagh is near other forest areas: **Seskinore Forest**, near Fintona, and **Dromore Forest**, further west. If you wish to strike across the moor country you can go by Mountfield on the A505 from Omagh, which will take you by the Black Bog, a nature reserve; any other little roads you encounter may take you past some of the many antiquities that testify to Bronze or earlier Stone Age inhabitants of this area.

At **Pomeroy**, 15 miles (24km) east of Omagh on the B4, high in the mountains and equidistant from Cookstown and Dungannon, are the remains of seven stone circles. More famous are the **Beaghmore Stone Circles**, outside Cookstown near Dunnamore; these intricate alignments on a north-east axis represent the remarkable architecture of the late Stone Age or early Bronze Age. Their formation has been likened to a clock pointing for the last 6,000 years towards the midsummer sunrise. They certainly look very impressive in the wild landscape that surrounds them. To get there, take a minor road off the A505 through Dunnamore and travel on a few miles, going north.

Near to Cookstown at 20 Wellbrook Road in Corkhill is **Wellbrook Beetling Mill** (*open Apr–June and Sept daily 11–6, July and Aug daily 2–6, Oct–Mar Sat, Sun and bank hols 1–5; adm; t (028) 8674 8210*), a water-powered hammer mill for beetling, which is the final stage of linen manufacture. The mill is situated in a lovely glen with walks along the Ballinderry River and the mill race.

Cookstown is in the middle of Northern Ireland, near the fertile heartland that traces its course beside the Bann in Londonderry and continues down by Lough Neagh. There are two Nash buldings in its environs. On the outskirts south-east of town is **Killymoon Castle**, a battlemented towered construction that contrasts with the simple Church of Ireland parish church, St Laurane's, at the south-east end of the main street. The conspicuous Puginesque Catholic church, on a hill in the middle of town, is a good landmark. Arriving at Cookstown, you will be impressed by the long, wide main street; cynics may think it a good street for leading a charge against insurgents. Cookstown has a strong Nationalist tradition, exemplified by the energetic Bernadette Devlin, now McAliskey, who was active in the Civil Rights Movement and elected to the British Parliament aged only 21 in 1969. There is also a strong Scottish Protestant tradition with the descendants of those who settled here in the 17th century.

Tourist Information

Cookstown: Burn Rd, **t** (028) 8676 6727
Dungannon: Killymaddy Tourist Information
Centre, 190 Ballygawley Rd, **t** (028) 8776 7259

Shopping

Crafts
Tyrone Crystal, Killybrackey, **t** (028) 8772 5335,
www.tyronecrystal.com. A glassworks where
you can take a guided tour, and buy seconds
very cheaply.

Sports and Activities

Fishing
There is fishing on the River Blackwater for
brown trout, sea trout and salmon. Licences
can be had from Foyle Fisheries Commission,
Derry, or local fishing tackle shops.
　For the Ballinderry River, you need a
Fisheries Conservancy Board game rod licence
and a permit (available from tackle shops or
tourist offices in Caledon, Cookstown, Omagh,
Moy and Aughnacloy).
Anderson's, 64 Market St, Omagh,
　t (028) 8224 2311
Killymaddy Tourist Information Centre,
　t (028) 8776 7259. An information source.
Loughs Agency, Derry City, **t** (028) 7134 2100.
　Information on fishing in Creeve Lough near

Benburb and White Lough near Aughnacloy,
and on brown trout fishing in Brantry Lough.
Treanor's, Main St, Gortin, **t** (028) 8164 8543

Golf
Aughnacloy Golf Club, t (028) 8555 7050
Killymoon Golf Club, Cookstown, **t** (028) 8676
3762. An 18-hole parkland course.

Open Farms
Altmore Fisheries, 32 Altmore Rd, 3 miles (5km)
south of Pomeroy, **t** (028) 8775 8977

Ponytrekking
Crocknagrally Forest Stables, 100 Croneen Rd,
　Fivemiletown, **t** (028) 8952 1991
Hilltop Stables, Eglish, **t** (028) 8775 3925
MoyRiding School, 131 Derrycaw Rd, Moy,
　t (028) 8778 4440

Shooting
Logue's Hill Clay Pigeon Club, near Cappagh,
　t (028) 8776 7259 (Killymaddy Tourist Centre)
Seskinore Game Farm, Seskinore,
　t (028) 8284 1243

Walking
　Forest parks with nature trails include
Favour Royal, just south-west of Caledon on
the Monaghan border, **Gollagh Woods,** and
Fardross Forest, near Clogher, where you
can see red squirrels. Riverside walks can be
enjoyed by **Wellbrook Beetling Mill,** which
lies close to Cookstown.

Places to visit nearby include the **Ardboe High Cross,** about 10 miles (16km) to the
east on the shore of Lough Neagh. This 10th-century monument has 22 remarkable
sculptured scriptural panels covered with scenes from the Old and New Testaments;
they are easily recognizable, unlike those on many of the other high crosses you may
see, which are usually so weathered you need to concentrate to read the theme. South
of Cookstown, **Tullaghogue Rath** (pronounced 'Tullyhog') is where the great O'Neill
chieftains were inaugurated. In 1595 Hugh O'Neill gave in to the British, and seven years
later the Lord Deputy Mountjoy had the throne smashed to prevent future ceremonies.
　At the foot of Tullaghogue hill, in what is now Loughry Agricultural College, is the
mansion where Jonathan Swift stayed while writing *Gulliver's Travels*; the portraits of
his two loves, Stella and Vanessa, still hang in the house. It is sometimes possible to
visit it; ask at the door. **Drum Manor Forest Park** (*open daily 10am–dusk; adm and
parking fee;* **t** *(028) 8676 2774, www.forestserviceni.gov.uk*) close by, to the east of
Cookstown on the A505, has a butterfly garden and a forest trail for the disabled.

Where to Stay

The Valley Hotel, 60 Main St, Fivemiletown,
t (028) 8952 1505, *www.thevalleyhotel.com*
(*expensive*). A comfortable and cheery
option despite the unprepossessing
modern exterior,

Charlemont House, 4 The Square, Moy,
Dungannon, t (028) 8778 4895 (*moderate*).
A Georgian townhouse boasting period
furnishings and lots of atmosphere. The
lovely garden has a view of the Blackwater
River at the rear.

Corick House, 20 Corick Rd, Clogher, t (028)
8554 8216, *www.corickcountryhouse.com*
(*moderate*). A 17th-century house full of
history, in lovely grounds, with a good
restaurant (see below).

Grange Lodge, 7 Grange Rd,
near Dungannon, t (028) 8778 4212,
www.grangelodgecountryhouse.com
(*moderate*). A comfortable Georgian
house situated by the Blackwater River,
offering outstanding breakfasts.

Braeside House, 23 Drumconis Rd, Coagh,
Cookstown, t (028) 8673 7301 (*inexpensive*).
Two B&B rooms in an old house.

Self-catering

Blessingbourne, near Fivemiletown,
t (028) 8952 1221, *www.blessingbourne.com*
(*inexpensive*). Three 2-bedroom apartments
with very comfortable rooms set around a
courtyard near an attractive Victorian
mansion in wooded grounds. It's the type of
place where you can imagine you're the
guest at a leisurely house party.

Eating Out

Corick House, Clogher, t (028) 8554 8216,
www.corickcountryhouse.com (*moderate*).
Good food made from the best local
produce, including vegetables and fruit
produced in the hotel's own early-Victorian
walled garden.

Tullylagan Country House, 40 Tullylagan Rd,
near Cookstown, t (028) 8676 5100, *www.
tullylagan.com* (*moderate*). Good cuisine made
from top local ingredients, including rack of
lamb with chive mash and rosemary jus.
Closed Sun eve.

Cookstown Courtyard, 56 William St, Cookstown,
t (028) 8676 5070 (*inexpensive*). Set lunches,
including home-made pies and puddings.

Rosamund's Coffee Shop, Station House,
Augher, t (028) 8554 8601 (*inexpensive*).
Home-made stew. *Closed eves.*

Suitor Gallery, 17 Grange Rd, Ballygawley,
t (028) 8556 8653 (*inexpensive*).
A place offering good home-baking.

Tommy's Bar, 9 The Square, Moy, t (028) 8778
4755 (*inexpensive*). An authentic pub serving
well-priced standards.

Tyrone Crystal Tea Shop, Killybracken Rd,
Dungannon, t (028) 8772 5335 (*inexpensive*).
A good café. *Closed eves.*

Dungannon and Along the Blackwater River

Dungannon, a city on a hill, looks like your average planter town; with a planned
main street and a Royal School founded in the time of James I of England. It was, in
fact, the centre for the O'Neills until the Flight of the Earls deprived the Gaels of their
native leaders (*see* **History**, p.12). It is now a quietly prosperous town with a long-
established textile industry specializing in Moygashel fabrics, and a glass factory
producing Tyrone crystal. At the beginning of the 17th century, in order to promote
good Protestant education, James I of England and Ireland (James VI of Scotland)
provided Royal schools as well as charters for land. You may notice the **Royal School,
Dungannon**, which is on Northland Row in the centre of the town. The present
building dates from 1786, and outside it is a statue of one of its most famous 'old
boys', Major General John Nicholson, whose exploits in India inspired such respect
that there was even a sect called 'Nikkul Seyn'. Another Indian connection is the
police station in the town centre, which looks like a castle with projecting apertures

for missile-throwing. Apparently it was built according to plans for a fort in the Khyber Pass because some clerk in Dublin got into a muddle. This is the usual explanation for many of the exotic-looking stations that are scattered about Ireland.

Tyrone has its River Blackwater, though it is not in the same league as the other Blackwater, which flows through Cork and Waterford. It creates a watery border with County Armagh and flows through **Moy** – with its Italian-styled square created by one of the Charlemont family – to **Benburb**, an ancient stronghold with a splendid ruined castle. The parish **church** (Church of Ireland) is 17th century, and there are some fine tombstones in the graveyard. In 1646 the Irish forces led by Owen Roe O'Neill gained a significant victory here over English Puritan and Scottish troops.

The Blackwater flows in a series of fine pools and little falls to **Caledon** on the A28, with its unspoiled Georgian look. Intriguing to the traveller is the **Clogher Valley**, which is border country with the Republic and so enjoys that anomalous status of being either frontier outpost or lost territory. This place evidently has a long history of habitation, for many ancient earthworks have survived. In the townland of **Gort**, between Ballygawley and Augher, is the ancient graveyard of Errigal Keerogue, with a fine high cross and a superb view over the countryside.

Just north of Augher, off the B83, is the **Knockmany Forest**, a government-run forestry plantation on Knockmany Hill. At the top, look for the **Knockmany chambered cairn**, said to be the burial place of Queen Aine, Queen of Oriel, a 6th-century kingdom the centre of which was Clogher. The cairn is a passage grave dating from Neolithic times. This type of monument consists of a stone-built passage leading to a terminal chamber, often cruciform in shape, and covered by a mound or cairn of stones. The remarkable thing about this grave is its incised decoration, in patterns of concentric circles, zigzags and other designs, which are similar in style to the great earthworks in the Boyne Valley, County Meath.

This country, besides being a fisherman's haunt, is well forested. The 19th-century landlords who once owned vast tracts of land have disappeared, but their old estates, such as Favour Royal and Fardross, gave their names to public parkland and forests where it is possible to camp and have picnics. At **Favour Royal**, you can walk from the river to St Patrick's Well and Chair at Altadaven – a secret, mossy place.

Augher and Clogher are both within striking distance. **Augher** lies between the Blackwater River and Augher Lake. You can see the 19th-century **Castle of Spur Royal** just to the west of the village as you pass by on the A4.

Clogher village is on a site of prehistoric importance, as well as being of great ecclesiastical significance. It was the original seat in the 5th century of the diocese of Clogher, one of the oldest bishoprics in Ireland. In the porch of **St MacCartan's Cathedral** there is a curious stone called the *Clogh-oir*, or 'Gold Stone'. There are two 9th-century high crosses in the graveyard, and you can climb the tower (*ask at rectory for access*) and get a stunning view of the Clogher Valley .

Behind this centre of ancient Christianity is the even older hill fort of **Ramore** (*always accessible*). Archaeologists have investigated it for evidence about the Iron Age, and perhaps the mysterious *Clogh-oir* comes from an idol of those times. It was

certainly the site of the palace of the kings of Oriel; the tradition of the dynasty
survives but not the dates, other than that they were pre-5th-century. The hill fort
itself is now just a grassy mound.

Benburb has a picturesque castle ruin on a cliff overhanging the Blackwater River;
this early-17th-century castle replaced an earlier O'Neill stronghold. The demesne
surrounding the castle is freely accessible, and the Servite Priory in the grounds has a
popular open day on the third Sunday in June. **Benburb Valley Heritage Centre** (*open
Easter–Sept Tue–Sat 10–5, Sun 2–5; t (028) 3754 9885*), on Milltown Road, operates from
the 19th-century linen mill on the banks of the Ulster Canal. You may like to take a
tour around the mill and learn about the linen industry in Ireland; the centre also has
a hostel and a café.

County Londonderry

This is a rich and varied region. The traditions of political argument and protest vie
with the gifts of learning and song in the people who inhabit this friendly land. The
countryside ranges from stormy sea coast and wild mountain ranges to sheltered
valleys, well wooded from years of far-sighted planting. The coastline from Magilligan
to Downhill is scattered with golden strands. Historic Derry is a spire-dreaming city
that arouses fierce passions in the hearts of its inhabitants.

The city and the whole county are fostering a renaissance of peace and heightened
business activity after suffering several decades of the Troubles, which started in the
1960s. New housing, sports centres and a £15-million theatre have been built, and
regeneration schemes have been implemented to replace destroyed shops with new
city-centre hotels, businesses and riverside apartments. Further rejuvenation has
come through its Craft Village, Heritage Centre, and award-winning Tower Museum.
People in the province are determined to live and work together harmoniously, and
the traditional tribal areas are becoming less so with each passing year. The economy
of County Londonderry is heavily subsidized by the British government, but there
is still high unemployment in places such as the Bogside. Several international
companies have set up factories and there are the traditional shirt-makers, although
these are now struggling in the face of competition from Third World countries.

Derry City

Derry (*Doire*: 'Oak Grove') is a symbolic city situated on the River Foyle. Before the 1960s
it was probably best known for its association with the pretty 'Londonderry Air' (better
known as 'Danny Boy'), but it has been one of Northern Ireland's troublespots until
recently. The strife is not unprecedented, for it has survived three sieges.

The city is a place well worth visiting. On most of the approaches to its centre you
will see its image across the water: a fine walled city, built around the curve of the
Foyle. Some ugly buildings have been allowed to mar its elegant profile, but not as

yet too many, and the docks are no longer crowded with thousands of folk sailing to a brand-new world, as they were in the 19th century. A walk around the historic walls gives you a good view of the docks and the wide River Foyle. Big ships still harbour in the port, three miles (5km) downstream of Derry, although in the days of the British

Getting There and Around

Derry, a terminus for trains and buses, is a halfway house for those heading east or west.

By Air

Belfast City Airport, t (028) 9093 9093, *www.belfastcityairport.com*
Belfast International Airport, t (028) 9448 4848, *www.bial.co.uk*
City of Derry Airport, t (028) 7181 0784, *www.cityofderryairport.com*. Flights to Dublin, Glasgow, Manchester and London Stansted.

By Sea

P&O ferries offer the shortest, fastest crossing (60mins) between Scotland and Larne. Seacat, Stena Line and Norse Merchant Ferries run crossings to Belfast. For details, *see* p.91.

By Rail

Translink, t (028) 9066 6630, *www.translink.co.uk*. Mainline services from Belfast to Derry, linking several coastal towns along the way.

By Bus

Airporter, t (028) 7126 9996, *www.airporter.co.uk*. An express bus service to Belfast City and International airports.
Belfast Europa Bus, t (028) 9066 6630. A daily, hourly service from Belfast to Derry.
Dublin *Busáras*, t (01) 836 6111. A Dublin–Derry Express bus service.
Londonderry and Lough Swilly Bus Company, t (028) 7126 2017. A firm that also goes into Co. Donegal.
Ulsterbus, t (028) 9066 6630. Derry–Belfast.

By Car

Desmond Motors, Derry City, t (028) 7136 7137
Europcar, City of Derry Airport, t (028) 7181 2773

By Bicycle

Happy Days Cycle Hire, 245 Lone Moor Rd, t (028) 7128 7128, *www.happydays.ie*

Festivals

March

City of Drama Festival, t (028) 7126 4455
Guth an Earraigh, t (028) 7126 4132. An Irish-language festival.
St Patrick's Day, t (028) 7136 5151. The 17 March celebration.

April

City of Derry Jazz Festival, t (028) 7137 6545, *www.cityofderryjazzfestival.com*

June

Walled City Cultural Trail, t (028) 7137 7577. An outdoor carnival.

July–August

Foyle Cup, t (028) 7126 7432. Youth soccer.
Gasyard Wall *Feile*, t (028) 7126 1916, *www.freederry.org/gasyard*. Music, workshops, exhibitions and more.
Maiden City Festival, t (028) 7134 9250, *www.maidencityfestival.com*. A celebration of Protestant diversity.
Orange Order Parades, t (028) 7126 7284. A famous 12 July event.

October

Banks of the Foyle Halloween Carnival, t (028) 7137 6545. Events on 17–31 Oct.

November

Craft Fair, Derry, t (028) 7137 6506
Foyle Film Festival, t (028) 7126 0562, *www.foylefilmfestival.com*
Sperrins Autumn Storytelling Festival, Rural College and Derrynoid Conference Centre, Draperstown, t (028) 7962 9100, *www.derrynoid.com*

December

Ferryquay Gate, t (028) 7126 7284. The anniversary (Sat nearest 18th) of the shutting of Derry's gates in the siege of 1689.

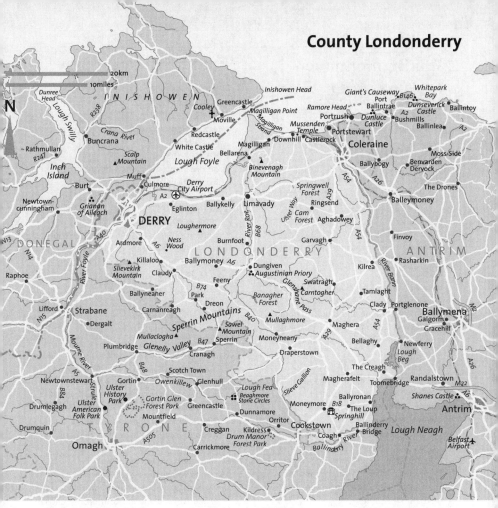

County Londonderry

[Map of County Londonderry showing towns and features including: Dunree Head, Inishowen, Lough Swilly, Crana River, Buncrana, Rathmullan, Inch Island, Scalp Mountain, Muff, Burt, Culmore, Newtowncunningham, Grianan of Aileach, Derry City Airport, Eglinton, DERRY, Loughermore, Ardmore, Ness Wood, Killaloo, Slievekirk Mountain, Claudy, Ballymoney, Ballyneaner, Park, Dreon, Carnanreagh, Sperrin Mountains, Sawel Mountain, Mullaclogha, Glenelly Valley, Sperrin, Plumbridge, Cranagh, Lifford, Strabane, Dergalt, Scotch Town, Owenkillew, Glenhull, Newtownstewart, Gortin, Ulster History Park, Gortin Glen Forest Park, Greencastle, Drumlegagh, Ulster American Folk Park, Mountfield, Drumquin, Creggan, Kildress, Drum Manor Forest Park, Carrickmore, Omagh, Tyrone, Donegal, Cooley, Greencastle, Magilligan Point, Moville, White Castle, Redcastle, Magilligan, Magilligan Strand, Bellarena, Lough Foyle, Binevenagh Mountain, Downhill, Castlerock, Mussenden Temple, Portstewart, Portrush, Ramore Head, Coleraine, Ballykelly, Limavady, Springwell Forest, Cam Forest, Aghadowey, Ringsend, Ulster Way, River Roe, Dungiven, Augustinian Priory, Feeny, Banagher Forest, Glenshane Pass, Carntogher, Swatragh, Garvagh, Mullaghmore, Moneyneany, Maghera, Draperstown, The Creagh, Magherafelt, Lough Fea, Beaghmore Stone Circles, Dunnamore, Moneymore, Orritor, Cookstown, Coagh, Ballindeny River, Giant's Causeway, Port, Ballintrae, Whitepark Bay, Dunseverick Castle, Ballintoy, Dunluce Castle, Bushmills, Ballinlea, Moss-Side, Benvarden, Dervock, The Drones, Ballybogy, Ballymoney, Finvoy, Rasharkin, Kilrea, River Bann, Tamlaght, Clady, Portglenone, Ballymena, Galgorm, Gracehill, Bellaghy, Newferry, Lough Beg, Toomebridge, Randalstown, Shanes Castle, Antrim, Ballyronan, The Loup, Springhill, Ballinderry Bridge, Lough Neagh, Belfast Airport, Slieve Gallion, River Foyle, Mourne River, Strule]

N

20km
10miles

Empire they carried exotic cargo such as silk from Bombay. To the north-west of the old city walls is the historical, Republican Bogside, with its much-repainted and photographed 'Free Derry' monument and murals. Irish nationalists and Catholics usually call the city 'Derry'; for Northern Irish Protestants it's 'Londonderry' (although in general both county and city are known as 'Derry'). One solution among the PC has been to write 'London/Derry', leading local jokers to label it 'Stroke City'.

History

The land on which the settlement of Derry grew up was granted to St Columba (St Colmcille) by Aimire, Prince of the O'Neills, in AD 546. The saint built a monastery on the oak-crowned hill. He eventually left and founded many other religious settlements, the most important of which was on Iona, the isle off the west coast of Scotland. From here Christianity spread over Scotland and the north of England. St Columba wrote, homesick for this place:

Tourist Information

Derry: 44 Foyle St, **t** (028) 7126 7284,
www.derryvisitor.com,
www.discovernorthernireland.com

Shopping

Antiques
The Whatnot, 22 Bishop St, **t** (028) 7128 8333

Art Gallery
The McGilloway Gallery, 6 Shipquay St, **t** (028) 7136 6011. Irish paintings, mainly landscape.

Books
Bookworm, 18–20 Bishop St, **t** (028) 7128 2727, *www.bookwormderry.com*. A shop with a terrific section on books of Irish interest.
Foyle Books, Craft Village, 12a Magazine St, **t** (028) 7137 2530. A second-hand bookseller.

Crafts
The Craft Village, Shipquay St, **t** (028) 7126 0329. A crafts-lover's paradise, including City of Derry Crystal (**t** (028) 7137 0042, *www. derry-crystal.com*).
The Donegal Shop, 8 Shipquay St, **t** (028) 7126 6928. Irish knitwear, pottery, traditional and contemporary jewellery and more.
Faller the Jeweller, 12 Strand Rd, **t** (028) 7136 2710
Tower Museum Gift Shop, Union Hall Place, **t** (028) 7137 4404

Sports and Activities

Golf
City of Derry Golf Club, 49 Victoria Rd, **t** (028) 7134 6369
Foyle International Golf Centre, 12 Alder Rd, **t** (028) 7135 2222, *www.foylegolfcentre.co.uk*

Indoor Leisure Centres
Brooke Park Leisure Centre, Rosemount Ave, **t** (028) 7126 2637
Lisnagelvin Leisure Centre, Ritchill Park, Waterside, **t** (028) 7134 7695
St Columb's Park Leisure Centre, Limavady Rd, **t** (028) 7134 3941

Templemore Sports Complex, Buncrana Rd, **t** (028) 7128 9200

Outdoor Activity Centre
Ness Woods, off A6 to Belfast, Derry. Nature trails and a waterfall.

Ponytrekking
Ardmore Stables, 8 Rushall Rd, Ardmore, **t** (028) 7134 5187

Walking Tours
City Tours, 11 Carlisle Rd, **t** (028) 7127 1996
McNamara's Famous Guided Walking Tours, **t** (028) 7134 5335. Tours of the city.
Northern Ireland Tours and Guides Ltd, 70 Marlborough St, **t** (028) 7130 9051

Where to Stay

Derry City
Beech Hill Country House Hotel, 32 Ardmore Rd, **t** (028) 7134 9279, *www.beech-hill.com*, (*expensive*). A manor-house hotel 2 miles (3.2km) outside the city walls, with lovely grounds and a reputation for its cuisine. There's a modern gym, a Jacuzzi, an aromatherapy steam room and a sauna, and massages, reflexology and Reiki treatments are available.
Hastings Everglades Hotel, Prehen Rd, **t** (028) 7132 1066, *www.hastingshotels.com* (*expensive*). A bland but comfortable choice overlooking the River Foyle, next to a golf course. There's a formal restaurant and the Library Bar, where you can enjoy snacks and a pint of Guinness in deep armchairs.
Ramada Da Vinci's, 15 Culmore Rd, **t** (028) 7127 9111, *www.davincishotel.com* (*moderate*). A modern 70 room chain-hotel complex a 10min walk from the city, including 21 serviced apartments.
The Trinity Hotel, 22–24 Strand Rd, **t** (028) 7127 1271, *www.thetrinityhotel.com* (*moderate*). A modern city-centre hotel.
Groarty House, 62 Groarty Rd, **t** (028) 7126 1403, *www.bandbnorthernireland.com* (*inexpensive*). A 200-year-old guesthouse 3 miles (5km) from the city, with views over it and the surrounding countryside.

Manor House, 15 Main St, Eglinton (near Derry City Airport), t (028) 7181 0222 (*inexpensive*). An attractive manor-house hotel.
Derry City Hostel, 6 Magazine St, Derry, t (028) 7128 0280 (*inexpensive*), *www. derrycityyouthhostel.com*. A purposebuilt facility next to the city walls, including family rooms and dorms, plus free parking for guests.

Eating Out

Derry City
Ardmore Restaurant, Beech Hill Country House, 32 Ardmore Rd, t (028) 7134 9279, *www. beech-hill.com* (*moderate–expensive*). A place serving delicious, imaginative food, including home-made tagliatelle, monkfish and sumptuous puddings.
Browns Restaurant, 1 Bonds Hill, t (028) 7134 5180, *www.brownsrestaurant.com* (*moderate*). A diverse menu based on good-quality lamb, fish and vegetables.
Fitzroy's, 2–4 Bridge St, t (028) 7126 6211, *www.fitzroysrestaurant.com* (*moderate*). A popular city-centre brasserie.
Indigo, 27 Shipquay St, t (028) 7127 1011 (*moderate*). A relaxed café-bar with a tasty Asian-influenced menu.
La Sosta Ristorante, 45a Carlisle Rd, Derry, t (028) 7137 4817 (*moderate*). A family-run Italian. *Closed Sun and Mon.*
Linenhall Bar, 3 Market St, t (028) 7137 1665 (*moderate*). A good place for lunch specials. *Closed eves.*
Oysters, 162 Spencer Rd, Waterside, t (028) 7134 4875 (*moderate*). A restaurant recommended for its warmth, good service and excellent, cosmopolitan menu.
India House, 51 Carlisle Rd, t (028) 7126 0532 (*inexpensive–moderate*). Spicy, well-cooked, reasonably priced food.
Badger's, 16 Orchard St, t (028) 7136 0763/3306 (*inexpensive*). A lively pub and restaurant offering grills and salads. *Closed Mon–Thur and Sun eves.*
Beckett's Bistro, 44 Foyle St, t (028) 7136 0066 (*inexpensive*). A popular place to come for pub lunches, afternoon bistro fare and evening meals.

Dungloe Bar, 41 Waterloo St, t (028) 7126 7716 (*inexpensive*). Pub grub and traditional music.
Metro Bar, 3 Bank Place, t (028) 7126 7401 (*inexpensive*). Soup and stews.

Entertainment and Nightlife
You can hear live traditional music in the pubs around Waterloo St.

Pubs and Clubs
Badger's, 16 Orchard St, t (028) 7136 3306. An award-winning pub.
Grand Central, 27 Strand Rd, t (028) 7126 7826
Henry Joy McCrackens, 10 Magazine St, t (028) 7136 0177. A self-described 'chapel of cocktails and monastery of music'.
Linenhall Bar, 3 Market St, t (028) 7137 1665
The Metro, 3 Bank Place, t (028) 7126 7401
Monico Lounge, 4–6 Custom House St, t (028) 7126 3121. One of Derry's oldest pubs, just beside the Walls.
River Inn Bar, 36 Shipquay St, t (028) 7137 1965

Theatre and Cinema
Orchard Street Cinema, Derry, t (028) 7126 2845. Mainly arthouse films.
The Playhouse, 5–7 Artillery St, Derry, t (028) 7126 8027, *www.derryplayhouse.co.uk*. A non-sectarian community arts centre with performances and workshops.
Strand Multiplex Cinema, Strand Rd, Derry, t (028) 7137 3900. A 7-screen cinema showing new releases.

Arts Centres
Comhaltas Ceoltóirí Éireann, 15 Crawford Sq, t (028) 7126 4177, *derryaoh@hotmail.com*. Traditional Irish culture, including music, singing, *ceilidh* and set-dancing.
The Nerve Centre, 7–8 Magazine St, t (028) 7126 0562, *www.nerve-centre.co.uk*. A multimedia centre complete with an in-house cinema.
The Verbal Arts Centre, Mall Wall and Stable Lane, Bishop Street Within, t (028) 7126 6946, *www.verbalartscentre.co.uk*. Northern Ireland's only centre devoted to literature and the storytelling tradition.

Derry, mine own small oak grove,
Little cell, my home, my love.
Oh. Thou Lord of lasting life,
Woe to him who brings it strife.

He never outgrew his love for the city, and would have sympathized with emigrant families who left Derry for America in the 18th and 19th centuries, among them the forebears of such famous figures as Davy Crockett and President James K. Polk.

Derry suffered at the hands of the Norsemen, and then an expedition burned the abbey in 1195. By the end of the 16th century, the English built a fort in Derry in order to attack the O'Neill of the time, and later a small town was constructed from the ecclesiastical ruins. This was completely destroyed in 1608 by Cahir O'Doherty and his supporters. It was after this that James I granted the city and the county to the London Livery companies, who rebuilt the walls and planned the streets, which remain. Derry thus acquired its 'London' prefix.

Derry is the most complete walled city in Ireland, with early-17th-century walls about a mile (1.6km) in circumference, pierced by seven gates, six bastions and many cannon. It was first besieged during the rebellion of 1641, then during the Cromwellian wars of 1649, and finally there was an historic siege in 1689. This siege still plays a very important part in the mind of the Ulster Unionist, for it sums up the courage and righteousness of the Protestant settlers who resisted with the cry 'No surrender.' The city was being assailed by James II, who had lost his throne in England and was trying to repair his fortunes in Ireland with the help of Louis XIV of France. Thirteen apprentice boys rushed to the gates of the city and shut them in the faces of his approaching army. This secured Londonderry for William III, who had been invited to take over from James II by the English parliament. The siege that followed resulted in many deaths, for the city had no stores of food. Citizens ate rats, dogs and even the starch for laundering linen. A boom was placed across the River Foyle to prevent food supplies reaching the city, but after 105 days it was eventually broken, and the city was relieved by the forces of the Lord Deputy Mountjoy, commanded by Captain Browning, at Shipquay on 28 July. Every year the anniversary of the shutting of the gates is celebrated on the Saturday nearest 18 December, and the Raising of the Siege on 12 August. There are marches around the city, with bands and drummers.

City Centre and City Walls

Derry has many attractions to offer the visitor: interesting museums and charming old streets. Great efforts have been made to improve the cultural life of the city, and its own spontaneous creativity in theatre, poetry and the arts has brought a welcome energy. One of the greatest changes has been the development of three huge retail complexes – Quayside, Foyleside and the Richmond Centre – which are a fair indicator of a newfound commercial confidence in a stable future for the city. Another major development is the relocation of **The Verbal Arts Centre** (*see* 'Arts Centres', p.367) to a building beside the city walls. The centre is a valuable resource, for it encourages and supports all forms of written and spoken creative expression.

The **walls** of Derry have been restored and make for a very interesting walk around the old part. They are entered by seven gates, and all along the circuit are views towards the Foyle, or into the Bogside and beyond to the hills. Information plaques mark every structure of note along the walls – accompanied by unofficial graffitti. If you start at **Shipquay Gate** opposite the Guildhall, you will see some of the cannon used in the siege of 1689. Walking on in a westward direction you come to **Ferryquay Gate**, where the gates were slammed and locked by the determined apprentice boys in the face of James II's troops.

Moving on, you soon come to the long low Plantation Church of Ireland **Cathedral of St Columb** (*chapterhouse museum open Mon–Sat summer 9–5, winter 9–1 and 2–4; adm; **t** (028) 7126 7313*), which lies between Fountain Street and Bishop Street on Clooney Terrace, and is an example of planters' Gothic. The building was founded by the Corporation of London in 1633, and restored in 1886. It was the first specifically Protestant cathedral to be built in the British Isles after the Reformation. The roof rests on stone corbels carved into heads that represent past bishops of Derry. The philosopher George Berkeley (1685–1753) was dean here between 1724 and 1732, and the well-known cleric, the Earl of Bristol, was bishop between 1768 and 1803. He was extremely rich and cultured, favoured Catholic Emancipation and opposed the tithe system. The bishop's throne incorporates the chair used at the consecration of the cathedral in 1633. There are a number of exhibits illustrating the spirit of the 17th-century siege; and the stained-glass windows depict incidents from it. The small museum inside is well worth visiting for its relics of the seige and mementos of Cecil Frances Alexander, composer of such famous hymns as 'Once in Royal David's City' and 'There is a Green Hill Far Away'.

Bishop's Gate, nearby, has fine stone carvings. It actually dates from 1789, when the original was replaced with this triumphal arch. The terraced housing area behind the walls here is the Fountain, a dwindling Protestant preserve, the only one this side of the city. Now, as you turn the corner, you can see the Double Bastion with its cannons that still point out over the Bogside, where the Jacobite army was camped. There is a wonderful view from here, and you can clearly see the Bogside's large wall murals. (The area immediately below the walls is a football pitch, well used by youngsters from the area.) If you continue, you come to **St Augustine's Church**, set among mature trees; somewhere here is the site of St Columba's (St Colmcille's) monastery, which, as the plaque proudly says, means 1,400 years of continuous Christian settlement.

On the corner opposite is the Apprentice Boys' Hall; along the walls here are plane trees planted to commemorate the apprentice boys. Overlooking the Bogside is the base of a monument to the Reverend George Walker, who rallied the dispirited Derry people to continue their defiance. The original statue was destroyed by an IRA bomb in 1973, and when a replacement was commissioned the IRA vowed they would blow that one up as well (it now resides safely behind a high fence, a few metres along the street past the Apprentice Boys Hall). The rest of the wall brings you back down Magazine Street, with its attractive 18th-century houses, to Shipquay Gate again; notice the fine **Presbyterian Church** in Upper Magazine Street with its classical lines.

This area has been much rebuilt, since hardly a single building was left undamaged in the ceaseless IRA bombing campaign of the 1970s. Off Shipquay Street, the **Craft Village** (*contact Inner City Trust for information,* **t** *(028) 7126 0329*), a representation of Derry between the 16th and 19th centuries, is worth a look, not least for a coffee break in one of the cafés, or a browse amongst the craft shops. **The Courthouse** (1813), in Bishop Street, is a good example of Greek Revival architecture; as the city's main symbol of British justice, it received a great deal of IRA attention, and the scars of numerous car-bombs are still evident.

To visit the **Bloody Sunday Memorial**, pass through the Butcher's Gate; it is down to the right, close by the road. This commemorates 30 January 1972, when a civil rights march ended in 13 deaths after the Parachute Regiment opened fire on the marchers (*see* p.30) – government inquiries into the incident continue even now in the Guildhall. Close by, just outside the city walls, is the 18th-century **Church of St Columba**, also called Long Tower Church, on the site of a 12th-century monastery, Templemore. St Columba is further commemorated in a boys' school of that name further down the street. **St Eugene's Roman Catholic Cathedral**, off Infirmary Road and Great James Street, has a fine east window and high altar. It was built in Gothic style in 1873. In Butcher Street, the **Calgach Heritage Centre** (*open Mon–Fri 9.30–4; adm;* **t** *(028) 7137 3177*) preserves genealogical data from 1663 in its heritage library, but its main attraction is a multimedia exhibition, 'The Fifth Province'. This tells the history of the Celts in the area, and is based on the mythical idea of a fifth Irish province: the shared heritage and state of mind that connects those of Irish descent, no matter where they live.

South-east across the Craigavon Bridge is the Waterside, which remains largely Protestant. The **Tower Museum** (*open July and Aug Mon–Sat 10–5, Sept–June Tue–Sat and bank hols 10–5; adm;* **t** *(028) 7137 2411, www.derrycity.gov.uk/museums*) in O'Doherty Tower, Union Hall Place, preserves the treasures of the Corporation of London, including a two-handed sword said to belong to Sir Caher O'Doherty, who raided Derry in 1608. This is an outstanding museum, winner of several awards, and it does help one grasp both the complex history of ancient Derry and the effects of the Troubles. Artefacts from the Spanish Armada ships wrecked off the coast in 1588 are also on display.

Leave time to go to the less fashionable but enthralling **Harbour Museum** (*open Mon–Fri 10–1 and 2–4.30;* **t** *(028) 7137 7331*) in Harbour Square, where ship models in glass cases, a replica of a currach in which St Colmcille (Columba) would have sailed to Iona, and items illustrating Derry's maritime history are set out on view.

Within the walls are attractive Georgian houses, some with medieval foundations. At the top of the hill on the Diamond, the central square of the old town, excavations were undertaken to try to uncover an early settlement, possibly the Columban foundation, but they only revealed domestic material from the early-17th-century settler population. The old workhouse in Glendermott Road is the **Workhouse Library Museum** (*open July and Aug Mon–Sat 10–4.30, Sept–June Mon–Thur and Sat 10–4.30;* **t** *(028) 7131 8328*), with exhibits on the famine; upstairs is the original workhouse dorm in the same condition as it was for the poor souls sent there. In another room, the 'Atlantic Memorial Exhibition' draws on the importance of the Foyle and Derry during the Second World War; Britain, Canada and the US all had navy bases here.

Other museums of interest include the **Foyle Valley Railway Centre** (*closed at time of writing; t (028) 7126 5234/7137 7331*) on Foyle Road, close to Craigavon Bridge. Here you can take a trip in a 1934 diesel railcar on a three-mile (5km) track beside the Foyle. At the **Amelia Earhart Centre** at Ballyarnett Country Park (*open Mon–Thur 10–4, Fri 10–1; t (028) 7135 4040*) is a museum commemorating the first woman pilot to fly solo across the Atlantic, who accidentally landed nearby in 1932 after mistaking the city for Paris. You may wish to trace your family history via the **Heritage Library** (*open Mon–Fri 9–5; t (028) 7126 9792*) at 14 Bishop Street, which holds all of County Londonderry's genealogical records.

Around the County

Eglinton to Magilligan

The A2 takes you along the Foyle Plain and bypasses Eglinton (the site of Derry City Airport) to travel through **Ballykelly**. This town was settled by people brought in by the Fishmonger's Company of London in 1618. There are two handsome churches here, the **Tamlaghtfinlagan Parish Church**, which is 18th-century Gothic with a graceful spire and fine tombstones; and the neoclassical **Presbyterian Church**. The next town along the coast, still following the A2, is **Limavady**, beautifully sited in the Roe Valley with fine mountain scenery to the north and south-east. Before the Fishermongers Company arrived, Limavady was an important centre of the territory of the O'Cahans, a *sept* under the lordship of the O'Neills, although no trace remains of their castle now. The town is associated with the famous 'Londonderry Air', noted down by Miss Jane Ross in 1851 from the playing of an itinerant piper. William Connolly, speaker of the Irish House of Commons before the Act of Union in 1800, and builder of Castletown House near Dublin, was the son of a Limavady blacksmith.

Precious gold representations of a masted boat, collars and a necklace fashioned in the Celtic La Tène style were found at **Broighter** close to the coastal marshes around the estuary of the River Roe. They are now in the care of the National Museum, Dublin. Further up the coast, underneath the forest-covered Binevenagh Mountain, is the triangle of **Magilligan Point**. A Martello tower, built during the Napoleonic wars, guards the entrance to Lough Foyle. The strand is well known for its shells, the herbs that grow among the dunes, the birds, and for the plagues of rabbits commemorated in a special Magilligan grace. The names of local villages such as Bellarena and the Umbra recall the foundering of the Armada; folklore would have you believe that some of the darker-hued Magilliganites are of Spanish descent. This part of the world also has connections with the Irish music tradition. At the end of the 18th century, interest in the Gaelic cultural achievement began amongst a group of scholarly men. Foremost among them was Edward Bunting, who did so much to preserve Irish airs and ancient music, and organized a great assembly of Irish harpists in Belfast in 1792. One of the oldest, a blind man called Denis Hempsey, or O'Hempsey (*c.* 1695–1807), lived near Magilligan, and provided Bunting with many old tunes and airs. **Benone Strand** is an extension of Magilligan, a glorious seven-mile (11km) sandy arc.

Tourist Information

Coleraine: Railway Rd, t (028) 7034 4723
Limavady: 7 Connell St, t (028) 7776 0307,
www.discovernorthernireland.com

Shopping

Antiques
Forge Antiques, 24 Long Commons,
Castlerock, t (028) 7035 1339

Crafts
Elements Pottery, 12a Mussenden Rd,
Downhill, t (028) 7084 9077,
www.elementsstudio.com
McCluskey Pottery, 11 Gortgarn Rd,
Limavady, t (028) 7776 4579
Patricia Gavin, Endymion, t (028) 7131 1060.
Elegant clothes created from tweed
and other textiles. Visitors need to call
ahead for an appointment.

Sports and Activities

Fishing
You'll find **coarse fishing** on the River Bann.
Deep-sea fishing is available between Lough
Foyle and Portrush. **Game fishing** for brown
trout and salmon is available on the Agivey,
Clady, Roe, Bann and Faughan rivers.
Foyle Fisheries Commission, 8 Victoria Rd,
Derry City, t (028) 7134 2100. A supplier of
game-rod licences.
Glenowen Co-operative, t (028) 7137 1544.
Guides, licences and package fishing trips.

Golf
Benone Golf Course, Downhill, t (028) 7775 0555
Castlerock Golf Club, 65 Circular Rd, Castlerock,
t (028) 7084 8314
Radisson Roe Park and Golf Resort, Limavady,
t (028) 7772 2222/776 0105.

Outdoor Activities
Roe Valley Country Park, t (028) 7772 2074.
A centre for walking, fishing, canoeing,
rockclimbing and orienteering.
The Ulster Gliding Club, Sea Coast Rd,
Bellarena, t (028) 7775 0301

Ponytrekking
Hill Farm, Castlerock, t (028) 7084 8629

Walking
The **Sperrins Sky Way**, a 20-mile (32km)
route, starts at Barony Bridge, Moydamlaght
Forest, near Draperstown, and runs along the
Sperrin Ridge, finishing at Eden, east of
Plumbridge, in Co. Tyrone.

Where to Stay

Ardtara Country House, 8 Gorteade Rd,
Upperlands, near Maghera, t (028) 7964
4490, *www.ardtara.com* (*expensive*).
A fine 19th-century house, comfortable
and welcoming, with a very good restaurant
(*see* opposite). The 8 bedrooms have king-size
beds, original fireplaces and panoramic
views across the grounds, and there is a
practice tee and an all-weather tennis court.
Brown Trout Golf and Country Inn,
209 Agivey Rd, Aghadowey, south of
Coleraine, t (028) 7086 8209, *www.
browntroutinn.com* (*expensive*). An inn in
pretty grounds near the river, with good food.
Self-catering cottages (1- and 2-bedroom)
are available (*moderate*).
Camus House, 27 Curragh Rd, Coleraine,
t (028) 7034 2982 (*moderate*). A listed
17th-century house with lovely views
over the River Bann.
Drumcovitt House, 704 Feeny Rd, Feeny, t (028)
7778 1224, *www.drumcovitt.com* (*moderate*).
A lovely 18th-century house set in scenic
countryside, plus 13 self-catering cottages.
Greenhill House, Aghadowey, Coleraine,
t (028) 7086 8241, *www.greenhill-house.com*
(*moderate*). A pretty Georgian farmhouse
with good home-cooking.
Laurel Villa, 60 Church St, Magherafelt, t (028)
7963 2238, *www.laurel-villa.com* (*moderate*).
A Victorian doctor's home, furnished with
antiques and run by a friendly Blue Badge
guide and his herb-growing wife. It is well
situated for day-trips to the Antrim coast,
Belfast, Derry and the Sperrin Mountains.
Guided tours of South Derry, based on poems
by Seamus Heaney, are the host's speciality.
Streeve Hill, 25 Dowland Rd, Drenagh, Limavady,
t (028) 7776 6563, *hidden.ireland@indigo.ie*

(*moderate*). A lovely early-18th-century house, with delicious food and walks in parkland and the 'moon garden'.

Ballycarton House, 239 Seacoast Rd, Limavady, t (028) 7775 0216, *www.ballycartonhouse.com* (*inexpensive*). A modern farmhouse located in a very scenic area close to Magilligan Nature Reserve.

Ballyhenry House, 172 Seacoast Rd, Myroe, Limavady, t (028) 7772 2657 (*inexpensive*). A farmhouse with good home-cooking and comfortable rooms.

Downhill Hostel, 12 Mussenden Rd, Castlerock, t (028) 7084 9077, *www.downhillhostel.com* (*inexpensive*). A most comfortable and sociable hostel, located right on a glorious stretch of beach west of Castlerock. Facilities include an old communal kitchen and laundry room. Dormitory and family rooms are available.

Dungiven Castle, Main St, Dungiven, t (028) 777 42428, *www.dungivencastle.com* (*inexpensive*). A well-restored Gothic Tudor style castle with hostel accommodation (ensuite family and dormitory rooms), a fully equipped kitchen, a reading room, a lounge area and 22 acres of parkland. It's brilliant for those on a budget, but note that breakfast is not served.

The Flax Mill Hostel, Mill Lane, Gortnaghey Rd, Dungiven, t (028) 7774 2655 (*inexpensive*). A converted stone mill with 16 beds. There's traditional music in a pub close by.

The Old Rectory, 4 Duncrun Rd, Bellarena, t (028) 7775 0477 (*inexpensive*). A pretty house at the foot of Binevenagh Mountain.

Self-catering

Lough Beg Coach Houses, Ballyscullion Park, Bellaghy, t (028) 7938 6235 (*inexpensive*). Six well-appointed cottages on a large estate bordering Lough Beg, each sleeping 6, with a communal games room, plus horseriding and lovely walks. Full Irish breakfasts and dinners can be provided.

Eating Out

Ardtara House, 8 Gorteade Rd, Upperlands, near Maghera, t (028) 7964 4490 (*expensive*). A dining room within a

lovely hotel (*see* opposite), offering a creative menu of dishes made using the freshest ingredients.

Brown Trout Golf and Country Inn, 209 Agivey Rd, Mullaghmore, Aghadowey, t (028) 7086 8209 (*moderate*). Good pub food in an established hotel (*see* opposite).

Gardiners, Garden St, Magherafelt, t (028) 7930 0333 (*moderate*). A popular place with locals, where the ambitious chef-owner's love of cooking shows in his creations at both lunch and dinner.

Radisson Hotel, Roe Park, Limavady, t (028) 7772 2222 (*moderate*). A golf-resort hotel serving sophisticated food in its two restaurants, the Coach House and Greens.

Strawberry Fayre, 1 Blagh Rd, Coleraine, t (028) 7032 0437 (*inexpensive–moderate*). Excellent lunches and teas made from fresh produce and natural ingredients – salads, fruit, local meats, home-baked breads and home-made desserts. *Closed eves.*

Café Slice, Rainey St, Magherafelt, t (028) 7963 3980 (*inexpensive*). A pleasant refuelling stop. *Closed eves.*

Ditty's Home Bakery, 44 Main St, Castledawson, t (028) 7946 8243 (*inexpensive*). Pies, lasagne and excellent bread. There's another branch in Magherafelt.

Lucille's Kitchen, 17 Catherine St, Limavady, t (028) 7776 8180 (*inexpensive*). Sandwiches and hot snacks.

Mary's Bar, 10 Market St, Magherafelt, t (028) 7963 1997 (*inexpensive*). Good pub food.

Morelli's, 54–57 The Promenade, Portstewart, t (028) 7083 2150 (*inexpensive*). Good ice cream and pasta dishes.

Salmon Leap, 53 Castleroe Rd, Coleraine, t (028) 7035 2992/7034 2992 (*inexpensive*). Good buffet lunches. *Closed eves.*

Entertainment and Nightlife

Arts and Theatre
Flowerfield Arts Centre, 185 Coleraine Rd, Portstewart, t (028) 7083 1400, *www.flowerfield.org*

Riverside Theatre, Cromore Rd, Coleraine, t (028) 7032 3232

Downhill to Coleraine

From Limavady you can cut inland through the Roe Valley to Dungiven on the B68 and pass through the Country Park, which has many fine picnic spots and walks by the River Roe. However, if you want to take advantage of the superb coastline you should go on from Magilligan, following the A2 to Downhill and on up to the pretty Victorian seaside resort of **Castlerock**, which has a superb sandy beach stretching for miles, a bowling green, a golf course and tennis courts. A really worthwhile expedition can be made to the **Palace of Downhill** and **Mussenden Temple** (*open mid-Mar–May and Sept Sat and Sun 11–6, June–Aug and Easter daily 11–6; glen and grounds always open; t (028) 7084 8728, www.ntni.org.uk*). This ruined castle, just off the A2 at Downhill village, was built in the late 18th century by Earl-Bishop Frederick Augustus Hervey (1730–1803), one of the most interesting and enlightened Church of Ireland bishops. The palace itself is sited on a windswept hill with wonderful views of the Inishowen hills and the Antrim headlands. Hervey was extravagant and well travelled. He built up a great art collection with the episcopal revenues from his Derry bishopric (which in the 18th century was the second-richest in Ireland), and had a second princely residence at Ballyscullion near Bellaghy, which is totally ruined. The landscaped estate that remains includes the Mussenden Temple perched on a cliff overlooking the sea, the ruins of the castle, family memorials, gardens, a fish pond, and woodland and cliff walks. The bishop was a great advocate of toleration, contributing generously both to Catholic and Presbyterian churches. One of his amusements was party-giving. If you go down to the Mussenden Temple, the story of the great race he organized between the Church of Ireland and the Presbyterian ministers is told. There was suspicion that he was more of a Classicist than a Christian: his temple, on a cliff edge, is modelled on the Roman temple of Vesta, and suggests a somewhat independent interpretation of religion.

Eastwards along the coast is **Portstewart**, a seasoned little resort town that is overlooked by the castle-style convent (*not open to the public*). Inland from here is **Coleraine** (*Cuil Raithin*: 'Fern Recess'), which is supposed to have been founded by St Patrick. Most of what you see was developed by the Irish Society of London. Whiskey from Coleraine is now made by Bushmills Distillery (*for tours of Old Bushmills Distillery, call t (028) 2073 3224*); it is still held with high regard and is supplied to the House of Commons.

The Coleraine campus of the University of Ulster is a centre for talks and tours during the summer, and there is a good **theatre** here called the Riverside. The campus has a rare collection of Irish-bred daffodils and narcissi (*always accessible*) that are in full bloom in mid- to late-April . The River Bann runs through the town and was the scene of early habitation. At **Mountsandel Fort**, on Coleraine's outskirts, Mesolithic flints have been found that indicate the presence of the earliest settlements in Ireland. There is much archaeological evidence to suggest that they date from 7000 BC. Later, the mound of Mountsandel became a royal seat of local Celtic kings, and finally, a Norman fort. If you visit the British Museum in London you will see some of those Bannside antiquities, the most spectacular of which is a huge hoard of Roman coins that were evidently seized by Irish pirates. On the A2, northwest of Coleraine, is **Hezlett House** (*open Apr, May and Sept Sat, Sun and bank hols 12 noon–5, June–Aug Wed–Sun 12–5; adm; t (028) 2073 1582, www.ntni.org.uk*), a thatched 17th-century cottage that was once a rectory, and has a cruck (or truss) roof.

The Bann Valley: Bellaghy to Moneymore

You can follow the River Bann through its valley by taking the A54. The valley is farmed by industrious farmers, many of them descendants of the Scots and English who were tenants of the London Companies and arrived in the region in the early 17th century. The countryside is very pretty in a cultivated way. At the **Garvagh Museum and Heritage Centre** (*open June–Aug Thurs and Sat 2–5, t (028) 2955 8188*) on Main Street, you can see farming implements and Stone Age artefacts.

The Lower Bann River broadens out into Lough Beg after leaving Lough Neagh. In the marshy area around the lake is **Church Island**, so called because of its ruined church and holy well. A spire has been constructed among the ruins – one result of Earl-Bishop Hervey's building ventures. He wanted to see the spire from his palace at Ballyscullion. The local people still leave offerings at the holy well on the island. The birdlife around the lake is superb; many waterfowl, snipe and swans can be seen.

Seamus Heaney, the poet, comes from this area, and the strength of his feelings for this land is apparent in his poetry. You can find out more about him at the **Bellaghy Bawn** (*open daily Apr–Aug 10–6, Sept–Mar 10–5; adm; t (028) 7938 6812*) in Castle Street, Bellaghy, a fortified farmhouse that was built for the London Vintner's Company around 1618. Inside this fine *bawn* are a series of rooms through which you are taken on a tour of local history since prehistoric times. There is a video presentation by Seamus Heaney, in which he explains how local places and experiences have influenced him. There is a café and library with some of Heaney's manuscripts and original works, as well as works by other Northern poets and artists.

Moneymore, further south, is a sister town to Draperstown, having been developed by the same London Company of Drapers. At 50 High Street is the **Plantation of Ulster Visitor Centre** (*open daily summer 10–5, winter 10–4; call in advance to arrange a guide; adm; t (028) 7962 7800, www.flightoftheearlsexperience.com*), an educational centre where you can learn about the Plantation period and see the 'Flight of the Earls' audio-visual show.

Located one mile (1.6km) outside Moneymore on the B18 is the most attractive of residences, **Springhill** (*open 1–6 Apr–June and Sept Sat and Sun, July and Aug daily; adm; t (028) 8674 8210*). This house was built in the late 17th century as a fortified manor house by the Lennox-Conynghams, a settler family, with its outbuildings in the Dutch style. It is a proper country gentleman's house, with soft, shadowed interiors, a lovely library and portraits, including one with a following gaze. There is a small costume museum (*t (028) 8674 7927*) and implements on show in the outbuildings. The grounds are beautiful; the yew thicket is said to be a vestige of the ancient forest of Glenconkeyne, and there is a herb garden, which was essential for any household in the 17th and 18th centuries.

Through the Sperrins: Maghera to Dungiven

Here you are on the edges of the Sperrin Mountains, which this county shares with Tyrone. **Maghera**, in the mountain heartland of the county, is a small and busy town that is situated at the foot of the Glenshane Pass. It is said to be the meeting place of the mountain- and plainspeople, rather like Dungiven on the other side of the mountain. It is also famous as the birthplace of Charles Thompson, who helped to draw up the American Declaration of Independence while he was Secretary to Congress. At the south-east end of the town you can admire the ancient **church of St Lurach** (*always accessible*), with a square-headed doorway that dates from the 12th century. The massive lintels are decorated with a carved, interlaced pattern, and a sculpture of the crucifixion.

The steep, straight road through the **Glenshane Pass** will take you on to Dungiven, or you can explore the charming countryside around Draperstown and go on to **Feeny**, travelling on the B40. You will pass by **Banagher Forest Glen**, which is a nature reserve. Close by, to the west, is **Sawel**, at 2,240ft (683m) the highest mountain in the Sperrin range. North of the forest, off the B74 from Feeny, is **Banagher Church**, founded by a St Muriedach O'Heney. The church itself is probably 12th-century, with a square-headed doorway and massive lintels. In the graveyard is a stone-roofed tomb or oratory with the figure of O'Heney in relief – the saint bequeathed to his descendants the power to be lucky with the sand from his tomb. The church is always accessible to the public.

On the south-eastern side of **Dungiven**, on the A6, is a fine ruin of an **Augustinian priory**; only the chancel with a Norman arch remains. The elaborate altar tomb erected in the late 14th century is very striking. It is carved with a figure in Irish dress grasping a sword, and commemorates an O'Cahan, whose family were the lords of this territory before the plantation.

County Antrim

The Antrim coast has a well-deserved reputation for being one of the loveliest and most spectacular in Europe. The coast road (A2) passes through exquisite little fishing villages and areas of protected beauty. The famous Giant's Causeway – one of the wonders of the natural world – the wild beauty of Fair Head and Torr Head, and the ruined Dunluce Castle, all contrive to make a trip here more than worthwhile. A little way inland are the Nine Glens of Antrim, which have been celebrated in poetry and song the world over because of their scenic beauty. Especially lovely is Glenariff, with its waterfalls, the 'Mare's Tail' being the most spectacular. The glen is an excellent example of a post-glaciation U-Valley; it is virtually geometric. The valley of the River Bann extends along the Londonderry border to Lough Neagh, the largest inland sheet of water in Britain: 150 square miles (388 sq km) in all.

The weather on the east coast is variable, as it is in all parts of Ireland, although it is more inclined to be sunny and dry with a brisk breeze off the sea. The traveller who can brave the cold Atlantic water will enjoy the breakers that roll into Whitepark Bay and the fine sandy beaches around Portrush. Cyclists will find the roads here quite strenuous, with hills and hairpin bends, but will be well rewarded by the views, while walkers can follow the Ulster Way, a marked trail that explores the Antrim Coast and Glens. A splendid adventure is to take the boat out to Rathlin Island and spend the day watching the huge sea bird population on the cliffs there, and revel in the island's unspoilt beauty.

Getting There and Around

By Air

Belfast International Airport, t (028) 9448 4848, www.bial.co.uk. An airport 25 miles (40km) from Larne.

By Sea

See also **Travel**, pp.90–1.

Isle of Man Steam Packet Company, Isle of Man, t 08705 523 523, www.steam-packet.com. Seacats between Troon and Belfast.

P&O Ferries, t (01) 407 3434. Ferries between Stranraer or Cairnryan in Scotland and Larne, taking about 2½ hrs.

By Rail

There are frequent train services from Belfast to Larne, which connect with ferries, as well as with buses travelling to the villages in the glens.

Translink, t (028) 9066 6630, www.translink.co.uk

By Bus

Ulsterbus operates the **Antrim Coaster**, which runs in summer between Belfast and Portstewart, stopping at most towns around the Antrim coast.

Ulsterbus and the Old Bushmills Distillery operate an **open-topped bus** between 27 June and 28 Aug from Coleraine along the Giant's Causeway, via Portstewart, Portrush, Portballintrae, Bushmills, and back.

Ulsterbus, t (028) 9066 6630, www.translink.co.uk

By Car

Avis, Ferry Terminal, Larne Harbour, t (028) 260799. Closed Sat pm and Sun.

Hertz, Aldergrove Airport, t (028) 9442 2533

By Bike

The Raleigh Rent-a-Bike network operates in Ballymena, through:

Ardclinis Outdoor Adventure Centre, 11 High St, Cushendall, t (028) 2177 1340, www.ardclinis.com

Cushendall Activity Centre, t (028) 2117 1340

Gibson's Bikes, 9 Abbots Cross, Newtownabbey, t (028) 9043 9959, ian.gibson@ntlworld.com

RF Linton and Sons, 31 Springwell St, Ballymena, t (028) 2565 2516

Portrush Tourist Office, t (028) 7082 3333. A source of information on cycle shops offering bike hire in the summer season.

Getting to Rathlin Island

There are daily boat crossings to the island, running from June to Sept. The rest of the year, a limited service is arranged by the Harbour Tourist Office in Ballycastle.

Ballycastle Harbour Tourist Office, 7 Mary St, t (028) 2076 2024, www.moyle-council.org. General information.

Rathlin Island Ferry, t (028) 2076 9299, www.calmac.co.uk. Four crossings daily June–Sept, at other times twice daily. The boat leaves Ballycastle at about 10.30am every day and returns in the afternoon.

Festivals

March

Ballymoney Drama Festival, t (028) 2766 2280, ext. 227

May

Ballyclare May Fair, t (028) 9034 0000. Horse trading, a community fair and a range of other events.

Feis na nGleann, t (028) 2076 2024. Gaelic music, crafts and sports in the Glens of Antrim during May and June.

Larne Irish Dancing Festival, t (028) 2826 0088. A week of Irish dance competitions for all age groups.

Northern Lights, Ballycastle, t (028) 2076 2024. A music festival and street entertainment, held late in the month.

July

Lughnasa Medieval Fair and Craft Market, Carrickfergus Castle, t (028) 9336 6455. An event held mid-month.

August

Heart of Glens Festival, Cushendall, t (028) 2076 2024. Traditional Irish music mid-month.

Ould Lammas Fair, Ballycastle, t (028) 2076 2024. Northern Ireland's oldest traditional market fair, the last weekend of the month.

History

Antrim lies very close to Scotland, with only a narrow strip of water between them, so it is not surprising that there are strong links between the two. Even the accents of the peoples are similar. Before the Celts invaded, the Scotti people moved easily between Scotland and Ireland, crossing the Moyle or North Sea Channel here. (This is the shortest ferry link to the mainland, and the same shifting of populations goes on today.) The word 'Scots' is derived from the 4th-century Irish verb 'to raid', and the Romans called Ireland 'Scotia' because it was from here that all the raiders came. It was not until the 12th century that its meaning was transferred to the country that is now called Scotland.

Up until the 6th century, the ancient Kingdom of Dalriada extended from the Antrim coast, including the islands of Rathlin and Iona, to the west of Scotland. By the late 14th century the clan MacDonnell held the balance of power, and their territory straddled both sides of the Atlantic up until the Elizabethan era. The time of the Dalriadic kings and the Scotti people is shrouded in half-myth and legend, but it has given rise to some interesting theories as to who the true natives of this land are – some of which have been used as cultural propaganda. The Scottish Presbyterians, whose forebears were settled here in the Jacobite plantations, have claimed they were coming back to their original home, and that the Catholic Celts who were driven into the mountains were in fact the interlopers who had come up from the south.

Whatever the theories of the past may be, today the Jacobite plantations continue to have an effect, in that there are pockets of staunch Presbyterians loyal to Britain who would man a Unionist army given half a chance. These Unionists live mainly in the rich plains, whilst there is a Catholic Nationalist fringe along the coast and in the glens; the two do not mix easily.

Stepping back into the mists and fantasy of legend, there are stories of Fionn MacCumhaill (Finn MacCool) and of Oisín, his son; stories of the sons of Uísneach who died for Deirdre's beauty; and of the Children of Lir, condemned to spend their lives as swans on the waters of the Moyle. The placenames of prehistoric remains, glens, mountains and caves abound with allusions to these myths.

Antrim's Eastern Coast

From Belfast to Larne

The Antrim Coast Road runs from Belfast to Larne. If you begin in Belfast, take the A2 loughside road passing the industrial districts and comfortable suburbs of Whiteabbey and Greenisland to the oldest town in Northern Ireland, **Carrickfergus**. The town takes its name from one of the Dalriadic kings, Fergus, who foundered off this point on one of his journeys between Antrim and Scotland. The kings of Scotland were descended from his line and, therefore, the kings and queens of England. He is said to have brought his coronation stone from Ireland to Scone. Certainly the rock of red sandstone, embedded with pebbles, is like rock found along the Antrim coast. The town is lovely, very well kept and pedestrianized in parts with some good craft shops.

Carrickfergus Castle (*open Apr, May and Sept Mon–Sat 10–6, Sun 2–6, June–Aug Mon–Sat 10–6, Sun 12 noon–6, Oct–Mar Mon–Sat 10–4, Sun 2–4; adm; **t** (028) 9335 1273*) is the most prominent sight in the town: a massive, rectangular, unbuttressed four-storey tower that was built by John de Courcy in the years after 1180. (John de Courcy and his kinsmen were very successful Normans who conquered much of Counties Down and Antrim.) In 1210, King John of England slept here during his tour of Ireland. The De Courcys renewed their oaths of allegiance to him at this time but in reality were very much a law unto themselves. The castle has been a museum since 1928, and houses an impressive array of weapons and armour, plus the history of such Irish regiments as the Inniskilling Dragoons. The video presentation and costumed guides give a lively insight into the 800-year history of one of the best examples of a Norman castle in Ireland. Beside this splendid fortification lies the grand marina, where there are pleasure boats for hire.

Carrickfergus has an old **parish church** that was founded by St Nicholas in 1185 and rebuilt in 1614. The famous Ulster poet Louis MacNiece (1907–63), who was associated with the group that included Cecil Day Lewis, W. H. Auden and Stephen Spender, wrote of the skewed alignment of the aisle:

The church in the form of a cross but denoting
The list of Christ on the cross in the angle of the nave.

Louis MacNiece's father was once the rector here. There's also a monument to Sir Arthur Chichester on the site – it's one of the loveliest pieces of 17th-century craftmanship to be found in Ulster. The Chichester family were given extensive lands in Ulster at the time of the Ulster Plantation in the 17th century. The **Knight Ride** (*open Apr–Sept Mon–Sat 10–6, Sun 12 noon–6; **t** (028) 9336 6455*), in Antrim Street, is a heritage exhibition and ride through history in the best Disney tradition. You can buy a joint ticket for this and the castle.

On your way north out of Carrickfergus you pass **Kilroot**. Here, in the ruined Church of Ireland church, Dean Jonathan Swift (1667–1745), best remembered for his satirical book *Gulliver's Travels*, began his clerical life. The road to Larne takes you along by the lough, which is almost landlocked by Islandmagee, a small peninsula with popular beaches such as Brown's Bay and Mill Bay. There is a ferry from Larne to Ballylumford on Islandmagee and it is fun to walk along the Gobbins – basalt cliffs on the east side of the peninsula. Before you get to Larne you pass one of the glens that break through the Antrim plateau – **Glenoe**, with four waterfalls. It is now under National Trust care. The little village of **Glynn** is actually on the shore of Larne Lough, and was the setting for a film called *The Luck of the Irish*.

Although there are some hideous buildings and unecological vistas created by the industrial sites round **Larne**, it is an important port and the gateway to the Antrim coast proper, so you cannot very well avoid it. There are railway services at regular intervals to and from York Street Station in Belfast. These connect with the sailing times of the boats between Larne and Stranraer and Cairnryan. It's the shortest sea crossing from Ireland to Scotland, taking only 70 minutes once you are in open sea.

Tourist Information

Ballycastle: 7 Mary St, **t** (028) 2076 2024
Belfast: Belfast Welcome Centre,
  35 Donegall Place, **t** (028) 9024 6609,
  www.visitnorthernireland.com
Carrickfergus: Heritage Plaza, Antrim St,
  t (028) 9336 6455, *www.carrickfergus.org*
Cushendall: 25 Mill St, **t** (028) 2177 1180. *Closed pm.*
Giant's Causeway: Visitor Centre,
  44 Causeway Rd, Bushmills, **t** (028) 2073 1855
Larne: Narrow Gauge Rd, **t** (028) 2826 0088
Portrush: Dunluce Centre, Sandhill Drive,
  t (028) 7082 3333. *Open Apr–Sept.*

Shopping

Crafts

Good places for crafts shopping are the
Giant's Causeway (*open Mar–Dec*) and the
Cushendun National Trust Shop (*open
Apr–Sept; other times by arrangement*).

Food and Drink

The good bakeries all over Co. Antrim sell
particularly good soda and potato breads.
  The local specialities, **Dulse** (seaweed) and
yellowman (confectionery), can be found in
Ballycastle grocery shops.
The Old Bushmills Distillery, Bushmills,
  t (028) 2073 1521. Whiskey tours and free
  sampling sessions.
Wysner Meats, 18 Ann St, Ballycastle, **t** (028)
2076 3224. Great sausages and black pudding.

Sports and Activities

Fishing

Fishing is very good all along the Antrim
Coast. For full information, contact Tourism
Ireland (*see* p.117) or the Ulster Cruising School
(*see* below).
  For local sea-fishing contact:
Red Bay Boats, Cushendall, **t** (028) 2177 1331
Tackle Shop, 74 Main St, Portrush,
  t (028) 7082 2209
Ulster Cruising School, Carrickfergus
  Marina, Carrickfergus, **t** (028) 9336 8818,
  ulstercruisingschool@hotmail.com

Golf

Ballycastle, **t** (028) 2076 2536,
  www.ballycastlegolfclub.com.
  A lovely seaside 18-hole course.
Bushfoot Golf Course, Bushmills,
  t (028) 2073 1317
Cairndhu Golf Course, Ballygally, Larne,
  t (028) 2858 3324. An 18-hole parkland
  golf course.
Royal Portrush Golf Course, **t** (028) 7082 2311,
  www.royalportrushgolfclub.com. Three links
  courses, including what is rated as one of
  the finest dunes courses in the world.

Open Farm and Ponytrekking

Watertop Open Farm, 188 Cushendall Rd,
Ballyvoy, Ballycastle, **t** (028) 2076 2576.
A hill farm that you can ride around on
horseback. *Closed Oct–late June.*

Steam Train Rides

Railway Preservation Society of Ireland,
  t (028) 9336 6455 (Carrickfergus Tourist
  Information Office), *www.rpsi-online.org.*
Excursions on vintage trains up the coast
as far as Portrush, on the *Portrush Flyer*,
departing from York St in Whitehead
every Sun June–Aug.

Tennis

Ballycastle Tennis Club, **t** (028) 2076 3022

On **Curran Point**, a promontory south of the harbour, you can see **Olderfleet Castle**,
a corruption of the Viking name *Ulfrechsfiord*. The castle is 13th-century and ruined,
with free access. If you have time to kill waiting for a ferry, a brisk 15-minute walk will
take you past the Cairnyan ferry dock to Chaine Memorial Road, where a replica of a
medieval round tower, 95ft (29m) tall, looks out to sea. Around here, so many Middle
Stone Age artefacts have been found that the term 'Larnian' is often used to describe
the Mesolithic culture of Ireland.

Where to Stay

Bushmills Inn, Main St, Bushmills,
t (028) 2073 3000, *www.bushmillsinn.com*
(*expensive–luxury*). An award-winning hotel,
comfortable and relaxing, with good service
and excellent food (*see* opposite).

Ahimsa, 243 Whitepark Rd, near Ballintoy,
Bushmills, **t** (028) 2073 1383 (*moderate*).
A tastefully modernized traditional cottage.
Organic garden produce is used in the
vegetarian meals, and yoga and reflexology
are available upon request.

Causeway Hotel, 40 Causeway Rd, Giant's
Causeway, Bushmills, **t** (028) 2073 1226/1210,
www.giants-causeway-hotel.com
(*moderate*). A delightful family-run hotel.

Colliers Hall, 50 Cushendall Rd, Ballycastle,
t (028) 2076 2531, *www.collliershall.com*
(*moderate*). A guesthouse a mile (1.6km)
outside Ballycastle.

Fullerton Arms, 22-24 Main St, Ballintoy,
Ballycastle, **t** (028) 2076 9613, *www.
fullertonarms.co.uk* (*moderate*). A family-run
B&B within easy reach of the coast.

Glenkeen Guesthouse, 59 Coleraine Rd,
Portrush, **t** (028) 7082 2279 (*moderate*).
A good value B&B just out of the centre of
town. All rooms are ensuite.

Glenluce Guesthouse, 42 Quay Rd, Ballycastle,
t (028) 2076 2914, *www.glenluceguesthouse.
com* (*moderate*). A welcoming family-run
guesthouse situated on Ballycastle's
main street, near the beach and marina.
It has its own tea-house.

The Londonderry Arms Hotel, 20 Harbour Rd,
Carnlough, **t** (028) 2888 5255, *www.
glensofantrim.com* (*moderate*). A coaching
inn that was built by the Marchioness
of Londonderry, whose mother was the
Countess of Antrim. It later came into
possession of her grandson, Sir Winston
Churchill, who sold it in 1926. In its
current incarnation, it retains a delightful
olde-worlde atmosphere.

Maddybenny Farmhouse, 18 Maddybenny Park,
Loguestown Rd, Portrush, **t** (028) 7082 3394,
www.maddybenny.com (*moderate*).
An easygoing atmosphere and great
breakfasts. Holiday cottages are available,
and horseriding can be arranged.

The Villa, 185 Torr Rd, Cushendun, **t** (028) 2176
1252, *maggiescally@amserve.net* (*moderate*).
A comfortable Victorian villa set off the road
in its own gardens, close to the beach.

Whitepark House, Whitepark Bay, Ballintoy,
t (028) 2073 1482, *www.whiteparkhouse.com*
(*moderate*). A 17th-century house on a hill
overlooking the Atlantic, luxuriously
furnished with mementoes from the
owners' Asian travels. It serves what are
probably the best full-Irish vegetarian
breakfasts you'll ever taste, along with a
version for meat-eaters. You're likely to
get involved in good conversations beside
the fire, accompanied by tea and biscuits.
Three of the rooms share bathrooms.

Ballycastle Backpackers Hostel, 4 North St,
Ballycastle, **t** (028) 2076 3612 (*inexpensive*).
A hostel occupying some seafront houses.

Black Bush Cottage, 34 Dickeystown Rd,
Glenarm, **t** (028) 2884 1559 (*inexpensive*).
A small country B&B on the coast road.

Cushendall Youth Hostel, 24 Layde Rd,
Cushendall, **t** (028) 2177 1344 (*inexpensive*).
A hostel in the glens, with some family rooms.

Manor Guest House, 23 Olderfleet Rd, Larne,
t (028) 2827 3305, *www.themanorguesthouse.
com* (*inexpensive*). A seafront guesthouse.

Rathlin Guesthouse, The Quay, Rathlin Island,
t (028) 2076 3917 (*inexpensive*). A very
friendly base from which to explore the
beautiful island.

From Ballygally to Ballycastle: Through the Glens of Antrim

Beyond Larne, still on the A2 coast road, some 60 miles (96km) of wonderful
maritime scenery stretches ahead of you. This area is like a pictorial textbook, with
examples of nearly every rock formation and epoch. For the average visitor this means
views of lovely mountains, looming white cliffs, glens, trout streams and beaches. For
the geologist it is fascinating: there are Archean schists more than 300 million years
old that formed the first crust over the once-molten earth, lava fields, glacial deposits,

Sheep Island View Hostel, 42a Main St, Ballintoy, t (028) 2076 9391, *www.sheepislandview.com (inexpensive).* A comfortable modern hostel with ocean views, handy for seeing the Causeway coast. Some dorms are in a camping barn. Bike hire is available.

Whitepark Bay International Youth Hostel, 157 Whitepark Rd, Whitepark Bay, Ballintoy, t (028) 2073 1745 *(inexpensive).* A hostel with excellent facilities, including family rooms, and views onto the beach.

Self-catering

See also *www.antrim.net/cottages* and *www.cottagesinireland.com.*

Briarfield, 65 Dickeystown Rd, Glenarm, t (028) 2884 1296 *(inexpensive).* A cottage for 4.

Rural Cottages Holidays Ltd, Tourism Ireland, t (028) 9024 1100 *(inexpensive).* A firm offering attractive traditional dwellings, restored and furnished to a high standard, including **Bellair Cottage**, a whitewashed farmhouse sleeping 6 in the glens above Glenarm, and **Strand House** in the pretty National Trust village of Cushendun, for 7.

Eating Out

Bushmills Inn, Dunluce Rd, Bushmills, t (028) 2073 2339, *www.bushmillsinn.com (moderate).* An excellent bistro-style restaurant where you can enjoy delicious cold salmon and salads.

Dobbins Inn, 6 High St, Carrickfergus, t (028) 9335 1905 *(moderate).* Rich à la carte dishes and bar meals.

Ginger Tree, 29 Ballyrobert Rd, Glengormley, Newtownabbey, t (028) 9032 7151 *(moderate).* A restaurant serving delicious Japanese food.

The Londonderry Arms, Carnlough, t (028) 2888 5255 *(moderate).* A place where you can enjoy good fish dishes, accompanied by wonderful views of the sea and glens.

Marine Hotel, Ballycastle, t (028) 2076 2222 *(moderate).* Simple but good cooking.

Smuggler's Inn Hotel Restaurant, 306 Whitepark Rd, Giant's Causeway, t (028) 2073 1577 *(moderate).* A la carte meals and high tea. B&B is also available.

Zio Restaurant, 21 Ballyreagh Rd, Portrush, t (028) 7082 4945 *(moderate).* A place serving Italian dishes in a dramatic setting overlooking the Antrim coastline.

Harbour Bar and Bistro, Harbour Rd, Portrush, t (028) 7082 2430 *(inexpensive).* A great atmosphere and excellent food, especially given the low prices.

McCuaig's Bar, The Quay, Rathlin Island, t (028) 2076 3974 *(inexpensive).* Pub grub.

National Trust Tearooms, Cushendun, Giant's Causeway and Carrick-a-Rede, t (028) 2282 1582 *(inexpensive).* Light meals. *Closed eves and Oct/Nov–Feb*

Rathlin Guesthouse, The Quay, Rathlin Island, t (028) 2076 3917 *(inexpensive).* Good snacks, sandwiches and high teas.

Sweeney's Wine Bar, Seaport Ave, Port Ballintrae, t (028) 2073 2404 *(inexpensive).* Grilled meats and vegetarian meals.

Entertainment and Nightlife

Traditional Music

The Central Bar, 12 Ann St, Ballycastle, t (028) 2076 3877

The Harbour Bar, Portrush, t (028) 7082 2430

McCarrolls Bar, Ballycastle, t (028) 2076 2123

raised beaches and flint beds. The red sandstone that colours the beaches was formed from the sands of a desert that existed 110–150 million years ago in the Triassic epoch. This was succeeded by a sea that formed Lias clays, which were in turn changed into chalk by a later invasion of the sea. This happened 120–170 million years ago, and now Fair Head's white headlands remind us of it.

After the Ice Age, the **Glens of Antrim** were formed by the movement of the inexorable glaciers that gouged out the valleys. It is best to imagine the glens as being part of a giant hand with ten fingers, with the spaces in-between forming a series of short steep valleys running out towards the sea. The glens drain in a north-easterly direction and look straight across to Scotland. They were isolated from the rest of County Antrim by the difficult terrain of the Antrim plateau with its bogs and high ground near Glenarm. Today on the Garron plateau it is still possible to lose oneself and to see wild ponies and goats grazing.

The A2 coast road links each of the nine glens. From south to north, they are Glenarm, Glencloy, Glenariff, Glenballyeamon, Glenaan, Glencorp, Glendun, Glenshesk and Glentaisie. The glens are rich in legend and history; most of the favourite characters of Irish legends make an appearance somewhere. The Children of Lir, who were changed into white swans by their wicked stepmother, were sentenced to spend 300 years swimming on the bleak Sea of Moyle – an ancient name for this stretch of the North Channel, which lies along the north-eastern shores of the glens. Thomas Moore (1779–1852) tells their sad story in the 'Song of Fionnuala':

> Silent, oh Moyle be the roar of thy waters,
> Break not ye breezes your chain of repose,
> While mournfully weeping Lir's lonely daughter
> Tells to the nightstar her sad tale of woes!

Deirdre and the sons of Uisneach landed near Ballycastle after they had been in exile, and were lured from there to their death at Emain Macha, near Armagh. Fionn MacCumhaill (Finn MacCool) mistakenly killed his faithful hound Bran in Glenshesk, and his son Oisín (Ossian) is buried in the glens. His grave is marked by a stone circle in **Glenaan**. Other relics of the past are the megalithic monuments that were built by agricultural people about 5,000 years back, and the *raths* dotted all over the area. These were lonely farmsteads 1,500 years ago.

The remoteness of the glens has caused the people of these parts to have a great sense of regional unity and an affinity with their neighbours on the Scottish coast. They also retained the Irish language until the last quarter of the 19th century. When the Gaelic League set out to revive the Irish language early last century, they held a great *feis* (festival) in 1904, at which people competed in Irish dancing, singing and instrumental music, storytelling, crafts and hunting. A summer *feis* has been held every year since, in one of the nine glens.

From Larne you follow the A2 beneath cliffs and through the Black Cave Tunnel to **Ballygally**. Here there is a very Scottish-style castle, now a hotel. It is well worth a look inside to see the interior of a Scottish *bawn* house. You can also have a drink in the bar, which is in the dungeon.

A couple of miles inland you can get a panorama of the Scottish coast, with the beehive outline of Ailsa Craig from the Sallagh Braes. **Glenarm**, 'Glen of the Army', is one of the oldest of the glen villages, dating from the 13th century. The castle here belongs to the MacDonnells, who are descended from Sorley Boy MacDonnell, Queen Elizabeth's great enemy. It is not open to the public, but if you go into Glenarm Forest you can look back at this turreted castle, which reminds many of the Tower of London. Those who are looking for folk music may well find it in the village itself.

This part of the coast is full of chalk and limestone. Glenarm exports it from the little harbour, and there used to be quarries at **Carnlough**, which is the town at the foot of **Glencloy** ('Glen of the Hedges'), although it is not particularly interesting. This area has long been inhabited and farmed, with dry-stone walls enclosing the land. Although Carnlough attracts local holidaymakers because of its sandy beach, solitude can be found on **Garron Moor** and in the other little glens.

On your way around the Garron Point to Red Bay, you will notice a change in the geology – from limestone to the Triassic sandstone exposed on the shore. All along the A2 coast road you will find breathtaking sea views. The road was built from 1834 to ease the hardships of the glens' people as a work of famine relief – but it also gave them a route out, resulting in a much-diminished population.

Glenariff ('Ploughman's Glen') is the largest and most popular of the glens, with its waterfalls: *Ess na Larach* ('Tears of the Mountain') and *Ess na Crub* ('Fall of the Hoof'). With names like these, you can understand how easy it was for poets to praise these valleys. **Waterfoot** is at the foot of the Glenariff River, by the lovely Red Bay, so-called because of the reddish sand washed by the streams from the sandstone. There are caves that were once inhabited in the cliffs above. The village is often the venue for the Glens of Antrim *Feis* (*Feis na nGleann; see* p.378). In the glen you will see steep climbing mountains and a narrowing valley floor that gives some aptness to Thackeray's description, 'Switzerland in miniature'.

This is perfect ground for nature rambles, with lovely wildflowers and the moorland of **Glenariff Forest Park** (**t** (028) 2955 6000). This magnificent national nature reserve has a campsite and a visitor centre in the glen. There is a beautiful walk beside the waterfalls and cascades of the glen. You can spend an hour or a whole day hiking here, and it is best to bring walking boots.

The MacDonnells, the McQuillans and the Rush Bush

The glens have had a turbulent history. Originally Richard de Burgh, Earl of Ulster, conquered them, and they were sold to the Bissetts in the early 13th century. Five generations later the last of the Bissetts, Margery, the daughter of Eoin Bissett and Sabia O'Neill, became the sole heir to the glens. At this time John More MacDonnell of Kintyre, Lord of the Isles, was looking for a wife, and he came to woo her. They were married in 1399, and from then on the glens have been in possession of the MacDonnells, who became known as the MacDonnells of Antrim.

The MacDonnells did not keep the glens easily however; they spent a lot of time fighting other claimants to their territory, particularly the McQuillans, the O'Neills and Sir Arthur Chichester. In 1559 Sorley Boy MacDonnell tricked the McQuillans by spreading rushes over the bog holes that lay between the hostile camps above Glendun. When the McQuillans and their allies, the O'Neills, led a cavalry charge, their horses sank into the swamps and their riders became easy prey to the arrows and axes of the MacDonnells. The MacDonnells still live at Glenarm Castle today (they were made earls of Antrim in the 17th century), and a traditional saying goes, 'A rush bush never deceived anyone but a McQuillan.'

Along the east flank of the valley you can see the remains of a narrow-gauge railway that a century ago transported iron. On the west side, at the Alpinesque cliffs of Lurigethan, you can look for the mound of **Dunclana Mourna**, the home of Fionn MacCumhaill and his son, the poet Oisín. According to legend, the warrior Fionn was the leader of a mighty tribe called the Fianna; he was renowned for his wisdom gained through eating the Salmon of Knowledge; for his shining beauty (Fionn means 'fair'); and for his bravery. His deeds are recounted in the legends and epics of Scotland, as well as Ireland.

Continuing on the coast road, we get to **Cushendall**, called the capital of the glens. It lies at the foot of the **Glenballyeamon** ('Edwardstown Glen'), a somewhat lonesome glen, and the two glens **Glenaan** ('Glen of the Colt's Foot', or 'Rush Lights') and **Glencorp** ('Glen of the Slaughter'). Cushendall is delightfully situated on the River Dall, and there is an excellent golf course and camping facilities and a good bar called Pat's. An interesting building is **Turnley's Tower** at 1 Millstreet, right at the crossroads of the town. Built in 1820 as a 'place of confinement for idlers and rioters', it had a garrison of one man, who lived in the tower until quite recently.

On **Tieveragh Hill** you can get marvellous views over the coast, and muse on the fact that you might be standing on the capital of the fairies – apparently they live inside it. (It is actually a rounded volcanic plug.) **Oisín's Grave** is at the end of a path on the lower slopes of **Tieve Bulliagh** about 2 miles (3km) to the west of Cushendall, in Glenaan. It is in fact a megalithic tomb and stone circle but, as usual in Ireland, it has a lovely story associated with it. The Celtic Orpheus, Oisín, was entranced by a vision of the golden-haired Niamh, and followed her to her father's kingdom of Tír na nÓg. He returned to find his companions dead and St Patrick preaching. He died unconverted, for the priests' music was not sweet to him after that of his father, Fionn MacCumhaill.

Further up the road is **Beagh's Forest**, which stands in splendid open country. From here you can look back at the mountains Trostan and Slievenanee, where St Patrick is said to have spent many lonely hours in his youth watching sheep. A mile out of the village, on the way to Cushendun and by the sea, are the ruins of **Layde Church**, which contains many MacDonnell monuments and was in use up to 1790.

Cushendun village and its beach are in the care of the National Trust. Clough Williams-Ellis, who designed the pretty cottages here, also designed the seaside village of Portmeirion in Wales. There are marvellous walks around the village and surrounding area. The River Dun is famous for salmon and sea trout, but you have to ask the local Cushendun fishing club for permission to fish.

Within the hidden glen of **Glendun** ('Brown Glen') and its wood, Draigagh, is a massive rock carved with a crucifixion scene, supposedly brought over from Iona. Poet John Masefield, whose wife came from here, was perhaps thinking of this glen when he wrote 'In the Curlew Calling Time of Irish Dusk', for it is full of wildlife and flowers.

Continue along the A2 northwards to **Ballypatrick Forest**, where there is a scenic drive, a campsite, a picnic area and walks. Opposite the entrance to Ballypatrick Forest is **Watertop Open Farm** (*see* p.381), where you can see the animals at close quarters and hire a pony for trekking.

You have not finished with the glens yet, but you have some wonderful views from the headlands coming up. Go by **Torr Head**, traversing a twisty road leading from Cushendun through Culraney Townland, which remained an enclave of Scots Gaelic speakers until about 75 years ago. Here you can look to the Mull of Kintyre, which is only about 15 miles (24km) away on the Scottish coast. You can understand why this part of Ireland felt nearer to Scotland than any other kingdom. Between here and Fair Head is **Murlough Bay**, where the kings of Dalriada had their summer residence. There are no remains, but the tree-fringed beach is charming. The best way to reach it is from Drumadoon. At **Fair Head**, which is reached from Ballyvoy, you can look down from the highest cliffs in the north-east, but still more impressive is the heather-covered top with its three lakes.

Ballycastle is a particularly attractive resort town. Although it's a fairly lively spot, complete with lawn tennis courts in the old harbour, golf facilities and various other forms of amusement nearby, this is the landscape in which two of the saddest Irish stories are set. According to legend, the Children of Lir, who were condemned to imprisonment as swans by their wicked stepmother, haunted these waters. At the eastern end of the Ballycastle sands there is a rock called *Carrig-Usnach*, where the ill-fated Deirdre landed with her lover Naoise and his two brothers, the sons of Uisneach, at the treacherous invitation of King Conor mac Nessa, who had lured them back from Scotland.

The Northern Coast: Ballycastle to the Giant's Causeway

Ballycastle is divided into the market end and the harbour end. The diamond-shaped marketplace is the site of the Ould Lammas Fair, which is held at the end of August (*see* p.378). Visitors from the nearby Scottish islands travel over for this famous ancient fair, which was given a charter in 1606 and is, therefore, the oldest of Ireland's big traditional fairs. It comprises large cattle and sheep sales, and about 500 stalls selling hardware, food and crafts. The fun goes on into the night, with dancing in the street. There is a rhyme that goes:

Did you treat your Mary-Ann
To dulse and yellowman
At the Ould Lammas Fair in Ballycastle?

Ballycastle Museum (*open July and Aug daily 12 noon–6, rest of year by appointment; t (028) 2076 2942, www.moyle-council.org/tourism*), which is situated in Castle Street, is worth a visit. Ballycastle was a stronghold of the MacDonnells, and at the ruined **Bonamargy Friary**, located to the east of the town, the great coffins of some of these redoubtable chiefs lie in the vault. Also associated with the town was the Boyd family, who developed the coal mines; the entrances to these may be seen if you go across the golf course to the foot of Fair Head.

The harbour has a memorial to Count Marconi and his assistant, George Kemp, who in 1898 established radio contact between Ballycastle and Rathlin Island. The town is also famous for its tennis tournament on the grass courts overlooking the sea. There is a fine beach, friendly pubs, and plenty of old-fashioned shops selling such seaside essentials as film, shrimping nets, and buckets and spades. There is a forest drive around the beehive-shaped **Knocklayd Hill** and good fishing in the River Margy.

County Antrim is very well endowed with home bakeries, and the potato bread known as 'fadge' is quite a speciality around Ballycastle. Also sold here are the 'dulse and yellowman' of the Fair rhyme; 'dulse' being dried seaweed, salty and chewy, and 'yellowman' being one of the most delicious confections you can imagine – a bit like the honeycomb inside a Crunchie bar. Ballycastle is a splendid touring centre, and the other glens that make the quorum of Nine Antrim Glens can be visited from here. **Glenshesk** ('the Sedgy Glen') is well wooded, lying east of Knocklayd Hill.

Breen Wood, at the head of the Glen, is a nature reserve with very old oaks that probably witnessed the fights between the O'Neills and MacDonnells for mastery of the area. On the other side of the Hill of Knocklayd lies the last glen, **Glentaisie**, named after Taisia, a princess of Rathlin. She seems to have been something of a warrior, having won a great battle on this broad glen that now carries the main road (A44) from Ballycastle to Armoy.

Another short expedition that can be made from the town is to **Kinbane Head**, a couple of miles to the north-west and a stronghold of Colla MacDonnell, Sorley Boy's brother. Now it stands as a picturesque ruin on its narrow white promontory, reached from the B15 going to the Giant's Causeway. A better-known tourist attraction is the swinging **Carrick-a-rede Rope Bridge** (*open daily mid-Mar–June, Sept and Oct 10–6, July and Aug 10–7; tea-room; adm; t (028) 2076 9839/2073 1582*), north of Ballycastle and about a mile (1.6km) on from Kinbane Head. The bridge is narrow, bouncy and made of planks with wire handrails, and it is thrilling to cross. The views are tremendous, and a small salmon fishery still operates on the ocean side.

One of the prettiest towns on the coast is **Ballintoy**: if you catch it on a good day it looks like a Mediterranean fishing village with its white church and buildings. You can walk west from here to **Whitepark Bay**, a great curve of beach with sand dunes that is a National Trust property. On the edge of the cliffs is **Dunseverick Castle**, of which only one massive wall remains. In under the cliffs is the little hamlet of **Portbraddan**, with a tiny church that is dedicated to St Gobhan (patron saint of builders), said to be the smallest church in Ireland. You will get a good close-up view of traditional salmon netting at this hamlet of four houses. The nets are set out to catch the salmon as they swim along the coast to find the river where they were spawned. You should take your time here; beachcombers can find fossils, flower enthusiasts can examine the dunes, and there is even evidence of a Stone Age settlement at the east end.

Rathlin Island

Fair Head gives you a good view of **Rathlin Island**, which is also called Raghery by the local people. It is said that Fionn MacCumhaill's mother was on her way to get some whiskey for him in Scotland, and she took a stepping stone to throw in on her way across the Moyle. This became Rathlin. The L-shaped island lies about 8 miles (13km) from Ballycastle and 14 miles (22km) from the Mull of Kintyre, and rises with white cliffs from the sea. It is populated by families who retained their Scots Gaelic longer than any other community, and it has a fascinating history, mostly of battles over the island's strategic position. Pirates and smugglers throughout the centuries have used it as a refuge and a hiding place for contraband. According to local legend, it was a good hideout for Robert the Bruce: he had to take refuge in one of the caves underneath the east lighthouse, and here he saw the determined spider that inspired the saying, 'If at first you don't succeed, try and try again.' This was in 1306 when, with renewed resolve, he fought for and gained the Scottish throne at Bannockburn. In early-Christian times the island's remote position provided a tranquil home for monks, until the Vikings came to plunder it in the 9th century. There are traces of a monastic settlement and a stone sweat house at Knockans, between Brockley and the harbour; and a prehistoric mound fort known as Doonmore, near the Stone Age settlement at Brockley. East of the harbour is a Celtic standing stone.

As you approach Rathlin in the boat, you will see the beautiful white cliffs of the island and the endless wheeling of the sea birds who rest all over it. The most dramatic place to watch them is from the west lighthouse, where the volcanic rock stacks are covered with puffins, fulmars, kittiwakes, razorbills, shearwaters and guillemots. Buzzards, waders, wild geese, ravens and peregrine falcons can be seen at different times of the year.

The island is otherwise inhabited by about 70 people who farm and fish, and there is a guesthouse and restaurant (*see* pp.382–3). If you decide to pitch a tent, do ask at the appropriate farmhouse first. There are no cars for hire on Rathlin, which is a blessing, and the roads are silent except for the odd tractor and car belonging to one of the families who live there. The island is small enough to walk around in a (long) day or, even better, you can hire a bicycle. The verges of the roads are starred with wild orchids and there are hardly any bushes, let alone trees, to block the magnificent views of mountainy bog and little lakes. You might hear a corncrake calling, which is rare enough nowadays. You should be able to arrange to go lobster-fishing with one of the locals; the best place to ask is in the pub on the quay. There is good sport to be had catching eels around the wreck of the cruiser *Drake*, which was torpedoed during the First World War. There is good shore fishing, and deep-sea angling boats may be hired at Ballycastle, Ballintoy, and Portballintrae. The journey to Rathlin takes just 45 minutes (*see* p.378), but bear in mind that if the weather turns bad you may not be able to return to the mainland the same day.

The Giant's Causeway and Environs

The **Giant's Causeway** is a UNESCO world heritage site (one of only two in Ireland), and this accolade only confirms what tourists have known for centuries: that the mix of black basalt columns, white chalk, sea, moorland and sandy beaches makes for a spectacular coastline. About 60 million years ago there was great volcanic activity, and basalt lavas poured out to cover the existing chalk limestone landscape. It actually baked the chalk into a hard rock – very unlike the soft chalk of southern England.

These lava flows and eruptions were separated by several million years, allowing tropical vegetation and soils to accumulate. The cooling of the basalt lavas was very variable. When exposed to the air or water, they cooled rapidly and formed skins like that on the top of custard. If they cooled slowly at depth, they shrank to form even polygonal columns like the Giant's Causeway. Here the Ice Ages eroded the cliffs, and graceful arches have been formed by the action of the sea and weather.

There is a 2-mile (3½km) circular walk past the strange formations. The National Trust, which manages the Causeway, has made great efforts to make the site accessible to the thousands of people who visit each year, retaining the beauty and natural habitat of the area. No souvenir shops and ice-cream vans mar the scenery as they do on other parts of this beautiful coastline. The Trust now owns 104 acres (42ha) of the North Antrim cliff path between the causeway itself and the ruins of Dunseverick Castle beside Whitepark Bay.

You will find the Giant's Causeway on the B146, a looproad off the A2 between Ballycastle and Bushmills. Car parking is provided, and a shuttle bus covers the two-thirds of a mile (1km) from there to the Causeway itself; otherwise access is by foot only. The **Visitors' Centre** (*open daily July and Aug 10–7, call for times rest of year; guided tours June–Sept, by appointment only at other times; car park fee; t (028) 2073 1855*) at the entrance includes a tea-room, a shop and information on the geology and history of the area. Next to the Centre is the **Causeway School Museum** (*open daily July and Aug 11–4.30; t (028) 2073 1777*), which takes you back to a small country school dating from around 1920.

You can walk a couple of miles north along another coastal path to **Portballintrae**, a picturesque fishing village, and past a huge strand with strong Atlantic rollers, called **Runkerry**. Here, a Spanish galleon, the *Girona*, was sunk off the Giant's Causeway. It contained the most valuable cargo yet found (now in the Ulster Museum, Belfast).

Bushmills, on the A2 inland from Port Ballintrae, is famous for its whiskey distillery, which claims to be the oldest in the world. Whiskey (from the word *usquebaugh*, or *uisce beatha*: 'water of life') is one word that the English have taken from the Irish. Before whiskey became a genteel drink, the 'best Coleraine' was admitted to be a connoisseur's drink. Peter the Great was amongst many to appreciate the Northern Irish liquor on his study tour of Europe in 1697. **Bushmills Distillery** (*open Apr–Oct Mon–Sat 9.30–5.30, Sun 12 noon–5.30, Nov–Mar Mon–Fri 9.30–5.30; tours take about 1hr; adm; t (028) 2073 3224, www.bushmills.com*) can be visited.

Move on via the A2 to Northern Ireland's biggest seaside resort, **Portrush**. Before you reach this uninspiring mecca of amusement arcades and fish and chips, visit **Dunluce Castle** (*open Apr, May and Sept Mon–Sat 10–6, Sun 2–6, June–Aug Mon–Sat 10–6, Sun 12 noon–6, Oct–Mar Tue–Sat 10–4, Sun 2–4; adm; t (028) 2073 1938*), sometimes translated as Mermaid's Fort; its bold ruins keep watch over the magnificent coastline. You can see it from the A2, three miles (5km) before you reach Portrush. Its long, romantic history is set out in a leaflet available at the entrance. Its kitchen actually fell into the sea while it was inhabited. Anyone approaching it along the shore (you can scramble from the White Rocks, a range of chalk cliffs accessible from the main road), may see the rare meadow cranesbill flower called the Flower of Dunluce.

The Legend of The Giant's Causeway

Irish myths are very clear about how the Giant's Causeway was created. It was built by the great hero, Fionn MacCumhaill (Finn McCool): a warrior, magician and poet more than 52 feet (16m) tall. Fionn had a feud with a Scottish giant, Benandonner, who lived on the Scottish island of Staffa. They challenged each other to a fight, and Fionn began to build the Causeway to get to his rival. He was so exhausted by this great labour, however, that he fell asleep as soon as he was finished. The next day Fionn's wife, the giantess Oonagh, saw the massive Benandonner pounding towards them down the Causeway, demanding to know where Fionn was. Quick-thinking Oonagh covered Fionn over and, pointing to his still sleeping form, told the Scot to stop being so noisy before he woke up the baby. Benandonner, unable to imagine how big Fionn had to be if this was the size of his child, turned tail and ran back to Staffa, tearing up most of the Causeway behind him.

Portrush is on a promontory jutting out into the Atlantic. It has a small harbour that is popular with yachters sailing in the west, and from here you can take boat cruises to see the Causeway Coast and the Skerries, a group of rocky islands where the great auk (now extinct) used to nest. Crowded in summer, it's not the most appealing place along the coast to stay – except for golfers, trying out the renowned Royal Portrush course. But the town's Victorian/Edwardian main buildings have their own contribution to make to the unique flavour of a Northern coastal resort.

Just west is the more personable resort of **Portstewart**, which also boasts excellent golf courses, as well as a huge stretch of sandy beach. An adventurous option in good weather is to hire a bike and cover a loop from Portrush to the Causeway, down to Bushmills for a well-earned whiskey, and back; it is possible to cover all of this in a single energetic but rewarding day.

Mid-Antrim

As you set off through mid-Antrim via **Ballymena**, you will be passing through the richest farmland in the North. The farmers here are among the most modern and hardworking in Ireland. If you are here during the summer you will see the Loyalist flag, with a white background and red hand on a red cross, fluttering from many a household. This area has also benefited from the linen industry, which was boosted in the late 17th century by the Huguenot weavers, who sought refuge here from the religious intolerance of Louis XIV of France. Louis Crommelin is credited with having started the industry; north-east of Ballymena is the village of **Newtown-Crommelin**, which is named after him. It is now a lonely sheep-rearing settlement, though in the past bauxite was mined on the moors around it.

Ballymena itself is a very prosperous town; the rumour is that all the farmers roundabout have bank accounts in the tax haven of the Isle of Man. (A riddle once asked, 'Why are pound notes green?', and answered: 'because Ballymena men pick them before they are ripe'.)

At the little Moravian settlement of **Gracehill**, just outside Ballymena, you can see some of the communal buildings dating from the 18th century around the green. These Moravians came from Eastern Europe. Their Protestant sect, also known as the United Brethren, was founded in Saxony before they came to Ireland in 1746. The village is linked to **Galgorm** by a bridge over the Main. You can glimpse the 17th-century Galgorm Castle, surrounded by a lawn and stately trees. The little village is delightful, with thatched cottages along one main street that runs by the river to the castle.

Off the A26 to Coleraine, on the outskirts of **Ballymoney**, is **Leslie Hill Open Farm** (*open Apr, May and Sept Sun and public hols 2–6, June Sat and Sun 2–6; July and Aug Mon–Sat 11–6, Sun 2–6; adm; t (028) 2766 6803*). The 18th-century farm buildings here include the Bellbarn (a threshing barn), a dovecote, a typical cattle byre and the

Tourist Information

Antrim: 16 High St, **t** (028) 9442 8331
Ballymena: 76 Church St, **t** (028) 2563 8494
Ballymoney: Ballymoney Borough Council,
t (028) 2766 2280
Belfast: Belfast Welcome Centre,
35 Donegall Place, **t** (028) 9024 6609,
www.visitnorthernireland.com,
www.gotobelfast.com

Shopping

Crafts
Forge Pottery, 18 Milltown Rd, Antrim,
t (028) 9446 5349
Irish Linen Centre, Lisburn, t (028) 9266 0074
Orchard Crafts, Castlecroft, Main St,
Ballymoney, t (028) 2766 7784

Food and Drink
Good bakeries all over the county sell especially tasty soda and potato breads.
Lough Neagh Fishermens' Co-operative Society,
Toomebridge, t (028) 7965 0618. Fresh eels.

Markets
Ballymena, car park beside leisure centre, on Larne Road link. Veg and clothes stalls, Sat.

Sports and Activities

Animal Sanctuary
TACT Talnotry Cottage, 2 Crumlin Rd,
Crumlin, t (028) 9442 2900,

www.tactwildlifecentre.org.uk. A sanctuary for injured birds and small mammals. Tea is available in the ornamental garden with advance booking. *Open Mon–Fri 12–3, Sun 2–5; other times by appointment.*

Fishing
The Bann, Main, Braid, Clough and Glenwhirry rivers all have an abundance of brown trout and salmon. Lough Neagh, meanwhile, has its own variety of trout, which is called 'dollaghan'.
The Inver, Glynn, Bush, Carey, Margy, Dun and Roe are all excellent for sea trout, salmon and brown trout.
Contact the relevant local tourist office for further information.

Open Farm
Leslie Hill Open Farm, Macfin Rd, Ballymoney,
t (028) 2766 6803/3109. A farm with a good tea-room (*see* opposite). *See also* above.

Pleasure Cruises
Cruises are operated on Lough Neagh and the River Bann.
Ulster Cruising School, Carrickfergus,
t (028) 9336 8818, *ulstercruisingschool@ hotmail.com*

Steam Train Rides
Railway Preservation Society of Ireland,
t (028) 2826 0803. Two-hour trips on the *Portrush Flyer* between Belfast and Portrush each summer. The fare is about £15 one way. Call for details and dates, which change every year.

payhouse. You can also see the old stables, which now house newborn piglets. The famous traveller and agriculturist Arthur Young visited Leslie Hill in 1776, and much admired the lovely grounds, pretty lake and island. The estate has been lived in by the Leslie family for 350 years, and the Big House (*only open to groups; advance booking advised; t (028) 2766 6803*) is a classic Georgian stone-cut building dating from 1760.

A few miles to the north in the tiny village of Benvarden Dervock, **Benvarden House and Garden** (*open June–Aug Tue–Sun 1.30–5.30; adm; t (028) 2074 1331*) has attractive 18th-century garden and pleasure grounds.

As you make your way down to Antrim Town and Lough Neagh you see the distinctive shape of **Slemish Mountain**, east of Ballymena, where St Patrick spent his youth after being captured by Irish pirates. To get to it, take the B94 from Broughshane; turn left

Where to Stay

Galgorm Manor, Ballymena, t (028) 2588 1001, *www.galgorm.com* (*expensive*). A spectacular 17th-century castle with lovely lawns, transformed into a plush hotel with a spa.

Keef Halla County House, 20 Tully Rd, Nutts Corner, Crumlin, t (028) 9082 5491, *www.keefhalla.com* (*expensive*). An award-winning little guesthouse 5mins from Belfast International airport, with free Internet access throughout the property and free long-term car parking.

Dunadry Hotel and Country Club, 2 Islandreagh Drive, Dunadry, Antrim, t (028) 9443 4343, *www.dunadry.com* (*moderate–expensive*). A comfortable hotel near Belfast International airport, with good food (see below), five acres of grounds and a fitness centre with a pool.

Adair Arms Hotel, Ballymoney Rd, Ballymena, t (028) 2565 3674, *www.adairarms.com* (*moderate*). An attractive old 23-room hotel.

Corr's Corner Hotel, 315 Ballyclare Rd, Newtownabbey, t (028) 9084 9221, *www.corrscorner.com* (*moderate*). A hotel, bar and restaurant with modern rooms.

Leighinmohr House Hotel, Leighinmohr Ave, Ballymena, t (028) 2565 2313, *www.leighinmohrhotel.com* (*moderate*). A pleasant family-run hotel.

Self-catering

Rural Cottages Holidays Ltd, Tourism Ireland, t (028) 9024 1100. Pleasant, well-furnished traditional properties, including **Slemish Cottage**, a 100-year-old farmhouse with lovely views and space for 6, in Broughshane; **Manns Cottage**, another attractive option in Broughshane. sleeping 10; and **O'Harabrook**, 3 apartments in stone outhouses on a large farm in Ballymoney, each sleeping 6.

Eating Out

Gillies Pub and Brasserie, Galgorm Manor, Ballymena, t (028) 2588 1001, *www.galgorm.com* (*moderate*). A traditional Irish pub serving local fare, under restoration as we went to press, with reopening scheduled for June 2006. A fine dining restaurant is due to open in the same hotel in early 2007.

Linen Mill Restaurant, Dunadry Hotel and Country Club, 2 Islandreagh Drive, Dunadry, t (028) 9443 4343 (*moderate*). An award-winning traditional restaurant. The hotel's more informal bistro is open all week. *Closed lunch and Sun–Fri eve.*

Manley Restaurant, State Shopping Centre, 70a Ballymoney Rd, Ballymena, t (028) 2564 8967/9360 (*moderate*). Cantonese and Peking cuisine.

Water Margin Restaurant, 8 Cullybackey Rd, Ballymena, t (028) 2564 8368 (*moderate*). Cantonese cooking.

Café Rio, Market Sq, Lisburn (*inexpensive*). Snacks and coffee.

Brown Jug, 27 Main St, Ballymoney, t (028) 2766 4212 (*inexpensive*). Salads and quiche. *Closed eves.*

Leslie Hill Open Farm, Ballymoney, t (028) 2766 6803 (*inexpensive*). Scones, cakes and teas. *Closed eves.*

after 1 mile (1.6km), right after 3 miles (5km) (signposted), right after half a mile (0.8km), and follow the road between dry-stone walls to Slemish car park. From the top – a steep climb of about 700ft (213m) – you get a wonderful view. This lonely, extinct volcano has been a place of pilgrimage on St Patrick's Day, 17 March, for centuries.

At **Dreen**, near Cullybackey, ancestral home of US president Chester Arthur (1881–85) is a restored thatched cottage (*open every afternoon Apr–Sept; adm;* **t** *(028) 2563 8494*).

Two miles (3.2km) south of Templepatrick on the A6, **Patterson's Spade Mill** (*open Apr, May and Sept Sat and Sun 2–6, June–Aug daily 2–6; adm;* **t** *(028) 9443 3619*) is the only water-driven spade mill left in Ireland. You can see a traditional forge where nine regional types of spades are produced, though in its heyday the Mill produced around 300 types. It has been restored by the National Trust and there is a fascinating guided tour of the glowing workshop. You can even go away with your own sturdy spade.

Antrim Town, a little way back from Lough Neagh, has an old nucleus with a 9th- or 10th-century round tower in almost perfect condition on Steeple Road (north of the centre), now being encircled by housing and shopping centres. **Antrim Castle and Gardens** (*open Mon–Fri 9.30–9.30, Sat 10–5, Sun 2–5;* **t** *(028) 9442 8000*), c. 1662, are worth a visit: the former stableblock is now an arts centre, but of the castle itself only a tower remains, the rest burnt down in 1922. The restored gardens include geometrical borders in the 17th-century Anglo-Dutch style and a wooded walk.

Shane's Castle, a ruin on a private estate outside Randalstown, is on the site of the ancient stronghold of Edenduffcarrick. The castle was for centuries associated with the O'Neills of Clandeboye; the sculptured head in the south wall of the tower is known as the Black Head of the O'Neills. There is a traditional saying that if anything should happen to the head, the O'Neill family will come to an end.

Lough Neagh, the largest stretch of inland water in the British Isles, is surrounded by flat marshy land. Legend tells how Fionn MacCumhaill took up a sod of land to throw at another giant, which left a hole. This became Lough Neagh, and the sod formed the Isle of Man. The lough is famous for its eels, which spawn in the Sargasso Sea, swim across the Atlantic, and struggle up the Bann in springtime, all 20 million of them (though now they are captured at Coleraine and brought to Lough Neagh in tankers). **Newferry**, at the top of Lough Beg, is a haven for coarse fishermen and water-skiers.

Lisburn, in the Lagan Valley, in the southern tip of County Antrim, has a Planters Gothic **cathedral**. Louis Crommelin lived here, and you will also find the excellent **Lisburn Museum and Irish Linen Centre** (*open Mon–Sat 9.30–5;* **t** *(028) 9266 3377*), which includes a re-creation of a linen-weaving workshop; specialist linen is produced here, and is available to buy (*see* also p.392). You might also visit the **Hilden Brewing Company** (**t** *(028) 9266 3863*), Ireland's oldest independent brewery, and taste its ales.

Belfast

Belfast is known to most people through the exposure brought by the Troubles. Press and TV reports have recorded the bombings, military involvement and sectarian murders, giving the sense of a war-torn city in a state of unrest, dangerous to visit.

Getting There and Around

By Air
Belfast City Airport, 4 miles (7km) from city, t (028) 9093 9093. This is only served by local UK airlines. To get here, take a train to Sydenham Halt from either of the railway stations, Citybus no.21, or a taxi from Donegall Square.
Belfast International Airport, 19 miles (30km) from city centre, at Aldergrove, t (028) 9448 4848. The airport coach leaves every 30mins from the Europa Bus Centre.

By Sea
Belfast–Douglas: Isle of Man Steam Packet, t 08705 523 523. May–Sept.**Belfast–Liverpool: Norse Merchant Ferries**, t (0870) 600 4321, www.norsemerchant.com
Belfast–Stranraer: Stena Line Ferries, t 08705 523 523, www.stenaline.co.uk. Four crossings a day, taking 1½hrs.
Larne–Cairnryan: P&O European Ferries, t 0870 242 4777, www.poirishsea.com. The Larne ferry service links in with trains to Belfast. The station is beside the terminal.

By Rail
Trains go to all destinations from **Belfast Central Station** on East Bridge St or **Great Victoria Street Station**.
Note there are **no left luggage facilities** in any Northern Ireland railway station.
Translink, t (028) 9066 6630, www.translink.co.uk. All rail enquiries.

By Bus
The **Europa Centre** on Great Victoria St serves destinations in counties Armagh, Tyrone, Londonderry, Fermanagh and West Down, the Republic and ferry services to the UK.
Go to the **Laganside Bus Centre** on Donegall Quay (east of the Albert Clock) for destinations in eastern Co. Antrim and North Down.
Ulsterbus runs throughout the suburbs and province; coaches also go to the Republic and mainland UK. **Metro buses** are pink and white and cover most routes. **City Stopper** buses nos. 523–538 also serve the Falls Rd and Lisburn Rd.
Ulsterbus, Europa Centre, Great Victoria St, t (028) 9066 6630, www.translink.co.uk. Enquiries and timetables.

Metro Bus Enquiries, t (028) 9066 6630, www.translink.co.uk

By Car
Parking is forbidden in the centre of Belfast; large notices are displayed on the pavements and there are double yellow lines at the edge of the roads. Excellent car parks and pay-and-display areas ring the centre of the city; the tourist office can provide you with a list and a map.
Avis, 69–71 Gt Victoria St, t (028) 9024 0404
Budget, 96–102 Great Victoria St, t (028) 9023 0700
Dan Dooley, 175B Airport Rd, Aldergrove, t (028) 9445 2522
Europcar, City Airport, t (028) 9045 0904; International Airport, t (028) 9442 3444
Hertz, International Airport, t (028) 9442 2533
McCausland Car Hire, 21–31 Grosvenor Rd, t (028) 9033 3777

By Taxi
Taxi **ranks** can be found at City Hall in Donegall Sq, Upper Queen St, Wellington Place and Castle St.
Belfast Taxi, t 0786 090 1899
Black Taxi, t (028) 906 2264

By Bike
See www.belfastandbeyond.com for further information about cycling in the city.
Bike Dock, 79–85 Ravenhill Rd, t 0845 062 5500, www.bikedock.com
Life Cycles, 36–7 Smithfield Market, t (028) 9043 9959, www.lifecycles.co.uk
McConvey Cycles, 183 and 467 Ormeau Rd, t (028) 9033 0322 and t (028) 9049 1163, www.mcconveycycles.com

Festivals

March
Belfast Film Festival, various venues, t (028) 9032 5913, www.belfastfilmfestival.org
The Best of Ireland, Ulster Folk and Transport Museum, Cultra, Holywood, t (028) 9042 8428, www.uftm.org.uk/whats-on. Traditional music and crafts.
Draíocht **Children's Festival**, West Belfast, t (028) 9024 6609

Belfast

500 metres
500 yards

N

To Belfast
International Airport

Yorkgate
Shopping
Centre

Yorkgate
Cinema

CLIFTON ST

CARRICK HILL

YORK STREET

PETERS   HILL

WEST LINK

Central
Library

St Anne's
Cathedral

Smithfield
Market

Castle Court
Shopping
Centre

Old Museum
Arts Centre

Linen Hall
Library

Grand Opera House

Europa Bus
Centre

Crown
Liquor
Saloon

Great Victoria
St Station

Ulster
Hall

Virgin
Cinema

City Hall

Royal Courts
of Justice

St Georges
Market

Central Train
Station

Maysfield Leisure
Centre

Sinclair Seaman's
Church

Seacat Terminal/
Isle of Man Ferry

Odyssey
Centre

SYDENHAM ROAD

Custom
House

Lagan Lookout Centre

LaganWeir

Albert
Clock

NITB

Laganside
Bus centre

Waterfront
Hall

Botanical
Train station

City Hospital
Station

SHAFTESBURY
SQUARE

DONEGALL ROAD

DONEGALL PASS

University
Sq Mews

University
Sq

Queen's University
Film Theatre

Queen's
University

Palm House

Ulster Museum

Botanical
Gardens
Park

Ormeau
Park

River
Lagan

Lagan Valley Walkway

Laganside Walkway

M2

NEWTOWNARDS
ROAD

QUEEN'S ROAD

BRIDGE END

SHORT STRAND

MOUNT
POTTINGER RD

ALBERT BR.

ALBERT BR. RD

RAVENHILL ROAD

RAVENHILL
AVE

RAVENHILL
ROAD

ARDENLEE AVE

PARK   ROAD

GROSVENOR ROAD

DIVIS STREET

PETERS   HILL

WEST LINK

CASTLE STREET

COLLEGE AV

COLLEGE SQ N.

GREAT VICTORIA STREET

SANDY ROW

DUBLIN ROAD

LISBURN ROAD

COLLEGE GDNS

WELLINGTON PARK

EGLANTINE AVENUE

MALONE ROAD

STRANMILLIS RD

UNIVERSITY ROAD

BOTANIC AVENUE

CROMWELL ROAD

UNIVERSITY STREET

FITZROY AVENUE

RUGBY AVENUE

AGINCOURT AVENUE

ORMEAU ROAD

ORMEAU EMBANKMENT

STRANMILLIS EMBANKMENT

ANNADALE EMBANKMENT

CLIFTON ST

YORK ROAD

CORPORATION STREET

PILOT ST

M2

QUEEN'S QUAY

DONEGALL QUAY

CORPORATION SQ

MIDDLEPATH ST

QUEEN ELIZABETH BR.

QUEEN'S BR.

DARGAN BR.

LAGAN BRIDGE

OXFORD STREET

VICTORIA STREET

EAST BRIDGE STREET

MAY STREET

CHICHESTER STREET

DONEGALL SQ. S.

ADELAIDE STREET

ALFRED STREET

CROMAC STREET

ORMEAU AVENUE

HOWARD ST

BRUNSWICK ST

BEDFORD ST

LINEN HALL ST

DONEGALL PLACE

ROYAL AVE

NORTH STREET

DONEGALL STREET

TALBOT STREET

DUNBAR LINK

NELSON ST

YORK STREET

HILL ST

WARING ST

BRIDGE ST

HIGH STREET

ANN ST

QUEEN'S SQ

CUSTOM HO

ALBERT SQ

SUSSEX PL

HAMILTON ST

GROSVENOR ROAD

GLENGALL ST

AMELIA ST

HOPE ST

WELLWOOD ST

BRADBURY PL.

UNIVERSITY SQ.

UNIVERSITY TERR.

LAGANBANK RD

April

Easter Celebrations, Ulster Folk and Transport Museum, **t** (028) 9042 8428, *www.uftm.org.uk*
World Irish Dancing Championships, Belfast Waterfront Hall, 2 Lanyon Place, **t** (028) 9033 4455, *www.waterfront.co.uk*

May

Balmoral Show, Kings Hall, Balmoral, **t** (028) 906 5225. A large agricultural show with showjumping, military displays and crafts.
Cathedral Quarter Arts Festival, **t** (028) 9023 2403, *www.cqaf.com*
Lord Mayor's Show, **t** (028) 9032 0202, *www.belfastcity.gov.uk*. May–June.

June

Shankill Festival, **t** (028) 9031 1333. Social, cultural and recreational events.
Storytelling Weekend, Ulster Folk and Transport Museum, **t** (028) 9042 8428, *www.uftm.org. uk*. Storytelling and traditional music.

July

Orange Order Parades, **t** (028) 9024 6609. A 12 July event.

August

Ardoyne *Fleadh*, **t** (028) 9075 1056. Local and international performers and *céilí*.
Feile an Phobail, **t** (028) 9031 3440, *www. feilebelfast.com*. Music, drama, Irish-language events, a carnival and a parade.
Rare Breeds Show and Sale, Ulster Folk and Transport Museum, **t** (028) 9042 8428, *www.uftm.org.uk/whats-on*. Rare, minority and re-established farm breeds.

November

Belfast Arts Festival, Queens University, box office **t** (028) 9097 1197, information **t** (028) 9097 1034, *www.belfastfestival.com*. Three weeks of music, films, plays, poetry and art exhibitions, including fringe shows from Edinburgh and international stars. Events take place mainly around the university area.

Tourist Information

Belfast Welcome Centre, Donegall Place, **t** (028) 9024 6609

NI Tourist Board, 59 North St, **t** (028) 9023 1221, *www.discovernorthernireland.com*, *www.tourismireland.com*
Belfast Visitor and Convention Bureau, 47 Donegall Place, **t** (028) 9023 9026, *www.gotobelfast.com*, *www.belfastconventionbureau.com*

Useful Contacts

Emergency Services, **t** 999
Belfast City Hospital, Lisburn Rd, **t** (028) 9032 9241
General Post Office, Castle Place and Shaftesbury Sq. *Closed Sun.*
AA, 108–110 Great Victoria St, **t** 08705 989 989; 24hr rescue service **t** 0800 887766
RAC, 14 Wellington Place, **t** 08705 722722; 24hr rescue service **t** 0800 828282
Youth Hostel Association, 22 Donegall Rd, **t** (028) 9032 4733, *www.hini.org.uk*
USIT/Belfast Student Travel, **t** (028) 9032 4073/7111, *www.usit.ie*

Internet Access

Internet Café, Welcome Centre, 47 Donegall Place, **t** (028) 9024 6609
Revelations Café, 27 Shaftesbury Sq, **t** (028) 9032 0337, *www.revelations.co.uk*

Shopping

Central Belfast is full of shopping arcades and pedestrian malls, and British high-street stores are well represented. More unusual shops are in Bedford St, Dublin Rd and Donegall Pass – design outlets, antiques and bric-à-brac. Expensive women's clothes are sold amongst the cafés and food stores on the Lisburn Rd. Shuttle buses service the car parks, and many city buses stop at the central City Hall.

Antiques

Alexander the Grate, Donegall Pass, **t** (028) 9023 2041, *www.alexander-the-grate.com*
Blue Cat, Bedford St, **t** (028) 9023 5204
Oakland Antiques, Donegall Pass, **t** (028) 9023 0176
Past and Present, 66 Donegall Pass

Books
Bookfinders, 47 University Rd, t (028) 9032 8269
University Bookshop, 91 University Terrace, opposite Queens College, t (028) 9066 6302
Waterstone's, 8 Royal Ave, t (028) 9024 7355, and 44 Fountain St, t (028) 9024 0159

Clothes
House of de Courcy, 487 Lisburn Rd, t (028) 9020 0250. Designer womenswear.
Paul Costelloe, 45 Bradbury Place, t (028) 9023 9496. A stockist of Irish designers.
Smyth and Gibson, Bedford St, t (028) 9023 0388, *www.smythandgibson.co.uk.* Top-quality Irish shirts made in Derry.

Crafts
Craftworks, Bedford St, t (028) 9024 4465
The Steensons, Bedford House, Bedford St, t (028) 9024 8269. Jewellery.
The Wicker Man, 12 Donegall Arcade, Castle Place, t (028) 9024 3550
The Workshops Collective, 1a Lawrence St, t (028) 9020 0707

Food and Drink
Feasts, 39 Dublin Rd, t (028) 9033 2787. Cheeses, charcuterie and home-made pasta.
French Village Bakery, 70 Stranmillis Rd, t (028) 9038 1671. Wheaten bannock, wheaten loaf, 'Belfast Baps' and more.

Irish Linen
Irish Linen Stores, Fountain Centre, College St, t (028) 9032 2727
Smyth's Irish Linens, 65 Royal Ave, t (028) 9024 2232

Markets
St George's Market, end of May St, t (028) 9043 5704. Fresh fruit, vegetables, fish, crafts, new and vintage clothes and other wares sold in the 19th-century 'Variety Market' building Tue and Fri 7–1.

Musical Instruments
Matchetts Ltd, Wellington Place, t (028) 9032 6695, *www.matchettsmusic.com.*

Sports Equipment
Graham Tiso, 12–14 Corn Market, t (028) 9023 1230

S.S. Moore, 6 Chichester St, t (028) 9032 2966
Surf Mountain, 12 Brunswick St, t (028) 9024 8877

Sports and Activities

Art Galleries
The Troubles seem to have generated a creative urge amongst Ulster artists that is both exploratory and introspective. Artists such as Tom Carr, T. P. Flanagan, Brian Ferran, Basil Blackshaw and Brian Ballard have produced excellent works on a variety of subjects, including Ulster scenery, nudes and interpretations of Irish myths.

Entry to commercial galleries is free.
Bell Gallery, 13 Adelaide Park, t (028) 9066 2998, *www.bellgalley.com*
Crescent Arts Centre and Fenderesky Gallery, 2–4 University Rd, t (028) 9024 2338. *Closed Sun and Mon.*
Emer Gallery, 467 Antrim Rd, t (028) 9077 8777, *www.emergallery.com*
Old Museum Arts Centre, 7 College Square North, t (028) 9023 3332, *www.oldmuseumartscentre.org*
Ormeau Baths Gallery, 18 Ormeau Ave, t (028) 9032 1402, *www.obgonline.net.* Good shows, usually by Irish and Ulster artists. *Closed Sun and Mon.*
Tom Caldwell Gallery, 429 Lisburn Rd, t (028) 9066 1890, *www.tomcaldwellgallery.com*
Townhouse Gallery, 125 Great Victoria St, t (028) 9031 1798. Prints and etchings.
Ulster Museum, Botanic Gardens (off Stranmillis Rd), t (028) 9038 3000, *www.ulstermuseum.org.uk*

Golf
Balmoral Golf Club, Lisburn Rd, t (028) 9038 1514. An 18-hole course.
Blackwood Golf Centre, Crawfordsburn Rd, Clandeboye, t (028) 9185 2706
Carrickfergus Golf Club, 7 miles (12km) northeast of Belfast on A2, t (028) 9336 3713. An 18-hole course.
Rockmount Golf Club, Carryduff, t (028) 9081 2279
Royal Belfast Golf Club, Station Rd, Craigavad, t (028) 9042 8165. The oldest of the 4 'Royal' clubs in Ireland.

Indoor Leisure Centres

Maysfield Leisure Centre, East Bridge St,
t (028) 9024 1633. A central centre with a
pool, gym, squash courts and sauna.

Tours

Guided **walking tours** include pubs, historic
Belfast, the University area and the Laganside
walk; **bus tours** are also available.

The Belfast Welcome Centre has a free
leaflet, 'Walk this Way', about the tours.
Belfast City Sightseeing, **t** (028) 9080 9009.
www.belfastcitysightseeing.com. Tours
taking in all the main sights of Belfast,
including Stormont and Belfast Castle.
There's also a 'Living History Tour' around
areas associated with the Troubles.

Where to Stay

Belfast

Luxury

The Culloden Hotel, 142 Bangor Rd, Craigavad,
t (028) 9042 1066, *www.hastingshotels.com*.
One of the best hotels in the area, situated
on the north-east of Belfast Lough. Very
plush, it has lovely grounds and luxurious
old-style furnishings.

Europa Hotel, Great Victoria St, **t** (028) 9032
7000, *www.hastingshotels.com*. A very
central modern hotel that was bombed so
many times that everybody lost count.

Expensive

Belfast Hilton, 4 Lanyon Place, **t** (028) 9027 7000,
www.hilton.com. A modern hotel up close to
the Waterfront Hall, with wonderful views.

Camera Guest House, 44 Wellington Park,
t (028) 9066 0026. A comfortably elegant
Victorian house with a friendly proprietress.

Malmaison, 34–38 Victoria St, **t** (028) 9022
0200, *www.malmaison-belfast.com*.
A trendy designer hotel opened in 2005,
with rather small rooms.

Ramada Hotel, 117 Milltown Rd, Shaw's Bridge,
t (028) 9092 3500, *www.ramadabelfast.com*.
A slightly souless but full-service hotel
with all mod cons, conveniently located for
travellers on the ring road 5 miles (8km)
from the city centre.

Moderate–Expensive

The Wellington Park Hotel, 21 Malone Rd,
t (028) 9038 1111, *www.wellingtonparkhotel.
com*. A modern and comfortable choice close
to the Botanic Gardens, with secure parking.

Moderate

Ash-Rowan Town House, 12 Windsor Ave,
t (028) 9066 1758/1983. A cosy and attractive
place 10mins from the city centre.

Blakely Manor Guest House, 67 Malone Rd,
t (028) 9066 2985, *www.blakelymanor.co.uk*.
A reasonably priced option set within its
own grounds less than a mile (1.6km) from
Belfast city centre.

Clandeboye Lodge Hotel, 10 Estate Rd,
Clandeboye, **t** (028) 9185 2500, *www.
clandeboyelodge.com*. A good-quality hotel
adjoining Blackwood Golf Course.

Dukes Hotel, 65–67 University St, **t** (028) 9023
6666, *www.welcome-group.co.uk*. A quiet
and central option close to restaurants.

The Old Rectory, 148 Malone Rd, **t** (028) 9066
7882, *www.anoldrectory.co.uk*. A lovingly run
old rectory 10mins from the centre, with very
good breakfasts.

Inexpensive

Belfast Palace Hostel, 68 Lisburn Rd,
t (028) 9033 3367, *www.paddyspalace.com*.
Centrally located budget accommodation,
including 8-person dorms and private
double rooms.

The following offer good-value B&B
accommodation in the quiet, leafy streets
of the university district. They are often busy
in summer, so book ahead.

The George, 9 Eglantine Ave, **t** (028) 9068 3212
Kate's B&B, 127 University St, **t** (028) 9028 2091
Liserin Guest House, 17 Eglantine Ave,
t (028) 9066 0769
Windermere Guest House, 60 Wellington Park,
t (028) 9066 2693

Self-catering

The Ark, 18 University St, **t** (028) 9032 9626.
A terraced house close to the city centre.

Queen's Elms, Queen's University,
78 Malone Rd, **t** (028) 9097 4525,
gehor@gub.ac.uk Mainly single rooms
with access to cooking facilities.

Eating Out

Belfast

Luxury
Restaurant Michael Deane, 36–40 Howard St, t (028) 9056 0000, *www.michaeldeane.co.uk*. A hugely popular, well-run restaurant. The more affordable **brasserie** in the basement also serves excellent food.

Expensive
Cayenne, Ascot House, 7 Shaftesbury Sq, t (028) 9033 1532, *www.rankinggroup.co.uk*. An imaginative menu and reasonable set lunches. Book ahead.

Moderate
Aldens, 229 Upper Newtownards Road, t (028) 9065 0079, *www.aldensrestaurant.com*. A well-established restaurant just outside the centre, serving contemporary cuisine.
Beatrice Kennedy, 44 University Rd, t (028) 9020 2290, *www.beatricekennedy.com*. A bistro popular with locals, offering good seafood. *Closed Mon.*
Café Vaudeville, 25 Arthur St, t (028) 9043 9160, *www.cafevaudeville.com*. A stylish Gallic-inspired café, all-day bistro and lounge, plus a cocktail and champagne bar.
The Cellar Restaurant, Belfast Castle, Antrim Rd, t (028) 9077 6925/9037 0133, *www.belfastcastle.co.uk*. Innovative and modern dishes made from fresh local produce, served in an historic atmosphere. *Closed Sun and Mon eves.*
Ginger's, 7–8 Hope St, off Great Victoria St, t (028) 9024 4421. Superb Southeast Asian inspired cooking, including freshly baked breads, vegetarian dishes and inventive recipes incorporating ginger. Book ahead, as its reputation has spread far and wide. There's a café section serving lunch daily. *Closed Mon eve and lunch Sun–Thur.*
Nick's Warehouse, 35 Hill St, Cathedral Quarter, t (028) 9043 9690, *www.nickswarehouse.co.uk*. A popular modern restaurant that is highly recommended for its gourmet dishes. *Closed Mon eve, Sat lunch, and Sun.*
Roscoff Brasserie, 7–11 Linenhall St, t (028) 9031 1150, *www.rankingroup.co.uk*. A new venue for modern and classical French food.

Scalini, 85 Botanic Ave, t (028) 9032 0303. Italian cuisine and grills. *Closed lunch.*
Shu, 253 Lisburn Rd, t (028) 9038 1655, *www.shu-restaurant.com*. A smart restaurant with a cocktail bar and bistro in the basement. The menu is eclectic. *Closed Sun.*
Sun Kee, 28 Donegall Pass, t (028) 9031 2233. The best Chinese restaurant in Belfast.

Inexpensive
Maggie May's, 50 Botanic Ave, t (028) 9032 2662. A place for big servings of good-value vegetarian meals.
The Other Place, 79 Botanic Ave, t (028) 9020 7200, and 537 Lisburn Rd, t (028) 9020 7300. Good burgers, chips and Ulster fries.
Scarlets, 423 Lisburn Rd, t (028) 9068 3102. Snacks and bistro fare
Speranza, 16 Shaftesbury Sq, t 9023 0213. Pizzas and pasta.
Villa Italia, 37–41 University Rd, t (028) 9032 8356. A lively, popular Italian. *Closed lunch.*
Wrap Works Co., 199 Lisburn Rd, t (028) 9022 1141. Mexican food, wraps and other dishes.

Cafés
Belfast has good cafés serving exotic, well-prepared food or simple, affordable meals, though some have yet to master the art of a good cappuccino.
Bonnie's Museum Café, 11a Stranmillis Rd. Pies, filled baguettes and soups.
Bookfinders Café, 47 University Rd, t (028) 9032 8269. Vegetarian meals in a bookshop.
Café Paul Rankin, 27 Fountain St, t (028) 9031 5090. A great place for breakfasts and snacks. There are also branches in Arthur St, the Castlescourt Shopping Centre and Belfast International Airport.
Cargoes, 613 Lisburn Rd, t 9066 5451. Med-style salads served in a café inside a delicatessen.
Equinox, 32 Howard St, t (028) 9023 0089, *www.equinoxshop.com*. A café in a sophisticated interior design and giftshop, with excellent salads, coffee and milkshakes.
Smyth & Gibson, Bedford St, t (028) 9023 0388. A coffee stop in the basement of the famous shirtmakers, with decent lattes and cappuccinos.
Zio, 23 University Rd, t (028) 9027 8788, *www.ziocafebar.com*. A café serving pasta dishes and pizza.

Entertainment and Nightlife

Pubs and Bars
The atmosphere in the bars listed below is warm. Traditional, folk and popular music is played in some places, and specialities such as champ and stew are served in others.

The best sources of information for music events are the *Belfast Telegraph* or *That's Entertainment* and *Artslink*, available from tourist offices and hotels.

Apartment, 2 Donegall Sq, t (028) 9050 9777. A hip and stylish bar in the centre, with coffee and cocktails, meals and snacks.

Crown Liquor Saloon, 46 Great Victoria St, t (028) 9027 9901. A Victorian extravagance (*see* p.402) restored by the National Trust, serving Irish stew and oysters at lunchtime.

The Duke of York, 11 Commercial Court, 103 Victoria St, t 9031 1088/9024 1062. Live music in the evenings.

Lavery's Bar and Gin Palace, 12 Bradbury Place, t (028) 9087 1106. An old favourite for a wide range of age groups, serving pub grub.

McHugh's, 29–31 Queen's Sq, t (028) 9050 9990. A charming bar and restaurant in Belfast's oldest building, popular with tourists and young professionals.

The Morning Star, 17 Pottinger's Entry, t (028) 9032 3976. An attractive old pub serving excellent meals.

Morrison's Spirit Grocers, 21 Bedford St, t (028) 9024 8458. A cleverly decorated theme bar.

White's Tavern, 2–4 Winecellar Entry, t (028) 9024 3080. Live music on Thur.

Live Music
Front Page, 106–110 Donegall St, t (028) 9032 4924. Food and live music.

Kitchen Bar, 16–18 Victoria Sq, t (028) 9032 4901. A traditional Irish bar with real ale and Ulster food, and Irish and Scottish music Fri nights.

The Rotterdam, 54 Pilot St, t (028) 9074 6021. Folk and traditional music.

Nightclubs
The Limelight, 17 Ormeau Ave, t (028) 9032 5968. A club that promotes new bands, and attracts a young crowd. U2 and Oasis have played here.

M Club, 23–31 Bradbury Place, t (028) 9023 3131
Robinson's Bar, 38–42 Great Victoria St, t (028) 9024 7447. Some truly awful duos and bands plus the occasional gem.

Arts Centres
Cultúrlann Macadam O'Fiach, 216 Falls Rd, t (028) 9096 4180, *www.culturlann.com*. An Irish-language arts centre, with performance and different forms of media.

Cinema
The Movie House, Yorkgate Centre, York Rd, t (028) 9075 5000.
Queen's Film Theatre, 7 University Square Mews, t (028) 9024 4857. Avant-garde, arthouse films.
Strand Cinema, 152–4 Holywood Rd, Strandtown, t (028) 9067 3500
UGC, 14 Dublin Rd, t 0870 155 5176. A multiplex.

Poetry
Ulster has produced poets of global renown; Seamus Heaney started writing at Queen's University in the 1960s, as did Paul Muldoon at a later date. During the **Belfast Arts Festival** in Nov (*see* p.397), you may be lucky enough to hear them and other talented poets read.

Theatres and Concert Halls
Belfast Waterfront Hall, 2 Lanyon Place, t (028) 9033 4455/9033 4400, *www.waterfront.co.uk*. A huge venue hosting concerts by classical and pop music stars.
The Grand Opera House, Great Victoria St, t (028) 9024 1919, *www.goh.co.uk*
Lyric Theatre, 55 Ridgeway St, off Stranmillis Rd, t (028) 9038 1081, *www.lyrictheatre.co.uk*. Serious Irish, European and American drama.
The Old Museum Arts Centre, 7 College Square North, t (028) 9023 3332. Avant-garde dance, theatre and comedy.
St Anne's Cathedral, Donegall St, t (028) 9032 8332, *www.belfastcathedral.org*. Occasional lunchtime recitals and wonderful sung services on Sun.
The Ulster Hall, Bedford St, t (028) 9032 3900, *www.ulsterhall.co.uk*. Concerts and comedy shows, including subscription concerts and lunchtime recitals in summer.
Whitla Hall, Queen's University, t (028) 9027 3075, Classical concerts all year, particularly during the Arts Festival (*see* p.397).

This is simply not the case. For visitors it is surprising how normal the streets are, full of people shopping at Marks & Spencer and other proliferous British chain stores. Military patrols and armoured police vehicles are now a rare sight, where once they were an everyday part of the city's life. Belfast people share a cautious optimism about the peace process, and while old sectarian divisions die hard, there is almost unanimous support for a permanent political resolution to the violence. They are very friendly, and will answer any queries with the characteristic good humour of the Irish.

There are many opportunities to see good theatre, art shows, classical and pop concerts, while the strong intellectual and historical atmosphere makes for good conversation and well-stocked bookshops. The well-educated young are still leaving for opportunities abroad, but many are coming back with a wealth of experience. Belfast is losing its parochial image and becoming more European-minded, and the bars and cafés more sophisticated. The Waterfront Hall and Hilton seem to be new symbols for Belfast, just as the Europa Hotel and the Opera House became symbols of surviving the bomb and bullet during the worst of the Troubles in the 1970s.

Belfast (*Béal Feirste*: 'Mouth of the Sandy Ford') is the administrative centre of the six counties that make up Northern Ireland. It has one of the most beautiful natural settings of any city, ringed by hills visible from most parts of the town, and hugging the shores of the lough. It has been a city officially only since 1888. In the 19th century it grew from an insignificant town by a river ford into a prosperous commercial centre and port, with great linen mills and the Harland & Wolff shipyards. The *Titanic*, built here and tragically sunk by an iceberg, was considered an outstanding engineering feat.

Architecturally, Belfast is made up of some grand Victorian public buildings and the red-brick streets that characterize many British towns. The prosperous-looking houses that make up the smart Malone Road area and line the lough on either side were built by the wealthy middle class who benefited from the linen industry. The workers in the factories and shipyards divided themselves between the Catholic Falls Road area and Protestant Shankill Road. Unemployment became worse as the linen and shipbuilding industries declined, nurturing the conditions in which terrorist armies could thrive. The division of these working-class areas from the centre was made explicit by the Westlink motorway, creating a boundary line through the west of the city.

Central Belfast

Central Belfast is pedestrianized, for security reasons, but you will see nothing else out of the ordinary unless you are extraordinarily unlucky. It has been spoiled by awful shopping arcades and British high-street shops. On the upside, shopping is convenient and there are a few decent cafés. There are also a few interior décor, furniture and Irish design shops worth looking out for (*see* 'Shopping', pp.397–8). The centre is quite compact and easy to walk around, and the area is often lively long after nightfall.

Belfast is a 19th-century town and lacks Dublin's grace; some say this is owing to the plutocratic city fathers. Two of the most attractive buildings are on Great Victoria Street: the **Grand Opera House** and the **Crown Liquor Saloon**, a gaslit High-Victorian pub decorated with richly coloured tiles. It has been preserved by the National Trust but not gentrified, and its old clientele still drink there (at night it can be noisy and a bit rough). The Opera House was also designed in the High-Victorian style (by Robert Matcham, the theatre architect) with rich, intricate decorative detail, including carved elephants. It was restored in the 1970s by architect Robert McKinstry, and the ceiling has a fine fresco by Cherith McKinstry. If you don't have an evening to spare, both are worth a quick look around, and the Crown is good for a quiet pint with lunch.

Although many of the splendours of Belfast date from its period of mercantile importance, there was a great quickening of spirit here in the 18th century. United Irishman Henry Joy McCracken, whose family first published *The Belfast Newsletter* in 1737 (the longest-running newspaper in the world), was a son of the city. Other 18th-century personalities include William Drennan, who coined the phrase 'the Emerald Isle' and founded the **Royal Academical Institution**. This distinguished building lies between College Square East and Durham Street, and was designed by Sir John Soane, the eminent London architect, classical scholar and collector. It was built between 1808 and 1810 in a style that is classical in proportion. The Institution is now a school, but it is possible to look around it. The prospect is a little spoiled by the great College of Technology, built on the corner of the lawn.

The **City Hall** (*guided tours available; t (028) 9027 0456*) in Donegall Square, built between 1896 and 1906 in Portland stone, is a grand composition with a central dome and corner towers borrowed from Wren's St Paul's Cathedral. Unfortunately the 18th-century Donegall Square has been replaced with a medley of different styles since the 19th century. The **Linen Hall Library** (*open Mon–Wed and Fri 9.30–5.30, Thur 9.30–8.30, Sat 9.30–4; t (028) 9032 1707; www.linenhall.com*) is one of the last survivors in the British Isles of the subscription library movement, so important to civilized Europe in the late 18th/early 19th century. Still a rich storehouse of books of Irish interest, it also has a comfortable room where you can sample periodicals, magazines and the day's flurry of newspapers. The librarians are polite and helpful, and the prints that line the walls echo the feeling of an earlier age.

Just along the way is the Robinson Cleaver Building, overlooking Donegall Place. This flamboyantly Victorian department store now houses a mixture of boutiques. The **Customs House** and **Courts of Justice** in Custom House Square and the **Ulster Hall** in Bedford Street with its impressive organ are all rather grey self-important buildings in a heavy Victorian style. In Corporation Square is the **Sinclair Seamen's Church**, designed by Charles Lanyon and built in 1853. The pulpit incorporates the bows, bowsprit and figurehead of a ship, the organ displays starboard and port lights, and the font is a binnacle. **St Anne's Cathedral** in Donegall Street was built in 1899 in Romanesque style, of the Basilican type. It is very imposing inside, with some fine stained-glass windows and mosaics. In the nave is the tomb of Lord Carson, the Northern Unionist leader, who died in 1935.

On the east bank of the Lagan River at Queen's Quay you'll find the **Odyssey Centre**. Inside there is an interactive children's museum, **whowhatwherewhenwhy – W5** (*open Mon–Sat 10–6, Sun 12 noon–6; adm; t (028) 9046 7700, www.w5online.co.uk*).

Kids can have great fun here making giant cloud rings, playing the Laser Harp and watching the Fire Tornado. Farther upstream, at the **Lagan Weir and Lookout Centre** (*open Apr–Sept Mon–Fri 10–5, Sat 12 noon–5, Sun 2–5, Oct–Mar Tue–Fri 11–3.30, Sat 1–4.30, Sun 2–4.30; adm; t (028) 9031 5444*) on Donegall Quay, you can take a platform view of the busy Lagan waterway, and find out about local industrial and folk history. South of here, following the Lagan, is the prestigious purposebuilt **Belfast Waterfront Hall**, a large concert hall and conference centre.

About 10 minutes' walk away from Donegall Square, going south down Great Victoria Street, is the leafy university area. This neighbourhood best reflects the character of the city, and is by far the most pleasant part of town in which to stay. Lisburn Road, in particular, has seen dozens of new cafés and art galleries spring up in the wake of the ceasefire, and the student population ensures the area's vitality.

You pass the imposing Tudor-style red-brick Queen's University building to go into the **Botanic Gardens** (*gardens open 8–sunset; Palm House open Mon–Fri 10–5, Sat and Sun 2–5*). The gardens are small but beautifully laid out with formal flowerbeds. The restored Victorian Palm House is a splendid combination of graceful design and clever construction. Richard Turner, the Dubliner whose ironworks produced it, was also responsible for its design. It is made of sections that comprise the earliest surviving cast-iron and curvilinear glass architecture in the world. Inside the Palm House are tender and exotic plants. Another building within the grounds worth visiting is the Tropical Ravine, which houses a large collection of tropical plants.

Set inside the Botanical Gardens is the **Ulster Museum** (*open Mon–Fri 10–5, Sat 1–5, Sun 2–5; adm for special exhibitions; t (028) 9038 3000, www.ulstermuseum.org.uk*). It has a variety of well-displayed and informative collections ranging from giant elk antlers to patchwork, jewellery and Irish antiquities. Of special interest is the outstanding modern art collection, with a good representation of Irish artists, including Sir James Lavery, whose wife was the Irish *cailín* (colleen) on the old Irish pound notes. The museum also has a unique collection of treasure from the wreck of the Spanish Armada vessel, the *Girona*. In 1588 Philip II of Spain ordered the greatest invasion fleet ever assembled to put an end to the growing power of England. Of the 130 ships that set sail, 26 were lost on, or just off, the coast of Ireland. In 1968 a fabulous hoard of gold and silver coins, heavy gold chains, rings, ornamented crosses, a beautiful gold salamander pendant set with rubies and a filigree brooch were all recovered off the coast of Antrim. As recently as 1999 a set of delicate gold and jewelled cameos was made complete by the addition of the 12th cameo. The temporary exhibitions are invariably excellent, and there is a programme of lectures, art films, talks and children's weekend activities. It also has a café overlooking the gardens. The streets leading off the University are attractive and tree-lined with some good restaurants and cafés, small art galleries and design shops – all a far cry from the wastelands of the 'other' Belfast, beyond the Westlink motorway.

If you want to have a look at the **Republican enclaves** in west Belfast, which are brightened by gaudy wall paintings and political slogans, take a black taxi. These run like miniature buses and serve areas such as the Falls, where public buses do not venture. Unemployment and poverty are obvious in the streets here, and although tourists are generally welcome, they do stand out, despite efforts to provide visitor facilities. These neighbourhoods are economically and socially depressed, and visitors should exercise caution, as they might in parts of London or New York. The communities are closed to strangers and it would not be wise to go drinking in the pubs or illegal clubs, nor to walk about these parts at night.

The **Unionist** working-class area in west Belfast lies beside the Falls, in the notorious Shankhill Road, which has political murals of its own. The so-called 'peace line', which is actually a high barrier, divides the two communities. **Sandy Row**, a short distance from Great Victoria Street and Shaftesbury Square, is another working-class Unionist area. It seems less threatening to walk around, and there are plenty of little bakeries and small shops, which gives it a bustling air. The bulk of the enclaves where the kerbstones are painted red, white and blue are over the river to the east, along Newtownards Road.

The Suburbs of Belfast

Parliament House, Stormont, can be seen from the Newtownards Road (A20) about 2 miles (4km) east from the city centre. It is a very imposing Portland stone building in English Palladian style, with a floor space covering 5 acres (2ha), and it stands in a park of 300 acres (121ha). Next door is **Stormont Castle**, built in the Scottish baronial style, which houses government departments.

There are many fine parks scattered around Belfast. In south Belfast, in the Upper Malone Road (B103) area, you will find **Barnett's Park**. Within the attractive parkland is an early-19th-century house with an art gallery, a permanent exhibition on Belfast parks and a restaurant (*open Mon–Sat 10–4.30*). Nearby is **Dixon Park** (*open daily till dusk; for information call City Council, t (028) 9032 0202*), where rose-fanciers get the chance to view the Belfast International Rose Trials, the finals of which take place in the third week of July. The park borders the River Lagan, and in summer about 100,000 roses are in bloom.

Continuing up the Malone Road, those visitors who are interested in Neolithic sites should visit the **Giant's Ring** (*always accessible*), near Ballylesson, about a mile (1.6km) south of Shaw's Bridge. The Giant's Ring is a circular grassy embanked enclosure more than 600ft (187m) in diameter, with a chambered grave in the centre. The dolmen in the centre is called Druid's Dolmen. The original purpose of the site is disputed but it was probably ritualistic; its date is unknown. The giant it is named after is possibly Fionn MacCumhaill, who is a favourite to tag onto such places (*see* **Old Gods and Heroes**, p.55). In old times, farmers used to stage horseraces in this enormous circle.

Shaw's Bridge, off the B23 and spanning the River Lagan, is very picturesque. It was originally built *c.* 1650. You can walk for 10 miles (16km) along the towpath of the River Lagan, past the public parks. Start at the Belfast Boat Club, Loughview Road, Stranmillis, and end at Moore's Bridge, Hillsborough Road, Lisburn.

On the northern side of the city, on the Antrim road (A6), baronial-style **Belfast Castle** appears unexpectedly from the wooded slopes of Cave Hill. It was built by the third Marquess of Donegall in 1870. His family, the Chichesters, were granted the forfeited lands of Belfast and the surrounding area in 1603; the Gaelic lords of the area, the O'Neills, lost everything and fled to the Continent. The planted grounds of the castle are always accessible to the public. There is a pleasant restaurant open for full meals or snacks in the castle itself, and a Heritage Centre (*call castle for more details, **t** (028) 9077 6925*) with exhibits on the flora and fauna of **Cave Hill** (1,182ft/368m). An easy climb to the summit gives stunning views over the city and Belfast Lough. There are five caves and the earthwork of MacArt's Fort, named after a local Gaelic chieftain of the Iron Age. It was here that the United Irishmen, Wolfe Tone and his followers, took their oaths of fidelity in 1798 (*see* **History**, pp.17–8).

Belfast Zoo (*open daily mid-Mar–Sept 10–6, Oct–mid-Mar 10–3.30; Metro bus nos.1A–F, 2A; adm; **t** (028) 9077 6277, www.belfastzoo.co.uk*), on the slopes below Cave Hill, is beautifully planted with flowers, shrubs and trees. The zoo has won awards for its emphasis on large enclosures, its breeding programme, and its mainly small-animal collection. It is great fun to view the penguins and sealions from underwater, and there is a rare opportunity to see a bespectacled bear and a red panda.

There are several interesting places within easy reach of Belfast that are worth a visit. About 6 miles (9km) north-east of the centre, along the A2 past some of the world's largest cranes in the shipyards, and the aircraft works at Sydenham, is the wooded suburb of **Cultra** near Holywood. Here, in a parkland of nearly 200 acres (80ha), is the **Ulster Folk and Transport Museum** (*open Mar–June Mon–Fri 10–5, Sat 10–6, Sun 11–6, July–Sept Mon–Sat 10–6, Sun 11–6, Oct–Feb Mon–Fri 10–4, Sat 10–5, Sun 11–5; adm; **t** (028) 9042 8428, www.uftm.org.uk; train from central Belfast stops at Cultra Station, in grounds of museum*). The museum, technically in County Down, provides a unique opportunity for visitors to explore Ulster's past. The best museum of its type in Ireland, it gives a wonderful insight into what life in the countryside was like all over Ireland until 60 years ago. It is open-air, with representative buildings of rural Ulster: a linen scutch mill, a blacksmith's forge, a spade mill and farmhouses built in different regional styles. These are all furnished appropriately, with real fires burning in the grates.

At **Helen's Bay**, a couple of miles (3.2km) north of Cultra, two lovely beaches joined by a path flank **Crawfordsburn Country Park**, with a stream flowing through the woods to the sea. The wooded demesne of Clandeboye Estate has protected this area from the work of housing developers. In the distance the delightful **Helen's Tower** can be seen, erected in Victorian times by the first Marquess of Dufferin and Ava to the memory of his mother. Some of the 19th-century English poet Alfred Lord Tennyson's lines are inscribed in the tower:

Helen's Tower, here I stand
Dominant over sea and land.
Son's love built me and I hold
Mother's love in letter'd gold...

It was erected at a time of destitution caused by the famine of 1845, and gave employment to many. It has become a symbol of Ulster; another Helen's Tower was raised in northern France near Albert to commemorate the appalling losses suffered by the men of Ulster in the First World War. The **Somme Heritage Centre** (*t (028) 9182 3202, www.irishsoldier.org*) on the A21 Newtownards– Bangor road carries on the theme. Clandeboye Estate is open from time to time for charitable purposes and specific events, but it is not possible to see inside the tower.

County Down

Sea-bordered and close to mainland Britain, this county has excited the envy and lust of waves of invaders. Its farmlands are amongst the richest in Ireland, and it has an attractive coastline, the famous Mourne Mountains, and a wealth of historical

Getting There and Around

By Air and Sea
See Belfast, p.395.

By Rail
Northern Irish Railways run a suburban service to Holywood and Bangor, and to Belfast via the Dublin Enterprise Rail Link, which stops in Newry.
Translink, t (028) 9066 6630, *www.translink.co.uk*

By Bus
Ulsterbus, t (028) 9066 6630. Excellent services to all parts of Co. Down.

By Bike
The Raleigh Rent-a-Bike network operates throughout Co. Down. The local dealer is:
Ross Cycles, 44 Clarkill Rd, Castlewellan, t (028) 4377 8029, and Unit 9, Slieve Donard Shopping Complex, Newcastle, t (028) 4372 5525

Festivals

March
St Patrick's Day, t (028) 4461 0800, *events@downdc.gov.uk*. Celebrations at Downpatrick, Newry and Cultra, on the 17th.

June
Castle Ward Opera Festival, Strangford, t (028) 9066 1090, *events@downdc.gov.uk*.

Green Living Fair, Castle Espie, t (028) 9187 4146. Ireland's biggest environmental event.
Ulster Harp Derby, Down Royal Race Course, t (028) 4176 2166. A day's racing at Ireland's oldest course.

July
Booley Fair, Hilltown, *events@downdc.gov.uk*. Demonstrations of vanishing skills such as weaving, stone-carving and smithy work, plus traditional music and dancing, street stalls and a sheep fair. Early–mid July.
Kingdom of Mourne Festival, Kilkeel, Cranfield and Annalong, t (028) 4176 2166/2525
Northern Ireland Game Fair, Ballywalter Park, Ballywalter, t (028) 2565 2349. A fair showing how farming, sporting and conservation can work together to preserve the countryside.
Orange Marches, *events@downdc.gov.uk*. All over Co. Down.

August
Fiddlers Green Festival, Rostrevor, *events@downdc.gov.uk*. A 5-day festival.
Ulster Pipe Band Championship, t (028) 4372 2222

September
Aspects, North Down Heritage Centre, Bangor, t (028) 9127 8032. A literary festival.

October
Brent Wildlife Festival, Castle Espie, t (028) 9187 4146. An arts and environmental festival.

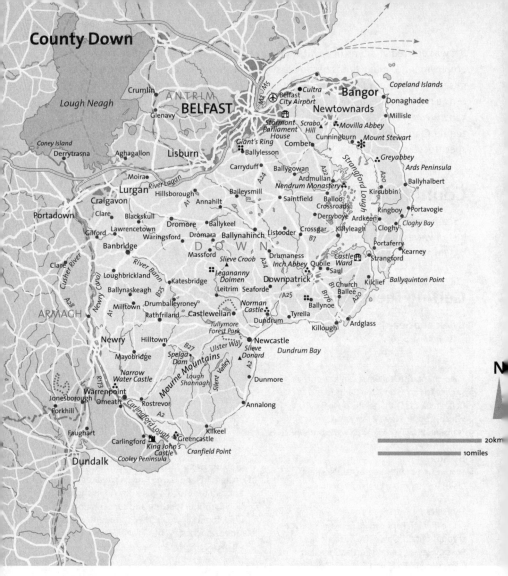

County Down

20km

10miles

buildings. For sailing enthusiasts there is the beautiful and sheltered water of Strangford Lough; for anglers there is exciting sea-fishing off Ardglass and Portavogie. And there are also plenty of opportunities for hill-walking, golfing, birdwatching and swimming. The climate has a reputation for being sunnier than in other parts of Ulster. There are many farmers and fishing folk, although, this close to the city of Belfast, there are quite a lot of dormitory towns, light industries and also big roads. The county is rich, however, in monuments from prehistory: there are cairns, standing stones, and dolmens dating from 3000 BC scattered around the Strangford Lough and Lecale district, and evidence of human settlement in the form of middens and flint tools dating from 6000 BC.

History

St Patrick is strongly associated with this county. After spending his boyhood as a slave in County Antrim, he passed 21 years in France preparing himself for his mission to bring Christianity to Ireland. In AD 432 he began his journey back to County Antrim, but was forced by bad weather conditions to land at the Slaney River between Strangford and the River Quoile. He founded an abbey nearby at Saul, near Downpatrick, where he died on 17 March AD 461. He is buried in the vicinity of Down Cathedral in Downpatrick. From St Patrick's work, and that of his missionaries in the following century, Christianity flourished and Ireland became a centre of great learning. In fact, during the Dark Ages in Europe, when the Roman Empire was in ruins, the monasteries of Ireland kept the light of Christianity alive. The monastery founded by St Comgall in Bangor in the middle of the 6th century boasted 3,000 students, but this famous place, like so many others in Ireland, was destroyed by the Norsemen (Vikings) in AD 824.

In the 17th and 18th centuries, County Down was planted with Scottish and English settlers, and the native Irish retreated into the hilly country around the Mourne mountains. North County Down remains, like Antrim, a cornerstone of Loyalist Ulster, flying the Ulster flag with its red hand against a white background.

The Ards Peninsula

The **Ards Peninsula**, which runs along the length of the east shore of Strangford Lough, takes its name from the rocky coast (*Ard*: 'Rock'). This finger of land curving round the Down mainland contains some of the most charming villages and towns created by the Scottish and English settlers. In-between these towns are earlier sites: *raths*, holy wells and monastic ruins. You are never more than three or four miles (5– 6km) from the sea. Prepare yourself for an exhilarating climate, for this is the sunniest, driest and breeziest bit of Ulster.

Start from **Bangor**, a seaside resort that was popular with the Edwardians, as you will see from the architecture. It was a famous centre of learning in the 6th and 7th centuries, and from here saints Columbanus and Gall set off to found Luxeuil Monastery in Burgundy and St Gall Monastery in Switzerland. St Comgall, who founded this monastery in the mid 6th century, trained men such as Columbanus and Gall to spread the word of Christ. Plundering Norsemen in the 9th century ravaged the town. All that remains from these times is the tower of the **Abbey Church** (*open Tue–Thur morning*), opposite Bangor railway station. The church has a pretty painted ceiling and ancient settler gravestones. An interlude can be spent in the Victorian castle, which houses the town hall and **North Down Heritage Centre** (*open Tue–Sun 10.30–4.30; t (028) 9127 1200*), with a permanent display on Bangor as an ancient place of learning. Apart from the Edwardian seafront, which has many B&Bs and small hotels, and a fine marina for yachters, there is not much to attract one to Bangor. The tacky shops and beach have an over-used look, though there is a lively market in the square on Wednesdays.

Tourist Information

Ards: t (028) 9182 6846
Bangor: t (028) 9127 0069
Groomsport: t (028) 9145 8882. *Open Apr–Sept.*
Newtownards: Kingdoms of Down, 40 West St,
t (028) 9182 2881, *www.kingdomsofdown.com*
Portaferry: Castle St, t (028) 4272 9882,
www.ards-council.gov.uk. Open Apr–Sept.

Internet Access

Emerald Tiger, 32–34 Main St, Greyabbey,
t (028) 4278 8453

Shopping

Antiques
Shops can be found in Main St in Greyabbey,
Portaferry and Holywood.

Crafts
See also *www.countydowncrafts.com.*
Ards Crafts, 31 Regent St, Newtownards,
t (028) 9182 6846
The Bay Tree Pottery and Gallery,
118 High St, Holywood, t (028) 9042 6414,
www.baytreeholywood.com
Iona, 27 Church Rd, Holywood,
t (028) 9042 8597. A lovely craft shop
that also sells organic vegetables.

Delicacies
There are excellent bread and cake shops
throughout the county.
Briggs Restaurant, Groomsport,
t (028) 9146 4288
Panini, 25 Church Rd, Holywood,
t (028) 9042 7774. An Italian delicatessen
selling good picnic fare.

Sports and Activities

Beaches
The beach at **Millisle** has a Blue Flag award
for cleanliness.

Fishing
There is sea-angling in **Strangford Lough** for
tope, skate, haddock and conger eel.
Fishing trips can be arranged at Portaferry
tourist centre (*see* above).
Nelson's Boats, 146 Killaughey Rd,
Donaghadee, t (028) 9188 3403,
www.nelsonsboats.co.uk
Norsemaid Sea Enterprises, 152 Portaferry Rd,
Newtownards, t (028) 9181 2081, *www.
salutay.com.* Shore-angling plus other
watersports (*see* opposite).

Golf
Carnalea Golf Club, Bangor, t (028) 9127 0368,
www.carnaleagolfclub.co.uk
Donaghadee Golf Course, Warren Rd,
Donaghadee, t (028) 9188 3624
Scrabo Golf Club, 233 Scrabo Rd,
Newtownards, t (028) 9181 2355,
www.scrabo-golf-club.org

Open Farms
Ark Open Farm, 296 Bangor Rd,
Newtownards, t (028) 9182 0445.
Rare breeds, including Irish Moiled Cattle.

Pleasure Cruises
Weather permitting, cruise boats leave
Bangor and **Donaghadee** in summer at 10.30,
2.30 and 7.30 for short cruises. Information is
posted on the piers, or call Bangor Tourist
Centre, t (028) 9127 0069.
For trips to the **Copeland Islands**,
call t (028) 9188 3403.

Donaghadee, a pretty seaside town with an attractive 19th-century harbour and a
good number of pubs, used to be linked with Portpatrick in Scotland by a regular
sailing boat. It has the feeling of an old port where generations of men and women
have waited for the wind and the tide to change. The poet John Keats stayed at Grace
Neill's Bar on the High Street, as did Peter the Great of Russia. ('Gracie's' is the oldest
pub in Ireland, established in 1611, and it is still one of the most attractive pubs in the
town; *see* box opposite) You can go stream-fishing at night in the summer with a
white feather as a lure. Or go out to the **Copeland Islands** – long, low islands covered

Watersports

Bangor and Strangford Sailing School, 13 Gray's Hill, Bangor, **t** (028) 9145 5967/9754 1592. Sailing on Strangford Lough.

Norsemaid Sea Enterprises, 152 Portaferry Rd, Newtownards, **t** (028) 9181 2081. Sailing, sub-aqua and scuba-diving, sea- and shore-angling.

Where to Stay

See also Belfast, 'Where to Stay', p.399.

Rayanne House, 60 Demesne Rd, Holywood, **t** (028) 9042 5859, *www.rayannehouse.co.uk* (*luxury*). Comfortable bedrooms, delicious breakfasts and an award-winning restaurant.

Clandeboye Lodge, 10 Estate Rd, Clandeboye, near Bangor, **t** (028) 9185 2500, *www.clandeboyelodge.com* (*expensive*). A luxury hotel with an 18-hole golf course.

Portaferry Hotel, 10 The Strand, Portaferry, **t** (028) 4272 8231, *www.portaferryhotel. com* (*expensive*). An old-fashioned yet well-appointed choice in a lovely situation.

Beech Hill Country House, 23 Ballymoney Rd, Craigantlet, Holywood, **t** (028) 9042 5892, *www.beech-hill.net* (*moderate*). A Georgian-style bungalow in a peaceful location.

Edenvale Country House, 130 Portaferry Rd, Newtownards, **t** (028) 9181 4881, *edenvalehouse@hotmail.com* (*moderate*). A pretty Georgian house in the countryside.

The Narrows, 8 Shore Rd, Portaferry, **t** (028) 4272 8148, *www.narrows.co.uk* (*moderate*). A modern building with sea views, a restaurant and a walled garden.

Adair's, 22 The Square, Portaferry, **t** (028) 4272 8412 (*inexpensive*). Simple and clean.

Barholm, 11 The Strand, Portaferry, **t** (028) 4272 9598, *www.barholmportaferry.co.uk* (*inexpensive*). A decent youth hostel.

Eating Out

See also Belfast, 'Eating Out', p.400.

The Bay Tree, Audley Court, 118 High St, Holywood, **t** (028) 9042 1419, *www. baytreeholywood.com* (*moderate*). A friendly place serving breakfast, salads, steaks, vegetarian dishes and cakes.

Fontana, 61a High St, Holywood, **t** (028) 9080 9908 (*moderate*). Excellent Mediterranean and Oriental dishes. *Closed Sat lunch, Sun eve, and Mon.*

Grace Neill's Bar and Restaurant, 33 High St, Donaghadee, **t** (028) 9188 4595, *www.graceneills.com* (*moderate*). Adventurous food served up in very generous portions.

Portaferry Hotel, 10 The Strand, Portaferry, **t** (028) 4272 8231 (*moderate*). Seafood straight from the fishing boats of Portavogie.

Villa Toscana, Toscana Park, West Circular Rd, Bangor, **t** (028) 9147 3737, *www.thinkitalian. co.uk* (*moderate*). A place offering superb Italian food.

Bay Restaurant, Mount Stewart House, Portaferry Rd, Newtownards, **t** (028) 4278 7807 (*inexpensive*). A place for light lunch and high tea on the Strangford Shore. *Closed Sun and eves.*

Bow Bells, 5 Bow St, Donaghadee, **t** (028) 9188 8612 (*inexpensive*). A coffee shop with good baking.

Briggs Restaurant, Groomsport, Bangor, **t** (028) 9146 4288 (*inexpensive*). Bar snacks and main meals. Good plain cooking.

Heatherlea Tea Rooms, 94 Main St, Bangor, **t** (028) 9145 3157 (*inexpensive*). Good quiche, pies and salads.

Roma's, 4 Regent St, Newtownards, **t** (028) 9181 2841 (*inexpensive*). Well-priced Italian food.

with spring turf and rabbit's trails, enchanting in spring and summer. It is possible to reach them and also to go out stream-fishing on a regular boat. Following the coast road through **Millisle** down to **Ballyhalbert**, you pass golden strands. There are pebbly beaches further on at **Cloghy Bay**. Notice the Scottish influence: snug, unpretentious houses and carefully worked fields. Many of the road names – taken from the townlands, early units of land-holding – are intriguing: Ballydrain, Ringboy, Balloo, Bright, and Scollogs Town. The National Trust maintains much of the little village of **Kearney**, which has pretty whitewashed cottages and coastal walks.

The most picturesque town on the Ards is **Portaferry**, situated where the tip of the Ards forms a narrow strait with the mainland of Down. On the waterfront you look across to **Strangford** village. The street here is wide, with brightly painted old houses. In Castle Street is the **Exploris Aquarium** (*open Apr–Aug Mon–Fri 10–6, Sat 11–6, Sun 12 noon–6, Sept–Mar closes 5; adm; t (028) 4272 8062, www.exploris.org.uk*), where in spacious tanks you can see many of the sea animals that inhabit Strangford Lough; there is also plenty of interesting background information on the geology and plantlife of the lough. On summer evenings you might be lucky and hear open-air music. A ferry runs between Portaferry and Strangford every half-hour, and the journey of five minutes is well worth it for the view up Strangford Lough. If you are an artist, you may be so won over by the charms of this part of the peninsula that you will want to enrol in one of the painting courses held here in the summer.

The Strangford Shore

On the A20, which hugs the Strangford Shore, you can enjoy the beauty of this nearly landlocked water. Scattered with small islands, this area is of special interest to naturalists. The National Trust has a wildlife scheme operating that covers the entire foreshore of the lough, totalling about 5,400 acres (2,000ha). Vast flocks of wildfowl gather here, as do seals and other marine animals. There are bird-watching facilities at Castle Espie, Mount Stewart Gashouse, and Island Reagh (*see* p.417). Strangford was named by the Viking invaders after the strong tides at the mouth of the lough (*strang* means 'strong'). In Norman times, the wealthy knights encouraged the monks to settle amongst the lovely scenery.

Grey Abbey (*An Mhainistir Liath*: 'the Grey Monastery'; *open Apr–Oct Mon–Sat 9–6 Sun 1–6, by request in winter; t (028) 4278 8585/9054 3037*) is one of the most complete Cistercian abbeys in Ireland. Built in the 12th century by Affreca, the wife of John de Courcy, it represented the new monastic orders that were introduced to repress Irish traditions. The Pope was determined to stop the independence shown by the Irish abbot-prince, who combined temporal and spiritual power and often ignored pronouncements from Rome. A Physick Garden has been developed, planted as it may have been in medieval times; it was a vital guard for the monks against illnesses (*adm*). The pretty 18th-century house, Rosemount, is not open to the public. **Kircubbin**, a fishing village much used by yachts and leisure boats, has the interesting ruined church of Innishargie and associations with the 1798 rising.

Approximately 15 miles (24km) east of Belfast, on the A20 to Newtownards, following the lough, the demesne wall of **Mount Stewart** (*house open for guided tours May–Sept Wed–Mon 1–6; temple open Apr–Oct Sun and bank hols 2–5; gardens open Apr–Oct daily 10–6; t (028) 4278 8387, www.ntni.org.uk*), the boyhood home of Robert Stewart, Lord Castlereagh, appears. The 18th-century house and grounds are now in the care of the National Trust. Edith, Lady Londonderry, 7th Marchioness (1879–1959) and one of the foremost political hostesses of her generation, created the wonderful gardens some 70 years ago for her children. There are some lovely topiary animals, colourful parterres and wonderful trees. If you ever come across her children's story *The Magic Inkpot*, you will recognize some of the place names from around here.

Also in the grounds is the **Temple of the Winds**, inspired by the building in Athens and built in 1780 for picnicking in style. In the Mount Stewart schoolhouse you can buy patchwork and hand-made cottage furniture. The tea-room in the house itself is painted beautifully with the animals from Noah's Ark. Lady Londonderry nicknamed all the famous men and women who were her friends after animals in the Ark – it is fun to guess who was who.

To complete the tour of the Ards, a quick visit to **Newtownards** will be rewarding, particularly for medievalists. The town square is also impressive and worth a visit. On the outskirts of the town, on the road to Millisle, is **Movilla Abbey** (*always accessible*), built between the 13th and 15th centuries. There was an earlier establishment here that was founded in the 6th century by St Finian, a contemporary of the great Irish saint, Columba (Colmcille). Unfortunately the two men did not get on; apparently St Columba stealthily copied St Finian's psalter, and they had a battle over it which caused many deaths (*see* **Connacht**, p.338). Columba was an O'Donnell prince as well as a cleric, and he was so dismayed at the bloodshed he had caused that he exiled himself and founded the famous church at Iona, an island off the coast of Scotland. From here Christianity spread to most of Scotland. The psalter he had copied became the warrior *Book of the O'Donnells* and was borne before them into battle; it is now in the National Museum, Dublin. The **Somme Heritage Centre** (*t (028) 9182 3202*) here examines Ireland's role in World War I, in particular the three volunteer divisions drawn from both traditions.

Newtownards has a 17th-century market cross and a fine town hall. You won't fail to notice the prominent tower on **Scrabo Hill**, a memorial to one of the Londonderry Stewarts and a good lookout point. The tower (*open Easter and June–Sept Sat–Thur 10.30–6; t (028) 9181 1491*) stands on a granite outcrop and has 122 steps to the top. All around are woodland walks and the remains of old quarries in which wildlife thrives. You might see a peregrine falcon. There is also a small visitor centre with an audio-visual show.

Close to the pretty little village of Saintfield is another wonderful garden in National Trust care. This is **Rowallane** (*open daily mid-Apr–mid-Sept 10–8, winter 10–4, adm; t (028) 9751 0131, www.nationaltrust.org.uk*), famous throughout the horticultural and botanical world for its shrubs and trees. The best time to see it is early spring, when the azaleas and rhododendrons are a riot of colour. There are also some interesting pillars and other structures in the garden made from Mourne stone, large round boulders of deep grey.

Mid-Down

Mid-Down is *drumlin* country until you reach Slieve Croob, around Ballynahinch. Harris, a local historian who described Down in the 18th century, had a rather droll phrase for the countryside contours, likening them to 'eggs set in salt'. Cap this with C. S. Lewis' recipe for his native county: 'earth-covered potatoes'. (The Belfast-born writer and critic became famous for his children's stories, *The Chronicles of Narnia*.)

To explore mid-Down you might start from **Comber**, a pleasant town with a prominent statue of Robert Gillespie, one of Ulster's military heroes in the Indian campaigns. Near here, off the A22 to Killyleagh, you can visit **Nendrum** (*open Apr–Sept Tue–Sat 10–7, Sun 2–7;* **t** *(028) 9054 3037, www.ehsni.gov.uk*). This is one of the most romantic of the monastic sites, founded by a pupil of St Patrick on Mahee Island and reached by a causeway through Island Reagh. It consists of a hilltop crowned with three circular stone walls, a church, a round tower stump, a sundial and cross slabs. It also has a small museum.

If you have time, it is worth taking a little detour at Balloo to **Ardmullan**. Whiterock yacht club is always a hive of activity, and it looks out onto the islands of Strangford Lough – including Braddock Island, where there is a bungalow designed by T. W. Henry, brother of the better-known painter Paul Henry. The little village of **Killyleagh** has a lovely-looking castle, still lived in by its original family, who came from Ayrshire in the mid 17th century. It is the oldest inhabited castle in Ireland, and is not open to the public, though pop concerts are sometimes held in the grounds.

On the A22, a couple of miles out of Killyleagh, is **Delamont** (*open daily 9–dusk;* **t** *(028) 4482 8333, www.delamontcountrypark.com*). This is a country park with fine views of Strangford Lough and the Mournes. Among its attractions is a heronry that you can view from a hide, some lovely walks and a restored walled garden. You can also go ponytrekking.

Going west on the B7, you come to the **Ulster Wildlife Trust** at Crossgar (*open Mon–Fri 10–4;* **t** *(028) 4483 0282, www.ulsterwildlifetrust.org*). Here you can learn about wetland raised bog and meadowland flora and fauna. The Victorian conservatory is planted to attract butterflies, and guided walks are available.

If you continue down the west side of Strangford, you cross the River Quoile and arrive at **Downpatrick**, an attractive Georgian town built on an old hill fort that reputedly belonged to one of the Red Branch Knights (*see* **Old Gods and Heroes**, p.58). It is at the natural meeting-point of several river valleys, and so has been occupied for a long time, both suffering and benefiting from the waves of settlers and invaders – missionaries, monks, Norsemen, Normans and Scots (the army of Edward Bruce). **St Patrick's gravestone**, a large bit of granite, may be seen in the Church of Ireland Cathedral graveyard, although this is not the reason why the town carries his name. The association was made by the Norman John de Courcy, a Cheshire knight who was granted the counties of Antrim and Down by Henry II in 1176, and who established himself here at this centre of St Patrick's veneration by promoting the Irish saint. De Courcy donated some relics of Sts Patrick, Columba and Brigid to his foundation and gave the town its name, adding Patrick to *Dundalethglas*, as it was previously called.

During the Middle Ages, Downpatrick suffered at the hands of the Scots: in 1316 it was burnt by Edward Bruce, and later it was destroyed by the English during the Tudor wars. In the early 18th century, stability returned to the town under the influence of an English family called Southwell, who acquired the Manor of Downpatrick through marriage. They built a quay on the River Quoile and encouraged markets and building. The **cathedral**, which had lain in ruins between 1538 and 1790, reopened in 1818. It is very fine inside, with some impressive stained-glass windows. On Market Street, the **Saint Patrick Centre** (*open Oct–Mar daily 10–5, 17 Mar and June–Aug Mon–Sat 9.30–6, Sun 10–6, Apr–May and Sept Mon–Sat 9.30–5.30, Sun 1–5.30; adm; t (028) 4461 9000, www.saintpatrickcentre.com*) uses the saint's own words to tell the story of his life and work in the context of the period in which he lived. The **Southwell Charity School and Almshouse** in English Street near Down Cathedral is a handsome early-Georgian building in the Irish Palladian style, and is now a home for the elderly. Nearby, in the old county jail in the Mall, is the **Down County Museum** (*open Mon–Fri 10–5 Sat and Sun 1–5; t (028) 4461 5218, www.downcountymuseum.com*), which contains some very interesting exhibits of Stone Age artefacts and local history. There are also useful starting points for leads on relics associated with St Patrick, which you might find elsewhere in the county.

Other Places Associated with St Patrick

Just a mile and a half (2.5km) north-east of Downpatrick, at the mouth of the Slaney, is **St Patrick's Church** in Saul, on the spot where St Patrick founded his first church after deciding to return to Ireland to convert the people. A memorial church of Mourne granite was built here in the 1930s to commemorate this. On Slieve Patrick nearby is a giant statue of the saint also made of granite. Another place of association with St Patrick is the 6th-century **Raholp Church**, between Downpatrick and Strangford village on the A25. It was founded by Tassach, a disciple of St Patrick, who gave him the last rites and carried his body to its burial place.

East of Downpatrick, off the B1 some 2 miles (3.2km) outside, are the **Struell Wells** (*always accessible*). There must have been worshippers at this pagan shrine, a group of holy wells, long before the arrival of St Patrick, who is thought to be closely associated with them; in all events, the waters are still well known for their curative properties. To the west of Downpatrick, on the A24, is the little village of **Seaforde**. In the grounds of the Big House here is an attractive **butterfly house** (*open Apr–Sept Mon–Sat 10–5, Sun 1–6; adm; t (028) 4481 1225, www.seafordegardens.com*). It also has a hornbeam maze and specialist nursery. It is fun to climb the modern Moghul Tower and look down on the richly coloured and patterned walled garden, shop and tea-room. The area is rich in bird- and plantlife.

Cloghy Rocks Nature Reserve on the coast, south of Strangford village, is particularly rich in inter-tidal plants, and has an ever-changing variety of seabirds and wildfowl. Common seals can often be seen basking on the rocks at low tide. Near Downpatrick, just off the A25 and guarded by Castle Ward at its southeastern end, is the **Quoile Pondage Nature Reserve** (*Wildlife Centre open Apr–Aug daily 11–5, Sept–Mar Sat and Sun 1–5; t (028) 4461 5520*). This was formed as the result of a barrage at Castle Island to prevent flooding caused by the tidal inrush of the sea from Strangford Lough into the river. The freshwater vegetation that has established itself here as a result is of great interest to the botanist. And for the ornithologist, a great variety of indigenous and migrant birds feed and nest here. In springtime you can see great crested grebes preening and displaying their crests.

Inch Abbey (*open Apr–Sept Tue–Sat 10–7, Oct–Mar Sat 10–4, Sun 2–4; adm; t (028) 9054 3034*), off the A7, is a very beautiful ruined Cistercian abbey on an island in the Quoile Marshes. It was founded in the 1180s by John de Courcy.

Going on the A25 in an easterly direction, 1 mile (1.6km) west of Strangford village, you pass **Castle Ward** (*open 1–6 Easter–Aug daily, Sept– Easter Sat and Sun; grounds open all year daily until dusk; adm, car park fee; t (028) 4488 1204*). The character and aspect of this house are worth a detour: it is a compromise between husband and wife, expressed in architecture. Built in the 1760s by Bernard Ward, later Lord Bangor, and his wife Lady Anne, it has a neoclassical façade and a Gothic castellated garden front. The interior echoes this curious divergence of tastes: the reception rooms are gracefully classical, following his Lordship, and the library and her Ladyship's rooms are elaborately neo-Gothic in the Strawberry Hill manner conceived by Horace Walpole. The ceiling in the boudoir caused poet John Betjeman to exclaim that it was like 'standing beneath a cow'. The property is in the hands of the National Trust and there are a number of other attractions: a Palladian-style temple that overlooks an early-18th-century lake, an early towerhouse and lovely grounds. A goldsmith's studio provides souvenirs for those looking for more valuable mementoes than snapshots. In June the rooms are full of music during the **Castle Ward Opera Festival** (*see* p.407).

Close by and just off the A25 is **Loughmoney Dolmen**, which is probably more than 4,000 years old. It is typical of dolmens round this district. **Strangford** village, reached by a coastal footpath, is a few miles on. This is where you can catch the ferry across to the Ards village of Portaferry. No less than five small castles are within reach of Strangford, testifying to its strategic importance: Strangford Castle, Old Castle Ward, Audley's Castle, Walshestown and Kilclief. The best way to see them is from the lough, when the ferry is in mid-stream. **Kilclief Castle** (*open July and Aug Tue–Sun 2–6; adm; t (028) 9054 3034*), easy to find on the A2 between Strangford and Ardglass, is very well preserved and in State care. Built before 1440, it is a grey-stone towerhouse.

More castles can be seen around the fishing village of **Ardglass**, an important port in medieval times, now a centre for herring fleets. The best-preserved among them is **Jordan's Castle** (*open July and Aug Tue, Fri and Sat 10–1, Wed and Thur 2–6; adm; t (028) 9054 3037, www.ehsni.gov.uk*), a 15th-century towerhouse with four storeys.

Also in the Strangford area is an 18-hole golf course, and there is good sea-angling off the coast here. The tree-lined village of **Killough**, about 1 mile (1.6km) from Ardglass, was developed as a grain port by the Ward family in the 18th century. There is a good beach here, and, further down at St Johns Point, an old ruined church. There are also some very good **strands**, notably Tyrella on the Dundrum Bay.

Interesting prehistoric monuments in this area are **Ballynoe Stone Circle** and **Rathmullen Mote**. They are both within easy reach of Downpatrick, situated amongst the maze of little roads in the triangle between the A25, A2 and B176.

Hillsborough and the Linen Homelands

Heading towards Belfast on the A25/A1, you'll find the town of **Hillsborough**. The Anglo-Irish Agreement was reached here. It is one of the most English-looking villages in Ulster, with fine Georgian architecture, several excellent antiques shops in

Tourist Information

Banbridge: Newry Rd, t (028) 4062 3322,
banbridge@nitic.net
Downpatrick: t (028) 4461 2233
Hillsborough: t (028) 9268 9717
Lisburn: t (028) 9266 0038

Shopping

Antiques
You will find antiques shops at Balloo House, Killinchy; in Killinchy St, Comber; and in Moira, Saintfield and Hillsborough.
The Gallery, Gilford Castle, Gilford; and Main St, Hillsborough

Crafts
Cowdy Crafts, Main St, Hillsborough, t (028) 9268 2455
Discovery Glass Workshop, High St, Comber, t (028) 9187 0181
Ferguson Linen Centre, Banbridge, t (028) 4062 3491. The world's only manufacturer of double damask linen. The centre has an exhibition and offers guided tours.
The National Trust, Castle Ward and Strangford, t (028) 4488 1204

Food and Drink
There are excellent bread and cake shops throughout the county.
James Nicholson, 27a Killyleagh St, Crossgar, t (028) 4483 0091. Excellent wines sold in an elegant shop.
McCartney's, 56 Main St, Moira, t (028) 9261 1422. A champion sausage-maker.

Sports and Activities

Beaches
Bathing is good at **Tyrella Strand** and **Dundrum Bay**.

Bird-watching
You can observe birdlife at the Castle Espie hide (*see* p.412), and at Salt and Green islands, Mount Stewart Gas House and Island Reagh (all on Strangford Lough).
For further information, contact:

Castle Espie, 78 Ballydrain Rd, Comber, t (028) 9187 4146, *castleespie@wwt.org.uk*
Delamont Country Park, t (028) 4482 8333
Strangford Wildlife Centre, t (028) 4488 1411
The Wildfowl and Wetlands Trust, 78 Ballydrain Rd, Comber, t (028) 9187 4146

Fishing
There's **coarse fishing** in the River Quoile basin. Contact the local tourist office for details. **Sea-angling** is available in Strangford Lough for tope, skate, haddock and conger eel. **Shore-angling** is available off Ardglass.
Captain R. Fitzsimons, Harbour Master, t (028) 4484 1291. Coverage for the Ardglass area.
Nelson's Boats, 146 Killaughey Rd, Donaghadee, t (028) 9188 3403. Fishing in Strangford Lough.
Norsemaid Sea Enterprises, 152 Portaferry Rd, Newtownards, t (028) 9181 2081, *www.salutay.com*. Sea- and shore-angling in Strangford Lough.

Golf
Ardglass Golf Club, t (028) 4484 1219, *www.ardgassgolfclub.com*
Downpatrick Golf Club, t (028) 4461 5947

Ponytrekking
Lime Park Equestrian Centre, 5 Lime Kiln Rd, Maghaberry, west of Lisburn, t (028) 9262 1139, *limeparkequestrian@5limekiln.fsnet.co.uk*

Sailing
Sailing is available in Strangford Lough. There is a sailing school on Sketrick Island in the lough with residential or day courses on all aspects of sailing.
Down Yachts, 37 Bayview Rd, Killinchy, t (028) 9754 2210. Sailing boat charter.
East Down Yacht Club, Comber Rd, Killyleagh, t (028) 4482 8375, *crockard@dnet.co.uk*

Tours
Leprechaun Tour Guiding, 6–8 Main St, Gilford, near Banbridge t (028) 3884 0054, *www.leprechauntourguiding.co.uk*

Walking
The **Ulster Way** goes through Comber and along the shores of Strangford Lough, around

the coast through Ardglass and Newcastle into the Mournes. There are lovely walks, too, on National Trust property in the Murlough Nature Reserve, near Newcastle, in the arboretum of Castlewellan, and at Tullymore Park, Newcastle.

Where to Stay

Pheasants Hill, 37 Killyleagh Rd, Downpatrick, t (028) 4461 7246, *www.pheasantshill.com* (*expensive–luxury*). A modern farmhouse on a smallholding, near a nature reserve.

Old Schoolhouse Inn, 100 Ballydrain Rd, Comber, t (028) 9754 1182, *www.theoldschoolhouseinn. com* (*expensive*). Comfortable rooms named after US presidents of Ulster descent, plus an award-winning restaurant.

Ballymote House, Killough Rd, Downpatrick, t (028) 4461 5500, *www.ballymotehouse.com* (*moderate*). A listed mid-18th-century Georgian house in fine grounds.

Dufferin Coaching Inn, 33 High St, Killyleagh, t (028) 4482 1134, *www.dufferincoachinginn. co.uk* (*moderate*). A rustic inn built in 1803.

Tyrella House, Clanmaghery Rd, Tyrella, Downpatrick, t (028) 4485 1422, *www. hidden-ireland.com/tyrella* (*moderate*). A Georgian country house with a private sandy beach. Riding and grass-court tennis are available.

Rosebank Country House, 108 Ballyduggan Rd, Downpatrick, t (028) 4461 7021, *www. rosebankcountryhouse.com* (*inexpensive–moderate*). A B&B in a rural setting in the heart of St Patrick country.

Self-catering

Killyleagh Castle Towers, Killyleagh, t (028) 4482 8261 (*expensive*). A 17th–18th-century castle.

Potter's Cottage, Castle Ward estate, Strangford, t (01225) 791199, t 0870 458 4400 or t (028) 4488 1204, *www.nationaltrustcottages.co.uk* (*moderate*). A cottage sleeping 4.

Eating Out

Balloo House, 1 Comber Rd, Killyleagh, t (028) 9754 1210 (*moderate*). A venue for traditional food, and live traditional music on Fri nights.

Cuan Bar and Restaurant, 6 The Square, Strangford, t (028) 4488 1222, *www.thecuan. com* (*moderate*). Venison and quail, plus hot and cold buffets.

Daft Eddys, Sketrick Island, Whiterock, Killinchy, t (028) 9754 1615 (*moderate*). A pub on an island reached by a causeway, serving good soups, steaks, seafood and veggie dishes.

Dufferin Arms, 35 High St, Killyleagh, t (028) 4482 8229, *www.dufferinarms.com* (*moderate*). A candlelit kitchen restaurant serving local produce, and a lively bar offering pub grub.

Hillside Restaurant and Bar, 21 Main St, Hillsborough, t (028) 9268 2765, *www.carmichaelgroup.com* (*moderate*). A well-reputed place for its soups, plus oysters in season.

The Lobster Pot, 9–11 The Square, Strangford, t (028) 4488 1288, *www.lobsterpotstrangford. com* (*moderate*). Very good set meals and pub grub, including oysters and other shellfish.

The Plough Inn, The Square, Hillsborough, t (028) 9268 2985 (*moderate*). Pub grub and an upstairs seafood bistro, both very popular with locals.

Slieve Croob Inn, 119 Clonvaragham Rd, Castlewellan, t (028) 4377 1412, *www. slievecroobinn.com* (*moderate*). A country restaurant close to the Mourne Mountains, offering both local fare and more exotic dishes. Accommodation is also offered, including self-catering.

Gilberry Fayre, 92 Banbridge Rd, Gilford, t (028) 3883 2098 (*inexpensive*). A welcoming spot for breakfast, lunch and afternoon tea, including freshly baked cakes and renowned shortbread. *Closed eves and Sun.*

Primrose Bar, 30 Main St, Ballynahinch, t (028) 9756 3177 (*inexpensive*). A good place for sandwiches.

Entertainment and Nightlife

Down Civic Arts Centre, 2–6 Irish St, Downpatrick, t (028) 4461 5283, *www.downartscentre.com*. An accessible venue with art exhibitions, music, theatre, comedy, children's events, and classes and workshops in fiddle, bodhrán and more.

the Main Street, tasteful craft shops and numerous restaurants. To the south of the town in parkland is a massive **fort** (*open summer Tue–Sat 10–7, Sun 2–7; winter Wed–Sat 10–4, Sun 2–4*) built by Sir Arthur Hill, an English settler, in the 17th century. **Hillsborough Castle**, which was the official residence of the Governor of Northern Ireland until 1973 and mostly houses various officials, stands in the parkland too. The wrought-iron gates that bar one's approach from the town are exquisite.

St Malachy's, the Church of Ireland parish church, is in handsome planter's-style Gothic and was built by the Hill family in 1774. If you are lucky enough to get inside, you'll see that it is typical of the cool, unadorned churches of that style, with box pews and 18th- and 19th-century wall tablets. It has a well-cared-for atmosphere, in contrast to the fate of so many Church of Ireland buildings in the Republic, which have become redundant because of dwindling congregations.

The **Linen Homelands** – Banbridge, Craigavon and Lisburn – is a convenient tag for an area of immense economic importance in the history of Northern Ireland. Nearly everybody in Ulster was involved in some way in the 19th and early 20th century in the growing and manufacture of linen, and especially so around the Upper Bann and Lagan River. The **Irish Linen Centre and Museum** (*open Mon–Sat 9.30–5, plus Apr–Sept Sun 2–5; t (028) 9266 3377*) in Lisburn, with its exhibition 'Flax to Fabric', is well worth a visit. If you have time, take the Linen Homelands Tour, which visits a water-powered scutching mill, a working linen factory, and the centre itself (*contact Banbridge Tourist Office, t (028) 4062 3322*).

South Down

South Down is a mainly mountainous area, and extends across to the south Armagh border, girded to the south and east by a beautiful coastline. The rather splendid fjord-like inlet, Carlingford Lough (a name of Scandinavian origin), cuts through the middle of the upland area. It follows a fault line forming the Gap of the North, the main north–south throughfare since ancient times.

In this trough, astride the ancient road from Armagh to Tara, lies the town of Newry. Within a 25-mile (40km) circle, 48 peaks rise in a purple mass of rounded summits. The scenery around these, the **Mourne Mountains**, is not wild or rugged (Bignian and Bearnagh are the only two craggy peaks); their gentle undulations inspire peace and solitude. Few roads cross the Mournes, so this is a walker's paradise: endless paths up and down through bracken and heather, unspoilt lakes and tumbling streams, the wild flowers of moor and heath, birds and birdsong, all under an ever-changing sky.

Of the many walks possible, perhaps the loveliest are up to **Silent Valley**; or to **Lough Shannagh** from above Kilkeel; to the glittering crystals of **Diamond Rocks**; to the summits above Spelga Dam; and to **Slieve Donard** itself, where on a fine clear day you can see across the water to England. For the benefit of the more hearty, it is worth mentioning the 20-mile (32km) **boundary wall** that links the main peaks. Quite a constructional feat in itself, it used to be followed on the Annual Mourne Wall Walk, until erosion by thousands of pairs of feet caused the event to be cancelled.

Perhaps the best place to start from when visiting this area is **Newcastle**, one of Ulster's more lively seaside resorts, although popularity has destroyed some of its charm. It has a lovely long sandy beach, and behind it there is the **Royal County Down Golf Course**, a fine championship course (*see* 'Sports and Activities', below). Near Newcastle lies the magnificent forest park of **Tollymore** (*open daily 10–sunset; t (028) 4372 2428*). It has many lovely – though well-trodden – forest trails and nature walks on the lower wooded slopes and along the River Shimna.

Before following the coast round, it is well worth heading northwards to visit one or two places. **Castlewellan** has two market places: one oval, one square. This neatly laid-out town is surrounded by well-wooded demesnes, one of which is **Castlewellan**

Tourist Information

Kilkeel: 6 Newcastle St, t (028) 4176 2525, *www.discovernorthernireland.com*
Newcastle: Newcastle Centre, 10–14 Central Promenade, t (028) 4372 2222
Newry: t (028) 3026 8877
Warrenpoint: t (028) 4175 2256

Shopping

Crafts
Blue Beans, 67 Main St, Castlewellan, t 028 437 70414, *www.bluebeans.co.uk*. A wide variety of craftwork and gifts.
Loch Ruray House, 8 Main St, Dundrum. A showcase for local crafts.
Parrot Lodge Pottery, 131 Ballyward Rd, Castlewellan. Fish and bird of paradise motifs, and objects both functional and surreal.

Delicacies
There are excellent bread and cake shops throughout the county. Try:
Victoria Bakery, Castle St, Newry. Delicious wholemeal loaves and barmbrack.

Sports and Activities

Fishing
There's **game fishing** for brown trout and salmon on the River Bann near Hilltown, on Spelga Dam, and on the Shimna River in Tullymore Forest Park; contact the local tourist office for more information.
For local knowledge of Carlingford Lough, contact:

Norsemaid Sea Enterprises, 152 Portaferry Rd, Newtownards, t (028) 9181 2081, *www.salutay.com*

Golf
Royal County Down (Links) Course, 36 Golf Links Rd, Newcastle, t (028) 4372 3314, *www.royalcountydown.com*

Open Farm
Slievenlargy Open Farm, 5 Largy Rd, Kilco, near Castlewellan, t (028) 4377 0083. A farm housing rare breeds of cattle, sheep, pigs and ponies.

Ponytrekking
Mount Pleasant Horse Riding, 15 Bannonstown Rd, Castlewellan, t (028) 4377 8651
Mourne Trail Riding School, 96 Castlewellan Rd, Newcastle, t (028) 4372 4351, *www.mournetrailridingcentre.com*
Ring of Gullion Centre, Lough Rd, Mullach Ban, t (028) 3088 9311. Horseriding, plus activities for young people on traditions and the environment.

Walking
Walking is good in the Mourne Mountains. The **Ulster Way** goes through Comber and along the shores of Strangford Lough, around the coast through Ardglass and Newcastle into the Mourne Mountains. The tourist office in Newcastle has details of Mournes walks.
There are also lovely walks on National Trust property in the Murlough Nature Reserve near Newcastle, in the arboretum of Castlewellan at Castleward, at Rowallane, and at Tullymore Park, Newcastle.

Park (with café and visitor centre; open daily 10–dusk; t (028) 4377 8664), home to the world's largest maze, and now a forest park renowned for its arboretum and lovely gardens. The arboretum was begun in 1740, and there are some magnificent trees. A sculpture trail created from natural materials from the park and lake makes a lovely walk. North of Newcastle, about 2 miles (3km) away, is **Murlough National Nature Reserve** (always accessible; t (028) 4375 1467, www.ntni.org.uk) where you can explore the sand dunes. Exposed to the wind, the dunes are a peaceful haven for waders, waterbirds and shore-birds. Sweet-smelling wild flowers grow unhindered, and in the summer wild strawberries weave across the sand. **Dundrum** is not far beyond. On the outskirts of this once flourishing fishing port, now more of a coal quay, a half-mile

Sports Council for Northern Ireland,
House of Sport, Upper Malone Rd, Belfast, t (028) 9038 1222. Contact the Field Officer for more details on walking in the Mournes.

Where to Stay

Hastings Slieve Donard Hotel, Downs Rd, Newcastle, t (028) 4372 1066, www. hastingshotels.com (luxury). An impressive Victorian building with wonderful views. close to golf links.

Burrendale Hotel, 51 Castlewellan Rd, Newcastle, t (028) 4372 2599, www. burrendale.com (expensive). An upscale modern option popular with bus tours.

Glassdrumman Lodge, 85 Mill Rd, Annalong, t (028) 4376 8451, www.glassdrummanlodge. com (expensive). A superb place to stay, with a wondeful restaurant (see below).

The Maggi Minn, 11 Bishops Well Rd, Dromore, t (028) 9269 3520, maggiminn@lycos.co.uk (moderate). A modern country house with views of the Mournes and delicious Ulster fry for breakfast. Dinner is also available.

Sylvan Hill House, Dromore, t (028) 9269 2321 (moderate). An 18th-century house with good food cooked by the proprietess.

Newcastle Youth Hostel, 30 Downs Rd, Newcastle, t (028) 4372 2133, www.hini.org.uk (inexpensive). A centrally heated apartment and family rooms beside the sea, at the foot of the mountains.

Rathglen Villa, 7 Hilltown Rd, Rathfriland, t (028) 4063 8090 (inexpensive). A decent B&B.

Ryan B&B, 19 Milltown St, Burren, Warrenpoint, t (028) 4177 2506 (inexpensive). Three reasonable ensuite rooms.

Self-catering

Hannas Close Cottages, Kilkeel, t (028) 4176 5999, www.travel-ireland.com/ hannas (inexpensive). Six traditional cottages sleeping 2–6 people, situated in a country lane and affording wonderful views of the Mournes.

Seeconnell Cottages, 104 Clanvaraghan Rd, Castlewellan, t (028) 4377 0050, www. seeconnell.com (inexpensive). A cluster of traditional cottages in a quiet mountain valley, sleeping 5–7.

Eating Out

Glassdrumman Lodge Restaurant, 85 Mill Rd, Annalong, t (028) 4376 8451 (expensive). Delicious, memorable food, especially the steak and fish dishes. The family who run the hotel (see above) grow their own vegetables and keep their animals in free-range conditions.

Bucks Head Inn, 79 Main St, Dundrum, t (028) 4375 1868 (moderate). A good place for seafood and steaks.

O'Reilly's Restaurant, 7–9 Main St, Dromara, t (028) 9753 2209 (moderate). Excellent seafood.

Brass Monkey Bar and Restaurant, 16 Trevor Hills, Newry, t (028) 3026 3176 (inexpensive). Coffee during the day, and good steak, chicken and fish dishes for lunch and dinner.

Deli Lites, 12 Monaghan St, Newry, t (028) 3026 1770 (inexpensive). A café offering lots of breakfast options, a good choice of soups and salads, and even fair coffee. Closed eves.

(0.8km) north-west of Dundrum on a wooded hill, are the extensive ruins of a Norman motte and bailey **castle** (*grounds always accessible; keep open Apr–Sept Tue–Sat 10–7, Sun 2–7; adm; t (028) 9054 6518*), enclosing a magnificent partly ruined stone castle with a circular keep. Staircases, parapets, towers and a massive gatehouse make this an ideal picnic spot and adventure playground for children. It was built in about 1177 as one of John de Courcy's coastal castles.

Newcastle to Rostrevor

Now travel along the coast from Newcastle to Rostrevor on the A2. From here there's a fine view of the Mournes, with Slieve Donard rising majestically as the centrepiece. Heading south out of Newcastle, past the now quiet harbour, you come to the **National Trust Mourne Coastal Path**, which runs for 4 miles (6km) from the very popular Bloody Bridge picnic site, along the rocky shoreline to Dunmore Head. The mountain path beside the Blood Bridge River is a starting point for hillwalkers into the Mournes. Here are the splendid mountains of Slieve Donard (2,796ft/850m) and Slieve Commedagh, which face each other, and the rockier peaks of Slieve Bignian and Slieve Bearnagh, between which lie Silent Valley and its reservoir of water for Belfast. A network of by-roads runs deep into the foothills behind Annalong and Kilkeel. Here you'll find the unspoilt, undisturbed Mourne way of life – stone cottages, people at work in their pocket-handkerchief fields, the elderly passing the time of day, children playing. It is not hard to imagine it all in the days before roads were made.

Back again on the coast road: round the corner lies the little village of **Annalong**, set against a backcloth of mountains. The little old harbour still flourishes: boats are being repainted, nets repaired; everyone is doing something, but no one hurries. You can visit **Annalong Corn Mill** (*open Feb–Nov Tue–Sat 11–5; adm; t (028) 4376 8736*), a working mill that overlooks the harbour and has a herb garden and café. **Kilkeel** is a surprisingly busy, prosperous town, home of the coast's main fishing fleet. It is on the site of an ancient *rath*, and the ruins of a 14th-century church still stand in the square. Just to the north-east of the town is a fine **dolmen** with a capstone measuring more than 10ft by 8ft (3x2.5m). The B27 road climbs up and across the Spelga Pass towards Hilltown. It has many vantage points for both the mountains and the coastal scenery. The A2 branches right about 4 miles (6km) out of Kilkeel; this unnumbered road, known as The Head Road, will take you to the Silent Valley and Ben Crom reservoirs. There is a visitor centre, craft shop and café here, and it is busy in the summer.

Continuing round the coast, the land levels out quite a bit. Leave the A2 and explore the peninsula of Cranfield Point and Greencastle, reached by narrow roads. Down to the left lies the long strand of **Cranfield**. Greencastle, the ancient capital of the 9th-century Kingdom of Mourne, is visible on the horizon and strategically sited at the entrance to Carlingford Lough. Its position was recognized by the Anglo-Normans, who built a strong castle here, **Greencastle Fort** (*keep open Apr–Sept Tue–Sat 10–7, Sun 2–7; grounds always accessible; t (028) 9054 3037*). The tall, rectangular, turreted keep and some of the outworks are all that remain of this impressive 13th-century stronghold. From the topmost turret of the castle there are splendid views across the lough to the Republic.

The road swings round still more, ever twisting and turning as it makes its way along the indented coast. The houses are larger, their gardens bigger and better kept. Clearly this was, and still is, a prosperous area. Sheltered by high hills and set against a purple and green backcloth of pine forests, the town of **Rostrevor** enjoys a mild and sunny climate, hence the profusion of brightly coloured flowers in the gardens, many of them of Mediterranean origin. It has a lovely long seafront and superb views across the lough, but sadly no sandy beach. It is a quiet place to use as a base for walking in the Mourne Mountains or in the pine-scented Rostrevor Forest. A mountain road climbs northwards, passing the little old church of Kilbroney with its ancient cross, and levelling out to follow the valley of the Bann and emerge at Hilltown. The many tumbling little streams, stony paths and patches of woodland make for excellent picnic sites en route.

Not far from Rostrevor is **Warrenpoint**, a lively and popular resort. It is spacious and well planned, with a very big square and a promenade more than half a mile (0.8km) long, the town being bounded by the sea on two sides. There is a well-equipped marina, golf and tennis facilities, and lots of live music in the pubs. Prior to the mid 18th century there was little here save a rabbit warren – hence its name. The **Heritage Centre** (*open Apr–Oct Tue–Sun*) in Bridge Road has items of local historical interest.

A little way to the north, on a spur of rock jutting out into the estuary, lies the square, battlemented towerhouse of **Narrow Water Castle** (*guided tours normally available July and Aug Tue–Fri 11–4.30; call Warrenpoint tourist office in advance, t (028) 4175 2256*), which is privately owned. It was built in the 17th century on the site of a much earlier fortification.

From here the road improves dramatically, and before long you reach **Newry**, an old and prosperous town sited where St Patrick planted a yew at the head of the strand – hence its name, which in Gaelic is *An tHúr*: 'Yew'. It enjoys a strategic site astride the Clanrye River. Newry has been a busy mercantile town for centuries, and trade was boosted in 1741 when the Newry Canal – believed to be the oldest canal constructed in the British Isles – connected Newry to Lough Neagh and Carlingford Lough. Today the canal is stocked with fish, and plans are afoot to open it up to boats, but a huge amount of work has to be done first. The long prosperity of this old town is clearly reflected in its large and imposing townhouses and public buildings, though many are now rather dilapidated.

St Patrick's Parish Church is possibly the earliest Protestant church in the whole of Ireland. The 19th-century **Cathedral of St Colman** boasts some beautiful stained-glass windows. The town hall is impressively sited astride the Clanrye River, which forms the county boundary. There is a good deal of Georgian architecture here, and many shops with small-paned windows and slate-hung gables. Some of Newry's oldest houses are to be found in Market Street. Remnants of far earlier centuries are the monastery, the castle and the Cistercian abbey. In the Arts Centre on Bank Parade you can explore the small **Newry Museum** (*open Mon–Fri 10.30–4.30; t (028) 3031 3138*), which contains many varied and interesting exhibits. Note that at the time of writing, however, the museum was scheduled to relocate to a new home in Bagenal's Castle in late 2006.

Two miles (3km) north of the town, near Crown Bridge, there is a very fine motte and bailey, giving rise to a crown-shaped mound. And at **Donaghmore** 3 miles (5km) on, in the parish graveyard, there is a fine 10th-century carved cross on the site of an earlier monastery, under which lies a souterrain. **Slieve Gullion Forest Park**, 4 miles (6.4km) south-west of Newry in County Armagh, has a wonderful 7-mile (11km) drive with views of lakes, which takes you nearly to the top of Slieve Gullion itself. A path continues upwards to 1,900ft (580m), where you can explore two Stone Age cairns.

Around Hilltown

Heading from Newry back across to Newcastle you pass just north of the Mournes. The view across to the mountains is superb and ever-changing. The road is very twisty, so it is good to stop and appreciate the many panoramic vantage points. There are two towns worth visiting. The first, **Hilltown**, the more southerly where the mountain roads from Kilkeel and Rostrevor converge, is a small angling village at a crossroads on top of a hill. The views are breathtaking. Just over 2 miles (3.2km) north-east of Hilltown, in Cloughmore on Goward Hill, is a huge dolmen known as **Cloughmore Cromlech**. Underneath its three massive upright supports and 50-ton granite capstone there is a double burial chamber in which traces of bones were once found. The road to Kilkeel (B27) passes close to the Silent Valley reservoir – a deep valley between the peaks of the Mournes. The road, known as the Spelga Pass, demands careful driving as it rises and twists amongst the spectacular scenery. However, if instead you decide to go north on the B25, you will come to a less dramatic landscape.

Easily spotted in the distance by its mushroom-shaped watertower lies **Rathfriland** – a flourishing market town high on a hill, commanding a wide view of the Mournes and the surrounding countryside. This area from Loughbrickland to Rathfriland is called Brontë Country, because here lived the aunts, uncles and, when he was young, father of novelists Charlotte, Emily and Anne Brontë. Emily is supposed to have modelled Heathcliff in *Wuthering Heights* on her wild great-uncle Welsh, who travelled to London with a big stick to silence the critics of his nieces' books. Nearby, at Drumballyroney school and church, is the small **Brontë Homeland Interpretative Centre** (*open Mar–Sept Tue–Fri 11–5, Sat and Sun 2–6; adm; t (028) 4062 3322*). Patrick Brontë, the father of the girls, was the parish schoolmaster here. The family homestead is at Emdale.

County Armagh

Armagh is the smallest county in Ulster, but its scenery is varied, ranging from the gentle southern *drumlins* to wild open moorland, and to the grander mountains and rocky glens further east. The Gaelic tradition of splitting land between all the family gives a familar pattern to the landscape. Here, an intricate network of dry-stone walls gathers what fertility may be had into fields with barely enough room for a cow to turn in. As you travel north towards the reclaimed wetlands on the shore of Lough Neagh, the orchards and dairy pastures become more extensive and are dotted with small lakes and the rivers that once turned the wheels of the flaxmills.

In general, the people here are fairly prosperous farmers, although the Troubles of the last 25 years have taken their toll of misery and death. People here feel extremely strongly about politics, and there is very little middle ground, so you may find it easier to avoid the subject altogether.

Highlights of the county include Ardress House and The Argory, both of which are National Trust properties that give visitors a great insight into the more settled times of the 18th and 19th centuries. For the fishing enthusiasts among you there are tremendous catches of bream in the Blackwater River, and walkers can enjoy the quiet tranquillity of Clare Glen.

You might be lucky and see a game of road bowls – an old Irish sport that is played here and in County Cork. The area has the reputation for being very rainy, but if you time your visit for May you will see the country at its prettiest, especially around Loughgall with its apple orchards in full blossom. Public transport is excellent throughout the county, and the main Belfast to Dublin railway line passes along its eastern border, stopping en route.

History

One of the most fascinating aspects of County Armagh is its history. On the outskirts of Armagh City is the legendary *Emain Macha*, also known as Navan Fort. This was the crowning place of the Sovereigns of Ulster (350 BC to AD 332), and it was from here that the legendary Red Branch Knights sallied out to display their prowess

Getting There and Around

By Train
A frequent service between Dublin and Belfast stops at Portadown and Newry. (Note that the express service does not stop at all). Translink, t (028) 9066 6630, *www.translink.co.uk*

By Bus
Ulsterbus Express buses run Belfast–Armagh Mon–Fri hourly 6.30am–6.30pm; twice Sun. **Armagh City Bus Station, t** (028) 3752 2266

By Bike
The Cyclery, Mount Zion House, 56 Edward St, Lurgan, t (028) 3834 8627
Raymonds, 65 Bridge St, Portadown, t (028) 3835 2828. A Raleigh Rent-a-Bike contact.

Festivals

March
St Patrick's Day, *www.visitarmagh.com*. A parade in Armagh City and concert in St Patrick's Hall.

May
Apple Blossom Festival, Armagh City, t (028) 3752 1800. *See* p.430.

June
Fleadh Ceol, Comhaltas Ceoltíorí Traditional Music Festival, *www.visitarmagh.com*. A county-wide event.

July
Scarva Sham Fight, t (028) 4066 0600. A symbolic reenactment of the Battle of the Boyne between 2 horsemen in period costume, representing William of Orange and James II.

August
All Ireland Intermediate Road Bowls Festival, *www.visitarmagh.com*. An event on roads around Armagh City.

November
William Kennedy Piping Festival, Armagh City, t (028) 3751 1248, *www.visitarmagh.com*

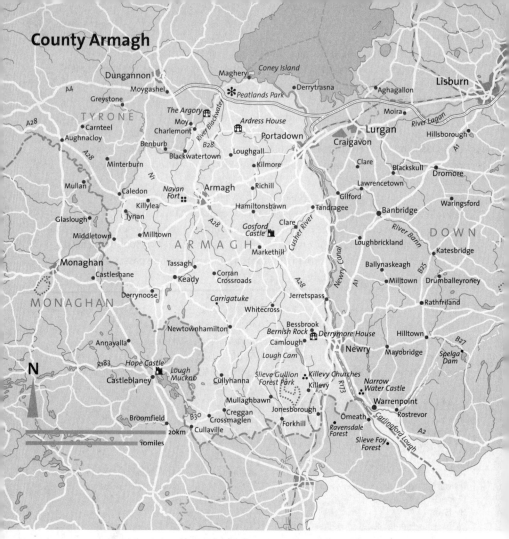

County Armagh

and do great deeds of chivalry. The greatest of these knights was Cú Chulainn, who is supposed to have received his training at the fort (see **Old Gods and Heroes**, p.54). Of course, this ancient history is clouded in mystery and legend; it is part of Ulster's mythology and identity, just as Fionn MacCumhaill and the Fianna are part of that of the rest of Ireland. Legends aside, we do know that when Fergus was King of Ulster in the 4th century, *Emain Macha* was burned and pillaged by forces from Tara, County Meath, and was never restored. Afterwards, the then-small city of Armagh established itself as the ecclesiastical capital of Ireland. In the 5th century, St Patrick constructed his first stone church here, and around it other churches, colleges and schools grew up. The city developed into a great centre of religion and learning until the 9th and 10th centuries, with the incursion of the Vikings. These days it is a fine city of attractive 18th-century buildings, built in settled, prosperous days, with an excellent museum.

Armagh City

Armagh (*Árd Macha*), now sprawled over seven hills, was a centre of Christian learning and tranquillity when Rome was in ruins and London glowed with endless fires started by the barbarians. Today there is little to show of the ancient city; its appearance is distinctly Georgian; yet it is still the ecclesiastical centre of Ireland. Armagh is a lovely city to walk around with its fine buildings, especially in the Mall and in Beresford Row. The **Courthouse** dates from 1809 and is the work of Francis Johnston, as are many buildings here; he was a local architect who later achieved fame in Dublin. It was bombed in 1993 but has since been completely restored. Many of the most interesting places to visit are just a brisk walk away.

A visit to the **Armagh County Museum** (*open Mon–Fri 10–5, Sat 10–1 and 2–5; t (028) 3752 3070, www.armaghcountymuseum.org.uk*) in the Mall East helps fill in the city's background. Here, a 17th-century painting shows the old wide streets, space for markets and the prominence of the early hilltop Cathedral of St Patrick. There is also a wide range of regional archaeological exhibits, a local natural history section, and an art gallery that has works by the Irish mystic poet and artist George Russell (1867–1935), better known as A. E. Russell. The **Royal Irish Fusiliers Museum** (*open Mon–Fri 10–12.30 and 1.30–4; adm; t (028) 3752 2911, www.rirfus-museum.freeserve. co.uk*), with displays of old uniforms, weapons and medals, is also in the Mall.

The two cathedral churches are unmistakable features of the city's skyline, for they each crown neighbouring hills. Founded by St Patrick, the ancient **Church of Ireland Cathedral** (*open daily Apr–Oct 10–5, Nov–Mar 10–4; adm free; t (028) 3752 3142*) is in the perpendicular style, with a massive central tower. Its present appearance dates mainly from the 18th century but its core is medieval. Before medieval times the city suffered terribly from the Viking raids, and the cathedral and town were sacked at least 20 times in 500 years. Inside the cathedral is a memorial to Brian Boru, the most famous high king of all Ireland, who visited Armagh in 1004 and was received with great state. The precious *Book of Armagh* (*c.* AD 807), which is now in Trinity College, Dublin, was placed in his hands and his visit was noted in the book. He presented 20 ounces of pure gold to the church. Ten years later he hammered the Vikings at the battle of Clontarf in 1014, which put a stop to their encroachment into inland areas (*see* **History**, p.10), but Brian Boru was killed in his tent after the battle was won. His body and that of his son were brought back to be buried here, and the memorial to them is in the west wall.

The other heirloom of those ancient days is St Patrick's Bell, which is enclosed in a cover dating from the 12th century; it can also be seen at the National Museum in Dublin. The moulding on the west door is very fine, and there is a good stained-glass window in the choir. Notice the carved medieval stone heads high up on the exterior and the mysterious statues in the crypt. The surrounding streets run true to the rings of the Celtic *rath* or fort in which St Patrick built his church – directed, it is said, by a flight of angels. On the corner of Abbey Street is **Armagh Public Library** (*t (028) 3752 3142, www.armaghrobinsonlibrary.org*), also known as Robinson's Library, which contains some rare books, maps and a first edition of *Gulliver's Travels*, annotated by

Tourist Information

Armagh: St Patrick's Trian Centre, 40 English St,
t (028) 3752 1800, www.visitarmagh.com
See also www.armaghandown.com

Shopping

Crafts

Appleby Connections, Armagh, t (028) 3751 0825
Cloud Cuckoo, Ogle St, Armagh, t (028) 3751 0771
Quinn's Antiquities, 27 Dobbin St, Armagh,
t (028) 3751 0947. Antiques and bric-à-brac.
St Patrick's Trian, 40 English St, Armagh,
t (028) 3752 1801

Markets

There are a couple of markets in Armagh City:
Shambles Market, Cathedral Rd.
Tue and Fri 9–5.
Variety Market, Market St. Tue and Fri 9–5.

Sports and Activities

Golf

County Armagh Golf Club, 7 Newry Rd,
t (028) 3752 5861. An 18-hole golf course.

Where to Stay

Armagh City

The Charlemont Arms Hotel, 63 English St,
t (028) 3752 2028, www.charlemontarmshotel.
com (moderate). A very cosy and restful
family-run hotel. The restaurant has a
special coffee menu (Illy is the brand of
choice), and there's also a bar and a
basement café and wine bar.
De Averell Guest House, 3 Seven Houses,
English St, t (028) 3751 1213 (moderate).
A Georgian townhouse with a good
basement restaurant.
Deans Hill, t (028) 3752 4923 (moderate).
A pretty 18th-century house with lovely
gardens, close to the Observatory. There
are 2 ensuite rooms, one with a 4-poster.
Drumsill House Hotel, 35 Moy Rd, t (028) 3752
2009 (moderate). A bland but comfortable
modern option.
Hillview Lodge, 33 Newtownhamilton Rd,
t (028) 3752 2000, www.hillviewlodge.com
(inexpensive–moderate). A reliable B&B with
6 ensuite rooms.
Armagh City Youth Hostel, 36 Abbey St, t (028)
3751 1800, www.hini.org.uk (inexpensive).
A purposebuilt, well-sited if sterile hostel
with good security and facilities.

Jonathan Swift himself. Richard Robinson, Archbishop of Armagh, was a highly
influential figure in the building of the 18th-century city. There is an exhibition and
historical centre in English Street, **St Patrick's Trian** (open Mon–Sat 10–5, Sun 2–5;
adm for exhibitions; t (028) 3752 1801, www.saintpatrickstrian.com); it derives this
name from an ancient division of the city. Inside, 'The Armagh Story' is illustrated
through the ages by an audio-visual show and an exhibition on the life and work of
St Patrick and his connections with Armagh. The 'Land of Lilliput' is a child-orientated
exhibition that has a giant model of Gulliver as the centrepiece. The centre also has
art exhibitions, tourist information, and is home to **Armagh Ancestry** (open Mon–Sat
9–5; t (028) 3752 1802), a central source for chasing up ancestors in Armagh county.

Across the valley are the twin spires of the Catholic **Cathedral of St Patrick**. This is a
complete contrast to its more sombre Protestant neighbour, with its profusion of
magnificent internal gilding, marbles, mosaics and stained glass. The building was
started in 1849 and finished in 1873; the passing of the years is marked by a collection
of cardinals' red hats suspended in the Lady Chapel.

Armagh has the most advanced facilities for astronomical studies in the British Isles.
The institution owes its pre-eminence to Archbishop Richard Robinson, who founded
and endowed the **Armagh Observatory** (t (028) 3752 2928) in 1790. It is complemented

Self-catering

Ballydougan Pottery Courtyard Cottages, 171 Plantation Rd, Craigavon, **t** (028) 38342201, *www.ballydouganpottery.co.uk*. Pretty cottages at a working pottery producing hand-thrown decorative stoneware. Choose from Bramley Apple Cottage, Wheat Loft Apartment and Gaskins Grove.

Eating Out

Armagh City

Manor Park Restaurant, 2 College Hill, The Mall, **t** (028) 3751 5353, *www.manorparkrestaurant. com* (*expensive*). French cuisine served in a centrally located 19th-century building.

D'Arby Byrne Restaurant, Palace Demesne, **t** (028) 3752 1801 (*moderate*). A restaurant in beautiful grounds, serving coffee, lunch and afternoon tea. *Closed eves.*

Rainbow, 13 English St, **t** (028) 3752 5391 (*inexpensive–moderate*). Morning coffee, lunch and afternoon tea, and bistro fare Sat evenings. *Closed Sun, eves exc Sat.*

Calvert Tavern, 3 Scotch St, **t** (028) 3752 4186 (*inexpensive*). Good pub grub: open sandwiches and grills.

Hester's Place, 12 Upper English St, **t** (028) 3752 2374 (*inexpensive*). Irish stew and great Ulster fry. *Closed Wed, Sun, and eves.*

Navan Centre, 81 Killylea Rd, **t** (028) 3752 5550 (*inexpensive*). Hot meals, snacks and coffee.

The Pilgrim's Table, 40 English St (inside St Patrick's Trian complex), **t** (028) 3752 1814 (*inexpensive*). Reputedly the best lunches in town, in pleasant surroundings.

Entertainment and Nightlife

Theatre and Cinema

Armagh City Filmhouse, Market St, **t** (028) 3751 1033. A 4-screen cinema complex.

Market Place Theatre and Arts Centre, **t** (028) 3752 1821, *www.marketplacearmagh.com*. An arts centre hosting drama, music and dance, with 2 theatres, a gallery and restaurants and bars.

Traditional Music

Charlemont Arms, Armagh, **t** (028) 3752 2028. One Thur a month.

Palace Stables Heritage Centre, **t** (028) 3752 1801. Performances by the Armagh Pipers Club once a month.

by the **Armagh Planetarium and Hall of Astronomy** (*open Mon–Fri 10–4, Sat and Sun 1.15–4; adm for shows and exhibition; t (028) 3752 3689, www.armaghplanet.co.uk*), which has Ireland's largest public telescope and hosts presentations in its star theatre. (Star shows are put on more frequently in the summer; it is advisable to ring and book for these.) In the grounds you'll find the Astropark, which is a scale model of the universe. The Observatory was designed by Francis Johnston, who is also responsible for the Georgian terrace on the east side of the Mall.

On the south side of the city is the Bishop's Palace demesne. The **Palace Stables Heritage Centre** (*open daily, call for times, t (028) 3752 1801; adm; www.visitarmagh.com*) is a restored 18th-century building in the demesne. The 'Day in the Life' exhibition features typical scenes of life as it was here in 1776, during the time of Archbishop Robinson. Craft exhibitions, fairs, lectures, art shows, music, dance and storytelling events are all held.

The ancient fort of *Emain Macha*, now called **Navan Fort**, dates from 600 BC and is about 2 miles (3.2km) west of Armagh City on the A28. The fort was a centre of pagan power and culture, and is famous for its association with the Red Branch Knights. When Fergus was King of Ulster in the 4th century, *Emain Macha* was burned, its timber structures completely destroyed. By the time St Patrick came to *Árd Macha*

(Armagh), this Bronze Age centre of power had lain in ruins for more than 100 years. Today, the grassy *rath* extends over about 12 acres (5ha). It is easy to walk or take a bus there from town, and you are rewarded with a pleasant view over the city when you arrive. Once in danger of being destroyed to make way for a quarry, the site has become a chief tourist attraction. Close by is the excellent interpretative centre, the **Navan Centre** (*open Mon–Sat 10–5, Sun 12 noon–5; adm; t (028) 3752 1801, navan@ armagh.gov.uk*), with a restaurant and shop. The centre is in the shape of a Bronze Age fort, and very unobtrusive; it is definitely worth a detour. The no.73 bus from Mall West in Armagh will drop you outside.

Around Armagh

The Shores of Lough Neagh to Tandragee

To the north-east of Armagh is the industrial part of the county, with the old linen town of **Portadown** and the new town of **Craigavon**. Though lacking in beauty, they do benefit from their proximity to Lough Neagh and the River Bann, with artificial lakes, boating ponds and a dry ski-slope. Craigavon's two large artificial lakes are used for watersports and trout fishing. There are also two golf courses. An interesting trip can be made to **Moneypenny's Lockhouse** (*open Apr–Sept Sat and Sun 2–5; t (028) 3832 2205*), Newry Canal, Portadown, which contains an exhibition on the history of this 18th-century canal and the lifestyle of the lockhouse keeper. It is a peaceful walk out of Portadown, along the banks of the canal from Shillington's Quay car park on Castle Street.

Near Portadown a network of little roads runs through a charming district, covered with fruit trees and bushes. In May and June the gentle little hills are a mass of pink and white apple and damson flowers. There is an **Apple Blossom Festival** in May (*see* p.425), featuring fairs, concerts, and exhibitions in Keady, Richhill, Tandragee and Loughgall. The orchards were a part of the old Irish agricultural economy long before the English settlers came here, although many of the fruit farmers are descended from Kent and Somerset families, well used to growing fruit. Their main crop is Bramley apples.

The retreating glaciers many millions of years ago left behind deposits of clay and gravel that form little hills known as *drumlins*, of which there are many in this area. The teardrop *drumlin* country is intersected by trout-filled lakes and streams, high hedges and twisting lanes. In **Richhill** you will find some furniture workshops and a fine **Jacobean manor** with curling Dutch gables. It is not open to the public, but the sight that it makes within the pretty well-kept village is worth stopping for. The village of **Kilmore** has what is probably the oldest church in Ireland. In the heart of the present little parish church stands the lower half of a round tower dating from the first half of the 3rd century.

Right in the centre of this fertile district is the quaint village of **Loughgall**, with, strung out along the main road, many little houses painted in the soft shades of blossom and gardens bursting with colour. At Sloan's House in Main Street, the

Tourist Information

Craigavon: Civic Centre, Lakeview Rd,
t (028) 3831 2400, *www.craigavon.gov.uk*
Crossmaglen: Community Centre, The Square,
t (028) 3086 1949. *Closed Sat and Sun.*
Lurgan: Waves Leisure Complex, Robert St,
t (028) 3832 2906/2205

Shopping

Antiques

Burnbrae Antiques, 77 Main St, Loughgall,
t (028) 3889 2003
The Curiosity Shop, 58 Dunbarton St,
Craigavon, t (028) 3883 2746
Four Winds Antiques, 66a Main St,
Craigavon, t (028) 9261 2226
Huey's Antique Shop, The Tavern,
43 Main St, Loughgall, t (028) 3889 1248

Crafts

Mullaghbawn Folk Museum,
Tullymacrieve, Forkhill, t (028) 3088 8108
The National Trust Shop,
The Argory, Moy, t (028) 8778 4753
Peatlands Park, t (028) 3885 1102,
www.peatlandsni.gov.uk. Hand-carved
figures made from compressed peat.

Markets

Livestock Market, Newtownhamilton.
Every other Sat.

Sports and Activities

Birdwatching

Oxford Island and Coney Island are good
for birdlife, as well as fishing. Note that there
is no ferry service to Coney Island: you have
to hire a boat from Kinnego Bay or Maghery
Country Park.
Lough Neagh Discovery Centre,
Oxford Island, Craigavon, t (028) 3832
2205, *www.oxfordisland.com.*
Birdwatching and walks.

Cycling

Craigavon Borough Council is developing
cycle routes on paths and minor roads.

Lough Neagh Discovery Centre,
Oxford Island, t (028) 3832 2205
McCumiskey Cycles, Dromintee,
t (028) 3088 8593

Fishing

Between Benburb and Blackwater town
there is an extensive river park where fishing
and watersports of all kinds take place.
Fishing is also available on the Cusher and
Callan rivers, which are tributaries of the
Blackwater River.
For more information contact the Armagh
Tourist Office on t (028) 3752 1800.

Golf

Craigavon Golf and Ski Centre,
Turmoyra Lane, Lurgan, t (028) 3832 6606
Tandragee Golf Club, Markethill Rd, Tandragee,
t (028) 3884 1272. An 18-hole course.

Open Farm

Tannaghmore Gardens and Farm,
Silverwood, Craigavon, t (028) 3834 3244.
A farm with rare animal breeds and a
Victorian rose garden .

Pleasure Cruises

There are cruises from Kinnego Bay in
Lough Neagh.
Paddy Prunty, Harbour Master, Kinnego Marina,
Oxford Island, t (028) 3832 7573. Sailing
courses are also offered here.

Ponytrekking

Crossmaglen Equestrian Centre,
t (028) 3086 1661
Greenvale Trekking Centre, 141 Longfield Rd,
Forkhill, t (028) 3088 8314

Walking

The **Ulster Way,** a signposted trail that
traverses the mountains and coastline of
Ulster, goes through Armagh. A large stretch
of it running along the Newry Canal between
Newry and Portadown is very scenic.
Carnagh and **Slieve Gullion Forest Park**
(*open 10–dusk*) have waymarked walks; ask for
details from the Tourist Office in Armagh.
Sports Council for Northern Ireland,
t (028) 9038 1222, *www.sportni.net.*
Details on the Ulster Way.

Watersports

Craigavon Water Sports Centre, Lakeview Rd, Craigavon, **t** (028) 3834 2669, *www. craigavon.gov.uk*. Watersports of all types.

Where to Stay

Planters Tavern, 4 Banbridge Rd, Waringstown, east of Craigavon on A26, **t** (028) 3888 1510, *www.planters.supanet.com* (*expensive*). A former coaching inn then bleach house, now a public house and guesthouse with 12 very comfortable rooms. Ask for one on the top floor, which benefit from views over the village church and gardens. Meals can be taken in either the restaurant or the lounge with its cricket memorabilia.

Ivanhoe, 10 Valley Lane, Waringstown, Craigavon, **t** (028) 3888 1287 (*moderate*). A country house in peaceful surroundings.

Ballinahinch House, 47 Ballygroobany Rd, Richhill, **t** (028) 3887 0081, *www.ballinahinchhouse. com* (*inexpensive–moderate*). A Victorian farmhouse with spacious rooms and an olde-worlde ambience.

Dundrum House, Dundrum Rd, Keady, **t** (028) 3753 1257, *www.dundrumhouse.com* (*inexpensive–moderate*). A well-preserved early-18th-century farmhouse.

Waterside House, Oxford Island, Lurgan, Craigavon, **t** (028) 3832 7573 (*inexpensive*). A hostel located in the conservation area overlooking Lough Neagh, offering a wide range of watersports and activities.

Self-catering

Benbree, Forkhill, **t** (028) 3088 8394 (*inexpensive*). Well-priced accommodation for up to 6 people.

Mountain View, Mullaghbawn, **t** (028) 3088 8410 (*inexpensive*). Another reasonable option for 4–6 people.

Eating Out

The Famous Grouse, 6 Ballyhagan Rd, Loughgall, **t** (028) 3889 1778 (*moderate*). A reasonably priced restaurant with a cosy ambiance, offering a selection of pub grub at lunchtime and an à la carte menu in the evening.

The Ferryside Inn, Maghery Rd, Dungannon, **t** (028) 3885 1903 (*moderate*). A characterful place serving meals such as good wild trout, eels and steak.

Loughview Brasserie, 235a Lough Rd, Lurgan, **t** (028) 3834 6611, *www.loughviewbrasserie. co.uk* (*moderate*). A place where you can choose between a grill menu, including steaks, and brasserie food such as salads and pasta dishes. *Closed Mon.*

Moneypenny's Restaurant, 9–19 Church St, Tandragee, **t** (028) 3884 0219 (*moderate*). International dishes served in a gracious atmosphere. Diners can choose between the bar and the restaurant. *Closed Mon eve and Tue.*

The Old Barn, 5 Mowhan Rd, Markethill, **t** (028) 3755 2742 (*moderate*). Both traditional local recipes and internationally inspired dishes served in a well-restored building. *Closed Mon–Thur eve.*

Seagoe Hotel, Upper Church Lane, Portadown, **t** (028) 3833 3076, *www.seagoe.com* (*moderate*). A restaurant serving good beef and Irish stews, within a hotel (*expensive*).

Ardress House, 64 Ardress Rd, Portadown, **t** (028) 8778 4753 (*inexpensive*). A restored National Trust manor house (*see* opposite) where you can enjoy picnic teas in the high season. *Closed exc Sun daytime in summer.*

Cafolla, 2 Carnegie St, Lurgan, **t** (028) 3832 3331 (*inexpensive*). A good place for a hearty fish and chip supper.

The Court Rooms Restaurant, 7 Main St, Markethill, **t** (028) 3755 2553 (*inexpensive*). A daytime venue the highlight of which is the scrumptious home-made desserts . *Closed eves and Sun.*

Old Thatch, 3 Keady St, Markethill, **t** (028) 3755 1261 (*inexpensive*). A handy spot for those looking to refuel on good cakes and coffee.

Hearty's Folk Cottage, Glassdrummond, near Crossmaglen, **t** (028) 3086 0086 (*inexpensive*). An atmospheric venue for afternoon teas, arts and crafts and traditional music. *Closed exc Sun afternoon.*

The Argory, Moy, **t** (028) 8778 4753 (*inexpensive*). A good tea-room, open 2–5.30pm only. *Closed exc June–Aug.*

small **Orange Museum** (*open by appointment; call Armagh Tourist Centre on* **t** *(028) 3752 1800*), displays mementoes commemorating the founding of the Orange Order here in 1795. Ireland in the late 18th century was a place of localized secret societies, mostly made up of poor agrarian Catholics, mobilized by land hunger, tithes and local issues. The ferment caused by the concessions of Grattan's Parliament towards Catholics in 1793, giving them the vote and more civil liberties, made sectarian tension in this part of Ulster particularly acute. A confrontation between the Protestant 'Peep o' Day Boys' and the Catholic 'Defenders' at Diamond Hill outside Loughgall led to the founding of the Orange Order, which has played such a large part in modern Ulster politics. **Dan Winter's Cottage and Ancestral Home** (*open spring and summer Sat, Sun and bank hols, call for times* **t** *(028) 3885 2777*) is at the centre of the site where the Battle of the Diamond took place in 1795; it bears the scorch marks where the building was set alight. Inside there are maps of and relics from the battle, and it is furnished in the vernacular style. (It may also be the longest thatched cottage in Ireland, at 94ft, or 29m)

Not far away is **Adress House** (*open Easter and Apr–Sept Sat, Sun and bank hols 2–6;* **t** *(028) 8778 4753, www.nationaltrust.org.uk*). This is a 17th-century manor that was much altered by George Ensor (who married the owner of the once-simple farmhouse), so that it is now Georgian in character. It is found in Annaghmore on the Portadown–Moy road (B28), 3 miles (5km) from Loughgall. Its elegant drawing room has one of the most beautiful decorative plasterwork ceilings in the whole of Ireland. The work is in Adam style, and both the ceiling and the mural medallions have been carefully restored and sympathetically painted. Set in lovely parkland, it is now in the care of the National Trust. There is a farmyard display, a picnic area, woodland walks and a small formal garden, and on Sundays in the summer months you can enjoy picnic teas here (*see* opposite).

Coney Island, which is one of the few islands situated in Lough Neagh, is also a National Trust property. It lies to the north, not far from the mouth of the Blackwater River, and can be reached by boat from Maghery. Apart from the excellent fishing on offer, this thickly wooded, reedy island covering 8½ acres (3.5ha) is also worth visiting for its huge and varied birdlife. St Patrick used the island as a retreat, and there is also a rather overgrown holy well. Be prepared for the Lough Neagh flies, which are food for the pollan, a fish that is unique to these waters – and that is absolutely delicious fried in butter.

Peatlands Park (*park open 9–dusk; visitor centre open Apr–Sept Sat and Sun 2–6, June–Aug Mon–Fri 2–6;* **t** *(028) 3885 1102, www.peatlandsni.gov.uk*), with its narrow-gauge railway, is close by on the Lough Neagh basin, and shows educational videos and outdoor exhibits on peat ecology.

Further east again you'll find the the **Lough Neagh Discovery Centre** (*open daily Apr–Sept 10–6, Oct–Mar 10–5; take exit 10 off M1 at Oxford Island;* **t** *(028) 3832 2205*), which explains the geology and natural history of the area; it is possible to do some birdwatching in the hides here, and to join guided nature walks. There are picnic areas, a café and a shop.

Returning southwards along the River Blackwater, which forms the county boundary, is **The Argory** (*open 1–6 mid-Mar–May and Sept Sat and Sun, June–Aug daily; adm; t (028) 8778 4753, uagest@ntrust.org.uk*), which lies 2½ miles (4km) from Charlemont on a tiny little road off the B28. Standing in woodland and parkland, this rather lovely early-19th-century neoclassical house overlooks the river. It is of particular interest in that its contents have remained almost completely undisturbed since the turn of the century. Much more of a home than a museum, it is full of treasures gathered over the years from all corners of the earth. The large cabinet organ at the top of the grand cantilevered staircase is unique. So too is the acetylene gas plant that still lights the house: every room has its own ingenious old light-fittings. Outside you can wander through the stable buildings and the semi-formal gardens and along woodland and river walks. The village of **Charlemont**, once an important parliamentary borough, is 2.5 miles (4km) upstream. It has an 18th-century cut-stone bridge and a 17th-century ruined fort with star-shaped walls typical of that period, built by Lord Mountjoy, Lord Deputy of Ireland in 1602.

Flax-milling has ceased, but flour-milling still thrives in **Tandragee**, a pretty, well-kept town with brightly painted houses. It is of considerable age and was founded by the O'Hanlons, chieftains of these parts before the plantations of James I. The old castle and the town were destroyed in the Civil War of 1641. The present castle is barely more than a century old and now houses the **factory** that produces Ireland's foremost crisp, 'Tayto'. It is possible to go on an intriguing free tour of what the locals call '**Tayto Castle**' (*open for tours Mon–Thur 10.30–1.30, Fri 10.30am; t (028) 3884 0249, www.tayto.com*).

Clare Glen and South to Slieve Gullion

Clare Glen, which is one of the prettiest glens in the country, is four miles (6km) away to the east of Armagh City. A fine trout stream winds under old bridges and past a now-silent mill. There are lovely walks around here, and it is on such country lanes as these that you might come across a game of 'bullets' or **road bowls**. This game is played with 28oz (795g) balls made of iron, which are thrown along a quiet winding road. The aim is to cover several miles in the fewest shots. Children are stationed along the course to warn motorists, and the betting and excitement among the onlookers is infectious.

On the Newry road (A28) you pass the village of **Markethill** on the right, and **Gosford Castle**, a huge early-19th-century mock-Norman castle (*open daily 10–dusk; adm; t (028) 3755 1277*), on the left. The magnificent grounds, also open to the public, are owned by the Forestry Commission. The walled cherry garden, arboretum, unusual breeds of poultry, nature trails and forest parks make it an enjoyable place to while away some time. Further south and keeping to the more attractive minor roads, you come across the village of **Bessbrook**. This model linen-manufacturing town, neatly laid out in the 19th century by a Quaker, still has neither pub nor pawn shop. The design of the model town of Bournville, near Birmingham in England, which is famous for its chocolate industry, is based entirely on Bessbrook. The remains of the huge mill, dams, weirs and sluices stand deserted, but nearby the impressive cut-stone Craigmore Viaduct still carries the main railway line to Dublin. Just outside Bessbrook is **Derrymore House** *(house open for guided tours Easter and May–Aug Thur–Sat 2–5.30; grounds open daily May–Sept 10–7, Oct–Apr 10–4; adm; **t** (028) 8778 4753, www.nationaltrust.org.uk)*, a small, thatched manor house set in parkland. Built in 1776, it was witness to the signing of the Act of Union in 1801, and is now in the care of the National Trust.

As you travel south from Bessbrook, the land becomes poorer, the fields smaller and the hedges higher, and the roads have more of a twist to them. Soon the hills of south Armagh appear in the distance, dominated by the peak of **Slieve Gullion**. This rugged group of hills is steeped in history and legend, and is described as 'the mountains of mystery'. The average tourist never hears of them, which is a pity, as the whole region has magnificent scenery, beautiful lakes, streams and unspoilt little villages. There have been many bloody incidents in this area, labelled 'bandit country'; the population is predominantly Catholic and Nationalist, and the situation here before the ceasefire was extremely tense. **Crossmaglen** has a dicey reputation, but with the ceasefire holding the situation has improved. In general, you can enjoy exploring the delightfully unkept countryside, so different from the tamer lands in the north. Caught between Camlough Mountain and Slieve Gullion lies the beautiful ribbon-like **Lough Cam**. The surrounding hedges and shorelines are the homes of many flowers and birds, and there is good fishing on the Fane River, Lough Cam and Lough Ross.

From the other side of Lough Cam, the road climbs up through the trees to the extensive, recently developed **Slieve Gullion Forest Park** *(**t** (028) 3755 1277)*. From the top of Slieve Gullion, panoramic views of the encircling mountains that make up the Ring of Gullion and the distant hills of Belfast and Dublin spread out before you. Slieve Gullion *(Sliabh gCuillin:* 'Mountain of the Steep Slope') is often shrouded in mist, and according to local folklore it is magical. Legend tells us that Culann was a chief who owned a fierce watchdog that was slain by a boy of 15, Setanta. The young hero was afterwards called Cú Chulainn ('Hound of Culann'). On the southern slopes is an ancient church known as **Killevy Church**. There are actually the remains of two churches here, each from different periods; this holy place was founded as a nunnery as far back as AD 450. Nearby is a holy well and prehistoric passage grave.

Close to the County Louth border, just off the N1 about 1.5 miles (2.4km) south of Jonesborough and east of the bridge, is one of the earliest datable Christian monuments in Ireland. The inscribed **Kilnasaggart Pillar Stone** is early 8th century and carved with crosses. It commemorates a local dignatory, and the inscription is in Gaelic. **Moyry Castle**, a three-storey ruin nearby, dates from 1601. It was built by Lord Mountjoy and ruined in the struggle between the English forces under him and the Irish forces under Hugh O'Neill during the Elizabethan wars. The villages of **Forkhill**, with its trout stream, and **Mullaghbane**, with its tiny folk museum, furnished as a south Armagh farmhouse, are picturesquely situated in their own valleys between the hills. This region is famous for its traditional music; one place you can be sure to find some is the **Ti Chulainn Cultural Centre** *(open July–Aug Mon–Sat 10–5.30, Sun 1–6; **t** (028) 3088 8828, www.ringofgullion.com/Eichulainn)* at Mullaghbawn, which has occasional live performances of traditional music, song and dance.

Crossmaglen and Through The Fews to Tynan

South-west from here is **Crossmaglen**, with its staggeringly large market square. The town is the centre of the recently revived cottage industry of lacemaking. Again, there are earthworks to explore: a superb example of a treble-ringed fort, remains of stone cairns, and a *crannóg* (artificial island) on Lough Ross. You are now actually following the old coach road from Dublin to Armagh, itself the ancient link between Emain Macha and Tara (another ancient centre of power), in County Meath. At Dorsey, east of the town, is the largest entrenched enclosure of its kind in Ireland. Constructed as a defensive outpost for *Emain Macha*, this huge earthwork encloses more than 300 acres (121ha) and lies astride the route. Some of the earth ramparts still remain. It is part of the ancient earth dyke known as the **Black Pig's Dyke**, which extends over most of the borders of Ulster.

On the B30, a short distance from Crossmaglen, an interesting stop can be made at the old church of **Creggan**. It dates from 1731 and the tower was added in 1799. The O'Neill vault contains more than 70 skulls from this ancient family, whose present clan leader is Don Carlos O'Neill of Seville. In the church grounds is a visitor centre with an exhibition on the poets and people of Creggan. Three 18th-century Gaelic poets are buried in the graveyard, one of whom, Art McCumhaigh (1738–1773), wrote a poignant *aisling*, or vision poem, 'The Churchyard of Creagán', in which the poet encounters the vision of a woman. They bemoan the decline of the Gaels of Tír Eoghain, and the ascendency of John Bull, while the poet's last wish is to be buried with Creagán's sweet Gaels. North of Creggan is **Cullyhanna** and the **Cardinal Tomás Ó Fiaich Heritage Centre** (*open Sun–Fri, call for times, t (028) 3086 8757*). This powerful and strong-minded prelate played his part in the recent history of Ulster, and there is an exhibition of his life, a collection of south Armagh songs and poems to listen to, and a research library.

Leaving behind the mountains of south Armagh, you enter the attractive upland country known as **The Fews**. The isolated village of **Newtownhamilton** was founded in 1770 but the neighbourhood is associated with the legendary story of Lir, for it was here that the ocean-god King Lir had his palace.

Do not go straight back to Armagh, but branch off the B31 to the west and climb **Carrigatuke Hill**. From the top an outstanding view of the area as far as Meath to the south and even Roscommon to the south-west lies before you. This small area across and down to the border is a miniature Lake District with lots of little irregular lakes caught between tiny hills, vestiges of glacial movement and deposition. Many of the lakes are studded with islands. **Lake Tullnawood** is very picturesque. Just north of boot-shaped Clay Lake is the small market town of **Keady**. It was once a very important linen centre, hence the number of derelict watermills in the district.

Nearby at **Tassagh Glen** is a mill and a huge viaduct that spans the wide valley. Under the viaduct's arches you can picnic among wildflowers, rose briars and red-berried rowan. From here it is only about 6 miles (10km) back to the city of Armagh. West of Armagh, beyond the little hilltop village of Killylea, lies the pretty village of **Tynan**. In the middle of the main street stands a fine sculptured stone cross more than 13ft (4m) high, dating from the 10th century. There are other ancient crosses in the nearby extensive demesne of **Tynan Abbey**; enquire at the estate if you wish to see them.

County Donegal

Donegal (*Dún na nGall*: 'Fort of the Foreigner') is a microcosm of all Ireland, and is the fourth largest county. In the west is the Gaeltacht, with its mountains, heathery moors and boglands, home of the dispossessed Celt. In the east, there are rich pasturelands, plantation towns, and long-settled families who were originally Scottish or English. It is set north-west against the Atlantic, and much of its beauty comes from its proximity to the sea: from the sweep of Donegal Bay, the maritime cliffs around Slieve League, the intricate indentations of the coast up to Bloody Foreland, and the northern peninsulas formed by long sea loughs – around 200 miles (320km) of coast in all. Donegal is a county of beautiful countryside; the ancient mountain ranges are older than any others in Ireland, and the light of Donegal brings alive the subtle greens and browns of the landscape, and the strength of blue in the sky and sea. There are some exciting walks and climbs for the experienced. Because of the mountains in central Donegal, the weather is often quite different in the south-west quarter.

Each part of Donegal has its own charm and beauty: the rocky flats of the Rosses studded with tiny lakes, the varied scenery of Inishowen, the curved beaches and mountains of Tirconnell and the rich cattle lands that border the River Foyle. Compared to many of the urban parts of Ireland, Donegal is still a land of wilderness and rock, where a lone farmhouse hugs the hill and its resident sheepdog hurtles out onto the road to chase the car that dares to intrude upon his kingdom.

Yet increasingly, as in other coastal parts of Ireland, there has been a growth in the numbers of homes and holiday chalets here, which are often built right along the coast. County Donegal has traditionally been the holiday destination of urban Northerners from Belfast and its surrounds; many leave their caravans in Donegal and, as prosperity grows, they are buying into the new developments. The uglier by-products of Ireland's more general prosperity and industrial development is apparent around **Letterkenny**, which grows rapidly every year. The baby boom in Ireland has been experienced in this county more than anywhere else, which (almost) makes up for the rural depopulation that scourged the countryside after the famine of 1845–49. This new generation is not being brought up on the old homesteads in lonely picturesque valleys but in the numerous bungalows and housing estates that line the roads near the factories that the Irish government has enticed in with substantial financial assistance.

Tourist attractions are being developed with the restoration of various buildings of architectural or historical interest, such as Lifford Old Courthouse and the Corn and Flax Mill at Newmills, not far from Letterkenny. The archeological and early-Christian remains found in County Donegal are numerous; St Colmcille, who is Ireland's most famous native saint (*see* p.47), was born here, at Gartan, and Glencolmcille is closely associated with him.

Some people say that Donegal is the 26th county in a 25-county state, meaning that there is an individuality and independence up here that Dublin likes to ignore. This Ulster county has the largest number of Irish native speakers of any county in Ireland,

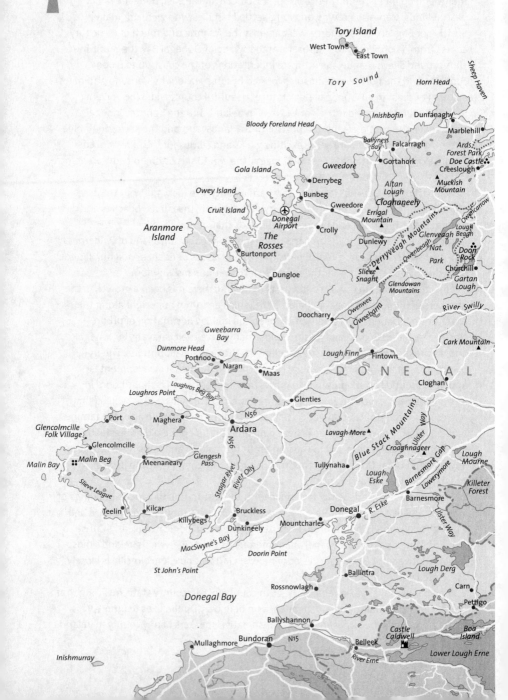

County Donegal

Malin Head
Ballyhilfin

Lag Sand Dunes

Fanad Head
Dunaff
Doagh Isle
Malin
Culdaff
Carrowblagh
Ballyliffin
Clonmany
Clonca
Gap of Mamore
Carndonagh
Gleneely

Melmore Head
Rosguill
Downings
Rosapenna
Carrigart
Tawny
Portsalon
Dunree Head
Knockalla Mountain
Magherabane
Slieve Snaght
Glentogher
Greencastle
Inishowen Head

Fanad

Portsalon
Lough Swilly
R238
INISHOWEN
Cooley
Moville
Magilligan Point

R242
Mulroy Bay
Carrowkeel
Buncrana
Crana River
Redcastle
Magilligan Strand
Downhill

Loughsalt Mountain
Millford
Rathmullan
R247
Lisfannon
White Castle
Magilligan
Bellarena

Barnes Gap
N56
Lough Fern
Inch Island
Inch
Fahan
Scalp Mountain
Muff
Lough Foyle
Binevenagh Mountain

Kilmacrenan
Rathmelton
Burt
Culmore
Derry City Airport

Newtown-cunningham
Grianán of Aileach
A2
Ballykelly
Limavady

Letterkenny
Manorcunningham
DERRY
Eglinton
River Roe
B68
Ulster Way

Newmills
N13
A40
Ardmore
A6
Ness Wood
Loughermore
Burnfoot

N14
Killaloo
LONDONDERRY
Dungiven
Augustinian Priory
Glenshane Pass

Drumkeen
Raphoe
Convoy
Beltany
River Deele
Ballindrait
River Foyle
Slievekirk Mountain
Claudy
R. Faughan
Ballymoney
B74
Feeny
Banagher Church
Park
Mullaghbash Mountain
Banagher Forest

Stranorlar
Lifford
Strabane
Ballyneaner
Carnanreagh
Dreon
B40
Mullaghmore

Ballybofey
River Finn
Dergalt
Mullaclogha
Sperrin Mountains
Sawel Mountain
Moneyneany

Mourne Beg
Mourne River
Plumbridge
Glenelly Valley
B47
Sperrin
Cranagh
Draperstown

Castlederg
A5
Scotch Town
Slieve Gallion

Newtownstewart
Gortin
Owenkillew
Glenhull
Lough Fea
Beaghmore Stone Circles

Killen
B84
Drumlegagh
Ulster History Park
Gortin Glen Forest Park
Greencastle
Dunnamore

Killeter
Ulster American Folk Park
TYRONE
Mountfield
Creggan
Kildress
Orritor

Lough Bradan Forest
Drumquin
A505
Drum Manor Forest Park
Cookstown

Omagh
Carrickmore
B4
Tullyhogue

Kesh
Camowen
Pomeroy
The Rock

White Island
A35
Dromore
The Diamond
Ballynchatty
Seskinore
Gortaclare
Sixmilecross
Galbally
Donaghmore

Getting There and Around

By Air

Daily services fly from Glasgow and Manchester to the City of Derry Airport, and there are also daily flights from Dublin to Sligo Airport, about 40mins' drive from Bundoran. There are numerous flights to Donegal Airport from Glasgow, and daily flights from Dublin.

City of Derry Airport, near Eglinton, t (028) 7181 0784, www.cityofderryairport.com. This lies about 40mins' drive from Letterkenny, and has connections with Paris and Brussels.

Donegal Airport, Carrickfinn (between Dungloe and Crolly), The Rosses, t (074) 954 8284, www.donegalairport.ie

Sligo Airport, Strandhill, Co. Sligo, t (071) 916 8280, www.sligoairport.com

By Rail

Daily services from Belfast to Derry, and Dublin to Sligo.

Translink, Belfast, t (028) 9066 6630, www.translink.co.uk

By Bus

Express bus services are operated between Dublin and Letterkenny by Bus Éireann. If you want to travel to less populous areas of Co. Donegal, you have to take local buses.

Bus Éireann, Letterkenny, t (074) 912 1309

Feda O'Donnell Coaches, t (074) 954 8114. A daily service to Galway and Belfast airport.

John McGinley, t (074) 9135201, www.johnmcginley.com. Buses between Inishowen, Letterkenny and Dublin, and Glasgow and Donegal.

Lough Swilly Bus Company, Derry and Donegal, t (074) 912 2863. A firm linking various towns, including Ballyshannon, Bundoran, Donegal, Killybegs and Letterkenny.

McGeehan's, t (074) 954 6150. Buses from Donegal town to Dublin, regular services to Glencolmcille and Dungloe, and also trips to Ardara, Killybegs, Kilcar and Carrick.

North West Busways, t (074) 938 2619. Buncrana–Letterkenny.

By Bike

The Raleigh Rent-a-Bike network operates here. The local dealers are:

The Bike Shop, Waterloo Place, Donegal Town, t (074) 972 2515

Church Street Cycles, Letterkenny, t (074) 912 6204

Getting to Tory Island

A passenger ferry operates daily between Tory and Bunbeg (75mins), Magheraroarty (40mins) and Portnablagh (Wed only). Contact Donegal Coastal Cruises for times of sailings, t (074) 953 1320/1340. Sailing is subject to the weather and tide.

though, curiously enough, 'Official Irish' is based on the Leinster dialect. The Ulster dialect has more in common with Highland Gaelic than with the southern strain. There are strong links with Scotland; many districts of Glasgow are reputed to be like parishes of west Donegal, and you will see buses going from places like Annagry all the way to Glasgow. Part of Donegal is officially Irish-speaking (the Gaeltacht).

History

The county of Donegal has a large proportion of Neolithic and early Bronze Age remains. The main monument that survives from prehistoric times is the Grianan of Aileach, near Burt, a superb structure dating in parts back to the Iron Age, 1700 BC and perhaps earlier. The northern Uí Néill kings occupied it as their royal seat c. AD 700. In Donegal the two important branches of this clan were the O'Neills and the O'Donnells, who became great rivals. The chief of the O'Donnells was known as the Prince of Tirconnell. In about 850, the Vikings settled in Inishowen and along the north-west coast (hence the Gaelic name of the county). The main County Donegal

Getting to Arranmore Island

There are roughly 6 sailings a day year-round, taking 25mins; call t (074) 952 0532.

Festivals

All dates vary from year to year. For details of those listed below where a number or website is not provided, contact the Letterkenny tourist office, t (074) 912 1160. For festivals in the Inishowen district, call t (074) 937 4933.

March

Hillwalking Festival, Ardara, t (074) 954 1518/ 41830. Mid-month.

April

Cup of Tae Festival, Ardara, t (087) 242 4590, www.cupoftaefestival.com. Traditional music.
Hillwalking, Glencolmcille, t (074) 973 0248, www.oideas-gael.com

May

Music, Poetry and Singing, Traditional Cottage, Muff, t (074) 938 4024

June

Buncrana Folk Festival, Inishowen. Late June.
McGlinchey Summer School, Clonmany, Inishowen, t (074) 9376110. A celebration of Inishowen's local traditions, history, folklore and music.

Portnoo/Rosbeg Seafood Festival, t (074) 954 5339
Weavers' Fair, Ardara, t (074) 954 1103

July

Buncrana Music Festival, t (074) 936 1397
Earagail Arts Festival, Letterkenny, www.eaf.ie
Killybegs Sea Angling Festival, t (074) 973 1137.

July

Donegal Town Summer Festival. July–Aug.
Dungloe Festival. Family-oriented music.
Orange Procession, Rossnowlagh (12th).
Rathmullan Community Festival, t (086) 245 3223

August

Ballyshannon Folk and Traditional Music Festival, t (074) 9851088, www.ballyshannonfolkfestival.com
Fiddle Festival and Fiddle Music Summer School, Glencolmcille, t (074) 973 0248
Kilcar Street and Sea-angling Festivals, t (074) 973 8337
Busking Festival, Milford, t (074) 915 3669

September

Harvest Fair, Glenties
Muff Festival. One of the largest country fairs for music and singing, north of Derry.
Traditional Music Festival, Carrick, t (074) 973 9297
Oyster Festival, Moville and Greencastle

clans clashed endlessly, and the Norman warlords laid waste to Inishowen, and constructed Greencastle on Lough Swilly. The wars between the O'Donnells, the O'Dohertys and other Irish *septs* continued for centuries, but towards the end of the 16th century two chiefs, Red Hugh O'Donnell and Hugh O'Neill, combined their powers in an effort to prevent the English from taking over. They were defeated at the battle of Kinsale in 1601 and made their way to the Continent in 'The Flight of the Earls'. This took place from the shores of Lough Swilly, near Rathmullan, in 1607 (*see* **History**, p.12). The Plantation began with Scots and English undertakers being given land and founding towns.

Between 1632 and 1636, the *Annals of the Four Masters* were compiled by Franciscan monks at Bundrowes, close to Bundoran. These annals have come down to us as a valuable source of Irish history. In 1841, the population of Donegal was at its height of 196,448. Then disaster struck with the Great Famine, which affected the west and north of Donegal very badly. In 1921 Ulster was partitioned, and Donegal was cut off from its natural hub of Derry.

South Donegal

Bundoran to Donegal Town

If you come up from Sligo along the superb sweep of Donegal Bay you will encounter one of Ireland's older seaside resorts, **Bundoran**. On its long main street you will find a typically uninspiring hotchpotch of hotels, amusements and souvenir shops, but nearby are wonderful beaches and the Bundoran Golf Course, one of the best-known courses in Ireland.

For those who are avoiding populous resorts, **Ballyshannon**, 5–6 miles (8–9½km) up the coast from Bundoran, is ideal. It is said to have been founded in 1500 BC when the Scythians settled a colony on a little island in the Erne estuary. The Scythians were an offshoot of the Phoenician peoples who were supposed, in one version of the early history of Ireland (there are many), to have colonized areas of the north. It has its own poet, the bard of Ballyshannon, William Allingham, whose lines –

Up the airy mountain,
Down the rushy glen,
We daren't go a hunting
For fear of little men

– must have been chanted by many generations of children. **The Lakeside Centre (*Ionad Cois Locha*)** on Belleek Road, on the shore of Assaroe Lough, provides wool-weaving demonstrations and lots of watersports. During the summer months a waterbus plies its way up and down the lough on storytelling trips for children; the trip lasts about one hour. **Abbey Assaroe Mill (*t* (071) 985 1580)**, just outside Ballyshannon and off the R231 Rossnowlagh road, was built by the Cistercians in the late 12th century, and has now been restored by local enthusiasts. It houses a local craft gallery, an interpretative centre and a coffee shop.

Nearby are the sands of **Rossnowlagh**. If you are here around 12 July you may witness the last-remaining Orange procession on this side of the Northern Ireland border. Otherwise, Rossnowlagh is known for its surfing. At the **Franciscan friary** (Centre of Peace and Reconciliation, *see* 'Sports and Activities', p.444), before you reach the pretty little town of Ballintra, you will find the diminutive **Donegal Historical Society Museum** (*open daily 10–6; **t** (071) 985 1342*), run by the Donegal Historical Society. It has a few interesting items, including a piece of Muckish glass made from mica mined in the Muckish Mountains, which you will see as you go further north.

Donegal Town is the meeting point of roads that travel into the heart of Donegal, to the north and west. On the River Eske, with a long history of habitation for its strategic site, it is a crowded, busy place even without the tourist buses that congregate near the hotels on the Diamond. (A diamond – or 'square' to most visitors – is an area where fairs and gatherings were held; in the Plantation period it was placed in the shadow of the castle to guard against the fighting that was a feature of these occasions.) The town is no one of the best places to buy Donegal **tweed**. Try Magee's shop in the Diamond, and the craft village on the Ballyshannon Road.

Tourist Information

Bundoran: t (071) 985 2683.
Closed Sun and Nov–Mar.
Donegal Town: t (074) 972 1148

Internet Access

The Blueberry Tearoom, Castle St,
Donegal Town, t (074) 972 2933

Shopping

Books
Four Masters Bookshop, The Diamond,
Donegal Town, t (074) 972 1526

China and Crystal
Barry Britton, Rossnowlagh, t (071) 985 2220.
Crystal wares.
Celtic Weave China, Cloghore,
Ballyshannon, t (071) 985 1844

Crafts
Donegal Town Craft Village (just outside town
on road to Sligo), t (074) 972 2225. Donegal
tweed, woodwork, batik, pottery, *uilleann*
pipes, stonework, ironwork and jewellery.
Glencolmcille Folk Village Shop,
t (074) 973 0017. Soaps, flower wines,
St Brigid's crosses and honey.
Laurence Herron, The Heritage Centre,
Donegal Town t (074) 974 1704.
Sculptures made of local bog wood.
Niall Bruton, Donegal Craft Village,
Donegal Town, t (074) 972 2225.
Hand-crafted jewellery.
The Present Company and Crooked
House Gallery, Quay St, Donegal Town,
t (074) 972 1999
Studio Donegal, Donegal Town,
t (074) 973 8194. Hand-weaving.
Taipéis Gael, Glencolmcille, t (074) 973 0325.
Naturally dyed, spun and woven tapestry.
Week-long tapestry courses are available.
Triona Design, Ardara, t (074) 954 1422. Tapestry.

Food and Drink
Simple Simon, The Diamond, Donegal Town,
t (074) 972 2087/2687. Health foods.

Tweeds and Knitwear
Bonners, Ardara
Cindy Graham, Handweaver, St John's Point,
Dunkineely, t (074) 973 7072. Subtle blends
of colours inspired by the Donegal landscape.
John Molloy Ltd, The Diamond, Donegal Town,
t (074) 972 2882; Ardara (factory), t (074) 954
1133; and Glencolmcille, t (074) 973 0282,
www.johnmolloy.com
Kennedy of Ardara, Ardara, t (074) 954 1106
Magee of Donegal, The Diamond,
Donegal Town, t (074) 972 1100,
www.mageeclothing.com
Studio Donegal Handwoven Tweed,
Kilcar, t (074) 973 8194
The Tannery, Mountcharles, t (074) 973 5675

Sports and Activities

Beaches
There are Blue Flag beaches at **Bundoran**,
Rossnowlagh and **Naran/Portnoo**.
Those best beaches in the area for
swimming are **Silver Strand**, at Malin Bay,
and **Glencolmcille**.

Courses
Oideas Gael, Glencolmcille, t (074) 973 0248,
www.oideas-gael.com. Courses in dancing,
flute and *bodhrán* playing, archaeology,
hill-walking, pottery, tapestry, weaving and
marine painting.
Taipéis Gael, Glencolmcille, t (074) 973 0325,
taipeisgael@eircom.net. Week-long arts
courses in summer.

Fishing
Sea-angling is available in most parts of
Co. Donegal, especially in the Killybegs region.
Boats are also available for hire in Ardara and
Portnoo. For charters, contact:
Bundoran Sea Angling, t (071) 984 1874
Donegal Bay Charters, Donegal Town,
t (074) 972 3191
Killybegs Angling Charter, t (074) 973 2007
Killybegs Boat Hire, t (074) 973 1288
West Donegal Sea Angling, Bunbeg, t (074)
954 8403, *www.donegalseaangling.com*
There are also many salmon and trout
rivers and loughs in Donegal. For information

on **game fishing** in the south and south-west area, contact:
The Northern Regional Fisheries Board,
Ballyshannon, **t** (071) 985 1435, *www.nrfb.ie*

Golf
Bundoran Golf Club, t (071) 984 1302, *www.bundorangolfclub.com*. One of the best courses in the country, dating back more than 100 years. It runs along the high cliffs above Bundoran beach.

Indoor Leisure Centre
Waterworld, Bundoran, **t** (071) 984 1172, *www.waterworldbundoran.com*

Outdoor Activity Centre
Malinmore Adventure Centre, Malin Bay, Glencolmcille, **t** (074) 973 0123. Scuba-diving, canoeing and boat trips.

Pilgrimages and Retreats
The Franciscan friary in Rossnowlagh, the Centre of Peace and Reconciliation (**t** (071) 985 1342/2035), offers guesthouse accommodation and retreats in a quiet, reflective ambiance.
On Lough Derg, **St Patrick's Penance** (**t** (071) 986 1518/1546), a place of pilrimage since early-Christian times, is open to pilgrims during the summer season.

Pleasure Cruises
There are hour-long waterbus cruises on **Donegal Bay**; sailing times are posted on Donegal Pier, **t** (074) 972 3666.
Nuala Star, Teelin,Carrick, **t** (074) 973 9365, Sightseeing trips to Europe's highest marine cliffs, at Slieve League.

Ponytrekking
Donegal Equestrian Centre, Bundoran, **t** (071) 984 1288, *www.donegalequestrianholidays.com*. Trail-riding holidays.

Walking
There is good hill-walking to be had on Slieve League (*see* p.447).
Details on walking the signposted **Ulster Way** are available from the Planning Department, DCC, Lifford, or the Long-distance Walking Route Committee, Cospair, 11th floor,

Hawkings House, Dublin 2. You do need to plan ahead, as landowners must be asked for permission first (they are very anxious about insurance claims against them).
The Blue Stack Way, Ardara, **t** (074) 973 5967, *www.thebluestackway.com*
Oideas Gael, Glencolmcille, **t** (074) 973 0248, *oidgael@iol.ie*. Walking holidays.
SOS Walking, Letterkenny, **t** (074) 913 5206, *info@sosdonegal.com*. Donegal walking tours and *céili* nights.

Where to Stay
Portnason House, Ballyshannon, **t** (071) 985 2016, *www.portnasonhouse.com* (*expensive*). A Georgian house close to the sea, which has elicited rave reviews. The antique brass beds and rolltop baths are a highlight.
St Ernans House Hotel, St Ernans Island, Donegal Town, **t** (074) 972 1065, *www.sainternans.com* (*expensive*). A lovely place in a charming situation on a wooded tidal island, though some might find the décor a little too colour-coordinated.
Sand House Hotel, Rossnowlagh, **t** (071) 985 1777, *www.sandhouse-hotel.ie* (*expensive*). An excellent manor-house hotel – friendly and comfortable, with delicious food and lots of opportunities for sporting enthusiasts, especially surfers.
Castlemurray House Hotel, St John's Point, Dunkineely, **t** (074) 973 7022, *www.castlemurray.com* (*moderate*). A small, comfortable hotel with fine French food prepared by its dedicated chef-owner, and lovely views.
Rhu Gorse, Lough Eske, near Donegal Town, **t** (074) 972 1685, *rhugorse@iol.ie* (*moderate*). A modern, family-run country house boasting views over Lough Eske and the Blue Stack Mountains.
Ardnamona House, Lough Eske, near Donegal Town, **t** (074) 972 2650 (*inexpensive*). A wonderfully hospitable place with magical views over landscaped gardens and superb food. It is famous for its rhododendrons, and for originally being the family home of 20th-century poet Rupert Brooke. Small functions and parties are catered for.

Campbell's Holiday Hostel, Glenties, t (074) 955 1491, *campbellshostel@eircom.net* (*inexpensive*). A decent youth hostel.

Dooey Hostel, Glencolmcille, t (074) 973 0130 (*inexpensive*). A large, friendly hostel.

Gallagher's Farm Hostel, Bruckless, t (074) 973 7057 (*inexpensive*). A hostel in converted farm buildings.

The Green Gate, Ardvally, Ardara, t (074) 954 1546 (*inexpensive*). B&B in a traditional cottage with a host who charms visitors into a sense of what life must have been like in Donegal a century ago (apart from the bathrooms and central heating). It's best experienced in the warmer months, when you can enjoy the glorious surroundings. Smokers are welcome.

Self-catering

Ardnamona Cottage, Lough Eske, t (074) 972 2650 (*inexpensive*). A pretty self-catering cottage in a traditional yard, surrounded by a lovely arboretum and scenery.

Bruckless House, Bruckless, t (073) 37071, *bruc@bruckless.com* (*inexpensive*). A charming 18th-century house with Oriental influences in its décor, overlooking Donegal Bay. The hosts, who speak French and Chinese, will point you in the right direction, whether your interest is walking, prehistoric monuments or just exploring. There's a mature garden.

Eating Out

Castlemurray House Hotel, St John's Point, Dunkineely, t (074) 973 7022 (*expensive*). Superb French cooking in a lovely hotel (*see* opposite) with beautiful views. It's very popular, so book ahead.

Harvey's Point Restaurant and Country Hotel, Lough Eske, Donegal Town, t (074) 972 2208, *www.harveyspoint.com* (*moderate–expensive*). Continental food in beautiful surroundings.

Bay View Hotel, Killybegs, t (074) 973 1950, *www.bayviewhotel.ie* (*moderate*). A hotel-restaurant serving mainly seafood.

Le Chateaubrianne, Sligo Rd, Bundoran, t (071) 984 2160 (*moderate*). A good place for seafood, steak and poultry dishes, and for Sunday lunch.

Harbour Restaurant, Quay St, Donegal Town, t (074) 972 1702 (*moderate*). Seafood, lasagne and the likes.

Kitty Kelly's, Killybegs Rd, Kilcar, t (074) 973 1925, *www.kittykellys.com* (*moderate*). A welcoming cottage restaurant that does tasty variations on Irish standards such as lamb stew.

The Smuggler's Creek Inn, Rossnowlagh, t (071) 985 2366 (*moderate*). Good fish and duck for dinner, Sunday lunches and traditional music (*see* below).

An Chistin, Ulster Cultural Foundation, Glencolmcille, t (074) 973 0213/0248 (*inexpensive*). Seafood, salads and soups. *Closed Nov–Feb.*

The Blueberry Tearoom, Castle St, Donegal Town, t (074) 972 2933 (*inexpensive*). Good vegetarian choices, including quiche and lasagne. Staff make a fair attempt at real coffee, and there's also internet access.

Glencolmcille Folk Village Tearoom, t (074) 973 0017 (*inexpensive*). Home-made scones, bread and soups. *Closed Nov–Easter.*

Nancy's Bar, Ardara, t (074) 954 1187 (*inexpensive*). Delicious oysters and burgers. *Closed winter.*

Entertainment and Nightlife

Traditional Music

Look in the local newspapers for traditional and popular music sessions, which change venue all the time.

Corner House, Ardara, t (074) 953 1078. Frequent sessions under the wing of the musician-owners, whose offspring are professional Irish dancers.

Glen Tavern, The Greenans, Glenties, t (074) 955 1170

Nancy's Bar, Ardara, t (074) 954 1187. Traditional music weekends after St Patrick's Day and almost nightly June–mid Sept.

Piper's Rest, Main St, Kilcar, t (074) 973 8205

The Scotchman, Donegal Town, t (074) 972 2022

The Smuggler's Creek Inn, Rossnowlagh, t (071) 985 2366. Traditional music Sat night and Sun afternoon.

Thatch Pub, Dorrian's Imperial Hotel, Main St, Ballyshannon, t (071) 985 1147

Donegal Castle (*open mid-Mar–Oct daily 9.30–6; adm; t (074) 972 2405*), which was once a stronghold of the O'Donnells, the Princes of Tirconnell, and was then taken over by the planter Brooke family, is a handsome stone ruin that dates from the 15th century. It incorporates a square tower and turrets built by the O'Donnells in 1505, and the Jacobean house constructed by Sir Basil Brooke in 1610. Also of interest is the monument in the Diamond to the Four Masters. *The Annals of the Four Masters* is a history of old Ireland written by three brothers called O'Clery and O'Mulconry, who were scholars and monks. The brothers were tutors to the O'Donnells and stayed for a while at the nearby abbey, situated where the River Eske and the sea meet. They wrote this great work between 1632 and 1636. It records an Irish society that was fast disappearing as the English and Scottish were settled in Ireland. Visitors might be interested in the **Donegal Railway Heritage Centre** (*t (074) 972 2655, www.cdrrl.com*), at The Old Station House, which takes a nostalgic look back at Donegal's narrow-gauge railways.

Further inland from Donegal Town lies the pilgrim's shrine of **Lough Derg**. Although most holy tradition in Donegal is associated with St Columba (Colmcille), the island is known as **St Patrick's Purgatory**, and between June and August it is the scene of one of the most rigorous Christian pilgrimages. People come here from all over the world to do penance, just as they did hundreds of years ago. The pilgrims stay on a small island on Lough Derg for 36 hours. They eat and drink only bread and water, stay up all night praying, and wear no shoes while making the Stations of the Cross. Information can be obtained from the Priory, St Patrick's Purgatory, Lough Derg, Pettigo (*t (071) 986 1518*). You can't actually visit St. Patrick's Purgatory unless you are a pilgrim, but it's quite a sight from the lough shore and certainly worth stopping for.

Closer at hand is the lovely **Lough Eske**, where there is good fishing for trout. It is close to beautiful walks in the low range of hills called the **Blue Stack Mountains**. Overlooking Lough Eske is a superb rhododendron garden at **Ardnamona House**, best seen from April to mid-June. Ardnamona is also a very good guesthouse, among the most memorable of places to stay in Ireland (*see* 'Where to Stay, p.444). There is an admission charge for the gardens.

Donegal Town is a few miles away from the **Gaeltacht**, which begins after Killybegs. The Gaeltacht forms the officially recognized Irish-speaking area where government grants encourage the local people to stay put. Here you can walk into a shop or bar and catch fragments of true Irish, one of the oldest recorded Aryan languages. It is a strange language: rich, almost soft, but shot through with harsher, guttural tones. It is poignant and moving but not melodious. The spoken English of Gaelic-speakers is, on the other hand, soft and poetic, as though through translation they have made a second language of it.

Around the Coast: Mountcharles to Glenties

Follow the N56 as it goes through **Mountcharles**, with its splendid view of Donegal Bay, **Bruckless** and **Dunkineely**. These towns were all centres of the now-defunct lace industry, and they are still good places to buy hand-embroidered linen and the subtly patterned Donegal jumpers and rugs. There is a fine collection of early Irish portraits that can be viewed at **Ballyloughan House** (*call t (074) 973 1507*) in Bruckless.

The narrow, winding and climbing road leads you to **Killybegs**; in the summer, bordering hedgerows bloom with honeysuckle and fuchsia, and as you get further west the sweet, acrid smell of peat hangs on the damp air. Here you reach the most important fishing port in Ireland, which is set to expand even further to the tune of 62 million euros so that it can accommodate even bigger fishing vessels. There are plenty of sea-angling boats for hire here, and in July the place is full of people come to enjoy the Sea Angling Festival. In the Catholic **church** there you can see the fine sculptured medieval grave slab of Noall Mór MacSwyne, which was found near St John's Point (this, by the way, is a lovely peninsula with a beautiful beach and views, signposted left from Dunkineely).

The highly paid fishing and processing industry has brought great prosperity to Killybegs. It is quite a sight to stand and watch the catches of haddock, plaice and sole being unloaded. The famous **Donegal Carpet Factory** started up here in the 1890s, headed by a Scottish weaver, Alexander Morton. The hand-knotted carpets were often designed for palaces and embassies all over the world. The factory (*on Kilcar road out of Killybegs, t (074) 973 9810, www.donegallusa. com*) re-opened and is producing some original designs in pure wool; the showroom is well worth a visit.

Beyond Killybegs, you will encounter some of the grandest scenery in Donegal; the great cliffs of Bunglass, Scregeigther and **Slieve League** are amongst the highest in Europe, rising to a height of 1,972ft (601m). If you walk along the cliffs from Bunglass along One Man's Pass, a jaggedy ridge, on a clear day you will be rewarded with fantastic views stretching right down to County Mayo. The determined bird-watcher should be able to see puffins and cormorants here, and the botanist should be able to find Arctic alpine species on the back slopes of Slieve League.

The village of **Teelin**, under Slieve League, is popular with students on Irish-language courses, while **Kilcar** is the site of the *Gaelterra Éireann* factory of fabrics and yarns. The wools are hard-wearing and flecked with soft colours, and you can buy them here in the craft shop and all over County Donegal. This is also a centre for hand-woven tweed, and you might also like to visit **Studio Donegal** (*t (074) 973 8194, www. studiodonegal.ie*), hand-weavers in the village.

Glencolmcille should be visited next. A local priest called Father McDyer established a rural co-operative here in order to try to combat the flight of youth from the village through emigration. He helped the local economy greatly, and there is now a craft shop where you can buy hand-made products such as jams, soaps and wines made from gorse or bluebells. The village has also become one of the most important centres for Irish culture and music, with its wealth of visitors who come in search of the best traditional pub 'session' in Ulster.

Glencolmcille Folk Village and Museum (*open Easter–Sept Mon–Fri 10–6, Sun 12 noon–6; tea-rooms open during season; adm; t (074) 973 0017, www. glenfolkvillage.com*) constitutes three cottages, each representing different periods of Irish life . There is also a 3½mile (5km) **pilgrimage walk** along the valley here, around 15 cross slabs and pillars, which is known as the Stations of the Cross. It includes many of the ancient sites of the area, and begins with a Stone Age court-grave, which is among other attractively carved gravestones in the yard of the 14th-century St Colmcille's Church. The Stations of the Cross are still performed on 9 June, which is St Columba's Day. Notice the beautifully built stone and turf sheds with their thatched roofs that abound in this area. The countryside is full of prehistoric antiquities, dolmens, cairns (including a famous horned cairn called Clochanmore), and ruins of churches connected with St Columba.

From Glencolmcille, an expedition can be made along a winding, narrow road to the tiny bay and long-deserted village of **Port**. The sea-cliffs here have been fashioned into wonderful shapes, including a huge sea-stack of 486ft (148m). For Ireland's most beautiful beach, however, you need to go 5 miles (8km) along the road south-west, following the clifftops to the Silver Strand at **Malin Bay**. This gorgeous bay is sheltered by high cliffs all around, and the water is as clear as Waterford crystal.

At the village of Malinmore is **Glencolmcille Woollen Mill** (*t (074) 973 0070, www. rossanknitwear-glenwoolmill.com*), known for its hand-woven traditional and modern knitwear, designer products and crafts; it also has a demo area and shop.

On the other side of the mountain, through the spectacular Glengesh Pass, you arrive at **Ardara**, another centre for Donegal tweed and Aran sweaters. Some lovely sweaters at very reasonable prices can be bought here (or at Glencolmcille). The **Andara Heritage Centre** (*open Easter–Oct daily 10–6; t (074) 954 1704*), on the Main Street, tells the history of tweed in the area. Nancy's Bar, also on Main Street, is famous for its fresh oysters and atmosphere.

If you follow the road to **Maghera Caves**, signposted just outside Ardara on the road to Donegal Town (N56), you will come to another of the most beautiful beaches in Ireland. The single-track road from here unfolds a series of wonderful views of mountains, the sea inlet of **Loughros Beg Bay**, traditional farms, and near the end, a waterfall. The walk to the caves and beach takes you through someone's farm and over sand dunes, so don't overload your picnic baskets.

If you travel a few miles on to the next little peninsula of Dunmore Head you will come to **Portnoo** and **Naran**, two popular beaches for holidaymakers from Northern Ireland. At Naran, you can park or hire caravans. There is a fascinating fort near here, built on an island in Doon Lough (beside Naran). It is more than 2,000 years old and is a very impressive sight – a circular stone fort that spreads over most of the island. It can easily be seen from the lough shore. At the neck of this peninsula you go from **Maas**, a small fishing resort, to **Glenties** (*Na Gleannta*: 'The Valleys' – so-called because of its position at the junction of glens), which is a good place for knitwear. There is a striking **church** designed by the innovative contemporary Irish architect, Liam McCormick, who is responsible for many fine churches in County Donegal. This one was built in the 1970s. Patrick McGill (1891–1963), novelist and poet, was born here; his semi-autobiographical novel *Children of the Dead End* sold very well in England but was considered anti-clerical in Ireland.

Northern Donegal

Gweebarra Glen to Gortahork

All along the north-west coast you will see mountain ranges broken by long river valleys that reach into the hinterland. Any route along these valleys brings you across the harsh mountainous areas where beauty is bleak and the cost of wresting a living from the poor soil is no longer acceptable.

There is a rather zigzag road from Fintown to Doocharry that brings you into the **Gweebarra Glen**. North-east of this, between the Derryveagh and Glendowan Mountains, the valley extends into **Glenveagh**, which is now part of a National Park. However, you should keep heading out towards the sea on the road to Dunglow (also spelled 'Dungloe' – the 'g' is silent) if you want to see '**The Rosses**', as this area is called. The Irish name is *na Rosa*, meaning 'Headlands', and is a good clue to the landscape. Although this area is going through a housing boom, it is still one of the most charming routes you can take to the north coast; loughs large and small are scattered through the hilly country, and the beaches are lovely.

If you make your way to Burtonport, which is an attractive fishing port, there is a regular ferry to **Aranmore Island**. You can enjoy a good day's exploration of the island: there is good cliff scenery to be viewed in the north-west, and it has a rainbow trout lake, Lough Shure. **Cruit Island** can be reached from the mainland by a connecting bridge. From here you can look out at Owey Island, and across at Gola Island with their deserted cottages. Despite the difficulties that the islanders had to face, such as hard weather conditions, no services and bureaucratic indifference to their needs, most of them did not want to leave their homes, and many return for the summer or for fishing. Several cottages are being restored as holiday homes. Boat hire must be negotiated with the local fishermen; none of them likes to be tied down to taking people out on a regular basis. Try the pubs and ask around. **Bunbeg** has an attractive 19th-century harbour and close by at **Carrickfinn** is Donegal airport, with daily flights from Glasgow and Dublin. The locals speak Irish and it is a favourite area for Irish summer schools.

Further north, past Bloody Foreland, in the heart of the *Gaeltacht*, is **Gortahork** ('Garden of Oats'), a small town on one arm of Ballyness Bay. It has a great strand that curves out into the sea, nearly locking the shallow bay in from the ocean. If you are here in the evening you can see cattle fording the waters back to the home farms. You might visit **Teach Mhici Mac Gabhann** (*t (074) 913 5555*), a 17th-century thatched cottage that was the birthplace of author Mickey McGowan.

Errigal and Muckish Mountains

Looking inland from Gortahork, you cannot help but notice the glorious outlines of the mountains. Errigal is cone-shaped, and Aghla More and Aghla Beg form a spaced double peak. Muckish means 'pig's back' in Irish, and you will see it is aptly named. You can approach these mountains from this angle, or take the road from Bunbeg, past the secret **Dunlewy Lough**, which is overlooked by a roofless white church.

Tourist Information

Letterkenny: Blaney Rd, t (074) 912 1160,
www.donegaldirect.com

Shopping

Crafts

Avalon Craft Shop, 19 Academy Court,
Letterkenny, t (074) 912 7939
Cavanacor Craft Centre and Gallery,
Ballindrait, Lifford, t (074) 914 1143. Crafts,
pottery and contemporary watercolours by
local, national and international artists.
Design Studio, Port Road, Letterkenny,
t (074) 912 5312
The Gallery, Dunfanaghy, t (074) 913 6224.
Paintings, antiques and knitwear.
Geraldine Hannigan, 4 Port Rd, Letterkenny,
t (074) 25312. Jewellery and crafts.
Lakeside Centre, Dunlewy, t (074) 953 1699
The Pottery and Tea Room,
Moyra, Falcarragh, t (074) 913 5330

Pottery

Cavanacor Studios, Cavanacor House,
Ballindrait, Lifford, t (074) 914 1143. Delicate
off-white bowls, plates and sculptures.
Robert Moore, Cashel, Creeslough,
Letterkenny, t (074) 391 8130.
Celtic-style pottery.

Tweeds and Knitwear

Falcara Ireland, Falcarragh, t (074) 913 5861
McNutts of Downings, t (074) 915 5314

Sports and Activities

Beaches

There are Blue Flag beaches at **Marblehill**
and **Portsalon**.

Fishing

Sea-fishing is good in most parts of
Co. Donegal, especially in Rathmullan. Boats
are available for hire in Dungloe, Dunfanaghy
and Falcarragh. For charters, contact:
Fisherman's Village Lodge, Downings,
t (074) 915 5080, *www.rosguill.com*
Port-na-Blagh, Dunfanaghy, t (074) 916 6197

Rathmullan Enterprise Group,
Rathmullan, t (074) 915 8131
There are many rivers and loughs in
Donegal for **game-fishing**; the Clady River,
which runs through Bunbeg and Gweedore,
is renowned. Out of season, call t (071) 985
1435. Or for information on areas in northern
Donegal, contact:
Loughs Agency, Northern Regional Fisheries
Board, t (048) 8166 2267.
Foyle Fisheries, Derry, t (028) 7134 2100.

Genealogy Centre

Donegal Ancestry, The Quay, Ramelton,
t (074) 915 1266, *www.donegalancestry.com*

Golf

Otway, near Rathmullan, t (074) 915 8319. A
fun 9-hole course on the edge of the Swilly.
Portsalon, t (074) 915 9459. A course running
above the beautiful Ballymastocker Bay.
Rosapenna, t (074) 915 5301. A championship
links course, the best part of which runs in a
low valley along the ocean.

Outdoor Activity Centre

Gartan Outdoor Education Centre,
Churchill, near Letterkenny, t (074) 913 7032,
www.gartan.com. Canoeing, rock climbing
and windsurfing.

Ponytrekking

See *www.finnvalley.ie/tourism* for
further information.
Black Horse Stables, Cashelshannaghan,
Letterkenny, t (074) 955 1327
Dunfanaghy Riding Stables, Arnold's Hotel,
Dunfanaghy, t (074) 913 6208
Finn Farm Hostel and Trekking Centre,
Cappry, Ballybofey, t (074) 913 2261
Golden Sands Equestrian Centre,
Rathmullan, t (074) 915 8124
Inishfree Equestrian Centre,
Atlantic View, Braade, Kincasslagh,
near Letterkenny, t (074) 954 8226
Tirconaill Stables, Kilmacrennan, t (074) 953 9252

Walking

Hill-walking is good on **Muckish** and **Errigal**.
Details about walking the **Ulster Way** can be
obtained from the Planning Department, DCC,

Lifford, or the Long-distance Walking Route Committee, Cospair, 11th floor, Hawkings House, Dublin 2. You need to ask landowners for permission first.

Walk with a ranger or by yourself on **Glenveagh Estate**; or take walking holidays organized by *Oideas Gael*, Glencolmcille, t (074) 973 0248, *www.oideas-gael.com*.

Co. Donegal now has **mountain rescue teams** based at Gortahork, Gweedore and Falcarragh; in emergencies, call **t** 999.

Watersports

Mevagh Dive Centre, Carrigart, Letterkenny, t (074) 9154708, *www.mevaghdiving.com*. A purposebuilt, year-round centre.

Where to Stay

Shandon Hotel, Spa and Wellness Centre, Marble Hill Strand, Port-na-Blagh, near Dunfanaghy, t (074) 36137, *www. shandonhotel.com* (*luxury*). A large family hotel with fine food and a spa and wellness centre, new in 2006, with a herb sauna, salt grotto, ice fountain and more. Most guestrooms overlook the sea, and for kids there's a playcentre and dedicated pool.

Arnold's Hotel, Dunfanaghy, t (074) 913 6208, *www.arnoldshotel.com* (*expensive*). A fine, old-fashioned hotel in a pretty village overlooking Sheep Haven.

Castle Grove Country House, Castlegrove, Letterkenny, t (074) 915 1118, *www.castlegrove. com* (*expensive*). A marvellous Georgian house in wooded grounds overlooking Lough Swilly, with well-appointed rooms and good food (*see* p.452).

Fort Royal Hotel, Rathmullan, t (074) 915 8100, *www.fortroyalhotel.com* (*expensive*). A fine period house with a family atmosphere.

Rathmullan House Hotel, Rathmullan, t (074) 915 8188, *www.rathmullanhouse.com* (*expensive*). An 18th-century country house on the edge of Lough Swilly, with beautiful gardens and excellent food in its dining room. There's also a cosy bar with a turf fire, a heated swimming pool and a sandy beach.

Frewin, Letterkenny Rd, Ramelton, t (074) 915 1246, *www.accommodationdonegal.net*, (*moderate–expensive*). A luxurious Victorian stone manor house, once a rectory. The elegant bedrooms have large bathrooms and woodland views. Dinner is available by prior arrangement.

Bunbeg House, The Harbour, Bunbeg, t (074) 953 1305 (*moderate*). A guesthouse with a restaurant and tea-rooms, overlooking Bunbeg harbour.

Glen Hotel, Aranmore Island, t (074) 952 0505 (*moderate*). A friendly family-run option by the sea. The restaurant offers kids' meals.

Ostan Thoraigh **Hotel**, Tory Island, t (074) 913 5920 (*moderate*). A cosy hotel on a wonderful island. Meals are available.

Viking House Hotel, Belcruit, Kincasslagh, t (074) 954 3295 (*moderate*). A modern hotel owned by a singer. An à la carte menu and children's meals are available.

Croaghross, Portsalon, t (074) 915 9548, *www. croaghross.com* (*inexpensive–moderate*). An elegant, modern country house overlooking Ballymastocker Strand, with good cooking. Of the 6 rooms, 1 is ensuite (and suitable for the disabled). A self-catering holiday cottage is also available.

Ardeen, Ramelton, t (074) 912 1819 (*inexpensive*). A comfortable, friendly house.

Baileant Sleibhe, Downings, t (074) 915 5661 (*inexpensive*). A well-priced B&B. One room has a 4-poster bed.

Corcreggan Mill Hostel, Dunfanaghy, t (074) 913 6507/6409 (*inexpensive*). A basic hostel in a renovated mill and mock railway station, 1¼ miles (2km) out of town. There is also an organic garden.

Errigal Youth Hostel, Dunlewy, Gweedore, t (075) 953 1180, *mailbox@anoige.ie* (*inexpensive*). A hostel rated by the tourist board.

Finn Farm Hostel, near Ballybofey, t (074) 913 2261 (*inexpensive*). A well-run, clean choice.

Greene's Hostel, Cornmare Rd, Dungloe, t (074) 952 1943/1021 (*inexpensive*). A decent hostel.

House on the Mall, The Mall, Ramelton, t (074) 915 1255, *m_bgallagher@yahoo.com* (*inexpensive*). A period home overlooking the River Lennon. Vegan breakfasts are available.

Pier Hotel, Rathmullan, t (074) 915 8115 (*inexpensive*). A small family hotel that's a favourite with locals and foreign fishermen, with plenty of atmosphere. The dining room serves à la carte dishes and children's meals.

Radharc na Mara Hostel, Tory Island, t (074) 916 5145 (*inexpensive*). A reasonable hostel.
Screagan Iolair Hostel, Crolly, near Gweedore, t (074) 954 8593 (*inexpensive*). A remote hostel with free pick-up from the N56.
Teach Campbell, Magheraclogher, Derrybeg, t (074) 953 1545 (*inexpensive*). A modern house by the pounding Atlantic, in the middle of the *Gaeltacht*, with excellent home-cooking.
Tra na Rosann, Downings, t (074) 915 5374 (*inexpensive*). The An Oige hostel.

Eating Out

Castle Grove Country House Hotel, Ramelton Rd, near Letterkenny, t (074) 915 1118 (*expensive*). First-rate cooking in a great hotel (*see* p.451).
Rathmullan House Hotel, Rathmullan, t (074) 915 8188 (*expensive*). Fresh, original cooking with vegetables from the hotel's walled garden. Sunday lunch here is good value.
An Bonnán Bui, Pier Rd, Rathmullan, t (074) 915 8453 (*moderate*). A small bistro offering excellent food with South American influences.
Bunbeg House, The Harbour, Bunbeg, t (074) 953 1305 (*moderate*). A cosy family-run place serving healthy snacks and simple vegetarian meals, plus heartier food. It also offers accommodation (*see* p.451).
Danann's Restaurant, Main St, Dunfanaghy, t (074) 913 6150 (*moderate*). A place worth visiting for its seafood specialities.
Danny Minnies, Teach Killindarra, Annagry, near Dungloe t (074) 954 8201 (*moderate*). Fish platters and à la carte dishes.
Jackson's Hotel, Ballybofey, t (074) 913 1021 (*moderate*). Excellent salmon and ham, and good bar lunches.
Kee's Hotel, Stanorlar, Ballybofey, t (074) 913 1018 (*moderate*). Wholesome food, good service and lower-priced bar food.
The Silver Tassie Hotel, Ramelton Rd, Letterkenny, t (074) 25619, (*moderate*). Good-value, large helpings of traditional fare, especially at lunch.
The Yellow Pepper Restaurant, Letterkenny, t (074) 91 24133, www.yellowpepperrestaurant. com (*moderate*). A converted late-19th-century shirt factory, offering a varied menu of tasty dishes served by friendly staff.

Acquolina Restaurant, Lifford, t (074) 914 1733 (*inexpensive–moderate*). A restaurant in the basement of the old courthouse, serving lunch and Italian cuisine in the evenings.
Bakersville, Church Lane, Letterkenny, t (074) 712 1887 (*inexpensive*). Yummy croissants, cakes, bread and sandwiches.
Cavanacor Tea Room, Lifford, t (074) 914 1143 (*inexpensive*). Home-made scones.
China Tower, Main St, Ballybofey, t (074) 913 1468 (*inexpensive*). Chinese and European food.
Dunfanaghy Workhouse, Dunfanaghy, t (074) 913 6540 (*inexpensive*). A coffee shop that turns into a wine bar in the evening.
Galfees Restaurant, The Courtyard, Letterkenny, t (074) 912 7173 (*inexpensive*). Set menus in the day and early evening, plus good dinners.
Lobster Pot, Burtonport, t (074) 954 2012 (*inexpensive*). Well-priced seafood.
Pat's Pizza, Market Sq, Letterkenny, t (074) 24901 (*inexpensive*). Good pizzas.

Entertainment and Nightlife

Live Music

Look in the local newspapers for traditional and popular music sessions, which change venue all the time. *Céilí* (traditional) music can be heard in the pubs of Falcarragh.
An Teach Ceoil, Fintown
The Bridge Bar, Ramelton, t (074) 915 1833
Central Bar, Main St, Letterkenny, t (074) 912 4088
Dunfanaghy Workhouse, Dunfanaghy, t (074) 913 6540. Summer only.
Ionad Cois Locha, Dunlewey, t (074) 953 1699. Traditional music sessions, June–Aug.
Leo's Tavern, Crolly (signposted *Croichsli*). A famous venue for traditional music; various members of Clannad learnt their skills here.
Mount Errigal Hotel, Ballyraine, Letterkenny, t (074) 912 2700. Dances and music.
Teach Hiúdaí Beag, Bun Beag, t (074) 953 1016

Theatre and Cinema

An Grianan Theatre, Port Rd, Letterkenny, t (074) 912 0777, www.angrianan.com
Balor Theatre, Ballybofey, t (074) 913 1840
Century Cinemas, Leckview Lane, Pearse Rd, Letterkenny, t (074) 912 5050

At Dunlewey, the ***Ionad Cois Locha*** or **Lakeside Centre** (*open Easter–Oct Mon–Fri 10–6, Sun 11–7; t (074) 953 1699*) has a fine craft shop and tea-room, a farm museum, animals and demonstrations in carding, spinning and weaving wool. You can also go on a storytelling trip on the lough, surrounded by its beautiful glens. Hidden behind this is the **Poisoned Glen**, so called either because the water in the lough is unfit to drink because of certain poisonous plants at the water's edge, or, so another story goes, because of the name some French travellers gave it, having caught some fish there. The hill and mountain climbs in this part are quite strenuous, but if you are fit you can tackle them.

Climb **Errigal** from the roadside, and after about an hour you will reach a narrow ridge of 2,400ft (731m), from which you will see Dunlewy Lough on one side and Altan Lough on the other side. Climb **Muckish** from the Gap or the western end. If you go straight for it from the Falcarragh side, you may find yourself going up by the old mine-works, for the mountain used to be worked for its mica, to be used in glass-making; this is a rather dangerous but interesting ascent. The people who lived in the cottages in these lonely sheep glens used to weave Donegal tweed in the evenings, and pass the time singing and composing poetry. The old weaver poets had a good phrase for Muckish, calling it 'an oul turf stack', and so it is: flat-topped, with its outline broken only by the remains of a cross. Looking across to Tory, you will see a huge hole, which is supposed to have been made when St Columba threw his staff from the top of Muckish.

Tory Island

It's possible to catch a regular ferry to **Tory Island** either from the pier at Magheraroarty or from Downings. Bad weather often makes the 7-mile (11km) journey impossible in winter, but if you have time to go, this windswept and barren island is endlessly fascinating. On a sunny day Tory feels rather like a Greek island, with its whitewashed cottages and bright blue and red doors.

The island has just two villages, which are called East Town and West Town. **East Town** is laid out in the traditional *clochan* or family grouping pattern of settlement (*see* p.61). Close to the shoreline in **West Town** are the remnants of St Colmcille's early-Christian monastery. Here you can see a decapitated round tower and a T-shaped cross, which is known as a Tau Cross. There is only one other in Ireland, and that is displayed in the Burren Centre in County Clare (*see* p.254). At the eastern end is **Balor's Fort**, a great rock sticking out into the sea. Balor was the god of darkness, with one eye in the middle of his forehead. Mythology says that he was one of the Fomorii leaders (*see* p.56).

In the summer months you can buy snacks at a tea-room and the café close to the island's only public bar. There is a small hotel, a hostel and several B&Bs here. The population is about 130 and thriving, with a school and a simple Catholic church. The island has become well-known for its fishermen artists, who mostly use house paints to create their naïve-style paintings of seascapes and birds. They were promoted by the landscape artist and portrait painter Derek Hill (1916–2000), whose house and collection of pictures were gifted to the State (*see* Glebe House in Churchill, p.457). You can purchase some of their work at a small exhibition gallery on the island, although a number of the more famous island painters exhibit and sell in Belfast and London.

Falcarragh to Doe Castle

Going back to the coast between Falcarragh and Dunfanaghy, you will see the great granite promontory of **Horn Head**. From a Falcarragh viewpoint, it does indeed look like a horn or rock. You can do a complete circuit by taking the little road that is signposted 'Horn Head Coastal Drive' by the bridge at the top of the main street in **Dunfanaghy**, an attractive village overlooking Sheep Haven, which is experiencing a rash of building as moneyed folk from Northern Ireland build new holiday homes. The road leads you past old **Hornhead House** (*not open to the public*), which was drowned by sand when the bent grass was cut, and then climbs around the rocky farms, giving you dazzling views across Sheep Haven to Melmore Head in the east and back towards Bloody Foreland Head. The road passes a 1940s military lookout post, and from here it is possible to walk to the **Little Horn**, a magnificent cliff that plunges down into the sea. From here there is a good walk ahead of you to an old tower, which takes about 40 minutes – you will need waterproof boots. You can peer over the 300ft (91m) cliff to see if the puffin population is in residence. There are also some caves and blowholes.

Dunfanaghy itself has a couple of good family hotels (*see* p.451) and, on the outskirts, the **Workhouse Heritage Centre and Art Gallery** (*open Mar–Oct Mon–Fri 10–5, Sat and Sun 12 noon–5; adm; t (074) 913 6540*), which tells the famine story and exhibits local artists' work.

Sheep Haven is a complicated indentation with beautiful golden sands and a wooded shore. **Marblehill**, with its special provision for caravans, is a favourite place for holidaymakers. The mystic poet-politician George (A. E.) Russell used to stay here in **Marblehill House**. It is possible to rent apartments in the house and stableyard that overlooks the marvellous long curving beach.

Further on, the **Forest of Ards** provides some scenic walks and splendid views. At **Creeslough**, you can admire another modern church designed by Liam McCormick. Its shape echoes the view of Muckish that you have from there. Otherwise it's a busy village with good shopping and pubs. On the road to **Carrigart** is one of the most romantic castles in Ireland: **Doe Castle**, set on the water's edge (*currently undergoing restoration*). It belonged to the MacSwineys (or MacSwynes), who came over from Scotland in the 15th century. They came to help the O'Donnells fight the encroaching Normans, and the constant small battles that took place with the O'Neill clan. They were part of the influx of mercenary soldiers known as 'gallowglasses' (*see* p.11). The castle was occupied right up until 1890. It had been taken by the English in 1650, and changed hands several times. In 1798 General George Vaughan Harte purchased it; he had been a hero in the Indian Wars, and his initials are carved over the main door. Scramble up the defensive walls for a superb view of Sheep Haven on one side, and on the other the pretty bridge and waterfall of Duntally.

Downings to Portsalon

To get to the **Rosguill Peninsula** you cross a neck of sand similar to the causeway at Horn Head, and arrive at **Downings**. This fishing village is in the holidaymakers' zone of **Rosapenna**, a long-established resort with a good golf course and harbour. You can sail out to the islands of Tory and Inishbofin from Downings; ask about boats in the local post office down by the harbour. Very good tweed is made in this area; try McNutt's shop above the harbour. The beach beside the golf course is huge and unspoilt, and is ideal for a long walk and a swim, if you are hardy. The coastal circuit (R245) leads to the spectacular **Atlantic Drive**. A branch road off this takes you past the **Trá Na Rossan Youth Hostel**, the only house designed by Lutyens in Ulster, and up to the wilder beaches of **Melmore Head**. There are several beaches along this road.

Leaving **Carrigart**, another centre for local crafts, the loughside road takes you down to Mulroy Bay, a narrow-necked lough bordered by the Fanad Peninsula on the opposite side and strewn with wooded islands. Behind Carrigart rises the Salt Mountain. A little moor-bound road crosses this range and comes out near Cranford. High in these mountains is the deepest lough in Ireland, **Lough Salt**. To take advantage of the panorama you should go up to the lough from the Letterkenny–Creeslough road (N56) and look out to the bays stretching from Horn Head to Fanad.

Down the road is **Millford**, a pretty town on a hill near some good fishing at Lough Fern. From Millford you can explore the **Fanad Peninsula** on the old road, which takes you past the Knockalla range by Carrowkeel and into the hidden reaches of **Mulroy Bay**, by Tawny. In this secluded land there survives a very idiosyncratic Gaelic – although it was not untouched by the settlements of the 17th century. Even in their isolation, the Irish and the Scottish settlers remained distinct. At the far eastern point you can see Fanad Lighthouse, which guards the entrance of Lough Swilly and looks across to the Inishowen hills.

The tiny village of **Portsalon** is beautifully situated over **Ballymastocker Bay**, an immense curve of strand. Like all the settlements on the Swilly, it is curiously linked to the opposite view on Inishowen by the water in its landscape, in a way reminiscent of the Greek idea of the sea being a bridge. Rita's Bar, with its blazing fire, is a famous place to retire to after a walk along the beach. The golf course here is well worth playing, and the views are wonderful, although Portsalon is being spoilt by a profusion of holiday houses and caravans.

Just a little way north, along the pretty road to Fanad Head, is the garden of **Ballydaheen** (*open May–Sept Thur and Sat 10–3; adm; **t** (074) 915 9091*). Protected by sheltering belts of trees, the garden's various 'rooms' and styles have flourished, and the views out to the Swilly are lovely. A planted walk leads down to The Seven Arches, a series of interconnecting caves on a tiny rocky beach. The house at the centre of the garden is Japanese in inspiration, and some of the planting and design reflects this.

Rathmullan to Newmills

A terrific coastal drive, which joins the R247, has been built with fabulous views over Lough Swilly and the Urris Hills. This brings you to Rathmullan, nestling in a sheltered plain that borders the Swilly as far as Letterkenny. The whole of **Lough Swilly** has played an important role in many of history's famous episodes. It is deep enough to accommodate modern war-fleets, as it did in the First World War. It has also been the departure route for the Gaelic aristocracy: in 1607 the earls of Tirconnell and Tyrone took their leave for France from here. Lough Swilly has been called 'the Lake of the Shadows' – an apt enough description, although from the Irish it means 'Lake of Eyes' or 'Eddies' (*Loch Suilagh*).

Rathmullan ('Maolán's Ring Fort') is a charming town complete with sandy beaches and lovely views across Lough Swilly. There are often fishing boats moored here as well as leisure craft, and, in the summertime, little boys dive off the barnacled sides of the pier. It is, however, also being rapidly spoilt by tightly packed holiday houses, constructed close to the beach. Kinnagoe Bay, which carries on from Rathmullan Beach, is losing its charm, and the Blue Flag status of the beach has been lost because of water pollution.

The ruined **Carmelite friary** in the town has a romantic air that is borne out by the story behind it. In 1587 Red Hugh O'Donnell was staying in a castle here owned by the MacSwiney clan from Fanad. A wine merchant's ship happened to be lying in the bay, and the reputation of its cargo enticed the young reveller onto the ship. Treachery became apparent as the ship slipped its mooring and carried young O'Donnell off to Dublin Castle, a prisoner of Queen Elizabeth I. He was a great hostage to have captured, for his father was the Lord of Tirconnell, the powerful Sir Hugh O'Donnell, and the son could be used to keep him loyal to the English. Further information is available from the excellent **Flight of the Earls Heritage Centre** (*open Easter–mid Sept daily, call for times* **t** *(074) 9158178; adm; www.flightoftheearls.com*), in the Martello tower by the pier.

One of the most lovely routes in Ireland is the road between Rathmullan and its neighbour, **Ramelton**. It is often spelt on maps as Rathmelton, which translates as 'Mealtan's Fort', but the town you will see is a relatively unspoilt Plantation town built by the Stewart family, one of the so-called undertakers of the Plantation (meaning that they undertook to supply fighting men and build fortified dwellings to subdue and keep the 'wild' Irish at bay). It developed as a prosperous market town, with goods coming up the Lennon estuary from as far away as Tory Island. Ramelton was nearly self-sufficient in the 18th century, with locally made whiskey, linen and leather goods and other small industries, and the Ramelton merchants built themselves fine houses in the Mall. (Letterkenny stole a march on the town fathers when the railway came, and now it is the boom town.) The town is famous for its annual **festival** in July, with its cheerful floats and Queen of the Lennon competition, and for its **pantomime** in February. It is also famous for its thriving bottling industry and a soft drink of cloying sweetness, called McDaid's Football Special. The bottling plant, in a fine 19th-century warehouse overlooking the River Lennon, was used for a recent film, *The Hanging Gale*, set in famine times. The foundations of the building date back to the original O'Donnell Castle. **The House on the Brae**, on the Tank road, has been restored by the local Georgian Society. It is sometimes used for temporary art exhibitions. American Presbyterians will be interested in the old **Meeting House** in the Back Lane, which is early-18th-century. It was here that the Reverend Francis Makemie (1658–1708) used to worship. He was ordained in 1682 and emigrated to America, where he founded the first Presbytery in 1706. It has been restored and houses temporary exhibitions, Donegal's **Genealogy Centre** and a library.

Letterkenny is a thriving town, with factories on the outskirts and new housing enclaves, yet it still manages to maintain a country town appearance, with one long main street that loops round into the Swilly Valley. You can use this town as a centre for expeditions east and west. The **Donegal County Museum** (*open Mon–Fri 10–4.30, Sat 1–4.30; t (074) 912 4613*) on the High Road has a permanent collection of artefacts from early history and folk life, as well as being a venue for travelling exhibitions.

In **Newmills**, 4 miles (6km) to the west of Letterkenny, an old **Corn and Flax Mill** (*open mid-June–Sept daily 10–6.30; adm; t (074) 912 5115*) has been restored, with a visitor centre and a riverside walk to a scutcher's cottage and forge.

Glenveagh, Churchill and Kilmacrennan

If you go through Letterkenny up the Swilly Valley, you reach the countryside where St Columba spent his first years. St Columba was the great Irish missionary who founded a church at Iona. He was born in about AD 521 on a height overlooking the two Gartan loughs. A large cross just on Glenveagh Estate marks the spot. Gartan Clay, which can only be lifted by a family who claim descent from the followers of Columba, has powerful protective properties; soldiers fighting in the First World War carried it. You should follow the road around the lough; if you take one of the forest trails on the Churchill side, a glorious prospect awaits you. The long glen that begins at Doochary on the west coast penetrates this far along the Derryveagh Mountains and into the scenic Glenveagh, parallel to the Valley of Gartan.

Glenveagh National Park (*Glenveagh*: 'Valley of the Birch'; *open 10–6.30 Easter–Sept daily, Oct and Nov Sat–Thur; last adm 5.15pm; restaurant, tea rooms and visitor centre; adm; t (074) 913 7090*), to the west of Churchill, is beautiful and isolated, with a 19th-century fairytale castle outlined against the mountains on the loughside . The gardens were developed by Henry McIlhenny, a millionaire whose grandparents came from these parts, and a visit is recommended. It would be difficult to find another such garden that combines the exotic and natural with so much ease. Henry McIlhenny gave the wild, heathery acres of Glenveagh to be used as a National Park. Deer roam the glen and peregrine falcons nest in the rocky ledges.

Close by in **Churchill** itself, the artist Derek Hill (*see* p.453) bequeathed his house and art possessions to the nation. Signposted from the village, **Glebe House** (*open May–Sept Sat–Thur 11–6.30; adm; t (074) 913 7071*) is a plain Georgian house packed with exquisite and curious *objets d'art*. The gallery's fine international collection includes paintings by Jack B. Yeats, Bonnard, Kokoschka, Basil Blackshaw, Annigoni and Victor Passmore. The gardens are beautifully laid out with shrubs and trees down to the lough's edge. It would be a great pity to miss Glenveagh, St Columb's and the Glebe Gallery, so make it a full day's outing. (If you feel that this may effect a surfeit of castles, galleries and gardens, make sure you tour Glenveagh.)

Close to Churchill, you may wish to drop in at the **Colmcille Heritage Centre**, situated next to the Gartan Outdoor Education Centre, which has a very informative display on days gone by.

On the way back from Glenveagh to Letterkenny you pass through **Kilmacrennan** ('Church of the Son of Enan'), which was named after one of St Columba's nephews. There are some ruins of a 15th-century friary here, but the fame of the place rests on the claim that it was here that Columba received his education. You can have tea at the traditional thatched cottage of **Lurgyvale**, with its displays of old rural implements.

Near here, the Princes of Tirconnell were inaugurated, at **Doon Rock**, about 2 miles (3.2km) on the road to Creeslough. At the curious **Doon Well**, those hopeful of being cured have left tokens; most of them are now rags, although there is a story that a visiting film star left her lipstick.

Raphoe, Lifford and Environs

If you are travelling east from Letterkenny bound for the North, you will find yourself passing through the more prosperous midlands of Donegal, the centre of which is south of here in **Raphoe**, an ancient town with a venerable cathedral, ruined bishop's palace and a pretty village green. Your fellow passengers on the road will probably be bound for the mart, the key of most Irish farmers' lives, and another indication of the importance of Raphoe. St Adomnan who lived in the 7th century founded an early monastery here. He was an O'Donnell like his ancestor St Columba. He wrote a life of Columba that reveals a lot about early-Christian society – at one synod they passed a law exempting women from regular military service. At **Beltany**, between Raphoe and Lifford, just beyond the River Deele, is a stone circle that has some kind of mystical alignment. Archaeologists who examined the site in 1921 suggested that the building had an astronomical purpose because the standing stone in the south-west is an almost perfect equilateral triangle. Its circumference measures 450ft (140m). There are 64 out of a possible 80 stones still standing, and a pleasant view from the top.

Lifford is the administrative centre of the county. The 18th-century courthouse with its **Seat of Power Visitor Centre** (*open Mon– Sat 10–6, Sun 2–6;* **t** *(074) 914 1733*) is attractive. It is open to the public and houses a genealogical centre, a café and a clan centre, which traces the importance of Lifford and the Plantation periods and the role of the dominant clans, including the O'Donnell princes, in the history of Donegal. If you find it open, go inside the **Clonleigh Parish Church** in the middle of the town. Here in an attitude of prayer are the Jacobean stone figures of Sir Richard Hansard and his wife, who gave money for the church to be built.

Outside Lifford, just off the Letterkenny Road at **Ballindrait**, is **Cavanacor Historic House and Craft Centre** (*open Easter–Sept Tue–Sun 12 noon–6; other times by appointment; pottery studio open all year; adm;* **t** *(074) 914 1143*). This 17th-century house, with its fortified yard, was the ancestral home of James Knox Polk, the 11th president of the USA. The house contains late-17th- and 18th-century furniture, and it is possible to tour some rooms and the small museum. Its exhibits are associated with the American Connection and with the historic visit of James II, who dined under the sycamore at the front of the house during the seige of Derry in 1689. The home-made teas here are splendid, and you may browse among the attractive crafts, pottery and watercolour paintings.

In Cloghan, near Ballybofey, you will find the **Isaac Butt Heritage Centre** (*opening hours erratic so call in advance; t (074) 913 3108*), which has a small exhibition on local life and an old school, restored to reflect the period in which Isaac Butt, the founder of the Home Rule movement, lived.

The Inishowen Peninsula

Inishowen (*Inis Eoghain:* 'Eoghain's Island') reaches out to the Atlantic between Loughs Swilly and Foyle, a kingdom of its own. As its name conveys, it forms a different territory to the rest of Donegal, which is part of Tirconnell. This is O'Doherty country. After leaving Letterkenny, you will pass through the rolling plains round Manorcunningham and Newtowncunningham to the neck of the peninsula at **Burt**. An unforgettable sight of this unexplored, almost islanded land can be obtained from the **Grfanán of Aileach** (or Grfanán Aílígh), an ancient stone hill fort. Turn right by an unusually roofed modern Catholic church, another of Liam McCormick's, and climb the unclassified mountain road that gives you views onto the Swilly. Why the Grfanán of Aileach is not as well known as Tara in County Meath, considering its spectacular position and its associations, must be one of the curious twists in the recording of history. Besides the circular stone fort and its terraces, there are three stone and earth ramparts, and underneath the Hill of Aileach there are said to be underground passages connecting the hilltop with Scalp Mountain, which overlooks the village of Fahan, about 6 miles (9.6km) further down the peninsula. There is an old story that the sleeping heroes of the past lie within the hill, to be wakened at Ireland's hour of need. The fort dates from about 1700 BC and, according to the *Annals of the Four Masters*, it was the seat of power for the Northern O'Neill kings from the 5th to the 12th centuries. It was destroyed by their enemies in AD 675 and 1101. The fort guards all approaches, which is the reason why it affords such good views over the Foyle and the Swilly.

Inch Island, signposted off the main Buncrana–Londonderry Road, is a beautiful place. At the crossroads by the local shop, take the right turn to **Inch Fort** and **Brown's Bay** and look across the limpid water to Fahan, or you might go for a swim. There is an O'Doherty Clan Centre here, the **Doherty Research Centre** (*t (074) 936 3998*). **Fahan** is famous for its St Mura's Cross in the Church of Ireland graveyard. This 7th-century two-faced cross with mythological birds and ecclesiastical figures is all that remains of the rich Abbey of St Mura. Here in the rectory in 1848, looking across to Inch Top Hill, Cecil F. Alexander wrote 'There is a Green Hill Far Away'.

There is a beautiful beach with lovely views all around that stretches up to **Buncrana**, a standard seaside resort with the usual run of amusement arcades. The Crana River is noted for salmon fishing and there are some pretty walks that

Tourist Information

Buncrana: t (074) 936 2600.
Open May–Sept exc Sun.
Inishowen: Carndonagh, **t** (074) 937 4933,
www.visitinishowen.com.
Closed Sat and Sun exc mid-June–Aug.

Shopping

Crafts

Crana Artists Network, Tullyarvan Mill,
Buncrana, **t** (074) 936 1613
Curious Glass, Burt, **t** (074) 936 8633.
Glassware.
Irish Knitting Centre, Lisfannon,
Buncrana, **t** (074) 936 2365. A centre
tracing the history of traditional patterns.
Mary Barr, Main St, Buncrana

Sports and Activities

Beaches

There is a Blue Flag beach at **Culdaff**.

Fishing

There are many salmon and trout rivers
and loughs in Donegal – the Crana River is
renowned for its salmon. **Sea-fishing** is also
available on Inishowen.
Inishowen Boating Co., Malin, **t** (074) 937 0605.
Sea-angling charters.
Loughs Agency, t (048) 8166 2267
Northern Regional Fisheries Board,
t (071) 985 1435

Golf

Ballyliffin, Inishowen, **t** (074) 937 6119,
www.ballyliffingolfclub.com. The most
northerly golf club in Ireland, with lovely
views over the Atlantic and 18 holes.
North West Golf Club, Fahan, **t** (074) 936 1027.
A gentle, rolling, sandy course overlooking
the Swilly.

Indoor Leisure Centre

Leisureland, Redcastle, **t** (074) 938 2306

Ponytrekking

Inch Island Stables, t (074) 936 0335
Lenamore Stables, Muff, **t** (074) 938 4022

Walking

Hill-walking is good on **Scalp Mountain**.
Contact the tourist office for details.
Oideas Gael, Glencolmcille, **t** (074) 973 0248,
www.oideas-gael.com. Walking holidays.

Where to Stay

Redcastle Hotel, Redcastle, Inishowen,
t (074) 938 2073, *www.redcastle.ie*
(*expensive*). An old Plantation house in
a lovely setting, with rather heavy décor
that has detracted from its charm. It's
popular with the Northern Irish.
Inishowen Gateway Hotel, Buncrana, **t** (074)
936 1144, *www.inishowengateway.com*
(*moderate*). A modern hotel on the shores
of Lough Swilly, with leisure centre and
fitness facilities.

lead close to the dilapidated early-17th-century Buncrana Castle and the O'Doherty
keep. Just outside Buncrana, at Lisfannon, on the Derry road, is the **Irish Knitting
Centre** (*t (074) 936 2355*), which traces the history of traditional patterns. Also of
interest is the restored **Tullyarvan Mill** (*t (074) 936 1613*), in Buncrana on the Crana
River; this is the base for Artlink, a community art group, and provides a space for
temporary art exhibitions and traditional music functions. It is to be found off the
scenic coast route signposted 'Inis Eoghain 100'; the mill is signposted on the right
after the bridge.

Close by at Dunree is the **Fort Dunree Military Museum** (*open June–Sept Mon–Sat
10–6, Sun 1–6; adm; t (074) 936 1817*), a restored coastal defence battery depicting
200 years of coastal and military history. It has a wonderful view and a fascinating
account of Wolfe Tone's plans to land with French help and take Derry in 1798.

Malin Hotel, Malin, Inishowen **t** (074) 937 0606, *www.malinhotel.ie* (*moderate*). A comfortable little family-run hotel.

Malin Head Hostel, Malin, **t** (074) 937 0309 (*inexpensive*). A clean and comfortable hostel, with an organic garden and orchard that visitors can use.

Sandrock Holiday Hostel, Malin Head, **t** (074) 937 0289 (*inexpensive*). Bunkbeds in ensuite dorms in a building overlooking the strand.

Trean House, Tremone, Lecamy, **t** (074) 936 7121, *www.treanhouse.com* (*inexpensive*). Farmhouse accommodation on a working farm a 5min walk from the beach.

Self-catering

Mamore Cottages, Clonmany, **t** (074) 937 6710, (*inexpensive*). Traditional Irish cottages with open fires, sleeping 7.

Rock Cottage, Goorey Rocks, Malin, **t** (074) 937 0612 (*inexpensive*). A cottage sleeping 2–4 people.

Eating Out

Kealy's Seafood Restaurant, Greencastle, Inishowen, **t** (074) 938 1010 (*expensive*). Award-winning seafood. Lunches are more moderately priced.

Holly Tree Restaurant, Ballyliffin Lodge, Ballyliffin, **t** (074) 937 8200, *www.ballyliffinlodge.com* (*moderate*). A hotel-restaurant with an award-winning head chef with a reputation for his gourmet fare. There's also a traditional Irish pub serving superior pub food.

The Niche Restaurant, Carndonagh, **t** (074) 937 4137 (*moderate*). A restaurant set in a restored 19th-century house, owned by a pair of chefs who met on the QE2. The cuisine is a tasty blend of east and west influences and flavours.

The Seaview Tavern, Ballygorman, Malin Head, **t** (074) 937 0117 (*moderate*). Seafood fresh from the local harbour, in a building at the most northerly point on the Inishowen 100 circuit.

McGrory's of Culdaff, Inishowen, **t** (074) 937 9104 (*inexpensive*). Bar food, traditional music Tue and Thur (*see* below), and accommodation.

Entertainment and Nightlife

Live Music

Look in the local newspapers for traditional and popular music sessions, which change venue frequently.

The Flough, Muff, **t** (074) 938 4024. A good place for songs, dances, poems and home-baking, mainly during the summer months.

McGrory's, Culdaff, **t** (077) 937 9104, *www.mcgrorys.com*. A well-known music venue (and guesthouse; *see* above), with performances Tue and Thur.

Teach Ceoil, Ballyliffin, **t** (074) 937 6124. A house of music and traditional entertainment on Tue and Thur evenings in July and Aug.

Buncrana to Muff

Take the R238 through the mountains to reach the spectacular **Mamore Gap**, from which you can gaze back at the view of the Fanad Peninsula. There are plenty of good beaches along the way if you take the longer coastal road, including **Linsfort** and **Dunree**. On the other side of the Mamore Gap, past **Clonmany**, are the beaches around the Isle of Doagh. This is truly unspoiled country, full of fuchsia hedges and little whitewashed cottages. At Clonmany you'll find the **Doagh Visitor Centre** (*open daily Easter–Oct 10–5.30; adm; t (074) 937 8078*), an outdoor museum of life as it was here in the 1870s.

In the Church of Ireland graveyard at **Carndonagh** you can look at some interesting monuments, including the Marigold Stone, which has the same ornamentations as St Mura's Cross. By the roadside opposite the church, meanwhile, is one of the most widely famed crosses in Ireland, because it is believed to be the oldest low-relief cross in the entire country, dating from around AD 650. This richly decorated and well-preserved cross must have been erected by a prosperous and settled community in those far-off times.

The most northerly village in Ireland, **Malin**, boasts a pretty green and has twice had the honour of being named 'Ireland's tidiest town'. It provides us with a good example of a well-preserved 17th-century Plantation village, with a fine church. Nearby is lovely **Five Fingers Strand**.

If you want to take a peek at the most northerly tip of Ireland, **Malin Head**, which will be familiar to those who listen to radio shipping forecasts, take a road that passes some extensive sand dunes and you will come to a pebbly cove where you can pick up semi-precious stones. The old signal tower located at Banba's Crown, at the very tip of Malin Head, was the last sight of Ireland for many of the emigrants as they left by ship. From Malin Head you can see lighthouse islands. From here to Glengad Head are cliffs rising to more than 800ft (246m). To the east of **Culdaff** are some fine sandy beaches.

All of this area constitutes fine walking country; the cliff scenery is interspersed with great stretches of sandhills. You can choose whether to walk around Malin Head itself, or head southwards towards **Inishowen Head**. Or visit yet another cross, 2 miles (3.2km) to the south of Culdaff in **Clonca**. This impressive shaft, which is called **St Boden's Cross**, is almost 12ft (4m) in height and is carved with a scene depicting the miracle of the loaves and the fishes.

On the road from Culdaff to Moville, in **Carrowblagh**, is an example of an ancient **sweat-house** – the Irish form of a sauna. The almost enclosed room was heated like an oven, and, having sweated thoroughly, you were next immersed in cold water. This was said to be the cure for aching bones and temporary madness.

Greencastle is a beach resort with the remains of a 14th-century castle built in 1305 by Richard de Burgh, the Red Earl of Ulster, who needed it as a strategic base from which to try to dominate the O'Donnells of Tirconnell (most of Donegal) and the O'Dohertys of Inishowen. The **Maritime Museum** (*open daily June–Sept 10–6; adm; t (074) 938 1363, www.inishowenmaritime.com*) in the old coastguard's house is full of interest, with a room on the Armada and Emigration. Further down the coast you come to **Moville**, formerly a point of departure for many emigrants to the New World. It is now a leisure resort with a well-planted green, lined with seats from which you can comfortably gaze at the sea or have a picnic.

At **Cooley**, 1½ miles (3km) to the north-west, is a 9ft-high (3m) cross and the remains of a chapel with a corbelled stone roof. The area between Moville and Muff has many planter castles. They are known as castles, but are actually Big Houses, and you get glimpses of them through the trees as you pass by. One of them, Redcastle, is now a luxury hotel; some would consider it ruined with all its modern embellishment. Behind them rise rather forbidding mountains, though if you venture on the mountain roads you will come across lost *clochans* and megalithic monuments, where yellow raspberries cluster beneath the hedges in July.

County Cavan

Cavan is a dreamy, unspoilt county. Although it is completely landlocked, there are attractive stretches of water everywhere, scattered as it is with lakes and rivers abounding with fish. It is a favourite county for coarse fishermen, many of whom come over from England for the huge catches. For the city-dweller in search of quiet, it is a perfect holiday place.

The countryside is pretty and interspersed with woods. The hills or *drumlins* that were left behind by a glacier in earlier times offer plenty in the way of wild glens. The highest mountain in the county is Cuilcagh, at 2,100ft (640m). On its southern slopes is the source of the great Shannon River, which flows out to the sea as far away as County Clare. Along the winding roads you will hardly meet a soul, for the population here is only 53,000. Most people are farmers, and many offer bed and breakfast accommodation.

Cavan is an undiscovered county to those who are not in the angling league, and this is undeserved. The ancient history of the county lingers on in the form of various charming, ruined castles and abbeys, and mysterious stone monuments

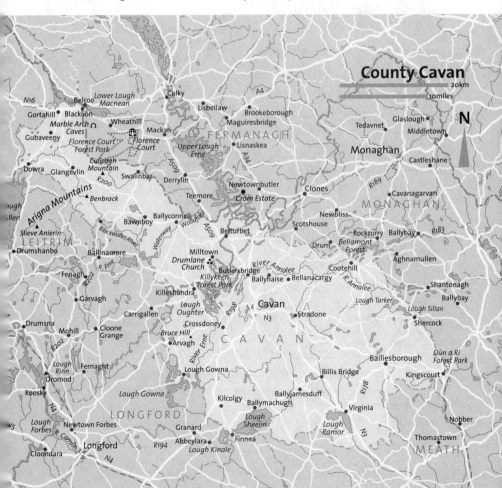

Getting There and Around

By Rail
There is no train service in Co. Cavan.

By Bus
Expressway buses stop in Cavan on their way between Belfast, Enniskillen, Galway and Dublin. The smaller towns are served by local buses.
Cavan Bus Depot, t (049) 433 1353/2533.

By Bike
Fitz Hire, Bridge St, Belturbet, t (049) 952 2866

Festivals

March
Cavan Drama Festival, t (049) 433 1942

May
County Cavan *Fleadh Cheoil*, t (049) 433 1942

June
Festival of the Lakes, Killeshandra, t (049) 433 4429. Music, dance, children's entertainment, powerboat racing and angling competitions.
Killinkere Whit Jamboree, Killinkere, t (049) 48102 or t 0863 112289. Car races, concerts and a busking competition.
Virginia Street Fair, t (049) 854 8299. Vintage cars, machinery and music.

July
Belturbet Festival of the Erne, t (049) 952 2781. A large family festival with watersports, music and heritage events, held late July–early Aug.

August
Knockbride Vintage and Heritage Festival, Bailiesborough, t (042) 966 5282. Displays of vintage cars and machinery.

October
Cootehill Arts Festival, t (049) 555 2150. Music, arts and crafts, drama and literature.

Tourist Information
Cavan: Farnham St, t (049) 433 1942, *www.cavantourism.com*. Open Mar–Oct.

Shopping

Crafts
Carraig Crafts, Mountnugent, t (049) 854 0179
Celtic Crafts, Ballyconnell, t (049) 952 6499. *Closed Sat Apr–Oct, Nov–Mar exc by request.*
St Kilian's Heritage Centre Craft Shop, Mullagh, t (046) 42433

Crystal
Cavan Crystal Factory, Dublin Rd, Cavan Town, t (049) 433 1800, *www.cavancrystaldesign.com*. Guided factory tours Mon–Fri.

Food and Drink
Back to Nature, Main St, Cavan Town, t (049) 436 1019. A health-food shop with good picnic supplies.
Corleggy Farmhouse, Belturbet, t (049) 952 2930, *www.corleggy.com*. Delicious goats' cheese flavoured with herbs and peppers, sold at an old-style farm where pigs wander about the yard.
Main Street, Kingscourt. Shops selling *Dun a Ró*, a Gouda-like farmhouse cheese.

Sports and Activities

Fishing
There is **coarse fishing** in most of Cavan's loughs. Particularly good spots are loughs Oughter, Inchin, Gowna and Bunn. The

dating from the Bronze Age and the Iron Age. Because it is in the lakelands, there are a number of *crannóg* sites and figures left over from pagan times. One of the most curious finds from west Cavan is the three-faced Corleck Head, a rare example of a pagan Trinity figure, which now resides in the National Museum in Dublin.

Woodford and Annalee rivers are also excellent. Look out for Hugh Gough's great book on coarse fishing in County Cavan.
Butlersbridge Trout Anglers, Annagh Lake, Butlersbridge, t (049) 437 8384
International Fishing Centre, Loughdooley, Belturbet, t (049) 952 2616. Tackle and bait.
Northern Regional Fisheries Board, Corlesmore, Ballinagh, t (049) 433 7174
Shannon Regional Fisheries, t (049) 433 6144.

Golf

Belturbet Golf Club, Erne Hill, t (049) 952 2287
Blacklion Golf Club, t (071) 985 3024
Cabra Castle Golf Course, Kingscourt, t (042) 966 7030. A 9-hole woodland golf course in an attractive setting.
County Cavan Golf Club, Drumelis, t (049) 433 1283, *www.cavangolf.ie*
Slieve Russell Hotel, Ballyconnell, t (049) 952 6444, *www.quinnhotels.com*. A championship golf course.

Pleasure Cruises

Shannon–Erne Waterway, t (078) 44855

Ponytrekking

Cavan Equestrian Centre, Shalom Stables, Latt, Cavan, t (049) 433 2017
Killykeen Equestrian Centre, Killeshandra, t (049) 61707
Redhills Equestrian, Killynure, Redhills, t (047) 55042

Steam Train Rides

Cavan and Leitrim Railway, t (071) 963 8599, *www.irish-railway.com*. An old-fashioned vintage train ride running Mon–Sat Sept–June 10–2.30, July and Aug 10–5, plus Sun all year 1–5.30.

Walking

The **Cavan Way** is a 15-mile (24km) marked trail that runs from Blacklion to Dowra and passes prehistoric monuments, a sweathouse

near Legeelan and wonderful views. It also goes close to the Shannon Pot, the source of the Shannon (350yds/300m south of the trail). Information and leaflets are available from West Cavan Community Council, Blacklion, t (049) 433 1799, Tourism Ireland and at Ballyconnell, t (049) 952 6121.

There are easier walks in **Killykeen Forest Park**, 2 miles (3km) north of Killashandra on the R201; at **Mulrick**, 1½ miles (2.5km) southwest of Lough Gowna village, on the edge of the lough; in **Dún a Rí Forest Park**; and at **Castle Lake**, a mile (1.6km) north of Bailieborough on the R178.

Where to Stay

Cabra Castle Hotel, Kingscourt, t (042) 966 7030, *www.cabracastle.com* (*luxury*). A 15th-century pile with landscaped gardens, stables and a golf course. The gastronomic restaurant serves all-Irish produce. Self-catering units are available.
The Slieve Russell Hotel, Golf & Country Club, Ballyconnell, t (049) 952 6444, *www.quinnhotels.com* (*luxury*). A hotel built by a local millionaire, with marble columns, fountains and Jacuzzis, a spa/leisure centre, 3 restaurants, and 300 acres of parkland with lakes and a championship golf course.
Park Hotel Virginia, t (049) 854 6100, *www.parkhotelvirginia.com* (*moderate–expensive*). An attractive old hunting lodge beside Lough Ramor, with a modern 9-hole golf course.
Sunnyside House, Lough Gowna, t (043) 83285 (*moderate*). A friendly, well-run B&B in what was, at the end of the 19th century, a doctor's residence. It has a rose, herb, fruit and vegetable garden, and is popular with fishing folk. Dinner is available.
Lisnamandra Farmhouse, Crossdoney, just west of Cavan Town, t (049) 433 7196, *lisnamandra@eircom.net* (*inexpensive*).

Christianity percolated slowly through this lakeland maze, and even up to the 17th century some of the recorded devotions to saints had a pagan flavour. A principal shrine of the Celtic gods in Ireland was at Magh Sleacht near Ballyconnell, but there is nothing left of it now.

An award-winning traditional-style farmhouse a 10min drive from Lough Oughter, offering its guests a very restful atmosphere, comfortable bedrooms and home-cooking.
Riverside House, Cootehill, t (049) 555 2150, *unasmith@eircom.net* (*inexpensive*). An old farmhouse overlooking the tree-lined River Annalee. It has high ceilings, elegant plasterwork and open fires in the main rooms. The hostess is an expert on fishing matters, and a boat with an engine can be used by guests. She also cooks delicious 5-course evening meals that are a bargain.
Rockwood House, Cloverhill, Belturbet, t (047) 55351, *jbmac@eircom.net* (*inexpensive*). Accommodation in a reconstruction of a rectory that stood here in the 1860s, surrounded by woodland and gardens.
St Kyran's, Dublin Rd, Virginia, t (049) 854 7087 (*inexpensive*). A simple B&B in a lovely setting on the shore of Lough Ramor.

Self-catering
See also Cabra Castle Hotel, p.465.
Killykeen Forest Chalets, Killykeen Forest Park, t (049) 433 2541, *www.coillte.ie* (*inexpensive*). Wooden chalets and log cabins in Killykeen Forest Park.

Eating Out
The opening of the **Shannon–Erne waterway** has been a boon for tourism, and more new restaurants and bars will no doubt appear.
MacNean Bistro, Blacklion, t (071) 985 3022/3404 (*expensive*). Imaginative cooking by renowned TV chef Neven Maguire, such as fillet of ostrich with *rösti*. Mostly locally grown organic produce is used. The desserts are highly lauded.
Casey's Steak Bar, Main St, Ballinagh, t (049) 433 7105 (*moderate*). The place to come for the best steaks in Ireland, according to some people.

The Imperial Bar, Main St, Cavan Town, t (049) 437 3027 (*moderate*). A very roomy and comfortable spot serving generous portions of good food on a daily menu, with steak a speciality. *Closed dinner exc Sat and Sun.*
The Olde Post Inn, Cloverhill, t (047) 55555, *www.theoldepostinn.com* (*moderate*). A renovated former posthouse with atmospheric gas lamps. The pork is always good, as the pigs are fed on the whey of Corleggy cheese. *Closed Mon.*
Park Hotel Virginia, t (049) 854 6100 (*moderate*). A hotel-restaurant serving imaginative and ambitious cooking.
Derragarra Inn, Butlersbridge, t (049) 433 1003 (*inexpensive*). An attractive pub by the river, serving lots of seafood, and hosting traditional music on Fri during summer.
Kloisters, Main St, Cavan Town, t (049) 437 1485 (*inexpensive*). A good atmosphere for pub grub..
White Star, White Star, Main St, Cavan Town, t (049) 433 1477 (*inexpensive*). Tasty pub lunches served amidst rustic, old-fashioned décor. *Closed eves.*

Entertainment and Nightlife

Live Music
Cathal Brady's, 1 Thomas Ashe St, Cavan Town, t (049) 433 1338. Traditional music Tue evenings at 10.
Louis Blessing's Pub, 92 Pearse St, Cavan Town, t (049) 433 1138. Occasional jazz.
McGinnity's, Bridge St, Cavan Town, t (049) 433 1236. A winner of the Regional Pub of the Year Award, hosting traditional music.
Ramor Theatre, Virginia, t (049) 854 7074
White Star, Main St, Cavan Town, t (049) 433 1477. A venue for traditional Irish music nights.

History
Cavan, created in 1584 by the British Lord Deputy, was part of the ancient Kingdom of Breffni, and its Gaelic rulers were the O'Reillys, who held on to power until the division of the county amongst Scottish and English settlers in the 1600s.

In the 19th century the county suffered greatly from the famine and the consequent mass emigration. It had a small linen industry, now defunct, as elsewhere in the north. Along with County Donegal and County Monaghan, it is separated politically from the rest of Ulster. This happened in 1921 with the division of Ireland into the 26-county state and the continuing allegiance of the other six Ulster counties to Britain.

Cavan Town and Around

Cavan (*An Cabhán*: 'The Hollow'), the inconspicuous county town, was important as an O'Reilly stronghold in the ancient kingdom of East Breffni. Their castle, **Clough Oughter** (pronounced 'ooter'), is a well-preserved Irish circular tower castle about 3 miles (5km) outside Cavan on an island in Lough Oughter. You approach it from the Crossdoney–Killashandra road and the wooded splendour of Killykeen Forest Park. It is possible to get out to the island if you hire a boat. This 13th-century tower is built over a *crannóg* and looks very romantic, viewed from the lakeside. Its history is more sinister. It was used as a prison by the Confederates in the 1641 rebellion, and Eoghan Roe O'Neill, the great leader of the Confederates, died here in 1649, poisoned, it is thought, by his Cromwellian opponents. North of Cavan Town, **Lough Oughter** is the name given to an entire region of small- to medium-sized lakes, an offshoot of the River Erne complex. This is a well-known coarse fishing area. **Lough Inchin** is noted for pike fishing, though recently roach have been introduced. The **Killykeen Forest Park** (*t (049) 433 2541*) is a good access point to the loughs.

There are some worthwhile diversions around Cavan, including **The Pighouse Collection** (*call in advance for guided tour; adm; t (049) 433 7248*), a vast accumulation of clothing, tools, kitchenware, and the other necessities of Irish rural life, some going back 300 years; the name comes from the pigsty where they used to keep it all. It is in Corr House, Cornafean, near Crossdoney (take the R198 west out of Cavan Town). On the road to Arvagh, continuing along the R198, is **Bruce Hill** (755ft/260m), worth climbing for the view. During the times of the Penal Laws, when Catholics were forbidden to build churches, Mass was celebrated here in the open air. If you like ornate cut glass, take the opportunity to buy a bit of Cavan crystal from the factory shop on the Dublin Road (N3), on the outskirts of town.

For those interested in prehistoric sites, a few miles out of Cavan on the R188 north-west to Blacklion on Shantemon Hill, off the Cootehill Road, are **Finn MacCool's Fingers** – standing stones within which the princes of Breffni, the O'Reillys, were crowned. (Many prehistoric standing stones are named after heroes of Irish legend.) **Ballyhaise** is a pretty, neat village on the River Annalee, reached by an unclassified road off the R198 going north out of Cavan Town. It has a rather grand arcaded market hall. Nearby is **Ballyhaise House**, built in 1733 and designed by Richard Cassels, who also designed Leinster House in Dublin. It is worth asking to go around it (it is now an agricultural college) to see the lovely oval saloon and plasterwork. It is also worth stopping in **Butlersbridge**, another pleasant village on the Annalee, to lunch at Derragarra Inn (*see* opposite). The fishing is reputed to be good here too.

North Cavan

Another lakeland town is **Belturbet** on the N3 north of Cavan. It is now a thriving angling and boating centre, and was once a depot for the traffic on the Ulster Canal, which might be somewhat revived now that the canal has been reopened. A boat trip along here is like driving on Irish roads fifty years ago, it is so unspoilt; you will barely even see a house. At **Milltown**, on the north end of the loughs, is a site associated with the 6th-century St Maodhóg; the site later became an Augustinian monastery, though today little remains but the ruined **Drumlane Church** and a truncated round tower. Look out for the faint carving, on the north side, of a cock and a hen. The church has a lovely Romanesque doorway.

Going north-west along the N87, you reach **Ballyconnell**, which is now a stopping place on the Shannon–Erne waterway, set on Woodford River. The 17th-century Protestant church here has a carved stone with a human head that came from a medieval monastery. In the grounds of the church it is possible to make out the outlines of two diamond-shaped fortifications dating from the Williamite Wars. The village is a pleasant base for fishing or hill-walking.

Three miles (5km) to the south-west, at **Killycluggin**, is a stone circle that once contained an ornamental phallic stone. You can see it on display at Cavan County Museum (*see* opposite).

For walkers, about 5 miles (8km) to the west on the N87 is the tiny hamlet of **Bawnboy**, which is on the way to some pretty glens and mountains. You can climb 1,148ft (350m) to **Glen Gap** between the peaks of Cuilcagh and Benbrack. For a panoramic view of the neighbouring counties, take the N87/R200 to Glangevlin (also known as Glengevlin), and go through Glen Gap to the summit of the Cuilcagh Mountains. **Blacklion**, a small village on the Fermanagh border, is delightfully situated between Upper and Lower Lough MacNean in the limestone foothills of the Cuilcagh Mountains. It has a frontier post into Northern Ireland but, more importantly for walkers, from here you can walk up to **Lough Garvagh**, **Giant's Cave**, and **Giant's Leap**. These names refer to legendary figures whose origins are lost in the mists of time. For instance, nobody knows who built the fine *cashel* 3 miles (5km) away at Moneygashel Post Office near **Burren**, south of Blacklion. It consists of three beautifully built stone walls. The central *cashel* is 82ft (25m) in circumference and has a rampart 10ft (3m) thick, with internal and external stairways. Inside the south *cashel* is a beehive-shaped **sweathouse** – a kind of Irish sauna that was still popular a century ago. Burren was an important Neolithic centre, and if you have the time to seek them out there are numerous dolmens in the neighbourhood, including the aforementioned 'Giant's Cave', and a 'rocking stone'.

The **Cavan Way**, a signposted trail, passes prehistoric monuments, a sweathouse and wonderful views (*see* p.465). It also goes close to the **Shannon Pot** (350yds/300m south of the trail), the 'eye', where an underground river surfaces to become the source of the mighty Shannon. Just over the border from Blacklion in County Fermanagh are the famous **Marble Arch Show Caves** (*see* 'County Fermanagh', p.351).

Swanlinbar, further to the south-east of this hilly country, is another frontier village. It was once known as the Harrogate of Ireland because of its sulphur baths. **Dowra**, at the western tip of Cavan, sits beside the Shannon at a point where the great river is still barely a stream; to the east of it you can inspect another long surviving section of the great ancient earthwork called the **Black Pig's Dyke** that stretches across much of northern Ireland.

Eastern Cavan: Cootehill to Ballyjamesduff

Cootehill, which is situated on the county border about 15 miles (24km) north-east of Cavan Town, is a market town that was named after the Coote family, who 'planted' the area with their followers in the 17th century. The Church of Ireland church at the end of its long main street is in the attractive planters' Gothic style. Nearby, to the north of the town in Bellamont Forest, is **Bellamont House**, built by Thomas Coote and designed by the famous Irish architect Sir Edward Lovett Pearce in 1730. It is a beautiful Palladian mansion which fell into decay and was lovingly restored by an Englishman. It has been claimed by an Australian descendant, but at the moment its future is uncertain and it is not open to the public. This is a great pity, since the interiors are spectacular.

The village next to Cootehill, **Shercock**, is rather pretty, with a fine plain Presbyterian meeting house set on the shores of **Lough Sillan** – a good lake for coarse fishing. This is a wooded and lake-studded country.

Seven and a half miles (12km) to the south-east is **Kingscourt**. Look in the Catholic church for the delightful stained-glass windows designed by the Dublin artist Evie Hone (1894–1955). Just over a mile (1.6km) away is **Dun a Rí Forest Park**, where you can picnic by the pretty Cabra River. There are planned walks and nature trails here. You might see a wild deer amongst the trees. It was the former demesne of the Pratts of Cabra – their castle home is now a hotel (*see* p.465).

Beautifully situated on the edge of Lough Ramor is **Virginia**, a village that was founded in the reign of King James I but named after his aunt, Queen Elizabeth I. It is the most southerly of the Ulster Plantation villages. Dramatist Richard Brinsley Sheridan lived here, and so did the parents of the other famous Sheridan, General Philip Sheridan of the American Civil War. Although the Protestant population has dwindled since pre-Independence, the centrepiece of the village is still the Protestant **church**, which is approached down a straight avenue of clipped yews. There are some pretty, rusticated cottages in the main street. It is a very attractive and well-planned town, with graceful trees; and the shops have traditional painted signs. The lough is beautiful, and is full of little islands.

To the north-west is **Ballyjamesduff**, home to the **Cavan County Museum** (*open Tue–Sat 10–5, Sun 2–6; adm;* **t** *(049) 854 4070, www.cavanmuseum.ie/ www.heritageisland.com*), set in a magnificent 19th-century building and containing various historical displays, medieval carvings, some of the clutter from The Pighouse

Collection (see p.467) and the ornamental phallic stone from the stone circle at Killycluggin (see p.468). Ballyjamesduff was made famous by a song written by the humorous writer and singer Percy French in the early years of the 19th century. At one time French worked as Inspector of Drains with the Cavan County Council. His songs are beloved of Irish emigrant communities all over the world:

> *There are tones that are tender, and tones that are gruff,*
> *And whispering over the sea*
> *Come back, Paddy Reilly, to Ballyjamesduff,*
> *Come back, Paddy Reilly, to me.*

County Monaghan

This pleasant, sheltered county is caught at the top betweeen the counties of Armagh and Fermanagh. There are no really high hills here – just lots of little ones that together form a gentle, rolling countryside. To the north of the country lies a small fringe of mountains. The central area is hillocky, with fairly rich farming land, and is in many ways reminiscent of County Down. Set among the hills to the south of Country Monaghan, at almost every bend of the road, lie small well-wooded lakes and sedgy bogholes. The little cultivated fields, the trimmed hedges, the tiny lakes, the profusion of wild flowers and the hordes of green and red dragonflies make it a land of satisfying detail.

In contrast to the smallness of scale, there remain a few large estates here, with their landscaped parks, lakes, formal gardens and age-old trees. You get glimpses of these Big Houses and of the forgotten ones, which are now, sadly, crumbling into ruins. Copper beech trees seem to have gone wild everywhere in Monaghan; they are quite a rarity elsewhere in Ireland. A native of the place swore to me that this was the last retreat of the Fir Bolgs, who were squeezed out of the rest of Ireland by the Dé Danaan and the Celts.

County Monaghan is well known to coarse fishermen because of the wealth of lakes here; otherwise it has been little visited by tourists. The locals are hoping to change this, and quite a few attractions have been developed. Lough Muckno, near Castleblaney, offers many sporting activities and accommodation. In the south-west the Rural and Literary Resource Centre in Innishkeen is a magnet for admirers of poet Patrick Kavanagh. To the northeast of the county, the pretty village of Glaslough has an excellent equestrian centre. Close by is Castle Leslie, a Victorian pile overlooking the lough and surrounded by beautiful trees. The north-eastern corner of County Monaghan, bounded by the Blackwater River and the N2 and known as the Parish of Truagh, is one of the most untouched areas in the county – the roads are so unused that the grass grows up the middle. Many of them would have led into County Tyrone or County Armagh before the Troubles began. You will find pretty mountain scenery and views that stretch over Ulster and beyond.

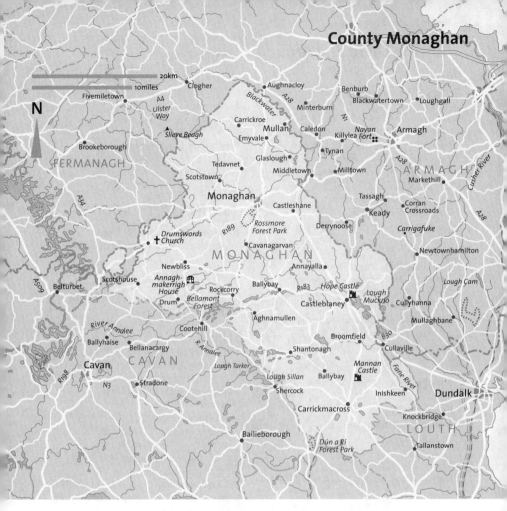

History

County Monaghan as it is now is a 16th-century creation. As the English conquered territory, they 'shired' it, hoping to make it easier to manage and more anglicized. Here, they joined the territories of the two ruling families, the MacMahons and McKennas. Other powerful families were the Duffys, O'Carrolls and Connollys, whose power was broken after the 1642 rebellion, when the lands of the Irish chieftains were divided between the English and Scots 'undertakers', who undertook certain duties to keep Monaghan loyal to the English crown in return for a grant of land. The descendants of those Gaelic families still live in the region today, whilst the undertaker families have disappeared or married into the local population. For more than 200 years, a smouldering resentment over land ownership made the relationship of peasants and landlord very uneasy, but this largely disappeared with the Land Acts of 1881, when the British government put up money for tenants to buy their own holdings.

Getting There and Around

By Rail
There is no rail service in Co. Monaghan.

By Bus
Frequent Bus Éireann express buses run from Dublin, Donegal, Armagh, Belfast and Derry. There are excellent local bus services to the smaller villages. Try also private operators, such as McConnons.
McConnons, Monaghan, t (047) 82020.
A daily service to Dublin.
Monaghan Bus Station, t (047) 82377.

By Bike
The Bicycle Shop, Shopping Arcade, Main St, Carrickmacross, t (042) 31967
The Cycle Shop, Ivy Lane, Carrickmacross, t (042) 63653
Emyvale Cycles, Knockafubble, Emyvale, t (047) 88108
Snipe Cycle Hire, Clones, t (047) 52125

Festivals

February–March
Castleblayney Drama Festival, t (042) 974 0454

June
Carrickmacross Festival, t (042) 966 1236/1618

July
Muckno Mania, Castleblayney, t (042) 974 6087. An arts and music festival.

August
Ballybay Celtic Festival, t (042) 974 1050
Clones Festival, t (047) 51718/52125.
A 4-day event.

September
Rhythm and Blues Festival, Monaghan, t (047) 71114, *www.harvestblues.net*

November
Castleblayney Heritage Week, t (042) 974 6087
Patrick Kavanagh Weekend, Inishkeen, t (042) 937 8560. Music, drama and poetry readings in the poet's birthplace.

Tourist Information
Monaghan Town: Market House, t (047) 81122, *www.monaghantourism. com*, *www.ireland-northwest.ie. Open Mar–Oct.*

Shopping

Crafts
Grainne O'Reilly, The Old Schoolhouse, Annalitten, Castleblayney, t (042) 974 3322. Fashion, textiles and lampshades.
Handwoven by Liz Christy, Annyalla, Castleblayney, t (042) 974 6614
Irish Celtic Art, Rockville, Creeve, Latton, Castleblayney, t (086) 880 0781. Woodcarving and repro art.
Killycracken Wrought Iron, Castleblayney, t (042) 974 9810. Iron furnishings.
Reimur Forged Crafts, Faragy, Shantonagh Post Office, Castleblayney, t (042) 966 9359. A blacksmith's work.

Food and Drink
Emyvale is famous for its duck; contact Monaghan Tourism, t (047) 71818.
Nature's World, Church Sq, Monaghan Town, t (047) 82882

During the 19th century County Monaghan benefited from the linen industry, and it also achieved fame for its trade in horses, many of which were exported as far as Russia for the use of the Imperial army. Now both the linen and the horse trade have disappeared, together with the old rail and canal links. However, the county is well served by express buses going to and from Dublin and County Donegal (*see* above), and there is a good local bus network, and these days Monaghan is noted for its furniture-making, poultry, and mushroom production.

Lace

Canal Stores, Clones Development, Clones, t (047) 51718

Carrickmacross Lace Gallery, Market Sq, Carrickmacross, t (042) 966 2506/2088

Clones Lace Guild, Fermanagh Terrace, Clones, t (047) 51729. A place to buy crocheted lace. There's also a display of antique lace and a coffee shop.

Sports and Activities

Courses

Cassandra Hand Summer School of Clones Lace, t (047) 51729, *mairelace@ eircom.net*. A course teaching traditional Clones lace-making in June.

Fishing

There is good **coarse fishing** in the numerous lakes, especially Lough Ooney, Muckno and the lakes beside Ballybay.
Game-fishing is good on the Finn, Fane and Monaghan Blackwater rivers (t (047) 81122).
Declan Loughman, Loughman Sports, Carrickmacross, t (042) 966 1714
Talbot Duffy, Ballybay area, t (042) 974 1692

Golf

Nuremore Hotel Golf Club, Carrickmacross, t (042) 966 1438,*www.nuremore-hotel.ie*. An 18-hole course.

Rossmore Golf Club, Monaghan, t (047) 81316. Another 18-holer.

Outdoor Activity Centres

Lough Muckno Adventure Centre, Castleblaney, t (087) 249 1305 or t (086) 313 1612. Sailing, canoeing, tennis, swimming, fishing and windsurfing.

Wildlife Educational Centre, Clontibret, between Monaghan and Castleblayney, t (047) 80632/80987

Ponytrekking

Carrickmacross School of Equitation, t (042) 966 1017

Greystones Equestrian Centre, Castle Leslie, Glaslough, t (047) 88100, *www.castleleslie.ie*

Walking

County Monaghan is a peaceful place for a walking or fishing holiday. For information on the **Monaghan Way**, contact James McMahan (t (042) 974 5173). For details of the signposted Ulster Way, see *www.sportni.net*.
Blaney Ramblers Hillwalking Club, t (042) 974 6554
Knockatallon Rambling Club, t (047) 81495

Where to Stay

The **Sliabh Beagh Rural Tourism Centre**, t (047) 89014, has information on local B&Bs.

Castle Leslie, Glaslough, t (047) 88109, *www.castleleslie.com* (*luxury*). Monaghan's most notable historic home (*see* p.475), with elegant rooms furnished with antiques. Dinner is available by request.

Hilton Park Country House, Scotshouse, Clones, t (047) 56007, *www.hiltonpark.ie* (*luxury*). A historic stately house set in the middle of luxuriant parkland, providing a superb place to stay if you are feeling extravagant. The rooms are furnished in keeping with the period of the house, and the food (*see* p.474) has a good reputation, with home-grown produce on the menu. Fishing and shooting are available in season, and golf and swimming in the lake can be enjoyed.

The local people are mostly involved in farming activities. Many of the country's chickens, ducks and even the rather exotic quail are produced for the table in County Monaghan – Emyvale in particular is well known for its Silver Hill ducks, which also provide down for luxury duvets and pillows. The people are fairly prosperous, and agriculture has been boosted tremendously by membership of the European Union. The moist and mild climate produces good grass for cattle rearing, and there are many small mixed farms. The population is currently about 51,000-strong.

Nuremore Hotel, Carrickmacross, t (042) 966 1438, *www.nuremore-hotel.ie* (*luxury*). A modern hotel in spacious grounds, popular with golfers for its fine 18-hole course, and also boasting a gym and a big indoor pool. The award-winning restaurant serves food with French-Irish influences.

The Hillgrove, Old Armagh Rd, Monaghan, t (047) 81288, *www.hillgrovehotel.com* (*expensive*). A similar proposition to the Slieve Russell in Cavan (*see* p.465) – comfortable and very welcoming.

Creighton Hotel, Fermanagh St, Clones, t (047) 51055, *creightonhotel@eircom.net* (*moderate*). A traditional 19th-century hotel on Clones' main thoroughfare, family-run. The restaurant offers children's meals.

Gleneven House, GlenevenInniskeen, t (042) 937 8294, *glenevenguesthouse@iolfree.ie* (*moderate*). A family-run Georgian country house in a peaceful setting by the River Fane.

Glynch House, Newbliss, Clones, t (047) 54045, (*moderate*). A highly recommended option with comfortable rooms in an 18th-century Georgian house designed by Richard Harrison. Dinner is available.

Shirley Arms, Main St, Carrickmacross, t (042) 966 1209 (*moderate*). A pleasant option in the centre of town.

Ashleigh House, 37 Dublin St, Monaghan, t (047) 81227, *ashleighguesthouse@ eircom.net* (*inexpensive*). A good and centrally located B&B.

Eating Out

Castle Leslie, Glaslough, t (047) 88100 (*expensive*). An old-world dining experience in truly opulent surrounds (see p.473), and a good choice for a special treat. Advance booking is required.

Hilton Park Country House, Scotshouse, Clones, t (047) 56007, *www.hiltonpark.ie* (*expensive*). A gorgeous restaurant in a stately-home hotel (*See* p.473), with views over the shimmering lake. The emphasis in on healthy eating, with herbs, salads, fruit and vegetables from the hotel garden wherever possible, and locally produced and personally selected meats. Advance booking is essential.

Nuremore Hotel, Carrickmacross, t (042) 966 1438 (*expensive*). Showy food served within a plush hotel (*see* above), including an 8-course gourmet menu.

Andy's Restaurant, 12 Market St, Monaghan Town, t (047) 82250 (*moderate*). All manner of very good dishes.

Avenue Restaurant, The Four Seasons Hotel, Coolshannagh, near Monaghan Town, t (047) 81888, *www.4seasonshotel.ie/ monaghan* (*moderate*). A modern setting for well-prepared cuisine. There's a less formal restaurant, **The Range**, within the same hotel.

The Hillgrove Hotel, Old Armagh Rd, Monaghan Town, t (047) 81288 (*moderate*). Traditional dinners and a carvery.

The Squealing Pig Bar and Restaurant, Monaghan Town, t (047) 84562 (*moderate*). A place with a good reputation for its seafood and steaks.

Entertainment and Nightlife

Arts

Garage Theatre, Monaghan Town, t (047) 81597

The Market House Venue & Gallery, Monaghan Town, t (047) 38158

Monaghan Town

Monaghan Town is a good place from which to start one's tour of the county. Constructed on an old monastic site, this market town has some very fine examples of urban architecture, especially round the market square, which is called the **Diamond**. The large, pedimented **Market House**, which now holds the tourist office and a gallery with varying exhibitions, dates from 1792. There is also a surprising amount of red brick in the smaller streets off the square. This is a very busy and prosperous town with lots of shops and a couple of good restaurants (*see* opposite). The small **Monaghan County Museum,** (*open Tue–Sat 11–1 and 2–5; t (047) 82928*), on Hill Street on the west side of Market Street, was founded in 1974 and won the EEC museum award in 1980. It has amongst its treasures the Clogher Cross – a fine example of early–Christian metalwork with highly decorative detail. There are objects collected from the nearby lake dwellings, including sandals and glass beads. There are also displays dealing with everything from lace-making to railways.

The 1860s Roman Catholic **St Macartan's Cathedral**, which is situated on the N2 to Dundalk, was designed by J. J. McCarthy, whose work is in the Gothic Revival style of Pugin – although an unfortunate modern 'improvement' has been the removal of the original altarpiece. You might also like to visit the **St Louis Convent Heritage Centre** (*open Apr–Oct Thur–Sun 2–4.30; t (047) 83529, stlouisheritage@eircom.net*), which traces the fascinating history of this order throughout the world. The building itself is beautiful, and there is a *crannóg* in the grounds.

Three miles (5km) to the south-west of Monaghan Town, on the R189 to Newbliss, you will find **Rossmore Forest Park** (*car park fee; t (047) 81968*), a former estate with beautiful grounds that are open to the public; there are picnic sites and forest and lakeside walks to be enjoyed.

North Monaghan

Only a small part of the county lies north of Monaghan town. It gently rises up from the flood plain of the Blackwater, to the high moorland of Slieve Beagh. Near the village of Glaslough, on the shores of a small grey lake, is the **Castle Leslie** demesne (*open May–Sept daily 12 noon–7; adm; t (047) 88100, www.castleleslie.com*). Sir Shane Leslie wrote superb ghost stories here in the early decades of the 20th century. The house, which is still lived in by the Leslie family, is in the Italianate style and full of art treasures, and it is possible to take a tour, or have an elaborate dinner (*see* opposite) and stay the night here (*see* p.473). After dinner, the cloaked mistress of the house will guide you by candlelight around its haunted rooms – a performance of fun and drama. There is also a pleasant tea-room in the conservatory.

To explore the tangle of little roads in this area known as Truagh Parish, you will need a detailed local map. To the west of Emyvale is pretty **Lough More** with its good stocks of brown trout; and the mountain scenery of Bragan, where local people go to cut their turf. North-east of here is the townland of **Mullanacross**, and in the graveyard of the ruined and ancient Errigal church are some superbly carved 18th-century gravestones. They depict the stag, the emblem of the McKennas, and biblical animals. Just across the road is a holy well, sacred to St Mellan, the patron saint of these parts. Further to the south-east you come across the deserted village of **Mullan**, which has some fine stone houses.

South Monaghan

To the south-east of Monaghan town lies **Castleblaney**, balanced on a narrow strip of land at the head of **Lough Muckno**. This is the county's largest stretch of water, with perhaps the best coarse fishing there is, though all the lakes around here vie for that award. Founded in the reign of James I, Castleblaney is now a prosperous town. The plain Georgian **Court House** is rather fine, and in the wooded demesne of **Hope Castle** (*car park fee*) there are nature trails and picnic sites . The castle once belonged to the 17th-century Blayney family, who developed the town, but it was bought in the 1870s by Henry Hope, who is remembered as the owner of the Hope diamond – the largest blue diamond in the world, but one reputed to bring ill luck to its owner. The Hopes sold up in 1916.

Heading west from Castleblaney on the R183, meandering between the hills and fish-filled lakes, you come down to the town of **Ballybay**, on the shore of Lough Major. The Catholic and Church of Ireland churches rise up attractively, each on its own hill overlooking the grassy lakes and farmland. Ballybay was noted for its horse fair, which sadly has become defunct with the age of the tractor. Flax-growing and tanning used to be very important industries here, but now they too have virtually disappeared.

Fifteen miles (24km) south-east of Ballybay is **Carrickmacross**, a market town famous for its hand-made lace, a cottage industry established at the beginning of the century. The very fine lace, appliqué work on tulle, is much sought after. Examples can be seen in **The Lace Co-operative** (*open Apr–Oct; book in advance for workshops and demonstrations; t (042) 966 2506*) at Carrickmacross. The Roman Catholic **church** here has ten splendid windows by the stained-glass artist Harry Clarke, whose work was inspired by the Pre-Raphaelite style.

About 3 miles (5km) to the north on the Castleblaney Road at Donaghmoyne, **Mannan Castle**, a great hilltop motte and bailey (*free access*), can be explored. This was constructed in the 12th century, and in 1224 it was encased in stone, some of which can still be seen. South-west of here, in County Cavan, is Dun a Rí Forest Park (*see* p.469), a great place for walks. The hilltop car park affords good views towards the Mourne Mountains.

About 5 miles (8km) to the south-east of Carrickmacross, near the border with County Louth, is the small village of **Inishkeen**. St Dega founded a monastery here in the 6th century, and you can see the remains of the old **abbey** and its 40ft-high (12m) round tower with a raised doorway. Poet Patrick Kavanagh was born here in 1904 and is buried in the graveyard of St Mary's church, which features **The Patrick Kavanagh Rural and Literary Resource Centre** (*open June–Nov Sat and Sun 2–6, Dec–May Tue–Fri 11–4.30, Sat and Sun 2–6; adm; t (042) 937 8560, www.patrickkavanaghcountry.com*). Kavanagh's masterly poem, *The Great Hunger*, is a very sad and ironic evocation of rural life in Ireland. The **Folk Museum** is now part of the Patrick Kavanagh centre, and deals with local history, folk life, and the old Great Northern Railway, which ran through the village.

Rockcorry to Clones

To the west of the county there are hundreds of small roads and lanes to explore, with lakes caught in between, so that they resemble a spider's web in the morning dew. Quite close to the County Cavan border on the R188 lies the small village of **Rockcorry**, which has some fine 19th-century stone dwellings that were constructed for destitute widows. Here too, on the south-western edge of the village, is the **Dartry Estate** with its open parkland, little lakes and large expanse of woodland, now all in the care of the Forestry Commission. This was once a very beautiful estate, but it is much less attractive now, with massive scars inflicted by tree-felling and a general air of neglect. There are some picnic sites and forest walks, but the Big House itself is a sad ruin. Nearby, lakes with names such as Coragh, Mullanary and Drumlona are full of fish.

Further west is the pretty riverside village of **Newbliss**, and 5 miles (8km) to the north-east again is the town of Clones. Between the two towns, near Kileevan, lies the country church of **Drumswords**. Dating from AD 750, it has now unfortunately fallen into disrepair, but one window still has the remains of fine basket tracery.

To the south of Newbliss, just off the R189, is **Annaghmakerrigh House**, which was once the home of Sir Tyrone Guthrie (1900–71). Sir Tyrone, a famous theatre, television and radio producer, left his estate to the nation on condition that it be used as a house for those who lived by the arts. A good many artists and writers come to spend some time in such a congenial place. Visitors may walk through the forest near the house, and carry on down to the lake. It is a very peaceful spot with some pretty parkland and trees.

Clones was once linked to Monaghan by the old Ulster railway and Ulster canal. In the days before the First World War it was a thriving town, but it is now rather rundown, although it is still an important agricultural centre. The town is, however, the main centre of traditional **hand-crocheted lace**. The tradition was brought here in the 1850s by Cassandra Hand, a local rector's wife, as a means of providing relief from the famine, and was based on Italian lace styles. Sadly, today the industry is in decline, but you can still buy Clones lace, which is thicker than its counterpart from Carrickmacross, through the **Ulster Canal Stores** (*t (047) 52125, clonesdevelopment@ eircom.net*) on Cara Street.

Built on an ancient site, Clones has some fine remains, some of which have been whisked away to the National Museum in Dublin. It does retain an overgrown *rath* with three concentric earthworks, an abbey, a well-preserved 75ft (23m) round tower, and a finely carved early-Christian sarcophagus, which is probably a MacMahon family tomb. In the church graveyard there are some fine 18th-century **gravestones** carved with skulls and crossbones. (The key is available from Pattons pub nearby.)

Presiding over Clones' triangular marketplace, which is perversely called the Diamond, is an ancient, much-inscribed **cross**. It is carved with scenes from the Bible, and probably dates from the 12th century. There are many fine old houses here too, particularly the imposing **market house**, which now houses the library. Charles Gavan Duffy (1816–1903), one of the leaders of the Young Ireland movement of the 1840s and later Prime Minister of Victoria in Australia, was born here. It's also the birthplace of Barry McGuigan, the former world champion featherweight boxer.

The Province of Leinster

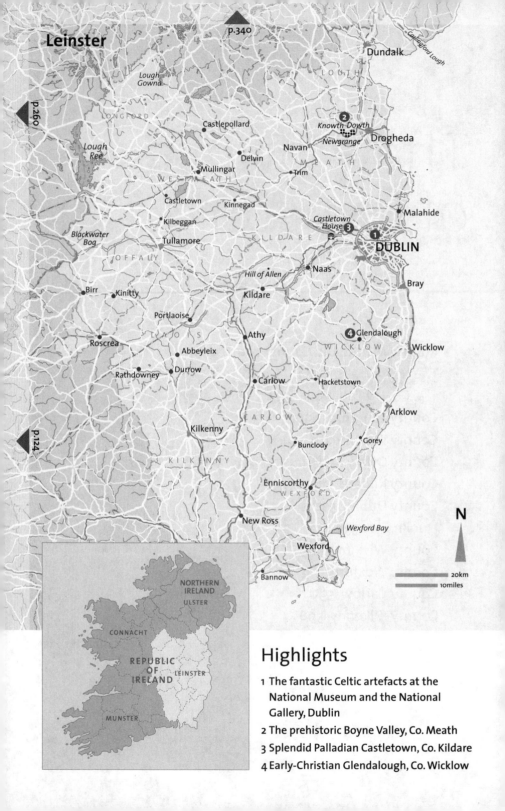

Leinster

p.340
p.260
p.124

Carlingford Lough

Dundalk

Lough
Gowna

LONGFORD

LOUTH

Lough
Ree

Castlepollard

Knowth · Dowth
Newgrange

Drogheda

Navan

Delvin

MEATH

Mullingar

Trim

Malahide

WESTMEATH

Castletown

Kinnegad

Castletown
House

Kilbeggan

KILDARE

DUBLIN

Blackwater
Bog

Tullamore

OFFALY

Hill of Allen

Naas

Bray

Birr

Kinitty

Kildare

Portlaoise

Roscrea

LAOIS

Athy

Glendalough

WICKLOW

Wicklow

Abbeyleix

Rathdowney

Durrow

Carlow

Hacketstown

Arklow

Kilkenny

CARLOW

KILKENNY

Bunclody

Gorey

Enniscorthy

WEXFORD

New Ross

Wexford Bay

Wexford

Bannow

N

20km
10miles

NORTHERN
IRELAND
ULSTER

CONNACHT

REPUBLIC
OF
IRELAND

LEINSTER

MUNSTER

Highlights

1 The fantastic Celtic artefacts at the
   National Museum and the National
   Gallery, Dublin

2 The prehistoric Boyne Valley, Co. Meath

3 Splendid Palladian Castletown, Co. Kildare

4 Early-Christian Glendalough, Co. Wicklow

Leinster (*Cúige Laighean*) has always had a reputation for wealth, because of its fertile land. Many aristocrats lived on estates here, within a day's ride of Dublin; the city, which is the symbolic centre of the province, grew larger as industry and people were attracted to it. The province includes the ancient Kingdom of Meath, and its pre-Christian kings were the most powerful in the land. Each successive wave of invaders since the Vikings have founded towns and built themselves strong castles in this beautiful and varied region. It has a long sea coast, stretching from Dundalk Bay in County Louth to Hook Head in County Wexford. Essential ports and trading places grew up along it, but Dublin, which became the centre of British rule, has always maintained its position as the most important. Today, the population of Dublin and its swelling suburbs is 1.5 million, so the farms of the province are engaged in supplying the huge city market with milk, vegetables, cattle and poultry. Brewing and other industrial ventures have grown up in the Greater Dublin area, but the rest of Leinster is comparatively rural, and the locals are either farmers or white-collar workers who commute to town.

The south-east coast has a reputation for being sunny, although the climate is fairly similar all over Ireland. Dublin is considered very cold and damp in winter. Tourist facilities are generally very good because restaurants and lodgings have responded to the sophisticated tastes of Dubliners. In fact, most travellers who come to Leinster head straight for Dublin City – a magnet that promises the most fun, history, culture and comfort. They might make a few sallies out into the countryside, perhaps to beautiful Glendalough in County Wicklow, the fascinating Boyne Valley burial grounds, or Tara, the seat of the high kings in County Meath. But Dublin City draws them all back, and the rest of Leinster pales into insignificance.

If you arrive in Ireland at Rosslare, in County Wexford, the province gets a fairer chance of being explored. There are many beautiful places in counties Wexford, Wicklow, Kilkenny and Carlow. Centuries of history are testified to by castles, monasteries, mansions and the more mysterious landmarks left behind by the Celts and those who went before. Leinster has more than its fair share of them, and many are open to the public. Castletown in County Kildare and Russborough in County Wicklow are the most impressive. The Bog of Allen, which takes up most of County Kildare and County Offaly, is counterbalanced by the gentle, rolling hills of the Blackstairs. The spiky mountains and rounded summits of the Wicklow range, the bogland and mountain pools make a happy contrast to the noisy crowds of Dublin. On a clear, blustery day it is not difficult to imagine yourself a million miles from civilization, even though the city is only an hour's drive away.

County Meath and County Louth

These two counties share many characteristics. Both are made up of rich farming land; both have some very exciting Neolithic, Celtic and early-Christian remains. And both were extensively settled by the Anglo-Normans, who built some fascinating castles and monasteries.

County Meath is drained by the River Boyne and its tributary, the Blackwater, and is planted with fine deciduous trees. Cattle and horses move about the fields of well-kept estates, and there are many Big Houses, built during the 18th century. The River Boyne is wide and slow and very beautiful. It is famous for the great Battle of the Boyne in 1690, when James II, relying on French and Irish forces to help him regain his English throne, was outnumbered and outflanked by the Protestant William of Orange. The low hills of Slane and Tara give lovely views over the countryside, and are vibrant with the memories of an ancient Ireland. Both figure in the mythology of the country and have been important since the Neolithic era. County Louth shares part of the Boyne Valley, and enters the sea at Drogheda. It too has its well-planted estates, especially on the grassy plain around Ardee. But it has a wilder side, too. To the north are the heathery slopes of the Cooley or Carlingford peninsula, while the rocky coastline of Clogherhead lies to the east.

Getting There and Around

By Rail
The main Dublin to Belfast railway line runs through Drogheda and Dundalk.
Drogheda Station, t (041) 983 8749

By Bus
From Dublin, Bus Éireann Expressway buses run hourly to Navan, Drogheda and Slane. Some Belfast–Dublin buses stop in Drogheda and Dundalk.
Bus Éireann, Drogheda, **t** (041) 983 5023

By Bike
The Raleigh Rent-a-Bike network operates here at the following shops:
Irish Cycle Hire, Enterprise Centre, Ardee,
t (041) 685 3772, *www.irishcyclehire.com*
Quay Cycles, 11 North Quay,
Drogheda train station, **t** (041) 983 4526

Festivals

Late May–June
Dundalk International Maytime Festival, Dundalk, **t** (042) 933 5253, *www. dundalkmaytime.com.* Cultural and sporting events, such as art, theatre, dancing and concerts. It also includes some children's events.

June
Blackrock Annual Raft Race, promenade/ beach, Blackrock, **t** (042) 932 1098. A local fundraising event with carnival and fancy dress.
Moneley Oyster Pearl Regatta, Carlingford, **t** (042) 937 3238. Races late in the month.

July
Kells Heritage Festival, t (046) 924 7840

August
Carlingford Oyster Fest, Carlingford, **t** (042) 937 3888. An oyster festival, with arts, crafts and fun for families.
Moynalty Steam Threshing Festival, Kells, **t** (087) 235 4763. A celebration of horse and steam power, with vintage displays, stalls, crafts, a funfair, music and dance.
Strand Races, between Laytown and Bettystown. Mid-month.

October
O'Carolan Harp, Cultural and Heritage Festival, Nobber, Meath, **t** (046) 905 2115

Both of these counties have experienced a huge rise in population over the last few decades, because they are within commuting distance of Dublin. Luckily, you can as often as not avoid the traffic on the major roads because there are lots of tiny country routes with few cars on them.

History

The ancient history of this area is rich and colourful; it has Tara and the passage graves of Newgrange. Since the Anglo-Norman invasion in the 13th century, events here have followed a pattern similar to that of the rest of Leinster. The Normans constructed for themselves some well-fortified castles, and later English settlers made themselves pleasant estates and farms amongst the rich agricultural land. The most famous confrontation between the Jacobite and Williamite armies took place along the Boyne river in 1690.

Louth and Meath suffered marginally less than other counties during the famine years of the 1840s, although, as was the case all over the country, the fate of the individual peasants depended to a great extent on whether or not they happened to have a good landlord. These days this area is prosperous with industry in the towns, while many of the locals in the countryside are earning their living working in the horse-breeding industry.

The Boyne Valley

The **Boyne Valley** is gloriously green, with a crumbling estate at every corner of the road, and ancient tumuli at every curve of the river. The valley was the centre of power in Ireland for thousands of years. The wealthy and organized farmers of Neolithic times built their burial chambers at Newgrange, Dowth, and Tara long before the Egyptians built their Great Pyramid. When the Celts arrived in waves, roughly between 500 and 100 BC, they recognized these burial mounds as very powerful and assimilated them into their culture. The Hill of Tara became a royal enclosure, while the burial chambers along the Boyne became the dwelling places of the Celtic god of love, Aonghus.

A bicycle tour is the ideal way to see the Boyne Valley. You can easily cover all the ancient places and monasteries in a few days at a leisurely pace; and in summer it is the most enjoyable way to travel along the country lanes, laced with cow parsley.

Kells

Kells (*Ceanannus Mor* on the road signs) is not actually in the Boyne Valley but in the wooded valley of the Blackwater. The village has a vast wealth of history behind it. Most people who come to Ireland go to see *The Book of Kells*, now in Trinity College, Dublin. The beauty and richness of this illuminated 8th-century manuscript never cease to amaze. **Kells Monastery**, in which it was so beautifully made, is no more, but there are many fine ruins to contemplate.

The High King of Ireland, Dermot (or Diarmuid) granted this defensive fort to St Columba in AD 550. (It is said to have been the residence of Cormac MacArt, a high king during the 3rd century AD.) St Columba (or Colmcille in Gaelic; *see* p.47) was the princely monk who founded the first monastery on Iona in AD 563, and whose missionary zeal subsequently converted most of Scotland to Christianity. The religious centre he established became very important, and in AD 807 the Columba monks moved back here from Iona after being repeatedly pillaged by the Vikings.

Today, in the graveyard of the Church of Ireland **church of St Columba**, you can see a 9th-century round tower that is in a good state of preservation; and the wonderful scriptural stone cross of St Patrick and St Columba, opposite. The circular ditch around the now-ruined monastery is reflected in the modern-day street patterns. The round tower at Kells has some dark associations, as a claimant to the high kingship of Ireland was murdered in it in 1076. The **high cross of St Patrick and Columba**, one of four in the graveyard, has a wealth of decoration and another Crucifixion scene. **St Columba's house** (*key kept at No.1 Lower Church View when closed*), nearby, is a high-roofed oratory with very early barrel-vaulting, and is similar to St Kevin's house at Glendalough in County Wicklow . It was probably built during the 9th century and is roofed with stone, the walls being at least 3ft (90cm) thick. Beside it is a well. There is a replica of *The Book of Kells* in the modern Church of Ireland church, the tower of which dates from 1578.

In the town, the landmark used to be a 10th-century **market cross** that had been moved there from the graveyard – until a car ran over it in 1996. There are plans to erect a replica on the spot, and the repaired original has been placed in the

Tourist Information

Brú na Bóinne: Brú na Bóinne Visitor Centre, Donore, t (041) 988 0305
Drogheda: t (041) 983 7070
Kells: Kells Heritage Centre, t (046) 924 7840
Trim: Town Hall, Castle St, t (046) 943 7227

Shopping

Antiques and Furniture
George Williams Antiques, Newcastle House, Kilmainhamwood, Kells, t (046) 905 2740
John McGrane, Delvin Farm Antique Galleries, Gormanstown

Crafts
Callan and Harte, 31 Railway St, Navan, t (046) 902 1459. Prints, ceramics and other gifts.
Claidhbh O'Gibne, Drogheda, t (041) 988 0095. Celtic wood carvings.
Courtyard Craft Centre and Café, Cookstown House, Kells, t (046) 924 0346. Locally hand-crafted ceramics, linen, textiles and more.
Elaine Hanrahan, Millmount Craft Centre, Drogheda, t (041) 984 1960. Jewellery.
Mary McDonnell Craft Studio, 4 Newgrange Mall, Slane, t (041) 982 4722. Quilts, wall hangings, ceramics and jewellery, plus an **organic food market** Fri 3–6 in winter.
McNulty Knitwear, 7 Millmount Craft Centre, Drogheda, t (041) 984 4199
Trim Visitor Centre, Mill St, Trim, t (046) 943 7227, www.meathtourism.ie. Hand-made silver jewellery, ceramics, textiles, leather goods, crystal glass and soaps.

Sports and Activities

Fishing
Beach fishing for bass and flounder is best at Laytown.
Sportsden, Trimgate St, Navan, t (046) 902 1130

Golf
Headfort Golf Club, Navan Rd, Kells, t (046) 924 0146/924 0857
Laytown, t (041) 982 7170
Royal Tara Golf Club, Bellinter, Navan, t (046) 902 5508/902 5244

Ponytrekking
Bachelor's Lodge Riding Centre, Kells Rd, Navan, t (046) 21736, lowryfam@eircom.net
Kells Equestrian Centre, Normanstown, Carlanstown, Kells, t (046) 46638 or t (046) 40313. Riding and instruction for all ages, 6 days a week.

Open Farms
Lily Angela Murtagh, Fordstown, Navan, t (046) 943 4135, www.causeyexperience.com. A re-creation of traditional life on a farm, with hands-on experiences.
Newgrange Farm, off N51 from Navan or Drogheda, near Slane, t (041) 982 4119. A working farm, offering tours around its 17th-century buildings and herb garden.

Walking Tours
Noel French, Meath Heritage Centre, Mill St, Trim, t (046) 943 7227. Guided tours of the area.

Where to Stay

Ardboyne Hotel, Dublin Rd, Navan, t (046) 902 3119, www.ardboynehotel.com (expensive). A modern, friendly choice.
Loughcrew House, 3 miles (5km) south of Oldcastle on Mullingar Rd, near Loughcrew Cairns, t (049) 854 1356, www.loughcrew.com (expensive). A luxurious country house set amid parkland and historic gardens, with 4 elegant guestrooms.
The Station House Hotel, Killmessan, t (046) 902 5239, www.thestationhotel.com (expensive). A very pleasant converted 1850s railway station.
Mountainstown, Castletown, Kilpatrick, Navan, t (046) 905 4154/905 4195 (moderate–expensive). A beautiful 17th-century house on a wooded estate, with delicious food. It even has peacocks on the lawn. There's a minimum 2-night stay.
Annesbrook House, Duleek, t (041) 982 3293, www.annesbrook.com (moderate). An 18th-century mansion with a Greek Revival portico. George IV once slept here. Closed Oct–Mar.
Conyngham Arms, Slane, t (041) 988 4444, www.conynghamarms.com (moderate). A snug hotel in the middle of the village.

Crannmor House, Dunderry Rd, Trim,
t (046) 943 1635 (*moderate*). A B&B
popular with those come to fish.
Old Mill Hotel, Julianstown, **t** (041) 982 9133,
www.oldmill.ie (*moderate*). A converted flour
mill on the River Nanny, with a pleasing
atmosphere and private fishing for guests.
The Gables, Dundalk Rd, Ardee, Co. Louth,
t (041) 685 3789 (*inexpensive*). Simple
accommodation, plus a fine restaurant
serving hearty food.
Seamrog, Tara, **t** (046) 902 5296 (*inexpensive–
moderate*). A B&B right beside the Hill of
Tara. The owner's family have owned the
nearby café, bookshop and tourist shop for
several generations.
Lennoxbrook House, Carnaross, Kells,
t (046) 924 5902, *lennoxbrook@ireland.com*
(*inexpensive*). A pleasant old farmhouse
owned by a welcoming family. Rooms are
full of pretty antique furniture, and the food
is good. Trout fishing is available locally.
Minnamurra House, Dublin Rd, Drogheda,
t (041) 984 1437 (*inexpensive*). A very
convivial option, with the owner's children
bouncing in every direction.

Self-catering
The Gate Lodge, Clonleason House, Fordstown,
t (046) 943 4111, *www.clonleason.com*
(*inexpensive*). A Georgian cottage combining
country-house elegance with cosiness in a
secluded lane. It sleeps 2.
Seabank, Laytown, **t** (041) 982 8104,
www.cottages-ireland.com (*inexpensive*).
Thatched cottages on the seashore. There is
a choice of other seafront houses as well,
from stately Victorian accommodation to
modern bungalows.

Eating Out
There are a few excellent eating places in
this region, but also a mass of vile hotel
menus and takeaways. The following should
stand you in good stead:
Forge Gallery Restaurant, Church St, Collon,
t (041) 982 6272, *www.forgegallery.ie*
(*expensive*). A delightful little restaurant
with an antiques shop, particularly good
for vegetarians. *Closed lunch.*

The Gables, Dundalk Rd, Ardee, **t** (041) 53789
(*expensive*). A small restaurant with an
imaginative menu and large portions.
Vanilla Pod, Headfort Arms Hotel,
Headfort Place, Kells, **t** (046) 40063, *www.
headfortarms.com* (*moderate–expensive*).
An international menu. *Closed Mon, and
lunch Mon–Sat.*
The Buttergate Restaurant and Wine Bar,
Millmount, Drogheda, **t** (041) 983 4759
(*moderate*). Good, plain food served with
imaginative sauces.
Dunderry Lodge Restaurant, Dunderry, Navan,
t (046) 943 1671 (*moderate*). A little restaurant
with a tremendous reputation – Dubliners
think nothing of driving out to sample its
Mediterranean-influenced food and wine.
Hudson's Bistro, 30 Railway St, Navan,
t (046) 902 9231 (*moderate*). A casual place
with an international menu. *Closed lunch.*
The Loft, Trimgate St, Navan, **t** (046) 907 1755
(*moderate*). Light meals and music.
Old Mill Hotel, Julianstown, **t** (041) 982 9133,
www.oldmill.ie (*moderate*). Irish and
Continental cooking using local produce.
The Station House Hotel, Kilmessan, **t** (046)
902 5239 (*moderate*). Tasty fish, lamb and
beef cooked with herbs and sauces, served in
in an old train station. *Closed lunch Mon–Sat.*
Bounty Bar, Bridge St, Trim, **t** (046) 943 1640
(*inexpensive*). The oldest pub in the county,
serving snacks.
Kieran Brothers Deli and Restaurant,
15 West St, Drogheda, **t** (041) 983 8728
(*inexpensive*). Self-service lunches, including
delicious ham and smoked salmon.
Newgrange Farm and Coffee Shop,
Slane, **t** (041) 982 4119 (*inexpensive*).
Home-made soups and sandwiches.

Entertainment and Nightlife

Traditional Music
Black Bull Inn, Dublin Rd, Drogheda,
t (041) 983 7139. Music at weekends.
Blackwater Pub, Kells. Traditional Irish and
modern country music on Mon nights.
Monaghan's, Carrick House, Kells,
t (046) 924 0100

Kells Heritage Centre (*open May–Sept Mon–Sat 10–5.30, Sun and bank hols 2–6, Oct–Apr Mon–Sat 10–5; audio-visual presentation every 30mins; adm; t (046) 924 7840*), at Headfort Place. In the 1798 Rising, this cross was used as a gallows. Its top has been broken off, but the fine carving of the scriptural scenes makes it well worth studying. On the head and shaft are scenes representing the Crucifixion, the Resurrection, Daniel in the Lion's Den, and the Fall of Man.

West of Kells, off the Crossakeel Road, is the **Hill of Lloyd Tower**, which looks rather like a lighthouse. It was built by the Marquis of Headford as a project to give relief to the needy in famine times. About 3½ miles (5.3km) to the north-west of Kells on an unmarked road near Castlekeeran, on the banks of a tributary of the Blackwater, is the ruined 14th-century **Church of St Kieran**. There is an ogham stone and two 9th-century crosses in the area around the church, and also a very attractive holy well. You may only drink from it, for if you wash in it the well would lose its holy properties – a rather sane law of hygiene. These remains are all that is left of an early hermitage called the 'Dysart of St Ciaran' – Ireland's first monks called their isolated monasteries 'deserts' in imitation of the lonely desert homes of the first Christian anchorites in the Middle East.

Sliab na Cailleach and Athboy

If you continue on the R163 out to the furthest reaches of County Meath, in the Loughcrew Mountains you can visit a Neolithic site that must have been as important as the Brú na Bóinne in its day, though it's one that gets little attention from either tourists or archaeologists.

Sliab na Cailleach (pronounced 'shleev nah cahloe', meaning: 'Mountain of the Hag') is known as the Hag's Chair, and is the highest part of the Loughcrew chain, offering views over several counties, the Irish Sea and the Atlantic. Neolithic people chose this conspicuous spot for three major groupings of passage-grave mounds, smaller mounds and standing stones. Locally the passage-graves are called cairns, for the rubble of stones that surround them; originally they must have gleamed like the one at Newgrange. Most of the sites are in open fields, and you may explore them at your leisure; in fact you could spend several days here. Some of the passages are locked; the key and a plan of the sites can be obtained from **Brú na Bóinne Visitors Centre** (*t (041) 988 0300*) in Newgrange. There are two major sets of monuments, called Carnbane East and Carnbane West. Of special interest at Carnbane East is 'Cairn T', oriented towards the equinoctial sunrises (on 21/22 September and 21/22 March); this is said to be the **Tomb of Ollamh Fódla** (pronounced 'Ola Fola'), a legendary king and high poet who was the first law-giver of Ireland, and who built some of the works at Tara and instituted the autumn festival there.

Athboy, to the south of Kells, was founded by the Plunketts, a Norman family who produced St Oliver Plunkett (1625–81), a wise and brave archbishop of Armagh who was hanged, drawn and quartered at Tyburn after being falsely accused of complicity in the popish plot of Titus Oates in England in 1678 (*see p.493*). About 2½ miles (4km) outside Athboy is **Rathmore Church**, which was built in the 15th century by a Plunkett. It has fine stone carvings and monuments, and a fragmentary 16th-century cross.

Trim

Trim is the usual starting point for a tour of the Boyne Valley. It was the capital of the Kingdom of Meath, which was granted to Hugh de Lacy by Henry II at the time of the Norman Conquest. You should approach it from the Dublin road (R154) if you can, for suddenly all the ruins, towers and moats through which the River Boyne winds burst upon you.

Trim Castle, also called King John's Castle (*open mid-June–mid-Sept daily 10–6, Nov–Mar Sat and Sun 10–5; adm; t (046) 943 8618*) was built in 1172 by Hugh de Lacy, and is the largest Anglo-Norman castle in Ireland. This imposing, well-preserved ruin dominates the town, covers 2 acres (0.8ha) and consists of a massive square keep, with side turrets in the middle of each face, and a huge curtain wall with circular towers at regular intervals. There are two gateways, one of which still has a drawbridge, portcullis and barbican. The castle was at the centre of every battle during the Middle Ages, and at one time the future King of England, Henry V, and the Duke of Gloucester were imprisoned here by Richard II.

The first Duke of Wellington went to school in Talbot Castle, off High Street. His father, the 1st Earl of Mornington, built **Dangan Castle** to the south of Trim, which is now completely ruined, and there is a handsome 15th-century tower attached to the 19th-century Church of Ireland **cathedral**.

About two miles (3.2km) away is the village of **Laracor**, where Dean Jonathan Swift and Stella lived for a while. He must have been a curious rector, or at least not the sort the locals felt at ease with.

Tara

The **Hill of Tara** (*Visitors' Centre open mid-May–mid-Sept daily 10–6; audio-visual presentation; adm; book guided tours in advance July and Aug, or on t (041) 988 4026 rest of year; t (046) 902 5903*) is to be found on a small road off the R154, just south of Trim. The turn for it is known as Pike's Corner, and you pass through the hamlet of Kilmessan. All that is left of Tara, the ancient palace of the high kings of Ireland, is a series of earthworks on a green hill in green fields, so do not be disappointed; the wooden buildings have long disappeared. Though the earthworks date to the second millennium BC, the site was taken over by the Celts and only seems to have been abandoned some time after Christianity came to Ireland in about the 6th century AD – it is said that the 6th-century Saint Ruadhan put a curse on it.

According to tradition, from the beginning of history Tara was the seat of kings who controlled at least the northern half of the country. It is central to many legends and mentioned in early annals, sagas and genealogies, such as the 12th-century *Book of Leinster*. One of the characters frequently mentioned in them is Cormac MacArt, a semi-mythical high king associated with the legendary time of Tara's great fame in the 3rd century AD (*see* p.54). Shut your eyes and imagine the pagan rites that were enacted, and later the great triennial *feis*, where tribal disputes were settled and laws were made. The *Book of Leinster* describes Tara in its heyday as being full of warriors who combined fierceness with elegance. The great wooden buildings resounded with the clamour of people going about their business, with music, feasting and the whinnying of the Fianna's sleek horses. The pastures around would have been thick with herds of cattle representing the wealth and importance of the high king. The Great Assembly Hall was built by Cormac, 'the Irish King Solomon', who presided over the massive banquets and laid down lists of protocol – even meat was portioned out according to rank: the king, queen and nobles of the first rank ate ribs of beef, buffoons got shoulder fat and chess-players shins, harpers and drummers got pigs' shoulders, and historians were entitled to the haunches.

The most important of the earthworks that remain are the **Mound of the Hostages** and the '**Banquet Hall**', a pair of long parallel banks that may have been a Neolithic processional avenue. There are a number of tumuli, including the **Rath of the Synods**, where Patrick and the early saints are supposed to have held the first church synods; another is called '**Cormac's House**', upon which stands the **Lia Fáil** (apparently the real 'Stone of Destiny', the coronation stone of the ancient kings). Sixty-odd years ago, one of the mounds was dug up by enthusiastic but misled British Israelites, who believed that the Ark of the Covenant was buried in one of the large mounds. They got the information from a second-hand bookshop in Charing Cross Road, and no one did anything to stop them.

Dunsany and Navan

Dunsany, near the Hill of Tara, is the family house of the Catholic branch of the Plunketts. They are an example of a Catholic Norman family, Barons of the Pale, who survived the vicissitudes of Irish political life because one branch of the family was Protestant and protected their interests. The **Church of St Nicholas** (*open June and July Mon–Sat 9–1, rest of year by advance booking; adm; t (046) 902 6202/902 5198, www.dunsany.com*), in the demesne of **Dunsany Castle**, is a 15th-century ruin . It has a beautifully sculptured fort with angels, apostles and saints on the basin and shafts. The castle, a 19th-century neo-Gothic mansion, is still lived in by the Dunsany lords. One celebrated Lord Dunsany (1878–1957), known for mystical short plays such as *The Glittering Gate* and *The Gods of the Mountain*, also wrote some very fine novels exploring his love for Ireland, its vanishing ways and the beauty of its countryside.

North of Tara, on the N3, is the busy town of **Navan**, which is Norman in origin. In **St Mary's Catholic Church** is a good wooden carving of Christ crucified dating from the 18th century. The sculptor, Edward Smyth, would have been at some risk carving such a subject during those penal times. The **Motte of Navan** dominates the town and the crossing on the River Blackwater. It is probably a natural mound of gravel deposited in the Ice Age, though legend says it was the burial tomb of a queen. The Norman baron of Navan built a bailey on top of it. There is a very pretty walk to Slane on the towpath of the old Navan to Drogheda Canal, which continues to Stackallen. The entrance to the walk is through a gateway on the left side of the Boyne road that leads from the market square. In this area are the pretty country roads leading to Balrath, Black Lion and the attractive Church of Ireland church at Kentstown, just off the R153.

Grove Gardens and Tropical Bird Sanctuary (*open Feb–Sept daily 1–-6; tea-room; adm; t (046) 943 4276*), at Fordstown, has one of Europe's largest collections of clematis roses within its 14 acres, along with the bird sanctuary and exotic animal mini-zoo.

Slane

Slane, situated just to the north-east of Navan on the N2 and the River Boyne, once belonged to other barons of the Pale, the Flemings. The Flemings lost out when they supported James II in the Williamite wars of the 1690s; their lands were forfeited, and a County Donegal family, the Conynghams, were awarded them in their stead. Burton Conyngham built the picture-book Gothic **Slane Castle** (*open May–early Aug Sun–Thur 12 noon–5; adm; t (041) 988 4400, www.slanecastle.ie*), with its fine gates, in the 1780s. It looks dreamlike when seen from the Navan–Slane road as you cross the River Boyne. It was designed by James Watt and Francis Johnston and has some magnificent rooms and a splendid circular library; the grounds are occasionally used as a venue for pop concerts. Look out, too, for the **four Georgian houses** in the village arranged in a square. Local legend has it that they were built for the four spinster sisters of one of the Conynghams, who could no longer stand their inquisitive chattering and quarrelling. They detested one another but could not bear to be parted, so he thought of this perfect solution; you can imagine them watching each other through lace curtains.

A few hundred yards outside Slane on the Ardee road (N2) is a very ancient site known as the **Hill of Slane**, famous in legend and as a site of early-Christianity. St Patrick is said to have kindled a fire here in the 5th century AD. The Druids forbade any but themselves to light a fire there, and by doing so St Patrick brought himself to the notice of the High King of Tara and converted him. The present monastic remains date from the 15th and 16th centuries. Some of the Flemings, barons of Slane, are buried here. On the Drogheda road (N51) just outside Slane is the **Francis Ledwidge Cottage and Museum** (*open daily Feb–Oct 10–1 and 2–5.30, Nov–Jan 10–1 and 2–3.30; adm; t (041) 982 4544*). Ledwidge was a labourer who wrote fine poetry, and although he was a Nationalist he joined up to fight in the First World War, 'neither for principle nor a people nor a law, but for the fields along the Boyne, for the birds and the blue skies over them'. He was killed in Belgium in 1917.

If you take the Slane–Drogheda Road (N51), and about 2½ miles (4km) from Dowth turn left off the main road, you will pass **Townley Hall**, a fine Georgian house that is now attached to Trinity College, Dublin. There is a lovely forest trail and walk in the grounds. Further on at the bridge at **Oldbridge**, you can follow the signposted route of the Battle of the Boyne, 1690 – a pleasant riverside drive.

Brú na Bóinne

On the other side of the river, along a twisting road, you will come to the most spectacular ancient site in Ireland, the burial sites known as **Brú na Bóinne**, 'the Palace of the Boyne'. This piece of land is enclosed by the river on three sides. There are at least 15 passage graves from Neolithic times, some of them unexcavated. The three main sites are called Newgrange, Knowth and Dowth. The **Visitors Centre** (*open daily Nov–Feb 9.30–5, Mar, Apr and Oct 9.30–5.30, May and 2nd half of Sept 9.30–6.30, June–mid-Sept 9.30–7; adm; last tours begin 1½ hours before closing; signposted from N51, t (041) 988 0300, www.heritageireland.ie*) is an attraction in itself – a striking piece of architecture with excellent exhibits on the creation of the monuments and the lives of their builders. Try to see it after your tour of the 'palace', because it has most of the answers to the questions you will want to ask about the sophistication of the building. And try to avoid going on weekends in summer, when the place is crowded: it is impossible to appreciate the age or the impressive atmosphere when you are squashed sideways against a sacred stone. Unfortunately, the visit to the actual sites is the most over-bureaucratized tourist experience to be had in Ireland; they'll stick a badge on you with a tour time, load you on a bus to the sites for a weak guided tour, and haul you back to the Visitors Centre before you've had time to look around. Newgrange and Knowth have separate tours and schedules.

Newgrange

Newgrange, on its hilltop, is visible for miles around: a mound 340ft (104m) in diameter, sparkling with white quartz like a beacon in the landscape. Somebody went to a lot of trouble to bring these white stones here; the closest place where they are found is in the Wicklow Mountains. Their use as a wall around the sides of a mound is unique to Ireland. Naturally, most of them fell down over the millennia, and restorers in the 1960s and 1970s had a long and careful task putting them back into place. The round stones that make such a lovely pattern among the quartz may not be in their original positions; here the restorers had to guess. Another change they made is the semi-circular bay faced with dark stone at the entrance, designed to accommodate large crowds of visitors. Originally, to enter, one would have to climb over the famous decorated slab that lies across the doorway, carved with an undulating pattern of spirals and lozenges. Like everything else at Newgrange, this stone has occasioned all manner of speculations: some see it as a kind of map of the Brú na Bóinne sites, others as an object for religious meditation, an obscure hint of what Newgrange might have meant to the people who built it.

Outside, a few standing stones remain from what was probably an unbroken ring around the mound, its purpose unknown. The tour will take you inside, down the narrow 62ft (19m) passage that does not quite reach the centre of the mound. At the end is a three-lobed chamber, typical of Neolithic constructions all over western Europe. It is covered by a cupola of corbelled stone that has kept the place dry for 45 centuries; the builders cut grooves in the upper side of the stones to carry away the water. Many of the stones in the chamber are carved with designs similar to those at the entrance – beautiful, exasperating designs that show serious intent and meaning, without allowing us to decipher it. Neither can we guess much about what went on here on Newgrange's big day, the winter solstice, when the first rays of the rising sun penetrated the artfully positioned 'roof box' over the entrance and illuminated the entire passage for a few minutes (on the tour they re-create the effect with artificial lighting). Right now, they say, there's a 10-year waiting list to visit on that occasion, and they have stopped taking names.

Built around 3500–3000 BC, Newgrange is not only one of the most impressive works of the Neolithic age but one of the oldest, antedating the great circle at Stonehenge by at least a millennium. In its layout, it resembles other passage-graves around Europe, notably Gavr'inis, near Carnac in Brittany, and its carved motifs echo those found in the temples of Malta, some of which were built at around the same time. When you visit Newgrange, try to think of it not as an isolated peculiarity from long ago, but as one of the finest monuments of a culture that stretched around the Atlantic and Mediterranean shores from Malta to Scandinavia – Europe's first great civilization, a world of remarkable artistic and scientific achievements that endured for more than 3,000 years.

Knowth, Dowth and the Battle of the Boyne

Knowth (*open Apr–Oct*), which can be visited on a separate tour from the Brú na Bóinne Visitors' Centre, is approximately the same size as Newgrange and contains a second, smaller passage in addition to the main one. Only part of the site is open to the public while archaeological excavations are completed, but you can see the wonderfully lavish kerbstones placed round the mound, decorated with spirals and lozenges. These may be common in Neolithic sites throughout Europe, but the Neolithic Irish carved many more of them than anyone else, and nearly half of the works so far discovered are at Knowth. Unlike Newgrange, Knowth is surrounded by nearly a score of smaller tumuli, and their placement is being studied closely for hints of astronomical or religious significance. Knowth seems to have been used for one purpose or another as late as the Middle Ages, and there are souterrains underneath that were probably dug by early-Christians. **Dowth**, the third of the great mounds, has a passage made diametrically opposite to the one at Newgrange so that it is illuminated by the mid-winter sunset. The archaeologists haven't done much work here yet, and the site is not currently open to the public. If they ever do reopen it, be prepared for a certain amount of scrambling if you want to see the two tombs inside and the early-Christian souterrain at the entrance.

Nearly in the shadow of these ancient relics lie fields that are known from a very different episode in Irish history. On the N51 as you go back towards Drogheda, near Tullyallen, you can see a marker commemorating the **Battle of the Boyne**, where the troops of William of Orange succeeded in crossing the river and routing a smaller army loyal to James II in July 1690. It wasn't the end of the struggle, but as a psychological turning point it is the event that is still celebrated each year by the Orange marchers in the north.

Drogheda

Drogheda, which is the largest town in County Meath, conjures up images of the cruelty of Cromwell, for which he is notorious in Ireland, but it has also been a famous place in Ireland since the Normans settled here in around 1180, and today it is bustling with energy (and eternal traffic jams). The old Drogheda Society has adapted some of the buildings of **The Millmount**, an 18th-century military barracks on a motte, as a museum (*open Mon–Sat 10–6, Sun 2.30–5.30; adm; t (041) 983 3097*). It has many interesting exhibits, including 18th-century guild banners, a 1912–22 room, information on the old industries of spinning, weaving, brewing, shoe- and rope-making, a folk kitchen and an extensive geological collection. **St Lawrence's Gate**, a twin-towered, four-storey gate, stands on the road going to Baltray. It is the best-preserved of all the remaining gates in this once-walled town. Off West Street, in the **Church of St Peter**, is the preserved head of St Oliver Plunkett, Archbishop of Armagh, who sadly became caught up in the panic of 'the Popish Plot' that was fabricated by Titus Oates in 1678. The 'Plot' was a smoke-screen manufactured by various powerful men in England in order to discomfit Charles II and his Catholic heir, James II. Plunkett was drawn into it because of his fearless pursuit of duty in a country full of treachery and unease, where Catholicism was essentially outlawed. He was canonized in 1975, becoming the first new Irish saint since St Lawrence O'Toole, more than 700 years ago.

Legal history in relation to Irish historic buildings was made here in 1989. Two of the finest 18th-century buildings in Drogheda were tumbled in spite of a court injunction to prevent the demolition. The judge then issued a High Court order, preventing any further demolition and requiring the owners to rebuild and restore the buildings. You can see them on Lawrence Street – one the townhouse of Lord Justice Singleton, the other Dr Clarke's Free School. Both of them were probably designed by Sir Edward Lovett Pearce in the 1730s.

Around Drogheda

Old Mellifont Abbey (*open May–Oct daily 10–6; adm; t (041) 982 6459*), a graceful ruin six miles (9.6km) west of Drogheda, was built in 1142 by the first Cistercians to come to Ireland from Clairvaux in France. Their arrival and the new ideas in architecture and church organization introduced here were the result of the efforts of St Malachy, who as Archbishop of Armagh did much to bring the Irish Church more in line with Rome. There is an interesting lavabo, a few arches of a Romanesque cloister, and a 14th-century chapterhouse. The Cistercians are still in the area at New Mellifont. **Monasterboice**, a 5th-century monastic settlement, contains the most perfect high cross, the **Cross of Muireadach**, made in the early 10th century. Nearly every inch of the cross is covered in scenes from the Bible – the only way the poor and illiterate could 'read' the scriptures. The West Cross is almost as handsome and less squat. You can climb the damaged **round tower** – the tallest ever built, at 358ft (110m).

Collon (pronounced 'cooh-lun'), a small place on the N2 south of Ardee, has a Church of Ireland **church** that is a miniature pastiche of King's College Chapel, Cambridge. It was at **Ardee**, now a very attractive market town, that Cú Chulainn slew his friend Ferdia in a four-day combat to stop the raiding party stealing the Bull of Cooley for Queen Maeve (*see* p.494). Ardee was an outpost of the Pale, often used by the English as a base for attacking Ulster; that is why you will find two old **castles** along the main street. One of them, Ardee Castle, is under restoration to house a new museum.

South of Drogheda, **Duleek** has a ruined 12th-century abbey, on the site of a church founded by St Patrick himself, as well as a medieval high cross. Between Drogheda and Dublin are numerous beach resorts. Laytown is the home of the **Sonairte National Ecology Centre** (*open Mon–Fri 11–5 and Sun 11–6; adm; t (041) 982 7572*), located at The Ninch, with an organic farm, environmental exhibits, a winery, a nature trail, an adventure playground and a wholefood coffee shop. The quiet, undiscovered village of **Termonfeckin**, along the coast, has its own 10th-century high cross.

The Cooley Peninsula

The Cooley Peninsula, located in the extreme north of County Louth, is one of the most beautiful and untouched places in Ireland. First go to **Carlingford**, which looks across its lough to the Mourne Mountains. This town is full of castellated buildings; it is said to have possessed 32 'castles' in the days of the Pale, when almost every house on the border was fortified in some way or other. The ruins of the Anglo-Norman **King John's Castle**, with arrow slits in the outer walls, is impressive. It was built in 1210 by John de Courcy and is similar to Carrickfergus Castle in County Antrim (*see* p.380). The Norsemen founded this town, and it was a place of great strategic importance in medieval times. Nowadays, it is nothing more than a little village with a 16th-century arched **Tholsel**, a **mint**, and **Taaffe's Castle**, which is multi-storeyed and attached to a modern house. The **Holy Trinity Centre**, situated within a restored medieval church, provides further local history.

You can have a marvellous walk across the **Cooley Mountains** (*for information call Dundalk Tourism: see opposite*) along the slopes of Slieve Foye and Ravensdale Forest. You will find Slieve Foye 2 miles (3.2km) to the north-east of Carlingford, on the R173 to Omeath. Omeath has a ferry to Warrenpoint in County Down, and fishermen sell shellfish in stalls by the boat. This is an area that is associated with the great story of the Bull of Cooley, otherwise known as 'The Táin Saga' (Táin is pronounced 'tawn'). The oldest vernacular epic in western literature, this was written down by monks in various versions from early-Christian times to the medieval period (*see* below, and **Old Gods and Heroes**, p.52). The stories that are contained in the 'The Táin Saga' are full of fantastic heroism and impossible deeds; Cú Chulainn defends Ulster, and through his 'warp spasm' is able to change from a beardless youth to a furious, blood-lusting warrior.

The *Táin Bó Cuailnge*, or The Cattle Raid of Cooley

Queen Maeve and her husband were measuring up their worldly possessions, and found that they were equal in all things except one: he owned the most magnificent white bull, which outclassed anything that she could produce. Maeve knew, however, that there was a fine brown bull in the Kingdom of Ulster that was its equal, and she was determined to have it. At certain times of the year the guardians of Ulster, the Red Branch knights, became as feeble as kittens because of a spell put on them. Choosing this time, Maeve and her raiding party thought the whole expedition would be easy. However, at a crucial fording point the young and untried hero, Cú Chulainn, who was free of the spell, challenged each Connacht man to fight, and slew them all. Maeve, undaunted, decided to get the bull for herself and succeeded. When she got the bull home, though, it went into a mad frenzy and fought with the white bull until the earth shook. Finally, the brown bull of Cooley caught the white bull by the horns and shook it to pieces, causing a loin to fall by the Shannon (and thus giving the town of Athlone its name).

Queen Maeve is said to be buried at the top of Knocknarea Mountain in County Sligo (*see* p.322).

Tourist Information

Carlingford: behind O'Hare's pub,
t (042) 937 3033
Dundalk: t (042) 933 5484

Shopping

Crafts

Ceramic Art, Tholsel Lane, Carlingford
Riverstown Old Corn Mill, Cooley, Dundalk

Food and Drink

The Continental Meat Centre,
Mullaharlin Rd, Dundalk, t (042) 932 6643

Sports and Activities

Fishing

Bellingham Castle, Castlebellingham,
t (042) 937 2176. Salmon fishing on
the River Glyde.
Peadar Elmore, North Commons, Carlingford,
t (042) 937 3239. Boat hire for trips on
Carlingford Loch.

Walking

The Tain trail is an 18-mile (30km) circular
signposted route running through the Cooley
Mountains. Tourism Ireland publishes an
information leaflet about it, available at any
tourist office.

Watersports

Carlingford Adventure Centre, Tholsel St,
Carlingford (take R173 from Dundalk, on
Cooley Peninsula), t (042) 937 3100.
A firm organizing windsurfing, sailing
and canoeing, as well as tours and hiking,
throughout the year.

Where to Stay

Ballymascanlon Hotel, Dundalk, t (042) 935
8200, www.ballymascanlon.com (expensive).
A Victorian country house set in an 18-hole
parkland golf course, much favoured by the
clergy as a venue for ecumenical conferences.
In the grounds you will find a fine example
of a portal dolmen, as well as a swimming
pool, gym and tennis courts. Those with
children are welcome.
Jordan's Town House & Restaurant, Newry St,
Carlingford, t (042) 937 3223 (expensive).
Guestrooms with views over the harbour.
Ghan House, Carlingford, t (042) 937 3682,
www.ghanhouse.com (moderate).
Very luxurious B&B accommodation in
an 18th-century manor house, with views
over the Lough and the Mournes.
Carlingford Centre and Holiday Hostel,
Tholsel St, Carlingford, t (042) 937 3100,
www.carlingfordadventure.com (inexpensive).
A basic budget option. Book well in advance.

Eating Out

Ghan House, Carlingford, t (042) 937 3682,
www.ghanhouse.com (expensive).
A renowned restaurant offering dishes
made from local ingredients.
Ballymascanlon Hotel, Dundalk, t (042) 935
8200 (moderate–expensive). Irish and French
cooking served in plush surrounds.
Jordan's Town House & Restaurant,
Newry St, Carlingford, t (042) 937 3223
(moderate–expensive). Good, simple
cooking using the best local ingredients,
including pigs' trotters.
Oystercatcher Bistro, Market Sq, Carlingford,
t (042) 937 3922 (moderate). The place to
come for tasty, well-priced seafood.

Make sure you seek out out **Faughart Hill**, which is just north of Dundalk; it is
signposted a few miles off the Dundalk to Newry Road on the left. From here, the
whole of Leinster spreads out below you. This is where Edward Bruce was killed in
battle in 1318. He had been sent by his brother, Robert Bruce, King of Scotland, to make
trouble for the Anglo-Normans in Ireland, thereby lessening the pressure on himself.
You can see the Wicklow Hills rippling across the plain to join the Slieve Bloom and
the Cooley Hills behind. This part too is touched by myth – Cú Chulainn was born in
these heather-coloured hills. In Faughart graveyard, there is a **shrine to St Brigid**,

patroness of Ireland. St Brigid (*see* also p.46) is a semi-mythical figure who has pagan associations; she was a powerful Celtic Goddess who was responsible for sacred wells, livestock, the home, poetry and learning. When the Christian missionaries arrived, they christianized Brigid, made her a saint, and her feast day was put on 1 February, which was the pagan Celtic festival of *Imbolc* ('Lactation of Ewes'), the beginning of spring. It was in such a way that the Christian monks were able to make themselves and their religion acceptable in Ireland. Her very garish shrine consists of a well, St Brigid's Pillar and a stone surrounding a bank. People still come here to do stations – prayers centring around devotion to the saint.

County Longford

For the coarse fisherman, this flat, watery county has a particular attraction. It is situated right in the middle of Ireland, and lies in the basin of the Shannon River. Many small streams make their way westwards through the county to join the Shannon, and the place is resplendent with lakes: Lough Gowna in the north and Lough Kinale near Granard. Both have some pretty islands, and the county is well planted with trees. The county also has strong associations for the literary-minded. Oliver Goldsmith (1728–74) was born in Pallas. He wrote 'The Deserted Village', the classic poem that is so beloved of anthologists, and the play *She Stoops to Conquer*, which took the London stage by storm in 1773 and is constantly revived. Maria Edgeworth (1767–1849) was a well-educated and thoughtful woman whose work was read with respect by Sir Walter Scott and Jane Austen. Her novels on Irish life in the 19th century are superb. Edgeworth administered a large estate and did much to help during the famine years of the 1840s in her area of Longford. Padraic Colum (1881–1972), a poet and dramatist who worked for the revival of Gaelic literature, was born in Longford Town.

In the past, Longford was known as Annaly, after a 9th-century prince who ruled over it. His tribe were the O'Farrells (one member of this famous family later became one of the founding fathers of Argentina). In 1547, the greater part of Annaly was formed into the new county of Longford. Today, the people of County Longford are mainly farmers or work in agriculture-related industries.

Northern Longford

Longford town is set on the River Camlin. It is a pleasant (if somewhat rundown) town, which grew up around a fortress that belonged to the O'Farrell tribe – this has long since disappeared. Visitors cannot fail to notice the dominating 19th-century limestone **Cathedral of St Mel**, with its lofty towers. There is a modern **public library** in the Annaly car park, boasting a good local studies section and a comprehensive collection of titles by Oliver Goldsmith, Maria Edgeworth and Padraic Colum. The town is the administrative centre of the county and has a number of quite good shops, particularly for those looking for picnic fare.

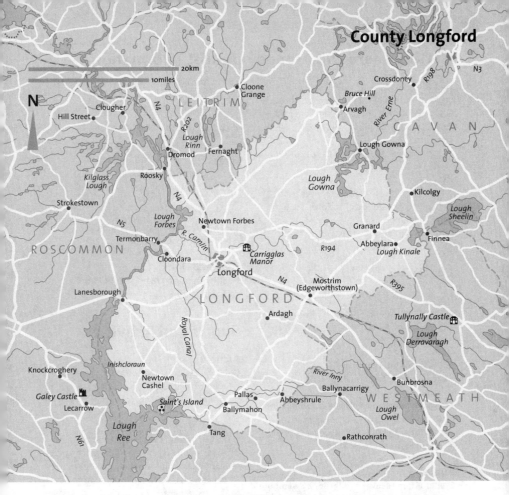

Five miles (8km) west, **Cloondara**, a pretty village on the Royal Canal, was formerly the Royal Canal terminal and the link with the River Shannon, and has a fine cut-stone canal harbour. In its *Teach Cheoil* (Irish music house), traditional Irish music, song and dance are performed in kitchen surroundings in summer. **Newtown Forbes**, 3 miles (4.8km) north-west of Longford, boasts a fine 17th-century mansion, **Castleforbes** (*grounds can be visited by writing ahead to Estate Office*), the seat of the earls of Granard. It overlooks Lough Forbes.

Carrigglas Manor (*open May–Sept daily 11–3; adm; t (043) 45165, www.carrigglas.com*), 3 miles (4.8km) from Longford Town on the R194 (Longford to Granard road), is a romantic Tudor-Gothic mansion with castellated turrets. It was built for the Lefroys, a French Huguenot family, in 1837 by Daniel Robertson. The ceilings in the main rooms are beautifully corniced and moulded. The stableyard was built in 1790 by James Gandon, the architect of the Dublin Four Courts. The Lefroys still live in the house and it contains most of its original furniture. Antique costumes are on display in a museum in the stableyard.

Getting There and Around

By Rail
The main Dublin–Sligo line passes through Edgeworthstown (Mostrim) and Longford Town, with 3 or 4 trains a day.
Longford, t (043) 45208
Iarnród Éireann, t (01) 836 6222, *www.irishrail.ie*

By Bus
There are expressway bus services from Dublin to Longford Town, Athlone, Granard and Ballymahon.
Longford Garage, t (043) 45208

Festivals

April
International Coarse Angling Festival, Abbeyshrule, t (043) 46566

July
Abbeyshrule International Fly-In Air Show, t (043) 57424. An annual air show complete with competitions.
Johnny Keenan Banjo Festival, Longford, t (087) 281 7825, *www.johnnykeenan.com*. Irish traditional and American Bluegrass music.
Longford Festival, t (043) 46566

August
Granard Harp Festival, t (043) 86643. A famous festival started in 1781, with competitions, held on the 2nd Sat of the month.

Tourist Information

Longford: Main St, t (043) 46566.
Open May–Sept.

Shopping

Books
The Longford Bookshop, Ballymahon St, Longford, t (043) 47698

Crafts
Tom McGuiness, Main St, Longford, t (043) 46305. Crafts and sweaters.

Food and Drink
Healthy Options, 3 Main St, Longford, t (043) 47776

Sports and Activities

Archery
Old Bond Estate, Killoe, Longford, t (043) 23327. Archery facilities within an attractive walled garden and woodland.

Fishing
The Cut in **Lough Ree** near Lanesborough is famous for its big bream, rudd, perch and pike. **Lough Gowra** is a coarse-fishing centre. An expedition may easily be made from here to Strokestown Park House, in Co. Roscommon (*see* p.314). For information, see *www.cfb.ie*.

Granard, on the R194 near Lough Gowra, is a bustling market town and angling centre for the River Inny, and for loughs Gowra and Sheelin. Its name, *Grian-ard*, suggests that it was a place of sun worship. A motte south-west of the town is crowned by a statue of St Patrick. Nearby at Abbeylara is part of an intriguing prehistoric earthworks, **Black Pig's Dyke**, which stretched from Donegal Bay to County Louth.

Southern Longford

Ballymahon, south of Longford Town, is Oliver Goldsmith country, and his connection with these parts is proudly remembered. Ballymahon itself is a good place from which to explore the River Inny and the Shannon. **Pallas**, 5 miles (8km) to the east of Longford Town, is Oliver Goldsmith's birthplace. All this countryside is

Denniston Edward & Co, Centenary Sq,
Longford, t (043) 46345. Equipment/supplies.

Golf
Longford Golf Club, t (043) 46310

Pleasure Cruises
For information on cruises on the Shannon
and Lough Ree, contact:
Athlone Cruisers, Jolly Mariner, Athlone,
t (0906) 72892

Ponytrekking
Chez Nous Riding Centre and Guest House,
Arva Rd, Drumlish, t (043) 24368

Where to Stay

The Longford Arms, Main St, Longford,
t (043) 46296, *www.longfordarms.ie*
(*luxury*). A plush, modern, central option
with a leisure centre and spa.
Shannonside House, Termonbarry, near
Cloondara, t (043) 26052 (*moderate*).
A comfortable house on the edge of
the Shannon. The owner is an expert on
fishing matters and has a boat available.
Toberphelim House, Granard,
t (043) 86568, *tober2@eircom.net*
(*moderate*). A pleasant old farmhouse,
family-friendly and run by a friendly family.
Viewmount House, Dublin Rd, Longford,
t (043) 41919, *www.viewmounthouse.com*
(*moderate*). A delightful Georgian house

with elegant bedrooms, woven rugs,
antique beds and beautiful views
over gardens and fields. Self-catering
accommodation is also offered.

Eating Out

There are also some good eateries over the
border, in Co. Westmeath (*see* p.504).
The Longford Arms, Main St, Longford,
t (043) 46296 (*moderate*). Pub lunches
and *table d'hôte* and à la carte menus.
Aubergine Gallery, 1 Ballymahon St (above
Market Bar), Longford, t (043) 48633
(*inexpensive–moderate*). Veggie lunches
very popular with locals. *Closed eves.*
Café au Lait, Main St, Longford, t (043) 47483
(*inexpensive*). Excellent salads, quiches and
soups. *Closed eves.*
The Rustic Inn, Abbeyshrule, t (044) 57424
(*inexpensive*). A good-value, family-run
restaurant offering plain food and steaks.
Torc Café and Shop, Ballymahon St, Longford,
t (043) 48277 (*inexpensive*). Light lunches,
snacks, cakes and chocolates. *Closed eves.*

Entertainment and Nightlife

Traditional Music
Camlin Lounge, Cloondara, t (043) 26039.
Twice-weekly in summer, weekly the rest
of the year.

charming, with soft green fields and hedges of hawthorn, sloe and holly. This area
is said to have had a seminal influence on Goldsmith's work. This is an extract from
'The Deserted Village':

Sweet was the sound, when oft at evening's close
Up yonder hill the village murmur rose;
There, as I passed with careless steps and slow,
The mingling notes came soften'd from below:
The swain responsive as the milkmaid sung,
The sober herd that low'd to meet their young;
The noisy geese that gabbled o'er the pool,
The playful children just let loose from school;
The watchdog's voice that bay'd the whisp'ring wind,

And the loud laugh that spoke the vacant mind;
These all in sweet confusion sought the shade,
And fill'd each pause the nightingale had made.
But now the sounds of population fail,
No cheerful murmurs fluctuate in the gale,
No busy steps the grass-grown footway tread,
For all the bloomy flush of life is fled.

Few are aware of Goldsmith's work in a field of even more lasting significance; as the editor of one of the first collections of nursery rhymes, John Newbury's *Mother Goose's Melody* of 1760, the poet may have invented some of the old standards himself. Certainly he recast many of them into the forms that we know today, and in the Newbury edition he added learned commentary and moral maxims to aid children with their studies. Of the Old Woman who lived under a Hill, he wrote: '...the very Essence of Truth. She lived under a hill, and if she is not gone she lives there still. Nobody will presume to contradict this'. And for the Three Wise Men of Gotham, in which had the bowl been stronger the song would have been longer, he adds, 'It is long enough'.

Abbeyshrule, near Pallas on the banks of the Inny, has the sad remains of a Cistercian abbey. To the north-east lies **Ardagh**, a lovely village surrounded by woods, where it is said that St Patrick founded a church, which is open to visitors. Not far from here at Kenagh is the **Corlea Trackway Visitor Centre** (*open Apr–Sep by guided tour only; adm; t (043) 22386, www.heritageireland.ie*), interpreting a timber trackway dating from 148 BC that was found in this area, beneath the bog.

Edgeworthstown (Mostrim), situated just outside Longford on the N4 running south, is not a very noteworthy place, except for the fact that Maria Edgeworth and her innovative father lived here. Richard Edgeworth reclaimed bogs and improved roads on his large estate, had four wives and a total of 22 children, advocated Catholic emancipation and educated his daughters. The quality of life for the peasant living in Ireland 150 years ago was miserable, and Maria cleverly showed the causes of this through the thoughts of the faithful servant Thady Quirk in *Castle Rackrent*. Uncaring greed, absenteeism and the exploitative methods of the middlemen are exposed in this great tale of moral fiction. She and her father are buried in the churchyard of St John's, as is Isolda Wilde, Oscar Wilde's sister. The Edgeworths' family home is now a nursing home and has been terribly altered.

Lanesborough is famous for its coarse fishing, and is on the northern tip of Lough Ree. You may tour the power station, which is fuelled by turf – one fossil fuel Ireland has a lot of. **Newtown Cashel**, a few miles south, is a pleasant town with a village green and stone walls. There is a lovely view of Lough Ree from the outskirts of the village, with the sympathetically restored **Abbey of Saints Island** to the south. This Augustinian monastery flourished in the 14th century, and today you can get to it by boat from Elfleet Bay, Lanesborough, in the summer. There are a variety of marsh birds around the lough, and good fishing. Another attractive island on the loch is **Inchcleraun** (also known as Inisclothran), which has the remains of a monastery founded at the beginning of the 6th century by St Diarmuid. On the highest point of the island is the Belfry Church, a Romanesque church with a square tower at the west end. There are the remains of several other churches grouped together and some early-Christian graves. The island is associated with the mythological Queen Maeve, who was killed by a stone fired from the sling of Forbai while she was bathing off the shore (*see* **Old Gods and Heroes**, p.57). It is easy to hire a boat out here during the summer from Coosan Point, Athlone or from Elfleet, Lanesborough.

County Westmeath

Westmeath (*Iarmhidh*) is one of the most fascinating counties for those who enjoy Irish history, fishing and exploring. The wooded lake country is scattered with magnificent old-fashioned pubs and ruins. It has a quiet beauty. The land is fairly level, with four large, spreading lakes: loughs Owel, Ennell, Derravaragh and Lene. It shares the beautiful Lough Sheelin in the north with County Cavan. The many other tiny lakes are humming with insect, bird and fish life, and are set amongst gorse and hazel-covered countryside. Untouched, unspoilt bogland makes up quite a section of the county, and it has its own unique bog flora and fauna. Coarse fishermen catch bream, rudd, pike, eels and tench, and, where the Shannon River expands into the islet-scattered Lough Ree, cruise boats can be hired. Many of the locals work as cattle-farmers, although there is some light industry around Athlone and Mullingar.

History

In pre-Norman times, the county was part of the Gaelic territory of Teffia and of the Province of Meath, and the Irish names that were recorded then are still common in the locality. These are the O'Flanagans, MacAuleys, MacGeoghegans, O'Dalys, O'Melaghlins and O'Fenelons. These *septs* were often at odds with each other, raiding cattle and encroaching on each others' territory. In approximately AD 300, the palace of the *árd rí* (high king) was at Uisneach, a small hill in the centre of the county from which you can see a long way over the surrounding countryside. Nothing remains of the palace. The *árd rí* moved back to Tara in County Meath in about AD 350. Yet this area was the chosen home of the high king again in the early 11th century, when Malachy II lived on the eastern shore of Lough Ennell. A large earthen mound marks the site of his fort, which is known as Dun-na-Sgiath.

Christianity came in the 5th century, and monasteries were founded by disciples of St Patrick in the following two centuries at Killare and Fore, and on Hare Island in Lough Ree. The Vikings raided up the Shannon and fought with the local Gaelic rulers. There is a story of how King Malachy slew the Viking chieftain, Turgesius, by throwing him into Lough Owel. When the Normans arrived after their successes in Waterford and Dublin in about AD 1170, they built themselves strongholds, and some of these can be seen today in the shape of mottes and baileys. Later they built stone castles and, from the 15th century onwards, towerhouses. The Gaelic tribes of the region did not allow the Normans to settle in peacefully: there were constant skirmishes and

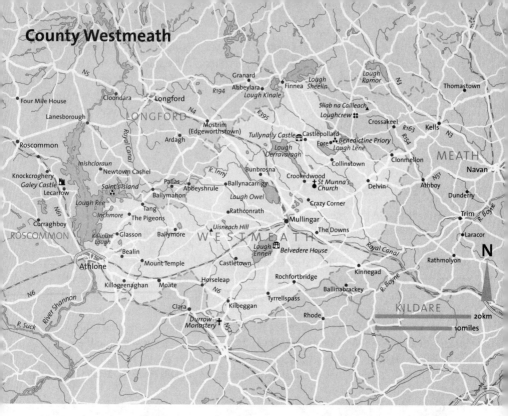

the usual muddle of complicated alliances between the Norman and Gaelic lords. Under the rule of the Plantagenet kings it had been administered as part of Meath, but in 1542 the part known as 'Westmeath' was split off from Meath because it was so difficult to control.

The 17th century bought great difficulties and much bitterness to the Gaels in the region. The Cromwellian wars of the 1640s resulted in huge amounts of land being confiscated, and as is the same all over Ireland, the local people still remember who the land once belonged to. The new landowners soon settled in and built themselves fine houses. But the last decade of the 17th century was fraught with the Jacobean/Williamite war. The war was a disaster for the Jacobites and the Catholic peasantry who fought with them; more land was confiscated and given to those who had supported William III, and the Penal Laws to control the Catholic population were passed (*see* **History**, p.16). There is a poem called *The Battle of the Aughrim*, written in 1927 by Richard Murphy; this is an excellent narrative poem from County Galway, which you should certainly try to read. It succinctly sums up the situation on the eve of the Battle of Aughrim in July 1691 by entering into the imagined thoughts and emotions of a Cromwellian landowner. Aughrim was one of the most decisive battles fought in the history of Ireland. William III's army of 18,000 men, under the command of Ginkel, met the Jacobite army of 24,000 men, under the command of a French general, St Ruth, and whipped them soundly.

Getting There and Around

By Rail
The county is served by 2 rail routes: the Dublin–Sligo line, which stops at Mullingar, and the Dublin–Galway line, which stops at Athlone. Both have 3 or 4 trains a day in either direction.
Athlone Station, t (09064) 73300
Mullingar Station, t (044) 48274

By Bus
Frequent express bus services stop at Kinnegad, Mullingar, Moate and Athlone. The local bus service stops at Killucan, Multyfarnham, Glassan and Kilbeggan.
Athlone Bus Station, t (09064) 484 406
Mullingar Bus Depot, t (044) 48274

By Bike
Buckley Cycles, Main St, Athlone,
t (09064) 78989

Festivals

May
All Ireland Amateur Drama Festival, Deane Crowe Theatre, Athlone, t (09064) 92129. A busy festival with many sideshows.

July
Brideswell International Celtic Festival, Brideswell, Athlone, t (09064) 94630. A popular folk music festival featuring musicians, singers and dancers from all over the Celtic world.
Mullingar Bachelor's Festival, t (044) 48650. A competition between eligible bachelors from around the world; 2nd week of month.

November
John McCormack, Golden Voice of Athlone, t (09064) 73173. An international classical singing competiton named after a local son who was the greatest lyric tenor of his day.

Tourist Information

Athlone: t (09064) 94630. *Open Easter–mid Oct*
Mullingar: Dublin Rd, t (044) 48650

Shopping

Antiques
Locke's Distillery Museum, Kilbeggan, t (0506) 32134, *lockesmuseum@iol.ie*

Crafts
Mullingar Pewter Limited, Great Down, The Downs, t (044) 48791, *mullingarpewter@ eircom.com*. Factory tours run weekdays.
Tom Birminghams Man's Shop, 37 Oliver Plunkett St, Mullingar, t (044) 40760. Tweeds and knitwear.

Food and Drink
Nuts 'n' Grains, Oliver Plunkett St, Mullingar, t (044) 45988

Sports and Activities

Boat Hire and Pleasure Cruises
Cruiser and rowing-boat hire is available from the following:
Adventure Viking Cruise, 7 St Mary's Place, Athlone, t (09064) 73383, *vikingtours@ ireland.com*. Cruises to Lough Ree and Clonmacnoise on a replica Viking ship, departing from the Strand Fishing Tackle Shop (*see* below).
Athlone Cruisers, Jolly Mariner, Athlone, t (09064) 72892
Greville Arms Hotel, Mullingar, t (044) 48563

Fishing
Brown trout fishing is good on **Lough Sheelin**. For coarse fishing try **loughs Owel, Ennell** and **Derravaragh**. There is also very good pike fishing all over **Lough Ree**.
O'Malley's, 33 Dominick St, Mullingar, t (044) 48300, *dpomalley@eircom.net*. Tackle and advice.
Strand Fishing Tackle Shop, St Endas Place, The Strand, Athlone, t (09064) 79277 or t (086) 8254141. Information, tackle, bait and boats for fishing on Lough Ree.

Golf
Athlone Golf Club, Hodson's Bay, t (09064) 92073
Mullingar Golf Club, Belvedere, t (09064) 48366

Ponytrekking

Ladestown House, Mullingar, t (044) 48218, www.ladestownhouse.com. Trail rides along the lake.

Mullingar Equestrian Centre, Athlone Rd, Mullingar, t (044) 48331/40569, www.mullingarequestrian.com

Where to Stay

Temple Spa and Country House, Horseleap, Moate, t (0506) 35118, www.templespa.com (expensive). A charming Georgian farmhouse with lovely bright rooms and an elegant dining room serving wholesome food, much of which is grown on its own farm or in its vegetable garden. The hotel has recently expanded its spa facilities, and residential breaks including relaxation therapies are now available

Greville Arms Hotel, Pearse St, Mullingar, t (044) 48563, www.grevillearms.com (moderate). A traditional-style hotel mentioned in James Joyce's Ulysses, with pretty hotels and suites.

Mearescourt House, Rathconrath, Mullingar, t (044) 55555, www.mearescourt.com (moderate). A family-run mansion house in pretty parkland, offering good home cooking and comfortable rooms.

Mornington House, Multyfarnham, near Mullingar, t (044) 72191, www.mornington.ie (moderate). A lovely country house within peaceful grounds, with two dogs who act as the welcoming party. Lake Derravaragh is within walking distance. Home-grown veg and herbs are served at dinner, which might be enjoyed in front of a log fire. The hosts are very knowledgeable about local history. Closed Nov–mid-Mar.

The Village Inn, Tyrrellspass, t (044) 23171 (moderate). A cosy, period townhouse hotel forming part of an elegant crescent around the village green. The service and the food are excellent.

Lough Derravaragh Camping and Leisure Park, Multyfarnham, near Mullingar, t (044) 71500 (inexpensive). A reasonable campsite.

Woodlands Farm, Streamstown, Mullingar, t (044) 26414 (inexpensive). A typical Irish farmhouse crammed with holy pictures, providing a warm welcome and delicious food.

Eating Out

Oscars Restaurant, Oliver Plunkett St, Mullingar, t (044) 44909 (moderate–expensive). A place highly recommended by locals for its menu of traditional and modern favourites. Closed lunch exc Sun.

Le Château, St Peters Port, Athlone, t (09064) 94517 (moderate). A friendly, good-value choice beautifully situated within an old church, specializing in game, fish and meat.

Conlon's Restaurant, 5–9 Dublingate St, Athlone, t (09064) 74376 (moderate). Traditional and modern fare, including vegetarian and children's dishes.

Crookedwood House, Mullingar, t (044) 72165 (moderate). A cellar restaurant that has won awards for its excellent, plain cooking. Closed Mon, and lunch exc Sun.

The Glasson Village Restaurant, Glasson, t (0902) 85001 (moderate). Lovely plain Irish cooking, including lots of seafood. Closed lunch exc Sun.

Tyrrellspass Castle, Tyrrellspass, t (044) 23105 (moderate). Medieval banquets and excellent Sunday lunches.

The Wineport Lodge, Glasson, t (09064) 39010, www.wineport.ie (moderate). A very popular spot in Ireland's first 'wine hotel', priding itself on its seasonally changing dishes made from local produce.

The Cottage, Kinnegad, t (044) 75284 (inexpensive). A good place for snack lunches and fresh scones. Closed eves.

Danny Byrne's, 27 Pearse St, t (044) 43792 (inexpensive). A Victorian-style pub and restaurant, good for lunch.

Entertainment and Nightlife

Live Music

The following offer both traditional and jazz music:

Anthony Hughes', Pearse St, Mullingar, t (044) 48237

Danny Byrne's, Pearse St, Mullingar, t (044) 43792

Three Jolly Pigeons, Tang, Lissoy, Athlone, t (09064) 85162

Athlone

Athlone, half of which is in County Roscommon but is dealt with here, is a good touring centre that straddles the River Shannon and immediately spreads into the lovely Lough Ree. Athlone (*Ath Luain*: 'Ford of Luain'), has always been important as the crossing place on the Shannon between the kingdoms of Leinster and Connacht; many raids were launched from here by the fierce Connacht men, who wanted the fat cattle of Meath. Later, when the Anglo-Normans had established themselves in Leinster, Athlone became the last strong outpost of that civilization, for behind it and around it stretched the world of the Gaels. Its castle was built by King John, and from it the English attempted to govern Connacht.

Over the centuries, the castle and walls had to be rebuilt many times, but the most memorable stories concern the Siege of Athlone, when the town was held for James II against the Williamite forces. Sergeant Custume (after whom the present barracks is named) and 10 volunteers gave their lives hacking down the temporary wooden bridge over which the enemy was about to swarm into the breach in the walls. Unluckily for the Irish, their leader, a French general called St Ruth, was a prize idiot, and, having secured what he thought was victory, decided to throw a grand party, even though Patrick Sarsfield, our Limerick hero, begged him to take the rumours of further attack seriously. Thus the Williamite forces were able to take the city while the Irish troops were drunkenly sleeping over their cups.

Today Athlone is a thriving market town, and a major rail and road terminus, and has a harbour on the inland navigation system. It is full of good food shops and places where you can have a good jar and listen to traditional or jazz music. One of the most striking buildings in the town is the enormous Roman Catholic **Church of St Peter and St Paul**, off Grace Road, built in the Roman Renaissance style. It was erected in the grounds of the old military barracks and opened for worship in 1937. On the west bank overlooking the bridge, almost opposite the church, is **Athlone Castle** (*open Easter–early Oct daily 10–6; adm; t (09064) 92912;visitors' centre t (09064) 42100*). This was built in the 13th century and has always been a strong military post. Although it has been strengthened over the centuries, it retains its classic Norman design. It was used as a military post until 1969, when it was declared a national monument, and a museum was established in the central keep. The museum has interesting exhibits on the folk life and the archaeology of the area, as well as exhibits on the siege of Athlone and on the town's favourite son, the great tenor John McCormack. For one week in late April/early May, Athlone is brimming with people who come for the All Ireland Amateur Drama Festival and its sideshows (*see* p.503).

If you decide that you would like to immerse yourself further in times past, wander into **St Mary's Church** in Church Street, where, frozen into stone statues, Tudor squires kneel with their ladies in perpetual prayer. The atmosphere inside is akin to that of a village church in England. The tower bell is one of those that were removed at the despoiling of Clonmacnoise.

The town's transport and heritage museum at Ballinahown, **An Dún** (*open Easter– Oct daily, call for times, t (09064) 30106*), contains a unique private collection of farm and transportation devices.

Lough Ree

If you are staying in Athlone, you may find time to explore the many islands in Lough Ree (*see* 'Sports and Activities', p.498). Ask down at the marina about hiring a boat to Hare Island, Inchmore, Inchbofin, Iniscleraun and Saints Island, all of which were homes to saints in ancient times. **Hare Island** is very attractive, and contains the ruins of a church founded by St Ciaran in the 6th century before he moved to Clonmacnoise in County Offaly. **Saints Island**, in the eastern part of the lake, has the ruins of a well-preserved monastery and church (*see* p.500).

If you follow the N55 to **Glassan** a few miles outside Athlone, you get a lovely view of inner Lough Ree and its wooded islands and shoreline. Glassan is a pretty little place where artisans' cottages are smothered with roses and clematis in summer. All the little country roads from here down to the left lead to Lough Ree and little coves such as Killinure and Killeenmore. Scholars and the tourist board have claimed the area between Glassan and Tang as 'Oliver Goldsmith Country'. Goldsmith (1729–74) was the son of a clergyman, and was actually born over the border at Pallas in County Longford (*see* p.496).

Bealin to Mullingar

If you follow the N6 east, you enter rich cattle-raising and dairy country. The little country roads around here are really rural and very enticing, with many fine demesnes and ruins set in wooded fields, and the roads are nearly empty of cars, so you can really enjoy driving or, even better, cycling.

At **Bealin**, on a little road between Athlone and Mount Temple, is a sculptured cross dating from the 8th century, called the **Twyford Cross**. It is almost 7ft (2m) high and was found in a nearby bog. **Moate** is an important market town, and is traditionally supposed to be named after the mound of **Mota Grainne Oige**, which rises beside it. (Mota was the wife of O'Melaghlin, an early Celtic chief of the district.) The mound was definitely used as a defensive site by the Normans when they arrived here in the 12th century. There are many small commercial sandpits in the esker – a long, winding ridge formed during the Ice Age – near Moate. Along the ridge runs one of the ancient roads of Ireland, going to Tara in County Meath; the surface of it is covered in hazel, hornbeam, bracken and gorse.

In Moate itself you'll find the **Dún na Sí Cultural Centre and Heritage Park** (*open Apr–Oct Mon–Thur 9–5; adm; t (09064) 81183*), a folk centre with old farm machinery and re-creations of traditional past life, including music, dancing and storytelling, alongside a genealogical centre where visitors can trace their roots.

If you are passing through these parts on your way to Dublin, you might like to stop in **Horseleap** on the N6. This place gets its name from an event that occurred when the Norman Baron de Lacy was being chased by a party of native Gaels (the MacGeoghegans, a ruling Gaelic family whose lands remained fairly intact up to the time of Cromwell in the 1640s), and made his horse jump over the castle drawbridge. Inside the village you can see a partly damaged Norman motte and bailey that dates back to 1192. There is also a well-preserved 16th-century towerhouse that was built by the aforementioned MacGeoghegans.

The next village along the N6 is **Kilbeggan**. It has an old distillery, founded in 1757 and restored as the **Locke's Distillery Museum** (*open daily Apr–Oct 9–6, Nov–Mar 10–4; t (0506) 32134, www.lockesdistillerymuseum.com*) by an enthusiastic local committee. The huge waterwheel is back in operation. On the Tullamore road a few miles out is the ruined **Durrow Abbey**, a famous monastery founded in the 6th century by St Columba. Amongst its attractions are a holy well and, in the disused graveyard, the **Durrow High Cross** (*see* 'County Offaly', p.515).

Back on the N6 to Dublin is **Tyrrellspass**, a very pretty village laid out as a crescent around the central green in the 18th century by the Countess of Belvedere. The area was ruled by an Anglo-Norman family, the Tyrells, until Cromwellian times. The castle, a private residence, was built by them in the 15th century. Richard Tyrell was a late-16th-century hero who annihilated a large Elizabethan force near here with the help of a small band of men. **Belvedere House, Gardens and Park** (*open Apr–Nov daily, call for times, t (044) 49060; adm; www.belvedere-house.ie*) lies between Tyrellspass and Mullingar on the shores of Lough Ennell. It was built for Robert Rochfort, Lord Belfield, afterwards 1st Earl of Belvedere, in about 1740. It was probably built by Richard Cassels, Ireland's foremost Palladian architect (*see* p.75). The house is small and comprises a three-bay recessed centre between projecting bay ends. The plasterwork on the ground floor is superb, with cherubs and classical figures amidst fruit, flowers, clouds and stars. The 1st Earl was a vindictive man who kept his young wife a prisoner in a nearby house for 31 years after her alleged adultery with his younger brother. The gardens are superb, with many old-fashioned shrubs, 18th-century follies and ruins.

Twelve miles (19km) to the west of Mullingar on the Ballymore Road, beyond Loughanavally, is **Uisneach Hill**, the 'Navel of Ireland', with an ancient boulder called the Catstone, or the 'Stone of Divisions', traditionally marking the spot where the four provinces of Ireland meet. *Uisneach* (pronounced 'Ush nock') in mythology was a seat of the high kings before Tara, but archaeologists have found nothing on the site but thick layers of ashes, suggesting that this was a place for important national ceremonies, perhaps Bealtaine (May Eve) with its fire festival. Uisneach would be the perfect spot for a bonfire; from the top of the hill you can enjoy a view said to take in no less than 20 counties.

Mullingar, which was a garrison town, has become a noted angling centre with a busy, brightly painted main street, several excellent pubs, and some grocery shops selling good picnic fare. It is one of the most pleasant market towns in Ireland, with a feeling of energy that is often lacking in some of the more dreary towns scattered through the middle of the country.

The area around Mullingar is great shooting, fishing and hunting country, and the new squires who lead the way are German and French. A lovely anonymous rhyme relates an episode in Mullingar:

There was an elopement down in Mullingar
But sad to relate the pair didn't get far.
'Oh fly,' said he, 'darling, and see how it feels.'
But the Mullingar heifer was beef to the heels.

The Seven Wonders of Fore and Castlepollard

Five and a half miles (8.9km) from Mullingar on the R394, east of Crookedwood village, is the fairy-tale **St Munna's Church** (*key kept at house opposite graveyard*), built in the 15th century and boasting a castle-like tower and battlements. In **Crookedwood**, at the southern tip of Lough Derravaragh, the scenery is really charming, as the village looks over the glittering lake.

Take the little road through Collinstown to **Fore**, which was once an important ecclesiastical centre, situated between loughs Lene and Bane and freely accessible. Fore has the same magical atmosphere as Glendalough in County Wicklow (*see* p.576) but it has not really been looked after. For a bit of blarney, make sure to stop in at the Seven Wonders Pub and ask about the 'Seven Wonders of Fore'; the staff there will send you on a tour of seven sites associated with miracles of St Feichin, including wood that will not burn, water that won't boil, and **St Feichin's Church** in the western graveyard, which dates from the 10th century and is remarkable for its enormous doorway; a cross in a circle marks the massive lintel, raised by the saint's prayers. The well-preserved Benedictine priory is one of the Wonders – the original church was constructed on a bog by St Feichin in AD 630. The one standing today was built by Walter de Lacy, a powerful Anglo-Norman, at the start of the 13th century on the remains of an earlier abbey. Another wonder, St Feichin's anchorite cell on the hillside, was occupied by a hermit as late as 1764, and later became a family vault for the Grenville-Nugents of Delvin. From the hills around Fore there are some lovely views of Meath, Cavan and Longford.

Castlepollard is an attractive 19th-century town with a triangular green. Close by, on the Granard Road (R395), are the beautiful grounds of **Tullynally Castle** (*open mid-June–July daily 10–6; gardens May–Aug daily 2–6; adm; t (044) 61159, www. tullynallycastle.com*), formerly Pakenham Hall, the seat of the earls of Longford. When viewed from a distance in its romantic setting, this makes you think of a castle in an illustrated medieval manuscript. The hall became a Gothick castle in the 1790s; the castellated additions were designed by Francis Johnston for the 2nd Lord Longford, whose family, the Pakenhams, bought the property in 1655. Inside you can see a fine collection of family portraits, furniture and memorabilia. Novelist Maria Edgeworth, an enthusiastic visitor, described it as, 'the seat of hospitality and the resort of fine society'. The present family are extremely literary: Lady Antonia Fraser is of this family, and her brother, the present viscount, is also a respected historian. The grounds are beautiful, and the castle looks down to Lough Derravaragh, which is one of the loughs associated with the story of the Children of Lir: it was here the children's jealous stepmother transformed them into swans.

County Offaly and County Laois

To many travellers, the only significance of these two counties is that you travel through them on your way to Tipperary or Cork. They lie in the centre of Ireland's saucer-shape, in the flat plains and boglands, separated from Galway and Roscommon on the west by the Shannon. Both counties are delightfully untouched by organized tourism, there are no bus tours to speak of; even travellers to the famous monastic site of Clonmacnoise will find it as quiet and still as did the 6th-century monks who sought out this island of tranquillity along the river.

Most of County Offaly is bogland, alive with its own special flora and fauna. It is bordered in the west by the River Shannon, and there is plenty of scope for cruising along its beautiful waters, and through the Grand Canal that divides the county in two. In the south-west, Offaly shares with County Laois the glens of the Slieve Bloom Mountains. They are not a great height – 2,000ft (610m) at their highest point – but they have a grandeur of their own, amongst the flat watery boglands around them.

Both counties have a great wealth of early-Christian sites, together with some superb examples of 18th-century Big Houses. The villages grew up around such landlord properties and are still, on the whole, very attractive. Birr is a gem of a planned 18th-century town, and the Parsons family who laid it out still own the magnificent gardens and arboretum their ancestors planted. You can spend hours in it, marvelling at the exotic species and grand design.

County Laois is bordered on its east by the Grand Canal, which runs alongside the River Barrow at Monasterevin, finally merging into the Barrow at Athy in County Carlow. The River Nore flows through Laois on its western side, so there is plenty of scope for the coarse fishing enthusiast.

Getting Around

By Rail

Portlaoise is on the main Dublin–Cork/Limerick line; there are at least 8 trains a day in each direction. Trains on the Dublin–Galway line pass through Portarlington and Tullamore.
Ballybrophy, t (0505) 46331
Portarlington, t (0502) 23128
Portlaoise, t (0502) 21303
Tullamore, t (0506) 21431

By Bus

Bus Éireann, Athlone, t (09064) 84406

By Bike

M. Kavanagh, Railway St, Portlaoise, **t** (0502) 21357 A Raleigh Rent-a-Bike scheme operator.

Festivals

June

Durrow Carnival Weekend, www.visitdurrow.com. Traditional music, *ceilidhs*, concerts and street entertainment.

July

French Festival, Portarlington, Laois, **t** (0502) 23128. A celebration of the French-Huguenot influence on the town.
Laois *Fleadh*, Clonaslee, **t** (0502) 21178 Music and dancing.

August

Birr Vintage Week, Offaly. **t** (0509) 20293. An 'Old Time Fayre' incorporating art exhibitions, antiques, parades, a variety of street entertainment, fireworks and singing competitions.
Stradbally Steam Rally, Laois, **t** (0502) 25444, *www.irishsteam.ie*. Working steam engines, carousels and stalls, early in the month.

October

John Keegan Weekend, Shanahoe, nr Abbeyleix, Laois, **t** (0502) 63355. An annual celebration of the life and works of the 19th-century poet, writer and storyteller.
Laois Arts Festival, Laois, **t** (0502) 63355, *www.laoisartsfestival.com*. A festival featuring music, all kinds of arts, literature and theatre performances

County Offaly and County Laois

History

Perhaps because of the bogland, our knowledge of Stone Age settlement in these parts is scarce. However, at Lough Boora near Kilcormac, excavations in 1977 revealed traces of nomadic activity from some 7000 years BC. There is plenty of evidence that humans were around in these parts during the Bronze Age (2000 BC), as weapons and ornaments have been found, those at Banagher being particularly famous. The Iron Age and the arrival of the Celts is marked by numerous hill-forts such as Aghancon, near Leap Castle. The *septs* that eventually emerged were the O'Connors, O'Molloys, O'Dempseys, MacCoghlans, Foxes and O'Carrolls in County Offaly; and the O'Moores, Fitzpatricks, and O'Dunnes in County Laois.

When the Anglo-Normans arrived in 1169, they could never establish themselves securely here and gradually retreated back to the Pale, a small area of land around Dublin, Meath and Louth. In the 16th century, the English started their experiment of planting disloyal parts of Ireland with loyal English. The boundaries of County Offaly and County Laois began to take shape with bits taken from the older kingdoms of Ossory (now Kilkenny), Meath, Thomond and Munster. When plantation did not work well enough, the Crown ordered the transplantation of the chief tribes and their followers to County Kerry, around Tarbert. By the 1620s, families such as the Parsons, now the earls of Rosse, had taken over the strongholds of the native Gaelic chiefs – in this case, the O'Carrolls of Ely in County Offaly.

Today, the people living in these counties work mainly in small industries such as the manufacture of vitrified clay pipes, or for Bord na Móna, the Irish turf development authority, which employs more than 5,000 people. Most of them have small farms that they work on a part-time basis.

Clonmacnoise

Clonmacnoise (*open daily mid-Mar–mid May, late Sept and Oct 10–6, mid-May–mid-Sept 9–7, Nov–mid Mar 10–5.30; guided tours; adm;* **t** *(0905) 74195, www.heritageireland.ie*), at Shannonbridge on the banks of the Shannon, is one of Ireland's most celebrated holy places . In AD 545 St Ciaran founded a monastery here which became one of the most famous of all monastic settlements in Ireland. T. W. Rolleston (1857–1920) adapted a beautiful early Gaelic poem, simply entitled 'Clonmacnoise', that suggests what a great centre of worship and learning it was, and the place it holds in the Celtic twilight view of history:

In a quiet water'd land, a land of roses,
Stands Saint Kieran's city fair;
And the warriors of Erin in their famous generations
Slumber there.

There beneath the dewy hillside sleep the noblest
Of the clan of Conn,
Each below his stone with name in branching Ogham
And the sacred knot thereon.

There they laid to rest the seven Kings of Tara,
There the sons of Cairbre sleep –
Battle-banners of the Gael that in Kieran's plain of crosses
Now their final hosting keep.

And in Clonmacnoise they laid the men of Teffia,
And right many a lord of Breagh;
Deep the sod above Clan Creide and Clan Conaill,
Kind in hall and fierce in fray.

Many and many a son of Conn the Hundred-fighter
In the red earth lies at rest;
Many a blue eye of Clan Colman the turf covers,
Many a swan-white breast.

Tourist Information

Birr: t (0509) 20110/20923, *www.elyocarroll.com.*
  Open May–Sept.
Clonmacnoise: t (09096) 74134. *Open Apr–Oct.*
Tullamore: t (0506) 52617

Shopping

Crafts

Banagher Brass and Copper,
  Cuba, Banagher, t (0509) 51381
Eric Stanley, Woodville Farm, Shinrone, Birr.
  Sheepskin slippers and jackets.

Food and Drink

Natural Stuff, O'Connor Sq, Tullamore,
  t (0506) 41308. Health foods.
Rudds, Busherstown House, Moneygall,
  t (0505) 45077. Home-made sausages
  and traditional smoked bacon.

Sports and Activities

Bird-watching

Look out for golden plover, wigeon, whooper
swans, curlews, lapwings and black-tailed
godwits in the flood meadows on either side
of the Little Brosna River.

Bog Tours

Five-and-a-half-mile (9km) circular tours of
the **Blackwater Bog** with the Clonmacnoise
and West Offaly Railway, t (09096) 74114,

www.bnm.ie, set out from the Bord na Mona
Blackwater Works, Shannonbridge every hour,
on the hour, daily 10–5 Apr–Oct.

Fishing

J. Hiney's Pub & Tackle, Main St, Ferbane,
  t (0902) 54344. Coarse fishing.

Golf

Birr Golf Club, The Glens, Banagher Rd, Birr,
  t (0509) 20082
Castle Barna Golf Club, Daingean,
  t (0506) 53384, *www.castlebarna.ie*
Esker Hills Golf and Country Club,
  Ballykilmurray, Tullamore, t (0506) 55999,
  www.eskerhillsgolf.com

Outdoor Activity Centres

Brendina O'Meara, Shannon Adventure
  Canoeing, Marina, Banagher, t (0509) 51411,
  advcaneo@iol.ie. Canoeing trips.
Outdoor Education Centre, Birr,
  t (0509) 20029, *birroec@indigo.ie.*
  Orienteering in the Slieve Blooms.

Pleasure Cruises

Celtic Canal Cruisers, Tullamore,
  t (0506) 21861. Cruiser hire.
Historic Cruising Tours, 17 Woodlands,
  Birr, t (0509) 51411, *advcanoe@iol.ie.*
  Cruises on Lough Derg.

Ponytrekking

Annaharvey Farm and Equestrian Centre,
  Tullamore, t (0506) 43544,
  www.annaharveyfarm.ie

The monastery was well sited on a major ford on the Shannon, on a huge esker
ridge that stands well above the boggy plain. It became a centre of great learning in
medieval times and was patronized by the O'Connor kings. Turlough and Rory were
buried there. The monastery suffered terribly from Viking raids and inter-dynastic
wars between different *septs*. The coming of the Normans spelt the decline of
Clonmacnoise, for they built a fort by the river, and an English garrison was built
at Athlone. It further fell into a decline after the Reformation, and was sacked in 1552
by the English garrison at Athlone.

Today the remains are extensive and include nine churches, a cathedral, three fine
high crosses, two round towers, and some decorated early grave slabs – they date
from the 8th, 9th and 10th centuries. Many of the names inscribed on them are found
in the annals, the ancient manuscripts of Ireland. A few of them are displayed in the

Kinnitty Castle Equestrian Centre,
  Kinnitty, Birr, t (0509) 37318
Noel Cosgrave, Birr Equestrian Centre,
  Kingsborough House, Fortal, Birr, t (0509) 21961

Swimming Pools
Banagher Outdoor Pool, Banagher.
Birr Indoor Pool, Roscrea Rd, Birr, t (0509) 20343

Walking
  The Slieve Bloom Way, a signposted circular
31-mile (50km) route, starts at Glenmonicknew
Forest car park. Ask for information at any
tourist office, or contact the following:
Ivan Sheppard Bus & Boot Tours, Kinnitty,
  Birr, t (0509) 37122 or t (086) 408 2118
Slieve Bloom Walking Centre, Kinnitty Village,
  t (0509) 37299, www.slievebloom.ie. A guided
walking tours programme and maps

Where to Stay

Kinnitty Castle, Kinnitty, t (0509) 37318, www.
kinnittycastle.com (luxury). An atmospheric
17th-century castellated mansion with a
Georgian restaurant (moderate).
Ardmore House, Kinnitty, Birr, t (0509) 37009,
www.kinnitty.net (moderate). A very
welcoming B&B in an historic house.
Moorhill, Clara Rd, Tullamore, t (0506) 21395,
www.moorhill.ie (moderate). A charming
Victorian house with a restaurant (see below).
The Maltings, Castle St, Birr, t (0509) 21345,
themaltingsbirr@eircom.net (inexpensive).
Converted 18th-century riverside maltings.

Self-catering
The Old Rectory, Coolbanaghe, Emo, Portlaoise,
  t (0502) 46538, www.oldrectoryemo.com
  (inexpensive). Renovated coachhouses.

Eating Out

Brosna Lodge Hotel, Banagher, t (0509) 51350
  (moderate). Bland but good-value cooking.
County Arms Hotel, Railway Rd, Birr,
  t (0509) 20791, www.countyarmshotel.com
  (moderate). Reasonable international
  cuisine served in a Georgian country-house
  hotel revamped in 2006.
Dooly's Hotel, Emmet Sq, Birr, t (0509) 20032,
  www.doolyshotel.com (moderate). A good
  coffee shop and a restaurant with adequate
  if rather pretentious global and local dishes.
Moorhill, Clara Rd, Tullamore, t (0506) 21395
  (moderate). An awardwinning restaurant in
  the converted stables of a Victorian country
  house (see above), using the best seasonal
  local produce.
Riverbank Restaurant, Riverstown, Birr,
  t (0509) 21528 (moderate). Fine food and
  wine, including the likes of pan-fried fillet
  of ostrich, on the banks of the Little Brosna
  River, a mile (1.6km) from Birr.
The Stables Restaurant, Oxmantown Mall, Birr,
  t (0509) 20263, www.thestablesrestaurant.
  com (moderate). A good place for seafood,
  meat and vegetarian dishes, including
  traditional Irish cuisine.
The Vine House, Banagher, t (0509) 51463
  (moderate). Good-value, simple cooking.

reception area as you enter the monastery. The ruins are dispersed in a large grassy enclosure, and each building is well described. Note that it takes at least an hour to walk around them.

Of particular note is the 10th-century **West Cross** with its decorative panels of figure-carving. The lowest panel on the east face of the shaft shows two figures clasping a post on which a bird perches. These have been interpreted as St Ciaran, the founder, and the local king, Diarmuid, who granted the land for the monastery. It is said that Diarmuid helped to build the first wooden church with his own hands, and was rewarded for his piety by the high kingship of Ireland. The largest church, the **cathedral**, has a fine north doorway (c. 1460) of limestone with foliate carvings and figure-sculpture. All the churches have Romanesque features; **Teampul Finghin** on the northern border of the site has a beautiful chancel arch in three orders, decorated with chevrons and animal heads. It dates from the second half of the 12th century. A small **round tower** rises from the chancel. There is a small tourist office in the car park, a coffee shop, and some picnic benches arranged around the entrance to the reception area. A pilgrimage is held here on 12 September, the feast of St Ciaran.

Southern Offaly and Tullamore

If you travel south towards Birr from Clonmacnoise and Shannonbridge on the R357, you will pass a lovely little castle at **Clonony**, built in Henry VIII's time. It is a four-storey towerhouse with a 19th-century reconstructed *bawn*. Gravestones uncovered here belonged to the Ormonde Butlers. **Shannonbridge** has a power station, artillery fortifications that date from the Napoleonic period and a superb reputation for coarse fishing. It also has an excellent pub and supermarkets to supply the cruiser trade.

Just outside Shannonbridge, Bord na Móna, the National Peat Board, has set up a unique attraction, converting one of its old working rail lines into the **Clonmacnoise and West Offaly Railway**, upon which you can travel on a 5½-mile (9km) guided tour of the Blackwater Bog and learn everything about the complex natural history of bogs and their importance to Ireland (*see* also 'Sports and Activities', p.512).

Nearby is **Shannon Harbour**, where the Grand Canal and the Shannon River meet. You moor your boat underneath the ruins of an old hotel. Many an emigrant said their goodbyes here before sailing to America. The boglands around **Ferbane** and **Boher**, just south of the river, are fascinating in their way, and the medieval church remains in these tiny places are very interesting. At **Banagher**, you will see a Martello tower guarding the western side of the river, built as a lookout to warn against a possible Napoleonic invasion. The attractive town is linked with the novelist Anthony Trollope, who was stationed here as Post Office Surveyor in 1841.

Just outside Banagher, the picturesque **Cloghan Castle** (*open by appointment only, call t (0509) 51650; adm*) was built in the 14th century on the site of a monastery that flourished seven centuries before. Now brought back to life by restorationist Brian Thompson, who lives here, it is furnished with a fascinating collection of antiques, weapons and armour going back to the time of Cromwell.

Birr is an absolute must on any tour of Ireland: the castle gardens are superb, and the town itself is beautifully laid out with wide, Georgian streets and squares. The hand of the Parsons family is obvious in this; it is the planned, landlord towns that have grown old gracefully. Birr stands on land granted to Laurence Parsons in 1620 and used to be called Parsonstown. In Emmet Square you will find Dooly's Hotel, a very old coaching inn (*see* p.513). The Galway Hunt were tagged 'The Galway Blazers' after setting fire to the hotel during a night of celebration in 1809. West of Emmet Square is **John's Mall** with its Georgian houses. Notice the fine fanlights above the doors. There is a pleasant walk downstream following the river, and right of Oxmanton Bridge is St Brendan's Church and the Convent of Mercy, designed by Pugin.

The entrance to **Birr Castle** (*grounds open daily 9–6; adm; t (0509) 20336, www.birrcastle.com*) is in William Street. Here you will find more than 100 acres (40ha) of pleasure grounds that were laid out by Laurence Parsons, the 2nd Earl of Rosse

(1757–1841). The castle itself is not open to the public, but various exhibitions are held in the gallery, in the grounds, during the summer, and you can see a gigantic reflecting **telescope** that was built in 1845, at which point it was the largest in the world; this is the centrepiece of the **Historic Science Centre** (*open daily 9–6; adm*), which is home to exhibitions on the contributions of the Irish to the various sciences. The 3rd Earl of Rosse planned and constructed it himself. The gardens, meanwhile, are famous for their elegant shrubs, magnolias and box hedges, which are as tall as trees, and the park for its variety of Chinese and Himalayan trees. There is a proper kitchen garden, which is a rarity nowadays. Birr Castle hosts a number of events each summer, ranging from concerts and astronomy weekends to a 'Georgian cricket match' in period costume.

In the southern corner of Offaly, near Gloster, you can visit **Leap Castle** (*open by appointment, call* **t** *(0509) 31115 or* **t** *0872 344064; adm*), which guards the valley from Leinster into Munster. This large towerhouse, which was restored in about 1750 by the Darby family, is a rather spooky place – parts of it have lain in ruins ever since a fire that raged in 1922. It is said to be the most haunted castle in the whole of Ireland, and one of its ghosts is renowned for being very smelly. The present owner has hopes to restore the property.

Tullamore is the county town of Offaly; it is a prosperous place that has grown up on the banks of a small river. The Grand Canal also passes through it, and it is a major cruiser base. Irish Mist and Tullamore Dew whiskey (*www.tullamore-dew.org*) are manufactured here, and there are some good shops and restaurants.

Seven miles (11km) west, at **Rahan**, is a lovely old canalside pub called The Thatch. Take the N52 out of Tullamore for 5 miles (8km) and take the second turning on the right. You can combine a drink here with a visit to the ancient **churches** of Rahan (*always accessible*). Two of them are 12th-century and in the Romanesque style. One of them is very well preserved, and is joined to a later church built in 1732. The chancel arch has some elaborate piers, carved into human heads with flowing hair.

About 5 miles (8km) north of Tullamore, off the N52, is the site where **Durrow Monastery** (*open daily 9–1*) was founded by St Columba (Colmcille) in the 6th century. It is most famous for the *Book of Durrow*, a 7th-century illuminated maunuscript, now housed at Trinity College, Dublin, and for the Crozier of Durrow, which is now in the National Museum, Dublin. Nothing remains of the monastery today except a 10th-century high cross and some fine early tombstones.

County Laois

County Offaly used to be known as 'King's County' after Phillip II, Spanish Consort of Mary Tudor. County Laois (pronounced 'Leash') was 'Queen's County', after Mary herself. She 'planted' this area with loyal supporters in 1556, but this policy did not bring peace, and early in the 17th century many of the rebellious Irish *septs* were banished to County Kerry. The new colonists built lovely houses and attractive villages. Houses of note include Abbeyleix, Roundwood House and Emo Court.

Tourist Information

Portlaoise: t (0502) 21178

Sports and Activities

Fishing
Ballaghmore Lake, Ballaghmore House,
Borris-in-Ossory, t (0505) 21366

Walking
For the Slieve Bloom Way, see p.513.

Where to Stay and Eat

Preston House, Abbeyleix, t (0502) 31432
(expensive). An ivy-covered stone B&B in
a former school, furnished with antiques

and housing a restaurant recommended
by locals. Closed Christmas and Feb.
Roundwood House, Mountrath, t (0502)
32120, www.hidden-ireland.com/roundwood/
(expensive). A 1740s Palladian mansion
run by a delightful family who instantly
make guests feel relaxed and comfortable.
Kids are welcome, and even have part of
the top floor in which to amuse themselves.
The food is delicious.
Ivyleigh House, Bank Place, Portlaoise,
t (0502) 22081, www.ivyleigh.com
(moderate). Four tastefully decorated
ensuite rooms in a luxurious Georgian
guesthouse in the centre of town.
Morrissey's Bar, Abbeyleix, t (0502) 31233
(inexpensive). A charming pub and grocery
with old cake tins and a stove. It's a good
place for stout and sandwiches.

Portlaoise to Portarlington

The county town is **Portlaoise**, which has nothing much to recommend it except
that it is an important rail junction. It has a certain notoriety, as there is a well-known
prison in the neighbourhood. Of great interest is the **Rock of Dunamase**, just outside
the town on the Stradbally road (N80). This is an ancient defensive fort, and the annals
record that it was plundered by the Vikings in AD 845. It came into Anglo-Norman
hands through the marriage of Aoife, daughter of the King of Leinster, to the warlord
Strongbow. It was blown sky-high by Cromwellian artillery in 1650. The climb to the
top is easy and the views are wonderful. At **Stradbally** there is a **Steam Traction
Museum** (call for opening hours, t (0502) 25114, adm). There is a steam rally every
August bank-holiday weekend. **Vicarstown** and **Monasterevin**, both on the River
Barrow section of the Grand Canal, are peaceful cruiser harbours.

To the north of Portlaoise is the canal town of **Portarlington**, which was founded at
the end of the 17th century and became an important centre for Dutch and French
Protestant refugees. In 1696 Henri de Massue, Marquis de Ruvigny, also the Earl of
Galway, was granted title to the lands round here; he was one of William III's foreign
favourites, who excited much jealousy among English courtiers. The connection is
commemorated by the so-called French style of the old townhouses; their gardens
stretch down to the river rather than into the street.

The magnificent neoclassical **Emo Court** (grounds open all year in daylight; house open
mid-June–mid-Sept daily 10.30–5; adm for house; t (0502) 26573/21450), on the Dublin
to Cork Road (N8) between Monasterevin and Portlaoise, was designed in 1795 by James
Gandon and has an impressive domed rotunda room. It was rescued by Mr Cholmeley
Harrison in the 1960s, and the house was further restored by the National Heritage
Service. The 18th-century gardens are laid out between the house and a large lough,
with grassy paths that lead you to a series of vistas.

Mountmellick, Mountrath and the Slieve Bloom Mountains

To the western side of the county you will find the Slieve Bloom Mountains, an island of true mountain wilderness with wooded glens, waterfalls, boglands and magnificent views, all of which are very well signposted. **Mountmellick** was founded during the 17th century by Quakers and grew prosperous on cotton, linen and wool industries. The town is curled into a bend of the River Owenass and today retains an 18th-century feel.

Mountrath, further to the south, is another attractive town that was founded in the 1600s by Charles Coote, an active entrepreneur, whose family built houses all over Ireland. He established charcoal-burning ironworks that ate up the natural forests. Today the State has planted thousands of acres of sitka spruce and pine in Laois, which, although rather monotonous, will one day yield a good cash crop.

Close to Mountrath is **Roundwood House**, a fine Palladian mansion that has won many awards as a first-class guesthouse (*see* opposite). The owners are always delighted to show people around. You get to it by following the N7 from Dublin to Mountrath, then following signs for the Slieve Bloom Mountains. It is situated about 3 miles (4.8km) out of town. The Irish Georgian Society rescued Roundwood House from ruin in the 1970s, and the Kennan family continue the good work. Notice the unusual staircase carved in Chinese Chippendale style. Beyond Borris in Ossory, following the N7 to Roscrea, is **Ballaghmore Castle**, which was a Fitzgerald outpost on the borders of old Ossory, and has a *sheela-na-gig* high up on its walls.

In the Slieve Bloom Mountains, the **Ridge of Capard** has outstanding views. It is reached from Rosenallis Village. **Glendine Gap** is also spectacular; from here you look over the four provinces of Ireland. One of the ancient highways of Ireland, the Munster Road, crosses the area from north to south through Glenlitter, Glynsk and the Tulla Gap. The pine marten, Ireland's rarest mammal, is found in these glens.

Southern Laois

In the southern tip of County Laois is the attractive town of **Durrow** (on the N8), which was owned at one time by the Duke of Ormonde. **Castle Durrow**, now a convent, was built in 1716. You can ask to look around it. To the south is the pretty village of **Cullahill**, which has a fine old gabled **castle** (*not open to the public*) built by the Fitzpatricks, lords of the area before the Normans arrived.

Back north again, as you follow the N8, is the town of **Abbeyleix**. Nothing remains of the Cistercian monastery founded here by Conor O'Moore in the 12th century, which became part of the Earl of Ormonde's vast possessions during Elizabeth I's reign. The town is well laid out, and in the south is the beautiful Adam house built by Viscount de Vesci after a design by William Chambers (*not open to the public*). On Main Street there is a lovely pub called Morrissey's (see opposite), which has a delightful old-fashioned stove that is used in winter.

At **Timahoe**, on the R426 between Portlaoise and Swan, there is a 12th-century **round tower** (*always accessible*), which is more than 100ft (30m) high, with a double door decorated with stone heads in a Romanesque style.

County Kildare

Kildare is a county of bog and plain, divided by the Liffey in the north-east, and the basin of the Barrow in the south. The Bog of Allen, a huge raised bog formed more than 5,000 years ago, spreads to the north-west. The county is crossed by the Grand Canal, which links Dublin and the Shannon River at Banagher; its towpath provides lovely walks away from the traffic and fumes of the roads, and excellent coarse fishing. Being so near to Dublin, Kildare is one of the most populated counties, yet it is possible to explore the canal villages and its many castles, stately houses and gardens, and still feel you are in the heart of the country. Do not linger too long in the towns, many of which tend to get jammed with traffic during the rush hours as they are situated on major through-routes to Dublin.

Most people have heard of The Curragh, a plain covering more than 5,000 acres (2,000ha) just east of Kildare Town, where some of the fastest horses in the world are bred and exercised. It was formed in the Ice Age, when the ice ground the surface of the limestone plain to a powder. This mixed with vegetable remains to produce a rich pasture, famed for making the bones of horses grazed on it very strong. You may wish to visit the National Stud and Irish Horse Museum at Tully near Kildare Town. Or there is great fun to be had attending the races, both at the Curragh and at Punchestown where, besides having a flutter, you can admire a Bronze Age standing stone, 23ft (7m) in height, which is in the grounds of the racecourse. This county also contains two of the grandest houses in the country: Carton House, ancient seat of the Earls of Kildare; and the next-door estate of Castletown House, a very fine Palladian mansion.

History

The history of the county is fascinating, for its fertile river plains have attracted many invaders. The first recorded inhabitants are a Celtic people, the Uí Dunlainge, who may have originated from Cornwall. They built great hill-forts, the remains of which can be seen at Mullaghmast in the south, Knockaulin in the centre, and the Hill of Allen in the west. Knockaulin, near Kilcullen, dates from the late Bronze Age, and shares with Tara in Meath and Emain Macha in Armagh a legendary importance in the folk memories of the Irish people. Christianity came in the 5th century, and the monks built their churches near the centres of Celtic pagan power. Moone, near the fort of Mullaghmast, has an 8th-century stone cross that is wonderfully carved with scenes from the Bible. The Uí Dunlainge split off into branches, becoming rivals and fighting for territory. The Norsemen arrived in early AD 900 and established their power in Dublin and the north-east of Kildare.

The Anglo-Normans under Richard de Clare, called Strongbow, came in the 12th century, invited by Diarmuid MacMurragh, King of Leinster, to help him regain his kingdom. Strongbow did indeed help him capture Dublin and defeat his enemies but, as the *Book of Leinster* records, 'he died after the victory of unction and penance; thence forward is the miserable reign of the Saxons, amen, amen' (*see* **History**, p.11). The Normans soon squeezed out the Celtic tribes, who took to the Wicklow Mountains, became the O'Tooles and mounted attacks on the Norman colony.

By 1300 Kildare was dominated by the Norman Fitzgerald earls of Kildare, known as the Geraldines. For a time in the late 15th century, they were so powerful and wealthy that they were the uncrowned kings of Ireland. Gerald, the 8th Earl, who was known as the Great Earl, was made Deputy of Ireland in 1481 by Edward IV, who reasoned that if all Ireland could not rule this man, he would let him rule all Ireland. Inevitably, however, the Tudor kings viewed the power of the Fitzgeralds with increasing resentment. By 1534 they had completely fallen out with the English government, and the 9th Earl died in the Tower of London. His son, Thomas, renounced his allegiance to Henry VII and attacked Dublin Castle. (He is known as

Getting There and Around

By Rail

Sallins, Kildare Town and Athy are on the main line from Dublin to Waterford. The main line to Sligo and Galway passes through Maynooth; trains are frequent. Iarnród Éireann, t 1850 366222, *www.irishrail.ie*

By Bus

Maynooth, Newbridge and Kildare are stops on many routes into Dublin. Bus Éireann, t (01) 836 6111, *www.buseireann.ie*

By Bike

For the Raleigh Rent-a-Bike network, contact: John Cahill and Son, Sallins Rd, Naas, t (045) 879655

Festivals

January–February

Féile Bhríde, St Brigid's Cathedral, Kildare, t (045) 522890. The Festival of St Brigid.

March

Kildare Drama Festival, t (087) 202 0241

April

Irish National Hunt Festival, Punchestown Racecourse, t (045) 897704

May

Leixlip Salmon Festival, t (01) 624 3085. A festival including a mock battle with Vikings, held in late May/June,
Robertstown Canal Festival, t (045) 875 0005. A canalside event held in the 1st week of May, and also the 1st week in Aug.

June

All-Ireland Turf Cutting Competition, Ticknevin, t (0405) 53660
Derby Festival, Kildare, *http://kildare.ie/ derbyfestival/*. A week of music and celebrations around the horse race.
Music in Great Irish Houses,various locations (see also **Practical A–Z**, p.102), t (01) 664 2822

July

Bluegrass Music Festival, Athy, t (059) 862 5266
Gerard Manley Hopkins Summer School, Monasterevin, t (045) 433613, *www. gerardmanleyhopkins.org*. A festival of poetry, music and the arts celebrating the Victorian poet.

August

For the second Robertstown Canal Festival, *see above*.
Monasterevin Canal Festival, t (045) 860427, Canalside fun for all over the course of the bank-holiday weekend.

'Silken Thomas' because his followers had silken fringes on their helmets.) His army was routed and he retreated to his stronghold at Maynooth. But in March 1535 Sir William Skeffington took it and the garrison was given the 'Maynooth pardon': in other words, they were executed. Thomas had escaped the bloodshed, but he eventually submitted and was given a guarantee of personal safety. This was not fulfilled and he too was sent to the Tower, and was hanged, drawn and quartered with his five uncles in 1537.

The Kildares lost much of their power again with the Cromwellian wars and plantation, although their estates were restored by Charles II. They survived the Williamite wars of 1689–91 and built Carton House. Many of the old Norman families did not fare so well and were replaced by new loyal colonists known as 'planters'. They were Protestant, and built themselves fine houses with beautiful craftsmanship. The Great Famine of 1845–49 and the various uprisings put an end to all of this. Dublin grew hugely in the last century, especially in the last 20 years, so that most of the villages of northern Kildare became dormitory suburbs of Dublin. People say 'we used to go to Dublin, but now Dublin has come to us.'

Northern Kildare

Naas and Around to the Grand Canal

Naas (pronounced 'Nace'), only 21 miles (34km) from Dublin, is a busy industrial town on the edge of the Wicklow Mountains, with good shopping and a hunting and horse-racing centre. In Irish it is known as *Nás na Ríogh*, meaning 'Meeting Place of the Kings'. It used to be one of the seats of the kings of Leinster, and was the centre of the Irish kingdom of Uí Dunlainge. All that remains of their fort is a motte: a large hill in the middle of the town. At **Kill**, 1½ miles (2.5km) away off the N7 to Dublin, is Goffs, the old established horse auctioneers who sell 50 per cent of all Irish-bred horses. John Devoy (1842–1928), the Irish-American newspaper man and Fenian, was born here. He was influential in organizing publicity in America, and worked in the early 20th century to help the Irish Freedom Movement with money and propaganda, through such organizations as Clan na Gael.

Jigginstown House, just one mile (1.6km) to the south-west on the Kildare Road (N7), is now a massive ruin. It was built by Thomas Wentworth, Earl of Strafford, when Charles I proposed to visit him. The visit never came off and 'Black Tom', who was one of the most unpopular men in Ireland, was executed in 1641 by the Roundheads before it was finished. It would have been the largest unfortified house ever constructed in Ireland, but only the cellars were completed. If you are in need of a little refreshment, an old-fashioned pub called Fletcher's, with cosy snugs and wooden floors, should fill that gap nicely.

Punchestown is famous for its standing stone and its races. The stone is 3 miles (4.8km) to the south-east of Naas, off the Woolpack Road, and is 23ft (7m) high with a Bronze Age burial chamber at its base. To the north-west are the quiet canal villages of Prosperous and Robertstown. The Grand Canal was built in the 1760s and carried agricultural produce between Dublin and the River Barrow at Athy. The railways destroyed the villages' passenger and commercial trade, but today the Grand Canal and the Naas Canal, a branch of the Grand, have been restored. The canalside has some very attractive walks and drives, and cruisers are for hire at Tullamore in County Offaly (*see* p.512).

Robertstown is an ideal place for a quiet and leisurely visit. The locals are very proud of the town's 18th-century associations, and the waterfront has been restored to look as it did in the days when travellers used to alight from their boats for an overnight stop. Some of the barges have been restored, and you can go for short trips on the canal. Eighteenth-century banquets are recreated in the Grand Canal Hotel, which no longer functions as a hotel but is used for all sorts of entertainments. The evening begins with a horse-drawn barge cruise and culminates with the feast. At weekends in July and August, there are concerts, lectures on the Georgian and canal eras, and lots of festivities.

Between Clane and Prosperous is a Victorian garden at **Coolcarrigan** (*open for groups by appointment; adm for house and gardens; t (045) 863527, www.coolcarrigan.com*). It is best seen in spring and autumn, as there are some magnificent trees.

Stucco Splendour: Castletown and Environs

Celbridge, 8 miles (5km) to the north of Naas, is a must-see for all lovers of Georgian country houses, for within a few miles of it lie both Castletown House and **Carton House**. Sadly, the future of the latter is rather precarious at the moment, and as a result it is difficult to view. It was once the seat of the earls of Kildare, a powerful Norman family who became very Irish, and the grounds were laid out by Capability

Tourist Information

Naas: 38 South Main St, t (045) 898888

Shopping

Crafts
Brenda O'Brien, Dun Buain Lodge, Kill, Naas. Pottery.

Food and Drink
Naturally, 29 North Main St, Naas, t (045) 871372. Health foods.
Friday Country Market, Town Hall, Naas. Fresh veg and herb cheeses, 10.45–12 noon.

Sports and Activities

Fishing
Fishing is good in Prosperous and all along the Grand Canal. Contact:
Countryman Angling and Game Supplies, Pacelli Rd, Naas, t (045) 879341

Horseracing
Look for details in the national newspapers, or in the racing calendar in the back of Tourism Ireland's annual *Calendar of Events*. See also *www.hri.ie* for horseracing information.
Naas, t (045) 897391, *www.naasracecourse.com*
Punchestown, t (045) 897704, *www.punchestown.com*

Pleasure Cruises
For boat hire/trips on the Grand Canal, call:
Grand Canal Hotel, Robertstown, t (045) 870005
Lowtown Marina, Robertstown, t (045) 860427

Ponytrekking
Kill International Equestrian Centre, Kill, t (045) 877333, *www.killequestrian.com*
Osberstown Riding Centre, Naas, t (045) 879074

Where to Stay

Barberstown Castle and Country House, Straffan, t (01) 628 8157, *www.barberstowncastle.ie* (*luxury*). An attractive jumble of Norman, Elizabethan and Edwardian architecture, recently expanded to include 36 new bedrooms and a restaurant where you can enjoy creative cuisine.
The K Club, Straffan, t (01) 601 7200, *www.kclub.ie* (*luxury*). One of Ireland's very finest country mansions, boasting a fitness centre, a highly rated restaurant (*see below*) and its own golf course, designed by Arnold Palmer.
Moyglare Manor, Maynooth, t (01) 628 6351, *www.moyglaremanor.ie* (*luxury*). An elegant Georgian house that is supposed to be the dower house to the Carton Estate. You can expect immaculately maintained bedrooms (including a garden suite), antiques, a friendly, clubby bar, delicious food (*see below*) and fresh flowers everywhere.
Leixlip House Hotel, Leixlip, t (01) 624 2268, *www.leixliphouse.com* (*expensive*). A Georgian house that has been converted into a plush modern hotel.

Eating Out

The K Club, Straffan, t (01) 601 7200 (*expensive*). A Michelin-starred restaurant offering sophisticated food.
Moyglare Manor Hotel, Maynooth, t (01) 628 6351 (*expensive*). A romantic ambience for seafood and more. *Closed lunch exc Sun.*
The Bradaun, Leixlip House Hotel, Leixlip, t (01) 624 2268 (*moderate*). Modern Irish fare served up in a bright, airy dining room. *Closed Mon, and lunch exc Sun.*
Michaelangelo Restaurant, Main St, Celbridge, t (01) 627 1809 (*moderate*). Irish/Italian food. *Closed lunch.*

Brown as a park where 'art and nature in just union reign'. The house was designed in the 1730s by Richard Cassels (*see* p.75), a French Huguenot who did a lot of work in Ireland. There is a shell house in the grounds. Mrs Delaney, who is still remembered for her diaries that recorded the privileged life of the Protestant ascendency, helped decorate the house when she stayed at one of the many house parties held at Carton during the mid 18th century.

Castletown House (*open mid-Apr–Sept Mon–Fri 10–6, Sat, Sun and bank hols 1–6; Oct Mon–Fri 10–5, Sat, Sun and bank hols 1–5; Nov Sun 1–5; adm; t (01) 628 8252*) lies at the eastern end of Celbridge village and is approached through a fine avenue of lime trees. This splendid Palladian mansion was built for William Connelly, speaker of the Irish House of Commons from 1715 to 1719, and contains some elaborate plasterwork by the Francini brothers, who taught Irish craftsmen the art of stucco. It has the only 18th-century print room in Ireland, and also contains some superb 18th-century furnishings. One of the hunt balls held during the week of the Dublin Horse Show takes place in its gracious rooms. From the windows of the Long Gallery you can see the extraordinary Connelly Folly, an obelisk supported on arches, built by the widow of Speaker Connelly to provide relief work after a particularly arduous winter. In 1994 Castletown became the property of the state and it is now run by the Office of Public Works. It is one of the venues for the Music in Great Irish Houses Festival, held in June (*see* **Practical A–Z,** p.102).

A few miles to the south-west of Celbridge between the N7 and the R403 is the pretty village of **Straffan**, which has a wonderful **Steam Museum** (*open June–Aug Wed–Sun 2–6; adm; t (01) 627 3155, www.steam-museum.com*), with rare examples of industrial steam engines and locomotives and a good tea-room.

Maynooth, a couple of miles to the north of Celbridge, has ancient associations with the great Geraldine family, the Fitzgeralds, later earls of Kildare and dukes of Leinster. The fine ruins of the 12th-century **Castle Fitzgerald** may be explored if you get the key from Castleview House, just across the road. A gatehouse, a massive keep and a great hall survive. This is where Sir William Skeffington, acting for Henry VIII, presided over the killing of the Geraldine followers when he took the castle in 1535. Today Maynooth is more closely associated with **St Patrick's College**, next to the castle, which has been turning out Catholic priests since 1795, although it is now a lay university as well. Funnily enough, it was established by the British, who did not like the idea of the Irish priests studying abroad where they might pick up revolutionary ideas. The buildings are late-Georgian in style, with a Gothic Revival addition by J. J. McCarthy, a pupil of Pugin, one of the architects who rebuilt the British Houses of Parliament. Visitors can see the **Ecclesiastical Museum** (*open Mon–Fri 11–5, Sun 2–6; adm*), which includes vestments made by Marie Antoinette for an Irish chaplain, gardens and an audio-visual presentation.

Just to the west of Maynooth, at Kilcock's **Larchill Arcadian Gardens** (*open May– end Sept daily 12 noon–6; adm; t (01) 628 7354, www.larchill.ie*), there is a rare example of an 18th-century style of garden called a *ferme ornée*, an 'embellished farm'. It may have been inspired by the famous one at Versailles where Marie Antoinette played milkmaid and enjoyed the Arcadian fantasies of that delicately jaded era. The owner of Larchill, Michael de las Casas, completed a loving restoration and won the annual Irish Conservation Award for his trouble. The work included rebuilding a lake, with 10 classical follies on islands, and a walled garden. Rare breeds of farm animals have been installed in quarters that are follies in themselves.

Leixlip (pronounced 'Leeks-lip') is on the banks of the Liffey; its name comes from the Danish *Lax-laup*, which means 'salmon leap'. Before the falls were utilized for hydroelectric power, it was a wonderful sight to see the salmon do just that. The 12th-century Norman **castle** is owned by Desmond Guinness, the force behind the Irish Georgian Society, which has done so much to preserve the rich treasury of 18th-century buildings in Ireland. It is not open to view. Leixlip has grown hugely as Dublin spreads ever outwards. The swift waters of the Liffey in this area are a great challenge to sports enthusiasts, and canoeists come here from all over the world.

Southern Kildare

The Curragh to the Bog

Kildare Town is on the edge of the Curragh, and is now an important centre for horse-breeding. It is said that St Brigid spread her handkerchief over enough land on which to build a convent, and the ruling king had to grant it to her. Her nunnery thrived during the 6th century, but by the 7th century it had become a monastery.

The Church of Ireland **cathedral** on the hill in the middle of the town dates in parts from the 13th century, and stands on the site of a 6th-century church. This venerable pile of stones has been pillaged and burned many times, and lay in ruins between 1641 and 1875. (A roof-restoration appeal is now being run.) The cathedral has some fine monuments, and a three-light west window with scenes from the lives of Brigid, Patrick and Colmcille, the three Patron Saints of Ireland. Beside it is a 10th-century **round tower** with an 18th-century top, which you can climb.

At **Tully**, the 1,000-acre **National Stud** (*open 12 Feb–12 Nov daily 9.30–6; adm for stud and gardens; t (045) 521617, www.irish-national-stud.ie*), located just outside Kildare Town on the R415, was started by Colonel Hall-Walker (later Lord Wavertree). He bred the famous Derby winner Minoru, and many other successful horses. In 1915 he presented the estate and horses to the Crown, and it was handed over to the Irish state in 1943. Its importance in the blood-stock and racing world is without parallel. The National Stud is open for guided tours in the summer, and there is a **Horse Museum**. Lord Wavertree, a Scotsman whose family made their money from beer, was brilliant with horses but a notable eccentric in his methods. On the tour the staff point out the skylights he had installed in all the stables; a firm believer in astrology, he wanted the stars to exert their influence on his horses to the full. Another thing that motivated him was a lifelong fascination with all things Japanese; he brought over two of that nation's most renowned landscape architects in 1906 to lay out a spectacular **Japanese Garden**, which is still perfectly maintained and is now one of the most popular attractions in Ireland. The gardens symbolize the life of humankind from cradle to grave, and include a Zen meditation garden.

Tourist Information

Kildare Town: Market House, Market Sq,
t (045) 521240. *Open June–Sept.*

Shopping

Crafts
Curragh Pottery, Lumville, Curragh,
t (045) 441630
Irish Pewter Mill and Craft Centre; *see* p.527.
Kildare Woollen Mills, Kildare, t (045) 522730

Sports and Activities

Horseracing
See the national newspapers, the racing
calendar in the back of annual Tourism Ireland
Calendar of Events, or *www.hri.ie.*
The Curragh Racecourse, t (045) 441205,
www.curragh.ie

Pleasure Cruises
Canalways Ireland, Spencer Bridge,
Rathangan, t (045) 524646

Ponytrekking
Red Hills Riding Stables, Kildare, t (045) 521570

Where to Stay

Kilkea Castle, Castledermot, t (059) 914 5156,
www.kilkeacastle.ie (*luxury*). The oldest
inhabited castle in Ireland, built by Hugh
de Lacy in 1180. Some rooms overlook the
tranquil grounds with their magnificent
rose gardens, and there are good health
and sporting facilities, including a golf club,
2 floodlit tennis courts, and a leisure centre
with an indoor pool, Jacuzzi, saunas, steam
room and gym.
Tonlegee House, just off Kilkenny road outside
Athy, t (059) 863 1473, *www.tonlegeehouse.com*
(*expensive*). An elegant 18th-century country
house with ensuite rooms and an excellent
restaurant (*see* below).
Ballindrum Farm, Athy, t (059) 862 6294
(*moderate*). Comfortable accommodation
on a working farm, with good breakfasts
and dinners available.

Doyles Schoolhouse B&B, Castledermot,
t (059) 914 4282 (*moderate*). A delightful
country inn with comfortable rooms and
excellent cuisine (*see* below).
Griesemount, Ballitore, t (059) 862 3158
(*moderate*). A genteel little B&B in a
Georgian house.
Kilkea Lodge Farm, Castledermot, t (059)
914 5156 (*moderate*). Accommodation in
a charming 18th-century farmhouse.
Riding holidays can be arranged.
Woodcourt House, Moone, Timolin, near Athy,
t (059) 862 4167, *www.woodcourthouse.com*
(*inexpensive*). A modern bungalow in quiet
countryside, near a good bar, the Moone
High Cross Inn. Evening meals are available
by advance request.

Eating Out

De-Lacy's, Kilkea Castle, Castledermot, t (059)
914 5156, *www.kilkeacastle.ie* (*expensive*).
Fine traditional and contemporary cuisine
made using seasonal local produce and
fresh vegetables, served in a dining room
with the ambiance of days gone by.
Les Olives Restaurant, 10 South Main St, Naas,
t (045) 894788, *www.lesolivesrestaurant.com*
(*expensive*). A restaurant where the emphasis
is on French gourmet cuisine, with fresh
seafood a speciality.
Tonlegee House, Athy, t (059) 863 1473
(*expensive*). A hotel dining room serving
imaginative and delicious cooking made
with organic vegetables grown in the
establishment's own garden, plus local fish
and game. *Closed lunch.*
Doyles Schoolhouse Restaurant,
Castledermot, t (059) 914 4282 (*moderate*).
A small and friendly restaurant with a
simple but delicious *table d'hôte* menu.
Moone High Cross Inn, Bolton Hill, Moone,
t (059) 862 4112 (*moderate*). A friendly,
old-fashioned pub where you can enjoy
better-than-average pub food, including
home-cooked roasts, sandwiches and
scrumptious apple pie.
The Red House Country Hotel and Restaurant,
Newbridge, t (045) 431657 (*moderate*).
A good place to come to sample French
dishes made from home-grown vegetables.
Closed lunch.

The green spring grass of the **Curragh** stretches for mile upon mile, with the blue hills of Dublin visible on the horizon. The pasture that grows on its limestone plain is said to be the best in the world for building horses' bones. But it is the skill of the breeders in choosing the sires that has made Curragh bloodstock so successful, and the excitement at the races when their skill is put to test is phenomenal: the chat is fast and furious, glasses of porter are downed in the tents, and the horses are splendid, thundering along in the green distance. Numerous meetings are held between March and November. The most famous are the Irish Sweep Derby in midsummer, the Irish 2,000 Guineas, the Irish Oaks and the Irish St Leger. The Curragh is also famous for housing the country's largest army camp.

The **Hill of Allen** (676ft/206m), situated to the south-east of Rathangan, is renowned in Irish legend as the other world seat of Fionn MacCumhaill (*see* pp.55–56). The summit is 15 minutes' walk from the road, and at the top you will find a 19th-century **folly** that was built by a Sir George Aylmer, 'in thankful remembrance of God'. The hill, together with Naas, and *Dun Aillinne* (Knockaulin), which is located just north-west of Kilcullen on the N9, was a residence of the kings of Leinster. Straight lines joining them form an equilateral triangle, with sides 9 miles (14.5km) long.

Rathangan, a quiet canal town, stands on the edge of the Bog of Allen, which is one of the largest raised bogs in this part of Ireland. At nearby Lullymore you can learn all you ever wanted to know about bogs at the **Lullymore Heritage and Discovery Park** (*open Mon–Fri 10–6, Sat and Sun 12 noon–6; adm; t (045) 870238, www.lullymorepark.com*).

Newbridge (*Droichead Nua*) to the east is an industrial centre on the Liffey. Outside it and near the Dominican College is an ancient motte.

From Athy to Kilcullen

Athy ('Ford of Ae'), situated to the south of Kildare Town on the R417, has developed from a 13th-century Anglo-Norman settlement at a fording point on the River Barrow. The Ae of the Gaelic name for the town was a king of Munster, who was killed while trying to take control of the ford in the 11th century. A privately owned 16th-century castle looks over Crom-a-boo bridge. (The name refers to the war-cry of the Desmond branch of the Fitzgerald family.) There is a lovely old **market house** in the town, which can be viewed from the outside only, as it is now a fire station. The pentagon-shaped modern Dominican church is built of massed concrete; it has attractive stained-glass windows. **Athy Heritage Centre** (*open Mar–Oct Mon–Sat 10–5, Sun and bank hols 2–6, Nov–Feb Mon–Sat 10–5, bank hols 2–6; t (0509) 8633075*), in the early-18th-century town hall, is worth a look for its multimedia displays on the town's history.

Half a mile (0.8km) outside of town on the R417, the 13th-century **Woodstock Castle** has survived in the form of a rectangular tower. A short expedition can be made from here to another historical spot, the **Ardscull Motte**, some 4 miles (6.4km) to the north of Athy off the N78. This was used by Edward Bruce in 1315 to defeat an English army. **Moone High Cross** (*always accessible*), one of the most famous and beautiful of all the high crosses, is 8 miles (12.9km) from Athy, in the demesne of Moone Abbey

House, beside the little village of Timolin on the N9. The cross, which is also known as St Colmcille's Cross, is 17½ft (5.3m) high and has 51 sculptured panels depicting various scenes from the Bible.

Castledermot, to the south of Moone on the N9, is famous for the remains of its **Franciscan abbey**, high crosses and round tower. The **tower** is tall and slender, and facing it is a lovely 12th-century Romanesque doorway. A modern copy of it in the church is in use. The two attractive sculptured granite **high crosses** are found in the graveyard. Castledermot was a place of great importance, once upon a time: a walled town in which Hugh de Lacy built an Anglo-Norman fortress. Edward Bruce fought for it in the 14th century but was defeated; and Cromwell sacked it in 1649. There are some remains of the stone walls, and Carlow Gate still stands. A few miles outside town is **Kilkea Castle**, once the home of the Earls of Kildare, now a luxury hotel and health farm (*see* p.525).

At **Timolin**, the art of pewter has been lovingly restored at the **Irish Pewter Mill and Craft Centre** (*open Mon–Fri 10–4; workshop open for visits Mon–Fri 11–5;* **t** *(059) 862 4164*). The neighbouring village of **Ballitore** was once a flourishing Quaker settlement; the old **Meeting House** has survived, and now serves as a library and museum, with a variety of exhibits on Quaker life. The nearby Ballitore School became famous for its high standard of education; Edmund Burke, the 18th-century political writer and orator; Napper Tandy (1740–1803), the United Irishman; and Cardinal Cullen (1803–78), who was instrumental in setting up a Catholic university in Dublin, were among its pupils. **Crookstown Mill** (*museum open Mon–Sat 11–6; mill open daily 10–6; adm;* **t** *(059) 862 3222*), situated by the river, has been restored and today hosts a collection of industrial archaeology and exhibitions on milling and the life of the community during the 19th century.

Not far from here, to the west of the village, you can see the **Rath of Mullaghmast**, an earthen Stone Age fort that is rich with folklore – it is claimed that Garret Óg Fitzgerald, the 11th Earl of Kildare, sleeps here, emerging once every seven years. A grisly massacre took place on this spot one day in 1597. This was also the setting for one of Daniel O'Connell's mass meetings in 1843, when he was campaigning for the repeal of the Act of Union, which had taken place between England and Ireland in 1801 (*see* p.19).

Close to the River Liffey and just to the south-east of the Curragh Camp are two tiny villages that are worth taking time to visit. **Old Kilcullen**, situated just off the N9, is the site of an early-Christian monastery, with fragmentary 8th-century crosses similar to those at Moone. There is also a ruined round tower. West of the tower, across the N78, is the Iron Age **Hill Fort of Knockaulin** (also called *Dun Ailinne*). From both of these sites you can get a wonderful view of the Barrow Valley. The petty chieftains of this area, who had ambitions to become kings of Leinster, associated themselves with the power and royal connections of the fort long after it had been abandoned as a royal centre in the first centuries AD. They referred to themselves as kings of Dun Ailinne. The monks were doing the same thing by building Kilcullen monastery so close to the mill.

County Dublin

Ireland's capital city sprawls over a large part of this county and threatens to dominate it completely, but if you wish to be guided by the example of fun-loving Dubliners you will follow them to the jaunty sea resorts along the coast, to the lavish gardens of Howth Castle, or to the unique collection of Irish furniture and portraits at Malahide Castle. When you are in the National Gallery, search out Nathaniel Hone's picture, *Cattle at Malahide*, for he has caught the glancing light of the east coast perfectly. James Joyce disciples who are travelling by themselves around the *Ulysses* landmarks in Dublin should not neglect the museum of Joyceana in the Martello tower, and Sandymount, where Gertie McDowell showed Mr Bloom her garters. Further to the south sweeps the lovely Killiney Bay, while to the north of Dublin,

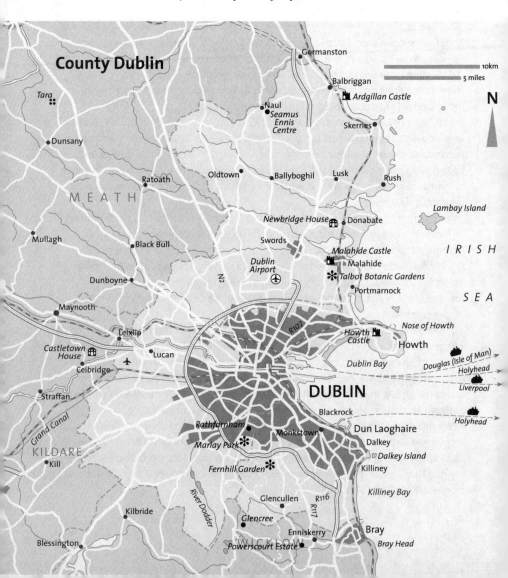

Getting There and Around

By Air

A variety of airlines fly into Dublin Airport, which is 8 miles (13km) from the city. A **bus service** runs between the Central Bus Station (Busáras) and Dublin Airport. The **Airlink** service on routes 747 and 748 runs every 15mins from early morning to 10.20pm between the airport and Heuston Station and Connolly Station, for train connections. At around €5, it's considerably cheaper than a taxi. You can also get the cheaper, but slower, **city buses** (routes 41 and 41B), circulating between the airport and Eden Quay, outside Busáras, and the 46X from Dun Laoghaire. *See also* **Travel**, pp.88–90.
Dublin Airport, t (01) 814 1111, *www.dublin-airport.com*
Aer Lingus, 40–41 Upper O'Connell St, flight enquiries **t** (01) 886 8888, bookings **t** (01) 705 3333, *www.aerlingus.ie*. This has several city offices.
British Airways, t 1800 626747, *www.ba.com*
BMI, Merrion Centre, Merrion Rd, **t** (01) 407 3036, *www.flybmi.com*
Ryanair, 3 Dawson St, D2, enquiries **t** (01) 677 4422, reservations (UK) **t** 0906 270 5656, *www.ryanair.com*. Probably the cheapest flights, depending on when/how you book.

By Boat

Ferries from Holyhead arrive at either **Dun Laoghaire** (Stena) or **Dublin ferry port** (Irish Ferries). Bus numbers 7, 7A, 7B and 7D run from Dun Laoghaire to O'Connell Bridge in the centre of Dublin; the No.7 continues over the bridge to Eden Quay outside the bus station. There is also a DART train from Dun Laoghaire to Pearse (rail) Station, on Westland Row, until around 12 midnight. If you arrive at the Dublin ferry port, you'll find buses to the bus station and city centre on the Alexandra Road – all buses with *An Lár* ('city centre') signs are going there.
Irish Ferries, Alexandra Rd, Ferryport, D1, **t** 0818 300400, *www.irishferries.com*
Stena Line, at Dun Laoghaire ferry port, **t** (01) 204 7777, *www.stenaline.co.uk*

By Rail

There are 2 main railway stations in Dublin city: **Heuston**, west of the centre on St John's Rd, serves the south, south-west and west of the country, as well as commuter trains to Co. Kildare. **Connolly** station, north of the Liffey on Amiens St, near the bus station, serves Wexford, Sligo and Belfast (where for Derry you must change trains), and has a connection with the main DART (Dublin Area Rapid Transit) line and commuter lines to Maynooth, Mullingar and Longford.
Iarnród Éireann Travel Centre,35 Lower Abbey St, D1, **t** 1850 444 2222, *www.irishrail.ie*. Your source for all rail information.

By Bus

All intercity Expressway buses run by Bus Éireann end up in *Busáras* (the central bus station), at Store St, on the north side of the Liffey, 3 streets east of O'Connell St.
The Travel Centre, Busáras, Store St, D1, **t** (01) 836 6111, *www.buseireann.ie*. Information on all services, including Eurolines for services to the UK and the rest of Europe. You can also contact the tourist offices.

By Bike

CGL, 9 Townyard Lane, Malahide, **t** (01) 845 4275. Bike hire.

Festivals

April

Howth Jazz Festival, t (01) 605 7700
Lots of gigs in local halls and bars, usually over the Easter bank-holiday weekend.

June

AIB Music in Great Irish Houses, *see* **Practical A–Z**, p.102. A festival of chamber music, with around 10 evening concerts held in great houses in the Dublin area.

July

Irish Open Golf Championship, Portmarnock, **t** (01) 846 2968

August

Festival of World Cultures, Dun Laoghaire, **t** (01) 230 1035, *www.festivalofworldcultures.com*. A family-friendly arts and culture festival comprising theatre, dance, film, circus and workshops.

the flat, tidy fields of Skerries and Rush slope down to the sea, and the wide arm of Dublin Bay ends at the beautiful peninsula of Howth Head. Most of the population of the county commute to Dublin City to work, although there is a certain amount of vegetable-growing and dairy farming. Many of the little villages described have become dormitory towns of Dublin. Some of the new developments are not particularly attractive: the poorer housing is traditionally badly built, but this has improved enormously. Dublin City has its beggars, housing ghettos and problems with theft and drugs, just like any other capital city, but it also has a wealth of Georgian architecture, a lively atmosphere and a charm that is peculiar to the city itself. Its beautiful setting beside the sea, within such easy reach of beaches and mountains, gives its people a great escape route when they need it, even if it is only for a few hours. Many Dublin writers – Flann O'Brien, James Joyce and Samuel Beckett to name just three – drew great inspiration from the countryside around them.

Around the County

North County Dublin

On the coast at the northern tip of the county, **Skerries** and **Balbriggan** are noted for their dry, sunny climate and their safe, sandy beaches. Many locals are involved in the fishing industry. Between Balbriggan and Skerries, **Ardgillan Castle** (*park open daily 10–dusk; castle open Apr–June and Sept Tue–Sun 11–6, July and Aug daily 11–6, Oct–Dec, Feb and Mar Tue–Sun 11–4.30, Jan Sun 2–4; adm to castle;* **t** *(01) 849 2212, www.fingalcoco.ie*) is a lush public park of 194 acres (78.5ha) of pasture, woods and gardens, amidst which is a well-maintained estate built in 1738. The main rooms are open to the public and are furnished in Victorian style; upstairs is an exhibition of historical maps of Ireland. At **Naul** (*An Aill:* 'The Cliff' or 'The Rock', after the cliff on which the Norman-built Black Castle stands), to the west, is the **Seamus Ennis Centre** (**t** *(01) 802 0898, www.seamusenniscentre.com*). Named after one of Ireland's most acclaimed traditional musicians, collectors of folklore and broadcasters, it is a focal point for traditional culture in the Fingal area of County Dublin.

Rush, another attractive fishing village, overlooks **Lambay Island** with its 500ft (152m) cliffs rising out of the sea. You have to get permission to land there from the owner, for it is the sanctuary of many rare birds, but the beauty of the island can still be seen by sailing around it. About 3 miles (5km) west of Rush is **Lusk Heritage Centre** (*open mid-June–mid-Sept Fri 10–5; adm;* **t** *(01) 647 2461*), including a round tower, a medieval tower with an exhibition on County Dublin churches, and an 1839 Church of Ireland church that contains some fine medieval tombs.

At **Donabate** off the N1 is splendid **Newbridge House** (*open Apr–Sept Tue–Sat 10–1 and 2–5, Sun 2–6, Oct–Mar Sat and Sun 2–5; adm;* **t** *(01) 843 6534, www.fingalcoco.ie*), one of the finest and most authentically maintained Georgian manors in Ireland. It was built in 1737 for Charles Cobbe, later Archbishop of Dublin. The authenticity extends to the restored dairy, forge, servants' houses and other buildings, all furnished as they might have been 200 years ago. There is also a working farm, managed according to

Tourist Information

Balbriggan: George's Sq, t (01) 841 4884
Dun Laoghaire: New Ferry Terminal,
  t (01) 605 7700, infoline t 1850 230330
Malahide: Malahide Castle, t (01) 845 0490
Tallaght: 3rd Level, The Square, t 1850 230330
See also *www.fingal-dublin.com*.

Internet Access

Net House, 28 Upper Georges St, Dun Laoghaire,
  t (01) 230 3085, *www.nethousecafes.com*
USurf.ie, 88B Lower Georges St,
  Dun Laoghaire, t (01) 231 9186

Shopping

Auctioneers
Mullen's Laurel Park, Woodbrook,
  t (01) 282 6107, *www.mullenslaurelpark.com*

Crafts
Malahide Castle Craft Shop, Seaview, Yellow
  Walls Rd, Malahide, t (01) 846 2184. Pottery,
  musical instruments and woven cloth.

Food and Drink
Cavistons Delicatessen, 59 Glasthule Rd,
  Sandycove, t (01) 280 9120, *www.cavistons.com*.
  Fresh fish, Irish cheeses and smoked salmon.
Country Cellar, 8 Patrick St, Dun Laoghaire,
  t (01) 280 3338. Health foods.

Sports and Activities

Beaches
Balscadden Beach, Howth: sandy but shallow.
Donabate: famous for its dunes.
Killiney: good for long walks; part of it is stony.
Malahide: long and sandy.
Portrane: has a bird sanctuary and lovely dunes.
Portmarnock: long and sandy;
  donkey rides in summer.
Rush: sandy and popular with Dubliners.

Fishing
Trout fishing is available on the River Dodder
and Bohernabrena Reservoir.

Golf
Luttrelstown Golf Course, Castleknock,
  t (01) 808 9988, *www.luttrellstown.ie*
Malahide Golf Club, south of Malahide Village,
  t (01) 846 1611, *www.malahidegolfclub.ie*
Portmarnock, t (01) 846 0611, *www.portmarnock.
  com*. A premier tournament course.
The Royal Dublin Golf Course,
  North Bull Island, Dollymount, t (01) 833
  6346/7153, *www.theroyaldublingolfclub.ie*
St Margaret's Golf Club, Newton House, off
  main Ashbourne–Slane road, next to airport
  t (01) 864 0400, *www.stmargaretsgolf.com*.
  A driving range, 27 holes and tuition.

Horseracing
Ireland's major tracks are close by in
Co. Kildare (*see* pp.518–527). Check *In Dublin*
and evening newspapers for details.
Fairyhouse Racecourse, Ratoath, Co. Meath,
  t (01) 825 6167, *www.fairyhouseracecourse.ie*
Leopardstown Racecourse, 6 miles (9.5km)
  south of Dublin city centre, t (01) 289 0500,
  www.leopardstown.com

Ponytrekking
Calliaghstown Riding Centre,
  Calliaghstown, Rathcoole, t (01) 458 8222,
  www.calliaghstownridingcentre.com

Watersports
Fingal Sailing School, Upper Strand Rd,
  Broadmeadow Estuary, Malahide, t (01)
  845 1979, *www.fingalsailingschool.com*.
  Junior, youth and adult courses in sail
  training and windsailing.
Wind and Wave Watersports, 16a The Crescent,
  Monkstown t (01) 284 4177. Windsurfing.

Where to Stay

Belcamp-Hutchinson Country House,
  Carrs Lane, Malahide Rd, Balgriffin, D17,
  t (01) 846 0843, *www.belcamphutchinson.com*
  (*moderate*). A charming country house
  offering a sense of comfortable elegance
  and guestrooms with all mod cons. The
  welcoming proprietress offers breakfasts
  from 4.30am for those catching an early
  flight. The relaxing surroundings include a
  maze, a walled garden and a tree-swing.

Marine Hotel, Sutton Cross, Sutton, D13,
t (01) 839 0000, *www.marinehotel.ie*
(*moderate*). A modern hotel convenient for
the pretty fishing village of Howth.
Coolfin House, 18 Clarinda Park East;
Dun Laoghaire, **t** (01) 280 5354 (*inexpensive*).
A B&B on on a Victorian square, convenient
for the harbour and DART trains to the city.
Evergreen, Kinsealy Lane, Malahide,
t (01) 846 0185, *www.evergreendublin.com*
(*inexpensive*). A B&B near the marina village
of Malahide and convenient for Dublin
airport and DART trains to the city centre.
Tara Hall Bed & Breakfast, 24 Sandycove Rd,
Dun Laoghaire, **t** (01) 280 5120 (*inexpensive*).
A B&B close to Sandycove DART station and
2mins from the seafront and Joyce museum.

Eating Out

Bon Appetit, 9 St James Terrace, Malahide,
t (01) 845 0314, *www.bonappetit.ie* (*expensive*).
An elegant restaurant arranged over
3 storeys of a Georgian house, with the
emphasis on elaborate seafood dishes.
King Sitric, East Pier, Howth, **t** (01) 832 5235,
www.kingsitric.ie (*expensive*). A place famous
for its seafood, also offering rooms (*moderate*).
The Red Bank Restaurant, 7 Church St, Skerries,
t (01) 849 0439, *www.redbank.ie* (*expensive*).
A superb fish place with rooms (*moderate*).
Bijou, 47 Highfield Rd, Rathgar, **t** (01) 496 1518
(*moderate*). A supper club meets bistro with
wonderful Asian/European fare. *Closed lunch*
The Bloody Stream, Railway Station, Howth,
t (01) 839 5076, *www.thebloodystream.com*
(*moderate*). A seafood bar and café by
Howth harbour, hosting regular music slots.
Caviston's Seafood Restaurant, 59 Glasthule Rd,
Sandycove, **t** (01) 280 9245, *www.cavistons.com* (*moderate*). A small restaurant attached
to a deli, serving great seafood. *Closed eves.*
Johnnie Fox's Pub, Glencullen, **t** (01) 295 5647
(*moderate*). A good seafood pub on the
Wicklow border.
Nosh, 111 Coliemore Rd, Dalkey, **t** (01) 284 0666,
www.nosh.ie (*moderate*). A trendy spot with
wholesome and uncomplicated food.
P.D.'s Woodhouse, 1 Coliemore Rd, Dalkey, **t** (01)
284 9399 (*moderate*). A friendly atmosphere
in which to enjoy oak-barbecued food.

The Purty Kitchen and Bar, Old Dun Laoghaire
Rd, Monkstown, **t** (01) 284 3576, *www.purtykitchen.com* (*moderate*). Good seafood,
salads and more, plus music nightly (**see**
below). There's a deli for takeout dishes.
Silks, The Mall, Malahide, **t** (01) 845 3331,
www.silks.ie (*moderate*). Good Chinese food.
Taylor's Three Rock, Grange Rd, Rathfarnham,
D16, **t** (01) 494 2999, *www.taylorsirishnight.com* (*moderate*). Traditional music and
dancing shows accompanied by a set menu.
Wong's, Main St, Castleknock, D15, **t** (01) 822
3330 (*moderate*). Another good Chinese,
with plenty of choice and pleasant staff.
Zen Garden. 2 Terenure Rd East, Rathgar, D6, **t** (01)
490 0206 (*moderate*). Asian fusion food.
Howard's Way, 8 Orwell Rd, Rathgar, D6,
t (01) 496 7821 (*inexpensive–moderate*).
A popular, good-value café/restaurant.
Malahide Castle, Malahide, **t** (01) 846 3027
(*inexpensive*). Good soups/snacks. *Closed eves.*
Outlaws, 62 Upper Georges St, Dun Laoghaire,
t (01) 284 2817 (*inexpensive*). A cheerful spot
serving good steaks, chicken and burgers.
The Queens, 12 Castle St, Dalkey, **t** (01) 285
4569 (*inexpensive*). A pub serving good
sandwiches and seafood chowder.

Entertainment and Nightlife

Cinema
UCI Cinema, The Square, Tallaght, D24, **t** (01)
459 8400/452 2611, and 84 Greencastle Rd,
Coolock, D17, Malahide, **t** (01) 848 5122,
www.uci.ie. Multi-screen complexes.

Live Music
Abbey Tavern, Howth, **t** (01) 839 0307. Cabaret.
Polly Hops, Lucan Rd, Newcastle,
t (01) 628 0295. Traditional music.
The Purty Kitchen and Bar, Old Dun Laoghaire
Rd, Monkstown, **t** (01) 284 3576, *www.purtykitchen.com*. Rock, country and traditional.

Theatre
Lambert Puppet Theatre, Clifton Lane,
Monkstown, **t** (01) 280 0974, *www.lambertpuppettheatre.com*. A suburban
venue with a puppet museum.

traditional methods. In the house, the drawing room and its early-Georgian furniture and curios are unique, as is the collection of antique dolls and a dolls' house with 14 rooms. There is also a small museum, made up of curiosities brought from all over the world and displayed in specially designed cabinets.

Malahide, a few miles further south, is another seaside resort, with a wonderful old castle that was the seat of the Talbots from 1185 to 1973. Today, **Malahide Castle** (*open Apr–Sept Mon–Sat 10–5, Sun 11–6, Oct–Mar Mon–Fri 10–5, Sat and Sun 11–5; adm; **t** (01) 846 2184, www.malahidecastle.com*) is publicly owned, and part of the National Portrait Collection is housed there. *The Boswell Papers*, which give us such an insight into 18th-century travel, were found here in a croquet box. The castle is made up of three different periods, the earliest being a three-storey towerhouse dating from the 12th century. The façade of the house is flanked by two slender towers built in about 1765. Inside is the only surviving original medieval great hall in Ireland, hung with Talbot family portraits. The display of Irish 18th-century furniture is fascinating and shows the sophistication of the craftsmanship and artistry existing in Ireland at the time. The grounds are superb, especially the part now known as the **Talbot Botanic Gardens** (*open May–Sept daily 2–5; guided tours Wed at 2; adm; **t** (01) 890 5629, www.fingalcoco.ie*), laid out with thousands of species, many of them exotic plants from the southern hemisphere brought here by Lord Talbot de Malahide between 1948 and 1973. Also on the grounds is the **Fry Model Railway Museum** (*open Apr–Sept Mon–Sat 10–5, Sun 2–6; adm; **t** (01) 846 3779, www.visitdublin.com*). Its hand-made models were built by Cyril Fry, a railway engineer and draughtsman in the 1930s. They are laid out on a track that passes many miniaturized Dublin landmarks, including Heuston Station and the River Liffey with all its bridges, trams, barges and boats. A final attraction in the Malahide Castle Demesne is **Tara's Palace** (*open Apr–Sept Mon–Fri 10.45–4.45, Sat and Sun 11.30–5.30; adm; **t** (01) 846 3779*), a magnificent dolls' house constructed by some of Ireland's best artisans, with Castletown House, Leinster House and Carton rebuilt to one-twelfth of their true size.

Swords, situated just inland from Malahide, boasts a very interesting monastic settlement that was founded by St Columba in AD 563. The monastery flourished, even though it was raided by the Norsemen, and became so rich that it was known as 'The Golden Prebend'. To protect their precious manuscripts and jewelled croziers, the monks built a **round tower**, 74ft (22.5m) high, the remains of which you can see in the Church of Ireland grounds. The church is 14th-century with a square tower. They can be viewed from the outside only. The archbishops of the 12th and 13th centuries were often as well armed as any baron, and the Archbishop of Dublin built a strong fortification at Swords for himself; the 12th-century **Archbishop's Castle** is five-sided and has been shored up against further ruin. Its courtyard is enclosed by strong walls, flanked by square towers.

Portmarnock, 5 miles (8km) further south along the coast, has a beach 3 miles (4.8km) long nicknamed the 'velvet strand'. Two miles (3.2km) inland at Balgriffin, just off the R107, is **St Doulagh's Church**, which incorporates a 12th-century anchorite cell and a small subterranean chamber covering a sunken bath, known as St Catherine's Well. The stone-roofed chancel dates from the 12th century. A square tower was added in the 15th century. The Velvet Strand stretches up the neck of the Howth Peninsula, while a mile (1.6km) out to sea is **Ireland's Eye**, a great place for a picnic; you can take a boat out there from the pier in Howth Harbour during summer. Its name comes from the corruption of *Inis Éireann*, which means 'Island of Éire'. The old stone church on the island is all that is left of a 6th-century monastery.

Howth (with the 'o' pronounced as in 'both') comes from the Danish word *hoved*, meaning 'head'. Before the Anglo-Norman family of St Lawrence muscled their way into the area, Howth was a Danish settlement. An important ferry port until it was superseded by Dun Laoghaire, its harbour today is full of pleasure craft. **Howth Castle** remains in the hands of the St Lawrence family. The public are allowed to walk around the bright **tropical gardens** (*open daily 8am–sunset; adm free*); in late spring the rhododendrons are a glorious colour. It is said that Grace O'Malley, the 16th-century pirate-queen from County Mayo (*see* p.300), stopped at Howth to replenish her supplies of food and water and decided to visit the St Lawrences. The family were eating however, and she was refused admittance. Enraged by this rudeness, she snatched Lord Howth's infant son and heir and sailed away with him to Mayo. She returned the child only on condition that the gates of the castle were always left open at mealtimes, and a place set at the table for the head of the O'Malley clan – a custom that is still kept today. The **National Transport Museum** (*open June–Aug Mon–Sat 10–5, Sept–May Sat and Sun 2–5; adm; t (01) 832 0427, www.nationaltransportmuseum. org*) in Howth Castle Demesne has specimens of everything that ever rolled on an Irish road, from Victorian-era carriages to early trams and fire engines.

South County Dublin and the Coast

Blackrock is a pleasant middle-class suburb south of Dublin, with a pretty public park overlooking the sea. In the 19th century, Martello towers were built all along this wharf to warn of a possible invasion by Napoleon. At **Monkstown**, about half a mile (0.8km) south, is the headquarters of *Comhaltas Ceoltóirí Éireann*, the cultural movement set up in 1951 to preserve and nurture traditional Irish entertainment (*see* p.71). In summer a variety of shows of traditional music, singing and dancing are held here every week. The building also includes a music library.

Dun Laoghaire (pronounced 'Dun Lay-reh' or 'Dun Leary', depending on who's doing the pronouncing), is a terminus for car ferry services from Britain. This Victorian town with its bright terraced houses was traditionally a holiday resort, and it is pleasant to stroll around before exploring the wilder delights of the Wicklow Mountains. Dun Laoghaire is named after Laoghaire, who was High King of Ireland when St Patrick converted him in the 5th century. For a time this busy port was called Kingstown, after George IV visited Ireland in 1821, but the name was dropped at the establishment of the Free State. The houses along **Marine Parade** are very handsome, painted different colours, and with intricate ironwork and Regency detail. The two great granite **piers** were built between 1817 and 1859. Both make for an invigorating walk; Sundays are especially good for people-watching. It is an important yachting centre, and the Royal Saint George and Royal Irish clubs are situated here.

The **National Maritime Museum** (*open May–Sept Tue–Sun 1–5; adm; t (01) 280 0969*) is in the Mariner's Church, Haigh Terrace. The **Sacred Heart Oratory Dominican Convent** (*access by appointment only*) on George's Street is a little gem of the Celtic Revival style, decorated by Sister Concepta Lynch in a combination of Celtic and Art Nouveau style. Marine Parade, laid out with trees and flowers, takes you to the **James Joyce Museum** (*open Apr–Oct Mon–Sat 10–1 and 2–5, Sun 2–6; adm; t (01) 280 9265/827 2077*) at The Joyce Tower in Sandycove. In fact this Martello tower, from the Napoleonic Wars, was rented by Oliver St John Gogarty, whose witty book *As I Walked Down Sackville Street* is a must for all true Hibernian enthusiasts. Joyce stayed with him for the weekend and used the visit in the opening scene of *Ulysses*. Gogarty ('stately plump Buck Mulligan') and Joyce later quarrelled – now their names are perpetually linked. Few people have actually read the whole of *Ulysses*, and for a long time it was banned by the Irish censor for revealing too much of the earthy Dublin character. But the tower is a shrine where visitors can worship and ponder over the collection of Joyceana. Just beside the tower is the Forty Foot Pool, where in *Ulysses*, Buck Mulligan had a morning dip. Made for the Fortieth Foot infantry regiment, it was traditionally a nude, men-only bathing spot, but now you have to wear a bathing suit after 9am. Aficionados swim here all year round, even on Christmas Day.

Dalkey, adjoining Dun Laoghaire, is a small fishing village where Bernard Shaw used to stay and admire the skies from Dalkey Hill. In the 15th and 16th centuries it was the main landing place for passengers from England. In the main thoroughfare, Castle Street, are the remains of fortified mansions from that time, plus **Dalkey Castle and Heritage Centre** (*open Mon–Fri 9.30–5, Sat, Sun and bank hols 11–5; adm; t (01) 285 8366, www.dalkeycastle.com*), where the history of the castle back to the Middle Ages is described by the area's famous resident author, Hugh Leonard. A boat may be hired from Coliemore Harbour to **Dalkey Island**, where there is a Martello tower and the remains of an ancient church. The Vico road runs along the coast, unfolding beautiful views of Killiney Bay. From the village centre you can walk to **Sorrento Point**, where you get a panoramic view of the distant coastline, the Sugar Loaf Mountains and the sweep of Killiney Bay itself. If you climb **Killiney Hill** you will have an even clearer view of the bay, the mountains and the Liffey Valley.

You pass through the little village of Glencullen on the R117 if you wish to go higher into the Dublin Hills, which merge into the Wicklow Mountains at Enniskerry. It is possible to take the old 'Military Road' up into the Wicklow glens, or go back towards Dublin on the R116 through forest and hill. On the way to Rathfarnham, a pleasant suburb about 25 minutes from the city centre, is **Marlay Park** (*gardens open daily Feb and Mar 10–6, Apr and Oct 10–7, May 10–8, June–Aug 10–9, Nov–Jan 10–5; t (01) 493 4059, www.dlrcoco.ie/parks/marlay*). Formerly the estate of David La Touche, an 18th-century banker, it was left to the county for public use. Dublin County Council has developed it, with a **crafts centre** in the converted stables, where you can buy some lovely things. The craft workers include a bookbinder, a harpmaker, a woodcarver, an antique restorer and a potter. The parkland is laid out with lakes, woods, a golf course and a miniature railway. The house itself is still being restored.

The Wicklow Way, a long-distance, signposted walking trail over the mountains, starts in Marlay Park. **Sandyford**, a neighbouring suburb, contains the green shades of **Fernhill Gardens** (*open Mar–Sept Tue–Sat 11–5, Sun 2–6; adm; t (01) 295 6000*), at Lamb's Cross. Giant Wellingtonia redwood trees form a sheltered walk, the front field is a wild meadow where cowslips grow, and in the walled garden is a Victorian vegetable and flower garden. There is also a rare example of a Victorian level garden and a fine rhododendron collection.

Lucan, a suburb to the west of the city, used to be a minor Bath, and is on a beautiful stretch of the Liffey. James Gandon (1743–1823), Ireland's most famous architect, lived here and is buried in Drumcondra graveyard. The village is now very built-up.

Dublin City

... The Dublin girl that's born an' bred,
Above all Ireland holds her head,
Still upper lip's her beauty.
No holy poke, she likes a joke,
She shies at nayther drink nor smoke,
An' at cards she knows her duty.

The Dublin boy that's born and bred,
Above 'em all high holds his head
For swagger, sport, an' cunning.
He's neither North, South, East, nor West,
But a blend of all that each holds best,
An' the tips he gets are stunning...

Here's Granua Aile, boys. Drink her down.
Quick end to all her troublin'.
May beauty, wit, and wisdom crown
Her Parliament in Dublin.
Dublin doggerel

Dublin, if not her parliament, has a worldwide reputation for culture, wit, friendliness and beauty, and this image perpetuates itself as the casual Dublin charm works its way into the heart of every visitor. Irish people themselves call it 'dear old dirty Dublin', and at first glance you may think that they are right and discount the affection in their voices when they talk about it. For there is no doubt that Dublin can be a bit of a disappointment, and you may ask yourself what all the fuss is about: the rosy Georgian squares and perfectly proportioned doorways are jumbled up with some grotesque modern architecture. Fast-food signs and partially demolished buildings mingle with expensive and tacky shops, and the housing estates can be depressing. The tall houses north of the Liffey were divided into rundown flats, though many have been done up and through doors and windows you catch glimpses of their former glory.

Modern Dublin was bent on knocking down the past or ignoring it so that it crumbled away on its own, especially during the 1970s. Should you ask about Wood Quay, official indifference reveals itself. This was the complete 9th- to 11th-century Danish settlement of houses, walls and quays that was recently excavated, giving great insight into the lives of those first Dubliners. The Dublin City Corporation actually built their ugly modern office block on top of it, despite sustained protests from those who felt the old city should be preserved. On the positive side, the Custom House Quay development, which also houses a financial centre, the IFSC, is a fine attempt at regeneration of the docklands area. And the last few years have seen a quickening of interest in preserving the lovely old buildings of the past. The Dublin Millennium Celebrations in 1988 caused a great sprucing up, and Dubliners took great pride in their city's history and heritage. In 1991 Dublin was the European City of Culture, which encouraged more refurbishment. There is still an amount of uncoordinated planning, though. Dublin is threatened with road-widening plans, and what amounts to a motorway has been built, cutting through the city centre.

You will find that gradually the charm and atmosphere of Dublin – and atmosphere is what it is all about – begins to filter through that first, negative impression. Get up early, explore the ancient medieval streets around Dublin Castle in the morning sunshine, and breakfast at Bewley's Café. Walk down Grafton Street, where noisy, laughing shoppers mingle with some genuine eccentrics. Relax, go with the flow and notice the pleasant things about Dublin that have been staring you in the face all along.

History

The Greek philosopher Ptolemy mentioned Dublin in AD 140, when it was called Eblana, but it really came to prominence under the Danes during the 9th century, because of its importance as a fording place and as a base for maritime expeditions. They established themselves on a section of ground between the River Liffey and Christ Church. The name Dublin comes from the Irish *Dubhlinn* – 'Dark Pool' – although the Irish form in official use is *Baile Átha Cliath*: 'Town of the Hurdle Ford', which refers to an ancient river crossing near the present Heuston Station.

The marauding Vikings arrived in AD 840 and established a fortress and settlement along the banks of the Liffey estuary. From a simple base for raiding expeditions, Dublin grew to a prosperous trading port with Europe. The local Gaelic rulers were very keen to grab it for themselves, but it was not until the Battle of Clontarf in 1014 that the dominance of the Danes was severely curtailed. They were finally driven out in 1169 by the Anglo-Normans under Strongbow (Richard de Clare), who took Dublin by storm and executed the Viking leader. The arrival of the Anglo-Norman foreigners began the occupation of Ireland by the English, which lasted 700 years. Dermot MacMurragh, King of Leinster, invited the invasion by asking Henry II of England for the help of Anglo-Norman mercenaries in his battle for the high kingship of Ireland. They came, and their military campaigns were so successful that they soon controlled not only Wexford and Waterford but most of Leinster and, of course, Dublin. Once here, the Normans had no intention of leaving. In 1172 Henry II came to Dublin to look over his kingdom, and to curb the powers of his warlike vassal lords.

Dublin City

To Dublin Zoo

To Phoenix Park

INFIRMARY ROAD

NORTH CIRCULAR ROAD

AUGHRIM STREET

PRUSSIA STREET

MANOR STREET

STONEYBATTER

GRANGE GORMAN UPPER

GRANGE GORMAN LOWER

PHIBSBOROUGH 11TH

CONSTITUTION ROAD

WESTERN

DOMINICK ST

King's Inns

BRUNSWICK STREET NORTH

CHURCH STREET UPPER

COLERAINE ST

KING STREET NORTH

KING STREET NORTH

St Michan's Church

MONTPELIER HILL

PARKGATE STREET

TEMPLE ST W

ARBOUR HILL

Collins Barracks

National Museum of Decorative Arts and History

ARBOUR HILL

BLACKHALL PLACE

BLACKHALL STREET

QUEEN STREET

MAY LANE

FRIARY AV.

SMITHFIELD

CHURCH ST NEW

Old Jameson Distillery

BERESFORD STREET

HALSTON STREET

ANNE ST N

GREEN STREET

GREEN ST LITTLE

MARY'S LANE

CUCKOO LANE

ST MICHANS

Market

ARRAN STREET

ST MARY'S

BENBURB STREET

Esplanade

SEAN HEUSTON BR.

WOLFE TONE QUAY

SARSFIELD QUAY

RORY O'MORE BR.

ELLIS QUAY

JAMES JOYCE BR.

MELLOWS BR.

ARRAN ST NEW

LINCOLN LANE

HAM LANE

CHANCERY STREET

GREEK STREET

CHARLES

ORMOND SQ

ORMOND

River Liffey

Heuston Station

VICTORIA QUAY

WATLING STREET

USHERS ISLAND

James Joyce House

ISLAND STREET

USHERS QUAY

USHERS QUAY

FATHER MATHEW BR.

INNS QUAY

Four Courts

JOHN'S ROAD WEST

MILITARY ROAD

Guinness Storehouse Brewery

BRIDGEFOOT STREET

AUGUSTINE STREET

River Liffey

MERCHANTS QUAY

WOOD QUAY

BOW LANE WEST

BOW BRIDGE

ECHLIN ST

St Catherine's Church

CRANE ST

THOMAS COURT

OLIVER BOND STREET

THOMAS STREET WEST

COOK STREET

CORN MKT

BRIDGE ST LOWER

BRIDGE ST UPPER

ST AUDOEN

St Audoen's Church

SKIPPERS ALLEY

ST MICHAEL'S HILL

HIGH STREET

WINETAVERN ST

Christ Church Cath.

Dublinia

CHRISTCHURCH PLACE

JAMES'S STREET

JAMES'S STREET

RAINSFORD STREET

Guinness Hop Store

BELLEVUE SCHOOL STREET

MARROWBONE LANE

THOMAS COURT

PIMLICO

MEATH PLACE

ENGINE ALLEY

SWIFTS ALLEY

T. DAVIS ST

NICHOLAS STREET

Tivoli Theatre

Iveagh Market

ANCES STREET

Tailors' Hall

BACK LANE

ROSS RD

BRIDE RD

ST NICHOLAS

To Irish Museum of Modern Art
Kilmainham Jail
Islandbridge

ST JAMES'S WALK

REUBEN STREET

MARROWBONE LANE

ARDEE STREET

CORK STREET

THE COOMBE

HANOVER LANE

BULL ALLEY

St Patrick's Park

St Patrick's Cathedral

PATRICKS CLOSE

DEAN ST

NEW ROW SOUTH

NEW ST SOUTH

KEVIN ST UPPER

CATHEDRAL VIEW WALK

SOUTH CIRCULAR ROAD

REUBEN STREET

DOLPHIN'S BARN ST

CORK STREET

DONORE AVENUE

DONORE AVENUE

CLARENCE MANGAN ST

O'DONOVAN ROAD

PETRIE RD

RAYMOND STREET

DUFFERIN AVENUE

BLACK PITTS

CLANBRASSIL STREET LOWER

LONG LANE

DOLPHIN'S BARN

PARNELL ROAD

R111

To Drimnagh Castle

CRUMLIN ROAD

DOLPHIN'S BARN ROAD

SALLY'S BR.

PARNELL ROAD

SOUTH CIRCULAR ROAD

DONORE AVE

SOUTH CIRCULAR ROAD

ROBERT EMMET BR.

CLANBRASSIL ST UPPER

M81

Grand Canal

SOUTH CIRCULAR ROAD

LOMBARD STREET WEST

VICTORIA STREET

GROVE ROAD

WINDSOR TERRACE

To Dillon Garden, Mus. of Childhood & Pearse Mus.

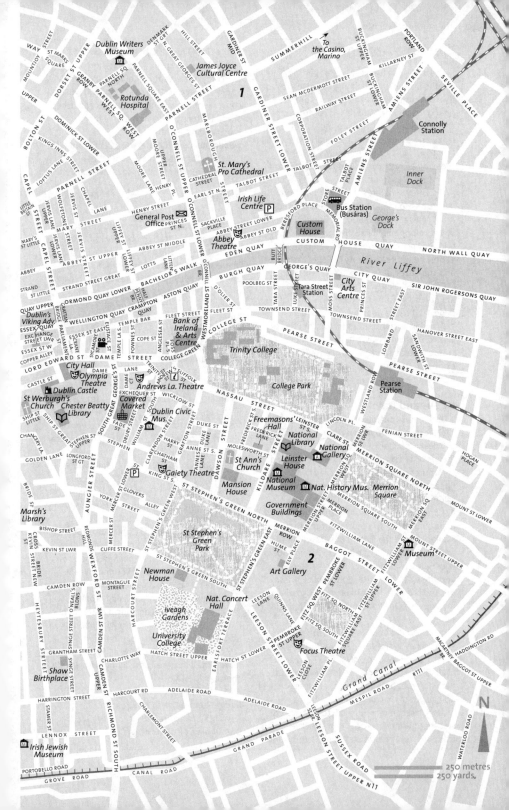

Getting Around

The best and cheapest way of getting around Dublin is by **walking**, because most of the museums, shops and galleries are fairly near to each other. Dublin is a compact city; the central area clusters around the River Liffey and occupies about 2 square miles (5 sq km). Most of the museums, galleries, theatres, architectural sights and restaurants are within this small area.

The **Liffey** separates the north side from the south. It is spanned by several bridges, the most central being **O'Connell Bridge**. The streets along the River Liffey are called quays, and they change names between bridges. St Stephen's Green, Trinity College, Grafton St and the Castle area are south of the river. O'Connell St, Henry St and Parnell Square are north. Grafton St and Henry St are both pedestrianized. **Phoenix Park** (1,760acres/712ha) is less than 2 miles (3km) from the city centre, to the north-west. The **Grand Canal** crosses the city and joins the River Liffey, enclosing the southern part of the city centre in a gentle curve.

By Bus and Train

Dublin Bus controls all public bus services in the Greater Dublin Area (which includes parts of Wicklow, Kildare and Meath). The DART feeder system is run by **Iarnród Éireann**, and commuter services are controlled by **Bus Éireann**. Their buses run until about 11.30 or midnight and are a very convenient way to get around, though you'll find the going slow enough through the centre. A route map is available from the Dublin Bus Travel Centre, and any of the tourist offices will help you find your way. Bus fares are based on distance, and there's a correct-fare only policy. A 1-day rail and bus pass is available for €8.50 and includes the DART. A combined bus and LUAS ticket costs €6.20.

DART (Dublin Area Rapid Transit) electric trains serve 25 suburban stations near the coast from Howth to Bray. A DART day ticket is available from Iarnród Éireann for about €6, but you probably won't need it unless you are doing a lot of exploring in the suburbs.

LUAS, the capital's light rail transit system, was inaugurated in 2004. Two street-level tramlines run from St Stephen's Green (south of the Liffey) to the suburb of Sandyford (Green Line) and from Abbey St (north of the Liffey) westwards to Tallaght (Red Line). There are several LUAS stops that you will find convenient for galleries, museums and other sites of interest. See *www.luas.ie* for route maps and other information.

Dublin Bus Travel Centre, 59 Upper O'Connell St, D1, t (01) 873 4222, *www.dublinbus.ie*
Iarnród Éireann, t (01) 836 6222, *www.irishrail.ie*

By Taxi

It's often rather difficult to flag down a cab on the streets. Taxis can be found outside hotels and train stations, however, and in special taxi parking areas in central Dublin. There are 24hr ranks at St Stephen's Green and O'Connell St. Taxis should always have meters. They charge extra per piece of luggage, per person and at night.
Blue Cabs, t (01) 802 2222
Metro Cabs, t (01) 668 3333/478 1111/677 2222
Pony Cabs, t (01) 661 2233
VIP Taxi and Courier Service, t (01) 478 3333

By Car

Parking is difficult (occasionally impossible) in the centre of town, but a computerized system with strategically placed screens tells you which car parks have spaces. The main **car parks** are in Drury St and the St Stephen's Green Shopping Centre, and there is metered parking around St Stephen's Green and Merrion Square. On the north side you might find a parking place in the Irish Life Shopping Centre (entrance off Lower Abbey St) or the Jervis Shopping Mall off Upper Abbey St.

Driving in Dublin is delightfully disordered, so be on your guard. It is mostly a matter of nerve and panache. Using your horn is the worst insult, so keep it as a last resort. Car theft and burglaries are an increasing problem, so it's a good idea when booking a hotel to check if it has secure parking. See *www.dublinks.com* under the 'Home' menu for details.

Most of the major **car hire** chains are represented at the airport, along with a wide choice of local firms:
AVIS, t (01) 605 7500, *www.avis.ie*
Budget Rent A Car, t (01) 844 5150, *www.budgetcarrental.ie*
Dan Dooley, t (01) 814 4043

Europcar, t (01) 614 2888, *www.europcar.ie.*
There's also a branch at Baggot Street
Bridge, D4, **t** (01) 614 2888
Hertz Rent-A-Car, t (01) 844 5466
National Car Rental, t (01) 844 4162

By Bike
The Bike Store Ltd, 58 Gardiner St, D1,
t (01) 872 5399
Dublin Bike Hire, 27 North Great George's St,
D1, **t** (01) 878 8473
Harding for Bicycles, 30 Bachelors Walk, D1,
t (01) 873 2455
Joe Daly Cycles, Lower Main St, Dundrum, D8,
t (01) 298 1485
Little Sport Ltd, 3 Merville Ave, Fairview, D3,
t (01) 833 2405

Festivals and Events

February–March
Dublin International Film Festival, t (01) 661
6216, *www.dubliniff.com.* A showcase for
Irish and world cinema, highly recommended.
Six Nations Rugby, Lansdowne Road Stadium,
Ballsbridge, D4 t (01668) 4601. A famous
event held over 2 Saturdays. There's always a
good party in the years when the Scots visit.

March
National St Patrick's Day Festival,
www.stpatricksday.ie. Lots of events and
music around the 17th, including celebrations
and parades starting on O'Connell St.

April
International Dance Festival, t (01) 679 0524,
www.dancefestivalireland.ie

May
Green Energy International Music Festival,
t (01) 456 9569. A huge event; past
headliners include the Cranberries,
Tracy Chapman and Joe Strummer.

June
AIB Music in Great Irish Houses, *see* **Practical
A–Z,** p.102. A festival of chamber music in
great houses in the Dublin area.
Bloomsday, t (01) 878 8547, *www.jamesjoyce.ie.*
Dublin's own peculiar holiday, on 16th June,

the anniversary of the day (in 1904) on
which all the action of Joyce's *Ulysses* took
place. Various events are held in the places
visited by Leopold Bloom, some scheduled,
some not. People wear Edwardian costume
and make recitations; some just come along
for the pub crawl. The day begins at 8am by
the tower in Sandycove.
Dublin Writers' Festival, t (01) 222 7847,
www.dublinwritersfestival.com. Four days
of readings and discussions by leading Irish
and international writers.

August
Kerrygold Horse Show, Ballsbridge,
t (01) 668 0866, *www.dublinhorseshow.com.*
An international equestrian event.

September
All Ireland Hurling and Football Finals,
t (01) 836 3222
Dublin Fringe Theatre Festival, t (01) 679 2320,
www.fringefest.com
Dublin Jazz Festival, t (01) 670 3885.
A week-long event held at a number
of venues in the city.
International Puppetry Festival, t (01) 280 0974

October
Dublin City Marathon, t (01) 623 2250
Dublin Theatre Festival, t (01) 677 8439,
www.dublintheatrefestival.com

December
Dublin Grand Opera Winter Season, Gaiety
Theatre, South King St, D2, **t** (01) 872 1122,
www.gaietytheatre.com, www.operaireland.ie.

Tourist Information
Dublin Tourism Centre, St Andrew's Church,
Suffolk St (off Grafton St, near Trinity
College), D2, **t** (01) 605 7700, toll-free
recorded information line **t** 1850 230 330,
www.visitdublin.com. Closed Sun.
This main office occupying an entire
restored church is all very modern and
efficient, but staff don't have a lot of printed
information to hand out and you could be
waiting forever. You have to take a number
and have a seat. Staff also change money,
and book hotels and theatre tickets.

Bord Failté Eireann/Tourism Ireland, Baggot Street Bridge (south of centre, on Grand Canal), D2, information line t 1850 230 330, *www.ireland.travel.ie*. *Closed Sat and Sun*. There's also an office at 14 Upper O'Connell St (north of the Liffey). **Dublin Airport** (*see* p.529) **Dun Laoghaire**: New Ferry Terminal. *Closed pm*. **Tallaght**: The Square, D24. *Closed pm*.

Practical A–Z

Banks
Mon–Wed and Fri 10–4, Thur 10–5.

Bureaux de Change
These can be found at the airport and in tourist offices and banks. Try:
American Express, 116 Grafton St, D2, t (01) 677 2874
Thomas Cook, 118 Grafton St, D2, t (01) 677 1307

Chemists
The following are open until 10pm:
Leonard's, 106 South Circular Rd, D8, t (01) 453 4282
O'Connell's, 55 Lower O'Connell St, D1, t (01) 873 0427

Emergencies
In an emergency, dial t **999** or t **112**.
Garda Confidential Line, t 1800 666111
Women's Aid, t 1800 341900

Hospitals
St James's Hospital, James's St, D8, t (01) 410 3000
St Vincent's University Hospital, Elm Park, D4, t (01) 221 4000

Internet Cafés
Central Cyber Café, 6 Grafton St, D2, t (01) 677 8298, *www.globalcafe.ie*
Does Not Compute, Unit 2 Pudding Row, Essex Street West, Temple Bar, D8, t (01) 670 4464
Global Internet Café, 8 Lower O'Connell St, D1, t (01) 878 0295, *www.globalcafe.ie*
Internet Exchange Café, 10 Fownes St, D2, t (01) 635 1680
Planet Cybercafé, 13 St Andrew's St, D2, t (01) 670 5183

Police (*Garda Síochána*)
Dublin Metropolitan Area HQ, t (01) 666 0000 and t 1800 666 111

Post Offices
The **GPO** (General Post Office; *open until 8pm*) is halfway along O'Connell St; there are branches in Parnell St and Summerhill, north of the Liffey, and south of it at Upper Baggot St, Lower Baggot St, Clare St, Earlsfort Terrace, Pearse St, Merrion Row, Montague St and South Anne St.

Student Travel Agency
USIT, 19–21 Aston Quay, D2, t (01) 602 1904. Staff here will also book accommodation, and run a hostel too. *Closed Sun*.

Telephones
Payphone centres are located in the GPO (*see* above), and beside the Gaiety Theatre on South King St. More and more of these are **cardphones**, the cards for which may be bought in post offices and selected newsagents. You will generally also find public phones in the big hotels.
The local dialling code for the whole of Co. Dublin is t (01).

YHA
Irish Youth Hostel Association (An Óige), 61 Mountjoy St, D1, t (01) 830 4555, *www.anoige.ie*

Media

Newspapers and Listings
In Dublin magazine (€1), started by students, is now sold at every newsstand. *Hot Press* is also essential, with good arts and music reviews. The *Evening Herald* contains cinema listings, while the *Irish Mirror* has a Friday supplement good for music and nightclubs. Read the *Irish Times* for reviews of plays, concerts and films. Every Saturday it also lists special happenings in Dublin and the provinces.

Websites
Good websites for information on city life include *The Dubliner* magazine's stylish website, *www.thedubliner.ie*, and *The Irish*

Times website, *www.ireland.com/dublin*, which lists events daily. Dublin Tourism's site, *www. visitdublin.com*, has excellent coverage as well.

Guided Tours

On Foot

Signposts erected around the city guide you through the historical sights on foot; there's the Georgian Trail, the Cultural Trail, the Old City Trail and the Rock 'n' Stroll Trail. Contact Dublin Tourism on Suffolk St (*see* p.541) for more details.

Dublin Tourism have also introduced **iWalks**, podcast audio-guides to themed walks around the city read by well-known Dublin author Pat Liddy. Each can be downloaded free from *www.visitdublin.com/iwalks*. At the time of writing, 2 walks were available and a further 9 were imminent.

There are also a selection of guided walking tours on offer:

Historical Walking Tour of Dublin, t (01) 878 0227, *www.historicalinsights.ie/tour*. Groups meet at the front gate of Trinity College at 11am daily.

The 1916 Rebellion Walking Tour, t (086) 858 3847. A tour departing from the International Bar, 23 Wicklow St, Sat at 11.30am, and taking you around all the sites linked with the traumatic event.

Old Dublin, t (01) 679 4291. Groups assemble at Bewley's, Grafton St or Dublin Writer's Museum, 18 Parnell Sq; call for times.

Revolutionary Dublin 1916–23, t (01) 662 9976. A daily tour conducted by Trinity College graduate students; call for times.

There are also several **pub tours**, where the walking becomes increasingly less steady; there is a fee, and you'll need extra cash for the Guinness.

The Dublin Literary Pub Crawl, 1 Suffolk St, D2, t (01) 670 5602, *www.dublinpubcrawl.com*. Groups meet at The Duke pub on Duke St Easter–Oct nightly at 7.30pm; Nov–Mar Thur–Sat 7.30pm; all year Sun 12 noon and 7.30pm. Tickets are sold on a first-come first-served basis.

The Musical Pub Crawl, t (01) 475 3313. A tour through several traditional music bars by 2 knowledgeable musicians; call for times.

By Bus

Dublin Bus, 59 O'Connell St (between Henry St and Parnell St), D1, t (01) 873 4222, *www. dublinbus.ie*. Open-top bus 'hop on-hop off' tours, meaning you can get on and off at any stop, and your ticket is good for the entire day. Buses run the circuit every 15mins. The firm also offer offers full- and half-day tours of north Co. Dublin, with a stop at Malahide Castle (*daily, 10am from O'Connell St*), and the southern coast into Co. Wicklow (*daily, 11 and 2, from O'Connell St*).

Sports and Activites

Greyhound Racing

Harold's Cross, D6, t (01) 497 1081
Shelbourne Park, D4, t (01) 668 3502 or t 1850 646566, *www.shelbournepark.com*

Hurling and Gaelic Football

The Gaelic Athletic Association's website, *www.gaa.ie*, gives detailed descriptions of these 2 games and their rules. You can see them both played in Dublin at Croke Park, Parnell Park and Phoenix Park.

See also **Topics**, pp.79–80.

Rugby and Football

Watch a game at **Landsdowne Road**, 1 mile (1.6km) south of the city centre, where in Feb or Mar you can catch the mighty Six Nations Rugby tournament (*see* p.541).

Shopping

The smartest and best shopping is in a small area around **Grafton St** and the little streets leading off it, just north-east of the river. North of the Liffey, **Henry St** is the busiest shopping street in Dublin – and generally cheaper than the upmarket Grafton St area. The flagship of this area is Clery's, on O'Connell St (*see* p.545).

Antiques

The antique shops in Molesworth, South Anne St and Kildare St are well regarded and sell top-quality furniture, silver and ornaments. For more junky stuff and bargains try Francis St, in the Liberties, where there are individual antique shops and an antiques arcade.

A Star is Born, Clarendon St, D2. Antique and second-hand items. *Closed Sun–Fri.*

Iveagh Market, just across road from Tivoli Theatre, Francis St, D8. A fine 19th-century covered market, now very shabby and occupied by second-hand clothes dealers.

Jenny Vander, George's Street Arcade, D2. Good second-hand clothes, lovely antique pieces of clothing and costume jewellery.

Auctioneers

De Vere's Art Auctions, 35 Kildare St, D2, t (01) 676 8300, *www.deveresart.com.* This sells mostly Irish paintings.

Herman and Wilkinson, 161 Lower Rathmines Rd, D6, t (01) 497 2245. Fortnightly auctions of silver, paintings and furniture.

James Adams and Sons, 26 St Stephen's Green, D2, t (01) 676 0261, *www.adams.ie*

Whyte's, 38 Molesworth St, D2, t (01) 676 2888, *www.whytes.ie.* Stamps and coins, old prints, maps, photos etc.

Books

An open-air **book market** is held in Temple Bar Square (*Sat and Sun 10–6*).

Books Upstairs, 36 College Green, D2, t (01) 679 6687. A wide range of Irish-interest books.

Cathach Books, 10 Duke St, D2, t (01) 671 8676, *www.rarebooks.ie.* A big indie bookseller.

Dublin Writers' Museum, 18 Parnell Sq, D1, t (01) 872 2077. A museum bookshop providing an out-of-print and antiquarian search service.

Eason & Son, Lower O'Connell St, D1, t (01) 858 3800. A general bookshop with several other branches in the city.

Fred Hanna's Bookshop, 28–29 Nassau St, D2, t (01) 677 1255. An independent bookseller.

Greene's Bookshop Ltd, 16 Clare St, D2, t (01) 676 2554, *www.greenesbookshop.com.* Rare and out-of-print books.

Hodges Figgis, 57 Dawson St, D2, t (01) 677 4754. A large general bookstore.

Winding Stair Books, 40 Lower Ormond Quay, D1, t (01) 873 3292. Three floors of second-hand books, plus an excellent café and a lovely view.

Clothes

Many of the UK's most prominent high-street clothing chains – Next, Principles, Marks & Spencer – have branches in Grafton St. (*See also* 'Department Stores', opposite.)

For **Irish tweed,** and for high-quality craft design, head for Nassau St, at the College Green end of Dawson St.

Avoca Handweavers, 11-13 Suffolk St, D2, t (01) 677 4215. Fashions and crafts, and a good café (*see* p.548).

A-Wear, 26 Grafton St, D2, t (01) 671 7200, *www.a-wear.ie.* Inexpensive diffusion ranges by Quin and Donnelly, appealing to all ages. There's another branch in Henry St.

The Blarney Woollen Mills, 21–3 Nassau St, D2, t (01) 451 6111, *www.blarney.com.* Tailored skirts and jackets, soft jersey dresses and jumpers, scarves and luxurious woollen coats, in a good range of colours – from the clear primaries to tweeds full of subtle shades inspired by the Irish countryside.

Cleo, 18 Kildare St, a little way off Nassau St, D2, t (01) 676 1421. A good designer tweed shop.

Design Centre, Powerscourt Townhouse Centre, D2, t (01) 679 4144. A plethora of contemporary design under one roof. *See* also opposite.

FX Kelly, 48 Grafton St, D2. Men's designerwear.

Kennedy & McSharry, 39 Nassau St, D2. Beautifully tailored suits in Donegal tweed.

Kevin & Howlin, 31 Nassau St, D2, t (01) 677 0257. Lovely tweed caps, scarves and suits for men.

Sé Sí Progressive, Temple Bar, D2. Inexpensive clubwear from young designer talent.

Commercial Art Galleries

The following galleries put on shows by Irish artists.

City Arts Centre, 23 Moss St, D2, t (01) 677 0643, *www.cityarts.ie.* A showcase for emerging young artists, with a pleasant café.

Graphic Studio Gallery, off Cope St, Temple Bar, D2, t (01) 679 8021. Fine art prints by Irish and international artists.

Green on Red, 26 Lombard St, D2, t (01) 671 3414. Contemporary paintings and sculpture.

Kerlin Gallery, Anne's Lane, off South Anne St, D2, t (01) 670 9093, *www.kerlin.ie.* A lovely gallery space for established and new talent.

Oriel Gallery, 17 Clare St, D2, t (01) 676 3410, *www.theoriel.com.* Mostly traditional and figurative early-20th-century work.

Rubicon, 10 St Stephen's Green, D2, t (01) 670 8055, *www.rubicongallery.ie.* Mostly modern work.

Solomon Gallery, Powerscourt Townhouse Centre, D2, t (01) 679 4237, *www.solomongallery.com*. A gallery showing pretty pictures that can occasionally verge on the twee.

Taylor Galleries, 16 Kildare St, D2, t (01) 676 6055. Work by established artists.

Crafts

Anthony O'Brien, 14a Ailesbury Road, D4, t (01) 260 4064. Pottery.

Designyard, Cow's Lane, Temple Bar, D2, t (01) 474 1011, *www.designyard.ie*. A hotspot for designer jewellery, ceramics, furniture and glass, located within a converted warehouse.

Irish Georgian Society, 74 Merrion Sq, D2, t (01) 676 7053. Historical placemats, books etc.

The Kilkenny Shop, Nassau St, D2, t (01) 677 7066 *www.kilkennyshop.com*. Excellent glass, pottery, jewellery, rugs and sweaters.

Louis Mulcahy Pottery, 46 Dawson St, D2, t (01) 670 9311, *www.louismulcahy.com*

Tower Craft Design Centre, Pearse St, D2, t (01) 677 5655, *www.ccoi.ie*. Craft-workers producing glass, jewellery, woodcarving, pottery, weaving and other lovely things.

Food and Drink

Asia Market, 18 Drury St, D2, t (01) 677 9764. Exotic ingredients.

Bretzel Kosher Bakery, 1A Lennox St, D8, t (01) 475 2724. A famous baker's near the Grand Canal, selling gingerbread men, walnut loaves, *challah* (shiny plaits of bread) and other treats.

Butler's, Grafton St, D2. Irish chocolates.

Caviston's, Epicurean Food Hall, Liffey St Lower, D1, t (01) 878 2289. An old-fashioned deli with fresh fish, Irish cheese and smoked salmon.

Down to Earth, 73 South Great Georges St, D2, t (01) 671 9702. Health foods.

Fitzpatricks, 40 Camden St, D8, t (01) 475 3996. A cheerful wholefood grocer.

Leonidas, Royal Hibernian Way, D2. Yummy Belgian chocolates.

Magill's, 14 Clarendon St, D2, t (01) 671 3830. A wonderfully old-fashioned place smelling of charcuterie and sourdough breads.

La Maison des Gourmets, 15 Castle Market, D2, t (01) 672 7258. A French boulangerie and deli in a pedestrianized area, with a café.

Patrick Guilbaud, 42 The Liffey Trust, Sheriff St, D1, t 855 5299. A French bakery.

Temple Bar Food Market, Meeting House Sq., D2. Local farmers' organic produce, home-baked breads and pastries, and exotic treats, every Sat morning.

Wallace's Food Shop, off Lower Ormond Quay, D1. An Italian deli in the trendy Quartier Bloom, a development near the Jervis Centre with Italian bars and cafes.

Department Stores

Brown Thomas, 88–95 Grafton St, D2, t (01) 605 6666, *www.brownthomas.com*. A first-class department store stocking Irish designers such as Paul Costelloe, Louise Kennedy, John Rocha and Michaelina Stacpoole. The excellent Wardrobe department has less expensive options, and there's a second shop, **BT2**, at no.28–9 of the same street

Clery's, O'Connell St, D1, t (01) 878 6000, *www.clerys.com*. A famous, old-fashioned, independent department store.

Powerscourt Townhouse Centre, 59 South William St, D2, t (01) 679 5718, *www.powerscourtcentre.com*. An innovative shopping mecca generally regarded as a showpiece marriage between conservation and commerce. The elegant building was constructed more than 200 years ago as a town residence for Lord Powerscourt, an 18th-century nobleman. A glass dome over the old courtyard makes a wonderful space for cafés and restaurants; try **Mimo** on the ground floor or the veggie **Café Fresh**. Small craft shops, fashion shops, antique shops and jewellers have spaces in the old house. Names to look out for include **Emma Stewart Liberty** and **Patrick Flood** (silversmiths), and the **Design Centre** (*see* also opposite), which sells clothes by up-and-coming and established designers, including Mariad Whisker, Louise Kennedy, Lainey Keogh and Deirdre Fitzgerald, who design gorgeous knitwear. A must for any serious shopper.

St Stephen's Green Shopping Centre, corner of St Stephen's Green and Grafton St, D2. A huge glass mall with a wide variety of small shops and a vast **Dunnes** store (a bit like Marks & Spencer). It is also home to the **Crafts Centre of Ireland**, t (01) 475 4526, *www.ccoi.ie*. The **Dome Restaurant** on the upper level is a good spot for coffee, with views out over St Stephen's Green.

The Westbury Centre, round corner from Powerscourt Centre, D2. A mall with an Aladdin's cave of a lingerie shop, leather studio, good coffee shop, and **Angles**, selling the best modern Irish jewellery.

Music

Celtic Note, 14-15 Nassau St, D2, **t** (01) 670 4157
Claddagh Records, 2 Cecilia St, D2, **t** (01) 677 0262, *www.claddaghrecords.com*. A specialist in traditional Irish music.
Waltons, 69–70 South Great Georges St, D2, **t** (01) 475 0661. A stockist of Irish and international musical instruments.

Street Markets

Cow's Lane Natural Food Market, Temple Bar, D2. A range of food stalls selling certified organic fruit, fish from the Atlantic, cheeses, breads and preserves, Sat 10–6.
Dublin Food Co-op, St Andrew's Centre, 114–16 Pearse St, D2, **t** (01) 873 0451. Whole and organic foods, every Sat.
Moore Street Market, off Henry St, D1. A generally good place to buy fruit and vegetables, and to observe Dublin life. Some of the veteran market traders, usually women, use prams up to 70 years old to carry jewellery, fish, turf, concrete blocks, flowers, evening newspapers and gaudy Taiwanese toys. These 'perambulators' are not strictly allowed, as the owners do not pay rent, unlike the proper stands, and melt away into the crowds if the police arrive.
Mother Redcap's Market, Back Lane, near Christ Church, D8. Pottery, books and bric-à-brac. Try the Gallic Kitchen for pies and cakes, and Ryefield Foods for farmhouse cheeses.

Where to Stay

Dublin

City Centre: South of the Liffey

Buswell's Hotel, Molesworth St, D2, **t** (01) 614 6500, *www.quinnhotels.com* (*luxury*). An old-fashioned, cheerful family hotel, very centrally located.
Clarence Hotel, 6 Wellington Quay, D2 **t** (01) 407 0800 9000, *www.theclarence.ie*

(*luxury*). A traditional 1930s hotel now owned by members of rock group U2, with lovely wood panelling, a fashionable bar (*see* p.550) and friendly staff. It's well situated at the edge of the Temple Bar area.
Conrad International Dublin, Earlsfort Terrace, D2, **t** (01) 602 8900, *www.conradhotels.com* (*luxury*). A top-of-the-range modern hotel in the Hilton group's luxury tier, with excellent facilities and a pleasant atmosphere.
Shelbourne Hotel, St Stephens's Green, D2, **t** (01) 633 4500, *www.shelbourne.ie* (*luxury*). A lovely old-fashioned building in which the Irish Constitution was drafted, with a very elegant drawing room and a gem of a bar. At the time of writing it was being refurbished, with reopening scheduled for Sept 2006 in time for the Ryder Cup.
Westbury, Clarendon St, off Grafton St, D2, **t** (01) 679 1122, *www.jurys-dublin-hotels.com* (*luxury*). A modern hotel, top of the range and conveniently central.
The Georgian Hotel, 18 Baggot St Lower, D2, **t** (01) 634 5000, *www.georgianhotel.ie* (*expensive*). A converted Georgian house with snug, pastel-coloured rooms. It's very central, so you can walk everywhere.
Longfields Hotel, Fitzwilliam St Lower, D2, **t** (01) 676 1367, *www.longfields.ie* (*expensive*). A quiet, intimate Georgian townhouse with period furnishings and an excellent restaurant.
The Morgan Hotel, 10 Fleet St, Temple Bar, D2, **t** (01) 679 3939, *www.themorgan.com* (*expensive*). Quiet, private accommodation in the heart of Temple Bar, with an elegant, modern, designer feel. Staff are helpful and discreet, and continental breakfast is served in your room.
Number 31, Leeson Close, D2, **t** (01) 676 5011, *www.number.ie* (*expensive*). A comfortable choice with stylish modern décor and a secure car park.
The Schoolhouse Hotel, 2–8 Northumberland Rd, D4, **t** (01) 667 5014, or **t** 1850 344000, *www.schoolhousehotel.com* (*expensive*). An excellent hotel with a good bar.
Leeson Inn, 24 Lower Leeson St, D2, **t** (01) 662 2002 (*moderate–expensive*). A stylish and conveniently located choice.
Earl of Kildare Hotel, 47 Kildare St, D2, **t** (01) 679 4388 (*moderate*). A good hotel in a perfect location near Grafton St and Trinity College.

Barnacle's Temple Bar House,
19 Temple Lane, Temple Bar, D2, t (01) 671 6277,
www.barnacles.ie (inexpensive–moderate).
A centrally located hostel with doubles and
twins, and cheaper dorms, plus self-catering
and laundry facilities.

Brewery Hostel, 23 Thomas St, D8, t (01) 453
8600, www.irish-hostel.com (inexpensive).
A well-equipped hostel near the Guinness
Brewery, with doubles, twins and dorms.

Kinlay House Hostel, 2–12 Lord Edward St, D2,
t (01) 679 6644, www.kinlayhouse.ie
(inexpensive). A large, well-equipped option
near Christ Church, with twins and dorms.

City Centre: North of the Liffey

Gresham, Upper O'Connell St, D1, t (01) 874
6881, www.gresham-hotels.com (expensive).
An hotel built in the days when a first-class
establishment had big bedrooms and huge
baths, and retaining the atmosphere of the
1920s and 1930s. The best bedrooms are at
the front, and there's a residents' car park.

Anchor Guest House, 49 Lower Gardiner St, D1,
t (01) 878 6913, www.anchorguesthouse.com
(moderate). A Georgian house B&B near the
bus station.

Castle Hotel, 2 Gardiner Row, D1, t (01) 874 6949
(moderate). Attractively furnished rooms
with televisions.

Jacob's Inn, 21 Talbot Place, D1, t (01) 855 5660,
www.isaacs.ie (moderate). A modern hostel
near the bus station, with dorms, doubles
and twins.

Dublin International Youth Hostel,
61 Mountjoy St, D7, t (01) 830 1766
(inexpensive). A central, clean, friendly choice.

Isaacs Hostel, The Dublin Tourist Hostel,
2–5 Frenchman's Lane, D1 (beside bus
station), t (01) 855 6215, www.isaacs.ie
(inexpensive). A very clean, hospitable place
in the centre, built as a wine warehouse on
the Liffey in the 1700s, with an excellent,
good-value restaurant and a patio garden.
The accommodation is in basic dormitories
and single rooms.

Outside the Centre: Dublin City South

Jury's, Ballsbridge, D4, t (01) 660 5000,
www.jurysdoyle.com (luxury).
A large modern chain hotel with an
executive wing and a leisure centre.

Ariel House, 52 Lansdowne Rd, Ballsbridge, D4,
t (01) 668 5512, www.ariel-house.net
(moderate–expensive). A charming Victorian
house with lots of antiques. Bedrooms in
the older part are more individual in feel.
Breakfast is served in the conservatory.

Waterloo House, 8–10 Waterloo Rd, D4,
t (01) 660 1888, www.waterloohouse.ie
(moderate–expensive). A small, friendly
hotel in a residential Georgian street within
walking distance of the centre, perfect for
those who require privacy, cleanliness and
efficiency. Carefully prepared breakfasts
are served in a plush garden dining room
by meticulous staff.

Aberdeen Lodge, 53 Park Ave, Ballsbridge, D4,
t (01) 283 8155, www.halpinsprivatehotels.com
(moderate). An 'urban estate' comprising a
graceful old lodge with private gardens.
Guestrooms have period furniture, whirlpool
baths and aromatherapy toiletries. Standards
are very high for this price range.

Andorra B&B, 94 Merrion Rd, Ballsbridge, D4,
t (01) 668 9666. A family-run B&B close to
the RDS (Dublin Horse Show venue) and
convenient for DART trains to the centre.

McMenamins Townhouse, 74 Marlborough Rd,
Donnybrook, D4, t (01) 497 4405, www.
irishwelcome.com (moderate). A welcoming
and peaceful choice in a residential street
not far from University College Dublin. The
helpful, hospitable host knows all about
Donnybrook's history, and his wife serves up
excellent home baking at breakfast (special
breakfasts are available for vegetarians).

Merrion Hall, 56 Merrion Rd, Ballsbridge, D4,
t (01) 668 1426, www.halpinsprivatehotels.com
(moderate). A friendly, family-run guesthouse
with pretty bedrooms and delicious breakfasts
including home-made yoghurt.

Avalon House, 55 Aungier St, D2, t (01) 475 0001,
www.avalon-house.ie (inexpensive). An old
building converted into a modern hostel
with twin, family and dormitory rooms.
It's central, clean and efficiently run.

Outside the Centre: Dublin City North

Fairview Lodge, 27 Philipsburgh Ave, Fairview,
D3, t (01) 836 8439, www.fairviewlodge.com
(inexpensive–moderate). A townhouse B&B
convenient for the airport and city-centre
bus routes. Parking is available.

Eating Out

Dublin

Dining out is a very popular pastime here, so always try to book a table in advance.

City Centre: South of the Liffey

L'Ecrivain, 109 Lower Baggot St, D2, t (01) 661 1919, *www.lecrivain.com* (*luxury*). A friendly little basement restaurant serving imaginative French food. Popular with local business people, it's particularly buzzy at lunchtime.

Patrick Guilbaud, 21 Merrion St Upper, D2. t (01) 676 4192, *www.restaurantpatrickguilbaud.ie* (*luxury*). Excellent classic French cuisine, awarded two stars by Michelin, served in a modern formal interior.

Clarence Hotel Tea Rooms, 6–8 Wellington Quay, D2, t (01) 407 0813, *www.theclarence.ie* (*expensive*). A fashionable and fun place to eat a set dinner (but not tea, despite the name). There's a good choice of salads.

Cooke's Restaurant, 14 South William St, D2, t (01) 679 0536 (*expensive*). One of the most pleasant and intimate restaurants in Dublin, with lovely Italianate interior and superb modern Italian/Californian cooking. The home-baked focaccia breads with olive oil dips and patisserie are to die for – don't miss the Calvados tart. There's also a very good-value early-evening set menu.

Jacob's Ladder, 4 Nassau St, D2, t (01) 670 3865, *www.jacobsladder.ie* (*expensive*). Modern Irish fare served in a dining room overlooking the grounds of Trinity College. *Closed Mon.*

La Stampa, 35 Dawson St, D2, t (01) 677 4444, *www.lastampa.ie* (*expensive*). A fashionable and graceful brasserie, set in the splendid rooms of the former Guildhall.

Thornton's Restaurant, Fitzwilliam Hotel, 128 St Stephen's Green, D2, t (01) 478 7008, *www.thorntonsrestaurant.com* (*expensive*). Modern Irish food and views over the Green.

Avoca Café, Avoca Handweavers, Suffolk St, D2, t (01) 677 4215, *www.avoca.ie* (*moderate*). An excellent café where organic produce is used whenever possible, producing tempting baked desserts. *Closed Sun and eves.*

Bad Ass Café, 9–11 Crown Alley, Temple Bar, D2, t (01) 671 2596, *www.badasscafe.com* (*moderate*). A diner-style place serving pizza, chops and burgers, famous because Sinéad O'Connor used to waitress here. It's a good place to bring kids.

Bewley's Café Bar Deli, 78–79 Grafton St, D2, t (01) 672 7720, *www.bewleyscafe.com* (*moderate*). A Dublin institution complete with Harry Clarke stained-glass windows. Dubliners have come here for breakfast, coffee and full meals for generations. Try the delicious barmbrack or almond buns, and catch some lunchtime theatre.

The Boulevard Café, 27 Exchequer St, D2, t (01) 679 2131 (*moderate*). A handy spot for shopping lunches. *Closed Sun.*

Caife Úna, 46 Kildare St, D2, t (01) 670 6087, *www.caifeuna.com* (*moderate*). A pleasant Italian café in the basement of a Georgian townhouse, with tasty vegetarian options and great soda bread. *Closed dinner exc Mar–Sept, and Sun–Fri Oct and Nov.*

The Chameleon, 1 Lower Fownes St, D2, t (01) 671 0362. A popular Indonesian.

Citron, Fitzwilliam Hotel, St Stephen's Green, D2, t (01) 478 7000, *www.fitzwilliamhotel.com* (*moderate*). A bright-yellow café where you can enjoy affordable Mediterranean food and speedy service.

Elephant and Castle, 18 Temple Bar, D2, t (01) 679 3121 (*moderate*). Burgers, omelettes and great bumper sandwiches. Always busy, this is a good place for brunch on Sundays.

Fitzer's, 42 Temple Bar Sq, Temple Bar, D2, t (01) 679 0440, *www.fitzers.ie* (*moderate*). A relaxed setting for eclectic global fare. There's another branch at 51 Dawson St.

Good World Chinese Restaurant, 18 South Great Georges St, D2, t (01) 677 5373 (*moderate*). A great spot for dim sum on a Sunday.

Gotham Café, 8 South Anne St, D2, t (01) 679 5266 (*moderate*). Pizza, pasta and more, including Sunday brunches.

Il Baccaro, Meeting House Sq, Temple Bar, D2, t (01) 671 4597 (*moderate*). Italian cuisine in a pleasant setting.

Imperial, 13 Wicklow St, D2, t (01) 677 2580 (*moderate*). A smart Chinese with good-value set lunches and dim sum.

Les Frères Jacques, 74 Dame St, D2, t (01) 679 4555, *www.lesfreresjacques.com* (*moderate*). An atmospheric and romantic French restaurant, with friendly staff. The lobster ravioli are recommended.

Mona Lisa, 16A D'Olier St, D2, t (01) 677 0499 (*moderate*). A reliable Italian.

Nico's Restaurant, 53 Dame St, D2, t (01) 677 3062 (*moderate*). A bustling, friendly Italian with a theatrical atmosphere. Book ahead.

Saagar, 16 Harcourt St, D2, t (01) 475 5060/5012 (*moderate*). One of the best Indian restaurants in Ireland, with innovative dishes alongside old favourites. *Closed lunch.*

Tante Zoe's, 1 Crowe St, D2, t (01) 679 4407, *www.tantezoes.com* (*moderate*). Cajun-Creole cuisine in Temple Bar. *Closed lunch.*

Yamamori, 71–75 South Great George's St, D2, t (01) 475 5001 (*moderate*). A good Japanese noodle house with bargain lunch specials.

Captain America's Cookhouse and Bar, 1st floor, Grafton Court, Grafton St, D2, t (01) 671 5266, *www.captainamericas.com* (*inexpensive–moderate*). Burgers, steaks, salads and shakes, all set to loud music.

Aya, Clarendon St, D2, t (01) 677 1544, *www.aya.ie* (*inexpensive*). Japanese sushi and bento.

Blazing Salads, 42 Drury St, D2, t (01) 671 9552, *www.blazingsalads.com* (*inexpensive*). Imaginative vegetarian cooking, including excellent soups, salads and home-made desserts. Yeast-/gluten-/sugar-free diets can be catered for, and there is organic wine, fresh-pressed vegetable juices and a deli for takeouts.

Cornucopia, 19 Wicklow St, D2, t (01) 677 7583 (*inexpensive*). A vegetarian restaurant serving wholesome bakes and soups, and catering for restricted diets.

Fitzers, National Gallery of Art, Merrion Sq, D2, t (01) 663 3500 (*inexpensive*). Tempting salads and pasta dishes. This is a great place to relax after exploring the gallery.

Govinda's, 4 Aungier St, D2, t (01) 475 0309 (*inexpensive*). A good vegetarian restaurant serving Indian and wholefood bakes, soups and mild curries.

Irish Film Institute, 6 Eustace St, D2, t (01) 679 3477 (*inexpensive*). A continental-style café with a self-service lunch bar offering salads and fresh breads.

National Museum Café, Kildare St, D2, t (01) 602 1269 (*inexpensive*). Simple and tasty coddle, salads and cakes.

The Old Stand, 37 Exchequer St, D2, t (01) 677 7220/677 5849 (*inexpensive*). Bar food, including famous steaks.

Pasta Fresca, 22 Chatham St, D2, t (01) 679 2402 (*inexpensive*). A crowded fresh pasta shop that serves its own produce at a handful of tables. The simple dishes come with a good choice of sauces.

The Queen of Tarts, Dame St and City Hall, D2, t (01) 670 7499 (*inexpensive*). Excellent patisserie/coffee shop.

Salamanca, 1 St Andrew's St, D2, t (01) 677 4799 (*inexpensive*). A good tapas restaurant.

The Stag's Head, Dame Court, D2, t (01) 679 3701 (*inexpensive*). The place to come for the likes of boiled bacon and cabbage, or Irish stew, plus live traditional music Wed–Sat from 9pm.

City Centre: North of the Liffey

Chapter One, Writers Museum, 18–19 Parnell Sq, D1, t (01) 873 2266 , *www.chapteronerestaurant.com* (*expensive*). A smart and atmospheric basement restaurant with French and modern Irish fare and efficient staff.

101 Talbot, 101 Talbot St, D1, t (01) 874 5011, *www.101talbot.com* (*moderate*). A cheerful setting for Mediterranean and Eastern-inspired cooking, with good options for vegetarians. It's popular with theatre-goers.

The Winding Stair, 40 Lower Ormond Quay, D1, t (01) 873 3292 (*inexpensive*). A charming café-cum-bookshop with a lovely view over the Liffey, serving soup and sandwiches.

Dublin City South

Locks Restaurant, 1 Windsor Terrace, Portobello, D8, t (01) 454 3391 (*expensive*). A cosy place overlooking the Grand Canal, with an assured, friendly feel. Some of the dishes are adventurous, and there is extensive use of organic produce from Co. Wicklow.

The Orchid Szechuan Restaurant, 120 Pembroke Rd, Ballsbridge, D4, t (01) 660 0629 (*expensive*). Excellent Chinese food popular with locals.

The Canteen Restaurant, The Schoolhouse Hotel, 2–8 Northumberland Rd, D4, t (01) 667 5014, *www.schoolhousehotel.com* (*moderate–expensive*). Good bistro food served in an impressive beamed hall.

Kitty O'Shea's Pub and Restaurant, 23–25 Grand Canal St, D4, t (01) 668 7172, *www.kittyosheas.com* (*moderate*). The original themed Irish pub that spread to Europe and then the States, good for Sunday brunch and Irish fare.

The Old Dublin Restaurant, 90–91 Francis St, D8, t (01) 454 2028 (*moderate*). A very appealing Oriental and Eastern European (mainly Scandinavian and Russian) biased menu, including lovely *kasha* barley, savoury rice and vegetarian *satsiv* (crispy curried fresh vegetables).

Roly's Bistro, 7 Ballsbridge Terrace, Ballsbridge, D4, t (01) 668 2611, *www.rolysbistro.ie* (*moderate*). A fun and fashionable café with a lovely interior and food to match. Advance booking is essential.

Ryan's, 28 Parkgate St, D8, t (01) 677 6097 (*moderate*). A cosy Victorian pub with a first-floor restaurant serving excellent Mediterranean-style cuisine.

Burdocks, 2 Werburgh St, D6, t (01) 454 0306 (*inexpensive*). Excellent take-away fish and chips to enjoy in the park around the corner.

Soup Dragon, 168 Capel St, D1, t (01) 872 3277 (*inexpensive*). A soup kitchen with an ever-changing menu – let the Thai chicken or haddock chowder tickle your tastebuds.

Entertainment and Nightlife

Bars and Pubs

Dublin's pubs and bars are famous for their warm, convivial atmosphere, their snugs, mirrors, food and whiskey – and, of course, their Guinness. If you haven't experienced them, you haven't experienced the true Dublin. The following are recommended.

The Bailey, Duke St, D2, t (01) 670 4939. A literary stop-off.

The Barley Mow Pub, Francis St, D8. A place where you can have a drink while a waiter The Old Dublin Restaurant (*see* above) next door takes your order.

Clarence Hotel Bar, Essex St, D2, t (01) 407 0813. A hit with with theatre and film people, with friendly staff.

Davy Byrnes, 21 Duke St, D2, t (01) 677 5217. A busy spot with tourists on the literary trail, offering good sandwiches.

Dawson Lounge, 25 Dawson St, D2, t (01) 677 5909. A quirky basement bar.

Doheny and Nesbitt's, 5 Lower Baggot St, D2, t (01) 676 2945. A place with Victorian décor, frequented by lawyers and politicians.

The Globe, 11 South Great George's St, D2, t (01) 671 1220/670 5765. A café popular with the young and beautiful crowd, serving good sandwiches and cappuccinos at lunchtime.

Grogan's, 15 South William St, D2, t (01) 677 9320. A magnet for aspiring writers, artists etc.

The International Bar, 23 Wicklow St, D2, t (01) 677 9250. A good spot to spend the afternoon. There's music in the evenings.

Kehoe's Pub, 9 South Anne St, D2, t (01) 677 8312. An offbeat, authentic place with a good snug.

Long Hall, 51 South Great George's St, D2, t (01) 475 1590. Knick-knacks, lovely mirrors and charming barmen.

McDaids, 3 Harry St, D2, t (01) 679 4395. A long-standing literary haunt hosting jazz some nights.

Mulligans, Poolbeg St, D2, t (01) 677 5582. A bar with a reputation for its Guinness, popular with journalists.

Neary's, 1 Chatham St, off Grafton St, D2, t (01) 677 7371. A theatrical spot serving up good sandwiches.

Palace Bar, 21 Fleet St, D2, t (01) 677 9290. A 1950s writers' haunt.

Ryan's Bar, 28 Parkgate St, D7, t (01) 677 6097. Well-preserved Victoriana, cosy snugs and very good pub food, especially at lunchtime.

Stag's Head, 1 Dame Court, D2, t (01) 679 3701. A cosy venue with friendly staff, good for sausages, chips and Guinness at tea-time.

The Shelbourne Hotel, Horseshoe Bar, 27 St Stephen's Green, D2, t (01) 663 4500. An elegant spot that's popular with lawyers, politicans and journalists, reopening in Sept 2006 (*see* p.546).

Toner's, 139 Lower Baggot St, D2, t (01) 676 3090. A place with Victorian fittings, serving good toasted cheese sandwiches and more to a mixed crowd.

Bars with Music

Folk, Jazz and Rock

Baggot Inn, 143 Baggot St, D2, t (01) 676 1430. Music 7 nights a week.

Bob's, 35–37 East Essex St, D2, t (01) 677 0945. Country.

International Bar, 23 Wicklow St, D2, t (01) 677 9250. Two floors hosting a variety of different musical forms.

J. J. Smyth's, 12 Aungier St, D2, t (01) 475 2565. Mostly jazz.

McDaids, 3 Harry St, D2, **t** (01) 679 4395.
First-floor blues.

O'Dwyers, 7 Lower Mount St, D2, **t** (01) 634 5460

Whelans, 25 Wexford St, D2, **t** (01) 478 0766.
Music almost every night: indie, rock,
bluegrass, country and some styles you
never dreamed existed. Legends such as
Leo O'Kelly play here.

Traditional Music

Traditional music sessions are free unless
a big name is playing; check in the local paper
or with the bar.

To learn more about traditional Irish music,
visit *Ceol*, the Irish Traditional Music Centre,
at Smithfield Village, Smithfield, D7, **t** (01) 817
3820, *www.ceol.ie*.

Brazen Head, 20 Lower Bridge St, D8,
t (01) 679 5186. The oldest bar in Dublin.

Harcourt Hotel, 60 Harcourt St, D2, **t** (01) 478
3677, or **t** 1850 664455. Sessions every night
with musicians from all over Ireland.

Hughes, 19 Chancery St, D7, **t** (01) 872 6540.
One of the best venues.

Kitty O'Shea's, 23 Upper Grand Canal St, D4,
t (01) 660 9965. A famous Irish bar.

Mother Redcaps, Back Lane, beside Tailors'
Guildhall, Christchurch, D4, **t** (01) 453 8306.
Traditional and folk music.

O'Donoghues, 15 Merrion Row, D2,
t (01) 676 2807

The Oliver St John Gogarty, Temple Bar, D2,
t (01) 671 1822, *www.gogartys.ie*

O'Shea's Merchants Bar, 12 Lower Bridge St, D8,
t (01) 679 3797. Traditional Irish and ballad
music and song, plus set-dancing.

Rumm's, Shelbourne Rd, D4, **t** (01) 667 6422.
Pub food and nightly music.

Slattery's, 179 Capel St, D1, **t** (01) 874 6844.
A very popular venue.

The Temple Bar, 47 Temple Bar, D2, **t** 672 5286,
www.templebarpubdublin.com

Cabaret and Comedy

The cabaret scene here is often a straggling
descendant of music hall, with old-time Irish
songs and jokes.

Ha'penny Bridge Inn, 42 Wellington Quay, D2,
t (01) 677 0616. Comedy some weeknights,
plus live music.

International Bar, 23 Wicklow St, D2, **t** (01) 677
9250. Mad Cow Comedy Club, Wed nights.

Jury's Hotel, Ballsbridge, D4, **t** (01) 660 5000.
A slightly touristy venue in summer.

The Laughter Lounge, 4 Eden Quay, D1, **t** (01)
878 3003, *www.laughterlounge.com*. Comedy.

Vicar Street, 58–59 Thomas St, D8,
t (01) 871 9390, *www.vicarstreet.com*.
A major venue for stand-up and music.

Cinema

Film is very popular in Dublin (the Irish go to
the cinema more than any other Europeans).
All cinemas are listed in the papers.

Cineworld, Parnell St, D1, **t** (01) 872 8444,
www.ugc.ie. First-runs.

Irish Film Institute, 6 Eustace St, Temple Bar, D2,
t (01) 679 3477, *www.irishfilm.ie*. Foreign and
art-house releases. The Dublin Film Festival
(*see* p.541) is organized from here, and it has
a good café (*see* p.549)

Savoy Cinema, Upper O'Connell St, D1,
t (01) 874 6000. First-runs.

Screen Cinema, D'Olier St, D2, **t** (01) 672 5500.
Independent films.

Classical Music and Shows

Big stars of whatever sort often appear at
the RDS Concert Hall in suburban Ballsbridge,
though some big rock acts use the Point
Theatre at East Link Bridge, or the Lansdowne
Road Stadium. Details of all are listed in *In
Dublin* (*see* p.542) or the newspapers.

Bank of Ireland Arts Centre, College Green, D2,
t (01) 671 2261, *www.boi.ie*. Classical music.

Gaiety Theatre, South King St, D2,
t (01) 677 1717, *www.gaietytheatre.com*,
www.opera-ireland.ie. Opera.

Hugh Lane Gallery, Charlemont House, Parnell
Sq North, D1, **t** (01) 222 5550, *www.hughlane.ie*.
Performances of classical music, including
lunchtime concerts, in a venue that has just
undergone major expansion (*see* p.565).

National Concert Hall, Earlsfort Terrace, D2,
t (01) 417 0000, *www.nch.ie*. The home of the
National Symphony Orchestra, also hosting
other concerts most of the year – classical,
jazz, pop and touring shows from abroad.

Nightclubs

Dublin at night can be fun, with most clubs
staying open until 2–3.30am. They are by their
nature fairly transient, so check *In Dublin*
before seeking out one of the following:

Club M, Anglesea St, D2, **t** (01) 671 5408. A lively choice in the heart of Temple Bar.

The Dublin Pod (Place of Dance), Harcourt St, D2, **t** (01) 478 0225. Dance music for posers, inside a train station.

Fitzsimons, East Essex St/Eustace St, Temple Bar, D2, **t** (01) 677 9315. A popular 3-storey club.

Gaiety Theatre, South King St, D2, **t** (01) 679 5622, *www.gaietytheatre.com*. A relaxed venue with several levels playing jazz, blues and salsa, dance and 60s/70s retro. There are also reggae nights.

The Kitchen, East Essex St, D2, **t** (01) 677 6635, *www.the-kitchen.com*. A hot, hip and friendly club owned by U2, with an open-house music policy – which means you get anything.

Lillie's Bordello, Adam Court, off Grafton St, D2, **t** (01) 679 9204. The longest-established of Dublin's currently fashionable clubs, frequented by models, visiting rock stars and other beautiful people of all ages. Be prepared to queue.

Olympia, 72 Dame St, D2 **t** (01) 679 3323. A delightful former music hall hosting a wide range of music.

The Red Box, Harcourt St, D2, **t** (01) 478 0166. A club with a huge dancefloor, hosting house, techno and disco nights.

Rí Rá, Dame Court, D2, **t** (01) 677 4835. A funky, unpretentious late-night drinking spot, with 2 floors of music and a quieter bar upstairs.

The Village, 26 Wexford St, D2, **t** (01) 475 8555. Live gigs and club nights. Indie, dance, rock and punk.

The Viper Room, 5 Aston Quay, Temple Bar, D2, **t** (01) 672 5566. A theatre bar and club.

Theatre

It is worth spending money on the theatre in Dublin. Things really take off during the **festival** in Oct (*see* p.541), with new plays by Irish authors, some of which may go on to become Broadway hits.

The most convenient place to **book tickets** is the stall in Brown Thomas's in Grafton St. You can also get them at the tourist offices on Suffolk St and O'Connell St, or from the theatres themselves. Student and pensioners can get a discount on tickets in some theatres.

Evening performances usually begin around 8pm, and the majority of theatres do not have shows on Sundays.

Abbey Theatre, Lower Abbey St, D1, **t** (01) 878 7222. The famous theatre founded by the indomitable Lady Gregory and W. B. Yeats. The old building burned down; the new one also houses the **Peacock Theatre**, which concentrates on contemporary playwrights, whereas the Abbey sticks predominantly to Irish classics. It has made the Irish turn of phrase famous throughout the world with plays such as *Playboy of the Western World* by J. M. Synge and *Juno and the Paycock* by Sean O'Casey. The new building is functional and modern, with an array of portraits of Dublin literati. It can be hard getting tickets, so book ahead.

Andrew's Lane Theatre, 12 St Andrews Lane, D2, **t** (01) 679 5720, *www.andrewslane.com*. A variety of dramatic fare, including adventurous, modern pieces in the **Studio**.

City Arts Centre, 23 Moss St, D2, **t** (01) 677 0643. Exciting productions.

Focus Theatre, 6 Pembroke Place, off Pembroke St, D2, **t** (01) 676 3071. Fringe theatre.

Gaiety Theatre, South King St, D2, **t** (01) 677 5622, *www.gaietytheatre.com*. A splendid, tiered Victorian theatre showing traditional plays, and providing a venue for opera (*see* p.541 and p.551), musicals and pantomime.

Gate Theatre, 8 Parnell Sq, D1, **t** (01) 874 4045, *www.gate-theatre.ie*. International and classic dramas. Famous names such as Orson Welles and James Mason began their acting careers here, and current productions often go on to New York.

The Helix, Dublin City University, Glasnevin, D9, **t** (01) 700 7000, *www.thehelix.ie*. A popular suburban venue.

Olympia Theatre, 72 Dame St, D2, **t** (01) 679 3323. A venue for drama, ballet, musicals and late-night concerts.

Project Arts Theatre, 39 East Essex St, Temple Bar, D2, **t** (01) 679 6622, booking **t** 1800 260 027, *www.project.ie*. Some of the most experimental and stimulating theatre in Dublin, with art exhibitions alongside.

Samuel Beckett Centre, Trinity College, D2, **t** (01) 608 1334, *www.tcd.ie/drama*. Exciting lunchtime theatre.

SFX City Theatre, 23 Upper Sherrard St, D1, **t** (01) 855 4090. Fringe productions.

Tivoli Theatre, Francis St, D8, **t** (01) 454 4472. Musicals and plays, usually excellent.

From then on, Dublin played a dominant role as the centre of English power. The Anglo-Normans fortified themselves with strong castles, and the area surrounding Dublin where they settled was known as The Pale. Anything outside was dangerous and barbaric – hence the expression, 'beyond the Pale'. For a short and glorious period in the late 18th century, Ireland had its own parliament here, 'Grattan's Parliament' (1782–1800); the élite who sat within it had many liberal ideas, such as the introduction of Catholic emancipation. One could speculate that the course of Ireland's history might have been happier if this independent parliament had been allowed to develop. A great surge of urban building took place during this time. Grattan was typical of the liberal landowners who wanted legislative reform, and is remembered for his powers of oratory. Unfortunately the influence of the French Revolution, and the growth of the United Irishmen, frightened the British Government. The 1798 Rising was a realization of their worst fears, and the British Parliament resumed direct control of Irish affairs in 1800. This meant that the resident and educated ruling class left Dublin, and took with them much of its dynamism and culture.

The struggle for independence from English rule manifested itself in violent episodes and street clashes in the 19th century, with violence becoming more common in the early 20th century. During the 1916 Rising, buildings and lives were shattered by Nationalists fighting with British troops, which erupted again during the Civil War that followed the peace with England. Many of those buildings, such as the Customs House, the masterpiece of James Gandon (1743–1823), have been restored to their former grandeur.

It was under the rule of the so-called Anglo-Irish Ascendency that Dublin acquired its gracious streets and squares, which amaze one with their variety. Many of the houses were built in small groups by speculators when Dublin was the fashionable place to be – hence the variety. Each door is slightly different, and the patterns of the wrought-iron balconies and railings change from house to house. You will not see ironwork like this in London, as most railings there were ripped up and melted down during the Second World War.

The size of Dublin increased very slowly during the 19th and early 20th centuries, due in part to the lack of countrywide industrialization, the famine and emigration. The population started to grow in the 1950s with a shift from rural to urban areas; today Dubliners suffer from a lack of housing, inadequate sewage treatment, increasing crime, and a huge traffic problem caused by urban sprawl and the neglect of public transport, which is now being addressed. The population of young people in Ireland, and in Dublin particularly, is high. Greater Dublin has a population of more than 1 million, and plenty of families are living on the dole; some of the suburban housing estates are among the poorest and most troubled in Europe.

Still, since the 1990s booming Dublin has become the power behind the 'Celtic Tiger' economy. It is a city full of new money and hi-tech industries, one growing outwards in all directions. Tourists pour in, drawn by the city's traditional charms and even more by the continuing worldwide popularity of all things Irish. Changes to the city itself are noticeable. New museums and attractions have appeared, and there is intensive redevelopment in the city's docklands and ongoing regeneration of the area around O'Connell Street. Dubliners are showing signs of finally reforming their notorious neglect of the inner city and its historic architecture; a symbol of this is Temple Bar, the riverfront area transformed by private initiative into a thriving and attractive entertainment district after the government tried – unsuccessfully – to demolish it. Dublin isn't a city given to grand gestures or showy mega-projects. Its people are cautious and mindful of traditions; they like things to stay as they are.

Throughout the centuries Dublin has produced great writers: Jonathan Swift (who suggested in his satirical yet frighteningly plausible essay *A Modest Proposal* that the ruling class in Ireland should eat all newborn babies to cure the problems of poverty and overpopulation), Bishop Berkeley, Edmund Burke, Thomas Moore, Sheridan, Le Fanu, Wilde and Goldsmith, to name but a few. Towards the end of the 19th century, Dublin became the centre of the Cultural Movement, which resulted in the formation of the Gaelic League, which became entangled with the Nationalists' aspirations of the time. How much influence this movement had on the next flurry of great writers it is hard to say, but George Bernard Shaw, George Moore, James Stephens, Yeats, James Joyce and later Samuel Beckett drew much of their inspiration from the streets of Dublin. This is an extract from *No Mean City* by Oliver St John Gogarty (1878–1957), a writer, wit and surgeon who details Dublin's famous men:

> Dublin, Dublin of the vistas. What names come to mind, names filling more than two centuries from the days of the gloomy Dean Swift, who left his money to found a lunatic asylum 'to show by one sarcastic touch no nation needed it so much', to Mrs Bernard Shaw, who left her money to teach manners to Irishmen; and some say (they would in Dublin) that, in spite of all his acumen, the man for whom it was principally intended failed to see the sarcastic touch; Oliver Goldsmith; Bishop Berkeley, who wrote 'Westward the course of Empire takes it way' and went his way to Rhode Island and gave his name to Berkeley, California; Hamilton, who discovered proleptically the Quaternion Theory by the banks of the Royal Canal; Burke, who thundered in defence of American liberation; Molyneaux, whose nationalism caused his books to be burned by the common hangman; Fitzgerald, who anticipated Marconi in the discovery of aetherial waves; Mahaffy, who was the greatest Humanist of his time as well as the expeller from Trinity College of Oscar Wilde to Oxford; down to Yeats, A. E., and lastly James Joyce, in whose Anna Livia Plurabelle the whole history of Dublin may be discerned by thought, this time cataleptic. All these men lived in Dublin, but most of them died elsewhere. Dublin, that stick of a rocket which remains on the ground while its stars shoot off to light the darkness and die enskied.

Trinity College

The **O'Connell Bridge**, the most important of the bridges that cross the River Liffey, is a good spot at which to get your bearings and to begin a tour of Dublin. On the riverbank the monuments of the city line up – the Four Courts on one side, the Custom House on the other. Across the river you'll find the famous O'Connell Street, while on the southern side, narrow, busy Westmoreland Street invites you into the heart of the city.

The former Parliament House stands where Westmoreland Street meets College Green, and is nowadays the **Bank of Ireland** (*open Mon–Wed and Fri 10–4, Thur 10–5; free guided tours of House of Lords Tue 10.30, 11.30 and 1.45 exc bank hols; adm; t (01) 677 6801*). The brainchild of Lovat Pearce, who designed it in 1729, it was finished in 1785 by James Gandon, Dublin's most notable architect. It was between these walls that Grattan stunned everybody with his oratory when he demanded constitutional independence from the English Parliament. Later, in 1800, a well-bribed House voted for the Union, and Parliament House became redundant. It is an imposing classical building with Ionic porticos. Inside you may see the coffered ceiling of the old House of Lords; a Waterford chandelier dating from 1765; and two fine 18th-century tapestries depicting famous Protestant victories, the Battle of the Boyne and the Siege of Derry, as well as the parliament's Golden Mace. The bankers celebrate their trade in the adjacent Bank of Ireland Arts Centre, Foster Place, with the **Story of Banking Museum** (*open Tue–Fri 10–4; t (01) 671 2261*).

Just opposite Parliament House is the entrance to **Trinity College**, through Regent House; in term-time students cluster around it, joking, chatting or handing out political leaflets. As you enter through the imposing 1759 façade, you leave bustling Dublin far behind and come upon a giant square with green lawn and cobbled stone, surrounded by gracious buildings. Stop to look at the **Museum Building** (which has only a small geological collection) for the stone carving by the O'Shea brothers; they also created the amusing monkeys that play round what used to be the Kildare Street Club, the brick palazzo on the north-east corner of Kildare Street.

The other buildings in the quadrangle are 18th-century and are described below, but first pass through the peaceful grounds into the second quadrangle, as your main objective will probably be to visit **Trinity College Library** to take a look at the priceless *Book of Kells* (*open June–Sept Mon–Sat 9.30–5, Sun 9.30–4.30, Oct–May Mon–Sat 9.30–5, Sun 12 noon–4.30; adm; t (01) 608 2320*). The library, on the right of the second quadrangle, dates from 1712. It has been a copyright library since 1801 and contains a vast number of manuscripts, including the diaries of Wolfe Tone and the manuscripts of John Millington Synge. The library is a fine building and contains the Long Room, which has a barrel-vaulted ceiling and gallery bookcases. The area underneath the Long Room, the Colonnades, has been remodelled, and the *Book of Kells* is permanently displayed there. Every day one of the thick vellum pages of the book is turned to present more fantastic and intricate designs. Someone once said the book was made up of imaginative doodles. The man who copied out the gospels and enlivened them with such 'doodles' was able to draw so perfectly that sections as small as a postage stamp reveal no flaws when magnified. The book is probably 8th-century and comes from an abbey in Kells, County Meath. Have a look too at the *Book of Durrow*, the *Book of Armagh* and the *Book of Dimma*, which are also beautifully illuminated.

Next door is the **Berkeley Library**, which contains more than 2 million books. It was built in 1967 to designs by Paul Koralek, who also did the skilfully designed **Arts Building**, erected in 1978. An audio-visual show, '**The Dublin Experience**' (*open late May–early Oct daily 10–5; adm; t (01) 608 2320*), is held in the Arts building. It tells the story of the city from its Viking beginnings to the present day.

Trinity College was founded in 1592, in the reign of Elizabeth I. The land on which it was erected had once been occupied by the Augustinian monastery of All Hallows, founded by Dermot MacMurragh in the 12th century. The squares are made up of a mixture of buildings, ranging from early-18th-century to the present-day. The red-brick **Rubrics**, beyond the campanile in the middle of the quad, is the oldest bit still standing, dating from *c.* 1700. Oliver Goldsmith had his chambers here, as do present-day students and professors. Trinity College has a long and venerable history; so many famous scholars, wits and well-known men of Ireland were educated here. It was freed from its Protestant-only restrictions in 1873, and Catholics were allowed to study here, but Paul Cullen, the Catholic archbishop of the day, threatened any that did with excommunication. The university remained the preserve of the Protestant gentry for some time (although that is far from the case now) but distinguished itself by admitting women students as early as 1903, as well as non-Christians. The **Provost's House** (on the left of the main entrance) is a fine 18th-century mansion. One of its most famous occupants was John Mahaffy (1839–1919) a great scholar and clergyman, as was essential for the fellowship of the college. He was also, in the last year of his life, a knight. His witty dinner talk was legendary, but he could also be very wounding. Apparently he impressed on Oscar Wilde the importance of good social contacts and brilliant conversation, and declared that James Joyce's *Ulysses* was 'the inevitable result of extending university to the wrong sort of people'.

On the right as you enter the first cobbled quadrangle is the **Theatre**, or Examination Hall, which was built between 1779 and 1791 with an Adam-style ceiling, and a gilt oak chandelier. On the left is the **Chapel**, built in 1798. Both buildings were designed by William Chambers, the Scottish architect who never actually set foot in Dublin. (*The Theatre and Chapel can be seen on request; ask at Porter's Lodge.*) Beyond the Chapel is the **Dining Hall**, designed by Richard Cassels in 1743. It was nearly destroyed by fire in 1984 and has now been restored. The quick responses of the staff and students ensured the survival of the portraits and other works of art that now grace its walls again: they formed a human chain to get them safely out. Quite often there is music of some sort in the Junior Common Room, and the **Douglas Hyde Gallery**, in the Arts Building, often mounts retrospective exhibitions of major Irish artists.

As it passes Trinity College, Westmoreland Street becomes **Grafton Street**, an attractive pedestrian way that is the choice shopping street of Dublin. On its way it passes the ornate **Bewley's**, a Dublin institution since 1840 (*see* p.548). On Suffolk Street west of Grafton, the **Dublin Tourism Centre** is a formidably busy tourist office with the air of an airport terminal, housed in an imaginative restoration of the long-abandoned Protestant St Andrew's Church (1860).

Powerscourt Townhouse in South William Street, built in 1771, was typical of Georgian townhouses of the Ascendency. It has fine Rococo and Adamesque plasterwork that has survived in the conversion of the house and surroundings into the **Powerscourt shopping centre** (*see* also p.545). This triumph of enlightened development is a pleasure to visit; it houses a large crafts co-operative and has a variety of restaurants including a very good vegetarian one, Fresh, right at the top. Here are Ireland's finest boutiques (including the Design Centre; *see* p.544) and speciality shops, enclosed under a great glass-roofed courtyard. Next to the Centre at 58 South William Street is the **Dublin Civic Museum** (*open Tue–Sat 10–6, Sun 11–2*; *t (01) 679 4260*), a collection of old newspapers, cuttings, prints, pictures and coins that build up a very clear picture of old Dublin. You can also see some Viking artefacts that were found in the recent excavations. Admiral Nelson's head – from the column the IRA blew up in O'Connell Street (*see* p.564) – has been relocated from the museum to Dublin City Library in Pearse Street.

St Stephen's Green

St Stephen's Green (*open 8am–dusk*), at the top of Grafton Street, is one of the loveliest and certainly one of the best-loved city parks you will ever see. In the middle is a romantic landscaped park with a lake and waterfall, ducks and weeping willows. Every age and type of Dubliner uses it to wander in, and enjoy the trees and flowers. Its cool, green gardens make a perfect setting for a picnic. At the western edge of the green is Henry Moore's graceful monument to W. B. Yeats. Another monument is to Lord Ardilaun – Sir Arthur Guinness, the fellow whose signature is on the bottle. He not only paid for the improvements but put through a bill in Parliament to purchase the park and open it to the public in the 1880s. Originally the area had been common land; in the 1660s the English fenced it in and converted it into a private residential square. The surviving Anglo-Norman aristocracy, Cromwellian adventurers and the new gentry (mainly composed of those who had profited from the seizure of forfeited lands) then built their grand houses around the square and adjoining streets.

Today, one of Dublin's biggest regrets is its many decades of utter carelessness in looking after its architectural heritage. This is certainly true in the streets around Stephen's Green. Two of the original houses that survive belong to University College Dublin, an institution founded by the Catholics in the 1860s as a counter to the Protestant Trinity College. **Newman House**, (*open June–Aug Tue–Fri 12–5, Sat 2–5, Sun 11–2; adm; t (01) 706 7422*) at 85 St Stephen's Green is named after Cardinal John Henry Newman, the great theologian of the 19th-century Catholic revival, who founded the University. These two buildings contain some of the finest late Baroque and Rococo plasterwork in Ireland; poet Gerard Manley Hopkins, who was a professor of Classics at the university, died here after many years' residence. No.85 was built in 1738, designed by Richard Cassels, and it contains the ravishing Apollo room, a masterpiece of stucco decoration by the Francini brothers. No.86 was built in 1765 for the MP Richard Chapell Whaley, father of the notorious Buck Whaley, whose memoirs of 18th-century Dublin are still a good read. The house has very good plasterwork by Robert West; the hall is decorated with motifs of musical instruments.

If you are passing the famous Shelbourne Hotel on St Stephen's Green (*see* p.546), you may notice a shuttered garden just left of it. The **Huguenot Graveyard** is a secret place – even Dubliners hardly know it is there. You can peer through the gates and see the mellow gravestones that mark the names of French Huguenots who successfully merged into the Irish way of life after a couple of generations. Ten thousand Huguenots arrived in Ireland to escape persecution for their religous beliefs, between the 1650s and 1700s. They had a great civilizing influence on early-18th-century Dublin, which was then very small and only just beginning to develop its own cultural activities after the turbulence of the 17th century. The Huguenots expanded the wine trade, started silk and poplin industries, and introduced a Horticultural Society, where they used to toast their favourite flowers.

Around Merrion Square

The beautiful Georgian **Merrion Square**, just east of St Stephen's Green, is one of the best-preserved in Dublin, and was the home of many famous literary people and politicians. Sir William and Lady 'Speranza' Wilde (Oscar's parents) lived at no.1; Daniel O'Connell at no.58; W. B. Yeats at nos.52 and 82; George Russell, known as A. E., at no.84; and Sheridan Le Fanu at no.70. With the Irish Parliament just next door, most of the square's homes have been converted into offices of the government, or interests that like to be close to it. **Leinster House**, on the western edge of the square, was finished in 1745, built to the design of Richard Cassels, who was responsible for so many lovely houses in Ireland – Russborough House in Wicklow, for instance (*see* p.577). Leinster House has two different faces, one looking out over Kildare Street and the other onto the pleasant garden of Merrion Square. It was the townhouse of the Dukes of Leinster and was originally known as Kildare House. Leinster House is now the seat of the Irish Parliament, which consists of the *Dáil* ('Lower House', pronounced 'doyle') and the *Seanad* ('Upper House', or 'Senate').

Just opposite the fountain stands **The National Gallery** (*open Mon–Wed, Fri and Sat 9.30–5.30, Thurs 9.30–8.30, Sun 12 noon–5.30; tours Sat 3pm and Sun 2, 3 and 4pm; t (01) 661 5133, www.nationalgallery.ie*). A statue of George Bernard Shaw greets you in the forecourt. He bequeathed one third of his estate to the gallery because he learnt so much from the pictures. Certainly this is one of the most enjoyable, first-class small galleries in the world. The Millennium Wing, designed by Benson and Forsythe, opened in 2002; its façade opens onto Nassau Street. There are more than 2,000 works on view here, including a small collection of superb work by Renaissance painters; Spanish, French and Italian 16th- and 17th-century painters; and Dutch Masters. The Irish Room includes some elegant portraits by Lavery, Orpen and many others, work by J. B. Yeats (father of W. B. Yeats) and well-regarded wild and colourful oils by Jack Yeats (brother of W. B. Yeats). Gainsborough is well represented with 10 major works. Upstairs in the Arts Reference Library is a good collection of Irish watercolours. The gallery restaurant in the Millennium Wing is a good place for lunch or early supper, and the shop selling postcards and art books is also excellent.

At 73 Merrion Square (south side), **The Irish Architectural Archive**, a wonderful example of a Georgian townhouse, admits the public to its reading room (*Mon–Fri 10–5; t (01) 663 3040, www.iarc.ie*).

The **National Museum of Ireland**, in a grand Victorian edifice, occupies two sites: most of the block south of Leinster House (*entrance on Kildare St; open Tue–Sat 10–5, Sun 2–5; t (01) 677 7444, www.museum.ie*) and Collins Barracks in Benburb Street, D7 (*see* p.567). It is the treasure house of Ireland, and absolutely vital for anyone who has not yet realized that Ireland between AD 600 and 900 was the most civilized part of northern Europe. It has the finest collection of Celtic ornaments and artefacts in the world, and items recently excavated from the Danish settlement in Wood Quay. The Historical Collection traces the history of Ireland from the 18th century to the mid 20th century. In the Antiquities Department you can see the beautiful filigree gold whorl enamelling and design that reached perfection in the Tara brooch and the Ardagh Chalice. The many beautiful torcs, croziers and decorated shrines on display will leave you amazed at the sophistication and skill of the craftsmen in those days. Also very interesting are the findings of the Stone and Early Bronze ages.

Linked to the museum is the **National Library**, which is also situated in Kildare Street. It contains more than half a million books and has a fascinating collection of Irish-interest source material. There is usually an exhibition on in the entrance hall, and the staff are very helpful. The **Genealogical Office** (*open Mon–Fri 10.30–12.30 and 2–4.30; t (01) 603 0200*) is across the street, in a stately building that was once an Anglo-Irish men's club .

The **Natural History Museum** (*open Tue–Sat 10–5, Sun 2–5; t (01) 677 7444*) on Merrion Street has barely changed in decades; it has a charming, musty atmosphere, with thousands of stuffed birds, fish and animals (including a new giraffe, 'Spoticus', replacing one that had been here since 1899), and some fascinating elk skeletons. The **Royal Irish Academy** (*open Tue–Fri 9.30–5; t (01) 676 2570*), at 19 Dawson Street, has one of the largest collections of ancient Irish manuscripts, one of which is on view.

Ely Place, a stone's throw away, between Merrion Row and Baggot Street, is more melancholy. It was once very grand but is now wrapped in a gloom that strip-lighting, glimpsed through the elegant windows, does nothing to dispel. **Ely House** is now owned by the Knights of Columbanus, a charity organization.

Fitzwilliam Square (1791), two streets south of Merrion Square, is the last of Dublin's residential squares, with more well-preserved examples of 18th-century architecture with pretty doors and fanlights above. Number **29 Fitzwilliam Street Lower** (*open Tue–Sat 10–5, Sun 2–5; guided tours; adm; t (01) 702 6165*), just off the square, is furnished in the style of a middle-class family of the period 1790–1820 . The house is owned by the ESB, the partially State-run electricity company, which restored it as a sort of penance after knocking down much of the rest of the neighbourhood for their unsightly office block in the 1960s.

Walk a street or two north-east from Merrion Square and you'll notice that the atmosphere changes rather dramatically. This is Dublin's docklands, a drab patch of abandoned wharves and gasworks. Like its London counterpart, this docklands is facing an inevitable recycling into a business centre; a few modest towers have already appeared, but so far there's little evidence that the transformation will bring any aesthetic improvement. Worth visiting, however, is the **Waterways Visitor Centre**, (*open June–Sept daily 9.30–5.30, Oct–May Wed–Sun 12.30–5.30; adm; t (01) 667 7510, www.waterwaysireland.org*) on the basin where the Grand Canal empties into the Liffey. This tells the story of the construction and architecture of the waterways, and their role in the history of Ireland, and describes their flora and fauna. The **Grand Canal** marks the extent of the Georgian city south of the Liffey, and the towpath that runs alongside it across the southern edge of the city centre takes you past wildfowl and over humpbacked bridges.

Around Dublin Castle

West of Trinity College and Stephen's Green, back towards the quays, you will come to an area lacking in governmental glitter and fancy shops that is nonetheless the true heart of the city, where Dublin began under the Vikings 1,000 years ago. On Dame Street, **Dublin Castle** (*open Mon–Fri 10–5, Sat, Sun and bank hols 2–5; adm; t (01) 645 8813, www.dublincastle.ie*), long the seat of British rule in Ireland, is well worth a visit, not only because of the place it has in Irish history but for the beautifully decorated State Apartments and for the Church of the Holy Trinity, designed by Francis Johnston, in the Lower Castle Yard. The various buildings that make up the castle complex are still reminiscent of a fortified city within its own walls. The original medieval walls and towers, begun under King John in 1204, may be gone, but the squares of faded red-brick houses with their elegant Georgian façades are a unity still. Many of the present buildings date from 1688, after the earlier castle was destroyed by fire, with most of the upper yard being built in the mid 18th century. From the 18th century onwards, a vice-regal court grew up around the Lord Deputy and his administrators, and there were receptions, balls and levees for the gentry and Dublin merchants. It was far removed from the lives of the ordinary people of Ireland. At that time Dublin Castle was the seat of an alien power, and to the young Republican activists of the 19th and early 20th century it was understandably a symbol of tyranny. It was handed over to the provisional government of Ireland in 1922, and is used today for rituals such as the inauguration of the President.

The guided tour starts out in the upper yard with the **State Apartments**. The lavish decoration, the grand chimneypieces and the beautiful antique furniture are a feast for the eyes. There is a Throne Room for visiting British monarchs, and a long Portrait Gallery containing their pictures. Particularly attractive are the blue and white Wedgwood Room and the Bermingham Tower with its Gothic windows. St Patrick's Hall, site of the inaugurations, has paintings of historical scenes; this leads to the newest – and oldest – attraction in Dublin Castle, the **Undercroft**. Foundations of the original Viking fort and parts of Dublin's first city wall were discovered here during recent excavation work.

The **Record Tower** is one of the oldest parts of the castle, although it was substantially rebuilt in 1813. It was from here that, in 1592, Red Hugh O'Donnell, who was one of the last great Gaelic leaders, managed to escape to the Wicklow Hills. The other blocks in the quadrangle have been refurbished inside and out, but sadly the proportions and the original woodwork have been mucked about. **The Church of the Holy Trinity**, which is also called the Chapel Royal, was designed by Francis Johnston in 1807. The outside is decorated with scores of sculpted heads of Irish saints and historical figures, while the interior has elaborate vaulting, exuberant plasterwork and oak carving.

Within the gardens of the castle sits the **Chester Beatty Library** (*open May–Sept Mon–Fri 10–5, Oct–Apr Tue–Fri 10–5, Sat 11–5, Sun 1–5; t (01) 407 0750, www.cbl.ie*). Sir Alfred Chester Beatty (1875–1968) was an American mining millionaire and collector who decided to make Dublin his home. The library and its art museum together contain one of the finest private collections of Oriental manuscripts and miniatures in the world, as well as albums, picture scrolls, and jades hailing from the Far East. The highlights of a visit are the Korans, the Persian and Turkish paintings, the Chinese jade books and the Japanese and European woodblock prints.

Just outside the Castle, facing Dame Street, **City Hall** (*open Mon–Sat 10–5.15, Sun 2–5; adm; t (01) 672 2204, www.dublincity.ie/cityhall*) occupies a building on Cork Hill, constructed in 1769 as the Royal Exchange. It houses a permanent exhibition on the history of Dublin, 'The Story of the Capital'. On the opposite side of the castle, facing Werburgh Street, **St Werburgh's Church** is worth visiting for the massive Geraldine monument and the pulpit, a fine piece of carving, possibly by Grinling Gibbons (*open by appointment Mon–Fri 10–4; donations invited; entrance by north door, 8 Castle St, t (01) 478 3710*). Lord Edward Fitzgerald of the United Irishmen and the leader of the 1798 rebellion is interred in the vault here. This church was for a long time the parish church of Dublin, and, before the Chapel Royal in the Dublin Castle complex was built, British viceroys were sworn in here.

Just across Lord Edward Street is **Christ Church Cathedral** (*open daily 10–5; adm; t (01) 677 8099, www.cccdub.ie*). The church was founded by King Sitric and Bishop Donatus in 1038, rebuilt by Strongbow in the 12th century, and heavily restored during the 19th century after part of the walls collapsed – there isn't much solid ground for building in central Dublin. The magnificent stonework and graceful arches are well worth a look, as is the effigy representing Strongbow, who was buried in the church – or at least, part of him was. The crypt is the oldest surviving portion of the building; it contains the old punishment stocks, the 'cat and mouse'. The arch that joins the cathedral to the Synod Hall frames a view of Winetavern Street and the River Liffey.

The Synod Hall in Christ Church is now home to **Dublinia** (*open Apr–Sept daily 10–5, Oct–Mar Mon–Sat 11–4, Sun 10–4; adm; t (01) 679 4611, www.dublinia.ie*), a multimedia exhibition of medieval Dublin life, with a model of the city as it has changed over the centuries, and life-size tableaux.

St Audoen's Church (*t (01) 677 0088; adm*), in Cornmarket, off High Street (the continuation of Lord Edward Street), is Dublin's only surviving medieval church. The belltower, restored in the 19th century, has three 15th-century bells. Note the beautiful Norman font, and make a wish at the lucky stone. **St Patrick's Cathedral** (*open Mar–Oct daily 9–6, Nov–Feb Sat 9–5, Sun 9–3; adm; t (01) 475 4817, www.stpatrickscathedral.org*), a short distance south in Patrick's Close, marks the site of a holy well associated with the saint. The largest church in Ireland, it was founded in 1190 and is Early English in style. It was built outside the city walls, on what was marshy ground, by a powerful Norman bishop who was also a baron, in order to outshine Christ Church (like Christ Church, it is Church of Ireland). In the 14th century it was almost completely rebuilt after a fire, and during the 17th century it suffered terribly from the fighting during the Cromwellian campaign, and was not restored until the 1860s. Benjamin Guinness, the drinks magnate, provided the initiative and funds for this great undertaking. It is an inspiring experience to attend a choir recital here, for its huge dimensions make a perfect auditorium for the song of red-frocked choir boys. It is here that Dean Swift preached his forceful sermons in an effort to rouse some unselfish thoughts in the minds of his wealthy parishioners; over the door of the robing room is his oft-quoted epitaph, 'He lies where furious indignation can no longer rend his heart.' Swift's death mask, chair and pulpit are displayed in Swift Corner, and nearby is the grave of Stella, Swift's pupil and great love. Notice the monument to Richard Boyle, 1st Earl of Cork, and the monument to the last of the Irish bards, O'Carolan.

Marsh's Library (*open Mon and Wed–Fri 10–1 and 2–5, Sat 10.30–1; adm; t (01) 454 3511, www.marshlibrary.ie*), near the cathedral in St Patrick's Close , is the oldest public library in the country. Founded in 1707, it has changed little since, and provides a rare example of an 18th-century library. Dean Swift once owned the copy of Clarendon's *History of the Great Rebellion*, and you can look at his pencilled notes. The entrance is very welcoming, with herbaceous plants softening the stone steps, and a feeling of hallowed learning inside. The library is classical in proportion and has a superb collection of Latin and Greek literature.

Temple Bar

Temple Bar is sold as Dublin's 'left bank' in the brochures; it is, but only if you're rowing upstream. The area is named after Sir William Temple, who was a provost of Trinity College in the 17th century. It was neglected for a long time and was once nearly razed by town planners to build a bus depot. While they were deliberating, a group of artists moved in and rented out studio spaces very cheaply, although now there is a continual battle with property developers, who want to oust the low-rent artistic element, even though the desirability of the area is mainly due to its bohemian atmosphere.

The area is home to various alternative bookshops, bars, clubs and restaurants, and the **Project Arts Theatre** on Essex Street, a cutting-edge theatre (*see* also p.552) that houses exhibitions and musical performances too. The **Irish Film Institute** (*t (01) 677 3477, www.irishfilm.ie*), on Eustace Street, shows the classics (*see* also p.551) and has a film bookshop as well as the National Film Archive. The **Temple Bar Information Centre** (*t (01) 677 2255, www.temple-bar.ie*) at 12 East Essex Street can tell you what's going on in the area.

The Guinness Storehouse and the Liberties

Where else but in Dublin would one of the main landmarks of the town be a brewery? In this case, they claim it is the largest one in the world, one that makes fully half of all the beer (stout, really) consumed in Ireland. **The Guinness Storehouse** brewery (*open daily Apr–Sept 9.30–7, Oct–Mar 9.30–5, adm; t (01) 408 4800, www. guinness-storehouse.com*), at St James's Gate, is just west of the city centre. An informative tour of the birthplace of Guinness is offered; you can visit a rooftop bar with panoramic views of the city of Dublin and try some of the stuff for free, watch a video of the processes that go into making it, and visit a museum in the old hop-store. A new part of the visitor experience opened in January 2006 focuses on the brewing and ingredients, taking visitors through every aspect of the Guinness production; it includes a Tasting Laboratory where visitors are taught to experience Guinness as professional tasters do. The shop sells all sorts of 'black gold' souvenirs.

The **Liberties** is the old residential area surrounding the brewery, and many of the workers come from this self-sufficient part of town. It was called 'The Liberties' because it stood outside the jurisdiction of the medieval town, and had its own shops and markets. In the late 17th century, French Huguenots set up a poplin and silk-weaving industry along the river valley (known as the Coombe) of the Poddle, a now-defunct river that used to flow through the Liberties and joined the Liffey at Wood Quay. The area still has great character; despite the new apartments and trendy shops springing up in places, it's very much a working-class district, and the people who live in it are the Dubliners of ballad and songs. Some families have lived here for many generations. In the late 18th century, faction-fighting was commonplace between the Liberty Boys, or tailors and weavers of the Coombe, and the Ormond Boys, butchers who lived in Ormond Market. Sometimes the fighting would involve as many as 1,000 men.

One landmark of the neighbourhood is **St Catherine's Church** in Thomas Street. This fine 18th-century church owned by the Dublin Corporation has a lovely Roman Doric façade. Although not generally accessible to the public, it is occasionally used as a venue for concerts.

A few streets west of Guinness and the Liberties is the Kilmainham neighbourhood and the **Royal Hospital and Irish Museum of Modern Art** (IMMA; *open Tue and Thur–Sat 10–5.30, Wed 10.30–5.30, Sun 12–5.30; t (01) 612 9900, www.modernart.ie*), on Military Road across from Heuston Station. The restoration of this wonderful classical building is one of the most exciting things to happen to Dublin in recent years. The government footed the enormous bill, and has earned much prestige through its role in saving it. The hospital was founded by James Butler, Duke of Ormonde, a very able statesman who survived the turbulent times of the Great Rebellion of 1640 and Cromwell's campaigns. He remained loyal to the Stuart kings, and was well rewarded by Charles II on his succession in 1660. The duke was a pragmatist, and was responsible for securing the passing of the Act of Explanation in 1665, that largely approved the Cromwellian land confiscations. But he also did some very charitable works, among them the building of this hospital for pensioner soldiers, similar in style to that of Les Invalides in Paris. The Royal Hospital is the largest surviving 17th-century building in Ireland and the most fully classical. Arranged around a quadrangle, it includes a Great Hall hung with rich and splendid royal portraits. The chapel has a magnificent Baroque ceiling of plasterwork designs of fruit, flowers and vegetables. The museum has a small permanent collection, mostly of contemporary artists. Temporary exhibitions of new artists and 20th-century greats are held in the long galleries.

Kilmainham Gaol on Inchicore Road, D8, where Parnell, De Valera and the leaders of every Irish revolt from 1798 to 1922 spent time, is now a historical museum (*open Apr–Sept daily 9.30–5, Oct–Mar Mon–Fri 9.30–4, Sun 10–5; adm; t (01) 453 5984, www. heritageireland.ie*). The leaders of the 1916 rising were executed (without trial) in the courtyard. Although rather a grim building, it is nevertheless interesting and quite moving; there are a guided tour, exhibits and an audio-visual presentation on the prison's history. Kilmainham was used as the prison in the film *In The Name of The Father*, starring Daniel Day-Lewis.

North of the Liffey

The broad thoroughfare of **O'Connell Street**, Dublin's Champs-Elysées, has, like its Parisian counterpart, come down in the world a little. After suffering considerable destruction in the Easter Rising, and more during the Civil War, it gradually ceased to be the swanky showcase of the city that it was intended to be. But despite the tatty shopfronts and the fast-food signs, it is still one of the most urbane and elegant streets you will find. And, as with Paris, Dublin is beginning to pay some attention to its famous boulevard once again, with a recently built plaza at the GPO, and trees and kiosks lining the street.

When O'Connell Street was created in the 18th century, it was purely residential, with a stately mall running up its centre to the Rotunda Hospital. The construction of the Carlisle (now O'Connell) Bridge over the River Liffey changed it into a main thoroughfare, and fine department stores, theatres and office blocks replaced the houses. The monuments lining the centre of the street still add glory to it, as do the variety of architectural styles, which you will notice if you lift your eyes above shop level. The (mainly Victorian) statues that you see are: Daniel O'Connell (1745–1833), the lawyer who won Catholic emancipation (the street was named after him in 1927; before that it was called Sackville Street); William Smith O'Brien (1803–64), the Nationalist leader; Sir John Gray (1816–75), owner of *The Freeman's Journal* and a Nationalist, who was knighted for organizing Dublin's water supply; James Larkin (1867–1943), the trade union leader; Father Theobald Mathew (1790–1856), who advocated and set up temperance clubs; and Charles Parnell (1846–91), a great parliamentary leader whose career was destroyed by the scandal of his affair with a married woman, Kitty O'Shea.

Lord Nelson, who defeated the French at Trafalgar, used to grace a column outside the GPO, but this was damaged by an IRA explosion in 1966 and subsequently demolished. In 2002 it was replaced by the 394ft (120m) **Spire**, an innovative and inevitably controversial landmark for the 21st century. It has generated a wealth of nicknames but is now most oftern referred to as 'the Spike'. Near the site there used to be a very different kind of monument, a modern sculpture of Anna Livia Plurabella, Joyce's eternal feminine personification of both the River Liffey and the women of Dublin, reclining in her fountain – artistic controversy surrounded her as soon as she was put here in 1988, and she was removed in 2001.

The **General Post Office** (*open Mon–Sat 8–8, Sun and bank hols 10–6.30; t (01) 705 7000, www.anpost.ie*), halfway along the street, is memorable not for its beauty but for the events of 1916, when Patrick Pearse and his men seized the building on Easter Monday and proclaimed the Irish Republic from its steps. The rebels held out for five days, while the British surrounded the building and shelled it from a gunboat in the River Liffey, wrecking it and much of O'Connell Street in the process. In the days that followed, the leaders of the rising, including Pearse and James Connolly, were summarily shot (*see* **History**, p.25–26). Inside you can see a memorial to the 1916 heroes that takes the form of a bronze statue of the dying Cú Chulainn. The GPO's historical role in the struggle for an independent Ireland has made it a venue for all manner of protest meetings.

Two streets behind, there is a colourful street market on **Moore Street** (*see* p.546), while on the other side of O'Connell Street, on Marlborough Street, the (Catholic) **Pro Cathedral of St Mary** is a Greek Revival Doric temple that was constructed between 1815 and 1825; the Catholics would have preferred to build it right on O'Connell Street, but times were still too bigoted for that. There is a lovely sung mass at 11am on Sundays that is a long-standing Dublin tradition; the great tenor John McCormack used to sing in it.

Down near the Liffey end of Marlborough Street is the famous **Abbey Theatre** (*see* also p.552) where the plays of Synge and O'Casey had their premières – often to the accompaniment of riots, carried out by moral-minded Catholics who packed the house just to break up the show. The current grim building replaced the original, which burned down in 1951.

The Custom House is just around the corner on the quay, near Butt Bridge. Many people consider this to be the most impressive building in Dublin. A quadrangular structure with four decorated faces, it now houses the Customs and Excise and Department of Local Government. It was designed by James Gandon and completed in 1791. Unfortunately, its impact on the waterfront is lessened by a railway bridge that passes in front of it and the IFSC (Irish Financial Services Centre) development behind. Gutted by fire in 1921 during the Civil War by the Republican side, it has been perfectly restored so that the graceful dome, crowned by the figure of commerce, still rises from the central Doric portico. Inside is a Visitors' Centre (*open mid-Mar–Nov Mon–Fri 10–12.30, Sat and Sun 2–5, Dec–mid-Mar Wed–Fri 10–12.30, Sun 2–5; adm; t (01) 888 2538*) with a small museum on Gandon and the history of the building .

Parnell Square

Found at the northern end of O'Connell Street, this square began its life as another of Dublin's residential squares; and in the 18th century it was the most fashionable address in town. These days it is known for its cultural institutions and for the conspicuous landmark of the **Rotunda Hospital**, which was set up in 1752 as the first specialized maternity hospital in the world.The Rococo Chapel within the hospital is very sumptuous, with some large-scale allegorical figures and curving plasterwork decorated with cherubs and putti. (Arrangements to view it must be made in writing to the Hospital Secretary, Rotunda Hospital, Parnell Square, D1.) The hospital has always had an unusual connection with the performing arts; its founder staged concerts to finance his project, including the first performance of Handel's 'Messiah'. The hospital's auditorium holds the Ambassador Cinema, and another part of the building is home to the Gate Theatre, an important venue for new Irish plays since the 1920s (*see* p.552). **The Garden of Remembrance** (*always accessible*), behind the theatre, commemorates Irish freedom. The central feature of the garden is a sculpture of the legendary Children of Lir, by Oisín Kelly.

The Hugh Lane Gallery of Modern Art (*open Tue–Thur 9.30–6, Fri and Sat 9.30–5, Sun 11–5; t (01) 874 1903, www.hughlane.ie*) in a fine Georgian house at No.1 Parnell Square, was extensively renovated in 2005. The bulk of the collection was formed by Sir Hugh Lane in the early 20th century (W. B. Yeats wrote a poem about his bequests), and the gallery has a small but wonderful collection of works by well-known artists: portraits of Yeats, Synge and other famous Irish figures, and a bust of Lady Gregory by Epstein. The magical stained-glass window by Harry Clarke, 'The Eve of Saint Agnes', is after a poem by John Keats. Within the gallery, the Francis Bacon Studio is a complete reconstruction of Bacon's studio at 7 Reece Mews, Kensington, London. The entire contents of the room were donated to the gallery after his death.

The **Dublin Writers Museum** (*open Mon–Sat 10–5, Sun 11–5, June–Aug until 6; adm, combined tickets with Joyce Museum and Shaw Birthplace available; t (01) 872 2077, www.writersmuseum.com*) is housed in another beautifully restored 18th-century building at No.18 Parnell Square North. The permanent displays introduce you to centuries of Irish literature, illustrated by letters, photographs, first editions and memorabilia. The **Irish Writers Centre**, within the museum, has a varied programme of lectures, readings and workshops. The museum also has a very good bookshop and restaurant, Chapter One (*see* p.549).

Yet another Georgian house in the area has become the **James Joyce Cultural Centre** (*open Mon–Sat 9.30–5, Sun 12.30–5; adm; t (01) 878 8547, www.jamesjoyce.ie*), at 35 North Great George's Street, housing exhibitions, a library, a bookshop and a café. On the same theme, the **James Joyce House** (*open daily 10-5, t 085 726 2855, www.jamesjoycehouse.com*) is at 15 Usher's Island, right opposite the recently built James Joyce Bridge by Santiago Calatrava, back towards the Guinness Storehouse. Dating from 1760, it has been carefully restored. It belonged to members of the writer's family and is the setting for Joyce's memorable short story *The Dead*, which John Huston adapted for the screen in 1987.

The Four Courts, St Michan's and the Collins Barracks

At the **Four Courts** (*open Oct–July Mon–Fri 10.30–4.30; t (01) 872 5555*), down by Ormond Quay, you get one of the most characteristic views of Dublin. The Four Courts was designed by Gandon, the architect of the Custom House, and completed by Thomas Cooley (1776–84). It was almost completely destroyed in the Civil War of 1921 but it has since been restored. The Law Courts were reinstalled here in 1931. The central block has a Corinthian portico and a copper green dome, and is flanked by two wings enclosing quadrangles. You can take a look inside the circular waiting hall under the dome. The **Public Record Office** next door was burnt down completely in 1921, with an irredeemable loss of legal and historical documents.

St Michan's on Church Street, west of the Four Courts, is a 17th-century structure on the site of an 11th-century Danish church. Most people are interested in getting to the **vaults** (*open Mar–Oct Mon–Fri 10–12.45 and 2–4.45, Nov–Feb Mon–Fri 12.30–3.30, Sat 10–12.45; guided tours; adm; t (01) 872 4154*), where bodies have lain for centuries without decomposing. Here the air is very dry due to the absorbent nature of the limestone foundations. The skin of the corpses remains as soft as in life, and even their joints still work. Layers of coffins have collapsed into each other, exposing arms and legs; you can even see a crusader from the Holy Land. The body of Robert Emmet, one of the leaders of the 1798 rebellion, is said to be buried here. The only things that do live down in this curiously warm and fresh atmosphere are spiders, who feed on each other. There are so many types that people come from afar to study them. It is said that a Dublin lad has honourable intentions if he brings his girl here. The interior of the church itself is very fine and plain. A superb wooden carving of a violin intermingled with flowers and fruits decorates the choir gallery, and is supposed to be by Grinling Gibbons. Whoever carved it was a genius, and it is sad that so many visitors, rather ghoulishly, go only to the vaults.

Just around the corner on Bow Street, recover from your experience, if necessary, in the **Old Jameson Distillery** (*open daily 9.30–6; adm; t (01) 807 2355*) at Smithfield. Though the big copper tanks are no longer in use, everything is kept as it was for the guided tours. There's also an exhibition on the history of Irish whiskey, a 15-minute film and, most important, a generous tasting of all the different Irish.

A few streets to the west, just north of the Liffey on Benburb Street, stands **The National Museum of Decorative Arts and History** at Collins Barracks (*open Tue–Sat 10–5, Sun 2–5; t (01) 677 7444*), an 18-acre site that was known as the Royal Barracks when it was the headquarters of the British military in Ireland. The main building, built in 1701, was restored by the National Museum to hold its collections of decorative arts, including furniture and relics of Irish history. In a sense this is Ireland's Smithsonian, and it holds a little bit of everything, from Etruscan vases to an oar belonging to one of the lifeboats from the *Lusitania*.

Phoenix Park

Phoenix Park, the largest city park in Europe, is just about within walking distance of central Dublin. (Cross the river northwards and walk west along the quays to Conyngham Road to get there; or catch a bus from O'Connell Street.) Dubliners are very proud of the park – with good reason. As well as sports fields, woodland, small lakes, duck ponds and Dublin Zoo (*see* p.568), it finds room in its 1,760 acres (712ha) to house *Áras an Uachtaráin* (the residence of the President), the residence of the American ambassador, the police headquarters and a hospital.

The name of the park comes from a corruption of the Gaelic *Fionn Uisce*, which means 'Bright Water', from a spring that rises near the Phoenix Column at the Knockmaroon Gate. To English ears the pronunciation of the Gaelic sounded rather like 'phoenix'. The Phoenix Column was put up in 1747 by Lord Chesterfield, who was the viceroy of the time, and who had the impetus and foresight to plant this part of the park with trees. The land was offered by Charles II to one of his mistresses, which illustrates to what degree Dublin, and indeed the whole of Ireland, was up for grabs in the 17th century. Luckily, the Duke of Ormonde (who built Kilmainham Hospital) suggested that it should be granted to the City of Dublin itself. Two hundred years later, in 1882, the Chief Secretary, Lord Frederick Cavendish, and the Under Secretary were stabbed to death by Nationalists in the park.

The park is memorable as a place where cattle still graze and deer can be glimpsed through the trees. It is open to the public at all times, and the **Visitor Centre** (*open Apr and May daily 9.30–5.30, June–Sept daily 10–6, Oct daily and Nov–Feb Wed–Sun 10–5, mid–end Mar 9.30–5; adm; t (01) 677 0095*), next to a 17th-century towerhouse, houses a multimedia exhibition on the history of the park over the last 6,000 years. Near the

main entrance to the park on Parkgate Street stands the **Wellington Monument**, a
211ft (65m) obelisk completed in 1861. The Duke of Wellington was born in Dublin,
though with his lifelong disdain for Ireland and the Irish he did not appreciate being
reminded of it. Beyond this lie the **People's Gardens**, and at the northern end is the
old **Phoenix Park Race Course**, which is no longer in use. Between lies **Dublin Zoo**
(*open Mar–Oct Mon–Sat 9.30–6, Sun 10.30–6, Nov–Feb Mon–Sat 9.30–dusk, Sun
10.30–dusk; adm; t (01) 474 8900, www.dublinzoo.ie*), one of the oldest zoos in Europe,
set in attractive grounds with artificial lakes. All the usual favourites are here, along
with a special Arctic section and a discovery centre for children.

Other Attractions in Dublin City

Shaw Birthplace, 33 Synge Street, D8, south of the centre near the Grand Canal
(*open May–Oct Mon, Tue and Thur–Sat 10–1 and 2–5, Sun 2–5; adm; t (01) 475 0854*).
It isn't much, this tidy middle-class home where the future genius George Bernard
Shaw spent a mildly unhappy childhood, but restored to what it might have looked
like in the 1860s it is a worthy introduction to the life of Victorian Dublin.

Irish Jewish Museum, 3 Walworth Road, D8, off the South Circular Road (*open
May–Sept Tues, Thurs and Sun 11–3.30, Oct–Apr Sun 10.30–2.30, adm; t (01) 490 1857*).
Ireland today may have a Jewish population of less than 2,000, but their long and
interesting history is recounted in this restored former synagogue.

The War Memorial Gardens, Islandbridge, off the South Circular Road (just before
Islandbridge; the gardens are signposted to the left). Designed by Edwin Lutyens in
1931, this is a very architectural garden. You approach it by formal avenues that centre
on the warstone at the heart of the garden. Circles and ovals commemorate the
49,400 Irish soldiers who died in the First World War. There are two sunken gardens,
surrounded by terraces, roses, flowers and shrubs.

National Wax Museum, Smithfield Square, D7 (*open Mon–Sat 10–5.30, Sun 12–5.30;
adm; t (01) 872 6340*). No big tourist city would be complete without one, and Dublin's
is neither more nor less grotesque than the average, except perhaps for the tableau
of Jesus and the apostles reproducing Leonardo da Vinci's *Last Supper*. Note that it's
closed until autumn 2006, when it will have relocated to its new premises.

Pearse Museum, St Enda's Park, Grange Road, Rathfarnham, D16 (*open Feb–Apr, Sept
and Oct 10–1 and 2–5, May–Aug 10–1 and 2–5.30, Nov–Jan 10–1 and 2–4; adm; t (01) 493
4208*). The poet-patriot ran an Irish-language school here before the 1916 rising. At the
time of writing, it was scheduled to be closed for renovation throughout 2006.

The Museum of Childhood, 20 Palmerston Park, Rathmines (*open Sun only, 2–5.30;
t (01) 497 8696*) has a charming private collection of antique dolls and toys.

Dillon Garden, 45 Sandford Road, Ranelagh, Dublin 6 (*open Mar, July and Aug daily
2–6, Apr–June and Sept Sun 2–6; adm; t (01) 497 1308, www.dillongarden.com*) is a
lovely city garden with secret areas of light and shade, clematis-draped arches,
borders filled with flowers, tubs of sweet-smelling lilies, and wildflowers and roses.

The Casino at **Marino**, north of the centre off the Malahide Road (*open June–Sept
daily 10–6, May and Oct daily 10–5, Nov–Mar/Apr Sat and Sun 12 noon–4; adm; t (01)
833 1618*). This 18th-century miniature classical temple of three storeys was designed

by Sir William Chambers, between 1762 and 1771, for Lord Charlemont. There isn't any gambling here – casino means simply 'cottage' in Italian, and fancy ones were a fad among 18th-century aristocrats. It is, in fact, one of Ireland's architectural gems. The public park nearby was part of Lord Charlemont's estate, the main house being demolished in 1921. It was exceedingly fortunate that this beautiful building did not go the same way. It is now restored and opened to the public. So ingenious was the architect that from the outside it only appears to be one storey high. The basement is actually below street level, whilst the ground and first floor are not distinguished in the façade. Inside are some splendid inlaid floors, delicate plasterwork ceilings and silk-covered walls. Not far away is **Croke Park**, the national temple of sport where the All Ireland hurling and Gaelic football finals are played, and where you can visit the **GAA Museum** (*www.gaa.ie/museum*).

National Botanic Gardens, Botanic Road, Glasnevin, D9 (*open summer Mon–Sat 9–6 Sun 10–6, winter daily 10–4.30; t (01) 804 0300*). Founded in 1795 by the Royal Dublin Society, this garden has a range of beautiful plants and mature trees that make it a wonderful place in which to walk. There is a magnificent curvilinear glasshouse more than 400ft (122m) long, built and designed by Dublin ironmaster Richard Turner between 1843 and 1869 and beautifully restored in 2004. Adjacent to the gardens is Prospect Cemetery, resting place of many famous Dubliners, including Michael Collins, Daniel O'Connell and Charles Stewart Parnell.

Drimnagh Castle, Long Mile Road, Drimnagh, D12, south-west of the centre (*open Apr–Oct Wed, Sat and Sun 12–5, Nov–Mar Sun 2–5; adm; t (01) 450 2530*). In a quiet suburban neighbourhood, this modest medieval castle, the only one in Ireland with a flooded moat, has an exquisite formal 16th-century garden.

County Wicklow

County Wicklow has everything that is thought of as Irish in its landscape: wild heather-covered glens and forests, high mountain peaks, deep loughs, ancient churches, stately houses and silvery beaches. Yet it is within only half an hour's drive of Dublin City. Dubliners call it 'the garden of Ireland'. Certainly it is their playground, and many come out to walk in the hills and picnic in the many beautiful places. Nothing could be more in contrast to the hustle and bustle of Dublin life.

In the winter months the Wicklow hills are severe and savage, with their bare conical shapes softened by snow. Throughout the summer these same hills are clothed in verdant oak, beech and fir trees; the loughs are blue, and the little streams that tumble from the hills create some delightful music. Pubs and restaurants here are of a high standard, and if you want to be organized into rockclimbing, canoeing or orienteering, there are some adventure centres hidden away in the glens. The coastline, meanwhile, has great charm. The Victorian resort towns of Bray and Greystones have a good number of amenities, and it is possible to walk for miles from Dalkey to Wicklow Town between the railway and the sea, with nothing much to interrupt the peace except the occasional train. The rugs that are produced in the

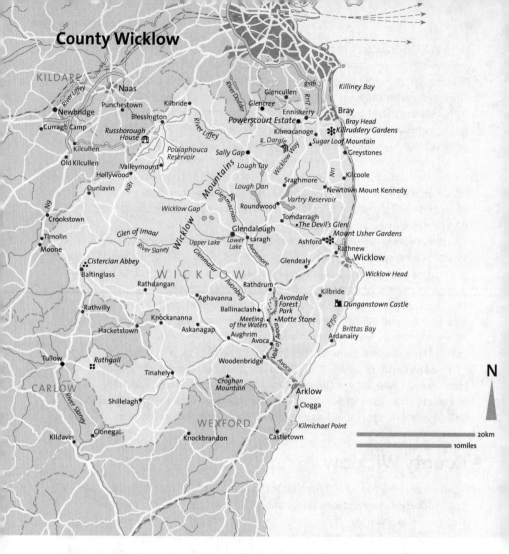

County Wicklow

KILDARE
Naas
Killiney Bay
River Liffey
Punchestown
Kilbride
Glencullen
R116
R117
Newbridge
Blessington
Glencree
Enniskerry
Bray
Curragh Camp
Russborough House
Powerscourt Estate
Bray Head
Kilmacanoge
Killruddery Gardens
River Liffey
R. Dargle
Sugar Loaf Mountain
Kilcullen
Poulaphouca Reservoir
Sally Gap
Greystones
Old Kilcullen
Valleymount
Lough Tay
Hollywood
Sraghmore
Kilcoole
N81
Dunlavin
Lough Dan
Newtown Mount Kennedy
N11
Crookstown
Wicklow Gap
Roundwood
Vartry Reservoir
N9
Glen of Imaal
Tomdarragh
The Devil's Glen
Timolin
Glenmacnass
Wicklow Mountains
Glendalough
Mount Usher Gardens
Moone
Upper Lake
Lower Lake
Laragh
Ashford
River Slaney
Avonmore
Rathnew
Cistercian Abbey
Glenmalur
Glendealy
Wicklow
Baltinglass
WICKLOW
Wicklow Head
Rathdangan
Rathdrum
Aghavanna
Kilbride
Avonbeg
Avondale Forest Park
Dunganstown Castle
Rathvilly
Ballinaclash
R750
Knockananna
Meeting of the Waters
Motte Stone
Hacketstown
Askanagap
Aughrim
Brittas Bay
Tullow
Avoca
Ardanairy
Rathgall
Woodenbridge
Vale of Avoca
Tinahely
Avoca
CARLOW
Croghan Mountain
Arklow
River Slaney
Shillelagh
Clogga
WEXFORD
Kilmichael Point
Kildavin
Clonegal
Knockbrandon
Castletown

N

20km
10miles

Avoca woollen mills (*see* opposite) are wonderful – a perfect combination of the colours you will almost certainly see around you in the countryside, and something to cherish when you go home.

The monastic remains of Glendalough are amongst the best in Ireland, as are the gardens at Powerscourt and the magnificent furniture and pictures at Russborough House. So, if you do not have much time in Ireland, County Wicklow might give you just a taste to bring you back again.

The county has a growing population of well over 100,000, many of whom work in Dublin. Greystones and Blessington are the main commuter towns. The towns of Bray and Arklow have a wide range of industries. In the mountains, hill-farming with sheep is practised, whilst the eastern coastal strip and the land in the south-west supports richer farms.

Getting There and Around

By Rail
The main line from Dublin to Wexford and Waterford runs through Wicklow via Bray, Wicklow, Rathdrum and Arklow. DART trains run to Dublin from Bray.
Iarnród Éireann, t 1850 366222, *www.irishrail.ie*

By Bus
Bus Éireann provides services to Co. Wicklow from Dublin, Rosslare Harbour and Waterford. Most towns in northern Wicklow are also served by Dublin Bus.
Bus Éireann, t (01) 836 6111, *www.buseireann.ie*
Dublin Bus, 59 Upper O'Connell St, D1,
t (01) 873 4222/872 0000, *www.dublinbus.ie*
St Kevin's Bus, t (01) 281 8119. Twice daily services running between Dublin and Glendalough, via Bray.

By Bike
Bray Sports Centre, 8 Main St, Bray,
t (01) 286 3046 or t (01) 282 8394
Tommy McGrath, Rathdrum, t (0404) 46172

Festivals

March
Arklow Music Festival, t (0402) 32732. Competitions.

April
Parnell Spring Day, Rathdrum,
www.visitwicklow.ie

May
Avoca Melody Fair, *www.avoca.com*.
A music and song festival.
Bray Jazz Festival, t (01) 287 3992
Wicklow Gardens Festival, t (0404) 20070,
www.wicklow.ie/tourism. A celebration of around 50 private gardens and heritage properties in the area.

June
Dunlavin Arts Festival, *www.dunlavinartsfestival.com*. A parade, flower and agricultural shows, crafts and plenty of *craic*.
International Cartoon Festival, Rathdrum,
t (0404)-46811

July
Arklow Seabreeze Festival, t (0402) 33356.
An event including a famous pig race.
Bray Summerfest, t (01) 286 7128. A family-run festival with races, a 'barney' show, a Festival Queen ball, hurling, live bands and fireworks.
Horticultural Rose Show, Delgany, t (01) 287 4400
Wicklow Town Regatta Festival, t (0404) 67526

August
Arklow Maritime Festival, *www.arklow.ie*
Evolution Music Festival, Kilruddery, Bray,
t (01) 284 7796
Greystones Arts Festival, t (086) 832 9686.
Bank-holiday weekend.
Tinahely Agricultural Show, t (0402) 867380.
Livestock, showjumping, crafts and music.

September
Music Under the Mountains, Holywood, t (045) 867380. Folk music. Past acts have included The Chieftains and Altan and Dervish.

October
Bray Seafood Festival, t (01) 286 7128
Oscar Wilde Autumn School, Bray, t (01) 286 5245. Readings and talks by leading writers.

Tourist Information
Arklow: t (0402) 32484, *www.arklow.ie*.
Open June–mid Sept.
Bray: t (01) 286 7128/6796, *www.bray.ie*
Glendalough: t (0404) 45688. *Open June–Sept*
Wicklow Town: t (0404) 69117, *www.wicklow.ie*

Shopping

Crafts
Avoca Handweavers, Millmount Mills, Avoca,
t (0402) 35105/35284, *www.avoca.ie*.
Tweeds, rugs and sweaters.
Ballinastoe Studio Pottery, Ballinastoe,
Roundwood, t (01) 281 8151. Quality work.
Belinda Brayshaw Pottery, Rathdrum,
t (0404) 46839.
Brian Keogh Pottery, Mount Usher Gardens,
Ashford, t (0404) 40313
Glendalough Woollen Mills, Glendalough,
t (0404) 45156

Handcrafted Irish Jewellery,
Blessington Business Centre,
Main St, Blessington, t (045) 865850
Harvest Loom Celtic Crafts, Laragh,
Glendalough, t (0404) 45721
Powerscourt House Shops, Enniskerry,
t (01) 204 6000. High-quality goods.
Rustic Works, The Square, Enniskerry,
t (01) 286 6820 www.rusticworks.com.
Pottery, jewellery, glass, lamps, shades,
ironwork, pictures and more.
Wicklow Vale Pottery, Arklow, t (0402) 39442

Markets

The movement to re-establish village
markets has really caught on in Wicklow.
Arklow, Masonic Hall, Sat 10.30–12 noon.
Avoca, Parish Hall, July and Aug Sun 2.30–5.
Blessington, Sat 2.30–4.30.
Macreddin Village, Brook Lodge Hotel,
Aughrim, 1st Sun of month.
North Wicklow County Market,
St Patrick's Hall, Kilcoole, 10.30–11.30am Sat
Roundwood Sunday Market, Parish Hall,
Roundwood. Home-baking, country butter
and flowers, Mar–Dec Sun 3–5pm.

Sports and Activities

Fishing

Dargle Anglers Club, Bray Sports Centre,
Main St, Bray, t (01) 286 3046. Salmon and
sea-trout fishing on the Dargle.
J. Byrne, t (0404) 67716. Advice.
Ray Dineen, Tara House, Redcross,
t (0404) 41645. Brown trout at Blessington.

Golf

Charlesland Golf and Country Club,
Greystones, t (01) 287 4350
Greystones Golf Club, Greystones,
t (01) 287 4136
Powerscourt Golf Club, Enniskerry, t (01) 204
6033, www.powerscourt.ie/golfclub/.
A championship 18-hole course.

Holistic Treatments

The Chrysalis Holistic Centre, Donard,
north of Baltinglass, t (045) 404713,
www.chrysalis.ie. Therapies such as Reiki
and Indian head massage.

Horsedrawn Caravans

Clissmann Horse-drawn Caravans,
Carrigmore Farm, Wicklow, t (0404) 48188,
www.clissmann.com. See also p.121.

Pony trekking

Bel Air Hotel Riding School, Ashford,
t (0404) 40109, www.holidaysbelair.com
Brennanstown Riding School, Hollybrook,
Kilmacanogue, Bray, t (01) 286 3778

Outdoor Activity Centres

Clara-Lara Funpark, Rathdrum, t (0404) 46161.
Waterslides and boats for children.
The Tiglin National Mountain and
White Water Centre, Ashford, t (0404)
40169, www.tiglin.com. Field courses in
mountaineering, orienteering, canoeing,
surfing and skiing.

Walking

The Wicklow Way starts in Co. Dublin at
Marley Park and climbs rapidly into the
Wicklow Mountains, switching from glen to
glen. The long-running Wicklow Mountains
Spring and Autumn Walking Festivals are run
by the Wicklow Tourist Office, t (0404) 69117.
For local walking trips, contact:
Barry Dalby, 155 Beachdale, Kilcoole,
t (01) 287 5990
Damien Cashin Outdoor Activities,
Tomdarragh, Roundwood, t (01) 281 8212

Where to Stay

The BrookLodge and Wells Spa,
Macreddin Village, near Aughrim,
t (0402) 36444, www.brooklodge.com
(luxury). A country hotel where fresh organic
produce is served for breakfast and afternoon
tea. The spa has an indoor-to-outdoor pool
and mud chambers.
Rathsallagh House, Dunlavin, t (045) 403112,
www.rathsallagh.com (luxury). A very
comfortable farmhouse where you can
enjoy good food (see opposite) and chat.
Facilities are in place for hunting, billiards,
golf, croquet, and a pool and sauna. Note
that children under 12 are not admitted.
Tinakilly House, Rathnew, t (0404) 69274,
www.tinakilly.ie (luxury). A very stylish
Victorian house, with delicious food.

Hunter's Hotel, Rathnew, t (0404) 40106, *www.hunters.ie* (*expensive*). An attractive coaching inn run by the same family for 5 generations.

Ballyknocken House, Glenealy, near Ashford, t (0404) 44627, *www.ballyknocken.com* (*moderate*). A pretty farmhouse welcoming children. There's a pony on the farm, and advice is given on walks.

Plattenstown House, Coolgreany Rd, Arklow t (0402) 37822 (*moderate*). A peaceful and comfortable country house.

Poulaphouca House, Poulaphouca, Holywood, t (045) 864412 (*moderate*). An attractive guesthouse with a traditional 1890s bar.

Powerscourt Arms Hotel, Enniskerry, t (01) 282 8903 (*moderate*). An attractive town hotel where they serve good Guinness.

Avonbrae Guesthouse, Rathdrum, t (0404) 46198, *www.avonbrae.com* (*inexpensive*). A family-run village guesthouse. Hill-walking and other activities can be arranged.

Lissadell House, Ashdown Lane, Wicklow, t (0404) 67458, *lissadellhse@eircom.net* (*moderate*). A comfortable house run by a friendly Irish-German couple.

Moneylands Farm, Arklow, t (0402) 32259, *www.moneylandsfarm.com* (*inexpensive*). B&B rooms in a Georgian farmhouse, plus 3 restored self-catering farm buildings.

Tynte House, Dunlavin, t (045) 401561, *www.tyntehouse.com* (*inexpensive*). An early-19th-century farmhouse with tennis facilities, a games room and a play area.

Self-catering

B McLoughlin, Glendalough, t (01) 459 1403, (*moderate*). An attractive 2-bedroom house.

Doyle's Lodge, Fortgranite Estate, Baltinglass, t (059) 647 3510 (*moderate*). An old stone house in a pretty setting, with 2 bedrooms.

Eating Out

Tinakilly House, Rathnew, t (0404) 69274 (*expensive–luxury*). Ambitious French cuisine served in an elegant dining room. Reservations are essential.

The Hungry Monk, Greystones, t (01) 287 5759, or t (01) 287 7892 (*expensive*). A family-run fish restaurant with an impressive wine list. It's a good spot for Sunday lunch. *Closed Mon, Tue and lunch exc Sun.*

Rathsallagh House, Dunlavin, t (045) 403112 (*expensive*). Top-notch country-house cooking, including seasonal game and fresh fish, in a luxurious farmhouse (*see* opposite). Most of the herbs and vegetables used are from the hotel's own organic gardens.

The Strawberry Tree, The BrookLodge and Wells Spa, Macreddin Village, near Aughrim, t (0402) 36444, *www.brooklodge.com* (*expensive*). An award-winning restaurant serving free-range, organic and wild foods. *Closed lunch.*

The Tree of Idleness, Seafront, Bray, t (01) 286 1498 (*expensive*). A long-standing restaurant run by a Greek-Cypriot, with a good reputation. Expect lots of feta cheese, olive oil and herbs. *Closed lunch and Mon.*

The Chester Beatty Inn, Ashford, t (0404) 40206 (*moderate*). A country inn with a restaurant with good seafood, a traditional Irish bar and log fires.

Hunter's Hotel, Rathnew, t (0404) 40106 (*moderate*). Famous cream teas and marvellous Irish cooking. The garden is lovely.

Mitchell's, Laragh, Glendalough, t (0404) 45302 (*moderate*). A restored schoolhouse where you can tuck into Wicklow lamb, and lovely home-baked cakes for afternoon tea.

Roundwood Inn, Roundwood, t (01) 281 8107 or t (01) 281 8125 (*moderate*). A 17th-century inn serving all-day bar food – from filling Irish stew to oysters – and à la carte dishes in its restaurant. Portions are enormous, and booking is essential. *Closed Sun eve and Mon.*

Avoca Handweavers, Millmount Mills, Avoca, t (01) 286 7466 (*inexpensive*). Home-made soups, vegetable bakes and cakes.

Poppies Restaurant, The Square, Enniskerry, t (01) 282 8869 (*inexpensive*). Salad lunches and home-baking. It gets lively at weekends.

The Stone Oven, 65 Lower Main St, Arklow, t (0402) 39418, *www.stoneoven.com* (*inexpensive*). A bakery and coffee shop specializing in German breads.

Entertainment and Nightlife

Esplanade Hotel, Bray, t (01) 286 2056. Country-rock and folk singing on summer eves, Thur–Sun.

History

Historically, County Wicklow was part of the kingdom of the Leinster kings, the MacMurraghs, whilst the Vikings established towns at Arklow and Wicklow. The modern boundary lines were drawn up by the English during the reign of Elizabeth Tudor. The mountain *septs* of Wicklow earned themselves a reputation for guerilla warfare when the Anglo-Normans arrived in 1167: they wore the Normans down with constant skirmishes, and contained them within the Pale – a small fortified area around Dublin where the English king had control. O'Byrne and O'Toole were the two clans who made life so awkward for the Normans, and they continued to do so for centuries. During the reign of Elizabeth Tudor in the 1570s, Fiach MacHugh O'Byrne constantly harried the English forces and won some small victories that rallied the Gaelic cause in these parts for 20 years.

The next great revolt was in 1798, and in Wicklow the Irish folk, led by Michael Dwyer (1771–1826), armed themselves with pikes to fight the English forces. The uprising was suppressed, and Michael Dwyer surrendered in 1803. He was spared execution because of the humanity he had shown in various engagements, and was sentenced instead to transportation to New South Wales, where he later became High Constable of Sydney. (You can go round his cottage home in the Glen of Imaal, *see* pp.577–78.) The English government then built the Military Road through the mountains from north to south, which is still in use today. It helped them to flush out the rebels. The Great Famine of the 1840s reduced the population from 126,000 to 100,000, and it further declined with emigration to America and Australia. Charles Stewart Parnell (1846–91) was the vigorous and effective voice of the Irish in the British parliament. His estate and house at Avondale is now a museum. The political campaigns he fought bore fruit in the Wyndham Land Acts, which made government loans available to tenant farmers to buy the land they had leased. Sadly, his career was bought down by his affair with Kitty O'Shea, a married woman; the scandal rocked Catholic Ireland, and he lost support.

Around Bray

Bray is one of Ireland's principal coastal resorts, and has golf, horseriding, swimming and cinema – all sorts of amenities, although it seems a bit rundown and seedy at the moment. **Bray Heritage Centre** (*open daily 10–4; t (01) 286 6796*) in the old courthouse contains a fine array of photographs, records, maps and artefacts relating to the area. The town has a safe beach of shingle and sand. There are good walks to Bray Head, and a cliff walk of about 3 miles (5km) to Greystones.

Greystones is a smaller resort, an old fishing village that's rather more attractive than Bray but is just as full of Dubliners and is slowly being swallowed up by the capital's sprawl. South of it, on the N11, home gardeners will enjoy the **National Garden Exhibition Centre** (*open Mon–Sat 10–6, Sun 1–6; adm; t (01) 281 9890*), with 16 individual gardens by noted designers to inspire the rest of us. **Killruddery Gardens** (*open May–Sept daily 1–5; house open May, June and Sept daily 1–5; adm; t (0404) 46024, www.killruddery.com*), between the N11 and R761 south of Bray, were laid out in the 17th century. Here a pair of long canals reflect the sky, and a high beech hedge encircles a pool and fountains. There is also a fine parterre edged with box and filled with pink moss roses. The house, which opens to the public at the same time as the gardens, is an 1820 Elizabethan Revival mansion built for the 10th Earl of Meath. It has some fine plasterwork.

The **Glen of Dargle** to the west of Bray off the N11 is another lovely place to walk. A narrow pathway runs beside the Dargle River, and a road follows the glen to the south. A huge rock, known as the 'lover's leap', juts out over the wooded gorge through which the river runs. Here, at Enniskerry, is **Powerscourt Estate** (*open daily Mar–Oct 9.30–5.30, Nov–Feb 10.30–dusk; adm; t (01) 204 6000, www.powerscourt.ie*), with one of the finest formal gardens in Ireland, with Italianate and Japanese-style gardens, and a Monkey Puzzle Avenue. Tragically, the house – which is one of the most beautiful in Ireland – was gutted by fire in 1976 after being carefully restored by the Slazenger family (of tennis-racket fame). However, the gardens remain and the setting of the house, facing the Sugar Loaf Mountain, makes it an unforgettable sight: you walk towards it thinking it is still intact, but it is in fact a mere shell. The Slazenger family have not given up on it, though, and are planning further restoration. On the Powerscourt Estate is the breathtakingly beautiful **Powerscourt waterfall**, the highest in Ireland. The water falls from 400ft (122m) into a fine stream, which winds its way through numerous walks. **Enniskerry** itself is a fine estate village with good food, shops and clothes boutiques. It is an excellent base for excursions into the surrounding hills. Nearby, **Coolakay House and Agricultural Display** (*open summer daily, call for times; t (01) 286 2423*) is a museum of Irish farm life over the centuries.

Wandering Along the Wicklow Way

From Enniskerry, follow the road through the Scalp, a glacier-formed gap. The forests surrounding the Scalp have some lovely trails. If you want to glut yourself on forest scenery take the Military Road, which runs through the mountains from Rathfarnham to Aghavannagh. This road bisects the county and takes you through some mysterious glens and remote valleys; you see turf-cutting country and some stupendous mountain scenery. One of the most spectacular glens is **Glencree**, which curves from near the base of the Sugarloaf Mountain to the foot of the Glendoo Mountain. Through it flows the Glencree River, which later joins the Dargle. The wild and beautiful **Sally Gap**, near the source of the River Liffey, is a crossroads from which you can follow the old Military Road to Laragh, the road to Roundwood or the valley road to Manor Kilbridge and Blessington. Dubliners come out at weekends to cut their turf at Sally Gap.

Laragh is a pleasant little village where roads from the north, south, east and west meet. Close to here, to the north-east on the R755, is the village of **Roundwood**, which is reputed to be the highest village in Ireland, at 780ft (238m) above sea level. It is close to the Vartry Reservoir, which supplies water to Dublin City, and to the wild scenery surrounding Lough Dan. The high ground in these mountainous areas was the realm of the 'mountainy men' – the Irish who had been deprived of their lands on the plain by the English settlers. Up here in the hills the rule of Dublin Castle had little influence.

Glendalough

The important early-Christian site of **Glendalough**, the 'Glen of Two Lakes', has overwhelmed people with its peace and isolation for many centuries, and is an enclave of holiness amongst the wilderness. Its setting is unforgettable and uniquely Irish, high in the hills, with two small lakes cupped in a hollow, a tall round tower and a grey-stone church. There are the remains of a famous monastic school, founded by St Kevin in the 6th century; and the remnants of churches spread between the upper and lower lakes; and the little river. There's a **Visitor Centre** (*open daily summer 9.30–6, winter 9.30–5; adm; t (0404) 45325*) beside the car park as you enter, with very interesting exhibits and an audio-visual show to enjoy before you explore the remains.

The churches, with a monastic gateway (the only one in Ireland) and a round tower, are clustered together by the little Glenealo River. At the south-east corner to the upper lake, by Poulanass Waterfall, is **Reefert Church**, where the O'Toole rulers were buried. On the southern shore is the **Church of the Rock**. Between Reefert Church and the lower lake are five crosses, which some say marked the boundaries of the monastic land and later became station crosses in the Pilgrims' Way. The story goes that St Kevin came here to recover from the effort involved in rejecting the advances of a beautiful girl named Kathleen. However, she chased him to the monastery, and he had to hit her with stinging nettles to lessen her ardour. Another version of the tale, recounted by Thomas (Tom) Moore, is that he cooled her off by pushing her into the lake. Despite Kevin's wish to be a hermit, his refuge became a centre of learning and later a place of pilgrimage. You can see **St Kevin's Kitchen**; the **church** with its corbelled roof; and the ruins of the **cathedral** with its 12th-century chancel. **St Kevin's Bed** is on the southern cliff-face of the upper lake; it is a very dangerous climb that is not recommended, since intrepid visitors who have attempted it have often had to be rescued. This is the cell where St Kevin stayed before the seven churches of the settlement were built. The views of the lakes are remarkable.

St Saviour's Monastery, about 430 yards (400m) north-east of the cathedral, is also very handsome. It is said to have been founded in the 12th century by St Lawrence O'Toole. The chancel arch is a lovely bit of Romanesque architecture: three orders resting on large clustered piers, decorated with dog-tooth, chevron and floral ornament. Human heads and animals decorate the capitals and bases.

Rathdrum and Through the Vale of Avoca

Continuing southwards for 5 miles (8km) on the Military Road, you go through **Rathdrum**, which has some good untouched pubs, such as P. Cullen's Bar in the Main Street, and some enchanting woodland in the Avondale valley. The 'big' **Avondale House** (*open Mar–Oct daily 11–6; adm; t (0404) 46111, www.coillte.ie*), to the south of town, was the birthplace and lifelong home of that great Irishman Charles Stewart Parnell, who fought for Home Rule and the land rights of the peasants during the 19th century. Now restored to its appearance as it was in Parnell's time, it is open as a museum, and the estate is a forest park, through which two nature trails have been signposted. Three rooms in the late-18th-century house are devoted to displays of Parnell memorabilia.

The scenery continues to be delightful as you travel south through the **Vale of Avoca**, which is where the Avonmore and Avonbeg Rivers meet, and was immortalized in the Romantic poetry of Thomas Moore's 'The Meeting of the Waters'. Copper is mined in the valley still. The meeting is marked by a very ugly pub with a glassy ballroom tacked on to its back wall; but the atmosphere inside is difficult to beat because everybody is there to have some fun. Traditional bands play here at the weekends; some of them are excellent.

You can understand the appeal of such scenery to the Romantic poets of the late 19th century, among them William Wordsworth, who did an Irish tour. About 2½ miles (4km) to the north-east of Avoca village and the rivers, and high above them, is the **Motte Stone**, a glacial boulder of granite perched on the summit of the 800ft (244m) Croneblane Ridge. It commands a spectacular view and used to be employed by travellers as a milestone because it is halfway between Dublin and Wexford. Along the valley road are shops selling the well-known Avoca-weave rugs, which make lovely presents. You can visit **Avoca Handweavers** (**t** *(0402) 35105, www.avoca.ie;* see *also p.571*) in Avoca village; this is the oldest working mill in Ireland and one of Wicklow's most popular attractions.

Woodenbridge, at the end of this 'sweet vale', was the site of a gold rush in 1796, and supplied much gold for Ireland's earliest goldsmiths. Nearby, the Croghan Mountain was the scene of another 18th-century gold rush.

Blessington to Baltinglass

West Wicklow is relatively unexplored, and ruggedly attractive. Travelling south-west out of Dublin on the N81, you come to **Blessington**, a small town on the northern arm of the **Poulaphouca Reservoir**. This huge reservoir, formed by the damming of the Liffey, is picturesque enough to warrant a visit. Other attractions are **Russborough House** and its art collection (*open 10–5 May–Sept daily, Easter and Oct Sun and bank hols; picnic area, tea-room, shop and children's playground; gardens with maze and rhododendron garden, but visits by appointment only; adm; **t** (045) 865239*). The house was designed by Richard Cassels in the 1740s for the Earl of Milltown, and its silvery Wicklow granite has aged magnificently. It is Palladian in style, with a central block and two semi-circular loggias that link the wings. The main rooms are decorated with elaborate plasterwork. The house was purchased by Sir Alfred and Lady Beit in 1952, and their art collection is one of the chief attractions of Ireland. It includes paintings by Rubens, Gainsborough, Murillo, Reynolds, Vernet, Velasquez and Guardi. Sadly, the house has been burgled on a couple of occasions (once by the IRA) and some of its treasures have been lost; others were given to the National Gallery in Dublin. It's a shame, too, that visits are limited to a 45-minute guided tour, as you don't get much time to look at the ones that are left.

Heading south from Blessington, you will come to **Poulaphouca Lake**, which forms the Wicklow Gap, and the lovely **Hollywood Glen**, before you arrive at Laragh. The nearby **Glen of Imaal** is also beautiful, although part of it is used as a military firing range, so you need to keep an eye out for the signs. Inside the Glen, at Derrynamuck on the Knockanarrigan to Rathdangan road, the **Michael Dwyer Cottage Museum** (*open mid-June–mid-Sept daily 2–6; adm; t (0404) 45325/45352*) commemorates the leader of the 1798 Rising. British troops had him surrounded in this old farmhouse, but he still managed to escape.

Baltinglass, which lies 19 miles (30km) south of Blessington on the N81, is in the Slaney Valley. The remains of a 12th-century **Cistercian abbey** lie to the north of the town. Six Gothic arches on either side of the nave remain to delight the eye. Above the town to the east rises Baltinglass Hill, at the top of which are the remains of a large cairn containing a group of **Bronze Age burial chambers**. It is an easy climb, and there is a splendid view over the countryside.

Wicklow Town to Arklow

The pleasant and resolutely sleepy county town, **Wicklow**, overlooks a crescent-shaped shingle bay. The English name is a corruption of the Danish *Wyking alo*, 'Viking Meadow'. Maurice Fitzgerald, a Norman warlord, built the ruined **Black Castle** on the promontory overlooking the sea at the eastern end of the town. He was granted the lands here by Henry II in the 12th century, but he did not have a very comfortable existence, for the castle was constantly raided by the O'Tooles and O'Byrnes. **Wicklow Gaol** (*open daily mid-Mar–end Sept 10- 6, Oct 10–5, adm; t (0404) 61599, www.wicklowshistoricgaol.com*) is fittingly dedicated to 1798, the famine, transportation of rebels and criminals, and all the other depressing events of Irish history this grim old building witnessed. The 18th-century Church of Ireland **church**, off the main street, has a fine carved Romanesque doorway in the south porch.

The ruined **Dunganstown Castle**, about six miles (9.5km) to the south on an unclassified road, is far more spectacular than anything in the town. At **Ashford**, a couple of miles north of Wicklow Town on the main Dublin to Wexford road, is **Mount Usher Gardens** (*open 15 Mar–Oct daily 10.30–6; adm; t (0404) 40116/40205, www.mount-usher-gardens.com*), a wonderful example of a naturalized garden. On the banks of the river Vartry, it is famous for its eucalyptus and encryphia, and the woodland walks provide beautiful vistas of azalea, rhododendrons and spring bulbs.

By taking the R750, it is possible to stay close to the coast all the way from Wicklow to Arklow, passing some lovely sandy beaches sheltered by dunes. Both Wicklow town and Arklow have beaches of their own; they are popular enough in summer, but you would be better off looking for the better ones in-between, especially the fine long strand at **Brittas Bay**.

Another Danish settlement in the 9th and 10th centuries, **Arklow** grew up at the mouth of the River Avoca. It is now a popular resort town, because the beaches surrounding it are safe for bathing. There is a golf course and a sports centre, and summer boat rides on the river, starting from behind the car park, off the main street. The remains of a 12th-century **castle** stand on the Bluff overlooking the river. It was constructed by Theobald Butler, and became one of the four strongest fortresses belonging to the Ormonde family. Later it was sacked by the Irish, then ruined by Cromwell in 1649. Father Murphy, the leader of the insurgents in the 1798 rising, was repulsed in Arklow with heavy losses, and there is a monument to his memory marking the site where he died. **Arklow Maritime Museum** (*open summer Mon–Sat*

10–1 and 2–5; adm; t (0402) 32868), in the Old Technical School on St Mary's Road, details this town's surprisingly rich career, which has involved boat-building, fishing and plenty of smuggling. There's everything a small-town maritime museum should have, down to the model ship made of matchsticks by an old sailor.

County Wexford

If you are invading Ireland from the south, as the Normans did, you will land at Rosslare Harbour, which is the warmest and driest part of the whole country. The countryside of Wexford is said to be rather similar to that of Normandy, with low hills, rich valleys and extremely tidy farms. Some of the thatched cottages here have upper floors, which is something you do not find elsewhere in Ireland. Perhaps this is a sign of the relative prosperity of the peasants in this area, and the influence of the English settlers in the 16th century. Vegetables and fruit are grown in the light, sandy soil, farm implements are manufactured, and bacon is cured. The population is approximately 100,000.

Along the coast there are gloriously sandy beaches and some old resort towns. Many Irish families still take their holidays here rather than in southern Europe. Towerhouses dating from the 14th century are a common feature; some are ivy-clad but others blend into the farmhouses and yards that have grown up around them. Happily, these centuries-old buildings have been treated with a bit more care than is usual in Ireland. There are some magnificent monastic remains and old castles to explore, as well as Kennedy Park, planted with shrubs and trees from all over the world to honour John F. Kennedy.

For the garden lover there are several small and beautiful gardens that are open by arrangement with their owners. Bird-lovers will be delighted to find herring gulls, kittiwakes, razorbills, puffin colonies, petrels, gannets, Greenland white-faced geese and terns in the numerous bird sanctuaries that have been established around the coast. Wexford is internationally famous for its Opera Festival, which was established in 1951 and specializes in rarely produced works. This week of first-class music and performers takes place in the autumn, and Wexford town buzzes with life.

History

County Wexford has a full history, due to its closeness to Britain and Europe. It has been the landing place of many; and in past centuries trade across the sea was constant. This brief sketch starts in about 350 BC, when the Celts arrived from Europe in waves. They absorbed many of the existing customs, but they also imposed their own legal, religious and cultural beliefs. Their ruling elite divided into hereditary royal families who ruled over small politically defined areas, and were often at odds with their neighbours. What is now Wexford had a hereditary enmity with the kingdom of Ossory, which roughly corresponds to County Kilkenny. The monks arrived in about the 5th century and with ease, it seems, took over the mantle of respect and power from their pagan predecessors.

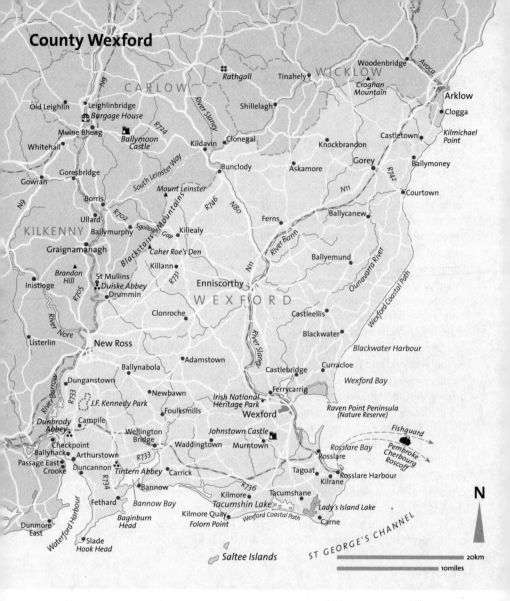

County Wexford

CARLOW

WICKLOW

KILKENNY

WEXFORD

Woodenbridge
Avoca
Rathgall
Tinahely
Croghan Mountain
Arklow
Old Leighlin
Leighlinbridge
Burgage House
Shillelagh
Clogga
Muine Bheag
Ballymoon Castle
Kildavin
Clonegal
Castletown
Kilmichael Point
Whitehall
River Slaney
R724
Knockbrandon
Goresbridge
South Leinster Way
Bunclody
Askamore
Gorey
Ballymoney
Gowran
Mount Leinster
R742
Courtown
N9
Borris
R702
R746
N80
Ferns
Ballycanew
N11
Ullard
Ballymurphy
Sgollogh Gap
Killealy
Blackstairs Mountains
Graignamanagh
Caher Roe's Den
River Bann
Ballyemund
Killann
R731
Ounavarra River
Brandon Hill
St Mullins
Duiske Abbey
Enniscorthy
N11
Wexford Coastal Path
Inistioge
Drummin
Clonroche
Castleellis
R705
River Nore
Blackwater
Listerlin
New Ross
River Slaney
Blackwater Harbour
Adamstown
Curracloe
Ballynabola
Castlebridge
Wexford Bay
Dunganstown
Newbawn
Ferrycarrig
River Barrow
R733
J.F. Kennedy Park
Irish National Heritage Park
Raven Point Peninsula (Nature Reserve)
Foulksmills
Dunbrody Abbey
Campile
Wellington Bridge
Wexford
Fishguard
Checkpoint
Waddingtown
Murntown
Johnstown Castle
Pembroke Cherbourg Roscoff
Ballyhack
Arthurstown
R733
Rosslare Bay
Passage East
Duncannon
Tintern Abbey
Carrick
Rosslare
Crooke
Tagoat
Rosslare Harbour
R734
Bannow
Kilrane
Fethard
Bannow Bay
Kilmore
R736
Tacumshane
Dunmore East
Baginbun Head
Kilmore Quay
Tacumshin Lake
Lady's Island Lake
Folorn Point
Wexford Coastal Path
Carne
Slade
Hook Head
Waterford Harbour
Saltee Islands
ST GEORGE'S CHANNEL

N

20km
10miles

The arrival of the Norsemen or Vikings in AD 819 was a blow to the rich monasteries, which were plundered and sacked. The Norsemen liked it here and stayed, establishing a settlement called *Waesfjord* ('Muddy Fjord'), now known as Wexford Town. All over Ireland, the story is the same: it is the Norsemen and the Anglo-Normans who founded the towns, never the Celts.

The *sept* that seemed to produce the most dynamic leaders was that of the MacMurraghs. They played a great part in Ireland's history, and made alliances with Norsemen, Welsh and Anglo-Norman mercenaries when it suited them. Surnames did not exist in Ireland until the 11th century, but it was a MacMurragh king who in

Getting There and Around

By Sea

Rosslare Harbour handles passenger and car ferries arriving from Fishguard, Pembroke and the French ports of Le Havre and Cherbourg.

There's not much of anything in Rosslare Harbour, though you'll find taxis for nearby Wexford (there are only a few, however, so disembark quickly if you need one), and often Bus Éireann coaches bound for Waterford or Dublin are timed to meet the boats.

See also **Travel**, pp.90–91.

By Rail

Mainline services from Dublin to Wexford and Rosslare stop at a number of smaller places en route.

Iarnród Éireann, t 1850 366222, *www.irishrail.ie*

Wexford Station, t (053) 22522

By Bus

Bus Éireann Expressway buses from Dublin go to Wexford Town and Rosslare hourly, and from there travel westwards as far as Waterford and Cork. For details of local services, call **t** (053) 22522.

Bus Éireann, t (01) 836 6111, *www.buseireann.ie*

By Bike

The Bike Shop, 9 Selskar St, Wexford, **t** (053) 22514

Hayes Cycles, 108 South Main St, Wexford, **t** (053) 22462, *hayescycles@eircom.net*

Kenny's, Slaney St, Enniscorthy, **t** (054) 33255 or **t** (087) 232 1137, *kennysfb@unison.ie*

Festivals

April–May

Viking Festival, Wexford, **t** (053) 23401
Wexford Book Festival, t (053) 22226

June–July

Duncannon Fort Re-enactments, **t** (051) 389454. Military re-enactments by the Munster Military Vehicle and Re-enactment Group.
Strawberry Fair, Enniscorthy, **t** (087) 263 7503. A 10-day celebration of the strawberry harvest.

July

Eileen Aroon Festival, Bunclody, **t** (086) 836 5265. Pub quizzes and talent competitions, free music on the square and more.
Kilmore Quay Seafood Festival, t (053) 29918. Fresh seafood, races and live music.
Wexford Hooves and Grooves Festival, **t** (053) 44634. An event featuring horseracing and live entertainment.

August

Blessing of the Fleet, Kilmore, **t** (053) 29922
Courtown Failte Festival, t (055) 22148
Gorey Summer Fair, t (055) 20640
Sandworld, Duncannon, **t** (086) 601 8892. A sand-sculpting competition between international teams.
Taghmon Mardi Gras, t (053) 34197

September

Blackstairs Blues Festival, t (054) 33747

October–November

Wexford Opera Festival, Theatre Royal, Wexford Town, **t** (053) 22400, *www.wexfordopera.com*

1068 laid siege to Bristol – the only Irish monarch to threaten an English city. His descendant, Diarmuid (or Dermot) MacMurragh (1110–71), is reviled in Irish history for having invited the Anglo-Normans over to help him in his territorial struggles. In fact, Diarmuid was following a well-used practice in hiring Flemish, Norman and Welsh mercenaries; but these ones stayed on, and laid claim to the whole of Ireland. The names Fleming, Prendergast, Fitzhenry and Roche are a reminder of these people, and can be seen around the county on shop and pub signs. The MacMurraghs produced another great leader in the late 14th century: Art MacMurragh Kavanagh became king of what is now Carlow, Wexford and the old kingdom of Leinster. He was so powerful that Richard II was forced into leaving his precarious throne in England to lead two campaigns against him in 1394 and 1399. Both were failures, and he lost his own throne into the bargain. The Normans were gradually absorbed into the Gaelic way of life. Up until the beginning of the 20th century, in the ancient Norman baronies of Forth and Bargy in the south-east corner, the locals spoke in the Flemish-sounding Yola dialect. Some words are still in everyday use – for example, *stour*, meaning a truculent woman. Later, settlers were brought in over the centuries by the British government and given land in payment for military services. Wexford is perhaps the most 'planted' of all the Irish counties; but the 'foreigners' moved in gradually, and not with the systematic force with which the Scots moved into the north. The Rebellion of 1798 is remembered in the many memorials placed around the countryside and towns; its 200th anniversary was a major event throughout Ireland, but especially in Wexford, where a new museum dedicated to it was opened in Enniscorthy. There is great emotive value placed on it still, because it was such a brave and pathetic struggle: thousands of peasants armed with pitchforks held off the well-trained forces of the English for six weeks, until they were defeated at Vinegar Hill with huge losses (*see* **History**, p.18).

Northern Wexford

Along the east coast is the pretty village of **Castletown** and the family resort of **Ballymoney**. There are numerous sandy coves here, perfect for bathing. **Courtown**, on the R742, is a harbour resort on the Ounavarra River with two miles (3.2km) of sandy beach. **Blackwater** is a very pleasant coastal village that has won numerous 'tidy town' competitions. This national award, run by the Tourist Board, inspires proud villagers to spruce up their paintwork and tidy their gardens each year. Courtown is said to be the *Ardladhru* ('Fort of Ladhru') frequently mentioned in the Gaelic sagas. (Ladhru was one of the principal Celtic leaders at the time of their first landings.) There is a fine hilltop earthworks just outside the village. **Curracloe Strand**, on the way back to Wexford, is superb for walking or bathing. It has 6 miles (9.7km) of golden beach and some pretty whitewashed houses. The **Raven Point Peninsula**, stretching from Curracloe to Wexford Harbour mouth, is a protected nature reserve, with 3 miles (5km) of sand dunes, forest, and bird- and plantlife.

Enniscorthy

Along the side of the Blackstairs Mountains you sometimes meet a lone deer making its way between here and the Wicklow Mountains. The tiny farms on these slopes are more reminiscent of the west than the neat prosperity of the rest of Wexford. Stop in **Killann** (on the R731 from New Ross) at **Rackards Pub**, one of the friendliest traditional pubs in Ireland; a local haunt, it has no hint of 'the singing pubs for tourists' theme. The Rackard family are famous for their skill at hurling – four of them were in the team that won the Leinster Trophy in 1951. Killann was an important ecclesiastical centre in medieval times, though nothing much remains.

Tourist Information

Enniscorthy: The Castle, **t** (054) 34699. *Open mid-June–Aug*
Gorey: Lower Main St, **t** (055) 21248

Shopping

Crafts

Badger Hill Pottery, Enniscorthy, **t** (054) 35060
Kiltrea Bridge Pottery Ltd, Kiltrea Bridge, Cairn, Enniscorthy, **t** (054) 35107

Sports and Activities

Golf

Courtown Golf Course, Kiltennel, near Gorey, **t** (055) 25166, *www.courtowngolfclub.com*
Enniscorthy Golf Club, Knockmarshall, **t** (054) 33191

Walking

Wexford coastal path, from Kilmichael Point to Ballyhack, stretches for 138 miles (221km). Ask for details from the tourist office.

Where to Stay and Eat

Marlfield House, Gorey, **t** (055) 21124, *www. marlfieldhouse.com* (*luxury*). A fine Regency country house. The modern restaurant serves *haute cuisine* (*expensive*), including lobster from a tank, oysters, scallops, veal, and other local fresh ingredients. Advance reservations are essential.
Ballinkeele House, Ballinkeele, Enniscorthy, **t** (053) 38105, *www.ballinkeele.com*

(*moderate–expensive*). An historic 19th-century country house, family run. Dinner (*moderate*) must be booked by 11am. *Closed Dec and Jan.*
Clohamon House, Bunclody, **t** (054) 77253 (*moderate*). This charming 18th-century house is set in an estate of 180 acres (40ha) in the lovely Slaney Valley, on a hill with a view of Mount Leinster. There is private fishing for salmon or trout on the Slaney River, a Connemara Pony stud, delicious food and comfortable period rooms with 4-poster beds. Lady Maria Levinge is a charming hostess with a good knowledge of local goings-on.
Salville House, Enniscorthy, **t** (054) 35252, *www.salvillehouse.com* (*moderate*). Large, simple bedrooms overlooking a pretty wood. Family-run, the place has its own restaurant.
Clone House, Ferns, **t** (054) 66113 (*inexpensive*). A pretty farmhouse with clean, attractive rooms and well-prepared, simple food.
Moss Cottage, Bunclody, **t** (054) 77828, *www.mosscottageireland.com* (*inexpensive*). A B&B in a courtyard setting with landscaped gardens. Self-catering accommodation is also available.

Entertainment and Nightlife

Ar mBreacha ('Our Roots'), Raheen, Ballyduff, **t** (054) 44148 or **t** (054) 83256. Evenings of Irish stories, music and dancing at the House of Storytelling on the first Tue of each month, and every Tue night in July and Aug. Call in advance.

Enniscorthy is the most attractive town in County Wexford. It is a thriving market town on the River Slaney, presided over by Vinegar Hill, from where there is a great view of the river and the rich farming land around. You might time your arrival for the Strawberry Fair in early July (*see* p.581). Enniscorthy was one of the hotspots of the 1798 rising, commemorated at the **National 1798 Visitors' Centre** (*open Mon–Sat 9.30–6.30, Sun 11–6.30; adm;* **t** *(054) 37596/7*), where you can learn the entire story through exhibits and audio-visual presentations. **Wexford County Museum** (*open summer Mon–Sat 10–6, Sun 2–6, winter exc Dec and Jan daily 2–5, Dec and Jan Sun 2–6; adm;* **t** *(054) 35926*) is in the **castle**, built by Raymond le Gros and later owned by the Roche family. It has an interesting folk section. All around County Wexford it is traditional for mummers (or rhymers) to act out the characters of Irish heroes by dancing to the rhythm of Irish reels. They dress in straw suits and tinsel and act out the perpetual struggle of good over evil. This tradition actually originated in England; in other parts of Ireland, custom differs. Like all country customs, it is in decline, but the mummers still 'visit' the houses of local people at Christmas time, and you might be lucky and see them perform at the Wexford Opera Festival (*see* p.581).

Bunclody (N80), on the borders with County Carlow in the north-west of the county, is a very pretty mountainside town. Many people stay here to go walking on the Blackstairs Mountains. It has a very attractive Church of Ireland church. Nearer to Enniscorthy, on the N11, is **Ferns**. This town is rather like Swords in County Dublin – full of memories and former glory. In the 12th century the King of Leinster, Dermot MacMurragh (the one who invited the Normans to invade), made it his capital and founded a rich abbey here, but after the Norman conquest the town declined. It has been pillaged and burnt so often that there is little left of it. Yet it is a fascinating place with a vast, ruined **cathedral**, a segment of which is now the Church of Ireland cathedral. A 13th-century Anglo-Norman **castle** built by William de Valence, which has a fine chapel in its south-east tower, was built on the site of the ancient fortress of the kings of Leinster. It was destroyed by the O'Connor and O'Rourke forces in their conflict with Dermot MacMurragh, and it was here that he waited for his allies, the Normans, sending guides to Baginburn to show them the way. Dermot is buried here in the ruins of the **Augustinian priory** that he founded. The High Cross covered in a fretwork pattern marks his grave. An interesting quirk of fate links Ferns with another man who may have changed the course of history: in the graveyard of the modern Catholic church is the grave of Father Ned Redmond, who as a young priest in France saved Napoleon Bonaparte from drowning during his student days.

Southern Wexford

Wexford Town

Wexford Town is one of the most atmospheric of all Irish places. It was originally settled by a Celtic Belgic tribe called the Manapii, about 350 BC, and later by the Vikings, who gave it the name *Waesfjord*. They ruled from the 9th to the 12th century and built up a flourishing port around the River Slaney and its outlet to the sea. Then the Normans, allies of Dermot McMurragh, captured it and built walls, castles and abbeys in their usual disciplined pattern. Many of the winding streets are so narrow that you could shake hands across them. Cromwell left as bloody a reputation behind him here as in Drogheda. He occupied the town in 1649 during his campaign to subdue the 'rebellious Irish', and destroyed many of the churches.

Most people come to Wexford for the Opera Festival, held every year in October (*see* 'Festivals', p.581). Programmes of lesser-known operas are produced with world-famous soloists, an excellent local chorus and the RTE Symphony Orchestra. Its reputation for originality and quality is held worldwide. Many fringe events, exhibitions, revues, and plays take place at the same time.

Tourist Information

New Ross: t (051) 421857.
Open mid-June–Aug Mon–Sat.
Wexford: Crescent Quay, **t** (053) 23111

Shopping

Crafts
You'll find good craft shops in Wexford Town and at the John F. Kennedy Park.
Basketry Studio, Saltmills, **t** (051) 397618
Bevel Country Furniture, Fethard,
t (051) 397463
Butlersland Craft Centre, Butlerstown,
New Ross
Ceadogán Rug Shop, Barrystown,
Wellingtonbridge, **t** (051) 561349,
www.ceadogan.ie
Kilmore Quay Country Crafts,
t (053) 29704/29885
Nicola Marray Knitwear, Waddington,
t (053) 39599
Paul Maloney Pottery, Ballindas, Barnstown,
t (053) 20188. *Closed Sun.*
Westgate Design, North Main St, Wexford,
t (053) 23787

Food and Drink
Carrigbyrne Cheese, Adamstown, **t** (054) 40560.
Delicious hexagonal Brie-type cheese.
Greenacres, 7 Selskar, Wexford, **t** (053) 22975,
www.greenacres.ie. Good veg, wholefoods
and a small but very good meat counter.
Rainbow Wholefoods, Walkers Mall,
North Main St, Wexford, **t** (053) 24624

Internet Access

FDYS Training Centre, Frances St, Wexford,
t (053) 23262
Wexford Library, Redmond Sq, Wexford,
t (053) 21637

Sports and Activities

Fishing
For **deep-sea fishing** charters, contact one
of the following:
Kilmore Quay Boat Charters, Kilmore Quay,
t (053) 29704
Southeast Charters, Duncannon, **t** (051) 389242

Golf
Rosslare Golf Club, Rosslare Strand,
t (053) 32203, *www.rosslaregolf.com*
St Helen's Bay Golf and Country Club,
Kilrane, **t** (053) 33669/33234,
www.sthelensbay.com

Open Farms
Ballylane Visitor Farm, New Ross (off N25),
t (051) 425666. A farm that also offers
orienteering courses.

Pleasure Cruises
Celtic Canal Cruisers, New Ross, **t** (051) 421723,
Cruises up the River Barrow Apr–Oct, or all
year at Tullamore, Co. Offaly (**t** (0506) 21861).

Ponytrekking
Horetown Equestrian Centre, Foulksmills,
t (051) 565786. Hunting courses, picnic
rides, hacking and beginners' courses, plus
accommodation in a lovely 17th-century
manor house.
Seaview Farmhouse Pony Trekking,
Seaview, St Kearns, **t** (051) 562239
Shelmalier Riding Stables, Forth Mountain,
Trinity, Taghmon, **t** (053) 39251

Walking
For information about the **Wexford coastal
path**, *see* p.583.
Summer evenings, a **walking tour** of Wexford
Town, led by a local historical society member,
departs from Whites Hotel and The Talbot
Hotel; contact the tourist office for full details.

The centre of town is a small square called the **Bull Ring** – a reminder of the Norman pastime of bull-baiting, which was held on this spot – and contains a figure of an Irish pikeman, commemorating the Wexford insurgents of 1798. Some bits of the Norman town walls remain, along with one gate, which now houses the **Westgate Heritage Centre** (*open May–Oct Mon–Fri 10–2 and 2.30–5, Sat 10–2; adm; t (053) 46506*). Here you can see an audio-visual presentation on the history of

Watersports

Ramsgrange Shielbaggan Outdoor Education Centre, New Ross, t (051) 389550. Sailing and snorkeling, canoeing, archery and rockclimbing.

Rosslare Sailboard and Watersports Centre, t (053) 32566. Sailboards, canoeing and more. *Closed Sept–May.*

Wexford Harbour Boat Club, t (053) 22039, *www.whbtc.com.* Water-skiing and sailing.

Where to Stay

Rosslare Harbour and the road leading north to Wexford have a vast number of hotels and B&Bs, so you shouldn't have too much trouble finding a place if you get off the ferry in the evening. Even so, in the summer months it's best to book ahead.

Note that the smart White's Hotel In Wexford is closed for renovation until spring 2007.

Dunbrody Country House, Arthurstown, t (051) 389600, *www.dunbrodyhouse.com (luxury).* A Georgian house set in a spacious park near the sea, retaining its period decoration. There is courteous service and superior cuisine (*expensive*), including breakfasts available 'til noon.

Ferrycarrig Hotel, Ferrycarrig Bridge, Wexford, t (053) 20999 or t 1890 516171, *www.ferrycarrighotel.ie (luxury).* A modern hotel on the Slaney Estuary, with good views and leisure facilities.

Kilmokea Country Manor, Campile, t (051) 388109, *www.kilmokea.com (expensive–luxury).* A near-perfect place set beside a walled garden in 7 acres on Great Island in the Barrow Estuary, offering private trout fishing and horse-riding grounds, cream teas and aromatherapy massages.

Newbay Country House, near Wexford, t (053) 42779. *www.newbaycountryhouse.com (expensive).* Log fires, excellent meals and pine/period furnishings in an 1820s house

2 miles (3.2km) from Wexford and 20mins from Rosslare. There are lovely gardens that you can stroll in.

The Talbot Hotel, The Quay, Wexford, t (053) 22566; *www.talbothotel.ie (expensive).* An elegant waterside hotel offering superb harbour views from many of its plush guestrooms, plus a health and fitness centre in a former grain mill, with a supervised play room so parents can get some pampering.

Monfin House, St John's, Enniscorthy, t (054) 38582, *www.monfinhouse.com (moderate–expensive).* A traditional Georgian country home built in 1823 and restored by the current owners. It's not suitable for children. Note that 24hrs' notice is required for dinner.

Clonard House, Clonard Great, near Wexford, t (053) 43141, *www.clonardhouse.com (moderate).* A late-Georgian house with a staircase that curves into the ceiling because money ran out for the top floor. There are perfect views and farmland to the sea, plus simple, delicious food.

Creacon Lodge, New Ross, t (051) 421897, *www.creaconlodge.com (moderate).* A cosy house with tiny mullioned windows and creeper climbing up the walls, close to the John F. Kennedy Park.

Glendine Country House, Arthurstown, New Ross, t (051) 389500/389258, *www.glendinehouse.com (moderate).* A Georgian country house built in 1830 and set in landscaped grounds with a view of the harbour.

Kilrane House, Kilrane, Rosslare Harbour, t (053) 33135 (*inexpensive*). A comfortable house 2mins from Rosslare Harbour.

Self-catering

Mill Road Farm, Kilmore Quay, t (053) 29633, *www.millroadfarm.com (inexpensive).* Six self-catering cottages with 2–4 beds, plus a family-run B&B.

Wexford. Near West Gate, off Abbey Street, is **Selskar Abbey**. It was built in the late 12th century, and the remains consist of a square, battlemented tower and a church with a double nave and part of its west gable. The 19th-century **church** (*always accessible*) stands on the spot where the first treaty between the Anglo-Normans and the Irish was ratified in 1169. Wexford's waterfront is a dowdy, long-neglected part of town that is currently being redeveloped. Notice the **Commodore John Barry**

The Old Deanery County House
Courtyard Cottages, Ferns, Enniscorthy,
t (054) 66474, *www.theolddeanery.com*
(*inexpensive*). Converted stone stables with
open log fires, plus garden apartments.

Eating Out

The Cedar Lodge Restaurant and Hotel,
Carrighbyrne, Newbawn, New Ross,
t (051) 428386, *www.prideofeirehotels.com*
(*expensive*). Good-quality food, including
oysters, mussels, lobster, crab, Slaney wild
salmon and lamb.

La Dolce Vita, 6/7 Trimmers Lane, Wexford,
t (053) 70806 (*moderate–expensive*).
Superb Italian food.

Clifford House, Rosslare Harbour, t (053) 33226,
www.cliffordhouse.net (*moderate*).
A small family-run restaurant overlooking
the sea. The home-cooking includes seafood
specialities. B&B accommodation is also
offered. *Closed Sun, and Oct–Easter.*

Galley River Cruising Restaurant,
The Quay, New Ross, t (051) 421723
(*moderate*). Six-course meals combined
with cruises on the River Barrow.

Heavens Above, The Sky and the Ground,
112 South Main St, t (053) 21273 (*moderate*).
A delightful restaurant above a well-loved
pub (*see below*). The excellent food,
including seafood platters, and the vast
wine list make it a must.

La Riva, Crescent Quay, Wexford, t (053) 24330
(*moderate*). A bistro-style restaurant
overlooking the harbour, serving superb
seafood, steaks and home-made pasta.

Lobster Pot, Carne, south of Rosslare,
t (053) 31110 (*moderate*). A cosy, popular
bar and restaurant serving great seafood
and pub grub all day. *Closed Jan and Mon
exc bank hols.*

Mange 2, 100 South Main St, Wexford,
t (053) 44033 (*moderate*). A simply but

stylishly furnished restaurant with red
walls and wooden tables, offering excellent
French-inspired cuisine served efficiently.

Oyster Restaurant, Strand Rd, Rosslare Strand,
t (053) 32439 (*moderate*). A place with scallops
and black sole as specialities.

Sqigl Restaurant, Duncannon, near New Ross,
t (051) 389700/389188 (*moderate*). A former
military building on the Waterford estuary,
serving contemporary cuisine and local
cheeses. *Closed Mon, Tue and lunch.*

Cappuccinos, 25 North Main St, Wexford
(*inexpensive*). A very popular lunchtime snack
spot, featuring hot ciabatta sandwiches
among the wide-ranging options.

Horse and Hounds Inn, N25, Ballynabola,
t (051) 428482 (*inexpensive*). Gargantuan
portions of simple food, including good
stew. Accommodation is available.

Kings Bay Inn, Arthurstown, t (051) 389173
(*inexpensive*). Good bar food.

Entertainment and Nightlife

Traditional Music

In Wexford Town it is difficult to stay bored
or sober for long. Try the following:

The Centenary Stores, Charlotte St,
t (053) 24424. Traditional music Mon
and Wed evenings and Sun mornings,
plus folk/blues Tue evenings.

The Sky and the Ground, South Main St,
Wexford, t (053) 21273. A convivial old
shop and pub where everything has been
left the way it was in the 1960s, including
the groceries. There's a snug and good
traditional music Sun–Thur nights.

Westgate Tavern, t (053) 22086. Folk and blues
(Thur pm), ballads (Sun pm), and pub theatre
July and Aug. Bar food is served all day.

Wren's Nest, Custom House Quay, Wexford,
t (053) 22359

Memorial on Crescent Quay: he was born 10 miles (16km) away at Ballysampson,
and is remembered as the father of the US navy, and the first to capture a British ship
in the Revolutionary War. A duplicate statue stands in front of Independence Hall in
Philadelphia. Lady Wilde (1826–96), the mother of Oscar and known as 'Speranza', was
born in the Old Rectory, Main Street. Sir Robert McClure (1807–73), who discovered the
Northwest Passage in the Arctic, is another famous Wexford son.

There are mudflats close to the town at **Ferrybank**, which were reclaimed from the sea in the 1840s. The **Wexford Wildfowl Reserve** (*open daily Apr–Sept 9–6, Oct–Mar daily 10–5; guided tours on request;* **t** *(053) 23129*) has more than 2,500 acres (1,000ha) of mudflats, or 'slobs', for an enormous variety of birdlife in winter. Vast numbers of Greenland white-fronted geese rest and feed here. There is a lecture hall, library and observation tower in the public area of the reserve.

About 2½ miles (4km) to the north of Wexford Town, at Ferrycarrig, is the **Irish National Heritage Park** (*open daily 9.30–6.30; adm;* **t** *(053) 20733, www.inhp.com*). Here you will find reconstructions of life as it was in the past, from 7000 BC to the medieval period. It is a scholarly and exciting exhibition, with full-scale replicas of the dwellings, places of worship, forts and burial grounds over the ages, and contains everything from a prehistoric *crannóg* to an incredible Viking ship.

Three miles (4.8km) south of Wexford, near Murntown, is **Johnstown Castle** (*open daily 9.30–5.30; adm in summer;* **t** *(053) 42888*). Built in the 19th-century Gothic style, it is now a state agricultural college, and visitors can tour the landscaped gardens and lakes but not the castle itself. There are three lakes and a walled garden, as well as the old estate farmyard, now home to the college's **Irish Agricultural Museum** (*open Mon–Fri 9–5, plus Apr–Oct Sat and Sun 2–5; adm;* **t** *(053) 42888*).

The Southern Coast: Rosslare to Hook Head

Five miles (8km) to the north of Rosslare Harbour, the ferry port, is the resort of **Rosslare**, boasting 6 miles (9.7km) of curving strand. The coastline beyond it, which is approached from the R736, is well worth travelling around. On **Lady's Island** you can see the ruins of an Augustinian priory and a Norman castle that was constructed in 1237. The rare roseate tern can be heard here, if seldom seen, and woolly cottonweed, a plant that died out on the south coast of England a couple of centuries ago, still grows on the sea bar. The island is sacred to the Blessed Virgin and is still a favourite place of pilgrimage.

In **Tacumshane**, which is a tiny village consisting of a few houses and a petrol station-cum-shop, you can see an example of a working **windmill** with an attractive thatched top. This is part of the ancient Barony of Forth, and the technology for the windmill was brought here by the families of Flemish and Norman mercenaries. Michael Meyler, who works at the petrol station, keeps the key to the mill, and will let you have a look round it. At Tagoat is **Yola Farmstead Folk Park** (*open May–Oct daily 9.30–5, Mar, Apr and Nov Mon–Fri 9.30–4.30; adm;* **t** *(053) 32611*), with a craft centre and a great tea-room.

Kilmore Quay is an attractive thatched fishing village from where you can take a boat, weather permitting, out to the **Saltee Islands**. Nobody lives on these islands, which are verdant with waist-high bracken. Although they are private property, with the result that visitors are prohibited, boatmen on the Quay will gladly take you out for a trip around them; just ask one of them. The puffins and other waterfowl here are magnificent, and there is a curious coronation place on the island, which was erected by the self-styled King of the Saltees in 1943. The view from Kilmore Harbour along the headlands looks rather like the 19th-century Dutch-influenced landscapes of the Norwich School of painters. The **Guillemot Maritime Museum** (*open Easter–end May and Sept Sat and Sun 12 noon–6, June–Aug daily noon–6; adm; t (053) 29655*) is housed in what was Ireland's last working lightship.

Keeping close to the sea on the R736, turn left after Carrick if you wish to visit historic **Bannow**, which was the first corporate town established by the Normans. The town is now buried deep under the shifting sands – a process that began in the 17th century, though the benighted steeple and a couple of chimneys still returned MPs to the Irish parliament until 1798. All that is left today of this proud Norman town is the ruin of St Mary's Church and an old graveyard.

Near Saltmills, on the way to Hook Head, at the crossroads of the R733 and R734, you will pass **Tintern Abbey** (*open mid-June–late Sept daily 9.30–6.30; t (051) 562650, www.heritageireland.ie*), which is said to have been founded in AD 1200 by William the Marshall, Earl of Pembroke, in gratitude for surviving a terrible storm in St George's Channel. 'Mastless, a wreck unhelmed', he and his wife vowed that if they were saved they would found an abbey wherever they landed. The vessel beached itself in this lovely creek. The Office of Public Works has not yet finished restoring the magnificent Cistercian ruin, but it is still accessible to the public.

Nearby **Fethard** is a quiet resort, and there is a lovely walk over the sea pinks and grass to the ruined ramparts at **Baginburn**, which the Normans hastily built to repel the Norsemen and the Gaels. The Normans won the day by driving a herd of cattle into the advancing army. It is claimed that at the Creek of Baginburn, Ireland was lost and won. Certainly, the Norsemen of Waterford and MacMurragh's Ossory enemies were slaughtered, and those captured were thrown over the cliffs. Raymond le Gros held the earthworks until he joined Strongbow before the siege of Waterford in 1170.

The road continues down to the tip of **Hook Head**, where the 700-year-old **Hook Lighthouse** (*open for guided tours daily 9.30–5.30; t (051) 397055*) still keeps the light burning. The colourful and lively village of **Ballyhack** has a five-minute car ferry across the river to Passage East in County Waterford and a large **towerhouse** (*open daily in summer*). At **Duncannon** there is a star-shaped **fort** (*open June–mid-Sept daily 10–5.30; guided tours by request; adm; t (051) 389 454*) that was built in 1588 as a defence against the Spanish.

Around New Ross

Near to **Campile**, on the R733 and beside the winding River Barrow, is **Dunbrody Abbey**. This is is one of the most underestimated ruins in Ireland. It was constructed by the monks of St Mary's, Dublin, in 1182. A vast pile of weathered grey stone, it was suppressed in 1539. The west door is magnificent, and so are the lancet windows over the high altar. A small **visitor centre** (*open May–Sept daily 10–6; adm; t (051) 388603, www.dunbrodyabbey.com*) can be found opposite the abbey, with a tea-room, a small museum, a picnic site and a fully grown maze.

Close by you will find **Dunmain House** (*open May–Sept Tue–Sun 2–5.30; adm; t (051) 562122*), a 17th-century building that has retained a good many of its original features. It is covered with slates, which are quite a common sight as you travel further south in Ireland.

Kilmokea Country Manor and Gardens (*open daily 10–6; guided tours by advance booking; adm; t (051) 388109, www.kilmokea.com*), near Campile, is a Georgian rectory with superb grounds. There is a rock garden, an Italian garden, a traditional herbaceous border, a lupin border, wide lawns with topiary hedges and a water garden set in beautiful woodland. Stay a few days if you can (*see* p.586).

The Kennedy ancestral home is in **Dunganstown**. In 1848 Jack Kennedy left his family homestead for a new life in America after the dreadful years of the famine. From there the success story needs no further telling: suffice it to say that his great-grandson is remembered all over the world but especially in Ireland. The house is now a museum, **Kennedy Homestead** (*open May, June and Sept Mon–Fri 11.30–4.30, July and Aug daily 10–5; adm; t (051) 388264, www.kennedyhomestead.com*), containing a unique collection of John F. Kennedy memorabilia and an audio-visual display,

New Ross on the River Barrow has some ancient gabled houses and a medieval feel to it. It was built by Isobel, Strongbow's daughter, and has seen fighting against Cromwell and during the 1798 rebellion. Although there was much brutality on both sides, the massacre of Scullabogue during the 1798 rebellion is still not forgotten. Hundreds of British prisoners were burnt alive by the frightened rebels after they had fled from the fight in New Ross. It is possible to cruise for two or three hours on the rivers Nore and Barrow over a meal (*see* 'Eating Out', p.587).

The Kennedy Centre, at the Quay in New Ross (*t (051) 425239*), provides genealogical records for those compiling family histories in the area, and the JFK Trust financed the building of the **Dunbrody** (*open daily Apr–Sept 9–6, Oct–Mar 10–5; t (051) 425239, www.dunbrody.com*), a 176ft (54m) replica of one of the ships that took immigrants to America during the famine. Early in 1999 the ship left the New Ross docks for its maiden voyage to Boston, and it is now docked here in the town. Also here is the **Berkeley Forest House Costume and Toy Museum** (*open May–Sept Sat, call for times, t (051) 421361; adm*), which has a collection of rare and delicate dolls and costumes. The lady who runs it makes tiny and exquisite dolls' hats.

To the south of New Ross, just off the R374, you can visit the **John F. Kennedy Park and Arboretum** (*open daily Apr and Sept 10–6.30, May–Aug 10–8, Oct–Mar 10–5; adm; t (051) 388171, www.heritageireland.ie*), which contains some marvellous young trees and more than 4,500 species of shrubs. The latter are grouped according to where they are found in the world.

County Carlow

County Carlow, the second-smallest county in Ireland, lies between counties Wicklow, Wexford and Kilkenny. It is flat, with undulating plains of rich farmland, though its borders to the south, east and west touch the hilly uplands of mountainous areas. To the south-east are the Blackstairs Mountains on the Wexford Border; in the west the River Barrow threads through a limestone region that forms the boundary with Kilkenny; in the north-east the River Slaney flows through the granite fringe shared with the Wicklow Mountains.

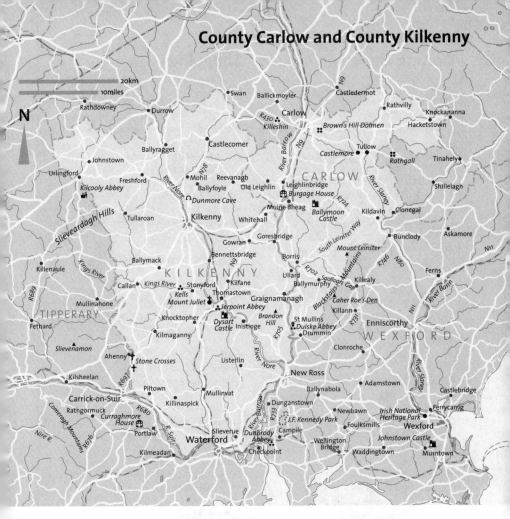

The rich river valleys contain many remains from the Anglo-Norman past in the form of castles and towerhouses. There are early-Christian monastic ruins as well. The wide, twisting rivers provide opportunities for salmon and trout fishing, and you can cruise on the River Barrow. There is unstrenuous walking in the Slievemargey Hills above Carlow Town, and the South Leinster Way, a signposted long-distance walk, starts in Kildavin and passes through some fine mountain countryside in the Blackstairs range, before dropping down to follow the towpath of the River Barrow, with all the different birdlife and tranquillity that the river world offers.

If you come from a highly industrialized country such as England, where farming is big business and where almost every inch of land has been ploughed up, Carlow is very appealing. It also seems to have escaped the indiscriminate building of modern bungalows, which so often mar the wild beauty of Connacht and the counties along the western seaboard. It is still far enough away from Dublin to be ignored by commuters. Most of the people who live in the county work in agriculture.

Getting There and Around

By Rail
Mainline trains to Waterford from Dublin pass through Carlow.
Carlow Station, t (059) 913 1633

By Bus
There are a few buses each day from Carlow Town for Dublin, Kilkenny and Waterford on Bus Éireann or Rapid Travel Express coaches. Private firms serve the other county towns.
Bus Éireann, Waterford, t (051) 879000, www.buseireann.ie
Rapid Travel Express Coaches, t (059) 914 3081

By Bike
Celtic Cycling, c/o Lorum Old Rectory, Bagenalstown, t (059) 977 5282, www.celticcycling.com
Coleman Cycles, 19 Dublin St, Carlow, t (059) 973 1273

Festivals

May–June
Carlow *Éigse* Arts Festival, College St, t (059) 914 0491, www.eigsecarlow.ie. Music, exhibitions, recitals and dances.

September
Fenagh Steam Rally, t (059) 9727233. One of the longest-running steam rallies in the country.
National & World Ploughing Championships, Grangeford, Tullow, t (059) 8625125. An event dating back 75 years.

Tourist Information
Carlow: t (059) 913 1554. *Closed Sun.*

Shopping

Crafts
John Kemp, Beech Lodge, Mortarstown Upper, Carlow, t (059) 9131010. A woodturner.
Pembroke Gallery, Pembroke St, Carlow, t (059) 914 1562
Wild Irish Crafts, Kilquiggan, Tullow, t (059) 915 6228

Herbal Supplies
Honeysuckle Products, The Watermill, Hacketstown, t (059) 647 1375. Shamrock seed.

Sports and Activities

Fishing
Try the **River Barrow** for brown trout and coarse fishing. Angling centres can be found in Muine Bheag (Bagenalstown) and **Tullow**.

Golf
Carlow Golf Club, Carlow Town, t (059) 913 1695, www.carlowgolfclub.com

Outdoor Activity Centres
Adventure Canoeing, t (087) 252 9700, www.gowiththeflow.ie. Canoeing on the Barrow.

Pleasure Cruises
Celtic Canal Cruisers, Tullamore, Co. Offaly, t (0506) 21861. Cruises and boat hire.

Ponytrekking
Carrigbeg Stables, Bagenalstown, (059) 972 1962

Walking
A good route is along the **South Leinster Way**; the tourist office can supply you with detailed maps. There is also a **forest walk**

History
In the 7th century Saint Moling founded a great monastic centre at St Mullins on the River Barrow. Later, many of the towns were Anglo-Norman strongholds, and were held for the king of England. In the 14th century, their position of power was challenged by a great chieftain, Art MacMurragh Kavanagh, who became King of Leinster and waged many successful battles against Richard II of England. MacMurragh was

by a canal at Bahana, 3 miles (4.8km) to the south of Barrow Bridge, Graignamanagh (on an unclassified road to St Mullins).

Where to Stay

Lorum Old Rectory, Kilgreaney, Muine Bheag (Bagenalstown), t (059) 977 5282, *www. lorum.com* (*moderate–expensive*). A great place for those with kids, with plenty to do on the farm, plus dogs, pet sheep, outdoor toys and croquet in the garden. The food is tasty and the rooms pretty and old-fashioned.

The Lord Bagenal Inn, Main St, Leighlinbridge, t (0503) 21668, *www.lordbagenal.com* (*moderate*). A small hotel with the owner's collection of paintings on the walls, helpful staff and generous breakfasts. It's another good option for families, as there's a children's playroom open until 8pm.

The Seven Oaks Hotel, Athy Rd, Carlow, t (059) 913 1308, *www.sevenoakshotel.com* (*moderate*). A reasonably priced option with traditional music on Monday nights.

Sherwood Park House, Kilbride, Ballon, t (059) 915 9117 (*moderate*). A peaceful Georgian house with extensive parkland, near Altamont Gardens. Rooms are furnished with brass-end canopy beds, and guests enjoy cosy open fires and good home-cooking.

The Watermill, Rathvilly, t (059) 916 1392 (*inexpensive*). A delightful restored 16th-century mill on the River Slaney, with home-cooking using home-grown veg, plus free fishing.

Self-catering

Rathlyon House, Rathanure, Tullow, t (059) 915 1824, *www.rathlyonhouse.com* (*inexpensive*). A large, imposing 19th-century farmhouse with 5 bedrooms – 2 doubles, a twin and 2 singles.

Eating Out

The Beams Restaurant, 59 Dublin St, Carlow, t (059) 913 1824 (*expensive*). A 300-year-old coaching inn with a bistro serving modern Irish cuisine: fresh seafood, game and home-grown vegetables. Booking is highly advised. There's an excellent wine and cheese shop attached.

Ballykealey Manor Hotel, Ballon, near Carlow, t (059) 915 9288 (*moderate*). A country-house-style restaurant.

The Carlovian, Tullow St, Carlow, t (059) 913 0911 (*moderate*). Formal dining, including a signature dish of herb-crusted rack of Irish spring lamb with rosemary jus.

The Lord Bagenal Inn, Main St, Leighlinbridge, t (059) 972 1668, *www.lordbagenal.com* (*moderate*). A very popular restaurant serving a good, varied menu, accompanied by an excellent wine list.

Brookes Bistro, Tullow St, Carlow, t (059) 913 3111 (*inexpensive–moderate*). A wine bar and restaurant favoured by locals.

The Green Drake Inn, Main St, Borris, t (059) 977 3116 (*inexpensive–moderate*). Simple meals made from local produce.

Teach Dolmain, Tullow St, Carlow, t (059) 913 0911 (*inexpensive*). Bar food accompanied by traditional music (*see below*).

Entertainment and Nightlife

Traditional Music

Lawlor's, Kilcarrig St, Muine Bheag, t (059) 972 1181. A venue for traditional *seisiún* on Thur nights.

Teach Dolmain, Tullow St, Carlow, t (059) 913 0911. Thur nights.

Tully's Bar, Tullow St, Carlow, t (059) 913 1862

initially put down by a huge expeditionary force led by Richard, but as soon as he had submitted and a treaty been agreed, he mounted another attack. He joined with the O'Neills of Ulster and the Earl of Desmond and, at the Battle of Kellistown in 1399, King Richard's heir, Roger Mortimer, was routed and killed. Richard's preoccupation with Ireland and his extensive losses gave his enemies in England a chance to organize against him, and Bolingbroke usurped his throne. Richard returned to imprisonment and death, and MacMurragh got his kingdom back.

For the next 135 years the authority of the English crown was reduced to the narrow 'Pale' around Dublin. Carlow Town was for a time its most southern outpost, and was heavily fortified. The Cromwellian confiscations of the 1650s, the Williamite wars of the 1690s and the penal laws had their dire effect on the Gaelic culture and society of Carlow, as they did elsewhere in Ireland. The 1798 rebellion against English rule claimed many lives, for the rebel army consisted of peasant mobs who were no match for the trained and well-armed British forces. Most of the leaders of this uprising are still remembered locally, among them Father John Murphy, who was executed in the Market Square of Tullow, a small place east of Carlow Town. There is a monument to him there, and he is still remembered by local folk. The Great Famine in the 1840s hit hard, and local life thereafter followed the usual pattern of death and emigration.

Carlow Town

Carlow Town is located at the crossing of the River Barrow in the north-west of the county, and is steeped in history. It used to be an Anglo-Norman stronghold, and much later it became the scene of a bloody scrimmage during the 1798 rebellion (*see* **History**, p.18). Nowadays it is involved in the processing of sugar beet, which was introduced in 1926 as part of the Irish self-sufficiency programme. Sights worth seeing include the **Norman castle**, probably constructed in the early 13th century, with its two drum towers. Its ruins were further reduced by a Dr Middleton, who built a lunatic asylum here in 1814. It is in private hands, but permission to look around it is readily given. (Ask at the house near the castle, which is right in the centre of the town near the east bank of the River Barrow.) There is also the prominent Catholic, Gothic Revival **Cathedral of the Assumption**, completed in 1833, off College Street, and a handsome **courthouse** (*open during working hours*) with a Doric portico, after the Parthenon, at the junction of Dublin Street and Dublin Road. You may like to visit **Carlow County Museum** (*open Mon–Fri 11–5, Sat and Sun 2–5; adm;* **t** *(059) 913 1759, www.carlow.ie*) in the Town Hall on Centaur Street , which has displays on folk life, archaeology and local history.

Around the County

Just outside Carlow, 2 miles (3.2km) over to the east, is the largest cap-stoned dolmen in Ireland, the **Browne's Hill Dolmen** (*always accessible*). Very impressive, it is estimated to weigh in excess of 130 tonnes. **Killeshin**, 3 miles (4.8km) to the west of Carlow town off the R430, is a ruined 12th-century church boasting an exception-ally fine Romanesque doorway. In the graveyard you can have a look at what is the oldest decorated font in Ireland.

Moving southwards, following the river Barrow, you come to Leighlinbridge and Old Leighlin on the N9. They are both pleasant spots. **Leighlinbridge** has a superb stone bridge with a Norman castle on its eastern side, which was built in 1181. On the unclassified road leading to Old Leighlin is **St Laserain's Church**, which has a very attractive belltower. **Old Leighlin** has the remains of a 7th-century monastery and fine cathedral. It was the centre of a bishopric from the 12th century until the diocese was joined with Ferns in County Wexford in 1600. The 12th-century **Cathedral of**

St Laserain has some fine 13th- and 15th-century architectural details, and in the graveyard are St Laserain's stone cross and a holy well. In the grounds of **Burgage House** near Leighlinbridge is a large *rath* known as **Dinn Righ**, an ancient residence of the kings of Leinster. You can ask to visit it.

If you want to do some inland water-cruising, all Ireland's rivers are beautiful and unspoilt. In Carlow, it is possible to cruise through Carlow Town, St Mullin's and Muine Bheag. The River Barrow connects with the Grand Canal to Dublin, and links up with the Shannon. **Muine Bheag**, formally Bagenalstown, was destined by Walter Bagenal to become an Irish Versailles – a plan that never came off (perhaps he ran out of money). About 2 miles (3km) away on the R724 is the impressive ruin of **Ballymoon Castle** (*always accessible*), built in the 14th century and one of the earliest Anglo-Norman strongholds built in Ireland. Legend says that it has never been conquered. It has two very strong square towers of enormous strength – the cut-granite walls are more than 8ft (2.5m) thick.

Borris is another pretty river town surrounded by the woods of Borris Castle. This is where the descendants of Art MacMurragh Kavanagh, 14th-century ruler of Leinster and scourge of Richard II, once lived. One of the famous members of his family, Arthur, who lived in the 19th century, was born without limbs yet was a great sportsman and could ride, fish, shoot and sail. He was also MP for Carlow. His daughter died in 1930 in the **Step House**, which is opposite the gates of the castle. The MacMurragh Kavanaghs are still well remembered here.

The kings of Leinster are supposed to have been buried at **St Mullins**, a very pretty village off the R729 on the way to New Ross. It is beautifully situated on the River Barrow and was once a site of great ecclesiastical importance. St Moling, Bishop of Ferns, founded a monastery here in the 7th century, and there are the remains of several ancient churches and an abbey. His little stone cell, the stump of a round tower, a holy well, the remains of a small nave and chancel church and an old weathered stone cross are grouped together around the abbey.

The Blackstairs Mountains to the south-east of the county are gentle and rolling; there is a pretty pass through the **Sgollogh Gap** (R702). The R746 leads to Bunclody in County Wexford at the north-east end of the mountain range. On an unclassified road to the north of Bunclody is **Clonegal**, a small village situated on the River Derry. In the centre of it is a fine Elizabethan building, **Huntingdon Castle** (*open June–Aug daily 2–6; guided tours; adm; t (054) 77552*), which has belonged to the Robertson family for centuries. The courtyard is rather fine, and it has a modern sculpture gallery. In the basement is a temple to the Goddess Isis, a rich medley of eastern statues and colour, and there's a magnificent yew walk in the grounds.

Following the N80/81 and the River Slaney northwards, you come to **Tullow**, which is the biggest town in the county and an angling centre for those fishing the Slaney for salmon and trout. If you are interested in archaeology, the *raths* ringing the town are worth a visit. **Castlemore**, the most important, lies a mile (1.6km) to the west. Three miles (4.8km) east of the town, just off the R725, there is the ancient stone fort of **Rathgall**. This has four ramparts; the outer ring is 1,000ft (300m) in diameter. Both sites are always accessible.

Altamont Gardens (*open Apr–Oct Mon–Thur 9–5, Fri 9–3.30, or by appointment; adm; t (059) 915 9444*), 5½ miles (9km) off the Tullow–Bunclody Road , is a superb place to spend a few hours, with a formal garden, herbaceous borders, a water garden, and good teas. In autumn there are masses of naturalized cyclamen.

A short drive north-east of Tullow lies **Hacketstown**, situated in the Wicklow foothills. This was the scene of a desperate engagement between the insurgents and the yeomanry in 1798. The tiny village of **Rathvilly** on the N81 to the west has a spreading view of the distant mountain ranges – the Blackstairs and the Slieve Blooms. It has a reputation to keep up, having won the All Ireland title for the tidiest town three times over.

County Kilkenny

The countryside that surrounds Kilkenny is lush and well cultivated, and in many ways it is reminiscent of that of England. So too are the villages, with their neatness and mellowed cottages. History colours the landscape wherever you are in Ireland, but in this county there is more visible evidence than in most of the interaction between Norman and Gael, and the later English landlords and Welsh miners. The Anglo-Normans invaded Ireland in 1169 and quickly established themselves as the ruling power. These lords of conquest built themselve numerous motte and bailey castles to hold their new territory, and as the centuries advanced and they grew ever more confident and wealthy, these large and fine castles served to proclaim their success. In Kilkenny, their dramatic castles standing along the river valleys of the

Getting There and Around

By Rail
Kilkenny City is on the main line from Dublin to Waterford, and there are about 4 trains a day in both directions.
MacDonagh Station, Kilkenny City, t (056) 7722107

By Bus
Bus Éireann has at least 6 buses a day to Dublin and Cork (via Clonmel), and less frequent ones to Waterford. Other Dublin–Waterford buses go through Thomastown instead. There's also 1 daily to Galway, in summer only. Contact MacDonagh Station in Kilkenny for details; *see* above.
Bus Éireann, t (056) 776 4933, *www.buseireann.ie*
Kavanagh's, t (056) 883 1189/1230, *www. bkavcoaches.com*. A private line with services between Kilkenny, Cashel and Thurles in Tipperary, as well as Carlow.

By Bike
J. J. Wall, 86 Maudlin St, Kilkenny, t (056) 772 1236

Festivals

May–June
The Cat Laughs, Kilkenny City, t (056) 776 3837, *www.smithwickscatlaughs.com*. A comedy festival in late May/early June.

June
Nissan Irish Open Golf Championship, Mount Juliet, Thomastown, *www.europeantour.com*. Ireland's premier international golf event.

August
Kilkenny Arts Festival, t (056) 775 2175, *www. kilkennyarts.ie*. One of the most important arts festivals in Ireland, with art exhibitions and music of all sorts, including opera. It's held during the last week of the month.

Nore and the Barrow, the splendid remains of Jerpoint Abbey and, more than anything else, the old city of Kilkenny itself make an exploration of this county a fascinating and rewarding occupation.

Apart from the ancient and stately buildings of Kilkenny, its wooded and well-tended countryside offers fishing, golf, horse-racing and riding opportunities. In Kilkenny City itself there is an arts festival, and good design and craft shops. The county's prowess also extends to hurling, a very ancient game recorded in Irish sagas: Nowlan Park, the hurling stadium in Kilkenny City, has great matches.

These days Kilkenny is a thriving agricultural county, with many craftspeople working in Kilkenny City and in small studios in the heart of the countryside, such as the Nicholas Mosse pottery at Bennettsbridge (*see* p.603). Here you can tour a small pottery museum and buy good-value seconds of lovely spongeware decorated with farmyard animals and flowers.

History

A brief survey of the history of Kilkenny inevitably centres on the Anglo-Normans, but before they arrived the county formed part of the old Gaelic kingdom of Ossory, an independent buffer state that sometimes joined with Leinster and sometimes with Munster. The old kingdom is remembered still in the diocese of Ossory, which stretches from near Waterford City in the south to the Slieve Bloom Mountains in the north. Its ruling family was called MacGiolla Phadruig, anglicized as Fitzpatrick. The kingdom of Ossory is said to date back to the 2nd century AD and it was such a stable force in the 11th century that the king of the time decided to try for the kingship of Leinster. The arrival of the Anglo-Normans, and the ease with which they triumphed over the ill-prepared Irish, eclipsed the Fitzpatricks. Soon the new name of Butler became all-powerful, and continued so for centuries. Theobald Fitzwalter was the first to carry the name. He came with Henry II on his great expedition in 1171, and in 1177 he was appointed Chief Butler in Ireland. Thenceforth his descendants were known as Butler, and by 1328 the head of the family was made Earl of Ormonde by Edward III. (Confusingly, in many of the places you will visit, the names Butler and Ormonde are interchangeable.) By 1391 the Butler family seat was in Kilkenny Castle, and many other castles in County Tipperary and Kilkenny became theirs as their clan grew in strength and numbers.

The Norman adventurers who first came to Ireland were brought to acknowledge the authority of the English crown by military expeditions staged by the monarch. But they frequently chafed at the restraint, and as time wore on they intermarried with the native Irish and became thoroughly Irish themselves. During the 14th century the colony went into a decline: there was the devastation of the Black Death, the native Irish began to reassert themselves, and the Norman families identified more and more with Gaelic Ireland. The effect of this was that royal authority was confined, apart from in a few walled towns, to an enclave on the east coast around Dublin – the Pale. In 1366 London reacted by calling a parliament in Kilkenny City that passed the Statutes of Kilkenny. These laws made it high treason for a Norman to marry an Irish woman, or for an Irish man to live in Kilkenny City. Normans were not allowed to wear

Irish dress (the long cloak), or adopt the customs, legal arrangements or language of the Irish. (Cahir Castle in County Tipperary, close to Kilkenny, has an excellent exhibition on the Brehon, or Gaelic, laws and customs; see p.234) The statutes were rigidly enforced for a while, but they came too late and soon fell into decline.

A mutual antagonism between the Butlers and the Fitzgeralds, another powerful Norman family, caused many a betrayal and pitched battle in the following two centuries. The Fitzgeralds in Leinster were the earls of Kildare, and the Fitzgeralds in Munster were the earls of Desmond. Both branches are often referred to as the Geraldines. The ramifications of the Butler dynasty and their feud with the Fitzgeralds spread far and wide. Anne Boleyn, the second wife of Henry VIII, was the grand-daughter of Thomas Butler, the seventh earl. Elizabeth I's cousin, Black Tom Butler, put down the late-16th-century revolt by the Earl of Desmond on behalf of the crown. The Bishop of Cloyne, a brave man, said at a requiem Mass for the wife of the fourth Earl of Desmond in 1391: 'Eternal God, there are two in Munster who destroy us and our property, namely the Earl of Ormonde and the Earl of Desmond with their followers, who at length the Lord will destroy, through Christ our Lord, Amen.' This prayer so incensed Butler and Geraldine that the bishop was compelled to pay Ormonde damages, and was deprived of his see. The feud was finally healed by the marriage of James Butler, first Duke of Ormonde, to his cousin Elizabeth Preston, heiress of the Earl of Desmond, in 1629.

Kilkenny City played a very important part in the Great Rebellion of 1641, which broke out in Ulster. The Norman and Gaelic families made an alliance, united in resentment against the new settlers – the Protestants 'planted' by James I – and the decades of economic, political and religious oppression. In May 1642 the city became the seat of the Confederate Parliament of the Catholics, with representatives from all the counties and main towns. Government was taken into their hands, taxes were levied, armies were raised, and weapons and powder were manufactured. Owen Roe O'Neill commanded for Ulster, Preston for Leinster; Munster was under Barry, and Connacht under Burke. The Confederation lasted until 1648.

But the alliance between the 'Old Foreigners' and the 'Old Irish' was complicated by their different loyalties as the Civil War in England between Charles I and Parliament spilled over into Ireland. The Butlers of Kilkenny were loyal to the Stuart crown; the old Gaelic families felt nothing for him and turned to France and Spain, the traditional enemies of England. But this split was overshadowed in turn by the rise of Cromwell, who began a ruthless campaign in Ireland. In March 1650, after five days' defence, Kilkenny City capitulated to him and his forces. James, Duke of Ormonde, was at this time deeply involved in the internal hostilities between the Confederates. He had supported Charles I and, after his execution, proclaimed Charles II King. The successes of Cromwell forced him to retreat to France, but he was later restored to his estates and given an English dukedom and peerage by Charles II. The Butler family was in any case probably destined to survive, for, as with many of the aristocratic families in Ireland, there were Protestant Butlers and Catholic Butlers, so they managed to keep a foot in each camp. In the more recent history of Ireland, the Butlers have ceased to play any part.

Northern and Eastern Kilkenny

Urlingford to Castlecomer

Places worth a visit in this area, running from west to east, include **Urlingford** on the border with Tipperary, where you will find a ruined 16th-century castle and the remains of a pre-Reformation church. The town itself dates back only as far as 1755; the site was established after the bog had been cut away. **Ballyragget** on the River Nore has more to recommend it to historians, besides being a pretty little place – it was the scene of a dramatic trial of strength that took place between Black Tom, Earl of Ormonde and Lord Lieutenant of Ireland in Elizabeth I's time, and Owen MacRory O'More, the head of the ruling Laois family. The battle culminated in the capture of the Earl in April 1600.

Tourist Information

Kilkenny: Shee Alms House, Rose Inn St, t (056) 775 1500

Internet Access

Compustore, Arcade James St, off High St, Kilkenny, t (056) 777 1200. *Closed Sun.*
Webtalk, Rose Inn St, Kilkenny, t (056) 775 0066

Sports and Activities

Fishing
There's good fishing at Graignamanagh, and also along the Lower River Barrow.
Hook, Line & Sinker, 31 Rose Inn St, Kilkenny, t (056) 777 1699. A place catering to all fishing needs.
Town and County Sports Shop, 82 High St, Kilkenny, t (056) 772 1517

Golf
Mount Juliet, near Thomastown, t (056) 777 3000, *www.mountjuliet.ie*. A Jack Nicklaus-designed course amidst woodland, used for top-notch international competitions.

Horseracing
This takes place at Gowran Park throughout the year; check the local newspapers or the back of Tourism Ireland's *Calendar of Events*, or contact:
Irish Horse Racing Authority, t (01) 289 2888

Pleasure Cruises
Valley Boats, Barrow Lane, Graignamanagh, t (059) 972 4945. A company offering cruises on the River Barrow.

Ponytrekking
Mount Juliet Equestrian Centre, Thomastown, t (056) 777 3000, *www.mountjuliet.ie*
Wallslough Equestrian Village, Sheestown, 3 miles (5km) south of Kilkenny, towards Thomastown t (056) 772 3838

Walking
For details of guided walking tours in Inistioge, call t (056) 775 8995.

Shopping

Crafts
Cushendale Woollen Mills, Graignamanagh, t (059) 972 4118. Tweed and woollen goods.
Duiske Glass, Graiguenamanagh, t (059) 972 4174
Jerpoint Glass Studios, Stoneyford, t (056) 772 4350. Thickly blown glass.
Toner's Bag Company, Thomastown, t (056) 772 4055. A place where you can see leather goods being made in their workshop.

Where to Stay

Mount Juliet Estate, Thomastown, t (056) 777 3000, *www.mountjuliet.com* (*luxury*).
A lovely stately house converted into a swish hotel and country club owned by

Conrad, the Hilton group's luxury tier, with beautiful grounds, friendly staff, good sporting facilities, including a golf course, riding and fishing, and 2 restaurants (*see* below). The spa offers traditional and alternative treatments, and the health club has a pool, sauna, steam room and gym.

Avalon Inn, The Square, Castlecomer, **t** (056) 444 1302, *theavaloninn@eircom.net* (*moderate*). B&B accommodation in an ivy-covered Georgian building.

Cullintra House, The Rower, Inistioge, **t** (051) 423614, *http://indigo.ie/~cullhse/* (*moderate*). A farmhouse set in beautiful grounds, with traditional furnishings and bohemian influences introduced by its lively proprietress. It's a paradise for cat-lovers, children and eccentrics who long for the timeless qualities of the old Ireland. The superb dinners are served by candlelight.

Garranavabby House, The Rower, Inistioge, **t** (051) 423613 (*moderate*). An old farmhouse in a lovely setting near Graignamanagh and charming Inistioge.

Kilrush House, Freshford, **t** (056) 883 2236 (*moderate*). A pretty 18th-century country house north of Kilkenny, with comfortable rooms, good simple cooking and a tennis court. Children under 7 are not admitted.

Waterside House, The Quay, Graiguenamanagh, **t** (059) 972 4246, *www.watersideguesthouse. com* (*moderate*). Modern rooms in a restored 19th-century granary on the riverfront. The atmospheric restaurant serves refined food, including especially good seafood. *Restaurant closed lunch, and Sun–Thur eve in winter.*

Eating Out

The Lady Helen Dining Room, Mount Juliet Estate, Thomastown, **t** (056) 777 3000, *www.mountjuliet.com* (*luxury*). Global fare made using produce and herbs picked daily from the gardens of this luxury hotel (*see* p.599). The dining room boasts impressive centuries-old stuccowork and panoramic views over the estate and the River Nore. *Closed lunch.*

The Motte, Main St, Inistioge, **t** (056) 775 8655 (*moderate–expensive*). A charming little restaurant situated in the most picturesque of villages, serving up adventurous food in a cosy atmosphere.

Kendals, Hunters Yard, Mount Juliet Estate, Thomastown, **t** (056) 777 3010, *www. mountjuliet.com* (*moderate*). A lower-priced option at the Mount Juliet Estate hotel, offering traditional Irish food in a relaxed setting with views over the golf course.

Circle of Friends, The Bank House, High St, Inistioge, **t** (056) 775 8800 (*inexpensive– moderate*). A café and restaurant in a converted house, offering excellent cakes and snacks downstairs, and fine dinners on the first floor.

The Lime Tree Bistro, The Square, Castlecomer **t** (056) 4440966 (*inexpensive*). A small family-run café serving lunch daily, plus breakfasts Mon–Sat. *Closed eves.*

Thomastown Water Garden and Cafe, **t** (056) 772 4690 (*inexpensive*). Teas served on the terrace of a lovely little water garden (*adm*) in Thomastown, beautifully planted with aquatic plants.

Further to the east, approximately 7 miles (11km) north of Kilkenny, just off the N78 near Ballyfoyle, is the dramatic **Dunmore Cave** (*open mid-Mar–mid-June and mid-Sept–Oct daily 10–5, mid-June–mid-Sept daily 9.30–6.30, rest of year Sat and Sun 10–5; guided tours; adm; t (056) 776 7726*). During the Viking raids people took refuge here, but they were found and nearly 1,000 were killed. Even so, the cave continued to be used afterwards as a refuge by local people. It is a fantasy world of coloured caverns, and you can spend a good hour down there. The Office of Public Works runs the cave, which is notable for its huge chambers and 'market cross' stalagmite column.

Nearby **Castlecomer** was laid out in the style of an Italian village by Sir Christopher Wandersforde in 1635. The area was once prosperous as a result of the coalfield situated in this region, which skilled Welshmen were imported to mine. The coalmines closed in the 1970s.

Gowran to Sheastown

Gowran deserves your attention if you love horseracing, for it has an excellent course. The town was an important fortress of the kings of Ossory until Theobald Fitzwalter, the first Butler and ancestor of the dukes of Ormonde, was granted it by Strongbow. Sadly, nothing remains of the castle he built, as Cromwell's troops burned it down in 1650. However, the Church of Ireland **church** has some interesting monuments, and is a mixture of 12th- and 13th-century architectural details. There is an effigy in armour of the first Earl of Ormonde (1327). On one of the gravestones is rather a witty couplet erected to a man and his two wives:

Both wives at once alive he could not have
Both to enjoy at once he made this grave.

Goresbridge is another attractive river village that joins County Carlow to County Kilkenny across the River Barrow. Many people come and fish for brown trout and a variety of coarse fish here. At Goresbridge you can also buy ornaments and other objects made out of a speciality of the county – the highly polished black limestone that had been used as paving in Kilkenny City itself. This 'marble' is no longer mined, although you may find Kilkenny marble chimneys pointed out to you in many Big Houses. Off the N9, just over a mile (1.6km) from Kilfane, is **Kilfane Glen** (*open May–mid-Sept Tue–Sun 2–6; adm;* **t** *(056) 772 4558*), with a waterfall adorned by a romantic garden laid out in the 18th century, and a thatched 'cottage *ornée*'.

Going south you reach lovely **Thomastown** (on the Waterford road), with its mellowed grey-stone buildings. Near here, on an unmarked road to the south of the town, is the ruin of **Dysart Castle**, the home of the famous idealist-philosopher George Berkeley (1685–1753), who gave his name to the city and university of Berkeley, California. The castle is not open to the public but can be viewed from the road.

West of Thomastown, near Stonyford, is one of the best-kept estates in Ireland, **Mount Juliet** (**t** *(056) 777 3000, www.mountjuliet.ie*). The house is a hotel (*see* p.599), and the gardens are beautiful, especially the delphiniums in the walled garden. Part of the grounds have become a Jack Nicklaus-designed championship golf course.

But the jewel of the area must be the fine monastic ruin of **Jerpoint Abbey** (*open Wed–Mon mid-Mar–May and mid-Sept–Oct 10–5, June–mid-Sept 9.30–6.30; adm;* **t** *(056) 772 4623*), just off the N9. Dating from the late 12th century, it follows a typical Cistercian plan, with two chapels in each transept. The ancient parts of the chancel and the transepts are in Irish Romanesque style, and appear to have been built by the same masons who raised Baltinglass in Wicklow. The abbey was founded in 1158 by Donal MacGiolla Phadruig, King of Ossory, and suppressed in 1540. Restoration work has been sympathetic and it is an impressive ruin. Make sure you take a look at the sculptured lords and ladies in the cloisters.

Due east rises the hill of Brandon, which gives you a clear view of this well-worked countryside, with the Blackstairs Mountains to the east on the Carlow-Wexford border. On your way here you will pass the charming town of **Inistioge**, home of the Tighes. This family was connected with a pair of remarkable ladies who exercised a great influence on taste in the 18th century. The 'Ladies of Llangollen', Lady Eleanor

Butler and Sarah Ponsonby, exemplified the Romantic and the Gothick by running away together to live in a Welsh cottage. Inistioge square is planted with lime trees, and there are wooded stretches surrounding the town, through which the River Nore runs. A Norman **motte** overlooks the river, and there are the fine ruins of an Augustinian **priory**, founded in 1210.

To the north of Inistioge is **Graignamanagh**, right on the Carlow border. It is picturesquely sited on a mountainous ravine and has the splendid early Cistercian **Duiske Abbey**, which survived the suppression of the monasteries in the 16th century, as did the Catholic **church**, which has some 9th-century crosses in the graveyard. Both are always accessible to the public. Notice the effigy of a knight in the church, lying crosslegged in 13th-century armour – this was medieval artists' way of expressing that the deceased had been a crusader. Before leaving the Graignamanagh district, take the opportunity to investigate the woolcrafts.

At **Ullard**, 3 miles (4.8km) to the north on the R705, there are remains of another foundation: a high cross and the remains of an old church, with granite carvings on the Romanesque doorway. St Fiachre set off for France from Ullard. He is one of the saints that chose the isolation of a foreign land in preference to a lonely island hermitage. He is the patron saint of Parisian taxi-drivers, because the first carriage conveyances in Paris used to congregate round the Hôtel de St Fiachre. About 3 miles (4.8km) south-east of Kilkenny City at **Sheastown**, on the way to Bennettsbridge, is a well dedicated to St Fiachre. *Patterns* are held here in late August around the time of the Arts Festival in Kilkenny.

Western and Central Kilkenny

Callan and Kells

West of Kilkenny City is the ancient town of **Callan**, which seems to have nourished a fair number of Ireland's great men. One of them, Edmund Ignatius Rice (1762–1844), a candidate for canonization, founded the influential teaching order of the Christian Brothers, who now educate not only most of Ireland's politicians but also some of the Third World's. He was born in a thatched cottage (marked by a plaque) at **Westcourt**, just outside Callan. Robert Fulton (b.1765), who designed the world's first steamship, and James Hoban (1762–1831), architect of the White House, came from near here.

Nearby on the Kings River is the complete, fortified, turreted and walled enclosure of **Kells** (*always accessible*). Since the early history of the Kingdom of Ossory, Kells has heard the murmur of prayer and the clash of warfare. Now it is a supremely peaceful place, and the impressive collection of early ecclesiastical buildings must make it a highlight of any Kilkenny tour. It was founded in the late 12th century by Geoffrey Fitzrobert de Marisco, who built a stong castle and an Augustinian priory. But it had been a centre of importance in the early history of Ossory, and most probably a mystical pagan site. St Kieran of Seer founded a monastery here in the 5th century, but it is the remains of the 12th-century **priory** that still impress. Its ruins cover 5 acres (2ha) and are divided into two courts by a moat and a wall. The north court is surrounded by a tall wall, and fortified with towers, and contains the church, cloisters and other monastic buildings. The south court is fortified, turreted and walled, but contains no buildings and was an enclosure for cattle in times of trouble.

Kilkenny City

Kilkenny City (*Cill Chainnigh*: 'St Canice's Church') was the focal point of the Anglo-Norman and Irish resistance to the Cromwellians in 1642, and was where they formed their Confederate Parliament. Before that it was the seat of power for the 'old English', the first foreign war-lords. The city (population: 17,700), takes its name from St Canice,

Tourist Information

Kilkenny: Shee Alms House, Rose Inn St, t (056) 775 1500

Shopping

Crafts
The Bridge Pottery, Chapel St, Bennettsbridge, t (056) 772 7077
Chesneau Design, Bennettsbridge, t (056) 772 7456. Mostly handbags and knapsacks.
The Kilkenny Design Centre, Castle Yard, Kilkenny, t (056) 772 2118, *www.kilkennydesign.com*. An excellent array of crafts from all Ireland; *see* also p.605.
Kilkenny Irish Crystal, Canal Square, Kilkenny, t (056) 776 1377. There's also the factory at Callan, which can be visited during the summer (call t (056) 772 5132).
Liam Costigan, Colliers Lane, off High St, Kilkenny, t (056) 776 2408. Jewellery.
Nicholas Mosse Pottery, Bennettsbridge, t (056) 772 7105, *www.nicholasmosse.com*. A contender for the title of loveliest pottery in Ireland: spongeware decorated with farmyard animals and flowers. Slight seconds are available, and there is an exhibition of pottery through the ages.
Rudolf Heltzel, 10 Patrick St, Kilkenny, t (056) 772 1497. Jewellery.
Stoneware Jackson Pottery, Ballyreddin, Bennettsbridge, t (056) 772 7175, *www.stonewarejackson.com*. Lots of swirly, bright patterns.

Food and Drink
The Good Earth, 43 Kieran St, Kilkenny, t (056) 775 2664. Health foods.

Mileeven Ltd, Owning Hill, Piltown, t (051) 643368. Honey and cider, and beeswax polish.
Shortis-Wong, 74 John St, Kilkenny, t (056) 776 1305. An excellent deli.

Sports and Activities

Golf
Kilkenny City Course, Lacken, t (056) 772 4725

Pleasure Cruises
Valley Boats, Barrow Lane, Graignamanagh, t (059) 972 4945. Cruises on the River Barrow.

Ponytrekking
Warrington Top Flight Equestrian Centre, Bennettsbridge Rd, Kilkenny, t (056) 772 2682, *www.topflightkilkenny.com*

Walking
Guided walks are available in **Kilkenny**; contact the tourist office, t (056) 775 1500

Where to Stay

Butler House, 16 Patrick St, Kilkenny, t (056) 772 2828 or t (056) 776 5707, *www.butler.ie* (*expensive*). A smart guesthouse in a restored Georgian building, central and comfortable, with muted modern interiors. Some of the superior rooms and suites have views of the castle.
The Club House Hotel, Patrick St, Kilkenny, t (056) 772 1994, *www.clubhousehotel.com* (*expensive*). The one-time headquarters of the Foxhounds Club, with many gracious features of another age. It is very central for all the sights of Kilkenny City.

who established a monastery here in the 6th century. The Church of Ireland **cathedral**, St Canice's, occupies its site off Vicar Street; it's a fine Gothic work completed in 1285, with an interior of beautiful Kilkenny stone. The second-largest medieval church in Ireland, it contains an exceptional collection of medieval sepulchral monuments. The 100ft (30m) **round tower** beside it also dates from this earlier time; ask in the church if you want to climb it (*adm*). The cathedral was much restored in the 19th century, and the nearby **library** houses some 3,000 books from the 16th and 17th century. This grouping of ecclesiastical buildings with the Church of Ireland vicarage is curious but charming, and represents the strength of the anglicizing influence in its best aspects.

Newpark Hotel, Castlecomer Rd, Kilkenny, t (056) 776 0500, *www.newparkhotel.com* (*expensive*). A large modern hotel with a leisure centre with a swimming pool, sauna, steam room and gym, a health spa, and golf and riding nearby.

Lacken House, Dublin Rd, Kilkenny, t (056) 776 1085, *www.lackenhouse.ie* (*moderate*). A family-run guesthouse in attractive grounds, offering good food prepared by the chef-owner.

Hillgrove, Bennettsbridge Rd, Kilkenny, t (056) 775 1453, *hillgrove@esatclear.ie* (*inexpensive*). A comfortable B&B with many amenities, and quite exceptional breakfasts.

Self-catering

Kilcoran House, Cuffesgrange, t (056) 772 8253 or t 0862 545618 (*moderate*). An attractive gatelodge and a 2-bedroom apartment on a farm 6.5 miles (10km) from Kilkenny.

Anne Murphy, Dreelingstown, Rathmoyle, t (056) 776 9281 (*inexpensive*). A 2-bedroom thatched cottage in a quiet location.

Eating Out

Lacken House, Dublin Rd, Kilkenny, t (056) 776 1085 (*expensive*). A popular, family-run restaurant serving imaginative, perfectly cooked food.

Newpark Hotel, Castlecomer Rd, Kilkenny, t (056) 776 0500 (*expensive*). A plush dining room offering Irish and Continental food.

Café Sol, William St, t (056) 776 4987, *www.cafesolkilkenny.com* (*moderate*). A popular café/restaurant with a lively atmosphere and a varied menu, including good vegetarian options. *Closed Mon.*

The Club House Hotel, Patrick St, Kilkenny, t (056) 772 1994 (*moderate*). A good place for steak-lovers.

Langton's Bar & Restaurant, 69 John St, Kilkenny, t (056) 776 5133, *www.langtons.ie* (*moderate*). An award-winning place serving good pub lunches and dinners.

Lautrec's, Kieran's St, Kilkenny, t (056) 776 2720 (*moderate*). A busy city-centre brasserie.

Rinuccini Restaurant, 1 The Parade, Kilkenny, t (056) 776 1575, *www.rinuccini.com* (*moderate*). A place serving both Irish and Italian dishes, including seafood and home-made pasta.

Kilkenny Castle, t (056) 772 1450 (*inexpensive*). A restaurant in the old castle kitchen, serving delicious lunches and teas. *Closed eves and winter.*

Kilkenny Design Centre Coffee Shop, Castle Yard, Kilkenny, t (056) 772 2118 (*inexpensive*). Good soups, cooked meats and salads. *Closed eves.*

Tynan's Bridge House Bar, St John's Bridge, Kilkenny, t (056) 772 1291 (*inexpensive*). An unspoilt Victorian pub retaining all its original fittings, serving well-priced pub fare.

Entertainment and Nightlife

Live Music

Kilkenny has several places that host music at least 1 night a week, including:.

John Cleere's, Parliament St, Kilkenny, t (056) 776 2573. Music, plus cabaret, comedy, plays and poetry readings at times.

The Pumphouse, Parliament St, Kilkenny, t (056) 776 3924

On the edge of the town centre, the great fortress of the Ormondes, **Kilkenny Castle**, (*open for guided tours Apr and May daily 10.30–5, June–Sept daily 9.30–7, Oct–Mar Tue–Sat 10.30–12.45, Sun 11–12.45 and 2–5; adm; t (056) 772 1450*) remains a dominant feature. William the Marshall, a Norman commander who married Strongbow's daughter, built the castle between 1195 and 1207. The building today is a mixture of Gothic, Classical and Tudor styles and is very dramatic, set above the River Nore. The skylit **Long Gallery**, an elegant example of the sort of space wealthy aristocrats of the 18th century built to display their paintings, is hung with superb Butler portraits, some of them going back to the 14th century. The sixth Marquess of Ormonde presented the castle and a portion of its grounds to the people of Kilkenny in 1967. Until 1935 it was the principal residence of the Butlers. Now you can go round it and enjoy the lovely gardens sheltered behind the castle walls. It has an art gallery with temporary exhibitions. The castle acts as an exhibition centre during the Arts Festival, and there is a good restaurant for snacks in the old kitchen.

Opposite the castle, on the parade, is the Castle Yard and **Kilkenny Design Centre** (*open Mon–Sat 9–6, Sun 10–6 exc winter; t (056) 772 2118, www.kilkennydesign.com*), which promotes Irish goods. Its label is almost a guarantee of good taste and quality. In the shop you will find china, glass, hand-knitted jerseys, tweed coats and jackets, kitchenware, ornaments, linen and jewellery. The National Crafts Council (*t (056) 776 1804, www.ccoi.ie*), based in the Yard, aims to develop and encourage designers through travelling scholarships. Their workshops are behind the Design Centre, in the converted stables of the castle.

Architecturally, the city is one of Ireland's most interesting, because it is so old. You should try to visit **Rothe House** (*open Apr–Oct Mon–Sat 10.30–5, Sun 3–5, Nov–Mar Mon–Sat 1–5, Sun 3–5; adm; t (056) 772 2893*), on Parliament Street, which is a unique example of an Irish Tudor merchant's house, constructed in 1594. It boasts an arcaded shopfront and consists of three buildings parallel to each other but separated by two inner courtyards and joined on one side by a linking passageway. Inside is a collection of period costumes and a genealogical centre. The Kilkenny Archaeological Society, a pioneer of its kind in Ireland and forerunner of the Royal Society of Antiquities in Ireland, also houses its collection there.

Further into the town, in the High Street, you can see the **Tholsel**, formerly the Toll House or Exchange and now the City Hall, which was built in 1761. It is built of black Kilkenny marble, and extends over the pavement to form an arcade made up of Tuscan pillars. It is possible to look inside if you ask.

On Rose Inn Street the **Shee Alms House** (*open Apr–Oct Mon–Sat 9–5.30, Nov–Mar Mon–Sat 9–4.30; also May–Sept Sun 11–12.30 and 2–4.30; hours may vary so contact Tourist Office before visiting, t (056) 775 1500; adm*), dates back to 1594 and contains an interesting 'Cityscope' show (*every 30mins during opening hours*) with a model of the medieval city.

Nearby in Abbey Street is the **Black Abbey** that gives the street its name. Wrecked by Cromwell, it was restored in the 19th century and is once more an active place of prayer. The **Black Abbey Gate**, known also as the Black Freyre (Friar's) Gate, is the only gate remaining from the former town walls.

Across the River Nore, in Lower John Street, is **Kilkenny College**, a handsome Georgian building where some of Ireland's greatest writers were educated, including the satirist Dean Swift, the philosopher Berkeley, and the dramatist Congreve. The building is now used as seat of the Kilkenny County Council.

The city acts as host to one of the finest cultural festivals in Ireland, the Kilkenny Arts Festival (*see* p.596). This takes place at the end of August and includes all the arts: visual, performing and gustatory (if you go by the number of people in the smarter pubs drinking the homebrew, Smithwick's – a beer that is as popular as Guinness). The castle and many other historic buildings are used as venues.

For a quiet jar after all this sightseeing, try Tynan's Bridge House Bar, close to John's Bridge, with views of the castle. Incidentally, many of the pubs in Kilkenny have hand-painted signs, which makes them attractive to look at.

Language

The Irish language is the purest of all the Celtic languages; and Ireland is one of the last homes of the prehistoric and medieval European oral tradition. The language was preserved by isolated farming communities, along with many expressions from the dialects of early English settlers. Irish was spoken by the Norman aristocracy, who patronized the Gaelic poets and bards. But with the establishment of an English system of land tenure and an English-speaking nobility, Gaelic became scarce, except in the poorer farming areas. The Famine in the 1840s hit those who lived here very hard; thousands died or emigrated, and spoken Gaelic was severely curtailed. The Gaelic League, founded in 1870, initiated a new interest and pride in the language and became identified with rising nationalism. In 1921 its survival became part of the new State's policy. It was decided that the only way to preserve Gaelic was to protect and stimulate it in the places where it was still a living language.

It is spoken today mostly in the west and around the mountainous coast and islands. These areas form 'the Gaeltacht'. Here, everything is done to promote Irish-speaking, in industry and at home. Centres have been set up for students to learn among the native speakers. There are special grants for people living in Irish-speaking areas, but the boundaries are a little arbitrary. In Galway there's a boundary line through a built-up area, so there's a certain amount of animosity between the two sides of the line, Irish speakers or no. There is also the problem of standardizing Irish, for the different dialects are quite distinct. The modern media tend to iron these out with the adoption of one region's form of words in preference to others. County Donegal seems to get the worst deal, being so much further from the centre of administration, although it has the largest number of native speakers.

One can appreciate all the reasons for promoting Irish, but it is only in the last few generations that the language has become popular. Before, it was left to Douglas Hyde and Lady Gregory to demonstrate the richness of Irish language and myth, and they had the advantage of being far away from the grim realities of hunger and poverty that the Irish speakers knew. Gaelic, like certain foods (usually vegetables), had associations with hunger and poverty, and belonged to a hard past. The cultural coercion of the 1930s had a negative effect on most Irish people. It was only in Ulster that Gaelic speaking and culture kept its appeal in the face of Protestant and official antipathy. Even now, people prefer to use English rather than stay in the Gaeltacht, existing on grants and other government hand-outs. Gaelic is a compulsory subject in schools in the Republic, and there is a certain amount in the newspapers, on TV, radio, signposts and street names (with English translations). The use of Gaelic among the more intellectual of the middle classes is now on the increase, and this is being reinforced by the establishment of Gaelic-speaking primary schools throughout the country. Irish Gaelic is one of the official languages of the European Union.

The carrying over of Irish idiom into English is very attractive and expressive. J.M. Synge captured this in his play *Riders to the Sea*. In fact, English as spoken by the Irish is in a class of its own. Joyce talked of 'the sacred eloquence of Ireland', and it is true that you could hardly find a more articulate people. Their poetry and prose is superb, and the emotions that their ballads can release is legendary. Great hardship and poverty have not killed the instinctive desire within to explain life with words. The monk who scribbled in the margin of his psalter wrote with Oriental simplicity the following poem entitled 'Winter':

My tiding for you: The stag bells
Winter snows, summer is gone.
Wind is high and cold, low the sun,
Short his course, sea running high.
Deep red the bracken, its shape all gone,
The wild goose has raised his wonted cry.
Cold has caught the wings of birds;
season of ice – these are my tidings.
              9th century, translation by Kuno Meyer

That hardship brings forth great poetry
is a theory strengthened by the school of
contemporary northern Irish poets who have
become known all over the world: Seamus
Heaney, James Simmons, Derek Mahon,
Medbh McGuckian. The cutting criticisms of
Brian O'Nolan (known as Flann O'Brien), the
gentle irony of Frank O'Connor and the furious
passion of Sean O'Casey, Patrick Kavanagh,
Liam O'Flaherty and John McGahern, to
name only a few, have become part of our
perception of the Irish spirit since
Independence. The list of recent writers could
go on and on. One can only urge you to read
them. There is a particularly good anthology
of short stories edited by Benedict Kiely
(Penguin) and an anthology of Irish verse,
edited by John Montague (Faber).

Even though the disciplined cadences of
the Gaelic bardic order were broken by the
imposition of an English nobility in the
17th and 18th centuries, the Irish skill with
words has survived, and is as strong as ever.
As a visitor to Ireland, you will notice this way
with words when you have a conversation in
a pub, ask the way at a crossroads, or simply
chat to the owners of the farmhouse where
you spend the night.

The Meaning of Irish Place Names

The original Gaelic place names have been
complicated by attempts to give them an
English spelling. In the following examples,
the Gaelic versions of the prefixes come first,
followed by the English meaning.
agh, augh, achadh a field
aglish, eaglais a church
ah, atha, áth a ford
all, ail, aill a cliff
anna, canna, éanarch a marsh

ard, ar, ard a height
as, ess, eas a waterfall
aw, ow, atha a river
bal, bel, béal the mouth (of a river or valley)
bal, balli, bally, baile a town
ballagh, balla, bealach a way or path
bawn, bane, bán white
barn, bearna a gap
beg, beag small
boola, booley, buaile, booleying
    the movement of cattle from lowland
    to high pastures (transhumance)
boy, buidhe yellow
bun the foot (of a valley) or mouth (of a river)
caher, cahir, cathair, carraig a rock
cashel, caiseal, caislean a castle
clogh, cloich, cloch a stone
clon, clun, cluain a meadow
derg, dearg red
doo, du, duv, duf, dubh black
dun, dún a fort
dysert, disert a hermitage
glas, glen, gleann a valley
illaun, oileán an island
knock, cnoc a hill
ken, kin, can, ceann a headland
kil, kill, cill a church
lis, liss, lios a fort
lough, loch a lake or sea inlet
ma, may, moy, magh a plain
mone, mona, móna turf or bog
monaster, mainistir a monastery
more, mór, mor big or great
owen, avon, abhainn a river
rath a ring fort
rinn, reen a point
roe, ruadh red
ross, ros a peninsula, a wood
see, suidhe a seat, e.g. Ossian's seat
shan, shane, sean old
slieve, sliabh a mountain
tir, tyr, tír country
tubber, tobrid, tubbrid, tobar a well
tra, traw, tráigh, trá a strand or beach

Some Ulster and Other Expressions

an oul sceach crosspatch
assay attention, as in Hi!
auld flutter guts fussy person
balls of malt whiskey

ballyhooley a telling off (in Cork)
blow-in stranger to the area
boreen country lane
brave commendable, worthy,
   e.g. a brave wee sort of a girl
bravely could be worse,
   e.g. business is doing bravely
caution (as in 'He's a caution'),
   a devil-may-care type
chawing the rag bickering couple
chick child
cleg horsefly
clever neat, tight-fitting, usually
   refers to a garment
coul wintry, cold
craic fun, lively chat
cranky bad-tempered
craw thumper a 'holy Mary' or hypocrite
cut insulted, hurt
dead on exactly right
deed passed away, dead
destroyed exhausted
dingle dent, mark with an impression
dip bread fried in a pan
dither slow
doley little fella he's lovely
dulse edible seaweed
eejit fool
fairly excellently, e.g. that wee lad
   can fairly sing
feed meal
fern foreign
in fiddler's green you're in a big mess
fierce unacceptable, extremely,
   e.g. it's fierce dear (expensive)
figuresome good at sums
fog feed lavish meal
foostering around fiddling about
guff impertinence, cheek
half sir landlord's son
harp six tumble
he hasn't a titter of wit no sense at all
jar a couple of drinks
lashins plenty
mended improved in health
mizzlin raining gently
mullarkey man
neb nose
nettle drive someone barmy
ni now, this moment
not the full shilling half-witted
oul or auld not young, but can be used about
   something useful, e.g. my oul car

owlip verbal abuse
palsie walsie great friends
paralytic intoxicated
plámás sweet words
playboy conceited fellow
poless police
put the caibosh on it mess things up
quare memorable, unusual
qurrier or cowboy bad type, rogue
rare to bring up, educate
rightly prospering, e.g. he's doing rightly now
scalded bothered, vexed, badly burned
she's like a corncrake chatterbox
skedaddled ran quickly
skiff slight shower or rain
slainte drinking toast
soft rainy, e.g. it's a grand soft day
spalpeen agricultural labourer
spittin' starting to rain
terrible same use as 'fierce'
themins those persons
thick as a ditch stupid
thundergub loud-voiced person
wean pronounced wain, child
wee little; also in the north means with,
   e.g. did I see you *wee* that man?
you could trot a mouse on it strong tea

Proverbs and Sayings

Wise, and beautifully expressed with a
delightful wry humour, these sayings and
proverbs have passed into the English
language. They highlight the usual Irish
preoccupations with land, God, love, words
and drinking, as well as every other subject
under the sun. These are just a few examples;
for a comprehensive collection read *Gems of
Irish Wisdom*, by Padraic O'Farrell.

On God
It's a blessing to be in the Lord's hand
   as long as he doesn't close his fist.
Fear of God is the beginning of wisdom.
God never closes the door without
   opening another.
Man proposes, God disposes.

On the Irish Character
The wrath of God has nothing on the
   wrath of an Irishman outbid for land,
   horse or woman.

The best way to get an Irishman to refuse to do something is by ordering it.

The Irish forgive their great men when they are safely buried.

It is not that the Ulsterman lives in the past... it is rather that the past lives in him.

Advice

No property – no friends, no rearing – no manners, no health – no hope!

Never give cherries to pigs, nor advice to a fool.

Bigots and begrudgers will never bid the past farewell.

When everybody else is running, that's the time for you to walk.

You won't be stepped on if you're a live wire.

If you get the name of an early riser you can sleep till dinnertime.

There are finer fish in the sea than have ever been caught.

You'll never plough a field by turning it over in your mind.

Don't make a bid till you walk the land.

A man with humour will keep 10 men working.

Do not visit too often or too long.

If you don't own a mount, don't hunt with the gentry.

You can take a man out of the bog but you cannot take the bog out of the man.

What is got badly, goes badly.

A watched pot never boils.

Enough is as good as plenty.

Beware of the horse's hoof, the bull's horn and the Saxon's smile.

Time is the best storyteller.

On Marriage and Love

Play with a woman that has looks, talk marriage with a woman that has property.

After the settlement comes love.

A lad's best friend is his mother until he's the best friend of a lassie.

A pot was never boiled by beauty.

There is no love sincerer than the love of food. (G. B. Shaw)

It's a great thing to turn up laughing having been turned down crying.

Though the marriage bed be rusty, the death bed is still colder.

On Argument and Fighting

Argument is the worst sort of conversation. (Dean Swift)

There is no war as bitter as a war amongst friends.

Whisper into the glass when ill is spoken.

If we fought temptation the way we fight each other, we'd be a nation of saints again.

We fought every nation's battles, and the only ones we did not win were our own.

On Women

It takes a woman to outwit the Devil.

A cranky woman, an infant, or a grievance, should never be nursed.

A woman in the house is a treasure, a woman with humour in the house is a blessing.

She who kisses in public often kicks in private.

If she is mean at the table, she will be mean in bed.

On Drinking

If Holy Water was porter he'd be at Mass every morning.

It's the first drop that destroys you; there's no harm at all in the last.

Thirst is a shameless disease, so here's to a shameless cure.

On the Family

Greed in a family is worse than need.

Poets write about their mothers, undertakers about their fathers.

A son's stool in his father's home is as steady as a gable; a father's in his son's, bad luck, is shaky and unstable.

On Old Age

The older the fiddle, the sweeter the tune.

There is no fool like an old fool.

On Loneliness

The loneliest man is the man who is lonely in a crowd.

On Bravery

A man who is not afraid of the sea will soon be drowned. (J. M. Synge)

On Flattery

Soft words butter no turnips, but they won't harden the heart of a cabbage, either.

Glossary

Anglo-Norman: the name commonly given to the 12th-century invaders of Ireland, who came in the main from south-west Britain, and also their descendants, because they were of Norman origin.

Bailey: the space enclosed by the walls of a castle, or the outer defences of a motte (*see* Motte-and-bailey).

Barrel-vaulting: simple vaulting of semi-circular form, such as in the nave of Cormac's Chapel, Cashel, Co. Tipperary, where the vault is strengthened with transverse arches.

Bastion: a projecting feature of the outer parts of a fortification, designed to command the approaches to the main wall.

Battlement: a parapet pierced with gaps to enable the defenders to discharge missiles at the enemy.

Bawn: a walled enclosure forming the outer defences of a castle or towerhouse. As well as being an outer defence it also provided a safe enclosure for cattle. There is a good example at Dungory Castle, Kinvarra, Co. Galway.

Beehive hut: a prehistoric circular building, of wood or stone, with a dome-shaped roof, called a *clochan*.

Bronze Age: the earliest metal-using period from the end of the Stone Age until the coming of the Iron Age in Ireland, 2500 BC.

Caher: a stone fort.

Cairn: a mound of stones over a prehistoric grave; they frequently cover chambered tombs.

Cashel: a stone fort, surrounded by a rampart of dry-stone walling, usually of late Iron Age date (*see* ring fort).

Chancel or choir: the east end of a church, reserved for the clergy and choir, and containing the high altar.

Chapter house: the chamber in which the chapter or governing body of a cathedral or monastery met. One of the finest Irish examples is the 14th-century chapter house at Mellifont, Co. Louth.

Chevaux-de-frise: a stone or stake defence work set upright and spaced. It occurs at Dun Aengus, Inishmore, Aran Islands, Co. Galway.

Cist: A box-like grave of stone slabs to contain an inhumed or cremated burial, often accompanied by pottery. Usually Bronze Age or Iron Age in date.

Clochans (I): little groups of cottages, too small to be villages, grouped in straggly clusters according to land tenure and the ties of kinship between families. The land around the *clochan* forms the district known as a townland. A familiar sight is deserted or ruined *clochans* in mountain and moorland areas where huge numbers of people left with the land clearances and the potato famine during the 19th century.

Clochan (clochaun) (II): a small stone building, circular in plan, with its roof corbelled inwards in the form of a beehive. There are many examples in the west, especially in Co. Kerry. The word *clochan* is from the Irish *cloch*, a stone. The structures were early monks' cells and nowadays they are used for storage.

Cloisters: a square or rectangular open space, surrounded by a covered passage, which gives access to the various parts of a monastery. Many medieval cloisters survive in Ireland, e.g. at Quin, Co. Clare.

Columbarium: a dovecote, as seen at Kilcooly Abbey, Co. Tipperary.

Corbel: a projecting stone in a building, usually intended to carry a beam or other structural member.

Corbelled vault: a 'false dome', constructed by laying horizontal rings of stones that overlap on each course until finally a single stone can close the gap at the centre. It is a feature of prehistoric tombs.

Corinthian: the third order of Greek and Roman architecture, a development of the Ionic. The capital has acanthus-leaf ornamentation.

Court cairn: a variety of megalithic tomb consisting of a covered gallery for burials and one or more open courts or forecourts for ritual purposes. They are very common in the north of Ireland.

Crannóg: an artificial island constructed in a lake or marsh to provide a dwelling place in an easily defended position for isolated farming families. Large numbers of *crannógs* (from *crann*, a tree) have been discovered as a result of drainage operations at Lough Gara, near Boyle, Co. Roscommon. These dwelling places would have been in use until the 17th century.

Curragh or *currach*: a light canoe consisting of skins or, in more recent times, tarred canvas, stretched over a wickerwork frame.

Curtain wall: the high wall constructed around a castle and its bailey, usually provided at intervals with towers.

Demesne: land/an estate surrounding a house that the owner has chosen to retain for their own use.

Dolmen: the simplest form of megalithic tomb, consisting of a large capstone and three or more supporting uprights. Some appear to have had forecourts.

Doric: the first order of Greek and Roman architecture, simple and robust in style. The column had no base and the capital was quite plain.

Dun: a fort, usually of stone and often with formidable defences, e.g. Dun Aengus, Inishmore on the Aran Islands, Co. Galway.

Early English: the earliest Gothic architecture of England and Ireland, where it flourished in the 13th century. It is characterized by narrow lancet windows, high pointed arches and the use of rib-vaulting.

Esker: a bank or ridge of gravel and sand, formed by sub-glacial streams. The most notable esker in Ireland stretches from the neighbourhood of Dublin to Galway Bay: Clonmacnoise and Athlone stand on offshoots of it.

Folly: a structure set up by a landlord to provide work for poor tenants in the 19th century.

Fosse: a defensive ditch or moat around a castle or fort.

Gallaun: *see* standing stone.

Gallowglass: A Scottish mercenary soldier hired by Irish clan leaders to fight their enemies.

Hill-fort: a large fort the defences of which follow a contour round a hill to enclose the hill-top. Hill-forts are usually early Iron Age.

Hospital: in medieval times, an almshouse or house of hospitality with provision for spiritual as well as bodily welfare, usually established to cater for a specific class of people. The foundation of the Royal Hospital, Kilmainham, at Dublin for aged soldiers, was in the medieval tradition.

Ionic: the second order of Greek and Roman architecture. The fluted column was tall and graceful in proportion and the capital had volutes (spiral scrolls in stone) at the top.

Irish-Romanesque: the Irish variety of the Romanesque style in architecture (*see* Romanesque). Cormac's Chapel, Cashel, Co. Tipperary; and Clonfert, Co. Galway, provide examples.

Iron Age: the early Iron Age is the term applied to the earliest iron-using period – in Ireland, from the end of the Bronze Age, *c.* 500 BC, to the coming of Christianity in the 5th century.

Jamb: the side of a doorway, window or fireplace. Early Irish churches have characteristic jambs inclined inwards towards the top. The incline is called the batter.

Keep: the main tower of a castle, serving as the innermost stronghold. There is a fine rectangular one at Carrickfergus, Co. Antrim, and at Trim, Co. Meath. Round keeps are rare in Ireland, but occur at Nenagh, Co. Tipperary. Castles with keeps date from the late 12th century until about 1260.

Kerne: an Irish foot-soldier of Tudor times.

Kitchen midden: a prehistoric refuse heap, in which many articles of bronze, iron, flint and stone have been discovered; also shellfish debris, which indicates what our ancestors ate.

Lancet: a tall, narrow window ending in a pointed arch, characteristic of early English style. They often occur in groups of three, five or seven, e.g. Cashel Cathedral, Co. Tipperary.

La Tène: a pre-Christian Irish classic ornamental style, which is linked to ornamental designs found in France.

Lunula: a crescent-shaped, thin, beaten gold ornament, of early Bronze Age date; it is an Irish speciality.

Megalithic tomb: a tomb built of large stones for collective burial, Neolithic or early Bronze Age in date.

Misericord or **miserere:** a carved projection on the underside of a hinged folding seat that, when the seat was raised, gave support to the infirm during the parts of a church service when they had to stand. Good examples can be found in St Mary's Cathedral, Limerick.

Motte-and-bailey: the first Norman fortresses, which were made of earth. The motte was a flat-topped mound, shaped like a truncated cone, surrounded by a fosse and surmounted by a wooden keep. An enclosure, the bailey, bounded by ditch, bank and palisade, adjoined it. The bailey served as a refuge for cattle and in it were the sheds and huts of the retainers. This type of stronghold continued to be built until the early 13th century.

Nave: the main body of the church, sometimes separated from the choir by a screen.

Neolithic: applied to objects from the New Stone Age, which was characterized by the practice of agriculture; in Ireland, between 3000 and 2000 BC.

Ogham stones: early Irish writing, usually cut on stone. The characters consist of strokes above, below or across a stem-line. The key to the alphabet may be seen in the *Book of Ballymote*, now in the library of the Royal Irish Academy, Dublin. Ogham inscriptions occur mainly on standing stones. The inscription is usually commemorative in character. They probably date from c. AD 300.

Pale: the district around Dublin, of varying extent at different periods, where English rule was effective for some four centuries after the Norman invasion of 1169.

Passage grave: a megalithic tomb consisting of a burial chamber approached by a long passage, covered by a round mound or cairn.

Pattern: the festival of a saint, held on the traditional day of his death.

Plantation castles: a name given to defensive buildings erected by English and Scottish settlers under the plantation scheme between 1610 and 1620, which were very common in Ulster.

Portcullis: a heavy grating in a gateway, sliding up and down in slots in the jambs, which could be used to close the entrance quickly. There is a good example at Cahir Castle, Co. Tipperary.

Rath: the rampart of an earthen ring fort. The name is often used for the whole structure.

Rib-vaulting: roofing or ceiling in which the weight of the superstructure is carried on comparatively slender intersecting 'ribs' or arches of stone, the spaces between the ribs being a light stone filling without structural function.

Ring fort, *rath* or *lis:* one or more banks and ditches enclosing an area, usually circular, within which were dwellings. It was the typical homestead of early-Christian Ireland, but examples are known from c. 1000 BC– AD 1000. The bank sometimes had a timber palisade. Some elaborate examples were defensive in purpose.

Romanesque: the style of architecture, based on late classical forms, with round arches and vaulting, that prevailed in Europe until the emergence of Gothic in the 12th century. *See* Irish-Romanesque.

Round towers: stone belfries, also used as refuges and built between the 9th and 12th centuries. They are a uniquely Irish form of architecture, tall and slender, with a conical top. The door is usually about 12ft (3.5m) from the ground.

Rundale: a system of holding land in strips or detached portions. The system has survived in parts of Co. Donegal.

Sedilia: seats recessed in the south wall of the chancel, near the altar, for the use of the clergy. A richly carved example may be seen in Holycross Abbey, Co. Tipperary.

Sept: in the old Irish system, those ruling families who traced their descent from a common ancestor.

Sheela-na-Gig: a cult symbol or female fertility figure, carved in stone on churches or castles. No one is sure of its origin.

Souterrain: artificial underground chambers of wood, stone or earth, or cut into rock. They served as refuges or stores and in some cases as dwellings. They occur commonly in ring forts and, like these, date from the Bronze Age to at least early-Christian times.

Standing stone: an upright stone set in the ground. These may be of various dates, and served various purposes, marking burial places or boundaries, or having a role as cult objects.

Stone fort: a ring fort built of dry-stone walling.

Sweathouses: an ancient form of sauna. Sometimes, mentally ill people were incarcerated in them for a while in an attempt to cure them.

Teampull: a church.

Torc: an ornament dating from the middle to late Bronze Age, made of a ribbon or bar of gold twisted like a rope and bent around to form a complete loop. Two very large examples were found at Tara, Co. Meath.

Tracery: the open-work pattern formed by the stone in the upper part of middle or late Gothic windows.

Transepts: the 'arms' of a church, extending at right angles to the north and south from the junction of nave and choir.

Tumulus: a mound of earth over a grave; usually the mound over an earth-covered passage grave, as in the case of Tara, Co. Meath.

Undertaker: one of the English or Scottish planters given confiscated land in Ireland in the 16th century. They 'undertook' certain obligations designed to prevent the dispossessed owners from reacquiring their land.

Vaulting: a roof or ceiling formed by arching over a space. Among the many methods, three main types were used: barrel-vaulting, groin-vaulting and rib-vaulting. Rib-vaulting lent itself to great elaboration of ornament.

Zoomorphic: decoration based on the forms of animals.

Chronology

BC
c. 8000 BC Humans arrive in Ireland
c. 3000 BC New Stone Age race build
Newgrange in Co. Meath.
c. 2000 BC Arrival of Beaker people.
c. 100 BC Arrival of a wave of Gaelic peoples.

AD
200 The Kingdom of Meath is founded, and
the high kingship at Tara, Co. Meath begins.
432 St Patrick starts his Mission.
700–800 Gaelic Christian Golden Age.
795 Viking raids begin.
1014 Battle of Clontarf and death of Brian Boru,
who won the decisive battle over the Vikings.
1170 The Anglo-Norman conquest begins with
the arrival of Richard, Earl of Pembroke.
1171 Henry II visits Ireland, and secures
the submission of many Irish leaders
and that of his own Norman barons.
1314 The Bruce Invasion fails
1366 Statutes of Kilkenny forbid English settlers
from speaking Gaelic, adopting Irish names,
wearing Irish clothes, marrying Irishwomen.
1394–99 Irish leaders war with Richard II.
1534–35 Rebellion of Silken Thomas
1541 Irish Parliament accepts Henry VIII as King
of Ireland.
1558 Accession of Elizabeth I. The Reformation
does not succeed in Ireland.
1562 on Elizabethan Conquest and settlement
of various counties.
1569–73 The first Desmond Revolt.
1579–83 Final Desmond Revolt and suppression.
1592–1603 Rebellion of the Northern Lords.
1601 Battle of Kinsale – a defeat for Hugh
O'Neill, Earl of Tyrone, and his Ulster chiefs.
1607 Flight of the Earls of Tyrone and Tyrconnell.
1608 Plantation of Ulster with Scots begins in
Derry and Down.
1641 Irish Rising begins. At this time, 59% of
land in Ireland is held by Catholics.
1642–49 Catholic Confederation of Kilkenny.
1649 Cromwell arrives in Ireland.
1650 Catholic landowners exiled to Connacht.
1652 Cromwellian Act of Settlement.
1660 Restoration of Charles II.

1680 Accession of James II.
1689 April to July, Siege of Derry.
1690 July, The Battle of the Boyne. A great
victory for William of Orange.
1691 September to October, Siege of Limerick.
1691 October, Treaty of Limerick.
1695 Beginning of Penal Laws. Catholics now
own 14% of land.
1699 Irish woollen industry destroyed by
English trade laws.
1704 Protestant nonconformists excluded
from public office by Test Act.
1714 Catholics own 7% of land.
1772 Rise of the Patriot Party in parliament,
known as Grattan's Parliament.
1778 Organization of Irish Volunteers.
1778 Gardiner's Relief Act for Catholics eases
the Penal Laws.
1779 English concessions on trade and the
repeal of most of the restrictive laws.
1782 Establishment of Irish Parliamentary
independence.
1791 The Society of United Irishmen founded.
1795 Orange Order founded.
1798 Rebellion of '98.
1801 Act of Union.
1829 Catholic Emancipation Bill passed.
1842–48 The Young Ireland Movement.
1845–49 The Great Famine that began with
the blight of the potato harvest.
1840s Emigration of thousands to New World.
1848 Abortive rising led by Smith O'Brien.
1867 Fenian Rising.
1869 Disestablishment of the Church of Ireland.
1875 Charles Stewart Parnell elected Member
of Parliament for Co. Meath.
1877 Parnell becomes Chairman of the Home
Rule Confederation.
1879–82 Land war.
1886 Gladstone's first Home Rule Bill for
Ireland defeated.
1890 Parnell cited in divorce case; he loses
leadership of the Irish Party in the Commons.
1892 Gladstone's 2nd Home Rule Bill defeated.
1893 Gaelic League founded.
1899 Beginning of the Sinn Féin movement.
1903 Wyndham's Land Act.

1912 Third Home Rule Bill introduced.

1913 Ulster Volunteer Force founded.

1914 Outbreak of the First World War. The third Home Rule Bill receives Royal assent, but is deferred until the end of the war.

1916 The Easter Uprising.

1918–21 The Anglo-Irish War.

1920 Amendment Act to Home Rule Bill, letting Six Counties in Ulster vote themselves out and remain with the rest of Britain.

1920–21 Heavy fighting between the Auxiliaries and the Irish Nationalist forces.

1921 July, King George V officially opens the Stormont Parliament in the Six Counties.

1921 December, the Anglo-Irish treaty signed.

1922 January, the treaty is ratified in Dáil Eireann. Start of the Irish Civil War between pro-treaty majority and anti-treaty forces.

1922 November, executions of anti-treaty leaders by Free State in Dublin.

1923 End of Civil War.

1926 De Valera founds Fianna Fáil.

1932 General Election. Fianna Fáil win.

1937 Constitution of Eire.

1938 Agreement with Britain; economic disputes are ended. Britain gives up tributary and naval rights in 'Treaty' ports.

1939 IRA bombing campaign in Britain. Outbreak of Second World War; Eire neutral.

1945 End of Second World War.

1948 General Election in Ireland. Defeat of Fianna Fáil, and De Valera out of office for first time in 16 years.

1952 Republic of Ireland declared and accepted by Britain, with a qualifying guarantee of support to the Six Counties.

1956–62 IRA campaign in the North.

1968 First Civil Rights march.

1969 January, democracy march, Belfast–Derry. Marchers attacked at Burntollet Bridge.

1969 August, British troops sent to Derry.

1971 February, first British soldier killed by IRA. August, internment of IRA suspects. Reforms to the RUC, and electoral system.

1972 'Bloody Sunday' (Jan): British troops kill 13 demonstrators in Derry. Direct Rule is imposed from Westminster: Stormont Government and Irish Parliament are suspended.

1973 The Sunningdale Agreement. An Assembly established with power-sharing between different political leaders.

1974 Ulster Workers' Strike brings down Assembly. Direct Rule reimposed.

1981 Bobby Sands dies after hunger strike.

1985 Anglo-Irish Agreement.

1993 Downing Street Initiative.

1994 August, IRA ceasefire.

1996 Canary Wharf bombing in London. IRA declares ceasefire over.

1997 IRA ceasefire renewed.

1998 Good Friday Agreement. May, Referendum Agreement. June, New Assembly elections by Proportional Representation. Unionist Party win most seats by a small margin. Sinn Féin and SDLP do very well. August, IRA dissidents kill 28 in Omagh bomb. October, John Hume and David Trimble are awarded Nobel peace prize for their work in ending the conflict.

1999 Patten Commission Report on RUC reform.

2000 Orange men protest at the banning of their traditional march through Drumcree for the seventh year running.

2001 January, Euro notes and coins go into circulation in the Republic June, Irish people vote against EU's Nice Treaty. In the British general elections, the Democratic Unionists and Sinn Féin are the main winners in NI, moderate parties lose ground. David Trimble resigns as First Minister of the Northern Ireland Assembly in protest against the IRA's refusal to decommission their arms, but is reinstated. November, the PSNI (Police Service of Northern Ireland) replaces the RUC.

2002 October, the Northern Ireland Executive and NI Assembly are suspended. The Republic's census reveals that returning emigrants outnumber non-Irish immigrants.

2003 April, devolution is suspended and the Secretary of State for NI is once again responsible for directing departments in the province. May, Joint Declaration by Irish and British governments of their commitment to return to normal security arrangements in NI. November, elections to the NI Assembly bring more gains to the DUP and Sinn Féin.

2004 December, a weapons decommissioning deal is almost brokered but fails on the issue of photographic evidence and remains an obstacle to the restoration of devolved government

2005 May, Peter Hain appointed Secretary of State for Northern Ireland.

Further Reading

Archaeology, Architecture and Art

Brennan, M., *Boyne Valley Vision* (Dolmen).

Craig, Maurice, *Dublin 1660–1860* (Allen Figgis), *Classical Irish Houses of the Middle Size: Lost Demesnes* (Architectural Press).

Crookshank, Anne and the Knight of Glin, *Painters of Ireland c. 1660–1920* (Barrie & Jenkins).

Day, Angélique and McWilliams, Patrick (ed.), *Ordnance Survey Memoirs of Ireland* (Institute of Irish Studies, Belfast).

De Breffny and Folliott, *Houses of Ireland* (Thames & Hudson), *Castles of Ireland* (Thames & Hudson), *Churches and Abbeys of Ireland* (Thames & Hudson).

Estyn Evans, E., *Prehistoric Ireland* (Batsford).

Guinness, Desmond, *Georgian Dublin* (Batsford), *Great Irish Houses and Castles* (Weidenfeld & Nicolson), *Palladio* (Weidenfeld & Nicolson).

Harbison, P., Potterton, H. and Sheehy, J., *Irish Art and Architecture* (Thames & Hudson).

Henry, Françoise, *Early Christian Irish Art* (Mercier).

Kennedy, Gerald Conan, *Ancient Ireland: The User's Guide* (Morrigan Books)

Maire de Paor, *Early Irish Art* (Aspects of Ireland Series).

O'Brien, Jacqueline and Guinness, Desmond, *A Grand Tour* (Weidenfeld & Nicolson).

O'Brien and Harbison, *Ancient Ireland* (Weidenfeld & Nicolson).

O'Riordain, S. P. O., *Antiquities of the Irish Countryside* (Methuen).

Sheehy, J., *Discovery of Ireland's Past* (Thames & Hudson).

White, James, *John Butler Yeats and the Irish Renaissance* (Dolmen).

Burkes Guide to Country Houses: Ireland (Burkes).

Historic Monuments of Northern Ireland (HMSO 1983).

Biography and Memoirs

Bence Jones, Mark, *Twilight of the Ascendancy* (Constable).

Chambers, Anne, *Granuaile: The Life and Times of Grace O'Malley* (Wolfhound).

Davis-Gough, Annabel, *Walled Gardens* (Eland).

Du Maurier, Daphne, *Hungry Hill* (Penguin).

Hunt, Hugh, *The Abbey, Ireland's National Theatre 1904–79* (Gill & Macmillan).

Joyce, James, *Portrait of an Artist as a Young Man* (Longman).

Kelly, A. A. (ed.), *Letters of Liam O'Flaherty* (Wolfhound Press).

Kenny, Mary, *Goodbye to Catholic Ireland* (Sinclair Stevenson).

Krause, David, *A Self Portrait of the Artist as a Man* (Sean O'Casey through his letters) (Dolmen).

Lyons, J. S., *Oliver St John Gogarty, A Biography* (Blackwater Press).

Moore, George, *Hail and Farewell* (Smythe).

Murphy, William, *The Yeats Family and the Pollexfens of Sligo* (Dolmen).

O'Crohan, Thomas, *The Islandman* (OUP).

O'Sullivan, Maurice, *Twenty Years a-Growing* (OUP).

Parker, Tony, *May the Lord in His Mercy Be Kind to Belfast* (Collins).

Shuilleabhain, E. H., *Letters from the Great Blasket* (Mercier).

Somerville-Large, P., *Irish Eccentrics* (Lilliput Press).

Taylor, Alice, *To School through the Fields* (Brandon).

Thomson, David, *Woodbrook* (Penguin).

Yeats, J. B., *Early Memories* (Irish Academic Press).

Yeats, W. B., *Synge and the Ireland of his Time* (Irish Academic Press).

All the Irish Heritage Series (Eason).

Cooking, Crafts, Flora, Fauna, Fishing

Allen, Myrtle, *Ballymaloe Cook Book* (Gill & Macmillan).

Davis-Goff, Annabel, *Walled Gardens* (Barrie and Jenkins).

Fitzgibbon, Theodora, *Cook Book*.

Heron, Marianne, *The Hidden Gardens of Ireland* (Gill & Macmillan).

Lewis, C. A., *Hunting in Ireland* (J. A. Allen).

O'Brien, Louise, *Crafts of Ireland* (Gilbert Dillon).

O'Reilly, Peter, *Trout & Salmon Loughs of Ireland* (Harper Collins).

O'Reilly, Peter, *Trout & Salmon Rivers of Ireland* (Merlin Unwin Books).

Reeves-Smyth, Terence, *Irish Gardens* (Appletree Press).

Webb, D. A., *An Irish Flora* (Dundalgan).

Bridgestones Guides, Where to Stay and Eat in Ireland (Estragon Press).

Traditional Irish Recipes (Appletree Press).

Gill & Macmillan publish a series of fishing guides on game, coarse and sea angling.

Fiction, Poetry, Plays

Banville, John, *The Untouchable* (Pan Books).

Beckett, Samuel, *Murphy* (J Calder).

Berry, James (ed. Horgan, M. and Gertrude), *Tales of the West of Ireland* (Dolmen).

Bowen, Elizabeth, *Elizabeth Bowen's Irish Stories* and *Bowen's Court* (Poolbeg).

Carleton, William, *The Black Prophet* (Irish University Press).

Carpenter and Fallon (ed.), *The Writers, A Sense of Ireland* (O'Brien Press).

Crone, Anne, *Bridie Steen* (Blackstaff).

Durcan, Paul, Yeats, W. B., Heaney, Seamus, Simmons, James and Clarke, Austin, *The Faber Book of Irish Verse* (Faber and Faber).

Edgeworth, Maria, *The Absentee* (OUP).

Farrell, J. G., *Troubles* (Penguin).

Joyce, James, *Ulysses* (Penguin).

Kickham, C., *Knocknagow, Or the Homes of Tipperary* (Mercier).

McGahern, John, *The Barracks* (Faber and Faber). Try any other novels by him as well.

McLiam Wilson, Robert, *Ripley Bogle* (Minerva).

The Penguin Book of Irish Verse and *The Penguin Book of Irish Short Stories* (Penguin).

O'Brien, Flann, *At Swim-two-Birds* (Penguin)

O'Connor, Frank, *Guests of the Nation* (Poolbeg).

Novels by Edith Somerville and Martin Ross, especially *The Great House at Inver* (Zodiac Press) and *The Real Charlotte* (Arrow Books).

Poetry by Michael Siadhail (bilingual)

All the plays by J. M. Synge.

Any stories by Mary Lavin (Penguin).

Any novels by George Birmingham (Blackstaff, BBC and others).

Any novels by Sam Hanna Bell (Blackstaff, BBC and others).

Any novels by Roddy Doyle.

Any novels by Kate O'Brien (Blackstaff, BBC and others).

Any novels by Colm Tóibín.

Any novels by William Trevor (Penguin).

Stories and plays by Brian Friel (Penguin and others).

Folklore, Music and Tradition

Cross, E., *The Tailor and Ansty* (Mercier).

Danaher, Kevin, *Folktales of the Irish Countryside* (Mercier).

Estyn Evans, E., *Irish Folk Ways* (Routledge).

Feldman, Allan and O'Doherty, *The Northern Fiddler: Music and Musicians of Donegal and Tyrone* (Blackstaff).

Flower, R., *The Irish Tradition* (Clarendon Press).

Gaffney, S. and Cashman, S., *Proverbs and Sayings of Ireland* (Wolfhound).

Gregory, Lady Isabella Augusta, *Gods and Fighting Men* (Smythe).

Healy, J. N., *Love Songs of the Irish* (Mercier).

Healy, J. N., *Percy French and his Songs* (Mercier).

Henry, S., *Tales from the West of Ireland* (Mercier).

Hyde, Douglas, *Beside the Fire* (Irish Academic Press).

Hyde, Douglas, *The Stone of Truth and Other Irish Folktales* (Irish Academic Press).

O'Boyle, Sean, *The Irish Song Tradition* (Gilbert Dalton).

O'Connell, James, *The Meaning of the Irish Coast* (Blackstaff).

O'Faolain, S., *Short Stories* (Mercier).

O'Farrell, P., *Folktales of the Irish Coast* (Mercier).

O'Flaherty, Gerald, *A Book of Slang, Idiom and Wit* (O'Brien).

O'Keeffe, D. and Healy, J. N., *Book of Irish Ballads* (Mercier).

O'Sullivan, Patrick, *A Country Diary* (Anvil).

O'Sullivan, Sean, *Folklore of Ireland* (Batsford).

Wilde, William, *Irish Popular Superstitions* (Irish Academic Press).

History and Literary History

Beckett, J. C., *The Making of Modern Ireland* (Faber and Faber).

Boylan, Henry (ed.), *A Dictionary of Irish Biography* (Gill & Macmillan).

Connolly, S. J. (ed.), *The Oxford Companion to Irish History* (Oxford University Press).

Corkery, Daniel, *Hidden Ireland* (Gill & Macmillan).

Cruise O'Brien, M. and C., *Concise History of Ireland* (Thames & Hudson).

Cruise O'Brien, Conor, *States of Ireland* (Hutchinson).

Edwards, R. Dudley, *A New History of Ireland* (Gill & Macmillan).

Edwards, R. Dudley, *An Atlas of Irish History* (Methuen).

Fitzgerald, Mairéad, *World of Colmcille* (O'Brien Press).

Foster, R. F. (ed.), *The Oxford History of Ireland* (OUP).

Foster, R. F., *Modern Ireland 1600–1972* (OUP).

Kavanagh, P., *The Irish Theatre* (The Kerryman).

Kee, Robert, *The Green Flag* (Sphere).

Lyons, F. S. L., *Ireland Since the Famine* (Fontana).

MacLysaght, E., *Surnames of Ireland* (Irish Academic Press).

MacLysaght, E., *Irish Families: Their Names and Origins* (Figgins).

Maxwell, Constancia, *Country and Town under the Georges* (Dundalgan Press).

O'Farrell, P., *How the Irish Speak English* (Mercier).

O'Grada, Cormac (ed.), *Famine 150 – Commemorative Lecture Series* (Teagasc).

Pakenham, Thomas, *The Year of Liberty: The Great Irish Rebellion of 1798* (Weidenfeld & Nicolson).

Stephens, James, *Insurrection in Dublin* (Colin Smythe Ltd).

Stewart, A. T. Q., *The Narrow Ground* (Faber and Faber).

Wallace, M., *A Short History of Ireland* (David & Charles).

Woodham Smith, Cecil, *The Great Hunger* (Penguin).

Burkes Irish Family Records (Burkes).

Burkes Landed Gentry (Burkes).

Maps

Historical Map (Bartholomew).

Ireland Map, by *Bord Fáilte* (Ordnance Survey).

Ireland Touring Map (Bartholomew).

Irish Family Names Map (Johnson & Bacon) – divided into North, East, South and West.

Ordnance Survey Holiday Map (1:250,000) for the south, useful for Cork and Kerry.

For greater detail, 89 Ordnance Survey maps cover the whole island with a 1:50,000 scale (2cm to 1km).

Photography

Daly, Leo, *The Aran Islands* (Albertine Kennedy).

Estyn Evans, E. and Turner, B. S., *Ireland's Eye: The Photographs of Robert John Welch* (Blackstaff).

Johnstone and Kirk, *Images of Belfast* (Blackstaff).

Walker, B. M., O'Brien, A. and McMahon, S., *Faces of Ireland* (Appletree Press).

Travelogues

Donegan, Lawrence, *No News at Throat Lake* (Penguin).

Duff, Chris, *On Celtic Tides: One Man's Journey Around Ireland by Sea Kayak* (St Martin's Press).

Hawkes, Tony, *Round Ireland With a Fridge* (Ebury).

McCarthy, Pete, *McCarthy's Bar* (Hodder & Stoughton).

McCrum, Mark, *The Craic* (Orion).

McKenzie, Richard, *Turn Left at the Black Cow* (Roberts Rinehart).

Moorhouse, Geoffrey, *Sun Dancing* (Orion).

Morton, H. V., *In Search of Ireland* (Methuen).

Murphy, Dervla, *A Place Apart* (Penguin).

O'Crohan, Tomas, *Island Cross-Talk* (Oxford Paperbacks).

Praeger, R., *The Way That I Went* (Figgins).

Robinson, Tim, *The Aran Islands* (the author).

Synge, J. M., *The Aran Islands* (Blackstaff).

Guides and Topography

Allen, F. H. A. (ed.), *Atlas of the Irish Rural Landscape* (Cork University Press).

Craig, Maurice and the Knight of Glin, *Ireland Observed* (Mercier).

Harbison, Peter, *Guide to the National Monuments of Ireland* (Gill & Macmillan).

Mason, T. H., *The Islands of Ireland* (Mercier).

A Literary Map of Ireland (Wolfhound).

Walking Guides

Fewer, Michael, *Irish Long Distance Walks*
  (Gill & Macmillan).
Lynam, Joss, *Best Irish Walks*
  (Gill & Macmillan).
O'Suilleabhain, Sean, *No. 1 South West*
  (Gill & Macmillan).

Whilde, Tony, *No. 2 West* (Gill & Macmillan).
Simon, Patrick and Foley, Gerard,
  No. 3 North West (Gill & Macmillan).
Boidell, Jean, Casey, M. and Kennedy, Eithne,
  No. 5 East (Gill & Macmillan).
Martindale, *No. 6 South East*
  (Gill & Macmillan).

Index

Main page references are in **bold**; Page references to maps are in *italics*.

Ireland touring atlas

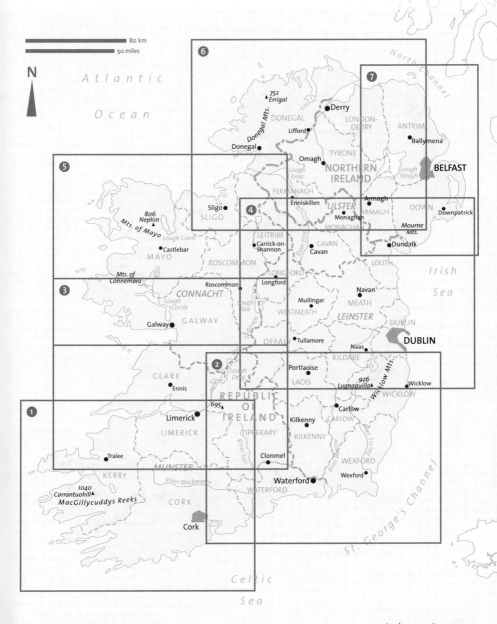

80 km
50 miles

N

Atlantic

Ocean

6

7

752
Errigal

Donegal Mts.

DONEGAL

Derry

LON-DON-
DERRY

ANTRIM

Lifford

Donegal

Omagh

TYRONE

NORTHERN
IRELAND

Ballymena

Lough
Neagh

BELFAST

5

Lough
Erne

FERMANAGH

806
Nephin

Mts. of Mayo

Lough Conn

Sligo

SLIGO

4

Enniskillen

ULSTER

Armagh

ARMAGH

Monaghan

MONAGHAN

DOWN

Mourne
Mts.

Downpatrick

Castlebar

MAYO

Mts. of
Connemara

Lough
Corrib

Carrick-on-
Shannon

LEITRIM

ROSCOMMON

Roscommon

LONGFORD

Longford

CAVAN

Cavan

River Erne

LOUTH

Dundalk

Irish

Sea

3

CONNACHT

Lough
Ree

Navan

Mullingar

MEATH

Galway

GALWAY

River Shannon

WESTMEATH

LEINSTER

DUBLIN

Tullamore

OFFALY

Naas

DUBLIN

2

Lough
Derg

Portlaoise

KILDARE

CLARE

LAOIS

Ennis

926
Lugnaquilla

Wicklow Mts.

Wicklow

WICKLOW

REPUBLIC
OF
IRELAND

695

1

Limerick

LIMERICK

River Suir

Carlow

CARLOW

Kilkenny

KILKENNY

River Barrow

TIPPERARY

Tralee

KERRY

River Blackwater

MUNSTER

Clonmel

Waterford

WATERFORD

Wexford

WEXFORD

River Slaney

1040
Carrantuohill
MacGillycuddys Reeks

CORK

Cork

St. George's Channel

Celtic

Sea

North Channel

REPUBLIC

Land 0–100 metres
Land 0–200 metres
Land 200–500 metres
Land 500–1000 metres
Land over 1000 metres

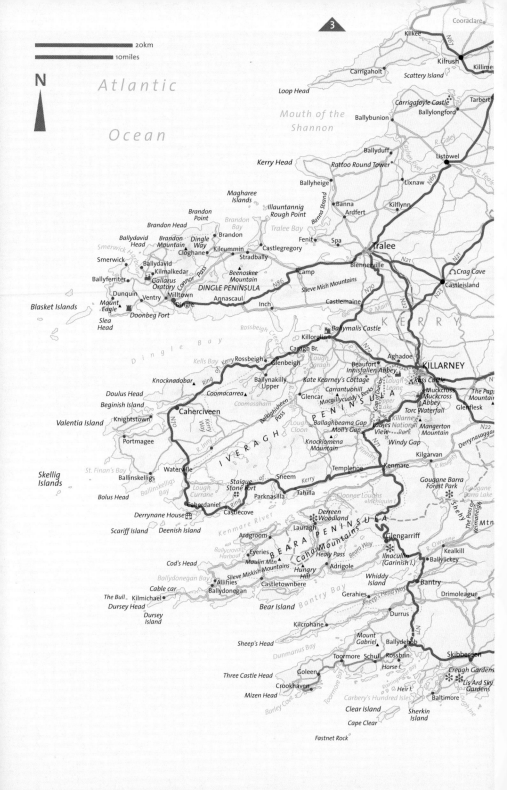

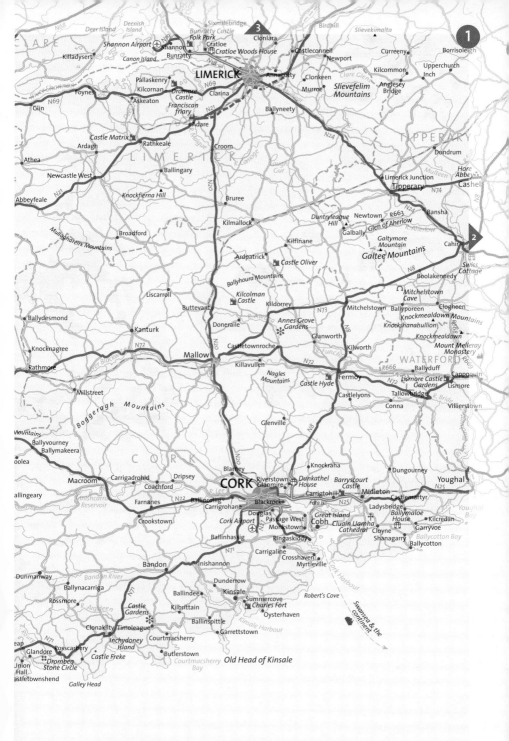

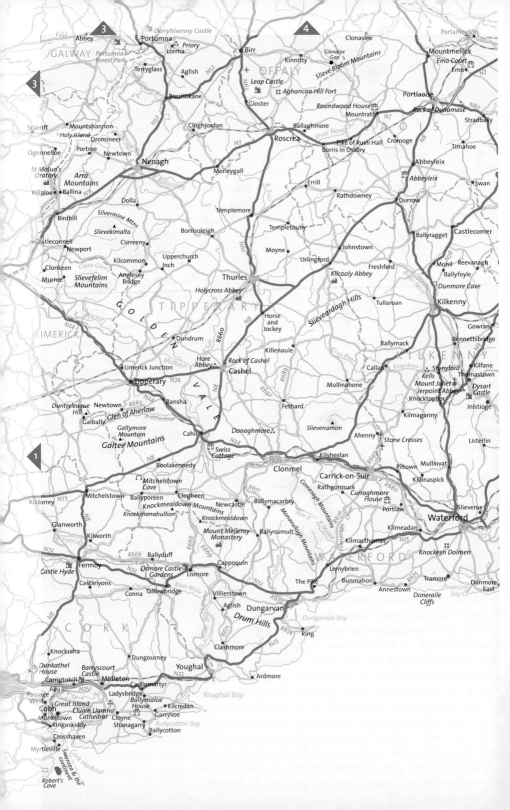

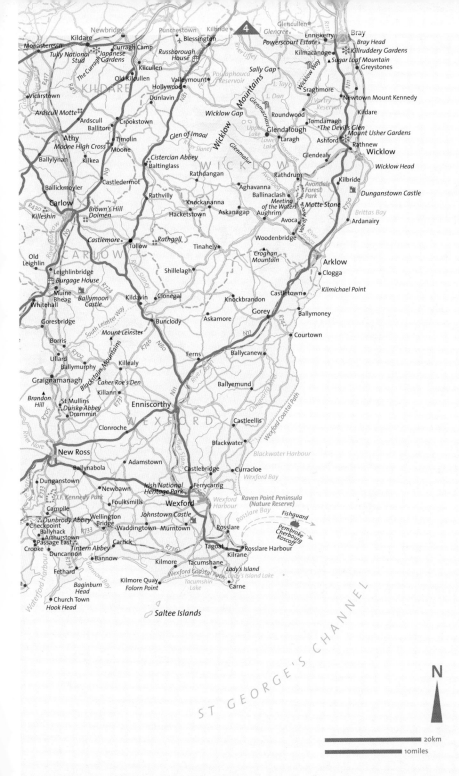

Newbridge
Kildare
Monasterevin
Tully National
Stud
Japanese
Gardens
Curragh Camp
The Curragh
KILDARE
Vicarstown
Old Kilcullen
Kilcullen
Hollywood
Dunlavin
Ardscull Motte
Ardscull
Ballitore
Crookstown
Athy
Moone High Cross
Timolin
Moone
Ballylynan
Kilkea
Ballickmoyler
Castledermot
Carlow
Brown's Hill
Dolmen
Killeshin
Castlemore
Tullow
Old
Leighlin
Leighlinbridge
Burgage House
Muine
Bheag
Whitehall
Ballymoon
Castle
Kildavin
Clonegal
Goresbridge
Bunclody
Borris
Mount Leinster
Ullard
Ballymurphy
Killealy
Graignamanagh
Caher Roe's Den
Killann
Brandon
Hill
St Mullins
Duiske Abbey
Drummin
Clonroche
New Ross
Ballynabola
Adamstown
Dunganstown
J.F. Kennedy Park
Newbawn
Irish National
Heritage Park
Foulksmills
Campile
Dunbrody Abbey
Wellington
Bridge
Waddingtown Murntown
Checkpoint
Ballyhack
Arthurstown
Passage East
Crooke
Duncannon
Carrick
Tintern Abbey
Bannow
Fethard
Baginburn
Head
Kilmore Quay
Folorn Point
Church Town
Hook Head

Punchestown
Blessington
Russborough
House
Valleymount
Wicklow Gap
Glen of Imaal
Cistercian Abbey
Baltinglass
Rathdangan
Aghavanna
Rathvilly
Knockananna
Hacketstown
Askanagap
Rathgall
Tinahely
Shillelagh
Clonegal
Knockbrandon
Askamore
Ferns
Ballycanew
Ballymund
Enniscorthy
Castleellis
Blackwater
Castlebridge
Curracloe
Ferrycarrig
Wexford
Johnstown Castle
Rosslare
Tagoat
Kilmore
Tacumshane
Kilrane
Lady's Island
Carne

Kilbride
Kildare
Glencullen
Glencree
Powerscourt Estate
Kilmacanoge
Sally Gap
L. Tay
L. Dan
Roundwood
Glendalough
Laragh
Glendealy
Rathdrum
Ballinaclash
Meeting
of the Waters
Aughrim
Avoca
Woodenbridge
Croghan
Mountain
Clogga
Castletown
Gorey
Courtown
Ballymoney

Enniskerry
Bray
Bray Head
Killruddery Gardens
Sugar Loaf Mountain
Greystones
Saghmore
Newtown Mount Kennedy
Kildare
Tomdarragh
The Devil's Glen
Ashford
Mount Usher Gardens
Rathnew
Wicklow
Wicklow Head
Kilbride
Avondale
Forest
Park
Motte Stone
Dunganstown Castle
Brittas Bay
Ardanairy
Kilmichael Point
Arklow

Poulaphouca
Reservoir
Wicklow
Mountains
Vartry
Reservoir
Wicklow Way
Upper
Lake
Lower
Lake

WICKLOW W

River Slaney

Wexford
Harbour
Raven Point Peninsula
(Nature Reserve)
Rosslare Bay
Fishguard
Pembroke
Cherbourg
Roscoff
Rosslare Harbour

Blackwater Harbour
Wexford Coastal Path
Wexford Bay

Lady's Island Lake
Tacumshin
Lake

Saltee Islands

ST GEORGE'S CHANNEL

N

20km
10miles

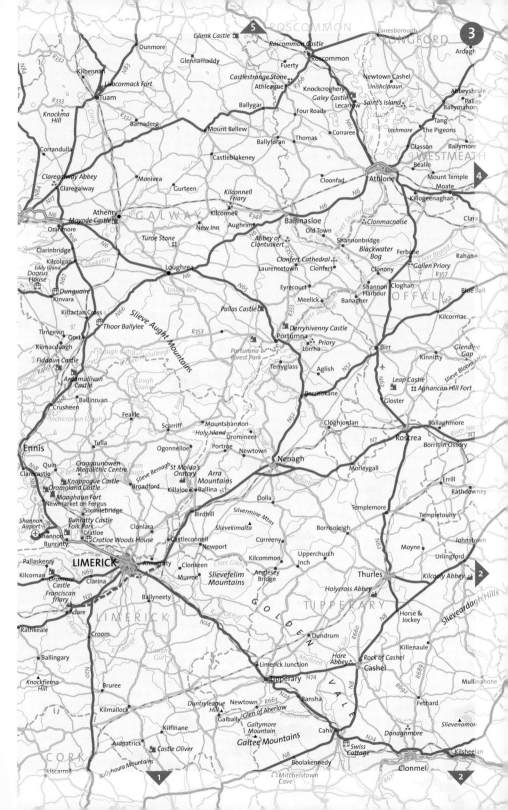

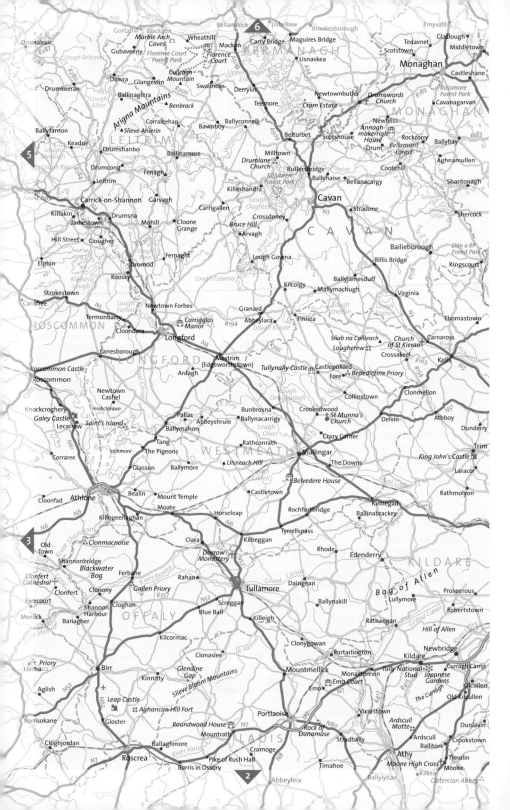

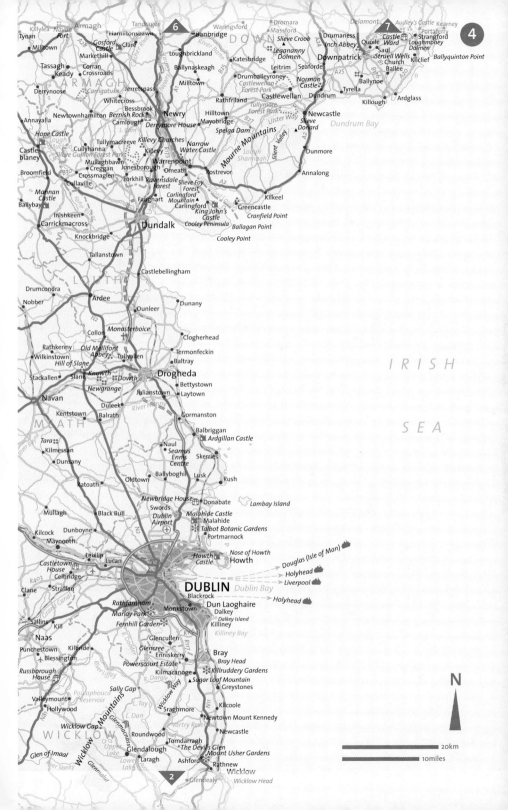

20km
10miles

N

Benwee Head
Erris Head · Broad Haven · Portacloy · Belderg Harbour · Downpatrick Head
Sruwoddacon Bay
Corclogh · Dooncarton Stone Circle · R314 · Céide Fields · Ballycastle
Inishglora · Belmullet · Pollatomish · Carrowmore
Corraun Point · R313 · Barnatra · Glenamoy · Rathfran Abbey
Mullet Peninsula · Drumreagh · R314 · Killala
Inishkea North · R313 · Bangor Erris · Belville
Aghlean
Inishkea South · Fallmore · Geesala · Bangor · Bellacorick
Duvillaun More · Blacksod Bay · N59 · Crossmolina
Nephin Beg Range
Slievemore · R312 · Castlehill
Croaghaun · Doogort
Keem Strand · Keel · Derreen · Nephin
Cathedral Rocks · Glen Nephin
Achill Island · Achill · Pontoon
Achill Sound · Corraun Peninsula · N59 · Lough Feeagh · Lough Cullin
The Atlantic Drive · Mulranny
Achillbeg Island · Rockfleet (Carrickahooley) Castle · Burrishoole Abbey
Clare Island · Ballytoohy · Clew Bay · Newport · M A
Knockmore Mountain · Castlebar
Westport Bay · Old Head · Murrisk Abbey · N5
Roonagh Quay · Louisburgh · Westport · N84
Carrowniskey · R335 · Croagh Patrick · Mace · Belcarra
Inishturk · Caher Island · Liscarney · Ballintubber Abbey
Killavally · Carrowkennedy · Cornanagh
M U R R I S K · Srah
Pass of Bundorragha
Inishbofin · Mweelrea Mts · Delphi · Ben Gorm · Partry Mountains · Slieve Carra
Inishark · Bofin · Killary Bay · Glenn Erriff · Trean · Lough Mask · Caher
Ballynakill Harbour · Renvyle · Salruck · Aasleagh Falls · Finny · Ballinrobe
Cleggan Bay · Tully Cross · Gowlaun · Kylemore Abbey · Leenane · Inishmaine Island
Cleggan · Dawros · Letterfrack · Maumturk Mts · Joyce Country · R334
Streamstown Bay · Moyard · Benbaun · Clonbur · Neal
Clifden Bay · Connemara National Park · The Twelve Pins · Finnisglin · Benlevy · Ashford Castle · Cong
Mannin Bay · Clifden · Bencorr · Benbreen · Teernakill · Maum · Cornamona · Inchagoill
Ballinaboy · Lettershea · Lissoughter Mountain · Leckavrea Mountain
Ballyconneely · Ballinafad · Recess · Maam Cross · Lough Corrib · Headford
Slyne Head · Errisbeg · Cashel · Oughterard · Aughnanure Castle
Roundstone · R342 · Lough Aroolagh · River Owenny · Ross Castle
Ballyconneely Bay · Bertraghboy Bay · Gortmore · Screeb · Rosscahill
C O N N E M A R A · Rosmuc · R340
St Macdara's Island · Carna · Kilkieran · Bealadangan · Moycullen
Mweenish Island · Lettermore Island · Costello
Casheen Bay · Lettermore
Gorumna Island · Carraroe · Rossaveal
Lettermullen Island · Ballynahown · R336 · Furbo · Salthill
Cashla Bay · Greatman's Bay · Inveran · Spiddal · Barna · GALWAY
North Sound · Galway Bay · Tawin Island
Brannock Islands · Onaght · Dun Aengus · Kilmurvey · Black Head · Aughinish
Inishmore · Kilronan · Burren
Arkin Castle

Atlantic

Ocean

3

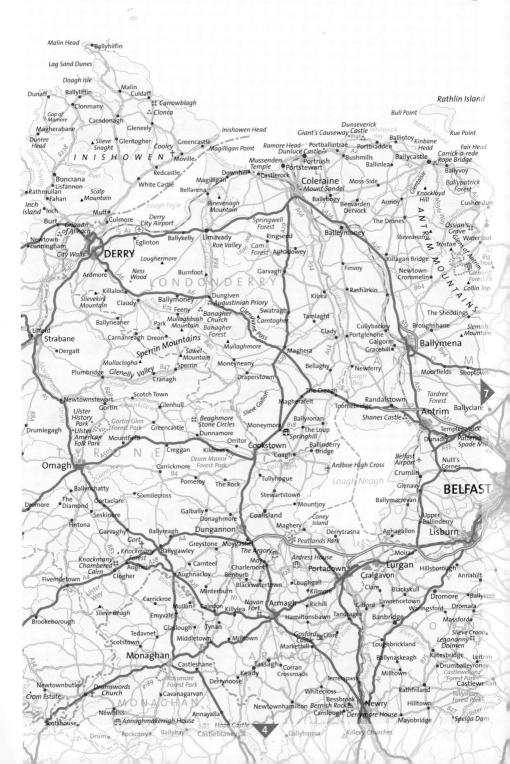

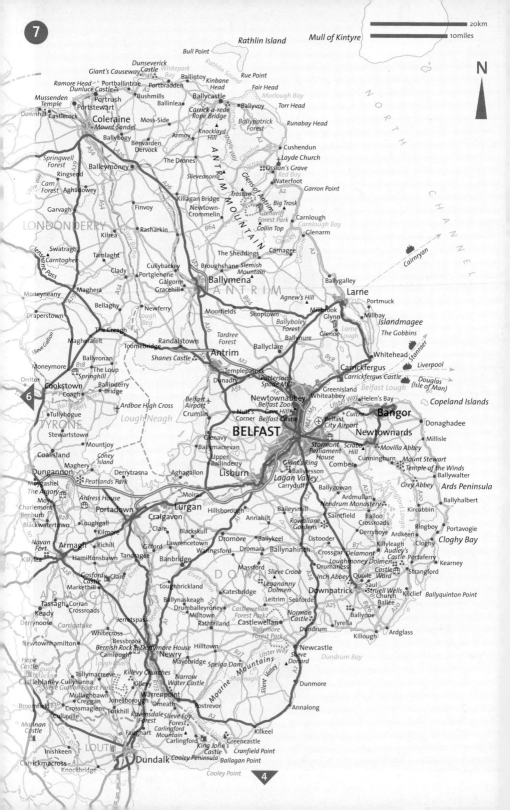

CADOGANguides SCOTLAND

'Excellently
written,
bursting with
character'
— *Holiday Which*

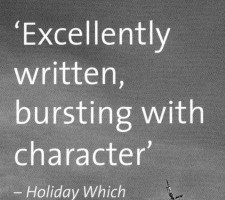

Edinburgh
Pick Your Brains Scotland
Scotland
Scotland's Highlands & Islands

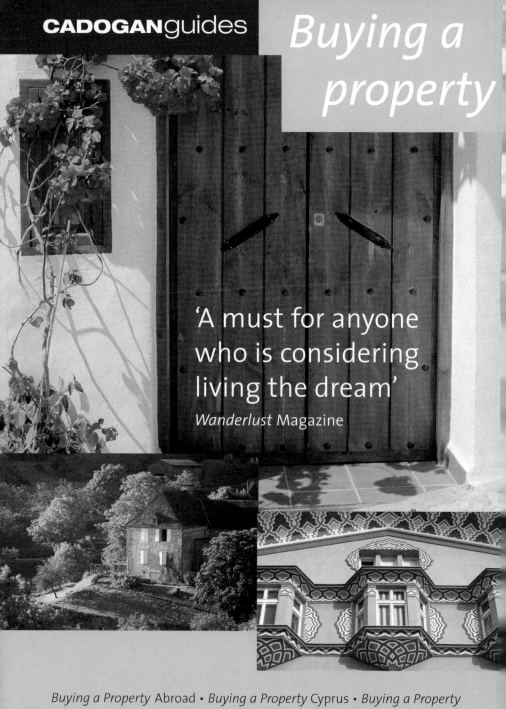

CADOGANguides

Buying a property

'A must for anyone
who is considering
living the dream'

Wanderlust Magazine

Buying a Property Abroad • *Buying a Property* Cyprus • *Buying a Property* Eastern Europe • *Buying a Property* Florida • *Buying a Property* France • *Buying a Property* Greece • *Buying a Property* Ireland • *Buying a Property* Italy • *Buying a Property* Portugal • *Buying a Property* Spain • *Buying a Property* Turkey • Retiring Abroad